GunDigest 2017

Edited by
JERRY LEE

Published by

Gun Digest® Books, an imprint of F+W Media, Inc.
Krause Publications · 700 East State Street · Iola, WI 54990-0001
715-445-2214 · 888-457-2873
www.krausebooks.com

To order books or other products call toll-free 1-800-258-0929
or visit us online at **www.gundigeststore.com**

CAUTION: Technical data presented here, particularly technical data on handloading and on firearms adjustment and alteration, inevitably reflects individual experience with particular equipment and components under specific circumstances the reader cannot duplicate exactly. Such data presentations therefore should be used for guidance only and with caution. Gun Digest Books accepts no responsibility for results obtained using these data.

ISSN 0072-9043

ISBN 13: 978-1-4402-4658-6
ISBN 10: 1-4402-4658-0

Cover & Design by Tom Nelsen & Dane Royer

Edited by Jerry Lee & Chris Berens

Printed in the United States of America

10 9 8 7 6 5 4 3 2 1

John T. Amber LITERARY AWARD

Congratulations to Charles E. Petty, recipient of the 35th Annual John T. Amber Literary Award. The award is given each year by *Gun Digest* in honor of an author's work that appeared in the previous year's edition. This year's award is for Charlie's fine historic profile of the King's Gunsight Company in the 2016 edition. He told the story of a company that started what eventually became a cottage industry in the gun business—providing adjustable sights for guns that came from the factory with fixed sights. From the end of World War I until the early 1950s, King's was the major source for adjustable sights, mainly for handguns, but for long guns as well. The company also offered numerous customizing services and today "King's" guns are highly sought-after by collectors.

Charlie Petty's love of guns and the outdoors began at the feet of his grandfather, a dedicated North Carolina quail hunter who was profiled by Charlie in "My Grandaddy's Shotgun," which appeared in the 1989 edition of *Gun Digest*. It was a wonderful story that touched many of us who grew up tagging along with their dad or granddad until we were old enough to shoot.

Charlie progressed through the NRA Junior rifle program and, following high school, joined the Air Force. He was assigned to Marksmanship School at Lackland Air Force Base in Texas where he was taught to accurize Model 1911A1 pistols to "AFPG" (Air Force Premium Grade) standards. Soon he became a serious competitor in NRA Bullseye Pistol and eventually earned a master card. Following the Air Force, Charlie went to UNC Charlotte and following school, got a job at Charlotte-Mecklenburg Utilities and retired after 30 years in 1993 as Chief Chemist. During the same time his interest in law enforcement led to service as a reserve police officer. He served in patrol and firearms training units, retiring with the rank of captain.

Without Uncle Sam's support, competitive shooting became prohibitively expensive and Charlie's interest shifted to gun collecting. This eventually led to his book, *High Standard Automatic Pistols—1932-1950*, which was published

Charles E. Petty

Photo by Mike Dendinger

in 1979 and launched a writing career that continues to this day. It is considered by many to be the standard text on High Standard pistols.

The first time the Charles E. Petty byline appeared in *Gun Digest* was in 1985 for his article "Little Known .22 Pistols of the Post War Era." In addition to several other stories in *Gun Digest*, he has written many articles and columns for the country's leading gun magazines including *American Rifleman, American Handgunner, GUNS, Shooting Industry, Shooting Times, Handgun Quarterly* and the *Hodgdon Annual Manual*. Currently he is a contributing editor for the NRA's *American Rifleman* and two Wolfe Publishing Company titles, *Rifle* and *Handloader*.

The John T. Amber Literary Award is named after the longtime editor of *Gun Digest* who was at the helm of the book from 1950 to 1979. Amber had instituted an award for the book's authors in 1967, named for the great shooting and hunting writer Townsend Whelen. In 1982, three years after Amber's retirement, the award was renamed in his honor. The winner of the award receives $1,000 and a handsome plaque honoring his achievement. Congratulations again to Charlie Petty, whose stories we look forward to presenting for your pleasure in future editions of *Gun Digest*.

Jerry Lee
Editor

WELCOME

to the 2017 71st Edition of *Gun Digest*!

Welcome to the *2017 Gun Digest*, the 71st annual edition of the complete go-to source for the firearms enthusiast. If you're new to *Gun Digest*, what you'll find in these pages are top writers in the shooting and outdoor fields sharing their experiences and opinions. Whether your interest in guns is for hunting, collecting, target shooting, personal protection or learning about the history of legendary models, there's something here for you. There are more than 30 feature articles, shooting tests, and Reports From the Field on the year's new guns, optics and handloading components, our comprehensive ballistics tables and a website directory to the entire firearms industry. The annual Firearms Catalog has descriptions and prices for virtually every handgun, rifle and shotgun currently in production, including muzzleloaders and airguns. All in all, our goal is to bring you the best all-in-one source for information on firearms and their uses.

We would like to welcome several new contributors to *Gun Digest* including Max Prasac, who wrote the "Revolvers and Others" report on the year's new revolvers, single-shots and derringers. Max was the author of *Gun Digest Book of Ruger Revolvers* that was published by Krause/Gun Digest Books a couple of years ago. Some other new bylines in this edition are Phil Shoemaker, Jerry Jacobson, Roger Smith and Doug Larson. Welcome to all.

Highlights of This Edition

One of the most famous handguns in the world, and some say the most famous, is the Luger. The former editor of a popular gun magazine told me a few years ago that every time they put a Luger on the cover, newsstand sales would skyrocket. It is still being made by various manufacturers 117 years after its introduction at the turn of the last century. Terry Wieland's story on the history, mystique and collectability of this famous pistol is a fine read and has some excellent photographs.

The year 2017 marks the 100th anniversary of the United States entering World War I, declaring war on Germany on April 4, 1917. Rick Hacker tells us about the weapons used by U.S. forces in what was supposed to be the War to End All Wars. Some became legends in firearms history, like the Springfield '03, the 1911 .45 pistol and the Winchester Model 1897 Trench Gun.

Tom Turpin takes a look at another piece of firearms history—the remarkable Model 98 Mauser rifle. Its roots go back more than 200 years and there have been a wide range of variants made by different manufactures. Recently the M98 has gone back into production in Germany and Tom provides a thorough review and test report on this most influential bolt-action rifle ever.

Wayne van Zwoll sorts out the growing list of 6.5mm rifles in his "Six-Five!" article. What once was a bore size often referred to as one that "never made it in America" is growing in popularity and moving out of the "cult" category. The newest is Weatherby's hot 6.5-300, with a velocity at 500 yards equaling that of the 6.5x55 at the muzzle. You'll find a lot more on the various .26's in Wayne's story.

Garry James knows more about three things than just about anyone I know: old guns, old movies – especially old movies that focus on guns, and European history. So no wonder his contribution to this edition is so good. It is a very well-researched story of the arms (not just the guns) of the "Gallant Six Hundred" in the infamous Charge of the Light Brigade in the Crimean War of 1854, when a British Light Cavalry made an ill-fated charge against Russian forces and faced many casualties. Garry explains the why and how of the charge, and why the sword and lance played a more effective role than the muzzleloading pistols and carbines of the time.

Some of the other features in this edition: One of the guns owned by Hank Williams, Jr., a double rifle, is now in the hands of Tom Tabor, who proudly tells us all about it in his story. John

Taffin explains why he believes Colt's finest single action is the current New Frontier; Nick Sisley and some of his world-class shooting pals share some good lessons for long-range shotgunning; Jim Wilson tells us why he loves the great Ruger No. 1 single-shot; Kevin Muramatsu reports on the growing popularity of suppressors; Phil Massaro says the .404 Jeffery is far from dead; Stan Trzoniec writes about Remington's role in the development and history of the semiauto shotgun; George Layman remembers the Auto Ordnance semiauto Thompson and Paul Scarlata has a nice story on the Winchester Model 1907. (These last three should serve as a reminder to certain politicians that the semiauto has been around awhile and is not some new "assault weapon.")

In our Testfire section, Doug Larson reviews the Ruger American Pistol, the latest in the American series of Rugers like the American Rifle and American Rimfire Rifle—so named to underscore the fact that all of its firearms are proudly made in the USA. The American Pistol is also on the cover of this edition. (See "About the Covers" on the following page.) Also in the Testfire department are three reviews that remind us that, for many, it is a .45 world. There's Dick Williams' report on the Ruger Redhawk revolver that handles both .45 Colt and .45 ACP cartridges, Steve Gash reviewing the Sharps .25-45 AR (a .223 case necked up to .25), and Jim Dickson's test of Charter Arms Pitbull, a compact revolver that handles .45 ACP ammo without half-moon or moon clips. Rounding out the Testfires is L.P. Brezny's review of the Smith & Wesson M&P 10 .308 rifle.

One of our most popular departments is the section called "One Good Gun," personal stories about specific guns during the writer's life. In this 2017 edition, we hope you enjoy Rick Hacker's "Colt 1860 Army," Robert Sadowski's "Shanghai Colt" and Will McGraw's "Remington Model 11."

Industry News

The firearms industry is doing quite well and according to a report by Frank Miniter in Forbes, is growing significantly to meet the continuing demand. The Bureau of Alcohol, Tobacco, Firearms and Explosives (ATF) reports that the number of gun manufacturers that make more than 50 guns per year grew from 318 in 2012 to 400 in 2014, an increase of more than 25 percent in two years. ATF always releases gun industry statistics a year after tabulating them. Not surprisingly many of these new companies are making AR-type rifles and parts. By now, virtually every major older manufacturer has a military style MSR (Modern Sporting Rifle) in its catalog, but the demand is still growing enough to support new start-ups.

Remington is celebrating its 200th anniversary as this edition goes to press. There are several special runs of iconic models like the Model 870 and 1100 shotguns, the Model 700 and 7600 rifles, and the 1911 R1 .45 pistol. Production is being limited to 2,016 guns during the year 2016 with C-grade American walnut stocks for the long guns and 24-karat engraving including a gold inlay portraying the founder, Eliphalet Remington, carrying a rifle. All of these may not be sold during 2016 but if you're reading this in 2017 and are interested, better act fast.

Winchester is also having an anniversary in 2016, its 150th, and is celebrating with several commemorative models, including the Model 1866 with a polished brass receiver, a grade V/VI satin-finished black walnut stock and fore-end, and a full-octagon 24-inch barrel. The famous Winchester Horse and Rider is on the receiver surrounded by lots of beautiful scroll engraving. Other classic Winchesters offered in 150th anniversary variations are the 1873, 1894 and Model 70 rifles, and the 101 over/under shotgun, all dressed up in high-grade wood and commemorative engraving. These are all limited-run models but Winchester has not announced what the total numbers will be.

Frank W. James 1946-2015

We are sorry to report that Frank James passed away in September of 2015, just a few weeks after our 2016 70th Edition was published. Frank wrote for several of the most popular gun magazines and had also contributed to *Gun Digest* in recent years. His articles and columns appeared in *Shooting Times, American Handgunner, Handguns, Guns, Combat Handguns* and other gun titles including several magazines that are published in Europe. Among his books were *Effective Handgun Defense* in 2004, and *The MP5 Submachine Gun* in 2003, both published by Krause/Gun Digest Books. His last contribution to *Gun Digest* was "The Machine Gun Investor" in the 2015 Edition. Frank lived in Indiana and was an avid Indy 500 fan, often covering racing for local newspapers. He was a fine storyteller, a great family man, an expert on guns and ammunition, and a good friend. Whenever you walked into a noisy, crowded party, you always knew when Frank was in the room from his joyful laugh. May he rest in peace.

Al Biesen 1918-2016

The custom gun world lost one of its best-known makers with the passing of Alvin Biesen on April 14, 2016, just a few weeks after his 98th birthday. Tom Turpin, our contributing editor for "Custom and Engraved Guns" was a friend of Al's and we asked him to give us his thoughts.

"Al Biesen was Jack O'Connor's favorite gunmaker and once told me that he had crafted well over 20 custom guns for the legendary outdoor writer, beginning with remodeling and re-stocking a 1903 Springfield in 1947 and ending when he delivered his final commission from O'Connor to his heirs after his passing in 1978. Al told me that first job did not overly please the iconic writer. As was the custom of the time, he adorned the stock with white line spacers and a high gloss finish. O'Connor had a case of his famous 'vapors' when he saw it for the first time. He kept the rifle with the admonition to Biesen to never do that again on his rifles. He didn't.

"Another story Al related to me was that when O'Connor passed away, Al of course attended the funeral. Jack had written on several occasions that his favorite rifle, the Biesen-crafted Model 70 that O'Connor called 'Number 2,' was so loved that he planned on having it buried with him. Al, not wanting the great one to run out of ammo, decided to smuggle a couple of .270 cartridges into Jack's casket at the funeral service. Thankfully, he learned just before dropping in the cartridges that the plans had changed and Jack was to be cremated. Al said, "Not wanting to send the old boy off with a bang, I took the cartridges back home with me."

The likes of Al Biesen are not apt to come our way again anytime soon. RIP —Tom Turpin"

Editor's note: O'Connor's rifle Number 2 and its companion Number 1 can be seen at the end of the "Custom and Engraved Rifles" story in this edition.

—Jerry Lee

Acknowledgements

The editor would like to thank our managing editor Chris Berens for his help and support in helping to create what we truly believe is The World's Greatest Gun Book. He plays a big role in the editing and production process and keeps us on schedule. We also appreciate the efforts and talents of designer Tom Nelsen for making *Gun Digest* one of the best looking books on the shelf.

ABOUT THE COVER

The newest Ruger with the proud, made-in-the-USA, all-American title is our cover gun, the Ruger American Pistol. It's a polymer-frame double-action-only striker-fired model with interchangeable backstraps. Put a flashlight on its integral rail and it makes an excellent home-defense weapon. It's available in 9mm or .45 ACP with magazine capacity of 17 or 10 rounds, respectively. The interchangeable backstraps make it easy to get a very comfortable ergonomic grip, making it an ideal handgun for the whole family. Other notable features include a trigger with a short take-up and positive reset, a barrel cam designed to reduce recoil, a low center of gravity and bore axis, Novak LoMount Carry three-dot sights, ambidextrous slide stop and magazine release, and a safe and easy takedown system with no tools required. An added safety feature is that the takedown does not require a trigger pull. Each pistol comes with two nickel-Teflon plated steel magazines. Suggested retail price for the Ruger American Pistol is $579.00.

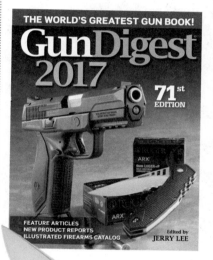

Also shown on the cover are two new product categories for Ruger, ammo and knives. Ruger ARX Ammunition is cutting-edge handgun ammo designed for personal defense. ARX bullets are a unique design that is engineered for maximum hydraulic displacement and terminal energy transfer to the target. Available in .380 ACP, 9mm and .45 ACP, Ruger has announced that a .40 caliber is coming soon. Light bullets made from a copper/polymer compound achieve higher velocities than traditional ammo. The .380 has a 56-grain bullet with a muzzle velocity of 1,315 fps, the 9mm is 80 grains at 1,445 fps, and the .45 Auto has a 118-grain bullet at 1,410 fps. Ruger ARX ammo is made in the USA by PolyCase Ammunition under license from Sturm, Ruger & Co.

The new Ruger line of knives are designed by five master knife-smiths and come in many varying styles and sizes. Shown on the cover and on this page is the Follow-Through folding model with locking liner and blade flipper. It features a stonewashed 3.75-inch drop-point, flattop blade. Ruger knives are manufactured by CRKT (Columbia River Knife and Tool), one of the most respected knife makers in America for more than 20 years. In addition to the Follow-Through, there are several other Ruger knife models, and here's important news: you can go to **www.gundigeststore.com** to check out the selection and place an order for one of six different Follow-Through models.

Gun Digest Staff

Jerry Lee, Editor
Chris Berens, Managing Editor

CONTRIBUTING EDITORS

John Haviland: Shotguns
Kevin Muramatsu: Handguns/Autoloaders
Max Prasac: Revolvers and Others
Wm. Hovey Smith: Muzzleloaders

Phil Massaro: Ammunition, Ballistics & Components
Tom Tabor: Optics
Tom Turpin: Custom and Engraved Guns
Wayne van Zwoll: Rifles

TABLE OF CONTENTS
2017 GunDigest®

2017 FIREARMS CATALOG

This DWM IP.08 with its 8-inch barrel was known as the artillery model.

The incomparably graceful, highly collectible, and most famous handgun in the world

LUGERS
"The Lure and the Lore"

By Terry Wieland

In 1987, Gun Digest Books published *Handgun Digest*, a volume similar to the one you are reading now, but devoted entirely to pistols. One of its chapters was contributed by the late Chuck Karwan, a noted handgun writer of that time who was also a keen gun collector. Karwan was looking at handguns as "collectible" items, and reflected on how prices had climbed, notably in the 30 years between 1957 and 1987.

In fairness, we could have picked from two dozen articles published since 1945 reflecting on climbing gun prices, and asking the same question: "How much higher can they go?" Those articles usually had a particular focus, such as Parker shotguns, Winchester Model 70s or Colt Peacemakers. But almost all came to the same conclusion: That the market had peaked. Almost all were wrong. The

actual answer to "How much higher...?" was virtually without exception, "A lot..."

Most articles about gun collecting ignore the larger world and why prices climb in the first place. Often, it has little or nothing to do with intrinsic value, and everything to do with financial and investment trends, the state of the U.S. dollar, and the plight of the mega-rich, desperately searching for a safe haven for their billions. In the 30 years since Karwan's article, the financial world has been rocked by many forces, but the dominant trend has been toward ever-lower interest rates. Karwan was writing as the high-inflation period of 1975 to 1985 ended, and interest rates began their downward path from 20 percent to — eventually — virtually zero.

For decades, the safest haven for large amounts of money was U.S. treasury bills and, for the average investor, money-

market funds. They might not pay much, but the money was absolutely safe and readily accessible. As this haven gradually disappeared, wealthy people looked for alternatives. Among these were Impressionist paintings, South Dakota farmland, and not least, collectible firearms. This trend has been particularly noticeable since 2008, when the financial crisis forced interest rates to zero. In the intervening eight years, the inflation rate has also been virtually zero, but you would never know it by looking at the prices of Impressionist paintings.

When a van Gogh sells for $200 million, it drags up the prices of lesser works in its slipstream; when prime South Dakota farmland hits $6,000 an acre, less desirable acreage also appreciates; and when the world's most coveted pistol sells for a million bucks, then others of the ilk will also rise. That is the way of the financial world.

From top: Luger carbine, IP.08 and 1908 commercial model, all by DWM. Until 1912, when production began at the Royal Rifle Factory in Erfurt, all Lugers were manufactured by DWM, the company that developed the pistol.

A financial analyst looking at gun collecting today, with interest rates beginning to rise and inflation allegedly stirring, and general unrest around the world, might conclude that this is another "top of the market" and that potential buyers would be wise to wait until prices settle. Our purpose here is not to argue one way or the other, but only to look at the trends of past decades. On that basis, it seems that making a shrewd gun buy here and there is almost never a bad investment, regardless of market tops and bottoms. Hold it long enough, and it will go up.

***

This is not to suggest that buying guns randomly will always make you money. Too many articles, such as John T. Amber's "My Triumphs in Gun Collecting" (GD #35, 1981) show how it is all too easy to lose money on bad investments, or throw away potential gains by selling too soon or for too little. For example, a man who in 1965 traded a nice vintage Colt Peacemaker for a spiffy new Winchester Model 59, with its aluminum receiver and fiberglass-wrapped barrel, would have thrown away, potentially, thousands. The man on the other end of that trade, who might have seemed the loser at the time, would have done very, very well if he had hung on to the Peacemaker.

This is the kind of broad statement that is easy to defend and difficult to disprove, and journalistic integrity demands some qualification. In the last 50 years, a gun buyer could well have ridden a trend, bought at the top of a market, and been left holding a gun now worth a fraction of what he paid. For example, the late 1990s saw a sudden resurgence in interest in external-hammer shotguns, and even a 1901 Sears clunker commanded a premium price.

The wave passed, and today hammer shotguns have fallen back to reasonable prices — still higher than in 1980, but considerably less than in 2000. The only real market now is for good hammer guns, not clunkers. By coincidence, you might have put the same money into NASDAQ in 2000, and not have recovered your money even now. It could well have disappeared completely, in fact, depending on how adventurous you were. If you had spent that money on a shotgun instead, you would at least have had the fun of shooting it for 17 years.

What are the good gun investments? Among others, there are Colt Peacemakers, Parker shotguns and anything with the name Winchester (well, almost

The distinctive, flowing "DWM" engraved on the toggle denotes the finest quality of manufacturing, fit and finish of *Deutschewaffen- undMunitionsfabriken.*

Commercial Luger made by DWM in 1908. As the earliest and most successful of the new semiauto pistols, the Luger found immediate admirers among the nonmilitary. Raymond Chandler's private eye, Philip Marlowe, often carried a Luger.

anything). Since 1990, double rifles have been almost unbeatable and original Mauser commercial bolt rifles are doing almost as well as pre-'64 Winchester Model 70s. Parkers have dragged the other American doubles up along with them, and the recent Colt 1911 craze has pumped up the prices of original military 1911s in their various iterations. In the last five years or so prices for Colt Pythons have doubled or tripled, depending on the configuration, and look to continue climbing.

However, the reigning monarch of the gun collecting world is the Luger. Now 117 years old, the Luger is the most collected firearm in the world, easily the most collectible (we'll explain shortly) and the best investment when viewed through a long lens. It is safe to say that, without exception, a mint Luger purchased in 1935 would be worth today thousands of times what was paid originally. That is completely aside from the effects of inflation, market tops or bottoms, or changing tastes. How many

other investments made in 1935 and left on their own for 80 years would have done as well, aside from a Monet?

From a collecting viewpoint, the Luger is unique. On its side it has history, variety, international interest and several substrata of collecting, including accoutrements, accessories and counterfeits. It also fits into subcategories of other areas of collecting, such as Nazi artifacts from the Second World War. An aeronautics enthusiast interested in the Luftwaffe might have a Krieghoff-made Luger as part of a larger collection that includes an airworthy Messerschmitt Bf 109. A far-fetched example, but not impossible.

The Luger, which was more or less perfected as a design in 1900 and reached its apogee with the 1908 German Army 9mm Parabellum, spans two world wars, the Spanish Civil War, the Russian Revolution and the re-arming of the U.S. cavalry after 1898. It was manufactured by some of the greatest names in gunmaking – DWM, Mauser, Krieghoff and Vickers, and includes everything from military sidearms to target pistols to hunting carbines with detachable stocks. There are presentation models, military-issue pistols, commercial models and hunting guns.

Lugers were owned by such notables as Kaiser Wilhelm II and President Theodore Roosevelt. It has appeared in literature (Raymond Chandler's private eye, Philip Marlowe, carried a Luger) and movies like Casablanca.

No one could have predicted when DWM ordered gun designer Georg Luger to rework the functional but awkward Borchardt, that he would create one of the all-time great pistols, but that is exactly what happened. In 1898, the great powers were all searching for semiautos to replace black-powder revolvers. Hugo Borchardt's design, a solid-lock breech mechanism employing a toggle, had proven mechanically sound but difficult to shoot. Borchardt, who considered his design perfect, refused to make any changes. Since DWM owned the patent, it was within its rights to assign Luger to the task.

Like Paul Mauser and Samuel Colt, Georg Luger was one of those rare individuals in the history of gun design who was almost a genius in his intuition for mechanics, who developed one pattern to perfection, and then stopped. Like Colt, Luger had charm, flamboyance and a talent for selling. After perfecting the broad design in 1900 Luger became DWM's foremost globe-trotting salesman for military arms-buying commissions around the world.

The first country to adopt the Luger was Switzerland. The Swiss model was chambered for the original .30 Luger (7.65mm) bottlenecked cartridge, and also employed the original grip safety. The Luger hung on as Switzerland's military sidearm until 1948, longer than

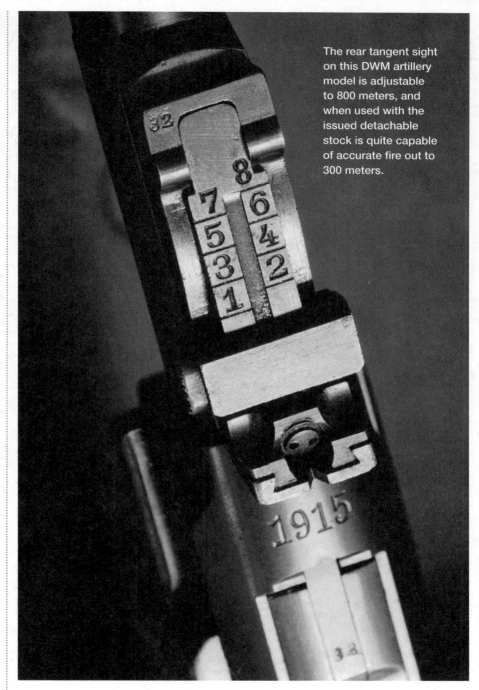

The rear tangent sight on this DWM artillery model is adjustable to 800 meters, and when used with the issued detachable stock is quite capable of accurate fire out to 300 meters.

any of the 20 or so other countries that eventually adopted it.

From 1900 through 1914 the Luger was modified to meet various requirements. The German navy, for example, wanted a 6-inch barrel, while the German army insisted on a more powerful cartridge and dispensed with the grip safety. The *Pistole '08*, or P.'08 as it came to be known, chambered for the 9mm Luger, remained the official German army sidearm until 1938, although it stayed in production until 1942 and in use through 1945.

Between 1900 and 1913, Georg Luger travelled the world, introducing his pistol to foreign armies. The U.S. considered it and even prevailed upon Luger to produce a couple in .45 caliber. In the end, it bought about a thousand pistols in .30 Luger and even issued them to some cavalry units (thereby making the Luger, at least briefly, an official U.S. sidearm) before adopting the .45-caliber Colt Model 1911.

Other notable Luger users included Czarist Russia, the Netherlands, Sweden,

DWM Luger carbine, built on the 1906 (pre-P.08) frame, with its handsome detachable walnut stock. Kaiser Wilhelm II particularly enjoyed hunting with his Luger because it was easily manageable with his damaged left arm.

Portugal, Bulgaria, Persia, Siam and various Latin American countries. Even the British considered the Luger, but rejected it as lacking the stopping power required for colonial policing operations.

Meanwhile, Luger had been pursuing commercial markets as well, producing Lugers in civilian models of different barrel lengths and configurations. Detachable stocks for pistols were popular at this time, and DWM marketed "carbines" with wooden fore-ends, detachable stocks and barrels varying in length up to 16 inches or more. These prestige products were used as presentation items (as with Kaiser Wilhelm and Theodore Roosevelt) as well as for general sale. Not many were made and sold, but by 1914 the Luger mystique was well established.

***

In any discussion of gun collecting one has to address the question of aura, romance, mystique. These are rather vague terms, but important nonetheless.

The Luger's rivals for the title of most-collectible handgun would be the Colt Peacemaker, foremost, with the Colt Model 1911 and maybe the Broomhandle Mauser getting some votes. At any given time, either a Luger or a Peacemaker will hold the distinction of being the most expensive pistol ever sold at auction, and these prices rise and fall with larger concerns, like the interest rate.

Why, then, is the Peacemaker (a.k.a., Colt Single Action Army, or SAA) not the most collectible? There are those who insist it is, but objective dealers generally give the Luger the nod. The Luger and the Peacemaker come from completely different backgrounds, but they have one thing in common: Ergonomically they are superb, and both have racy, attractive lines that are still distinctive more than a century (117 years for the Luger, 144 for the Colt) after they were introduced.

In his article on gun collecting, Chuck Karwan referred to the Luger as "incomparably graceful," and it is impossible to come up with a better description. The Luger is instantly recognizable, even to non-gun people. It was designed when

"art nouveau" dominated the age and designers of everything from bicycles to bath tubs sought to make their creations "usable art." At the same time, it was the golden age of craftsmanship, especially in gunmaking. Hugo Borchardt may have had no eye for graceful lines (witness the Sharps-Borchardt rifle) but Georg Luger certainly did. Not only did he create a technological marvel of ingenious assembly, he gave it sculpted lines that would please da Vinci.

No one can pick up a Luger and not run his hands over it, marveling at the sheer feel of it. The same is true of a Purdey shotgun, a Holland & Holland double rifle, some of the early Mannlicher-Schönauer bolt actions and the Colt Single Action Army — but none more so than the Luger. Although it survived in serious military use into the 1950s, it is really an artifact from a bygone age. On most Lugers, the fitting and finishing of the parts, inside and out, is on a par with the lockwork of a Rigby or the workings of a Swiss watch. No admirer of precision machinery can resist the Luger.

From Greta Garbo onward, admirers of beautiful women have looked for two qualities: Physical beauty and an element of mystery. And again, like Garbo, the Luger has both.

It is estimated that about 3.5 million Lugers were produced during its 48-year initial life span by seven major companies. This total is only an estimate because no one will ever know for certain. Up to 1914, as the Luger was adopted by the German military and international tensions rose, aspects of Luger production were either proprietary industrial information or a military secret. After 1918, the Treaty of Versailles severely limited Luger production, dictating such things as caliber and barrel length. As DWM sought to get around trade restrictions, and later as the German government began to circumvent Versailles and rearm, production figures and details were deliberately obscured. Finally, large chunks of Germany's military archives were destroyed by the Allied bombing of Potsdam in the final weeks of the Second World War, while other records fell into the hands of the Red army.

As a result of 45 years of secrecy, obfuscation, deception and wartime destruction, many questions about Luger production numbers, models, barrel lengths and individual design features can never be documented. Its history is pieced together like a puzzle. Over the years many books have been written about the Luger. Some are more accurate than others, yet all offer the opportunity to quote previous works, thereby quite often perpetuating myths, misinformation and outright lies.

For any Luger collector, these mysteries are both a gold mine and a mine field. They produce rarities, but also provide opportunities for unscrupulous dealers and collectors to "create" rarities where none exist. The collector's best defense against this is knowledge, and understanding of Luger history begins with the companies that made it.

DWM (*Deutschewaffen- undMunitionsfabriken*) was part of the industrial empire of Ludwig Loewe of Berlin. He was an early investor in Mauser and eventually owned the company; he also owned munitions factories in the Austro-Hungarian Empire, and Loewe financed the start-up of Fabrique Nationale (FN) in Belgium, to produce Mauser rifles for the Belgian army.

From 1900 to 1910, all Lugers had DWM's graceful, flowing initials stamped on the toggle. As tensions rose and war was imminent, it became obvious to the German government that DWM would not be able to produce enough Lugers, so production capacity was added at the Royal Rifle Factory in Erfurt, outside Berlin, in 1910. Erfurt Lugers were made until 1918.

In 1916 the Germans developed a high-capacity magazine (32 rounds) for the lP.08 that came to be known as the "snail drum" because of its shape. Original snail drums are serious collectors' items in themselves. Use of the snail drum and shoulder stock in the trench warfare of 1917-18 led directly to the development of the submachine gun.

Luger carbines were never a production item but were manufactured one at a time, in various factories, over many years. As such, although they are a valued collector's item, they are difficult to categorize. This also makes them a ready target for counterfeiters. This one is a genuine DWM, circa 1906.

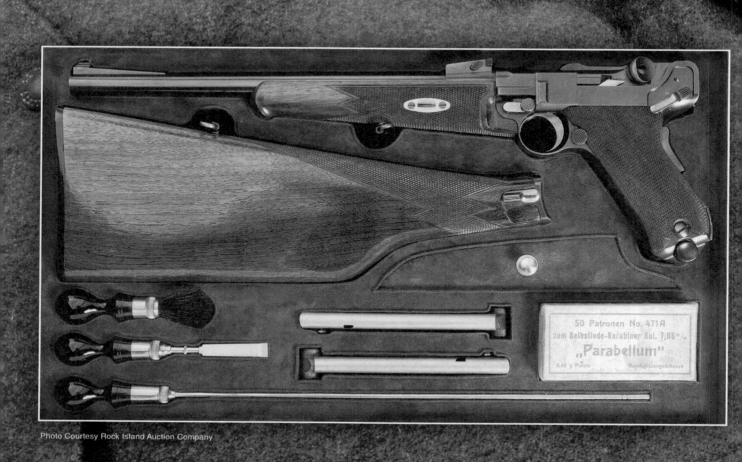

50 Patronen No. 471A
zum Selbstlade-Karabiner Kal. 7,65 m/m
„Parabellum"

0,40 g Pulver   Rundspitzengeschosse

Photo Courtesy Rock Island Auction Company

Since it was a government arms plant, Luger lore contends that Erfurt guns are not as finely finished as DWMs, but that is a question best left to the experts. However, Erfurt pistols do provide a subcategory for collectors. After 1918 the situation became confused with former army pistols being reworked for police issue, DWM producing certain models allowed under the Versailles Treaty, and most military production allocated to Simson & Co., of Suhl. Simson Lugers were produced until the early 1930s, at which time the company was "Aryanized" because of its Jewish ownership.

Ironically, Ludwig Loewe was also Jewish, but that corporate breakup occurred at Allied insistence after 1918. The name was changed, but reverted to DWM around 1930.

By this time, the last major remaining arms-making operation from the former Loewe/DWM empire was Mauser. Mauser became the sole maker of Lugers in 1932. Production continued until 1942 when the last German Luger came off the assembly line.

Heinrich Krieghoff of Suhl was the only other German manufacturer, having received a contract to produce Lugers for the Luftwaffe during the 1930s.

Two non-German companies were involved in Luger production. Vickers Sons & Maxim, of England, had corporate ties to the Loewe empire before and after the Great War. When the Dutch needed replacement parts and guns in the late 1920s DWM was forbidden to produce them even though they had supplied the neutral Dutch all through the war. To get around the rules, DWM produced semi-finished guns, shipped them to England to be finished and proofed by Vickers, and then shipped on to the Netherlands. This accounts for the Vickers name and English proofmarks on some Lugers.

Finally, the Swiss began making their own Lugers at Bern in 1918, and production continued there until the Luger was replaced by the SIG in 1948.

Given this history, the opportunities for collecting and specialization are almost endless. Some specialize in DWMs, others in Erfurts, or Swiss Lugers; some collect by year, looking for examples of every Luger made in 1908, or 1915; others want only Lugers with Nazi proofmarks; still others want guns from the Great War.

By comparison with this embarrassment of riches, the rival Peacemaker seems almost one-dimensional. Its records are mostly intact, its origins limited to one company, its history largely confined to the American West. Colt collectors have divided and subdivided, as collectors will, and now even identify the individual inspector who approved a gun before it left the plant, with some being more finicky than others. Even so, compared to the multifaceted Luger, this is grasping at differentiating straws.

The Colt Model 1911 is better off, with various companies from Ithaca to Singer to Remington-Rand producing guns under government contract, but still it was used by only one major army (the U.S.) and interest is limited largely to the United States.

This brings up another aspect of collecting. The Luger has been collected virtually since it was introduced, but serious, widespread interest in the Peacemaker began only in the 1950s with television Westerns. This also sparked interest in Winchester lever actions. Suddenly, inspired by Matt Dillon and Wyatt Earp, gun nuts began buying Colts and quick-draw rigs, and interest in old Colts began to take off. It has never stopped. The question is, how long will it go on?

The generation of collectors that watched those TV Westerns is dying off. Will interest in the Colt SAA survive their departure? No one can say for sure, but when you are counting on someone to step up and bid one or two million dollars for an arcane SAA made in 1892, it becomes a matter of more than academic interest. It has long been a truism of the collecting game that any gun is worth *only* what someone else is willing to pay you for it. If the number of collectors with a particular interest dwindles, so will prices paid.

Another consideration, as collectors depart and their collections are put on the market, is the effect of dilution. As this is being written, several large and important Luger collections have been sold off, and this has resulted in some prices being depressed, or at least leveling off. If the market is big enough and diverse enough, then it should be what the stockbrokers call a "buying opportunity," rather than the beginning of the end.

* * *

The question of who you will get to buy your collection is a real consideration after a certain age. After all, you may have accumulated guns instead of putting money into real estate or a 401(k). There is always the risk that you will end up with an accumulation of scrap metal that is of interest to no one except the police.

There is no foolproof advice for gun collectors to make money, any more than a stockbroker can guarantee to make you rich on Wall Street. However, there are a few rules that can make life less risky.

When he was living in Paris in the 1920s, Ernest Hemingway became interested in art and wanted to buy paintings. He turned to his friend Gertrude Stein, herself an art collector, for advice, complaining that no matter how much he economized on food and clothing, he could never afford the Picassos he wanted. Miss Stein advised him to buy the works of painters of his own age, his own "military service group."

With a few twists, this advice can be applied to firearms. Those who invested in like-new military rifles when they were cheap and plentiful in the 1960s, and kept them in good, original condition, now have some serious collectors' pieces. The same is true of those who bought English double rifles in obscure calibers. In 1977, Abercrombie & Fitch listed new Purdeys in their catalogue at $2,700. A Purdey .470 Nitro Express would be worth, today and conservatively, $100,000? More? But, in 1977, $2,700 looked outlandish.

Closer to home, when I was a kid, I hungered for a Marlin Model 62 Levermatic in .256 Winchester Magnum. True to form, when I reached an age of nostalgia for youth, I started looking for one to fulfill the dream at long last. Finally, I found one about five years ago, bought it for $300, spent another $300 on a scope and mounts and a little repair work. For the next few years I kept track of Marlin Levermatics in their various models (56, 57, 57M, 62) and found that prices were climbing steadily. Today, the rifle I bought for $300 commands about $600, and I have even seen one dealer with a pair of them, asking $1,995 apiece!

As a company, Marlin does not attract a fraction of the attention given to Winchester, even though it has a comparable history and products. Remington and Smith & Wesson could make the same complaints, and who can explain it? However, it is a fact that if you can't afford to collect Winchesters, you turn to Marlins or Savages or Remingtons, and if you can't afford Colts, there is always Smith & Wesson. This is another manifestation of the slipstream effect.

From this, it is obvious that the route to a collection that is affordable today, but which will be valuable tomorrow, is to buy what will be popular, not necessarily what is popular. Since no one can predict the future this advice is questionable at best, but look at it this way: If you buy what is out of favor today, you won't be risking much money. If the value of my Levermatic dropped to zero, I would not be out much.

Recognizing the role of gun collections as places to park money, some dealers have begun advertising in terms of "investment-grade" guns, which is as good a reason to flee as I can think of. If nothing else, you will be paying "investment" prices. Moving in such circles requires a level of expertise that most gun collectors wish they had, but generally do not.

But let's go back to Lugers for a moment. It is an accepted principle of collecting that two qualities are paramount: Rarity and condition. Condition includes factory originality, and condition trumps rarity except where rarity trumps condition. Say you were offered a 1916 DWM Luger, all original, good bluing, good bore and all the numbers matched. Military contractors stamped the last two digits of the serial number on all the minor parts including grips, sideplate, extractor, toggle, etc., so that when the gun was dismantled by an armorer he could match up all the right parts. A Luger with mismatching numbers could be a gun assembled from parts, or at the very least, not factory original or "as issued."

A gun in good condition with matching numbers, if kept this way, will go up in price as sure as the sun rises in the east. Essentially, it has no choice. If you pay $1,500 for it today and sell it in five years for $2,500, you've done well. Alternatively, say you are offered a real rarity for $50,000, and go to sell it in five years only to find that the market for that particular oddity has stagnated. You've tied up a large (for me, anyway) sum of money, for no return. Taking this a step further, if you have $50,000 to spend on collectible guns, you are better off to buy 20 good ones at $2,500 apiece than to spend the whole roll on one gun. It spreads your risk in many ways.

Also, one should keep in mind that counterfeiting does take place — in Lugers, Peacemakers, Rigby doubles and anything else you can name that is very valuable — but rarely is a piece of low to medium value counterfeited. Why? Because it's more effort than it's worth. There is safety in the middle of the pack. I lose no sleep worrying that some charlatan is going to counterfeit my Marlin Levermatic.

* * *

The IP.08 (*langePistole '08*), commonly called the artillery model, has an 8-inch barrel and comes equipped with a detachable shoulder stock that is combined with a special holster. The IP.08 was manufactured by DWM and Erfurt, from about 1913 to 1918.

In any area of gun collecting, knowledge is your best defense, and knowledge comes primarily from books and credible magazine articles. There are many more authoritative, comprehensive, accurate firearms reference works today than there were 20 or 30 years ago. Dr. Geoffrey Sturgess, probably the world's foremost Luger collector and authority, co-authored (with Joachim Görtz) a three-volume work on Lugers. The first edition was published in Canada and the second in the U.S. by Simpson, Ltd. of Galesburg, Illinois. Robert Simpson also happens to be the world's largest Luger dealer.

Sturgess' book runs to near 2,000 pages; the table of contents alone is 42 pages. At close to $400, it's not cheap, but for a prospective Luger collector there is no better investment.

The second investment I would make is to buy a (relatively) inexpensive, mismatched, noncollector-type Luger (what is often referred to as a "shooter") and learn how to take it apart, put it together, make it run and see exactly how it works. Familiarity with the mechanism and actual shooting pays dividends. It gives you a basis of comparison. This will probably cost another $1,200 or so at today's prices.

The third step is to establish a relationship with a solid, reputable dealer. Again, with Lugers, Robert Simpson would be a good place to start. He knows them inside out and guarantees the authenticity of everything he sells, not just for a few days, but for the time you own the gun. If you find that Simpson sold you something that later turns out not to be as described — and it happens occasionally with everyone — he will make it good.

The Internet has had a huge influence on gun collecting generally, both through gun sales and the proliferation of "information" that may or — far more likely — may *not* be accurate. From gun dealers' websites to collector forums, to Wikipedia entries, the Internet is a minefield of misrepresentation and misinformation. This is not to say that every dealer's website is a trap, only that a guy operating out of a back room, or no room at all, can, with a good web page, make his shoestring operation look like the second coming of Griffin & Howe.

On the positive side, a site like Gun Broker can show you, in real-life terms, what a particular gun is likely to sell for. Any gun is worth *only* what someone else is willing to pay you for it. If you are looking for something in particular, these sites can give you real insight into both availability and prevailing prices.

A final good investment at the beginning is to buy books like the *Standard Catalog of Firearms* and *Standard Catalog of Military Firearms* from Gun Digest Books. More important, keep them, and even look for older editions on eBay, Amazon or used-book stores. Knowing what a gun was worth in 1987 can be extremely valuable when buying one in 2017. They are part of a gun collector's essential reference library.

For confirmation, all I need to do is pull Handgun Digest off the shelf and read what Chuck Karwan had to say 30 years ago, or John T. Amber a few years before that. What Karwan had to say about 1957, we can now say about 1987. How much higher can they go? Very likely, a lot. But of course, there are no guarantees.

SIX-FIVE!

What's in a number? Rich history and a host of cartridges—including the latest big-game hotrods!

By Wayne van Zwoll

I'd ordered a Ruger Hawkeye in 6.5 Creedmoor, but hunting season arrived first. Todd Seyfert at Magnum Research scrambled to deliver a test rifle on a long Remington 700 action. Its long carbon-fiber barrel had a stainless core rifled by Kreiger and chambered for the Creedmoor. GreyBull Precision sent a stock and a 4.5-14x Leupold with GreyBull elevation dial to match the arc of Hornady 129-grain bullets.

A few days later on a frosty morning, a pal coaxed a hungry coyote across a sunny mesa. As the dog skidded to a halt 250 yards off, I began a measured crush from the sit. The coyote collapsed.

The elk that season proved less compliant. After John and Phil and I joined outfitter Ray Milligan near his Chama, N.M., digs, we saw plenty of animals; but branch-antlered bulls were scarce.

Then, one evening on the hem of a sprawling sage basin, we caught a break.

A band of elk sifted through the purple shadows half a mile distant. They were moving away.

"We can get closer." Ray Milligan tried to inject optimism.

"Let's do it fast," I hissed, picking up the pace. Only minutes of legal light remained.

The others stayed on my heels through the pinions. We scooted up a spine until it fell abruptly to the sea of sage below. The elk loafed toward its far shore.

"Six hundred." Ray's Leica Geovid binocular confirmed John's read.

"Too far." I shook my head, gulping wind.

"Get ready." Ray urged. It was good advice. Whatever the range, you make final decisions after you're ready to fire, not before.

Sliding the sling up my arm, I flopped prone and chambered a round, then spun the elevation dial to six. Dead-still air promised zero drift. Confident in rifle, scope and load, I hesitated. This elk was twice as far as any I'd shot at in 35 years of hunting. I had passed shots at many closer bulls, hewing to my "90 percent" rule. Only when sure I could make the shot nine times in 10 tries, would I fire. Here, 600 yards from my target, the smallest error in hold or execution would likely cause a miss or crippling hit. Follow-up hits would be difficult when the elk moved, trailing in the dark at least as challenging.

Still, my position was solid, the air absolutely still. I felt excuses slipping away.

"Trust the dial," John whispered. "Remember, you kept all the bullets in a 12-inch gong at 500."

The raghorn bull was quartering to. Not yet. My finger came taut. The cross-wire quivered in the shoulder crease. The bull turned slightly and stopped, tawny ribs gold in the orange slanting light of dusk.

The 6.5 Creedmoor is an unlikely star. Announced in 2009, it was named after Creed's Farm in New York, birthplace of long-range rifle matches in the U.S. This short-action cartridge was developed by Hornady's Dave Emary in consultation with 1,000-yard competitors. Rather than imply Winchester's .308 case, Dave chose the shorter .30 T/C, whose neck kept long pointed bullets within limits imposed by short magazines. He used powder from the company's Superformance project. This 6.5 hurls sleek bullets that exit on

the heels of 130-grain spitzers from a .270 Winchester. Past 400 yards, their superior ballistic coefficient narrows the gap, then erases it. The Creedmoor's modest recoil has broadened its appeal. Sales have jetted past those of magnum cartridges that gulp twice as much powder and launch the 7mm and .30-caliber bullets so popular with American hunters.

I adore the Creedmoor. I've used it

on deer, elk, pronghorns and African antelopes. I've fired it in competition to 1,200 yards. This cartridge is easy to shoot well; its bullets (120 GMX, 129 SST and 140 ELD) fly very flat at the far end of their arc and gamely battle wind. It seems inherently accurate, deadlier than its size suggests. Short rifle actions feed it smoothly. Here's what to expect downrange:

The 6.5 Creedmoor (left) is based on the .30 T/C, trumps the 6.5x55 with long bullets in short actions.

FACTORY LOADS FOR THE 6.5 CREEDMOOR (EXTERIOR BALLISTICS)

120 A-MAX (HORNADY)	MUZZLE	100 YDS.	200 YDS.	300 YDS.	400 YDS.
Velocity, fps	2910	2712	2522	2340	2166
Energy, ft-lbs	2256	1959	1695	1459	1250
Arc, inches	–1.5	1.6	0	–7.1	–20.5

129 SST (HORNADY)	MUZZLE	100 YDS.	200 YDS.	300 YDS.	400 YDS.
Velocity, fps	2950	2756	2570	2392	2221
Energy, ft-lbs	2492	2175	1892	1639	1417
Arc, inches	–1.5	1.5	0	–6.8	–19.7

140 A-MAX (HORNADY)	MUZZLE	100 YDS.	200 YDS.	300 YDS.	400 YDS.
Velocity, fps	2710	2557	2409	2266	2128
Energy, ft-lbs	2238	2032	1804	1596	1408
Arc, inches	–1.5	1.9	0	–7.9	–22.6

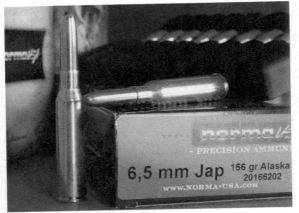

The 6.5 Arisaka appeared in 1897, but wasn't adopted by the Japanese army until 1905, in the M38 rifle.

You might ask why such a cartridge didn't arrive sooner. Good question.

There's no magic, or inborn failing, in the diameter of a rifle's bore or bullet. But 6.5s have long struggled for acceptance stateside. It's not that they can't kill. A century ago, explorer Frederick Courtney Selous and W.D.M. Bell used the mild 6.5x54 Mannlicher-Schoenauer to down elephants. Its long, solid bullets penetrated thick pachyderm skulls to reach the brain. Both hunters were fine marksmen. Charles Sheldon also liked the 6.5x54, and carried it for Alaskan brown bears and moose. The trim Mannlicher-Schoenauer carbines popular in this chambering endeared themselves to far-ranging hunters.

Superior ballistic coefficients flatten the arcs of bullets at extreme range and reduce their wind drift.

Initially a Greek military cartridge, the 6.5x54 M-S joined a bevy of similar rounds following the arrival of smokeless powder in the 1890s. Italy snared the 6.5x52 Mannlicher-Carcano for its infantry in 1891. The rimmed 6.3x53R Mannlicher was picked up by Dutch and Romanian military units in 1892. Sweden's 6.5x55 armed that country's soldiers in 1894—and endures as a popular big-game round. The 6.5x50 Arisaka came along in 1897 in a rifle deemed unsuitable, but was adopted by the Japanese army in the Model 38 rifle eight years later. The 6.5x57 (and 6.5x57R) never made its way into uniform, but after its 1894 introduction began a long history in the hunting field. Several other 6.5s developed in Europe in the early 20th century flamed out. The high-octane 6.5x68 Schuler, introduced by RWS in 1939, did not.

Years ago, hunting in Spain for ibex, I was down to my last hours with no prospects for success. A local sportsman, hearing my sad story, insisted I hunt with him one more afternoon. "You can use my rifle." I consented. Late that day, we spied a big ram hundreds of yards off. "Shoot from here," he urged, assuring me his 6.5x68 shot so flat I didn't have to hold high. Politely I demurred, and suggested a stalk. We paused on a rock ledge across from the ram, where my amigo again told me to fire. "Too far," I said, offering to go on alone. He threw up his hands. But fortune favored me; some minutes later I made a 200-yard shot, prone, dropping the ibex. It was a memorable hunt, the only one I've made with a 6.5x68.

The much more common 6.5x55 Swedish has joined me on several trips. Less potent than long-action 6.5s, it's still a versatile cartridge and has no doubt killed more moose in its native country than any other round. Once, poking through Wyoming lodgepoles with a Howa rifle in 6.5x55, I bounced two elk from a finger ridge. They crashed off into the canyon below, one sweeping right, one left. I dashed forward, veered left and found a shot alley as that bull paused. Lung-shot, the animal plunged downslope. I stumbled after it, and tagged it once more, ending the hunt. My 140-grain softpoints clock about 2,650 fps; traditional 156-grain roundnose bullets loaf along at 2,550. Swedish hunters say that's fast enough.

The 6.5x55 feeds smoothly. It performs well in short barrels and recoils gently. My 1896 Swedish military carbine with

Wayne got this bull with a 129-grain Hornady SST from a Magnum Research rifle in 6.5 Creedmoor.

Wayne used a modified Swedish military carbine in 6.5x55 to take this pronghorn in winter weather.

Winchester's .264 Magnum still excels for mule deer. It dates to 1959 with 140-grain bullets at 3,200 fps.

in 1959, gave shooters a high-octane 6.5. Based on the belted .458 (circa 1956), the .264 was touted as a hotrod deer/varmint round. "It makes a helluva noise and packs a helluva wallop!" claimed the ads—without noting its suitability for elk-size game. Shooters were not impressed. Claims of rapid throat wear hamstrung the .264. The similar 7mm Remington Magnum (same case, just .02" bigger in diameter at the mouth) was, at its 1962 debut, cleverly described and loaded as a deer and elk round. It almost killed the .264. Winchester put a nail in the coffin when it reduced .264 Magnum starting velocities in its ballistics tables from 3,200 fps to 3,030 for the 140-grain Power Point. The .270 Winchester had better numbers.

Many moons ago, after concluding my $35 Short Magazine Lee Enfield didn't reach far enough to kill every deer I wanted to bag, I got hungry for a .264. Months of milking cows left enough coin in my jeans for a Mark X barreled action and a walnut blank from Royal Arms. Months later, I thumbed three shiny cartridges into the rifle's belly. But I had neglected to bed the lug tighter than the tang. The figured Claro splintered at my first shot. My long road back finally yielded a whitetail buck.

Loaded to its potential and fired in a 26-inch barrel, the .264 Magnum can launch 140s faster that even original factory claims. With slow powders like IMR 7828 and RL-25, I've clocked Sierra spitzers at 3,300 fps. No pressure signals. The superior ballistic coefficients of 140- and 150-grain 6.5mm bullets give the .264 Winchester an edge on same-weight bullets in Remington's 7mm Magnum.

Remington entered 6.5 territory in 1966, with its 6.5mm Magnum, which appeared (with sibling, the .350 Remington Magnum) in Models 600 and 660 carbines, built from 1965 until 1971. This 6.5 has a 2.15-inch hull, shorter than 2.50-inch "short magnum" cases like the .264 Winchester's, fashioned for .30-06-length rifle actions. These belted rounds have a common parent: the 2.85-inch .375 H&H, from 1912. Ballistically, the 6.5 Remington Magnum matches the .270.

The .260 Remington on the .308 Winchester case appeared in 2002. Its modest success at market is partly the fault of the similar 7mm-08, which preceded it by a decade. With 120-grain bullets, the .260 has an edge downrange. On the final day of a Colorado hunt, I sneaked to within 270 yards of a cow elk, bellying

18½-inch barrel wears an aftermarket aperture sight and handles like a wand. The effective reach of Norma's 120-grain Ballistic Tip load far exceeds my iron-sight range. Once, in a fit of dim-eyed confidence, I carried that rifle on a pronghorn hunt. After I'd declined several pokes at ordinary pronghorn distance, a hapless buck wandered by at 75 yards and dropped at the shot.

As 6.5s proliferated in Europe, American shooters tried other sub-30 cartridges. Charles Newton, trained as a lawyer but hopelessly intrigued by rifles, was wildcatting. While his aspirations to establish a rifle company were repeatedly doomed by circumstance, Newton developed big-game rounds far ahead of their time. The .250 Savage, a .25-06 and the .30 Newton all appeared before the Great War! In 1913 the .256 Newton

became the first commercial 6.5 sold in the U.S. Unlike the .250 Savage and other .25s, it did not use a .257" bullet. Its original load launched a 129-grain .264 missile at 2,760 fps. Modern powders would have added 150 fps. Slightly shorter than the .30-06, the .256 Newton shared its .473" base. A few years ago, talented riflemaker Buzz Fletcher loaned me a Mauser he'd barreled to .256 Newton—a lovely rifle with a slim, elegant prewar profile. It was a joy to shoot. Buzz eventually pried it away.

With .25s on one side and the .270 and 7x57 Mauser on the other, even the most endearing 6.5s had a devilish time wooing American hunters. Following World War II, surplus Swedish Mausers sold at steep discount along with battle-weary .303 SMLEs and 8mm German Mausers. Winchester's .264 Magnum, introduced final yards in deep snow. At the report of my .260, the cow dashed downhill, then somersaulted in a cloud of snow.

Inspired by its long-range target-shooting credentials, hunters are drifting to the 6.5/284. VLD (very low drag) bullets have boosted its fortunes in long rifle actions. Norma and Black Hills list ammo for the 6.5/.284. Lapua has brass. My rack holds two 6.5/284 rifles: a heavy sporter with Savage action and fluted stainless E.R. Shaw barrel, and a synthetic-stocked welterweight by Ultra Light Arms. Melvin Forbes at ULA designed his M20 action to feed midlength rounds like the 7x57 and the .284 Winchester. Its magazine accepts 3-inch cartridges. Both of these 6.5/284s shoot nickel-size groups with hunting loads.

A fine big-game cartridge, the 6.5/284 is a ballistic twin to the 6.5/06, a wildcat that never caught on. Why not? It's no better than the .270. The 6.5/284's short-action advantage is pretty much canceled by the deep seating necessary with long bullets, and by its rebated rim, a design that permits hiking case capacity on a base of standard diameter – but

that detractors claim impairs feeding. The 6.5/284 has served me well. Once while easing down a steep Idaho canyon toward a five-point bull, I ran out of cover at 300 yards. The elk fed into timber on the cusp of a draw. In my Zeiss scope I found a small alley to the shoulder. My bullet sped true. The bull flipped over dead, four feet aloft. Who says this short 6.5 isn't an elk round?

Wildcatter John Lazzeroni came up with a series of cartridges on his own rimless case. Those that have faded away are two potent 6.5's – the short 6.71mm Phantom (2.05-inch case) and the 6.71 Blackbird (2.80-inch case). Other Lazzeroni rounds remain, chambered in John's excellent rifles.

While 6.5s have appeared mainly in bolt actions, the rising tide of AR-15s has inspired cartridges sized for that mechanism. In 2002 the PPC Benchrest birthed the 6.5 Grendel, its 1.52-inch

hull a tad shorter than the .223's. Loaded length is the same. It was fashioned by Bill Alexander of Alexander Arms and by Arne Brennan, who'd chambered a prototype in an AR in 1998. (Lou Palmisano had set this stage in 1984 with the first 6.5 PPC.) Using a bolt rifle, Arne

Upper Right: Better bullets for both hunting and competitive shooting have boosted the popularity of frisky 6.5s.

This New Ultra Light rifle from Melvin Forbes has a mid-length magazine, ideal for the 6.5/284.

Wayne killed this Idaho bull with one 300-yard shot from his Savage/E.R. Shaw rifle in 6.5/284.

Les Baer's .264 is essentially the same as the 6.5 Grendel. Both were designed for AR-15 rifles.

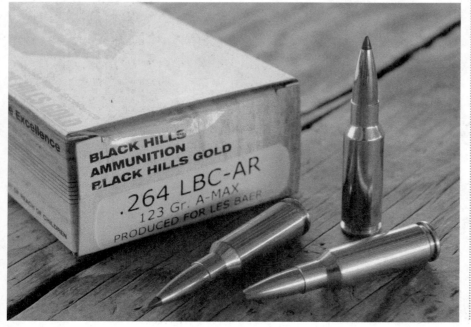

BLACK HILLS AMMUNITION BLACK HILLS GOLD .264 LBC-AR 123 Gr. A-MAX PRODUCED FOR LES BAER

fired a 600-meter group with the Grendel that miked just under 1.2 inches! Speeds reach 2,500 fps with 129-grain bullets. Les Baer's .264 LBC AR is essentially the Grendel with a different label. Chamber dimensions differ slightly.

It's fair to say high-performance 6.5s first appeared in Europe with the 6.5x68 Schuler in 1939. Two decades later Winchester offered hunters its .264 Magnum. The hiatus since then has been of epic length. But at the SHOT Show in 2014 Nosler trotted out a high-octane 6.5 that handily trumped both its predecessors. The .26 Nosler derives from the .404 Jeffery, a British number released in 1910. Don Allen used the .404 case early on for his Dakota line (through .375). Rims on these cartridges and kin fit bolt faces sized for the .532" rims of most belted rounds. But ahead of the extractor groove, a belt-free design yields larger brass diameter, which means greater capacity to the shoulder.

With a loaded length of 3.34 inch, Nosler's .26 fits a .30-06-length action. The hull is 2.59 inches long—between the common 2.50-inch short-belted-magnum measure, and the 2.62-inch .300 Winchester Magnum's. The Nosler's 35-degree shoulder is set well forward, almost as far as that short-necked .300's. Nosler brass is beautifully finished, though pockets of .26 cases are snug for CCI Magnum Rifle primers.

Nosler notes that it fashioned the .26 to push its 129-grain AccuBond Long Range bullets at 3,400 fps, and to hurl 140-grain Partitions at 3,300. With 3,385 ft-lbs of energy at the muzzle and an even ton at 400 yards, the 140s carry a haymaker punch. On the charts, it out-classes original .264 Magnum loads by 100 fps—and Winchester's current anemic listing by 270 fps.

As I had no Nosler factory ammunition, I handloaded Nosler brass with what seemed appropriate powders. The company's 120-grain Ballistic Tips joined the 129s and 140s on my bench. Mason Payer at Nosler suggested 82 grains Retumbo, 93 grains US 869 as maximum for the 129. He listed 86 grains US 869 as tops for 140s. I didn't have that powder on hand, but scrounged Retumbo and several other super-slow fuels. My Oehler chronograph recorded these average speeds for selected loads.

CAUTION: These are observed results, not recommendations! Reduce charges by 5 percent to start!

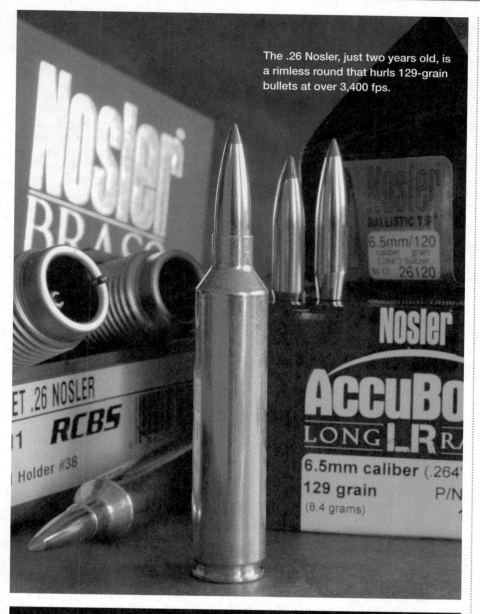

The .26 Nosler, just two years old, is a rimless round that hurls 129-grain bullets at over 3,400 fps.

HANDLOADS FOR THE .26 NOSLER	VELOCITY
129 AccuBond LR, 83 grains Magnum	3449 fps
129 AccuBond LR, 81 grains H1000	3403 fps
129 AccuBond LR, 80 grains RL–25	3474 fps
140 Partition, 78 grains Retumbo	3318 fps
140 Partition, 85 grains Accurate 8700	3339 fps
140 Partition, 81 grains Magnum	3431 fps (maximum!)

The 129 AccuBond LR in front of 81 grains H1000 came in at almost exactly the target speed of 3,400 fps and drilled a tight .8-inch group with my first trio of bullets. I figure 3,650 is about as fast as a 120-grain bullet should go, 3,400 fast enough for 140s. While these ambitious loads left primers a bit flat, neither they nor any other load gave me a sticky bolt lift. The rifle fed, extracted and ejected without fault.

Perhaps the .26 influenced Weatherby's decision to end a 16-year pause in cartridge design with a hot 6.5. But, I suspect the 6.5-300 Weatherby Magnum was on the drawing board in Paso Robles before Nosler's announcement. Indeed, a 6.5 on blown-out .300 H&H Magnum brass dates back to the wildcat developed by Paul Wright of Silver City, N.M., for 1,000-yard competition. In his *Handbook for Shooters and Reloaders* (1962), P.O. Ackley wrote of the 6.5/300 Weatherby-Wright Magnum, listing velocities of 3,400 fps with Hodgdon 202 and 870 powders. He noted that Bruce Hodgdon found almost no velocity boost when the huge .378 Weatherby case was necked to 6.5. It "required 106 grains of IMR 6915 for a velocity of 3,440 fps…."

Shooters whose memory goes back as far as mine should recall a 6.5/300 Wright-Hoyer. This is the same cartridge as the .300 Weatherby-Wright Magnum. Alex Hoyer ran a gunshop in Mifflintown, Penn., where he built several rifles for the round.

Weatherby's interest in a 6.5 may have had little do with my suggestion that the company neck the .240 case to .264. "You'd have, essentially, a 6.5/06 in a case that would fit the Mark V Lightweight action. It would out-shine the 6.5 Creedmoor ballistically, and approach Winchester's listed speed for the .264 Magnum." A salesman I'm not. Ed Weatherby and his staff smiled politely and thanked me. Then they did what shooters have come to expect of Weatherby: they fashioned a magnum that drives bullets faster than its competition. All of its competition.

In the early '40s Roy Weatherby had trimmed the .300 H&H hull to 2.50 inches for his .257, .270 and 7mm Magnums. But now a 6.5 on that case would yield little if any more speed than Winchester's same-size .264 Magnum. No, the world didn't need another 6.5 of that measure—any more than it would welcome a 6.5/06 with a belt.

If there's any way to earn the fealty of a skeptic, it's to make him a participant. But the invitation to build a Mark V in 6.5-300 came as a surprise. With so few manual skills that even the pear-pickers in my orchard keep me off ladders, I've no place around costly machinery. Ed Weatherby must have known that. "You'll have help," he added.

Ed and son Adam, now Weatherby's Executive VP and COO, welcomed me with an introduction to a new Mark V. "It's not new just because we've added a cartridge," Adam said. "For 2016 all Mark Vs have been upgraded. The Criterion barrels are lapped. Walnut and

Weatherby engineer Vince Pasco, who designed the new Mark V trigger, checks out Wayne's 6.5-300.

hand-laminated synthetic stocks have a trimmer profile, plus a modest palm swell." There's still a full-length alloy rail in synthetic stocks. A new LXX trigger (for the company's 70th anniversary) was designed by engineer Vince Pasco. It adjusts down to 2.5 pounds. Now Weatherby guarantees sub-minute accuracy from all Mark Vs.

In the cage, an assembly area on the expansive shop floor, Clint Nicholson drew the short straw. Of the handful of invited guests, he got me. His consolation: he'd host my colleague Craig Boddington, too. Neither of us, it turned out, had ever built a rifle from scratch. "Both rookies?" Clint smiled grimly.

The project took most of a day.

Clint Nicholson secures a Mark V in Weatherby's proof fixture for a test with a "blue pill" load.

Without help from Clint and other patient people, and preparation that included matching finished parts for sub-assemblies, it might have taken a month. We bead-blasted and roll-marked the fluted, stainless barrels, then torqued them to receivers. We gave the bolts their serial numbers, installed strikers and triggers, checked headspace and fired proof rounds that left ejector marks on case heads. Back at the bench, we checked headspace again, polished bolt bodies and adjusted trigger pull. While we fumbled through the complex task of re-assembling bolt sleeves, the blueing tanks imparted a rich, dark finish to receivers and bolt components.

Fixtures and tooling specific to each operation helped a great deal. The safety seems a simple device but comprises small parts and must be tuned to ensure easy but positive operation. Experienced hands, a jig and a high-speed grinder brought our safeties "to spec."

"The new stocks hew closely to the shape and dimensions of Roy's original Mark V stocks," Ed told me as he joined us at another bench. Glass bedding in the recoil lug and at the rear tang ensure secure action seating. The barrel floats. We torqued the screws and shouldered the rifles. I must say, the tweaked shape is an improvement. We finished the day installing Leupold VX-6 scopes. Relieved that I'd not lost any parts, damaged any machinery, set off the sprinkler system or otherwise revealed my incompetence, I looked forward to my turn in the shooting tunnel the next morning.

Weatherby's tunnel leaves you no excuses. The bench is solid, the target well lit, with electronic sensors that show strikes on a computer grid at your elbow. Of course, there's no wind. Last in line to test my 6.5-300, I shot it poorly. The dime-size knot Craig fired from his rifle was salt in that wound. "Maybe the barrel is fouled," said Jim Davis, bless his charitable soul. During lunch, he scrubbed the bore. While my cohorts motored out of Paso Robles to bang distant plates in the hills, I went to the tunnel. My second trio of LRXs drilled a .7-inch group. In the echoes of that last shot, I heard sigh of relief from behind the spotting scope. Weatherby's crew had managed to shepherd a rookie through 36 operations to come up with a functioning sub-minute rifle!

The 6.5-300 is a hotrod. Its 127-grain LRXs, factory loaded at this writing in Paso Robles, clock 3,537 fps from my rifle (extreme spread: just 17 fps!). At 500 yards they match the muzzle speed of 156-grain bullets from a 6.5x55! Point-blank range for this new Weatherby, on a 5-inch target, is 305 yards. Zero a 6.5-300 Mark V at 200 yards, and bullets will strike within 2½ vertical inches of point of aim to 305 yards. They hit hard too, delivering 3,100 ft-lbs at 100 yards, or about what you'll land with a frisky 180-grain load in a .300 Winchester Magnum. The 127 LRX delivers 1,800 ft-lbs to 500 yards. It carries 1,000 almost to the 900-yard mark. You can also choose a 130-grain Swift Scirocco or a 140-grain Swift A-Frame bullet (muzzle velocities 3,476 and 3,395). Recoil? The AccuMark I assembled, with 26-inch barrel, scales 8¼ pounds and isn't at all uncomfortable to fire. At 6¾ pounds, the Ultra Lightweight Mark V will hop a bit.

Is the 6.5-300 a barrel-burner? That concern, emphasized at the .264 Winchester's debut 57 years ago, might have merit for competitive shooters firing many rounds in timed matches. But a 6.5 magnum generating a ton and a half of energy is properly a big-game cartridge. On any hunt, shots are infrequent. Few hunters who've criticized "over-bore capacity" cartridges have worn out barrels. Roy Weatherby's .257 Magnum endured that same indictment, as has

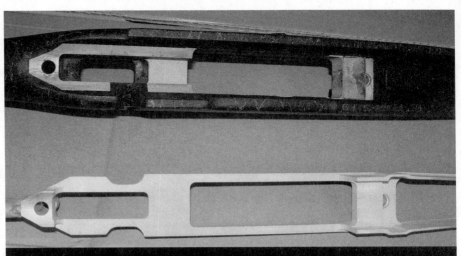

The Weatherby Mark V owes some of its sub-minute accuracy to the full-length alloy rail in its hand-laid stock.

the later .30-378. All of these rounds were designed for that one long poke you hope will salvage a costly hunting expedition. Unless you run a 6.5-300 barrel to egg-poaching temperatures, you'll look hard to find throat erosion until you're too old to care about it.

Mark V Magnum rifles in this chambering—AccuMark, Arroyo, Outfitter,

TerraMark and Ultra Lightweight—have 1-in-8-twist bores. It's a faster spin than listed for the 139-grain Norma match bullets Paul Wright used, and better suited to the long ogives of modern missiles. Some barrels wear a brake. If, like me, you loathe blast, you'll get one without.

Here's what to expect from Weatherby's factory loads:

Weatherby's hot 6.5-300 Magnum appeared late in 2015, with 127-grain LRX bullets at 3,530 fps.

EXTERIOR BALLISTICS FOR THE 6.5–300 WEATHERBY MAGNUM, 100–YARD ZERO

127-GR. BARNES LRX	200 YDS.	400 YDS.	600 YDS.	800 YDS.	1,000 YDS.
Velocity, fps	3099	2706	2347	2015	1740
Energy, ft-lbs	2707	2065	1553	1145	828
Arc, inches	-1.7	-16.4	-50.3	-109.6	-203.6

130-GR. SWIFT SCIROCCO II	200 YDS.	400 YDS.	600 YDS.	800 YDS.	1,000 YDS.
Velocity, fps	3084	2726	2394	2087	1804
Energy, ft-lbs	2746	2145	1655	1257	939
Arc, inches	-1.7	-16.7	-50.4	-108.6	-199.0

140-GR. SWIFT A-FRAME	200 YDS.	400 YDS.	600 YDS.	800 YDS.	1,000 YDS.
Velocity, fps	2866	2394	1970	1597	1293
Energy, ft-lbs	2552	1781	1206	793	520
Arc, inches	-2.0	-19.4	-60.3	-135.1	-260.4

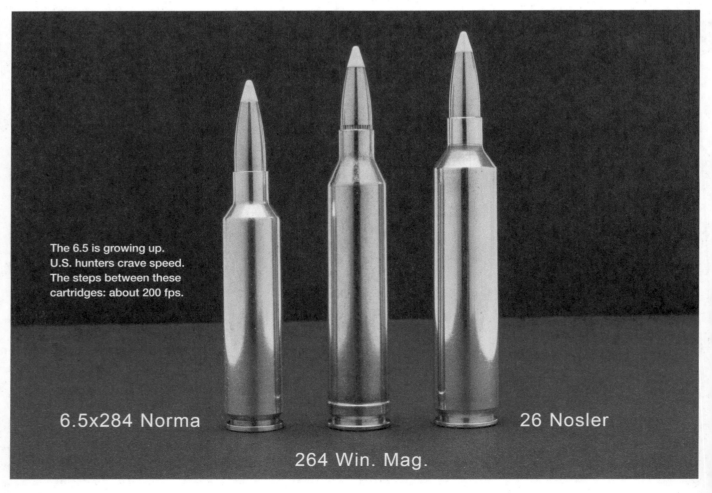

The 6.5 is growing up. U.S. hunters crave speed. The steps between these cartridges: about 200 fps.

6.5x284 Norma

26 Nosler

264 Win. Mag.

The limits of any cartridge are ever in question. You can't legally use a 6.5x54 on elephants, nor is it a practical choice. Only a solid through the brain with a 6.5 bullet will kill such a beast humanely. In the current debates over maximum reach, yardage trumps animal size as the measure of a load. Honestly, that's a flawed way to assess cartridges. I once fired a .264 Winchester Magnum at a target a mile away. Shifting breezes pushed many bullets wide. Eventually I scored. That shot would have killed a deer—but I was unable to ensure a hit. All the previous bullets would have missed or crippled a deer. Was that .264 load a 1,700-yard option? Not in my hands under those conditions. Neither is it a 100-yard killer if the shot comes offhand on a windy ridge I've just climbed fast, my heart still pounding. I've declined shots as close as 30 yards when the target, my position or the conditions put odds of a lethal hit below 90 percent.

And of course, you must consider the terminal effect of your bullet and the tenacity of the animal. Once, after an arduous hunt, I sent a 120-grain GMX quartering toward the off-shoulder of an eland bull. The animal galloped off. Its great splayed prints led into heavier thorn. Andrew and I kept to the track. An hour passed. Then, just ahead, above the bush, spiral horn tips! We raced forward. The bull dashed into a canyon, then suddenly reappeared, lunging up the far side. "Two hundred," hissed Andrew. Jamming the rifle onto the sticks offhand, I fired.

Wayne fired this knot with Ruger's American, 6.5 Creedmoor. Light recoil helps you hit consistently!

Behind! I flicked the bolt, shot again as the bull vanished.

We found him dying. I stood to the side. My final 6.5 Creedmoor bullet had had driven forward between the hams, slicing the dorsal aorta near the spine. "A perfect hit," said Andrew. We both knew it was a lucky shot. "Eland take some killing."

Worldwide, the 6.5 family is one of the biggest and oldest cartridge clans. Its newest members are wooing U.S. shooters, who find their downrange performance and manageable recoil appealing—on the hunt as well as on the range. It's about time.

SIFTING THE NUMBERS

When enthusiasts talk of classic sports-car engines or the diameters of hunting bullets, numbers take on personality. Bullet sizes followed custom as cartridge firearms replaced muzzleloaders after the Civil War. Diameters shrank and velocities increased with the development of smokeless powder during the 1890s. But the diameters of bullets that armed the world's powers at that time seemed to come from nowhere. Great Britain armed itself with the .303 British and its .311" bullet, in 1888. That year, Germany adopted the 7.92mm (8mm) Mauser with a .318" bullet; it switched to the .323" "JS" bullet in 1905. The U.S. fielded the .30-40 Krag in 1892, the .30-03 in 1903, the .30-06 in 1906. All used a .308" bullet. Italy, Sweden and Japan chose 6.5mms. So did Holland, Greece and Portugal.

By the way, bullet diameter is not bore diameter. It instead matches groove diameter, the measure across spiral grooves cut into the bore to spin the bullets. For 30-caliber rifles (and .300s), bullet diameter is .308". Oddly enough, the .308 Winchester uses the same bullets, as it is named for bullet diameter, not for the bore. European smokeless cartridges are labeled by bullet diameter and case length in millimeters. The 7x57 has a 7mm (.284) bullet in a case 57mm long, the 6.5x55 a 6.5mm (.264) bullet in a 55mm hull.

WINCHESTER'S
MODEL 1907
SELF-LOADING RIFLE

By Paul Scarlata • Photos By James Walters and Becky Scarlata

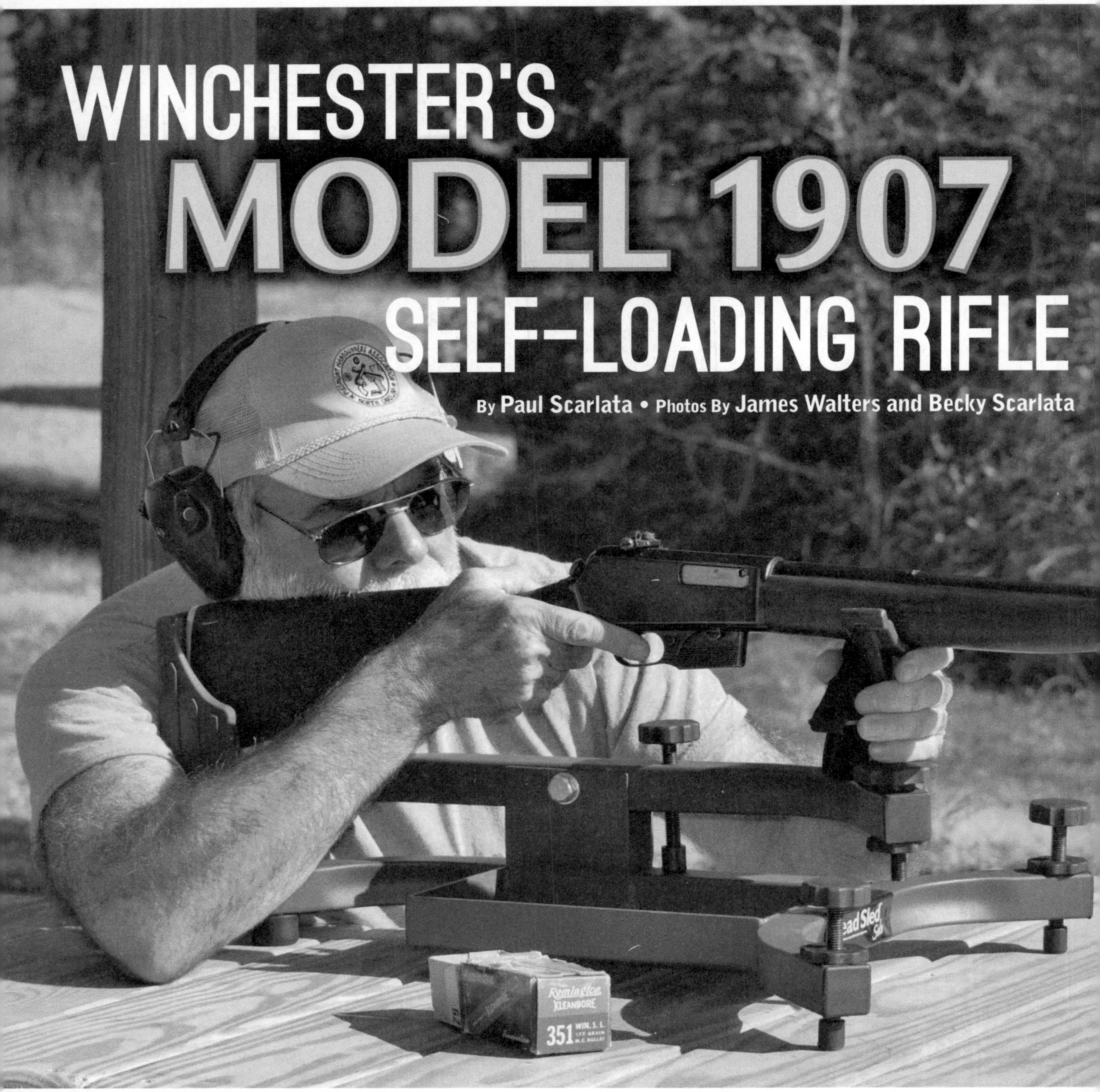

While many of our uninformed "friends" in government and the media consider them a modern scourge, the concept of the semiautomatic rifle goes back to the late 19th century. In fact, the first practical ones were introduced by American gunmakers before the first decade of the

last century was half over.

In 1891 Winchester began a long-term research and development program to develop such a rifle, and for over a decade their engineers, William Mason and Thomas Johnson, examined several operating systems. While the former developed a rifle that used a Luger/Maxim-style toggle joint to lock the breech, the

latter approached the problem from a different — and simpler — direction.

Johnson developed an operating system in which a relatively light bolt was attached to a counterweight that "balanced" it during recoil. This system was later referred to as a "blowback" operating system. When a cartridge was fired, the rearward forces of the

Test fire ammunition consisted of Remington .351 WSL cartridges loaded with 177-grain FMJ bullets. Shown next to the .351 WSL cartridge is a .30 M1 Carbine round for comparison.

The Semi-Automatic Rifle Has Been Part of Firearms History for Well Over a Century

powder gas had to first overcome the inertia of the bolt, counterweight and recoil spring, which kept the bolt closed until the bullet had left the barrel and pressures had dropped to the point where the it was safe to extract the spent cartridge case. While relatively simple in theory, the tricky part was calculating the amount of force needed to reliably cycle the action.

Johnson located the counterweight forward of the bolt, under the barrel where it reciprocated in a cutout in the wooden fore-end. As the bolt reached the limit of its rearward travel, it impacted against a spring-loaded buffer in the buttstock that not only prevented undue stress to the receiver, but also provided a bit of forward impetus to the bolt to insure proper functioning. The recoil spring then pulled the bolt forward where it picked up the next cartridge from the magazine and chambered

it as it went into battery.

After comparison testing, it was decided that Johnson's rifle would be markedly easier to manufacture then Mason's. The Model 1903 Self-Loading Rifle — the first commercially manufactured semiauto rifle — was chambered for Winchester's proprietary .22 Winchester Automatic rimfire cartridge. It was an immediate success on the market, encouraging Winchester to introduce a centerfire version — the Model 1905 Self-Loading Rifle.

The Model 1905 was basically an enlarged Model 1903 and, as did its predecessor, used a rather small, square-shaped receiver with separate butt and fore-end made from walnut. While the Model 1903 had a tubular magazine located in the buttstock, the Model 1905 utilized a detachable, five-round magazine that was released by pressing a catch in the front of the magazine well while a push-button safety was located in front of the triggerguard. Pressing on the knurled end of a rod (called the "operating sleeve") that extended from the front of the fore-end retracted to bolt to charge the rifle or extract an unfired cartridge.

Model 1905s could be had chambered for two new cartridges, the .32 and .35 Winchester Self-Loading (WSL). Both used straight-walled, semi-rimmed cases; the former's was 1.24 inches long and loaded with a 165-grain bullet moving at 1,400 feet per second (fps), while the latter's shorter 1.154-inch case contained a 180-grain projectile at a slightly faster 1,450 fps. The pair's performance was unimpressive to say the least, being sorely underpowered for hunting deer-size animals — a fact that customers quickly realized.

Johnson's operating system was severely limited in that the unlocked bolt prevented the use of high-pressure cartridges. This became glaringly obvi-

Winchester's first semiauto rifles were the .22-caliber Model 1903 (bottom) and .35-caliber Model 1905.

(Photo courtesy of Rock Island Auction Co.)

ous when Remington introduced their Browning-designed Model 8 Semiauto Rifle the following year. Chambered for the .25, .30, .32 and .35 Remington cartridges, it provided performance far superior to its Hartford-made rivals and proved more than suitable for game animals like deer, black bear and moose.

In an attempt to counter Remington's new rifle, Winchester had Johnson redesign his rifle to accept a more powerful cartridge. Known as the Model 1907 Self-Loading Rifle, it was little more than a beefier Model 1905 rifle. While all major parts looked identical, only a dozen of the smaller components were, in fact, interchangeable.

As were the earlier Self-Loading rifles, the Model 1907 was a takedown design. Unscrewing a knurled bolt at the rear of the receiver allowed the buttstock and trigger unit to be separated from the receiver and barrel unit for cleaning, storage or transport.

The new rifle was chambered for the .351 WSL cartridge. This round also used a straight-wall, semi-rimmed case, but was .24 inch longer than the earlier .35-caliber offering, allowing enough extra propellant to give its 180-grain bullet a rated velocity of 1,850 fps.

On paper that translated to 1,370 ft-lbs of energy, still well below that of the .30-30 Winchester cartridge and the competition's .30, .32 and .35 Remington. Most American ammunition companies offered the cartridge with a choice of softpoint or full-metal-jacket bullets, and it was also produced in Canada and Europe.

Unlike the 1905, the Model 1907 proved a more attractive proposition to American sportsmen for hunting medium-size game and varmints, especially in heavy cover. In addition to a small, but loyal, clique of

hunters the 1907 attracted the attention of law enforcement agencies, which felt that its short overall length and high rate of firepower made it an excellent choice for use by officers in patrol cars, prison guards and security details. To address this segment of the market, beginning in 1914 Winchester offered the option of a 10-round magazine.

With the outbreak of World War I, the Model 1907 attracted the attention of the European Allies who needed a weapon to equip observers in the newly developed "aeroplanes." Between 1915 and 1918 the British, French and Russians purchased in excess of 5,600 rifles, and millions of rounds of .351 ammo from Winchester. Model 1907s used by aircrews were often fitted with a wire mesh cage to catch ejected

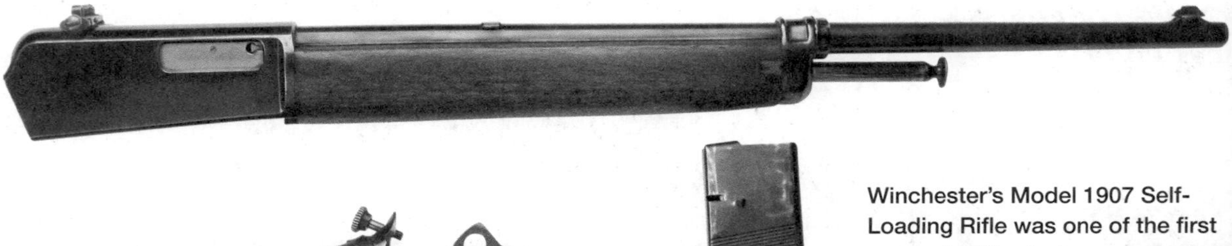

Winchester's Model 1907 Self-Loading Rifle was one of the first semiauto rifles to be commercially successful. The left side view shows the Lyman aperture rear sight and takedown screw on the rear of the receiver. To separate the butt/trigger and receiver/barrel units, one merely unscrewed the knurled takedown screw.

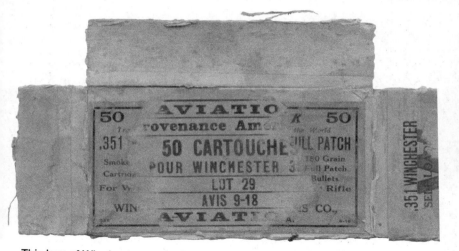

This box of Winchester-made .351 cartridges has a French language label pasted over it. (Photo courtesy of Yves Etievant collection)

French-made .351 WSL cartridges produced in 1918. (Photo courtesy of P. deCoux collection)

SPECIFICATIONS — WINCHESTER MODEL 1907 SELF-LOADING RIFLE	
CALIBER:	.351 Winchester Self-Loading
OVERALL LENGTH:	39.5 inches
BARREL LENGTH:	20 inches
WEIGHT (UNLOADED):	7.75 pounds
MAGAZINE:	5- and 10-round detachable box
SIGHTS:	Front: Blade with bead
	Rear: U-notch adjustable for elevation
STOCK:	Walnut
SPECIAL FEATURES:	The receiver tang was drilled and tapped to accept an aftermarket aperture sight.

Photographed in 1911, Maderista supporters Senior Herculano de la Rodia and his daughter Clara. She is armed with a Winchester Model 1907 rifle and what appears to be a Colt Model 1905 pistol.

cartridge cases to prevent them from damaging the cloth covered fuselage of early airplanes. Local manufacturing of the .351 cartridge took place in France at the Ecole Centrale de Pyrotechnie in Bourges, and bore head stamps "ART.VV, 351 EOP" and dates of 1916, 1917 and 1918 have been observed.

The French designation for the Model 1907 was *la Winchester carabine semi-automatique* and on July 19, 1915, Capitaine Antonin Brocard, commandant of the Escadrille des Cigognes, is credited with shooting down a German Albatross DIII fighter with a Model 1907.

With the development of practical aircraft machine guns, the French and Russians transferred most of their Model 1907s to infantry assault units where they,

Members of the 1st Aero Squadron serving in Mexico circa 1916. Observers in some of the planes were armed with Model 1907 rifles. (U.S. Army photo)

This Nebraska Safety Patrol Model 1907 with a 10-round magazine was rifle #30 issued to the Nebraska Safety Patrol.

(Photo courtesy of James D. Julia Auctioneers, Fairfield, ME, www.jamesdjulia.com)

reportedly, provided excellent service. While it has been reported that some of the French rifles were modified to be capable of full-auto fire, French collector and ammunition expert Jean Huon has informed me that this was not the case. French rifles were fitted with sling swivels and lugs to accept a bayonet and some continued in service until the 1930s.

Despite this record, when Winchester attempted to interest the U.S. Army's fledgling air wing in the Model 1907, they were told that it was "not satisfactory for aeroplane work." Although in 1916 the Army relented and purchased a dozen Model 1907s to arm observers of the Curtis Jenny biplanes of the 1st Aero Squadron of General John Pershing's Mexican Punitive Expedition that pursued Pancho Villa after his raid on Columbus, N.M. During WWI a small number of Model 1903s were purchased by the Army for training purposes.

Additional Model 1907s also showed up on the both sides of the Rio Grande during Mexico's *la Revolución de 1910,* and there are photos of them being used by Texas Rangers, Mexican rebels and American soldiers of fortune serving

Right: A gaggle of gangster guns confiscated from 1930s-era criminals include a Winchester Model 1907, Savage 99, a pair of Thompson submachine guns and a Colt 1911 pistol.

with Pancho Villa's *Division del Norte.*

The Roaring Twenties, Prohibition and the resultant crime waves made the handy, fast-shooting Model 1907 an attractive proposition, and it was adopted by a number of police agencies and penal systems. According to John Henwood's book, *The Forgotten Winchesters*, among these were the Nebraska Safety Patrol (predecessor of the Nebraska State Patrol), Maryland State Police, Santa Rosa County (FL) Sheriff's Department, South Bend (IN) Police Department, Calcasieu Parish (LA) Sheriff's Office, Oak Ridge (TN) Police Department, Asotin County (WA) Sheriff's Department, North Dakota State Prisons, Texas Department of Corrections and Louisiana State Penitentiary. All of these departments issued Model 1907s, some of which remained in service well into the 1980s.

U.S. Border Patrolmen serving on the Mexican border found the Model 1907 especially useful in combating bootleggers and smugglers but, since the Depression-era Patrol's budget could not provide them to field officers, according to the late Col. Charles Askins, many patrolmen carried privately purchased 1907s.

In the late 1920s the FBI purchased a number of Model 1907s for issue to their agents, but it is reported that the .351 cartridge's performance against the heavy steel bodies of the automobiles of the day was found to be lacking. Accordingly, in 1938 the bureau replaced their Winchesters with .30-caliber Remington Model 81 rifles.

In the 1930s a gunsmith in San Antonio, Texas, Hyman Lebman, modified a number of Model 1907s for selective

The Winchester Model 10 was a slightly upsized Model 1907 built to handle the larger and more powerful .401 Winchester Self-Loading Cartridge.

(Photo courtesy of James D. Julia Auctioneers, Fairfield, ME, www.jamesdjulia.com)

fire, shortened the barrels to 16 inches, installed a muzzle compensator of his own design and a Thompson submachine gun forward pistol grip. Reportedly several were of these were purchased by the infamous gangsters John Dillinger, Pretty Boy Floyd and Homer Van Meter.

A display at the FBI Museum of weapons captured from John Dillinger's gang includes two Model 1907s – a customized Lebman gun with 10-round magazine and a standard model.

Winchester avidly pursued the law enforcement market and in 1935 introduced the special order Model 1907 Police Rifle. It came standard with the 10-round magazine, steel buttplate, sling swivels and sling while the tip of the operating rod was enlarged to make it faster and more positive to chamber a round or clear a misfire. Other options included a fixed rear sight and an adapter to accept a bayonet. The latter device consisted of a metal sleeve with an integral front sight that was slipped over the muzzle, was secured by two bolts and had lugs to accept surplus U.S. Krag-Jorgensen bayonets.

In addition, the George F. Cake Company in Dallas offered 15- and 20-round magazines for the 1907 into the late 1950s. It was said that these extended magazines had functioning problems and were not popular with patrol officers, although some were used by tower guards at prisons.

The final member of the family we will discuss is the Winchester Model 1910 Self-Loading Rifle, which was a scaled-up version of the Model 1907 that was designed to fire the .401 WSL cartridge.

The Model 1910's cartridge utilized a straight-walled, semi-rimmed case 1.5 inches in length with a 200-grain bullet propelled to 2,135 fps, making it a practical big-game rifle. But it proved less popular than its .351-caliber cousin and only about 20,000 were produced before production ended in 1936.

Winchester factory records show an order placed in 1915 for 150 Model 1910 rifles, spare magazines and 25,000 rounds of .401 WSL ammunition by the firm of Andre, Schaub & Pioso as an

agent of the French government. A subsequent Dec. 7, 1917, order of 400,000 cartridges is believed to indicate additional Model 1910 rifles were acquired by the French through other means. Winchester records also show orders for about 500 Model 1910 rifles for the Imperial Russian government dating to 1915 and 1916. Further details are not available.

The Model 1910 never proved as popular as the Model 1907 and manufacture of it ended in 1936 after a total production of 20,787 rifles. Manufacture of the standard and Police Rifle versions of the Model 1907 continued until 1957 with a total of 58,000 rifles leaving the factory.

Test Firing the Model 1907

My brother Vincent has been the source of many of the firearms I have written about, and he recently provided me with a Model 1907 that, even though its serial number indicates it was produced in 1909, is in excellent condition. Some previous owner had swapped the original open rear sight with a Lyman #41 aperture sight and replaced the factory front sight for one with a larger, nonmatching base.

Fortunately, Vincent also provided me with a supply of 1950s vintage Remington .351 WSL ammunition for test firing purposes. These were loaded with 177-grain FMJ bullets, and when fired across my chronograph provided an average velocity of 1,834 fps.

Keeping in mind the Model 1907's intended role, the wide rear sight and its ballistically sedate .351 cartridge, I felt there was little to be gained by trying to shoot 100-yard groups. Accordingly, I set a target out at 50 yards and proceeded to see what this self-shucking Winchester was capable of when fired from my Caldwell Lead Sled rest.

Despite a rather heavy trigger, the aperture sights made the M1907 a very user-friendly rifle, and after a slight windage adjustment every one of the 15 rounds I sent downrange formed a 2-7/8-inch group – with every one of them in the 10 ring.

We then spent a pleasant half hour engaging "targets of opportunity" (rocks, sticks and clods of dirt on the 50-yard backstop). The Winchester functioned perfectly during these games and it was only the lack of ammunition that forced Becky and I to pack up and head home. My only complaint was that

To chamber the first round from the magazine in the 1907 family of Winchester rifles, you depress the "operating sleeve" to the rear and then release it.

Accuracy testing was performed at 50 yards from a Caldwell Lead Sled shooting rest. The author placed 15 rounds into a very nice 2-7/8-inch group.

SPECIFICATIONS — WINCHESTER MODEL 1910 SELF-LOADING RIFLE

CALIBER:	.401 Winchester Self-Loading
OVERALL LENGTH:	38 inches
BARREL LENGTH:	20.5 inches
WEIGHT (UNLOADED):	8 to 9 pounds
MAGAZINE:	5-round detachable box
SIGHTS:	Front: Blade with bead
	Rear: U-notch adjustable for elevation
STOCK:	Walnut
SPECIAL FEATURES:	The receiver tang was drilled and tapped to accept an aftermarket aperture sight.

it took an inordinate amount of effort to load the magazine to capacity.

All in all, I came away with a favorable impression of the Winchester Model 1907. It was reliable, well balanced, soft recoiling and could send bullets downrange quickly and accurately. It brought me to mind of a later — and much better known — Winchester product: the M1 Carbine. But — as I am wont to say — that is another story altogether.

I would like to thank the following persons and companies for supplying materials used to prepare this report: Vincent Scarlata, Walter Shipman, Herbert Houze, Gary James, Lou Behling, Bob Hunnicutt, Jim Curlovic, Yves Etievant, Jean Huon, Peter deCoux, Lisa Warren, Joel Kolander, James D. Julia Auctioneers of Fairfield, Maine, and Rock Island Auction Company.

SURVIVAL GUNS

ONE MAN'S CHOICE OF THE BEST SURVIVAL RIFLE AND HANDGUN

By **Dick Williams**

Lining up the Springfield M1A Scout Squad for the first shot on Gunsite's Scrambler, or for us older guys, "The Ambler." The author didn't set any new time records for course completion, but did take all but one target on the first shot.

An often heard bit of wisdom at the various firearms self-defense training schools is that, "In a crisis, we do not rise to new levels of performance, but rather resort to our basic level of training." My basic military training with a rifle occurred several decades ago and involved a .30-caliber battle rifle that had a wood stock with a semi-pistol grip and aperture sights. That was followed by several decades of civilian life using conventional rifles with wood stocks and a variety of iron sights and scopes. My brief competitive bull's-eye pistol career also took place while I was in the military, where my primary centerfire weapon was a .45-caliber Model 1911 with iron sights. The Model 1911 pistol was one of the "man guns" that served the U.S. military through two world wars, an incredibly nasty police action involving some very bad weather, and a prolonged support engagement in tropical weather, not to mention several excursions into violent places around the world. It was .30-caliber rifles that got our guys through both world wars, Korea and stood ready at the beginning of the Vietnam conflict. However, in the 1960s the classic battle rifle was phased out for the new breed of plastic rifle chambered for what many considered a "varmint" round, and in the 1980s the mighty .45-caliber fight-stopper was replaced by a smaller European caliber and higher capacity, lighter weight pistol also of European ancestry.

While I was not an early believer in either of the new weapons, in the last 20 years I'll admit I have succumbed to the lure of the plastic rifles and lightweight pistols with their smaller calibers, reduced recoil and increased round capacity. In fact, until recently, I thought I had truly made the emotional transition and become a 21st century plastic, tactical guy. Then in February of 2016, we gathered a group of six writers and editors for three days at Gunsite Academy and allowed each participant to bring what he considered the best defensive/survival rifle and pistol. There were no firearms sponsors to influence our thinking; Gunsite provided the ranges, the Range Masters and the bunkhouse for quarters.

After a great deal of thought, the Ne-anderthal reactionary in me re-emerged and I showed up with a Springfield M1A Scout Squad in 7.62 NATO and a Model 1911 chambered in the venerable .45 ACP. As you might expect, I was not in step with my younger, brother scribes. In summary, the other five guys chose one of the newer, wide-body polymer pistols that held something like 17 rounds in the magazine, and four of the five selected a variant of the AR-style rifle chambered in .223/5.56. The fifth participant selected the Ruger Mini 14 rifle (kind of a downsized M1A) in .223. They all had some excellent arguments to support their choices, such as the weapons and ammo were lighter in weight allowing you to carry more rounds and move faster, the pistols were simpler and required less maintenance, the pistol and rifle magazines held more ammo, the rifles were equipped to handle helpful accessories and were easier to carry in the "ready to fight" position, etc. So what was I thinking?

First of all, I'm not young, and I don't move fast. Quite the opposite – I'm getting old and slow. In the event of a national emergency that becomes life-threatening and then erupts into a fight for survival, one-shot stopping power is much more important to me than rate of fire. Perhaps it's old-school thinking, but I have more confidence in the .308 and .45 cartridges stopping a fight quickly than I have in the lighter weight calibers. And in the event of an emergency/survival situation, I'm not going anywhere. Where I live in southern California, it's difficult traveling the freeways at any time of day. I can't imagine trying to evacuate this area with the state's entire population on the run. My bug out bag is my house, which can hold considerably more guns and ammo (and other equipment) than any duffel bag I can lift or carry in my truck. The designated safe room in my house is much more defendable than my pickup truck heading down the freeway. My house, and even my safe room, will keep more ammo readily accessible than my truck.

The only gun I constantly have on me loaded and ready to fight is a pistol, because that's the gun I carry concealed every day. A rifle and some loaded magazines stored in my gun vault could be made quickly available depending on the nature of the emergency and the manner in which it evolves. As Clint Smith, President and Director of Thunder Ranch firearms training, is quoted as saying, "The purpose of your pistol is to fight your way to your long gun." Whether that's a shotgun in the closet or a rifle in the vault, defense starts with the pistol because that's what most of us are likely to have with us. As an emergency is defined, the .308 Springfield would be brought from the safe and kept more immediately accessible, but neither it nor a lighter AR is something I would wear constantly. I've attended a couple of rifle and shotgun events at Gunsite where I've carried a long gun hanging from my neck and learned I don't move smoothly or quickly thus armed.

The author's old Springfield 1911 with some refinements provided by Wayne Novak and a weapon light from SureFire. Of course it's chambered in .45 ACP; it's a Man Gun!

For the serious "Gentleman Handgunner" as he travels through his urban domain: a totally reliable 1911 loaded with Ruger's new ARX .45-caliber ammo, a minimalistic plastic holster that provides quick access, and an elegant, razor sharp Spyderco pocketknife.

A small rail mount was added to the right side of the M1A to allow for a SureFire M600 Scout light. Size and output of your light will dictate maximum range at which you can engage.

Both of my selected guns have been modified, but only one change was made on the Springfield M1A Scout Squad rifle. On the right side of the stock near the muzzle I added a very short rail, just long enough to hold a SureFire M600 weapon light. Among my other emerging symptoms of old age is a noticeable degradation in vision, particularly in low light. The SureFire light has a push-button switch on the back end that can be operated by the thumb of my support hand. It's mounted on the right side of the stock so it is the first part of the gun exposed if I'm shooting around a corner. If I were left-handed, I would have mounted it on the left side of the rifle. Since the Springfield weighs about 9 pounds, even with the short 18-inch barrel, I did not add any optics and stayed with the factory aperture sights. Even in low-light conditions, the SureFire's 500 lumens output adequately illuminated

the target, and depending on the range, permitted me to clearly see the front sight blade against the body of the threat. It's possible some kind of night-sight front blade would work even better, and that's something I will explore in the future.

The Springfield .45 is an older gun, a Model 1911-A1, and it has received a number of modifications from famous pistolsmith and inventor Wayne Novak. The most noticeable of these changes includes a set of Novak night sights, a Novak accessory rail and the one-piece, no-grip-safety backstrap that Wayne calls "The Answer." The rail is for a SureFire X300 weapon light, the night sights are so I can see my sights in a dark encounter if I don't have the weapon light, and the one-piece backstrap is to insure that no matter how I grasp the pistol in a life-threatening situation, there will never be a failure to deactivate

the grip safety. This all-steel handgun also features a flared magazine well since total concealment is not a priority requirement in this kind of scenario. OK, the Springfield's action has also received the Novak touch since I'm a bit of a snob when it comes to 1911s. The pistol is not especially pretty when you first see it, but it becomes a thing of beauty when you've operated it for any amount of time.

The Gunsite instructors ran us through one day of drills each for pistol and rifle followed by some play time and optional exercises with our weapons of choice. Throughout the three days I had zero failures of any kind with either weapon. The rifle was fed a mix of Black Hills 168-grain Match Hollow Points and Hornady's steel case 155-grain JHPs. The pistol devoured Black Hills' and Double Tap's 230-grain FMJ rounds along with a couple boxes of Ruger's new 118-grain ARX ammo. Regardless of the ammo type used, paper targets consistently displayed large holes while steel targets rang out like Quasimodo's church bells. On the third day I went through the Gunsite Scrambler (for guys my age it's referred to as the Gunsite Ambler) with both rifle and pistol during daylight hours. The Scrambler features seven silhouette steel targets (some full size, some the skinnier, popper-style target) at distances from about 80 to 130 yards. Engaging all targets from the standing position I missed one with the rifle, a called shot high and right. The added weight and stability of the heavier M1A was advantageous in this kind of shooting. With the pistol, three of the targets out at 100 yards and beyond escaped unscathed. I was actually pretty pleased with this performance

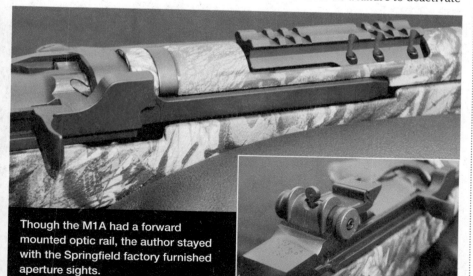

Though the M1A had a forward mounted optic rail, the author stayed with the Springfield factory furnished aperture sights.

This 9-pound necklace didn't help the author's mobility or reaction time. A conventional shoulder-slung carry using old-style swivels worked much better.

Getting down on the ground for a rest may not be a good solution for an older guy with limited mobility and flexibility. The author is obviously not comfortable without a backrest, plus he will now require additional time to change locations.

A 10-round magazine compared to a 20-round magazine. The rifle handled well with either magazine installed, but depending on the state you live in, anything over 10 rounds can get you some unwanted attention, even if your magazines are grandfathered in by law.

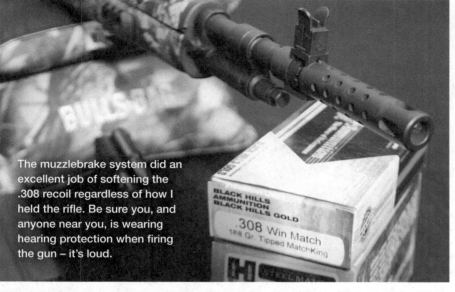

The muzzlebrake system did an excellent job of softening the .308 recoil regardless of how I held the rifle. Be sure you, and anyone near you, is wearing hearing protection when firing the gun – it's loud.

Although this trip through Gunsite's Fun House was made during afternoon sunlight, both photos demonstrate the poor light conditions that can occur even during daylight hours. You never know when or where you'll need a good light, and there's no alternative action plan once confronted by a demon of darkness.

A good weapon light allows early identification of friend or foe while leaving both hands on the gun for best weapon control. Although the light's main beam is still pointed down, it's clear that this home invader has a gun.

given that some of the targets are rather indistinct in the shade of Arizona juniper trees, and 100 yards is a long way for a 1911 pistol.

Some of the guys gave their rifles a workout at longer ranges, but for me longer distances require shooting positions other than standing, and by day three, I wasn't about to undertake some up-and-down calisthenics with any rifle regardless of its weight. I did hit the Fun House with the pistol where I re-verified the value of a pistol light. Even in daylight hours, houses have dark spots and a good weapon light does double duty in identifying people and determining whether or not someone is a threat. Despite years of working with handheld lights, I remain a two-handed pistol shooter, something that can't be done with one hand devoted to manipulating a separate flashlight.

A final note on weapon selection as influenced by geography. Some of us do not live in "free states." In an all-out "Armageddon" kind of survival situation, no sensible person is going to worry about political rules involving magazine capacity, special magazine release buttons or the shape of the grips allowed on your weapon. In fact, many of the politically restricted devices on defensive weapons can be removed and replaced in minutes by more sensible and effective options. Still, if you live in one of the government-care regions, acquiring your weapons in advance of a survival situation could pose risks if you break the rules. The Mini 14 owner and I (both California residents) recognized that our state hasn't shown the same irrational hysteria toward our older style rifles as it has toward the "assault weapon" lookalikes. Magazines on these two rifles are released by pressing a lever, and no one has yet dictated or invented a "lever button." California (and other states) ban magazines with capacities greater than 10 rounds, but there are some grandfather provisions regarding older guns, and both M1As and Mini 14s have been around long enough to have been owned by many grandfathers. As I said, I'm impressed with the more modern plastic rifles and pistols, but I'm comfortable with my two choices. Of course, the real issue isn't what you choose, but rather that you have made some choices and prepared yourself for those kinds of emergencies that were once unthinkable, but seem to be occurring with disturbing frequency these days.

ARMS OF THE
LIGHT BRIGADE

A look at the fascinating blades and firearms carried by Britain's legendary Light Brigade on its ill-fated charge down **"The Valley of Death."**

By **Garry James** • Photography By **Jill Marlow**

Paradoxically, it remains one of the most celebrated military disasters in history. The ill-fated cavalry charge of almost 700 men of Britain's Light Brigade against massed Russian guns on October 24, 1854, at the Battle of Balaclava during the Crimean War, provided the inspiration for one of the

most popular, oft-recited poems of the 19th century, the writing of countless histories and novels, and the production of at least four motion pictures. Quite an achievement for an action that resulted in no tactical gain, casualties of over one-third of the attacking force and controversy that has continued to this day.

What then, accounts for the popularity of such a debacle? Certainly the bravery and indomitability of the officers and men of the units of the four cavalry regiments that took part in the action are partly responsible. Alfred, Lord Tennyson's lines extolling of the achievements of "The Gallant Six Hundred" as they made their way down "The Valley

A TRUMP CARD (IGAN).

of the Shadow of Death," appealed to his typically romantic Victorian audience—and thus added luster to what was, in fact, a blunder of the first magnitude.

Today, students of the Crimean War (1854-56) tend to look more at the whys and wherefores of the action (not that there weren't plenty of investigations, and recriminations during the period to go around), and while studying the personalities and reasons for the action is a popular pastime, there is also an active interest in the weaponry issued to the participants.

But before we get into the arms themselves, perhaps it might not be amiss to go over some of the events that led up to the disaster and some of the principal characters involved in this celebrated blunder.

From 1815 until 1854 Britain had not been involved in a European war. She had become the foremost power in the world and was extremely protective of her newly acquired territories. Russia had coveted naval access to the Mediterranean in territories controlled by Turkey for some time. This, combined with England's paranoia concerning real or imagined Russian interests in British territories, formed a bed of tinder waiting for a handy spark.

The flash came in the form of a squabble among Orthodox and Roman Catholic monks over the custodianship of the key to the Church of the Nativity in Bethlehem, then under Turkish control. Scuffles resulted in the death of some Orthodox monks and Czar Nicholas blamed the Turkish police for allowing it to happen. Using this as an excuse, he marched into the Turkish provinces of the Danube and declared himself the

protector of Orthodox subjects under Turkish rule.

France, after being assured of British support, championed the Roman Catholics and declared war on Russia. England soon followed suit.

But the British were not really ready for such an adventure. The proper uniforms, weaponry, and hospital and commissary support were terribly lacking.

At this time British officers in infantry and cavalry regiments mainly acquired their ranks by purchase. Thus it was possible for landed individuals, lacking in military acumen, to obtain high rank in fashionable regiments, while poorer and often more capable officers had to be content with subordinate roles. The Duke of Wellington wholly subscribed to the system, feeling the upper classes had more of a stake in the nation than the lower ones.

The Commander of the British Army in the Crimea was 65-year-old Lord Raglan,

James Brudenell, 7th Earl of Cardigan, one of the richest men in England and commander of the Light Brigade was arrogant and difficult. Scandal-ridden and unpopular with his officers and men, nonetheless he was brave and led his men gallantly to the Guns at Balaclava. More than anyone Cardigan seems a symbol of the changing attitude toward the Charge. Here he is portrayed left to right: The first two illustrations are from *Punch* magazine, a lampoon offered early in the war; the third illustration a romantic view after The Charge made in an attempt to legitimize the debacle; and finally, as portrayed by Trevor Howard in the 1968 antiwar "Charge of the Light Brigade" film, full circle as a haughty satyr.

whose main distinction had been that he was Wellington's military secretary for many years, and later, Master-General of the Ordnance. Raglan was basically a kindly, considerate man who hated to offend anyone. His bravery and determination, however, were unquestionable. At Waterloo he had lost his right arm, and as it was being carried away at the operating station, he beckoned the orderly to bring it back so he could retrieve a signet ring from one of the fingers.

The Cavalry Division, composed of the Heavy and Light Brigades, was led by Lord Lucan. He was an insensitive, infuriatingly punctilious officer whose over-attention to trivial details drove his subordinates to distraction.

Commander of the Light Brigade was James Brudenell, 7th Earl of Cardigan. One of the richest men in England, he had purchased himself the colonelcies of fashionable regiments, only to repeatedly be undone by his own pettiness

CHARGE AT BALACLAVA, AND DEATH OF CAPT. NOLAN.

Captain Louis Edward Nolan, who delivered Lord Raglan's fateful order sending the Light Brigade on its ill-fated charge, was the first casualty of the action. An officer in the 15th Hussars, he was a great proponent of cavalry, thinking it, under the right circumstances, was virtually omnipotent on the battlefield. He had little use for the lance as a weapon.

and arrogance. A martinet and stickler for military detail, Cardigan's wealth ensured that his men were the best dressed and mounted in the army.

Unfortunately his brother-in-law was Lord Lucan, and after Cardigan left his wife, his relationship with Lucan deteriorated to the point that neither man would even to speak to the other—not the best situation for a commander and subordinate. Raglan was often heard to remark that the pair must be kept apart, and would often give orders to Cardigan and neglect to inform Lucan. It was, at best, a difficult situation.

This clash of personalities, coupled with a vague order that was probably misinterpreted by Lucan or misconstrued by Raglan's messenger Captain Louis Nolan (who was also the first casualty in the charge, when an explod-

ing Russian shell tore open his chest), resulted in the ill-fated and unsupported advance of the Light Brigade directly down a valley toward massed Russian artillery. As well as having to contend with the guns at the end of the valley all along the "half a league" of the charge, the cavalrymen were subjected to musket, artillery and rifle fire from the heights flanking the valley.

The Light Brigade consisted of five regiments of light cavalry: the 8th and 11th Hussars (Cardigan's old regiment), the 4th and 13th Light Dragoons, and the 17th Lancers. Each regiment was required to furnish two squadrons of 250 men for service in the Crimea. By the time of the charge, however, disease and other causes had pared the command down to less than 700 officers and men. The trooper's mounts also suffered terribly,

and replacements became increasingly difficult to obtain.

Despite their ride, as Tennyson aptly put it, "into the mouth of Hell," a good number of the officers and men actually reached the guns where they engaged in a brief affray with the gunners and a counterattack by Russian cavalry, before withdrawing back down from whence they came. Of the 673 or 661 men (depending on the source) that started down the valley some 271 were either killed or wounded. A number of cavalrymen were also taken prisoner. Over 300 horses were lost.

Almost immediately a series of charges and countercharges were launched concerning who was to blame for the disaster. It has yet to be satisfactorily resolved. One thing that cannot be doubted, however, is the bravery of the officers and men who probably realized the futility of the action, yet still charged down the valley to their almost certain doom.

Arms carried by officers and troopers varied between ranks and units, though items such as swords remained universal. While probably few, if any, firearms were employed during the Charge, they did come into use during patrol and picket duties. Other ranks in the light dragoons and hussars carried carbines and sabers.

The percussion carbine used by the British cavalry at this time was termed the "Victoria Pattern" in honor of the Queen. Introduced in 1836 (though it didn't go into production until two years later) with a back-action lock and sliding safety, this "First Model" was altered by the addition of a side-action lock in 1843. The caliber was .73, overall length 41¾ inches with a 26-inch barrel. Like many earlier carbines it was fitted with a captive ramrod that permanently attached to the gun at the muzzle so it could be more easily loaded on horseback. The buttplate, triggerguard and nose cap were of brass. Opposite the lock on the other side of the stock was a long bar and ring for a carbine sling swivel. This "Second Model" Victoria Carbine, designed under the auspices of Inspector of Small Arms, Francis George Lovell, was certainly a well-made, sturdy, rugged arm, but its musket-bore was felt by many to be excessive for a mounted arm. Troops complained of excessive recoil, which was understandable as the gun's load consisted of a .68-caliber, 483-grain round ball backed by a stout charge of 2½ drams (68 grains) of gunpowder con-

All regiments of the Light Brigade, with the exception of the 17th Lancers, carried the Pattern 1842 Victoria Carbine. This rugged smoothbore was criticized because of its musket-bore and excessive recoil.

tained within in a white paper wrapper. Cartridges were distributed in paper packets of 10 rounds each.

Percussion caps were issued in tin "magazines," which troopers initially kept in their cartridge boxes, though by the time of the Crimea a buff leather cap pouch that could be attached to the front of the sword belt was also available. Percussion caps were provided in a ratio of five to each cartridge.

To load and fire a Victoria Carbine the soldier withdrew a paper cartridge from his pouch, bit off the rear and poured the charge down the barrel. He then withdrew the ramrod and rammed the bullet, enveloped in its wrapper, down the bore. After the ramrod was returned to its channel beneath the barrel, the gun was leveled, capped, shouldered and fired. Being a smoothbore, accuracy was only so-so — but cavalrymen were rarely required to fire at targets at any great distance. In fact, many of the carbines didn't even

The 2nd Model Victoria Carbine, and the one carried in the Charge had a sturdy side-action lock. The last year the guns were made was 1854.

BELOW: Like most carbines of the period, the Victoria had a long bar, the ring of which could be clipped to the swivel on the trooper's carbine sling.

The 17th Lancers' primary weapon was the Pattern 1846 Lance. It had a 9-foot-long ash shaft and wicked fluted steel tip. A metal cap on the butt protected the lance as it was carried in a stirrup-mounted socket. This original 1846 is lacking its red and white pennon as well as rear leather sleeve and white buff leather wrist strap.

STEP 1.

STEP 2.

STEP 3.

STEP 4.

STEP 5.

Loading a Victoria Carbine (the same method is also used for the P42 Pistol) is simple and relatively fast. First one bites off the cartridge and pours the charge down the barrel. The bullet, paper and all, is pushed into the muzzle, the rammer withdrawn and the ball seated on the charge. The gun is then capped and it's ready to go.

have a rear sight and only a small blade front, though some did have fixed rear notches. When not in use, carbines were carried in leather "buckets" on the sides of the saddles.

The lancer's primary weapon was the pattern 1846 lance. Its 9-foot shaft was made of ash and coated with a mixture of tar and linseed oil. The wicked, fluted 9-inch steel head was secured to the pole by means of long, flanking languets. On the base was a metal ferrule that fitted into a leather socket on the saddle stirrup. A jaunty red and white swallow-tailed pennon was affixed to the languets—the colors, which were those of Poland, chosen in tribute to Polish lancers the British first encountered during the Napoleonic Wars and which were the inspiration for the later establishment of English lancer regiments. The lance was also fitted with a leather sleeve on its after-portion as well as a white buff wrist strap at around midpoint.

By the time of the Crimean War this archaic weapon was losing its luster in some circles. In his book, *Cavalry: Its History and Tactics,* Captain Louis Edward Nolan (yes, the same chap of Light Brigade fame) noted, "The lancer's pennons attract the fire of artillery. If the lances be such good weapons, surely those who wield them ought to acquire great confidence in them, whereas it is well known that in battle, lancers generally throw them away and take to their swords."

Though the primary weapons for the lancer regiments was the lance, and the troopers were not provided carbines, they were given a pistol – albeit one of the most ungainly handguns ever to be

The Victoria Carbine, while rugged, was not particularly accurate, being a short-barrel smoothbore. Still, at the ranges it was meant to be used, it was relatively effective. Recoil is stout but not prohibitive.

Interestingly enough, the Pattern 42 Pistol and Victoria Carbine used the same lockwork and were the same .733 caliber. Both were smoothbores.

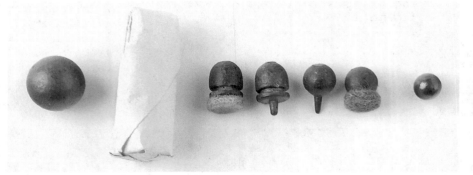

BELOW: Ammunition used in the firearms of the Light brigade included left to right: .68 ball and cartridge for the Victoria Carbine and Lancer Pistol; .442 conical and round balls (one with wad attached) for the Deane, Adams and Deane; and .375 ball for the Colt Navy.

The butts of the P42 Lancer Pistols were usually engraved with unit designations. This one was carried by a trooper in the 12th Lancers. The 12th was not present at the Charge, but did serve in the Crimea later on.

issued to any soldier. The pattern 1842 musket-bore pistol employed the same lock as the Victoria Carbine, and its 9-inch .73-caliber sightless barrel was little more than an abbreviated version of the carbine's barrel. Embellished with brass furniture, the walnut stock was ungainly and extremely awkward to hold. The 1842 used the same cartridge as the carbine, so recoil was beyond prohibitive. The author has fired his own pattern 1842 using a service load and found it to be simply nasty.

A small number of pattern 1842s were also issued to hussar and light dragoon regiments for use by sergeants major and trumpeters. That a Russian was killed or even wounded by one of these guns is extremely doubtful. Curiously, the P42 has a small swivel on the front of the trigger guard, the utility of which has not been adequately explained. While logic indicates it might have been the attachment for a snap-cap similar to those used on the pattern 1853 Enfield, these accessories were simply not available in 1842. These little swivels are also seen on some early East India Company longarms, so the mystery of their employment continues.

The principal weapon used in the Charge of the Light Brigade was the sword. Most troopers carried the 1821 Light Cavalry Trooper's pattern. It had a three-branch steel guard and wire-bound leather grip. The slightly curved blade terminated in a double spear point. Scabbards were of steel and featured two carrying rings. Some troopers, it is suspected, had been issued the newer Pattern 1853 Sword—which was primarily built under contract by Kirschbaum in Solingen, Germany. It also had a three-branch steel guard and its blade was the same length (35½ inches) as that of the 1821, but was slightly different in configuration. Weighing 2 ounces more than its predecessor, the '53 featured a checkered, two-panel leather grip.

This latter sword had the distinction of being issued to both light and heavy cavalry. Both patterns came in for their share of criticism. Troopers complained that the swords could not cut through the Russian gunners' heavy overcoats—but, on the whole, they proved to be serviceable and generally adequate to the tasks they were asked to perform. A white buff leather sword knot secured the weapon to the user's wrist.

Officers of all regiments sported the 1821 Light Cavalry Officer's sword. This blade was in use by the British service until 1896, with a blade style change in 1850, and had a three-branched steel guard and silver wire-bound ray skin grip. Its slender, spear-pointed blade measured 35½ inches. A gold and

Samuel Colt established a London factory anticipating orders from the British Board of Ordnance.

Colt revolvers made in or sold in Britain had to be proofed. Proofmarks appear on barrel and cylinder chambers.

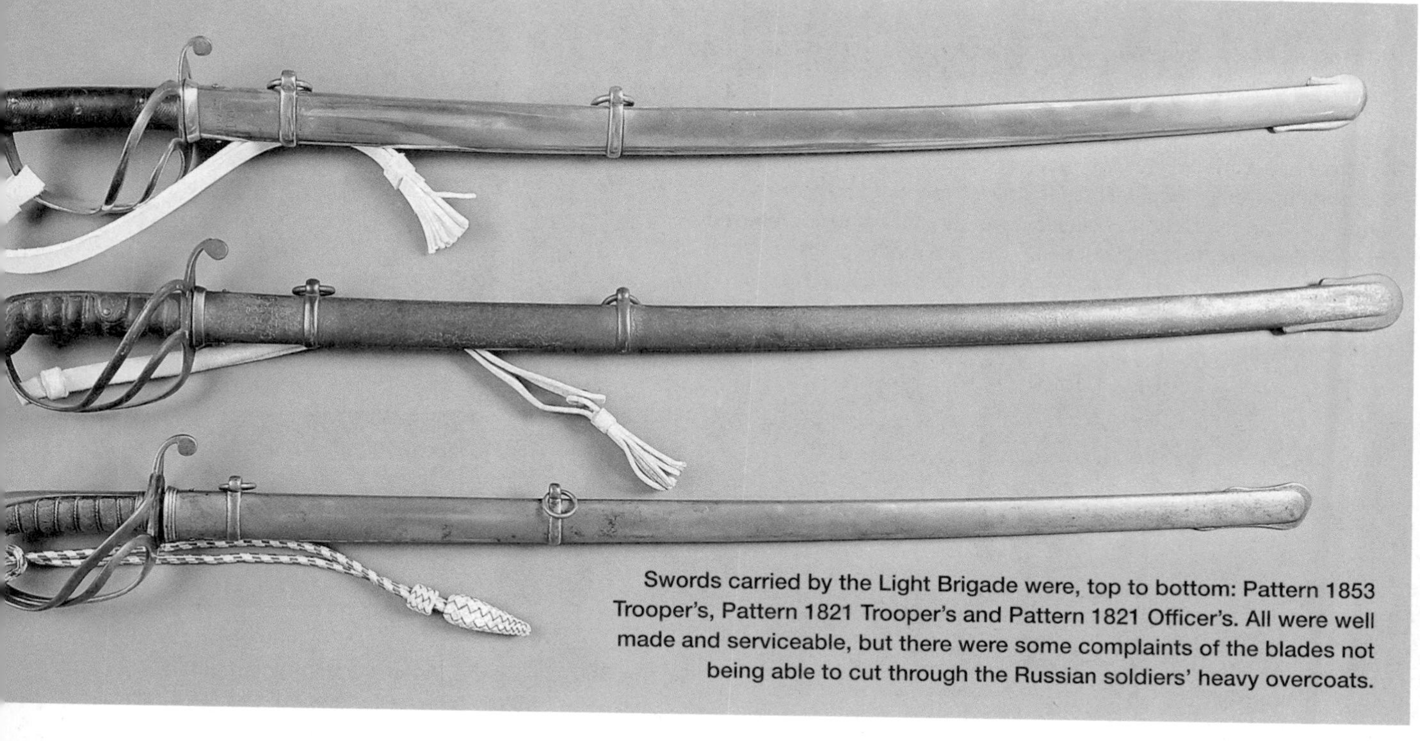

Swords carried by the Light Brigade were, top to bottom: Pattern 1853 Trooper's, Pattern 1821 Trooper's and Pattern 1821 Officer's. All were well made and serviceable, but there were some complaints of the blades not being able to cut through the Russian soldiers' heavy overcoats.

The Colt 1851 Navy was a .36-caliber single action and basically machine-made. It was rugged and reliable and saw considerable use during its long career.

The Colt Navy rear sight was a simple notch on the hammer nose. The front sight was fixed.

crimson sword knot with an acorn end was used by all regiments. Often these swords will be found with elaborately etched blades with regimental or armorial distinctions. Like the trooper's swords, they were intended more for thrusting than slashing.

Officers fielded any number of different types of single- and multibarreled personal handguns of varied quality and practicality, such as a faulty "rotten old pistol" used by Lieutenant Henry Fitzhardinge Berkely Maxse (of the 21st Foot, the only infantry officer to ride in the Charge) to defend himself on his trip back from the guns. But with revolvers becoming vogue, commissioned ranks were sensibly encouraged to supply themselves with repeaters. The two most popular at the time of the Crimean War were the Colt Model 1851 Navy and the 1851 Deane, Adams and Deane.

The Colt Navy, a .36-caliber follow-on to the smaller .31-caliber Pocket and larger .44-caliber Dragoon models (all of which logically also could have seen service in the Crimea, though to date there is no reliable information attesting to this one way or the other) was a superb arm. A single-action with a 7½-inch barrel, it was simple and reliable. The gun was manufactured using interchangeable parts,

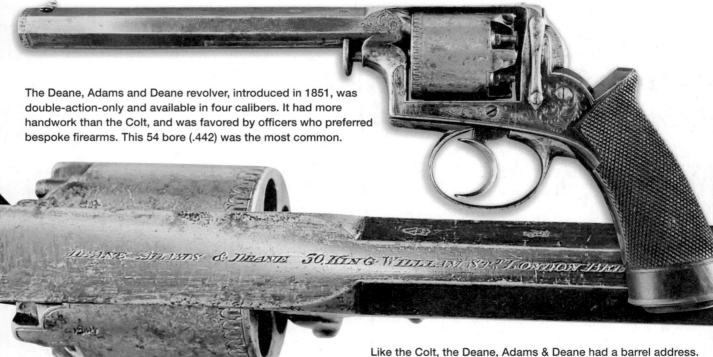

The Deane, Adams and Deane revolver, introduced in 1851, was double-action-only and available in four calibers. It had more handwork than the Colt, and was favored by officers who preferred bespoke firearms. This 54 bore (.442) was the most common.

Like the Colt, the Deane, Adams & Deane had a barrel address. But unlike the Colt's, which was stamped, this is engraved.

ABOVE: As well as a half-cock safety, the Colt cylinder had pins between the chambers that mated with a notch in the hammer. This way the gun could be carried loaded with the hammer down.

LEFT: Since it had a solid frame the Adams had a fixed notch rear sight. The front dovetailed blade was drift adjustable for windage.

To free the cylinder and carry the revolver safely loaded, the Adams had a frame-mounted retaining spring that held the hammer away from the nipples. Some versions actually had push-on safeties that kept the cylinder from rotating.

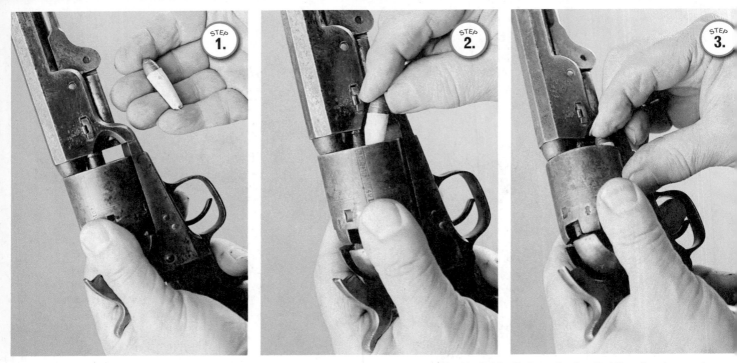

Like the Adams, the Colt was a percussion firearm and chambers had to be loaded individually from the front of the chambers using loose powder and ball or a combustible cartridge. The gun was first put on half cock, a load inserted and then rammed down with the loading lever. Finally, the nipples on the rear of the cylinder were capped. This photo sequence is continued on the next page.

so under the proper circumstances repair was easy to effect. Featuring an integral under-barrel loading lever, the Navy loaded easily using loose powder and ball or, as was more commonly seen in the field, even more efficiently with prepared combustible cartridges. A rear sight consisted of a notch on the nose of the hammer, which became completely visible when the gun was on cocked. The front sight was either a thin blade or post.

Samuel Colt had exhibited his revolvers at the Crystal Palace Exhibition in London in 1851. Their enthusiastic reception led him to establish a London factory. Prompted by the promise of mass-produced arms, the Royal Navy ordered a quantity of the 1851 Navy revolvers. Some '51s were also provided to the 12th and 17th Lancers, though they

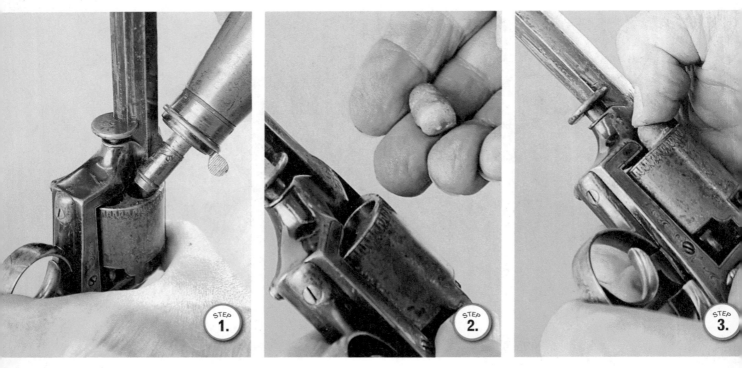

STEP 4.

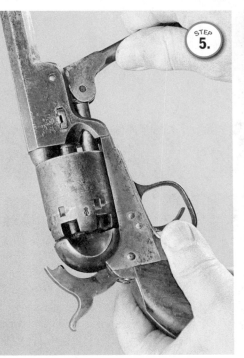

STEP 5.

STEP 6.

were principally given to officers and regimental sergeant majors. Despite being reliable and well made, the Colt was felt to be not as nicely finished as the English gentry was used to — it was a Yankee product, after all.

On the other hand, the

38-bore (.500-caliber), 54-bore (.442), 80-bore (.380) and 120-bore (.320) self-cocking (double-action) Deane, Adams and Deane revolvers, which were the brainchild of engineer Robert Adams, were all British and built by craftsmen using traditional methods. Offering five shots in double-action only, they did not even have hammer spurs, nor did they sport loading levers. Bullets with attached, lubricated wads were pressed into the chambers with the fingers. This practice, while simple, resulted in an imperfect seat and it was found loads had a tendency to move forward under recoil. After the war Adams would modify his arms with different rammer systems, and in short order came out with a single-double-action version—the highly regarded Beaumont-Adams. Still, the D, A&D had many positive features. The action was smooth and reliable. It was a solid frame and the cylinder could be removed by simply sliding out an arbor beneath the barrel. It also had more traditional sights—a fixed rear notch and drift adjustable front. Fit and finish was superb and all guns left the makers exhibiting some degree of engraving.

While the Colt employed a simple half-cock notch on its hammer, which allowed

the cylinder to spin free, the Adams featured a manually activated spring catch that was applied to the space offered between the frame and hammer when the trigger was pulled slightly to the rear. This also functioned as a sort of safety, inadequate as it might be. Accordingly, some later guns were fitted with a slender push-on wedge that fitted into spaces on the cylinder, freezing it in place and keeping the trigger from being accidentally pulled. Colt's revolver had a safety half cock as well as pins, which accommodated a notch in the nose of the hammer allowing it to rest securely between chambers. Unfortunately, these pins had a tendency to wear or become battered over time, which reduced their effectiveness.

The Deane, Adams and Deane was offered in heavier calibers than the Colt, but the mechanism was more likely to go out of order and it had only five chambers to the Colt's six. The Colt Navy had the advantages of simplicity, ruggedness and reliability. Both of these arms were popular with departing officers and each had its champions. Those who wanted to be able to fire quickly generally chose the Adams and those who liked to take deliberate shots opted for the Colt. The Adams' rapid-fire advantage was attested

STEP 4.

The Adams had a unique loading system. First the cylinder was freed and a charge of powder poured in the chamber. Then a bullet with a lubricated wad was pushed into the chamber with the shooter's finger. Lastly, the pistol was capped. Though quick and simple, bullets had a tendency to move forward under recoil.

THE CHARGE IN THE CINEMA

Director Tony Richardson's 1968 antiwar film, "The Charge of the Light Brigade," provided a brilliant depiction of England in the 1850s. Costuming was excellent as were the performances and dialogue. The uniforms, for the most part, were well researched and would have been perfect if Richardson hadn't fooled around with some of the details. Unfortunately, the Charge itself was somewhat disappointing.

Beginning with Alfred, Lord Tennyson's immortal poem, "The Charge of the Light Brigade" written in 1854, a scant two months following the action, The Charge has been fair game for purveyors of popular culture. Songs, marches, fashion, ephemera, toys, literature— all are fodder for enthusiasts and hucksters.

Probably no medium has had a greater influence than the cinema – especially as we get further and further away from the time of the

actual event. At least four films have had The Charge as the major theme and a number of others have at least touched upon it peripherally.

The first movie of note concerning The Charge of the Light Brigade was, appropriately enough, filmed in England in 1928—first as a silent and then modified later with a soundtrack. "Balaclava," was a typical melodrama of the period, and like the later 1936

American film, "The Charge of the Light Brigade," used the Charge itself as a spectacular climax. The Charge was portrayed handsomely and excitingly mounted. And depicts some real participants in the War—Generals Raglan and Cardigan and Captain Nolan.

In 1936 Warner Brothers pulled out all the stops with their version. A first-class production directed by Michael Curtiz, "The Charge of the Light Brigade" starred two of Warner's

In the 1936 film the troopers carried Victoria Carbines prop fabricated from Springfield Trapdoor rifles along with an officer's sabertache for the "27th Queens Own Lancers" and an undress cap worn by actor Patrick Knowles.
Photograph by Phil Schreier.

top players, Errol Flynn and Olivia de Havilland. As entertaining as it was, any attempt at historical accuracy was thrown to the wind. Starting out with events in India, inspired by the Sepoy Mutiny of 1857, which took place after the Crimean War, it builds up to one of the most spectacular action sequences ever filmed—The Charge itself. Led by Flynn ("Major Geoffrey Vickers of the fictional "Queen's Own 27th Lancers") it is simply fabulous. No CGI computer animation here—just lots and lots of extras riding toward the guns for all they're worth.

It is the only "Charge" film that makes liberal use of firearms—albeit they are of questionable authenticity. Seen are pistols and carbines fabricated from Springfield Trapdoor rifles and a circa 1871 Remington Rolling Block pistol wielded by C. Henry Gordon who plays the films archvillain "Surat Kahn." Blades range from Model 1904 Austrian cavalry officer's swords to U.S. Model 1860 sabers. And the bamboo lances that are shown prominently were not used in the regular British Army until some years after the Crimea. Correct the film may not be, but it's a helluva lot of fun and possesses the added benefit of a rousing Max Steiner score.

"The Charge of the Lancers" from 1954 is simply a dreadful film. Starring Paulette Goddard at the absolute nadir of her career, and Jean-Pierre Aumont, the so-called "Charge" seems to be simply thrown in as an after-thought to justify the movie's title. Possessed of a remarkably silly plot and directed with considerable ineptitude by William Castle, it is really best forgotten. Certainly not worthy to be in the company of the other three listed here, it is included only for the sake of completeness.

The most accurate film of the batch, director Tony Richardson's 1968 "The Charge of the Light Brigade," is a superb slice of mid 19th century Victoriana. Blessed with an excellent (if occasionally somewhat "creative" with the truth) script, superb performances and meticulous attention to period details (with some lapses, which will be noted later), the movie, though ostensibly an antiwar film, makes a real attempt to cover the basics of the Crimean War and The Charge itself. Blessed with a clever bridging device consisting of animated period-style *Punch* magazine cartoons crafted by Richard Williams of "Who Framed Roger Rabbit" fame, and a cast of real-life characters —Lord Raglan portrayed by Sir John Gielgud, Lord Lucan by Harry Andrews, Lord Cardigan by Trevor Howard, Captain Nolan by David Hemmings and, to provide the requisite love interest, Vanessa Redgrave as Clarissa—it is a beautifully mounted feature.

Drawbacks: Though the uniforms were meticulously researched by costumers John and Boris Mollo, Richardson had to fiddle around with them and as a result there are some considerable inaccuracies in Light Brigade attire. Too, the weaponry is only so-so, with the British infantry at the Battle of the Alma carrying a combination of wooden dummy rifles and the inevitable Trapdoor Springfields and Hemmings shooting a skulking Russian with a circa 1878 Mark II cartridge Adams. The main letdown is The Charge itself, which ended up being a rather skimpy anticlimax. Still, overall, it's a great film and comes highly recommended.

to by one officer, Lieutenant J. G. Cross of the 88th regiment of Foot, who wrote to the inventor:

"I had one of your largest sized Revolver Pistols at the bloody battle of Inkermann, and by some chance got surrounded by the Russians. I then found the advantages of your pistol over that of Colonel Colt's, for had I to cock before each shot I should have lost my life. I should not have had time to cock, as they were too close to me, being only a few yards from me; so close that I was bayoneted through the thigh immediately after shooting the fourth man."

Other ranks' sword belts, cartridge boxes and other personal items were pretty much standard issue throughout the regiments. The sword belt was of pipe-clayed buff leather with a brass plain rectangular buckle fastening. Swords were attached via a pair of

The Adams' trigger pull is smooth and not too heavy, though the gun is lacking in being double-action-only. Still, it was reliable and serviceable. This was the gun that legitimized the double-action revolver.

Pouch belt/carbine sling as worn by the hussars and light dragoons. Lancers, having no need for the sling and carbine swivel only had a pouch and more abbreviated shoulder belt.

straps. A black leather sabertache pouch was also authorized, but it appears this latter accessory was only worn by the hussars in the Crimea.

The carbine sling/cartridge box strap was also of white buff leather. Black leather cartridge boxes, holding 20 rounds of ammunition were slung to small straps, which were stitched to the inner side of the sling. The buckle and tip were of brass and the sling swivel, which clipped on to the saddle ring on the carbine to prevent the trooper losing his weapon in battle, was of steel. Lancers, having no need of the full sling or swivel had simpler pipe-clayed crossbelts, which held only their cartridge boxes.

Generally speaking, the Light Brigade was as well armed as most other mounted units of the period. Though experiments with breechloaders would ultimately sound the death knell for the Victoria Carbine, it hung around for a time as different weapons underwent testing and evaluation.

The success of revolvers during the war led to the universal issue of repeaters. Buying British, in 1856 H.M. Board of Ordnance began purchasing, issuing and testing the Beaumont-Adams, the government officially adopting it a few years later. Colt, thwarted in his attempt to interest the English in his wares and seeing the handwriting on

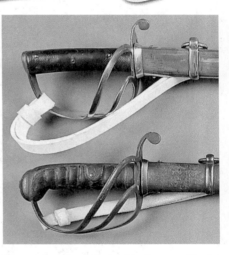

Reconstruction of a trooper's sword belt. By the time of the war, percussion cap pouches were common. The large black sabertache was only worn by hussars in the Crimea.

the wall, ceased production at his London factory in 1856.

Certainly at the time of the Crimean War, "The Gallant Six-Hundred" felt their tools were at least up to the tasks they would be called upon to perform. That the disaster that was "The Charge of the Light Brigade" resulted in devastation was no fault of the arms or the men. To quote Tennyson one final time, "Someone had blunder'd."

The Mauser Brothers and the
Model 98

One of the world's great rifles returns to its roots

By **Tom Turpin**

What eventually became the Mauser company began in 1811-1812 as a Royal Arsenal in Oberndorf, Germany, a small village in the Black Forest region. The Mauser brothers, Wilhelm and Paul, came on the scene in about 1867 when they invented a vastly improved rotating bolt system for breechloading rifles, and in 1871 their Model 71 rifle was adopted by the German army as its standard rifle.

Between that event and 1898, the brothers developed several different improvements featured in succeeding models, culminating in the development of the standard upon which just about all bolt-action rifles today are based in one manner or the other, the Model 98. In 1897, the old Royal Arsenal was turned over to the Mauser brothers, becoming Waffenfabrik Mauser AG. In 1898, the German army bought the Mauser design and its 7.92×57 cartridge as their standard combat rifle. It was the most important arm in the hands of German troops in World War I. It went through a few modifications to eventually become

Top of page: Black and white photo shows Paul (left) and Wilhelm Mauser.

These components were used to craft a lovely hunting rifle chambered for the 9.3x64 cartridge. The DWM-made 1909 Argentine Mauser action was about as pristine as one is apt to find these days. The trigger and bottom metal are from Blackburn-Swift and the three-position safety from Dakota Arms.

the K98, the main battle rifle of the German army in World War II. In addition to manufacturing rifles for the German army, Mauser also produced a line of sporting rifles during the period between the World Wars. These rifles, if in original condition, are highly desirable collectors' items today.

This is a modern representation of the Mauser Magnum Square Bridge action from Granite Mountain Arms. Quite a number of rifles chambered for the massive .505 Gibbs cartridge have been crafted using this action.

A very popular Mauser action to use for a lightweight hunting rifle these days is the Czech-made G33/40 action. They are getting a bit hard to find and pretty pricey when one can be found. This one has already had a fair amount of custom work done on it including new bottom metal, a new bolt handle, a two-position side swing safety and some polishing of the action has begun. Much remains to be finished, however, before it is ready to make into a hunting rifle.

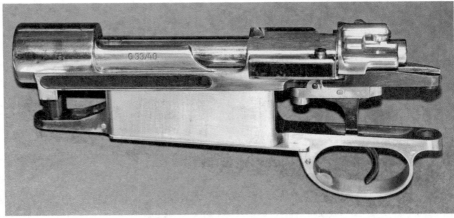

One of our best metalsmiths, the late Tom Burgess, turned this military G33/40 into a really great action to be used on a lightweight sporting rifle. They just don't get much better than this.

They also made and sold actions to the trade. Mauser's agent for the United Kingdom for many years was the respected firm of John Rigby. Rigby custom rifles built on Mauser actions became renowned among big-game hunters around the world.

The factory in Oberndorf was gutted after the war ended and the equipment confiscated and much of it moved to France. Most of the records were destroyed, although some were saved by former Mauser employees. Three Mauser engineers, Alex Seidel, Theodor Koch and Edmund Heckler went on to establish the firm of Heckler & Koch, which is still going strong today. Like most of the German arms companies, Mauser kept going during the postwar period and its prohibition against arms production by producing other products. In the case of Mauser, they made precision measurement instruments and tools such as micrometers. When they were permitted to do so, Mauser resumed producing hunting and sporting rifles.

In 1966, the Mauser plant introduced a rifle to the sporting market of a totally new design. It was not a Mauser design, but rather one by Walter Gehmann, a well-known inventor, competitive shooter and firearms dealer in Germany. Mauser acquired the production rights to the Gehmann design and began production. The Mauser Model 66 featured a very short action, quick interchangeability of barrels and calibers. It offered many advantages over standard sporting rifles, but – typical of German fascination with engineering – contained a zillion parts, was expensive, overly heavy and was ugly as sin. That's my personal opinion of course, but apparently most in the marketplace agreed with me. I don't know how popular it was on the Continent, but in the U.S. market it went over like the proverbial lead balloon. The few Model 66s that were sold in this country went mainly to guys named Müller, Schmidt, Fenstermacher and the like.

In the mid-1970s, Mauser entered into an agreement with the old German firearms manufacturer F. W. Heym, to produce a series of rifles—the Models 2000, 3000 and 4000—which were more or less of traditional design. Unlike the controlled-round feed of the Model 98, however, it was a push-feed action. They were available in a wide variety of calibers and marketed in the U.S. under the banner of Mauser Bauer. These rifles did enjoy a degree of success in the U.S. for Mauser. When the agreement was terminated, Heym made a few modifications and marketed the rifle worldwide as the Heym Models SR-20, 30 and 40.

Mauser introduced a new rifle and a new design in 1977 called, what else, the Model 77. The Model 77 was also pretty much conventional in design. It was a push-feed action that had a few new features. I had one of these rifles for a while chambered for the .30-06 cartridge. It shot well and was a good solid rifle. It also did not do well in the U.S. market.

The company was taken over by the Rheinmetall Group in 1995 or thereabouts, and from then until about 2000 or so Mauser built and marketed a series of rifles, namely the Model 96 and 97. In celebration of the 100th birthday

The author started this fine rifle with a 1909 Argentine Mauser action made by DWM. The stock is by ace stockmaker Gary Goudy.

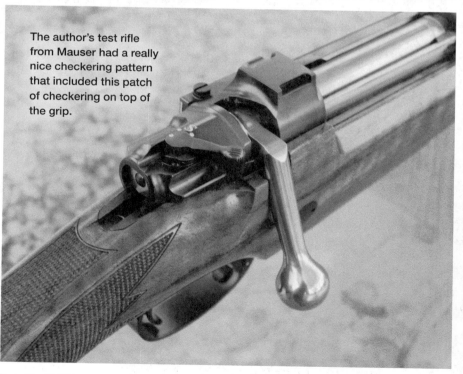

The test rifle would be a fine choice for hunting most anything. Chambered for the .375 H&H, it was exceptionally accurate using Federal factory ammunition loaded with Barnes 300-grain TSX bullets. Mauser provided quick-detachable scope mounts with the rifle, but the test shooting was done with the iron sights.

The author's test rifle from Mauser had a really nice checkering pattern that included this patch of checkering on top of the grip.

of the Model 98 in 1998, they produced a few military Model 98s and also a few original Model 98 sporting rifles.

In about 2000, give or take a year, Rheinmetall sold the civilian arms portion of Mauser production to the Lüke-Ortmeier group of investors who then formed Mauser Jagdwaffen GmbH. The group also owned the firms Blaser, SIG and Sauer. They moved the company from Oberndorf to Isny, Germany, and co-located it with Blaser and Sauer. It is still a separate company with separate manufacturing facilities, but co-located.

In the interim, the company marketed a few very nice Model 98 sporters, however, I believe that these early 98s were produced by someone else in Germany and marketed by Mauser. A couple of companies had been making and marketing copies for a few years. Two that I'm aware of are Johannsen and Prechtl, and recently I've learned of another, FZH. The prestigious firm of Hartmann & Weiss also makes its own actions.

The Lüke-Ortmeier group also introduced the Model 03 in 2003 and the Model 12 in 2013. The M 03 had a suggested retail price starting at around $4,500 and went up from there depending on the variation, and the M 12 starts at around $1,500 and goes up from that figure. The flagship of the Mauser line, the M 98, starts at a base price of $12,495.

The Lüke-Ortmeier group also purchased the old London firm of John Rigby after numerous ownership changes and tremendous confusion about the company, finally consolidating both the company and its historical records under one ownership. Rigby is now, once again, producing rifles in London using genuine Mauser actions from Germany.

I am not a big fan of modern European firearms design in general, but the return of Mauser to its roots, the Model 98 action as the basis for production, was super interesting to me. The Teutonic fascination with engineering apparently above all else has resulted in some interesting designs, to say the least. I tend to follow the guidelines my dad taught me many years ago. One of his most important lessons was, "if it ain't broke, don't fix it." The 98 Mauser has never been broken, and is in no need of fixing.

I prepared a wish list to send to Mauser requesting a test rifle. Before doing so, however, I waited a couple years to ensure this was not a pipe dream, but rather a serious effort at resurrecting the previous glory of the name Mauser. It is, and I sent in the request.

The company sent me a Magnum Model chambered for the .375 H&H cartridge. It features all the bells and whistles of a London-built Express rifle. It has a slightly extended magazine to permit loading an additional cartridge. It holds four in the magazine and one in the chamber. It also features express sights consisting of one standing leaf for 50 yards and two folding leaves, one for 100 yards and the second for 150 yards. The action features double square bridges, which are milled to accept Recknagel quick release scope rings. It features a banded ramp front sight with a relatively small bead. My tired old eyes and a small bead do not go well together, so I asked my son Jeff to come along to the range and do the shooting for me. Anytime I have some serious range work, I usually ask Jeff, likewise an avid hunter, shooter and gun nut like his dad, to tag along just

The Mauser M98 uses a barrelband front sight ramp with a brass bead insert. For young eyes this bead size is fine. For the author's old eyes, however, he'd replace the insert with a larger bead if the rifle was his.

The express sights on the test rifle were of a pretty standard configuration, one standing leaf and two folding ones. They were regulated for 50, 100 and 150 yards.

in case I have an off day. The older I get, the more off days I seem to have.

It really is a beautiful rifle. The stock is crafted from a very nice stick of European walnut, well figured and with nice pleasing color. It is styled like a typical English Express rifle, which is to say, pretty near perfect. It is nicely checkered in a point pattern in what appears to be about 24 LPI and is exceptionally

Mauser uses a nicely shaped steel grip cap with the Mauser logo and coat of arms.

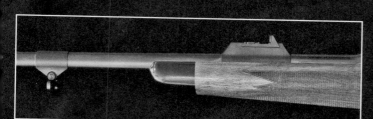

This photo highlights the black fore-end tip and the excellent checkering, both in the pattern and in the execution.

A cheekpiece side view of the Mauser M98 Magnum. Rifle styling just doesn't get much nicer than this one.

The bolt side of the Mauser Magnum M98. The styling is excellent, more reminiscent of a fine English Express rifle than a German made one.

executed, some of the best I've ever seen on a German-made rifle. It features nondetachable sling swivels, with the front swivel on a barrelband base. There is a steel grip cap with the Mauser logo, a black fore-end tip, apparently of ebony, and a black recoil pad. It also features two through-bolts to reinforce the stock. On the downside, however, I noticed a fair number of unfilled pores in the wood

finish, indicating that the finisher had quit his chore a mite too soon.

The rifle has a three-position wing-type safety that locks the firing pin when on safe. The trigger is fully adjustable and the test rifle has a fantastic trigger that fits the old saw "releases like breaking glass." According to my trigger scale it releases at 3 pounds. The rifle will soon be available in .375 H&H, .416 Rigby,

.450 Dakota, .458 Lott and .500 Jeffrey. Plus, it will eventually be offered in standard calibers, I am told, but exactly when I've not been able to find out. The best I've been able to determine is "next year at the earliest."

Having said all that, all positive, the rifle is not perfect, at least not by my standards, whatever they might be worth to anyone else. My first criticism is a simple fix. My test rifle has a stock length of pull of 14¾ inches. That would be about right for Shaquille O'Neal. I'm over 6 feet tall, weigh 205 pounds and wear a 34-inch sleeve length, and my rifles are 13⅞-inch LOP.

Since I lived in Germany for a bunch of years, and have worked with the German firearms industry for about four decades, I understand why this happens. Why are German scope mounts always too high for American shooters? It is simply that Germans shoot differently than we do. They hunt a great deal from high seats. They usually have lots of time to make their shot. They are taught from an early age to hold their head high when shooting.

Americans, on the other hand, are taught to weld their cheek tightly on the stock. As a result, American shooters demand very low scope mounts, and the German shooters much higher. That also affects the LOP. The higher the cheek, the longer the LOP required. Simple solution, a hacksaw!

The next problem is also not difficult to solve. For my use, the barrel is about 2 inches too long. There is no advantage

The authors's son Jeff Turpin is often called upon these days by his dad to assist with range sessions. His much younger eyes and nerves provide for a more accurate test of a rifle's capabilities. Plus, he really likes doing it. The author often brings his grandson along as well and makes a day of it.

that I am aware of to a 25-inch barrel on a .375 H&H, over one that is 23 inches long. I can think of a couple disadvantages, in particular. If you've ever wrestled through the alders and willows in Alaska, or the mopane scrub in Africa with a long-barrel rifle, you know what I mean.

Some of the ultra high velocity cartridges benefit from long barrels,

sometimes significantly so. The .375 H&H, however, is not one of them. This is just my personal opinion though, as some shooters do prefer longer barrels.

Being an ounce or two shy of 10 pounds for a .375 H&H rifle is too heavy by 1 to 1½ pound. It is particularly so when the rifle is empty and unencumbered with a scope and mounts. Scoped, with a sling and fully loaded, it wouldn't miss the 12-pound mark by much, if any. I suspect the reason for this is that the magnum calibers that Mauser chambers for are most likely all on the same platform. By that I mean the same action, same barrel contour, etc. If that is the case, naturally, the .375 would weigh the most, as the hole in the barrel is smaller, thereby causing it to weigh more. That is certainly understandable from a manufacturing perspective, but not from a functional one.

Another thing that I would change, had I the power to do so, is the finish on the middle of the bolt release, the bolt knob and bolt long extractor. These three items are polished to a high gloss finish and reflect light like a mirror. Aside from aesthetic objections, I suspect the reflections could spook game from a long distance away.

Before leaving for the range with my son Jeff, I went through my stash of ammo. I was working on a very tight deadline and had no time to order in a bunch of new ammo. I found a couple boxes of handloads, one box loaded with

260-grain Ballistic Tip bullets and IMR 4320 powder, and the other 285-grain Speer bullets, pushed along by IMR 4064 powder. I also had one box of factory ammo, Federal Premium Cape-Shok loaded with Barnes 300-grain TSX bullets.

We first set up at 50 yards since the standing leaf rear sight was adjusted for that distance. We learned quickly that the rifle liked neither of our handloads. While the groups would have killed any large game at that distance, we knew the rifle could do better. Jeff fired a group with the Federal factory ammo and bingo, we found in short order what this rifle preferred.

We moved back to the 100-yard range and shot the remaining Federal ammo. Considering we were shooting with open sights, the accuracy was outstanding. Jeff shot the best group that measured 1.062", a great group shooting with a scope – let alone just open sights. None of the three-shot groups exceeded 2 MOA. To say this rifle is a shooter is a gross understatement. If it belonged to me, I wouldn't even waste time developing handloads for it. I'd just lay in a supply of Federal 300-grain TSX ammo and go hunting. A 300-grain slug leaving the muzzle at 2,470 fps is sufficient to lay most anything low.

Welcome back to the fraternity Mauser. Paul and Wilhelm would be proud.

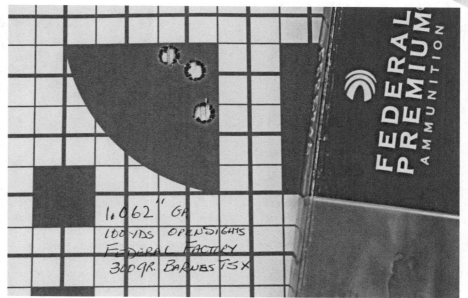

1.062" GR
100 YDS OPEN SIGHTS
FEDERAL FACTORY
300 GR. BARNES TSX

The best group Jeff fired at 100 yards using Federal factory ammo and only the iron sights. The author believes this rifle is ready to go hunting anywhere in the world as is right from the factory.

My Love Affair with the Ruger No. 1

By Jim Wilson

The author's combination for Cape buffalo: A No.1-H in .375 H&H with 1.5x5 Leupold scope and Leupold binocular.

The year is 1966 and American hunters are taking to the woods with their favorite hunting rifles, namely bolt actions from Winchester and Remington, or lever actions by Marlin, Savage or Winchester. Without question, Bill Ruger would like to have his company's name in the mix, too. But he doesn't bring his Model 77 bolt action out for a couple of more years. Instead, Mr. Ruger hands the hunting public something that

they probably hadn't thought about in quite some time, if at all. His offering is the Ruger No. 1, a single-shot rifle.

An interesting fellow was this William Batterman Ruger. He was a student of history and he was very interested in the classic versions of cars and guns. What was revolutionary about Ruger was that he found ways to improve the old firearms designs through the use of such modern techniques as investment casting and coiled springs. Regardless, his

love of tradition and the old stuff is apparent when you consider that his No.1 rifle is most usually compared to the Farquharson single-shot that was made famous by such international hunters and explorers as Frederick Courteney Selous.

The Farquharson rifle was designed by John Farquharson, of Doldhn, Scotland, in 1872. Farquharson soon partnered with English gunmaker George Gibbs and they manufactured the rifle until 1910, when their patent ran out. Following that, the rifle was manufactured by numerous gunmakers and, in fact, is still being produced today. Quite popular throughout the world, the Farquharson is a stout rifle that features an internal hammer and a falling-block action that is activated by a lever that functions integral with the triggerguard.

However, it is incorrect to say that Bill Ruger copied the Farquharson rifle in creating the Ruger No.1. He obviously appreciated the style and design of this British single-shot but, just as with his other guns, he found ways to improve the design while still honoring it. In so doing, he came up with a smaller action that was just as strong as the Farquharson.

Custom stockmaker Len Brownell was brought into the Ruger plant to work with engineers Larry Larson and Harry Sefried. While maintaining a traditional look to the No.1, this team was able to design a short, lightweight action that was still tough enough to handle just about any centerfire rifle cartridge. To begin with, they centrally located the internal hammer and moved the mainspring to the front of the receiver. This forward mainspring assembly then became the fastener for the fore-end and the ejector spring.

A quarter rib was designed and attached to the rifle barrel just in front of the action and also included integral scope bases. It was decided to utilize a tang-mounted safety that would be equally handy for right- and left-handed shooters. Len Brownell contributed a classic-design stock configuration that featured a schnabel fore-end, called the Alexander Henry, on some models. What has made the Ruger No.1 so popular over the years is the combination of traditional looks with modern, up-to-date manufacturing techniques that resulted in a rugged hunting rifle that was also quite pleasing to the eye.

In the 50 years since its birth, the Ruger No.1 has been chambered for right at 50 different calibers. The stout action handles everything from the .204 Ruger, on the light end, right on up to such bruisers as the .458 Winchester Magnum, .458 Lott, .416 Rigby and the .450/400 Nitro Express. In addition, the action has been re-barreled to handle just about every wildcat cartridge that one can imagine. In addition to the large caliber selection, the No.1 has been offered in several stock and barrel variations.

The No.1-A Light Sporter features a checkered walnut stock with the Alex

Henry fore-end. The rifle has a folding rear sight mounted on the quarter rib and a ramp front sight. While the rear sling swivel is mounted in the buttstock, the front swivel is attached to the barrel with a barrelband. The No.1-A utilizes a 22-inch barrel and has an average weight of 7¼ pounds. For the most part, the No.1-A has been chambered for non-magnum rifle cartridges.

The No.1-B Standard sports a beavertail fore-end and has the sling swivels mounted in the buttstock and the fore-end. This rifle also makes use of the quarter rib for scope mounting but does not have iron sights. Barrel lengths are 22 and 26 inches, depending upon the particular caliber. Average weight of this model runs from 8 to 8¼ pounds, depending upon caliber and barrel length. Over the years the No. 1-B Standard has been chambered for numerous popular rifle cartridges, including various magnums.

The No.1-H Tropical Rifle has the same contours and looks as the No.1-A, including iron sights and barrelband mounted front swivel. Designed for use against large and often dangerous game, the Tropical Rifle has a heavier contoured 24-inch barrel. The longer, heavier barrel helps the Tropical Rifle handle powerful cartridges that run the gamut from .375 H&H right on up to the .458 Lott.

The No.1-RSI International rifle is set apart due to its full-length Mannlicher-style stock. It utilizes the integral scope mount-rib along with iron sights. In

The author's update of a famous photo of Frederick Courteney Selous and his Farquharson rifle. The single-shot is still going strong. Original photo courtesy of Africahunting.com.

Jim's son, Ryan Wilson, with his Texas mule deer taken with No.1-A in .270 Winchester.

addition, a complete sling swivel is installed on the fore-end portion of the stock. The incorporation of a 20-inch lightweight barrel, chambered for many standard rifle cartridges, makes this model an especially light, handy hunting proposition.

No.1-A in 7x57 is just about the perfect combination for white-tailed deer hunting.

The No.1-S Medium Sporter has the looks and features of the No.1-A and No.1-H rifles. It utilizes a medium-weight barrel in 22- or 26-inch lengths, depending upon the cartridge that it is chambered for. The weight on this model runs from 7 to 8 pounds depend-ing upon the caliber chosen.

The No.1-V Varminter has a heavy-contoured barrel that is devoid of iron sights and quarter rib. In their place are found target scope blocks for mounting the larger varmint scopes. Barrel lengths run 24 and 26 inches and average weight is 8¾ to 9 pounds. Stock design is much like that on the No.1-B Standard rifle, with the forward sling stud mounted in the fore-end.

These are the standard model variations of the Ruger No.1 rifle. From time to time, stainless rifles have been offered that correspond to these various blue-steel guns. In most recent news, Lipsey's Inc. of Louisiana has become the exclusive distributor of the Ruger No.1 rifles. They currently offer each model of the No.1 in one caliber, with that caliber changing from year to year. Sources say that this is not an indication that Ruger is slowly working toward a discontinuation of this fine rifle, as Lipsey's is the exclusive distributor of a number of different guns and not all of them are Rugers.

The above descriptions of the various models of the Ruger No.1 are not meant to be all inclusive. Over the years a number of variations and special rifles have been produced and it is difficult to list them all without inadvertently leaving some out. In addition, the rifle has become quite a collector's item over the years. Experts note changes in stock design, sights and even the color of the recoil pad, all of which can designate a particularly collectable variation of this popular rifle. Those interested in the collectability of the Ruger No.1 rifle are well advised to consult *Ruger No.1* by J.D. Clayton (Blacksmith Corporation Publishers, 1983) and *Standard Catalog Of Ruger Firearms* by Jerry Lee (Gun Digest Books, 2014).

My own interest in the Ruger No.1 has been as a hunting rifle. And I have always been partial to the various models with the Alexander Henry fore-end and iron sights. My first one was a No.1-A in .270 Winchester, which I topped off with a 4X Leupold scope. My whitetail load consisted of the 130-grain Sierra softpoint bullet over a suitable amount of H4831, switching to a 130-grain Nosler Partition bullet for heavier game. With that handload, the rifle would deliver 1-inch groups at 100 yards and forever disabused me of the idea that the Ruger single-shot was not an accurate rifle.

This particular Ruger was used to collect quite a number of white-tailed and mule deer, feral hogs and javelinas over the years. My son killed his first few deer with the rifle. In fact, it was what he asked for as his high school graduation present. It's the only deer rifle he has ever owned or shot, and he continues to bring home the venison with it to this day.

In the meantime, I filled the gap in my hunting battery with a No.1-A in 7x57, a No.1-H in .375 H&H and a No.1-S in .45-70. The 7x57 has been my choice for hunting deer and other medium-size game. The .375 H&H is used for the big stuff that will often fight back. And the .45-70 is – well – it's just around because a fella just ought to own at least one .45-70.

Hunting with a single-shot rifle is not for everyone, nor should it be. In fact, it is often difficult to explain to other riflemen why a single-shot like the Ruger No.1 holds such appeal to a dedicated hunter. I suppose that the best way to explain it is in the restrictions that we place upon ourselves as hunters, the challenges that we impose.

Some enjoy the challenge of hunting game with a bow and arrow. Others, myself included, like to improve our stalking and woodcraft skills by getting close enough to collect game with a handgun. And let's not overlook those who honor the pioneer and mountain man tradition by hunting with a black-powder rifle. So long as our choices are legal and our goal is to make clean, humane kills on game, it really just comes down to personal preference.

In my case, I learned early on that I would have starved to death if I had to rely on a bow and arrow to bring in the venison. And burning black powder never did really excite me. Ah, but the single-shot cartridge rifle certainly did. One simply can't go into the hunting field without thinking just a bit about those American frontiersmen and their trusty Sharps and Winchester High-Walls. And to hunt Africa with a single-shot is to honor the traditions of men like Frederick Courteney Selous with his bigbore Farquharson single-shot.

Regardless of what type of rifle we choose to hunt with, we know that the first shot is the most important shot to be fired. It is rare that, with the failure of the first shot, subsequent shots will be able to resolve the matter in favor of the hunter. Knowing that the rifle only holds one shot encourages the serious hunter to take extra measures to insure a proper sight picture and to pay special attention to the trigger press in order to ensure that the one bullet goes just where it needs to.

Still, there are times when a quick second shot is needed. Most serious single-shot hunters have worked out a technique for getting a fresh cartridge into their rifle. Probably the earliest of these methods was to hold a couple of extra cartridges in the fingers of the support hand. Others make use of wristbands that fit on the wrist of the shooting hand and hold two or three extra cartridges. Either method works well with just a little bit of practice.

My preference is to use an open-topped cartridge carrier that is mounted on my belt just next to the belt buckle. The best that I have found is the leather C-2 shell holder from Murray Custom Leather in Aledo, Texas. Dick Murray has hunted all over the world and understands the needs of serious hunters. His gear is properly designed and made of the best quality materials. Still, good gear is one thing, knowing how to use it is quite another matter.

When getting my .375 H&H Ruger No.1-H ready for my first Asian buffalo hunt in northern Australia, I realized that being able to deliver a second shot to an 1,800-pound wounded buffalo might be a really good thing. So I worked out a speed-load technique much like the one that we use with defensive handguns.

Using my speed-load on the Ruger No.1, the butt of the rifle should always stay in the shoulder pocket. After the shot, the muzzle is dipped slightly to facilitate loading the second cartridge. When this is done properly, the shooting eye looks right over the top of the scope and keeps track of the target. The shooting hand flips the Ruger's lever, ejecting the empty, and then goes down for the shell holder on the front of my body. This second cartridge

The author's choice for a speed reload are the ammo pouches from Murray Custom Leather.

Australian Professional Hunter Simon Kyle-Little and the author with a nice Asian buffalo taken with the No.1-H in .375 H&H using Barnes bullets.

is snatched from the holder and dropped into the empty chamber, the lever raised, the muzzle raised, and the shooter is back on target.

To accomplish this speed-load effectively, the cartridge holder should always be worn in the same place. The entire operation can and must be performed without looking down. The hunter must always keep his eyes on the game animal and this is especially true with dangerous game. Purchasing dummy rounds from Brownells and doing a lot of dry-fire practice at home prior to the hunt is the way to perfect the technique. While I have never run a stopwatch on this method, it can be fast enough to compete with running the bolt or lever on a repeating rifle. The two times that I have had to use it in the field both resulted in putting the animal down for the count.

The first experience with the speed-load came on that initial buffalo hunt in Australia. My outfitter, Simon Kyle-Little, had shown me the big red bovine that they called the Australian Wild Ox. Actually, these are descendents of the original wild European cattle that were brought to Australia in the 1850s. They run at the sight of humans, prefer to spend most of their time in the thickest brush, and can get a bit perturbed when they are disturbed.

Accordingly, we drove to a swamp located near the ocean and crawled into the thick stuff looking for a good bull. We spooked a big one, close to 2,000 pounds, that had heard us but not smelled us. He didn't go far before turning and watching his back trail. At 25 yards, I could just see enough of him to make out his chest and realize that he was facing me. My first Barnes 350-grain TSX bullet hit him in the center of his chest. As he lunged forward, not really charging, he turned just enough to his left that I could see the point of that left shoulder. Having completed my speed-load, I was able to put another of those good Barnes bullets into his shoulder and bring him down. He came to rest only about 10 yards from me.

In 2012, I took the same rifle to Mozambique for a cape buffalo hunt. They had been telling me that we would hunt in

The moment of truth. We are just out of the mud and sawgrass, up on the sticks and sighting in on a Cape buffalo bull some 40 yards away.

a swamp. Now, when you say swamp to me, I am thinking of cyprus trees, vines and lots of water, but such was not the case. In eastern Mozambique the swamp is actually coastal prairie, wide open and with very few trees. The area is, however, crossed by numerous freshwater streams that run to the nearby Indian Ocean. Cape buffalo congregate in huge herds to graze on the lush, abundant grass in this region.

The game plan was to spot a herd and then begin a stalk using a water course with its tall sawgrass and papyrus for cover. When wading through one of these water courses, it is best not to spend too much time thinking about the hippos and crocodiles that also inhabit the streams. Just cuss the deep mud and slop through it as quickly as possible.

On the morning that I connected, we came out of one of those streams and into the sawgrass within 40 yards of a herd of over 200 cape buffalo. I got on the shooting sticks and kept my eye on the particular bull that my Professional Hunter suggested that I shoot, waiting for him to give me a clear shot. When the bull had moved so that there were no buffalo immediately behind him, I put a 300-grain Barnes TSX on the point of his shoulder. The bull staggered like a drunk about six steps and disappeared into the sawgrass very near to us.

Again, the speed-load came in handy and my No.1 was recharged while I kept my eye on the tall grass where I'd last seen the buffalo. Fortunately, he was down and dying. That second shot, between the shoulder blades, through the spine, and into the heart, was what is called "paying the insurance."

For whatever reason, I am simply one of those who gains a good deal of satisfaction from taking game with a single-shot rifle. The Ruger No.1 is a relatively light, handy rifle that is well balanced and a joy to hunt with. Its stout action will handle virtually any rifle cartridge and is strong enough to deal with any reasonable handload. And the single-shot is what was used by all of those early hunters in the days before repeating rifles were perfected. In the end, I suppose it gives me an opportunity to honor those who have gone before us.

Speaking of honoring people, I only met Bill Ruger on a couple of occasions. Given the chance to speak to him again, I would simply thank him for building an elegant, rugged hunting rifle, the Ruger No.1.

Moving in on a Cape buffalo. He may be down, but not out. About to make the important insurance shot.

GUNS OF THE GREAT WAR

The Colt 1911 was the epitome of a 20th century fighting handgun.

The Fighting Weapons of Uncle Sam's Army during World War I

Story and Photos By **Rick Hacker**

t was called The Great War, or more euphemistically, The War To End All Wars. But of course, we now know that Pollyannaish title was not correct, for there were other wars that came after it and in fact, it wasn't called World War I until much later, when there was a World War II. Nonetheless, what is now known as the First World War was a game-changer in more ways than one. It saw the introduction of mechanized armored vehicles replacing horse-drawn caissons, and the advent of aerial warfare that had little resemblance to the balloonists who dropped crude bombs on the troops below them during The War Between the States.

World War I also made us rethink our battlefield strategies, which still clung to the old cavalry tactics. And it introduced the horrors of trench warfare. But perhaps most importantly, WWI saw an amalgamation of weaponry that combined the old with the new, and gave our American doughboys an impressive array of one-on-one combat arms that spanned both 19th and 20th century technologies. Indeed, World War I could just as easily – from an individual firearms standpoint – have been called the Battle of Two Centuries.

But this diversification of fighting weapons for Uncle Sam's Army did not come about because we were taken by surprise, as was the case years later during WWII with the bombing of Pearl Harbor. And back around the turn of the last century, it wasn't as if we didn't know a worldwide inferno was about to explode. In fact, what became known as WWI had been smoldering in Europe for over a decade, as military and political factions of countries – many of which don't even exist today – fought for supremacy while we watched from afar.

Ironically, although countless millions of small arms rounds from a variety of guns were fired during the four years, three months and two weeks timespan that encompassed The Great War, the entire conflagration was started by just two shots from an FN Model 1910 chambered in .380 ACP. They were fired on June 28, 1914, by a 19-year-old Yugoslavian anarchist named Gavrilo Princip at

almost point blank range to assassinate Austrian Archduke Franz Ferdinand, heir to the Austro-Hungarian throne, and his wife Sophie, Duchess of Hohenberg, in Sarajevo, the capital city of Bosnia. One month later Austria-Hungary invaded Serbia, which caused Russia to come to its defense, while Germany invaded France, which caused Great Britain to declare war against Germany.

Meanwhile, President Woodrow Wilson had adopted an isolationist philosophy of non-intervention, even when a German U-boat sank the British passenger ship Lusitania on May 7, 1915, killing 128 Americans on board. Already unpopular, Wilson barely got re-elected in 1916 with the slogan, "He kept us out of war" … but not for long. Germany relentlessly resumed attacks on other civilian vessels. The turning point came when German submarines sunk seven U.S. merchant ships. Around that same time, British intelligence intercepted a German plan to finance Mexico's revolution and join forces with it to take back Arizona, New Mexico and Texas from the United States.

Once this became public knowledge, Wilson could no longer utter the words, "America is too proud to fight." On April 6, 1917, Congress declared war

against Germany. Immediately thereafter the Selective Service was enacted to draft civilians into the armed forces and Major General John J. "Black Jack" Pershing was put in charge of what became known as the American Expeditionary Forces (AEF), which would soon be fighting alongside British and French troops, although the AEF retained its identity as a separate army under American command, thanks to Pershing's insistence.

In addition to American pride, and understandably not wanting to diminish control of his troops, no doubt another factor motivating Pershing to keep his command separate was that the weapons carried by our soldiers were far superior to those used by our allies. First and foremost was our primary battlefield rifle, the Model 1903 Springfield, more formally known as U.S. Magazine Rifle, Caliber .30, Model of 1903, which had been approved on June 30, 1903, to officially replace the then-current .30-40 Krag-Jorgensen bolt action. But unlike the Krag-Jorgensen, which existed as both rifle and carbine, the new Springfield was only made as a 24-inch barrel rifle, weighing 8½ pounds (unloaded) and featuring a full length walnut stock with a distinctive elongated finger groove fore-end and "humped" handguard to protect the rear sight.

The Model 1903 Springfield was one of our two primary battle rifles during WWI. The magazine's Cut Off Lever was designed to disengage the magazine follower, thus turning the rifle from a repeater into a single-shot.

The British P14 Enfield (top) was "Americanized" (bottom) by Winchester and Remington (and their Eddystone subsidiary) by chambering it for the .30-06 service round.
Photo courtesy Garry James.

Instead of the rather awkward-appearing side loading, hinged magazine of the Krag-Jorgensen, the Springfield featured a five-round, internal magazine that was loaded via a stripper clip, with the cartridges thumb-pressed into the magazine through the opened receiver.

Ironically, the Springfield inherited many of its features from the 1893 Spanish Mauser that had been used against our troops during the Spanish-American War. This included the aforementioned stripper clip, as well as safety and extractor improvements. In addition, the Springfield featured a non-rotary extractor that prevented double feeding of cartridges, and a bolt-cocking plunger that enabled the rifle to be de-cocked by pulling the trigger while holding back and manually releasing the plunger.

But, perhaps the most unusual feature (I would hesitate to call it useful because it wasn't from a practical fighting gun point of view) was the '03's magazine Cut Off Lever, a steel tab located on the left side of the receiver that effectively could prevent rounds from being fed into the chamber. In its downward or "off" position, which nestled the tab into an inlet in the stock, the cut off lever disengaged the magazine follower, thus turning the rifle from a bolt-action repeater into a single-shot. But in its "on" or upward position, the rifle functioned as a bolt action should, ejecting and feeding rounds with the operation of the bolt.

It is hard today to image why such a device would be installed on a bolt-action rifle that would normally have a cycling rate of 15 to 20 shots per minute. But "back in the day," as they say, there were certain individuals in the military hierarchy who remembered the older Trapdoor Springfield single-shots and were fearful that with a fast-firing repeater such as the Springfield '03, there would be a tendency to waste ammunition. Thus, newly-inducted recruits were instructed to put the magazine Cut Off Lever in the "On" position and to use the rifle as a single shot, saving the cartridges in the magazine as reserves. I have no doubt this practice was quickly forgotten when our doughboys got into their first firefight. (For a frightening story of a brown bear attack blamed on the magazine Cut Off, see "The Sporting 1903 Springfield" elsewhere in this edition. -Editor)

Just as interesting as the magazine Cut Off Lever is the almost immediate switch to ammunition for the newly adopted Springfield. Originally the rifle was chambered for the .30-03, which was heralded as an improvement over the .30-40 Krag. Unfortunately, it used the same 200-grain roundnose bullet, which resulted in a rainbow trajectory and also produced excessive chamber pressures and recoil. Obviously someone in the Ordinance Department R&D section had not done their homework. As a result, in 1906 the Springfield's caliber was changed to what has since become one of the most famous cartridges of all time, the .30-06 Government.

Designated "Cartridge, Ball, Caliber .30, Model of 1906," it fired a 150-grain spitzer bullet (changed to a 172-grain boat tail in 1926), which left the barrel at 2,800 feet per second (fps), resulting in a flatter trajectory and vastly improved accuracy. Consequently, this new cartridge required a slight redesign of the rifle, which included altering the rear flip-up battle sight, which was optimistically calibrated for 2,850 yards. With the leaf folded down, however, the sight was set for a slightly more realistic 525 yards. Practically all of the early 1903 Springfields in .30-03 were altered to chamber the .30-06, and today an '03 Springfield in its original .30-03 configuration is a rarity.

The development of the Springfield set a precedent for the M1 Garand and M1 Carbine that came after it, because like these two shoulder weapons, the rifle and its cartridge had been developed before we had to send our troops into battle. By the time the U.S. entered World War I, Springfield Armory and Rock Island Arsenal had already manufactured 843,239 Springfield rifles and production quickly ramped up once war was declared.

It should be noted that early heat-treating problems resulted in a small number of rifles with serial numbers below 800,000 (Springfield Armory) and under 286,506 (Rock Island Arsenal) malfunctioning and causing potential damage to both gun and shooter. *These guns should not be considered safe to fire without extensive examination of the metallurgy and inspection by a qualified gunsmith.* After the Armistice, manufacturing was halted at Rock Island, but the 1903 continued to be made at Springfield Armory until 1927, with many variations, including the 1903A1 with semipistol grip stock.

In addition to the Springfield, our other primary battle rifle in WWI was the British .303 Pattern 1914 Rifle, or the P14 Enfield, as it was known. Unlike the Springfield, this was a British design – but also with a Mauser-type

A Smith & Wesson Model 1917 is shown here. Like the Colt version, this revolver was adapted to the .45 ACP cartridge by the use of half-moon clips.

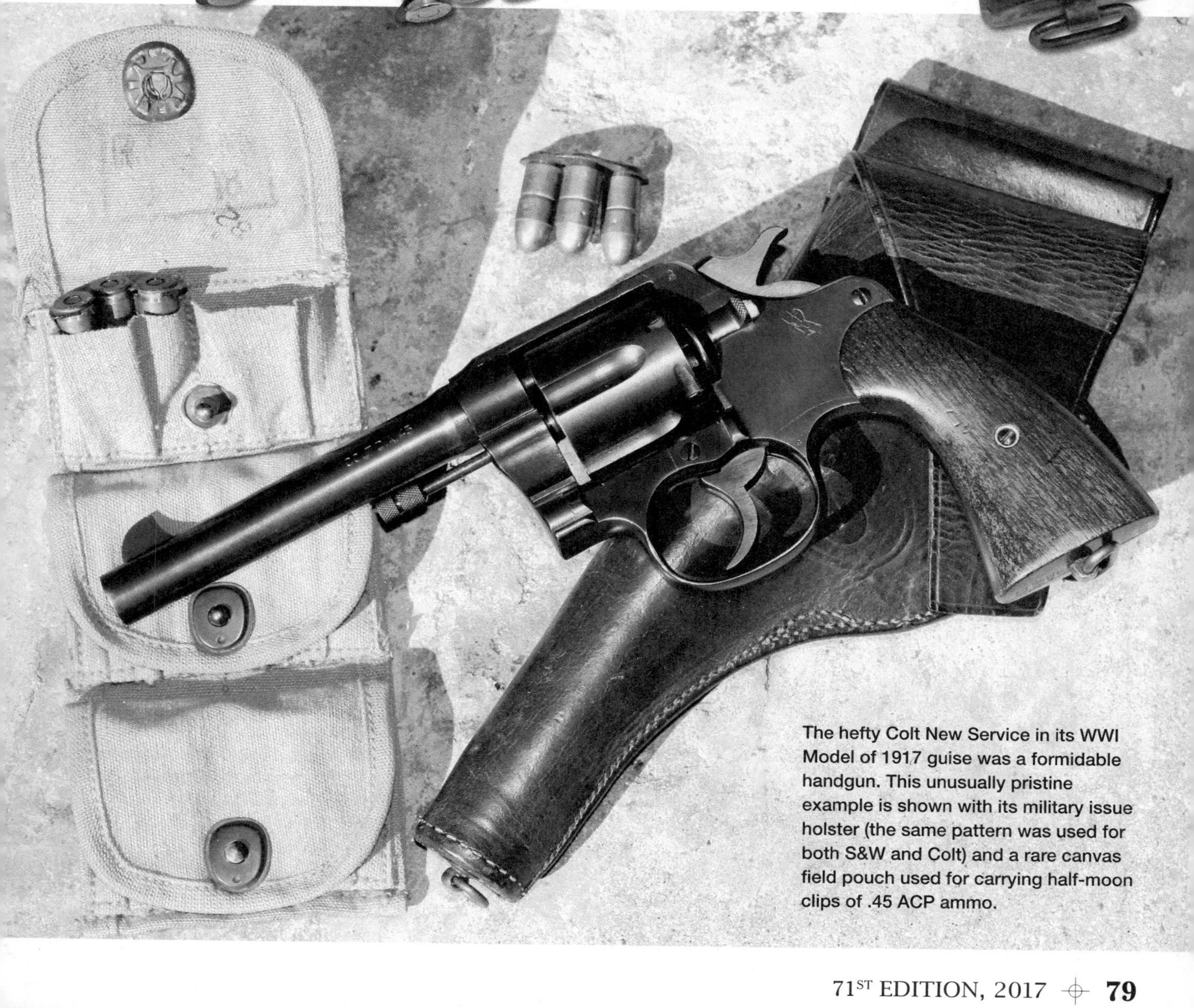

The hefty Colt New Service in its WWI Model of 1917 guise was a formidable handgun. This unusually pristine example is shown with its military issue holster (the same pattern was used for both S&W and Colt) and a rare canvas field pouch used for carrying half-moon clips of .45 ACP ammo.

The Model 1917 revolvers were stamped on their butt with an Army service number, which had no relationship to their serial number. This is the butt of the 1917 New Service version.

action – that Winchester, Remington and their Eddystone subsidiary had been making for Great Britain's troops due to the inability of the Royal Small Arms Factory in the north London borough of Enfield to keep up with demand. After all, during this period the Brits were already fighting the Germans; we were not. But in 1917, with our entry into the war, things changed. After completing their contracts by producing 1,235,298 Enfields for our British Allies, Winchester and the two Remington factories continued making the P14 Enfield, but instead chambered them for the government's .30-06 cartridge. Thus, the American Enfield, or U.S. Rifle, Caliber .30, Model of 1917 was born.

With its humpbacked rear sight and sharply curved pistol grip, it was not as graceful as the Springfield. Nonetheless, weighing in at 8 pounds and sporting a 26-inch barrel, the American Enfield balanced well. However, its six-round magazine could only be loaded five rounds at a time, as the P14 used the same stripper clip as the Springfield. But the unique dog-legged angle of the bolt handle placed it close to the trigger, which made for faster cocking. By the end of the war, more Enfields had been produced – a total of 2,193,429 rifles – than Springfields. One of its greatest tributes is the fact that Sergeant Alvin York was armed with an American Enfield when he single-handedly killed 20 German soldiers and captured 132 others, recalling "...all I could do was touch the Germans off just as fast as I could. I was sharp shooting. I don't think I missed a shot..."

Perhaps not as accurate but certainly as prolific was our Army's official side-arm during WWI, the Colt Automatic Pistol, Caliber .45, Model of 1911. American Expeditionary Forces commander General "Black Jack" Pershing was certainly no stranger to the slab-sided semiautomatic, having carried one as he rode across the Mexican border in pursuit of Pancho Villa a few years earlier. That was just about the time the Army was making its changeover from smallbore double-action revolvers to bigbore single-action semiautomatics. And like the advent of the Springfield, thankfully the 1911 had been adopted by the Army on March 19, 1911 – well before we entered the war.

So much as been written about the Model 1911 by myself and others – hitting a crescendo in 2011 in an unrelenting 100th anniversary celebration of this great gun – that it would be superfluous to repeat the same details again. Suffice to say the 1911 descended from a John Browning design that began in 1897 and gradually evolved from the ungainly .38 ACP Colt Automatic Pistol of 1900 (Colt's first successful semiauto), to the 1902 Model Colt Automatic Pistol, the Model 1905 (which featured an angled grip with built-in safety, a 5¼-inch barrel and seven-round magazine – all of which would eventually find their way into the 1911) and the gradually improved Models of 1907, 1909 and 1910.

By the time the Model 1911 beat out all of the other competitors in the final Army field trials of March 15, 1911, after a grueling 6,000-round test in which the Browning design did not incur a single failure to function, it had become the epitome of what a 20th century military handgun should be. Features included not one, but three safeties (grip, thumb-operated slide/hammer lock and half cock), and a lanyard loop on both the gun and its magazine to prevent losing them if either were dropped. If there was one fault with the Model 1911, it was its anemic front and rear sights, which made aiming a challenge, at best. The 1911's loose-fitting parts, which made field assembly and disassembly a cinch, didn't help accuracy either. But both of these criticisms were offset by the cartridge that the pistol fired, for you didn't really have to make a direct hit to topple a target that was hit with a 230-grain roundnose .45 ACP bullet.

Coming off of repeated battlefield failures involving its .38-caliber wheelguns, the Army demanded that their new semiautomatic pistol be chambered in .45 caliber, a proven manstopper. But the rimmed .45 Colt cartridge of Indian Wars fame, while effective, was not adaptable to the new semiautomatic. Browning decided to update the cartridge into an ACP (Automatic Colt Pistol) version, just as he had done with the .38 for his previous semiautomatics. Working with Colt and Brigadier General John Taliaferro Thompson of the Army Ordnance Corps, a 230-grain, full-metal-jacket cartridge was

developed that was ballistically similar to the .45 Colt, and would become just as famous. It became known as the Caliber .45 Automatic Pistol Ball Cartridge, Model of 1911, or more popularly, the .45 ACP. Together, the Model 1911 and its .45 ACP chambering would go on winning victories long after WWI.

However, just as with the Springfield, production for the Model 1911 was unable to keep up with wartime demand. Thus, in spite of the Army's adoption of the semiauto, it found it had to resort to revolvers for officers and others who needed a close range means of defense. And of course, these revolvers had to be able to chamber the new rimless .45 ACP cartridge. Although such wheelguns didn't exist, there were two strong and reliable revolvers that were chambered in .45 Colt and could be adapted with a little judicious factory reaming to accept the 1911's round. Enter the Smith & Wesson Second Model Hand Ejector and the slightly heftier Colt New Service, both with 5½-inch barrels.

This was not the first time the Colt New Service had become an official U.S. Army sidearm. It had been briefly known as the Model 1909 for a two-year period before the Army's adoption of the 1911. Then it was back to being the New Service. But now, neither of the two revolvers kept their civilian names once they were drafted into service. To make things confusing, they were both given the same nomenclature of "U.S. Model 1917."

To enable both revolvers to chamber the .45 ACP, and suspecting that the U.S. would soon be entering the war, in 1916 Smith & Wesson and Springfield Armory began working in tandem to develop a half-moon steel clip that held three .45 ACP cartridges and enabled them to be engaged by the cylinder's extractor. Naturally, two clips were required to fill the six chambers. In addition, the chambers were machined so that the .45 ACP cartridges would have the proper headspace to be fired even without half-moon clips. This, of course, meant that the empties would have to be punched out individually, as the extractor couldn't engage the rimless cases without the clip.

The compact size of the Colt Pocket Hammerless Models of 1903 (.32 ACP) and 1908 (.380 ACP) made them ideal for issuing to general officers during WWI. This is a later version featuring walnut grips rather than the hard rubber of First World War guns.

The Winchester Model 1897 Trench gun was a formidable weapon, but its regulation 1917 issue bayonet made it awkward to use in close quarters. All of the WWI guns were solid frames. Takedown versions were used in WWII.

Although the Colt Model of 1917 exhibited a brushed blued wartime finish, without any of the smooth external polishing of the civilian versions of the gun, the Smith & Wesson Model 1917 sported a polished blued finish with case-hardened hammer and trigger – unusual quality for a wartime firearm. Both the Colt and S&W revolvers sported two-piece walnut grips and the bottoms of their barrels were stamped "United States Property." Their butts featured a lanyard and were stamped, "U.S. Army Model 1917," followed by an Army service number, which had nothing to do with the revolver's serial number. Most of the Colt and Smith & Wesson Model 1917s were shipped to Springfield Armory or U.S. Army depots, where they were subsequently deployed to active duty. In all, by the time World War I ended 163,476 S&W Model 1917s had been produced, compared with 151,700 of the Colt version.

But there were other pistols involved in the Great War as well, including the Colt Pocket Hammerless Models of 1903 and 1908, in calibers .32 ACP and .380 ACP respectively. These were marked "U.S. Property" and were issued to general officers. Interestingly, unlike the parkerized versions issued during WWII, these First World War guns were given a lustrous blued finish, indicating that perhaps they really weren't destined for front line use.

But one weapon that was very much in the trenches – quite literally – was the Winchester Model 1897 Trench Gun, which was basically a militarized version of the pump-action Model 97 Riot Gun. Featuring a 20-inch open-choke barrel and a five-round tubular magazine, the gun was chambered in 12 gauge only. Military loads of 00 buckshot, coupled with the Model 97s ability to be "slam-fired" by keeping the trigger depressed while working the pump, proved to be so devastating that Germany tried unsuccessfully to have the shotgun outlawed from The Great War.

Already a popular sporting arm among civilians, the Model 97 Trench Gun, with its short barrel, sling swivels and ventilated heat shield became indispensable for our doughboys fighting in the open, chest-high trenches of No Man's Land, where they might turn a corner and literally come face to face with the enemy. In fact, although the '97 Trench Gun was outfitted with a bayonet lug, the standard military M-1917 bayonet's

Above: The regulation Army bayonet features a 16½-inch blade. Many of these early bayonets were cut down during WWII.

16½-inch blade interfered with the otherwise excellent balance of the Trench Gun, and was especially cumbersome in close quarters. Nonetheless, it looked menacing when affixed to the Trench Gun, although it was mainly used for last-ditch fighting.

Another last-ditch weapon that many do not associate with The Great War was the Remington Double Derringer, a .41 rimfire over/under pistol that is more often identified with riverboat gamblers and "painted ladies" of the old frontier. But these little two-shot pocket pistols could be slipped into an Air Service pilot's jacket and provided an emergency means of self-defense for flying aces who found their biplanes shot down or otherwise were forced to land behind enemy lines.

Of course, there were many more firearms that entered a war that started, for the U.S. at least, 100 years ago, but these are some of the more notable ones. Suffice it to say that by the time World War I ended on November 11, 1918, a diverse array of American guns had joined ranks to effectively preserve our precious freedoms.

Left: A number of Air Service pilots in WWI slipped the tiny Remington Double Derringer into their flight jacket pocket as a last ditch self-defense tool in case their biplanes went down behind enemy lines.

FIVE EXPERT SHOTGUNNERS SHARE THEIR
WINGSHOO
BEYOND THE BASICS

By **Nick Sisley**

n the 10 to 30 years prior to World War I, shotgunners were in the midst of their heyday, especially in England and Scotland. Those were the years when the Marquis of Ripon (Lord de Grey) and Lord Walsingham, as well as others, accounted for some unbelievable game bags. The shooting world never figured to see that era's equal in the numbers of game shot – as well as the expertise of those doing this massive wing gunning.

But in the early 1970s the doves of South America were discovered, first in Colombia, but by the early 1980s Argentina had emerged with more aerial targets than Ripon or Walsingham could ever have imagined. Today, more than 40 years later, there are even more doves

than there were in 1984. Further, those dove populations have expanded dramatically into Uruguay and Bolivia. Thus, the opportunity for today's wingshooters has expanded far beyond what was believed in 1920, 1950 and beyond.

Many have experienced this South American shooting 20 and more times during their life. Some stay to shoot for extended periods. So move over Lords de Grey and Walsingham, because you are being replaced by wing gunners who have shot as much or nearly as much – plus the expertise of handling a shotgun properly and wonderfully have been perfected to the figurative nth degree.

One of the Argentine lodges where I've shot frequently is called Pico Zuro. It's in the fabled Cordoba area, and it was there

South America can produce more shooting opportunities than Lords DeGrey and Walsingham ever saw.
Photo by Jorge Piper Molina.

SECRETS ON LONG-RANGE SHOOTING

The author reloads his Perazzi MX8 as he watches the sky for approaching doves.

I met Horacio Dartiguelongue, Manager of the David Denies Wingshooting operations. One day he asked why I was shooting those 25- to 35-yard doves. "You hardly miss those easy shots. Why don't you stretch your abilities – try some really long shots?" Horacio introduced me to the 60-yard and even longer dove shots and started imparting the techniques to help me become very successful in that type of demanding shooting. Of course, those techniques are just as effective in shooting doves and other winged targets at any range.

Horacio also told me about Simon Ward. Even Horacio shakes his head at what Simon is able to do at long ranges with a shotgun. On that same trip I also met Bill Anderson, and over the years

since then we have become close friends – at least via email. Finally, Horacio introduced me to two other super dove shooters that have frequented Pica Zuro repeatedly for years, Peter Bassnett and Kevin Jobling. So what follows is the expertise from these five gentlemen on what it takes to make the really long shots.

SIMON WARD

When Horacio started giving me advice about shooting doves farther and farther distant, he told me it was Simon Ward who showed this Pico Zuro manager that such shotgunning was not only possible, but with some special techniques, consistency was also in the

shooting cards. Horacio speaks almost reverently about Ward's shotgunning skills. Simon hails from England and has spent his life shooting and teaching others to wing gun in the United Kingdom.

Simon is a freelance shooting instructor and gun fitter who works with five shooting schools within an hour of London. *Field Magazine* lists him as Britain's finest all-around game shot and also one of the country's top 100 game shots of all time. His shotgun of choice is a 12-gauge Perazzi 2000S with 32-inch barrels – both barrels choked Full. His favorite shells for long-range doves are Fiocchi 28-gram #7. Just a guess, but I'm thinking Ward prefers the #7s over #7½ and #8 because a tad more striking energy at the longer distances.

To get started, Simon first suggests focusing on footwork and balance. "If you don't get your feet into the correct position you can't keep the gun moving. If your balance is too far over the front foot you will tend to shoot underneath long-range doves.

"For long-range crossing doves I prefer a 50/50 balance on each foot. This type of balance allows me to hold the line on the bird with a free-moving gun. However, for high driven or high crossing shots I prefer to take such birds more off my back foot – say 40 percent front, 60 percent rear foot. Again this enables me to stay on the line of the target and with a free moving gun."

Note Simon's remarks about "staying on the line" of the bird. As you read on you will see the other experts remark repeatedly about the "line." Ward does not refer to "gun mounting" but to "precision gun mounting."

He suggests, "To consistently shoot long-range doves your gun mount must be perfect every time. Your consistency in connecting your eyes and the muzzle of the gun with the bird has to be pinpoint accurate every time to achieve consistent success.

"Use the front hand to do the pointing. There is no room for error because the target is so far away – so if your gun pointing is the least bit erratic, especially with the 'line,' you will struggle to shoot these birds with any degree of consistency.

"When shooting at extreme range your technique – from your footwork and balance to your gun-mounting skills to the fit of the gun – all these come under scrutiny."

Ward continues, "I've spent a lifetime of shooting – striving to perfect the art of being able to consistently kill the long-range birds – doves, pigeons, pheasants, partridge and grouse. There is a limit (with a shotgun) and one of the great skills to killing long-range birds is learning where the cutoff point is – i.e. where your shotgun pattern and the striking energy of your cartridge and your gun runs out. Also, don't forget that you can kill a crossing dove much farther than an overhead dove due to the law of gravity."

How about lead on the target at long range? Simon picks this up with, "Firstly, perfect your footwork and balance. A smooth and pinpoint accurate 'moving' gun mount on to the bird (with 'moving' gun mount I think Simon means starting the move of the barrels as you simultaneously start the stock to your shoulder) – your perceived lead will become natural

Simon Ward is one of Britain's top shooting instructors. To consistently shoot long-range doves, he says your gun mount must be perfect every time. He also stresses the importance of the shooter's footwork.

for whatever the range of your shots. Every gunner sees a different 'picture' as we all move the gun at a different speed. Make your mantra 'make the speed of the gun the same as the speed of the bird for all ranges of shots.' This helps the shooter feel as one with the gun and what appears to be a fast bird appears to slow down – but lead will be automatic.

"The sign of a master at work is that such wing gunners seem to have all the time in the world, and they show the utmost respect for their quarry."

"What about visual focus?" I asked Simon Ward.

"For all ranges of dove shooting, once you have picked out your target use soft focus to start with (What does soft focus mean? Shooting instructor John Shima in his book *Moment of Truth* suggests that soft focus is occurring when driving a car. You're sort of looking at everything and your peripheral vision is wide) and only as you start to lock on to the bird switch to hard focus at this point and look in front of the beak – cheek glued to the stock.

"Once you have completed the connection to your chosen bird and moved to the space in front and taken the shot I can't emphasize enough the concept of keeping your cheek glued to the stock even after you have killed the bird. By doing this you will receive a visual message sent back up the barrel to your lead eye (and brain) – of what you saw when you killed the bird. To achieve the same success time and time again, repeat this staying-in-the-gun process to build your memory bank of sight pictures."

PETER BASSNET

Peter lives on the south coast of England with his wife and three spaniels. In the UK he shoots wood pigeons, his favorite, but in addition to his more than 20 trips to Argentina he has shot in Uruguay, Morocco, South Africa, Croatia, Spain, Portugal, France, Ireland and more. During his many trips to Argentina alone he feels he has pointed his gun at doves over 100,000 times. While he has killed many extremely high birds, the reason he returns to Pica Zuro is for the variety of shots and the constant challenge of always finding something a little more difficult than the last time.

For starters, Peter feels too many shooters spend too much time thinking or creating "lead," when they should be concentrating more on the "line." As the

Peter Bassnett shooting high-flying doves in Argentina.

shotgun is swung and mounted it's very easy to move the gun off the line – usually downward from the bird's flight path. "There is no right way for every shot. Each shot must be treated individually, but certain principles must always be brought into play.

"Over a long life of shooting I've watched many great shooters who always seem to have one thing in common. They never rush a shot. They always seem to have plenty of time. These great shooters also seem to take a lot of time looking at the bird before the gun is started. During this time the muzzles of the yet unmounted gun go to the bird – as the feet are moved to the appropriate point for a killing shot."

For his shooting in the UK, Peter Bassnett enjoys working and shooting over his three spaniels – two springers and a cocker.

Bassnett has a shooting mantra he follows. "HANDS – make sure the hands are in the perfect spot for the upcoming shot – slightly forward on the fore-end for a lower incomer or outbound bird – slightly farther out on the fore-end for a high incomer or crosser. FEET – make sure the feet are in the direction that the shot will go. EYES – look at the bird intently and do not shoot at the entire bird – try to see the beak, some plumage – even an eye – practice this hard focus on small objects to make doing what I'm suggesting easier. FACE – pointing the muzzle at the bird whilst raising the gun – the stock coming into the shoulder pocket and the face at about the same time – I want to feel my cheek bone on the stock."

So Bassnett's shooting mantra HANDS, FEET, EYES, FACE is what he tries to accomplish every shot. If his shooting slips he puts his mindset back into that mantra. Another mantra – he loads his own over/under. After shooting a box he takes a bit of a break – watches the eagles, the mountains, other birds and the sky before starting on another box of shells. This stopping insures no hurry, no worry and a "don't forget to smell the flowers" attitude.

Finally, Peter advised, "Most shooters could improve their performance if they wrote MMFF on the back of their hand – which means 'move my friggin' feet!'"

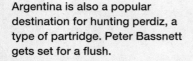

Argentina is also a popular destination for hunting perdiz, a type of partridge. Peter Bassnett gets set for a flush.

While Bassnett shot a Beretta Jubilee 20 gauge for many years, about five years ago he switched to a Caesar Guerini Maxum model – a 20 gauge with 30-inch barrels and screw-in chokes. For the very long-range doves he tends to rely on Improved Modified and Full chokes.

KEVIN JOBLING

Kevin Jobling also calls the United Kingdom home. His wingshooting experience not only spans decades, he has also pulled the trigger a figurative zillion times – with numerous trips to Argentina and driven shoots at home, plus he's a champion clay target shooter – in fact he won the United Kingdom F.I.T.A.S.C. Championship in April of 2015 at Park Lodge. Jobling is also the Director at the Jervaulx Game Farm, plus he raises game birds that are sold all over the UK and is Area Manager for the Work Stores, Ltd.

Jobling's favorite shooting method on very long targets is maintained lead. Why? He says because gun speed is slower – the result being more control of the gun – perhaps more control of the target as well. "This method allows me to place the shot string very accurately and consistently – especially on the very distant birds. But on driven-type birds I prefer the pull away. Swing through and pull away methods require perfect timing as gun speed is faster than the bird (at trigger-pulling time)."

He goes on, "Unfortunately many things can affect your timing – like both mental and psychological states of mind, even tiredness."

Let's say he has bagged the first bird, but for the second shot his gun is already behind that second bird. Kevin says not to fret for this is an ideal situation. So dismount the gun to allow your eyes and mind to acquire a clear picture of the bird and what it's doing – like speed, angle, distance and so forth. "The brain is a very efficient tool that enables me to adjust foot position and having worked out the necessary lead picture, remount on the bird without consciously thinking through the process."

He suggests never moving the feet during the shot. When he focuses on the bird he's mentally calculating where he's going to take the shot – so if he needs to move his feet his mind does that for him automatically. This is a very important tip, and one the typical wing gunner never does – decide where the shot is going to be taken before the gun mount even begins. So readers must work on

Preparing for the shot means so much. Figure out the bird's flight path. Move the feet to where you are going to pull the trigger – before you start the gun mount.

Kevin Jobling, and all the other experts interviewed by the author, says gun fit is extremely important for successful wing shooting, and even more important when shooting extra-long-range doves.

this critical aspect of shooting before it becomes automatic.

This foot movement thing allows the shoulders to remain square – parallel to the target. If the shoulders don't stay square the gun can't stay on the line – the muzzles will dip down away from the target. Further, when Jobling selects the bird he wants to shoot he has the muzzle on the bird's tail before even mounting. As the bird approaches the area where

he wants to shoot, he starts the mount and shoots very soon after the mount is completed.

His move comes from the hips – not the arms – so it's a turn rather than a swing. Foot position is so important and here's why. "If you stand under some overhead cables and try to swing the gun down those cables using only your arms and not your hips you would find that the barrels come away from those cables

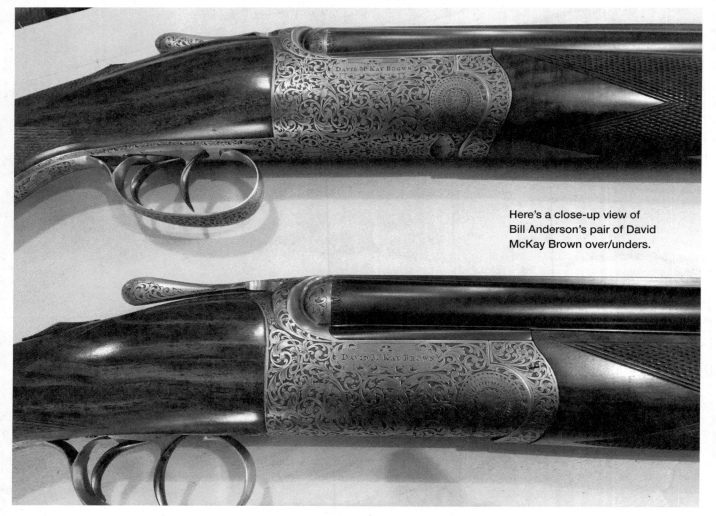

Here's a close-up view of Bill Anderson's pair of David McKay Brown over/unders.

– downward. But if you take your hand off the fore-end (thus eliminating the use of the arms) you will have to swing with your hips. You will then find how easy it is to keep the muzzles on the cables."

Mentally, Kevin has total confidence in his preparation for the shot. He thus trusts his capability. He admonishes any doubts about missing from his mind. He tries to get in the "zone" in clay target competition because he's trying the break every bird. But in dove or other types of live bird stuff, missing is not as important since this is for enjoyment. If he does lose confidence he thinks back to his past achievements, tries to regain the "feelings" he had when shooting well, plus reverts back to the basics of timing, foot position and shot preparation.

Five years ago he went to Italy for his SC3 Perazzi that was built to his specifications, which he says is a great service when buying a new Perazzi. He prefers a gun with a balance point that is behind the hinge. For him this creates a gun that feels light and is "fast handling." Jobling

also told me such a gun balance provides for more effortless shooting, and helps reduce the possibility of head lifting. His SC3 Perazzi has two sets of barrels – one set choked Half and Half - which he uses on clays, the second set choked Half and Three-Quarters that he uses on game.

"I don't honestly think that I could shoot any better than I can with this Perazzi."

As with many sports, top shooters make it look easy. It usually looks like they have time to spare. This is because they have prepared for the shot properly. The worst flaw he sees is bad gun fit. "Properly, a gun should nestle into the shoulder with the shooter looking down the barrels, *without* lowering the head. The shotgun should never be aimed, but should be an extension of your body pointing where you are looking."

Finally, Jobling offered these four tips; (1) get some professional instruction, (2) get professionally fitted to your gun, (3) give yourself time on your shots and

prepare early, and (4) go to the Cordoba area of Argentina – the greatest training ground in the world – where you can practice every shot imaginable over and over and over.

BILL ANDERSON

I get the impression that Bill has worked very hard all his life, but when we email back and forth it's never about anything but shotguns and shooting them – not about his business ventures. When we first met at Pica Zuro it took a few days before he confided some of the shotguns he owned. He mentioned that he had a pair of David McKay Brown over/unders. (Bill corrected me saying, "David pronounces that middle name Mc-eye.") I had an idea how many pounds sterling it would take to buy one, so I knew Anderson was serious about his shooting. He, too, tries to shoot Argentina every year, but he has formed a shooting syndicate that shoots in England and Scotland, plus he makes a yearly trek to Spain for driven red-legged partridge. He shoots about 75 days a year with this shooting syndicate – red grouse, gray partridge and pheasants, the emphasis probably on the latter.

Bill begins, "I've always shot maintained lead. This allows me to best judge both the speed and the 'curl' of the bird." Pheasants are known for the curl of their flight, but this can apply to all game birds in flight. Speed and lead are important, but the curl cannot be minimized.

He continues, "Whilst awaiting the birds I stand with the butt of my gun on my hip – the muzzles thus pointing upward, not only for safety but also the muzzles are up in the direction the birds are expected to appear. Thus the gun's muzzles can already be trying to track the bird as the gun is raised to the shoulder. This is a natural movement using the least effort whilst giving more control over the gun. This also means you are getting your body in the proper shooting position."

Another tip from Bill is that his left foot is always forward, but just as important is right foot is pushing forward. He believes that we can't shoot successfully without a bit of aggression – or maybe he could call it determination. "You have to remove all doubt from your mind when pulling the trigger. If I lose confidence with the high birds I shoot some closer ones – then move a bit higher to get where I was before. Most shooters I'm with do this."

But let's back up a bit. The bird first appears in front. Bill's first move is not with the gun but with his feet – yes his feet. You've read that in this treatise previously. The feet move to where they need to be when the trigger is pulled. As this is occurring the muzzles are doing what they do, but Bill is watching the "line" of the bird. The amount of lead is important, but one instructor after another has told me the "line" of flight is equally important, and Anderson says the same. Feet first. Mount next.

"Longer shots and longer barrels require greater accuracy. This can only be accomplished by a correct and consistent gun mount." Bill's current pair of David McKay Browns wear 32-inch barrels and very Full chokes. At 60 yards the barrels' patterns are 4 feet wide – at 45 yards about 2 feet 6 inches. "The latter is not a big area to center a moving target."

Bill believes "a proper gun fitting, along with a correct and consistent gun mount cannot be stressed enough. Let's say you try Argentina or another top wing gunning destination. Look at the

Pica Zuro Lodge manager Horacio Dartiguelongue gives some shooting instruction to a guest shotgunner.
Photo by Anastasia Votekova.

cost of not just the trip and the airfare but also the shells. You are going to be a lot more successful with a perfectly fitting gun." Bill is also impressed with how today's shotguns, properly choked, and with very good ammunition, how far a good shooter can reach out. Since Bill does so much shooting, the proper cartridge for him and his gun may not be suitable for you. He's adamant about both. The cartridges must perform great in his gun, but they must be comfortable to shoot. Of course, the gun and how it is stocked has plenty to do with felt recoil.

"The good shots – there's almost a casual air about them and their shooting. They are not casual. They see everything that's going on during the day. They are very keen without show-ing it – a trait any wingshooter might want to emulate."

HORACIO DARTIGUELONGUE

Horacio is the guy who got me going with extending my ranges while dove shooting on one of my trips to Pico Zuro Lodge. I guess he challenged me with, "You can do this – pointing to a bird that I thought was way out of range. Then he patiently stood behind and gave me advice. I offered him my Perazzi to try his luck. He not only killed plenty of distant doves, I was also impressed with his shooting style; smooth, no hur-rying, staying in the gun beautifully. As head man for David Denies Wingshoot-ing he gets to watch some of the world's outstanding shooters, plus he coaches neophytes in dove shooting – and all shooter types in between. I asked him a number of questions, and here's how he responded.

He told me clay targets are one thing. "You know the flight path, the speed, and you can get all set up for such birds. Live feathered game is a different story. They can change direction, increase or decrease their speed, dive downward, rise upward, take the wind. While sus-tained lead, swing through, pull away and other shooting methods can work I prefer the move, mount, shoot."

What if the dove is in front of the gun? Horacio comes back, "Such a bird is the wrong choice. In Argentina there will be plenty of other chances, usually within seconds." He suggests that "reading" the bird is very important. He's talking about what the bird is doing; crossing,

The author tries for a very long dove, reaching out with a Caesar Guerini Summit Sporting with 32-inch barrels.

diving, turning, whatever. So choose the bird that allows enough time to get the body in a good position before mounting.

"After reading the bird footwork comes next – getting your body in the best position to make the shot. Only then is the gun mounted. To the uninitiated this might look like jerky separate movements, but really there's a smoothness and beauty to watch this unfold. The feet/body must be in a good position at trigger pulling time – so the swing doesn't slow – plus the muzzles tend to get below the bird's flight path as the shooter runs out of swing."

He suggests not thinking about the gun. Instead focus hard on the bird, your body in good balance while concentrating on smoothness. Try not to think too much. Don't try too hard. Don't care if you miss. If one is missing don't think lead, think more about increasing the speed of the gun. Allow the gun to travel more in front of the bird. Delay the trigger pull. All this helps increase the lead, which, of course, is so important in shooting the truly long doves.

When Horacio is really shooting well he feels like he's dropping the birds with little effort (The Zone?). "I'm reading the birds well, naturally getting my body in the right position. If the bird takes a new direction or increases speed I often find I still go to such a bird naturally. It's hard to explain."

Like all of us sometimes he falls out of The Zone. What then? Take a break. Take more care in watching the birds and what they are doing. Are you sure you are reading the birds correctly?

"This gives me a chance to relax and help me know that when I miss – the birds have to win sometimes," he said.

Regarding gun suggestions, Horacio is certain that the brand does not matter nearly as much as a properly fitting gun, and the longer the ranges you will be shooting the more important proper fit becomes. He goes on, "Most of our shooters at Pica Zuro have never been coached so it's easy to make them better with simple basics. Some of the faults I see and try to correct would be stopping the gun, lifting the head off the stock and simply snap shooting hoping the shot will somehow arrive properly with the bird. Because we have so many birds our shooters can keep repeating – getting the body in a good position, staying in the gun and keeping the momentum of the swing. When they try all three they see doves tumbling."

There is the chance that there will be detractors of shooting long range at the doves of South America – perhaps on moral grounds or whatever. But the fact is a few very experienced and very good wingshooters have been and are perfecting the techniques that allow them to be very consistent in this shooting. Further, as Simon Ward has pointed out there are cutoff distances – where it does not pay to try shooting at some distance – always dependent upon one's skill, techniques, gun and load. Further yet, the techniques suggested in this article will also work on any bird and at any useful distance – not merely long-range doves. Finally, Simon Ward also pointed out that these expert gunners have the ultimate respect for their quarry, and we all should. I know I do.

Nick Sisley is no stranger to shooting South America. Beginning with his first trip in 1972 when the wing gunning in Colombia began its heyday Sisley has shot there, Ecuador, Argentina, Uruguay, and Bolivia a total of over 50 times. A full-time freelance writer since 1969 Nick has sold thousands of magazine articles. He's also the author of 13 books. His latest is a Gun Digest Books publication, Shooter's Guide to Shotgun Games. *Four of his e-Books are on* www.amazon.com.

Photography by Anastasia Votekova, www.pvphotography.com.ar *and Jorge Piper Molina,* www.boliviaadventures.com. *To learn more about Pica Zuro Lodge contact* Santiago@daviddenies.com.

COLT'S FINEST SINGLE ACTION—
THE NEW FRONTIER

By **John Taffin**

"Pick up a seashell and it is said that one can hear the sea as the shell is placed over the ear. Pick up a Colt Single Action and you can hear the tickling of piano ivories in the saloon on Main Street in Dodge City. You can smell wet cattle as they are driven north through wind and rain and dust. You can taste fresh cooked bacon and beans over a campfire in the mountains of Montana, and you can see the history of our country stretching over a century.

"Pull back the large hammer, sight down the hog wallow trough that serves as a rear sight, and slowly squeeze the trigger. As the gun roars and gently bucks in recoil of a .45 Colt or .44 Special or .44-40, you feel the mild but business-like recoil of the heavy bullet as it settles its business with finality. No heavy kickin' Magnum here, but a load that has served sixgunners for over 100 years.

"Countless numbers of deer, black bear, cougars and even grizzly have fallen to the old Colt. A young rancher friend of mine here in Idaho still carries a 4¾-inch .45 Colt as his every day ranch sixgun and he has taken everything that walks hereabouts with it, and he does it with black-powder loads. This man will never suffer from the stress of modern life. He has discovered one of the real keys to happiness.

"Watch a group of Colt Single Action devotees gather and start talking about the big Colt. You can tell 'em easily. A big Stetson, a $300 pair of boots and a nickel's worth of clothes in between. They have a contented look on their faces no one else can understand. Their eyes mist over as they talk in reverential, almost mystical, tones about the virtues of the Single Action Colt. Yes, they will look down their noses at your wonder-nine and maybe even politely laugh a little at your poor choice of handgun. Call 'em throwbacks if you will, but don't call 'em out!

"Handguns are my passion, and Colt Single Actions are my ultimate consum-

The stainless steel Freedom Arms Model 97 in .44 Special (top) bears a striking resemblance to the Colt New Frontier. Both have 5½-inch barrels.

Below: The late legendary gun writer Skeeter Skelton was directly responsible for the resurrection of the .44 Special Colt. He especially favored the 7½-inch New Frontier model.

ing love. When I want to shoot silhouettes, I reach for a Dan Wesson revolver. For big-game hunting my first choice is one of the excellent five-shot revolvers from Freedom Arms. Knocking about the woods, a virtually indestructible Ruger—preferably an old Flat-Top Single Action suits me just fine. And for defensive use, I can think of no finer choice than a 4-inch double action big-bore sixgun from Smith & Wesson. BUT when I want to stir my soul, quicken my spirit, or make my heart beat just a little faster. I'll reach for a Colt Single Action Army and head for the hills."

The preceding words were written by me nearly 25 years ago and they are shared here once again to show my deep affection for the Colt Single Action, an affection I might add which has only deepened with the passing of time. The Colt Single Action is so perfect it is still being produced with very little change more than 140 years after it first arrived way back in 1873.

In the 1890s the Colt Single Action Army was improved to the Colt Flat-Top Target. These handsome replicas were made by the now defunct U.S. Fire Arms Company. The rams horn stocks are by Roy Fishpaw.

It is said William Mason is responsible for the Colt Single Action; I'm skeptical. Colt had submitted an 1871-72 Open-Top .44 for the Army tests to select a new sidearm. Just as the name implies, the Open-Top Colt followed the lines of the 1860 Army, which did not have a top strap. The Army rejected the new Colt saying they wanted a "top-strap" pistol and wanted the caliber enlarged to .45, so it was back to the drawing board. And it is here I become somewhat skeptical.

Oh, I'm not questioning the fact William Mason went back to work, completed the drawings for the new pistol, turned the drawings over to the factory workers, and the result was the Colt Single Action. However, I think deep down in my sixgunning soul something is missing. I question the fact that any mere man could've come up with such a magnificent design as the Colt Single Action Army. At least in my heart I can envision William Mason sitting at his drawing board and thinking just what to do next. I want to think he fell asleep and when he woke up something supernatural had happened and the plans for the

new sixgun were finished and in front of him. Perhaps, it didn't happen this way. But then, perhaps it really did.

The Colt Single Action would originally be produced from 1873 to the eve of World War II. These are known as First Generation Colts. The Second Generation Colts began in late 1955 and ran until the early 1970s when they were shut down again, and then came back as the Third Generation Colts in the mid-1970s. The production was shut down for a brief interval a couple of times since then, however it is still being produced, though in somewhat small quantities.

There is no agreement on exactly how many different chamberings were made in the original run, but it is at least 30, and probably more. When the Second Generation appeared the only chamberings were .45 Colt, .44 Special, .357 Magnum and .38 Special. With the arrival of the Third Generation we also returned to the old frontier chamberings of .44-40, .38-40 and .32-20.

The Colt Single Action Army is Perfection in a Pistol. It is a natural pointer, chambered in cartridges powerful

enough to get the job done, more than sufficiently accurate, and has a grip that fits more hands than any other. So how do we improve on perfection? Improvement comes by changing the sights from the fixed hog wallow rear sight across the top strap, matched up with a blade front sight which in most earlier guns was very narrow and hard to see – especially when matched up with a narrow "V" rear sight. Current Colt Single Actions have a square-cut rear sight matched up with a blade of uniform width, both of which are a tremendous improvement from the originals; however, they are still fixed and not easily adjusted for windage or elevation.

Improvement came as Colt engineers sought to make perfection even more perfect with better sights. Target shooting was very popular in the closing decade of the 19th century and Colt added target sights to the Single Action Army. Actually, Colt first started with target sights on the then new Bisley Model, which was the Single Action Army with a target hammer and trigger, and a grip frame more conducive to target shooting.

The so-called target sights of the time were a square notch rear sight set in a dovetail, which could be moved for windage, and a screw adjustable front sight for elevation. Very crude, but better than the original for target shooters. Those Flat-Top Targets did not stay in production very long.

The next improvements came not by Colt but by men like Elmer Keith and companies like King Gun Sight Co. Keith wrote of several Single Actions he had fitted with adjustable sights. His gunsmiths used Smith & Wesson rear adjustable sights matched up with more visible post front sights sometimes using gold bars inlaid in the front sight for different elevations. King Gun Sight Co. added fully adjustable sights and target ribs to the tops of barrels to make it much easier to shoot the Colt more accurately. Keith also redesigned the grip frame to what he called the Number Five SAA by combining the backstrap of the Bisley Model with the triggerguard of the Single Action Army. Keith tried to convince Colt to add his improvements to the SAA but his pleas fell on deaf ears.

When the Single Action Army was reintroduced in late 1955 it was basically the same Colt that first arrived in 1873. The sights had been squared but were still fixed sights and might or might not have

A 5½-inch .44 Special New Frontier is flanked by .45 Colts with 4¾- and 7½-inch barrels.

shot to point of aim. Finally, someone at Colt decided it really was time to improve on perfection and the result, at least to my mind, is the finest Colt Single Action ever produced, the New Frontier model.

The feeling of the country in 1960 was much different than it is now. We had a new young president, a president who spoke of country and what we can all do for the country – not what the country could do for us. Optimism and hope ran high; we seemed to be on the threshold

New Frontiers are shown here in George Lawrence #120 Keith holsters from the 1950s.

of a new era. In late 1961, Colt introduced its New Frontier model in honor of President John F. Kennedy's ringing declaration, "We stand at the edge of a New Frontier…" To further honor the new young president Colt went to work on a special engraved presentation model New Frontier to present to JFK, however the dark days of November 1963 occurred before the Colt was finished and it was never presented.

To come up with the New Frontier, Colt basically took the standard Single Action Army, now in its Second Generation, generously and beautifully flat-topped the frame as Bill Ruger had accomplished with his new .357 Blackhawk in 1955, fitted it with a fully adjustable rear sight matched up with a ramp-style front sight, and the New Frontier was born. Finish on those Colts, which I consider the most beautiful single actions ever factory produced, consisted of a case-hardened frame as only Colt could do, with the balance of the gun being Colt's Royal Blue finish, as found on .357 Magnum Pythons of the same era.

The Colt Single Action Army is perfection in a pistol and definitely the choice of traditionalists, however the New Frontiers have everything the SAA has, the beautiful looks, feel and balance of the Single Action Army with the added advantage of adjustable sights. It is a rare fix-sighted sixgun that shoots perfectly to point of aim, and even if it does so it may be with only one particular load. If such a sixgun shoots low it is an easy fix to simply file down the front sight.

The sixguns are 4¾-inch .45 Colt New Frontiers and the leather is El Paso Saddlery's 1930 Austin.

However, if it shoots high that means the front sight has to be made taller which is not such an easy fix. If the windage is off the barrel must be turned using a special vise.

Four years ago we spent considerable time checking over 100 traditional single actions of various manufacturers and spent several days turning barrels to bring point of aim to point of impact. The adjustable-sighted Colt New Frontier requires nothing more than a proper fitting screwdriver to change point of impact. The addition of adjustable sights not only improves on the perfection of a Colt Single Action it also, when chambered in .45 Colt and .44 Special, even .357 Magnum when used with common sense, turns into a viable hunting handgun.

The first run of Colt New Frontiers, all Second Generation guns, began at serial number 3000NF and finished in 1974 at serial number 72XXNF. Four chamberings were offered in this first run of magnificent modernized Colt Flat-Top Target sixguns: .45 Colt, .44 Special, .357 Magnum, and very rarely, .38 Special. Standard barrel lengths of 4¾, 5½ and 7½ inches were cataloged – but not in every caliber. For example there were no 4¾-inch .44 Specials.

In 1962 the Single Action Army sold for $125 and the new New Frontier sold for $15 more. Both were totally out of my reach as I was in my third year of college, married with two babies and a

third one on the way, and working full time while going to college full time so we could survive and my wife could stay at home and take care of our family. Not only could I not afford either one of those sixguns, I had to sell my very early production Second Generation .45 SAA to provide living expenses. Our local store had a New Frontier .44 Special that I wanted really badly, however family and school took precedence. It would be more than 25 years before I would have a Second Generation .44 Special New Frontier.

Colt expert Don Wilkerson provided the information in the chart below to show the production numbers of the Second Generation New Frontier by caliber and barrel length.

From this chart it is easily seen just how rare the .44 Special Second Generation New Frontier is, and how especially rare the .38 Special is. I am fortunate to have examples of everything except .38 Special when it comes to Second Generation New Frontiers. Three of these are chambered in .45 Colt, with two of them having 4¾-inch barrels. However, both started as .357 Magnums and were then re-chambered to a tight .45 Colt and re-barreled with Colt original Second Generation 4¾-inch New Frontier barrels. Most Colt .45 cylinders will be found with chamber throats of .454" or, sometimes more, unfortunately; these new cylinders are cut to .451" to .452" and are especially accurate. Using the old Lyman/Keith #454424 cast bullet over 20 grains of #4227 results in one-hole groups at 25 yards. Or I should say, did result this way when I was a little younger.

BARREL LENGTH				
Caliber	4¾"	5½"	7½"	Total
.38 Special	0	39	10	49
.44 Special	0	120	135	255
.45 Colt	85	520	1,020	1,625
.357 Magnum	78	795	1,035	1,918

My other Second Generation .45 Colt New Frontier is a 7½-inch version and somehow came out of the factory with a barrel/cylinder gap you could almost stick your finger through, well, almost. This .45 Colt shot slower than my Single Actions with 4¾-inch and 5½-inch barrels and it was also not what one would call a very accurate

This current production 7½-inch .45 Colt New Frontier carries easily in El Paso's Tom Threeperson's holster.

sixgun. It was sent off to Hamilton Bowen who set the barrel back to a minimum barrel/cylinder gap and the result was not only the gaining a significant amount of muzzle velocity, the groups also tightened up significantly.

My .44 Special Second Generation is also a 7½-inch version and is just about perfect in every way. I have always been particularly drawn to 7½-inch single actions so it's no surprise my .357 Magnum Second Generation New Frontier is also of the longer barrel version. Another Second Generation Colt is my "Almost New Frontier." I came upon a Second Generation 4¾-inch Colt Single Action Army chambered in .357 Magnum and I just could not pass it up. However, it did not shoot real well and actually shot several inches to the left. When we tried to turn the barrel we found it was too tight and metal would have to be removed to make this happen. As I was contemplating this I remembered I had two things that would really improve this .357 Magnum, namely a 5½-inch Second Generation New Frontier barrel and a Smith & Wesson adjustable rear sight. Everything was turned over to my gunsmith Tom at Buckhorn Gun Shop and I now have an Almost New Frontier which not only shoots more accurately, the sights are fully adjustable.

The New Frontiers were dropped from production in 1974. In 1978, they went back into production as the Third Generation New Frontier. This time the serial numbers began at 01001NF using five digits instead of four; this is the easiest way to tell which generation a particular New Frontier belongs to. This time four chamberings were offered. The same three, .45 Colt, .44 Special and .357 Magnum of the Second Generation run were again produced, however, the .38 Special was replaced by the .44-40. While all of the original Second Generation New Frontiers had case-hardened frames with the balance of the metal finished in bright blue, Third Generation New Frontiers will be found this way as well as some in all blue and some nickel-plated. During the Second Generation run of New Frontiers a few .45 Colt Buntlines were offered, but during the Third Generation production Buntlines were offered in .44 Special, .44-40 and .45 Colt, with some of them being fully nickel-plated.

Don Wilkerson gives the information in the chart below for the Third Generation New Frontiers, which officially ended in 1982 with a few assembled in 1983 and 1984.

Third Generation New Frontiers have different barrels that were changed from 20 tpi to 24 tpi, just as the Third Generation SAAs have a different thread pattern on their barrels. I have no idea why Colt did this since new barrels could no longer be easily fitted to older Colts. The upside is that Third Generation New Frontier barrels will fit Ruger Three-Screw .357 Blackhawk Flat-Tops (as well as all other Ruger single actions – except the Single-Six and Bearcat) making for a very neat conversion by r-chambering these old Rugers to .45 Colt, .44-40 or .44 Special and installing a New Frontier barrel.

The official production of the New Frontier Third Generation ended in 1982 as we have mentioned previously. I was told by the people at Colt that they would never come back, however, I'm glad this is one instance where we should never say never. The year 2011 marked the 175th anniversary of Colt Single Actions going all the way back to the first one – the percussion Paterson of 1836. To help celebrate this anniversary Colt resurrected the New Frontier, and all New Frontiers produced in 2011

THIRD GENERATION NEW FRONTIER BY CALIBER AND BARREL LENGTH				
Caliber	4¾"	5½"	7½"	Total
.44 Special	0	783	2,761	3,544
.45 Colt	1,106	57	7,407	8,570
.357 Magnum	0	0	1,046	1,046
.44-40	519	0	1,046	1,565

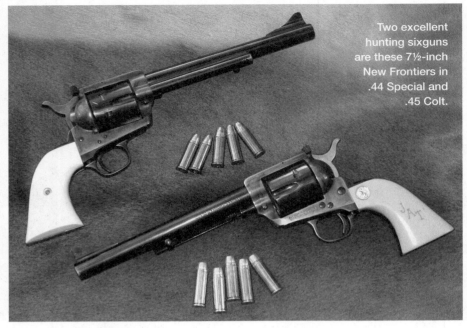

Two excellent hunting sixguns are these 7½-inch New Frontiers in .44 Special and .45 Colt.

have a special anniversary marking on the barrel consisting of "1836 – 175th Anniversary – 2011" and serial numbers began at 20000NF. Colt announced all three standard barrel lengths, 4¾, 5½ and 7½ inches in three chamberings of .357 Magnum, .44 Special and .45 Colt.

Colt may have announced three barrel lengths in three chamberings, but the first two production runs consisted of the .45 Colt with 7½-inch barrel and the 5½-inch .44 Special, with also apparently a very few being made a with a 4¾-inch barrel, none of which I have seen yet, nor have I heard of any .357 Magnums being produced as this is being written. Colt is producing some of the best 1911s and Single Actions ever and most of their production is probably taken up with semiautomatic pistols and rifles.

As previously mentioned, I had a long acquaintance with both Second and Third Generation New Frontiers including all three barrel lengths and chamberings of .45 Colt, .44 Special .357 Magnum and .44-40. These are wonderful "Perfected Pistols," but they actually pale in comparison to the resurrected New Frontiers. This early new production pair are unequivocally the most beautifully finished Colt Single Actions I have ever experienced. Not only is the finish absolutely stunning, consisting of a case-hardened frame and the balance in a blue you can see your ancestors in, but both of these sixguns are also exceptionally well fitted with no sharp edges. Grip frame to mainframe fit is as it should be and running a finger over the seams shows a nice smooth transition.

Lockup is tight and trigger pulls, while not perfect, are certainly more than adequate.

Grip panels are nicely fitted to the grip frame, and although a very plain wood, they are shaped to fit my hand perfectly. I'll take proper fitting and shape over fanciness anytime, however, they have already been replaced with custom grips worthy of the metal finish. I purchased two pair of single action stocks from Hogue and my friend Tony finished the job by fitting them perfectly to these two New Frontiers.

As a bullet caster I have a great advantage, namely being able to custom-tailor bullet diameters to fit each particular sixgun. There have been many variations found over the years in the chamber throats of both .45 Colt and .44 Special sixguns. This is not only true of Colt but other manufacturers as well. Applying a pin gauge to the .45 New Frontier gave me a uniform reading of .455" for all six chambers. I keep a generous supply of reloads on hand with both .452" and .454" diameter bullets so for the most part I chose the latter. However, I was pleasantly surprised to find the smaller bullets also shot well, as did factory loaded ammunition.

Most of the Colt Third Generation .44 Specials I have encountered have been in the .433" category, while earlier guns from the Second Generation run were normally tighter. I was pleasantly surprised this time to find chamber throats at a uniform .429". Reloads were used with both .429" and .430" cast bullets and results show this is the most accurate Colt Single Action I have ever encountered in 55 years of shooting sixguns. Several loads were under one inch for five shots at 20 yards with one of my favorites, the RCBS Keith bullet #44-250 over 17.5 grains of #4227 placing five shots in an astounding 1/2 inch. This is a whole lot better than I can normally shoot.

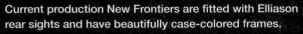

Current production New Frontiers are fitted with Elliason rear sights and have beautifully case-colored frames.

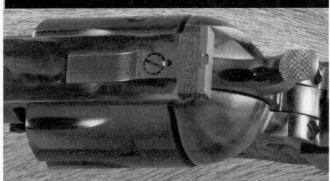

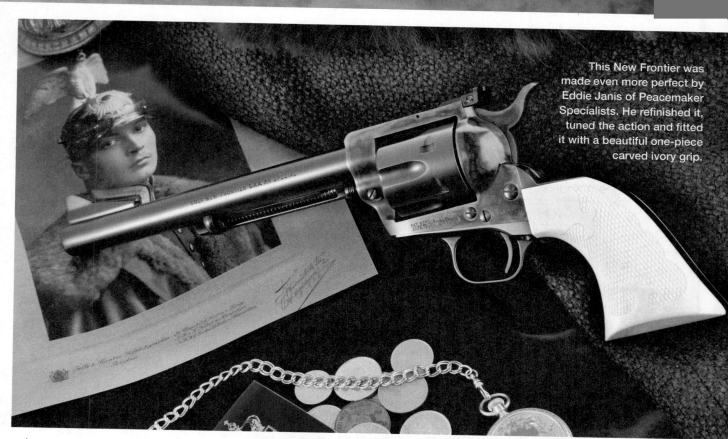

This New Frontier was made even more perfect by Eddie Janis of Peacemaker Specialists. He refinished it, tuned the action and fitted it with a beautiful one-piece carved ivory grip.

As mentioned in the beginning of this article, one of the great attributes of Colt Single Actions chambered in .45 Colt and .44 Special is how user-friendly they actually are. Loads in the 800 to 1,000 fps range are exceptionally pleasant to shoot with felt recoil at a minimum. When the trigger is pulled the hammer begins its long arc to strike the primer and as the sixgun fires, instead of heavy recoil one experiences a gentle nudge. The original Colt Single Action grip frame has always been comfortable. Things change a little, but not much, as one creates heavier hunting handloads. Using 250- to 260-grain cast Keith bullets at 1,100 fps in the .45 Colt, and sneaking up on 1,200 feet per second in the .44 Special, results in more felt recoil – but certainly nothing punishing. Both of these cartridges are more than a century old, and are still viable for hunting in sixguns such as these New Frontiers. I have taken deer with the .45 Colt and some very large feral hogs with the .44 Special. There was no question as to the immediate results.

All Colt Single Actions and the New Frontiers have the traditional action which means they can only be safely carried with five rounds and the hammer down on an empty chamber. In this day

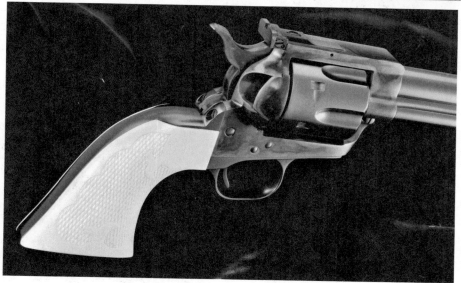

of high-capacity semiautomatic pistols sneaking up on being able to hold a half a box of cartridges, this may seem to be very dinosauric. Keep in mind, no less a sixgunner than Texas Ranger Frank Hamer, who was called out of retirement to stop Bonnie and Clyde, was once asked about the fact that he carried a .45 Colt with five rounds and no backup cartridges. The answer was if he could not get it done with five rounds he was guilty of sloppy peace officering. Have

things changed so much this doesn't apply today?

When Colt resurrected the New Frontiers as the Third Generations it originally did away with the full-length cylinder bushing and instead switched to a button in the front end. With the new guns, which are still considered Third Generation sixguns, the full-length bushing is back. More importantly, the rear sight has been changed. The original adjustable rear sight was certainly

SPECIALLY SELECTED LOADS FOR THE NEW FRONTIER

COLT NEW FRONTIER .44 SPECIAL 5½-INCH BARREL

LOAD	MUZZLE VELOCITY	FIVE SHOTS AT 20 YARDS
Hornady 240 XTP/ 7.5 gr. Unique	877 fps	7/8"
Speer 240 Gold Dot/7.5 gr. Unique	880 fps	7/8"
Speer 240 JHP/17.0 gr. #4227	882 fps	1"
Speer 225 SWCHP/17.0 gr. #4227	1,001 fps	1"
RCBS #44-250 KT/ 7.5 gr. Unique	889 fps	1-1/8"
RCBS #44-250 KT HP/17.5 gr. #4227	986 fps	

COLT NEW FRONTIER .45 COLT 7½-INCH BARREL

LOAD	MUZZLE VELOCITY	FIVE SHOTS AT 20 YARDS
Lyman #454424 KT/ 10.0 gr. HS-6	825 fps	1-1/4"
Lyman #454424 KT/20.0 gr. #4227	997 fps	1-3/8"
RCBS #45-255KT/10.0 gr. HS-6	841 fps	1-1/4"
RCBS #45-250 FN/10.0 gr. HS-6	884 fps	1-3/8"
Oregon Trail 250 RNFP/8.0 gr. Unique	917 fps	1-1/8"
Oregon Trail 250 RNFP/6.0 gr. Red Dot	818 fps	1-1/8"

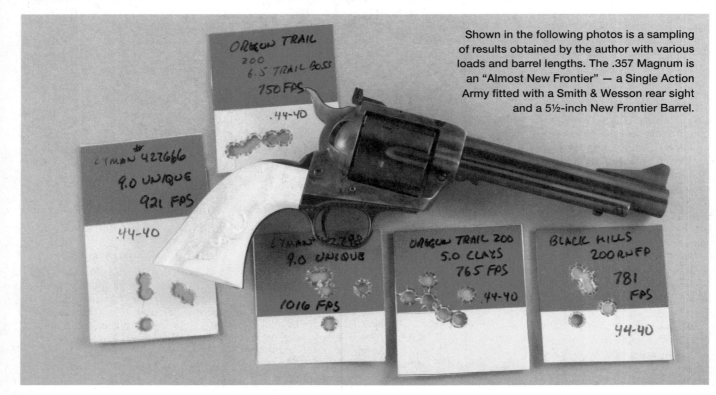

Shown in the following photos is a sampling of results obtained by the author with various loads and barrel lengths. The .357 Magnum is an "Almost New Frontier" — a Single Action Army fitted with a Smith & Wesson rear sight and a 5½-inch New Frontier Barrel.

.45 COLT RCBS 45-255 KT
18.5 H 4227

.45 COLT
OREGON TRAIL
255 SWC
20.0 IMR
4227
1,013 FPS

821 FPS

.38 SPECIAL
LYMAN # 358429
11.0 # 2400
1216 FPS

.357 MAGNUM
38-150 KT RCBS
14.5 # 4227
1137 FPS

1196
FPS

← 4
SHOTS

.357 MAGNUM
CPBC 187GC
13.5 WW 296

COLT NEW FRONTIER .44-40 7½-INCH BARREL

LOAD	MUZZLE VELOCITY	FIVE SHOTS AT 20 YARDS
Lyman #427666/9.0 gr. Unique	993 fps	1-1/4"
Lyman #42798/9.0 gr. Unique	1,066 fps	1-3/4"
Meister 200 RNFP/7.1 gr. HP38	919 fps	1"
Oregon Trail 200 RNFP/9.0 gr. Universal	939 fps	1-1/8"
Oregon Trail 225 RNFP/8.0 gr. Universal	966 fps	1-1/8"
Oregon Trail 200 RNFP/6.5 gr. Trail Boss	817 fps	1"

DISCLAIMER: Any and all loading data found in this article or previous articles is to be taken as reference material *only*. The publishers, editors, authors, contributors and their entities bear no responsibility for the use by others of the data included in this article or others that came before it.

A new production New Frontier is flanked by Second and Third Generation examples.

adequate and acceptable, and a tremendous improvement over the original fixed sights. Now Colt has improved the improvement by stepping up to the excellent Elliason rear sight. Adjustments are more precise and the back of the rear sight is totally flat and serrated to block glare. Perhaps someday I will equip all my New Frontiers with Elliasons.

One glaring minus applicable to all New Frontiers – be they Second or Third Generation examples – is the fact they have all been equipped with some of the most nondescript, plain-Jane walnut grip panels possible; function is fine but form not so much! If ever a sixgun deserved nice stocks it is the New Frontier with its beautifully blued finish and case-

hardened flat-top frame. Perhaps Colt realizes anyone smart enough to buy a New Frontier is also dedicated enough to fit it with beautiful custom grips. Any New Frontier certainly is deserving of ivory stocks or staghorn or even exotic wood. One-piece ivory stocks especially add to the beauty of the New Frontier.

Both of my "New" New Frontiers were acquired in 2011. In finishing up this piece five years later, I called Colt to find the current status of the New Frontier. I talked to my old friend Tim Looney who informed me a large batch of New Frontiers were just run the previous week. Currently the New Frontier is offered in both .45 Colt and .44 Special with 5½-inch and 7½-inch barrels, as well as the .45 also offered with the 4¾-inch Perfect Packin' Pistol barrel length.

Colt New Frontiers are still made the old way, which among other things means no key locks, no transfer bars and definitely no lawyer warning labels on the barrels. Sometimes lack of progress can be a wonderful thing.

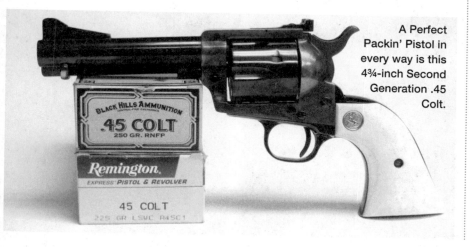

A Perfect Packin' Pistol in every way is this 4¾-inch Second Generation .45 Colt.

By **Tom Tabor**

SAVAGE ARMS®
SEMIAUTO SEVENTEEN

A Safe and Reliable Semiauto rifle for the .17 HMR

Many rimfire shooters prefer the versatility and speed of cycling that comes from a semiautomatic. In 2002 when Hornady introduced their new .17 HMR cartridge it was quite natural that the rifle manufacturers started working on plans to produce a semiauto chambered for it. Considering the fact that the .17 HMR is essentially nothing more than a .22 Magnum cartridge which has been necked down to accept a .17-inch diameter bullet it was also natural to assume that it could easily be accommodated within some of existing semiauto rimfire rifle designs. Stick a .17-caliber barrel on an existing .22 Magnum rimfire model rifle and you should be good to go, right?

Well, that was what some firearm manufacturers obviously thought. We now know, however, that assumption turned out to be akin to dangling your feet in a pond plagued by half-starved alligators.

The folks at Ruger were possibly the first to be drawn into the fray, thinking that they could utilize the very popular 10/22 design for the conversion. Attempting to get ahead of their competition, Ruger struck out early in January 2004 with a series of announcements introducing what they called their new 10/17 semiauto, a look-alike 10/22 but chambered for .17 HMR. Those announcements were well received by the shooting public and included both paid advertising as well as a listing in the company's catalog. In reality, however, I'm not sure that a single one of those rifles ever reached the hands of a consumer before the company ran headlong into major problems resulting in the abandonment of the concept in its entirety.

The .17 semiauto fiasco wasn't limited to Ruger. Remington also took a bite of that same poison .17 apple thinking they too could simply utilize the existing semiauto straight-blowback Model 597 design. But unlike Ruger, Remington jumped even farther into the alligator-infested pond by actually putting those rifles on the market, which eventually resulted in considerable embarrassment for the company, followed by a costly recall effort.

The problem that both Ruger and Remington eventually discovered was the fact that the common straight-blowback action designs used on many semiauto .22 rimfire cartridges is not always safe when applied to the .17 HMR, or even for that matter for the smaller .17 Mach 2 cartridges. It is believed that when those cartridges are shot in one of these style actions it could result in an early ignition of the cartridge, before the action has had time to fully close from the rifle's previous firing. Or in other instances, the action

Savage Arms achieved something several other gun manufacturers attempted to do—produce a dependable semiautomatic rifle chambered in .17 HMR.

Small-game hunting is a perfect match for the Savage A17. The A17 tested by the author was light in weight and well balanced.

may open too quickly before the cartridge has fully discharged. To counter those difficulties inherent in the straight-blowback designs a few manufacturers like Volquartsen Custom and Magnum Research utilize heavier bolts and springs to assist in keeping the bolts closed during the firing process.

Savage Arms took an entirely different approach when developing the new Model A17 semiautomatic .17 HMR rifle. After throwing around ideas in the company's new products meetings for a full seven years a plan eventually began to emerge for an entirely new rifle design. But, even then it took Savage an additional 2½ years before the final plan came fully to its fruition. The curtain was first raised at the 2015 SHOT Show in Las Vegas where Savage Arms introduced the new A17 (for Automatic .17 caliber) to the anxiously awaiting public. I attended that show as well as many before that one and have

never encountered so much interest in a new rifle.

At the heart of the A17 design is a delayed ejection concept that utilizes a unique interrupter lug to lock down the bolt until after the peak chamber pressure has passed and the bullet has fully cleared the muzzle. When firing, most shooters would never recognize that there is an actual delay taking place, but this slight pause in the ejection process assures that the bolt stays closed long enough so no out-of-battery discharges take place.

In addition to the introduction of Savage's new A17 rifle, company officials felt it was time to usher in a new and more powerful .17 HMR cartridge. Working with sister company CCI Ammunition a new and faster velocity .17 HMR cartridge made its debut as well at the 2015 show, which the company appropriately dubbed the CCI A17. That new CCI ammunition comes loaded with Varmint Tip 17-grain

bullets and is said to produce muzzle velocities 100 fps faster than the other currently available cartridges. While Savage feels its A17 rifles perform best when shooting the new CCI A17 ammunition, any of the current produced .17 HMR cartridges will function in the rifle.

Aside from the unique delayed ejection design of the A17 rifle there are other characteristics that set it apart from other rimfire semiautos. For example, its oversized bolt handle makes opening the action much easier than most other designs. Its 10-round rotary magazine assures smooth and consistent feeding of its cartridges and it comes equipped with Savage's user-adjustable AccuTrigger, allowing the shooter to adjust the trigger pull down to very light weights and still remain safe for use in the field.

As I mentioned earlier, my first exposure to Savage Arms' A17 rifle came as part of the 2015 Las Vegas SHOT Show. Every year writers and editors are able to get together the day before the actual show begins in order to experience some hands-on exposure to the new products. That event generally takes place at the

While shooting off the bench the author found that the Savage A17 performed exceptionally well.

Boulder Rifle & Pistol Club that is located just a few miles from the busy Vegas strip. Hearing about Savage's phenomenal new .17 HMR A17 rifle I immediately headed to that area of the range and took my place in line to give the rifle a try. Unfortunately, even though I found the A17 to be an impressive and accurate shooting rifle, my time behind the trigger was quite limited as it always is at such events. So I did the most logical thing – I placed an order for a rifle. Once it arrived I quickly mounted up a Konus Pro 275 3-10x44mm scope using a set of 1-inch Warne Maxima Quick Detach rings, and headed out back to my private rifle range in order to conduct a more thorough evaluation.

In order to complement the A17 rifle Savage joined forces with sister company CCI to produce a high-velocity .17 HMR load.

Removal of the trigger assembly can be done by simply knocking out a couple of retaining pins.

Lifting off the top cover of the action exposes the recoil spring and its guide rod, allowing easy access for cleaning purposes.

The A17 comes equipped with the famous and very favorable AccuTrigger, which is adjustable for trigger pull weight.

Over the next few weeks I ran the A17 through its paces, possibly firing more rounds of ammunition than many shooters fire in their entire lifetime. A significant portion of that included simply punching holes in paper targets at 50 yards, but I can never seem to resist the urge to turn the muzzle in the direction of my various rimfire silhouettes positioned at distances out to 100 yards. Those tar-

gets include a variety of different shaped Champion DuraSeal designs, metal swingers and even golf balls that I'd hung from wires around a horizontal spindle. I quickly found the A17 was equally deadly on all of those targets as well.

For the accuracy testing portion of my review I shot four different types of

ammunition: The new CCI A17, Federal V-Shok, Hornady V-Max and CCI FMJ. The accompanying chart provides a detailed look at how those cartridges performed and the average muzzle velocities that each type of ammunition generated. In summary, I felt that all of the ammo achieved very good results with one group measuring less than ¼ inch. While the actual measured average muzzle velocity of the CCI A17 ammunition was very close to the factory reported level of 2,650 fps, it did not completely live up to the claim in every instance of being "100 fps faster than other .17 HMR loads of the same weight." When compared to the Federal ammo loaded with the same weight 17-grain bullets, I found the A17 cartridges averaged only 44 fps faster. Nevertheless, when a comparison was made between the CCI A17 and the Hornady V-Max ammo, I found that the A17 far exceeded that 100 fps promise. And obviously when bullet weight is increased as in the case of the 20-grain CCI FMJ ammo, you must expect the velocities to decline.

The Savage A17 rifle functioned perfectly throughout the live-fire testing, ejecting the empty cases smoothly every time with the cartridge cases showing no visible signs of excessive pressure. As a side issue, I did find that the ejection was a very powerful one, more powerful than any semiauto I've ever witnessed. The empty cases were frequently tossed distances from about 30 feet all the way out to 60 feet from the rifle. I must assume that is a side trait of the delayed ejection concept. I can't really see any disadvantage in this but I nevertheless found it to be an interesting characteristic.

The rifle's AccuTrigger is a great feature that I found to be crisp and without slop or creep in its movements. My own rifle came from the factory preset to the moderate trigger pull of 3 pounds, 4 ounces (from an average of five pulls), which I felt was a good setting for general use. Nevertheless, knowing that I could easily reduce or increase that setting if I so desired was certainly a benefit.

A few months after receiving the Savage A17 rifle I was invited to tour the Westfield, Mass., Savage Arms factory. There I witnessed the actual manufacturing and assembly of the A17 rifles and came away quite impressed by all of the performance, functionality and procedural checks that the company employs. One of the most unique of

The magazine release is located in front of the magazine.

The removable rotary magazine holds 10 rounds of .17 HMR ammo.

At the Savage Arms factory the author assisted in the testing of a new run of A17 rifles.

This rack of freshly assembled A17 rifles await their live-fire testing before being certified and packed for shipment to dealers.

The oversized operating handle on the side of the bolt makes opening the action much easier than with the smaller handles found on most semiautomatic rifles.

The bolt locking lever is located in front of the triggerguard. To lock the bolt in the open position you simply need to draw the bolt back and while in the open position, press the locking lever.

those processes involves Savage's barrel straightening procedure. All metal has built-in stress factors that can result in twisting and distortion of the end product, and rifle barrels are no exception. For that reason every barrel produced by Savage Arms, including those used on the A17s, are carefully inspected and expertly straightened. Only three individuals are considered fully qualified for that work, which combines those workers' decades of experience and expertise with uniquely designed hydraulics to get the job done.

The process begins by first mounting the barrel in a cradle with the muzzle pointing to a white illuminated screen. From there the operator peers down the bore to locate and analyze the distortion before repositioning the barrel so hydraulics can be used to bring the barrel into absolute perfect alignment.

In addition to finding the shooting accuracy of the A17 to be very good, the rifle functioned perfectly throughout the testing period. I was also impressed by the high luster blueing job on the rifle. Blueing of this quality is seldom encountered on anything other than very high-end firearms. I also liked the oversize bolt handle, which made opening the action much easier than the style of handle found on most rimfires.

The ribbed, skeletonized synthetic stock on the A17 is lightweight and strong.

The channel in which the barrel resides is a separate piece that screws to the inside fore-end of the stock.

The detachable rotary magazine of the A17 holds 10 rounds of ammo and I found its feeding to always be smooth and effective. I did find, however, that the magazine seemed to lock into place a bit easier when the rifle action was in the open position. I have found this to be fairly common on many detachable magazine designs, and for that reason I have simply gotten in the habit of opening the action before attempting to feed the magazines in. I don't see this to be a negative issue; it is just a trait that is easily accommodated.

The A17 carries an MSRP of $473 and comes drilled and tapped for scope mounts. The bases are included with the rifle, but rings are not. Its carbon steel 22-inch button-rifled barrel has a 9:1 twist rate. Savage manufactures all of their own barrels in-house, which provides them with the best control over the final product.

At a weight of only 5.41 pounds the A17 is a pleasure to carry in the field, and the rugged synthetic stock is assured to stand up against adverse weather conditions and potential rugged handling. If you prefer a wood stock, Boyds Hardwood Gunstocks just recently announced that they are producing an aftermarket laminated wood thumbhole version specifically for the A17.

Contacts:

Savage Arms
100 Springdale Rd.
Westfield, MA 01085
(413) 568-7001
www.savagearms.com

CCI Ammunition
2299 Snake River Avenue
Lewiston, ID 83501
(800) 379-1732
www.cci-ammunition.com

Boyds Hardwood Gunstocks
25376 403rd Ave.
Mitchell, SD 57301
(605) 996-5011
www.boydsgunstocks.com

For the person who prefers a wood stock, Boyds Hardwood Gunstocks is now making an aftermarket thumbhole laminated stock specifically for the Savage A17.

Savage A17 Range Results
All test shots were fired at 50 yards in three-shot groups.

CCI A17, 17-grain Varmint Tip

Average Muzzle Velocity	2,647 fps
Smallest Group	.49"
Largest Group	1.44"
Average Group	1.12"

Federal V-Shok, 17-grain Speer TNT Hollow Point

Average Muzzle Velocity	2,603 fps
Smallest Group	.3"
Largest Group	2"
Average Group	.93"

Hornady V-Max, 17 grains

Average Muzzle Velocity	2,406 fps
Smallest Group	.43"
Largest Group	.96"
Average Group	.68"

CCI FMJ, 20 grains

Average Muzzle Velocity	2,389 fps
Smallest Group	.23"
Largest Group	1.64"
Average Group	.97"

OLD IS NOT DEAD —
THE .404

The morning sun was just showing her face over the steep hill of the escarpment that ran northeast, when we spotted the bull. It's strange how your senses achieve a heightened state when a hunter gets close to dangerous game; I can clearly remember the weaver birds singing their morning song, and the way the slight breeze was rustling the mopane leaves when we checked the wind.

However, it was the immense bull elephant that had the majority of my attention, and as we closed the distance between us as quietly as possible, my mouth felt as dry as my bank account usually is, yet for some reason my hands were sweating profusely. The sticks were spread, and Professional Hunter Tim Schultz whispered three words: "In

the heart." I had watched the cigarette smoke from his head tracker M'Butha, and knew the wind was good. At 16 strides, the bull seemed as big as Zimbabwe itself, but I swallowed harshly and slid the fore-end of the Heym .404 Jeffery into the sharp V of the shooting sticks. I could see the temporal gland leaking, staining the cheek of the enormous beast, and I clearly remember thinking how a bull elephant in musth can create one hell of a mess in no time at all.

I picked a crease in the gray hide, on the rear portion of the shoulder, so as to reach the top of the heart and lungs. That smooth trigger broke cleanly, and the shot went true, driving a 400-grain Woodleigh Hydro solid into 6 tons of N'dlovu, nearly setting him down on his haunches, and then waited what seemed

like an eternity for him to come clear for the follow-up shot. Twenty yards later, with the bull on the ground, I got the shakes to the point that I couldn't light the Dunhill cigarette offered to me. I paid respects to that beautiful bull, knowing that an entire village would be provided with protein for the winter.

I sat, now sweating in the morning heat, and ran my hands over the Heym rifle, grateful for its accuracy and for the cartridge it was chambered for: the .404 Jeffery Rimless Nitro Express. Elephants are elephants, and there are times when no cartridge or bullet is big enough to bail you out of trouble. Volumes of material have been published on cartridges suitable for dangerous game, citing over a century of field experiences from the mouths of safari clients as well as

This handsome .404 Jeffery Heym Express rifle is shown with Swarovski optics and Woodleigh ammunition.

By **Phil Massaro**

Still a smart choice for the all-around African rifle, including for dangerous game.

JEFFERY

The .404 Jeffery is a true classic African rifle, a favorite of hunters for over a century.

Professional Hunters. While we all know the similes that opinions receive, it is safe to say that the .404 Jeffery, while not winning the modern popularity contests among rifle companies and ammunition manufacturers, has a stellar reputation.

The History of the Jeffery

The actual year that the .404 Jeffery was released is a source of debate and even argument among those who study cartridge history, and particularly African hunting cartridges. Most research will indicate that 1909 was the official release date, yet Phil Shoemaker — the famous brown bear guide from Alaska — has a rifle that dates back to 1907, clearly original and clearly chambered for the .404 Jeffery.

It doesn't really matter; let's agree that the latter portion of the first decade of the 20th century saw the .404 burst onto the scene. Its purpose was to replicate the ballistics of the steadfast .450/400 3-inch Nitro Express in a bolt-action rifle, and it worked. The bullet diameter was changed from .410" to .411" for the .450/400 to .423" for the .404 Jeffery — for reasons I can't quite figure out — and the new case drove a 400-grain bullet at a muzzle velocity of 2,125 fps for 4,020 ft-lbs of energy, as well as a 300-grain copper pointed bullet at 2,625 fps, designed for long-range work. The .404 has an 8-degree shoulder; usually a cartridge that doesn't feature a rim or a belt features a much more prominent shoulder in order to facilitate good headspacing. That said, I've never had a single problem with headspacing in the .404 Jeffery, and that slight shoulder allows the cartridge to feed like a dream — and that's an important feature on any dangerous-game cartridge. While it became very popular among British rifle makers, it was also embraced by German rifle makers, designated as the 10.75x73mm.

That early muzzle velocity of 2,125 fps may seem sedate when compared to the .375 H&H Magnum or the .416 Rigby, which run at 2,550 fps with a 300-grain bullet and 2,410 fps with a 400-grain bullet, respectively. But it is enough to ensure reliable expansion and penetration with the standard cup-and-core softpoints and steel jacketed solids. All this in a cartridge that has, possibly,

The author with a Zimbabwe elephant bull taken with the Heym Express rifle.

the mildest perceived recoil of any of the dangerous-game cartridges I've used. The combination of mild recoil and the ability to place those bullets where they need to be is tantamount to quickly dispatching game animals. It was so effective, in fact, that the game departments of both North and South Rhodesia (now Zambia and Zimbabwe), Tanzania and Kenya chose the Vickers bolt-action rifle chambered in .404 Jeffery as the standard-issue rifle. In my opinion, if it was good enough for those guys required to handle the problem animals, it is good enough for me. The .404 Jeffery has the distinction of taking what many consider to be the greatest North American trophy ever taken — the Chadwick ram — the world record stone sheep taken in British Columbia in 1936 by Dr. Chadwick.

The original .404 load quietly made a fantastic reputation among those who had the opportunity to use it on a daily basis — folks like John "Pondoro" Taylor, who in his classic book, *African Rifles and Cartridges*, would testify to the effectiveness of the Jeffery cartridge. But, that original load didn't stick around for long. Kynoch bumped the muzzle velocity from 2,125 fps to 2,225 fps, also increasing the muzzle energy by almost 400 ft-lbs, recognizing the fact that the .404 Jeffery case was capable of more than what was being loaded. More about that in a minute…

The early part of the 20th century saw many great safari cartridges introduced; some would fade into obscurity and some would go on to become undeniable classics that few hunters would not insist on having in their collection. The .375 Holland & Holland Magnum certainly heads that list; it is perhaps the single most useful cartridge ever invented, and while it may not be perfect for everything, it will certainly get the job done on any game animal, anywhere. The writings of Robert Ruark brought the proprietary .416 Rigby into the spotlight, and I'd confidently say that without that book, the Rigby cartridge and the .416-inch bore diameter would've walked off into the sunset. The prestigious firm of Westley Richards answered the .404 Jeffery by releasing the .425 Westley Richards, using a .435" diameter bullet at 2,350 fps for just over 5,000 ft-lbs of energy. However, the severely rebated rim of the .425 didn't give reliable extraction, so it didn't gain a huge following, and is a rarity today.

THE NEW ·404 RIFLE.

JEFFERY MAUSER MAGAZINE ACTION.

1905 MODEL. RIMLESS CARTRIDGE.

Charge, 55 or 60 grains of Cordite, velocity 2,200 feet per second. Striking force nearly 4,000 foot pounds. With the new flat strip cordite the velocity and striking force are about 20 per cent higher, without increase in pressure. 400 grain Nickel Covered Bullets. Flush Magazine, holding three cartridges, and admitting of the bolt being closed on one cartridge in the barrel, thus enabling four cartridges being fired without re-charging.

(The illustration represents a Rifle with Hair Trigger.)

No. 1 Model, ·404 Jeffery Mauser Action Rifle, plain finish, Pistol Grip Stock, Chequered Grip, 24-inch Steel Barrel, Standard, Two-leaf, and Tangent Back-sight, Ivory Bead Fore-sight on Socket Block, Roughened Iron Heel-plate with Trap for Cleaning Rod, Eyes for Sling, accurately sighted   £15 0 0

No. 2 Model, ·404 Jeffery Mauser Best Quality Rifle, with 24-inch O.S. Nickel Steel Barrel, best quality Back-sight with Standard and Four Leaves, or with Standard, Four Leaves, and Tangent, Ivory Bead Fore-sight on Socket Block, Selected Walnut Stock, Chequered Pistol Grip, and with Roughened Iron Heel-plate and Trap in Heel for Rod, Eyes for Sling, Ordinary Trigger   £25 0 0

No. 3 Model, ·404 Jeffery Mauser Rifle, with perfectly plain Straight Grip, Military Pattern Butt, Standard, Two-leaf, and Tangent Back-sight, Platina Tipped Bead Fore-sight, Ordinary Trigger   £12 12 0

The No. 3 Rifle is designed for those sportsmen who require a sound rifle, of military finish, at a moderate price.

These Rifles can be had with Jeffery Peep-sights fitted on the tail ends of the bolts. Price of Sight, including fitting, 21/-
(See Page 59).

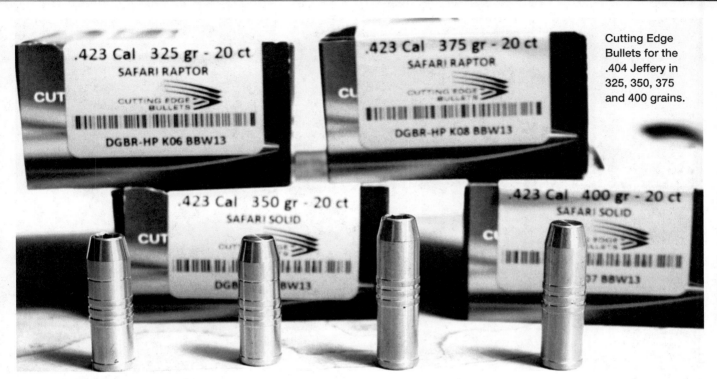

Cutting Edge Bullets for the .404 Jeffery in 325, 350, 375 and 400 grains.

The .450-400 3" NE was, and still is, a wonderful choice for a hunter, but the rimmed cartridge is usually reserved for the double rifles and single-shots; the former became very expensive to produce and the latter fell out of vogue until the advent of the Ruger No. 1 in the 1960s. By the middle of the 20th century, much of Africa had begun the plunge into political turmoil, and ammunition for many of the big double rifle calibers like the .450 NE and .470 NE became increasingly harder to find.

To fill the void, the .458 Winchester Magnum came on the scene in the 1950s in the affordable and reliable Winchester Model 70 bolt-action rifle, reproducing (at least in theory) the ballistics of the venerable .450 Nitro Express. For many years, a sportsman didn't have much choice for a safari; you either grabbed a .375 or a .458. Still, there were those few who quietly hoarded .404 rifles and ammunition, using the vintage rifles with great effect on all shapes and sizes of game.

The Rise of the Phoenix

Recent years have seen a small, but steady resurgence of the .404 Jeffery, and I'm happy it has. Perhaps it has something to do with the development of the Remington Ultra Magnum and Winchester Short Magnum series of cartridges, both being based (in one fashion or another) on the .404 case. Or

perhaps, rifle makers have realized the fact that the .404 is a cartridge that has yet to come into its own, at least in the hands of the sportsman. Comparisons and quantifications will always be a huge part of the campfire cartridge debate, and we should, perhaps, address some of the more important points regarding the Jeffery. Many hunters are devoted fans of the .375 H&H (I love it, myself), and feel that with the modern bullets there is nothing you can't do with a three-seven-five. Recent loadings incorporate 350-grain bullets, as well as some fantastic 235-grain slugs and a whole lot in between, so there's merit to that argument. Others feel that hunting dangerous game where the potential exists to be charged and possibly killed, warrants the use of a true stopping rifle, say of .45 caliber or larger. I can also see the wisdom in that argument, especially when things get up close and personal. Those guns throw heavy bullets — usually at or over 500 grains — but come with some serious recoil, sometimes more than the average guy or gal can handle.

Me? I've always appreciated the tradeoff offered by the cartridges in the lower .40s, for a few reasons. One, they can throw bullets of up to 450 grains — to bring them closer to the true stopping rifles — yet there are some great lighter bullets available to extend the trajectory for shots out a bit further than normal. The traditional choice of a 400-grain bullet with these calibers will still give a

flat enough trajectory to make a 300- to 350-yard shot, and yet have the horsepower up close to effectively handle the big boys. The .416 Rigby is definitely a classic in this power range, and I'm a fan of that big, sharp-shouldered case, even though it takes a whole bunch of powder (and generates some impressive recoil) to push the 400-grain bullets to 2,400 fps.

I have had a decade-long, multicountry, multicontinent love affair with the .416 Remington Magnum. It makes a whole bunch of sense to me; the recoil is more comfortable than that of the Rigby, yet the muzzle velocities are identical. I've taken many different species of North American and African game with it, including my first Cape buffalo. I have nothing bad to say about the .416 Remington, provided it's chambered in a good controlled-round-feed rifle, and I wouldn't hesitate to grab my Model 70 out of the safe and board a plane to anywhere. However, while the .416s are a wonderful choice for any sportsman (or Professional Hunter for that matter), it's nice to have the choice of something, well, "outside" the common chamberings, which will be just as effective.

An Unexpected Introduction

I found the .404 Jeffery Rimless Nitro Express pretty much by accident. The elephant hunt I told you about earlier happened to be booked at the same time I was talking with Chris Sells of

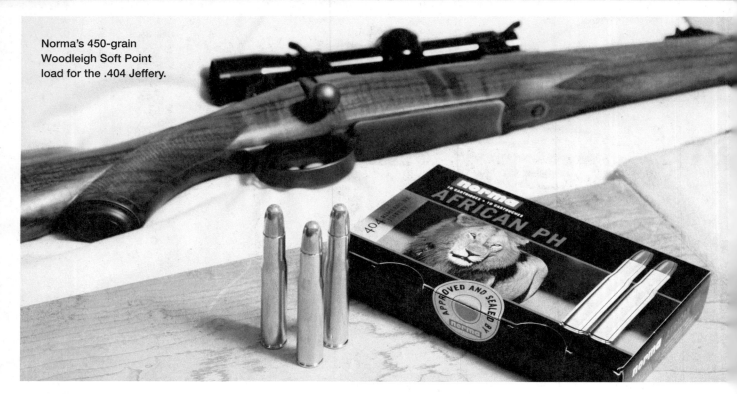

Norma's 450-grain Woodleigh Soft Point load for the .404 Jeffery.

Heym Rifles, discussing their Express bolt-action rifle, when Mr. Sells was kind enough to offer the use of that rifle for the hunt. We talked about the different calibers that would possibly cover both the plains game I intended to hunt and the elephant bull, when Chris informed me that he had "a rifle we use at the shows, chambered in .404 Jeffery." I didn't exactly hesitate to jump at the opportunity to use it. There wasn't a lot of time to develop a load for the rifle, so I grabbed a pair of bullets that I thought would fit the bill: the 325-grain Cutting Edge Bullets Safari Raptor for lighter

game and the 400-grain Woodleigh Hydrostatically Stabilized Solids for the elephant.

The range work showed me two things; first, that the .404 can be very accurate, and secondly, that the Heym Express rifle is quite possibly the finest bolt-action rifle I've ever used. The Woodleigh Hydro clocked in at 2,280 fps and gave me just under MOA accuracy, while the Cutting Edge Raptors moved out at 2,550 fps and three-shot groups printed exactly minute-of-angle. Best of all, the two bullets printed a collective six-shot

group measuring under two inches. Alliant's Reloder-15 powder and Federal's GM215M large rifle magnum primer, in Norma cases, provided accuracy that most people would be pleased with from their deer rifle, let alone an elephant gun. The Heym rifle, with my own handloaded ammunition, accounted for the elephant bull in Zimbabwe, as well as an impala and blue wildebeest in South Africa. Simply put, I was in love. So much so, I sent a check to Heym instead of returning the rifle.

Upon my return from Africa, I had a chance to test some factory ammo in the .404, namely the Norma African PH line with 450-grain Woodleigh softpoints at 2,150 fps, and the Nosler 400-grain solid at 2,350 fps. Both gave excellent results, with the Norma stuff printing ¾-inch groups at 100 yards, and the Nosler stuff putting three bullets into 1¼ inches at the same distance. You really can't ask for more than that. I tried that same load of Reloder-15 with one of my favorite big-game bullets — the Swift A-Frame — and it shot just as good as the Woodleigh solids, so I wouldn't hesitate to use that bullet on anything shy of elephant. The Hornady pair of dangerous game bullets, the 400-grain DGX and DGS, gave good velocities and accuracy, clocking in at 2,255 fps and just over 1 MOA. It seems that the Heym Express isn't hard to please.

Nosler's impressive .404 Jeffery ammo with 400-grain solids.

There are other powders that will work just fine in the .404 Jeffery, like Hodgdon's VARGET and H414, IMR4064 and IMR4350, Norma's URP and Reloder 17. You'll want a good large rifle magnum primer, like the Federal GM215M or CCI250, to spark those large powder charges. New component brass cases are available from Hornady, Norma and Nosler, and I like both the Redding and RCBS reloading dies. The neck of the .404 Jeffery is sufficiently long enough that roll crimping isn't necessary — and I don't crimp my cartridges — but it wouldn't hurt if you did.

Kynoch still offers a factory load for the .404 Jeffery, using a 400-grain solid at a sedate velocity of 1,975 fps, and that load will still work just fine. In my opinion, it's a better choice for the recoil sensitive shooter pursuing dangerous game than the .375 H&H; the speed is much slower and that 400-grain bullet will make a larger wound channel. Modern factory ammunition loaded by Hornady, Norma and Nosler usually runs between 2,300 and 2,350 fps when using a 400-grain bullet, and Norma loads the 450-grain Woodleigh Solid and Softpoint at 2,150 fps for 4,620 ft-lbs of energy. That is a load I'd recommend for those who appreciate the heavy-and-slow approach, and as I said, it was plenty

accurate enough. However, the 400-grain Woodleigh Hydro Solid penetrated (and exited) the entire body of that huge bull elephant, not once, but twice, so I'm not really sure that much more bullet weight is needed.

The updated factory ammunition with a muzzle velocity of 2,250 to 2,350 fps brings the venerable .404 Jeffery into the same arena as the classic .416 Rigby and Remington. The slight variance in bullet diameter (.416" vs. .423") is small enough not to really make any appreciable difference. The frontal diameter crowd will embrace the .404, and the sectional density crowd will champion the .416s. Yet, the 400-grain .423" diameter bullet still has a sectional density figure of .319, and any bullet with a SD figure better than .300 is considered a good dangerous-game bullet. If you have a .404 Jeff that will print good groups with one of the premium softpoints—like the Swift A-Frame or Woodleigh Weldcor—and a good solid, you've truly got a combination that will handle anything, anywhere.

One Gun to Hunt Them All

An African safari can be a rather unique situation in that unlike most of our North American hunts where we generally pursue one species at a time, a

multitude of huntable species may present themselves at any given time. When I'm hunting in a dangerous game block, as I did in Zimbabwe, I prefer to carry a rifle fully capable of taking the biggest species I may encounter, not worrying about being over-gunned for the smaller antelope. The .404 Jeffery is a fine example of a caliber that falls into that category. Does it shoot as flat as a .300 Magnum? No, but that's OK. If you are concerned about distant shots you can zero your .404 at 200 yards, being just 3.3 inches high at 100 paces. Just remember that you'll need to hold a touch low for closer shots. At the 300-yard mark, most loads will strike 12 to 14 inches low, which is totally fine for an accomplished marksman.

If the hunting block is rather thick with longer shots being a rarity, I zero the Jeff at 100 yards, knowing that it'll hit 3 inches low at 150 yards and 8 inches low at 200. That 100-yard zero allows me to confidently "thread the needle" through small holes in the bush without worrying about hitting a branch and risking bullet deflection. My iron sights are set to hit dead-on the bull's-eye at 50 yards, and my Heym will print tight groups at that distance, even with aging eyes. Obviously, the lighter bullets like that 325-grain Cutting Edge Raptor at a

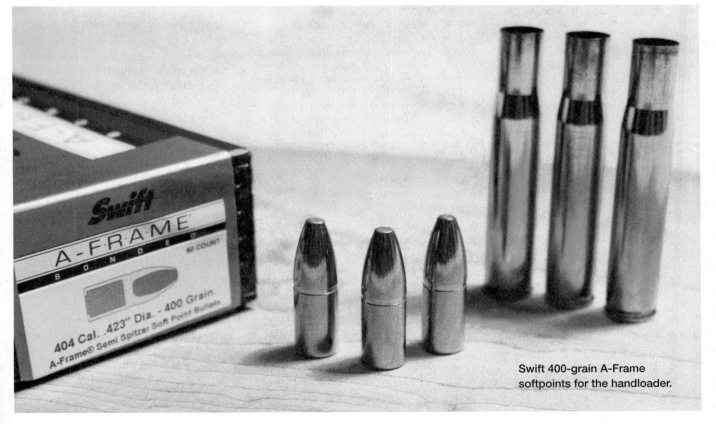

Swift 400-grain A-Frame
softpoints for the handloader.

The .404 Jeffery is capable of excellent accuracy.

higher velocity will give an even flatter trajectory, making the .404 a versatile cartridge that could be used for the larger ungulates of North America. The impala and blue wildebeest that I hunted in South Africa were both taken between 160 and 170 yards, and making the shot was no problem at all. The 1-6x Swarovski scope was plenty of magnification, and I'll happily report that even the diminutive 90-pound impala was none too dead.

The .404 Jeffery has suffered from one huge marketing ailment: no major U.S. rifle manufacturer has ever chambered for it. No Winchester 70, no Remington 700. The Heym Express is an incredible rifle, and I'm more than happy with that gun. The .404 Jeff was available from the Winchester Custom Shop, and Ruger made a limited run of their excellent No. 1 in .404, but the cartridge may have had a different history if there was a standard U.S.-made rifle chambered for

it. The CZ550 has been a safari favorite and is available in .404, as is the Dakota Model 76 African. Cooper Firearms from Montana is now producing their beautiful Model 58 Dangerous Game rifle in .404, and Legendary Arms Works from Pennsylvania has added the .404 Jeff to their lineup in the Big Five rifle, a fine rifle that is suitable for any climate, on any continent.

I like to set up my dangerous-game rifles with a riflescope mounted in removable rings so I can quickly use the iron sights, or, if while pursuing dangerous game with the scope removed, I can quickly install the scope should a distant trophy antelope present a shot. My Heym Express wears removable Talley rings, and they perform flawlessly.

To me, a rifle of this quality, with the option of quickly deciding between a scope or iron sights, chambered in a cartridge as cool as the .404 Jeffery, makes me a confident and happy hunter. If you enjoy the classic African cartridges, yet want a rifle fully capable of taking all the world's game with no handicap whatsoever, take a long, hard look at the .404 Jeffery. I think you'd be as happy as I am.

The interesting backdrop for these .404 Jeffery cartridges is the ear of an elephant.

QUIET GUN

Silencer Primer For the "I'm Not a Silencer Person" Pers

By Kevin Muramatsu

If you have been reading any of the usual gun rags on the store shelves or happen to subscribe to them, you may have noted the increasing frequency of articles or even just pictures of firearms that have been fitted with a silencer, or sound suppressor. There is a very good reason for this odd phenomenon, and that is the increasing frequency of silencer ownership in the general public.

While these accessories have always been legal, for most of their extant lives they have been rather heavily restricted.

AMTAC Suppressors offer both standard en mount suppressors ar reflex-style suppresso that fit over the end of the barrel too. Many g operated autoloading rifles experience increased gas leakage into the shooter's face when a silencer is mounted. Reflex-style suppressors significar reduce the extra gas blowback effect, at the cost of some of the baffling at the muzzle.

Nowadays, the burden of paying the tax necessary to acquire any item under the purview of the 1934 National Firearms Act has lessened, probably because of 80 years of bad fiscal policy. Well, I suppose every cloud has a silver lining. The result is that there are, every year, an ever-increasing number of silencers legally purchased by members of the public.

The PC wing of gundom (and there is one, but for generally good reasons, and

not to an extreme) will insist that these devices are not really silencers because the guns upon which they are mounted still make a very discernable noise. I'm going to continue to use the term "silencer" since that's the legal name for them and that's the term that the inventor used so many years ago. The gun silencer is nothing more than a device similar to the muffler on your car. It is a device used to reduce the objectionable

sound to a more acceptable level. Like a muffler on your car, using a silencer is simply good manners.

It's ironic that so many complaints made by those who live around gun ranges involve the "horrible noise" because that noise would be barely discernable, if at all, if those guns had this simple accessory attached to the end of the barrel. While it is likely that those folks will simply find something

Some silencers use quick-detach mounts to attach to a barrel. If an owner wishes to use the same silencer on multiple rifles, this is a quick and easy way to transition. In fact, many owners do not purchase a .223-caliber can and simply get a .308. Similar to other manufacturers, this SilencerCo SpecWar 762 model on top mounts on the flash hider that came with the SpecWar 556 silencer below. A .30-caliber silencer will still be very effective on a .22-caliber barrel.

else to complain about, this would take that intentionally spurious argument and burn it away.

A bill has been introduced in Congress called the Hearing Protection Act, which unfortunately stands little chance of passing or being signed under the current administration. It would remove most of the restrictions currently applied to silencers and treat them as regular firearms that you can currently purchase in your local gun shop. Go to store, do an FBI NICS background check, pay for item and take it home, just like a handgun or rifle. Should this legislation be adopted, one could expect the number of legally owned silencers to grow significantly and become much more socially acceptable to own.

Let's be honest here. The last time I took one to the range I got the "is that legal?" and "nobody needs one of those" looks from a couple of the others there. Hollywood and the political left in this country have successfully demonized beyond reason the most logical piece of gun safety equipment available for the shooter. As the hoops to jump through are reduced and the punitive tax is removed there will be more in circulation. This will lead to several points which I'll now address which would be good to ruminate upon a bit.

Firstly, the number of NFA regulated silencers used in crimes is so damn low

Shooting in a tunnel or indoor range makes silencers look or sound even better. Enclosed walls that echo loud noises amplify gun shot reports and make the perceived sound seem worse. Rifle silencers in this situation are still quite loud – but the concussion that is normally enhanced by walls is practically eliminated, resulting in far fewer sinus-clearing range events.

that there's no point in even mentioning it. Anyone going through the process to get one legally isn't going to commit a crime with it. It should be expected, unfortunately, if they are deregulated, that there eventually will be some number used in crimes going forward. After all, if they are more readily available they are going to be more commonly stolen by

the worthless lowlifes who populate our criminal element. However, it is a canard to then blame the silencers themselves, even more than blaming guns (as the left continues to illogically do) since the only way to hurt someone with a silencer is to put a stick in it and hit someone upside the head with it. Someone who reckons to kill somebody is going to do it

This is the Brevis II silencer from Delta P Design. It is very short, but quite a bit larger in diameter than most cans and has no seams or welds, making it very structurally sound. It's quite effective for its length.

SilencerCo is developing an integrally suppressed pistol called the Maxim. This is highly anticipated.

whether or not the gun makes a bang or a "phoosh," or for that matter, whether he has a gun or a knife or a stick.

It should be noted that there is already legislation on the books that makes the punishment worse if you use a silencer in the commission of a crime. Furthermore, effective silencers are very easy and cheap to make. Nothing is currently preventing criminals from making their own, other than the effort to do so. Again, if they are criminals, they by definition are not going to obey the law, regardless of

whether you yourself, the noncriminal have to jump through legal hoops or not.

Secondly—and this is the central point of the Hearing Protection Act—the long term consequences of shooting on the ears of shooters, particularly hunters, will be greatly affected. Every single gunshot over 140 decibels causes permanent hearing damage to the human ear. Every single one. It's small per instance, but it's cumulative and will add up over time. You can ask anyone who served in the military, particularly in the infantry, to confirm this. If it's a centerfire rifle or pistol, a standard gunshot far exceeds 140 decibels (150-160 or more), and many rimfire pistol shots will do so as well. A silencer (and this is why the term "sound suppressor" is so well liked) will reduce

those gunshot reports to 110–130ish decibels, depending on the cartridge. You might think that isn't much; but be it known that when you are sitting quietly in your home reading a book the background noise that you don't even consciously notice is around 50 decibels. When a person whispers in your ear, the noise level at your ear is around 70–80 decibels. A good clap approaches 100. It's not a linear scale.

Very few hunters use ear protection, since they want to be able to use their ears to help detect game. Many would say that you don't even notice the sound anyway. Well that may be partially true at the moment (because I sure as hell noticed it, every time), but I guarantee you will definitely notice it when your kid says something to you 20 deer seasons later and you start yelling at him to speak up and speak clearly so you can understand it, and your wife gives you a chastisingly dirty look because *she* heard him just fine because your child isn't the one with the problem.

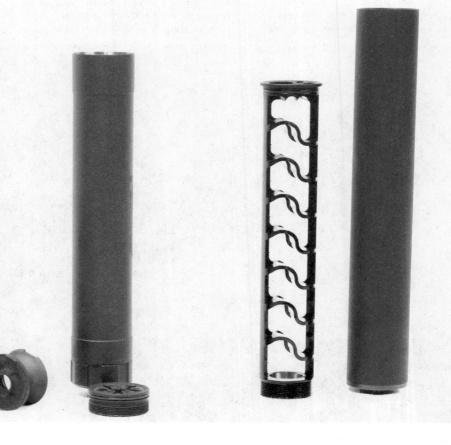

Two examples of baffle cores from two different manufacturers' pistol silencers – the Yankee Hill Manufacturing Sidewinder with a monocore (a single piece machined baffle), and an Advanced Armament Corp. Ti-Rant with a core consisting of several "K" baffles (shaped loosely like a K). Different concepts, both effective.

It's actually you. It's ironic that the one piece of safety equipment most useful for firearms is more restricted than the firearms themselves. The fact that OSHA hasn't shoved their nose into this area of safety equipment sometimes confounds me.

Thirdly, in my opinion silencers are currently rather badly overpriced, a state exacerbated by the punitive taxation. Yes, I know the exotic high-wear metals are expensive, but there is an economy of scale that currently is rather small. Should the HPA pass, I'd expect the cost of silencers to drop significantly. This and the reduction in restrictions will make them more popular to own and create a positive feedback loop.

Finally, and this may initially sound a bit corny, there's a freedom aspect. For the last 80 years we have "compromised" our way into thousands of gun laws whose primary purpose seems to be to send otherwise good law-abiding citizens to jail, but have no net effect on reducing violent crime. I for one am sick of giving up liberties and getting nothing of consequence back. This is why many of us have gotten to the point of saying "No more!" Even if it sounds good on the surface, it rarely is beneficial below the surface. Ultimately it doesn't matter. When someone espousing "common sense" gun control demands that we compromise, what they really mean is for us to turn around and grab our ankles. You want universal background

This is a .22-rimfire silencer, specifically a YHM Stinger. Rimfire silencers get very dirty, very quickly. This one has baffles that are pretty well caked after only about 100 rounds. Something to remember when you have rimfire cans, and to a lesser extent centerfire pistol cans, is that you have to clean them regularly.

checks (code for de facto universal registration)? Okay let's do a real compromise and deregulate silencers and short-barreled rifles—because that's the only way that I will even consider supporting that kind of backdoor universal registration.

Alright, look. Beyond the obvious safety issues, it really is more fun to shoot a gun with a silencer attached than without. You won't bother anyone else with the noise, and you will be supporting a section of an industry that is well divided politically between hunters and shooters. These two groups need to start supporting each other unquestioningly and nonjudgingly. If they don't, then in the foreseeable future the elitists that run this country will be talking about banning all of the left-handed bolt-action muzzleloaders.

That's about the extent of the topic that I wanted to address. I could go on and on about the science and tech involved, which I find to be fascinating, but that would be a big digression. If you don't own a silencer, please find someone who does and try one out. I think you will like it a lot, particularly the rimfire models. You may even find the benefits outweigh the hassle of the red tape. Oh, and you should know that it's pretty difficult to stop at one. You will want at least one rifle, one pistol and one rimfire silencer each.

Just like with guns, manufacturers release new models of silencers at SHOT Show every year. This is an example of a new, partially modular can called the Slingshot. The length can be modified with a longer end cap.

Winchester Model 94 Big Bore rifles are not only elegant, they are capable hunting tools.

BIG BORE 94s

The plight of the .307, .356 and .375 Winchester — they deserved a better fate.

By **James E. House**

he Winchester Model 94 lever action has been immensely popular for well over a century. However, the current suggested retail price of a Winchester Model 94 varies from $1,199.99 to $1,459.99 depending on the version of the rifles, which are produced under license in Japan. That is some rather

serious money for a rifle that not many years ago had a list price of less than half that amount. Not long ago, it was a regular occurrence to see many good used specimens that could have been bought for under $200. As they say, you never appreciate something until it is gone. When Winchester discontinued the Model 94 at the close of the New Haven, Conn., plant, the price increased drasti-

cally in keeping with this principle.

With so many cartridges carrying the word "magnum" as part of the name and other descriptors such as super, ultra, etc. used in various combinations with magnum, it is not surprising that a caliber such as the .30-30 Winchester, which has been used effectively by hunters, explorers and settlers for well over a century, does not get a lot of attention. At times, one often sees bags of new cases for some of the "rage" calibers on a clearance sale when .30-30 brass may be nowhere in sight. It is reported that reloading dies for the .30-30 Winchester are perennially among the largest sellers. The .30-30 may not get a lot of *attention*, but it does get a lot of *use*.

It is safe to say that the .30-30 Winchester will outlive several of the mighty awesome magnums. Many hunters realize that for certain types of hunting a cartridge such as the .30-30 is all that is needed. The fact that ammunition companies now offer reduced-power loads in several popular calibers that just about duplicate the performance of the .30-30 should be adequate proof.

By modern standards, the .30-30 Winchester does not offer stellar performance. In an effort to attract customers who liked lever-action rifles, Winchester introduced a new version of the Model 94 in 1978 known as the Big Bore with a retail price of $199.95, along with the .375 Winchester cartridge. The receiver of Big Bore rifle was greatly strengthened to handle loads producing around 50,000 psi, and serial numbers for the rifles were preceded by the letters "BB."

Initial .375 Winchester loadings included 200- and 250-grain bullets at advertised velocities of 2,000 and 1,900 fps, respectively, from a 24-inch barrel. Bullet velocity from the 20-inch barrel of the Model 94 was slightly lower. Although the original Big Bore was a fine rifle, it was somewhat inconvenient to use with a scope. Since cases were ejected from the top of the receiver of the Model 94, a scope had to be offset with a side mount. This was corrected in 1982 with the introduction of the Angle Eject model that ejected cases from the right side of the action. All of the Big Bore rifles were provided with open sights.

The .375 Winchester case is very similar to that of the old .38-55 Winchester cartridge, but the former operates at approximately twice the pressure of the latter. The current Winchester load for the .38-55 is listed as producing only 1,320 fps with a 255-grain bullet – so the .375 is in quite a different class. At moderate ranges, the .375 is considered to be a cartridge for use on game larger than deer, the traditional target for .30-30 rifles. However, the .375 Winchester did not replace significant numbers of .30-30s or .35 Remington lever actions that were widely used by hunters. Interestingly, the .375 is now touted

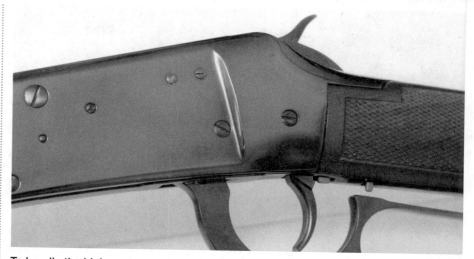

To handle the high pressure of the .307, .356 and .375 Winchester cartridges, the sidewalls of the Model 94 action were greatly strengthened.

Above: All of the Winchester Big Bore rifles were provided with open sights. This type of sight was utilized on the .375 Winchester rifles.

Left: A hooded ramp front sight was used on all Big Bore rifles.

Below: Winchester Big Bore rifles generally had nice walnut stocks and polished metal parts.

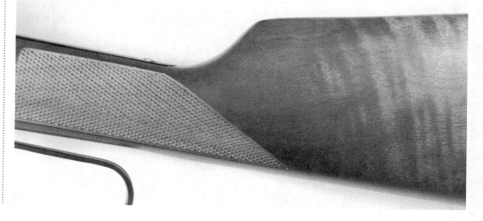

On top-eject Big Bore rifles, a side mount such as this one on a Model 94 .30-30 is necessary.

as a wonderful caliber for hunting when used in single-shot pistols with a barrel length of 14 inches. Somehow, it seems to be overlooked that the same cartridge fired from a rifle with a barrel measuring 20 inches would be even more effective.

In anticipation of a scope being mounted on Angle Eject rifles, a folding rear sight was provided.

With the introduction of the Model 94 Angle Eject in 1982, empty cases were ejected from the action horizontally to the right. This change allowed a scope to be mounted directly above the action. Very early Angle Eject rifles were drilled and tapped so that the screws for attaching the front sight base entered the receiver on either side from an angle. Later versions were constructed so that the screws are placed in-line. Other variations included the addition of a crossbolt safety in 1992. The safety moves laterally and blocks the hammer when in the "on" position. Space does not permit a complete review of Winchester Model 94 variants, but they are numerous even in the Big Bore models. One variant of note is that a few rifles were produced around 1983 with a raised comb, which looked somewhat unusual on a lever-action rifle.

Initially offered in the .375 Winchester caliber, the Big Bore was later produced in .307 and .356 Winchester. Whereas the .375 has case dimensions that are very close to those of the old .38-55

Winchester, the .307 and .356 cartridges are based on the .308 Winchester case with a rim. At this time, factory loads for the .375 and .356 are produced with only 200-grain Power Point bullets at velocities of 2,200 and 2,460 fps, respectively, although both .375 and .356 loads were formerly produced with 250-grain bullets at 1,900 and 2,160 fps, respectively. Initially, factory loads for the .307 Winchester were offered with 150- and 180-grain Power Point bullets with velocities of 2,760 and 2,510 fps, but only the 180-grain load is still available. As a result, if you want to do anything innovative with any of these three calibers, you must reload your own.

Doing creative things with loading .307 and .356 Winchester ammunition is an attractive proposition. All of the Model 94 Big Bores in those calibers are the Angle Eject version. Therefore, mounting a scope directly above the action is a simple process unlike that of older Model 94s that had top ejection and required a scope to be mounted on the side of the

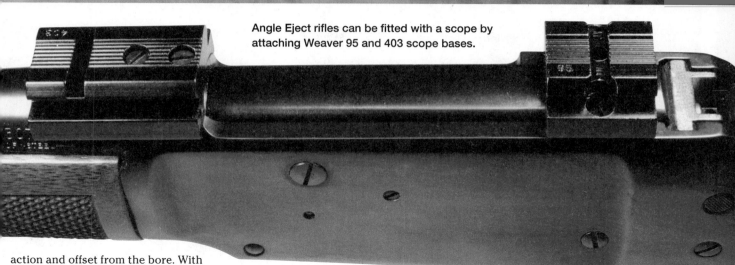

Angle Eject rifles can be fitted with a scope by attaching Weaver 95 and 403 scope bases.

action and offset from the bore. With light loads and a scope mounted, the .307 and .356 can even be used as moderate-range varmint rifles.

As a result of the .307 and .356 cases having external dimensions that duplicate those of the .308 and .358 Winchester, respectively, reloading dies for the .308 can also be used to load .307 cartridges. Similarly, .358 Winchester dies can be used to load .356 cartridges. It is generally stated that the cases of the .307 and .356 have thicker walls, which reduces internal volume, and one *cannot* use .308 Winchester loading data for the .307, or .358 Winchester data for loading the .356. The .307 and .356 utilize bullets with diameters of 0.308" and 0.357", respectively, so there are many bullets available *as long as one does not use pointed bullets in a tubular magazine.* However, handloading still offers almost limitless options.

Loading the Big Bore calibers is no different than loading other cartridges with similar types of cases. The .375 Winchester is a straight-walled case so it requires a case mouth expanding die in addition to the resizing and decapping die, and bullet seating and crimping die. Both the .307 and .356 cases are of the bottlenecked type so loading them requires the usual two die set.

The .375 Winchester case has a relatively small volume for the bullet diameter so fast-burning powders work best. These include Alliant Reloder 7, IMR 4198, Hodgdon H332 and H335, and Winchester 748. When it comes to loading .375 ammunition, the choice of bullets is somewhat limited, but excellent options with flat softpoints are available from Sierra (200 grains), Hornady (220 grains) and Barnes (255 grains). For plinking loads, one can even load round balls of .375" diameter.

Powders that generally work well in the .307 and .356 are those that also work well in the .308 Winchester. Therefore, IMR 3031, 4895 and 4064, Hodgdon H335, LEVERevolution, Varget, H322 and Winchester 748 are

These boxes represent the range of loads originally offered in .307, .356 and .375 Winchester.

Below: From left to right, these cartridges are 150- and 200-grain .307, 200- and 250-grain .356, and 200- and 250-grain .375 Winchester.

This .307 Winchester factory load is shown with a few bullets that can be handloaded in the .307 case. They vary from 90 to 170 grains for use on game ranging from varmints to large animals.

Right: Adding a rim to the .308 Winchester (center) is the starting point for producing the .307 Winchester (left) and the .356 Winchester (right).

suitable. For loading the .307 Winchester, any of the flatpoint bullets of .308" diameter can be utilized. Moreover, Hornady offers the 160-grain polymer-tipped FTX, both in some factory loads and as a component bullet for reloaders. Numerous other bullets are available that weigh from 90 to about 180 grains. For hunting, it is hard to beat either the Hornady FTX bullet or the 170-grain Nosler Partition that is also used in the .30-30 Winchester. A .307 Winchester can be used effectively as a varmint rifle at moderate ranges by loading the excellent 110-grain Speer hollow flatpoint bullet, a 110-grain roundnose or the 125-grain Sierra flatnose hollowpoint bullet.

Loading the .356 Winchester is a most interesting proposition because in addition to such game bullets as the 180- and

220-grain Speer, or 200-grain Hornady FTX, one can load any bullet having a diameter of .357" including those normally used for loading handgun ammunition. Therefore, for preparing ammunition for plinking or varmint shooting, the entire range of bullets used in .38 Special or .357 Magnum handguns can be utilized, although with these short bullets the length of the overall cartridge will usually require such cartridges to be loaded singly.

The Winchester Big Bore lever-action rifles are no longer in production, but they are not forgotten by those who own them or others who want to. Not long ago, the author contacted the last large manufacturer that offered the .358 Winchester in a bolt-action rifle hoping to find one. The .358 Winchester is a wonderfully effective game caliber so not surprisingly the response was that no rifle in that caliber was available. It is interesting to note that rifles such as the .307, .356 and .358 Winchester did not make it in the marketplace, but

every one listed for sale anywhere that the author has seen is sold very quickly and they command premium prices. The old saying "speed kills" is applied to driving – but apparently velocity kills when it comes to rifles. As the author has been informed, some of the highly touted magnums are not exactly setting sales records.

From published information, it appears that the .308 Marlin Express – which is almost a ballistic twin of the .307 Winchester – and the .338 Marlin Express – which approximately duplicates the 200-grain load in the .356 Winchester – are not in great demand. Probably the newer Marlin cartridges were created more on the perception of *name* rather than *need*. The issue is that many hunters seem to believe that pointed bullets at high velocity are necessary, but that is simply not true for a lot of hunting. Most game is taken at no more than 200 yards. The author just read a field test of a new piece of equipment in which a deer was taken with one shot at 142 yards. A short,

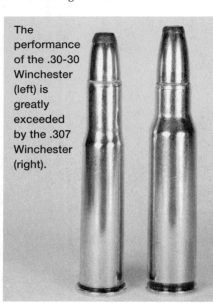

The performance of the .30-30 Winchester (left) is greatly exceeded by the .307 Winchester (right).

Finding ammunition such as this .375 Winchester load can be difficult.

Outstanding results can be obtained by loading the 160-grain Hornady FTX bullet in the .307 Winchester.

With handloading, the versatility of the .356 Winchester can be greatly increased. The three bullets on the left are intended for use in handguns but are good varmint bullets, whereas the three on the right are big-game bullets – the 200-grain Hornady FTX, 180- and 220-grain Speer.

handy lever-action rifle in any of the Big Bore calibers or even the .30-30 would have performed just as well. There is also a perception that lever-action rifles are not accurate. With one of the author's lever actions in .30-30 Winchester, 22 three-shot groups with seven types of factory ammunition averaged 1.9 inches at 100 yards. Such accuracy is perfectly adequate for shooting at medium-size game within the effective range of the caliber.

The Winchester Big Bores did not have catchy names and the ammunition for them was offered in limited types by Winchester only. How different things might have been if Hodgdon LEVERevolution powder and polymer-tipped Hornady FTX bullets had been available in .307 and .356 Winchester. We will never know, but the Winchester Big Bores are still highly prized rifles. The Winchester Big Bores have become decidedly collectible and a nice .307 or .356 will cost around $700 to $800 or more. Prices for the Big Bore in .375 Winchester are usually somewhat higher. The author recently saw one of the relatively rare .356 Winchester rifles with the raised comb priced at $1,499.

Although the Winchester Model 94 Big Bore rifles are collectible, they are much more. Winchester Model 94 rifles are legendary for their portability and ease of handling. In Big Bore calibers, they are eminently capable hunting rifles that are completely satisfactory for a lot of hunting. I think that E. Kreps summarized it very well in the delightful little book *Camp and Trail Methods* (A. R. Harding Publishing Company, Columbus, OH, 1950, p. 64): "… yet there are many hunters who can find fault with and will condemn every style or brand of arm except the one they are using at the time." In some cases, that also applies to specific calibers.

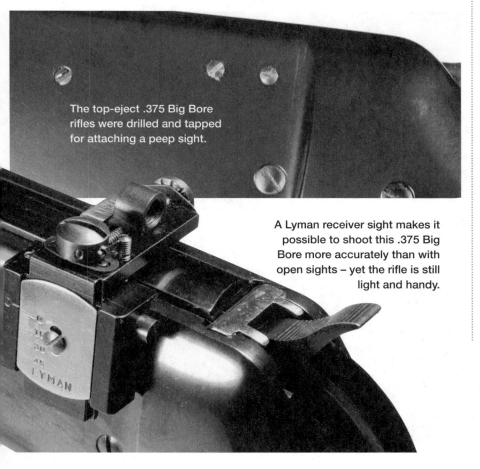

The top-eject .375 Big Bore rifles were drilled and tapped for attaching a peep sight.

A Lyman receiver sight makes it possible to shoot this .375 Big Bore more accurately than with open sights – yet the rifle is still light and handy.

DISCLAIMER: Any and all loading data found in this article or previous articles is to be taken as reference material *only*. The publishers, editors, authors, contributors and their entities bear no responsibility for the use by others of the data included in this article or others that came before it.

Smith & Wesson & Cops

For much of the 20th century, the Smith & Wesson revolver was America's top cop gun.

By **Robert K. Campbell**

This revolver is marked with Police Department numbers, although the agency is lost to history.

The most successful revolvers ever made are the Smith & Wesson double actions, from the break-top designs of the 1880s to the swing-out cylinder models of today. Small double-action "pocket revolvers" chambered in .32 S&W and .38 S&W were immensely popular in the early 1880s. Many of those guns were carried in the uniform tunic of police officers in the Northern cities. It was considered bad form in those days to expose the revolver to the public eye.

The first Smith & Wesson Hand Ejector .32 had novel design features. Note the script engraved on the cylinder.

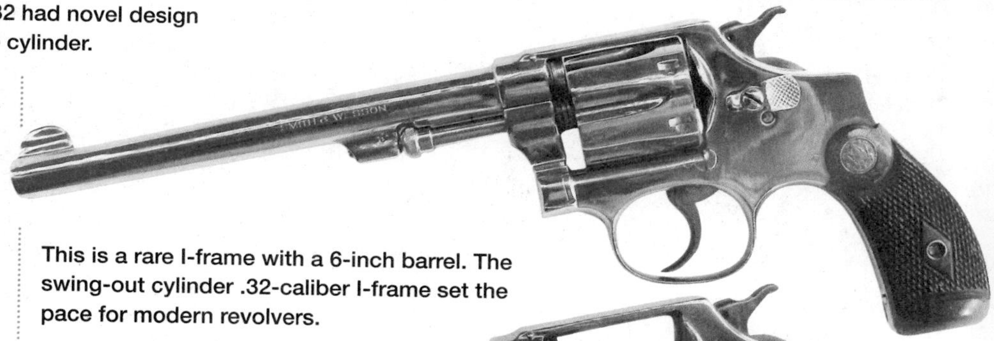

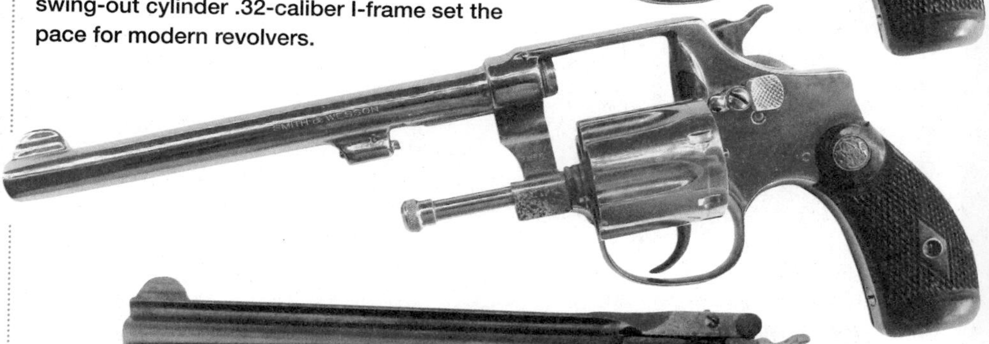

The Smith & Wesson models were high quality and more reliable than the cheap break-top models from other manufacturers – which were often "out of time" and soon ready for the junk box. Technology proceeded and the next step was to the double-action revolver with a swing-out cylinder. Smith & Wesson did not manufacture the first revolver of the type, but arguably they were the best of the day.

Smith & Wesson introduced the swing-out cylinder Hand Ejector .32 on the new I-frame in 1896. The cylinder swings out by pulling forward on the ejector rod, which does not lock at the front. The bolt stop is contained in the topstrap. Each time the cylinder rotates, the spring-loaded bolt stop actually moves above the topstrap, along with the rear sight. Yet, the internal mechanism is easily recognizable as similar to the most modern Smith & Wessons.

The 1896 Hand Ejector was chambered for the .32 Smith & Wesson Long cartridge. Without the limitations of leverage imposed by a break-top action, the new swing-out cylinder revolvers could be chambered for longer cartridges. The I-frame evolved into a much-improved Hand Ejector. With a conventional frame, an ejector rod that locked at the front, a push-type cylinder release and a bolt stop located in the frame – these were modern revolvers.

This is a rare I-frame with a 6-inch barrel. The swing-out cylinder .32-caliber I-frame set the pace for modern revolvers.

These Smith & Wesson revolvers were a result of customer demands. The lower revolver is the Safety Hammerless and the upper is the Perfected Double Action.

The Regulation Police five-shot .38 is a nicely proportioned revolver that is easy to carry all day.

The .32-caliber revolvers are a joy to fire and use, and are often quite accurate. I have fired both the 1896 and a later 1910 version with Fiocchi's 98-grain RNL load with excellent results. An important variation on the six-shot .32 frame was a five-shot version firing the .38 Smith & Wesson cartridge. With a square butt and 4-inch barrel this revolver was known as the Regulation Police. These revolvers are well balanced, accurate and offer a butter-smooth action.

They are ideal for carry in a deep pocket, and the short-barrel versions were popular for concealed carry. The problem was the power of the cartridge. Both the short .38 and .32 have poor records in personal defense. As Chick Gaylord reported in his book, *The Handgunners Guide*, a New York City detective once fired several .32s into a robber's face with no effect and the con escaped. The short .38 with standard loads was little better, although Ed McGivern sang its praises in his *Fast and Fancy Revolver Shooting*. However, McGivern never actually shot anyone.

A rather curious revolver was produced combining the break-top revolver and the I-frame. Smith & Wesson listened to the public and this is a large reason for the company's success. They had developed the Safety Hammerless revolver with a grip safety, in order to address the issue of a child who had injured herself with a revolver. The break-top had been criticized on a number of occasions because in a struggle thugs had been able to grasp the lock and unload the revolver. Smith & Wesson's Perfected Double Action revolver combined a break-top upper with an I-frame. The break-top lock and the cylinder release had to be simultaneously operated to unload the revolver. While odd in appearance, these revolvers are smooth in operation and surprisingly accurate.

The Most Famous Smith & Wesson

In 1899 the Smith & Wesson Military and Police revolver was introduced. Smith & Wesson now offered, as the late Tom Ferguson remarked, "the gunfighter's gun of the 20th century." In terms of sheer numbers, the Military and Police .38 saved more cop's lives than all of the rest of the service revolvers put together. At one time the Smith & Wesson .38 Special armed some 75 percent of American law enforcement officers. The revolver also enjoyed strong foreign sales, particularly in the British Commonwealths.

When you examine the revolver the quality of design and manufacture are evident, even in parkerized wartime versions. I think that much of the success of the M&P revolver lies in its size and weight. The 4-inch barrel, six-shot .38 Special weighs about 34 ounces. It is the ideal size, and is well balanced. Many years after the introduction of the Military and Police revolver the FBI conducted a study that found that a handgun weighing over 35 ounces was too heavy for all-day carry.

As one example, despite the reams of pages written in favor of the .41 Magnum it seems incredible today that anyone seriously believed this heavy revolver would be adopted by the police, particularly with the light and fast-handling Combat Magnum .357 available to solve every police problem. The K-frame .38 Special is light enough, fits most hands well in either the square or round-butt version. With a 5-inch barrel, the Military and Police is possibly the best balanced revolver of all time, offering a good natural point, but the introduction of the 4-inch heavy barrel version pretty much killed the 5-inch version.

When introduced, the Military and Police revolver had a great advantage. It was seen as a replacement for the trouble-prone Colt 1892 revolver. While the Colt's main failing may seem to be the .38 Long Colt cartridge, the action itself was less than robust. The new Smith & Wesson revolver was clearly superior to the Colt. The .38 Special cartridge was more powerful than the .38 Long Colt, and more importantly had much more development potential.

While the .38 Special may not be a powerhouse by today's standard, the cartridge was more powerful than the common police cartridges of that time period. Most Northern agencies issued

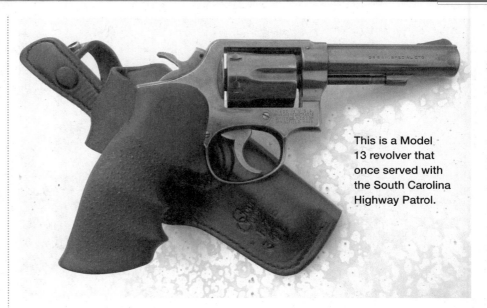

This is a Model 13 revolver that once served with the South Carolina Highway Patrol.

some type of .38 S&W chambered break-top revolver. The .32 Colt was also popular. While western officers may have preferred the .44 and .45 revolver, many town agencies carried .38-caliber revolvers. As late as 1938,

motorcycle cops in small towns carried the .32 Regulation Police. The .38 Special was seen as a powerful cartridge that was reasonably easy to master with a minimum of training. Nothing has changed on that count.

Smith & Wesson had competitors, but no equals. Left to right, Colt, Miroku, Smith & Wesson.

This very nice 1905 Military and Police revolver still sees outdoors use.

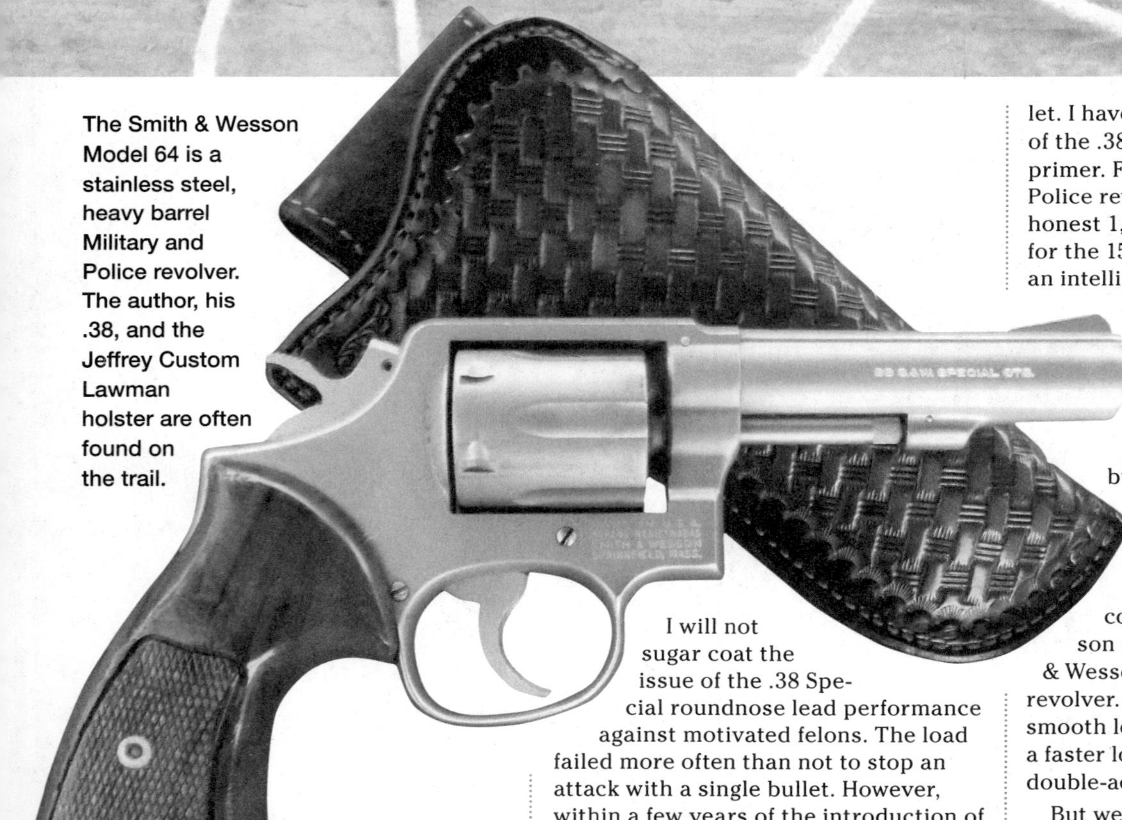

The Smith & Wesson Model 64 is a stainless steel, heavy barrel Military and Police revolver. The author, his .38, and the Jeffrey Custom Lawman holster are often found on the trail.

I will not sugar coat the issue of the .38 Special roundnose lead performance against motivated felons. The load failed more often than not to stop an attack with a single bullet. However, within a few years of the introduction of the cartridge, handloaders developed loads for the .38 Special that moved it into a different category. By the 1930s the factories offered high-speed loads rated at 1,100 fps with a 158-grain bul-

let. I have fired the Remington version of the .38-44, complete with large pistol primer. From a 5-inch Military and Police revolver the load clocked an honest 1,050 fps compared to 755 fps for the 158-grain standard load. With an intelligent and motivated user the .38 Special became a fine cop cartridge.

As a badge of office, the .38 Special was ideal to arm semi-trained officers. Smith & Wesson had some competition, but by the 1950s there was no real equal. Prior to World War II companies such as the D.W. King Gunsight Company experimented with short-action conversions of the Smith & Wesson revolver. After the war, Smith & Wesson introduced the short-action revolver. While some bemoaned the old smooth long action, the new gun offered a faster lock time and was the better double-action revolver.

But we are getting ahead of the story. During the war Smith & Wesson supplied more than half a million Military and Police revolvers to the allies and our own armed forces. For the most part, the British guns were chambered

The most highly evolved Military and Police revolver is the Model 19 .357 Magnum Combat Magnum. This one wears Ahrends grips.

The author keeps his hand in with the Military and Police Model 13, chambered for the .357 Magnum and .38 Special.

in .38-200 and the American revolvers in .38 Special. While most of our .38s were issued to aircrews or defense plant guards, the British considered their revolvers front-line weapons. These revolvers featured a V prefix in the serial number and were known as the Victory Model. They certainly contributed to victory over the Axis powers.

In 1954 Smith & Wesson managed the engineering feat of adapting the .357 Magnum cartridge to the K-frame revolver with the Combat Magnum, later known

as the Model 19. The Combat Magnum was a target-sighted revolver, but it was a simple matter to produce it with fixed sights and what amounted to a .357 Magnum Military and Police revolver – thus was born the Model 13 in 1974. I have carried the Model 13 on a professional basis and regard it as my first choice in a "go-to" revolver. My revolver is comfortable to fire with its load of choice, the Black Hills 125-grain JHP .357. Many of these revolvers were loaded with the .38 Special +P during their service life. When

loaded with Magnum rounds and in the hands of a well-trained and practiced individual the Model 13 was a formidable service revolver. This revolver, along with the stainless steel Model 64 .38 Special and Model 65 .357 Magnum, were among the last Smith & Wesson models designed for police officers.

Far from being a relic of days gone by, these are hard-working revolvers ready to serve. They remain excellent choices for personal defense or security work.

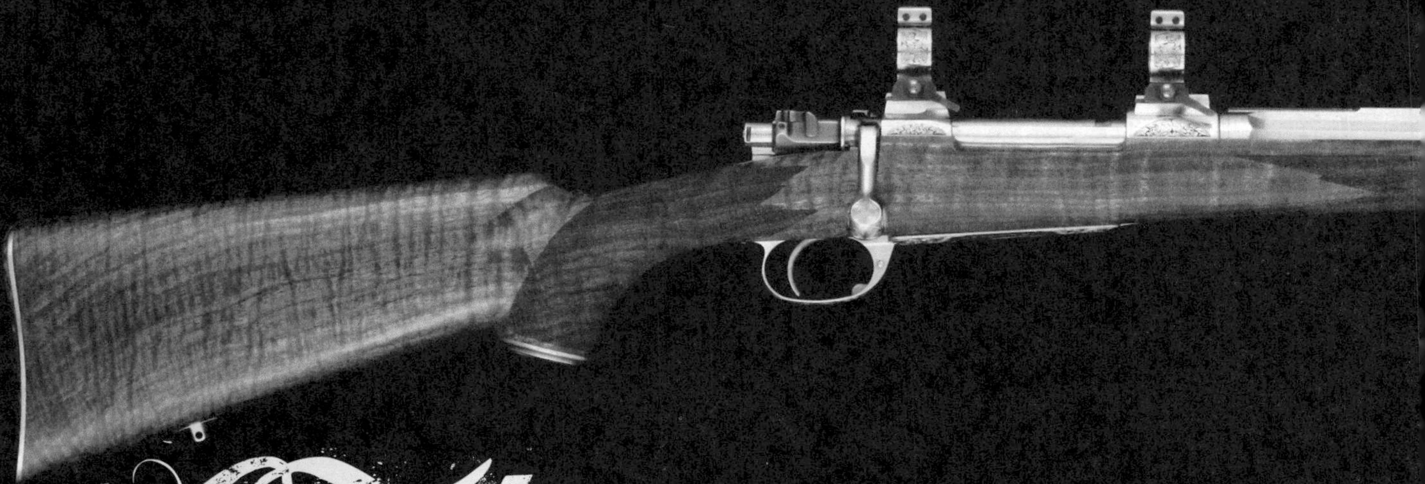

Custom & Engraved Guns

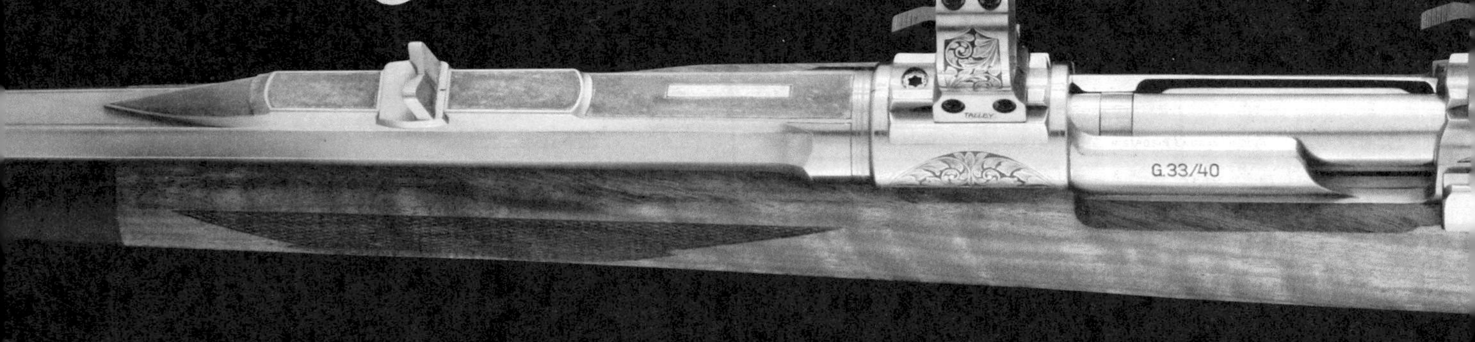

Martini, Wesbrook, Strosin

A few years back at the American Custom Gunmakers Guild show in Reno, a gentleman well known to the firearms industry approached Dave Wesbrook with a request. It was simply for Wesbrook to assemble a team of craftsmen to, in essence, build for him the best G33/40-actioned rifle ever made. Such a commission doesn't come up very often and Dave jumped at the chance.

He marched the client to Ralf Martini's table and they discussed metalwork options. Wesbrook had wanted to collaborate with Ralf on a project for many years, but by the time this came along, Ralf was mainly doing complete projects. However, he agreed to join in this venture.

No detail was spared on this project. The list of the various tasks accom-

plished is far too long for this report. It is sufficient to say that everything that could be done to enhance the project was done, including a Martini half-round, half-octagon barrel with everything integral on the barrel.

For the stock, Wesbrook selected the finest example of quarter-sawn fiddleback European walnut that he had ever seen, let alone owned. It was

Our Annual Review of the Finest Examples of Beauty and Artistry in the World of the Custom Gun

BY **Tom Turpin**

dense with perfect grain flow, and expensive. From this blank, he crafted the stock. The photos show the stock much better than I can explain in mere words.

Finally, Robert Strosin was selected and accepted the challenge to do the engraving on this extra-special rifle. The client and Strosin finally met at a

Firearms Engravers Guild of America show in Las Vegas and decided on the engraving theme.

The results of this all are shown in Wesbrook's wonderful photography. It is

quite simply, a masterpiece. We won't see its likes again anytime soon.

Photos by Dave Wesbrook

Jesse Kaufman

Jesse is a friend of mine of long standing. I met him a bunch of years ago on a trip to visit Dakota Arms in Sturgis, S.D. Jesse worked for Dakota, and there was very little that he couldn't do extremely well. For a long time, he worked days at Dakota and in the evenings and on weekends, he did checkering and stock work at home for private clients. A few years back, in what little spare time he had available, he took up engraving. His progression as an engraver is mind-boggling to me. He was pretty well established as a stockmaker and checkerer, but now an engraver too! You bet.

The accompanying photos are of a Parker shotgun that Jesse stocked, checkered and engraved. About the only thing he didn't do on this fine Parker was to smelt the steel! Watch out in the future for this young man and his tremendous talents.

Photos courtesy of Jesse Kaufman.

C.J. Kai

C.J. is an engraver that leans toward the extra ornate motif. He would have been a Rocco master in medieval Europe. His work is clean and superb. It is also not for the faint of heart. Shown here is a folding knife that he engraved. It is typical of his work, regardless of the canvas. Not only is he a heck of an engraver, he's also a peach of a guy. His work makes a statement, loud and clear. Photo by Sam Welch.

Mike Dubber

One of the best and most prolific engravers that I know is Hoosier native Mike Dubber. He is a longtime member of the Firearms Engravers Guild of America (FEGA) and also a longtime Colt Master Engraver. The Colt Single Action Army pistol shown here was commissioned as a presentation piece honoring the Willys Jeep. Fantastic work from a terrific engraver. Photos by Mike Dubber.

David Miller Co.

The Classic Rifle

A very recent example of a David Miller Co. Classic rifle. This one is chambered for the .416 Remington cartridge and is ready for Africa. The Miller Classic rifle is as good as human hands and the best materials can produce. He starts with a recent Winchester Model 70 Classic action, which, by the way, he and his associate Curt Crum helped design for Winchester. He uses Krieger cut rifled barrels almost exclusively. He also uses Sunny Hill bottom metal and most everything else is made in house. The English walnut blank was specifically chosen for this rifle as it is, according to David, the perfect blank for this rifle. Every square inch of a Miller Classic rifle is worked over by either David or Curt, and sometimes both. Photo by Tom Turpin.

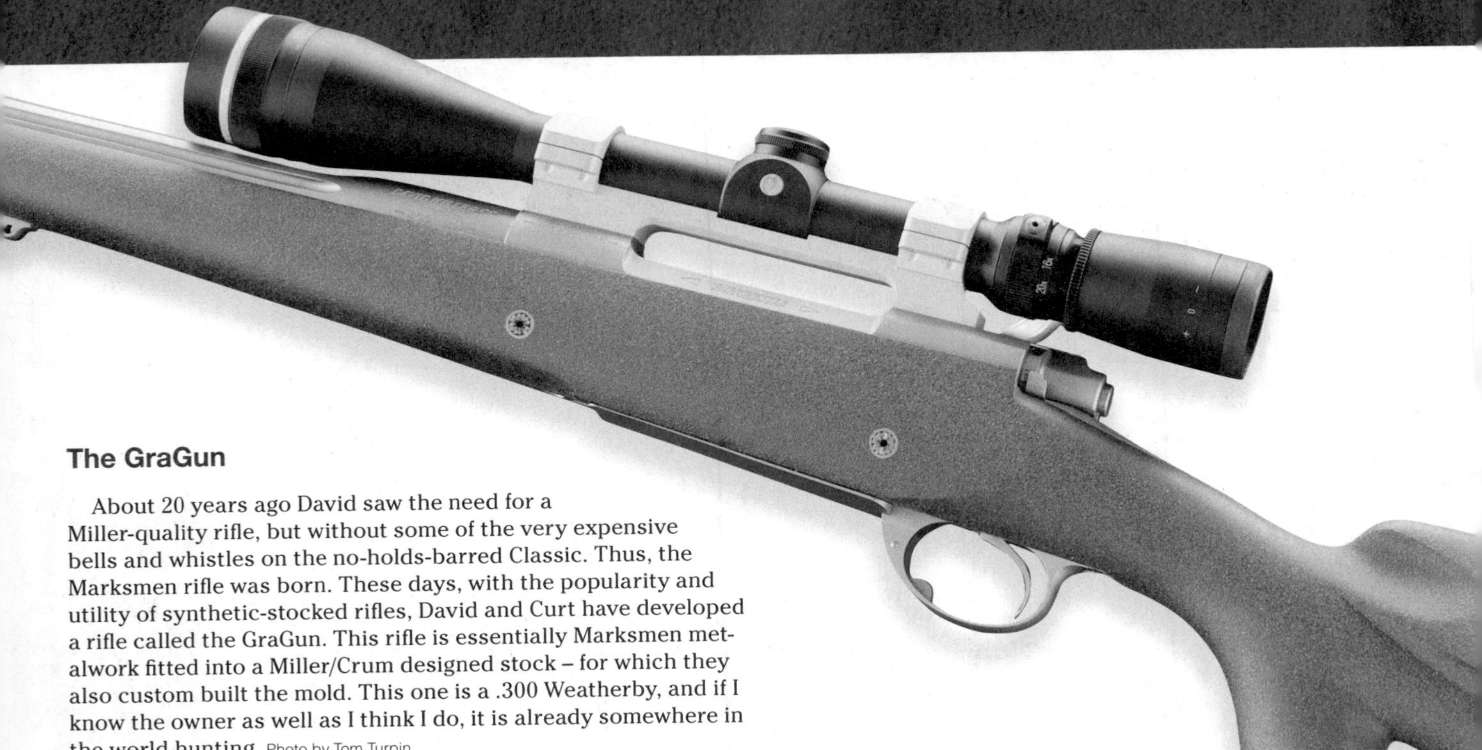

The GraGun

About 20 years ago David saw the need for a Miller-quality rifle, but without some of the very expensive bells and whistles on the no-holds-barred Classic. Thus, the Marksmen rifle was born. These days, with the popularity and utility of synthetic-stocked rifles, David and Curt have developed a rifle called the GraGun. This rifle is essentially Marksmen metalwork fitted into a Miller/Crum designed stock – for which they also custom built the mold. This one is a .300 Weatherby, and if I know the owner as well as I think I do, it is already somewhere in the world hunting. Photo by Tom Turpin.

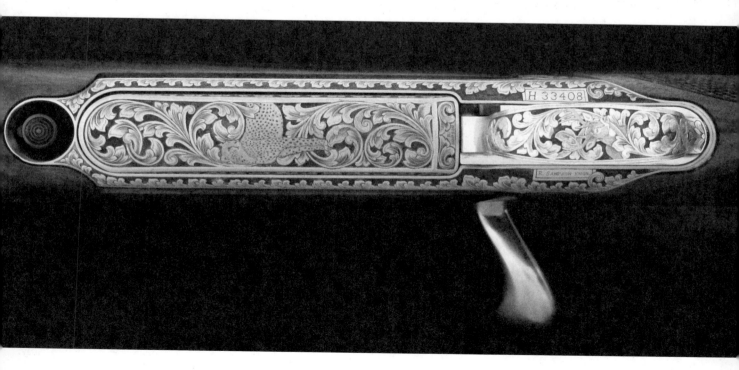

Roger Sampson

Roger Sampson has been a mainstay within the Firearms Engravers Guild of America (FEGA) since long before I became involved in reporting on their activities, and that has been more than two decades. When I first met him, his forte was engraving miniature firearms. I marveled at how he could do that. These days, however, he has broadened his engraving horizon into doing full-scale engravings. Shown here is an example of his current work. It is superb. Photos by Roger Sampson.

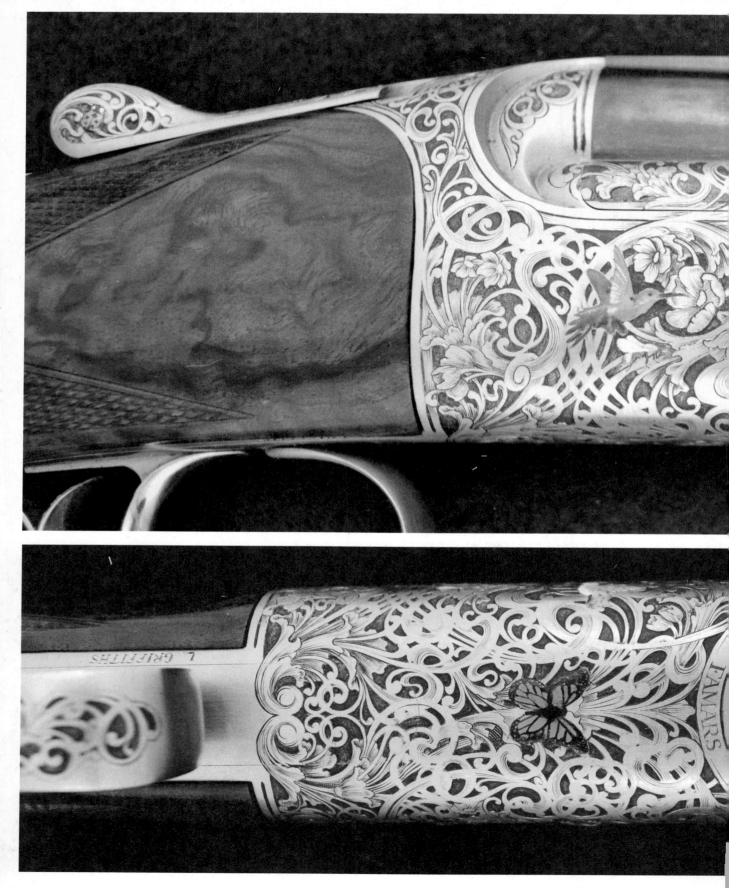

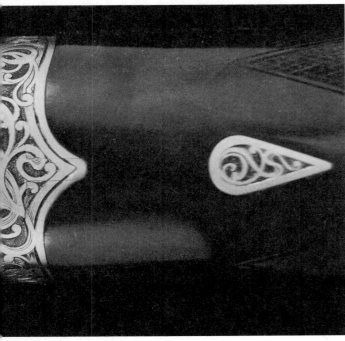

Lee Griffiths

Lee Griffiths is an amazing fellow. A few years back I had the pleasure of looking at his first engraving job. I remember it well; it was on a Parker shotgun. It was also wonderfully done. Even though it is a bit out of the ordinary, I wanted to show his first oil painting, a portrait of three generations of Brownells – Bob, Frank and Pete. It is equally amazing, perhaps even more so.

Since this is not an art class, I've included three photos of a Famars over/under shotgun that Lee engraved and inlaid. He has become an old master at this aspect of his career. We'll have to wait and see how his portraiture career proceeds.

Photos courtesy of Lee Griffiths.

Barry Lee Hands

Sharps Arms Co. Rifle

This rifle above was originally built by the Sharps Arms Co. of Big Timber, Mont., as a display piece illustrating their capabilities. Master Engraver Barry Lee Hands was commissioned to do the wonderful scroll engraving and gold inlay work. In addition to being tied to his engraving bench taking care of commissions, Barry is currently serving as the President of the Firearms Engravers Guild of America (FEGA). Sharps Arms donated the rifle to FEGA, which sold it at auction as a fundraising effort. Photos courtesy of Sharps Arms Co.

Fogarizzu Knife

Found on the opposite page this is a very special folding knife by a master knife-maker, Tore Fogarizzu, engraved by master engraver Barry Lee Hands. The scales are mother-of-pearl, a beautiful but not so durable material. As far as I know, Hands is the only one out there doing this type of engraving and inlay work; I've not seen any such stylish inlay done by anyone else. Gold inlaid and diamond encrusted throughout, including into the pearl scales, this knife is truly for the one who has everything else. A simply fantastic piece. Photo by Francesco Pachi.

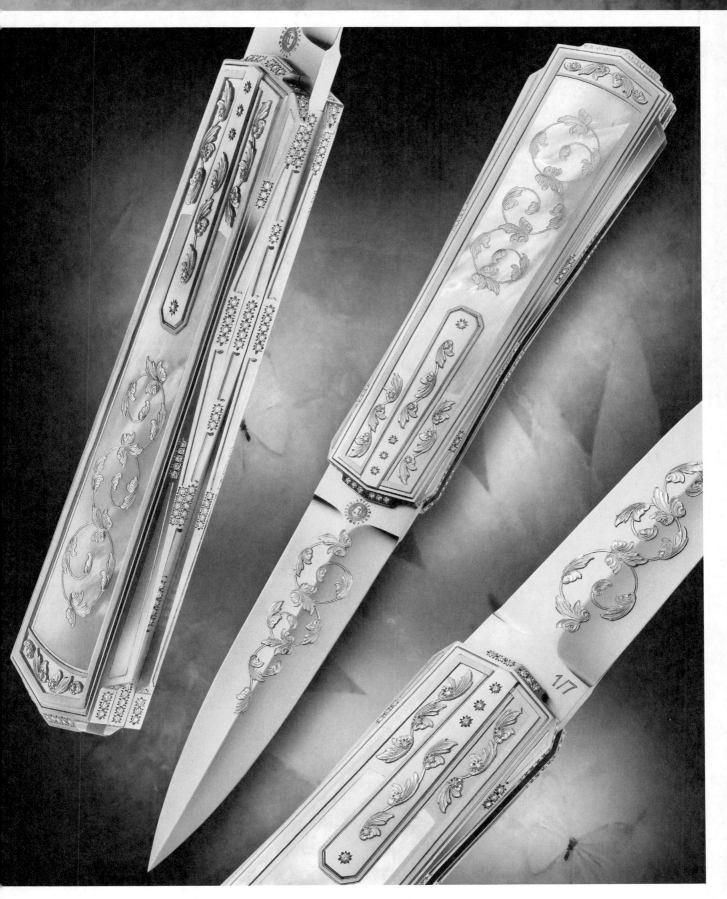

Jim Blair

Roger Green performed his magic and built this sidelock double gun with two sets of barrels – one set in .410 bore and a second set in .22 Hornet. He chose Jim Blair to do the engraving. The accompanying photos illustrate just what a wise decision that was. Blair can work in many different styles but his approach on this canvas seems to be his favored styling. Photos by Jim Blair.

Custom Rifles from the Past
RIFLES OF JACK AND ELEANOR O'CONNOR

Jack's Favorite Rifles

Although he has been gone now for 38 years, Jack O'Connor is still considered the dean of outdoor writers by many, including me. He is credited with "making" the .270 cartridge with the shooting and hunting public, and while I believe it is good enough to have made it on its own, there is no question that O'Connor helped it along immeasurably. Shown here are his two favorite rifles of all time, his Number 1 and Number 2 Winchester Model 70 .270 rifles as done up by Al Biesen. The Number 1 rifle is on the top and the Number 2 is below. Naturally, the Number 1 rifle came first, and O'Connor was so enamored with it, he feared shooting out the barrel since he was using it so much. As a result, he ordered a second one a few years later to match the first as a backup. As it turned out, he liked the Number 2 even more than Number 1, so the roles were reversed. The Number 1 rifle is in private hands and the Number 2 is still in the O'Connor family. If only these two rifles could talk, the tales they could tell!

Photo by Tom Turpin.

Eleanor's Favorite Rifles

The two rifles shown at the left were most often used by Eleanor O'Connor, wife of the dean of outdoor writers, Jack O'Connor. The rifle on the left is one that Jack had built for himself, but Eleanor shot it, loved it and took it for her own. The metalwork was done by Tom Burgess and the stock created by Russ Leonard. Chambered for the 7x57 cartridge, she used it for just about all of her hunting after talking Jack out of its ownership.

The rifle on the right is what Eleanor called her "big" rifle, one she used sparingly and only when it was necessary. Chambered for the .30-06, it was crafted for her by Wyoming gunmaker Len Brownell prior to her and Jack departing for India on a tiger hunt. She used it on a couple of tigers, and later in Africa brained an elephant using 220-grain solids. Photo by Tom Turpin.

Hank's DOUBLE RIFLE

By **Tom Tabor**

A rare find for the author's collection: an elegant English double by way of Nashville royalty

There was a time not too long ago when craftsmanship and quality took precedence over speed of production. It was an era when gunmakers were looked upon as artisans that displayed their work proudly and with a high degree of reverence to their craft. Few could argue that William Jackman Jeffery wasn't one of those prestigious individuals. And as such, the firearms carrying the name of W. J. Jeffery frequently found them-selves in the hands of nobility on driven pheasant hunts in the British Isles, and other times they were the firearm of choice for safari hunters embarking on the Ivory Trail to face the dangers,

The author found the balance of the W.J. Jeffery double to be superb.

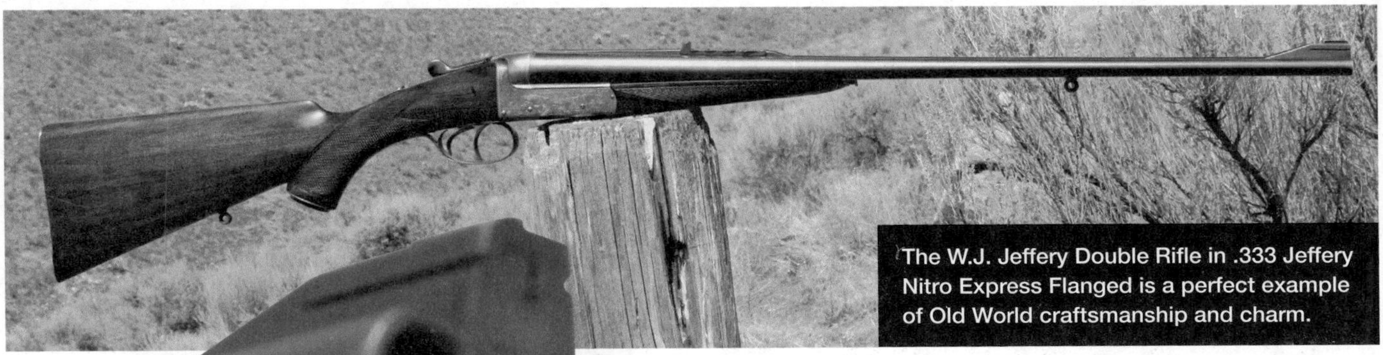

The W.J. Jeffery Double Rifle in .333 Jeffery Nitro Express Flanged is a perfect example of Old World craftsmanship and charm.

rigors and rewards of the Dark Continent.

Jeffery built a variety of different types of shotguns and rifles, but to me the most impressive were the double rifles. Like many avid hunters, gun collectors and gun lovers in general, I dreamed of someday owning one of these rifles that has been so heavily immersed in the African and Asian hunting culture of the past. So, when I heard that famed country singer Hank Williams Jr. decided to sell his coveted W.J. Jeffery double chambered in the somewhat unusual rifle caliber of .333 Jeffery Nitro Express Flanged, I simply had to have a closer look.

Hank's main residence is understandably located in Tennessee where he has unfettered access to Nashville, but he also has a place in Montana just a few miles from where I reside. Plus, he owns a gun shop, Deadly Nostalgia, which is manned by his personal gunsmith, Dan Coffin of Coffin Gunsmithing, who does the vast majority of Hank's gun repair and customizing work. While visiting with Dan one day he mentioned to me how surprised he was that Hank had decided to sell his Jeffery double .333 rifle. Even though Hank's interest typically lies heavily in the guns of the American west, he had become quite fond of this particular rifle, likely because of the historic significance and ambiance that surrounded it.

Like most of Hank's huge collection of firearms the Jeffery was in phenomenally great condition, especially considering it had over eight decades of use to its credit, with a very large portion of that time being smack dab in the corrosive era of the cordite days. Upon seeing it I knew I had to find a way for it to take up resi-

DEADLY NOSTALGIA

285 MAIN STREET VICTOR, MT. 59875

INVOICE/STATEMENT

DATE OF ORDER 9/18/14

CUSTOMER'S ORDER NO	PHONE	SOLD BY	TERMS	STARTING DATE
				/ /

BILL TO Tom Tabor

ORDER TAKEN BY

ADDRESS

CITY STATE ZIP

☐ DAY WORK
☐ CONTRACT
☐ EXTRA

SHIP TO: LOCATION

JOB PHONE

DESCRIPTION

Jeffery Double Rifle
.333 Cal.
Ser #

Hello Tom
enjoy the "sweet shooting"
Jeffery Double
Hank Williams Jr

TOTAL MATERIALS
TOTAL LABOR
TAX
TOTAL AMOUNT

DATE COMPLETED / / ORDERED BY

I hereby acknowledge the satisfactory completion of the above described work.

Signature

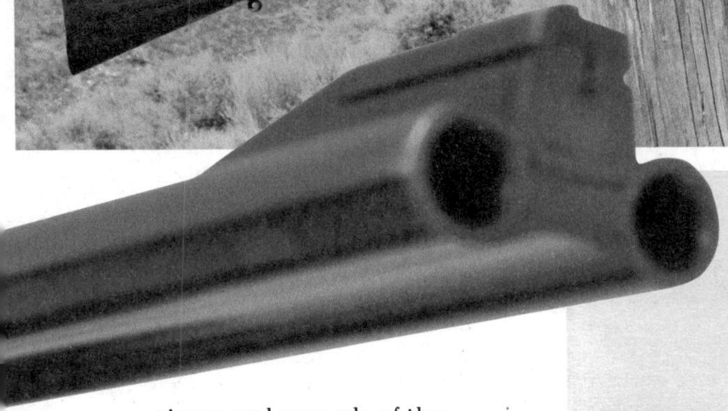

Hank's endorsement on the receipt adds a bit of creditability as to his fondness of this particular rifle.

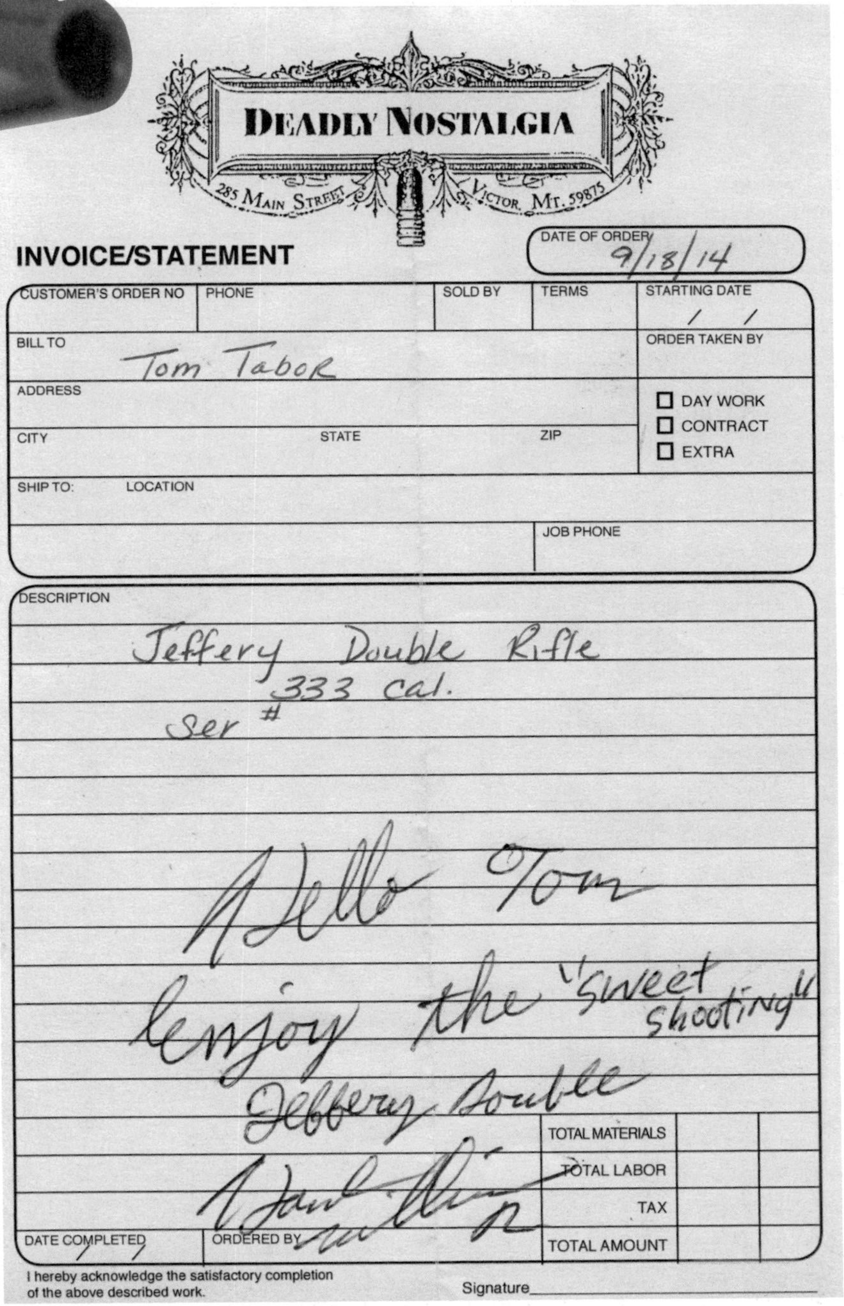

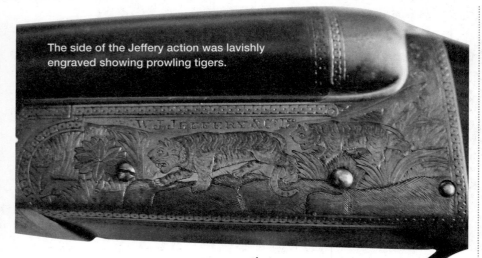

The side of the Jeffery action was lavishly engraved showing prowling tigers.

dency in my own gun safe. At the time, Hank was on a dove hunt in Tennessee so communication was done through a cell phone. A deal was struck and I proceeded to write out a check before packing up the Jeffery and heading home with it.

W.J. Jeffery learned at least some of his expertise from Cogswell & Harrison and P. Webley & Son, who at that time were some of the most well-respected gunmakers in Great Britain. Eventually he formed a partnership with a man by the name of Davies, but that union was short lived and the two men soon parted company. That gave Jeffery the opportunity to form the W. J. Jeffery & Company. By 1900 the operation had developed into a full-blown gunmaking business

that soon progressed into one of the most influential of the era.

The years that followed brought with them a variety of important patents and a broad array of proprietary rifle cartridges, many of which bear Jeffery's name. Some of the best known include the .600 Nitro Express, .400 Jeffery N.E., .404 Jeffery, .500 Jeffery Rimless, .433 Rimless and the flanged cartridges of the .280 Jeffery, .255 rook rifle and—while not necessarily frequently encountered—my own .333 Jeffery N.E. Flanged.

On the Ivory Trail of Dark Continent the .333 Jeffery Nitro Express Flanged

was considered to fall into the classification of a light rifle in the normal battery of weapons carried by those stalwart safari adventurers. In India it was sometimes considered a good choice when it came to hunting tigers, whether those exploits took place from a howdah on the back of a large Asian elephant, or from a high-positioned machan platform possibly overlooking a staked-out goat for bait. The engraving on the action of my Jeffery depicting a couple of prowling tigers would seem to indicate that Jeffery felt that this particular rifle and caliber were perfect for that task.

A .333 Jeffery N.E. Flagged chambered double rifle is a fairly rare thing to find today. Double rifles have always been labor intensive to construct, which always translates into expense to the customer. That being the case, many ivory and safari hunters chose bolt actions for what they considered their light rifles, then dedicated more of their available funds in order to purchase their bigbore doubles.

This particular .333 was built in 1933 and at that time it sold for what may seem today to be a paltry sum of only GBP sterling 53 pounds, 12 shillings and sixpence. Adjusted to today's monetary standard that would be equivalent to only about $83.00 U.S. It is important to keep in mind that this was smack dab in the heart of the World Depression when jobs and money were exceedingly scarce. Now, more than eight decades

Safari hunters frequently use shooting sticks to steady their wavering rifle.

later, I can assure everyone that Hank Williams Jr. demanded a bit more than that initial $83.00 for me to add that rifle to my collection.

There were actually two commercially made .333 cartridges during this era. The .333 Jeffery N.E. Flanged was developed in 1908 specifically for chambering in break-open rifles, whether those came in the form of single-shots or as doubles. The second of those cartridges was not flanged and was designed specifically for use in bolt rifle designs. Both cartridges share similar ballistics, but what little reloading data there is available should not be interchanged.

At first glance most observers would recognize that both .333 cartridges share the common trait of being loaded with very long bullets possessing a common weight of up to 300 grains. In John (Pondoro) Taylor's excellent book, *African Rifles and Cartridges,* he discusses use of the .333 in Africa at length. He is quoted as saying, "The plain softnose slug for the .333 is excellent for all the heavier types of soft-skinned game." Taylor went on to say that he feels those results are at least partly due to the higher than normal sectional densities of those characteristic long bullets.

When compared with the more common cartridges of today, I would say that ballistically the .333 Jeffery N.E. Flanged is close to the performance of the wildcat .338/06, or the improved version of that same cartridge and is only slightly less powerful than the .338 Winchester Mangum. Historically, and even today, it seems that a 300-grain bullet is most favored for loading, but Woodleigh Bullets and Hawk Bullets both make 250-grain and 300-grain bullets in .333 diameter, and loaded ammunition is still available from the United Kingdom based Kynoch. The factory cartridges produced by Kynoch and loaded with 250-grain bullets are said to generate a velocity of 2,150 fps and 3,090 ft-lbs of energy at the muzzle, and the 300-grain loads produce 2,400 fps and 3,200 ft-lbs.

This particular rifle came with many unique and interesting traits and clearly projects the image of quality for which W.J. Jeffery has become known. First off, it possesses selective automatic ejectors, which are considered an upgrade on many doubles and an added expense to the production costs. Many rifles of this era possessed multiblade rear sights, but in this case the Jeffery came with a fixed V-blade and four additional hinged blades marked in 100-meter increments.

The front blade sight came with an ivory bead insert and a ramp, which allows the replacement of the sight by removing a single screw located in the top of the ramp. The ramp was grooved in order to accommodate a hood, but unfortunately none came with the rifle, possibly because few safari hunters in those days favored using a hood.

I found one trait particularly interesting and that was the tiny storage compartment located inside the pistol grip of the stock. The metal pistol grip cap had been heat treated and still retained a great deal of its original color striations. In the center of that cap was a hinged compartment door providing access to a tiny compartment inside the hollow pistol grip. On many of Jeffery's other rifles the caps were made of horn or other types of material, making me assume this too may have been an upgrade for this particular rifle. I was anxious to find out if anything was stored inside but found the compart-

The .333 Jeffery N.E. Flanged is shown in the center and flanked on the right by the wildcat .338/06 Ackley and on the left by the .338 Winchester Magnum. For ballistic comparison purposes these cartridges are fairly similar in performance.

One thing that makes this particular double rifle unique is its unusual caliber, the .333 Jeffery Nitro Express Flanged.

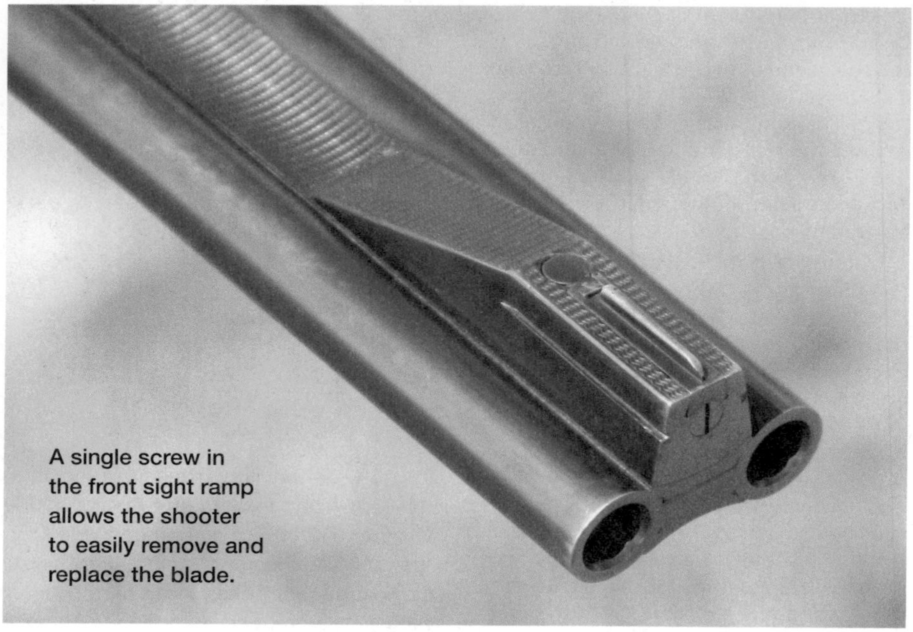

A single screw in the front sight ramp allows the shooter to easily remove and replace the blade.

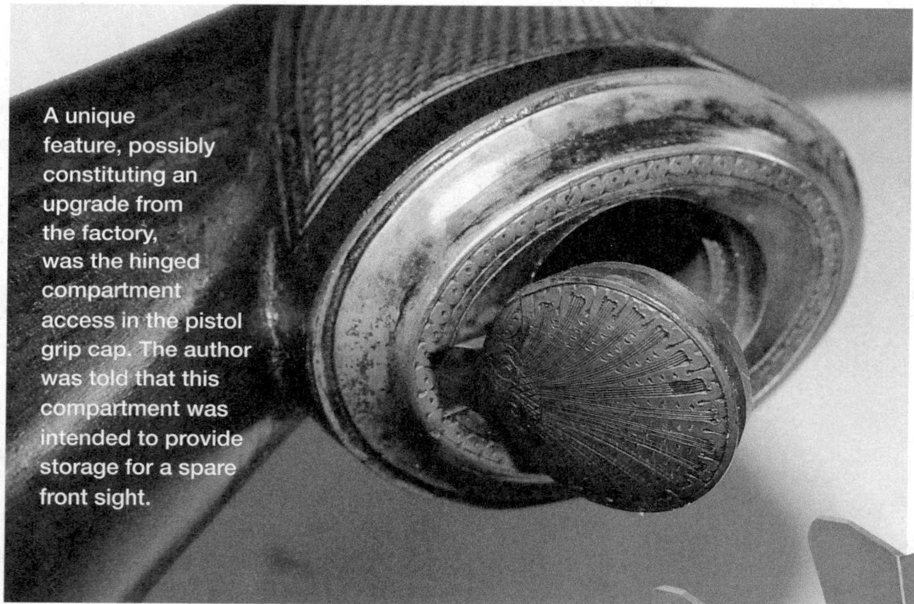

A unique feature, possibly constituting an upgrade from the factory, was the hinged compartment access in the pistol grip cap. The author was told that this compartment was intended to provide storage for a spare front sight.

The rear sight is the typical safari style comprised of multiple hinged blades. In this case there was one fixed blade and four hinged blades marked in 100-yard increments.

ment empty. That got me to wondering what this area was meant to store. Clearly it was too small to even hold a single round of spare ammunition, but possibly a cleaning cord might fit.

Eventually my curiosity got the best of me and I contacted J. Roberts and Sons and Charles Williams in England and was told that typically that compartment was used to store an extra front sight blade. I'm also thinking that possibly in some instances it might have been used to store a hood for the front sight. When hunting the thick bush, sight hoods have a tendency to get knocked off and damaged, so this would be an excellent place to store a spare unit.

Rather than possessing the usual recoil pad or buttplate, this Jeffery has what I would characterize as a type of skeleton buttplate. Rather than the metal portion of the plate surrounding the entire butt, it was comprised of a small piece of metal located at the heel and a separate piece on the toe. These two metal pieces were delicately inlayed into the end grain of the wood and the exposed wood portion was finely checkered.

While W.J. Jeffery & Company constructed both sidelock and boxlock action doubles, this particular rifle was of the latter design. The action was case colored and lavishly engraved with Indian tiger scenes on both sides, and the lower plate and triggerguard were blued. The other metal parts had also been engraved with various floral patterns. The stock was comprised of what I would characterize as a medium grade

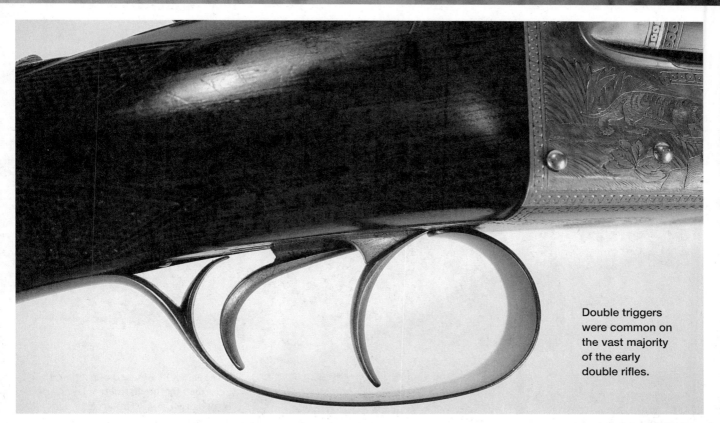

Double triggers were common on the vast majority of the early double rifles.

of dense grain walnut and contained the typical finish of that era projecting a rich brownish red tint.

The construction of double rifles is a dying art form. It takes true gunsmithing craftsmen well schooled in their art to properly construct these rifles. The artisans doing that work must have decades of experience under their belt. One of the largest challenges to that construction is the ability to regulate the barrels so that both shoot to approximately the same point of impact when firing a specific type of ammunition. Since most double rifles were considered primarily short-range weapons, most were regulated at 50 yards and frequently included engraved loading data inside their actions. In this particular case the .333 Jeffery was engraved with the phrase "Cordite 40½–300 Max." Obviously, cordite is no longer available and there is little published reloading data for the modern-day smokeless powders, which leaves anyone wishing to continue shooting these rifles at a bit of a quandary. Hank Williams, however, had shot the rifle and accompanying it was a box of handloads

The notation on the inside of the action indicates "Cordite 40½–300 Max," meaning that the barrels had been regulated to a load of 40½ grains of Cordite powder backing a 300-grain bullet. No indication was present as to the appropriate range.

The buttstock came with a skeleton-style buttplate, so rather than the butt being encircled completely with metal, a small piece of metal had been inlayed at the toe and another one at the heel of the stock with the center finely checkered.

In most cases the English double rifles came supplied with a suitcase-style gun case. Unfortunately, the original case for this rifle has long since been lost. The only alternative was to purchase a reproduction case, which was close to the original style.

W.J. JEFFERY & Co. Ltd
GUN & RIFLE MAKERS
9, Golden Square, Regent St.,
LONDON. W.1.
CLOSE TO PICCADILLY CIRCUS.

Virtually every area of the metal contains at least a small amount of engraving.

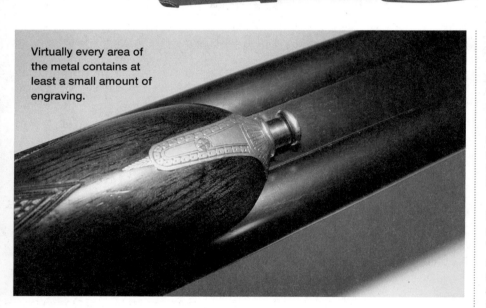

Date 10/4/99
Cartridge 333 Flanled
Case Bertram
Primer WiN
Powder ReL15 50 gR.
Bullet Woodleigh 300 gR.
Remarks Jeffrey Double Rifle
Home Brewed By Hank

To get the author started shooting, the Jeffery came with some of Hank Williams Jr.'s own handloads, which had been characteristically marked "Home Brewed by Hank."

he specifically devised himself as characterized by the distinctive label: "Home brewed by Hank." Those cartridges were loaded with 300-grain Woodleigh bullets, Winchester primers and 50 grains of Reloader 15 powder stuffed in Bertram brass. That load seemed to shoot well and I eventually was able to work up some of my own loads using Reloader 25, with both barrels printing close to the same point at 50 yards.

The attention to every detail abounds in this rifle, just as they did in every rifle and shotgun that W.J. Jeffery produced. The trigger pull was amazingly crisp and sharp with virtually no sign of creep in its movements. Weighing in at 9 pounds, 10½ ounces, it is not excessively heavy for a 24-inch barrel double rifle, and its balance is nothing short of superb. Surely this rifle will reside permanently within the confines of my gun safe until I have an opportunity to meet up with W.J. where all devoted gun lovers meet in the afterlife.

DISCLAIMER: Any and all loading data found in this article or previous articles is to be taken as reference material only. The publishers, editors, authors, contributors and their entities bear no responsibility for the use by others of the data included in this article or others that came before it.

Remington® AUTOLOADING SHOTGUNS

By Stan Trzoniec

Setting the Standard Since 1906

Chances are that if you have never picked up a Remington semiautomatic shotgun you will, eventually. With all the models manufactured over the last century, even if you don't want a new gun like the famous 1100, there are plenty to pick from on both the used and secondary market. They are fun to shoot, easy on the shoulder, made in America and they last. I have always had more than one in my gunroom, and I've used them from the hefty 10-gauge magnum ascending downward to the 12, 20 and 28 gauges.

When it came to the game of trap shooting, I purchased a Model 1100 Trap gun made years ago. Remington always had a knack for making guns that niche shooters needed and this gun with its longer barrel, specially designed stock dimensions and fancy wood, suited me to a tee. It still does. I love the sport of quail hunting and taking my Special Field 20 gauge around the fields of Georgia is always a highlight of my year. With a good bird dog at my feet and the anticipation of a flush, there is nothing better in to-day's world to relax any field hunter. The gun was especially made for me at the Remington Custom Shop and includes a nice piece of fancy wood complete with an English-style stock. With a shorter barrel and its lighter weight, the gun tracks like radar and never disappoints me (or the dog), if I do my part.

One of the features of the Remington autoloaders is their ability to soften the blow to one's shoulder with the gun operated via recoil, or gas as in the later Remington guns. With the long recoil operation found in Remington's Model 11 and 11-48, both the bolt and barrel recoil toward the rear. This movement has to

There is nothing to compare with a day of fine quail shooting carrying a Remington Model 1100 autoloader.

be longer than the host shell as to allow room for the spent (and extended) shell to clear the receiver and be ejected out of the gun so the rearward distance that both must travel is considerable. While the Model 11 was a great seller, the Model 11-48, a gun that used interchangeable parts and stamped components with a completely new design, superseded it. It would turn out to be the precursor of today's modern guns, especially the receiver.

Gas-operated guns, on the other hand, are not new. They have been in the military for many years, so it's a good reason to incorporate the design features for consumer use. However, while a design on paper looks good, it has to work — and work without fail — in the field, year after year. Since you are dealing with high pressure driving the mechanism to the rear to operate the gun, you are looking at only a brief moment in time to accomplish all of this.

For example, on the majority of guns the pressure buildup of the cartridge firing and dumping a specific amount of the pressure into the gas system happens within thousandths of a second. While this sounds simple, engineers have to calculate all of this as it relates to the gas port, its distance forward from the chamber, the weight of the shotgun, varying temperatures the gun will be used at and

how long (or short) the rearward thrust should be to extract, eject and load the gun for the next shot. Additionally, design factors include the safe unlocking of the gun during the ejecting cycle, the size of the piston and how easily shells feed from the magazine tube. Years back, you could adjust the gun for the load you were using; now guns are self-compensating and handle both regular and magnum loads with aplomb. In the past, all this information was done on a slide rule. Today, computers handle this data with ease.

The lineage of Remington shotguns is as interesting as it is diverse. Guns produced by the company within models included many gauges, grades and barrel lengths to suit all sportsmen. In looking at a multitude of sources, to me there are literally thousands of combinations over the years that include hunting, trap and skeet shooting and lately, sporting clays. Remington, in short, has rallied to the cause over the decades to produce something for everyone. So while I have labored to give the reader a list as complete as possible, I am sure that deep in the contents of history I have missed something. With that said, let's begin with first of the first, the Model 11.

The Model 11 had the honor of being the first autoloading shotgun made and produced in the United States. Through a few misfortunes it ended up in the hands

of Remington Arms. The Model 11 (aka Auto-5) would become one of the best sellers of a long line of shotguns. At its inception, John Browning designed the gun and proudly took it to Winchester, where the management had taken a kind heart to his previous gun designs by producing and marketing them. However, on this trip he tried to convince Winchester executives to a new royalty based fee system on the sales of this new design.

Even though the design was sound, Winchester refused his new system of compensation, so heavy hearted he journeyed to Remington in Ilion, N.Y. Seemingly riding on a string of bad luck, Browning found that the president of Remington had an untimely heart attack, putting the gun on hold awhile longer. At this time Browning was getting weary of the present situation and moved on to Fabrique Nationale, a company that in the past had taken a liking to his semiautomatic pistols and manufactured them in Belgium.

Looking on the brighter side, Remington restored their interest in the gun and in 1906 agreed to produce it under the name of the Remington Autoloading Shotgun. Some five years later, in 1911, this impressive shotgun was renamed the Remington Model 11. Some 300,000 Model 11s were manufactured from 1911 to 1947, chambered for the 12, 16 and

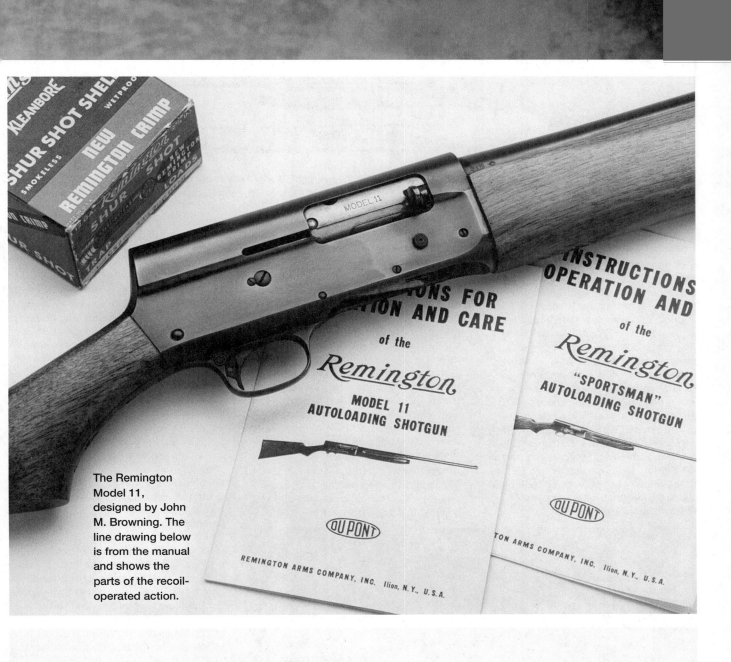

The Remington Model 11, designed by John M. Browning. The line drawing below is from the manual and shows the parts of the recoil-operated action.

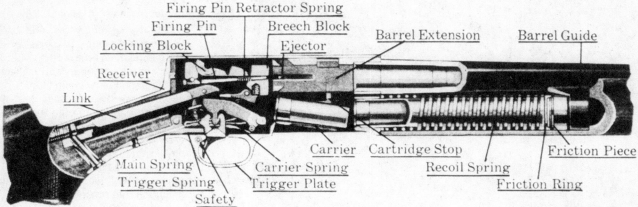

Firing Pin Retractor Spring
Firing Pin   Breech Block
Locking Block   Ejector   Barrel Extension   Barrel Guide
Receiver
Link
Carrier   Cartridge Stop   Friction Piece
Main Spring   Carrier Spring   Recoil Spring   Friction Ring
Trigger Spring   Trigger Plate
Safety

ACTION OPEN

The "humpback" Model 11 was succeeded by the streamlined 11-48 in 1948. Both are recoil-operated guns.

20 gauges, plus about 65,000 made for Browning during World War II.

In appearance, whether the gun was produced by Browning, Remington, Savage or Miroku, it had the distinct pleasure of having that trademark "humpback" complete with a high rear edge to the receiver, which, as told by many, aided its sighting ability for fast moving upland or waterfowl. I had a Browning Auto-5 that I found great to use in the field, although uncanny to shoot because of the long recoil system and noise it generated with all of those moving parts. In appearance, while the receiver did blend in with the vent rib and barrel, many shooters didn't particularly enjoy that annoying design feature at the rear of the receiver. There it took a sharp dive downward just before the wrist of the stock.

In operation, you pull the operating lever to the rear exposing the rear of the chamber and follower. Dropping a shell into the receiver and pushing the button under the bolt pushes the round into the chamber. All additional shells go into the magazine for follow-up shots. It's interesting to note that the gun had a set of friction rings that in effect controlled the rate of recoil. As stated in the manual, setting or positioning these rings is vital to the care and performance of the weapon. In short, they are there to control excessive recoil within the gun ensuring a long usable life of the weapon and to allow adjusting the various settings for different loads.

Specifications of the Model 11 included a blued finish, steel barrels in 26 or 28 inches, with later options going up to 30 or 32 inches. There was an optional solid or ventilated rib, and full, modified or cylinder chokes. The action was hammerless, blued and relatively easy to take down. Magazine was set for four rounds with an open position on the bolt and side ejection. The stock was walnut, checkered or uncheckered depending on the grade. The fore-end matched the buttstock, had a deep groove near the top with a removable takedown cap on the very front of this piece of wood. Those interested in the deep history of this gun will find all sorts of models and grades to please all types of shooters.

Like the guns produced today by Remington, the Model 11 came in many variations and it seemed the parent company was eager to please those with deep pockets. For example, there was the Standard or Sportsman (11A) grade with a plain stock. Moving up the Special (11B) had imported wood, the Trap (11C) grade had fancier wood, as did the Tournament (11D) grade but with a hint of scroll engraving. Still ascending, the Expert (11E) had better wood, more engraving and checkering. Finishing up, we move into the Premier (11F), which was the most elaborate in the series with full coverage engraving on the receiver and exquisite checkering on the best Circassian wood they could find. In 1914 the Model 11 Premier had a list price of $125.00.

Naturally, nothing stands still, especially in the shotgun game, so the next gun to appear was the Model 11-48. Just looking at the photos recently taken at the Remington Museum in Ilion, N.Y., it's not hard to see Remington had an eye to the future. Although the Model 11-48 was another recoil-operated gun, the overall design with its "New Generation" receiver that tapered down to the wrist of the stock was pleasing and right in tune with 1949. In a 1953 retail handout, Remington told prospective buyers the gun was light, streamlined and fast pointing. Adding more to the pot, not only was the gun chambered in 12, 16, 20 and .410 bore, but for the first time in shotgun history you could get one in .28 gauge.

The Model 58 (bottom) was Remington's first gas-operated shotgun and was introduced in 1956. The 1100 (top) was an improved version of the Model 58 design and came along in 1963. The Model 1100 is the most popular autoloading shotgun ever made and today, more than a half-century later, is still in production.

In many respects, this Model 11-48 was a breakthrough for the company. To help lower the cost of assembly, stamped steel components were employed and along with consistently made parts, made interchangeability between guns a reality without the aid of a gunsmith. Again, looking toward the future, the 11-48 had an aluminum trigger assembly that was removable for cleaning or repair, something we would see in later 1100 and 11-87 models.

Like the Model 11, this gun used a system of rings to control recoil – but in a different way. First, there was a pair of return springs, one of which was located in the buttstock that served to add some resistance to the bolt. The second was on the magazine tube itself and served as a barrel recoil spring that allowed the barrel to move into the receiver, a distance long enough to allow flawless ejection of the spent shell. One nice feature of the 11-48 is that the design of the friction ring allows it to be self-adjusting to make the gun work with a variety of hunting loads.

When it came to models, the 11-48 had the field pretty well covered. For example, with the four gauges there were models for skeet shooting — all with a skeet choke and fancy hand-checkered wood. Barrels were available in 26-, 28- and 30-inch lengths, but with the 28 and .410, only the 25-inch length was standard. A crossbolt safety was standard and the guns came with either a three or four-shot magazine depending on the gauge.

The 11-48 was classified as a takedown, side ejection and hammerless autoloading shotgun. And, like the Model 11, various grades were listed, much on the same order as its predecessor. There was the usual Standard grade, and for law enforcement, a Riot gun was offered with a plain 20-inch barrel. Moving up in grades, you had the Special with select wood, a RSS (Rifled Slug Special) in 12 gauge with a 26-inch barrel. Competition shooters were not forgotten as the Tournament had a ventilated rib, engraved receiver and fancy wood. The Premier was, of course, the top of the line, and in 1963 a Duck Gun was added in 12, 16 and 20 gauge.

Finally, as mentioned, Skeet shooters had their guns with ventilated ribs in a SA grade. In addition, a Sportsman-48 was in production from 1949 to 1959 with slight modifications that mildly separated it from the parent Model 11-48. In all, the guns were discontinued in 1968 with a total run of almost 456,000 units.

To me, the big turn for Remington was in 1956 when it introduced the Model 58. This was its first fully functional gas-operated shotgun. Looking at the photographs taken at the museum, when laid next to a Model 1100, you could see where the company was going. The two guns separated by years were basically the same in size, dimensions and outward appearance. I have the catalog sheet for the model's introduction and it seems like Remington had to hold itself from bursting as witnessed by the amount of copy on just this one page! Features by the dozens were listed as Remington wanted to get this gun in the hands of serious hunters and competition shooters without delay.

Called the "Power-Matic" action, and being gas operated, the apparent recoil effect was softened by means of a gas system that bled off pressure tapped from the barrel and routed into a larger chamber. From here, a piston pushed the action bar to the rear, which ejected the spent shell and cycled the action via an action spring. In addition, any excess gas was released by the operation of a venting device on the end of the magazine cap. Here, Remington added another name to the fray, which was known as the "Dial-A-Matic" load control.

While the Model 11 and 11-48 used a set of friction rings to control the action with various loads, the new Model 58 used this "Dial-A-Matic" system located on the front of the magazine cap that

had letters denoting "L" for light loads and "H" for heavier hunting loads. With a slight twist of the dial, the shooter could see the setting at a glance with large letters to depend on reliable functioning of the gun no matter the ammunition used.

With this system, Remington could now claim it had the fastest loading system, bar none. In its 1956 sell sheet, you could load three shells in as little as three seconds! To single load, all you had to do was drop a shell into the port, press the action release and go. While you had the angled gun in your hand, you could for an instant admire the inscribed game scenes on both sides of this streamlined receiver complete with a top matte finish to cut down glare while shooting. They go on to say that to make this a standout gun, Remington mentions it has "NEW beautiful wood and metal finishes," perfect hand-fitting grip and puts the balance where it belongs.

In looking at the specifications, at its introduction the Model 58 was available in nine different models from the Sportsman-58 ADL Deluxe to ascending grades much like the other models and now also included Target, Tournament and Premier grades for both trap and skeet shooters. Retail prices started on the low end of $129.95 on up to $946.65 for the big-ticket Premier models.

Ordering a gun gave one many options. Aside from the various grades, extra barrels were there at the ready with various chokes, lengths up to 30

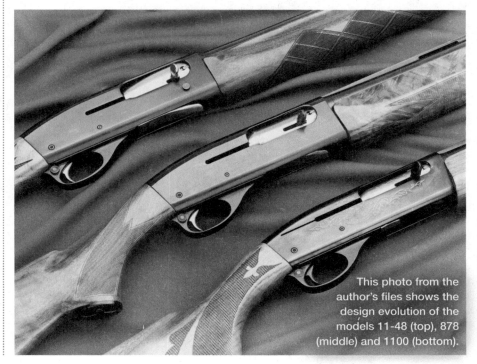

This photo from the author's files shows the design evolution of the models 11-48 (top), 878 (middle) and 1100 (bottom).

A cutaway model at the Remington Museum shows the inner workings of the Model 1100.

inches and with or without a ventilated rib. Only 12, 16 and 20 gauge were available, nothing noted for the .410 bore. On the Sportsman 58 SX, Remington offered a Sun-Grain maple stock, which was a light, yellow colored stock.

Some three years after the Model 58 was introduced, the Model 878 came out. Often missed by collectors and the public, it was very similar to the Model 58. According to history, it was called the "Automaster" and for some it was easy to remember when it came to model numbers. For example, the 87 could be linked to the Model 870 pump gun, while the last digit reminded folks of the Model 58. For those on a budget, it filled the void of a working autoloader with a plain barrel and no checkering for only $119.95. Up the ante a bit and you could get it with a ventilated rib and a checkered stock for only $20 more.

Only available in 12 gauge, it had the option of a 26-, 28- or 30-inch blued

barrel in three chokes, but the receiver had no roll engraving until you moved up to the higher grade of gun. Following the lead of other Remington guns, there were high-grade guns available in skeet and field guns in 878D, 878F and 878 Expert with engraving. Deep in the history of this gun, just like some of the guns before it, was listed in an SX grade that included a Sun Grain stock and fore-end.

Reference material shows that the same three engineers who worked on other Remington autoloaders — L.R. Crittendon, Ellis Hailston and Harold Hameister — would get credit for the Model 878. It contained the same "Power-Piston" affair that offered a self-adjusting mechanism that could tell the difference between low- and high-based loads. It was quite a novel design in the fact that the front part of the piston would move to the rear (and against a strong spring) cutting off pressure, thus insuring a safe- and soft-operating shotgun.

Additionally, it was available in 12 gauge only for use with 2¾-inch shells. During its brief stay of three years in the line, around 62,000 were made until 1962, as in 1963 Remington autoloaders would alter the course of history for the company.

While 1962 brought the famous Remington Model 700 rifles, it seemed Remington was doing well because the following year the Model 1100 shotgun was brought into the line. Looking over the material relative to this gun, I came up with reams of information, much too much to be covered in this article, so allow me to hit on the high spots of this historic gun.

While digging around with the help of Dick Dietz, former public relations manager at Remington, aside from all the photos we took at Ilion, we came upon some interesting files. We found the initial release to get the gun going from 1958, plus the chronology of most of the 1100 models starting in 1963 with ads from that same year touting the guns' features and specifications. In compiling all of this data, one could see how easy (read time consuming) it would be to dedicate a full-size rewarding book project to this shotgun.

In any event, in a Remington newsletter dated 1963, then editor J.P. Linduska relates on how in 1958, "the management of Remington Arms issued a challenge to the company's research and development department." It goes on to say, "to design a shotgun that will shoot like no shotgun ever produced before. A gun with that any shooter, novice or expert, can shoot better, hunting game or breaking targets. Make a gun anyone would be proud to win and proud to show his friends and make it rugged enough to last a lifetime of shooting." It should be noted that along with this request, "no limitations on the design of the new model were imposed and any type of action could be used, along with any system of operation."

A tall order for sure, and to head up this new era for Remington was Wayne Leek. At that time, Remington was fielding three different shotguns (Models 11-48, Sportsman 58 and Model 878) and looking at the bottom line did not make any sense to the company's bean counters, so a new gun was on the minds

On a pheasant hunt, the author with friend and longtime Remington public relations man, Richard Dietz.

Remington Model 1100 factory photos, from the top: Light 20 – the forerunner to the Special Field, Deer Gun with rifle sights and TA Trap gun.

of many in upper management. Leek took the lead in engineering and came up with some personal parameters for design that I found interesting. For certain he wanted a new look with improved wood, checkering and finishing, the ability to handle all types of shotgun shells without time consuming adjustments, a larger capacity of five shots, some increased muzzle weight and, of course, a marked reduction in recoil.

Leek and his team had their work cut out for them. For example, the breech bolt went through several designs to make it lighter, and for testing they made an ad-hoc Model 1100 run by compressed air that hammered the action day and night for endurance testing. They worked on the recoil system to stretch it out to reduce the apparent recoil, while allowing easy maintenance on the system in the field if necessary.

The gas system was self-adjusting and self-cleaning, a boon to those who shoot many shells at a time like competition shooters. Leek and his men designed the system with just the right amount of gas to operate the action while still reducing the recoil up to 55 percent.

While some might call the Model 1100 over-engineered, the genius of Remington's R&D is demonstrated where the gas is taken off to operate the action. The engineers

decided to bleed gases closer to the chamber where pressures are higher and generally more consistent. Using a smaller gas port, it featured a piston located outside of the magazine tube allowing escaping gases freer movement while curtailing carbon deposits for cleaner operation. For cleaning, all you have to do is remove the fore-end, pull the barrel out of the receiver, and with the gas system outside of the magazine tube, cleaning is a chinch.

As for dependability, you simply can't beat a Model 1100. I've been in tournaments and seen them shot so hard that you could get a serious burn by just touching the barrel. I've also witnessed them in the hunting fields, in blinds and sporting clays going through hell but still chugging along at the end of the day.

With the internal operating system all set, the next step was for appearance, function and handling. At first, the walnut stock had acceptable impressed checkering and a fleur-de-lis pattern. Later on as CNC machines came about, cut checkering was included with the gun, some-

Machine cut checkering on the Model 1100 Special Field added a custom touch to the English-stocked upland gun.

thing that helped it vault into the custom class, especially with a higher grade of wood. To keep the guns looking sharp through a lifetime, Remington (at that time part of Dupont) applied a tough, clear-coat they labeled RKW. This polyurethane product made the walnut stand out no matter the grade and was resistant to scratches and hard use. I remember the ads that mentioned this finish "is similar to that used on bowling pins," assuring the new owner of a gun with a stock that would last no matter the use or weather.

The Model 1100 receiver is made from a solid block of steel machined for strength and durability over the long run. I've personally been to Ilion, N.Y., to watch the production of these guns and I can attest to the fact everything — and I mean everything — is done with precision and longevity in mind. It is highly polished and blued, making it that much more resistant to wear and weather. There is a crossbolt safety, and while the trigger is not made to target standards, competitors everywhere have more than received it. Decorative scrollwork adorns this receiver and bolt giving it that custom look right out of the box.

When it came to gauge selection, the 12 gauge came in 1963, 16 and 20 gauges in 1964, and the .410 bore introduced in 1969. Along with all of these choices, there were also matched pairs, lightweight and magnum guns – all designed with the shooter and shooting in mind. From there the sky was the limit, with limited editions for such organizations as Ducks Unlimited, and special magnum models and field stocks to fit just about any personal taste in any gauge. As an example from the 1974 Remington catalog, I count 80 different models in field, trap and skeet with 61 additional choices in extra barrels in all gauges!

A Remington print advertisement from 1970 for the Model 1100 showing all four gauges.

Model 1100 Trap & Skeet Guns
12, 20, 28, & 410 Gauges

The Model 1100 stands alone as the most popular automatic shotgun for trap and skeet. At the 1973 World Skeet Championships, there were more Model 1100s on the line than all other brands and models combined. Model 1100 SA grade skeet guns come in 12, 20, 28, and 410 gauges with left hand versions in 12 and 20 gauge. SB grade skeet guns with specially selected wood are available in 12 and 20 gauge. All have special skeet-bored barrels.

Model 1100 TB trap grade guns have won more championships at the Grand American, state, and zone shoots in the last ten years than any other automatic. Their minimum recoil sensation reduces fatigue during long shoots, and their reliability makes every shot count. TB grade 1100s are available with regular or Monte Carlo stocks in full or modified trap chokes. Left hand models in full choke only.

	12 Ga.	16 Ga.	20 Ga. Stand.	20 Ga. Lwt.	28 Ga.	410 Ga.	Retail Prices
Extra Barrels, Plain							
30" Full Choke	9500						$49.95
28" Full Choke	9502	9530	9546				$49.95
28" Full Choke				6578			$52.95
25" Full Choke					9588	9574	$52.95
28" Mod. Choke	9504	9532	9548				$49.95
28" Mod. Choke				6580			$52.95
25" Mod. Choke					9510	9576	$52.95
26" Imp. Cyl. Choke	9508	9536	9552				$49.95
26" Imp. Cyl. Choke				6582			$52.95
25" Imp. Cyl. Choke					6584	9578	$52.95
22" Imp. Cyl. Rifle Sights	9548		9572				$60.95
Extra Barrels, Vent. Rib							
34" Full Choke	6576						$84.95
30" Full Choke							$74.95
29" Full Choke	9514	9538	9564				$74.95
28" Full Choke				9590			$77.95
25" Full Choke					6586	9580	$74.95
29" Mod. Choke	9516	9540	9566				$74.95
29" Mod. Choke				9592			$77.95
25" Mod. Choke					6588	9582	$77.95
26" Imp. Cyl. Choke	9520	9544	9560				$74.95
26" Imp. Cyl. Choke				9594			$77.95
25" Imp. Cyl. Choke					9590	9584	$77.95
Extra Barrels, Vent. Rib, Trap & Skeet Grades							
26" Skeet Choke	9522		9562				$79.95
26" Skeet Cutts Comp	9524		9564				$104.95
25" Skeet Choke					6692	9586	$82.95
34" Full Choke	6854						$80.95
30" Full Choke	9526						$79.95
30" Mod. Trap Choke	9570						$79.95
29" Full Choke							$79.95
29" Mod. Trap Choke	9566						$79.95
Left Hand Extra Barrels, Vent. Rib							
30" Full Choke	5682						$76.95
29" Full Choke			5692				$76.95
29" Mod. Choke	5694		5696				$76.95
26" Imp. Cyl. Choke	5686		5696				$76.95
30" Full Choke Trap	5690						$81.95
26" Skeet Choke	5688		5698				$81.95

Model 1100 SA Skeet: 12 Ga., 26" $229.95 A smooth-swinging competitor. Ivory front, metal rear sights. Checkered composition butt plate. Also available in left hand model or with Cutts Compensator.

Model 1100 SA Skeet: 20 Ga., 26" $229.95 The class of 20 gauge skeet events. Ventilated rib barrel is specially skeet-bored. Left or right hand models.

Model 1100 SA Skeet: 28 Ga., 25" $239.95 All of the same 1100 features and performance in a smaller gauge. Perfect balance at 6¾ pounds.

Model 1100 SA Skeet: 410 Ga., 25" $239.95 Reliable gas-operated action. Weighs in at 7¼ pounds. Match-weight skeet caps, optional for 28 and 410 gauge guns, will add up to 12 ounces.

This 1975 print advertisement shows Trap and Skeet 1100s in all four gauges.

When the 3,000,000th Model 1100 came around in 1983, the author had the privilege of photographing it for an article.

Custom guns are part of the Model 1100 heritage and the Remington Custom Shop routinely produces some fine examples of the engraver's art. I had the outstanding 3,000,000th Remington for photos and an article denoting the occasion. To celebrate the 200th Anniversary of Remington Arms, a special edition of the Model 1100 of only 2,016 (for the year 2016) units is being produced. They will feature a highly polished receiver, barrel and all metal parts, gold inlays, "C" grade American black walnut stock with fine-line, fleur-de-lis cut ribbon checkering all finished up with a special serial number range and commemorative packaging.

However, the new Remington literature shows that apparently the Model 1100 is being phased out slowly with only a few competition and Classic Edition models available. Surely, a small shadow of what this great gun used to be. In its place, you will see the new V3 Field Sport and Versa Max autoloaders with modern updates like a Cerakote receiver and synthetic camo stocks. No match for the variety of models we had with the 1100, but with factory mergers and a wide technology sweep, new guns are on the horizon.

Looking back, perhaps now I see how the writing was on the wall for the Model 1100 back in 1987. In that year, the Model 11-87 was introduced in a wide variety of models with the new Rem-Choke as part

Model 1100 Automatic Shotguns
Field Grade in 20 Gauge Lightweight, 28 & 410 Gauges

Remington makes smaller gauge Model 1100s to match any hunter's game and personal preferences. All hold the dependability, handsome appearance, and performance features you expect from America's oldest, most experienced manufacturer of automatic shotguns.

Model 1100 field grade guns in 20 gauge Lightweight versions give hunters less weight to carry. Built on a special weight-saving design with high-strength receiver, they point fast and smooth. A 3" Magnum model handles 20 gauge 2¾" or 3" Magnum loads only . . . as effective as a 12 gauge gun shooting standard field loads. At 6½ pounds, these lightweights really pay off in all-day carrying ease in the field.

The 28 and 410 gauge 1100s are available in a wide selection of chokes with plain or ventilated rib barrels. Exceptionally fine handling and pointing qualities put these Model 1100 automatics in a class by themselves. Remington extra barrels give all of these 1100s extra versatility. 20 gauge Lightweight barrels interchange only on 20 gauge Lightweight receivers.

Model 1100: 20 Gauge Lightweight Special weight-saving design with maximum strength and dependability. Handles all 2¾" loads. Ventilated rib or plain barrel. Mahogany stock and fore-end.

Model 1100 3" Magnum: 20 Gauge Lightweight At 6¾ pounds, this 1100 weighs less, but delivers maximum power and performance. Chambered for 2¾" or 3" 20 gauge Magnum loads only. Rubber recoil pad.

Model 1100: 28 Gauge Classic 1100 styling and performance on a smaller frame and receiver. Plain or ventilated rib barrel is 25" long. A sporting gun for smaller, faster gamebirds . . . and fine first shotgun for younger hunters.

Model 1100: 410 Gauge The automatic that all other 410s are gauged by. Full, Modified, or Improved Cylinder choke. Chambers 2½" or 3" shells.

4

A 1975 advertisement for Model 1100s with detailed descriptions of the guns. This ad is for the smaller gauge guns in 20, 28 and .410 bore.

When a milestone comes around, Remington does it in a big way. This is the left side of the 2,000,000th Model 1100, made in 1977. On the right side of the same gun the engraver carried the theme with more dogs and engraving on the bolt.
More than 4 million 1100s have been manufactured.

When you engrave a gun, you might as well finish it off with some fancy checkering. Complete with a border, it does the gun proud.

of the package. Additionally, Remington was still looking for a design that would digest both 2¾- and 3-inch shells interchangeably without any manual adjustment by the owner. This was particularly important as we were into the age of steel shot, and for the dedicated waterfowler, this was a huge plus.

Still keeping the "11" in the number, Remington assured future customers this new model was still in the family of the 1100, but with some important upgrades. Most important was the new "Pressure-Compensating" (PC) gas system that, when the shell was fired, it helped to maintain a controlled bolt velocity. With this new addition to the gun, no matter the load, the gun would operate smoothly. Internal parts were also beefed up to include the extractor that was designed to be around 25 percent thicker for strength and reliability. Both the piston and piston seal were heat-treated and nickel-plated, again, for strength and durability, and the magazine tube was made from

Warming up before the hunt, Remington's former marketing guru Richard Dietz picks away at clay targets with a Model 11-87.

Gun Digest Editor Jerry Lee getting the feel of the 11-87 shotgun before heading to the skeet range.

stainless steel for ease of maintenance, to fight corrosion and was termed self-cleaning.

It was in the same model year that the Rem-Choke was introduced so instead of having many different barrels with various chokes and lengths, this new invention allowed the shooter to just remove one choke tube and replace it with another. Perfect for the all-year hunter, who could go from duck to dove to quail hunting with one gun, one barrel and a set of removable choke tubes. The only drawback was that barrels were not interchangeable between the Model 1100 and the Model 11-87, but those who carried the former in the field were not forgotten, as Remington thoughtfully made barrels with the Rem-Choke feature for the faithful of that time tested

semiautomatic shotgun.

Seems that over the years the Model 11-87 was in production, like previous guns in the Remington shotgun line, it was tuned to the American hunter. The stocks went from a satin to a glossy finish, the receiver was tastefully filled with fine-line engraving, left-hand models were available and with a model line to include over two dozen variations, there was indeed something for everyone. Remington made sure of that! In fact, one of the guns that made an impression on me was the Model 11-87 Sporting Clays gun with 28-inch barrel, four Rem-Choke tubes and a receiver furnished in a soft, nickel-plated, low-luster finish complete with fine-line engraving.

The Model 11-87 had a top version Remington simply called the Premier.

This best seller was available with 26-, 28- or 30-inch ventilated rib barrels that included the Rem-Choke system, and a left-hand model. The Premier Trap gun was also a big hit with those who love the sport, available with either a classic or Monte Carlo stock and tournament checkering, and the addition of a Trap Super Full Rem-Choke. Like the Premier Skeet model, internally they were adjusted to handle and perform flawlessly with 2¾-inch 12-gauge target loads only. Years later, the Model 11-87 included the SPS series, a cantilever scope mount Deer Gun and a model with a Light Contour barrel to keep the gun in the 7-pound range.

Interesting to note that while the Model 1100 was still very much in production, it was pushed back in the catalog a few pages, in fact after the pump-action Model 870. It was obvious then that Remington was indeed moving on with the newer Model 11-87. There were still plenty of replacement barrels to be had, and although the model line was severely compressed, those interested in the Model 1100 could still purchase one.

As a sidebar to the Model 11-87 run, in among the pages of the catalog was the mention of the 11-96 Euro Lightweight. As far as I can see, it was a twin to the Model 11-87 – including the operating mechanism except for the slimmed down receiver, three-shot magazine and the addition of a light contour barrel. While the specifications show it is lighter than comparable Model 11-87s by a quarter of a pound (12-gauge), it came with a fancy Claro walnut stock and fore-end and a receiver decorated with fine-line engrav-

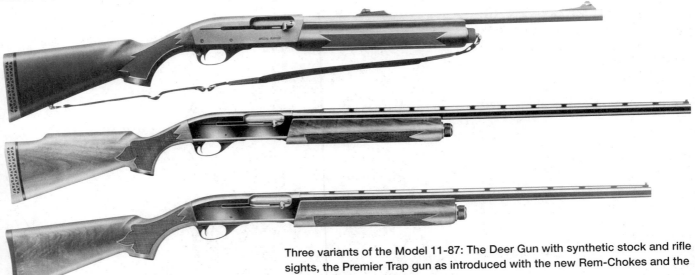

Three variants of the Model 11-87: The Deer Gun with synthetic stock and rifle sights, the Premier Trap gun as introduced with the new Rem-Chokes and the Premier Skeet gun.

ing. It did have the Rem-Choke feature and a 6mm ventilated rib suitable for the upland hunter, but alas, it only lasted from 1996 to 1999.

As innovative as Remington can be, the next step in the progression of the autoloading shotgun came as a complete surprise at a Remington writer's conference in 1989. In a giant move, Remington purchased the production rights to the Ithaca Mag-10 and after a year of massaging it to the company's specifications and improvements, offered it to the shooting public in the second half of 1989. The new name would be the Remington SP-10 Magnum.

The SP-10 came with a long list of new features, but one of them did not change — the weight. As a 10-gauge gun, it checked in at a hefty 11 pounds with the standard 26-inch tube; if you wanted a longer 30-inch barrel, it moved up to 11½ pounds. Hefting the gun for the first time made one think of an African safari rifle, but once you touched off a 10-gauge shell, the extra weight was a blessing. After using the gun on pass shooting in Texas, the weight was of no consequence because once you got the gun moving, it kept right on moving!

Overall finish on the gun was excellent with its express metal and satin stock. The stock is more than generous and profiled from straight-grained walnut with cut checkering. A camouflage sling was included with the gun as were sling swivels and a soft recoil pad to help tame the level of recoil down close to seemingly 12-gauge levels. At the Texas shoot, I recall using two boxes of 10-gauge ammunition and walking away with no ill effects. Most of this is due, I'm sure, to the fact that Remington went through the gun, redesigning the gas system with twin gas ports, an elastomer buffer and a new bolt buffer to absorb the recoil in a most civilized manner.

Further improvements included a new feeding and extraction system with all major gas components necessary to the operation of the gun like the bolt, carrier, shell stop latch and the operating handle made from quality stainless steel. In fact, looking over the spec sheet supplied to writers that week, I was in awe at the work Remington went through to improve that gun. I count almost two dozen improvements from the fire control system to smaller components like the firing pin and spring, a new 10-gauge choke system, new magazine follower assembly and even an improved fore-end cap. The list is endless and Remington

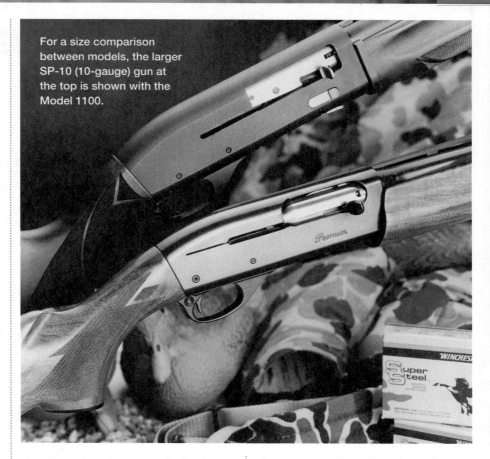

For a size comparison between models, the larger SP-10 (10-gauge) gun at the top is shown with the Model 1100.

should receive a big pat on the back for what they undertook with that big autoloader.

For the collectors out there looking for something unique from a new production gun, at the time in 1989, the first 5,000 guns had a special block of serial numbers starting out with the prefix LE-89. I use the past tense because Remington discontinued production of the SP-10 in January 2011. To further note, at the time of its demise, the SP-10 was available as a Thumbhole, Magnum Synthetic or Wood model, as well as the SP-10 Waterfowl model complete with three Briley extended and specially made waterfowl choke tubes.

In the "for what's its worth" department, in the last quarter of 2005, Remington introduced a Model SPR453 autoloading shotgun in the Spartan (read Russian-made) line. According to my sources, it is a variation of a Russian MP-153 shotgun made by the Ishevsk Mechanical Plant for export under the common Baikal name. Remington was the distributor for the gun; it was only available in 12-gauge and its stock was standard fare synthetic. Five models were available including camouflaged versions with a variety of barrel lengths,

choke tubes and a self-regulating gas system. Reasonably priced starting at $390, these models were short lived and were imported for two years.

Moving into the more recent autoloaders, in 2007 Remington introduced the Model 105 CTi, their first autoloading shotgun with bottom ejection. By doing this, Remington saved on machining two guns—one for right-hand and one for left-hand shooters, making the gun ambidextrous. With the Model 11-87 starting to get a little worn around the edges, it was time, according to upper management, to introduce a new gun worthy of the rigors of competition.

If you were looking for a high-tech gun, this would have been your match. For one, it had a space-age carbon-titanium receiver that was far different than most shooters were accustomed to on the formidable Model 1100. With this new autoloader it seemed the main objective was to cut the overall weight, and by adding a bit of carbon fiber to the rib and receiver they knocked off a pound overall from the gun.

In addition, Remington engineered an oil-filled shock absorber installed in the buttstock to reduce recoil. A friend of mine mentioned that compared to

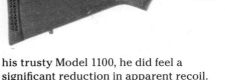

his trusty Model 1100, he did feel a significant reduction in apparent recoil. Additionally, the CTi 105 had a specially engineered R3 recoil pad, which in concert with the shock absorber quelled the rearward push even more. Even though all of this redesigning was done in good faith by the company, many of the shooters that I queried had not even heard about the gun, and those who did look at it decided to just keep their Model 1100 or 11-87.

Now to more modern times—and while the Model 1100 and Model 11-87 are still available in very limited models—the big push at Remington now seems to be with the V3 Sport and the Versa Max autoloaders. Separated by minor details and pricing, both have taken the lead in Remington's marketing program. The V3 is the lower priced shotgun in the series with a current list of around $900. With a novel system that regulates internal gas pressure to operate the gun depending upon the length of the shell, it adjusts the operation of the gun without much trouble. Inside the gun, a tray of sorts has a number of holes machined into it. If you insert a 3-inch shell into the

chamber, only four ports are open, while a 2¾-inch shell will allow eight ports to be exposed, therefore the gun is set up for both lengths of shotgun shells. Quite a departure from the popular Model 1100 for sure.

The Remington V3 Sport has four different models including one with a traditional walnut stock, plus choices in black synthetic, camo and sport camo. Barrel lengths are 26 and 28 inches, depending upon the model. Cast and drop are adjustable. A crisp trigger set at the factory to 3½ pounds and a Super Cell recoil pad complete this gun.

The Remington Versa Max shares no parts with the V3, even though they look somewhat alike, and their methods of operation are different. While the V3 can use two shell lengths, the Versa Max operating system will accommodate three sizes – from the 2¾-inch to the 3-inch and 3½-inch magnums – by uncovering the number of ports inside the gun. In addition, the Versa Max has a rotating bolt head, Teflon-coated internal parts, special HiViz sights and oversized controls for the waterfowler who wears heavier cold weather gear.

The Versa Max is all business for those who like to hunt the flyways of America with the Waterfowl Pro model.

The author is ready to move out to a duck blind with the Remington SP-10 shotgun.

Features include a distinctive Shadow Grass camo pattern, enlarged feeding port and extended choke tubes. Overall, I count nine models to cover everything from Competition Tactical, Turkey, conventional black synthetic and more. List prices today run from $1,066 to $1,765 for the Waterfowl Pro. At the present time, both the V3 and the Versa Max are available only in 12 gauge.

Remington's presence in the semiautomatic shotgun field has been nothing less than extraordinary. From its beginnings over a century ago, millions upon millions of guns have been produced for field hunters, waterfowlers and competitors. While some of the guns mentioned here are mere memories, my Remington's are still here with me enjoying countless hours by my side as partners in the field and on the trap range. Presently, we don't see many of the past models in the catalogs, but newer guns like the V3 Sport and the high-tech Versa Max continue to keep the legacy of the Remington autoloader alive and well today.

For this, we applaud Remington. Keep 'em coming!

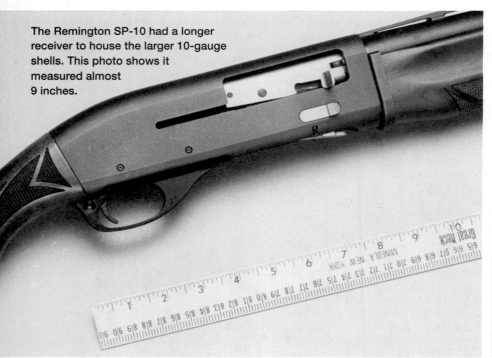

The Remington SP-10 had a longer receiver to house the larger 10-gauge shells. This photo shows it measured almost 9 inches.

The .327 FEDERAL
–The Thoroughly Modern Magnum

The most versatile and powerful of the .32s

By Steve Gash

Handgun design and usage have been strongly influenced by .32-caliber cartridges for well over a century. The majority of the .32-caliber cartridges of the past were pretty anemic, but still, most of them were quite popular for personal defense. Nowadays, if you go out armed with a .32, folks think you're demented.

Bad guys seem to have gotten a lot tougher in the past few decades, too. Back in the 1920s and 1930s, folks thought it was perfectly logical to arm themselves with a slim, hammerless automatic pistol or a small revolver chambered for one of the many .32-caliber cartridges available (see page 174). Back then, good guys didn't worry too much about shooting a bad guy, and if you shot a crook, they'd probably give you as medal rather than throw you in the juzgado. There were no powerful antibiotics then, so anyone whacked in the gizzard with a .32 (or any) slug, was probably going to get an infection, and be headed to the last roundup.

Evolution works with cartridges, too, and today we have what is perhaps the quintessential expression of the .32-caliber in the .327 Federal Magnum. Introduced in 2008, the new .327 is one of the most powerful .32-caliber rounds to ever be chambered in a handgun. Federal currently offers three factory loads for the .327 and their performance is impressive. This ammo includes tough, jacketed hollowpoint and softpoint bullets at velocities unheard of only a few years ago. The .327 fires 85-grain bullets at

MAGNUM CARTRIDGES COMPARED

Cartridge	Bullet Wt. (Grains)	Muzzle Velocity (fps)	Muzzle Energy (Ft-Lbs)
.32 H&R Magnum	85	1,120	237
.327 Federal Magnum	100	1,450	467
.357 Magnum	158	1,240	540
.44 Magnum	240	1,270	860

The new .327 Federal Magnum is the latest in a line of popular .32-caliber cartridges dating from the turn of the last century. From left: .32 S&W Long, .32 H&R Magnum and .327 Federal Magnum.

.327 FEDERAL MAGNUM

Bullet Brand and Type	Bullet Wt. (grains)	Case	Primer	Powder (type)	Powder (grains)	Velocity (fps)	Deviation (fps)	COV (%)	ME (ft-lbs)	Accuracy (inches)
Sierra JHC	90	Federal	F-200	Univ.	4	940	39	4.15	177	2.75
Sierra JHC	90	Federal	F-200	CFE-Pistol	6.4	1,260	13	1.03	317	1.5
Hornady XTP	100	Federal	F-200	2400	10.0	1,161	38	3.27	299	2.09
Hornady XTP	100	Federal	F-200	Power Pistol	6.5	1,278	22	1.72	363	1.67
Federal American Eagle, 85-grain SP, #AE327A						1,529	21	1.37	441	4.25
Federal American Eagle, 100-grain SP, #AE327						1,522	101	6.64	514	3

.32 H&R MAGNUM

Bullet Brand and Type	Bullet Wt. (grains)	Case	Primer	Powder (type)	Powder (grains)	Velocity (fps)	Deviation (fps)	COV (%)	ME (ft-lbs)	Accuracy (inches)
Sierra JHC	90	Federal	F-100	Blue Dot	7	1,189	23	1.93	283	2.5
Hornady XTP	100	Starline	F-100	2400	7.5	966	16	1.66	207	2.5
Hornady XTP	100	Federal	F-100	Blue Dot	6.9	1,115	18	1.61	276	2
Cast DEWC	107	Federal	F-100	W-231	2.3	813	15	1.85	157	1.95
Hornady Critical Defense, 80-grain FTX, #90060						1,059	13	1.23	199	1.96
Federal American Eagle, 85-grain JHP, #C32HRB						1,014	15	1.48	194	2

.32 S&W LONG

Bullet Brand and Type	Bullet Wt. (grains)	Case	Primer	Powder (type)	Powder (grains)	Velocity (fps)	Deviation (fps)	COV (%)	ME (ft-lbs)	Accuracy (inches)
Cast roundnose	78	Winchester	F-100	TiteGroup	2.3	771	20	2.59	103	2.01
Cast roundnose	78	Winchester	F-100	Viht. 3N37	3.2	898	20	2.23	140	1.53
Cast DEWC	107	Winchester	F-100	Universal	2	838	26	3.1	167	1.99
Cast flatpoint	115	Winchester	F-100	Viht. 3N37	3.4	791	13	1.64	160	1.54
Federal Champion, 98-grain lead roundnose, #C32LB						684	15	2.19	88	2.22
Federal Champion, 98-grain lead wadcutter, #C32LA						650	12	1.85	80	1.77
Winchester Super-X, 98-grain roundnose, #X32SWLP						630	31	4.92	75	2.66

NOTES: All loads tested in a Ruger Model SP101 with a 4.2-inch barrel. Accuracy is the average of three, five-shot groups at 25 yards from a sandbag rest.

ABBREVIATIONS: JHC, Jacketed Hollow Cavity; XTP, eXtreme Terminal Performance; DEWC, wadcutter; COV, coefficient of variation.

DISCLAIMER: Any and all loading data found in this article is to be taken as reference material ONLY. The publisher, editors, author and their entities bear no responsibility for the use by others of the data incuded in this article or others that came before it.

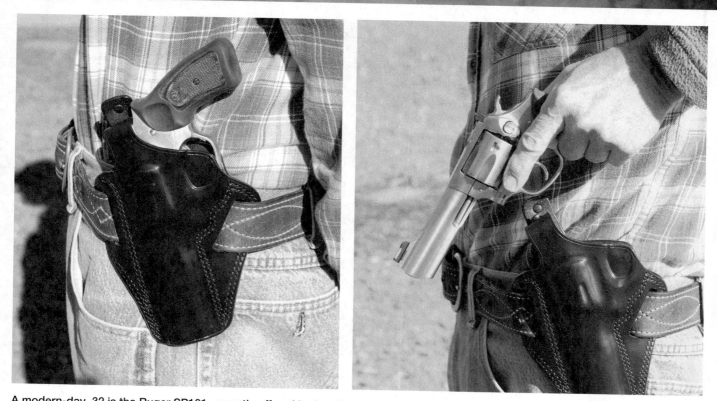

A modern-day .32 is the Ruger SP101, recently offered in the .327 Federal. It is comfortably carried in this custom Fletch belt-slide holster from Galco Gunleather, available in a number of finishes and left-hand models.

1,500 fps and 100-grain bullets at about 1,450 fps. Muzzle energy of the latter round is about 467 ft-lbs. By comparison, the .357 Magnum generates 540 ft-lbs and the .44 Magnum, 860 ft-lbs.

The early .32s were low powered and designed to fit in small semiautos or revolvers. The first attempt at a high-powered .32 was in 1984 with the introduction of the .32 H&R Magnum. This was a joint development of the Harrington & Richardson Company and Federal Cartridge. While a big improvement over the old-timers, it was still of modest power.

Like the .357 and .44 Magnums before it, the .32 H&R followed the example of lengthening an existing case and upping the pressure for more velocity. The .32 H&R case is .155 inch longer than the .32 Long, and the .327 is .128 inch longer than the .32 H&R. Plus, the .327 operates at much higher pressures than other .32s.

Although the .32 H&R languished, the .327 built on the example, and after a slow start, six-gunners have recognized the ballistic virtue of the

The sturdy SP101 holds six rounds and has ample steel around the high-pressure .327 rounds.

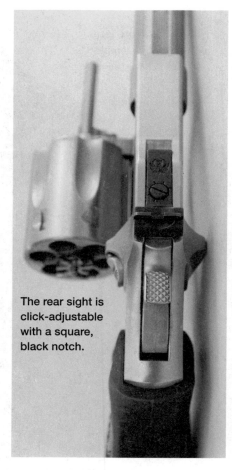

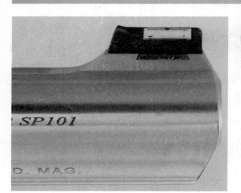

The Ruger SP101 has a unique green fiber-optic front sight. It's great for self-defense, but less than optimum for precise shooting.

The SP101 stocks feature semi-soft rubber with nicely checkered walnut inserts.

The rear sight notch (top) is properly sized for the fiber-optic front. The green fiber-optic front sight (bottom) shows up like a beacon in the night, and would definitely be comforting in low-light situations.

The rear sight is click-adjustable with a square, black notch.

.327 and the trim guns that shoot it. It finally seems to have caught on, but interestingly, with two distinct groups of shooters. This is reflected in the types of firearms the gun companies have built for it, aimed at two some-times disparate groups.

In one camp are the traditional outdoorsmen who would no sooner go out of the ranch house without their sixgun than without their pants and boots. It's just a part of getting dressed. The .327 is eminently suitable for hunting a variety of small game and medium-size varmints, protection from venomous snakes, or tacking up wanted posters, so it's right at home on the trail. Everyone would agree that in the field a rifle is better in almost all instances, but a long gun is most unhandy to tote around. A compact yet powerful revolver, however, rides nicely in a belt holster, barely noticed until it's needed. Then, with one quick hand motion, it's ready for service.

For these folks, Ruger and others have brought out revolvers that are about perfect field guns. Many of these new guns have medium-length barrels and adjustable sights that allow the shooter to fit the gun to the load, rather than the other way around with fixed sights.

Many in the other group of .327 aficionados could care less about roaming the backcountry. For them, it's the urban jungle that presents their challenges, as the members of some tribes are not always friendly. For these urban road warriors, the powerful .327 in a trim, lightweight revolver is a godsend, since it can be carried unobtrusively until needed for protection.

A .327 revolver offers a lot of power in a small package, and this translates into a fight-stopping combination for the armed citizen and has subtly changed the perception and reality of armed carry. Faced with the realities of today, many citizens have chosen to arm themselves with a .327.

Both groups are right. The .327 Federal Magnum is perfectly comfortable in either situation, and offers the best of all worlds. Not only is it sufficiently powerful to be a self-defense round in its own right, it will handily dispatch game as large as coyotes, and light loads make for a delightful afternoon of good ol' plinking fun.

The revolvers in .327 available at this writing include the Ruger Single Seven in 4.62-, 5.5- and 7.5-inch barrels; the compact LCR; and the midsize SP101 with a 4.2-inch barrel. Taurus offers a couple of snubnose guns – one with a 2-inch barrel and the other with a 3-inch ported tube. The bottom line is that a diverse selection of quality .327 guns is available to the urban shooter or outdoorsman.

I was unable to resist the tug of the .327 (OK, I admit it, I'm a weak person),

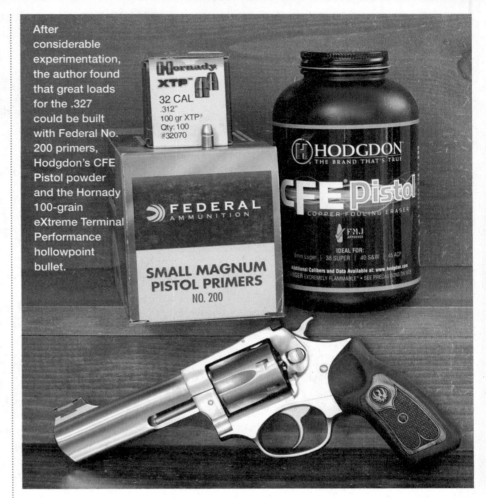

After considerable experimentation, the author found that great loads for the .327 could be built with Federal No. 200 primers, Hodgdon's CFE Pistol powder and the Hornady 100-grain eXtreme Terminal Performance hollowpoint bullet.

so I purchased a new Ruger SP101. It is a beautiful little gun with a brushed stainless finish, and the action is a smooth as silk. The trigger pull was a

little heavy, but a set of Wolff springs fixed that in about 10 minutes. The only thing I don't like about it is the fiber-optic front sight. As soon as I can find a plain black blade it's getting replaced.

I checked .327 and .32 H&R factory loads in the SP101, then brewed up some representative handloads to see what the round would do. The results are shown in the accompanying load table. Basically, the groups at 20 yards were quite good, especially considering that I had a hard time holding that green blob of a front sight the same for each shot.

I also tried some .32 S&W factory loads from Federal and Winchester, and the results were also excellent. They would be perfect for bunny busting, potting fool hens or dispatching rattlers. I didn't shoot any .32 ACP loads, but the SP101 chambers and ejects them A-OK. Those results are also shown in the load table.

Factory fodder for the .327 is good ammo, but it isn't cheap, so the economical answer is handloading. This,

Handloads for the .327 Federal are easily assembled with readily available die sets. The same dies can load a variety of .32-caliber rounds (see text). A very useful add-on tool (right) is the Lee Carbide Factory Crimp Die that applies a firm roll crimp and ensures that all handloaded rounds will chamber in any gun so chambered.

CHRONOLOGY OF THE .32s

Cartridge	Year Introduced	Bullet Weight (Grains)	Velocity (Fps)	Muzzle Energy (Ft-Lbs)
.32 Smith & Wesson	1878	98	705	108
.32 ACP	1899	71	905	129
.32 Smith & Wesson Long .32 Colt New Police	1896 1903	98	780	132
.32 Short Colt .32 Long Colt	1873 1875	80 82	745 755	99 104
.32 North American Arms	2002	60	1,200	192
.32 H&R Magnum	1984	85	1,100	228
.327 Federal Magnum	2008	85 100 115	1,400 1,500 1,300	370 500 432

The history of .32-caliber cartridges opens an interesting window on their ballistic phylogeny. While many were used for small-game hunting, it is interesting to note that virtually all of the early .32-caliber rounds were highly regarded for personal defense, a concept that today is considered ridiculous. Let's take a look at .32-caliber cartridges that presaged the modern .327 Federal Magnum.

.32 ACP

Introduced by Colt in 1899, it was a big hit, and was chambered in a number of small, lightweight semiauto pistols by several manufacturers. One of the more popular was the Colt Model 1903, a slim hammerless pistol that could be carried in a pocket without dislodging your britches or shooting your appendix off. In fact, Colt called its pistol the Pocket Automatic. It fired a 71-grain FMJ bullet at about 905 fps. As a testament to the enduring qualities of the .32 ACP, ammo is still available. I have an M-1903, and it's just cute as a bug's ear and very fun to shoot.

.32 SMITH & WESSON

This ancient round started life as a black-powder cartridge and was later loaded with smokeless. It and the .32 ACP were equally popular in their day, and its ballistics are about like the .32 ACP – in other words – puny.

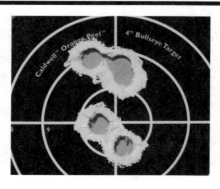

Handloads slightly under maximum pressure were pleasant to shoot yet still offered a considerable boost in power over the older .32s. This cluster was shot with the Sierra 90-grain JHC over a charge of 6.4 grains of CFE Pistol at 1,260 fps.

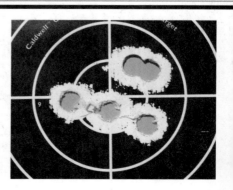

The .327 Federal proved very accurate with Federal factory loads. This group was made with the American Eagle 100-grain Soft Point at 1,522 fps.

.32 SMITH & WESSON LONG

This revolver round appeared in 1896 (or 1903, depending on the source). It fired a 98-grain lead bullet at about 780 fps and was extremely accurate. In fact, some specialty target semiauto pistols appeared in Europe for ISU competition. The .32 S&W Long was used by many police officers back in the 1920s and 1930s, and they obviously felt well armed. Numerous firms made high-quality revolvers chambered for it, and arms of lesser quality were made in Europe. Never one to miss out on a good thing, Colt loaded the .32 S&W Long with flatnose bullets and called it the .32 Colt New Police. The two rounds are interchangeable. My Model 31 has a 3-inch barrel and fixed sights, and really lays 'em in there.

.32 SHORT AND LONG COLT

These were both originally black-powder cartridges loaded with outside-lubricated bullets. In Europe it is called the .320 Revolver. The ballistics are similar to the .32 S&W and .32 S&W Long.

.32 NORTH AMERICAN ARMS

This unique little round is made by necking down the .380 ACP to .32 caliber. COR-BON makes ammunition loaded with a 60-grain jacketed hollow point at over 1,200 fps.

.32-20 WINCHESTER

The .32-20 was first chambered in the Winchester Model 1873 lever-action rifle, but quickly became popular for revolvers as well, as folks saw the utility of having one round for both a rifle and handgun. It propelled 80- or 100-grain bullets at velocities that made it suitable for small game, varmints and the occasional unsuspecting deer.

.32 H&R MAGNUM

The .32 Harrington & Richardson Magnum was introduced in 1984 and is one of the modern .32s that has sufficient power to be credible for hunting small game as well as for self-defense. Although the cartridge is an excellent performer, its popularity was initially limited somewhat by the lack of high-quality handguns to shoot it. That changed when Ruger chambered the Single-Six for it in 1984 and Smith & Wesson the Model 16 in 1990, though both were discontinued after a few years. I had one of each of these revolvers and both shot wonderfully. Federal introduced the first ammunition for the cartridge, and a diverse selection of loads is still made by Hornady, Double Tap, Black Hills Ammo and Buffalo Bore.

.327 FEDERAL MAGNUM

The .327 is the current culmination of the .32 line. It was introduced by Federal in 2008, and its supporters claim that it closely matches the .357 Magnum in practical power. This may be debatable, but the .327 has a modest following of fanatics that regard it very highly. Ruger offers three different models chambered for the .327: the Single-Seven single action, the LCR concealed-carry gun and the SP101. Taurus also produces a couple of short-barrel carry guns, and Federal makes three loads.

The American Eagle 85-grain Soft Point also grouped nicely at a sizzling 1,529 fps.

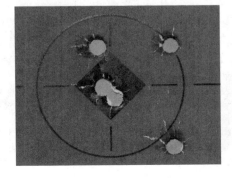

The Hornady 100-grain XTP Hollow Point bullet shot well using 6.5 grains of Power Pistol. Velocity was 1,278 fps.

The .32s offer considerable versatility, as shown by the variety of bullets suitable for them. From left: 78-grain cast roundnose, Hornady 90-grain hollow-base wadcutter, 115-grain cast semiwadcutter, Sierra 90-grain Jacketed Hollow Cavity and Hornady 100-grain XTP (eXtreme Terminal Performance) hollowpoint.

fortunately, is a snap, and the same dies and shell holders used for the .32 Long and .32 H&R will work just fine for the .327, too. Federal uses their No. 200 small pistol magnum primers, and I did likewise in my .327 handloads, though I used Federal No. 100s for the other two cartridges. I lucked into a good quantity of Federal nickel-plated .327 cases, so used them for my test loads. I used Starline cases for the .32 H&R and Winchester for the .32 Long.

Suitable powders for the .327 really fall into two categories. For the highest velocities with 100- to 115-grain bullets, Winchester 296 (aka Hodgdon 110), and Lil'Gun are good choices. For medium-power loads, you just can't beat Hodgdon's new CFE Pistol, although HS-6, Universal and AutoComp are also good. For what used to be called "gallery loads," Bullseye, Winchester 231 and TiteGroup with cast bullets are the ticket to low recoil, a mild report and small groups.

When it's all said and done, my solution to loading the .327 was very simple. I just kept the charges a bit under maximum. Accuracy and velocity were fine, and I had not a single case failure or any trouble ejecting a case. However, if you find yourself with a lot of .32 H&R cases and few .327s, it's no problem, as

the H&R brass makes up into accurate and powerful ammo for use in a .327 wheelgun.

The .327 Federal is a great little cartridge, but it is not without its foibles. It offers a lot of performance, but at a price. Yes, factory ammo is expensive, but that's not what I'm talking about. Chamber pressure and noise are the costs. The Maximum Average Pressure (MAP) allowed for the .327 by SAAMI is 45,000 psi. By contrast, MAP of the .357 Magnum is 35,000 psi and 36,000 psi for the .44 Magnum. So, reloaders should not use powder charges heavier than those in the loading manuals. Actually, handloads a bit below maximum offer plenty of power and trouble-free functioning.

Another cost of the .327 is a very loud muzzle blast. Unless a grizzly is chewing on your leg or a bad guy is closing fast, the .327 should never be fired without hearing protection. However, this is not an insurmountable problem for the industrious .327 shooter.

A tremendously useful attribute of a .327 revolver is its ability to shoot a variety of shorter rounds. The .32 H&R, .32 S&W, .32 S&W Long, and even the .32 ACP (because it's actually a semi-rimmed case) can be safely fired in a .327. Hornady makes a .32 H&R round

with an 85-grain XTP bullet at 1,150 fps that is a terrific load for the .327. Federal also makes .32 H&R ammunition.

But, the real solution is to handload the .327 to match the shooter's need. Cases, bullets and powders are readily available, so a load for just about any purpose can be tailor-made. Plus, handloads are extremely inexpensive compared to factory fodder.

So, in the .327 Federal Magnum we have the most versatile and powerful modern-day .32-caliber cartridge to achieve broad-based popularity. Modern ammunition and new firearms are available for it, and it can be handloaded to suit the shooter's needs and pocketbook. While the .32 ACP and .32 S&W Long in classic pistols like the M-1903 Colt and S&W M-31 are fun to shoot, the .327 can be easily loaded to the power levels of most of those earlier rounds, in addition to power levels unheard of for those older rounds.

The .327 offers a broad spectrum of performance, is economical to handload and shoot, and at the same time is a powerful round for personal protection. The shooter looking for a small or midsize handgun with pizzazz would do well to consider the versatile .327 Federal Magnum.

THE SMALL-GAME RIFLE

These rifles have a rich tradition and a place in any hunter's collection

By Walt Hampton

If there is a better way to spend a bright fall morning than sitting in a stand of hickories with a trim and accurate squirrel rifle, I don't know what it would be. I'm sure there are some in the antler-insanity camp who would argue that statement, and yes, I like to hunt deer; but for sheer fun and true relaxation give me small game every time. And, the two are not mutually exclusive, given the right gun-in-hand.

It might come as a surprise to most hunters today but at one time, the small-game rifle was a true art form, perfected by every gun manufacturer in our great country. In the 100 years before 1970 it was small game, not deer, that drew the most attention, and that's where young hunters got their start. If you consider yourself a rifleman today, you owe a debt of gratitude to the small-game hunters of yesteryear that drove the demand for firearms innovation.

The Rimfires

Since most folks associate small-game rifles with the .22-caliber rimfire cartridge, we will dispense with it first. In constant production since its inception as the first commercially produced self-contained metallic cartridge, the .22 rimfire is the round that wrote the book. I began my hunting career with a .22 rimfire Remington rifle, and luckily I still have it and I still shoot it. Everyone who shoots should own a .22.

Small-game rifles from left: Winchester Model 61 in .22 Magnum; Remington Model 25 in .32-20; Remington-Hepburn in .38-56; Winchester 1885 Hi-Wall in .32-40; Ballard in .44 Rimfire; Remington #4 in .22 Long Rifle; Remington #2 in .22 WRF; Marlin 27S in .25 Rimfire; Marlin 27S in .25-20; and Marlin Model 37 in .22 Long Rifle.

The .22 begat a storm of rifles in every action type. The .22 Short cartridge was introduced in 1856; over time the rolling-block and falling-block guns gave way to the bolt, pump and semiautos, and soon every gunmaker was putting their own personal touches on a wide array of .22-caliber rifles for the hunting public. Parenthetically, this is fertile territory for the gun collector; literally hundreds of models and variations exist within each action type and some of the finest gun collections I have seen were dedicated to .22 rimfire rifles of some sort or the other.

The .22 rimfire cartridge comes in several guises and power levels. From the diminutive CB cap to the hyper-velocity magnum loadings, within this spread of power the cartridge is capable of taking a surprising range of game; but it is at its best restricted to squirrels, rabbits and pests up to the size of the fox. It has of course been used on larger game. I remember reading about a record-book grizzly killed by an Indian girl using a .22 Long as it strolled by her while she was

The Ballard in .44 Rimfire is a classic small-game rifle in a great caliber. Factory ammunition is unobtainable, but perfectly usable ammo can be made with a steel case and a .22 Short cartridge (without the .22 bullet) for ignition. As a turkey or squirrel gun, and for animals up to the size of the coyote, it may have been the best small-caliber rimfire ever developed.

hunting spruce grouse, but that was a matter of necessity and not preference. Her name was Bella Twin and the kill was made in 1953 in Alberta.

I have used the .22 Long Rifle and .22 Magnum loadings to kill farm-raised hogs and cattle. The penetration of the 36-grain lead bullet at velocities between 1,200 and 2,000 fps will surprise you.

Probably the best of all rimfire small-game cartridges was the now-defunct .25 Stevens Long, a superb killer on turkeys and coyotes within its range restrictions, using the 65-grain lead slug at about 1,200 fps. If I could have one wish in the firearms and ammunition world it would be for some manufacturer to bring back this wonderful cartridge. Some of the most beautiful rimfire rifles built over the years were chambered for this round.

My wish was echoed by none other than Elmer Keith. At his behest, just before World War II, Remington was gearing up to bring out what they would call the .267 Remington Rimfire that was essentially the .25 Stevens, but the idea was shelved with the Pearl Harbor attack. No, the .25 rimfire is not the

The Winchester Model 61 (top) in .22 Magnum Rimfire was a popular, reliable gun for small game and varmints. The Remington Model 25 (bottom) in .32-20 was one of the most accurate pump rifles ever built.

The concept of the "boy's rifle" was established with the Remington #4 rolling-block rifle (top). In .22 Long Rifle it is responsible for starting thousands of hunting careers. The Remington #2 (bottom) is chambered in .22 Winchester Rimfire. These are precision shooters made for squirrels, rabbits and head shots on turkeys.

This case holds .44 Rimfire rounds made with steel cases and .22 rimfire shells for primers. In the upper left side of the box is a .25 Rimfire round made in the same manner. The close-up of the .44 Rimfire case shows the index cut and the .22 Short case used as the primer.

gee-whiz super-speed new .17 caliber, but for the careful hunter it was an effective and accurate round. The Marlin 27S pump action pictured in these pages is still taking small game with some of my carefully hoarded original ammunition.

At one time rimfire cartridges ruled the woods and they were available in virtually every caliber you could imagine. Very popular in those old days were the .32- and .38-caliber guns, and we all know that the .44 Rimfire Henry rifle and its large diameter, heavy slug worked on man and beast alike. A moderate velocity, heavy slug in those guns was quiet and effective for small-game work. Today our new high-velocity .17-caliber rimfire rounds offer flatter trajectory, but their killing power and penetration cannot match what was obtainable with the older, now-obsolete loads. If you chest-shoot an adult gobbler at 75 yards with a high-velocity .17 rimfire you might end up with a handful of feathers and a lost bird; taking the same shot with the .25-, .32- or .38-caliber rimfire guns shooting lead bullets, my guess would be that the bird would be waiting for you when you walk up. Faster isn't necessarily always better.

The idea of the "boy's rifle," a term deemed politically incorrect in our insane world, was best represented by the Remington rolling-block rifle and the Winchester and Stevens falling-block single-shot rifles. The Number 4 Remington and the Winchester 1885, and the many Stevens "Favorite" variations, are also classic small-game guns. Still found today in obsolete rimfire calibers at flea markets and gun shows, they can be very affordable. If you don't have access to the original ammo there are alternatives, such as relining the barrels and chambering them for modern calibers, or if you like a challenge, you can make your own fodder.

Many fellows have come up with steel cases in the proper dimensions using the .22 Short for ignition, properly indexed in the gun for firing pin strike, to load their own. My friend Jansen Cox has accomplished this in both the .25 and .44 Rimfire calibers, taking what was considered to be near-worthless old guns and putting them back into service. Where there is a will, there is a way.

Small-game hunting means small targets, and while in the old days open sights ruled the woods, a good scope on your rifle makes sure hits easier. I started with open sights on the .22 for squirrels but as soon as I could put together enough hay money I bought a Weaver C-4

for Dad's Remington. Now I could better pick out the little fellows in that early season foliage and I tried to specialize in head shots. My great-aunt, May Pearman (I called her "Ain't May) had an 800-acre farm in Wythe County, Va., with plenty of hickory in the woodlots and from one of these I proudly brought her a limit of grays one fall morning. She said I ruined them; it seems she liked squirrel brains in her scrambled eggs, so from then on it was body shots for her and noggin shots for me. A good .22 with a quality scope is a great combination for squirrels.

The Centerfires

When the centerfire cartridge was introduced it effectively killed the rimfire, because of one reason — it was reloadable. In the rifle world we now saw the "dual purpose" gun emerge, chambered for calibers that, with the proper load, could be used effectively on small game and bigger critters alike. Some centerfire calibers were marketed as small-game rounds specifically and there were rifles built for these calibers and this use. Many of the guns originally made for rimfire cartridges were then offered by the factories in the new configuration (the Marlin 27S and the Remington Model 25 in .25-20 and .32-20 are good examples). Gun people began their climb up the performance ladder and increased velocity was gaining more attention.

In the beginning, of course, these cartridges were loaded with black

powder, but now it is easy to safely duplicate these black-powder loads with smokeless propellant. The .25-20 can be easily loaded down to .25 Stevens Long performance, just as the .32-20 can be loaded to .32 Rimfire velocity. It wasn't too long ago that I sat beside a friend when he took a fall turkey with a beautiful 175-yard shot through the open timber with his .38-56 Hepburn, the lead slug punching a neat caliber-size hole and damaging nary a smidgeon of meat. That same gun and load accounted for many squirrels and a few big fat doe deer. For the handloader these old calibers can be just as useful today with judicious use of SR4759 or IMR4198 and a cast lead bullet. Low recoil, low noise, accurate and deadly; can't ask for more than that from a small-game rifle.

Most often these days when we think of small-game centerfire guns we immediately think of the .22 centerfire cartridges such as the Hornet, Bee or even the .222 and .223. My .218 Bee was a Martini Cadet action and with it I was the fox squirrel's worst nightmare, particularly late in the season with the leaves off of the trees and stalking into shotgun range impossible. Albeit a bit loud for the squirrel woods, it shot so flat and so accurately that head shots at 100 yards, with a good rest and of course a good scope, were easy. This rifle even clipped the heads off of a couple ruffed grouse that made the mistake of meandering to by my squirrel stand; I love to hunt grouse with a shotgun and my black lab, Buck, but I also love to eat them so the opportunity was gladly taken. No regrets.

The centerfire deer rifle can also be a small-game gun with the proper load. Using either jacketed or cast lead bullets and reduced loads, I have used my .308, .25-06, .260, 7x57 and .30-30 to fill the game bag with squirrels and turkeys during the deer season. Most deer hunters never imagine their pet rifle as being used in this manner, but if you handload there is a whole new world awaiting you with reduced loads. There is no better rifle practice for the deer woods than using that same deer rifle for squirrels, and we all could use more practice.

Recently when testing a new Savage rifle in .260 Remington caliber, in addition to the full-performance handloading I was doing with various jacketed bullets, I ran through some 143-grain cast lead bullets in reduced loads and found once again that with the proper attention to detail, the modern centerfire rifle can be very useful for small game.

Jansen Cox takes the nearly imperceptible recoil from firing a 240-grain lead slug through the Ballard .44 Rimfire.

Top Left: These three beautiful rifles can pull double duty for small game and deer, under their range constrictions. Top, the Hepburn in .38-56; center, the Winchester Hi-Wall in .32-40; and the Ballard in .44 Rimfire. **Above:** The author's .218 Bee is built on a Martini Cadet action. The grouse was an unexpected bonus on a squirrel hunt. **Right:** The Marlin 27S is the author's favorite pump-action small-game rifle. The one on the left is a .25 Rimfire, the right is the .25-20. Some of the most elegant and useful pump-action rifles ever produced were made for the rimfire calibers — slick and fast, accurate and deadly little guns that were a joy to carry and shoot.

I built my dedicated small-game rifle using an original Winchester 1885 low-wall with a shot out .32-20 barrel. My son Wade cut for me a new half-round, half-octagon 28-inch tube and chambered it for .357 Magnum. I had a piece of Grayson County burl walnut that had too many flaws to sell and was really too small for any other purpose. Using the original stocks as patterns, I turned out a new buttstock and fore-end, repaired the many flaws in the new wood with Acraglas, and fit up the wood to the metal. Shooting 148-grain lead .38-caliber wadcutters at about 900 fps, this rifle is a joy to carry and use, much to the chagrin of the Buck Mountain squirrels and turkeys. It has no recoil and is so quiet that repeated shots in a small woodlot won't spook the squirrels into hiding.

On the bench at 50 yards it will put 10 shots into one ragged hole just barely over the diameter of the slug; my son started calling these loads "waddle-cutters" because of the way they treated our turkey population. One afternoon last year during the deer gun season on the ridge behind our hunting cabin, I was trying to fill out a limit of bushytails with this rifle when a big, meaty doe came down the trail at about 45 yards. The lead wadcutter passed through her head and she simply wilted in place, a

welcome addition to our meat supply. A very satisfying day, with a good rifle.

A Short Tirade on Turkey Hunting with the Rifle

It makes absolutely no difference what firearm is used to kill turkeys. Virginians have been killing turkeys with rifles, shotguns, handguns and archery tackle since European settlement more than 400 years ago. Currently all of these listed weapons are legal for use in the spring and the fall turkey seasons in Virginia. But, like some in the fly fishing fraternity that view bait fishing as akin to child molestation, there is a noisy bunch of hunters that think only shotguns should be allowed in turkey hunting. This has been carried so far that even some states restrict turkey hunting to shotguns only. This is, of course, nonsense.

When this question is argued the most often given reason for the use of the shotgun over the rifle is safety. The implication is that for some reason the rifle is the more dangerous of the two. Right here, at the start, is where we find ourselves wrapped around the axle looking at the wrong aspect of the hunting accident: the problem, gentlemen, is not the gun (The obvious parallel here, with the current political debate over "gun violence" versus just plain old criminal violence, is clearly intended). Only in densely populated, flat-terrain areas, where the rifle is already restricted from use for all hunting, should any shotgun-only restriction for turkey hunting be valid.

Vivid in my memory of the 10 rules of safe gun handling is the tenet "KNOW YOUR TARGET AND BEYOND." These five simple words place the responsibility of the shot exactly where it should be, with the shooter. It does not make any difference what firearm you are shooting at game, if you fail to follow this rule. The shotgun folks claim that the shotgun wound would be more survivable than that inflicted by the rifle, that somehow it would be okay if you are only blinded or crippled by a shotgun blast instead of shot dead with a rifle. Of the four people I have personally seen that have been shot with the shotgun, one was a spring turkey hunter who tried to sneak in between a gobbling turkey and another hunter who was working the bird. In addition to his other wounds, the victim had 11 hits on the front of his camouflaged hat. The load of magnum 12-gauge copper plated #4 killed him as dead as any rifle could have. This shooting was later determined to be intentional but you see the point; if you follow the safety rules you will not accidentally shoot another hunter.

The fall-back position for the shotgun-only supporter is the question of ethics, their argument being that the turkey hunt is only ethical if the bird is called in and killed at close range, and the turkey hunting firearm should be restricted by law for this reason. There are so many things wrong with this line of thinking I find it hard to know where to begin in my argument against it.

Of course I love to call in spring gobblers and shoot them at close range; of my 70-something spring gobbler kills, the vast majority have been laid down in this manner, most within 20 yards, most with the 20-gauge shotgun, and I prefer to do it this way if given the chance. But I have also called spring gobblers in to hand-shaking distance and killed them with the rifle, muzzleloader and handgun; I don't think the turkey was aware of the difference. I also like eating turkey and in the fall seasons, when hunting turkeys specifically or if I get into them when after other game, I will shoot them with the rifle (or the handgun, or the muzzleloader) if given the legal opportunity, whether I have called them, stalked them, blundered into them or had them stagger by.

Let us remember, fellow hunters, if the game department did not want you to kill turkeys, there would be no season on them. Ethics cannot be legislated. Within the constraints of law, how the hunter conducts the hunt is up to the hunter.

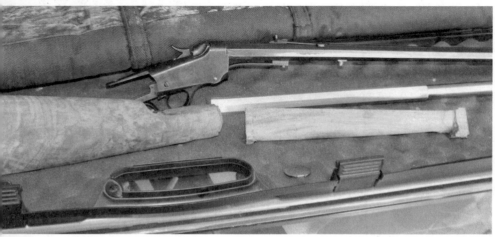

The author built his dedicated small-game rifle using an original Winchester 1885 Low-Wall with a new half-octagon, half-round barrel chambered for .357 Magnum and a piece of flawed Grayson County burl walnut. Shooting 148-grain wadcutter lead bullets at approximately 900 fps, it works beautifully for squirrels and turkeys.

Turkeys with the rifle: what's the problem? This .30-30-caliber 1893 Marlin took this monster spring gobbler with a 180-grain lead bullet at about 1,100 fps. Spring or fall, turkey hunting with the rifle can be safe, challenging and rewarding.

To a lesser degree I have heard some shotgun-only guys say that the rifle destroys the bird or ruins the meat. Well, duh, how about don't shoot the bird in the damn breast? The crippling loss from the shotgun far outweighs this argument, as most rifle shooters are much more precise in targeting the bird. I have never lost a bird I have shot with the rifle – I cannot say this about the shotgun.

As far as I am concerned, if you want to take a whack at a spring gobbler with your hunting handgun or your squirrel rifle, or be able to take a turkey while rifle or muzzleloader deer hunting (if the season is open), if you bought the expensive license, you should be able to do just that. There is no biological, ethical or safety reason to restrict the use of any modern, legal firearm in turkey hunting. OK, off the soapbox.

Modern small-game rifles marketed today are almost exclusively the .22- and .17-caliber guns, and once again, mostly rimfire. The new rifles from Savage in particular are very nice, married with new chamberings from Hornady and Winchester, and the .17 Hornet centerfire might be one of best small-game chamberings we've seen in many years. The single-shot and pump guns of old are now mostly a memory, replaced with the bolt actions, but the Marlin lever .22 rimfires are still with us. Sadly, there is not much emphasis on small-game rifles these days, replaced by the headlong rush to better deer guns.

Small-game hunting started many hunting careers back in the days before the deer explosion we experienced in the 1970s. I honestly believe that starting out young or novice hunters on small game instead of jumping right in on deer is the best way to introduce new people to our pastime, and both of my boys got their start in the hunting world with squirrels and turkeys. Watching the boys develop their shooting skills with my small-game rifles, and seeing their ethics and gun etiquette evolve was a great pleasure, directly related to the amount of practice shooting they had with the little small-game rifles in hand. Small-game rifles have a rich tradition and history and a place in any hunter's collection.

Most people think of the .22 Rimfire when talk turns to small-game rifles. This classic Remington Model 550 semiauto started the author on the hunting road.

DON'T MESS WITH MY *Marlin!*®

By Wayne van Zwoll

While "deer rifle" brings to mind whitetails in hardwoods, Marlin's 336 is at home on the prairie too.

It was everyman's deer rifle. Like a car that always starts and a dog that always obeys, you don't miss it until it's gone.

The Wind River Range had become the Big Lonely. Elk rut had sputtered to silence. Early snow had frosted meadow and forest, then softened and froze. It crunched in dawn's knife-edge chill. A raven stirred the air overhead. Whoosh. Then it left, a dot receding into dishwater sky.

I walked, with everywhere to look and nowhere to go. Elk could lie in the next 'pole thicket. Or in a drainage two ridges over.

Sometimes luck favors the lost. Far away, a young bull gave voice. I didn't wait for an encore. A 20-minute hustle later, I crept into a herd scattered across a hump nudging a broad meadow. A rag-horn quartered away. I knelt, thumbed the hammer and settled the bead. The trigger broke as the bull turned. *No!* Seconds later I lost the race. He bled little from the forward nip, and showed no limp. I tracked him until the prints

vanished in the braided path of the herd.

Seeing no elk is dispiriting but not an indictment. Muffing a shot is much worse. I climbed fast to leave my failure behind. It dogged me onto elk sign snaking up a draw. I kept the track to my side, but the snow crunched. They exited high. A window opened to the bull's ribs. I didn't fire. One botched attempt was enough.

Noon came. Spent, I swung toward a saddle and sat near a trail crossing, my back against a rock. Idly I glassed the ridge above, a monochrome of burned black 'poles over patchy snow under gray cloud. Then I saw an upturned limb – the only one that didn't droop.

The carbine steadied itself. I kissed the tree with the bead. It covered what little of the elk's vitals I could see. The bull spun at the shot and jetted away. My climb led to great splayed tracks in aerosol red spray, the bull lay dead a stone's toss beyond, lungs pulped by the .32 Special.

Three hunts in one morning. Well, that Marlin was due. Passed over for years

as scoped bolt rifles snared my eye, it deserved better.

While North America's first successful bolt rifle waited for rimless cartridges, smokeless powder and jacketed bullets, John Mahlon Marlin had a slick-shucking lever action hard on the heels of Custer's loss at the Little Bighorn. Marlin's career in firearms design had begun much earlier. In 1853, at age 18, the Connecticut youth apprenticed as a machinist. He agreed to work for no wages for six months, after which he would earn $1.50 a week!

Honing his talents in "gun valley" during the most productive period in the U.S. firearms industry, Marlin first built derringer-style pistols, then Ballard rifles. The top-ejecting Model 1881 lever action followed in .40-60 and .45-70. Designer L.L. Hepburn came up with Marlin's short-action 1888 for the .32-20, .38-40 and .44-40. In the Model 1889 Marlin introduced side ejection and a more reliable carrier. Hepburn's 1893 accepted longer cartridges: the .32-40 and .38-55, then the .25-36, .30-30 and

.32 Special. As troops returning from the Great War turned their sights on deer, Marlin's 1893 competed vigorously with the Winchester 1894.

Meanwhile, Marlin had upscaled the '93 to take the potent .45-70-405, adopted by the U.S. Army in 1873 and popular with hunters. The Model 1895 also came in .38-56, .40-65 (.40-60 Marlin), .40-82 and .45-90. In 1897 the .40-70 WCF joined this list, in 1912 the .33 WCF. Various configurations of the 1895 were sold through 1913; only the lightweight version that appeared in 1912 showed up afterward. The company priced the 1895 at $27 in 1917, its final year of production. It would lie dormant 55 years.

In 1937 Marlin introduced "a new gun especially for American big game." The Model 1936 had a "solid frame, 20-inch round tapered special smokeless barrel [and] Ballard-type rifling." A handsome rifle with case-colored receiver, it boasted a pistol grip buttstock for steady aim. All variations, in .30-30 and .32 Special, listed for $32. A year later the Model 336 supplanted the 36 with a new extractor in a round bolt "encased … by a solid bridge of steel." The 36's flat mainspring gave way to a coil spring.

Marlin's 336 fared well against Winchester's 94 at market, largely because the 336 offered side ejection, so scopes – increasingly popular, even on woods rifles – could be mounted low over center. Less celebrated was Marlin's chambering of the .35 Remington. It offered a bit more punch than the .30-30 and .32 Special, popular in both the 94 and 336. In Michigan camps during my youth, Marlin carbines turned up as often as Winchesters. Both could be had for under $100. I should have hocked my first automobile.

In 1972 Marlin announced a New Model 1895 in .45-70. It had the 336 receiver and mechanism, modified for bigger cases. Later the re-introduced 1895 would be chambered for modern cartridges: the .450 Marlin and .308 and .338 Marlin Express, all developed in Hornady's ballistics lab. The .450 Marlin hurls 325-grain bullets 200 fps faster than the same missiles from the .45-70. The .308 Marlin starts 160-grain FTX bullets at 2,600 fps. They clock 2,000 fps at 300 yards, and pack 1,200 ft-lbs of punch at 400. In north-slope timber in New Mexico, I carried one of the first .308 MEs. The forest floor had been flayed by elk traffic; bull-scent hung heavy in the air. The snick of a twig stopped me. Then – a wink of antler! I side stepped, found a shot alley as the bull quartered to me

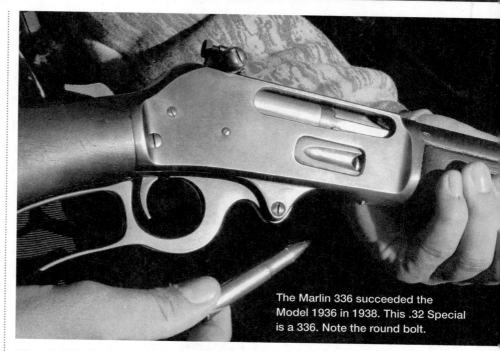

The Marlin 336 succeeded the Model 1936 in 1938. This .32 Special is a 336. Note the round bolt.

Side ejection and a solid top receiver permit centered scope mounting or uninterrupted aim with irons.

Wayne made six first-round hits, prone, from 100 to 600 yards with this Marlin 1895 in .338 Marlin Express.

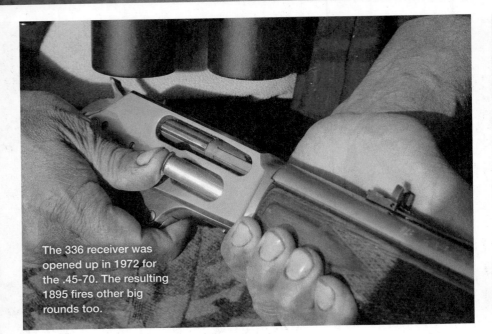

The 336 receiver was opened up in 1972 for the .45-70. The resulting 1895 fires other big rounds too.

and drove a bullet through the near shoulder. Cycling the Marlin quickly, I followed with three more hits. The elk died after a few steps.

Hornady's point man in this effort, Dave Emary, was pleased with that performance but thought the 1895 had more potential. Back in Grand Island, he fashioned an even more potent round, based on the .376 Steyr. At 2,565 fps, a 200-grain bullet from the .338 Marlin Express scribes an arc all but identical to that of the '06 out to 300 yards, and hits harder. "But of course, a lever rifle won't match a bolt-action for accuracy at distance," a pal declared. It was a challenge not to be ignored.

I replaced the aperture sight on that .338 ME rifle with a 4.5-14x Leupold. Don Ward at GreyBull scribed an elevation dial to match the bullet's arc. On the Wyoming prairie I bellied into the grass, sling taut, and fired at a 12-inch steel bull's-eye 100 yards off. To no one's surprise, the bullet struck center. I moved back to 200 and fired again. Another middle hit. At 300 I dialed up and hit. At 400 the plate looked tiny. But the Hornady landed with a "thwock." Frankly, 500 seemed a stretch. But the plate shivered. I almost stopped. That's farther than I fire at game, farther than lever rifles are supposed to hit vitals. But

I hiked back to 600, dialed a handful of clicks and tried to steady the rifle. The bullet struck a hand's width from center. Six first-round hits to 600 steps – as solid a performance as I can manage with *any* hunting rifle!

But lever-action mystique has less to do with power and precision than with the history – stories of the frontier that bred these rifles, and exploits of the colorful characters who used them.

Beyond that, the lever gun pulls you into cover. Even a modern Marlin begs its turn in timber, where shots come close and fast. So when I had a chance to hunt black bears on Alaska's Prince of Wales Island, I grabbed a 336.

Our wake bleached by a pair of 330-horse diesels, we motored out of Wrangell on sun-shot water, hitting light chop as, hours

later, we began the long swing around the island's western shore. A red dusk settled onto the Pacific, its reflected light a shimmering aisle to Japan. At 7 knots, "Bear Necessity" muscled through the waves. We'd need our 1,200-gallon diesel reserve, as even in quiet seas this 52-foot boat drank a gallon a mile. Circumnavigating Prince of Wales Island is a 400-mile trip. "Alaska's 40,000 miles of shoreline exceeds that of the entire Lower 48," Mark Gala reminded me.

He's hosted countless hunters on his boat, skirting coastal mountains that

The 1895, dropped in 1917, reappeared in 1972 in a 336 receiver. This late SS model is in .308 Marlin Express.

Much of the lever-rifle mystique comes from history. Annie Oakley used Marlins in her exhibitions.

MISS ANNIE OAKLEY,
(LITTLE SURE SHOT.)
BUFFALO BILL'S WILD WEST.

vault from jagged black rock beaches hemming forest that gets 18 *feet* of rain annually. He glasses for bears that prowl tidal flats in search of fresh grass.

Mark told me he'd never guided anyone with a .30-30. "To tell you the truth, I'm not crazy about it. Our bears are big. Cover's thick. We want a quick kill. Some clients bring .375s."

We anchored in a cove ringed by an abandoned fishing village. Next evening, when the seas laid down, Mark and I launched a skiff and motored up a small stream. Alaska's tides can rise and fall 20 feet in six-hour swings, so we moored the craft with a long line on a tall rock. Donning backpacks, we pushed inland through tidal grass. At timber's edge, 150 yards off, Mark spied two bears. I dropped to hands and knees and led, clutching my Marlin. When the wind swung, the sow vanished. The boar paused. I pegged his elbow. "Ninety yards," I thought. The 170-grain flatnose smacked home. Trees swallowed the bear.

We inched ahead in dripping foliage. No blood. And, of course, no track. Then: a red smear! The trail was suddenly painted. We came upon the heart-shot bear at close range. I fired the Marlin again, just to be sure.

Such success breeds confidence. In mid-September after that Alaskan hunt I hiked into Utah's Uinta Mountains with the same Marlin carbine. As dawn blushed above a shadowed north slope, I heard elk sifting through aspens. Playing the wind, I angled up toward the herd,

now moving steadily to bedding cover. It's hard to stay undetected trying to catch elk traveling with purpose. You make too much noise or expose yourself once too often. I throttled back, hoping for a straggler. Luck came my way. A young bull, keeping a safe distance behind the herd's patriarch, minced along the track. A thicket separated us. Delay was risky in the capricious wind. I stepped to an alley. At 19 yards, as he stopped, wide-eyed, I fired into the bull's throat. He wilted at the blast.

Encouraged again by the Marlin's lethal sting, I slipped that saddle gun into a scabbard for an elk hunt in Montana's Bob Marshall Wilderness. A leap of faith? Certainly. The Bob's great swaths of timber hide widely scattered elk. Broad prairies test the hunter's reach. I might get one long shot. Watching John Way's linebacker shoulders rock to the rhythm of his pony, I thought of the scoped .300 I had left behind.

Flashlight beams danced in the dark as we wolfed toast under stars not yet fading. Hooves sucked mud, and limbs swiped my face as I trailed Darrell up a forested canyon, where in cold drizzle we swung stiffly from our saddles.

Eight hard hours later, saturated and tired, we got back on the ponies. We'd seen nothing. Darrell turned. "Want to try one more hill?"

It quickly became too steep for the horses. We tugged them on, into Ponderosas grimly gripping the slope below a knife-edge ridge. Darrell pulled pipe and grunt tube from his pack and loosed a lungful, drawing out the scream.

We were stunned by an immediate reply. Darrell bugled again and had barely finished when the bull answered, closer! Fire in my lungs, lead in my legs, I scrambled uphill as my partner crouched by a tree. The bull brayed again, the blast so strong, it seemed to shake the trees. I threw myself prone. Black and tan winked between the boles. Hooves snapped limbs as the great arc of an antler parted the pines. I steadied the Marlin and quartered his chest with the 2½ X Leupold. He spun at the report and vanished in second-growth. Suddenly all was quiet. I waited to hear him fall.

Two minutes later he hadn't. I inched to the side, spied a patch of rib and triggered another shot. The bull boiled out of the trees on shaky legs. I fired again. He toppled.

"Experts" these days tell us the .30-30 isn't adequate for elk. Balderdash! This old favorite, with the similar .32 Special, .35 Remington and .303 Savage, has killed many truckloads of elk. A 1939 survey of 2,200 elk hunters in my home state of Washington showed it and the .30 Remington (think rimless .30-30) were hugely

In north-country alders where grizzlies live, many guides prefer fast-shucking Marlin big-bores.

Wayne's late Marlin from North Haven shows the classic lines, tight wood-metal fit 336 fans adore.

Below: Wayne killed this Alaskan bear with his 336 in .30-30. "Some hunters bring .375s," said his guide.

popular. Yes, that was another time. And if you're bent on killing an elk as far as you can aim with a scope from an improvised rest, pick a stronger round. But my last three elk fell at an *average* distance of 26 yards. Oddly, hunters who'd fire a .30-06 at elk with a top-of-the-withers hold dismiss the .30-30 even at woods ranges, where it actually delivers more energy than the '06 brings to 400!

That Marlin 336 finished the year with a Wyoming pronghorn and a Montana mule deer, felled with a shot apiece at about 160 yards. Hardly surprising. The rifle punched 1½-minute groups on paper.

Not long ago I made my way into a Cabela's Gun Library, mainly to chat with the clerk. But a Marlin lever rifle caught my attention. It was an 1893, in .32 Special. No alterations. Only light wear. A couple of special-order features. As I expected, the tag showed Cabela's was mighty proud of this rifle. But the fellow in charge was pleasant, and let me put a patch and light through the bore. He must have seen me grimace, as the price immediately fell. After appropriate deliberation, I bought that 1893. Its 2-minute groups are much better than the bore promised, and as good as I can produce with iron sights.

If there's a more enduring deer rifle than the Marlin 336, I can't name it. Enduring through 80 years of production,

Southpaws can use a 336 without awkward accommodation. That flat receiver is scabbard-friendly.

Wayne killed this big bull at 55 yards with his 336 in .30-30. Ideal elk rifle? "No. But certainly underrated."

and also afield. My .30-30 proved that on a Colorado prairie when a pal and I were checking zeros. I was prone. He fired over the hood of his Suburban. When time came to change targets, I trotted toward 200-yard paper. He fired up the Chevy to set distant steel. He apparently forgot about my rifle and spotting scope. The Suburban ran over the 336, generously distributing its tread over buttstock, tang, receiver and lever. I returned to find the wrist in pieces, the lever askew, my friend trembling. But I'm a charitable lad, and after counting to 10 (or was it 1,010?) I fetched up some tape to wrap the wrist. The lever required a tug, but the action then cycled silkily. I bellied onto the mat, prepared for gross sight adjustment. Instead, my shots centered the bull's-eye. Nary a hiccup in feeding.

On Dec. 26, 2007, Remington Arms announced a plan to buy Marlin Firearms. The sale took place Jan. 28, 2008. On Mar. 25, 2010, Marlin's old North Haven factory was shuttered, most of its machinery bound for Remington's Ilion, N.Y., digs. "Some supervisors moved," said Eric Lundgren, product manager for Marlin rifles at Remington. "But we underestimated the handwork required on rifles manufactured with that equipment." The first lever actions from Ilion lacked the quality of North Haven Marlins. Remington scrambled, investing manpower and tooling to build better Marlins.

The move forced a hiatus in production of more than a dozen Marlin rifles. Some are now back in the line. "We won't release rifles prematurely," Eric tells me, adding that Remington – now Remington Outdoor Group – is "over the hump" getting Marlins back to original standards of fit and finish. "We're minding the details and getting things right." In addition, Remington has just announced a custom-built line of lever guns to be assembled in the Sturgis, S.D., facility that produces Dakota and Nesika rifles. The custom Marlins I've seen are handsome; the actions cycle like race-car pistons.

Still, the North Haven 336 is gone. Recently, in the second-hand rack of a local gunshop a Marlin caught my eye. A 336. A .30-30 dating to the '60s. No damage. The stock showed honest wear; the steel had nearly all its original blue. I recalled when such rifles languished on gun-show tables. Now, at triple their price, this one had me by the lapels. I pulled away.

But I may go back. The 336 has done well by me. And after having fired many, its one gun I can't seem to leave alone.

Pronghorns are a challenge with iron-sighted lever rifles! Try to pry that Marlin from Wayne's hands!

A 1939 survey of Washington elk hunters showed the .30-30 and rimless .30 Remington most popular.

Durable! After a Suburban ran over this 336, it took a pronghorn at 160 steps. No sight adjustment needed.

THE TRIPLE SAGA OF THE
THOMPSON

The early Auto-Ordnance company developed
the world-renowned Thompson submachine guns,
but an obscure member of its lineup
was the semiautomatic Model 1927.

By **George Layman**

The ubiquitous silhouette of the Thompson submachine gun has made it one of most well-known firearms in the world. Its concept was the brainchild of U.S. Army Brigadier General John T. Thompson, who saw to its research and development that began in the middle of the First World War. His idea was for a portable, lightweight machine gun primarily geared for sweeping trenches on the battlefields of France by U.S. Expeditionary Forces. However, by the time the first production prototypes were slated for an unofficial delivery to the U.S. Army, the Armistice was signed on November 11, 1918. Even at this time, however, the final product was yet to be perfected and significant modifications were still on the table.

At the end of the war Auto-Ordnance Corporation immediately began to set its sights on other markets for what was to eventually become the Model 1921 Thompson submachine gun. This piece of late World War I technology was chambered for the .45-caliber Automatic Colt pistol cartridge. It was equipped with a sloped, detachable buttstock, angled vertical fore-end with finger grooves, barrel cooling fins, and adapted to either a 20-shot box or 50- and 100-round drum magazines. Cosmetically, it was a radical appearing firearm that some observers felt was too far ahead of its time. With the company's motto "On the Side of Law and Order," it was obvious that Auto-Ordnance intended to primarily zero in on the United States law enforcement trade.

The first and only run of 15,000 Model 1921 Thompsons were made under contract by Colt's Patent Firearms Company in Hartford, Conn., in a 16-month period during 1921 and 1922, and was expeditiously advertised and demonstrated both in the U.S.A. and abroad. Contrary to popular belief, the Thompson got off to a rocky start. It was considered by

Flanked by the 1923 Thompson catalog and copies of original Bureau of Investigation purchase orders (the predecessor of the FBI), a modern copy of the Model 1927 adds a touch of romanticism to the mystique of this world-renowned design.

The first full production Thompson submachine gun made by Colt Patent Firearms Company was the Model 1921. This variant was the basis of the Model 1927 modification simply because it was more cost effective to use existing inventory than to manufacture a completely new firearm. With 15,000 Model 1921 Thompson guns made, there were still plenty on hand to rebuild. Responsible for repair and modifications, Colt soon tired of Auto-Ordnance Corporation due to negative publicity in its direction, and would never make the Thompson again.
Photo courtesy of Tracie Hill.

both military and police officials as somewhat of a novelty that fit in a category between a rifle and pistol and offered selective fire in both full and semiautomatic. Even before completion of the 15,000 Thompson guns, many visualized that the effective handwriting of the future was already on the wall. Unfortunately for Auto-Ordnance, bad publicity would precede the good.

The first quantity purchase of 495 of the Model 1921 Thompson guns were delivered to anxiously awaiting American-based agents for the Irish Republican Army. To the chagrin of all parties concerned, they were seized by federal authorities who learned of the botched smuggling plot aboard a ship in Hoboken, N.J., bound for Ireland via Norfolk, Va. Although Auto-Ordnance was desperately seeking sales contacts, this affair temporarily became more than what was desired and was front page news in the New York papers. In spite of this, it is interesting to note that as early as 1920, pre-Colt prototypes of the Model 1921 (known at this time as the Model 1919) had been presented to police departments in New York City, Chicago, Cleveland and others for evaluation.

Purchases were minimal in the following three years. By 1925 sales of the Thompson were nowhere close to the expectations originally anticipated by Auto-Ordnance vice president, Marcellus Thompson (the son of John T. Thompson). Even with a high-powered, convincing sales campaign, the market for submachine guns was still a limited one with a mere 4,000 sold by 1926. The company was treading on bankruptcy.

On the flip side, scores of motorized bandits began plaguing the nation and violent foreign revolutions were sprouting up in the Spanish-speaking Americas. As a result, both American and military and police abroad, began to take another serious look at the Thompson gun. Its 800-900 rounds-per-minute rate of fire could easily deal with domestic armed criminals and troublemakers on foreign soil, making it unparalleled for the time.

Soon, various state and local police forces in Connecticut, Massachusetts, West Virginia and Illinois, as well as clients in Mexico and Cuba, commenced purchasing them in conservative quantities. The U.S. Post Office even bought 250 Model 1921 Thompson guns in 1926 to deal with a rash of robberies in the crime-ridden post WWI era.

Interestingly, the Marine Corps was tasked with guarding the U.S. mail, and in turn were later allowed to retain a number of the Postal Service Thompson guns when the Marines were ordered to deploy a force to deal with political agitators in Nicaragua in 1926-27. U.S. Marine after-action reports on the Thompson's efficiency noted the guns had performed admirably in the guerilla-infested jungles of Central America and continued to do so during the various "banana wars" in other locations, such as Haiti. The Thompson was also hailed by the Marines protecting U.S. interests in Shanghai in 1932.

Earlier on, the Marine Corps, along with the U.S. Navy, pushed for limited adoption of the Thompson, providing that Auto-Ordnance would re-design the action to reduce its rate of fire to a more manageable 600 to 700 rounds per minute. The end result was the U.S. Navy

A very rare sight, indeed, is this view of the original, and very scarce, Colt Model 1927 Thompson. It can plainly be seen where the Model 1921 markings were machined over in order to create this semiautomatic-only version. The lightly countersunk "Model of 1927" and "Thompson Semi-Automatic Carbine" re-stampings vividly show this. In addition, the word "full" was machined over, just adjacent to the front selector paddle. With only an estimated 50 guns assembled, it is truly a key piece for a serious Thompson collector. Practically all but forgotten, it took nearly 47 years to finally see it recreated.
Photo courtesy of Tracie Hill.

Model of 1928 that was modified from existing Model 1921 Thompson guns in stock, with a heavier bolt actuator to accomplish this reduction. In addition, the vertical fore-end was replaced with a far more durable, finger grooved, horizontal type. Incidentally, the U.S. Coast

Guard also purchased the Model 1928 for dealing with coastal rumrunners. In the late 1920s, however, another question surfaced regarding the Thompson in its full-automatic mode; a safety issue so to speak. The Auto-Ordnance Corporation received feedback that some American law enforcement organizations were apprehensive in issuing the Model 1921 to rank and file patrolmen not thoroughly trained with such arms, simply because some inexperienced officers did not know when to let go of the trigger.

Enter the Model 1927

In the early 1960s, author William J. Helmer corresponded with longtime Auto-Ordnance employee George Goll, and among the topics was the reasoning behind the creation of a semiautomatic-only version of the Thompson gun. According to Mr. Goll, there was hardly any notable discussion of this among the Auto-Ordnance staff in the late 1920s. However, it did become a reality when a decision was made to take the fully automatic Model 1921 and create the Model 1927 Thompson Semi-Automatic Carbine. Aside from factory broadsheets issued in late 1928, it is believed to have been officially unveiled in the highly illustrated Auto-Ordnance catalog of 1929, and was first coined the Model 1927 "Anti-Bandit Gun." Again, no historical background information in early Auto-Ordnance factory records provides details on the hows and whys of this new addition.

Mechanically speaking, what made the arm unique from the selective-fire Model 1921 was the altering of the rocker and rocker pivot by which the paddle selector remained only in the "single fire" or semiautomatic position. Externally, the Model of 1921 markings were machined over and remarked "Model of 1927" along with "Thompson Semi-Automatic Carbine" stamped over the machined-out markings "Thompson Sub-Machine Gun" located on the left receiver side. Though Colt management had washed their hands of any future production after their first and only contract of 15,000 of the Model 1921, they were apparently responsible for the repair of existing guns, and obviously undertook modification of transforming it into a semiauto-only version. From about 1925, Colt sorely wished to distance themselves from Auto-Ordnance once the news media's stream of negative publicity began stereotyping the Thompson's "gangster affiliation" during Prohibition on a

regular basis, especially since it wore the Colt hallmark on its frame.

Of worthy mention is the fact that from 1921 to 1936, practically all Auto-Ordnance catalogs gave a rundown of which state, local and international law enforcement organizations had purchased the Thompson gun along with photographs. The 1929 catalog in particular has a captioned illustration showing a guard at New York's Sing Sing prison carrying the semiautomatic Thompson Model 1927 at sling arms. Other known state institutions that purchased it included the Montana State Prison at Deer Lodge, and the Clinton Prison at Dannemora, N.Y. In regression, other former Auto-Ordnance staff members interviewed by Helmer (along with George Goll), bluntly stated the Model 1927 was a total flop and surviving sales records positively reflect that. The fact that very few were ordered or even assembled can be proven by the number of examples in the hands of modern-day collectors and museums. Original Auto-Ordnance documentation indicates a mere 42 Model 1927 Semi-Automatic Carbines had been sold by 1934, with modern Thompson historians almost certain that no more than 50 were assembled in all.

Keep in mind that the Thompson was never an inexpensive firearm, and most factory literature listed the Model 1927AC Anti-Bandit Gun at $200 with Cutts Compensator, and the Model 1927A without the compensator at $175. The Cutts Compensator located on the muzzle, helped reduce climb of the Thompson during full-automatic fire and was a valuable extra; on the semiautomatic Model 1927, however, it was a rather useless addition. In realistic terms, all Thompson guns were probably some of the most overbuilt American firearms that were embellished with features that were otherwise unnecessary for such an arm of its intended purpose. In a nutshell, the pre-existing Colt manufactured Model 1921 was the basic organ donor for modification of the Model 1927 Semi-Automatic Carbine and the later Model 1928 series of submachine guns. Finely finished high-quality walnut stocks complimented by beautiful Colt quality blued frames and barrels, roll stamped markings on the upper frame along with precision windage adjustable Lyman rear sights with raised leaf, seemed more at home on a fine sporting rifle. In essence, it was no more than a product of high-handed over-expenditure, all footed by the Auto-Ordnance Corporation's inves-

tor, Mr. Thomas Fortune Ryan; but such elegance nevertheless fit perfectly into the period of the Roaring Twenties.

The last known Auto-Ordnance catalog to offer the Model 1927 was the 1936 edition, which interestingly reflected identical prices from the 1929 and 1934 catalogs. Of worthy mention, most surviving Model 1927 Thompson semiautomatic carbines show evidence that the rocker pivots in the fire control system were converted back to the selective-fire mode. All in all, an original, untouched, factory correct, semiautomatic Model 1927 is quite scarce and can reap prices well into five figures. Due to this capability of being readily converted back to full automatic, an original Model 1927 Thompson today still requires registration with the Bureau of Alcohol, Tobacco, Firearms and Explosives as a Class III firearm, along with the $200 transfer tax stamp.

The Rise and Fall of the Thompson "Trench Broom"

Retired U.S. Army Brigadier General John T. Thompson was very fortunate to have a circle of friends who knew people with money to help make his dream of a light, portable, fully automatic "trench broom" a reality. Without having secured a $1,000,000 chattel mortgage from the wealthy New York investor Thomas F. Ryan, the story of the Thompson submachine gun might never have come off the drawing board. Ryan's itemized investment included all research and development work, advertising and payroll, all commencing in 1916 into actual production by Colt in 1921. It is important to note that in the beginning, the Auto-Ordnance Corporation had no real property – no offices, no bank accounts, nor any assets whatsoever. Financially, it relied solely on operating funds in the form of personal checks supplied by its investor that were made out to Auto-Ordnance's chief engineer, Theodore H. Eickhoff, who applied all monies into day-to-day business expenses. A year after Prohibition was enacted, the Model 1921 Thompson submachine gun began rolling off Colt's assembly line, and a lucrative future for this revolutionary new firearm seemed to be anticipated.

Problems for Auto-Ordnance's vice president Marcellus Thompson soon surfaced in June 1921 following the aforementioned sales of submachine guns to Irish Republican Army purchasers, and again in later years when the Thompson gun fell into domestic criminal hands. A great deal of Thomas F. Ryan's money was spent on demonstrating and promoting the Thompson gun worldwide, but the sales persuasion at any cost using other people's money was slow to reach the expected profit margins. The first four years were disappointing for Auto-Ordnance, but when business picked up in 1926-29, the horizon appeared much brighter. However, what really hurt sales of the Thompson was the Depression of 1929, and more so, the death of Thomas F. Ryan that same year. Ryan's heirs never really approved of his involvement in the arms business, nor were they impressed with Marcellus Thompson heading the company.

The Ryan estate forced Thompson out of the management chain and installed their own people to run what remained of Auto-Ordnance assets. The Thompson family and their associates were suddenly reduced to minority stockholders. The Ryan family with their agents, Federal Laboratories of Pittsburgh, continued to sell the leftover stock of all Thompson guns and parts that remained in storage at the Colt factory in Hartford. From 1930 on, they wanted to quickly dispose of the company, of which by 1938 saw 4,700 of the original 15,000 Colt Thompson guns still in inventory. In 1939, the Ryan estate sold Auto-Ordnance to Connecticut industrialist Russell Maguire for $529,000.

A near broken man, Marcellus Thompson died of a stroke that same year, with John T. Thompson passing away in 1940. Russell Maguire took the company into World War II where the Thompson submachine gun finally gained its deserving reputation, and of course the rest is history. After the war, however, there was practically no interest in this now very obsolete piece of first-generation technology of its kind. Moreover, the Thompson Model 1927 Semi-Automatic Carbine was almost completely forgotten.

Numrich Arms and the Return of the M1927

For nearly six years following World War II, the Auto-Ordnance inventory was a stagnant subsidiary of Maguire Industries, with no market for this long obsolete submachine gun, an antique at best. Maguire was anxious to sell Auto-Ordnance as he had long since made his money off the venture. The corporation existed once again as nothing more than boxed up, crated assets of parts and prototype guns, including 86 complete Thompson guns also in storage. But, out of the blue in 1949 Maguire received an offer from one-time toy gunmaker Kilgore Manufacturing Company that quickly bought Auto-Ordnance for the fire sale price of $385,000. Gross miscalculations by the Kilgore company saw them want-

ing to unload A.O.C. as soon as possible. They succeeded in selling it in 1951 at an even lower bargain price to one-time Auto-Ordnance executive Frederick A. Willis. That same year Willis sold it to the Numrich Arms Corporation in Mamaroneck, N.Y., a now well-known company which has since been re-designated as Gun Parts Corporation located today in West Hurley, N.Y.

The new owner of Auto-Ordnance Corporation, George Numrich, suddenly became the world's source for those wishing to find parts or to have their Thompson submachine guns repaired and serviced. On request, Numrich also built new Thompson guns from scratch, using old, original Auto-Ordnance parts for customers desiring to purchase the real deal. Realistically, the Thompson was not for everybody, thus sales were never that profitable. In the late 1950s, Numrich pondered remanufacturing a legal-to-own, semiautomatic version that could be had by anyone. The plan to carry this out was very slow in getting off the ground as it would take a great deal of experimentation, but all too often, Numrich considered his gun parts business a far higher priority. Finally in the mid-1960s, Numrich assigned two employees, Bill Kaye and Werner Vogel, to make an attempt at building a modified M1927 using existing, original Auto-Ordnance parts. It would have to meet BATF specifications as a

The right frame on the West Hurley made Model 1927 Semi-Automatic Thompson has the Auto-Ordnance address, along with the original Thompson patent markings. Note the older West Hurley style bolt handle on top was a non-original, cylindrical-type affair made for ease of efficiency in pulling back the heavy resistance of the double-spring operated bolt.

legal, not convertible to full automatic, semiauto .45-caliber carbine. By the fall of 1967 they had a prototype design that was unveiled at several gun shows and sporting exhibitions.

The reception by the shooting public was phenomenal, but it wouldn't be until late 1974 when all became a reality. That same year, longtime Numrich employee Ira Trast bought a portion of the Auto-Ord-nance subsidiary from George Numrich. A new plant was built on the land that Numrich leased, and soon saw the set up of all assembly operations while awaiting BATF approval on a new design of the .45-caliber Model 1927 semiautomatic.

It was on the second try that every-thing began rolling. On March 20, 1975, a letter from the BATF was received approving the internally redesigned new sample and thus began the "second generation" of the Thompson Model 1927. After a hiatus of 40-plus years, a now fully legal variation was born. Catalogued as the Model 1927A1 Thompson Semi Automatic Carbine, it was at first offered in both a Deluxe and Standard variation. Each featured the classic Thompson roll-stamped, marked receiver, but clearly indicated it was manufactured by Auto-Ordnance in West Hurley, N.Y.,

and not Hartford, Conn. The Deluxe Model included the classic cooling fins on the barrel, with some original surplus and remanufactured copies of the Cutts Compensator, and provisions for only a "safe" and (semiautomatic) "fire" selector on the lower fire control group.

The Standard Model was supplied with the horizontal, 1928-style fore-end, and was made without cooling fins or the compensator. However, two noticeable cosmetic differences from the earlier 1920s variant were obvious — a nondetachable buttstock and a legal 16.5-inch barrel length. The internals of the new M1927A1, however, presented a whole different ball game as compared to the old Colt-made original. The BATF practically demanded that this new version must not fire from an open bolt like the original Thompson guns. Thus, an entirely unique closed bolt, blowback firing system was implemented with the sear connecting directly to rear of the firing pin, as opposed to the original where the sear held the open bolt in the ready to fire position. Such an arrange-ment prevented readily converting the M1927A1 to full-automatic fire.

The new product was well received and advertised in the elegant, textured

beige and white West Hurley Auto-Ordnance catalogs that presented a very nostalgic format. The catalog listed several accessories including an optional vertical fore-end, classical carrying equipment such as a violin case, as well as a replica of the classy FBI hard case. In addition, original Thompson 20- and 30-round magazines were available, as well as a new Type XL 39-round drum magazine. Noteworthy is that the maga-zine stop on the 1927A1 was larger than on original Thompson guns, requiring enlargement of the engagement hole on the spine of older surplus Thompson magazines. This modification was under-taken by the factory in West Hurley.

From 1975 to 1990, it appears there were various quality control issues for the Thompson Model 1927A1 warrant-ing further improvement. One of the most commonly noted was that several bugs regarding firing pin designs should have been eliminated at the onset of production. Complaints of firing pin breakage forced Auto-Ordnance to redesign the bolt face on two occasions to alleviate the problem. In all, there were three types of firing pins fitted to the West Hurley Thompson Model 1927 series throughout its 24-year production. By 1990, the company settled on its "Type 3" pin that had a solid nub milled on the nose of the firing pin bar that appeared to solve the breakage problems. The author, having spoken with former Numrich employees involved in production of the 1927A1, was told that manufacturing of most components of this arm was farmed out to different subcontractors, and then were merely fitted and assembled by the West Hurley plant. Furthermore, the use of out-of-date tools such as bench grinders and other older equipment was commonplace.

In 1977, Auto-Ordnance introduced a pistol variation of the Model 1927A1 that was catalogued as the Model 1927A5 Thompson Semi-Automatic Pistol. This new addition is, and was, perhaps as close to the old originals by virtue of a shorter 13-inch barrel and was produced sans buttstock, with no provision to attach one to the lower frame. To do so would put the pistol in the "short-barrel rifle" category, requiring federal registration. The barrel length of all early Thompson guns was 10.5 inches, thus the Thompson M1927A5 barrel still exceeded the length of the genuine Prohibition-era variants. Made without the Cutts Com-pensator, the '27A5 almost resembled the

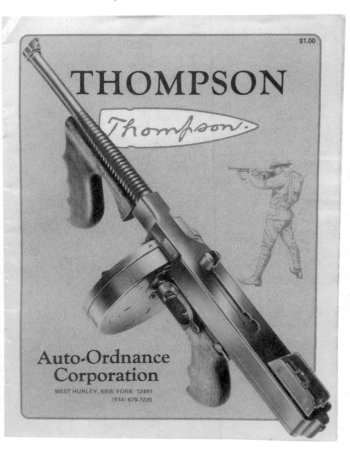

Until the early 1990s, Auto-Ordnance of West Hurley, N.Y., supplied very nostalgic factory literature that was reminiscent of catalogs issued during the 1920s. This 1979 edition of textured white and beige features the Thompson Model 1927A5 on the cover.

THOMPSON

Thompson.

Auto-Ordnance Corporation

WEST HURLEY, NEW YORK 12491
(914) 679-7225

$1.00

The author found that the offhand, two-hand hold with the '27A5 Thompson Semi-Automatic Pistol produced impressively tight groups at 25 yards using the Winchester-Western .45 Auto 230-grain standard roundnose cartridge. Both the new Kahr and the older West Hurley Thompson Model 1927A1 should be used with standard G.I. hardball ammunition to preclude jams and hang-ups between the magazine and feed ramp. Original, early Thompson guns were designed solely for this cartridge. Photo courtesy of Shawn Kelly.

old Thompson Model 1919 that preceded the Model 1921, and was originally made without a buttstock. At 6¾ pounds, with an even lighter than normal aluminum alloy upper frame, essentially made the 1927A5 a two-handed pistol. Offhand accuracy is chancy at best, but fired from the hip using instinctive point fire shows impressive results. To compound this, loaded with a full 39-round or an original 50-round drum magazine makes it prohibitively overweight for anything but, again, two paws!

Few modern owners of West Hurley 1927A1 Thompson guns realized that many original parts left over from George Numrich's 1951 acquisition of Auto-Ordnance Corporation were used throughout production from 1975 to the late 1990s. Approximately 932 first-year production Deluxe Model 1927A1 Thompsons have the surplus, original Lyman rear sights, which today are very expensive. These beautifully made precision sights are marked with the Lyman address as well. It was only until

they were exhausted and a reproduction was manufactured and installed on the remainder of 1927A1 production. The workmanship of the new rear sight was not up to the qualities of the Lyman-made example.

There was yet another addition to the West Hurley Auto-Ordnance semiautomatic line – the .22 rimfire Model 1927A3. Introduced in 1979, it was made of ultralight alloys with a slightly undersize frame. Intended for those who wished to have a Thompson that digested far

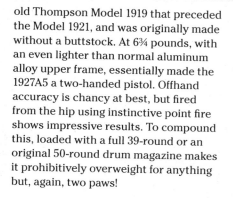

This is the Auto-Ordnance Thompson Model 1927A5 with 20-round magazine, produced in West Hurley from 1977 to 1995. Manufacturing was terminated due to the 1994 Assault Weapon Ban because its 13-inch barrel, weight and other restrictions found it included among weapons on the banned list. Those made prior to the 1995 cut-off date are grandfathered in by federal law.

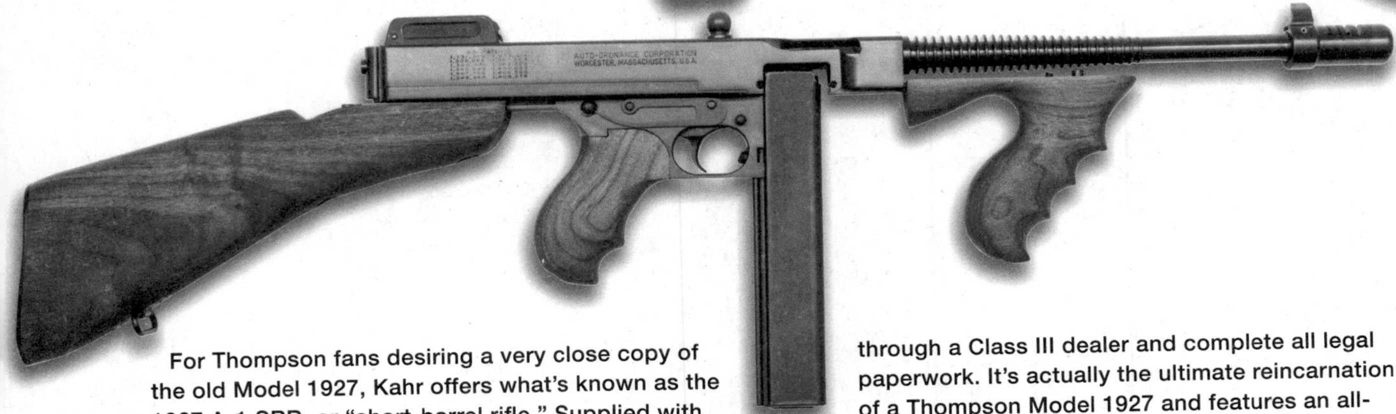

For Thompson fans desiring a very close copy of the old Model 1927, Kahr offers what's known as the 1927 A-1 SBR, or "short-barrel rifle." Supplied with a 10½-half inch barrel and detachable buttstock, it's as close to the real thing that one will ever find made today. The only catch is the buyer must go through a Class III dealer and complete all legal paperwork. It's actually the ultimate reincarnation of a Thompson Model 1927 and features an all-steel frame. Some states prohibit short-barrel rifles entirely, so one must check their state laws before purchasing.

more inexpensive fodder, it was sold with a very unoriginal appearing 30-shot curved banana contour magazine, and weighed less than 7 pounds. A 120-round drum magazine was also available at extra cost. Reports from many indicate it had a limited popularity with several mechanical issues as time went on. Though it is beyond the scope of this story, Auto-Ordnance also introduced a semiautomatic version of the World War II M-1 Thompson that had a side-mounted bolt handle just like its ances-tor. Physically, it too practically copied the original – except for the 16.5-inch barrel and closed bolt action.

It was in the mid-1990s that the West Hurley era of Auto-Ordnance slowly came to an end. The only one of the series to be discontinued for legal complications was the Thompson Model 1927A5 Semi-Automatic Pistol. Purposely made with the 13-inch barrel to meet the overall length requirement of 26 inches, it abruptly fell into the BATF's "Any Other Weapon" category 17 years after introduction. The 1994 Assault Weapons Ban put the screws to continued production of the '27A5 as it did not comply with the new length and weight criteria as a pistol, as well having a detachable magazine ahead of the triggerguard along with a vertical fore-end. However, those guns produced before the 1995 cut-off date have been automatically grandfathered in by federal law. Production of West Hurley manufactured Model 1927 Thompson guns were discontinued in 1997. But,

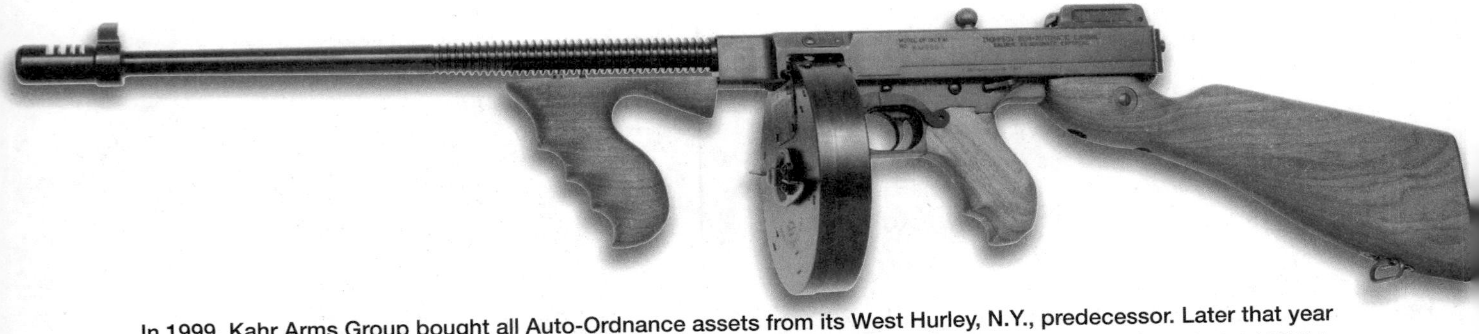

In 1999, Kahr Arms Group bought all Auto-Ordnance assets from its West Hurley, N.Y., predecessor. Later that year it introduced most of the variants of the former company. This included the well-established Deluxe Model 1927A1, in a lightweight version, and also with a detachable buttstock. Unlike the earlier company, Kahr had a complete machine shop with up-to-date equipment to manufacture all components, since few original Auto-Ordnance parts remained. Production has continued in Worcester, Mass.

Photo courtesy of Tracie Hill and Kahr Arms Group.

The lightweight Kahr Arms Thompson 1927TA5 Semi-Automatic Pistol is a re-introduction of the old West Hurley Model 1927A5, and joined the Kahr line in the mid-2000s. The catalog illustration shows many differences – such as the required legal, horizontal fore-end, original-style 10.5-inch barrel, rear sling swivel on the rear of the frame, and the unique addition of the WWII-era M1 Thompson sight protector ears. The original Thompson-style upper bolt handle appears far more authentic than what was found on the West Hurley versions.
Photo courtesy of Kahr Arms Group.

The 20- and 30-round magazines, and the 50-round drum magazine were standard for early Thompson guns, just as they are for the new Kahr Arms M1927A1 series and the older West Hurley guns. The 30-round Thompson magazine, however, was a product of World War II production arms. Though not shown, Kahr offers an exact reproduction of the 1920s-era 100-round drum as well. Fully loaded, it puts the overall weight of the '27A1 carbine at about 14 pounds.

they would not be off the market for very long.

Kahr Continues the Legend

Due to lack of in-house manufacturing capability, not to mention that pre-existing original surplus Thompson parts were beginning to dry up, Auto-Ordnance Corporation of West Hurley, N.Y., was sold to Kahr Arms of Blauvalt, N.Y., in 1999. It was apparently a cost-

effective move for the West Hurley firm to sell the company as they envisioned that being forced to outsource all parts and components would cause retail prices of the 1927A1 to become far out of reach for average buyers. Early that same year, existing equipment and inventory was moved from New York to Kahr's production facility in Worcester, Mass.

Engineers at Kahr Arms Group were determined not to make the same mistakes made during the West Hurley

years. Some improvements upon the older versions began immediately, and production of the 1927A1 commenced in late 1999. Most importantly, a new durable, short stem, firing pin tip of thicker diameter was introduced and has remained the standard to this day. From past experiences the author has concluded – they do not break!

In the beginning, Kahr continued to manufacture all of the catalogued versions of the Thompson 1927A1 as sold by

The author, shown here back in 1986 firing his A.O. Deluxe Model 1927A1, has long been a fan of the legal-to-own Thompson since its introduction. Its practicality has some limitations, but to the more nostalgically inclined, it will forever be the ultimate classic among American firearms. Photo courtesy of George J. Layman Sr.

their predecessor, and slowly expanded the line to nine different models. One cosmetic addition that Kahr added is the original-style bolt knob of the older Thompson guns. The West Hurley series was supplied with a non-original, cylindrical-type affair that always appeared somewhat out of place. What's more exciting is that Kahr even had a fully legal version of the old West Hurley Model 1927A5 Thompson Pistol back on board. In order to meet BATF specifications as a pistol, the barrel was shortened to the same 10.5 inches of the original Thompson guns, and the weight was further reduced with a lighter aluminum space-age alloy frame. Catalogued by Kahr as the Thompson 1927A1 Deluxe Pistol TA5, the primary feature that puts into the legal category as a pistol is its 1928-style horizontal fore-end. To maintain legal status, it cannot be swapped out with the older 1927A1/A5 Thompson-style vertical front grip. To do so would deem it illegal as a handgun.

In addition to offering both a full and lightweight version of the standard 1927A1 Thompson Semi-Automatic Carbine, there is also a nostalgic variation with the old original-style detachable buttstock. Going a step further, they have reintroduced authentic copies of the 50- and 100-round drum magazines that are mechanically true to the first generation original. But, Kahr has not stopped there. If the true Thompson aficionado wishes to spend a few more bucks, one can purchase the ultimate reincarnation of the old Model 1927 – a "Short Barrel Rifle" version with the original 10½-inch tube, Cutts Compensator and detachable buttstock. Actually, Kahr introduced this concurrently with a fixed stock configuration as well. Listed as their Thompson 1927A-1 SBR, one must be certain to understand that again, a short-barrel rifle must be processed and transferred through a Class III license holder. The catalog specifies the factory will work directly with authorized dealers for such transactions.

There is one point to be reiterated, and that is that Kahr no longer services any of the older West Hurley manufactured 1927 Thompson guns, as all have warranties that long since expired. For those who need to have their West Hurley Thompsons serviced, they would do well to contact Las Cruces, N.M., gunsmith Tom Hanson at hudsontradingpost.com. A former Numrich employee, he is very well versed on repair of the older family of the Model 1927A1/A5 Thompson guns.

From a quality control standpoint, we are quite fortunate that Kahr Arms has kept the workmanship and true tradition of this now third generation example of the Thompson Model 1927 on par with its original ancestor. No, you may not be getting black walnut figured stocks, Lyman sights or early Colt blue finish from years gone by. But, you will have the very best in today's legal recreation of one of the most recognizable firearms of all time.

BIBLIOGRAPHY:
The Gun That Made the Twenties Roar, William J. Helmer, 1969, The Gun Room Press, Highland Park, N.J.
Auto Ordnance Corporation Catalogs 1923, 1929, 1934 and 1936 Editions; Auto Ordnance Corporation Catalogs (West Hurley, NY) 1979 and 1980' Auto Ordnance Corporation Catalogs (Kahr Arms Group) 5th and 6th Editions.
A very special thanks goes out to Thompson author Tracie Hill and to Frank Harris of Kahr Arms Group for providing information and assistance.

WEST HURLEY AUTO ORDNANCE MODEL 1927 THOMPSON		
MODEL	**YEARS OF PRODUCTION**	**SERIAL NUMBERS**
M1927A1 Semi-Automatic Carbine		
Deluxe and Standard	1975 to 1997	1 to 29,585
Model 1927A3 Semi-Automatic Carbine		
Deluxe and Standard	1978 to 1995	T9 to T5444 (.22 rimfires had a T prefix)
Model 1927A5 Semi-Automatic		
Pistol	1977 to 1995	100P to 3359P (All had a P suffix)

THOMPSON–LYMAN REAR SIGHT

By **Jerry L. Jacobson**

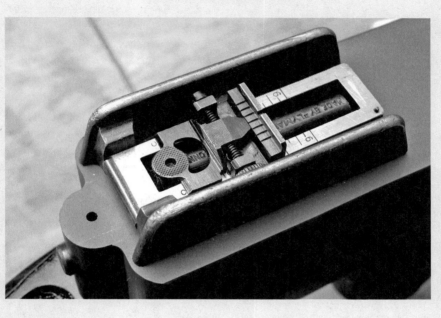

Much has been written about the Thompson submachine gun, and one of the most distinguishing features of the earlier models, including many of the military contract M1928 and M1928A1s, is the rear sight. Everyone calls it the Lyman sight, which makes some sense since the base of each one is conspicuously marked:

"MADE BY "LYMAN" MIDDLEFIELD CONN U.S.A."

In fact, though, the Lyman Company was only the manufacturer and was not the designer; the sight was designed by Theodore H. Eickhoff, who was responsible for much of the design of the gun. In other words, the sight was an original Thompson design – not a Lyman design. But, for a submachine gun sight, it was unique in at least one respect: it was designed as if it were to be used for competitive target shooting and not as if it were to be used in combat at submachine gun ranges.

In the beginning, the Thompson didn't have *any* sights, front or rear. When the hooked actuator handle was replaced with the centrally mounted knob, the groove in the knob was designed to function as a rear sight as described in patent number 1,338,866, filed on May 4, 1920, by Oscar Payne. This patent describes a "centrally located combined actuator and rear sight." The slot in the actuator knob was intended from the beginning to serve as the rear sight. The actuator slot would have been quite adequate as a rear sight within the confines of a trench, which was the original intended use of the gun. Figure 1 shows what the gunner would have seen using the actuator slot as his sight on a gun also equipped with a front sight.

It wasn't very long before the gun designers went to work to create a proper rear sight for the gun, and the result was the famous

FIG. 1

Figure 1: Actuator knob used as rear sight.

Thompson-Lyman rear sight. The sight patent was granted on Feb. 28, 1922, and its number is 1,408,276. This number can be found as the last number engraved in the right-hand column on the right rear of the receiver. Some current dummy receivers also display this patent number in its correct location.

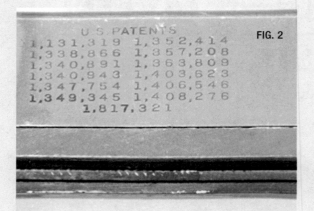

Figure 2: Patent numbers on the receiver.

Design

Gun writers always note how well designed and well manufactured the Thompson- Lyman sight is, but it possesses some unique or even odd features that probably reflect its having been designed by Auto-Ordnance engineers and not by the Lyman Company, which already had long experience in the design of small arms sights.

As with many other adjustable military sights, the Thompson sight offers more than one sighting option, including the adjustable folding leaf assembly and a simpler, nonadjustable battle sight. The battle sight consists of a small square notch to be used when the sight leaf is in its lowered position. When this sight is used with a conventional sight picture (more on this later), the gun will hit its point of aim at 50 yards. By modern standards, the battle sight is much too small for quick target acquisition or low-light use, although this was common to a large proportion of rifle sights of its era.

Figure 3: Tiny battle sight notch.

The adjustable elements of the sight are more interesting. The top end of the folding sight leaf is grooved, apparently to provide a better gripping surface when raising the leaf. The leaf is graduated from 0 to 600 yards, with additional reference marks between the 100-yard increments. Some sights were calibrated from 0 to 600 *meters* for some foreign buyers. The word "meter" is marked on the leaf. When elevated, sighting is done through an aperture instead of a notch, and the position of the aperture is adjustable vertically for range and horizontally for zeroing.

Although the leaf is graduated to 600 yards, one of the peculiarities of the Thompson- Lyman sight is that the range cannot be set at 600. The longest range the sight can be set at is 550 yards. This does not seem to have been noted by any of the many commentators on the Thompson, although the trajectory and drift data in the original manuals all stop at 500 yards. And at another point in U.S. Army Field Manual FM 23-40, it is indicated that the gun should not be used beyond 500 yards.

Another unusual feature of the sight leaf is the correlation between the elevation serrations machined onto the left side of the sight leaf and the distance graduations on the front of the sight. Most folding leaf military sights have notches that correspond to the distance graduations on the front of the sight leaf. The Thompson, instead, simply provides a column of finely but uniformly spaced notches about .02

Figure 4: Sight set at maximum range.

inch apart that are not coordinated with the range markings. A spring-mounted stud on the movable sight slide engages one of these fine notches to retain the slide at the desired elevation. In practice, the fine cut of the serrations does not prevent the operator from setting the sight close to a specific desired distance, but it does make it easy to slip into a notch or two above or below the desired distance, especially under stressful conditions.

The square-notch open sight does not have any windage adjustment provision, sighted as it is at a very short range of 50 yards. The aperture sight does have a windage adjustment, however, and the most interesting feature of this unusual sight is this adjustment. The aperture moves laterally for windage on the sight slide, which provides a series of seven evenly spaced reference marks. The marks are simply straight lines and have no numerical designation. The approximate distance between the marks is .075 inch. Refer to the photograph at the top of this article.

The windage adjustment screw has about 10½ turns from one extreme to the other, and there are about three turns from one windage reference mark to the next. There are no click stops to hold the windage screw in place or to assist with sighting. It is interesting to note that both commercial and military manuals include a table indicating right drift due to the rifling and provide some discussion of it, but do not indicate how to apply the information to the Thompson sight:

"b. Windage and Drift.—One point of windage will change the point of strike 1 foot at 100 yards. At ranges of 300 yards or more, lateral correction is also made for drift. The drift table shows drift to the right from line of bore with 230-grain bullet is as follows:"

Range in yards	Drift in Feet
50	0
100	.1
150	.25
200	.5
250	.85
300	1.4
350	2.3
400	3.25
450	4.5
500	5.9

Assuming that "1 point of windage" would be equal to 12 minutes of angle (1 minute of angle = 1 inch at 100 yards), none of the manuals explain how to translate that into sight settings. The meaning of the windage index marks is not defined, nor are the number of turns of the windage screw defined in terms of angle of fire. The data sounds nice and scientific, but is meaningless in application because it does not translate to specific sight adjustments. Moreover, although paragraph b. says "One point of windage will change the point of strike 1 foot at 100 yards," the table below indicates the drift will be only .1 foot at 100 yards. A mystery.

But the most intriguing feature of the sight is that there is no reference mark on the eyepiece index finger to allow the windage to be accurately reset to the same position or to allow the operator to gage the amount of deflection right or left required under windy conditions. The original Auto-Ordnance manual explains the idea behind this design, an idea worthy of the most demanding competitive shooter:

"The personal element of holding the gun greatly affects the accuracy of fire, and consequently there may be a considerable variation in hits when the same sight setting is use by different persons.

"The index line on the eyepiece to 'zero' for lateral adjustment is omitted in manufacture to allow for individual determination of this point. After this point has been satisfactorily determined, it is suggested that a line be placed on the index finger with a sharp knife or other sharp instrument."

The absence of an index mark can be seen in Figure 5. To put into perspective exactly how sophisticated this concept is, it is good to remember that at this time, throughout the Second World War and as late as the original U.S. M16 rifle, most infantry rifles did not have windage adjustments on the rear sight. Most had lateral adjustment of the front sight for zeroing, but this adjustment was rarely used after the piece left the factory. This situation extended a *fortiori* to submachine guns.

The eyepiece index finger of the sight is divided into two parts, an upper part that is smooth and a lower section that is grooved, prob-

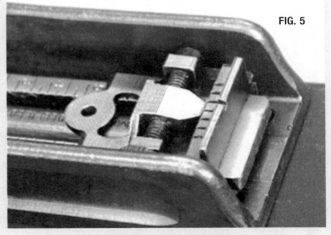

FIG. 5

Figure 5: The index finger.

ably to reduce reflective glare. According to the original A.O. instructions, the person to whom the gun was assigned was supposed to sight the gun in to his own requirements, just as competitive shooters do, and then make a scratch or other mark on the clear area of the index finger to indicate the shooter's individual windage zero. (The author has seen very few Thompson-Lyman sights with any windage zero marking on the index finger, so apparently this refined feature was little used.)

The Original Auto Ordnance Instructions

To make some sense out of the Thompson-Lyman sight, let's look first at the instructions from the original Auto-Ordnance Corporation Handbook, First Edition of 1940, page 12:

"For rapid firing with the sight leaf down a 50-yard open sight is provided (Point Blank).

The sight is graduated up to 600 yards for the 230-grain bullet cartridge. With tracer ammunition very good results can be secured up to the 600 yards range. The extreme accurate range of the weapon is 600 yards with this standard ammunition."

Later, the A.O. manual refines this specification:

"Caliber .45 tracer ammunition can be used in conjunction with the 230-grain bullet to indicate ranging of shots at the longer ranges from 350 to 600 yards." (page 24)

It becomes clear that A.O. is telling the user that the 600-yard range is practical only with tracer ammunition mixed in with ball, and that the practical range using ball ammunition alone is about 300 yards.

The Fine Sight

The natural tendency of all automatic rifles is to raise the muzzle; that of the average marksman is to shoot high; consequently the submachine gun should be sighted slightly low with a fine sight (the top of the front sight just appearing in the bottom of the peep or open sight) in order to obtain maximum accurate results. The slightly upward and

FIG. 6

Figure 6: Simplified Thompson sight.

to the right tendency of this gun, especially during automatic fire, can be corrected by a small amount of practice on the part of the gunner, in holding steady. (A.O. 1940 First Edition, page 13.)

The idea of the "fine" sight is important, since the military manuals pick it up later but do not explain it as did the original A.O. manual. It is also important because modern sighting practices contradict it.

The modern standard for sighting with iron sights is as follows:

The front sight is centered in the rear sight notch, and the top of the front sight is level with the top of the rear sight notch. For peep (aperture) sights, the top of the front sight is level with the center of the aperture.

However, the "fine" sight picture, as described in the original Thompson manual, has the front sight just barely visible in the bottom of the notch or aperture.

The Second Generation Thompson-Lyman Sight

As fine as it was, the original Thompson-Lyman rear sight required a great deal of manufacturing time and resources, which were in short supply after World War II began. So the sight went from what was undoubtedly the most sophisticated and misunderstood submachine gun sight to what was one of the absolute simplest. The new sight was a simple stamped L-shaped piece of sheet metal with two sighting options. One was a very small square open notch for use at about 250 yards, and the second was a small aperture set for 100 yards. No adjustment of any kind was available. This version also featured a checkered circular area on the rear face of the sight to reduce glare.

Two variations were manufactured. The earlier of the two was marked: "LYMAN MIDDLEFIELD, CONN. USA". The second variation was simply marked "LYMAN".

In spite of the Lyman name being on these stamped sights, however, when someone refers to the Lyman sight on the Thompson, they are always referring to the earlier adjustable sight.

Return To The Actuator Knob

The British manual for the Thompson submachine gun recognized the actuator slot as the proper rear sight for close combat. Figure 7, which is an illustration from that manual, shows the gun being aimed at a drawing of a German paratrooper. This illustration was so popular that it has shown up in a wide range of Thompson literature. It seems likely, though, that the authors of the British manual didn't actually try sighting with the actuator knob, since if a shooter brings his or her head down far enough to use the knob slot as a sight, the knob can't be seen. It is obstructed by the adjustable Thompson-Lyman rear sight, as shown in Figure 8, and Figure 9 shows how the later stamped rear sight also obstructs any view of the actuator knob slot. Oh well, so much for little details.

FIG. 8

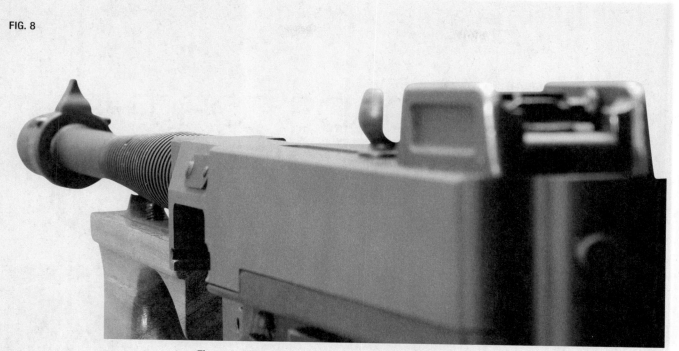

Figure 8: Adjustable sight blocks view of actuator knob.

Conclusion

The Thompson captured the imagination of the world soon after it was introduced, and that fascination persists today with a large body of collectors. There are good reasons for this: it was probably the first appearance of the configuration that is now nearly universal for handheld automatic small arms – vertical pistol grip, vertical magazine in front of the pistol grip, and separate vertical or horizontal fore-end.

FIG. 9

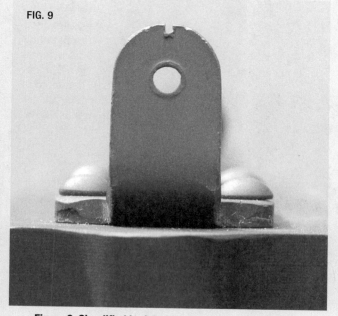

Figure 9: Simplified L-sight blocks view of actuator knob.

FIG. 7

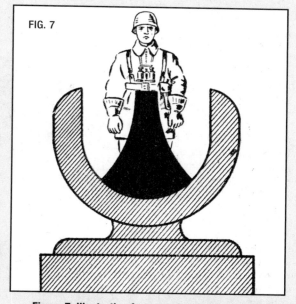

Figure 7: Illustration from wartime British manual.

The British innovation of locating the sling on top of the buttstock and on the left side of the fore-end was probably the very first appearance of the assault rifle sling concept. And there are other Thompson influences that have endured. But this article is just about the sights, in particular, the Thompson-Lyman adjustable rear sight. It is a beautifully machined device, but there are a number of unexplained mysteries about its design. We will probably never get to be privy to the thoughts of the designers, but the mysteries may be explainable by the fact that the designers were gun designers, not sight designers.

LIGHT LOADS FOR THE
.45-70

It's a shame the versatility of this grand old cartridge has been ignored by many and forgotten by most.

by **Roger Smith**

Dueling dual digital devices: Velocities reported are the average of the readings provided by a Shooting Chrony Alpha and a Gamma mounted in tandem, 10 feet from the muzzle.

For 20-plus years now, all of the emphasis on handloads for the .45-70 has seemed to be on the heaviest possible loads for use on the biggest, toothiest and nastiest-tempered beasts. That's all well and good, but when you light up one of those babies, you know you've set fire to something! How do you become smoothly proficient and confident with your rifle when all of the fun has gone out of it and the flinching begins by the time you've launched the third 500-grain dinosaur-dropper?

Reduced power practice loads using lightweight bullets and small powder charges are the obvious answer, of course, and have been for well over 115 years. I wanted to shoot cast bullets lighter than 300 grains at speeds near the traditional 1,340 fps range for 405-grain bullets. The goal was to enjoy plinking and practicing at 50 yards or less. I quickly discovered such loads are not easy to come by. Yes, Hodgdon publishes low power Trail Boss loads for 300- to 485-grain cast bullets, but those are not a satisfactory substitute for what we need.

Unfortunately, Lyman's molds for lightweight bullets were discontinued at least 50 years ago. They once offered four good candidates for the .45-70. Probably best known of the old lightweights is the 140- to 146-grain "collar button" bullet, 457130. The next best known is the Lyman 195- to 210-grain 457127 roundnose, which the 1897 Ideal Hand Book said, "has become very popular for light charge, small game, short range or gallery practice." In addition, there is (or was) the Himmelwright-looking 193-grain pointed nose wadcutter 456401/457401 intended for the .455 Webley, and the button-nosed wadcutter 457326. Rapine used to make nice collar button molds, numbers 458130 and 460130, but they closed up shop in 2009.

All loads were developed with a Marlin 1895XLR equipped with a 4x Leupold FX-II scope.

Fortunately, however, Lyman brought back the 457130 in 2014. Western Bullet Company (westernbullet.com) sells sized and lubed bullets cast with an original Lyman Ideal mold. I bought some unsized bullets from Western, which measure .459" at the front band and .458" at the rear; I used them as-cast. NEI (neihandtools.com) still offers a collar button mold, .458-150-PB #332C. Both of these designs are pointed bullets, which I wouldn't consider safe for use in a tube-fed gun, despite the low recoil of the loads.

In September 2010 I lucked into a group buy through castboolits.gunloads.com for a gorgeous four-cavity brass-collar button mold, the MP 460 Collar from MP Molds (MP-Molds.com). It took until February 2012 to receive it, but it was worth the wait. This modernization of the old design offers wider driving bands than the original 457130 for an even better grip on the rifling. Its 152-grain wheel-weight bullets measure .459" at the front band and .460" at the rear. In addition, it has a .105" meplat on its nose, making it safe to use in tubular magazines. I used them as-cast as well. MP Molds told me they had a few left, and if there is sufficient interest, they will make more.

In lieu of the unobtainable 457127, I was able to buy a short-lived variation and improved four-cavity version, a 462-210-PB mold from BRP Products shortly before they sold their machine shop business in 2011. It delivers very nice 220-grain bullets with a .125" meplat that fall from my mold at .462" when cast from BHN 12 wheel weights. The Marlin has a .457" bore, so I size them down a little bit to .460" with a custom Lee Lube and Sizing Kit.

I've never seen a 456401 or 457401 mold for sale, but was able to buy 100 nice 20:1 alloy bullets from Pb Boolits during their bottle-rocket-brief existence in 2011. Also, 457326 molds and bullets have been as elusive as Sasquatch. John at Western Bullet Co. says he actually had one in captivity for a while, and sent me a photo as evidence.

Top, Lyman 457130; Center, MP 460 Collar; Bottom, N.O.E. 460-186-CB.

From the left: Lyman 457130, MP 460 Collar, N.O.E. 460-186-CB.

Everything I shot, whether purchased or homemade, was lubricated with Liquid Xlox from White Label Lube Co. (lsstuff.com). It's very similar to what Lee sells in 4-ounce bottles as Liquid Alox, but comes in a quart bottle for $10.50.

I fired several groups with four holes touching, or nearly so, and a flyer spoiling the group. When Ken Waters wrote his ".45-70 Pet Loads" article for the May 1974 issue of *Handloader* dealing with both jacketed and cast bullets 300 grains and up, he reported, "...despite the utmost care, cast bullet groups frequently included one flyer that spoiled an otherwise good group of four shots." Some things just never change.

Prior to the 2014 resurrection of the 457130 collar button mold cut with new cherries, Lyman offered a run of 100 molds in 1999 cut with the old original cherry, with a data sheet for high-speed loads (up to 2,032 fps!). Other than that, the last time Lyman published reloading data for the 457130 and 457127 was in the first edition of their *Handbook of Cast Bullets* in 1958. Frank C. Barnes included loads for them and the 457401 in his 1973 *Gun Digest* 100th anniversary article about the .45-70. The fastest powder

Table 1

Charge (grains)	Lyman 1958 Estimated Velocity (fps)	Barnes 1973 Reported Velocity (fps)	Smith Recorded Velocity (fps)
457130 Bullet and Unique Powder			
5	900	—	679 (2012)
8	—	1350	972 (2012)
9	1200	—	1082 (2012)
14.5	1638 (2014)	—	1650 (2015)
17	1907 (2014)	—	1806 (2015)
457127 Bullet and Unique Powder (462–210–PB bullet)			
7	1100	888	868
7.5	—	—	905
8	—	—	932
10	—	1330	1096
12	1550	—	1278
13	—	—	1363
457401 Bullet and Unique Powder			
10	—	1330	—
12	—	—	1280

Table 2 – 457130 Bullet and Powder Charges and Velocities/Extreme Spreads

Powder weight (grains)	Unique	Red Dot	Bullseye	Clays	Trail Boss
			Velocities/Spreads (fps)		
5	679/105	770/77			
5.5					
6	797/88		1006/87		
6.5		1017/58	1085/36		
7		1059/75		937/64	923/91
7.5		1095/102		1044/64	943/56
8	972/61			1120/48	
8.5	1040/98				1065/61
9	1082/50		1385/38		1113/52
9.5					
10		1348/111	1482/36	1401/48	
10.5				1455/72	
11			1448/43		
11.5		1513/68			1288/65
12	1388/30				1376/74
12.5					
13					1460/55
13.5					1518/64
14					1550/72
14.5	1638/49				
17	1806/125				

listed from both sources was Unique.

My results with Unique were notably different from what Lyman estimated and Barnes reported. For example, Lyman estimated 1,550 fps using 12 grains with the 457127. I recorded only 1,278 fps with my 462-210-PB in the Marlin (and 1,295 fps with an H&R single-shot). Nonetheless, it shoots gratifyingly small groups. Its useful range is 10-13 grains of Unique. Other comparison results can be seen in Table 1.

If I weren't so darned curious, I could have quit right there. But then, I wouldn't have found several other loads that shoot such small groups that they're worth re-setting the sights, and we wouldn't have this article.

Low-pressure loads of Unique in any caliber leave too much soot and unburned powder in the barrel to suit me. Uninterested in belching fireballs of unburned rifle powders, I next went for pistol powders at the fast end of the scale for less "boom" at the muzzle. I chose Clays, Red Dot and Trail Boss for their bulkiness, and good ol' Bullseye; Winchester standard primers were used for everything.

A Hornady Lock-N-Load Auto Charge Powder Scale and Dispenser was used for all loads. Velocities were measured with Alpha and Gamma model Shooting Chronys mounted in tandem.

I started this project using a Lyman neck-sizing die on my mixed vintage, well-used WW cases, which were trimmed to 2.085", but later switched to a Lee sizing die because it sizes the cases .004" smaller at the neck. I used a Lee Powder Through Expanding Die, which flares the case neck, and the .455"-diameter Lyman neck expanding M die which comes as part of their .45-70 die set. When it became available, I switched to a .460"-diameter expander plug from N.O.E. Bullet Molds (noebulletmolds.com) designed to convert a Lee Universal Expanding Die

Illustration of the Ideal/Lyman 457127 from the *Lyman Cast Bullet Handbook*, 2nd Edition, left, compared to a photo of the BRP 462-210-PB design.

Table 3 – 462–210–PB Bullet and Powder Charges and Velocities/Extreme

Powder weight (grains)	Unique	Red Dot	Bullseye	Clays	Trail Boss
		Velocities/Spreads (fps)			
5		751/56			
5.5					
6		850/16		814/28	
6.5			1002/16		
7	868/28	950/18			
7.5	905/19	964/32		1039/29	
8	932/31	1060/42			
8.5					
9	990/55	1126/54			1020/55
9.5					
10	1096/28	1230/33			
10.5			1333/13		
11	1197/77	1282/31	1400/37	1333/13	
11.5				1360/41	
12	1278/60	1375/27			
12.5					1272/26
13	1363/58	1469/21			
13.5					1281/50
14					1339/22
14.5					1362/43
15					1415/31

A Hornady Lock-N-Load Auto Charge Powder Scale and Dispenser was used for all loads.

Table 5 – .45–70 Best Loads with Light Bullets

Lyman 457130 and MP 460 Collar	
12-14 grains Trail Boss	1376-1550 fps
10-10.5 grains Clays	1400-1455 fps
10-11.5 grains Red Dot	1348-1513 fps
9-11 grains Bullseye	1385-1448 fps

Lyman 457127 and BRP 462–210–PB	
10-13 grains Unique	1096-1363 fps
7.5 grains Clays	1039 fps
8-12 grains Red Dot	1060-1375 fps
9-14 grains Trail Boss	1020-1339 fps

Lyman 457401	
14 grains Trail Boss	1407 fps

N.O.E. 460–186–CB	
10 grains Bullseye	1394 fps
12.5 grains Unique	1364 fps
13 grains Clays	1572 fps
14 grains Trail Boss	1392 fps

to work like a Lyman M die for my .460" to .462" cast bullets. A Lyman seating die was necessary for these short bullets, and the 457401s received a separate roll crimp with a Lee die.

Powder charges are the same and there is no discernible on-target difference between the 457130 and the MP 460 Collar bullets, so you may never need to go beyond buying 457130s from Western

Table 4 – 460–186–PB Bullet and Powder Charges and Velocities/Extreme Spreads

Powder weight (grains)	Unique	Bullseye	Clays	Trail Boss
		Velocities/Spreads (fps)		
8.5				1015/81
9	1077/79			
9.5				1070/80
9.6	1086/73			
10		1394/36		
12.5	1364/76			
13			1572/49	
14				1392/28
14.5				1469/47

Bullet. The single outstanding load of this whole test was 13 grains of Trail Boss with either version of this bullet; its useful range seems to be 12-14 grains. I also got excellent results using 10 and 11½ grains of both Clays and Red Dot, and 9-11 grains of Bullseye. They all shot 1½-3 inches high and slightly right at 50 yards, but it would be worth re-adjusting the sights or scope. Velocities ran in the 1,335-1,480 fps range. The 462-210-PB bullet mentioned earlier also shoots very well using 7.5 grains of Clays, 8-12 grains of Red Dot and 9-14 grains of Trail Boss.

Since I had so few 195-grain 457401s, I started with the very best loads for the 462-210-PBs, and tested only three rounds each instead of five. Unique and Trail Boss showed promise, and the clear winner was 14 grains of Trail Boss at 1,407 fps, delivering frequent near-cloverleafs.

About the time I figured I was finished with this article, I discovered N.O.E. had come up with a new version of the collar button bullet, which was not available when I began the project. Their 460-186-CB gains its extra weight within the same outer dimensions by having a much shallower lube groove.

The 457130, dating from the 1890s, has a wasp-waisted lube groove with an inner diameter of .283" to hold a huge amount of grease for use with the filthy burning low-pressure black-powder loads recommended back then. The MP 460 Collar has a flat-bottomed lube groove with an inner diameter of .274". It holds even more lube, which is totally unnecessary with smokeless, but keeps the improved bullet close to the original's weight.

The N.O.E. 460-186-CB's flat-bottomed lube groove is .404" in diameter and holds far less lube – just right for smokeless. It also has a more generous .125" meplat. Considering its updated design and increased weight, it may well be the better bullet as a compromise between the 146- to 152-grain collar buttons, and the rare and expensive old 210-grain 457127 roundnose as an all-around plinking and small-game bullet. In the Marlin 1895XLR it shot excellent groups with 10 grains of Bullseye, 12.5 grains of Unique, 13 grains of Clays and 14 grains of Trail Boss.

These lightweight bullet designs do not incorporate a crimping groove. A simple taper crimp is fine for single-shot use but that isn't safe with a spring-loaded, tube-fed lever gun. One solution is to simply roll crimp beneath the front driving band, which will work in most rifles. The motivation for switching to Lee sizing dies is that when you seat a .460" bullet in the tighter cases, you can see the large bullet bulging above the smaller diameter case body creating a shelf or ledge beneath the bullet, effectively preventing the bullet from

being pushed deeper. You can use either method alone, or together.

While working on another project, it finally dawned on me that a third method is to crimp your own cannelures into your cases like the factories do to prevent bullets telescoping back into the case. You say there is no such crimping tool on the market? Ah, but there is, cleverly disguised as the collet-type Lee Factory Crimp Die for rifle cases. They will make custom case crimping dies to whatever case length you want, for any caliber. Simply measure where you want the cannelure to be with whatever case trim length you use and which bullet you want to use. Then carefully cut off a couple of .45-70 cases to that exact length. For the collar button bullets, I used 1.778". For the 458127-type bullets, I sent 1.625" sample cases. Seat jacketed bullets so the case mouth exactly covers the bullets' crimping cannelures. Send your dummy cartridges to Lee Precision with a check for $25.00 for each crimping die plus $6.00 shipping, wait patiently for six weeks, and you will have the slickest case canneluring tool(s) ever.

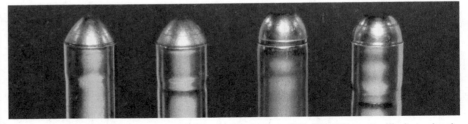

From left: 460-186-CB squeezed into Lee sized case; 460-186-CB seated in Lee sized case after case was cannelured with custom Lee rifle crimping die and expanded with N.O.E. .460 expander plug; 462-210-PB squeezed into Lee sized case (note how you can see the driving bands through the case); 462-210-PB seated in Lee sized case after case was cannelured with custom Lee rifle crimping die and expanded with N.O.E. .460 expander plug.

Above: New cases cannelured with custom Lee Factory Crimp Dies: left, for 457130; right, for 457127.

Right: The powders used to develop light loads for the .45-70 were Trail Boss, Red Dot, Unique, Bullseye and Clays.

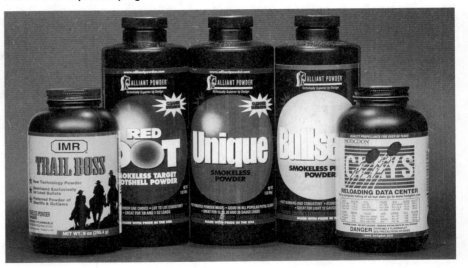

TARGET 1

7-16-12 95°
1895XLR 50 YDS
457130
  5 SHOTS
1450 Fps ES 68
13.0 gr. TRAIL BOSS

TARGET 2

7-19-12 89°
1895 XLR 50 YDS
W 457130
13.0 gr. TRAIL BOSS
1434 Fps
    ES 93

TARGET 3

460-186-PB
14.0 gr. TRAIL BOSS, WLR
1405 Fps ES 68

TARGET 4

2

7-20-12 77°

140$ Fps
ES 27

1895XLR 50 YDS
457401
14.0 gr. TRAIL BOSS
1406 Fps
    ES 29

Target 1: 457130, 13 grains of Trail Boss, five shots.

Target 2: 457130 from Western Bullet, 13 grains of Trail Boss, three shots.

Target 3: 460-186-PB, 14 grains of Trail Boss, three shots.

Target 4: 457401, 14 grains of Trail Boss.

No more need to roll crimp case mouths, and case length ceases to be critical. Just seat the bullets so the case covers however much of the top driving band your rifle likes. With my 1895XLR there doesn't seem to be any discernible accuracy difference with any of the crimping methods.

Finding the best light loads for the .45-70 was well worth the effort, and I would expect very similar results using them in the slightly smaller capacity .450 Marlin case. With just a little bit of sight or scope adjustment, or practice holding off, now we can have some *real* off-season fun with our bad boy big boomers without the physical or financial pain!

DISCLAIMER: Any and all loading data found in this article or previous articles is to be taken as reference material *only*. The publishers, editors, authors, contributors and their entities bear no responsibility for the use by others of the data included in this article or others that came before it.

THE MODERN "TRUCK GUN"

THOUGHTS ON GUNS FOR THE ROAD

By Al Doyle

"Truck gun" is a popular (but vague) American term. Those who don't own pickups tend to refer to such firearms as truck guns even when they ride in the trunk or under the front seat of a car. So what exactly is a truck gun or trunk gun? Filling this unglamorous but potentially crucial role involves some contradictory requirements.

As with any gun, these traveling pieces need to be dependable and trouble free. No one wants to tote the equivalent of a large paperweight around to defend life and limb. On the other hand, a typical truck gun comes in at the lower end of the price scale for logical reasons.

Guns in vehicles may bounce around on a regular basis and will be stored in conditions ranging from the blast-furnace heat of the Desert Southwest to the subzero cold of the Upper Midwest

and New England. Only those with more money than brains would toss a pristine Browning Hi-Power or a prized bolt-action hunting rifle with a high-priced scope and an exquisite black walnut stock into a truck and expect it to remain in the same condition.

If anything, a typical truck gun has picked up some dings or faded blueing along the way. Some say it "gives 'em character." More importantly, signs of typical wear lowers the price on the purchase of a used weapon. What's a little cosmetic decline as long as the gun functions reliably with decent accuracy when called into service? Vehicles are popular targets for thieves, and that's another reason not to invest too heavily in a truck gun.

The Second Amendment has no income test, and many Americans who have a genuine need to carry a weapon don't spend their free time at the country

club. In numerous situations, it's not a matter of how much money will be lavished on a name-brand pistol. The real issue is scraping together enough cash to obtain some reliable protection.

Handguns often end up as truck guns due to their size, but a fair number of rifles and shotguns ride around in the "just in case" role, or serve double duty as plinkers when the opportunity for some informal practice presents itself. Very few would recommend a rimfire as the ideal choice, but .22s can be found in vehicles with some frequency. Perhaps the best of the bunch for toting around is the Marlin Papoose. This takedown rifle comes in a handy zippered case for easy storage. The Papoose is basically a shortened version of the Marlin 795, and it combines accuracy, dependability and low weight (3 pounds, 4 ounces). Weight may not be much of a consideration during normal times, but what if a person

An ideal trunk gun should be sturdy and can be inexpensive. This Mosin-Nagant rifle and Hi-Point pistol meet those requirements. But it takes a full-size trunk to carry a full-length military surplus rifle like the Mosin-Nagant.

has to hike long distances in a crisis? Fewer pounds and even ounces could be quite helpful.

Dealing with reality again, some will insist on carrying a .22 pistol. There are dozens of good options, but which model is the best for truck/trunk gun status? The utterly reliable Ruger Mark II/III would be a logical choice, but the company has an even better piece for

For those who are more comfortable with a .22, you can't go wrong with the Ruger Mark III pistol or a carbine like the Marlin Papoose below.

toting around. Ruger's SR22 has earned a reputation for gobbling a wide range of ammunition. Many semiautomatic rimfires are picky when it comes to which brands of ammo they feed, but that hasn't been a problem for the SR22. Why go with the newer pistol over the gun that has been around since the company's debut in 1949? At 17.5 ounces, the SR22 is exactly half of the 35-ounce weight of the all-steel Mark II.

What about a low-priced .22 revolver? Look for a used Harrington & Richardson, but shop patiently. Prices are all over the map.

The concealed-carry movement has become a major force in the gun rights issue. Some CCW holders will go to great lengths to tote and hide a full-size handgun, but many prefer ease of carry to more rounds and larger calibers. Here is a pair of smaller pistols that are accurate, dependable and easy on the wallet:

If your funds are in the $200 range, the blued Taurus 738 is a clear choice. The pair I have tested have eaten five different brands of ammo and reloads without a hiccup, and accuracy was somewhat better than what might be expected from a 10.2-ounce pocket pistol with small sights.

When it comes to combining value, quality and options, the CW series by Kahr Arms more than gets the job done. Available in .380 ACP, .9mm, .40 Smith & Wesson and .45 ACP, the stainless slide/polymer frame Kahrs carry MSRPs of $419 (figure $325 to $350 retail) and weigh anywhere from 10.2 to 19.7 ounces.

Almost every gun owner has sold a few pieces for financial reasons, with the regrets lingering long after the cash was spent. In my case, a Kahr CW 45 is at the top of the list. The single-stack pistol never jammed while displaying fine accuracy. What about a budget .38 Special snubnose revolver? Wheelgun prices have jumped in recent years, but the Armscor and Taurus .38s can fit into an average person's budget.

Why not pick up a Glock if money is an issue? I'm not referring to a new in-the-box piece with a $550 to $600 price tag. Used Model 17s (9mm) and 22s (.40 S&W) are common items at retail shops, shows and online. These are police trade-ins with varying degrees of holster wear and usage. If owning a Glock seems like the impossible dream, check the price of former cop guns before deciding to look at a different brand. Creativity can help make up for limited funds.

There is another name-brand pistol that routinely sells for $350 or less. If you like your guns new in the box (NIB), the Smith & Wesson SD9 VE in 9mm and the SD40 VE in .40 S&W combine high capacity (16 + 1 in the SD9, 14 + 1 in the SD40), dependability and well-designed ergonomics in an affordable package. Add in the venerable Smith & Wesson logo, and you've got a piece that makes the list of good values for the money spent.

How many Americans have longed for a full-size .45 ACP pistol, but feel that such a desirable item is beyond their modest budgets? Don't give up just yet, as the cure for .45 fever isn't always expensive.

If the classic Model 1911 is your dream, check out the GI Standard series from Rock Island Arms. Available with 4¼- or 5-inch barrels, these no-frills pistols are as retro as it gets. Think wood grips, parkerized all-steel frames and plain sights. That combination might not appeal to those who want to be trendy,

Size matters for concealed carry, but in a vehicle there's a place somewhere for a full-size handgun like the Hi-Point .45. However, the Taurus 738 .380 might be a better fit for a tight spot in your sports car.

but who can argue with over a century of unbroken popularity and happy owners? Plan on spending $450 or less minus sales tax or any background check fees for a fistful of Americana.

What if your budget is really tight, as in nickels and dimes? Could there be a full-size .45 ACP in that price range? Hi-Point's JHP 45 make be heavy and even clunky, but these blowback pistols have developed a loyal following thanks to their ammo-gobbling ability and accuracy. NIB prices range from $150 to $190, which includes a lifetime warranty. These are American-made products, as all Hi-Point guns are built in Ohio.

When it comes to a low-cost rifle in the trunk, your best option could be gathering dust in the closet. Remember the good old days of the early 1990s when Chinese-made and other SKSs could easily be had for $69 to $150? Many shoppers picked up an SKS or several as bargain-basement impulse purchases. These rifles cost somewhat more today, but countless NIB pieces have been untouched for 20 years or more after being obtained for little cash. Perhaps it's time to take that unused SKS out of retirement and put it into service as a highly dependable semiautomatic "just in case" firearm.

Likewise, millions of used Mausers and Enfields have been purchased in the past for prices that seem unbelievable today. Rather than spending time and money searching for a solid truck gun, it might be wiser to reach into the gun safe or closet for something that has been tested and proven to work.

What about the person who wants to buy a sturdy old war-horse today? Various Russian-made Mosin-Nagants are the obvious choice. At $100 to $150 retail, this isn't the time to skimp on condition. Check the bore to make sure that corrosive ammo hasn't turned the barrel into a sewer pipe. The Mosin that Igor or Ivan carried decades ago will serve well as a no-nonsense truck gun in the 21st century.

Shotguns can be the solution in tense situations. The pump-action Maverick 88 is Mossberg's no-frills line. Made in 12 or 20 gauge, the Maverick has proven to be a dependable performer for a blue-collar price. At least one national sporting goods chain was selling Mavericks for $169.95 during the 2015 Black Friday weekend, and similar pricing should be available during future discounts and promotions.

The saying "Don't bring a knife to a

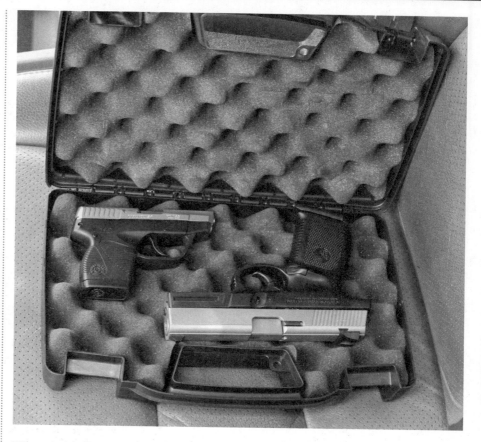

Why not arm two people with the contents of one hard case? A Smith & Wesson SD9 VE and a Taurus 738 are pictured.

The Kel-Tec Sub 2000 folding carbine easily fits into a medium-size backpack as well as any trunk. It's light and easily concealed, comes in 9mm or .40 S&W, and it accepts Glock magazines.

gunfight" applies to even the skimpiest of budgets. What can a person do if they have $100 or less to spend on a firearm for the road?

Used single-shot shotguns by H&R and other manufacturers are often available for a Ben Franklin or less. Many of these pieces haven't been used much, although they can have some dings in the stock along with faded blueing. It pays to do

some word-of-mouth advertising if you're looking for an inexpensive single-shot in 12 gauge, 20 gauge or .410, as these weapons often lie forgotten in closets. In such situations, the owners may be willing to sell the neglected item for a nominal price.

A gun-savvy friend who earns a modest wage and has a large family to support keeps an H&R 12 gauge in his car.

Slugs, buckshot and birdshot accompany the weapon. Even with the one-at-a-time loading method of his chosen firearm, my friend is confident that it will serve well if needed. I wouldn't argue with a determined man who is pointing the business end of a single-shot in my direction.

What else is needed for a long gun in the truck or trunk? A sling is essential to keep your hands free when walking.

How about a rifle that can fit into a duffle bag or even a backpack? Kel-Tec's Sub 2000 in 9mm or .40 S&W easily folds in half. The 16¼-inch barrel makes this carbine light and supremely handy with little recoil. Most Sub 2000s are built to accept Glock magazines, and Kel-Tec also offers Sub 2000s designed to use Sig, Beretta and Smith & Wesson pistol magazines.

Could there be a drawback to a very popular gun that has proven to be accurate out to 100 yards? The Sub 2000 may not work for the 10 percent of the population that shoots left-handed. As a member of that minority, I was catching brass in the face while testing the carbine. Switching to the right hand and closing my left (dominant) eye produced groups that were surprisingly tight, as I don't practice enough with weak-handed shooting.

If you're preparing to deal with unexpected emergencies, carrying a trunk gun is just part of the equation. Water, food, comfortable boots or shoes, warm clothing, the ability to make a fire and a blanket should also be at hand. Are you expecting communications or the grid to break down? Prepare accordingly. Keep some cash and small silver coins in the backpack just in case the ATM machines don't function.

Even with typical financial obligations, finding the money needed to obtain a gun specifically for the car or truck is a realistic goal. Even a small investment in protection could prove to be a lifesaver when trouble rears its ugly head.

It goes without saying that state and local gun laws *must* be considered and taken *seriously* when there's a firearm in your vehicle. What's legal in Indiana or New Hampshire could lead to grief and trouble a few miles away in Chicago or Massachusetts. And these days, gun laws are changing all the time. Before carrying a gun in your vehicle, do some research on the most current legislation for your area.

Obvious locations for quick handgun access are the center console or driver's side door.

The Smith & Wesson SD9 VE is a good example of a moderately priced 9mm car or truck gun.

SPRINGFIELD SPORTERS

A Salute to the Sporterized 1903 Springfield

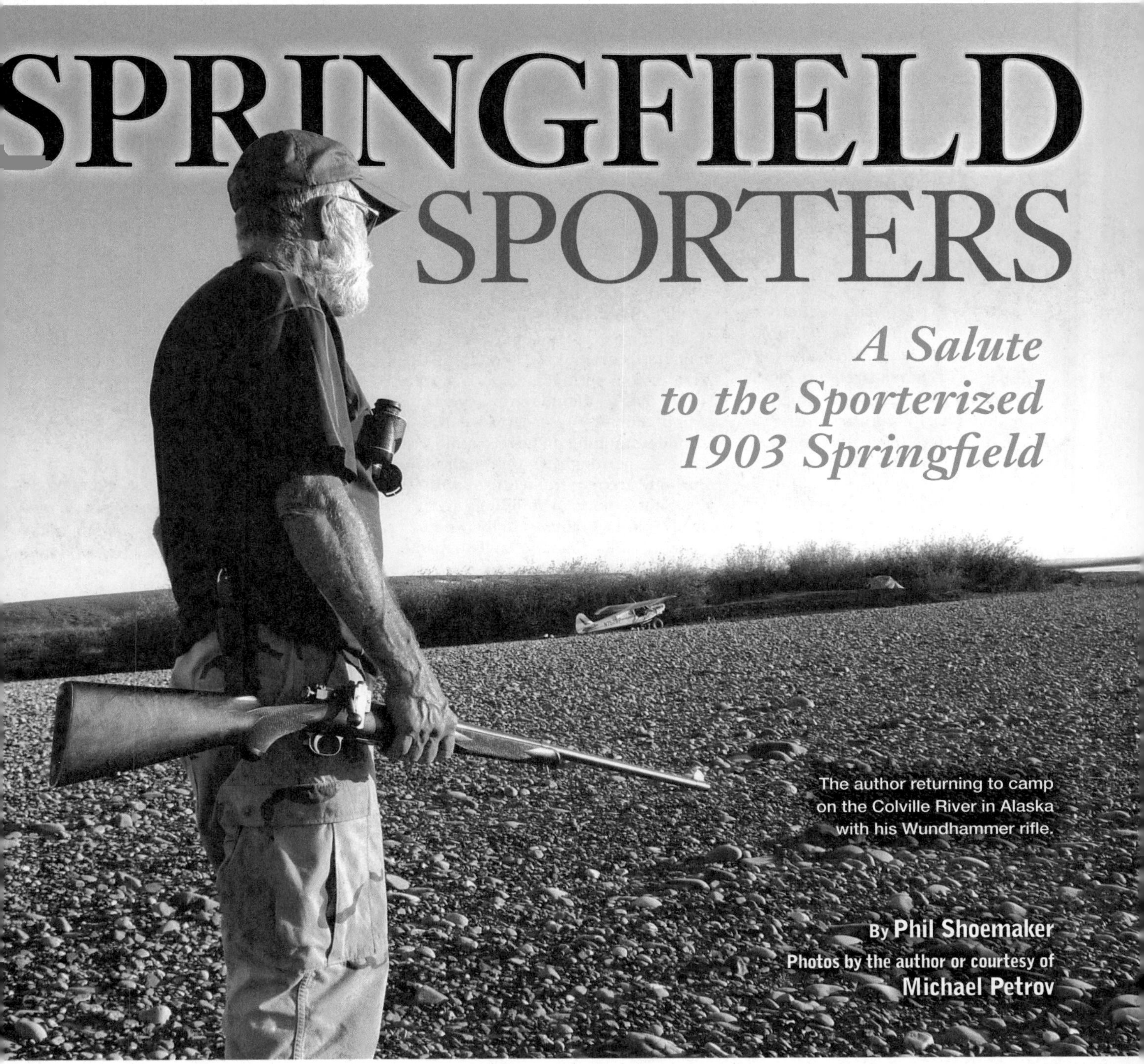

The author returning to camp on the Colville River in Alaska with his Wundhammer rifle.

By **Phil Shoemaker**
Photos by the author or courtesy of
Michael Petrov

At the turn of the 20th century Theodore Roosevelt was a wildly popular president. He also happened to be an avid outdoorsman and hunter and in 1903, the year a new military bolt action rifle was introduced, he ordered a modified sporting version directly from the U.S. Springfield armory. Rifle serial number 00009 was stocked similar to one of Roosevelt's favorite Winchester lever actions and delivered the following February. It was chambered for a newly designed, rimless .30-caliber cartridge referred to as the .30-03. The cartridge was a typical government compromise as it incorporated a modern rimless case but saddled it with the same long neck and roundnose 220-grain bullet used by the outdated .30-40 Krag. Three years later the military re-assessed the cartridge's design and reconfigured the case with a shorter neck and a 150-grain spitzer bullet that offered less recoil and a much improved trajectory. Although it was possible to fire the new 1906 version in the older .30-03 chamber, accuracy proved unacceptable and all existing rifles in inventory had their barrels sent back and rechambered for the .30-06.

As a serious hunter and rifleman, President Roosevelt remained abreast of the newest rifle developments. According to Clark S. Campbell, author

The author's Wundhammer rifle. Wundhammer had a wealth of understanding of how a rifle should fit. "Never a rifleman tried one of Wundhammer's sporting Springfields that did not marvel at the perfect hang of the rifle and the perfect proportions of the stock."
Photo courtesy of Michael Petrov.

Wundhammer's first Springfield sporting rifle was built for author Stewart Edward White.
Photo courtesy of Michael Petrov.

of the authoritative book, *The '03 Springfield Rifles' Era*, Roosevelt had his rifle rebarreled to .30-06 immediately prior to leaving on an extensive 11 month East Africa safari. In his well-publicized account, *African Game Trails,* Roosevelt wrote that he was, "desirous of testing the small, sharp-pointed army bullet on the big beasts." He also noted that, "the sharp pointed bullets penetrated well, and not splitting into fragments, but seeming to cause a rendering shock." Both statements indicate that he was using the most current 150-grain military ball .30-06 ammunition.

Published in 1910, *African Game Trails* became an immediate best-seller and sparked a keen interest in both the powerful, flat-shooting .30-06 as well as in sporterizing the new Springfield bolt-action military rifle. Although unimaginable today, Public Law No. 149 passed in March of 1905, made the current military rifle available for purchase by civilian members of the National Rifle Association. The best custom gunbuilders of the time—men like Fred Adolph, Seymour Griffin,

Barney Worthen and Ludwig "Louis" Wundhammer—soon began receive orders to build sporting rifles from the Springfield Model 1903.

California craftsman Louis Wundhammer is credited with building the first custom Springfield sporting rifles. Trained as a gunbuilder in Bavaria, Wundhammer possessed a wealth of understanding on how to build a first-rate hunting rifle. He required no Baroque arcitectural features with convoluted flutings, moldings and shadow lines to illustrate his wood-working skills. Like the English master John Rigby, Wundhammer'a rifles were slim, lightweight hunting tools devoid of all plethoric excesses. Each rifle incorporated first-class craftsmanship; including sculpted metalwork, his unique, subtle "Wundhammer grip" palm swell and differential cast-off at heel, toe and grip.

Edward C. Crossman, a popular and prolific gunwriter of the era, wrote glowingly of Wundhammer's work. "Never a rifleman tried one of Wundhammer's sporting Springfields that did not marvel at the perfect hang of the rifle and the perfect proportions of the stock, the shape of the grip, the sharp, even checkering and the finish of the wood." Crossman placed an order for five Wundhammer sporting rifles, one for himself

and the others as gifts for influencial friends, including wealthy adventurer and author Stewart Edward White, who immeditely packed his off to Africa.

The late Anchorage gun collector, photographer and author Michael Petrov possessed an encyclopedic knowledge and extensive collections of early custom 1903 Springfield sporters. He was exceedingly generous about sharing his knowledge and collection, and at the end of each hunting season I would stop in to visit. Although he possessed a number of ornate and finely finished rifles, the six Wundhammer rifles in his collection were our favorites. They were as lithe, lively and finely balanced as any rifles I have ever thrown to my shoulder.

Inspired by Roosevelt's African exploits, Seymore Griffin,

German immigrants like Fred Adolph utilized their wood carving talents on sporting rifles.
Photo courtesy of Michael Petrov.

The "war to end all wars" had proven the rugged superiority of the bolt action over the popular lever-action rifles like the Savage M-99.

Sporting Springfields

MR. Stewart Edward White has already killed 24 head of big game with one of my rifles on his East African trip. If you own a New Springfield service rifle, or can obtain a set of the parts for this rifle, and want an American sporting Mauser like Mr. White's, write me. Stocking guns of any sort and building rifles de luxe my specialty.

Prices right, but quality of workmanship and finish always the first consideration.

LUDWIG WUNDHAMMER, Bullard Block, Los Angeles, Cal.

Wundhammer advertisement in 1911 issue of *Outer's* magazine. Isolated trappers and homesteaders would thumb through well-worn issues of the *Alaskan Sportsman, Forest and Stream* and *American Rifleman* magazines, lusting after the sleek Springfield sporting rifles.

a New York cabinetmaker by trade, decided to try his hand at building rifle stocks. In January of 1910 he purchased his first Springfield rifle and very quickly earned an enviable reputation for his classic designs and impeccable workmanship. In 1923 he joined with James Howe, a toolmaker who had been in charge of the Small Arms Experimental Department at the Frankford Arsenal, to form the legendary American firm of Griffin & Howe.

Fred Adolph, another old-world craftsman renowned for the excellence of his stock carvings, built a rifle for writer Townsend Whelen in 1910 and another for Roosevelt. Those, and a few other obscure, but highly talented gunmakers, started the trend of the American sporting bolt-action rifle.

Alaska then, as now, was one of the world's greatest game fields and reliable, solidly built rifles were a coveted commodity. By the close of World War I, the population of the Alaskan territory began to swell as homesteaders, hunters, miners and trappers trekked north. The "war to end all wars" had proven the rugged superiority of the bolt action over the popular lever-action rifles. Isolated trappers and homesteaders would thumb through well-worn issues of the *Alaskan Sportsman, Forest and Stream* and *American Rifleman* magazines, lusting after the sleek Springfield sporting

rifles being advertised by men like Fred Adolph, Griffin & Howe, A.O. Niedner, Bob Owens, R.F. Sedgley and Ludwig Wundhammer. The attractive photos and glowing recommendations were carefully scrutinized during the long, dark winter nights. In the spring, if fur sales were good or the paydirt looked rich, an order would be placed in the mail. Photos of the era show a fair percentage of Northern hunters holding sporterized Springfields.

Astute Alaskan riflemen and early territorial guides were quick to recognize the quality and benefits of the new sporters. Alaska's first licensed guides Andrew Berg, Charlie Madsen (the dean of Kodiak guides) and others like Slim Moore and Jay Williams carried Springfield sporters the majority of their careers. In his book,

Photos of the era show a fair percentage of Northern hunters holding sporterized Springfields. Harry Staser, hunting for railroad construction crews near Kenai Lake circa 1915-16 is shown here with what appears to be an early Wundhammer rifle.

Bruce Staser photo used with permission of Jack Staser.

Alaskan Adventure, Williams writes, "My little Springfield sporter, fashioned by Ludwig Wundhammer, was picked up in the morning as regularly as my hat." It became his daily companion for 30 years until eventually lost in a boat fire. By then, Wundhammer had been dead for over 25 years so he ordered another Springfield sporter chambered in .35 Whelen from a skilled Wisconsin gunbuilder by the name of Alvin Linden.

The popularity of the Springfield was such that soon hundreds of local gunsmiths across the country began "sporterizing" military models. They were held in high esteem as a result of their smooth, reliable feeding, target-grade accuracy, as well as for the flat trajectory and game-smashing power of the .30-06 cartridge. The Philadelphia firm of R.F. Sedgley was the most prolific producer of sporterized Springfields and eventually even chambered them in calibers as powerful as the .375 H&H. Moderately priced, Sedgley sporters found favor with a large number of Alaskan hunters.

As beloved as the 1903 Springfield sporters were, however, they had a few design features that could bite the unwary. In 1933, Alaskan game warden and territorial hunter Hosea Sarber, accompanied by Jay Williams, was taking photos of a brown bear on Afognak Island. Hosea was holding his Springfield in his left hand with the safety off. Focused on the bears he was unaware that, with the safety off, the bolt handle had been slightly raised. Both Sarber and Williams were comfortable around

bruins but they must have pushed a bit too close as the bear decided it had had enough. When the bear charged, Sarber raised his rifle to fire but all he heard, in his words, was a "snick" rather than the heavy blast he anticipated. When the bolt handle of a Springfield is not in the fully down and locked position it reduces the tension on the mainspring and does not have power to propel the firing pin with enough force to ignite the primer. Being an old hand at bear killing, Sarber swiftly chambered another round and dropped the bruin.

Not having the bolt handle down in the fully locked position will cause failures in most bolt actions, but on the Springfield action there is a solution. Barney Worthen, another superb gunsmith and machinist working out in San Francisco in the early part of the century, installed a spring-loaded pin in the rear safety lug that snapped into an indentation on the back of the claw extractor. That made it considerably less likely for a cocked bolt to accidentally get bumped out of position.

The 1903 Springfield had another feature, the magazine cut-off, that could also cause problems. Many military rifles of the era, including Krags and early British Lee-Enfields, suffered the same affliction. The cut-off was an anachronism insisted upon by hidebound generals who had come up through the ranks during the era of single-shot rifles. Its purpose was to isolate all the rounds in the magazine for use in an emergency, while in normal use the soldier was expected to load, aim and fire the rifle as a single-shot. It was an unnecessary complexity that could become a fatal flaw in the hands of the unwary.

In early September of 1952 Alaskan hunter Henry Knackstedt was moose hunting near his cabin on the Kenai Peninsula. A steady wind was blowing and Henry was slowly stalking into it when he surprised a brown bear sow with cubs. Greeted by "a low, ominous growl" not 15 feet to his left, Henry instinctively swung his rifle up, operating the bolt as he did. As he slammed it forward he realized it had not fed a round. The magazine cut-off had accidentally been bumped into the down position, preventing the bolt from moving far enough rearward to capture a round from the magazine.

The bear was immediately upon him and Henry raised the rifle in front of his face to protect himself from the gaping jaws. He said, " I was conscious for three,

Magazine cut-offs were an unnecessary complexity that, in the hands of the unwary, could become a fatal flaw. Many turn of the century military rifles had them and they remained on sporters like this .303 Lee-Speed and 1903 Springfield.

perhaps five seconds—I have a faint memory of smelling rotten fish—and I was out as though a 10-ton truck had hit me. I lay unconscious in a pool of blood with my left eye gone and the left side of my face and head a gory mess. Part of my skull had been bitten or clawed away exposing brain tissue to open air. There was a hell of a big hole in the back of my neck and my rifle had been tossed 30 feet into the brush. I was on my face with the packboard shifted well forward and I thank that old moose board for saving my life. The sow had taken a few healthy bites out of it before deciding I was dead and departed."

Henry came to an hour later and began to slowly crawl and drag himself toward his cabin. Twice he fired a few evenly spaced shots hoping to attract attention. Eventually one of his neighbors heard them and came to investigate. Henry spent 70 days in the hospital before finally returning to his Kenai homestead.

Although considered a quaint, historical anachronism today, the slim,

slick-feeding 1903 Springfield remains an attractive and useful hunting tool. I am custodian of a number of fine early Springfield sporters and continue to hunt with them. I was fortunately able to obtain Michael Petrov's favorite Wundhammer rifle after his untimely death and carried it on a two-week hunt along the remote Colville river on Alaska's North slope.

I also own and hunt with a georgous Springfield sporter built in the early 1930s by stockmaker Adolph G. Minar. Gunwriter Jack O'Connor proclaimed Minar "one of the finest craftsmen to practice the trade of stock-making," who, "turned out some of the most beautifully checkered and shaped stocks ever made in this country." Late in his life, after owning rifles crafted by many of the nation's top builders, O'Connor still proclaimed his Minar sporter as "one of the handsomest, fastest-handling rifles I have ever had."

Measured in years, the era of the sporterized Springfield rifle did not last

By the time the first Pasque flowers have bloomed the black bears are out foraging in Interior Alaska.

The author on an Alaska Interior spring black bear hunt with a 1930s vintage Adolph Minar sporter. Jack O'Connor claimed his Springfield was "one of the handsomest, fastest-handling rifles I have ever had."

A fine Springfield sporter built in the early 1930s by Adolph G. Minar.

long. Like the best British-built African rifles, however, their reputation far exceeded their actual numbers. After using them in the field one quickly understand the attachment and reverence that the early hunters developed for their Springfields.

When Winchester designed its Model 54 sporting rifle in 1925, it adopted the Springfield's coned breech, as well as the schnable fore-end tip and slim, lithe features of the early custom Springfield sporters. When Winchester decided to refine the design in the 1930s it sought input from knowledgeable Alaskan riflemen including Jay Williams and his close friend, Alaskan game commissioner Frank Dufrensne. They also solicited advice from popular gunwriters of the era like Townsend Whelen and Elmer Keith. The resulting rifle, the now iconic Winchester Model 70, quickly earned a reputation as "the rifleman's rifle" and owes much of it's existence to the early Springfield sporters.

The availability of the well-designed and reasonably priced Winchester Model 70 rifles pretty well stifled demand for custom-built Springfield sporters. By the end of World War II, customers wanting something a step above a standard-grade rifle could simply order a Super Grade M-70 from the factory. If they really wanted something extra special they could contact a number of custom makers like Griffin & Howe, which would build anything they wanted, but by 1950 were primarily using new M-70 actions rather than surplus Springfields.

Anyone further interested in the fascinating history of the 1903 Springfield rifle, and the talented gunsmiths who built our nation's first bolt-action sporting rifles, can find more information in a number of excellent books. *The Springfield 1903 Rifles,* by Lt. Col. William S. Brophy and *The '03 Springfield Rifles'Era,* by Clark S. Campbell are still available. And although recently out of print, Michael Petrov's books, *Custom Gunmakers of the 20th Century,* volumes 1 and 2, are must-have books for riflemen interested in the Springfield's past.

The author's Wundhammer rifle is shown here as a size reference to brown bear tracks, a not so uncommon sight near the author's Alaskan hunting camp.

The author's stag handled Colt .32-20 fits in well with other Old West accoutrements. The holster is from 45maker.com.

The Modern
.32-20

By Robert K. Campbell

When I look over the firearms in my gun safe I find a number that perform well at a given task. The .308 Winchester is represented and the .22 Long Rifle as well—and there is a single humble rifle and cartridge that does things the others cannot, the .32-20.

It will reach varmints and small game past rimfire range. The .32-20 will also give a day's enjoyment, firing hundreds of cartridges, without producing eddies in the arm or a sore spot for a day or two. The combination of efficiency, economy, accuracy and historical significance is practically unequaled. Add the ability to use the cartridge in a revolver and you have a cartridge that clearly deserved its status in the Old West.

I am at a point now in my life where every firearm and cartridge doesn't need a well-defined task. Some are owned for historical or recreational value, but the .32-20 is a versatile cartridge perfect for many chores. The cartridge is a great bridge between the .22 and the .308 in the game field, and while there are better choices for deer, the .32-20 has taken plenty of game that we might find better suited to larger cartridges.

I may be nearing old-timer status but I am not going to tell you I grew up using this "old-timer" cartridge. I have been using the .32-20 Winchester Center Fire for only a few years. As a good match against squirrels, rabbits and predators up to the bobcat and coyote size, it stands alone in my opinion. The .32-20 will not perforate a boar hog and leave a divot in the ground behind him, but it is certainly useful for other game. It isn't overly destructive on small game with careful shots but does reach out to snag larger animals cleanly.

When firing any firearm for accuracy the most important variable is the person behind the sights. Light recoil is an aid to keeping the gun steady. There is no good reason to knock yourself off of the bench at the range. I have to admit that if factory performance were the sole criteria for choosing the

.32-20 I would probably pass, but I am a handloader and you should be as well if you want to get the most from this cartridge.

A Bit of History

The area west of the 98th meridian where the line bisects Kansas and out to the Sierras was labeled the Great American Desert in geography books well into the 20th century. The primary story in that country told of the times of the cowboy. The cowboy lived in the dramatic grinding reality of the day. Most were young and took to the hard-fisted reality of the frontier. They herded cattle, mended fences, rescued strays in all types of weather, and rustlers and Indians were often a concern.

While many cowboys chose the .45 Colt revolver or the .44-40 rifle and handgun combination, it is interesting to note that there were some years during which the .32-20 was the best seller in the Single Action Army. It also remained a popular caliber during the entire run of the Winchester 1892 lever-action rifle.

My affinity with the cartridge began with the purchase of a Colt Single Action Army that was manufactured in 1899. When I examined the revolver I

The author's Winchester Model 1892 (center) is still reliable and accurate as it approaches its 97th birthday. He believes the .32-20 WCF provides a good bridge between the rifles like the .308 Savage 99 (top) and Marlin .22 Long Rifle (below).

If you like period gear, then the Colt .32-20 is a must-have addition to your shooting battery.

Left to right: .32-20 WCF, .38-40 WCF and .44-40 WCF cartridges. All good calibers!

found it was in great condition, but not so fine a piece that I couldn't afford it. I mentioned to my wife I would have preferred the .45 and she said, "Are you going to carry it for personal defense? No? So the caliber doesn't matter." The rest is history and the sixgun was mine. Soon I had an opportunity to purchase a Winchester 1892 rifle in the same caliber. Neither is a museum piece but both are solid working firearms.

The .32-20 WCF was introduced in the Winchester Model 73 rifle in 1882. Soon afterward Colt chambered the Peacemaker for the cartridge. The primary advantages of the cartridge were its light weight and economy. You could carry more .32-20 ammo than the larger .38-40 or .44-40 and it was less expensive. When loaded with a 115-grain flatpoint over 20 grains of black powder the .32-20 would break about 1,200 fps from a carbine barrel and 900 fps from the 7½-inch revolver. This gave over

350 ft-lbs of energy from the carbine and over 200 pounds from the revolver. That level of power proved useful when combined with a bullet capable of good penetration. Many deer, and even elk, were taken with a .32-20 rifle. I'm not recommending such a course—far from it—but the frontiersman made do with what he had and likely was an excellent shot and knew his rifle well.

When smokeless powder became popular there was the inevitable experimentation with the cartridge. Fortunately, my Single Action Army is a smokeless-powder version and the Model 1892 rifle was manufactured in 1919. While I am not bound to black powder, neither do I experiment with Elmer Keith Memorial loads. There is a consensus that the .32-20 whetted the appetite of American shooters for high velocity. The thick cylinder walls of the Colt Single Action revolver allowed for loads that pushed the 115-grain bullet to about 1,200 fps.

The rifle cartridges could be loaded to 1,500 fps or more. Much of this improvement was possible due to the Winchester 1892 rifle's strong action. In handling the rifle, leverage is excellent due to the relatively short cartridges. The 1892 features a solid bottom receiver. The bolt recesses and the twin locking bolts are designed for strength. The receiver walls are thick, and the rails and slots are also made of good steel. Both the vertical and longitudinal supports are good, and each locking bolt is held strongly against the bolt when the rifle is locked.

As for the revolver, the strength of the Colt Single Action is very well-known. With a solid locking base pin keeping the cylinder firmly in place the revolver has excellent accuracy potential.

The rifle is useful as issued with its original sights. However, both nostalgia and practical accuracy requirements led me to mount a Lyman aperture sight on it. The Lyman Gun Sight Company was

The .45 Colt's cylinder (top) doesn't have as much steel for safety as the smaller .32-20 (bottom), which allows the latter to be loaded much hotter.

The Lyman tang sight is a great addition to any lever-action Winchester. Not only does it allow for quick shooting, it also gives the rifle a classic appeal.

founded in 1878 on the basis of its tang-mounted peep sights. After all these years shooters have found nothing better for fast and accurate shooting. The rear sight offers excellent speed; the eye tends to center the front sight in the aperture and the result is not only accuracy but an unobstructed view of the target. I personally find the Lyman sight superior to standard sights in practically any application.

Loading the .32-20

The .32-20's gently rolling shoulder and limited powder capacity doesn't fit well into the sharp-shouldered rifle cartridge family of today. Just the same, this limited capacity means real economy for the handloader. In a broad sense the .32-20 WCF is similar to the .30 Carbine. The .32-20 may use heavier bullets and the average Model 92 rifle is more accurate than the .30 Carbine, but whatever the .30 Carbine will do the Winchester will as well.

My example is an octagon-barrel rifle and will develop greater velocity than the carbine. It is also more accurate than most. Like many modern shooters I did not have a specific purpose in mind when I began shooting the .32-20, but it

The '92 Winchester features a short throw and plenty of leverage.

That's a full-size Colt Peacemaker all right but the beast isn't kicking very hard. It is a .32-20 and the lady loves shooting it.

XTP I was able to work safely to 1,700 fps. With the Sierra 90-grain JHP, 1,680 fps; the Hornady-100 grain XTP, 1,550 fps. I have not encountered sticky extraction or flattened primers and will not pursue higher velocity. Accuracy hovers around 2 inches at 50 yards.

I am certain that this load will prove effective against coyotes and hope to be getting one in my sights soon. The .32-20 is a fine old cartridge and one that is still useful for the modern shooter.

is such a good cartridge I found several uses. Recoil is light, and that definitely means something to my wife. The initial firing sessions were conducted with Black Hills Ammunition's 115-grain loading. This load breaks 780 fps from the revolver. From the rifle it isn't too far off original specifications at 1,090 fps. Accuracy is excellent.

Original loads used a bullet that was one part tin for 20 parts lead. The BHA bullet is similarly soft enough to slug up but hard enough to limit leading. Sometimes hard-cast bullets do not provide the best accuracy, while others may be brilliantly accurate. I have enjoyed good results with the Rim Rock 115-grain bul-

let. A modest charge of Titegroup, Winchester 231 or Alliant Unique powder breaking about 1,100 fps gives good accuracy in the rifle. It isn't difficult to work up a load in the revolver that gives 900 fps, a useful improvement and nicely suited for field use.

To begin assembling .32-20 hand-loads I obtained a set of Lee Precision dies. Small rifle primers may be used with heavy charges but in the end small pistol primers worked fine with every load. The Lee die resizes the neck for use with jacketed bullets, and I wanted to see how the rifle performed with the Hornady XTP bullet. I ordered the XTP in both 85- and 100-grain examples.

Next, and perhaps most important, I obtained a quantity of 500 Starline brass cases. These cartridge cases are strong, made to exacting procedure, and are ideal for repeated loadings. The .32-20 is a small cartridge case with thin walls and a well-deserved reputation for crushed case walls.

I enjoyed good results with cast bullets in the revolver and felt no need to push the envelope with jacketed bullets. The lead bullet loads were used in the rifle for practice. On the other hand, searching for a good load for the jacketed bullets was more difficult. I elected to concentrate on Winchester 296 and Hodgdon H110 powder. No need to pursue light loads for practice; the full-power loads are light enough. With the 85-grain

The Model 92's classic crescent buttstock can be a kicker with some calibers, but not with the .32-20.

This classic holster by 45maker.com carries the author's Colt .32-20 when he's hiking in the woods.

DISCLAIMER: Any and all loading data found in this article or previous articles is to be taken as reference material *only*. The publishers, editors, authors, contributors and their entities bear no responsibility for the use by others of the data included in this article or others that came before it.

MEANINGFUL TESTING FOR RIFLE ACCURACY

Author at the bench with Ruger 77V .25-06. Front rest is the heavy but stable Hart pedestal described in the article.

WHAT YOU NEED TO KNOW ABOUT SHOOTING FOR GROUPS

By **Mike Thomas**

How many shots in a centerfire rifle group and how many groups are necessary to provide valid, meaningful information? Lots of thoughts on this subject; upon mentioning it to a respected veteran of the gun writing trade he countered with the simple explanation that the topic is of little importance since only the first round or two are of any consequence to a hunter. From his perspective, the assessment was correct. Some shooters have little or no interest in group shooting or experimentation. They feel that once a rifle is zeroed and a shot is fired occasionally to verify the zero, no other work is necessary. Certainly, for these persons, there is nothing wrong with such an outlook. Others, however, are no less than fanatical on the matter.

This project was born of both necessity and frustration. For years, shooters have read about and listened to discussions

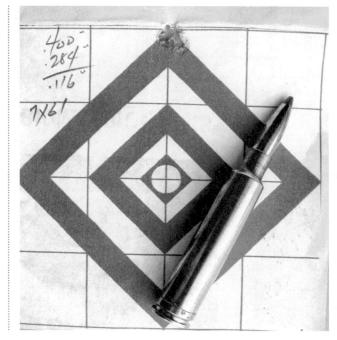

Three-shot group fired using the author's New Ultra Light Arms 7x61 Sharpe & Hart. One three-shot group, regardless of size, is of little use for accuracy evaluation. It serves only to indicate that additional groups need to be fired.

and arguments regarding three-shot vs. five-shot groups and the alleged conclusions that can be drawn from analyzing each. On occasion, there is mention of the four-shot group. However, it appears there is presently no great advocacy for what may be a practical alternative to three- and five-shot groups.

When it comes to accuracy and group shooting, there are hunters, shooters, handloaders, accuracy enthusiasts and combinations of these with different expectation levels ranging from minimal to extreme. I began reading gun publications in the early 1960s when five-shot groups were the norm. Average group sizes were generally larger for several reasons, not the least of which was the quality of barrels, bullets and scope sights. Other factors included stock material and bedding, front and rear rests, etc.

Despite technological advances that contributed to overall accuracy improvements, the three-shot group eventually became the new informal but generally accepted standard for evaluation purposes. Additionally, and importantly, a three-shot group is generally smaller than a five-shot group. It became easier to make a claim of excellent accuracy. Not only is the "luck" factor in a tiny three-shot group greater than in a five-shot group, the three-shot group will often effectively mask such deficiencies as a barrel that throws wild shots after it warms up a bit, as in shots number four and five.

There is some validity to the often repeated justification that a hunting

RIFLES AND LOADS TESTED

Ruger 77 MK II

Caliber:	.223 Rem.
Barrel:	22", .650" contour
Scope:	Burris 6X Compact
Handload:	50-grain Sierra Blitz, 23 grains Reloder 7, Federal brass, CCI-400 primer
	OAL = 2.235"
	Muzzle Velocity = 3,200 fps

Winchester M70 FWT

Caliber:	6.5x55
Barrel:	22", .555" contour
Scope:	Leupold FXII 6X
Handload:	140-grain Sierra GameKing, 46 grains H4831, Norma brass, CCI-200 primer
	OAL = 3.06"
	Muzzle Velocity = 2,591 fps

FN Mauser

Caliber:	.22-250 Rem.
Barrel:	24", .710" contour
Scope:	Lyman 6X Silhouette
Handload:	50-grain Sierra Blitz, 33 grains Varget, Remington brass, CCI-200 primer
	OAL = 2.39"
	Muzzle Velocity = 3,520 fps

Cooper M52

Caliber:	.270 Win.
Barrel:	24", .660" contour
Scope:	Leupold VX-3 2.5X-8X
Handload:	130-grain Barnes TXS BT, 54 grains H4350, Remington brass, Federal 210M
	OAL = 3.29"
	Muzzle Velocity = 3,056 fps

Cooper M54

Caliber:	6mm Rem.
Barrel:	24", .605" contour
Scope:	Leupold VX-3 2.5X-8X
Handload:	100-grain Sierra ProHunter, 44 grains H4831, Remington brass, Winchester brass, Federal 210M primer
	OAL = 2.83"
	Muzzle Velocity = 2,835 fps

Win. M70 Extreme Weather

Caliber:	.308 Win.
Barrel:	22", .615" contour
Scope:	Leupold FX-3 6X
Handload:	150-grain Hornady SP, 44 grains H4895, Winchester brass, CCI-200 primer
	OAL = 2.74"
	Muzzle Velocity = 2,760 fps

Ruger 77V

Caliber:	.25-06 Rem.
Barrel:	24", .750" contour
Scope:	Leupold FX-3 6X
Handload:	117-grain Sierra ProHunter, 53.5 grains H4831, Winchester brass, CCI-200 primer
	OAL = 3.13"
	Muzzle Velocity = 2,950 fps

Win. M70 Extreme Weather

Caliber:	.30-06 Springfield
Barrel:	22", .620" contour
Scope:	Leupold FX-3 6X
Handload:	180-grain Sierra ProHunter, 53.5 grains H4350, Remington brass, Federal 210M primer
	OAL = 3.24"
	Muzzle Velocity = 2,620 fps

situation seldom requires even three shots, let alone five. However, a rifle capable of firing tight five-shot groups on paper may well provide an increased level of confidence to a hunter. Some may argue this as being nothing more than intangible. However, it can be worth a lot in the field, particularly when making a long shot under adverse conditions. Consistently small five-shot groups are evidence that all is right with a rifle and load. Here, even the "no one fires more than three" faction have little basis for argument.

There were, and are, other aspects, too. Less time and ammunition are expended firing three-shot groups. With a heavy recoiling rifle it is not as unpleasant to fire a three-shot group from a bench rest as it would be to fire a five-shot string. For people sensitive to recoil, and that probably includes far more of us than would make the admission, such a reason makes good sense.

Other arguments in favor of the three-shot group include potentially decreased variation in wind changes and reduced shooter fatigue. Closely related to the

Rifles used in the group shooting project include (from left): Ruger M77 MK II .223 Remington, FN Mauser .22-250 Remington, Cooper Model 54 6mm Remington, Ruger 77V .25-06 Remington, Winchester Model 70 6.5x55 Swedish Mauser, Cooper Model 52 .270 Winchester, Winchester Model 70 Extreme Weather .308 Winchester and Winchester Model 70 Extreme Weather .30-06 Springfield.

latter is ordinary human error. Prime examples include jerking the trigger and sloppy rest or bag positioning. If using a rifle with a history of excellent accuracy with many different load combinations, three-shot groups may be sufficient if the shooter has already fired many such groups. Little is gained for the purpose of evaluation if five-shot groups are the same as or only minutely larger than three-shot groups. Same goes for a rifle that isn't particularly accurate with any load, i.e., barely capable of decent 100- to 200-yard hunting accuracy. Anything more than three-shot groups would probably be a waste of ammunition.

One side note on light triggers and high magnification scopes—some shooters reason that these will compensate for a lack of ability. Such rationalizations are always a mistake. One must become an experienced shooter first.

American Rifleman continues to evaluate centerfire rifle accuracy much as it has for decades by averaging five, five-shot groups, usually fired at 100 yards. Some of the groups are small, others larger, but the average is what is important. It is imperative to remember that even the pros and competitive shooters must deal with human error – it happens. Sometimes the error may be too small to notice while shooting, but may be blatantly displayed in group size.

Some firearm publications publish handloading data tables that depict many loads, each followed with a group size. If not noted, one can normally assume these were three-shot groups. Another safe assumption is that only one group was fired for each load. If the majority of groups are small, it's a good bet the rifle is an accurate one. However, should there be considerable variance in the size of single groups (some small, others large), one can assume nothing. Rather, the reader is forced to speculate on many factors: a "finicky" rifle, mechanical (bedding, scope, etc.) problems, the evaluator's benchrest technique is lacking and/or inconsistent, conditions were windy or any combination of the above. Such information is little more than worthless. Rests are important. Any front rest that moves on the bench when a shot is fired contributes to the worthlessness.

If a group size is recorded by not counting the shot farthest from the rest of the group, the figure is nothing short of skewed. This is useless information unless the errant shot was known to the shooter when the trigger was pulled and noted as such. To do things right, a re-fire is necessary.

What about waiting between each shot for a barrel to cool when shooting a group? It is difficult to understand the reasoning behind this or what is to be gained from it other than perhaps an unrealistic result.

How many groups need to be fired to verify the accuracy of a particular load? First, let's assume a knowledgeable shooter capable of consistent bench techniques and a rifle without mechanical problems. The correct answer is always however many groups it takes for the shooter to feel comfortable in knowing he has an accurate load combination for a particular rifle, but this will likely be several groups. The aforementioned admonition regarding limited group firing for the very experienced shooter using a rifle that shoots small groups with practically any load could be applied here. Regardless, the more groups averaged, the more meaningful the results.

What about four-shot groups? I used this approach for the first time about 15 years ago with a cast bullet article. Five-shot groups using cast bullets are seldom a problem from the "hot barrel" perspective, unlike high-velocity jacketed bullet loads. However, the particular article included a great deal of load data. Approximately 1,000 rounds were fired. Not only were a lot of components used, some of the heavier loads produced sufficient recoil to quickly cause shooter fatigue. Twenty percent fewer rounds fired seemed to make sense. Since then, four-shot groups have been used for evaluation with a number of rifles shooting jacketed bullets as well.

An advantage of the four-shot group over the three-shot variety comes to light particularly during group shooting in the initial load development stage. How often does a handloader put together several batches of three rounds, each with some variance in powder charge, overall cartridge length, primer, etc.? Or, what about the factory ammo shooter who does the same using different brands and bullet weights and styles? One may often get a group with two shots clustered together and a third round away from the group. Shooter error or something else? A four-shot group makes the analysis much easier.

To illustrate the points made thus far, eight bolt-action varmint and game centerfire rifles, each chambered for a different cartridge, were selected. Various barrel contours are represented. Muzzle diameters are listed next to barrel length. Handloading data for each cartridge is included.

The Ruger .223 was purchased new in 1991 and has been shot a great deal. It has served mostly for load development and as a coyote rifle. The FN Mauser was bought used more than 25 years ago, but

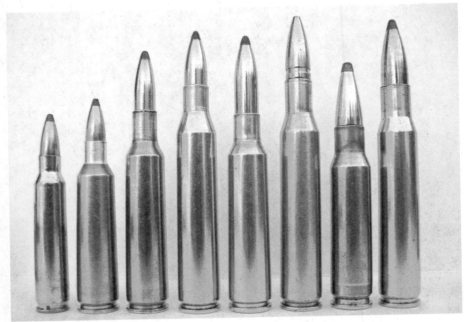

Cartridges, all handloads, used in this group shooting experiment include (from left): .223 Remington, .22-250 Remington, 6mm Remington, .25-06 Remington, 6.5x55 Swedish Mauser, .270 Winchester, .308 Winchester and the .30-06 Springfield. See text for details on components and loads.

has fewer than 1,000 rounds through its second .22-250 barrel (Lilja). The Cooper 6mm Remington was acquired new in 2012. An estimated 500 rounds have been fired in it. The Ruger 77V .25-06 was bought new in 1990, but has not been fired in excess of 1,000 rounds. The M70 6.5x55 Featherweight was purchased from a longtime friend a few years ago. He bought it new and performed a popular break-in routine on the barrel. However, it was shot little after that until I bought it. At least 500 to 600 rounds have been fired during the last couple of years in load development work.

The Cooper .270 was purchased new several years ago for use in an extensive load data update article. As a result of this work and continued load development subsequent to the article, it is a "high-mileage" rifle. Accuracy has fallen off a bit. Bullets must now be seated to a longer OAL to maintain decent accuracy. Both Winchester Model 70 Extreme Weather rifles were new guns on loan from the manufacturer.

With the noted exception of the Model 70 6.5x55, none of the rifles were subjected to any sort of barrel break-in procedure. All listed scopes are the ones customarily used on the rifles; each has a common "plex-type" crosshair reticle.

All group shooting for this endeavor took place during several range sessions. While windless days are truly a rarity in North Texas, wind velocities are often around 5 mph, sometimes less, during the early morning hours. Shooting during such favorable conditions was not always possible. Nevertheless, no shooting was done when known wind speeds exceeded 10 mph or when range temperatures were greater than 90 degrees.

Group shooting was performed with each rifle from a 100-yard bench rest in the following manner:

Five, five-shot groups	=	25 rounds
Six, four-shot groups	=	24 rounds
Eight, three-shot groups	=	24 rounds
Total for each rifle	=	73 rounds

Shots for each group were fired in a normal sequence, not allowing for barrel cooling between rounds. Two groups were never fired back-to-back with the same rifle. Barrels were allowed to cool after every group. Any blatant error on my part (jerky trigger release, etc.) necessitated a re-firing. Front rest was a 17-pound Hart pedestal with a Protektor sand-filled leather bag. A Protektor "bunny ear" leather sand-filled bag was used for a rear rest.

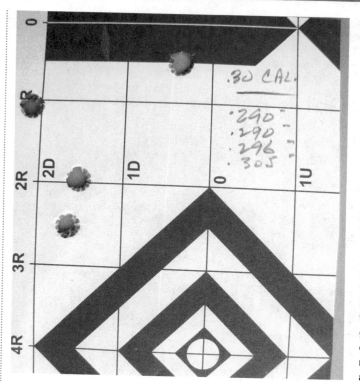

Left: Bullet holes in targets are generally undersized and not particularly uniform in diameter. None of the .30-caliber holes depicted measure as large as .308".

Below: Except for competitive use (as in benchrest) where a group measuring device is employed, a ruler graduated in tenths of an inch is far more useful for measuring groups than a dial caliper. Such measurements are also repeatable.

There are a couple of significant factors that need addressing regarding "conventional and accepted" methods of measuring bullet holes in targets and in the measuring of group sizes. Most of us compute group size by measuring center to center of the two most distant holes, or measuring outside to outside of the two most distant holes and subtracting bullet diameter. Results should be similar.

A problem with measuring bullet holes is that the holes in the paper are generally smaller than bullet diameter and not necessarily consistent in size. Contributory factors include – but may not be limited to – the type of target paper and the backing the target is affixed to.

With the exception of formal benchrest competition, where a group size can be extremely small and a group measuring device is employed, it is pointless to use a dial caliper for measuring the size of a group. Those who do may be unaware that it is all but impossible to find the center of a bullet hole or the exact edge of the same. Yet, these shooters "compute by inference" such measurements to a thousandth of an inch. Also of importance is the fact that these measurements are not repeatable. If one insists on measuring groups with a dial caliper, a group measuring device is a must for reasonably factual figures.

Again, except for benchrest competition, measuring to the nearest eighth of an inch, or even one-sixteenth of an inch with a standard ruler is plenty precise and measurements are repeatable. However, for easy reading and record keeping, these figures should be converted to decimal equivalents (3/8" = .375", etc.). To simplify all of this, rulers graduated in tenths (or twentieths) of an inch are available. It is difficult to imagine a practical need for

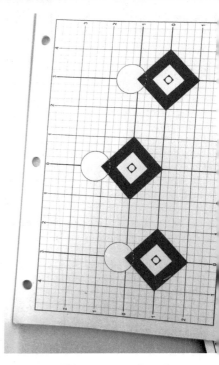

Model 70 6.5x55 (top) is equipped with a Leupold FXII 6x36mm scope while the Model 70 Extreme Weather has Leupold's FX-3 6x42mm. Scopes of 6x magnification are more than adequate for most hunting situations, even long-range use. Many contemporary enthusiasts, however, have never tried them, preferring more powerful variable models.

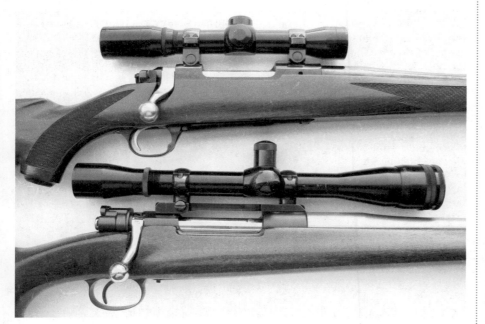

The only variances from Leupold scopes on test rifles were the 6x Burris Compact on the Ruger .223 (top) and the 6x Lyman Silhouette on the .22-250 FN Mauser. Long out of production, these scopes still work well after many years of use.

greater repeatable precision than this in measuring group sizes. I prefer to use 1/10" increments. Such a method was used for the group sizes measured here. Each group size measurement was rounded to the closest tenth.

One good group is nothing more than an indication that more groups need to be fired. Something seldom mentioned with regard to the single, lucky miniscule group (that often cannot be duplicated) is that a flyer can land inside the group just as it can land outside. While it takes some time, effort and a good supply of ammunition, averaging multiple groups, whether they are of the three-, four- or five-shot variety is the only reasonable and realistic approach to assess the accuracy potential of a rifle.

Some may use a multiplying factor in hopes of predicting what a five-shot group will be based on three-shot group averages. However, the method may just as likely provide meaningless results. Better figures can be obtained by simply firing an adequate number of five-shot groups.

Targets. There are more than a few choices here, particularly when one considers the current variety of commercial targets and downloadable examples available from various Internet sources. Target selection is subjective, but there is much truth in the adage, "small targets for small groups." Regardless of target design, any shooter is best advised to use the smallest target compatible with scope power and vision

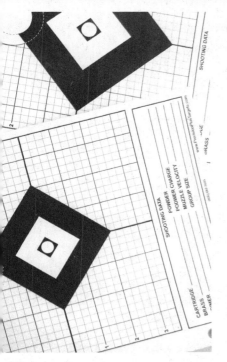

Depicted targets (produced and marketed by Mountain Plains Industries) are excellent examples of those commercially available for group shooting. Diamond-shaped centers have become increasing popular, and colors other than black are far better for visually locating bullet holes with spotting scopes.

SHOOTING RESULTS

Ruger 77 MK II, .223 Remington

Five-shot groups: .5", .7", 1.5", .5", 1.6"	Average = .96"
Four-shot groups: .9", .6", .9", .8", 1.0", .9"	Average = .85"
Three-shot groups: 1.3", .8", .7", 1.0", 1.0", .8", .8", .3"	Average = .84"

FN Mauser, .22-250 Remington

Five-shot groups: .6", 1.0", 1.4", .9", .6"	Average = .90"
Four-shot groups: 1.1", 1.1", .4", .7", .6", .9"	Average = .80"
Three-shot groups: .8", .9", .9", .5", .7", .6", .5", .8"	Average =.71"

Cooper 54, 6mm Remington

Five-shot groups: .6", .8", .8", .8", .5"	Average = .70"
Four-shot groups: .7", 1.2", 1.0", 1.1", .9", .7"	Average = .93"
Three-shot groups: .8", .9", .3", .8", .5", 1.0", .8", .3"	Average = .68"

Ruger 77V, .25-06 Remington

Five-shot groups: .8", .6", .7", .9", .8"	Average = .76"
Four-shot groups: .8", .5", .9", 1.0", .6", .4"	Average = .70"
Three-shot groups: .4", .7", .7", 1.0", .8", .9", .7", .6"	Average = .73"

Winchester 70 FWT. , 6.5x55 Swedish Mauser

Five-shot groups: 1", 1.7", 1.2", .8", .9"	Average = 1.12"
Four-shot groups: 1.1", 1.7", 1.2", 1.3", 1.7", 1.5"	Average = 1.42"
Three-shot groups: 1.3", .9", 1.4", .8", .5", 1.3", .3", 1.4"	Average = .99"

Cooper 52, .270 Winchester

Five-shot groups: .6", 1.1", 1.2", .5", .8"	Average = .84"
Four-shot groups: .6", .7", 1.1", 1.4", .9", 1.1"	Average = .97"
Three-shot groups: .5", .8", 1.5", .8", .4", 1.0", .7", .7"	Average = .80"

Winchester M70 Extreme Weather, .308 Winchester

Five-shot groups: 1.4", 1.8", 1.4", 1.1", 1.6"	Average = 1.46"
Four-shot groups: .6", .8", .9", .8", .6", 1.1"	Average = .80"
Three-shot groups: .5", .8", 1.0", 1.3", .9", .5", .7", 1.3"	Average = .88"

Winchester M70 Extreme Weather, .30-06 Springfield

Five-shot groups: 1.4", 1.0", 1.7", 1.7", 1.7"	Average = 1.50"
Four-shot groups: 1.4", 1.0", 1.4", 1.0", 1.7", 1.5"	Average = 1.33"
Three-shot groups: .6", .9", .8", 1.5", 1.1", 1.3", 1.1", 1.1"	Average = 1.10"

acuity. No aspect of either target or scope should induce even minimal eye fatigue or strain, and the view should be clear. Many shooters have come to see a distinct advantage in diamond-shaped targets, available in various sizes, and target colors other than black. While some may find a diamond-shaped target 3 to 4 inches on a side perfectly adequate for 100-yard shooting with most scopes between 4x and 10x, others may prefer something else.

The figures provide far more information than could be conveyed in a written explanation. The rifles and accuracy levels combine to form a cross section that is representative of what can reasonably be expected by experienced shooters performing the same lengthy (tedious?) chore. Clearly, the rifles used vary considerably in accuracy results.

It would have been easier and faster to fire three, five-shot groups; four, four-shot groups, and five, three-shot groups for a total of 46 rounds per rifle instead of 73. This routine was seriously considered

and results may have been similar. However, in support of the selected method it remains a fact that, within reason, one can't fire too many groups for the purpose of evaluation. Duly noting exceptional circumstances mentioned earlier, too few groups simply do not provide much in the way of useful information.

How BULLET COATING Affects Performance

By Brad Miller

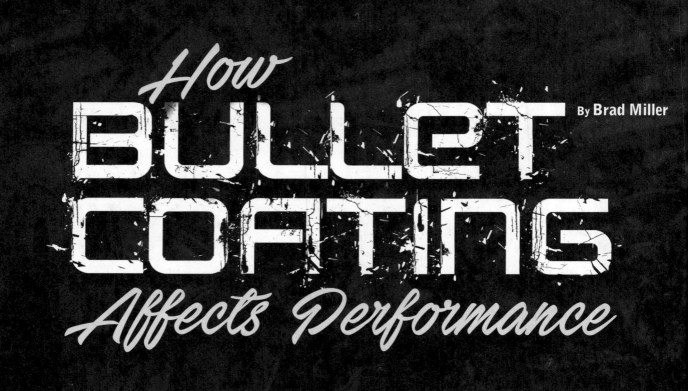

Handloaders have a wide range of bullets to choose from these days. Selection usually depends on the intended use (plinking, target, hunting, defense) as well as type (lead, plated, jacketed), design (RN, FN, HP), feeding reliability and cost. As many handloaders know, different bullets might produce a different velocity with the same load even though they are the same weight and shape.

Six different types of .45 ACP 230-grain RN bullets were compared to see how they responded to the same load of gunpowder. They were FMJ (Full Metal Jacket), plated, swaged, cast, moly (molybdenum disulfide) coated and polymer-coated cast bullets. Moly and polymer coatings are replacements for the traditional waxy lubes applied to lead bullets. These coatings generally reduce the amount of smoke produced by waxy lubes.

The bullets used in the testing were Remington FMJ, Berry's copper plated, Hornady swaged, Oregon Trail cast, Bear Creek Supply proprietary moly coated cast and Bayou Bullets Hi-Tek polymer coated cast bullets (Figure 1). Bullets were loaded in the same headstamp Blazer brass with CCI 500 primers to 1.240" cartridge overall length (COL).

Four different charge weights of Winchester 231 were used. Ten rounds were loaded with each charge weight for a total of 240 rounds (6 bullets x 4 charge weights x 10 rounds = 240). They were fired from a Para Ordnance P14 .45-caliber pistol. Velocity was measured with a Shooting Chrony chronograph at about 10 feet.

FIGURE 1

.45 ACP

Shown are the 230-grain RN bullets used in this comparison. Ten bullets of each type were weighed and their average values are shown here.

	Berry's Plated	Remington FMJ	Hornady Swaged	Bear Creek Moly	Bayou Coated	Oregon Trail Cast
Weight (gr) →	230.3	230.2	230.1	235.4	231.8	227.5

SHOOTING RESULTS

FIGURE 2

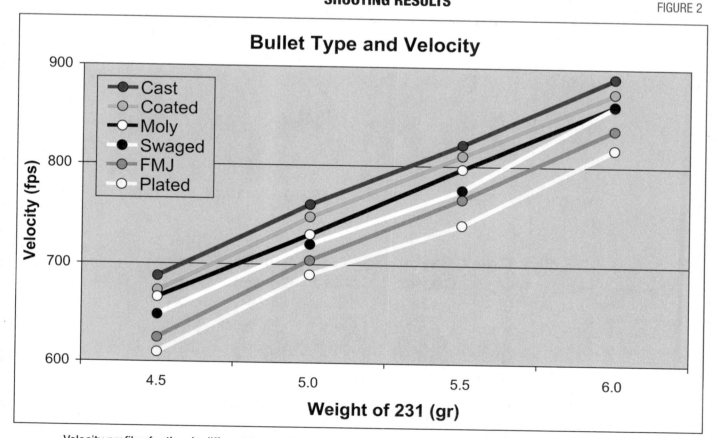

Velocity profiles for the six different types of bullets with four different charge weights of Winchester 231 powder.

TABLE 1

Gunpowder Weight (gr)	
Cast	5.3
Coated	5.4
Moly	5.5
Swaged	5.6
FMJ	5.7
Plated	5.9

This table shows the different gunpowder weights of Winchester 231 for each type of bullet to reach 800 fps. Values were calculated with linear regression.

The different bullet types produced different velocities that were consistent at every charge weight tested (Figure 2). Cast bullets were the fastest, followed by the polymer-coated bullets, the moly coated bullets, the swaged bullets, the FMJ bullets, and the plated bullets were the slowest.

The average difference in extreme spread of velocity between the fastest (cast) and slowest (plated) bullets with the same amount of gunpowder was 75 fps. That is not a trivial number, and translates into a difference in power factor of 17.25.

Producing different speeds with the same amount of gunpowder means that they require different amounts of gunpowder to achieve the same velocity. The cast bullets, because they were the fastest, required the least amount of gunpowder for a given velocity, while the slow plated bullets required the most (Table 1). For example, the plated bullets required .6 grains more gunpowder than the cast bullets to reach 800 fps.

To test the generality of the results with the .45 bullets, an additional comparison was made with a .38 Super and 124/125-grain bullets. They included cast, jacketed, plated, moly and polymer-coated bullets. However, this test consisted of a wider variety, with several brands of plated, FMJ and coated bullets (Figure 3). Ten rounds of each type were loaded in Starline .38 Super Comp brass (a rimless version of .38 Super) with CCI 500 primers and seated to 1.250" COL. Just a single gunpowder charge weight of 5.3 grains of 231 was used. They were fired from a Para Ordnance Pistol with a 5-inch Kart barrel.

Results with these bullets were similar to the .45 results, but the use of multiple brands showed that where a type of bullet ranked could depend on its brand (Figure 4). The plated (yellow bars) and FMJ (orange bars) bullets produced the lowest velocity, as they did in the .45, but the plated bullets were not the slowest. In this sample, the slowest bullet was the Montana Gold FMJ.

FIGURE 3

.38 SUPER

	Berry's Plated 124	Speer Plated 124	Montana Gold FMJ 124	Remington FMJ 124	Sierra FMJ 125
Weight (gr) →	124.0	125.2	124.0	124.8	125.0

Bullets used in the .38 Super. Their average weight is shown below each bullet. Several different types of coatings are available and are described at the maker's website.

Bear Creek Moly 125	Bayou Coated 124	Eggleston Coated 125	Blue Bullets Coated 125	Suter's Choice Cast 125
125.9	124.7	127.1	125.2	124.2

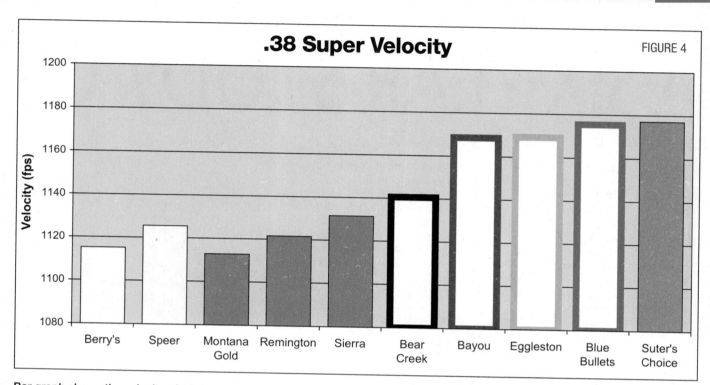

.38 Super Velocity

FIGURE 4

Velocity (fps)

Berry's · Speer · Montana Gold · Remington · Sierra · Bear Creek · Bayou · Eggleston · Blue Bullets · Suter's Choice

Bar graph shows the velocity of 124/125-grain bullets tested in the .38 Super. All bullets were loaded with the same powder charge weight. Bullets are color coded for type: the plated are yellow, the FMJ are orange, the coated are white, the cast are gray. The colored border of the coated bullets match the bullet color in Figure 3.

The moly coated (white/black bar) bullets were faster than the plated and jacketed bullets, but slower than the other polymer-coated (white/colored bars) and cast (gray bar) bullets, just as they were for the .45 caliber. The cast bullet was the fastest, but it was only an average of 1.6 fps faster than the polymer-coated Blue Bullets. The extreme spread between the slowest and fastest bullets in this group was 64 fps. In this weight range (124/125 grains), that translates into a difference in power factor of eight.

Conclusions

Different types of bullets can produce different velocities with the same load. Different brands of the same type, such as FMJ, can produce different velocities as well. In these tests, the cast bullets were faster than the other types. Plated and jacketed bullets were the slowest. Swaged and coated bullets produced intermediate velocities.

Moly significantly reduces friction, which decreases pressure and velocity, and explains why they had the lowest velocity of the cast bullets. However, the manufacturer of Bear Creek's bullets notes that while moly coated lead bullets tend to shoot slower than their non-coated counterparts at low pressures, he has observed that they can produce significantly faster velocities than their noncoated counterparts when loaded to high pressures.

Handloaders might need to make adjustments in their charge weights if they are aiming for a particular velocity and switch to a different bullet, so long as their loads stay within safe operating pressures. Always consult a handloading manual.

How velocity with different bullet types affects accuracy is difficult to predict and requires testing. Several factors can affect accuracy. These include details of the specific bullet design, such as shape (roundnose, flatnose, hollowpoint, etc.), length of bearing surface, hardness, diameter, weight, as well as details of the reloading process such as overall length, bullet alignment and crimp. Some gunpowders seem better suited for the task than others, and this might vary by bullet and caliber. Different barrels have preferences, as well. In the final analysis, you have to test different loads in your gun to see what it likes.

It's prudent to find load data for the specific bullet used, but this is not always possible since some bullet manufacturers do not publish load guides. Check the manufacturer's website for their recommendation. Start load development at the starting charge weights and work up slowly. Watch for pressure signs to make sure it is safe in your gun. Results of this test are specific to the particular guns used. Your results might be different. Only testing can determine what velocity your gun will produce.

A special thanks to Mr. Miller of Bear Creek Supply (no relation to the author) for his insightful discussion of moly coated cast bullets.

DISCLAIMER: Any and all loading data found in this article or previous articles is to be taken as reference material *only*. The publishers, editors, authors, contributors and their entities bear no responsibility for the use by others of the data included in this article or others that came before it.

RESOURCES:

http://www.thebluebullets.com/
http://www.bayoubullets.net/
http://www.egglestonmunitions.com/
Bear Creek moly coated bullets: no website, phone: 209-874-4322.

A SIX-YEAR STUDY OF

By **Ken Walters**

How does practice affect marksmanship? And how much practice? I wanted to know.

The plan was simple—yearly shooting studies. The same shooting studies would be run over and over again all year long. Each day the targets would be scored and the results computerized.

The results have been fascinating—nothing like what I expected but fascinating. Though it was never intended, I ended up with a way to tell not only how well your practice is going but also when, or maybe if, better equipment would help. This technique, which I will examine, works with any firearm, not just .22s.

Federal Value Pack ammunition was used in the shooting because cost was an issue. Also I used Dixie Gun Works EA8200 targets.

Figure 1 shows my longest study. Each circle is the score from one gun for one day. The black line is a 10-day running average. So we have two ways of looking at the data and both are helpful.

Let's start with the running average, i.e. the black line. If you look at just the high points of this line in each of these nearly seven years, you see that they are pretty much the same. Years 2010 and 2012 are a bit low because not much shooting was done in those two years. The really odd year, however, was 2013. A lot of shooting was done that year but up until the very end the scores were pathetic. Oddly enough, however, 2013 is the key to understanding a significant problem. Why do the scores bounce all

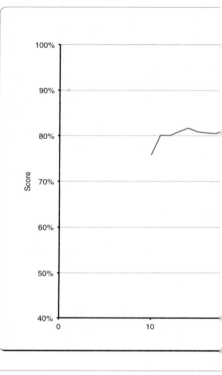

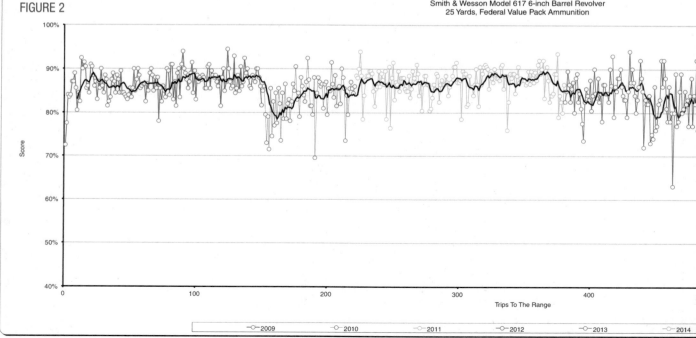

FIGURE 2

Smith & Wesson Model 617 6-inch Barrel Revolver
25 Yards, Federal Value Pack Ammunition

Score

Trips To The Range

—○— 2009   —○— 2010   —○— 2011   —○— 2012   —○— 2013   —○— 2014

MARKSMANSHIP

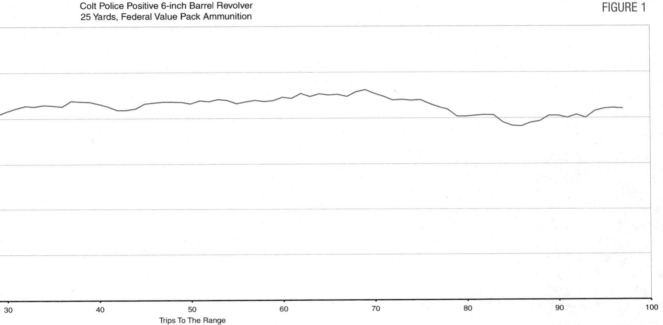

Colt Police Positive 6-inch Barrel Revolver
25 Yards, Federal Value Pack Ammunition

FIGURE 1

Trips To The Range

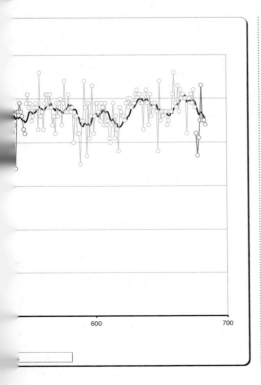

over the place? Because of the number of low outliers.

Look at the black line. I'd say that 2009 and 2011 were my best two years. Fewest outliers and hence more consistent scores. And 2013 was my worst. There was no reason for this. It just happened. That's odd. I can understand having a bad day. I would never have believed, however, that I could have a bad year if I didn't, literally, have graphic proof.

Equally weird is the fact that a bad year can be gun specific. Studies like this were done again with a Smith & Wesson Model 41 target pistol and then with a Ruger Competition target pistol. These two guns did just fine in 2013. So you can have a bad year with one gun while having a normal year with another.

There is another key point here. My scores don't improve over time. I thought that I would see slow but steady improvement. Doesn't happen. What does hap-

pen is that you hit an upper limit with a particular gun and ammunition and then you just stay there.

And there is another oddity. There wasn't much difference in the accuracy of the S&W Model 617, S&W Model 41 and Ruger Competition. That struck me as odd until I realized that none of these guns were limiting my ability so switching between them wasn't going to give me any improvement.

So how much does the choice of gun limit your ability? Oddly enough quite a bit. Also price doesn't have a lot to do with it. I tried four inexpensive semiautomatic pistols and one very old and small lightweight Colt 6-inch barrel target revolver. The pair of Ruger Mk III's, one with a 4.75-inch barrel and one with a 6-inch barrel, did just fine. Only a little less accurate from what we saw in Figure 1. I was surprised because the sights on these guns aren't anything special and they cost a whole lot less. The old Colt wasn't quite as good, so here, finally, is

FIGURE 3

Walther P22 Semiautomatic Rimfire Handguns
25 Yards, Federal Value Pack Ammunition

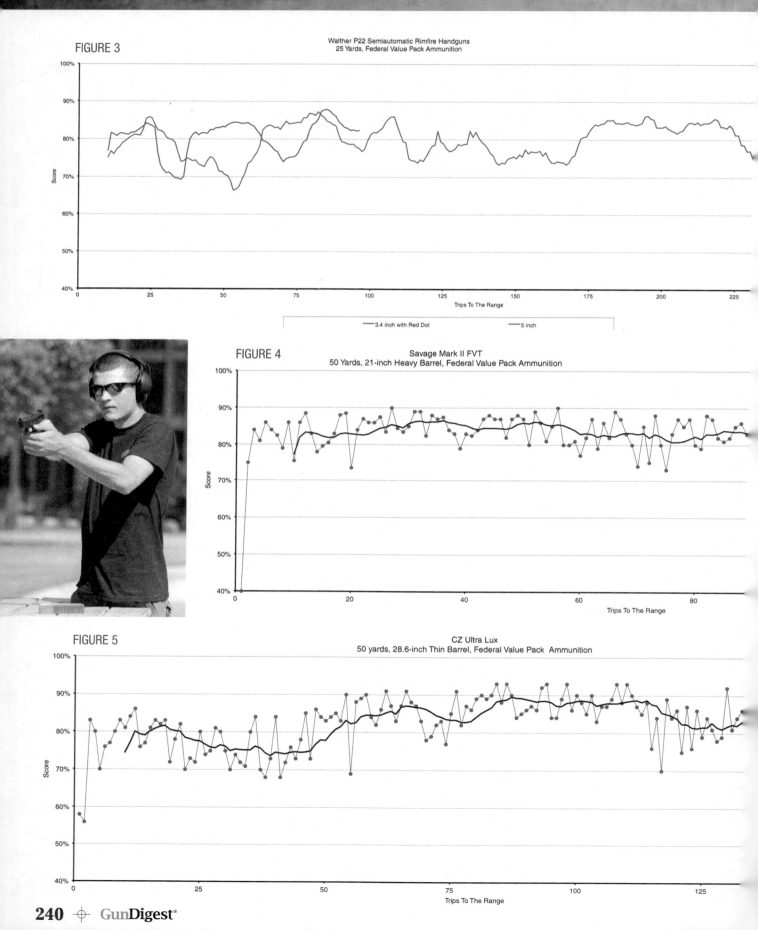

Trips To The Range

——— 3.4 inch with Red Dot   ——— 5 inch

FIGURE 4

Savage Mark II FVT
50 Yards, 21-inch Heavy Barrel, Federal Value Pack Ammunition

Trips To The Range

FIGURE 5

CZ Ultra Lux
50 yards, 28.6-inch Thin Barrel, Federal Value Pack Ammunition

Trips To The Range

275

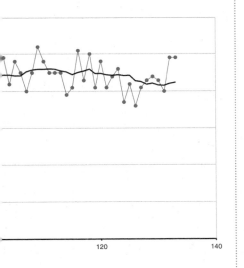

120   140

a gun that was limiting my ability. I was beginning to wonder if that was possible. (See Figure 2)

I believe that one thing that limits accuracy is the gun's weight. To see if this was true I studied two Walther P22's (see Figure 3). These two pistols weigh next to nothing. Obviously my scores were the worst yet. Actually they were the worst ever.

There is a consistent theme across all this. The lighter the gun the more outliers. More outliers mean that the scores will not be as consistent and inconsistent scores will be lower. So it isn't that a lighter gun is more inaccurate. Rather it is much harder to control. So if I wanted to be a really top-of-the-line .22 target pistol shooter I'd get a very lightweight semiautomatic

pistol, something that would minimize my possibility of doing well, and practice with it a lot. Improvement here would not be easy but any improvement would not be subtle. You would see improvements, clearly.

Now let's move on to rifles. I wanted an excellent but inexpensive .22 bolt-action rifle. I found two, the Savage Mk II FVT, see Figure 4, and the CZ Ultra Lux, see Figure 5.

Which one is the more accurate? Well, clearly the Savage produced the more consistent results. However, the CZ was capable of higher scores but, unfortu-nately, also higher inconsistency. Figure 4 tells me that I've reached the upper limit of what I can do with the Savage. Figure 5 suggests that I could do a great deal better with the CZ *if* I can learn to control the outliers. So if I wanted to be really great rifle shot, the CZ would be the better selection because it has more room for improvement.

I've always liked experiments. When the experiments are over and you start writing the stuff up it is like putting the pieces of a jigsaw puzzle together and the pieces never fit the way you expected. I seriously thought, for ex-ample, that I would slowly but steadily improve. It never occurred to me that at some point my scores would flatten out. It never occurred to me that a simple graphical technique would allow me to decide when, or even if, better equip-ment was called for.

But that is exactly what happened. What I found was a way to know when bet-ter equipment would be worth the invest-ment. If you have a graph like Figure 3 you really aren't ready for better equipment. If you have progressed to the point that your scores look like Figure 2 then better equipment will almost certainly help. When you have progressed to something like the results shown in Figure 1, there is no way to know if better equipment will help. If you want to find out you just have to spend the money and see what hap-pens. Obviously, this will work for either pistols or rifles. This graphical technique will also work with centerfire guns.

So the key to doing well with a .22, or any gun, is in these graphs. All you need are your scores and a piece of graph paper. If you use this graphical technique not only will you literally see how your shooting is progressing – you will also have the key to knowing when, or if, better equipment would be justified. All by just making a very simple graph.

150

BY **Wayne van Zwoll**

FEW NEW MODELS ARE TRADITIONAL "CLASSICS." BUT SURELY SOME WILL BE REMEMBERED THAT WAY!

The initial roster of 2016 Republican presidential hopefuls was long indeed. Ditto the list of rifles I'm obliged to sift for *Gun Digest's* annual rifle roundup. While ordinarily high-volume manufacturers gobble many column inches, a surprising dearth of innovative rifles from major brands, but fetching new models from small companies, have skewed my coverage. So be it. Equal coverage appears an outdated custom in presidential debates. I won't say it's gone from this section; but for 2016, rifles that evidenced clever design or excelled in function or drilled tiny groups or drew the eye with fine fit and finish earned their paragraphs. Space constraints

dictated I omit several makers of worthy but largely unchanged rifles – Heym, Hill Country Rifles and H-S Precision, to name a few starting with "H." My apologies.

Bergara

The name is that of a town in northern Spain, where a factory builds accurate rifle barrels for BPI Outdoors, which in 1999 bought CVA (Connecticut Valley Arms) and is now owned by the Spanish firm, Dikar. In 2003, BPI CEO Dudley McGarity looked for ways to make CVA more profitable. Expanding the Bergara factory to make barrels CVA previously had to buy, McGarity and company had

the fortune to land other barrel contracts when President Obama's election triggered a stampede to gunshops. Bergara has since evolved into a rifle brand with its own action on a Remington 700 footprint. A Custom Series comprises eight rifles, a Premier Series four, in tactical and hunting configurations. Prices: $2,100 to $4,100, with top-rung components from the likes of McMillan, Badger, Shilen. But there's a new, more affordable B-14 action too. It comes in two lengths: short for the 6.5 Creedmoor and .308 (with 22-inch chrome-moly barrels), long for the .270, .30-06 and 7mm Remington and .300 Winchester Magnums (24-inch). The B-14's coned bolt nose has a sliding plate extractor, a plunger ejector. There's

Bergara's new B14 includes this Woodsman with straight-comb stock, floorplate, adjustable trigger.

The B14 bolt has a cocking indicator, an enclosed face with sliding plate extractor, plunger ejector.

a two-position safety, adjustable trigger, traditional hinged floorplate. For 2016, the walnut-stocked Woodsman joins the Timber (walnut with Monte Carlo comb) and Hunter (synthetic) B-14 rifles. The .270 Woodsman in my rack is awaiting time at the range. I like its profile and heft, its trigger and the way the SIG 2-10x42 sits low for quick aim over the straight comb. Price: $945, same as the Timber. The Hunter lists for $825. (www.Bergarausa.com)

Blaser

Several configurations of the R8 have appeared since this straight-pull bolt rifle supplanted the R93 as Blaser's flagship. On both, the bolt head locks with a collett forced into a circumferential groove in the barrel shank. But the R8 is stronger. Its locking angle is steeper than the R93's. A bushing slides into the collett's center upon lock-up, for added support. In tests, the R8 endured pressures of 120,000 psi. The R8 has hammer-forged, switchable barrels with screw-less scope mounting, a single-stack magazine tucked into a compact trigger group. The thumb-piece that cocks the R8 is the only safety. So you can carry an R8 safely with a round in the chamber. Thanks to its telescoping, radial-head bolt, the action is about 2 inches shorter than that of a standard bolt rifle!

Stocks for R8s – walnut, synthetic and laminated – include European and American profiles, thumbhole grips and leather appointments. Most recent: a laminated prone stock with a vertical wrist, adjustable comb and rail-equipped fore-end. That's what Blaser installed on its new R8 in .338 Lapua. Based on the .416 Rigby, this rimless round is longer even than full-length magnum cartridges fashioned from .375 H&H brass. It's bigger in diameter too: .588" at the web, compared to .532" at the .375's belt. The flat-shooting Lapua is gaining favor in long-range matches. Its 250- and 300-grain BTHP bullets (Scenars and Sierra MatchKings) sail with miserly concessions to gravity and wind. For plates beyond 1,000 yards, there's arguably no better choice in rifles you can carry with one hand. Indeed, this Blaser is lighter than it looks. (The Schmidt & Bender PM II 5-25x56 scope I used to check accuracy added considerable heft.)

An aggressive brake hikes muzzle weight and blast but tames kick and barrel jump. A lighter R8 in this chambering has a midweight barrel with Blaser's Dual Brake, a Professional Success stock. I chose the GRS with laminated prone stock because the .338 Lapua has the legs for prone shooting. Whichever you pick, you can readily switch barrels, bolts and magazines. With three brands of ammunition, all with 250-grain BTHP bullets, this Blaser drilled snug groups. Black Hills took top honors with a .7" knot. The comfortable stock was a great assist; ditto the crisp 2¼-pound trigger. The action cycled silkily, without fault. Cost? With a scope like the S&B PM II, this R8 dings you as deeply as a divorce attorney's retainer. It's worth the price. (www.blaser-usa.com)

Browning

Only the Medallion and Left Hand Stainless Stalker rifles remain in Browning's once burgeoning line of A-Bolt rifles. Replacing them, X-Bolts proliferate. Among the most interesting of late arrivals – the Stalker Long Range with braked 26-inch barrel and Dura-Touch stock finish. Striking by virtue of a Burnt Bronze Cerakote metal finish and McMillan Game Scout stock is an upscale rifle ideally suited for prone shooting at distance. North of $2,100, it's more than double the price of the Stalker LR.

Browning offers many X-Bolt variations, a deep roster of chamberings. The recent addition of Combos (rifles with scopes) includes Carbine (green synthetic) and Desert Tan X-Bolts with Leupold VX 1 3-9x40 optics. They retail for $1,070. The X-Bolt line is proving fluid; 13 rifles have been dropped as new variations rush the stage. Combos have also appeared in the modestly priced AB3 stable. These rifles feature Redfield's Revenge 3-9x42 or, for more money,

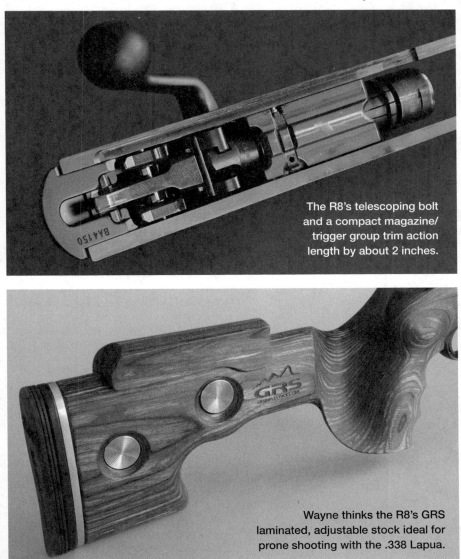

The R8's telescoping bolt and a compact magazine/ trigger group trim action length by about 2 inches.

Wayne thinks the R8's GRS laminated, adjustable stock ideal for prone shooting with the .338 Lapua.

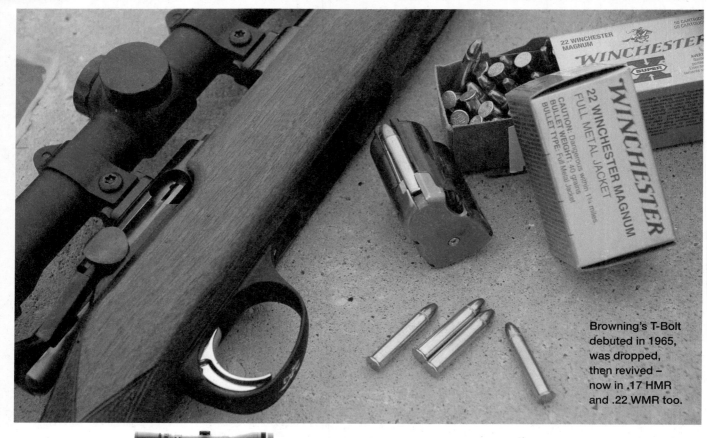

Browning's T-Bolt debuted in 1965, was dropped, then revived – now in .17 HMR and .22 WMR too.

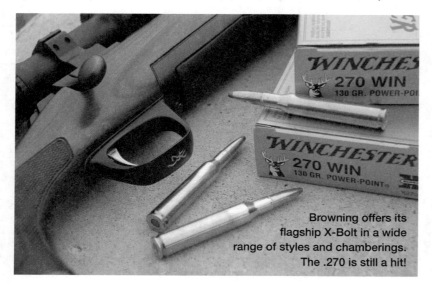

This thumbhole Eclipse Hunter is one of many Browning X-Bolt rifles. The A-Bolt is almost gone.

Browning caters to budgets with a growing stable of AB3 bolt rifles, including Combos with scopes.

Browning offers its flagship X-Bolt in a wide range of styles and chamberings. The .270 is still a hit!

Nikon's 4-12x40 Buckmaster II.

This spring I noticed a new BLR lever action. The Black Label Takedown, with 16- or 18½-inch barrel has a gray laminate stock, a top rail and side rails up front on the fore-end. A flash hider and suppressor threads are standard; the 18½-inch barrel can be had without them.

Browning rimfire rifles include two of my favorites: the T-Bolt (nine versions) and the BL-22 (seven). Introduced in 1965, then built for a decade in Browning's Belgian factory, the T-Bolt was costly to make and vanished. It then reappeared, with changes. In 2008 Browning offered a new Miroku-built T-Bolt in .17 HMR and .22 WMR, as well as .22 LR. It has a 10-shot "double helix" detachable box. You can now order the T-Bolt and the BL-22 with maple stocks, a fetching option! (www.browning.com)

CZ

The push-feed Model 557 action has largely supplanted CZ's 550 with its Mauser claw. Notable exceptions: Safari-class rifles, and the new Badlands and Sonoran, built for extended-range shooting and chambered, like dangerous-game models, for long magnum cartridges.

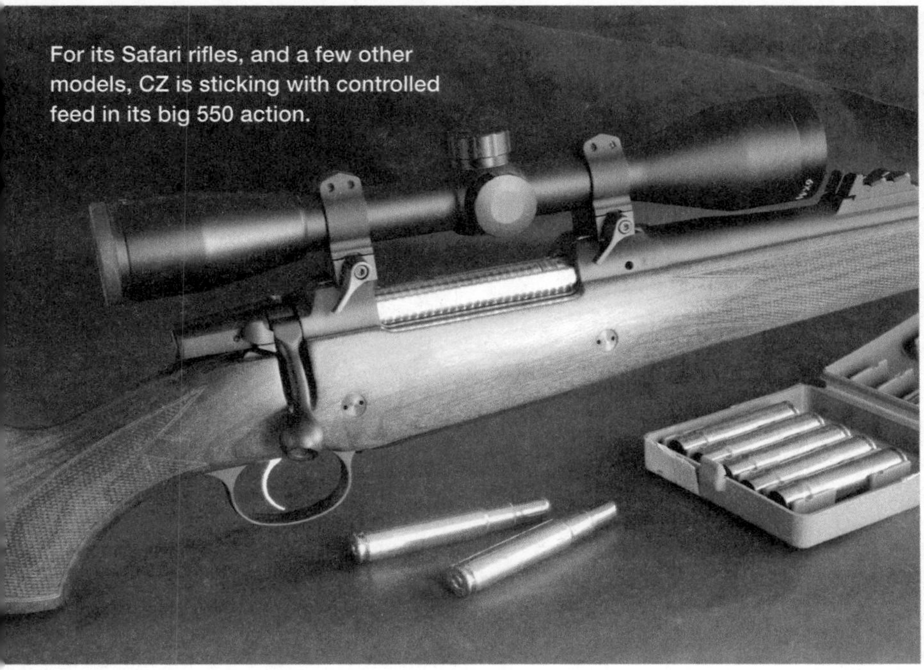

For its Safari rifles, and a few other models, CZ is sticking with controlled feed in its big 550 action.

sights) and American (walnut stock) also come in .22 WMR. (cz-usa.com)

Dakota

True to the vision of the late, talented Don Allen, the company he established decades ago builds bolt rifles that look and function like early M70 Winchesters but offer refinements, better fit and finish. Model 76 Dakotas were later joined by the similar 97, with a tubular receiver and a more palatable price. Last year a synthetic-stock Professional Hunter appeared, with a quarter-rib and banded front sight and swivel. Chamberings: .375 H&H to .450 Dakota. The 97 series got a new Varminter, its Claro artfully shaped. I like the blind magazine it shares with the iron-sighted 97 Outfitter. As Dakota's elegant Model 10 single-shot isn't getting any cheaper, I'm about to spring for one to keep my .280 company. The 10 is to my eye one of the most attractive hunting rifles ever!

The Nesika brand, born in benchrest competition, is now in Dakota's family too. Sporter, Tactical and Long Range Nesikas offer affordable accuracy from Douglas stainless air-gauged barrels, and Bell and Carlson stocks. Chamberings run to .338 Lapua. By the way, Dakota's Sturgis, S.D., headquarters now serves Remington (which owns the brand) as its Custom Shop. I'm told it will build not only Remington rifles, but gussied-up Marlins. (www.dakotaarms.com)

Howa

Under the shingle of Legacy Sports International, the Howa action (used by Weatherby and other firms) has spawned

The Safari Classics stable handles the burly .500 Jeffery and .505 Gibbs, as well as the popular .416 Rigby; the Badlands chambers the .338 Lapua, the Sonoran rounds as big as the .26 Nosler. CZ still catalogs the 550 FS (full-stock), Composite Carbine and Ultimate Hunting Rifle, all for standard-length rounds. But the 557 is steadily gobbling more of the bolt-market pie. This year, the short-action rifle announced last spring in .243, and .308 is shipping. Like the 557 Sporter in 6.5x55, .270 and .30-06, it has a receiver machined from a steel billet, with 19mm dovetails for CZ bases. Its steel bottom metal boasts a hinged floorplate under a four-shot magazine. The two-detent

safety permits bolt cycling "on safe." The trigger adjusts for weight, take-up and overtravel; 22-inch barrels are hammer forged and lapped. My favorite 557 is the Carbine with 20½-inch barrel. It is perfectly balanced and points instantly to the iron sights. A Manners Sporter trims 8 ounces from the 7¼-pound walnut 557, but hikes the price from $800 to over $1,250.

CZ continues with its line of rifles on the .223-size 527 action. For 2016 there's a new .22 rimfire: the 512. An autoloader of modular design, it has an alloy upper receiver, a polymer lower half housing the trigger group and detachable box magazine. The Carbine (synthetic, with

Dakota slowly grows its bolt-action lines. Lug bedding in this 97 stock shows expert workmanship.

The author killed this British Columbia goat with a Dakota 97 in .30-06. The round action distinguishes it from the 76.

This Howa rifle points well for the author. The stiff, finely machined actions appear in myriad rifles.

a growing line of Howa rifles. Legacy has packaged some with scopes. The push-feed action has a twin-lug bolt, two-stage trigger, three-position safety. The straight-stack detachable box isn't my favorite, as on many models it protrudes, and the latch is easy to trip accidentally. Still, some Howas have fixed magazines. Stocks of walnut, wood laminates and synthetic materials (the latter mostly from Hogue) come in thumbhole, varmint and tactical, as well as traditional hunting profiles. Chamberings run from .223 to .338 Winchester. Last year the Howa Mini Action appeared, with a mechanism an inch shorter than standard short actions. First in .204 Ruger and .223, it's now available in 6.5 Grendel. Howa has tweaked its rifles to yield eight new variations for 2016. But biggest news for me is the Empire Rifle, a Howa with a pillar-bedded, checkered stock of Italian walnut and classic lines. It has a flush, detachable steel box. Legacy has revived the British brand, Webley & Scott ("gunmakers since 1790") to market this rifle in .243, 7mm-08, .308, .270 and .30-06. That name also distinguishes a new synthetic-stocked rimfire bolt gun, in .22 LR, .17 HMR and .22 WMR. (legacysports.com)

Kilimanjaro

In 2007 Erik Eike explored a new line of rifles based on those of Serengeti's Mel Smart. Twenty prototypes later, he bought the name and its equipment to establish Kilimanjaro Rifles. Then he recruited the industry's best craftsmen to build semicustom rifles under that shingle. Eight styles of rifles emerged, in chamberings .22-250 to .500 Jeffery. The Leopard and Tigercat are trim lightweights. The Artemis is a svelte bolt action proportioned for women. The Kodiak and African bring what hunters value in stopping rifles. Another fetching big-bore, the distinctive Doctari, is now a best seller. These patterns give clients freedom to make each Kilimanjaro rifle a custom project. Erik uses barrels from PacNor, Douglas, Shilen, Lilja, Krieger. My Kilimanjaro is bored to 7mm Weath-

erby Magnum. A midweight Walkabout, it's on a Dakota 76 action with PacNor barrel. A banded NECG front sight mates with a pop-up aperture below the 6x Zeiss. The figured walnut responded beautifully to shaping, finishing and the Diamond Fleur full-wrap checkering. If you've dreamed of a rifle built to your specs, shop Kilimanjaro! (kilimanjarorifles.com)

Kimber

At the 2016 SHOT Show, I chatted up Kimber engineer George Hawthorne, pretty sure the firm had reached a practical limit in paring down rifle weight. The Adirondack, new in '15, weighs just 4¾ pounds with its 18-inch barrel, threaded for Kimber's brake. Now available in .300 Blackout and 6.5 Creedmoor (the .300 Blackout with standard threads for aftermarket brakes), this short-action 84M complements the Mountain Ascent with 84L action and 24-inch barrel. Different camo patterns on the stocks. Both rifles include lightweight Talley scope rings. For years Kimber's line – including wood-stocked and tactical rifles – has built on a trim two-lug bolt action with Mauser-style extractor for controlled feed. New this year: the Kimber Hunter, a short-action rifle designed mainly by Hawthorne with important features and high-quality components at a blue-collar price. It has the 84's lugs, extractor and three-position safety, and an adjustable trigger – plus Kimber's first detachable box magazine. The molded polymer stock with pillar bedding incorporates the triggerguard. The receiver and 22-inch barrel are satin-finished stain-

Despite their light weight, Kimber 84-series rifles shoot well – as does this Black Hills .30-06 load.

Kimber 84 L Black Hills 168 BTHP .30.06

less steel. In .243, .257 Roberts, 6.5 Creedmoor, 7mm-08 and .308, it scales 6½ pounds. (www.kimberamerica.com)

Legendary Arms Works

Last fall I hunted with a spanking-new LAW rifle. In a Montana 'pole thicket, I fired offhand at an elk. The animal spun, staggered and collapsed. At 9 yards I certainly didn't need the reach of Nosler's .280 Ackley load, but I couldn't imagine a more versatile rifle for Western big game. Now in production, the LAW rifle is the brainchild of Pennsylvanian Mark Bansner and partners who've tapped into his long experience building semicustom rifles. (Mark's High Tech rifle-stocks are industry favorites.) The Model 704 LAW action boasts the best of Remington's 700 – plus a .25"-thick recoil lug, an extractor to permit controlled feed and an M70-style safety that works with a Timney trigger. The tubular receiver is CNC machined from 416 stainless true with the bolt's axis. It has 8-40 scope base holes (hooray!). A stainless follower lifts each round to the middle. Hinged bottom metal is alloy for The Closer and The Professional versions, steel for The Big Five. Stocks are High Tech, of course. Short and long actions accommodate 18 chamberings to .458 Lott (in the Big Five, with brake). Prices start around $1,600. (www.legendaryrifles.com)

Marlin

Born in 1836, Connecticut native John Mahlon Marlin apprenticed as a machinist at 18, working unpaid for six months, then for $1.50 per *week*. His first guns were rimfire pistols. His first tube-fed lever rifle, of under-hammer design, sold poorly. John took a new direction with the Model 1881 and submitted it for military trials. It fired 10 shots in seven seconds, but when a cartridge exploded in the magazine, the Army dismissed it. Fast-forward 120 years across a landscape of lever-action successes: Marlin's 1893, 1894, 1895, Models 36 and 336. On January

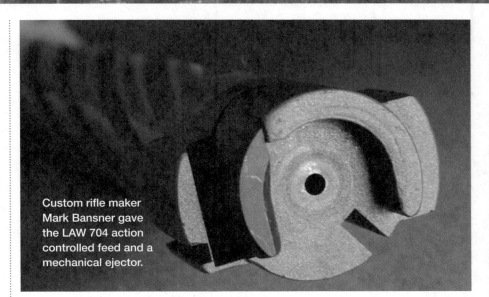

Custom rifle maker Mark Bansner gave the LAW 704 action controlled feed and a mechanical ejector.

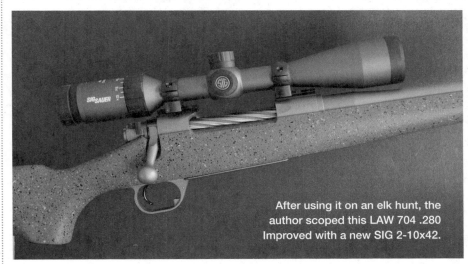

After using it on an elk hunt, the author scoped this LAW 704 .280 Improved with a new SIG 2-10x42.

28, 2008, Remington Arms bought the company. By March 25, 2010, Marlin's North Haven factory had closed. Remington moved most machinery to its Ilion, N.Y., plant. But few Marlin employees followed. And Remington underestimated the hand fitting required on lever-action

rifles built on WWII-era tooling.

The first Marlins from Ilion were of substandard quality. Remington has since invested in the brand.

Top: Commemorative and custom Marlins are slated for building at Dakota's Sturgis, S.D., shop.
Bottom: This new, large-loop, stainless Marlin 1894 with laminated stock wears a rail and a ghost-ring sight.

John Mahlon Marlin first made rimfire pistols. He started building rifles on Ballard actions like this.

I'm told all major parts are now produced on CNC centers. To mollify Marlin fans, the line has been expanded to include custom rifles hand finished at the Dakota shop in Sturgis. A dozen rifles have been temporarily dropped, notably those in .308 and .338 Marlin Express. The 1894 is returning – not so the bolt-action X7 that went to Remington's Mayfield, Ky., factory (which produces Marlin rimfire rifles). Remington insists Marlin lever actions are getting better. Custom Marlins I've seen show attention to detail and are surprisingly affordable. (www.marlinfirearms.com)

Mauser

Arguably, every modern bolt rifle owes its genesis to Paul Mauser's masterpiece of 1898. Last year the Mauser factory (now in Isny, Germany) reintroduced the most celebrated hunting rifle on the original 98 action. Essentially a grown-up '98, the double-square-bridge Magnum Mauser swallows the longest dangerous-game rounds. This heart of archetypal 20th century sporting rifles has been resurrected in an eye-popping new hunting rifle. While Granite Mountain Arms and a few other shops have produced exquisite actions and rifles faithful to the type, this Magnum 98 is a *Mauser*. Pillar bedded with double recoil lugs, it features a deep magazine, three-detent, side-swing safety, 24½-inch barrel with banded stud. The height-adjustable, banded front sight pairs with a three-leaf express sight on an island. The straight-comb, fancy walnut stock has point-pattern checkering, shadow-line cheekpiece, black fore-end tip, steel grip cap. In .375 H&H or .416 Rigby – five- and four-shot boxes, with a heavy barrel option in .416 – this Mauser will make any rifle enthusiast grab the checkbook – after confirming the balance. (www.mauser.com)

Montana Rifle Company

If you're a fan of Winchester Model 70s, you know about Montana rifles, built on the outskirts of Kalispell, Mont. Investment-cast receivers on the pre-'64 M70 pattern are mated to barrels produced on site by Brian Sipe's shop, which has also supplied high-quality barrels to the industry. I've carried Model 1999 Montana rifles in Alaska and Africa, as well as in western elk cover – and am impressed! One has become my go-to .375. Under the guidance of Brian's son Jeff, Montana is adding CNC equipment to its shop and is growing its line.

The American Legends Rifle boasts a classy, wrap-checkered walnut stock, an upgrade of the American Standard Rifle and partner to the American Vantage rifle with iron sights for big-bore rounds to .458 Lott. The new Prairie Runner features a laminated thumbhole stock on stainless metal. The Seven Continent Rifle is a synthetic-stocked muscle gun with new Professional Hunter action for cartridges as big as the .338 Lapua, .416 Rigby, .378 and .460 Weatherby, and .505 Gibbs. You'll also find the PH action on Montana's walnut-stocked Dangerous Game Rifle. Other synthetic-stock rifles, in stainless and chrome-moly, have joined the Montana line. Marksman and Tactical rifles too. The long list of Montana chamberings includes the 6XC and .280 Ackley. (montanarifleco.com)

Mossberg

From the popular rimfire rifles of my youth to the hugely successful Model 500 pump shotgun, to the less celebrated Model 800 centerfire rifle, Mossberg has evolved to serve North American sportsmen. I've used its 464 lever action for deer, its affordable synthetic-stock bolt rifles on pronghorn hunts. The best Mossberg rifles, in my view, just appeared. This Patriot line features fluted bolts, Lightning triggers and flush detachable boxes. There's an iron-sighted dangerous-game rifle in .375 Ruger. Like the .375's laminate, the walnut and synthetic stocks of other Patriots boast straight combs, stippled grips. Pick from 11 chamberings with 22-inch barrels.

Wayne's go-to .375 is the Leupold-scoped Montana 1999 rifle he's aiming here. It's fast and accurate.

Combo packages feature Vortex scopes. (www.mossberg.com)

New Ultra Light Arms

There's been another change at New Ultra Light Arms. When Melvin Forbes handed off part of his business to a team at the Westbrook, Maine, firm of Titan Machine Works, it was to offer less costly versions of his semicustom Models 24 and short-action 20 light-weight bolt-action rifles. The new 20B and 24B were to be production-line variants – 5½-pound rifles with E.R. Shaw barrels, blind magazines, Timney triggers, two-position, three-function safeties and Talley scope rings. Like original Melvin Forbes rifles from West Virginia, the receivers at Forbes Rifles, LLC, were machined in house from steel billets, then paired with straight-comb, hand-laid stocks of the lightest materials. They looked and handled like Melvin's originals, minus custom features and the long list of chamberings at New Ultra Light Arms. I'm using the past tense for the Maine venture because Melvin tells me it no longer ships Forbes rifles. But he is still building and servicing New Ultra Light Arms rifles at his Granville, W.Va., shop. The M20 in my rack shoots into a nickel. Melvin thoughtfully engineered this short action to accept the mid-length 7x57 and .284 families. (www. newultralight.com)

Nosler

Joining the fast-stepping .26 Nosler, the .28 and now the .30 Nosler also nudge the top of velocity charts. Nosler's 48 Heritage rifle, a twin-lug, push-feed bolt action, comes in 18 other chamberings too. A side-mounted extractor and plunger ejector yield an enclosed bolt face. The trigger is adjustable, well shaped and positioned to the rear of the guard. A traditional magazine has an alloy floorplate. The stainless, hand-lapped 26-inch barrel is slim but not whippy. All steel parts are Cerakoted satin black. The conservatively shaped walnut stock is point-pattern checkered 20-lpi. Nosler's Heritage is one of three M48s. The others wear synthetic stocks, pillar and glass bedded, with alloy bedding rails. The Nosler Patriot comes in 17 chamberings, .22-250 to .35 Whelen. The Outfitter, built for hunting dangerous game, is fitted with open sights, has a blind magazine and comes in seven

This mule deer fell to a Mossberg 464 in .30-30, an affordable rifle with a popular profile and action.

chamberings – .308 to .458 Winchester. (www.nosler.com)

Proof Research

Bring together Jense Precision with its custom-rifle resume, and Advanced Barrel Systems with a patented process for making carbon-fiber-wrapped barrels. Then invite Lone Wolf Rifle Stocks to the party in a 27,000-square-foot facility with a million-frame-per-second ballistic camera, and you have the beginnings of Proof Research. The northwest Montana firm specializes in synthetic-stocked bolt rifles and AR-style autoloaders with CF barrels "10 times stronger than stainless steel" – and nearly six times stiffer. Three bolt rifles – the lightweight Summit, long-range Terminus and braked Tac II with adjustable stock – are truly custom rifles. You can specify dimensions within reason, and chamberings to .375 H&H. In 2012 Proof joined with Lawrence Barrels and now lists both stainless and composite barrels. The company partners with Advanced Composites Division in

Dayton, Ohio. ACD provides resins, adhesives and composite materials for applications in the defense and aerospace industries. (proofresearch.com)

Quarter Minute Magnums

In my youth, benchrest shooters and woodchuck hunters tested long-range accuracy across green Pennsylvania hills. Scott and Vickie Harrold began gunsmithing there, then moved "closer to elk hunting" in Lewiston, Idaho. There Scott builds super-accurate hunting rifles for flat-shooting cartridges. He calls them Quarter Minute Magnums. That's his accuracy standard – half-inch groups at 200 yards! But these aren't ponderous rifles. His lightest weighs less than 8 pounds with a #5 Krieger barrel and HTG McMillan stock. Scott uses Remington 700 actions but prefers BATs from Bruce A. Thorne. The integral rail has 20 minutes gain. Scott installs cut-rifled barrels, carefully lapped and rifled to give long bullets "just enough spin to fly straight." He'll ream for fac-

Quarter Minute Magnum rifles get the best barrels, chambered for factory loads to minimum specs.

tory ammo but prefers chambers snug around neck-turned hulls. He has Dave Manson reamers for more than 40 cartridges. Allowing that brakes can affect accuracy, he adds them on magnums at client request. To ensure concentricity, Scott buys BAT brakes undersize, then bores them .02" over groove diameter. Most QMM rifles wear McMillan stocks. His rifles have magazines, but he notes that single-shot actions are stiffer. Clients have a choice of triggers. (quarterminutemagnums.com)

Remington

On this, the 200th anniversary of America's oldest gunmaker, you'd expect commemorative rifles to dominate the catalog. Well, there aren't many. The perennially popular Model 700 bolt action and the 7600 pump get special treatment (engraving, gold inlay, fancy walnut). But the rest of Remington's stable remains pedestrian. New for 2016 is the 700 CDL SF in .35 Whelen, one of my favorite chamberings. It's a stainless rifle, in checkered

walnut. Other 700s for hunters include Long Range and VTR, an SPS with a left-hand action and a muzzleloader. Last fall I saw a whopper of an Illinois whitetail that had dropped to one of these accurate front-loaders. Four Tactical 700s round out that series. It's clear Remington wants sportsmen to notice its modestly priced 783, now in camo dress. At the other end of the price scale, it has throttled up its Custom Shop, most of which has moved to Sturgis, S.D. You can still get Model 547 rimfires, and 700 and 40-X centerfires built to order there. Biggest news for 2016 may be the return of a hard-copy Remington catalog, last year absent for the first time in decades! (www.remington.com)

Rifles, Inc.

Lex Webernick specializes in building trim rifles, mainly on Remington 700 actions. Visiting his rural Texas digs, you'll see an immaculate machine shop where he finishes his own lightweight synthetic stocks. They make Lex's rifles handle like wands! Soft-spoken but well-traveled, Lex *uses* the rifles he builds; he knows what works best afield. Accuracy matters at Rifles, Inc., where light sporters routinely punch benchrest-tight groups. With acoustical electronics, Lex designed his own brakes. They mate so perfectly to the barrel, you'll look hard to find the seam. Rifles, Inc. has offered special edition rifles, but not every year. The discriminating hunters who keep orders coming to Lex Webernick's shop know the difference between "new this year" and "so good we didn't change it." (www.riflesinc.com)

Rigby

In Dublin in 1775, John Rigby started gunsmithing at age 17. He built flintlock smoothbore guns, including dueling pistols. Long-range target rifles and double-barrel hunting rifles followed. Generations later, at the turn of the 20th century, Thomas Bissell and Paul Mauser collaborated on a Rigby that would become the most celebrated of African bolt actions. In 1912 it chambered the potent, elegant .416 Rigby. But not all Rigby rifles were big-bores. W.D.M. "Karamojo" Bell reportedly owned six Rigby Mausers in .275 (7x57). In India, the great tiger hunter Jim Corbett used a .275. It once saved his life. On the trail of the man-eating Chowgarh tigress, Corbett paused to pick up a couple of rare bird eggs. In a sandy wash he stepped clear of a rock, turned and "looked straight into the tigress's face" *8 feet* away. In his left hand

Remington trimmed its bolt-action line, but Custom Shop rifles like this Model Seven are still made.

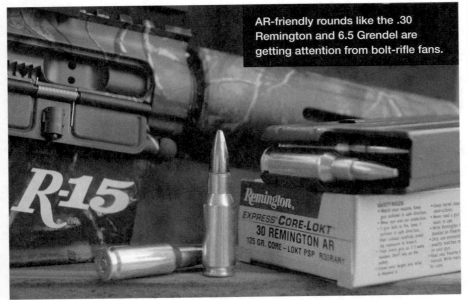

AR-friendly rounds like the .30 Remington and 6.5 Grendel are getting attention from bolt-rifle fans.

Nesika, benchrest-bred, is now part of Remington's family. Rifles are built in Sturgis, S.D.

Remington is in its 200th year – and still making hunters smile! This warthog fell to a 700 in 7mm-08.

Corbett still held the eggs. They may have prevented sudden reaction, he later wrote, which would almost surely have triggered a charge. Slowly he eased the .275 across his chest. "My arm was now at full stretch and the weight of the rifle was beginning to tell." The tigress had not taken her eyes from his. It seemed "that my arm was paralyzed, and that the swing would never be completed." At last the muzzle covered the beast. Corbett fired. The 7mm bullet shattered the cat's spine, and her heart. She had killed 64 people.

Since then, Rigby has traveled a tortuous path. But now its classic big-bore has returned. Built in Germany on Magnum Mauser actions, it's marketed by the Blaser-Mauser-Sauer triumvirate of Isny. The Single Square Bridge model, in .416 or .450 Rigby, wears a 22-inch barrel and express sights. This 10½-pound rifle has a three-position flag safety. The Double Square Bridge model, .375 H&H or .416, weighs a half-pound less with 24-inch barrel. Its Winchester 70-style safety moves easily under scopes. Quarter rib, barrelband swivel, deep magazine and checkered, figured walnut stock is the same. At the Dallas Safari Club and SCI shows this January, it was hard to tell which drew the most traffic – Corbett's .275 Rigby rifle (yes, the original; it points to the sights!) or Rigby's new big-bores! (www.johnrigbyandco.com)

Rock River Arms

No manufacturer I know builds a wider variety of AR-15s than this Illinois company – or offers more value. These midpriced rifles have high-end features. I've used both the LAR-15 (5.56) and LAR-8 (7.62). Among my favorites is a trim carbine in 6.8 SPC. The LAR-15 X-1 has a cryo-treated barrel with Wylde chamber for both .223 and 5.56 loads. Its 1-in-8 rifling delivers subminute accuracy with leggy bullets popular for long-range shooting. The 9½-pound LAR-8 X-1 offers equal precision in .308. This year, X-1 rifles also come in .458 SOCOM, .300 Blackout and 7.62x39.

There's an LAR-15 LEF-T for southpaws. Want a piston-driven AR? Pick Rock River's PDS. You'll find RRA rifles in 9mm and .40 S&W too. Myriad barrel and stock options – and accoutrements – can give your rifle a custom look. Full-length Picatinny rails on floating handguards over low-profile gas blocks permit countless sight options. The firm's Beast and Hunter muzzlebrakes tame recoil. (www.rockriverarms.com)

Ruger

A major design departure from Ruger's Model 77 rifle, the American has been a hit. The debut price of $449 made it a bargain. But this rifle is *good* too. A three-lug, full-diameter bolt has dual cocking cams to ease bolt resistance during the 70-degree lift. A detachable rotary box fits flush. The trigger, with tab, adjusts to 3 pounds. Steel V-blocks in the stock

Wayne thinks the extensive line of Rock River ARs includes some of the best values on the market.

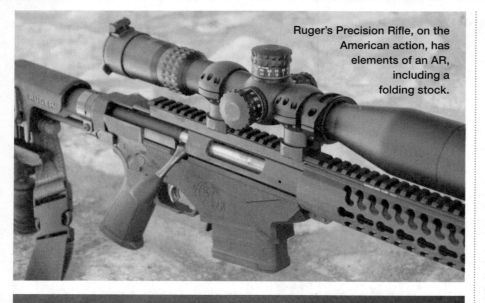

Ruger's Precision Rifle, on the American action, has elements of an AR, including a folding stock.

The durable Ruger American Magnum in .300 Winchester delivers tight groups, feeds smoothly.

Alas, the Ruger No. 1 now goes to only one distributor, in limited numbers. A costly rifle to build!

magazine well accepts a variety of boxes: M110, SR 25, DPMS, Magpul and AICS. Dual latches engage side or rear lips.

The midweight 24-inch barrel on my RPR in 6.5 Creedmoor is of hammer-forged 4140 steel, rifled 1-in-8 and threaded 5/8-24 at the muzzle. Headspaced with an external nut, the barrel can be replaced easily with AR wrenches. But you'll want to keep the original. Its 5R rifling, with minimum bore and chamber dimensions, yielded .8-minute averages *for five five-shot groups* at the factory! While the RPR's mechanism defines it as a bolt gun, the lower and its vertical grip, with the ventilated metal fore-end, are clearly AR. The stock folds to the left and can be locked there. Fold and lock latches, with length-of-pull and comb-height cams, are finger-friendly. I've fired this rifle to 1,200 yards for fun and in competition. It brings back the pure joy of hitting! (ruger.com)

Sako

Suojeluskuntain yliesikunnan asepaja was established April 1, 1919. Nearly a century later, Sako (pronounce it "Socko," not "Sayko") has two main rifle lines. The 85 comprises eight configurations, in chamberings from .223 to .375 H&H. Its three-lug bolt has a fixed ejector and an external extractor that controls case rims from the detachable box magazine. Sako hammer forges its barrels, which have a long-standing reputation for fine accuracy. Triggers adjust from 2¼ to 4 pounds. Stocks include carbon-fiber material on the Carbonlight stainless 85, walnut on the iron-sighted Bavarian and laminated wood on the .375 Kodiak, the braked Long Range and the versatile Grey Wolf. (The Kodiak strikes me as one of the best .375s on the market!) Choose from four M85 action lengths, each sized to the chamberings.

The new A7 Roughtech, now in Long Range, Coyote and Big Game variations, has many features of the 85, with a synthetic stock stiffened by aluminum. Fluted barrels are bored for eight top-selling chamberings – .243 to .300 Winchester. In tactical rifles, Sako lists the TRG 22 (.308) and TRG 42 (.338 Lapua) with heavy, braked barrels and adjustable stocks. The TRG M10 has all the features you could wish on a sniper rifle, and some you couldn't imagine – including interchangeable bolts, magazines and barrels in .308, .300 Winchester and .338 Lapua. If loud rifles give you headaches, check out Sako's Finnfire II in .22 LR and .17 HMR, with a checkered walnut, hunting-style stock. Beretta

engage angled mortises. A couple of seasons back, I hunted with an American Magnum, killing a Colorado elk. Early this year the Magnum joined Ruger's growing American stable – along with a rifle on the American action but with features of the firm's SR-762 AR autoloader. The Ruger Precision Rifle's upper receiver and bolt are CNC machined from 4140 chrome-moly. Its lower comprises halves machined from 7975-T6 aluminum. The Picatinny receiver rail, secured by stout 8-40 screws, has 20 minutes of gain. It slopes up to the rear so you can zero far without hitting dial stops or cranking the erector tube steeply off axis. The AR-style safety is reversible. With an allen wrench cleverly stowed inside the bolt shroud, you can adjust the Marksman trigger down to 2¼ pounds. No disassembly. No lost wrenches. The oversize bolt knob is threaded and easily replaced – though I wouldn't switch this one. The beveled handles Sako sales stateside. (www.sako.fi and www.beretta.com)

Sauer

Sauer shares a manufacturing site in Isny, Germany, and a U.S. marketing team in San Antonio, Texas, with Blaser and Mauser. Michael Luke and Thomas Ortmaier control the L&O Group that owns all three brands, plus SIG SAUER in northern Germany. Bernhard Knobel, who runs Blaser, is CEO of the three Isny enterprises. Matthias Klotz oversees the Sauer plant, a trot across the parking lot. Hunters who use rifles hard appreciate the Sauer 101. Choose synthetic, walnut or laminate stocks. My pick of eight configurations is the iron-sighted Scandic carbine, with 20-inch barrel. In green/brown laminate, this 6½-pound wand cheeks to the sights and has a fine trigger. The 101's long list of chamberings includes the hard-hitting 9.3x62 I used in Africa last year.

In Europe shortly thereafter I hunted with a new Sauer, the 404. It has a sliding cocking switch instead of a safety. Thumb it forward to cock, release and ease it back to de-cock. You can carry a loaded chamber without fear of accidental discharge. Available in five versions, with two-piece walnut or synthetic stocks cradling an alloy receiver, the 404 has a six-lug bolt that locks directly into the barrel. The bolt head and barrel are easy to switch out. Change both to accommodate 13 chamberings – .243 to .375 H&H. Insert the correct magazine (three-shot for standard cartridges, two for magnums), and you're done! Sauer cleverly incorporated the takedown wrench in the front swivel. The 404's trigger adjusts from 1¼ to 2¼ pounds. Slide it forward and back .3 inch to fit your finger. On the rain-lashed steeps of Scotland, 404s in .308 and .300 Winchester rang steel plates to 1,000 yards. Twin ejectors spilled cases briskly.

Sauer's Universal Mount gripped Leica's newest variable scope firmly. It detaches in a wink, returns the sight reliably to zero when you reattach. Though smitten by the figured Turkish on walnut 404s, I hunted with a synthetic thumbhole version. When my stalker (gamekeeper) spied a heavy antlered red deer, we splashed across an icy stream and climbed fast to beat gathering dusk. In a squall that drove rain into lenses, eyes and teeth, I bellied atop a ridge, found the stag's ribs with the Leica and fired. Hornady's ELD-X bullet quartered to the stag's off shoulder. I like the 404! (www.sauer.de)

Sauer's newest rifle, the 404, got a workout on a stag hunt in Scotland. Hard rain didn't affect it.

Savage

In 2015 Savage's A17 autoloader appeared, cycling the .17 HMR with a hard-chromed bolt in a case-hardened receiver. What makes this rifle function with rounds that stymie actions designed for the .22 Long Rifle is its *delayed* blowback design, with a rising lug to hold the bolt closed just long enough to dissipate some pressure. This spring, Savage has applied that design (actually, it's chambered that rifle) to the .22 WMR. The synthetic stock, alloy receiver, 10-round rotary box and Savage AccuTrigger appear on both the A17 and A22. The A17 now comes in two new laminate versions: Sporter and Target/Sporter Thumbhole. Also in the small-bore category, Savage has added three variations to its B.Mag in .17 WSM. Target Beavertail, Heavy Barrel and Sporter rifles share the rear-lug, cock-on-close bolt and AccuTrigger. They differ in stock design and material, and barrel contour.

Big game rifles? The 6.5 Creedmoor (one of my favorites!) has joined other chamberings in Axis bolt rifles, and in the new 16/116 Lightweight Hunter, a synthetic-stock sub-6-pound rifle with 20-inch stainless barrel. Savage has a new utility gun too – the Model 42 Takedown. It's a modern version of the Model 24 .22/.410 over/under that in my youth beguiled every youngster with a trapline. This takedown O/U also comes in .22 WMR too. (savagearms.com)

Shiloh Sharps

In 1876 Charles Overbaugh, exhibition shooter and chief salesman for Sharps Rifle Co., had an idea for a lightweight version of the 1874 action. Firing the 1,000-yard Creedmoor match, shooters leaned to long, heavy barrels for their generous sight radius, thick, stiff walls and recoil-absorbing mass. Given the 10-pound weight ceiling, a lighter action would permit a longer barrel. Overbaugh's 1877 Sharps has now joined the Shiloh Sharps line. In January of this year, I spoke with the Big Timber, Mont., people responsible for these exquisite rifles. Waiting time has been shaved for the 1877 and the plethora of 1874 Sharps reproductions. Choose from heavy and standard-weight barrels, 26 to 34 inches, in all traditional chamberings. You'll spend a couple grand for a basic rifle – more if like me you're sweet on fancy wood, tang and globe sights – other Shiloh options. Consider the grim total a grand investment! (www.shilohrifle.com)

Springfield Armory

In 1974 the Reese family's company, Springfield Armory, began offering a semiauto version of the M14. Relabeled the M1A, it has evolved into 34 versions. Six are new for 2016. The SOCOM 16 with CQB five-position AR-style stock accounts for two of them, differing only in their sights. Rails top and front (M-Lok) accommodate various attachments. The ported 16¼-inch barrel in .308 is rifled 1-in-11. Three other SOCOM rifles feature more traditional stocks in black, green and flat dark earth. They pair .135" aperture rear sights with XS posts (tritium inserts) up front. Scout carbines with 18-inch barrels and M1A Standard rifles with 22-inch wear walnut as well as synthetic stocks. Two new M1A

Loaded rifles are N.Y. compliant, without muzzle devices. Two new M1A Loaded Precision Adjustable rifles with 22-inch stainless and carbon-steel barrels have FDE adjustable composite stocks nicely configured for prone shooting. National Match and Super Match lines are unchanged. Ditto the M21 Tactical. I adore the Super Match with its heavy stainless barrel and oversize walnut stock. The long, steep wrist and beefy fore-end add control. This 11¼-pound rifle features 1-in-10 rifling, a 4½-pound trigger. (www.springfield-armory.com)

Tikka

Built at Finland's Sako plant, Tikka rifles boast many of the same features – even the same barrels – for less money. Established in 1893, Tikka predates Sako by 26 years, but it has manufactured a wide variety of items, from sewing machines to submachine guns. After WWII it turned to hunting rifles and collaborated with Sako on a Model 555 Tikka. Later, Sako acquired Tikka and the shotgun firm, Valmet. By 1989 production at Tikkakoski Works had moved to Sako's Riihimaki plant. Tikka marketed its bolt-action Whitetail rifle stateside during the 1990s. In 2003 Tikka began importing a T3. Much like the Sako 75, the T3 comes in eight versions, with wood, laminate and synthetic stocks, in chamberings from .204 Ruger to .300 Winchester. The twin-lug bolt is remarkable for its simplicity and smooth cycling. It strips cartridges from a single-stack polymer box. Trigger pull adjusts from 2 to 4 pounds. A two-detent safety locks bolt and trigger. I've used several Tikkas and found all but one more accurate than I had any right to expect. The 6¼-pound T3 Lite with synthetic stock, the T3 Laminated Stainless and the T3 Hunter with checkered wood stock are my favorites. Behind a Norwegian elkhound in a Finnish forest, I spied a cow moose and fired offhand with my T3. Steam blew into the shadows. She spun and dropped. On another hunt, a bull paused after running through brush that prevented a shot. I found a thin alley and triggered the T3. Down he went. That rifle later took a whitetail for me. On paper and in the woods, I've had good luck with Tikka rifles and, truly, can't find even a detail to criticize! T3s are handled by Beretta. (www.tikka.fi and www.beretta.com)

Volquartsen

Forty-two years ago Tom Volquartsen began gunsmithing. Blueing jobs led to rebarreling. Within 12 years, he'd begun building custom firearms. Volquartsen Custom remains a family owned business, its focus now on glitzy, super-accurate rimfire rifles. It builds its own actions, CNC and wire-EDM machines turning steel into slick-cycling autoloading mechanisms. Last year the firm introduced a rifle in .17 WSM – the only self-loading rifle I know that chambers this 3,000-fps rimfire. Its tungsten alloy bolt runs in a stainless receiver with an integral rail. The sleek, bright laminated stock cradles a beefy 20-inch stainless barrel. The rotary magazine holds eight rounds.

Volquartsen's line of blowback rimfire autos includes the takedown Fusion with tubular AR-style handguard. Switch barrels from .22 LR to .22 WMR to .17 HMR in seconds without tools! A counterweighted bolt ensures faultless function with WMR and HMR ammo. A 2¼-pound trigger pull helps you hit. The new Evolution self-loader in .204 and .223 is gas-driven, its stainless receiver housing a black-nitrided bolt, carrier and extractor. You can buy barreled actions, also stainless and carbon-fiber barrels. Volquartsen lists accessories too – and parts to upgrade Ruger's 10/22. Volquartsen's stocks strike me as the best-handling, best-looking laminates around. (www.volquartsen.com)

Weatherby

Last spring, its 70th, Weatherby announced, to no one's surprise, a 70th Anniversary Mark V rifle. All 70 sold out quickly, each with a leather case and handmade knife and sheath by Roy's grandson, Dan Weatherby. A new Mark V Arroyo RC (Range Certified) followed, in 14 chamberings. For us commoners there was the Vanguard Synthetic, an under-$800 .375 with iron sights. It's one of the most "pointable" and comfortable .375s I've fired lately. For 2016 Weatherby adds another Vanguard in .375 – a Dangerous Game Rifle. Its hand-laminated stock is an upgrade, also its NECG sights. The Vanguard clan has grown to 25 versions, including the H-Bar with a fetching, adjustable laminated stock. The Modular Chassis rifle will please shooters addicted to AR-style grips and buttstocks. Three Vanguards wear the Wby-X label, until now marketed separately as a line for young shooters.

This year, after a 16-year hiatus in cartridge design, Weatherby reached back several decades to a wildcat developed by Paul Wright for 1,000-yard competition. In his 1962 *Handbook for Shooters and Reloaders,* Parker Ackley reported the 6.5/300 Weatherby Wright Magnum reached velocities of 3,400 fps. Alex Hoyer, who operated a gunshop in Mifflintown, Pa., built rifles for it. Now, with the moniker 6.5-300 Weatherby Magnum, it is available in a new Mark V. Choose the AccuMark, Arroyo, Outfitter, TerraMark or Ultra Lightweight. Some wear brakes; for this round I'll do without. A 1-in-8 spin stabilizes the leggy bullets popular with long-range shooters. Ed Weatherby and his son Adam, now

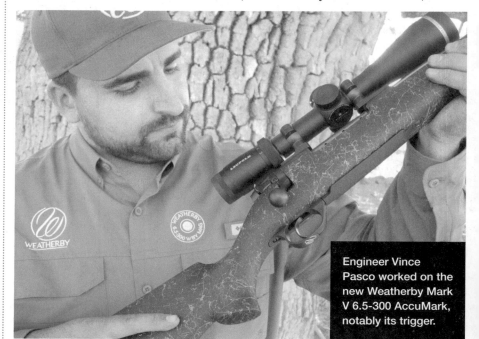

Engineer Vince Pasco worked on the new Weatherby Mark V 6.5-300 AccuMark, notably its trigger.

RUGER® 10/22 TAKEDOWN®

CONVENIENT FOR STORAGE AND TRANSPORTATION

The Ruger® 10/22 Takedown® combines all of the features and functionality of the 10/22® rifle, with the ability to easily separate the barrel from the action for convenient storage and transportation. The simple reassembly of the barrel and action yields a rock-solid return to zero for consistent, reliable performance. Packed in a convenient carry-case (included), the Ruger® 10/22 Takedown® makes it easy to keep America's favorite rimfire rifle by your side.

Patented, Detachable 10-Round Rotary Magazine

Barrel and Action Easily Separated and Reassembled for Ease of Transportation and Storage

Recessed Locking Lever

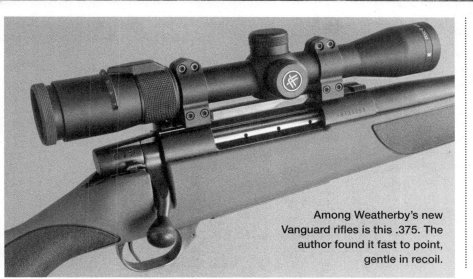

Among Weatherby's new Vanguard rifles is this .375. The author found it fast to point, gentle in recoil.

covered the splatter from all three hits. While I once thought all ARs differed by about as much as the shade of black on their uppers, the fine machining on Wilson Combat rifles distinguish them – even before you belly up to the bench. Introduced in 1999, they comprise a major part of the business Bill started by building pistols. These ARs cycle with Swiss-watch precision. Triggers adjust to bolt-rifle break. The .223 and .458 SOCOM dominate in sales, albeit Bill's 7.62x40 (a necked-up .223 hull) endeared itself to me on a pig hunt around Wilson's Texas retreat.

Want more muscle? Bill now builds a plus-size AR for the .308. Commonly, if not universally, called the AR-10, such an action adds thump, but also weight and

Executive VP and COO, introduced me to the 6.5-300 at the company's Paso Robles Mark V assembly cage. In fact, they invited me to *build* a 6.5-300. With help from patient people, I fumbled through every step without triggering alarms or sprinklers, jamming machinery or injuring employees. The rifle charitably sent three shots into a .7-inch knot, meeting Weatherby's subminute guarantee. You won't get a Mark V assembled by a green recruit like me, but you *will* get one unlike any built since 1958. "We've upgraded the rifle," said Adam. All versions and chamberings. Walnut, laminated and synthetic stocks have a trimmer profile in grip and fore-end, plus a modest palm swell. Criterion barrels are lapped. The LXX trigger (for the firm's 70th anniversary) adjusts to 2.5 pounds.

The 6.5-300 Weatherby Magnum is a long-range marvel. Factory loaded 127-grain Barnes bullets clock 3,537 fps from my rifle. At 500 they match the *muzzle* velocity of 156-grainers from the 6.5x55! If you zero a 6.5-300 at 200 yards, bullets will hit within 2½ vertical inches of point of aim to 305. They'll strike hard too, unloading 3,100 foot-pounds at 100 yards – the same that you'll get with a frisky 180-grain load in a .300 Magnum. Despite its raw power, the 6.5-300 Magnum is civil in recoil. Norma still produces ammo for other Weatherby Magnums; 6.5-300 cartridges are currently loaded in Paso Robles. (www.weatherby.com)

Wilson Combat

When the Aimpoint's dot steadied on the 200-yard target, I loosed a third 300-grain TTSX from Bill Wilson's .458 SOCOM . *Whop!* A walnut would have

Hog hunting in Texas, the author used a suppressed carbine from Wilson Combat to take this big boar.

Wayne fires a new AR rifle in .308 from Wilson Combat. The firm makes top-end ARs and pistols.

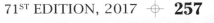

This Winchester 1892 Short Rifle is nicely reproduced by Miroku. The '92 was popular worldwide.

Classics offered by Winchester (Miroku) include this 1885, the first Browning-designed Winchester.

bulk. I snared one of the first of Wilson's .308s. It arrived in a soft case thick as an Angus haunch, herringboned with magazine pouches. Upper and lower are machined from billets. Flats are ripple-free under satin black Armor-Tuff coating, edges crisp, seams airtight.

This AR has a direct-impingement gas system. It's simple and reliable and incrementally lighter in weight than piston-driven bolts. The one criticism of DI systems, that they run a bit dirtier, is countered in Wilson rifles by NP3 bolt surfacing. NP3 combines tiny particles of Teflon with electroless nickel for lubricity so high, there's no need for lube that gathers grit. This .308's bolt runs like a race-car piston. Fire controls are easy to reach. There's no forward assist. Wilson's single-stage trigger breaks at a clean 3¾ pounds.

The 1:10-twist barrel tapes 14¾ inches, a pinned and welded flash hider bringing it to a rifle-legal 16¼ inches. Wilson Combat button-rifles its own barrels. Wilson offers a host of attachments for the integral top rail that abuts the receiver rail. My test rifle came with a one-piece mount/ring assembly (optional) secured by one star-shaped nut. The six-position Rogers Super Stock adjusts from 11-3/8 to 14-3/8 inches. Short but also trim, this .308 feels like an AR-15. No dietary snob, it cycled perfectly with a variety of loads. Even Remington Managed Recoil ammo (a 125-grain bullet at 2,660 fps) printed a .9" group. Hornady Whitetail 150-grain InterLocks shot into .5", Black Hills Gold with 165-grain Ballistic Tips .8". Sierra 175-grain MatchKings in Federal and Setpoint loads an even inch. (www.wilsoncombat.com)

Winchester

The first cataloged Winchester rifle, the Model 1866, appeared 150 years ago. After the 1873 and 1876 models, Winchester vice president (and Oliver Winchester's son-in-law) Thomas Bennett discovered a rural Utah gunsmith who, with his brothers, was building his own dropping-block single-shot. Bennett bought the rifle and put it in Winchester's line as the Model 1885. Over the next 17 years he bought three dozen more designs from John M. Browning. For 2016, Winchester is listing a new Deluxe Rifle version of the 1886, one of Browning's most popular lever actions. A case-colored receiver complements the checkered pistol grip stock. It's my pick of the crop. Winchester also has a new 1873 octagon-barrel Sporter with cased receiver. There's an embellished 1873 150th Commemorative – and one on a '94 action. Fanciest is a 150th Commemorative 1866, with engraved brass receiver, octagonal barrel. Like the other two, it wears a gold muzzle band and figured walnut. In bolt rifles, Winchester has added seven chamberings to the XPR introduced last year in .270, .30-06, and .300 and .338 Winchester Magnum. A new XPR Hunter (camo) comes in all 11 chamberings, .243 to .338. Hardly as appealing as the Model 70, the XPR competes in a crowded field of sub-$600 hunting rifles. It push-feeds from a detachable box; its M.O.A. trigger adjusts for weight and overtravel. (Claims of "zero take-up, zero creep and zero overtravel" are applesauce, albeit to me, the trigger feels as good as most.) The two-position safety has a button that permits unloading with the safety on. The M70, which starts at a daunting $940, carries on. I'm sweet on the Featherweight and the recently revived Alaskan. The only new '70 is a handsome 150th Commemorative. Sadly, Winchester lists no .22 rimfires in its current catalog. The company that produced the Models 1890, 52, 61, 63, 9422 and other .22s many of us lusted after in our youth – where has it gone? (www.winchesterguns.com)

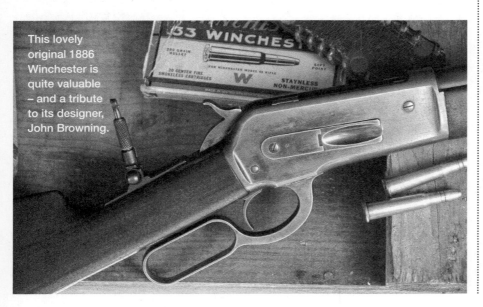
This lovely original 1886 Winchester is quite valuable – and a tribute to its designer, John Browning.

NEW SHOTGUNS

BY **John Haviland**

No matter if your shotgun shooting passion is cottontails hidden in a local woodlot, grouse in a hardwood bog, gobblers strutting among the pines or a rousing game of clays, there are new shotguns this year to satisfy your desires.

Benelli

Benelli and its sister companies Franchi and Stoeger have new small-gauge guns, guns to celebrate an anniversary, guns for women and a budget pump. Benelli teamed up with Fiocchi Ammunition to develop a 3-inch 28-gauge shell awhile back and is now chambering the shell in its ETHOS autoloader. The gun weighs 5.3 pounds with a 26-inch barrel that has C (cylinder), IC (improved cylinder), M (modified), IM (improved modified) and F (full) Crio choke tubes. The magazine holds two of the long 28 shells.

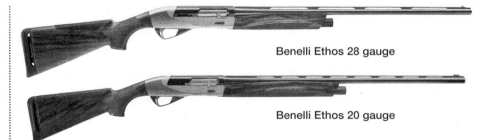

Benelli Ethos 28 gauge

Benelli Ethos 20 gauge

Benelli recommends at least 7/8-ounce loads to reliably cycle the action.

The ETHOS is also now made in 20 gauge. The 20 gauge has a fiber-optic front sight with red, green and yellow inserts and bead midsight. Like the 28, it has an engraved nickel-plated receiver that accents the walnut stock and fore-end. The 20 is available with a 26- or 28-inch barrel with C, IC, M, IM and F Crio choke tubes, and up to four shotshells fit in the magazine. The gun weighs 5.7 pounds.

The Super Black Eagle II celebrates its 25th anniversary with a limited edition model and Pacific, Central, Mississippi and Atlantic Flyway models. The limited addition model features a nickel bolt, oversize bolt handle and bolt release, elongated front sight and extended chokes. It is available with a Realtree MAX-5 camo finish or with a black Cerakote finish. The Flyway models have a blued 28-inch barrel with a ventilated rib. Gold inlaid flyway specific waterfowl scenes decorate each side of the

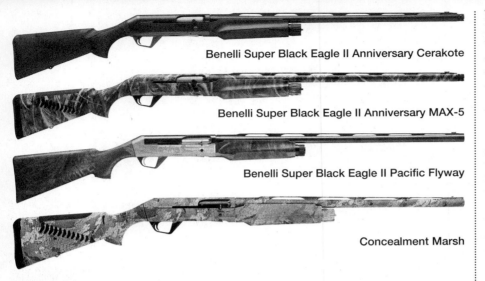

Benelli Super Black Eagle II Anniversary Cerakote

Benelli Super Black Eagle II Anniversary MAX-5

Benelli Super Black Eagle II Pacific Flyway

Concealment Marsh

nickel-plated receiver. New camouflage patterns for regular Super Black Eagle II guns include Gore Optifade Marsh, and Timber and Mossy Oak Bottomland.

The Franchi 12-gauge Affinity Catalyst autoloader and Instinct Catalyst over/under have stocks with drop, cast, pitch and length of pull tailored to a woman's build. The Affinity Catalyst has a 28-inch barrel and weighs 6.6 pounds. The Instinct Catalyst has 28-inch barrels and weighs 7.2 pounds. The Instinct L is now chambered in 28 gauge and .410. Each over/under weighs 6 pounds.

The Stoeger P3000 is an economically priced 12-gauge pump with lots of

Browning Citori 725 Grade VII Small Gauge

Browning A5 Sweet Sixteen

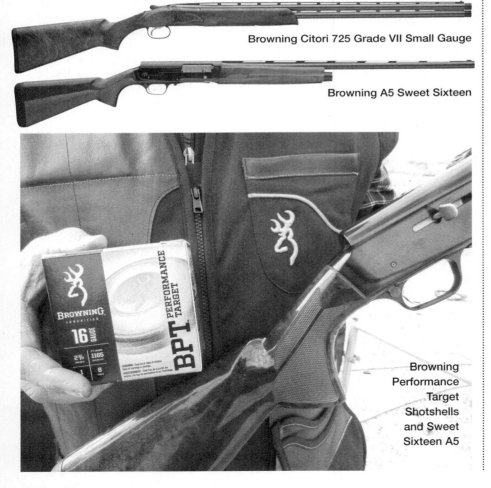

Browning Performance Target Shotshells and Sweet Sixteen A5

features. Its anodized aluminum receiver has a crossbolt safety at the rear of the triggerguard. The black synthetic stock and fore-end have molded checkering and sling loops. A modified choke tube and a wrench are included.

Browning

Every few years requests for the never-say-die 16 gauge builds to the point that it's worthwhile building shotguns to meet the demand. Browning has done it this year with the

Sweet Sixteen A5 autoloader. Like the classic Auto-5, the new A5 Sweet Sixteen is built on a smaller and lighter aluminium receiver that weighs a pound less than the 12-gauge A5.

The A5 works with a recoil-operated Kinematic Drive System that is guaranteed for five years or 100,000 rounds. The stock and fore-end are gloss-finished walnut with a close radius grip and 18 lines-per-inch checkering. The stock is adjustable for length of pull with ¼-inch and ½-inch stock spacers, and with shims to adjust cast and drop. Three Invector-DS chokes are supplied for a 26- or 28-inch length barrel.

I shot the Sweet Sixteen at clay targets with Browning's new shotshell ammunition this past winter. Browning offers 16s loaded with 1-1/8 ounce of #6 shot with a muzzle velocity of 1,295 feet per second and 1 ounce of #8 at 1,185 fps. Maybe it was all in my mind, but I could not miss with either load – and shooting the A5 was, well, sweet.

Browning has expanded its Citori 725 Sporting and Field over/under lineup to include the 28 gauge and .410. Both feature a FireLite Mechanical Trigger. Sporting models include 30- or 32-inch ventilated rib barrel lengths with five extended Standard Invector choke tubes. The receiver has a silver nitride finish with gold accented engraving to highlight the gloss oil finished Grade III/IV walnut stock and fore-end. Weight is 7 pounds 4 ounces for the new Citori 725 Sporting small gauges. The Citori 725 Field features a silver nitride finished receiver with engraving. Stock and fore-end are Grade II/III walnut with a close radius pistol grip in gloss oil finish. Ventilated rib barrels are 26 or 28 inches.

Browning's High Grade Program continues with Citori 725 Grade VII shotguns offered in 20 and 28 gauge and .410 bore. These over/under shotguns receive as much as 30 hours of hand deep-relief engraving and gold accent engraving on their blued receivers. The Grade VI/VII walnut stock features a close radius pistol grip and palm swell. Barrels are 28, 30 or 32 inches with five black extended choke tubes, all in a fitted case.

CZ-USA

CZ has new guns in just about every category. The 712 Green G2 autoloader adds color to the 712 line with a green anodized receiver. The CZ 712 3-Gun G2 is easier to operate with an extended bolt handle and oversize bolt release. Its magazine extends just past its 22-inch barrel and holds nine 12-gauge shells. Three extended black choke tubes are included. The 712 Synthetic is dipped in Mossy Oak Shadow Grass Blades camouflage.

The CZ over/under line has two new guns. The economy Drake 12 and 20 gauge are based on the same CNC machined receiver as other CZ shotguns, and feature a single selectable trigger and laser-cut checkering. The 28-inch barrels come with five choke tubes. The Redhead Premier is CZ's flagship over/under. It has a one-piece CNC machined receiver, single selectable trigger and 28-inch barrels with five choke tubes. The 12- and 20-gauge guns have ejectors, while the 28 gauge and .410 have extractors.

The All-American Trap Combo ships with two barrel sets. One set is a single-shot "un-single" with a dial-adjustable aluminum rib that regulates shot impact from 50/50 up to 90/10. The set is a standard set of barrels with stepped rib and 50/50 point of impact. An adjustable comb, competition trigger and auto ejectors make the gun ready to step up to the line at the trap range.

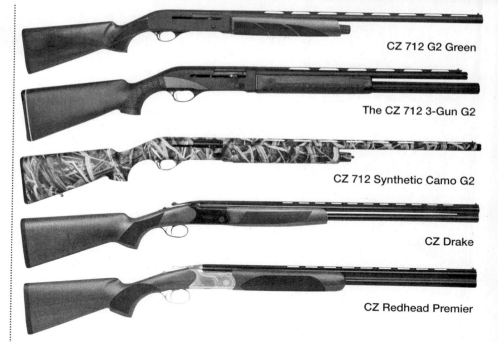

CZ 712 G2 Green

The CZ 712 3-Gun G2

CZ 712 Synthetic Camo G2

CZ Drake

CZ Redhead Premier

Legacy

The Pointer Synthetic over/under and break-action single-shot are Legacy's new shotguns.

The Pointer Synthetic Over/Under 12-gauge guns have 3-inch chambers with chrome-lined bores in either a field model with 28-inch barrels, or home defense gun with a 18-inch barrels. Actions are single trigger, select fire with an auto-reset safety. Both guns are equipped with F, M, IM, IC and C choke tubes. The field model features a full-length, raised ventilated rib with a fiber-optic front bead. The home defense gun is also equipped with a fiber-optic front bead, plus a Picatinny rail on the top for mounting optics, and a second rail beneath the front of the bottom bar-

rel for lights and such.

The Pointed Break Action Youth models are chambered in 20 gauge and .410. These single-shots come with a 26-inch barrel and fixed modified choke. Metal parts are matte black and the synthetic stock is also black. A brass bead is the front sight. The guns have a manual push button safety, hammer safety and a transfer bar safety. The 20 gauge has a 3-inch chamber and weighs 5.2 pounds, while the .410 has 2½-inch chamber and weighs 4.8 pounds.

Mossberg

Mossberg's new guns include a tricked-out 500 pump, new stocks and fore-ends on the SA-20 autoloader, and competition and hunting 930 autoloaders.

Mossberg 500 ATI T2 Scorpion

Mossberg 590 Seven-Shot Ghost Ring

Mossberg 590 Nine-Shot Tri-Rail

Mossberg 930 Pro-Series Sporting

Mossberg has partnered with Advanced Technology International to create a specialized 12-gauge 500 ATI Scorpion. The pump gun features an ATI T2 TactLite six-position adjustable stock with 3-7/8-inch length of pull (LOP) adjustment, and 1-inch adjustable cheek riser with a Scorpion recoil-reducing rubber grip and rear pad. The Scorpion also has an ATI steel Halo Heatshield around the 18.5-inch barrel. On each side of the front of the Heatshield is a dovetail rail for mounting accessories and a front post sight on the top. A top rail provides a base for mounting optics or other sights. Completing the Scorpion is an ATI Halo Side Saddle, mounted directly to the tapped 500's receiver. The aluminum saddle comes with three Add-A-Shell units that can flip 180 degrees to present shells for a quick grab.

The SA-20 autoloading shotgun now has the choice of a walnut-stocked All-Purpose Field or a Turkey model with a camo stock and fore-end. The Field is checkered on the fore-end and grip and has polished blued metal. The 26-inch vent rib barrel is equipped with a front bead and set of C, IC, M, IM and F choke tubes. The Turkey has an extended turkey choke tube screwed into a 22-inch ventilated rib barrel topped with a fiber-optic three-dot sight. The receiver is topped with a rail for mounting optics. The synthetic stock and fore-end are hidden with Mossy Oak Obsession camo. The metal finish is matte blue.

Five versions of the 590A1 and 590 pump shotguns feature a seven-round magazine with cylinder bore 18.5-inch barrel. Options in these 12-gauge, 3-inch tactical shotguns include Ghost Ring sights and interchangeable Accu-Choke system with a Parkerized, Kryptek Typhon or Marinecote finish.

Mossberg collaborated with professional shooting instructor Gil Ash on the design features of the 930 Pro-Series Sporting shotgun. Every 930 Pro-Series Sporting shotgun purchase comes with a free 60-day trial subscription to the Ash's *Knowledge Vault*, a collection of instructional articles and videos on clays and wing shooting by Gil and his wife, Vicki. The Pro-Series shotguns feature boron nitride coatings to resist corrosion on the gas piston, piston ring, magazine tube, hammer, sear, return spring plunger and return spring tube. The shell stop, bolt slide and elevator receive additional finishing to reduce friction. The Pro-Series Sporting 12 gauge has a dual vent-gas system. The semigloss-finished walnut stock and fore-end were designed with measurements formulated by Ash for proper fit and eye alignment.

The 930 Stock Drop System provides a custom fit with drop-at-comb adjustment shims. The slim contoured fore-end has laser stippling. The complementing Tungsten-finished receiver is treated with a durable Cerakote™ protective coating and the 28-inch vent rib, ported barrel has a blue finish. The shotgun is ready for competition with a beveled loading gate for quick reloading, a HIVIZ TriComp fiber-optic sight with LitePipes of varied shapes and colors, and extended Briley Skeet, M and IC choke tubes.

Mossberg 935 Pro-Series Waterfowl

Weatherby Element Waterfowler

Weatherby SA-08 Compact MAX-5

The 930 and 935 Magnum Pro-Series Waterfowl autoloading shotguns are available with Mossy Oak Shadow Grass Blades camo. Boron nitride coat on nearly all internal parts protects against corrosion in the damp of duck blinds or the goo of goose pits. A quick-empty release button conveniently unloads shells from the magazine. A fiber-optic bead is the front sight on the ventilated barrel and a Stock Drop System adjusts comb height. Choke tubes include F, M and IM for the 28-inch barrel.

Remington

Remington celebrates its 200th anniversary in 2016 with commemorative edition Model 870 Wingmaster and 1100 guns. The 12-gauge guns have C-grade walnut stocks and fore-ends with fleur-de-lis pattern checkering paired with engraving and gold inlay on the receivers. The 870 has a 26-inch barrel and the 1100 at 28-inch barrel.

A more straightforward 870 is the Hardwood Home Defense Model with a dark stained hardwood stock and fore-end. The 18.5-inch barrel has a cylinder choke tube with an extended magazine underneath that holds six rounds.

Remington introduced its V3 autoloader in 2015, but shipments of guns were delayed until this year. The V3 is similar to its big brother the Versa Max, which uses the Versa Port operating system to regulate gas pressure based on shell length to reliably cycle light 12-gauge 2¾-inch shells on up to 3-inch magnums. Three versions of the V3 include a black synthetic stock and fore-end, American walnut woodwork or dressed butt to muzzle in Mossy Oak Break Up Country or Blades Camo. All are equipped with an adjustable stock shim system, SuperCell Recoil Pad and magazine cutoff. Barrel length is 26 or 28 inches. Weight is 7.2 pounds.

Savage

Savage's Model 24 shotgun-rifle combo was available in a range of cartridges and gauges when it was introduced in 1950, but the gun was discontinued in the late 1980s. Savage reintroduced the over/under a few years ago, and this year a Takedown (35.75-inch) and Takedown-Youth (34.75-inch) versions of the shotgun-rifle combo gun break down with the push of a button. The Takedown's bottom 20-inch barrel is chambered in 3-inch, .410 bore to shoot birdshot, buckshot or slugs. The top barrel is chambered in a choice of .22 LR or .22 WMR and equipped with open sights. The gun stores in an Uncle Mike's Go Bag for compact transport.

The Stevens 320 12-Gauge Field Grade Waterfowl camo pump shotgun is made with dual slide bars, a rotary bolt, synthetic stock and fore-end, and five-round magazine. Compact and standard length-of-pull models are available. The Waterfowl is finished with Mossy Oak Shadow Grass Blades camo patterns.

The S1200 12 Gauge is Steven's first autoloading shotgun. The S1200 features an inertia operating system with walnut, black or camouflage synthetic stock and fore-end. It's offered with a 3-inch chamber and a 26- or 28-inch vent rib barrel that accepts Beretta Mobilchoke tubes.

Weatherby

The Element and SA-08 autoloading lines have three new editions. The inertia-operated Element has a Griptonite synthetic stock and fore-end available in black synthetic, and Waterfowler with Realtree MAX-5 camouflage. The guns are available in 12 or 20 gauge with 3-inch chambers and 26- or 28-inch barrels. Integral Multi-Choke System tubes include Improved Cylinder, Modified, Full and Long Range Steel.

The gas-operated SA-08 Waterfowler MAX-5 Compact has a short 12½-inch length of pull. The 20-gauge gun weighs 5¾ pounds with a 24-inch chrome-lined barrel. The Waterfowler comes with Improved Cylinder, Modified and Full choke tubes. The gun is concealed in Realtree MAX-5 camo.

Winchester Repeating Arms

Winchester is celebrating its 150th anniversary with a Model 101 150th Commemorative over/under 12 gauge. The 101 is showcased with a gloss finish High Grade IV/V walnut stock and fore-end with 24 lines-per-inch checkering. Metalwork features deep relief scroll engraving with gold embellishments on the silver nitride finished receiver, triggerguard, top lever, fore-end bracket, latch lever and safety/barrel selector. The Winchester 150th Anniversary logo and WRA trademark enhance the aesthetics of the shotgun.

Winchester's Super X pump 12-gauge shotguns have been expanded for deer and turkey hunting. The Super X Pump Extreme Deer and Long Beard both feature a synthetic pistol grip stock with textured gripping surfaces and a Mossy Oak Break-Up Country camo finish. Two interchangeable combs allow adjusting comb drop for use with optical sights or the supplied TRUGLO fiber-optic front sight and an adjustable rear sight. Two length-of-pull spacers permit changing the LOP of the Inflex Technology Recoil Pad. The Extreme Deer has a 22-inch barrel that is fully rifled. The Long Beard has a 24-inch barrel with an Invector-Plus Extra-Full Long Beard turkey choke tube.

Winchester 101 150th Anniversary Commemorative

BY **Kevin Muramatsu**

New
Semi-Auto Handguns

As in previous years, and as will be in the future, the gun companies continue to offer new models of, or expansions to the existing lines of, their diverse selection of handguns. This is evident particularly with the large companies such as Walther, Smith & Wesson and Kimber. Not to be left out, the smaller companies (where much innovation takes place) such as DoubleTap or Les Baer will almost always have a new model or edition, just as the big boys do. As the golden age of firearms ownership continues, so does the difficulty in finding just what you want. Fortunately, there is something to satisfy anyone, whether it be the fantastic color case-hardened samples from Turnbull or Republic Forge, or the starkly utilitarian models offered by FMK or New Order Firearms, both relatively new or very new to the industry; the big-bore expansions like the Walther PPQ .45 or something smaller like the 5.7mm versions from Excel Arms.

Let's take a look at what's new. Most of this information is necessarily gleaned from SHOT Show 2016, as that's when most manufacturers unveil new models. However, some info will have originated in the later mists of 2015, and not have been noticed or otherwise included in this article from the previous edition of *Gun Digest 2016*.

Beretta

Beretta unfurls the new M9A3. It's not black, has a threaded barrel, a Vertec-style grip, oversized mag release, convertible safety/decocker, an accessory rail, front and rear grip checkering, night sights and comes in a fun plastic ammo box. Price tag is $1,099. Also new are the M9 Centennial, Exclusive and Limited models. These are dressed-up pretty guns. The Centennial commemorates the 100th year of military pistols starting with the M1915. The Commemorative is single action with a frame-mounted safety, with wood grips and a Brigadier style slide. The Limited commemorates 30 years of the M9 pistol and functionally is more traditionally M9 but with wood grips and, I daresay, some rather gaudy writing on the side of the slide. The Exclusive is much like the Limited but the writing has been upgraded to gold inlay and the wood grip panels are a thing of beauty. Prices on these three are $3,000, $1,099 and $3,500.

Also new is an M9-22. It is full sized and shoots .22 LR and retails for $420. A Compact Carry PX-4 Storm is also new, mating a subcompact-length gray Cerakoted slide with a slightly taller frame and lower profile controls. A grip with much more "grippage" is also standard on this model, as is the inclusion of three 15-round magazines.

CZ-USA

CZ has delivered a number of upgrades to their current line of pistols. For example, several of the CZ 75 B Omega models now have the ability to "quick change" swap the decocker for a safety in a manner similar to the P-07 and P-09, allowing the traditional double-action pistols to be carried cocked and locked. They are identified by the word "Convertible," with an MSRP starting at $570. CZ has addressed the increasing prevalence of silencer ownership by unveiling a line called the Urban Grey Suppressor Ready guns. This line contains a P-09, P-07, CZ 75 SP-01 Tactical, CZ 75 B Omega and a CZ 75 P-01. All are an attractive light gray color with high-profile sights and threaded barrels for use with sound suppressors. These pistols retail from $537 to $723.

A strangely attractive piece is the new CZ 75 Tactical Sport Orange. Meant for

One of CZ's new Urban Gray suppressor-ready models, in this case a CZ 75 SP-01.

The CZ 75 Tactical Sport Orange single-action match pistol.

full-size .22 LR versions of the larger K100 and K100 X-Trim models. The K22S has an open Beretta-like slide and a threaded barrel. The X-Trim has a heavily slotted slide and threaded barrel. Both models' slides and frames are made of steel, a rarity for a .22, though they do still have polymer grips, and like the others in the Grand Power line, are manufactured in Slovakia. The K22S retails for $528 and the K22 X-Trim retails for $735.

The Bersa Thunder 9 Pro XT is a sport shooter derived pistol with a fitted

showy competition, it has a number of minor upgrades and mods, not the least of which is a single-action trigger. The Tactical Sport Orange has a $1,784 price tag and if it doesn't make your scores go up, it will at least draw some attention. Finally, the CZ Scorpion Evo 3 S1 (a bit of a mouthful) that has proven to be quite popular, is now available in Flat Dark Earth, and should you want to file a Form 1 and make it a legal Short Barreled Rifle, an SBR kit is available now from CZ to make it simple and easy.

EAA

Importers of Tanfoglio pistols, there are a couple new models of note. Tanfoglio is making a Witness full-size 1911 pistol, which intriguingly fires a .45 ACP cartridge out of a polymer frame, and this year compact and officer models join the line.

Eagle Imports

Eagle Imports handles the importation for a number of gun companies. The Llama brand has been resurrected and Eagle is bringing the Micromax back, and a "standard" 1911 called the MAX-1. These are sub-full-size 1911-style pistols chambered in .380 ACP, the former replicating the "Government", and the latter looking like a bob-gripped "Commander." MSRPs are $468 and $543.

Grand Power has a new K22S and K22 X-TRIM. Both are

Grand Power K22S.

Grand Power K22 X-TRIM. Note the many lightening cuts on the slide to reduce the weight.

The EAA Witness 1911 Compact.

Llama is back courtesy of Eagle Imports and one of their offerings is the Micro Max, another entry into the miniature 1911 market.

5-inch barrel, adjustable rear sight and Cerakote finish, and a $923 MSRP.

FMK Firearms

The FMK pistols are made in California and are designed to be protrusion free, highly ergonomic and proudly American. The G2 model of the C1 is now available and can be had in .40 and 9mm. The FMK pistols have low felt recoil due to a very low bore axis and rubber backstrap. These pistols can have a double-action trigger or the newer FAT (Fast Action Trigger), which has a shorter pull and reset. Multiple frame color options can be chosen. MSRP starts at $409.95, which is quite affordable and has a lifetime warrantee on materials and workmanship.

Glock

Last year Glock introduced the MOS adaptation to their line, which incorporated a removable top panel behind the ejection port for the mounting of a micro red-dot sight. This year the MOS feature has been expanded to variants of the Glock 17 Gen4 and the Glock 19 Gen4. It was almost a given that these two very commonly purchased models would receive the upgrade after the competition models had been MOSed. We will see how soon the holster manufacturers offer MOS (with red dot attached) compatible holsters for these guns. MSRP for the Glock 17 and 19 with MOS is $750.

Heizer Defense

Heizer Defense is making a .45 ACP pistol called the PKO-45, apparently the thinnest .45 on the market. It has a very low mounted barrel and feeds from 5- and 7-round magazines, is entirely made of stainless steel and titanium, and sports a significant carry bevel treatment. As of this writing, MSRP had not yet been determined.

Honor Defense

This is a very new company that takes very obvious pride in the fact that everything on its new pistol is made in the U.S.A. The Honor Guard pistol is available in multiple configurations. They come standard with a 7-round magazine, ambidextrous magazine release and a

Honor Defense Honor Guard pistols. The model on the right has the extended FIST frame.

short reset 7-pound trigger. One model is available with a manual safety. A unique model is the FIST frame. This model has an odd projection on the front of the frame. It almost looks like they forgot to cut the thing off before it left the factory. It has a reason. FIST stands for Firearm Integrated Standoff. The point is that body contact can be made with the muzzle on a perp and it will not result in making the Honor Guard pistol's slide move out of battery. You can shove the thing into

This is Heizer Defense's PKO45, or Pocket .45.

Here are the Ithaca Pro-Fit on the left and the Short-Block user-finishable model on the right.

someone's belly and be assured that his fat gut will not disable your gun. Honor Guard pistols start at $499.

Inland Manufacturing

This is the new 1911 from the new Inland Manufacturing Company.

Not the same company, but a successor to the GM subsidiary that manufactured M1 Carbines in WWII, Inland is doing the same thing as its predecessor. Now it also builds 1911 pistols as well. It is available in a standard Government model, a 1911A1 Match model and a 1911 Custom Carry. The Custom Carry is made of Stainless steel. These guns start at $759.

Ithaca Gun Company

The resurgent Ithaca has been making 1911 pistols for several years. They have all been reasonably high-end, hand-fit models that ran over $2,000. New this year is the Pro-Fit series that has been manufactured specifically to reduce hand fitting. These guns are tight and feel and look like their hand-fitted models, but are substantially cheaper at $1,575.

In this gunsmith's opinion, even more shiny and neat are the new short-block kits. These kits come from the factory for $1,175 and have, in addition to the frame and slide, the barrel, fire control internals including the trigger, and a perfectly blended and fit grip safety. All that is missing are the thumb safety, grips and sights, which to be honest, are the things that most people tend to personalize on their 1911s anyway. You can also finish the gun in pretty much whatever means you like.

Kahr Arms

The new Gen 2 Premium series of Kahr pistols is also shipping in 2016. The KP9 and KP45 are shipped with TRUGLO tritium fiber-optic sights. The TP9 and TP45 come with 4-, 5- or 6-inch barrels. The 4-inch model has identical sights to the previously mentioned KP series. The 5-inch model has standard sights but has a removable plate for mounting a micro red-dot sight. The 6-inch adds the red-dot in the form of a Leupold

Kahr TP9 6-inch barreled, micro-red dotted, compensated pistol. A far cry from the original concealed carry models.

DeltaPoint standard, as well as a compensated barrel. All of these guns come with the short trigger installed. MSRP for the KP9 and KP45 is $976. The 4-, 5- and 6-inch TP9 and TP45 are $976, $1,015 and $1,566, in that order.

Kimber

A number of Kimber product upgrades were released in 2016 and late 2015. Of the most notable is the Kimber Micro chambered in 9mm. For those not completely in the know, the Micro was released previously in .380 ACP, roughly in conjunction

Kimber's Micro 9 pistol with the laser in the grip.

This .380 Micro Carry RCP from Kimber has sights that are as low profile as you can get, combined with a Crimson Trace Lasergrip.

with similar offerings from Colt and SIG SAUER. Hearkening back to the original Mustang, the Micro proved to be a fine resurrection of the theme. Now that it is in 9mm, it should prove to be a more potent offering for those not comfortable with .380, but who like the Micro-size Kimber 1911. Other renditions in .380 such as the RCP with trench-cut sights, or the DC and RCP models equipped with a Crimson Trace Lasergrips are also new.

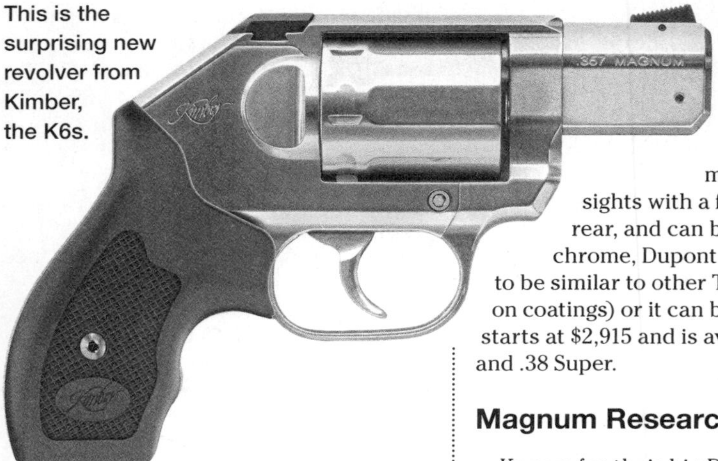

This is the surprising new revolver from Kimber, the K6s.

The Custom TLE and Pro TLE have also received RL upgrades to include a threaded barrel and elevated tritium sights for use with silencers.

One of the more unexpected developments was the release of the K6s revolver. It is a very small, "hammerless" .357 Magnum sixshooter with a really nice match trigger and very comfortable grip. Sights are low profile and this gem sells for $899.

Kriss USA

Sphinx pistols finally are coming into the USA in full-size flavors. The SDP Standard Alpha with polymer lower frame and the SDP Standard with aluminum lower frame are both available in 9mm at the time of this writing. Several options, including different Cerakote colors or threaded barrels can be chosen as an alternative to the stock models with PVD coating. There was no MSRP at the time of this writing, however, the compact carry models are about $1,000, so these full-size models ought to be comparably priced.

The Kriss Vector series has matured into a Gen II line and is now available with more features, such as an AR-compatible interface so a pistol brace can be mounted. Different color finishes are now available as is the 9mm chambering, again using Glock-style magazines. Retail prices range from $1,350 to $1,600.

Les Baer Custom

In honor of his new Shelby 1000 sports car, Les Baer has introduced the GT Monolith Stinger. In short, it is an Officer-size frame with full-length dust cover, mated to a Commander (or Comanche) length slide and barrel. Unlike most carry guns that only come with one, or maybe two, magazines, the GT Monolith Stinger properly comes with three mags. It has night sights with a fully adjustable rear, and can be finished in hard chrome, Dupont S (which appears to be similar to other Teflon-based spray on coatings) or it can be blued. MSRP starts at $2,915 and is available in .45 ACP and .38 Super.

Magnum Research Inc.

Known for their big Desert Eagle pistols, seen most often in movies, MRI modified these big heavy buggers and released an interesting alternative at the end of 2015. The Mark XIX L5 and L6 models are "lightweight" models with aluminum frames and shorter barrels. The weight is shaved on the .357 L5 by a good 1½ pounds, and 3/4 of a pound from the .50 AE L6. Both include Hogue rubber grips

New Order Firearms

Yet another newcomer to the market, New Order Firearms has what few others have. A true, fully left-handed pistol. The NO9 comes either right- or left-handed and has a 30 percent glass-filled polymer frame. A rather light and very smooth 5-pound trigger is standard and it uses off-the-shelf Beretta 92 style magazines. This is another fully 100 percent made

Magnum Research's new lightweight Desert Eagle L5 in .357 Mag.

New Order Firearms is a new company. This is their new pistol, the NO9, fully and completely made in the USA. This pistol can be purchased as a true left-handed pistol.

in America pistol. It lists at $675, though this is an introductory MSRP and may change. The usual alternate calibers and compact/subcompact varieties are planned in the near future.

Remington

Remington has its 200th anniversary this year and has released a number of commemorative versions of their iconic rifles and shotguns. The R1, a 1911 model, is also now available as a commemorative. It features a fair amount of classic "American" engraving and some gold inlay, and is patterned along the 1911A1 style with standard grip safety and short trigger. A flat mainspring housing and dovetailed sights differentiate a bit to keep it from getting boring. It's rather attractive, really, and is limited to 2,016 examples. Retail price is $1,649.

The RM380 released late in 2015 is a small subcompact .380 pistol. It is recoil operated for felt recoil reduction and has an ambi magazine catch. It is also available with a Crimson Trace Laserguard so you can scare the crap out of someone before you hopefully don't have to shoot them. MSRP is $638 for the Laserguard model and $436 for

the standard model. Both models have a six-round magazine.

Republic Forge

This is another relatively new 1911 company. These guys make some really pretty guns, particularly their new Defiant variant with color case-hardened frame and slide, with ivory grips. This model sells for $3,275. It also has a checkered front strap, top slide serrations and all the modern upgraded parts.

Ruger

It was only a matter of time before Ruger added a pistol to the "American" lineup. It's currently available in 9mm and .45 ACP and is a completely new design from Ruger. A wrap-around grip insert is interchangeable for larger or smaller hands, and the grip will contain nickel-teflon plated magazines that hold 17 rounds of 9mm or 10 rounds of .45. Regardless of caliber, the grip width is the same. When I played with this gun at the SHOT Show I was impressed, particularly when the lead designer took it apart for me to drool over the insides. Unlike most semiauto pistols, no trigger manipulation is required to fieldstrip the American.

SCCY CPX-3 with the Roebuck Quad Lock for accuracy and security. It's a new .380.

MSRP is comparable to competitors' designs and is set at $570.

SCCY Firearms

New for SCCY is the CPX-3. Very similar in appearance and size (but a bit smaller) to the existing CPX-1 and CPX-2 models, it also uses a new and unique locking system enhancement called the Roebuck Quad-Lock system, designed to improve accuracy and barrel stability. Currently available in all black or in a two-tone arrangement, it uses a 10-round magazine to hold its .380 ACP ammo. MSRP is $334.

SIG SAUER

SIG SAUER's new Legion pistol, the P226 SAO Legion. Thus far, it is only available in 9mm, and it has a single-action-only trigger. That's what SAO means. It also means "sweetness."

SIG announced in the middle of 2015 the Legion series. This selection of pistols, two versions of the P226 and a P229, have upgrades requested by some professional users of firearms. Such upgrades include low-profile decocker and slide stop pads, special night sights, a reduced and recontoured beavertail to prevent snagging, and a short-travel trigger that

Remington's 1911 R1 Bicentennial pistol, one of 2,016 made.

This beautiful pistol is the Republic Forge Defiant. Probably the only 1911 I've seen with a color case-hardened slide. Wish I could afford it. But then I'd buy it and probably never shoot it.

The SIG SAUER P250 modular pistol is now available in the form of a .22 LR.

Due to customer demand, SIG SAUER has brought back the P225-A1.

was previously only available as an aftermarket upgrade. A PVD finish (like on its new silencers) and enhanced checkering on the grip and triggerguard are also present. The P226 Legion can also be purchased with a single-action-only trigger. All three are available in 9mm, .357 SIG and .40 S&W. MSRP on all three is $1,428.

A .22 model of the P250 pistol, in the compact size, was released in November of 2015. While it is set up from the factory as a .22 LR, like the previous iterations of the P250 it is modular and can be upgraded with a centerfire barrel and slide to 9mm, .357 Sig or .40 S&W. Practice in .22 and then carry in 9mm or whatever floats your boat. MSRP is $434.

The P225-A1 is a reintroduction of the classic P225 pistol used by the West German police. The new model, produced on modern equipment, should prove popular in the concealed carry market here in the U.S. MSRP is $1,175 with two eight-round magazines and night sights.

P229 carry models in .357 SIG and .40 S&W were also added last year in Nitron or SAS styles. The SAS has carry "melting" anti-snag treatment and a short reset trigger mechanism, both having G10 grips and night sights. MSRP is $1,142 for the Nitron and $1,176 for the SAS model.

Smith & Wesson

Smith has added a couple of new minor models, such as an M&P BG380 without a safety, and an M&P Shield with night sights. What really interested me was the new SW22 Victory pistol. It's a .22 semiauto, and while it closely resembles the old 22-A cosmetically, it is an entirely new animal (the guts are completely different). It costs $409. It has an extra Picatinny top rail for optics and is pretty much a modular firearm. Aftermarket items such as a Volquartsen barrel were promoted side by side with S&W, so the support should be quite strong. Target-type upgrades on the gun include a slightly faster than normal 1:15 rifling twist (standard .22 is 1:16), an overtravel trigger stop and a fully adjustable rear sight. While the grip appears to be quite large, it does feel somewhat smaller than the handful that was the 22-A. It's also available from the factory with a threaded barrel or concealed beneath Kryptek Highlander camo.

Springfield

Several years ago Springfield released the EMP pistol, a slightly smaller version of the 1911 chambered in 9mm. This year the EMP4 joins the club with a 4-inch barrel and slightly taller grip. The extra inch increases muzzle velocity and the

Smith & Wesson's new SW22 Victory.

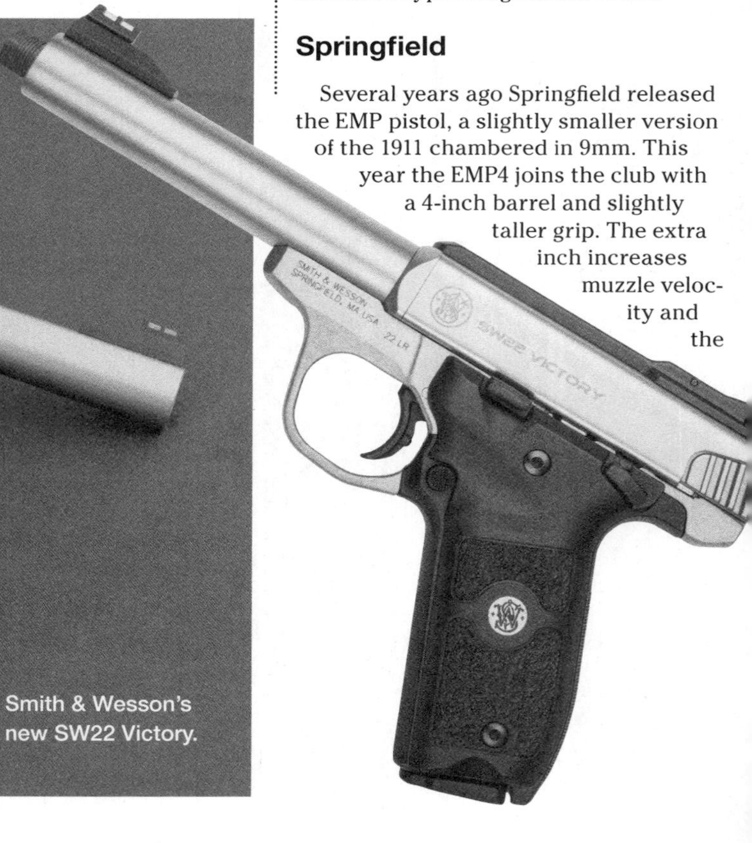

Springfield Armory's new full-size 5-inch barrel XD9 Mod.2 with Grip Zone.

The Springfield Armory XD-S, now available with the CT Laserguard.

Springfield finally released a Range Officer in 9mm this year. Yay.

extra height adds one more round to the magazine, which now stores 10 rounds. It retains the same smaller grip circumference, low-profile sights, checkering and cocobolo wood grips as the earlier, smaller EMP.

The XD Mod.2 in 9mm is also new. Featuring a full 5-inch barrel, but retaining a slim grip with a 16-round magazine, it makes a very comfortably shooting full-size 9mm pistol. It's available in Melonite finish or as a two-tone stainless steel slide model. Prices are $608 and $651. The standard XD Mod.2 has expanded to include the usual caliber suspects.

XD-S models are also now available with a Crimson Trace Laserguard, as are 1911 Loaded models. Suppressor-ready XD-M models with threaded barrels from the factory are new this year as well. XD-Ss can now be purchased in Flat Dark Earth finish so you can lose your gun in the desert after it falls out of your holster.

The Range Officer Operator is the classic Range Officer optimized for self-defense purposes, notably with low-profile combat sights. At $1,029 in both 9mm and .45 it should sell pretty well. The classic Range Officer now can wear stainless steel too at $1,045.

STI

STI is adding a Classic model and a 3-Gun model to their DVC line of competition guns. The Classic is chambered in 9mm, .40 S&W and .45 ACP while the 3-Gun model can only be had in 9mm. The Classic, which MSRPs at $2,799, has a hard chrome finish, a number of parts built by Dawson Precision (well desired in the comp community) and VZ grips. It

The DVC Classic single stack from STI. Note the large mag funnel at the base of the grip.

has a single-stack magazine. The 3-Gun has a black DLC (Diamond Like Carbon) finish, a somewhat longer 5.4-inch barrel and an MSRP of $2,999. It uses a double-stack magazine and has lightening cuts in the slide. Both models use a TiN coated barrel for hard use.

The new Hextactical cocking cuts on the pistol of the same name are pretty cool. Rather than traditional serrations, or the much newer scales commonly seen on slides, the Hextactical uses machined hexagons in place of the older cuts. It's quite eye-catching and works just as well as the traditional methods. Both 1911 and 2011 models are HEXed and run $2,099 and $2,599, respectively. Grip upgrades to VZ grips made of G10 are now available for the Lawman, Sentinel Premier, Tactical SS and Nitro 10 models.

Traditions

Traditions added several samples to its Black Powder Revolvers series. Specifically, they are engraved models of the 1858 Army (blued), 1851 Navy (blued), 1851 Navy (nickel) and the 1860

The STI DVC 3-Gun in all its dark glory.

Army (blued). Pricing goes from $299 up to $399. These BP percussion cap pistols really look nice and are all in .44 caliber.

The Frontier series also has a couple new members. The 1873 Sheriff's model has a short 3.5-inch barrel. It has a color case-hardened finish and is chambered in .357 Mag. The 1873 Oversized grip model has a longer and beefier grip and a 5.5-inch barrel to offset the larger look of the grip. Also chambered in .357 Mag., and with color case-hardening, all of the new Oversized grip models sell for $574. The Sheriff has an MSRP of $499.

A wall of engraved Traditions black-powder revolvers at the SHOT Show.

Turnbull Manufacturing

Turnbull adds to its fascinating collection of highly finished pistols with the Government Heritage and Commander Heritage models, and Turnbull 1911 Government and Commander models. The former have a color case-hardened frame with blued slide. The latter are fully blued and come standard with nitre blued small parts. Both are fitted with modern parts such as extended beavertail safeties, flat mainspring housings and checkered front straps.

New from around the middle of last year are the BBQ Heritage models that are essentially an ode to well-prepared meat, sporting a crossed 24K gold spatula and fork inlay, and standard engraving on the slide. The frames are color case-hardened and elk grips. MSRP begins in the $5,000 range.

UA Arms

UA Arms is known for its 1911 pistols that use the explosive welding technique to join steel rails to aluminum frames. Now the company has released a 1911 called the MagnaT5, which uses a very hard Magnesium frame and slide. This material is stronger than aluminum but is also 35 percent lighter. This is an extremely light pistol. Chambered in .45 ACP it is relatively inexpensive (for such a specialty alloy) at $1,499.

Walther Arms

Walther Arms has shown itself to be very productive in the last few years. This year's most anticipated delivery was the PPQ chambered in .45 ACP. Having shot this pistol at the range I can say that most people will be pleasantly surprised with this item. Felt recoil is much less than I expected and is easily comparable to that felt from a full-size 9mm pistol. Like the previous models of the PPQ, the trigger is wonderful and the grip is comfortable. The $699 MSRP is not onerous and it will hold 12 rounds of good US of A old reliable.

A new version of the PPS, the M2 was also released, and updated that gun to address the average American shooter (who likes thumb button mag releases), and the current Walther trend to make all of its pistols look as much alike as possible. It's getting to the point that I have to look twice to determine which model of Walther pistol I'm seeing when I am seeing one. $469 if you want to pay full price for one of these.

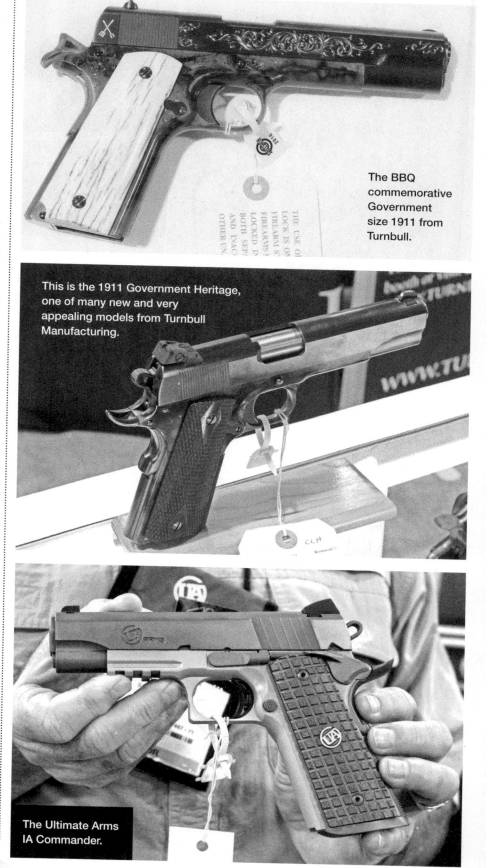

The BBQ commemorative Government size 1911 from Turnbull.

This is the 1911 Government Heritage, one of many new and very appealing models from Turnbull Manufacturing.

The Ultimate Arms IA Commander.

REVOLVERS & OTHERS

BY **Max Prasac**

Photo courtesy of C. Magera.

If you are anything like me, I suspect you are reading this out of more than just idle curiosity, but more likely that you probably have a deep love and fascination with all things Western. There was a time in America when the Western genre of movies and television shows was very popular.

Those were simpler times, the world was seen through two lenses, one good, one bad, with nothing gray in between. The good guys on television always wore white and carried a Colt Peacemaker (and maybe even two of them) slung low on their hips. Well, the bad guys also carried the same revolvers, giving the public a double dose of Single Action Army!

There is something unexplainably special about single-action revolvers. They are simple, aesthetically pleasing to the eye and ergonomic to the hand. But most importantly, they have a soul, something other handguns fail to possess. A soul that harkens back to the days when men settled their differences face to face on a dusty street with gun play. The faster, more accurate shooter was able to keep his life and live to fight another day. It was a dangerous existence for saloon dwellers, gamblers, lawmen and even innocent bystanders who simply wound up in the wrong place at the right time — a time punctuated with names like Wild Bill Hickok, Billy the Kid and Doc Holiday, and places with names like Boot Hill, Dodge City and OK Corral. It was a time that conjures up romantic notions of driving cattle, robbing stagecoaches and settling the western territories.

All of those heady images are encapsulated by 3 pounds of steel with a wooden grip. When you hold it in your hand, close your eyes and pull back on the hammer, you can almost envisage a time long ago, with each click of the hammer moving back. The single-action revolver, even in modern times is a throwback, a piece of history and even a relic of a bygone era, where rugged individualism paved the way to the modern existence we enjoy today, through blood, sweat, and an indomitable spirit and grit.

Fast forward to the 21st century and not only is the single action alive, and thriving, it has been joined by a whole slew of modern double-action revolvers that still uphold and preserve the spirit of the wheelgun. Revolvers represent pure unadulterated Americana, particularly in single-action form, but that is merely one aspect of this chapter. The same can be declared about the derringer – another piece of pure Americana. As you will see, there are contemporary takes on the theme that are being built and still serve the intended purpose of the originals, but with a modern twist of flavor.

We are a consumer nation in no uncertain terms, where "More's Law" rules the trappings of the daily grind of life. If some is good, more must be better, right? For some time, great amounts of energy and research dollars were expended on increasing the capacity of semiauto pistols to enable the shooter to hold off mass waves of zombies for stretches of time without ever changing magazines. I asked myself where it would end. I have big mitts, but some of

these auto pistols feature such big grips to accommodate the highest of capacity magazines, that I have trouble reaching the trigger without some extreme contortionist maneuvering. I again asked myself where it would end. Revolver manufacturers also got in on the action, with some models featuring a round or two of increased capacity, but design limitations make really high capacity a physical impossibility. This isn't a bad thing, just an observation.

In this day and age of bottom feeding, plastic-frame pistols in small calibers that are stuffed into Kydex drop holsters, I am happy to report revolver manufacture remains vibrant. As you are aware, this segment is a celebration of revolvers, derringers and single-shot pistols. We will examine what is currently available and highlight what is new. Some exciting models have been introduced recently and I think you will agree, these are good times!

American Derringer

Founded in 1980 by Robert Saunders, American Derringer set out from the beginning to create handmade derringers. When Robert passed, wife Elizabeth took the helm and to this day ensures that American Derringer stays true to Robert's vision. A full line of single- and double-action derringers are available in a variety of calibers ranging from .22 LR to .45 Colt/.410. American Derringer also produces small semiautomatic pistols. New this year is the LM4 Simmerling, purportedly the smallest .45 ACP ever made, this single-action pistol boasts a magazine of five-shot capacity (plus one in the chamber). It weighs in at a paltry 24 ounces and is handmade – like all of American Derringer's products. These are limited-quantity, handmade high-quality firearms that are not mass produced. (www.amderringer.com)

Armscor

Four defensive-type revolvers are available by Armscor. Designed with durability in mind, defensive revolvers cannot chance compromise from a reliability standpoint, and for this reason Armscor has chosen "bulletproof" design parameters. All Armscor revolvers feature an all-steel construction and thus uncompromising strength. All four wheelguns are chambered in .38 Special and three of the four come with a Parkerized finish, the last one with a matte nickel finish. All feature a conceal-friendly 2-inch barrel length, and the M200 features a 4-inch barrel option. The M280 and M289 are equipped with spurless hammers. (www.armscor.com)

Bond Arms

In the business of building high-quality derringers for more than 20 years, Bond Arms manufactures its firearms in the great state of Texas. From the outset, Bond Arms set out to create what was once considered a symbol of the Old West into a modern, safe and dependable defensive handgun for predators of the two-, four- and no-legged slithery variety. We would say Bond Arms succeeded in spades.

The newest Bond Arms derringer is called the Patriot. Proud Americans can have this double-barrel powerhouse with laser-carved grips prominently fea-

Cimarron Eliminator .45 Colt with octagon barrel. Author photo.

turing the American flag and bald eagle. The Patriot is chambered in the popular .45 Colt and .410 shotgun (2.5-inch), and features an all stainless steel construction (barrels and frame), automatic spent casing extractor and a patented rebounding hammer. The patriot weighs in at only 21.5 ounces. (bondarms.com)

Charter Arms

Known for producing double-action revolvers for more than half a decade, Charter Arms entered the gun-building fray with the Undercover, a five-shot .38 Special that weighed in at only 16 ounces. Today, Charter Arms produces a full line of double-action revolvers for many purposes. Why choose Charter Arms? There are a number of great reasons to include one-piece frames (stronger than screw-on sideplate designs), a safe and completely blocked hammer system, three place cylinder lockup, and Charter Arms revolvers are 100 percent American made and owned.

Charter Arms revolvers are available in a variety of models to suit your personal defense needs, to include the original Undercover (still in .38 Special), the Pitbull in 9mm, .40 S&W and .45 ACP, the lightweight Undercover Lite coming in at 12 ounces, the Bulldog in .44 Special, as well as the Pathfinder in

.22 LR and .22 Magnum. There is something here for everyone serious about personal defense.

New for Charter Arms is the Nitride finish, a proprietary process that adds a scratch- and wear-resistant finish that is also attractive. The Nitride finish is available on three Pitbull models and one Undercover model revolver. (www.charterarms.com)

Cimarron

Cimarron is an importer of both Uberti and Pietta revolvers from Italy and offers a complete line of replica Single Action Army revolvers, as well as black-powder percussion revolvers, open-top revolvers and conversion revolvers. New this year is the Eliminator series of 1873 Single Action Army revolvers that are made exclusively for Cimarron by Pietta. The Eliminators feature a 25 percent shorter hammer stroke for even faster action manipulation, and can be had with the Cowboy Comp U.S. action job. One model is equipped with an attractive 4¾-inch octagon barrel, a color case-hardened frame with blued barrel and cylinder, and is available chambered in .357 Magnum or .45 Colt, another is available in stainless steel in .45 Colt. These are ideal for competition use and are not only high performers – but they look great while performing as well. (cimarron-firearms.com)

Cobra

Cobra produces derringers and double-action revolvers that are 100 percent American made, keeping your

The Bond Arms Patriot derringer.

hard-earned money at home. While they also produce small semiautomatic pistols, it's their single-action double-barrel derringers and compact double-action revolvers that have our interest here. Cobra derringers are available in several different configurations, to include different finishes in calibers ranging from .22 LR for some models, all the way to .45 Colt/.410 shotgun. The "Shadow" series double-action revolver is available as a five-shot .38 Special +P only, but in a variety of finishes. (www.cobrapistols.net)

Colt

The company that really started it all still produces a version of the famous Single Action Army (SAA) today. Sometimes called the "Peacemaker," virtually all modern single-action revolvers are loosely based on Colt's classic design. One of the most iconic pieces of Americana, the Colt Single Action Army is probably the most recognizable gun in American film history. Three generations of Colt SAAs have been produced since its inception in 1873.

The first generation was produced from 1873 through the start of World War II. During this time frame, the classic Army style revolver was available and later joined by the Sheriff and Storekeeper models that featured shorter barrels and no ejector housings. In the late 1880s, a flattop SAA target model was added to the lineup. The Bisley model, a competition-style revolver, was introduced in the early 1890s that featured a distinct vertical grip frame and low-spur hammer, fixed or adjustable rear sight, and a removable front sight blade. Production ceased during the war and didn't begin again until 1956.

The Army-style model continued to be produced and the only variation

was the New Frontier model that was a target-style revolver with modern adjustable iron sights. Production ended in 1974, only to resume in 1976. Significant changes in design marked the third generation guns including a different barrel shank thread pitch, and a solid cylinder bushing. By 1982, regular production faltered even though the factory custom shop continued producing revolvers on a special order basis.

By 1993, the Single Action Army was back in Colt's catalog, and is available today in .44 Special and .45 Colt in the three standard barrel lengths: 4¾, 5½ and 7 ½ inches. The fixed-sight SAA is also available in blue and color case-hardening, or nickel plated, in .357 Magnum or .45 Colt, with the same barrel lengths. The Colt Custom Shop will build you a Single Action Army with a variety of different grip material options and custom engraving, enabling you to personalize your Colt sixshooter.

The granddaddy of all modern single-action revolvers is alive and well. (www.colt.com)

Dan Wesson

Founded by the great grandson of D.B. Wesson, co-founder of Smith & Wesson, Daniel B. Wesson established Dan Wesson Arms in 1968. Born in 1916, Daniel worked in the family business (Smith & Wesson) from 1938 to 1963, when Smith & Wesson was acquired by Bangor Punta.

Featuring a number of innovations, Dan Wesson's revolvers were known for quality, durability, and most importantly, accuracy, an asset that made them a favorite in metallic silhouette competition. Dan Wesson big-bore revolvers were inherently accurate, strong and on the heavy side, making them among the

most pleasant to shoot even with hot loads.

Certain innovations set Dan Wesson revolvers apart from others, most particularly switch-barrel capability. Imagine purchasing a revolver that comes with a number of different, replaceable barrels enabling you to turn your revolver into a carry piece, and then switching barrels out for a longer unit for a silhouette match the same day! Imagine switching barrels yourself in a matter of minutes. Ingenuity was a trademark of Dan Wesson Arms.

Dan Wesson also offered stretch-frame revolvers specifically designed for the ever more popular long-range metallic silhouette of the late '70s and early '80s, chambered in .357, .375 and .445 SuperMags. Only a small number of .414 SuperMags made it out the door before Dan Wesson closed shop.

By 1983, Dan Wesson Arms, no longer family owned, was in financial trouble. Quality suffered as a result and there was a decline in popularity of silhouette shooting to contend with. Looking more and more like Dan Wesson Arms would close their doors for good, Seth Wesson – son of Dan and Carol Wesson – took control of Dan Wesson Arms and renamed it Wesson Firearms Company. But, the company soon faltered and after a few years the name was purchased by New York International with the intent of producing Dan Wesson designed revolvers once again. Included in the acquisition were the necessary tooling, patents, trademarks, intellectual properties and all remaining inventories. The old manufacturing machinery wasn't purchased as not only was it dated, it was also worn out. What was soon evident was that producing the same high-quality firearms would require new tooling.

The new Wesson Firearms tooled up anew and by December of 1997, the first revolvers were shipped. The fit and finish of the first run were of an excellent quality. The production process continued to improve and 1999 marked a year of growth for the company with two new large-frame revolvers added to the lineup, as well as the reintroduction of the .414 SuperMag. The Pistol Packs and Hunter Packs returned to production at this time as well, but with new refinements. The Pistol Packs bear mention as they really set Dan Wesson apart from other manufacturers. Your revolver came with three different barrels in three different lengths and the accompanying barrel shrouds, two sets of grips, and

The Colt New Frontier in .45 Colt. Author photo.

the necessary feeler gauge and barrel wrench for swapping barrels. This was truly a great innovation.

Then 2005 rolls around and CZ-USA purchases Wesson Firearms with the desire to add its excellent products to CZ's impressive line of firearms. CZ-USA offered a .445 Alaskan model, but generally dialed back on revolver production instead focusing on semiautomatic pistols, including the ones designed by Wesson Firearms prior to CZ-USA purchasing the company. A number of years later and CZ-USA had shelved all revolver production. However, the 715 .357 Magnum double-action revolver is now back in production just like it was before. You can expect the highest of quality and unparalleled accuracy just as was the case before. The 715 ships with a 6-inch barrel with a vent, and as was a feature of the Dan Wesson revolvers of yore, barrel assemblies and grips are easily swapped. Are more calibers going to be offered in the future? Only time will tell, but we will certainly keep our fingers crossed. (cz-usa.com)

DoubleTap Defense

DoubleTap produces what could best be described as a modern-day derringer made in the USA. The pistols are small, light in weight and hammerless, making carry in a pocket possible with no hammer to snag. These double-barrel pistols come in two calibers, .45 ACP and 9mm (standard pressure). Barrels are interchangeable and frames are made from aluminum or titanium. The titanium version buys you two ounces of weight over the aluminum frame. Two spare rounds can be carried in the grip on a speedloader, enabling fast reloads. Optional ported barrels are available, cutting muzzle flip. All DoubleTap pistols are fully CNC machined and come with a lifetime warranty. (www.doubletapdefense.com)

European American Armory Corporation

European American Armory produces a line of single- and double-action revolvers. While the single actions are Colt Single Action Army reproductions, the double-action "Windicator" series is geared toward personal defense. The Windicator is a dependable, quality firearm in .38 Special or .357 Magnum with fixed sights and rubber grips, and is made in Germany. This is a no-frills, no-

compromise double-action revolver with either a 2- or 4-inch barrel, in a blued alloy frame or a nickel-plated frame (.357 Magnum only).

The Bounty Hunter single-action revolvers are also manufactured in Germany, and have been sold in the United States for more than 20 years. They are chambered in a number of calibers ranging from .22 LR through .45 Colt, including the powerful .44 Magnum. These are traditional single actions with the added safety benefit of a transfer bar. The cylinders are counter bored and the revolvers can be had in a number of different finishes such as blue, color case-hardened or nickel. (www.eaacorp.com)

Freedom Arms

Freedom Arms has the distinction of making some of the finest single-action revolvers in the industry – period. Demand is so high in Freedom, Wyo., that Freedom Arms currently isn't releasing anything new.

These revolvers are the Cadillacs of the single-action revolver world. Freedom Arms was started by entrepreneur Wayne Baker with a revolver design brought to the table by the veteran designer and originator of the modern, high-pressure, five-shot revolver, Dick Casull, in 1978. The first guns manufactured by Freedom Arms were actually mini revolvers of Casull's design. The biggest and most notable result of that union was the Freedom Arms Model 83 released in – you guessed it – 1983, and chambered for Dick Casull's wonder cartridge, the .454 Casull. The introduction of the Model 83 also debuted the .454 as an honest-to-goodness production cartridge. Freedom Arms takes its name from the location of its plant in Freedom, Wyoming.

Though a traditionally styled single-action revolver, the FA 83 is all modern

on the inside and produced of modern materials (17-4PH stainless steel), though in a five-shot configuration (a lesson learned by Dick Casull after decades of experimentation and development). When handling a Freedom Arms revolver, the lack of cylinder play becomes readily apparent. The company prides itself on hand assembling each and every unit to tight and exacting tolerances. It is true custom-built production revolver, and the tolerances are tight enough to necessitate regular cleaning to avoid problems like moving parts, well, not moving (a condition that could prove detrimental when facing an angry furbearer higher up on the food chain than the user).

Unlike other commercial revolver producers, Freedom Arms has the distinction of performing machine work that is normally a custom shop-only proposition, a procedure known as line boring. With the cylinder placed in the frame of the revolver, a face-boring fixture is fitted where the barrel will attached, and each chamber is drilled through this fixture (which is mimicking the barrel). Thus, each hole is bored in precise alignment with the barrel, and it is one of the reasons Freedom Arms revolvers shoot as well as they do. All of this extra attention will cost the buyer more, but perfection never comes cheap.

Fast forward to 2016, and Freedom Arms not only continues to produce the Model 83, but it does so in a number of different calibers and in two different grades, Field and Premier. The FA 83 is available in the following calibers: .22 LR (Field grade only), .357 Magnum, .41 Magnum, .44 Magnum, .454 Casull, .475 Linebaugh and .500 Wyoming Express.

One can also opt for cylinders in compatible calibers like .45 Colt (with .454 Casull), and .480 Ruger (with .475

The FA83 in .500 Wyoming Express.
Photo courtesy of L. Martin.

Linebaugh). The Premier grade revolvers feature a brighter brushed finish, fully adjustable rear sight, laminated hardwood grips and a limited lifetime warranty. Field grade revolvers have a matte finish, a rear sight that can only be adjusted for elevation, a one-year warranty, and rosewood or rubber grips.

Freedom Arms also produces a smaller framed revolver, more in line with the size of the Colt Single Action Army, the Model 97, for those who wish for a trimmer package on their hip. The 97 is available in the following calibers: .17 HMR, .22 LR, .224-32 FA (a wildcat of Freedom Arms' design), .327 Federal, .357 Magnum, .41 Magnum, .44 Special and .45 Colt.

As the Model number suggests, the 97 was introduced in 1997. This revolver is a departure from the Model 83 mechanically, in that it features a transfer bar safety system similar to that of Ruger's design, which allows for safe carry with a round under the hammer. Also of note is the size difference between the 97 and the 83. When newly introduced, the 97 was only offered as a six-shot .357 Magnum, the line was later expanded to include the .41 Magnum and the .45 Colt in a five-shot configuration. The Model 97 makes for a really fine packing revolver.

Freedom also produces fine breakopen, single-shot pistols designated the Model 2008. Available in 11 different calibers, and three different barrel lengths – 10, 15 and 16 inches – the Model 2008 defines practical. All barrels are interchangeable, making caliber switches simple. What sets the FA 2008 apart from other specialty, single-shot pistols is the excellent grip frame borrowed directly from the FA Model 83, a grip that lends itself well to heavy recoil. Non-catalog barrel lengths are available for an extra fee.

In summary, these revolvers and pistols have no equals with regards to fit and finish. Tolerances are very tight and the grip frames are superb. Just like single-action Colts of old, the FA 83 should not be carried with a cartridge under the hammer.

Loading and unloading is performed with the hammer in the half-cock position, allowing the cylinder to spin – another nod to the Colt Single Action Army. Freedom Arms recommends carrying the Model 97 with an empty chamber under the hammer as well, to eliminate any possibility of an accidental discharge. In all, Freedom Arms produces true modern-day classics. (www.freedomarms.com)

Heizer Defense

If you desire a whole lot of punch in a small package, look no further than Heizer Defense and their PS1 Pocket Shotgun in .45 Colt/.410. The single-shot PS1 is svelte package that weighs a mere 21 ounces, is less than 5 inches long and a lean .7-inch wide. As if that wasn't enough, the PAR1 or "pocket AR" as it is so lovingly referred to, is a single-shot pistol chambered in 5.56. This model can be had with or without porting. New this year is the PAK1, and as the name suggests, the "pocket AK" is chambered in 7.62x39 and comes with a ported barrel to keep muzzle flip to a bare minimum. Rumor has it that a .300 Blackout version is on the horizon. Also new for 2016 are interchangeable "accessory barrels" enabling the owner of any of the above mentioned pocket pistols to be chambered in any of the available calibers with a simple barrel swap, adding to the versatility of these pocket powerhouses. (heizerdefense.com)

Heritage Manufacturing

Heritage Manufacturing offers two different Rough Rider revolver versions, the Big Bore and the scaled-down Small Bore. The Small Bore revolvers are chambered in either .22 LR or .22 Magnum (some models are available as combos with two cylinders) in a variety of barrel lengths, finishes and grip materials from cocobolo to wood laminates. A flat, low-glare black finish is available on some models, giving the buyer many options to choose from when selecting a revolver. One version comes equipped with birdshead grips for a compact package. The Big Bore revolvers are available in .357 Magnum and .45 Colt. (www.heritagemfg.com)

The PAK1 or "pocket AK," single-shot pistol in 7.62x39 by Heizer Defense.

Kimber

Not really known for revolvers, Kimber surprised the industry and the shooting world in early 2016 with the introduction of the Kimber K6s double-action revolver. The K6s is purportedly the world's lightest small-frame six-shot .357 Magnum revolver for concealed carry. Equipped with a 2-inch barrel and a 1.39-inch diameter cylinder of stainless steel, the K6s features a match-grade trigger, an internal hammer, and smoothed and rounded edges ensuring smooth holster extraction, weighing in at a svelte 23 ounces. Compact, lightweight, great ergonomics and high quality. What's not to like about the New Kimber K6s? (www.kimberamerica.com)

Magnum Research

Magnum Research entered the revolver building business in 1999, with the introduction of the BFR – the "Biggest Finest Revolver" – chambered in the ubiquitous .45-70 Government. Magnum Research has since redesigned its revolvers and changed the moniker to stand for "Big Frame Revolver." As you are well aware, it takes a large cylinder and equally large frame to house a cartridge as big as the .45-70. Today, Magnum Research produces both long- and short-frame revolvers in a range of calibers to suit just about everyone's needs.

Magnum Research of Minnesota, a subsidiary of Kahr Arms, offers a whole line of long-frame and short-frame stainless steel single-action revolvers in standard caliber configurations and a plethora of custom Precision Center offerings. New in its long-frame configuration are two chamberings, .300 AAC Blackout and .458 SOCOM. Also available as a custom option from Magnum Research's Precision Center is a new Bisley style grip frame for the enthusiast who prefers the handling of a more vertically profiled grip.

New rubber Hogue overmolded grips designed specifically for the BFR have replaced the old rubber grips, and a new LPA adjustable rear sight (in place of the previous Ruger adjustable rear sight) adorns all BFR revolvers now. These are big, no-compromise, well-built revolvers that offer unparalleled accuracy and strength at a reasonable price point. BFR – Bang For the Revenue! (www.magnumresearch.com)

The Big Framed Revolver in .45-70 from Magnum Research.
Author photo.

BFR available in .500 JRH from the Precision Center.
Photo courtesy of V. Ricardel.

North American Arms

Miniature revolvers are the name of the game for North American Arms. These small, well-crafted, stainless steel single-action revolvers are available in three rimfire calibers – .22 Short, .22 LR and .22 Magnum. A cap-and-ball version of the mini revolver is also available for the enthusiast wanting something very different. The .22 Short version comes equipped with a 1-1/8-inch barrel and has to rank as the smallest five-shot mini revolver in production with its diminutive stature. Probably the most serious of North American Arms' mini revolvers is the "Magnum Mini Masters Black Widow" series that can be had in .22 Magnum, with a heavy vented 4-inch barrel, adjustable sights, a bull cylinder and oversized rubber grips. (northamerica-narms.com)

Rossi

With the same family at the helm of the company for 117 years, not many firearms manufacturers can claim the rich, deep and continual history of Rossi, founded in the late 1800s by Amadeo Rossi in Brazil. The company still offers a full line of double-action sixguns in .22 LR, .38 Special and .357 Magnum in stainless and blued steel, as well as the Ranch Hand, a shortened lever-action pistol available in .357 Magnum, .44 Magnum and .45 Colt. A single-shot "Matched Pair Pistol" in the popular .45 Colt/.410 shotgun configuration is also available, with the added flexibility of a switch-out barrel in .22 LR. Both barrels are 11 inches in length and finished in blue. This pistol should prove a versatile combination for a variety of purposes to include plinking, target shooting and small-game hunting.

New from Rossi are two Plinker eight-round double-action revolvers in .22 LR. As the name implies, these just might be the ultimate plinking revolvers for the handgun enthusiast. Both feature an all carbon steel construction, and the R98104 and R98106 are fitted with a 4-inch and 6-inch barrel, respectively. The rear sight is adjustable and both revolvers are finished in a deep blue. (www.rossiusa.com)

Smith & Wesson

Smith & Wesson builds no single-actions, only double-action revolvers, but it has the distinction of building some of the finest double-action revolvers in the world. Smith & Wesson revolvers are known for their quality fit and finish as well as their distinctive actions. Distinctive how? The word "superb" comes to mind. They are characteristically smooth and only become smoother with use.

The newest revolvers to come out of Smith & Wesson are the Model 642 LaserMax edition, a lightweight aluminum J-frame, double-action-only revolver in .38 Special +P, and the 460 XVR Bone Collector model from the Performance Center. As a handgun hunter, I take particular interest in revolvers like the Bone Collector as their design intent is big-game hunting. Like all X-frames, this is a big revolver, weighing in just shy of 5 pounds unloaded. Chambered in the high-velocity .460 Smith & Wesson Magnum, the Bone Collector is fitted with a 7½-inch barrel (with integral optic rail) featuring a fully adjustable rear sight with a green fiber-optic sight up front. As a Performance Center model, the already exceptional action is tuned for even smoother performance. (www.smith-wesson.com)

Sturm, Ruger & Company

Sturm, Ruger and Company obviously needs no introduction here.

Probably the most produced modern single-action revolver in circulation is Sturm, Ruger & Company's Blackhawk and its .44 Magnum derivative, the Super Blackhawk. Strongly built and affordable, this is the single-action revolver for the masses. These revolvers have a number of innovative design features that set them apart from other makes in modern form, particularly the transfer bar safety system – introduced with the "New Model" designation in 1974. The transfer bar allows the revolver to be safely carried with a live round under the hammer.

Ruger is a company the revolver enthusiast should always keep an eye on. Having one of the most active dealer exclusive programs in the industry, Ruger often releases interesting variations on existing themes and even more one-offs.

The big news last year was the introduction of two new Super Blackhawks in .454 Casull and .480 Ruger in five-shot configurations. These are the revolvers handgun hunters have been asking for and

Ruger, through Lipsey's, has made it happen. Available in stainless steel only with a 6½-inch barrel and a Bisley grip frame.

Ever since Sturm, Ruger & Company released the .480 Ruger in the love-it or hate-it Super Redhawk back in 2001, revolver aficionados have been browbeating Ruger to release this cartridge in their popular single-action revolver lineup. The combination of Super Blackhawk and .480 Ruger is debated incessantly on gun websites yet Ruger's reticence to actually make this happen has frustrated handgun hunters who have long wanted to see this marriage come to fruition. Basically a shortened .475 Linebaugh, the .480 Ruger is a serious big-game hunting round that even when loaded to spec isn't too abusive to the one pulling the trigger. Ruger has finally relented by offering not only their .480 Ruger in the Super Blackhawk line, but also the raucous .454 Casull. Ruger has offered the double-action Super Redhawk in .454 Casull since the late '90s. Handgun hunters everywhere have reason to rejoice as two of their favorite calibers can be had in the revolver they love in an affordable package. Available as a Lipsey's (lipseys.com) distributor exclusive, I cannot imagine supplies will last long.

Here's what you need to know. The new revolvers are based on the old revolvers. Ruger used the standard Super Blackhawk frame in stainless steel (415 stainless steel). The barrel is 6½ inches in both models and made from 15-5 stainless steel, with a 1:24 and 1:18 rifling twist for the .454 Casull and .480 Ruger, respectively. The barrel is straight, without a taper, and features a front sight base that is silver soldered on with a pinned-in sight blade, and a standard Ruger adjustable sight in the rear. The cylinder is carved from 465 Carpenter steel, the super-strong, hard-to-machine material that first made an appearance in the late '90s in the Super Redhawk in .454 Casull (and later in the .480 Ruger version). The cylinder is a five-shot configuration, with counter-boring to encapsulate the case heads. The new revolvers were fitted with an extra-long ejector rod housing that made its first appearance on the limited run of stretch-frame .357 Maximum revolvers of the early 1980s. A Bisley grip frame is the only one offered and the only one Ruger deemed acceptable for these applications. A locking base pin guards against the base pin walking out under recoil, a nice touch.

Also new is the Davidson's dealer exclusive .41 Magnum Redhawk. Replete with a 4.2-inch long barrel, the six-shot double-action Redhawk is what we have come to expect from the platform – and that is strength and a bit of heft to go along with it. The sample I tested proved accurate with a number of factory loads out to 25 yards. Recoil is negligible in this package, and would make for a good starter pistol for the recoil sensitive.

Another new revolver that caught my eye was the Talo dealer exclusive Birdshead Vaquero in .44 Magnum. You read that right, this Vaquero is chambered in .44 Magnum. Confused yet? Ruger brought back the old, full-size Vaquero for this model, making it the first new old Vaquero in years, not to be confused with the mid-frame Vaquero that is also still being produced. Equipped with a 3¾-inch barrel and a highly polished stainless steel finish, the little powerhouse is rather easy to pack. (ruger.com)

Taurus

Taurus has a revolver for every season, and every reason, from personal defense to big-game hunting. Manufactured in Brazil, Taurus offers a full line of revolvers for many uses, with a plethora of models of differing frame sizes and calibers. At Taurus, variety is evidently the spice of life!

Taurus produces small-frame revolvers in .22 LR on up through .357 Magnum and everything in between, with many variations on the theme. The medium-frame revolvers can be had in .38 Special as well as .357 Magnum in a variety of barrel lengths to suit your needs. The Tracker series is my favorite of the Taurus offerings. It is considerably smaller in stature than the Raging Bull, and also of a five-shot configuration. The Tracker is available in .357 (a seven-shot) and .44 Magnum calibers and offers an easy packing alternative for field use. Available in matte stainless steel or blued steel, with a 2.5- or 4-inch barrel, the Tracker is quite an attractive package. The 4-inch .44 Magnum version weighs in at a light 34 ounces empty. Trackers also come equipped with Taurus' excellent "Ribber" rubber grips.

The last step before the Raging Bull is the large-frame line of revolvers. Available in two calibers, the .357 Magnum – an eight-shot, and .44 Magnum – a six-shot revolver. The .357 version can be had with either a 4- or 6½-inch barrel, while the .44 Magnum can be had with a 4-, 6½- or 8-3/8-inch ported barrel. Built on a full-size

Ruger's five-shot .454 Casull Super Blackhawk available through Lipsey's. Author photo.

The Ruger Super Blackhawk in .480 Ruger. Author photo.

frame only available in stainless steel, the heaviest of the large frames weighs in at 57 ounces (.44 Magnum with 8-3/8-inch barrel).

While the most powerful Raging Bull currently in production is the .454 version, the Raging Bull can be purchased new in a six-shot configuration in .44 Magnum, and in a five-shot platform in .454 Casull. Introduced in 1998, the Raging Bull is all business. Available in high-polish stainless, matte stainless or blue finish, Taurus made sure there was something for every enthusiast, even with the most discerning taste. The largest Raging Bull is fitted with a bull barrel available in 5-, 6½- and 8-3/8-inch lengths, with a full underlug and a vented rib, adjustable sights and effective rubber grips – effective in that they provide a good cushion to the shooter's hand. Barrels all feature porting to cut down on felt recoil even from the stoutest of loads. The Raging Bull certainly looks the part and lives up to its name.

Taurus also produces an answer to Smith & Wesson's scandium-frame lightweight revolvers in its Ultralite series of revolvers. These are large-frame .44 Magnums featuring a construction of a titanium alloy. Available with a 2¼-inch or 4-inch barrel in either a Titanium Blue or Titanium Stainless Steel finish, these lightweights weigh 27.3 and 28.3 ounces for the 2¼ incher and 4 incher, respectively. The six-shot revolver can be carried day and night without even the slightest burden, and would make for a great backup, protection revolver for the outdoorsman.

Another Taurus revolver that has exceeded all expectations as far as popularity is concerned, is the Judge. This long-frame revolver is chambered in .410 bore and .45 Colt. A variety of different configurations are available to the public, culminating in the Public Defender Polymer Judge, the ultra high-tech revolver, with a steel frame and polymer exterior that is over-molded onto the steel frame. The popularity of the Judge series of revolvers has spurred the design and production of "Judge only" .410 shotgun loads to accommodate the short-barrel revolver with a focus on home defense, something the .410 has never been loaded for commercially.

Taurus offers a wide range of quality revolvers for a wide range of usage. (www.taurususa.com)

Taylor's & Company, Inc.

There's plenty of interesting products in the Taylor's & Company catalog starting with reproductions of the famous Howdah pistols that were used in the second half of the 1800s. The Howdah was designed to stop tigers from dragging poor unsuspecting individuals off of the backs of elephants. The Howdah Hunter is a faithful reproduction side-by-side, external-hammer pistol available in .20 gauge or .58 caliber. Also of interest is the

The .41 Magnum Ruger Redhawk with a 4.2-inch barrel.
Author photo.

Talo dealer exclusive .44 Magnum Ruger Vaquero with birdshead grip frame.
Author photo.

The Taurus Tracker in .44 Magnum.

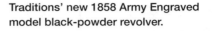

Traditions' new 1858 Army Engraved model black-powder revolver.

Traditions Performance Firearms' Frontier series 1873 model revolver.

reproduction Le Mat Cavalry pistol, featuring a nine-shot .44-caliber cylinder and a 20-gauge barrel in the cylinder center pin.

The company's black-powder line of revolvers is rather extensive with a number of famous models including the 1836 Paterson, 1848 Dragoon and the 1847 Walker. The cartridge revolver segment of the Taylor's catalog is even more extensive with large a variation in 1873 Single Action Army replicas as well as 1858 Remington Conversions, and Schofield revolvers. An entire chapter could easily be dedicated to Taylor's & Company offerings, so we suggest taking a look at the website. (www.taylorsfire-arms.com)

Thompson/Center Arms

Thompson/Center Arms is known for a number of differing firearms, from bolt-action rifles to muzzleloaders, and single-shot rifles and pistols. It's the pistols we are most interested in and Thompson/Center produces two different pistol frames for the target shooter or hunter, the Encore Pro Hunter and the smaller G2 Contender.

A wide variety of options are available at Thompson/Center where the pistol enthusiast can choose from a number of different configurations of G2 Contenders or Encore Pro Hunters. You can specify fore-end and grip material (rubber or walnut), blued or stainless steel frame and barrels, and in the case of the Encore Pro Hunter – calibers ranging from .223 Remington all the way up to

.460 Smith & Wesson Magnum. The G2 Contender can be had in calibers ranging from .17 HMR through .45-70 Government. (www.tcarms.com)

Traditions Performance Firearms

Traditions, well known for their muzzleloader rifles and historic replica muzzleloading pistols, also offers a line of imported Single Action Army replicas in two series – the Frontier, and for the more cost conscious, the Rawhide series. Both feature a transfer bar safety system enabling safe loaded carry in the field. Traditions also sells a full line of black-powder revolvers that are fully functioning, dedicated replicas.

New to the black-powder revolver lineup are four new models all featuring laser engraving, available in .44 caliber. They are the 1851 Navy Engraved model, the 1860 Army Engraved, the 1858 Army

Engraved model and the 1851 Navy Engraved model.

New on the Frontier series single-action cartridge revolver front are two new 1873 models. The new Sheriff's model comes equipped with a 3.5-inch barrel chambered in .357 Magnum, with attractive walnut grips and color case-hardened finish. Also available this year is an oversize-grip model with a barrel length of 4¾, 5½ or 7½ inches, chambered in .357 or .44 Magnum. (www.traditionsfirearms.com)

Uberti

Oddly enough, some of the finest reproduction American Old West guns are produced in Italy. Strange but true. Uberti, a subsidiary of Benelli, offers a whole line of reproduction Colt 1873 Single Action Army revolvers (the Cattleman series) made of modern materials. These fine reproductions are economical, pleasing to look at and of good quality. Like their progenitor, the Colt Single Action Army, you have to place the hammer on half cock in order to rotate the cylinder for loading and unloading. Included in the lineup is the Callahan revolver chambered in .44 Magnum. Many finish and barrel length options are available. Open top cartridge revolvers are available in .38 Special and .45 Colt. Black-powder revolvers are also prominent in the Uberti catalog, including reproductions of the 1849 Pocket Revolvers, 1847 Walkers and the 1851 Navy revolver. (www.uberti.com)

The Uberti Callahan Target in .44 Magnum.
Author photo.

The Remington Ultimate Muzzleloader took this deer at 85 yards with a 100-grain load of two Triple Se7en pellets and Thompson/Center Arms' 240-grain lead Cheap Shot Bullet. A second deer was shot a few days later at 200 yards with the same load. The Lab, Diana, was instrumental in recovering both deer.

MUZZLE LOADERS
BUILDING ON OLD FOUNDATIONS

BY **Hovey Smith**

The closer I examined Diana, my senior Lab, the more the damning evidence accumulated. There was blood staining her chin fur, her stomach was bulging to the full mark, and the clinching bit of evidence was a deer tick working its way down her snout. She had found the deer that I had shot at 200 yards with the Remington Ultimate Muzzleloader,

and apparently decided not to tell me about it.

I dislike making shots right before dark, but during the last days of Georgia's deer season I had a chance to take a deer with the Remington at a much longer range than the previous one I had shot at about 85 yards. I knew the range, was in a stable position in my built-up stand and squeezed off the shot. With the smoke

and dim light I could not tell where the deer ran. I returned with my dogs and started my search in the dark. I did not find it, but apparently Diana had not only found it, but also sampled it, as is her want. Returning after a business trip a day and a half later, I found and salvaged the mangled remains of the deer.

Billed as "The Ultimate Muzzleloader" and capable of shooting a 200-grain

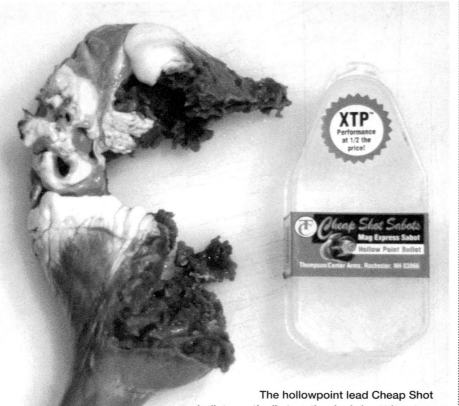

The hollowpoint lead Cheap Shot bullet practically tore the doe's heart into two pieces, but even so the doe ran 30 yards before it fell.

weight of nearly 10 pounds with scope gives it excellent stability, it is easy to clean, has a precision trigger, is well stocked and ideal for a situation where it can be taken to a fixed stand and shot across a field. It does not, however, shoot flat to 300 yards. With my 100-grain powder charge and 240-grain bullet, I had to compensate for about 18 inches of drop at 200 yards. The maximum Remington load drops about 21 inches at 300 yards with a 100-yard zero, according to Remington's data.

Hunting With Degraded Loads

Georgia's unusually wet hunting season produced adverse effects on loads of granular charges of Hodgdon's Triple Se7en powder in both a .75-caliber Brunswick Rifle and Uberti Super Walker Revolver. After being assembled from salvaged Nepalese parts and restocked, I had an adjustable rear and higher front sight installed on the Brunswick Rifle to allow better shot placement. I shot over the top of a deer using a patched belted ball and charge of Triple Se7en powder. The gun had been loaded for two weeks in wet weather, and subsequent shooting revealed that the degraded charge had thrown the bullet more than a foot over the point of aim at 50 yards.

Shooting the Super Walker (see *Gun Digest 2016* for details on the gun) revealed similar results. The degraded loads shot significantly higher than the point of aim. Reloading with GOEX FFg black powder in the rifle and FFFg in the pistol, I found that these loads shot closer to the sighting-in points than Triple Se7en. The old-time African hunters had their guns unloaded, dried and cleaned to be

charge of powder, this single-shot variant of the Remington 700 was tried on a variety of game this season; but warm, rainy weather offered few opportunities. I did not like the heavy recoil generated by the 200-grain load, and took both of the deer with two of Hodgdon's Triple Se7en pellets and Thompson/Center Arms' 240-grain pure lead hollowpoint Cheap Shot bullets. These expanded

well and passed completely through my smallish Georgia does.

Outfitted with a Leatherwood 4-16x44 scope, this is a precision-shooting instrument that can work very well with low-end black-powder-substitute loads and has demonstrated capabilities at long ranges with its advertised 200-grain charges and 250-grain jacketed copper bullets. The gun is very accurate – its

The author's rebuilt Brunswick rifle shown here on Georgia's Cumberland Island with a wild hog's skull, was completed this year, but failed to take any game.

The Super Walker with a sight-in target. Modifications to the Walker were completed by Michael Brackett of Goon's Gun Works in Marietta, Ga., who specializes in action work on single-action and percussion revolvers.

loaded fresh before each day's hunt. This was good practice then – and now. If you are hunting in a continually wet or damp environment, as I was, black powder degrades less rapidly than the Triple Se7en. Should you have doubts about the stability of your load, aim low for a heart shot. Even if the powder has lost some strength, the high-flying bullet may still strike in the vital area of your deer with sufficient energy to kill it.

For more details see my video, "Stability of black-powder loads in revolvers and a .75-caliber Brunswick rifle" at: https://youtu.be/Jh6i-TGpMt4.

2016 SHOT SHOW REPORT
Muzzleloaders are Still Muzzleloaders

A steam-powered automatic 1858 Remington-pattern revolver with scope and monopod exhibited in the NRA Museum Section of the SHOT Show was a remarkable exhibition of 19th century engineering technology, although apparently modern made. A gauntlet, strapped on the arm, contains the mechanism, which was operated by articulated

Constructing a steam-powered automatic revolver was not out of bounds for the inventive individual whose creation includes a scope mount and supporting monopod under the front of the barrel. The articulated wooden fingers worked and powered the mechanism.

WORLD'S FIRST AUTOMATIC HANDGUN

Operating this steam-powered device involves donning the brass and leather gauntlet, complete with its gauges for trigger pull. Fitted with a telescopic sight, this innovative single-action handgun is based on a six-shot .44 Remington percussion revolver and even includes a forward monopod for firing stability.

Loaned by John Belli.
On display at the NRA National Firearms Museum in Fairfax, Virginia.

Range day at the SHOT Show in January 2016 was clear and pleasant, but windy, in comparison to some very cold days in Las Vegas in the past.

wooden fingers to cock and fire the gun. Beautiful in design and execution, this gun indicates that muzzleloading gun technology still may have new, and surprising, things in store.

Modern muzzleloading rifles remain predominantly single-shot guns for which charges must be loaded one component at a time down the muzzle. While there have been improvements in ballistics, many historic individuals knew their long guns could kill just as far, and nearly as effectively, as any modern replica – given adequate quality guns, skills, shooting conditions etc. The modern replicas are easier to learn to shoot, easier to clean, have a flatter trajectory for a longer point-blank range and will give several lifetimes of service. Progress was and is being made in advancing muzzleloading technology in providing better bullets

and powders. However, the essence of muzzleloading remains killing an animal with a one carefully loaded and aimed large-diameter projectile. The particular configuration of the gun has become increasingly less important to many shooters than having a reliable hunting tool that gives consistent results.

The new single-shot rifle introduced this year by Thompson/Center Arms, the first muzzleloading gun since the firm's purchase by Smith & Wesson, is the Strike. This hammerless muzzleloader uses an externally threaded breech plug to enable the break-open gun to be easily cleaned without resorting to breech-plug wrenches and vises to free stuck plugs. Its futuristic lines are somewhat different, the break-open action is no longer novel and the entire appearance is

unlike traditional sidelock guns, yet it is still rightly classified as a muzzleloading gun. It is a single-shot, loads from the muzzle, shoots a .50-caliber bullet and, although easier to use than traditional guns, has the same basic attributes as its historic ancestors.

Another new hammerless drop-barrel muzzleloading rifle has been introduced by Woodman Arms. This New Hampshire company was started by designer Mark Woodman who seeks extreme accuracy in lightweight muzzleloading guns. He uses hand-lapped barrels, a patented trigger and other modern design features to get maximum accuracy from his hunting-weight .45- and .50-caliber rifles.

By contrast, the new percussion 1805 Harpers Ferry single-shot pistol made by Davide Pedersoli is a smoothbore gun in .54-caliber, and is a truer replica of a percussion-converted original than the flintlock version that the company has made for decades that used a .58-caliber rifled barrel to offer a little more accuracy and versatility. As a hunter I prefer the version with the larger caliber rifled barrel, and I featured it as an example of a big-bore flintlock handgun in my E-book, *Hunting Big and Small Game with Muzzleloading Pistols.*

Chiappa

Chiappa retained all of their black-powder products in this year's line and introduced a modern case with accessories for those shooters who wanted to take their Le Page duelers to the range. This modern foam-fitted case and accessories are ideal for the shooter who wants to get the most out of the gun.

The CVA .50-caliber Optima pistol remains one of the most popular guns in the CVA line.

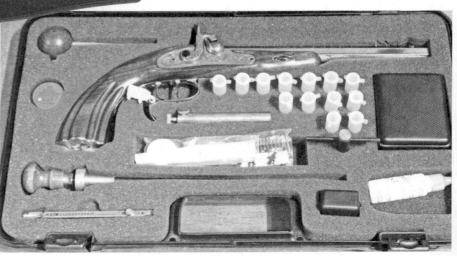

Chiappa's cased Le Page pistol provides the shooter with a modern case and reasonably priced accessories to take this gun to the range.

Connecticut Valley Arms (CVA)

With the large-scale adoption of nitride-treated barrels last year, CVA made almost no additions to their product line for 2016. Dudley McGarity, the company's owner, said that one of the most surprising sales was of the Optima .50-caliber single-shot big-game pistols, which were moving off the shelves as fast as he could make them.

Davide Pedersoli

This Italian firm specializes in producing replicas of historic firearms and includes a staggering line of arms from Europe, the U.S. and Asia. Thanks to modern production techniques, its machines can make a run of 1873 Winchester rifles one week and some of its new 1805 Harper's Ferry percussion .54-caliber smoothbore pistols the next. These guns use barrels with a smaller bore than the company's previous .58-caliber rifled flintlocks and employ a new drum-and-nipple firing mechanism. True to the originals, they are bright finished and have only a front blade sight on the 10-inch barrel. A second unusual handgun, also a .54-caliber smoothbore, is their Mamelouk pistol, which was carried by North African mercenary cavalry in Europe during the Napoleonic wars. These come with a bronze medallion in the stock showing one of the turbaned horsemen swinging his curved saber. This pistol is not generally sold in the U.S., but may be ordered through IFG, the company's American distributor.

After several years, Navy Arms has also brought back the Smith Carbine, which was among the more common of the Civil War era carbines. Show here are upgraded versions with American-made barrels and American walnut stocks.

Dixie Gun Works

Among many other items, Dixie imports the full line of Davide Pedersoli guns and was among the first to advertise its new .54-caliber smoothbore 1805 Harper's Ferry percussion pistol ($495). Although a flintlock rifled .58-caliber version has been available for years ($565), the new version is truer to the percussion conversions carried during the Civil War when finances or scarcity prevented the combatants from acquiring revolvers. The original pistols were all made as flintlock .54-caliber smoothbores with bright finishes. Many consider the 1805

the most elegant military sidearm produced by a U.S. arsenal, and a crossed pair of pistols is the insignia of the U.S. Military Police.

Knight Rifles

Knight Rifles did not exhibit at the 2016 Shot Show, but calls to the company indicated that they are still very much in business and continuing with the same line they offered in 2015.

Navy Arms Co.

Val Forget's Navy Arms Company was one of the pioneers in the replica muzzleloader business, and his firm has now returned to the muzzleloader market with the reintroduction of the Parker-Hale Enfield Whitworth rifle with its .451-caliber hexagonal bore, and the round-bored Volunteer rifle in the same caliber. These were recognized as the best replica muzzleloaders of the period. Although always more expensive, and now priced at $1,499, they provided precision shooting tools for the reenactor and hunter. These guns are stocked in American walnut and made in the U.S. High production costs have always put them on the edge of economic viability, and if you want to own a new example of one of the finest replica muzzleloaders ever, get it while it is still available.

Also available from Navy are the Smith Artillery and Cavalry model carbines

Navy Arms' hexagonally bored Parker-Hale Enfield Whitworth rifle on top and round-barrel bored Volunteer rifle on the bottom. Navy has recently re-introduced these replica guns. They were the best made of the replica Civil War era rifles and are highly desired for long-range muzzleloading shooting and hunting.

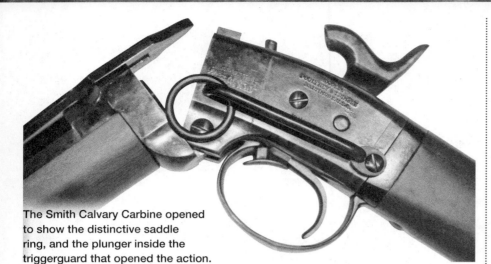

The Smith Calvary Carbine opened to show the distinctive saddle ring, and the plunger inside the triggerguard that opened the action.

Brass cases for the Smith Carbine. The preloaded powder and bullet are contained in this case and fired by a percussion cap placed on the nipple of the gun.

($1,499). These replicas are made with modern shooters in mind and are .50 caliber, with a separate brass loading chamber and a short conical bullet. The cases sold by Navy are different from the composition or brass cases sold by Dixie. These were among the handiest, but weakest, of the Civil War carbines. The replicas are typically shot with 30 to 40 grains of FFg black powder and .515-caliber round ball or lightweight conical, according to the Navy catalogue.

Although the same design, the Navy Smith carbines are better versions of the same Pietta-made gun that has been available from other sources and feature American-made barrels and Grade 1 American walnut. A prominent plunger inside the triggerguard pushes up a spring lock on the top of the action to open

the breech to allow the preloaded brass chamber-bullet to be inserted. A musket cap placed on a nipple fires the bullet.

Remington Arms Company

Remington continues to offer the Model 700 Ultimate Muzzleloader. In a conversation with a designer at the SHOT Show we had a nice chat about the gun. One feature that I noted was a primer set back in the special cartridge case used to prime the gun. Regardless of the load, the primer would be backset about 1/16 inch. In most cartridge guns, this would be considered a sign of excessive headspace and or too hot of a load, although I never experienced blown primers or gas leakage. Asked about this happening, he

replied that this was not a problem, and all of the Remington Ultimate Muzzleloaders would backset primers.

The specialized case used to prime the Ultimate Muzzleloader is a rimless case based on the .30-06/.45 ACP family of cases. Anyone who reloads cases in this family can easily re-prime the used brass with Remington Large Magnum Rifle Primers. I found that my old Lyman Tong Tool in .45 ACP de-primed and re-primed these cases very effectively at home and at the range.

I like the gun as a precision shooter, but even with a scope and weight of 10 pounds, I found that the much advertised four-pellet charge and 300-yard range was not of much significance to the average shooter. I found it much more comfortable to shoot with a three-pellet charge and achieve the same result by holding a little higher on the target. A Remington representative confirmed that at 300 yards the difference in bullet drop between a 150-grain load and a 200-grain load was only 4 inches with his test bullet. In short, don't beat yourself up with a four-pellet load when a three-pellet load with the same bullet will do nearly as well. With a 100-yard zero you are working with over 20 inches of bullet drop and you must know your load and wind drift to make effective hits.

A lighter weight version of this gun with a slimmer barrel and stock is planned for introduction next year, the Remington representative said. As with all muzzleloaders of similar weight, this

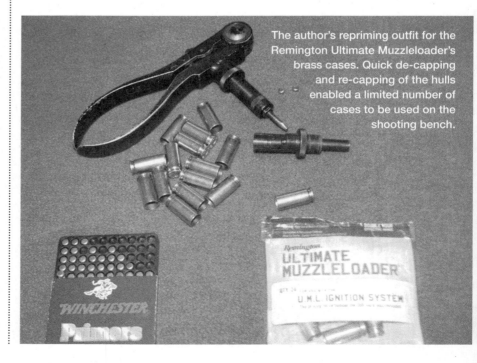

The author's repriming outfit for the Remington Ultimate Muzzleloader's brass cases. Quick de-capping and re-capping of the hulls enabled a limited number of cases to be used on the shooting bench.

version of the Ultimate Muzzleloader will be best used with 100- to 150-grain powder charges. This lighter gun will also kill at 300 yards, if you know your load and can adequately compensate for bullet drop and wind drift.

Thompson/Center Arms

The first new muzzleloading gun produced by Thompson/Center Arms since its purchase by Smith & Wesson four years ago is the Strike .50-caliber hammerless, break-open rifle with an externally threaded breech plug. This new breech plug prevents fouling from seizing internal plugs, and a rubber gasket and shroud prevents gas blowback. Although I had seen the gun at other events, my first chance to shoot it was at the 2016 SHOT Show where it was demonstrated by designer Karl Ricker, who first sold the rifle as the LHR Redemption Rifle, and now has rejoined T/C. It is uncommon when a former employee quits a company and was later invited back after going out on his own.

When asked why he designed the gun Ricker replied, "I wanted to make one of the simplest guns that we could produce so far as function and ease of use was concerned." Advanced features on this gun include a hammerless, striker-fired ignition operated by a sliding tang button, while the externally

Thompson/Center Arms' Strike drop-barrel, hammerless muzzleloader with externally threaded breech plug as introduced in Eufaula, Ala., during the SEOPA Writers' Conference.

The Strike disassembles very simply for storage and transport, much like a conventional break-action shotgun.

Karl Ricker shooting the Strike rifle during a range day demonstration. The photo captures it in full recoil from shooting a 300-grain bullet and charge of 85 grains of Hodgdon's Triple Se7en powder.

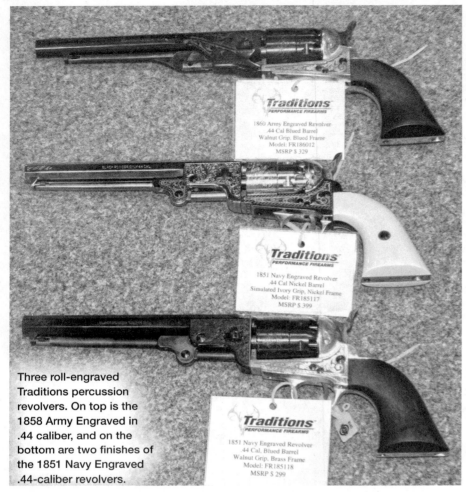

Three roll-engraved Traditions percussion revolvers. On top is the 1858 Army Engraved in .44 caliber, and on the bottom are two finishes of the 1851 Navy Engraved .44-caliber revolvers.

tion of conventional muzzleloading guns, Traditions continues to offer a line of reasonably priced sidelock muzzleloaders. The company has also expanded their line of Northwest Guns with exposed ignitions to include the popular break-action Buckstalker ($269-$369) and Pursuit ($339-$399) .50-caliber rifles. This modification allows hunters in Idaho, Washington and Oregon to use these guns during their states' muzzleloader seasons when only guns with exposed ignition systems are allowed. The Buckstalker has a 24-inch barrel with Truglo fiber-optic sights, and the more expensive Pursuit features a 26-inch Cerakote barrel with Williams fiber-optics sights.

Three upgraded .44-caliber percussion revolvers with roller-engraving were added to the line. The most distinctive is the 1851 Navy Engraved with a nickel finish and synthetic ivory grips ($399), but this treatment is also extended to the brass-frame 1851 ($299) and Remington 1858 Army ($399). These are ideal for those wishing to display fancier versions of Civil War revolvers at relatively inexpensive prices.

Woodman Arms Inc.

Mark Woodman has introduced a new design of hammerless, drop-barrel muzzleloading rifles featuring custom match-grade nitride-coated barrels. Woodman's 24-inch barrels are button rifled and hand lapped to .0003 inch. They shoot extremely well, indeed, with his patented trigger and new cocking mechanism. Aluminum or steel frame options are available, along with laminated wood, walnut and graphic-dipped walnut stocks. Sights may be 1-inch or 30-mm scope mounts, a Picatinny rail with a choice of open sights built into the rail, or peep sights. All guns are equipped with a crossbolt safety, are guaranteed for life and have a suggested retail price of $899, depending on the options. Dealer and individual orders are accepted.

threaded breech plug takes interchangeable 209 primer holders for optimum performance for pelletized or loose powders, and an easy take down for transport to hunting locations.

During the all-day range event, the gun functioned flawlessly and gave good accuracy at short and long-range targets. The gun was mostly shot with a load that appeared to be about 85 grains of Hodgdon's Triple Se7en and a 300-grain bullet, although it's rated for 150-grain charges and heavier bullets.

The base price for the synthetic-stocked rifle with fiber-optic sights is

$499, which is $120 less than LHR's price for the same rifle. The new rifle will be available with a synthetic black, synthetic camo or walnut stock, match-grade trigger, ambidextrous cocking system, 24-inch nitride-coated barrel with Weaver scope bases and a weight of 6.25 to 6.75 pounds, depending on stock materials. This gun is made in the U.S. and carries T/C's factory warranty.

Traditions Firearms

Unlike other manufacturers that have largely abandoned the produc-

Woodman Arms Patriot muzzleloading rifle. The Patriot features a newly patented trigger, hand-lapped nitride-coated barrel, a selection of optic and iron sights, and choice of stock materials and finishes, with either an aluminum or stainless steel frame.

Alliant's Blue MZ pelletized muzzleloading .50-grain pellets in blister packs. This is advertised to be a cleaner burning, less corrosive pelletized powder for muzzleloading use.

Powders, Bullets and Accessories

Alliant has introduced a new black-powder-substitute powder, Blue MZ, in 50-grain pelletized form. Like other pelletized powders, this is sold in blister packs and may be used in muzzleloading rifles and pistols. The pellets are a distinctive blue and are not to be confused with the company's Blue Dot, which is a granular powder intended for cartridge guns. Blue Dot is NOT the granular equivalent of Blue MZ, although colored the same in blister packs and cans.

Federal Premium Ammunition introduced a Premium B.O.R. Lock MZ lead bullet that has a pure lead projectile using the same capsulated sabot technology used last year in the Trophy Copper muzzleloader bullet. These bullets have a hard base to help break the crud ring left by some pelletized powders, and are designed for rapid expansion and good weight retention in deer-size game. The copper bullet weighs in at 270 grains and the denser lead bullet at 350 grains.

FEDERAL PREMIUM®
.50 CAL 350 GRAIN LEAD BULLET WITH B.O.R. LOCK MZ™

FEDERAL PREMIUM®
.50 CAL 270 GRAIN TROPHY® COPPER WITH B.O.R. LOCK MZ™

Federal's lead and copper muzzleloading bullets compared.

OPTICS

From A to Z — Aimpoint to Zeiss — and Many Others in Between, Here is Our Annual Review of the Latest in Optical Gear for the Shooting Sports.

The new model Aimpoint Micro H-2 sight worked out to be the perfect sight for the author's AR-15.
Photo by the author.

BY **Tom Tabor**

Aimpoint

For over 40 years Aimpoint has been providing high-quality optics for the world's shooters. They were the originator of the very popular electronic red-dot sighting technology and are one of the main producers of red-dot sights today. In 2007 the company came out with their very first micro sight, which is favored by hunters due to its lightweight, compact size and its long battery life.

Aimpoint prides itself in listening to its customers and when shooters and hunters began offering ideas for improvements, the company responded, giving way to a new model micro sight called the H-2. A few of the enhancements over the earlier H-1 Model include: a new sight housing that allows the addition of front and rear protective flip covers, additional physical protection for the sight's adjustment

turrets, an increased ruggedness for the internal electronic components, better light transmission and increased clarity. The H-2 can be mounted on most rifles,

shotguns, handguns or crossbows and can be used with most existing mounts that fit the earlier model, including the Blaser saddle mount. From a single 2032

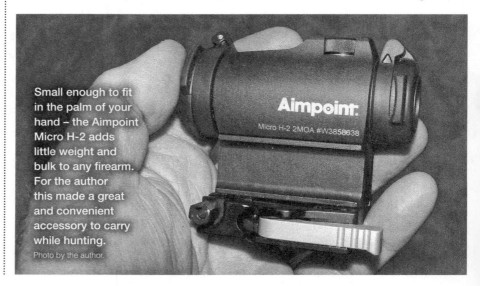

Small enough to fit in the palm of your hand – the Aimpoint Micro H-2 adds little weight and bulk to any firearm. For the author this made a great and convenient accessory to carry while hunting.
Photo by the author.

battery the user can expect up to five years of constant usage.
www.aimpoint.com

Bushnell

Bushnell has been in the performance sports optics business for more than 65 years. I still personally own and use on a regular basis a Bushnell Ensign 7x35 binocular that I purchased probably 45 years ago, and it continues to perform much as it did when it was new. But certainly there have been major improvements made in Bushnell's optics over the years; a classic example of those enhancements can be found within the expanded Legend Binocular Series. Today there are three models available: the E-Series, L-Series and the M-Series, all of which are available in either 8x42 or 10x42 configurations. These models include a chassis constructed of strong, lightweight magnesium, and come with fully multicoated optics with Ultra Wide Band Coating that is customized to encourage maximum brightness and truer colors across the light spectrum. The E-Series comes with premium objective covers and a fine-click diopter adjustment. The L-Series feature an additional locking eyepiece diopter and ED prime glass, and are available in black or the 10x model can be purchased in Realtree Xtra camo. MSRPs range from $179.99 for the E-Series 8x42, up to $399.99 for the M-series 10x42.

Also new within Bushnell's Equinox Z product line are two new night-vision binoculars that come packed with a host of features including digital zoom, image capture and video recording, and are available in either 2x40mm or 4x40mm configuration. Both models come in a rugged water-resistant housing, glass objective lens with multicoated optics and feature

1-3x zoom, adjustable IR setting and daytime color viewing. They are powered with common AA batteries for added cost savings and convenience. After the still images or video have been captured they can be easily downloaded for later viewing on your computer. The Equinox Z 2x40mm binoculars are expected to carry a MSRP of $499 and the 4x40mm would run $549.

In recent years the Bushnell Elite 6500 series riflescopes have in many ways become the centerpiece of the company's hunting riflescope market. Capitalizing on that basic success Bushnell is now offering two new series of scopes, the Elite 3500 and the Elite 4500. These new additions feature Ultra Wide Band (UWB) coatings, an antireflective coating that allows better light transmission through the glass to the eyepiece and optimum brightness and true color across the light spectrum. The lenses are protected with the patented RainGuard HD coating, which causes the moisture to bead up and scatter less light. The 3500 and 4500 were designed to be more compact and like the 6500 Series, their tubes are one-piece cold mold constructed and argon purged. Both the 3500 and 4500 series scopes come with 1-inch main tubes while the 6500 series have 30mm tubes. The 3500 series scopes range from 2-7x32mm to 4-12x40mm and the 4500 series come in configurations from 2.5-10x40mm to 8-32x40mm.

Bushnell is proud to announce that all of the company's riflescopes, binoculars and spotting scopes within the Trophy, Trophy Xtreme, Legend, Elite and Elite Tactical lines now carry lifetime warranties. In the words of Jordan Vermillion, Bushnell's Global Director for Optics, "It's our absolute, everlasting pledge to honor our customers. We're proud of our products and we are willing to guarantee complete satisfaction. We promise to repair or replace our product and ship it back at absolutely no charge."

Bushnell Legend M Series binoculars are available in either 8x42 or 10x42 (as shown here) configurations. All of the Legend M Series come in a lightweight and strong magnesium chassis.

Bushnell Elite 4500 8-32x40mm riflescopes come in a variety of variable powered models from 2.5-10x40mm to 8-32x40mmm. The one-piece cold mold construction is argon purged to help ensure waterproof and fogproof performance.

This new No Questions Asked Lifetime Warranty was launched at the 2016 Archery Trade Association Show in Louisville, Ky. It is fully transferable and covers accidental damage as well as defects in materials and workmanship, and no receipt or warranty card is needed to take advantage of that service. Bushnell will simply repair or replace the product with one of equal or similar value and or specifications. Plus, unlike many of the Bushnell competitors, they will return the product with no shipping or handling charges to the customer.
www.bushnell.com

Celestron

Over the years Celestron has established itself as one of the foremost leaders in star-gazing equipment. But this California-based operation has now branched out to include not only astronomy based products, but also sporting optics, including spotting scopes, monocular and binocular units. The new Celestron Granite ED Series binoculars come with extra-low dispersion (ED) glass objective lenses for edge-to-edge sharpness and color correction, fully multicoated optics and dielectric-coated Bak-4 prisms. Its magnesium alloy exterior housings are waterproof and nitrogen purged and come with strong metal twist-up eyecups. Six full-featured models are available to choose from, including 7x33, 9x33, 8x42, 10x42, 10x50 and 12x50, which range in price from $319.95 to $459.95.

For those folks looking for even greater magnification, Celestron offers a new Echelon 10x70 binocular specifically designed for low-light use. The Echelon 10x70 binos are assembled in the USA and utilizes premium Japanese optical components. The lenses are fully multicoated, contain BaK-4 prisms and include XLT coating for maximum light transmission through the entire optical path. Packaged in a rubber-armored aluminum housing, the Echelon 10x70 is designed to withstand rugged use in the field. They come with objective lens caps, RainGuard protection, a neoprene neck strap and a waterproof hard case. MSRP for the Echelon 10x70 binoculars is $749.95.

www.celestron.com

Leica's new Ultravid HD Plus 12x50 binocular is constructed of durable titanium and magnesium materials and covered by a robust layer of rubber armor.

Leica

Leica's new ER 6.5-26x56mm LRS Premium Long-Range Riflescope is the latest in a large selection of fine optics meant for the sportsmen. Boasting high magnification, this scope could be a good match for long-distance shooting and includes long-range reticles with stadia lines and wind hash marks, as well as ballistic turrets. Like all Leica ER riflescopes, the ER 6.5-26x50 LRS features precision-ground HD glass elements and cutting-edge glass coatings. Its strong monobody main tube is made of aerospace-grade aluminum and includes a highly durable anodized metal finish and a waterproof, fogproof exterior. In addition, it comes with low color fringe/high contrast optics, parallax compensation, AquaDura coating, a lifetime limited warranty and a three-year Leica Passport Protection Plan.

Also new from Leica are the extremely compact Ultravid HD-Plus 50mm series binoculars, which are available in 8x50, 10x50 and 12x50. Created with new objective HD/HT glass elements, these binoculars are meant to provide brighter and clearer images and include precisely formulated SCOTT HT glass, which is created using a new, high-temperature

plasma-coating process that deposits thin films of high-quality materials on the lens surfaces. The company says these features combine to increase the light transmission by up to 92 percent. Construction consists of durable titanium and magnesium materials covered by a heavy layer of rubber armor, and an AquaDura coating to protect against damage from water, dirt and fogging. MSRP for the Ultravid HD-Plus 50s binos run from $2,499 up to $2,749.

us.leica-camera.com/Sport-Optics

Leupold & Stevens

Leupold & Stevens' Gold Ring optics have long been recognized as some of the best sporting optics in the business, but making a good product even better is what the Leupold company strives to do. The latest of those upgrades includes a re-design of the Gold Ring Spotting Scope Line. These modifications were made to enhance the scopes' ruggedness and include the addition of the Impact Reticle in the 12-40x60mm HD and the 20-80x60mm models. The MOA-based front focal-plane reticle design allows guides or spotters to better call impacts and offer quicker shot corrections. A minute-of-angle based grid set in the lower half of the viewing field is intended to allow for faster and more accurate measurements at any magnification. In addition, the mil-radian dots allow the Impact Reticle to be used with mil-based reticles. A new armor coating offers superior protection in the field, while the prism-less Folded Light Path System significantly reduces the overall length of the scope. The Gold Ring Spotting Scopes are completely backed by the Leupold Gold Ring Full Limited Guarantee.

The Leupold Carbine Optic (LCO) 1X red-dot sight.

With the increased interest in red-dot optics today and in particular for

Leupold's DeltaPoint Pro is constructed with a lightweight aluminum housing that is shrouded by spring steel to provide the ultimate in ruggedness, yet only weighs a mere 1.95 ounces. Leupold's patented Motion Sensor Technology discerns any movement of the sight and automatically activates the illumination feature.

carbine shooters, Leupold developed the Leupold Carbine Optic (LCO). This compact 1x red-dot sight encourages quick and natural target acquisition. The 1-MOA dot reticle of the LCO has 16 brightness settings with the most intense of those being appropriate for bright day use, while the lower settings can be used in conjunction with night-vision optics. The manually controlled on/off switch is of a push-button design and is integrated with the brightness control to make changing the intensity quick and easy. The LCO is waterproof and backed by Leupold's Gold Ring Full

Leupold BX-3 Mojave Series open bridge binoculars are available in models covering a wide variety of different magnifications and objective sizes ranging from 8x32 up to 10x50.

Lifetime Guarantee. MSRP for the LCO is $1,249.99.

Also new to the Leupold red-dot sight line is the DeltaPoint Pro. Its lightweight aluminum housing is shrouded by spring steel for enhanced ruggedness, yet only tips the scale at a mere 1.95 ounces. Leupold's patented Motion Sensor Technology discerns any movement of the sight and automatically activates the illumination feature when motion is detected. Tested to a water depth of 33 feet assures its ability to resist moisture in the toughest and wettest of environments. From handguns to ARs, and from rimfires

The large 56mm objective diameter and the 8x magnification of Meopta's new MeoPro 8x56 HD binocular would be ideal in low-light situations, and with a 7mm exit pupil it is about the maximum pupil dilation of a normal human eye.

to big-bore .458 rifles, the DeltaPoint Pro has been designed to function well and comes with windage and elevation adjustments of 60 MOA. The MSRP for this sight is $749.99.

New to the Leupold binocular line are the open-bridge designed BX-3 Mojave series models. Cold-mirror-coated prisms combine with a fully multicoated lens system to provide peak brightness and resolution and true-life color fidelity. Rugged, waterproof and dependable, the BX-3 Mojave binoculars come covered by the Leupold Limited Lifetime Warranty and in magnification choices ranging from 8x32 up to 10x50 and carry MSRPs from $439.99 to $714.99.

www.leupold.com

Meopta

Meopta USA has expanded its popular MeoPro HD binocular series to include a new MeoPro 8x56 HD model. The large objective lens, advanced fluoride high-definition optics and MeoBright multicoated lenses helps to enhance glassing in low-light conditions. Meopta's General Manager, Reinhard Seipp, expounded on that point in his own words by saying: "Its large, 56mm objective diameter and 8x power create an exit pupil of 7mm, which is about the maximum pupil dilation of a normal human eye. The large exit pupil of this binocular floods the eye with light, allowing hunters to see fine detail in extremely low light. This is why most wild boar hunters in Europe use 3-12x56 riflescopes set on 8x in combination with their 8x56 binoculars because if they can see the boar with the binocular, they can see it through their scope."

The external lenses of MeoPro HD are treated with Meopta's proprietary MeoShield abrasion-resistant coating that meets military specifications for durability and surface hardness. Twist-up eye caps feature four click-stop positions to accommodate users wearing eyeglasses, and a right side ocular diopter control provides +/- 3D adjustment for simple individual optical tuning. Joining the newly released 8x56 HD binoculars, MeoPro HD binoculars are the 8x32, 10x32, 8x42 and 10x42 models. MSRP for the new 8x56 HDs are $1,034.99.

Meopta has also added to its popular 1-inch MeoPro riflescope line a new 6.5-20x50 and a 6.5-20x50 HTR (Hunt/Tactical/Range) model. These scopes were specifically designed for long-range hunting and precision shooting applications and feature a side parallax adjustment. The MeoPro 6.5-20x50 is available with capped style hunting turrets and the MeoPro 6.5-20x50 HTR version features exposed target-style turrets. Four different reticle options are offered to meet a variety of shooters' needs: Z-Plex, BDC, McWorter HV and Windmax 8. All are backed by Meopta's North American Lifetime Transferrable Warranty. MSRPs range from $1,092.49 to $1,149.99.

Meopta has also added a new MeoStar R2 8x56 RD riflescope to the company's R2 line. This is a fixed power 30mm scope, which would be a good match for moderate-range hunting in low-light conditions. It is available in a choice of illuminated 4C or 4K reticles that are in the second focal plane and come with 8 levels of reticle intensity. Like all Meopta riflescopes, the MeoStar R2 main tube has been machined from a solid block of aircraft-grade aluminum alloy and built to withstand extreme conditions. MSRP for the MeoStar R2 8x56 RD scope is $1,494.99.

www.meoptausa.com

Left Top: Meopta's new 6.5-20x50 comes with a 1-inch main tube and is one of the newest additions to the company's MeoPro line.

Left Middle: The new 6.5-20x50 HTR (Hunt/Tactical/Range) scope comes with exposed target style turrets and side turret parallax adjustment.

Left Bottom: Meopta has added this MeoStar R2 8x56 RD to its premium line of R2 riflescopes.

Nikko Stirling

Nikko Stirling is known for its reasonably priced sporting optics and accessories. The company's riflescopes include a wide variety of magnifications and come with limited lifetime warranties. The new Panamax Series include models ranging in magnification from 3-9x up to 4.5-14x, and in most cases are available in either 40mm or 50mm and with a 1-inch main tube. Some models come with illuminated reticles and have parallax adjustable objectives. One of the unique features of this series of scopes is the fact that even though they are all based on a 1-inch main tube, they offer an extremely wide angle of view, which results in 20 percent larger viewing potential than most other 1-inch scopes.

All lenses are coated with the company's own proprietary Micro Lux ETE Gen III coatings to encourage a higher level of ambient light transmission. The glass surfaces are multicoated to provide a higher definition picture and increased clarity. The main tubes are high-grade aluminum and come with a hard anodized coating. All of the Nikko Stirling Panamax series scopes possess the new Half Mil-Dot (HMD) Reticle designed to make precise holdover and wind corrections quick and easy. MSRP ranges from a low of $129.00 up to $245.00.

If you are looking for a higher degree of magnification Nikko Stirling has introduced the new Mountmaster 4-16x50mm Illuminated Scope. Designed to be light-weight, durable and attractively priced at only $115.00 MSRP, the Mountmaster could possibly be a good match to your hunting needs. It is shock tested and dry

Nikon's new P-308 4-12x40mm BDC 800 riflescope is intended to match precisely the ballistics of the .308 Winchester/7.62x51mm NATO round when loaded with a 168-grain HBT Match bullet at a muzzle velocity of 2,680 fps.

Nikon's new Buckmasters II series riflescopes come in two very popular variable magnification models: 3-9x40mm and 4-12x40mm (shown here). Both come in matte black finish and include Spring-Loaded Instant Zero-Reset turrets to make in-the-field adjustments easy and effortless.

nitrogen purged at the factory to make it waterproof and fogproof. Duel red/green illuminated reticles provide versatility when hunting at dusk and dawn. The fully coated lenses are designed to reduce the reflection of light, enhance clarity and provide more vibrant color retention. The Mountmaster comes with a Mil-Dot reticle and each scope comes with a set of Weaver-style rings. The AO lens offers parallax adjustment from 10 to 750 meters and is accompanied by a Nikko Stirling Limited Lifetime Warranty. www.nikkostirling.com

Nikon

Nikon Buckmasters riflescopes have been available to shooters for more than a decade. That line, however, has now been expanded under the name of the Buckmasters II and includes two new additions in the very popular sizes of 3-9x40mm and 4-12x40mm. Both come in matte black finish and have Spring-Loaded Instant Zero-Reset turrets to make in-the-field adjustments easy and effortless. The Buckmasters II scopes come with the parallax adjusted at the factory to 100 yards and are waterproof, fogproof and shockproof.

Each comes with the popular BDC reticle, which utilizes a unique set of circles as aiming points. When used in conjunction with the company's Spot On Program, it provides the shooter with exact aiming points for virtually any load or ammunition at a specified range. It contains the ballistic information for more than 5,000 different loads and can also accommodate custom handloads. MSRP for the Buckmasters II 3-9x40mm BDC is $129.95 and for the 4-12x40mm BDC is $149.95.

Also new to the Nikon line and an expansion of their existing precision .308 Winchester riflescopes, is the P-308 4-12x40 BDC 800. This scope is intended to ballistically match the .308 Winchester/7.62x51mm NATO round when loaded with a 168-grain HBT Match bullet sent on its way at 2,680 fps. This scope also comes with the Nikon Spring-Loaded Instant Zero-Reset turrets and is waterproof, fogproof and shockproof. MSRP for the P-308 4-12x40 BDC 800 is $249.95.

At no other time in our history has rimfire shooting been more popular than it is today, and Nikon has capitalized on that interest with the new PROSTAFF Rimfire II line of riflescopes. There are currently two new scopes within this series that have been specifically dedicated to .22 LR shooters. These include a 3-9x40 and a 4-12x40 model, both of which feature Nikon's own BDC 150 reticle. They come with the parallax set at the appropriate range of 75 yards and reticle adjustments equal to ¼ inch at 50 yards per click. Both scopes come with Nikon's Spring-Loaded Instant Zero-

Left Top: With the increased popularity of rimfire shooting today the Nikon PROSTAFF Rimfire II could be a perfect match. There are currently two new scopes in this series dedicated to the .22 Long Rifle caliber: 3-9x40 (shown here) and the 4-12x40, both of which feature Nikon's own BDC 150 reticle.

Left Bottom: There are currently two new riflescopes in Nikon's new PROSTAFF Rimfire II series: 3-9x40 and 4-12x40 (shown here).

Reset turrets and are optimized for use with Nikon's Spot-On Ballistic Match Technology in order to provide exact aiming points at varying ranges. The PROSTAFF Rimfire II scopes are waterproof, fogproof and shockproof, and carry MSRPs of $119.95 and $139.95.

www.nikonsportoptics.com

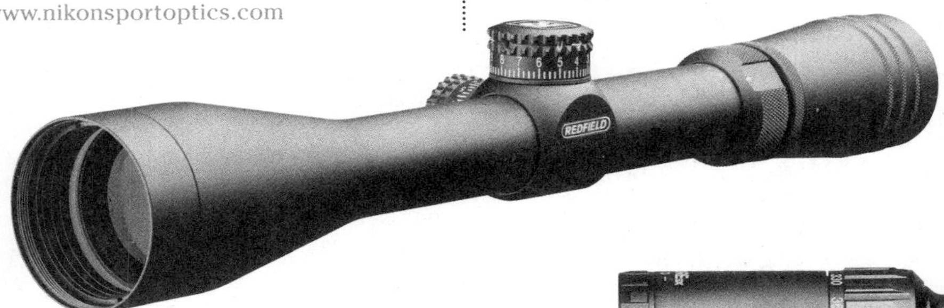

Redfield's Revolution /TAC scope was designed for tactical use and comes equipped with many functions and features that tactical shooters prefer.

Redfield

The new Revolution and Revolution/ TAC riflescopes by Redfield can provide the shooter quality and dependability at a reasonable price. The Illuminator Lens System includes premium lenses, vapor deposition and dielectric coatings. They also come with a generous degree of eye relief and Rapid Target Acquisition eyepieces. The Accu-Trac adjustments components are made from stainless steel and have 1/4 MOA per click finger adjustments dials. These scopes are 100 percent waterproof and fogproof and nitrogen purged. There is a selection of reticles to choose from and carry MSRPs ranging from $249.99 up to $314.99.

www.redfield.com

Sightmark

Sightmark is offering a new series of Core SX scopes that have been specifically designed for unique hunting applications, including crossbow, handgun and shotgun applications. Each scope in this series comes specifically dedicated to one of those uses. The Core SX 1.5-4.5x32 Crossbow Scope was designed for hunting medium-size game such as white-tailed and mule deer. It provides arrow drop compensation tuned to 250-400 fps crossbow velocities. This scope is equipped with a red/ black VXR-M reticle that comes with 11 brightness settings and arrow drop compensation allowances. Its counterpart, the Sightmark Core SX 3x32 Crossbow Scope is intended for use on larger size game such as elk or moose, and was

The Sightmark Core SX 1.5-4.5x32 Crossbow Scope was designed for use on medium-size game, such as white-tailed and mule deer. It provides arrow drop compensation tuned to 250-400 fps crossbow speeds.

The Redfield Revolution would make a great choice for the hunter that wants to couple economy with dependability.

Right Top: The Sightmark Core SX 3x32 Crossbow Scope is intended for use on larger game such as elk or moose, and was engineered with kill zone rangefinding capabilities and fixed power magnification.

Above Middle: The Sightmark Core SX 1x24 Shotgun Scope provides extra-long eye relief capabilities for effective use on shotguns, muzzleloaders and high-recoil firearms. It comes with a duplex reticle and a wide field of view, making it a good choice for hunting turkeys, rabbits, squirrels and wild boar.

Above Bottom: The Sightmark Core SX 4x32 Pistol Scope was engineered for use on dangerous game where large-bore pistols are used in the category of .40 or .50 calibers. It offers up to 17 inches of eye relief and a tapered duplex reticle for quick target acquisition.

engineered with kill zone rangefinding capabilities, but comes with fixed power magnification. The ballistic compensation characteristics of the Core 3x32 are keyed to 320 fps crossbows. Plus, it comes with a red/black VXR-L reticle with 11 brightness settings.

The Core SX 1x24 Shotgun Scope provides extra-long eye relief capabilities for effective use on shotguns, muzzleloaders or high-recoil firearms. This scope comes with a duplex reticle and possesses a wide field of view, making it a good choice for turkey, rabbit, squirrel or wild boars. And last, the Core SX 4x32 Pistol Scope was engineered for

Steiner's Miniscope is a great product for those of us that like to keep the size and weight of our field equipment to a minimum. Measuring only 2 inches high and 2 inches wide, and weighing only 2.8 ounces, it is convenient to carry, yet comes with an impressive 8x magnification.

dangerous-game hunting where large-bore pistols are used in the category of .40 or .50 caliber. It offers up to 17 inches of eye relief and has a tapered duplex reticle for quick target acquisition. The compact and lightweight nature of this scope is well suited for handgun use. MSRPs are: $179.97 for the Core SX 1.5-4.5x32 Crossbow Scope, $119.97 for the Core SX 3x32 Crossbow Scope, $89.97 for the Core SX 1x24 Shotgun Scope and $119.97 for the Core SX 4x32 Pistol Scope. www.sightmark.com

Steiner

Keeping gear size and weight down while hunting is a major consideration for many shooters. That is why Steiner's new Miniscope should have a lot of appeal to hunters and other outdoors people. Its pocket-size design, measuring only 2 inches high and 2 inches wide, and with a weight of only 2.8 ounces, in my personal opinion makes it a near perfect accessory to carry in your pocket or purse. Yet, with a magnification of 8x it permits great long-distance viewing possibilities. The Miniscope features the company's Sport-Auto-Focus, which after the unit has been adjusted to the user's own eyes, everything from 65 feet to infinity will be in clear focus. I personally used one of the new Miniscopes and found it very useful for viewing all types of game from ducks to elk. I found the optics to be crystal clear and absolutely loved the lightweight and compact nature of the unit. The Steiner Miniscope comes with a 10-year company warranty, a plastic carrying case and carries a modest MSRP of $114.99.

Steiner's new XC Series Binoculars are designed for rugged use in the outdoors, but double as a great accessory for taking along to the ball game or for concert viewing. There are four models currently available, consisting of two compact versions – the 8x32mm and 10x32mm, and two midsize models – the 8x42mm and 10x42mm. MSRPs run from $530.00 to $580.00. Also new is the roof prism, open-bridge design Wildlife XP Series, which incorporates premium German fluoride glass and classic European styling. These lightweight binos carry MSRPs ranging from $2,299 to $2,414. www.steiner-optics.com

Swarovski

Austrian-based Swarovski is considered by many to make the best optics in the world and their North American subsidiary, Swarovski Optik North America, provides the link to those products for the sportsmen of the Western world. This year there are a couple of new riflescope models that assuredly will be well received. The new X5(i) comes with newly designed turrets allowing for a full 20 MOA per revolution and has a viewing window to show the user what revolution he or she is on. At the heart of the X5(i) is its Spring Retention and Lever System that exerts the same pressure on both turrets from the inversion system regardless of positioning. This helps to assure maximum accuracy and repeatability. There is up to 116 MOA of elevation adjustment inside its 30mm main tube that yields a 5x zoom range. The X5(i) also features a new Subzero Function that allows the shooter to shoot at closer distances if the zero is set at farther than the usual zero. This allows the shooter to come down to 10 MOA (equivalent to 40 clicks) from a preset zero. The illuminated reticle versions have fully illuminated reticles

with 10 brightness settings. Second focal plane long-range reticles in one or two MOA increments are available in both illuminated and non-illuminated models. Two magnification levels are available: 3.5-18x50 and 5-25x56 that carry MSRPs of $3,666.00 and $3,888.00, respectively.

Swarovski introduced its EL Range series binoculars in 2011, but recently made improvements to their ergonomic design. Two models are available: 8x42 and 10x42. The improvements start with the development of the FieldPro package. The new and easy to use rotating strap connector with cord adapts better to the user's movements. Its bayonet catch allows the carrying strap to switch and fit silently and more easily to accommodate different carrying and use positions. The new objective lens and eyepiece covers attach securely, while blending into the overall design of the body. As a result of a more slip-resistant design it allows easier use of the focusing wheel and diopter adjusting rings. The EL Range binoculars are said to be the lightest in their class and carry MSRPs ranging from $2,433.00 to $3,188.00.

www.swarovskioptik.com

The Swarovski X5(i) riflescopes come with a 30mm main tube and up to 116 MOA of elevation adjustment. Shown here is the Model 5-25x56mm.

The author found the optics of the Swarovski X5(i) 3.5-18x50 scope to be crystal clear and as such made long-range shooting a breeze.

The new EL Range Binoculars offer new and improved ergonomics. Two models are available: 8x42 and 10x42.

Trijicon

Trijicon recently introduced the new AccuPower series of riflescopes intended for long-range competition use and big-game hunting applications. Generated from the success of the LED-powered Trijicon VCOG and TARS, the AccuPower series was designed for versatility and come in the variable magnifications of: 1-4x24, 2.5-10x56, 3-9x40 and 4-16x50. The construction consists of an aircraft-grade aluminum housing, high-quality glass lenses and advanced application-specific illuminated reticles. The adjustable intuitive reticle brightness settings have 11 choices to select from and an "off" position located between each of those choices. The AccuPower series incorporates a hybrid black chrome/etch and fill illuminated-reticle system that is available in either red or green. Four reticle choices are available: an intuitive MOA, MIL-square, Duplex crosshair and the popular competition segmented circle crosshair with BDC capabilities. All are located in the second focal plane, meaning the reticle size and appearance remains the same as when the magnification setting is changed. Power is provided by a single, long-lasting CR2032 battery. MSRPs for the AccuPower scopes range from $699.00 to $999.00.

Trijicon takes red-dot sight technology to the next level with the new Miniature Rifle Optic (MRO). The MRO was specifically designed to be tough enough to withstand the rigors of law enforcement, as well as the environmentally tough conditions encountered while hunting. The MRO mounts easily, zeros quickly and functions well in a variety of different shooting scenarios. Its short optical length and large objective lens help to eliminate the "tunnel vision" or "tube-effect" that is sometimes commonly encountered in similarly designed sights. Its 2 MOA dot was sized to encourage fast target acquisition. It comes with eight brightness settings, including two that are night vision compatible, plus one extremely bright setting for use in full and intense sunlight conditions. Power is provided by a single 2032 battery, which can last as long as five years in continuous use. The MRO sight adjustments are made in increments of a half minute and

Right Top: The aircraft-grade aluminum main tube, high-quality glass lenses and advanced application-specific illuminated reticles make the new Trijicon AccuPower series riflescopes a great choice for hunting applications.

Right: The Trijicon AccuPower series scopes are right at home on AR-style rifles.

The compact and lightweight characteristics of the Trijicon Miniature Rifle Optic (MRO) red-dot sight would make it a likely candidate for law enforcement, hunter or target shooter use.

The Trijicon Miniature Rifle Optic (MRO) is powered by a single 2032 battery, which can last as long as five years on continuous use.

have a full range of 70 MOA potential. Adjustments are easily made and if a screwdriver isn't readily available for that purpose, the rim of a 5.56mm casing can be utilized. The MRO is functional under extreme temperatures ranging from minus 60 degrees Fahrenheit to more than 160 degree Fahrenheit. Its 7075-T6 aluminum housing is waterproof and tested to a depth of 100 feet to ensure total watertight integrity. MSRP is $629.00 with mounts or $579.00 without.

www.trijicon.com

Zeiss

The German technology of Zeiss has been in existence since 1846. After WWII, however, the company was forced to split into two separate manufacturing operations, but in 1990 those two facilities merged and grew into an even more influential leader in the optics business. Today the plant operates with more than 24,000 employees. An example of that progress can be seen in the company's entirely new Victory SF series triple-link bridge binoculars. At the heart of the Zeiss Victory SF binoculars is the Ultra-FL lens that has been designed to achieve a high level of resolution, brilliance and color reproduction. This is accomplished as a result of the company engineers developing a new, highly innovative optical system that is comprised of two fluoride lenses made

Generated from the success of the LED-powered Trijicon VCOG and TARS, the AccuPower series was designed for versatility with variable magnifications of: 1-4x24, 2.5-10x56 (as shown here), 3-9x40 and 4-16x50.

with SCHOTT glass. In addition, the Victory SF comes with what the company calls its "Smart Focus" concept, which shortens the needed movement of the user when making the focusing adjustment. Conventional binoculars typically require the focusing wheel to be turned 2.5 times in order to change from close viewing to maximum distance viewing. The Smart Focus function shortens those required movements by 39 percent, or to only 1.8 times. Two models of the Victory SF binoculars are currently available: 8x42 and 10x42. Both are lightweight at only 27.5 ounces and carry MSRPs of $2,888.87 and $2,944.43 respectively.

In the mountains and on the trail every ounce counts and that is where Zeiss' new TERRA ED Pocket Binoculars provide a real advantage. Weighing in at only 10.9 ounces and equipped with ED glass, the new TERRA ED Pocket bino couples compactness with a high level of

optical excellence. They are operational within the temperature range of minus 4 degrees Fahrenheit to more than 145 degrees Fahrenheit – and are waterproof. The double-link bridge design allows the tubes to be quickly and easily folded together for convenient storage inside the user's pouch or pocket. They come in two sizes, 8x25 and 10x25, carrying MSRPs of $333.32 and $366.66, respectively, and are backed by the Zeiss U.S. limited lifetime transferable warranty.

With the current popularity of crossbow hunting Zeiss has addressed those activities in a big way with their new TERRA 3x XB75 2-7x32 Crossbow Scope. This scope is based on a 1-inch main tube design that is lightweight, rugged and comes with MC anti-reflective lens coatings to produce bright, high-contrast images. The reticle design provides the ability to shoot at distances up to 75 yards in 2.5-yard increments.

Right: At the heart of the Zeiss Victory SF binoculars are the Ultra-FL lenses, which are designed to achieve new levels of resolution, brilliance and color reproduction.

Left: Binoculars other than the Zeiss Victory SF typically require the user to turn the focusing wheel 2.5 times in order to change the focus from close objects to maximum distance objects. The Smart Focus function of the Victory SF, however, accomplishes the same thing in 1.8 times, or 39 percent less movement. This permits the user to get on target more quickly.

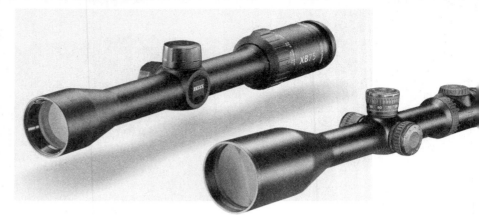

The new Zeiss TERRA ED Pocket Binocular provides a real advantage when it comes to weight and compactness.

The reticle design of the Zeiss 3x BX75 Crossbow Scope provides the ability to shoot at distances up to 75 yards in 2½-yard increments. This is accomplished by having six separate reticle crosshairs.

Zeiss' management is justifiably proud of the new Victory V8 line of riflescopes – including this 4.8-35x60 model.

This is accomplished by having six separate crosshairs, the main cross section of each representing whole yardages (20 to 70 yards). The dot in between each crosshair set represents the half yardage marks and the top and bottom of each represent the 2.5-yard marks. The scope's ocular ring has been engraved representing arrow speeds of 275 fps to 425 fps and magnifications from 2x to 7x. To program the scope you simply mount it on the rail of the crossbow using high-quality rings then set a target at 10 yards. Then using the 20-yard mark (first crosshair from the top), you adjust the scope and continue to shoot until you hit center, then repeat at 20 yards. Once the main 20-yard reticle is sighted in, the user turns the speed indicator on the ocular to the manufacturer's advertised speed. Once

the 30-yard crosshair is sighted in, the scope is now calibrated to your crossbow and all of the other aiming points will be correct.

The Zeiss TERRA XB75 is built tough and is backed by the Carl Zeiss U.S. limited transferable warranty. I had an opportunity to use one of these scopes and found the optics to be crystal clear and extremely easy to compensate for the trajectory drop of the crossbow bolt. I particularly liked the circle-style reticle, which worked perfectly for me in a crossbow-shooting environment.

Zeiss is also quite pleased to announce the new illuminated Victory V8 Series riflescopes, which are available in four models: 1-8x32, 1.8-14x50, 2.8-20x56

and 4.8-35x60. Of these there are select models that include the new bullet-drop compensator ASV, which is a nine engraved ring system allowing the user to match the appropriate ring to their specified long-range ballistics. Also included is a certificate for a free custom engraved KENTON ballistic turret ring ($149 retail value) that will be built exactly to match the shooter's chosen caliber and load, a set of Talley signature rings (another $149 retail value), and a Switchview magnification "high-speed" throw ring ($60 value) for extremely fast magnification change and target acquisition. The Victory V8 scopes come in a 35mm tube design and include fluoride lenses HT glass.

The multifunction illumination button on the Victory V8 scopes is intended to allow the user to quickly, silently and intuitively operate the illumination control system even when wearing gloves. The illuminated dot is automatically deactivated as soon as the rifle is put down and is reactivated as soon as the shooter takes aim, a feature that helps to significantly save time and energy. MSRP for the Victory V8 riflescopes runs from a low of $2,888.88 up to $4,111.10.

www.zeiss.com/us/sports-optics

The author had an opportunity to try out the new TERRA 3x XB75 2-7x32 Crossbow Scope on the range at the 2016 SHOT Show, and found the optics to be excellent and very easy to drop the crossbow bolt on target at 30 yards. The crosshair design essentially took the guesswork out of where to hold.

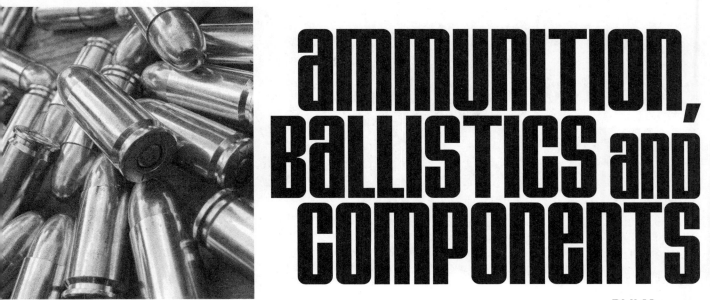

AMMUNITION, BALLISTICS AND COMPONENTS

BY **Phil Massaro**

As if 2015 didn't hold a gaggle of new products for us hunters and shooters, the gun industry decided to raise the bar for 2016. Some companies – with very familiar names and reputations – have thrown their respective hats into the ammunition ring, and I think it'll be a very good thing for the shooting community. There are a couple new cartridges of note; one expected, one totally unlooked for, and both are welcome additions. There are new powders for the reloaders, new bullets in both loaded and component form, and some innovative new reloading tools to help keep our ammunition as accurate as possible. Things continue to evolve, and that has greatly benefitted the hunters and shooters; the advancements in both component projectiles and loaded ammunition will make any rifleman smile, and shotgunners as well as pistoleros will have something to be happy about. From radical new designs, to vintage collectable pieces, the industry has something for all. Sit back, dear reader, and enjoy the new offerings for 2016.

Alliant Powder

The Alliant Reloder series of powders have been, for decades, a reliable source of fuel for some of the most

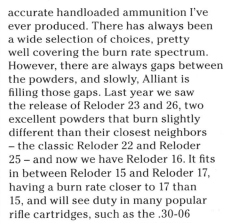

Reloder 16 powder

accurate handloaded ammunition I've ever produced. There has always been a wide selection of choices, pretty well covering the burn rate spectrum. However, there are always gaps between the powders, and slowly, Alliant is filling those gaps. Last year we saw the release of Reloder 23 and 26, two excellent powders that burn slightly different than their closest neighbors – the classic Reloder 22 and Reloder 25 – and now we have Reloder 16. It fits in between Reloder 15 and Reloder 17, having a burn rate closer to 17 than 15, and will see duty in many popular rifle cartridges, such as the .30-06 family, as well as the 6.5-284 Norma.

Like Reloder 23 and 26, the new Reloder 16 has been engineered to be insensitive to temperature fluctuations, and the pressure and velocity changes that are associated with it. I can see this powder working very well with the .270 Winchester and .280 Remington, as well as the .338 Winchester Magnum, the .375 Holland & Holland and the .404 Jeffery.

Alliant has announced that it is offering Blue MZ muzzleloader pellets. Giving reliable ignition and a consistent burn rate, the pellets come in 50-grain equivalent size, and come 48 to the pack. The Blue MZ pellets will work with just about any muzzleloader bullet, and the residue cleans

Alliant Blue MZ

up well with soap and water. For the muzzleloading hunter who wants the reliability of the Alliant powder line, Blue MZ pellets may just make your season that much better.

Berger Extreme Outer Limits

Berger Bullets

Are you a long-range shooter and/ or hunter? Does distance intrigue you? Then you know you need the absolute best gear you can get your hands on, and that includes your projectiles. Berger bullets have long been revered for their match-grade target bullets and J4 jackets. For 2016, they have introduced the Extreme Outer Limits line of bullets; a series of very heavy-for-caliber boat-tail hollowpoints. The first of the series is a 195-grain 7mm bullet, with a G1 B.C. of .754. No, that's not a misprint, that's a Ballistic Coefficient of .754. The second in the series, which literally just arrived today, is a 170-grain .277" caliber, with a G1 B.C. of .662. Both of these bullets are from the Elite Hunter series, and the high B.C. and heavier weight will help to hold onto velocity and kinetic energy at extreme ranges. Just be sure of the twist rate of your rifle; these longer bullets require a fast twist, sometimes faster than is normally produced. The 7mm pills need a minimum of 1:9" twist, and preferably 1:8.3" or faster. The .277"

bullet needs a 1:8" twist rate or faster, instead of the traditional 1:10". Hey, maybe these bullets warrant a new rifle build? You can't have too many...

Browning

The company that bears John Moses Browning's name and has introduced so many fine rifles, shotguns and pistols, has delved into the ammunition game. Not just one or two loads, they've like, seriously entered the ammunition business. Centerfire rifle, centerfire pistol, shotshell and rimfire are all available this year. The Browning BXR Deer ammunition uses the Rapid Expansion Matrix Tip bullet, giving a good blend of quick expansion for hydraulic shock and a large wound channel. It's available in seven popular deer calibers, in sensible bullet weights. The Browning BXC Big Game ammunition uses the bonded-core Controlled Expansion Terminal Tip, for deep penetration on tough game. Available in six different time-proven calibers that are well suited to North American game and African plains game. Browning's BXP Personal Defense pistol ammunition features the X-Point bullet, designed to protect the hollowpoint through intermediate barriers. The Browning Target pistol ammunition is loaded to the same specs and weights as the Personal Defense ammo, but is loaded with full metal jacket bullets, designed to be a practice counterpart to the Personal Defense line. Available in .380 Auto, 9mm Luger, .40 S&W and .45 ACP. Browning's BXD Waterfowl shotshells are available

Browning Ammunition

in both 12- and 20-gauge loads, and the BPT Target loads will make breaking clay birds easier than ever. The BPR Performance Rimfire line of .22LR rimfire ammunition comes in 50-round packs, in both 37- and 40-grain loads. The bullets are a bit different, designed to fragment into four pieces upon impact to deliver all kinds of trauma on pests and small game. Browning now offers an ammunition choice for the multitude of firearms they produce, and I think there will be some happy hunters and shooters in the coming months.

CCI

I'm a big fan of CCI handgun shotshells; I watched my dad dispatch a snake with one as a small boy, and I've been intrigued by them ever since. I still carry them in my S&W Model 36 in the summer, when the threat of rattlesnakes is a reality. Now CCI offers those shotshells stoked with No. 4 shot, extending the range and increasing the striking power of your .38 Special or .357 Magnum. The plastic shot caps are red for the No. 4 shot, as opposed to the light blue color of the shells loaded with the finer shot size. Ballistic gel tests have shown that the Big 4 shotshells

CCI Big 4

CCI
Copper-22

will penetrate up to 6¾ inches into bare gel when fired from a distance of 10 feet. CCI packs the Big 4 shells 10 to the box. I need these.

A new .22 Long Rifle load is available from CCI, using a 21-grain bullet. The new projectile, while lighter than normal .22 Long Rifle bullets, is made of a combination of compressed copper particles and a polymer to hold it all together. The resulting hollowpoint projectile will fragment upon impact, making it a perfect choice for small game and varmints. The high muzzle velocity – 1,850 fps, if you must know – will ensure a flat trajectory, and plenty of hydraulic shock for a humane kill. Accuracy tests have shown this new load will print very tight groups. I look forward to testing this load on the nasty little woodchucks that plague my garden every spring and summer.

Federal Cartridge

For 150 years, cast lead bullets have been embraced by the handgun community; initially as the only game in town, and later – once the jacketed bullet was fully embraced – as an inexpensive option for the high-volume shooter. The problem with lead bullets is as old as the lead bullets themselves – while the lead bullet is perfectly soft enough to take the rifling and seal the gasses, it also soft enough to leave a smear of lead in the bore of the rifle or pistol. This phenomenon, called 'leading', will require additional cleaning efforts, in addition to ramping up the frequency of cleaning sessions. That, dear friends, is no longer a problem. Federal's Syntech bullet is a lead bullet wrapped in a red polymer coating that not only virtually eliminates the leading problem, but also reduces friction. Because the lead-to-barrel contact is removed, the powder charge required to propel the Syntech bullet to the common velocities associated with popular pistol cartridges is reduced, resulting in a lower pressure load, without sacrificing velocity. The lead bullet is completely encapsulated in the polymer

American Eagle Varmint & Predator ammunition

coating, so it also reduces the amount of vaporized lead in the air, perfect for an indoor range situation. The new Catalyst primer is also completely lead-free, combining with the new bullet for one of the cleanest burning cartridges available to shooters today. Less cleaning, less recoil, less muzzle jump, and just about as green as it gets. Available in 9mm Luger, .40 S&W and .45ACP.

The American Eagle line of ammunition has always represented a great value to the hunter/shooter. That tradition continues with the Varmint & Predator line. Offered in 40- or 50-rounnd packs, depending on caliber, it offers either Tipped Varmint bullets or jacketed hollowpoints for the quick and devastating expansion that works best for hunting varmints and predators. The American Eagle line is made in the same plant as the

Federal Premium ammo, so you can count on reliable feeding, consistent primer ignition and great accuracy. Available in .17 Hornet, .22 Hornet, .22-250 Remington, .243 Winchester, 6.8 SPC and .308 Winchester.

Last year's release of 3rd Degree Turkey ammo – with its three-shot blend payload – quickly garnered the respect of those who live for the springtime chess game that is turkey hunting. However, it was only available in 12 gauge; but that's all over. There are many turkey hunters who have embraced the specialty turkey guns in 20 gauge; Federal has heard the call and is introducing the 3rd Degree ammo in 20 gauge. The 1-7/16 ounce payload is comprised of 20 percent No. 6 Flitestopper pellets, 40 percent copper-plated No. 5 shot and 40 percent No. 7 HEAVYWEIGHT shot. 20-gauge turkey hunters, rejoice!

For those who enjoy hunting with MSR chambered in 6.8 SPC, Federal is loading the Fusion bullet for you in a 90-grain hunting load. The Fusion bullet has the jacket chemically bonded to the core, so even at

Federal Fusion 6.8SPC ammunition

Federal American Eagle Syntech

Federal 3rd Degree 20 gauge

Federal Power Shok Copper

lighter weights the shooter doesn't have to worry about bullet breakup. The 6.8 SPC – .277" diameter – can use the lighter bullets in that caliber with good effect, and the Federal Fusion load pushes the 90-grain pill at a muzzle velocity of 2,850 fps. Even at 400 yards it will stay above 1,500 fps, and at 300 yards, the Fusion bullet still has 750 ft-lbs of energy. This makes it a perfectly viable load for most deer, feral hogs and even close-range black bears.

The Power Shok line of centerfire rifle ammunition from Federal represents an affordable, yet completely reliable product – one I've used with great effect. Traditionally, the Power Shok line was loaded with, well, inexpensive cup-and-core bullets. Not that they are bad in any way, but sometimes they paled in comparison to the top-shelf projectiles in the Federal Premium line. Well now, all that has changed, with the introduction of the Federal Power Shok Copper. You still get the trusted Federal brass and primers, but now you have an affordable means of shooting a mono-metal hollowpoint bullet – which is

also compliant with the "lead-free" zones of a particular ocean-front state in the southwestern U.S. Available in most popular hunting rifle calibers, the Power Shok Copper should prove to be a winner.

Subcompact handguns are extremely popular lately, and while they are an absolute pleasure to carry, sometimes they don't quite agree with traditional ammo. The shorter barrels can be unhappy with ammo designed to satisfy a number of different barrel lengths, so Federal has decided to solve the problem with ammunition designed specifically for the subcompacts. They introduced the Personal Defense Micro HST line last year with the .380 Auto, and now have extended it into the highly popular 9mm Luger. Using a 150-grain HST bullet – my personal favorite bullet in my carry gun – Federal has tweaked the load to perform best in the subcompact handguns. The deep penetration and consistent expansion that is associated with the other HST loads are here as well; the result of testing is the familiar 'metallic flower' that the HST forms. I've been to the Federal plant, and I've done some testing of the HST bullet into ballistic gel; to be honest I can't pick a better bullet for righting a situation that has gone horribly wrong.

Federal Micro HST ammo

Hodgdon Powders

The Hodgdon line of Extreme Powders has earned an impeccable reputation over the last couple of decades, and last year the Enduron line of IMR powders brought the temperature insensitivity of the Hodgdon Extreme powders over to the IMR line. The original trio - IMR4166, IMR4451 and IMR7977 – have a new baby brother this year. IMR4955 is a powder that falls close to the burn rates of IMR4831 and H4831, while offering the same resistance to the effects of temperature extremes. Falling between the burn rates of IMR4451 and IMR7977, the new IMR4955 will work well in the smaller members of the .30-06 family of cases, from the .25-06 Remington up through the .280 Remington, as well as the belted magnums like the 7mm Remington Magnum, .300 Winchester and .338 Winchester Magnum. I'm especially interested about using IMR4955 in my pet 6.5-284 Norma. The small kernel size – which aids in good metering and measuring – and a copper fouling reducer built in to the powder make IMR4955 and the entire Enduron line of powders worth a try.

IMR4955

Hornady

This year, Hornady expands the Dangerous Game Series to include two more cartridges: the .500-416 Nitro Express and the .450 Rigby. The Dangerous Game line features both the DGX (Dangerous Game eXpanding) bullet, as well as the

Hornady Dangerous Game

DGS (Dangerous Game Solid) bullet, and the two complement each other very well. When it comes to thick-skinned game, which is more often than not measured in tons, you need dependable ammunition. Hornady's Dangerous Game Series has always delivered the goods, and for those fans of the .500-416 and .450 Rigby, they can count on that reliability. While the .450 Rigby is almost always produced in a bolt-action rifle (and if you haven't checked out the new Rigby rifles, you should), the .500-416 Nitro Express is becoming a favorite among double rifle shooters. I can tell you for a fact that several companies use the Hornady Dangerous Game ammunition to regulate their double rifles, so there's good reason to give it a try. The .500-416 uses 400-grain DGX and DGS, while the .450 Rigby uses 480-grain DGX and DGS bullets.

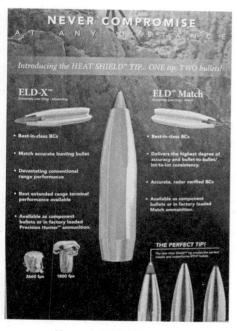

Hornady ELD-X Bullet

The Hornady team of engineers has always been on the cutting edge of bullet development, and this year they have unveiled something I find very intriguing: the ELD-X (Extremely Low Drag – eXpanding) bullet with the Heat Shield Tip. The story behind the bullet is this: While doing some Doppler radar testing on now-traditional polymer tipped bullets, Hornady discovered that at distances beyond 500 yards the bullets – especially at high velocities – started acting rather erratically. The result of further investigation determined that the polymer tips were actually melting, and therefore drastically reducing the bullet's ballistic coefficient. While I've never recovered a polymer tip bullet that was not upset so badly that the tip was deemed melted, I don't doubt the Hornady theory. The new Heat Shield Tip will avoid this long-range issue by using a polymer that has a melting point twice as high as the conventional polymer used for bullets, making the ELD-X bullet a perfect choice for true long-range hunting work. Hornady is also offering the ELD in a match bullet, for competitive shooting without the worry of terminal ballistics. Hornady loads these bullets in their Precision Hunter line of ammunition, as well as offering them in component form. Available in 6.5mm (143 grains), 7mm (162 and 175 grains) and .30 caliber (178, 200, 212 and 220 grains). If you're serious about long-range hunting, the Hornady ELD-X may just be for you.

I've been a fan of the 180-grain bullets in the .30-06 Springfield and .300 Winchester Magnum for decades, and now Hornady has released a Superformance load for each, using the 180-grain GMX. The monometal GMX (standing for Gilding Metal eXpanding) has proven itself for quite some time now, and at 180 grains, it will handle all but the largest and most dangerous game on earth. The .30-06 load pushes that 180-grain GMX out of the muzzle at 2,820 fps, for over 3,100 ft-lbs of energy, and when zeroed at 200 yards it will only drop 7.6 inches at 300 yards. That's performance that you could expect from the .300 Holland & Holland, and certainly isn't your grandpa's "ought-six" load. The .300 Winchester Magnum load delivers a muzzle velocity of 3,070 fps, for over 3,700 ft-lbs of muzzle energy. Even at the 400-yard mark, the .300 Winchester load still delivers over 2,000 ft-lbs and only drops 18 inches when using a 200-yard zero. Combine those ballistics with the high weight retention of the GMX bullet, and you've got some serious elk, bear and moose medicine, at just about any sane hunting distance. As

with all of the GMX bullets, that polymer tip will guarantee expansion even at long distances and lower velocities.

The Big Red H is offering some new calibers in their lineup of excellent brass cases for 2016. For those who handload ammunition, Hornady cases have long represented an affordable, yet reliable source of brass. Hornady has offered a wide selection of calibers, including some of the rarities like .450-400 NE, .404 Jeffery and .300 Remington Ultra Magnum. I've depended on Hornady to supply cases when I couldn't get any other brand. I like the brass because it's often annealed, keeping the brass soft for many firings. New for 2016, Hornady is offering the following calibers to its already impressive lineup: 6mm Hagar, 6mm Creedmoor, .25-35 Winchester, .250 Savage, .264 Winchester Magnum, .270 Weatherby Magnum, .30 Carbine, 7.62x36mm and (heaven be praised!) .35 Remington.

Little Crow Gun Works

I absolutely love the ingenious ways in which some of the smaller companies create tools for reloading; it's nice to see an innovative design that makes the tedious steps we reloaders must take in case preparation just a little bit easier. Little Crow Gun Works, from Minnesota, has a pair of well-thought-out tools that will make trimming your brass and preparing your cases a quick and accurate process. The WFT, or World's Finest Trimmer, is a simple, yet precise means of trimming brass cases to proper length, using a standard drill and the LCGW trimmer. Simply adjust the set screws to achieve the proper length of trim, and spin the drill

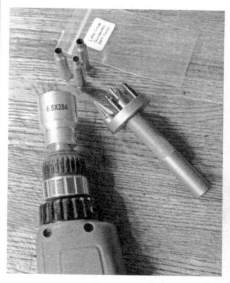

Little Crow Gun Works

and your cases will be uniformly trimmed to a consistent length. The WFT is case-specific, so I ordered two of my favorites: 6.5-284 Norma and .300 Winchester Magnum. Within minutes, I used a master case (at the appropriate length) to set the depth of the trimmer, and I was happily trimming cases. Once trimmed, we all know the case mouth must be deburred and chamfered. Again LCGW has a tool for that. While there are many hand tools on the market – many of which require that twisty wrist motion that can become fatiguing – the Precision Prep Tool uses an anodized aluminum handle and an offset design that changes the twisty wrist to more of a fishing-reel, forearm-operated motion. The tool head has four threaded holes, so you can easily clean the primer pocket, chamfer, deburr and uniform the primer pocket without fumbling for tools. Well played, Little Crow, well played.

Lyman

Lyman Deluxe Anodized Aluminum Loading Blocks. We reloaders all have them – the homemade loading blocks made of wood and cut out with a drill bit, or, at best, the ancient, cruddy and warped plastic case blocks that are filled up with bits of brass and lead residue. Well, guys and gals, throw 'em out! The days of nasty old case blocks are over.

.30 Nosler

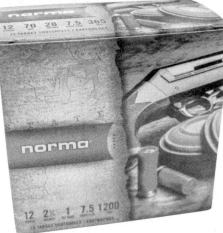

Norma shotshells

Lyman has introduced the Cadillac of case blocks: The Deluxe Anodized Aluminum Loading Blocks. A solid block of aluminum, with accurately machined holes to hold three different case head sizes, and attachable rubber feet to prevent annoying rattle on the bench. The very weight of them prevents them from toppling over (and dinging the necks or shoulders), and they look very, very cool on the bench, in all their burnt-orange glory.

Norma

At the 2016 SHOT Show, Norma of Sweden, long famous for its excellent ammunition and component brass, announced the release of Norma shotshells. The product line includes 12-gauge ammunition at first – Norma had display boxes showing 1 ounce of 7½ shot at 1,200 fps – and should expand to most popular hunting loads. Given the successful history of the Norma rifle ammunition line, I have no doubt that the Norma shotshell line will be a winner.

Nosler

Hot on the heels of the two previous Nosler developments – the .26 Nosler and the .28 Nosler – comes the next logical development: the .30 Nosler. Part of me wants to say that we don't need yet another means of launching a .30-caliber bullet, but I definitely see the wisdom of the .30 Nosler design. Offering the velocity of the .300 Weatherby Magnum in a long-action rifle, the .30 Nosler squeezes out just about all the velocity that any sane shooter could expect from a .30-06 length action. Again, Nosler has embraced the idea of a shortened

Remington Ultra Magnum case, based on a blown-out .404 Jeffery, with a slightly rebated rim. The .30 Nosler design, along with its older siblings, will give magnum performance in a cartridge without a belt and the case stretching associated with the belted magnums. The 180-grain AccuBond bullets will achieve 3,200 fps, and the 210-grain AccuBond Long Range – a great choice for maximizing any cartridge's velocity potential – will still attain 3,000 fps. I look forward to spending some time behind the trigger of the new .30 Nosler; if it will better the performance of the .300 Winchester Magnum without overly punishing the shoulder, it'll stick around for quite some time to come.

Redding

We reloaders spend an awful amount of time

Redding Master Hunter Die Sets

prepping our cases; we use precision dies to deliver just the right amount of shoulder bump, we uniform the flash holes and trim them to exact lengths. We also chamfer the inside of our case mouths, but that step usually comes with a hand tool. At best, the concentricity of the chamfer – especially a VLD chamfer – is as uniform as we can hold it. The good folks at Redding have solved that issue, and while it may seem like a minor issue, it is one more step in the never-ending pursuit of accuracy. The Model 15P Chamfer Tool uses a hardened steel guide to center the cutting bit in the flash hole of the case, so that your VLD chamfer will be completely even. The tool comes on an accessory handle – looking like a screwdriver handle in Redding green – and the 15 degree cutter locks down via a set screw. For those of you who continue the pursuit of the ultimate accuracy, the Model 15P is for you.

Redding has expanded their line of

Master Hunter reloading dies sets to include four new calibers. The Master Hunter set includes a standard Redding full-length resizing die, and a micrometer adjustable seating die, to produce some of the best and most consistent ammo available. For 2016, you can now purchase these sets in 6.5-284 Norma (a particular favorite of mine), the .280 Ackley Improved (an old long-range favorite), .338 Winchester Magnum, and the brand spanking new .30 Nosler. Just like other Redding die sets, a spare decapping pin and Allen wrench are included in the heavy duty plastic die box.

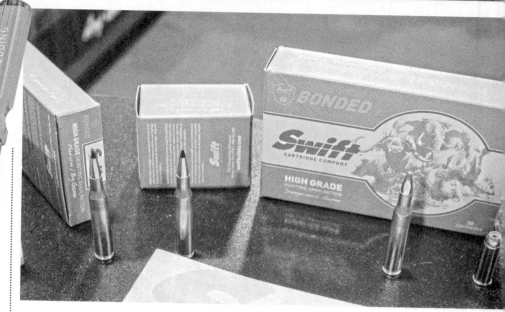

Swift Ammunition

Redding Model 15P Precision Neck Chamfering Tool

Ruger

Sturm, Ruger & Co. has also decided to enter the ammunition business this year, announcing the release of the ARX line of handgun ammunition. Using a compressed copper-polymer blend (that seems to be all the rage this year) and very light-for-caliber bullet weights, the Ruger ARX bullet has three spiral "flutes" in the front end of the projectile to maximize the hydraulic displacement. The .380 Auto load uses a 56-grain bullet at 1,315 fps, the 9mm Luger pushes an 80-grain at 1,445 fps and the .45 ACP load uses a 118-grain bullet at just over 1,300 fps. Ruger has also announced an upcoming .40 S&W load that will use a 107-grain ARX at 1,320 fps, coming later this fall.

Sierra

Last year's release of Sig Sauer ammo caught quite a few people off guard, and after a bit of testing, it proved to be good stuff. Loaded with the V-Crown bullet, it lived up to expectations. This year Sierra, which produces the V-Crown for Sig, is offering the handgun bullet in component form. Available in 9mm, 10mm and .45 caliber, these stacked hollowpoint bullets will retain their weight well, yet give good expansion and deep penetration. As we've grown to expect from the Bulletsmiths, Sierra has delivered a great new product, and given us reloaders a new toy to play with for 2016. Available in 9mm (90, 124 and 125 grains), .40/10mm (165 grains) and .45 (200 grains).

Swift Ammunition

The Swift Bullet Company, long famous for its pair of fantastic projectiles – the Swift A-Frame and Swift Scirocco II – is now the Swift Ammunition Company, offering this dynamic duo of bullets, along with the Swift Breakaway Solids in loaded form. While there are some companies who will load the Swift bullets in their lineup – namely Remington and Federal – the choices are often limited. Swift's new ammunition line will offer many popular hunting calibers – both for big game and truly big game – giving the hunter who doesn't reload the option to try what I consider to be three of the best hunting bullets on the market. I've used Swift bullets for close to 15 years, and I've used them all over the world on game that varies in size from the 25-pound steenbok in Africa, to the American bison and African Cape buffalo, both approaching a ton. Swift bullets have never let me down, and I'm looking forward to trying their new factory loaded stuff.

Weatherby

This was something I didn't see coming. The 2013 release of the .26 Nosler – a case based on a shortened Remington Ultra Magnum – showed just how interested the shooting market was in both the fantastic 6.5mm bullets

Sierra V-Crown handgun bullets

6.5-300
Weatherby

maintaining all sorts of downrange energy. Barrel life – as with any of the hyper-velocity cartridges – may be shorter than expected, but for a hunter who wants to reach out and touch something, the 6.5-300 Weatherby may be well worth it.

Winchester

The sesquicentennial anniversary of Winchester is a big deal. Actually, it's a huge deal. To celebrate the event, Winchester has produced several anniversary rifles and a shotgun: the Model 1866 comes in .44-40 Winchester, the Model 1873 comes in .44-40 as well, the Model 1894 comes in .30-30 Winchester, the Model 70 comes in .270 Winchester, and the Model 101 in 12 gauge. In addition to the really nice firearms, Winchester is making a commemorative line of ammunition, with vintage artwork and labeling, to accompany the limited series of firearms. The .44-40 uses the 200-grain Winchester Power Point bullet, the .30-30 WCF load uses the classic 150-grain Power Point, the .270 Winchester uses the heavy 150-grain Power Point, and the 12-gauge load is 1¼ ounces of No. 2 steel shot. Now, while this ammunition may be nothing special on the surface, I firmly believe the stuff will be collectable, as so many commemorative issues are. While the firearms are limited to 500 of each model – individually numbered One to Five Hundred of Five Hundred – I'm not sure how much of the Winchester ammunition will be produced. Nonetheless, I'd like to have a couple of boxes for my collection. Last year we talked about the Winchester Rooster XR shotshells with the ShotLok technology, and now they've extended that same idea to the Varmint X shotshell line. Hunting coyotes and foxes with a tight choke makes all kinds of sense, especially in the thick brush or the hemlock woods, where shots tend to be on the close side. The new Winchester Varmint X line uses BB shot instead of 00 or 000 buck, giving more pellets per shot and a greater chance of ending the predator's career. With 1.5 ounces of shot – held in position by the same resin that the other Winchester shotshells have used so well – I've seen pattern tests that show the effectiveness of this load out to 60 yards. And with a muzzle velocity of 1,300 fps, there should be plenty of energy to stop even larger Eastern coyotes.

and the pursuit of high velocity and flat trajectory. Since last we spoke, Weatherby answered the Nosler development by taking the veteran .300 Winchester case and necking it down to hold .264" diameter bullets, driving them to as-of-yet impossible velocities. Pushing a 127-grain bullet at a muzzle velocity of over 3,500 fps,

you can guarantee this will be a serious long-range cartridge with a very flat trajectory. Given the stellar reputation of the 6.5mm bullets for more than a century – both in the hunting fields and the target community – and the latest bullet technology, the 6.5 Weatherby will represent a cartridge capable with the trajectory of a frozen rope, while

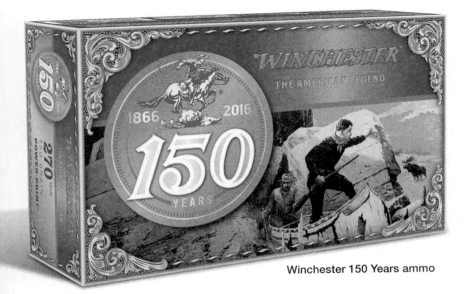

Winchester 150 Years ammo

The Shanghai Colt is a Model 1911A1 pre-WWII Colt Commercial manufactured between 1925 and 1942.

A SHANGHAI COLT

Fairbairn and Sykes' Pistol of Choice When Shooting to Survive

BY Robert Sadowski

Above: A typical street scene in 1925 on Nanking Road, Shanghai, in a shopping district near the former Wing On (Yong'an) department store.

Photo courtesy of Historical Photographs of China (hpc.vcea.net).

I didn't need to have my arm twisted when Bill Wilson asked if I wanted to see his private firearms collection. Naturally I expected 1911s, and there was nearly a boxcar full; pre-1970s Colts, custom 1911s built by gunsmiths from a decade or more ago, new Wilson Combat models and literally in the corner, a Colt 1911 .45 that was well used—battered and worn is more like it—along with a rather small book. I was told that this Colt, with hardly any finish remaining and looking its age, had a fighting past.

Then came the "ah-ha moment." I read the stamping on the side of the gun: Shanghai Municipal Police. You can probably guess the title of the book: *Shooting To Live*. This pistol and the techniques described in the book shared a moment in history. Their two paths crossed in the 1920s and 1930s. Shanghai was a city plagued with violence and crime, a lawless place quite foreign to Westerners where gunfights were as common as rickshaws and trolley cars. It was a time when the 1911 pistol continued to build upon its legend. At the same time, cutting-edge shooting techniques were

being developed that would later be described as point shooting or instinctive shooting.

The hellhole of Shanghai was the perfect environment for the tool and the method to literally be baptized under fire. This is the story of a Colt Model 1911 .45 oddly modified to suit the needs of the Shanghai Municipal Police (SMP) force, and a new combat pistol training developed by two SMP firearm instructors, William Ewart Fairbairn and Eric Anthony Sykes, who revolutionized the way we fight with handguns.

First, the place. Shanghai back then, just as today, was a bustling cosmopolitan city on the south bank of the Yangtze River in eastern China with all the glamour and excitement the bright lights of a big city could offer—a city where the East met the West. The underbelly, however, was ugly. Violent

gangs and many independent operators preyed on each other and the public. Streets seeped in greed, corruption, vice, robbery, rape and murder. Drugs and other illicit commodities like gold and ivory flowed through Shanghai.

Now the pistols. Not knowing a lot about the SMP or the pistols they used, I contacted an acquaintance at the National Firearms Museum, Doug Wick-

These are members of the SMP circa 1930. Note both M1908 and M1911 pistols and the use of body armor.

Note the "Shanghai Municipal Police" markings and the "No. 69" indicating that this is an early model acquired by the SMP.

Another feature is the checkered short trigger.

lund, Senior Curator. Wicklund had, in fact, been a collector of SMP Colts and Fairbairn and Sykes paraphernalia. "My personal examples from my collecting days back in the 1980s," says Wicklund, "including headstamped SMP rounds, guns and ephemera were sold off many years ago when I needed grad school funds. Some were bought by Rex Applegate, but his collection was scattered to the winds long ago after his death. I had an autographed photo of Fairbairn, but supposedly there exists only a passport photo for Sykes." As I picked his brain the story of Wilson's Shanghai Colt came into focus.

At the time, the Colt M1908 .380 and M1911 .45 pistols had reputations as well-made, reliable firearms, and were considered two of the best pistols of the day. The SMP issued both types of Colt semiautos. Without seeing Bill Wilson's Shanghai Colt, Wicklund deduced it most likely made its way into the hands of the SMP by one of two routes. It could have been left over from World War I or bought new. "Both M1908 .380 and 1911 Commercial Government Model and ex-military .45 pistols were acquired by the SMP," says Wicklund. " The commercial .45 handguns may have been more expensive than former military pistols surfacing on the Asian market after WWI and, bear in mind," he explains, "that other handguns were also used by the SMP. Webley revolvers were widely used by certain sections of the force." Fairbairn and Sykes used semiautomatics for a reason. "Fairbairn felt ammunition reliability was better with a semiauto pistol than a revolver. He also felt it took five times the ammo to train someone with a revolver," adds Wicklund.

The Colt M1908 was basically identical to the earlier Model 1903 Pocket Hammerless except it was in .380 ACP, while the 1903 was chambered for the .32 ACP. Both models were named after the year in which they were introduced. The 1903 had a capacity of eight rounds in the magazine and one in the chamber, and the 1908 was seven plus one. These pistols are not actually "hammerless." The hammer is concealed by the rear of the slide. At the time the 1903 and 1908 were both popular with law enforcement agencies in the States. Criminals also favored the pistols. Bonnie and Clyde, Al Capone and others plied their trade at one time or another using these compact pistols. John Dillinger had one in his pocket when he was killed. General George Patton carried one as a backup piece in WWII.

This is an example of a SMP Colt M1908. Like the Model 1911 shown below, it has the thumb safety pinned and deactivated.

Photos courtesy of Rock Island Auction Company.

SMP M1908s typically wore checkered rubber grips and most specimens were refinished by the police arsenal. Nearly all of the SMP were reblued due to the harsh Chinese climate and daily use.

The 1911 doesn't really need an introduction. At first glance Wilson's Shanghai Colt could have started out as a "Black Army" 1918/1919 production M1911 from the Colt factory. "The original finish on these pistols was pretty lousy," says Wicklund, and Wilson's specimen shows little to no finish. It also has an arched mainspring housing and short trigger, something that could have been retrofitted into an ex-military pistol. WWI U.S. issue 1911s had a flat mainspring housing and long trigger. Somewhere along the line the SMP modified their Colts to better suit their purpose, just like the U.S. military modified the M1911 into the 1911A1. Soldiers were shooting low with flat mainspring

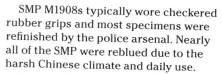

It may seem odd to modern shooters but the Shanghai Municipal Police deactivated the thumb safety using either a pin or screw to lock the safety in the off position.

housing pistols, and an arched mainspring helped remedy the situation. "Readily replaceable components and finish," Wicklund says, "like the arched mainspring housing could have been added or swapped out at any point after 1926."

Looking at that serial number, however, and after doing a bit of digging in firearm guides, it became clear to me how the SMP acquired this pistol. The letter "C" precedes the serial number, which indicates Wilson's Shanghai Colt is a Commercial variant. In fact, it is a Model 1911A1 pre-WWII Colt Commercial. These pistols were manufactured from 1925 to 1942, in the same time period Fairbairn and Sykes were part of the SMP. The finish was either blue or parkerized with an arched and checkered mainspring housing, a longer grip safety spur and cut outs in the receiver behind the trigger, characteristics similar to the design changes found on the U.S. Military 1911A1.

Fairbairn joined the SMP force in 1907 and it is likely he began obtaining Colts for himself and fellow officers soon thereafter. According to Wicklund, "A major order for 1,200 of the M1908 pistols is recorded in 1925. A total of 4,185 M1908s were ordered from 1925 to 1938." There are stories of earlier acquisitions of M1903 .32 Colts, but he has never encountered any with SMP markings. Fairbairn likely ordered both models after joining the SMP force, and Sykes was the agent for Colt and Remington in the Far East.

"Sykes would have had samples early on in production runs," explains Wicklund. "We know Sykes met

Fairbairn in 1919, so the orders from Colt might have gotten easier to procure at that point." Sykes was Fairbairn's connection to the pistols and even though logistically speaking for ammunition procurement and training, it would have been better to have one pistol model and one caliber, there was a reason for a compact M1908 and full-size M1911A1—each had an advantage. Fairbairn thought the M1908 was better suited to smaller stature officers—both Europe and and Chinese—rather than the larger and more powerful 1911.

Some officers were better served with the .380 pistol," Wicklund explains, "but Fairbairn worked with many officers and friends to get them more familiar and better shooters with a .45 pistol." Obviously the 1911 had the firepower. The two men liked Colt pistols, but they did change a few things.

According to Wicklund, ownership markings were placed on both M1908 and M1911 pistol models, reading "Shanghai Municipal Police," and components—slide, barrel and frame—were all numbered. Bill Wilson's SMP 1911 is stamped on the right side of the receiver with "Shanghai Municipal Police" and it also has "No. 69" stamped on the receiver, slide and barrel. A modification made to Wilson's Shanghai Colt and all other SMP pistols, for that matter, looks unusual to a modern shooter. A small screw is used to deactivate the thumb safety. Fairbairn and Sykes didn't trust any safety feature on their guns and actually wrote in *Shooting To Live*, "We have an inveterate dislike of the profusion of safety devices with which automatic pistols are regularly equipped." It was thought at the time officers would forget or become confused with the thumb safety. We need to remember that at this time revolvers were still the main handgun used by police agencies and many militaries.

Shooting To Live pioneered a new shooting technique; many instructors today use some aspects of what Fairbairn and Sykes created.

The SMP procedure was to carry the pistol with an empty chamber. The pistol was drawn from a flap holster and the slide racked to chamber a round. Not exactly the cocked-and-locked method used today, but techniques ferment and evolve over time and experience.

Other changes were also made. "Modifications are believed to have been made at the SMP," says Wicklund. "Inquiries to Colt on specific pistols for factory 'letters' have not revealed any factory work or modifications." Additional modifications included a side lanyard loop, which repositioned the original loop. This position worked for SMP lanyards and SMP carry policy. Magazines on the pistols had additional witness holes added to the front and back to show that loaded cartridges were in place. One reason for the extra holes on the magazines

was to verify actual rounds during shift changes. Ammunition had a very high street value and some Chinese SMP officers were known to have supplemented their salary by selling cartridges.

In addition, the slides on M1908s were fitted with a spring-loaded fixture to better stabilize barrels and ejectors, and magazine safeties on these pistols were deactivated. Another modification, this to the ammunition, was to help keep track of shooting incidents. Since Shanghai had literally hundreds of fights and armed robberies each year, the SMP issued cartridges with the letters "SMP" stamped on the bullet to aid in identification at crime scene shootings.

Now the technique. Fairbairn and Sykes began to teach SMP officers a fast method of shooting a pistol. "Fairbairn stressed serious pistol use and was not interested

in competition, just training," explains Wicklund. Most violent encounters then are like today—occurring within four yards, when speed is key to win a gunfight. They taught officers not to use the pistol's sights, but to keep both eyes open and raise the pistol until it covers the target then pull the trigger. "It was thought that the poor sights of that era might have contributed to the technique Fairbairn employed," speculates Wicklund. "His emphasis was on speed."

Fairbairn and Sykes also taught officers to shoot with a two-hand grip, much like instructors teach today. They also stressed the use of cover to exposed as little of your body to your adversary as possible. Sound familiar? They also used what we commonly call today a shoot house, basically a structure where students walk through encountering targets. Fairbairn and Sykes made sure the targets were exposed for only a brief time so officers were forced to react and shoot fast at bobbing and moving targets. Unknown to students, dummy rounds were at times loaded into magazines forcing students to manipulate and clear the pistol.

Fairbairn and Sykes would both move on to train British Commandos during WWII using the methods they crafted and honed in Shanghai. When Fairbairn was chief instructor for the SMP he wrote an article titled "Pistol Shooting" that was published in a 1927 edition of *American Rifleman* magazine. *Shooting To Live* was not published until 1942. "His work wasn't appreciated in the U.S. until many years later," adds Wicklund. To say this small book was influential is an understatement. Fairbairn and Sykes pioneered modern combat pistolcraft, and the 1911 pistol – a design now more than 105 years old – is still considered an excellent combat handgun.

Acknowledgements

Special thanks to Bill Wilson (wilsoncombat.com) for access to his private collection, Rock Island Auction Company (rockislandauction.com) for images of the SMP Colt M1908, the Historical Photographs of China (hpc.vcea.net) for images of Shanghai during the Fairbairn and Sykes era, and especially to Doug Wicklund for his keen knowledge and generosity.

References

"2015 Standard Catalog of Firearms" 25th Edition, edited by Jerry Lee, 2015.

"Blue Book of Gun Values" 35th Edition, by S.P. Fjestad, 2015.

"Gun Traders Guide" 37th Edition, edited by Robert A. Sadowski, 2015.

"Shooting To Live With The One-Hand Gun," by W.E. Fairbairn and E.A. Sykes, 1942. Reprint Paladin Press, 2008.

W.E. Fairbairn (left) and E.A. Sykes (right) wrote *Shooting To Live*, the groundbreaking book that pioneered modern pistolcraft.

The author's brother Matt finds that the old John Browning design is a natural pointer and quick on the mount.

REMINGTON'S
MODEL 11
SPORTSMAN

BY Will McGraw

ow does one begin the story of one good gun? This particular humpback shotgun is now doing duty in its fourth generation. According to the unique barrel date code on this Remington shotgun, it was manufactured in 1934 and quickly found its way to the rolling farm country of western New York state.

Way back in the early 1930s the awakening conservation movement was taking hold throughout the country and the hunting community was trying to emphasize the fair chase aspect. Remington had the popular Model 11 shotgun with a four-round magazine. Remington's in-house staff conceived the idea of taking the popu-

lar model 11 and designing a magazine holding only two shells plus one in the chamber. For the knowledgeable hunter, that was plenty for anything that you cared to shoot. With new waterfowl hunting regulations that mandated a three-shot limit, this put on the gun market a shotgun ready for the local duck pond right out of the box. In fact, Remington dubbed their new modified design the "Sportsman" and along with a nice engraved receiver with pheasants on one side and ducks on the other, it was ready to enter the uplands or the duck blinds.

My grandfather was the first to acquire this particular 20-gauge smoothbore with its factory 26-inch barrel choked modified. With it he prowled the

ridges and valleys of New York's Steuben County and harvested a few deer, and an occasional ruffed grouse in the game bag. Several decades later when I had possession of the shotgun, I benched it at 50 yards and it always shot tight groups with Winchester 1-ounce Foster-type slugs.

Of course, anyone familiar with John Browning's long-recoil shotgun design knows that the humpback has a distinctive "double shuffle" upon firing. I always had a purple bruise mark on my right shoulder after shooting slugs with the gun, which never had a rubber recoil pad.

Along about the mid-1960s, my dad became the caretaker of this smoothbore and he had one of his police bud-

Simple engraving patterns show pheasants on the right side of the receiver, ducks on the left. The fast-handling 20 gauge was always at home in the field as well as in the duck blind.

dies refinish the original walnut stock to a beautiful luster. Dad was a small-town police chief in upstate New York and would take the shotgun on deer hunts in the surrounding woodlands. When I reached about 10 or 11 years of age, I was fortunate to be asked if I wanted to tag along. What kid wouldn't jump at the chance to prowl the oak and hickory hillsides in search of big game? This was before the widespread use of hunter orange, and I distinctly remember my grandmother and mother sewing some square patches of yellow cloth to the front and back of Dad's red checkered wool hunting jacket. Along with extended family, I participated in

the hunt for deer, but the deer were safe from this slim, square-back 20 gauge for a couple more seasons. Then, my father got a job in a different state and the Remington Sportsman went into long-term storage for several years in the back of his closet. It would be several more years after high school and a stint in the Air Force before I would once again be reunited with this old shotgun.

After my four-year enlistment and return to familiar surroundings, I got the itch to try my hand at some informal trap shooting. Perusing a nearby sporting goods store, I picked up a small, portable trap machine,

and with my younger brother Mark commenced to busting clay pigeons at the Rod & Gun Club. By this time I had acquired my own Mossberg 500 12-gauge pump, but we brought along the vintage 20-gauge humpback for an afternoon bang fest. Truth be told, the little Remington hummed right along and the higher percentage of targets hit with it attested to its handling, design, balance and optimum choke configuration. Heck, I was so good with that shotgun that I could shoot at several flying targets with just one hand like a pistolero! One time, we even brought along my brother's girlfriend who had never fired a gun before, and in no time at all she was smoking the birds. The little 20 was that good.

In the late 1980s, with my college studies completed and a few years of civilian government service accomplished, I accepted a customs inspector position on the remote northern border of Vermont. Lots of big woods up that way with large tracts of paper company land open to hunting, plus private lands welcoming to hunters. Posted signs were still few and far between at that time. I wasn't new to hunting, but the land of tall firs and big spruce trees was unfamiliar to this cornfield nimrod.

My good friend Ivan was an avid partridge hunter and patiently explained

The familiar square back silhouette indicates that the Remington is a cousin to the Browning Auto-5 recoil-operated autoloader.

the methods for finding and taking these explosive "thunder chickens" of the Northern woods. I didn't have the Mossberg anymore, but I did quickly snatch the 20-gauge Sportsman from my parent's attic that fall and got to tromp the old logging trails that laced the regions of northern New Hampshire and Vermont. Though a good hunting dog would certainly help, I had no trouble most chilly mornings just strolling along some long-forgotten skidder trail and getting frequent shots that first year.

Notice I said shots – and not necessarily birds in the game bag. As any veteran grouse hunter knows, this game bird is wily and super fast after it unexpectedly explodes from hiding and zooms off to safety. Good thing that Sportsman only held three rounds or else I would've been making more trips to the local gun store to stock up on shells. It is amazing how fast one can crank off three shots on a single flush.

The local game birds were not the only pursuit that I was engaged in with that 20-gauge shotgun. One year I found myself without my recently acquired .30-30 deer rifle and had to make do with the old shotgun. It was the third day of the Vermont rifle season and only a dusting of snow was on the ground. With my dear wife Kate off to her teaching job and the kids safely on the school bus, I slipped out the back door and up the wooded hillside immediately behind our

house at about 8:15 a.m. On that day, I didn't have to be at work until 3:30 p.m., so my plan was to just mosey around in a big circle until midafternoon, then head back to the house and off to work.

After about 10 minutes of slow, quiet walking, I heard something crashing through the woods coming in my direction. I froze like a statue and readied my shotgun for anything that might appear. About five seconds later a large doe literally vaulted out of the trailside brush and stopped on the old woods road. She stared at me for what seemed like minutes then sprang off and continued her escape. Now, I had heard from many an old whitetail hunter that if you see any does during the rut, well, a buck could be trailing behind. Putting this bit of knowledge to the test, I decided to hold my position and see if anything would show up. Sure enough, after a few more minutes passed, I head another something crashing through the dry limbs and crunchy leaves. Even before appearing, I knew that this had to be a buck and raised the shotgun to my shoulder in preparation for firing. I was well rewarded for my patience when almost in the same spot, a good-size spike horn popped out into view and paused for just a second in the middle of the trail. Off went the safety, the trigger squeeze completed, and the .62-caliber Winchester rifled slug found its mark at about 20 paces. Lowering the shotgun, I glanced at my watch and noted the time as 8:30 a.m. Not too bad for 15 minutes worth of effort and literally out my back door!

To this day, that remains the shortest deer hunt of my life. In no time at all I had that deer dressed, dragged downhill to the garage and was well into my second cup of coffee when the wife called to check in on my day around midmorning. Needless to say, she was astounded that I had been out to the woods and back so soon. Hanging up the phone and grabbing a rag, I gave the patina-covered shotgun a quick wipe down and shoved it back into the gun case. After many years out of the deer woods, the ol' Remington had spoken once again.

Another memorable hunt with the family heirloom occurred a couple of years later when my son Chris and I headed to the back side of Brownington Pond in the northeast kingdom of Vermont for a mid-winter snowshoe hare hunt. In years past, Chris had used the Remington Sportsman, but for this jaunt he carried a dandy little Remington 870 shotgun in 20 gauge. Fortu-

A 26-inch barrel choked modified has served as a fine general-purpose shotgun for several generations of the author's family. Note the original factory front bead sight.

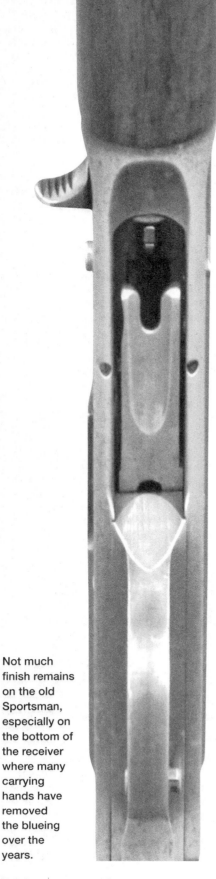

Not much finish remains on the old Sportsman, especially on the bottom of the receiver where many carrying hands have removed the blueing over the years.

SPORTSMAN
THREE SHOT AUTOLOADER

MODEL 11
FIVE SHOT
AUTOLOADER

Remington DUPONT

Both Sportsman and Model 11 are made in 12, 16 and 20 gauges. All chambered for 2¾" shells. The only autoloading shotguns made in 20 gauge.

nately the snow wasn't too deep that year and stalking through the woods was fairly easy. We started near the shoreline and in no time at all kicked up a white rabbit, and Chris got it on the first shot.

Now for my turn. Despite many years of small-game hunting in warmer climes, I had never scored on a rabbit of any description. I was hoping my luck would change. We continued hunting in a wide circular pattern up the mountainside away from the pond for some time before taking a rest. Lots of tracks were about, but I had not so much as seen a white rabbit. As we moved out after the break, I had gone scarcely 15 steps when suddenly a white ball of fur zipped off to my left at lightning speed. Quickly I shouldered the Remington squareback, popped the safety off and slapped the trigger all in the same millisecond. It was kind of an instinctive snap shot, as I didn't calculate any lead into the target at all. The hare was well within 20 yards and the ⅞ ounce of number 8s found their mark. One shot was all it took. Again, I was impressed by the design and gracefulness of this quick-into-action shoulder-thumper. Two rabbits were in the pot that night, and once again the practicality of a 20-gauge shotgun repeater for upland hunting was proven.

When the long-recoil Sportsman was not out hunting it was a favorite pastime for the family in midsummer to shoot some informal trap at the nearby Fish & Game club. My daughter Stephanie showed quite a bit of aptitude to hitting flying targets and my wife Kate could smash those little orange clay pigeons to dust. It was not uncommon for a friend to show up and an impromptu shooting lesson would be followed with easy, "folly floaters" sent airborne to ensure a positive experience. A 20 gauge makes a wonderful tool for introducing novice shooters to the sport since it's easy on the recoil, but can still easily bust clay birds within reasonable range. No fancy AA target loads were utilized, just whatever promo loads that I could scrape up at the local big box store.

As the 21st century dawned, I got the bug for a 12-gauge Remington Wingmaster for some future turkey and pheasant hunts that might be on the horizon. I got a good deal on a new Light Contour model and decided that it was also just right for upland birds and rabbits. The old family Remington Sportsman was retired to the back of my closet that day and was rarely pulled out for several years thereafter. I viewed myself as the current custodian of this family heirloom and over the next several years only occasionally unsheathed it from the frayed canvas case to fire a few slugs for an infrequent deer hunt. For the most part, I had already transitioned to the 12-gauge pump for all my hunting needs.

After a decade of only occasional use, and wanting to clean out my overstuffed closet of all items that were taking up much needed space, I decided that it was time to pass along the Sportsman to the fourth generation of the family. By this time I was working and living in the Southeastern U.S. and I wanted my nephews who were coming of shooting age to have the same opportunities for fun and memories that I enjoyed over the years with this particular gun. So, a couple of years ago I gave her one last cleaning, smeared some Hoppe's gun oil over the fading blue finish, and wiped down the dinged and scarred walnut stock for one last time.

You bond with a gun when you clean it. A thousand memories come rushing back into your mind of endless days afield. The shot that almost was, the crunch of frozen mud under your boots, the feel of cold steel in your hands on a frosty October morning. If only an old shotgun could talk, and the tales it could tell. Such was this gun.

When the boys are ready, it will be there for them and their adventures on clay target ranges or nearby game lands. I'm confident that when called upon, this one good gun will be doing the double-shuffle and thumping the shoulders of their children for decades yet to come.

With its elongated grip and graceful profile, the 1860 Army was the inspiration for the gun that spelled its demise, the .44-caliber Colt 1871-72 Open Top. This replica Open Top presentation engraved version was made for the author by Cimarron Firearms; the accompanying holster is by El Paso Saddlery.

STORY AND PHOTOS BY Rick Hacker

COLT MODEL 1860 ARMY

I have often written that for those of us who gravitate toward cap-and-ball revolvers, specifically of the open-top Colt design, we live in a Golden Age. After all, if we actually had been around during the 19th century, as so many of us wish, if it was 1849, the most advanced Colt you could have purchased would have been the diminutive .31-caliber Model 1849 pocket pistol, or its antithesis, the hefty 4½-pound .44-caliber First Model Colt Dragoon – neither of which was optimum for carrying in the field. And if it were 1851, the Third Model Dragoon and the .36-caliber Colt Navy

would have been the newest kids on the block. The better-balanced Navy was a scant but viable alternative to its predecessors, combining vastly improved firepower over the Model 1849 but falling far behind the Dragoons in that respect, although the handling qualities of the '51 Navy were a welcomed improvement.

Today, of course, thanks to a virtual plethora of well-made and relatively affordable replicas and a still adequate supply of not-quite-as-affordable originals, we have the option of choosing any of Sam Colt's cap-and-ball wheelguns, ranging from the 1836 Paterson to the 1860 Army. In fact, entering a well-

stocked gun store, flipping through the pages of firearms catalogs, or surfing the Internet under "replica cap-and-ball revolvers" is tantamount to walking into a fictional Samuel Colt's Emporium back in the 19th century and being able to select practically any of his cap-and-ball revolvers.

But therein lies a dilemma, which one of his company's many revolvers would you select to buckle on your hip and face the challenges and adventures that might await you just around the next corner or behind the next boulder? Or in today's more practical scenarios, which one gun would you most closely identify

The one-line address of an authentic Colt re-issue. Italian replicas do not carry this mark.

Below: Due to the popularity of the 1860 Army, Colt re-issued the gun as Second and Third Generation revolvers. This is a Third Generation Signature Edition, circa 1996. These guns are no longer in production and have assumed a collectability of their own, although not on a par with original First Generations.

with and which would you most enjoy owning and shooting?

For me, that answer has always been the .44-caliber Colt 1860 Army, or "The New Model Holster Pistol," as it was originally called. Even as a kid during the 1950s, I was mesmerized by the hefty Hubley Colt .45 Revolver cap gun, which, even though it came with removable "bullets," and caliber notwithstanding, nonetheless featured the same elongated grips and smooth flowing under-barrel lines of the 1860 Army. While for a brief period as an adult shooter I was lured away by the crisp, squared-off lines of the octagon-barrel 1851 Navy, but I always came back to the much more graceful design of the 1860 Army, with its harder-hitting caliber.

The 1860 Army has always struck me as something that could have very well been created by industrial designer Henry Dreyfuss during the 1930s, rather than on the eve of the American Civil War by the combined talents of Samuel Colt and his chief engineer, Elisha King Root. But the 1860 Army was Colt's answer to the government's need for a .44-caliber revolver that was not as cumbersome as the company's First, Second and Third Model "horse pistols" that were currently used by the U.S. Mounted Dragoons. Of course, Colt was selling all of the .36-caliber Navies the company could turn out, but Samuel Colt, already one of the 10 wealthiest men in America, knew that if he wanted to keep the coffers flowing he had better land an Army contract.

The solution of creating a large-caliber handgun on a belt pistol-size frame was a rather ingenious one, made even more so by the fact that this was still an era of rather crude metallurgy; you couldn't just substitute a lighter, stronger material such as aluminum or titanium, which of course, didn't exist for gunmaking back then. Instead, Colt started with the already proven .36-caliber 1851

Navy frame. But how to get a .44-caliber cylinder to fit onto it?

This was accomplished by milling and lowering the front two-thirds of the frame slightly, just enough to clear the larger forward portion of a newly designed, rebated cylinder. Thus, the rear of the cylinder was akin to a .36-caliber version. But, the front two-thirds of the cylinder, with its slightly larger diameter, stepped up to accommodate six .44-caliber chambers, which were slightly tapered towards the rear of the cylinder to meet its narrower diameter. Consequently, the .44-caliber cylinder was able to fit on a .36-caliber frame. And somewhat appropriately, the 1851 Navy's Ormsby-engraved May 1843 naval battle scene between Texas and Mexico was repeated on the 1860 Army's rebated cylinder.

As a further improvement, the hinged under-barrel rammer of the '51 Navy, which would sometimes bind under hard use, was redesigned as a smoother operating "Patent Creeping Lever," a steel knobuled rack and pinion system that Root had previously employed on Colt's 1855 Sidehammer Model. To further modify the new gun, the barrel was rounded, which enabled it to flow gracefully into an area protecting the rammer, giving the 1860 a sleek appearance unlike anything the Colt factory had previously produced. But perhaps even more dramatic, and certainly distinctive as far as handling characteristics were concerned, was the 1860's elongated grip, a feature that was added after the first few thousand guns were made.

This initial run of 1860s also sported 7½-inch barrels, but the Army requested that the barrels be lengthened to 8 inches, along with the adoption of the drop-grip profile, ostensibly to aid in the gun's balance and tame the recoil of the heavier .44-caliber loading. As someone who has shot both replicas and originals of the 1860 Army, I can say that the longer barrel does indeed give the gun better balance and pointability. But the real ben-

efit of the elongated grip is to nestle the gun more securely in the hand and help reduce muzzle flip, while also positioning the hammer closer to the thumb during recoil for a faster repeat shot.

Needless to say, the 1860 Army met with immediate acceptance by soldiers and civilians alike, with the Army stating in its May 19, 1860, report from the first U.S. Ordnance trial, "...The improvement, as claimed by Mr. Colt, consists of diminishing the weight of his revolver known as the Dragoon or Holster Pistol, and retaining the same caliber, thereby securing the same efficiency of fire without the disadvantages of heretofore found in handling the heavier pistol... the New Model Revolvers, with 8-inch barrel, will make the most superior cavalry arm we have ever had..."

Between the firing upon Fort Sumter in 1861—that signaled the start of The Great Rebellion—and 1863, the Army purchased 119,300 Model 1860 Army revolvers, some of which had detachable shoulder stocks. Guns destined for this accessory are identified by a cutout in the recoil shield and a fourth screw that projected from both sides of the frame for anchoring the stock to the gun. Johnny Reb also took a liking to the New Model Holster Pistol, and hundreds were ordered by the Confederacy before Union blockades put a halt to this activity. As a result, the 1860 Army remained a coveted prize whenever one could be procured on the battlefield, and Quantrill's Raiders were said to have been armed with four 1860 Armies per man —two carried in holsters and two more in pommel scabbards. But unlike other Yankee sidearms, the South never counterfeited the 1860 Army, as its rebated cylinder and ratchet rammer were deemed too complicated to reproduce.

After The War Between The States was over, the Model 1860 went west in both military and civilian guises. Even with the advent of the self-contained metallic cartridge, the 1860 continued to blaze away as Thuer, Richards and Richard-Mason conversions. It also became the inspiration for the Colt 1871-72 Open Top, which eventually begat the Single Action Army. In all, 200,500 Model 1860 Army revolvers were produced, with production finally stopping in 1872, thanks to the introduction of the Colt Open Top.

Yet for all its attributes, the 1860 had some faults. For one thing, like all Colt cap-and-ball revolvers, its miniscule front sight was less than adequate, especially when coupled with the shal-

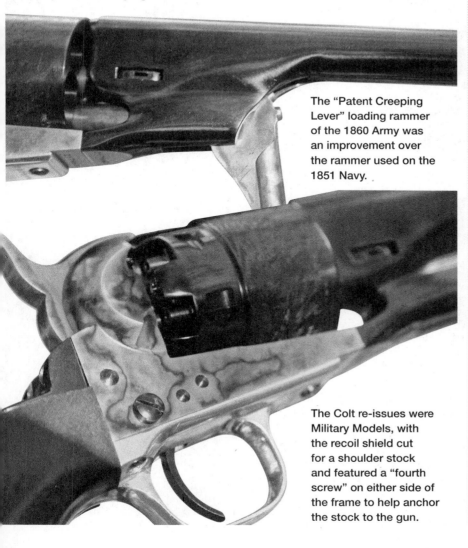

The "Patent Creeping Lever" loading rammer of the 1860 Army was an improvement over the rammer used on the 1851 Navy.

The Colt re-issues were Military Models, with the recoil shield cut for a shoulder stock and featured a "fourth screw" on either side of the frame to help anchor the stock to the gun.

The author fires his original 1860 Army with a standard military load of 25 grains of 3FG black powder. Recoil is minimal.

Below: The only safe way to carry an 1860 Army – or any cap-and-ball revolver – with all six chambers loaded is with the hammer resting between the nipples. Otherwise, only load five chambers, with the hammer resting on the nipple over the empty sixth chamber.

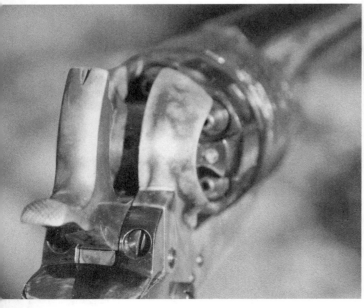

Yes, that little notch cut into the top of the hammer is actually the rear sight.

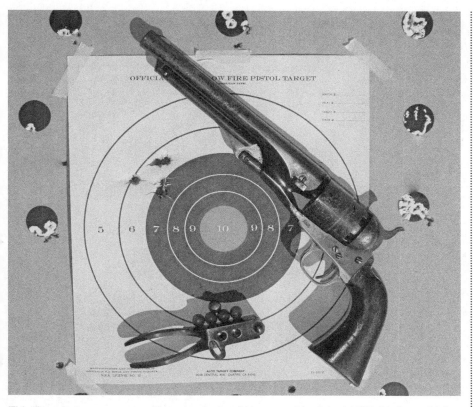

This five-shot group proves there is plenty of accuracy in original 1860 Armies, which unlike today's replicas, featured progressive rifling.

low notch milled into the hammer, which ostensibly served as a rear sight. Consequently, these guns shoot high and to the left, the actual point of impact depending on how worn the hammer notch was and how far the barrel-retaining wedge had been driven in. As a result, it is not uncommon to find original guns with rear sights dovetailed or brazed onto the breech end of the barrel, and more than a few 1860s have had their front sights built up or otherwise altered.

Still, with the Army's recommended charge of 25 grains of black powder and a .44-caliber lead ball, the 1860 Army was a proven manstopper and had more than enough of what today is known as "battlefield accuracy." Although I own a few replicas of this gun, including a 1996 Colt re-issue, I often shoot my original 1860, which unlike the reproductions features progressive rifling. With Hornady's swagged lead round balls behind 25 grains of GOEX 3FG black powder, I have fired five-shot, 1-1/8-inch to 1½-inch groups at 25 yards, which typically print 4½ inches high and 2½ inches left of a 6 o'clock hold. Trying to stretch the gun's capability out to 100 yards one day – test enough for any handgun, let alone one designed well over a century ago – I aimed at a gong, and by holding 8 inches over the top and about a foot to the right, was actually able to hit it more than once.

I purchased my original 1860 Army many years ago from the late Turner Kirkland, founder of Dixie Gun Works of Union City, Tenn. Interestingly, this gun has some old blood etching on it, which Turner swore was from a Yankee. However, the gun's serial number is 169XXX, which puts its date of manufacture at 1867, two years after General Lee's surrender at Appomattox. Thus, if my 1860 was once owned by a Yankee, I suspect he was a Civil War veteran who simply wanted to pack the best Colt cap-and-ball revolver ever made.

The author's original 1860 Army, which was made in 1867 and sports some purported "Yankee blood etching," even though it was made after the Civil War.

The one-line barrel stamping of an original 1860 Army Colt.

Proud American!

Built for sporting use and self-defense, the new Ruger American Pistol is available in 9mm and .45 ACP. Th[e] polymer-frame, strike[r]-fired handgun boasts [a] felt recoil reducing ca[m] system and short tak[e] up trigger.

RUGER AMERICAN PISTOL

BY Doug Larson

Ruger's new full-size, striker-fired, polymer-frame pistol is a rugged gun ready to serve in all capacities.

If you are a gun enthusiast or if you simply want a gun for sport or self-defense, you are living in probably the best time in history because the selection of guns is greater now than ever. Ruger has just added another choice with the introduction of the American Pistol.

If you are one who doesn't think another polymer handgun is necessary because there are enough to choose from already, consider that for every model on the market today, there are people who find it to be the best one for their needs. While the differences between brands and models are sometimes subtle, most

people who grasp a particular handgun find that it either feels good in the hand, or that it doesn't. And while some people like a particular feature on a gun, others despise it. So having a large selection of guns to choose from makes it more likely that each shooter will find a gun he or she likes.

To assure that the Ruger American Pistol suits as many shooters as possible, the engineers and designers at Ruger spent a great deal of time studying the likes and needs of shooters, and requested input from law enforcement and military trainers from around the country.

FEATURES

Although not obvious, it is not a typical polymer frame gun. Instead, the nylon-filled grip frame houses a modular chassis that contains the fire control group and has rails on which the slide reciprocates. The chassis is made of precision-machined steel with a black nitride finish that is extremely tough and corrosion resistant. And because it is the part that has the serial number on it, there is the potential to replace the grip frame and slide to modify the size and contours of the gun. Presumably, Ruger or another company will eventually offer

The Ruger American Pistol disassembles like most others. The recoil spring assembly uses a flat-coiled spring, and the gun has a specially designed locking cam to help reduce felt recoil.

such conversion kits, but that is merely speculation at this time.

The grip frame has different size wraparound grips that are easily swapped out to fit many different hand sizes. The 9mm version has three sizes, and the .45 ACP version has two. These one-piece grips include not only backstraps, but also side panels so that with each one, trigger reach and size of the palm swell change. The front and backstraps are heavily textured with diamond-shaped bumps, and the sides are stippled to help obtain a nonslip grip. Changing the grip requires only a quarter turn of a retention screw with the aid of a supplied wrench. Plus, the gun is equipped with a lanyard attachment point at the heel, something that is seeing a comeback on pistols lately.

At the front of the grip frame where there is often nothing more than a dust cover to keep dirt out of the recoil spring assembly, Ruger included a Picatinny

When the slide is removed, the chassis is visible. Made of machined steel, the chassis is the part that bears the serial number, so if other grip frames and slide assemblies become available, the caliber and size of the gun could be changed without government paperwork.

With three interchangeable grip modules, the Ruger American Pistol in 9mm can be configured to fit almost any hand. All controls are truly ambidextrous making it easy for right- or left-handed shooters to use.

The backstrap has raised diamond-shaped bumps and stippled side panels to help the shooter obtain a nonslip grip. Serrations at the rear of the slide are designed to give the shooter a positive grip when racking it.

accessory rail for the attachment of a light or laser. For a gun that will be used for personal protection, those are good items to consider, since most deadly force confrontations occur in diminished light. Remember that lasers are not gimmicks or toys — they serve a very useful purpose when employed properly after competent training.

Each American Pistol is supplied with two stainless steel nickel-Teflon plated magazines. The 9mm version holds 18 rounds, while the .45 ACP magazine holds 10. Lower capacity 10-round 9mm magazines are available for those who live in jurisdictions where the right to use full-capacity magazines has been restricted.

Controls are simple and will be familiar to anyone with experience shooting striker-fired, semiautomatic polymer-frame pistols. However, Ruger has made an improvement not found on all other pistols in this class. The magazine release and slide stop are both ambidextrous so that both right- and left-handed shooters are on equal footing with the pistol's controls.

While prominent and easy to activate, the slide stop is not obtrusive and does not interfere when the shooter racks the slide. The magazine release is located at the junction of the front strap and the triggerguard, the location preferred by most. It is a triangular button that is prominent enough to easily activate, but not enough so that it is prone to accidental activation during carry or shooting. Just to its rear is an irregular quadrilateral-shaped bump to partially protect it from being accidentally pressed.

Since the striker is partially cocked after the slide is racked, Ruger was able to develop a short-take-up trigger. The trigger on the test gun did have a relatively short take-up and broke cleanly at just less than 7 pounds with almost no creep and no discernible overtravel. A right-angle ledge built into the rear of the triggerguard stops overtravel. For those readers interested, reset was distinct.

TOP END

The slide is manufactured of stainless steel that has been finished in black nitride because it creates a very hard surface, and is extremely corrosion resistant. Instead of the square, blocky appearance of most semiautomatic pistol slides these days, this one has the square corners cut off so — but not

At the bottom of the dustcover, Ruger placed a Picatinny rail for the mounting of accessories like a light or laser, which are excellent options for a gun to be used for self-protection.

Genuine Novak LoMount three-dot sights are standard on the Ruger American Pistol. These are very rugged sights and are drift adjustable for windage. The serial number is located at the rear just below the slide on the back of the fire control chassis.

rounded — so it does have a more pleasing appearance. At the rear of the slide are serrations that do a good job of affording a solid purchase when racking the slide by hand. At the front of the slide there is a slight bevel on each side near the muzzle that should help to guide the gun into the holster.

Atop the slide, Ruger has installed genuine Novak LoMount Carry sights with the familiar three-dot configuration. The sights are extremely rugged, used by many manufacturers as original equipment, installed by many as an aftermarket accessory, and because of their configuration are less prone to snagging on clothing or slicing a finger when racking the slide under stress in an emergency.

This striker-fired pistol from Ruger has no external safety, but it is equipped with a trigger-lever style safety that prevents the trigger from moving all the way to the rear unless the trigger is pressed. The trigger overtravel stop is at the bottom rear of the triggerguard.

The slide stop, magazine release and trigger on the Ruger American Pistol are in familiar locations, but unlike many other pistols, these really are ambidextrous.

ON THE RANGE

Due to the different sizes of interchangeable backstraps, most shooters will probably find the gun comfortable to grasp. That is one of the first criteria most people use in selecting a handgun. Reliability, though, is the most important feature in a gun used for self-protection, and the gun ran without any malfunctions during testing for this article.

Ruger stated that it has designed a special barrel cam for the American Pistol that reduces felt recoil by spreading the unlocking of the slide, barrel and frame over a longer period of time. Without the same pistol built

The Ruger American Pistol in 9mm was easy to shoot and exhibited low felt recoil, making it easy to get back on target for follow-up shots.

PERFORMANCE

| LOAD | VELOCITY (FPS) | ACCURACY (INCHES) | |
		AVERAGE	BEST
Black Hills 124-grain JHP	1,136	2.8	2.15
Federal 147-grain Hydra-Shok JHP	981	3.25	2.53
Winchester 147-grain PDX1 JHP	993	3.32	3.03

Bullet weight measured in grains, velocity in feet per second 15 feet from the muzzle by chronograph, and accuracy in inches for three five-shot groups at 25 yards.

with a standard cam system to compare against it, though, there is no way to positively prove that felt recoil is reduced. However, in testing the gun, recoil was quite manageable. In the end, how comfortable a gun is to shoot is a subjective observation and is unique to each shooter.

The Ruger American Pistol is another new product by Ruger that is redefining the company compared to what it was in its early years. The gun is affordably priced, and if it turns out to be as robust as so many of the company's other guns, it will probably be well accepted.

RUGER AMERICAN PISTOL

SPECIFICATIONS

CALIBER:	9mm (reviewed), .45 ACP
BARREL LENGTH:	4.2 inches, 1:10 RH twist
OVERALL LENGTH:	7.5 inches
WEIGHT:	30 ounces
GRIPS:	Glass-filled nylon
SIGHTS:	Novak LoMount three-dot
ACTION:	Semiautomatic, striker-fired
FINISH:	Black nitride
CAPACITY:	17 + 1
PRICE:	$579

Rapid-fire strings at 7 yards were not difficult with the Ruger American Pistol due to the 9mm chambering, polymer-grip frame and easy recovery from recoil.

THE SHARPS .25-45 AR

An exciting new option for America's most popular rifle platform, the AR-15

BY Steve Gash

TEST FIRE

SRC offers new brass cases made by Federal, as well as factory ammo loaded by SRC.

The new .25-45 Sharps cartridge is one of the many rounds based on the .223 Remington case, and has a lot to offer the rifleman. Where others have tried and stumbled, the .25-45 looks like a winner.

The popularity of the .223 has spawned the development of a host of new cartridges based on the case. Would-be cartridge designers and wildcatters have necked the case up and down and "improved" it, with each presented as the NBT (Next Big Thing) to fill a micro-niche then bereft of the PBS (Perfect Ballistic Solution).

In all fairness, we must admit most of these NBTs were not PBSs. Some mirrored the parent round and offered little in the way of new or unique performance, or ballistically duplicated existing cartridges. But they fulfilled the designer's heart with warmth and cheer, and made some gunsmith some dough.

A perfect example is the 6x45, the .223 necked up to .24 caliber. I worked with not one, but two 6x45s a few years back. Its claim to PBS was that it could shoot heavier bullets than the .223, which would buck the wind better. But then folks started using .223 barrels with 7-inch twists and 77- to 90-grain bullets, and, dare I say it, got almost the same velocities as with the 6x45.

Then there was the embarrassing problem of bullet expansion, or lack thereof. Game-weight bullets launched out of the 6x45 were barely fast enough at close ranges to reliably expand in lightweight big game, and at long ranges, they frequently slipped through tissue almost like a solid. I like the 6x45, but in an honest side-by-side comparison, I had to eventually admit that it offered little over the standard .223.

The .25-45 Sharps was recently developed by the Sharps Rifle Company (SRC) of Glenrock, Wyo., and is another matter.

No, SRC doesn't make breechloading .45-70s, but the company name was chosen to reflect the heritage started in 1848.

SRC makes spiffy ARs in numerous configurations and offers complete uppers, conversion kits, or just new barrels, in case you want to upgrade your existing shootin' iron. In addition, they make numerous critical components for ARs, such as the Relia-Bolt and Balanced Bolt Carrier.

The .25-45 is named for the bullet diameter (.257 inch) and the case length in millimeters (45, the same as the .223). Almost all new cartridges formed from existing cases remain "wildcats," as there is usually no pressure-tested load data or "standard" specifications for them. SRC went through the effort of having their new round approved by SAAMI, so the .25-45 is truly a "factory" round. This allows companies to safely produce ammunition and rifles for the round.

When different cartridges are made from the same base case, it's good to have the proper headstamp, as with these SRC factory new cases produced by Federal.

New cases with the proper headstamp are made by Federal, and are available from SRC. In addition, SRC produces factory ammunition (also in Federal cases).

There is a dual problem with the .22- and .24- (6mm) caliber bullets for cartridges formed from .223 cases. Bullets that are heavy enough to be considered "game" bullets fired by either round just cannot be driven fast enough to ensure reliable expansion. These heavier and longer bullets require a faster twist, too. Conversely, bullets light enough to attain sufficient speed are usually a "varmint" design with a thin jacket that expands violently and lacks sufficient penetration for big game.

The clever folks at SRC avoided this two-headed conundrum. Their factory ammo is loaded with the Speer 87-grain Hot-Cor bullet that has been around for at least 50 years, and which has earned an excellent reputation for reliable expansion and good penetration. The lead alloy core material is melted and the molten metal is poured into the jacket, which is relatively thick and tough.

The subsequent bonding keeps the core and jacket together after impact; actually, the Speer Hot-Cor might be considered the original bonded bullet. After the core cools, the bullet is shaped into a softpoint with a small exposed lead tip. For years I used either the 180- or 200-grain .30-caliber Hot-Cors in my .300 H&H Magnum for mule deer and elk, and had nary a bullet failure.

Another attribute of the Speer 87-grain Hot-Cor that endears it to the .25-45 is its ogive. Many spitzer bullets have long skinny points, and if seated to work in an AR magazine, the major diameter of the bullet can end up below the case mouth. However, the Hot-Cors are just a little bit less pointed. In an AR magazine, this makes for a perfect fit with an overall cartridge length of 2.25 inches. So this bullet has the right shape and design to function in the AR platform and perform reliably on big game, as SRC intended.

The inventors claim that the .25-45 matches the real-world ballistics of the once popular but now moribund .250 Savage, which was invented by the well-known cartridge designer Charles Newton. He originally designed it to drive a 100-grain bullet at 2,800 fps when it was adopted by Savage in 1915 as a high-velocity round for the Model 99. But Savage saw the marketing benefits of a velocity of (then astounding) 3,000 fps, so in 1932 the bullet weight was reduced to 87 grains. Factory loads with this bullet weight usually gave the desired velocity, and Savage called the round the .250-3000 Savage. The name

was later changed to .250 Savage. The .250 is still a terrific round, and was immensely popular until about 1955 when the .243 Winchester and the .244 Remington were introduced. The resulting sales saga of this pair is well known, and together they sealed the fate of the .250.

SRC's goal for the .25-45 was to duplicate, in an AR, the real world ballistics of the famous .250 Savage with an 87-grain bullet at a velocity of about 3,000 fps. As usual with factory-listed velocities, this included some blue sky, and the actual speed out of sporter-length barrels was somewhat less. I happen to have a Savage Model 14 American Classic with a 22-inch barrel chambered in .250 Savage. The Western Super-X 87-grain Soft Point factory load was listed at 3,030 fps, but registered 2,958 fps 10 feet in front of the Model 14's muzzle. Such speeds can be almost duplicated in the .25-45, as we shall see.

The more I read about the .25-45, the more I had to have one. Since I already had other ARs, I ordered an SRC upper in .25-45 for testing. For testing, I pinned it onto a Match Target lower receiver assembly. The result is a striking outfit. The SCR unit has a 20-inch barrel, a flat top, a sexy Diamondhead handguard and a futuristic muzzlebrake. My Olympic lower receiver has been upgraded somewhat by the addition of an oversize charging handle and a Timney trigger.

Factory ammo from Sharps Rifle Company is loaded with OEM powders not available to handloaders. The cartridge shown here has the reliable Speer 87-grain Hot-Cor Soft Point.

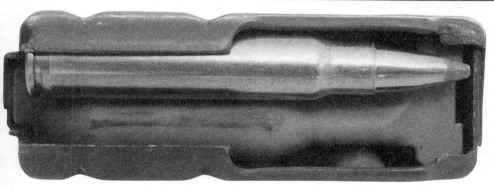

Loaded .25-45 rounds with an overall length of 2.25 inches or less fit in standard AR-15 .223 magazines.

A Sharps Rifle Company upper assembly is mounted here on an Olympic Arms lower. The Nikon Prostaff 5 4.5-18x40 scope perfectly complements the outfit.

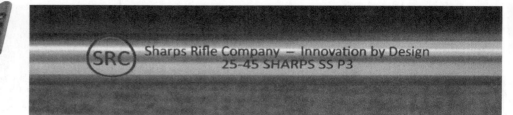

The barrel of the SRC .25-45 is stainless steel and features three-groove polygonal rifling, as indicated by the barrel markings.

The barrel of the tested upper came fitted with a high-tech muzzlebrake.

For sights, I mounted a new Nikon Prostaff 5 4.5-18x40 in a Nikon P-Series mount. This excellent scope has the Nikoplex reticle, a side-focus parallax adjustment, crystal clear optics, and positive ¼-minute elevation and windage click adjustments. It also has an elevation turret that can be reset to zero after zeroing in.

SRC forwarded a couple of boxes of their factory loads, and out of the rifle's 20-inch barrel the velocity was 2,910 fps. This is a mere 48 fps slower than the 87-grain .250 Savage load from the 22-inch barrel Model 14 noted above.

The .25-45 is the .223 case necked up to .25 caliber with no other change, so handloading it is pure pleasure. While the factory ammo is perfectly fine for deer and antelope hunting, handloading adds immeasurably to the round's versatility. Forming cases for the .25-45

SRC's logo is engraved on the Relia-Bolt carrier and the dust cover has the cartridge laser engraved on its inside.

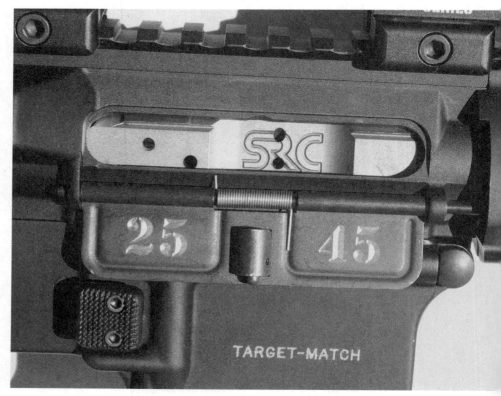

is simple. First, round up a bunch of .223 cases. If you don't have a bucket of them handy, plenty are available. While fired military brass is widely useable, I recommend using commercial cases as they have a bit more powder capacity. All you have to do is expand the neck of the .223 case to .25 caliber, full-length size it, and you're set. Oh, one more thing: If using military brass, don't forget to ream or swage the crimp around the primer pockets. Both RCBS and Redding make die sets for reloading the .25-45 Sharps.

I had a large quantity of once-fired Federal .223 cases, so I used them exclusively for my .25-45 handloads. This small case calls for standard small rifle primers and I used CCI-400 primers throughout.

Powders suitable for the .25-45 fall in the fast to medium-fast categories. The problem with the .25-45 (as with the .223 and rounds based on it) is that one runs out of powder capacity before enough (relatively) slow powder can be stuffed into the case. As a result, many of the loads shown are compressed. For ease of loading, the least grief approach is to use a relatively fast spherical powder, or a fast extruded one. Good choices are Accurate Arms 2200, X-Terminator, 2015 and Alliant's Power Pro 1200R.

I tried seven different bullets with 11 powders. Ballistic consistency was excellent, as the average coefficient of variation (the standard deviation expressed as a percentage of the mean velocity) of all loads was .52 percent. Appropriate charges fill the .25-45's small case to the brim and this aids uniformity, too.

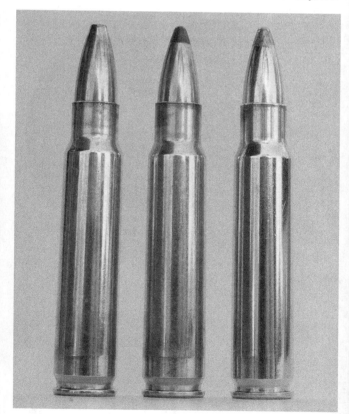

The .25-45 Sharps is the .223 Remington case necked up to .25 caliber without any other change. These three handloads performed great in the .25-45. The bullets are from left: 75-grain Hollow Point and 87-grain Spitzer from Sierra, and the Speer 87-grain Hot-Cor Soft Point.

SHARPS RIFLE COMPANY
.25-45 SHARPS AR UPPER RECEIVER
(As tested assembled to Olympic Arms Match Target Lower Receiver)

SPECIFICATIONS

TYPE:	Direct gas impingement semiautomatic repeater
CALIBER:	.25-45 Sharps
MAGAZINES:	Uses standard 5-, 10-, 20- and 30-round magazines for AR-15
BARREL:	20-inch 416K stainless steel, three-groove polygonal rifling, 10-inch twist, muzzle threaded 5/8-24, 3-inch muzzlebrake provided
OVERALL LENGTH:	40¾ inches (with muzzlebrake)
WEIGHT:	8 pounds, 11 ounces without magazine; 10 pounds with scope, mount and magazine, as tested
UPPER RECEIVER:	Forged aluminum, M4 feed ramp; SRC Relia-Bolt and Balanced Bolt Carrier standard
TRIGGER:	As tested with Timney trigger, weight of pull 3 pounds, 13.6 ounces
SIGHTS:	None. Flattop receiver for standard scope/optic mounts. Tested with Nikon Prostaff 5 4.5-18x40 SF Custom Turret scope with Nikoplex Reticle
MOUNT:	Nikon P-Series 1-inch mounts, as tested
FINISH:	Barrel polished stainless steel, receiver matte black
HANDGUARD:	Free-floated 15-inch Diamondhead, ventilated, with 24 threaded holes for accessory attachment
STOCK:	A2, as tested, various other stocks available
ACCESSORIES:	Soft case, owner's manual
MSRP:	$1,379.99 complete rifle, $649.99 upper only, depending on features
MANUFACTURER:	Sharps Rifle Co., 1195 U.S. Highway 20-26-87, Glenrock, WY 82637; 877-256-4794; srcarms.com

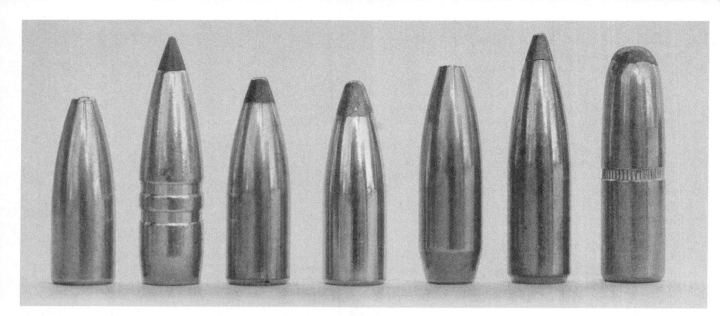

A good selection of .25-caliber bullets is available to the handloader. From left are: Sierra 75-grain Hollow Point, Barnes 80-grain Tipped Triple Shock-X Bullet, Sierra 87-grain Spitzer, Speer 87-grain Hot-Cor Soft Point, Sierra 90-grain Hollow Point Boat Tail, Nosler 100-grain Partition, Hornady 100-grain Round Nose InterLock.

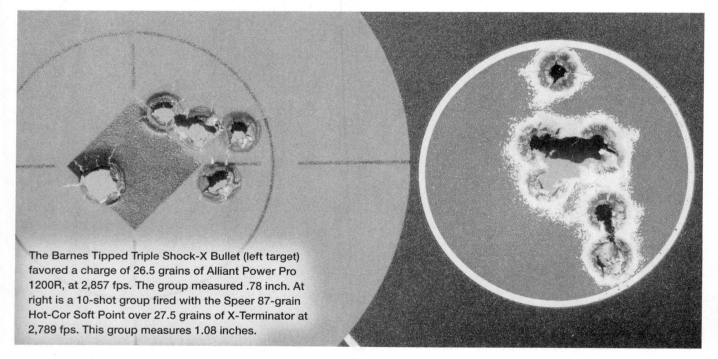

The Barnes Tipped Triple Shock-X Bullet (left target) favored a charge of 26.5 grains of Alliant Power Pro 1200R, at 2,857 fps. The group measured .78 inch. At right is a 10-shot group fired with the Speer 87-grain Hot-Cor Soft Point over 27.5 grains of X-Terminator at 2,789 fps. This group measures 1.08 inches.

COMPARATIVE .25-CALIBER BALLISTICS

ALL LOADS WITH 87-GRAIN SPEER HOT-COR BULLET	MUZZLE VELOCITY (FPS)	VELOCITY OF 2,450 FPS AT	ENERGY OF 1,165 FT-LBS AT	TRAJECTORY AT 200 YARDS
.25-45 handload	2,810	120 yards	120 yards.	-2.05 inches
.25-45 factory load	2,910	150 yards	150 yards	-1.84 inches
.250 Savage handload	2,950	165 yards	165 yards	-2.10 inches

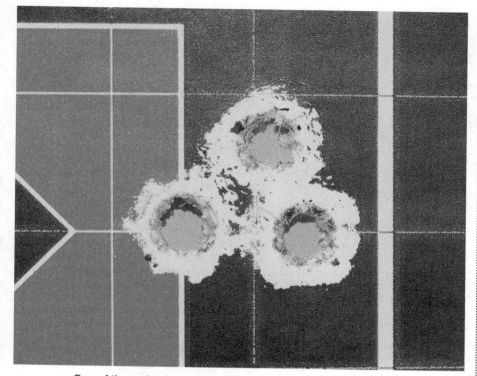

One of the author's best handloads was with the Sierra 87-grain Spitzer and 27.5 grains of H-335. Velocity was 2,835 fps.

The loads were accurate, too. The average group size of all 29 loads was 1.07 inches, and almost half of the loads tested came in under an inch. Best of all, the SRC barrel clustered bullets into nice, round groups.

With the Speer 87-grain Hot-Cor bullet used in SRC factory loads, I came within 109 fps of the factory offering, and 157 fps less than the .250 Savage load in the Model 14. The Sierra 87-grain Spitzer came in a little faster with a top speed of 2,835 fps. So, one can come pretty close to duplicating factory fodder.

Let's look at the ballistics of these 87-grain loads for a minute, all with the Speer 87-grain bullet. While the .25-45 handload is slightly slower than the SRC factory fodder, in the field this is of little consequence to the prudent hunter. A quick comparison of the two loads with the Oehler Ballistic Explorer program shows that the .25-45 factory load is going about as fast at 150 yards as the handload at 120 yards. The .250 Savage handload is about the same velocity at 165 yards. Trajectories are likewise similar, with a total difference between the .25-45 and .250 handloads at 200 yards of .26 inch. Thus, it would appear that the SRC wizards pretty much accomplished their goal.

But the .25-45 isn't just for use where the deer and antelope play. The varmint hunter can spice up the deadly Sierra 75-grain hollowpoint bullet to almost 3,000 fps with a charge of 27 grains of AA-2200 with 1.1-inch groups. Only slightly slower at 2,866 fps was 26 grains of AA-LT32, which had a group average of a mere .7 inch. Then, we must add, there what are euphemistically called the "tactical applications." In addition, a Bob Sled single-shot adapter can be used in place of a magazine with sleek target bullets seated out longer than magazine length for long-range work.

The hunter can hardly go wrong with a Nosler Partition, whatever the size or weight, but try as I might, I just couldn't find a recipe that this rifle liked. Your rifle may love it, of course, and other 100-grain bullets cry for equal time. Velocities were fine, though. With the 100-grain Partition, a charge of 26.5 grains of X-Terminator produced a velocity of 2,642 fps.

Okay, bear with me. I know that long, pointy bullets are the modern thing, but I had to try one of my favorite bullet designs, the Hornady Round Nose Inter-Lock, because it works so well in many calibers. In the .25-45, a dose of 24 grains of AA-2200 gave the respectable velocity of 2,467 fps, and a sub-inch group average. At reasonable ranges, it would be a great deer load.

When the dust settled and all the data was analyzed, I had to conclude that the .25-45 Sharps is not just another flash in the pan. Here we have a well-balanced cartridge that utilizes game-weight bullets at respectable velocities. With the judicious selection of bullets and propellants, the .25-45 can bite as well as bark. And in the Sharps Rifle Company's high-quality ARs, it is not only accurate, it is just a delight to shoot.

DISCLAIMER: Any and all loading data found in this article or previous articles is to be taken as reference material *only*. The publishers, editors, authors, contributors and their entities bear no responsibility for the use by others of the data included in this article or others that came before it.

Reloading dies are available through SRC from RCBS and Redding. This set from RCBS includes the traditional sizer and seater dies, and an expander die to open .22-caliber case necks to .25 caliber

BY L.P. Brezny

SMITH & WESSON M&P 10

The Smith & Wesson M&P 10 dressed to drill 1,000-yard steel. There are many options in added features with this advanced and flexible rifle – including a Dakota Silencer.

TEST FIRE

HPR

Unless you have been living in a cave for the past 40 years you most likely are well aware that the little black rifle dubbed the M-16 has made quite an impression among shooters, both positive and negative. For a very long time the M-16/AR-15 variants were considered spray and pray bullet hoses, plagued with problems, and not worthy of being found in an operational state.

For the most part, the post-1980s as a timeline started to press home the fact that with careful manufacturing methods, quality materials and great production detail to receivers, bolts and barrels, the basic AR-15 was starting to turn in some impressive scores on paper and warm targets downrange. Smith & Wesson, not to be left on the bench at the range, took notice of this change in performance standards and brought forth the M&P 15-T. I still own a very low numbered early model of that rifle today.

It was only natural that the M-15 would over time evolve into a high-power rifle clearly capable of harvesting big game

and drilling targets at some very long ranges. Enter the AR-10 series rifles that quickly moved into the military M110, and today a massive number of

heavy caliber variants among many gun manufactures. Here again, Smith & Wesson was watching with keen eye, and as such enters this discussion via their .308

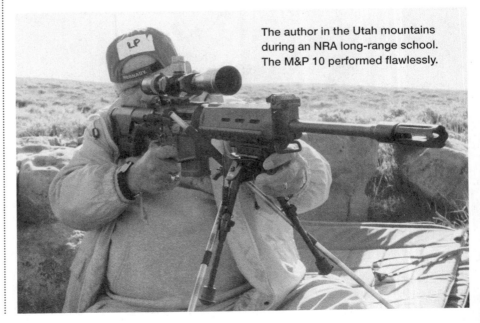

The author in the Utah mountains during an NRA long-range school. The M&P 10 performed flawlessly.

Winchester (7.62x51) in the M&P 10.

My first exposure to the M&P 10 came about during a long-range NRA school sponsored by Smith & Wesson during the late summer of 2015. At a location high in the Wasatch mountains of Utah, the .308-caliber black rifle was subjected to days of shooting from 4,000 feet in elevation to 10,000 feet, and just about every kind of weather you can dream up for a gun test. In terms of range extension, on steel targets the rifle was pressed to a close range of 500 yards, then stretched to 1,000 yards based on Hornady Match .308 ammo with the A-Max 168-grain bullet.

I must admit that at first I was very skeptical of the rifle choice as applied to the long-range school. The M&P 10 retained a short 18-inch barrel, standard gas block operating system, and with its proprietary conventional birdcage muzzlebrake, would present itself as somewhat of a nuisance to the guy, or spotter, next to you in a shooting lane. Not only was I a bit taken aback by the selection in rifles, but our professional military grade instructors looked flat out horrified at the sight of the AR-style

black rifles. In effect, where were the turn-bolt, sniper-class long-range tools?

With rifles at the ready, spotters in position and instructors covering everyone, the first rounds went downrange at the 500-yard warm-up steel targets. But with the M&P 10's Russian-designed 5R coated rifling, the outstanding barrel-to-receiver match, and the Huskemaw Optics 3x12LR optic system with custom elevation turret and Best Of The West style windage adjustments in the reticle, nothing but the slap of bullets on steel was returned from downrange. The rifle's sights were calibrated exactly for the elevation adjustments required of the Hornady .308 168-grain Match A-Max cartridge, and simply turning the elevation turret to the exact range indicated by the spotter put bullets on steel with ease. Shooters with very sharp skills regarding long-range shooting were able to place bullets out to 1,000 yards into sub-MOA groups. All this from a standard .308 rifle built as an out-of-the-box system from Smith & Wesson.

It can be stated that two days of shooting does not make an evaluation complete. One of the M&P 10's came home

with me to enter its rightful place in the gun vault. Now, a real extended test of the rifle's ability to face the local conditions of a western South Dakota winter would come to light, and a complete overview of the new AR-LR .308 rifle would be pressed toward full volition.

Smith & Wesson's M&P 10 as chambered in the .308 Winchester 7.62x51 NATO is above all a fully developed military/police niche rifle. Not that it can't handle sport shooting, whether big game or varmints, but the rifle is designed with a dual set of receiver controls that allow complete function from the right or left side of the receiver. With the cartridge assist still located on the right side of the receiver the rifle is not completely ambidextrous, but the design is about as close as it gets in this department.

Making use of the 4140 steel barrel with that 5R rifling, the accuracy of this .30 caliber is excellent. I won't say that the rifle I tested back in Dakota always shot sub-MOA groups, but for the most part the loads listed in the accompanying table illustrate that the rifle is in the ballpark of the military M110 assault/sniper rifle. Chamber tolerances were

Results on the 1,000-yard steel targets. Note the tight groups on some targets. The one on the upper right is sub-MOA.

The shooters show off their 900-yard steel results at the NRA long-range school in Utah. The M&P 10 made short work of these targets.

Cold weather testing the M&P 10. The rifle never failed the author down to 16 degrees Fahrenheit. However, as dressed, the rifle has started to feel more like a Russian Dragunov PSL-54C.

so tight that at one point when group-shooting U.S. Army Camp Perry match ammunition I had an unfired case freeze in the chamber that required a rather complicated extraction be undertaken. That means that the M&P is built very close in terms of chamber dimensions, but other than that single round, everything else I fired ran with ease.

The rifle I tested was set up with Magpul stocks, whereas the over-the-counter rifle retains the standard six-position CAR stock and standard fore-end furniture, so there was some handling difference to be sure. When the M&P 10 reached me it was quickly fitted with a Dakota Silencer "can", and an aftermarket fore-end grip. Again, weight and balance changed with these modifications. The overall weight of the factory standard rifle comes in at 7.71 pounds, while the aftermarket additions brought its weight up to almost 13 pounds, and that makes it a static shooting system.

Torture testing of this rifle consisted of stressing the 9310 steel bolt and hard chrome firing pin in terms of their fail points when lacking any general maintenance. The .308/7.62 NATO round, being much larger then the AR-15 5.56 NATO,

LOAD	SMALLEST (INCH)	LARGEST (INCH)
Hornady Match Superformance: 178-grain BTHP	.478	1.124
Lake City Government M 852, 168-grain BTHP	.903	1.211
Winchester Power Max Bonded: 150 grain	1.330	1.509
HPR S.P. 150 grain	1.426	N/A*
Winchester Ballistic Silver Tip 168 grain	.760	N/A*
Hornady 168-grain Match A-Max	.685	.960
Norma Manual: 168-grain Sierra MK N-201	1.04	1.205
Norma 165-grain ORYX N-202	1.406	N/A*

* None recorded.

All measurements were based on three-shot groups.

Wind:	0-5 mph 30/following percent left to right.
Temperature:	45 degrees Fahrenheit
Elevation:	3,000 feet above sea level
Rest:	Bench
Range:	100 yards

tends to fowl gas systems, chambers and all related receiver parts very quickly due to the increased amount of powder used in the larger cartridge. This became clear at about the 200-round point when the M&P 10 flipped a few spent cases end around and stove piped them, requiring a magazine dump to clear the jam. Case conditions also turned quickly to totally black carbon covered brass, and an unusual amount of residual burn (white smoke) that also took place when the bolt remained open even during single-round firing. In effect, I had almost shut down the M&P 10 in terms of being a reliable operating system. That stated, however, the rifle never did fail to fire regardless of how fowled the receiver group was.

As offered in the box, the Smith & Wesson M&P 10 has a heavy 6.5-pound trigger pull according to my Timney trigger scale. These are military and police specifications, and when shot in Utah during the NRA long-range school program, I didn't give that trigger weight much consideration at all. While working with instructors, spotter partners,

Jim Smith (right) and Brock Gasper warming up for a calling contest and looking over the suppressed M&P 10 as tested by the author. The system got high marks from these coyote hunting professionals.

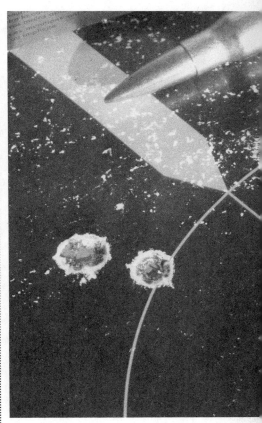

A sub-MOA group at 100 yards. Note that two bullets went into the same hole. This happened often with high-grade ammunition.

altitude adjustments from 4,000 to 10,000 feet, and almost every kind of weather and temperature range you can think of (including an oncoming hail storm at 10,000 feet that walked straight through our 800-yard targets during firing), triggers come in a distant second on the list of considered downrange issues. However, back in South Dakota and on the bench rest with time to burn, and minor details all settled out, trigger control got to be a serious issue. Now, that 6.5-pound pull weight felt like a tow truck cable being pulled when trying to settle in and shoot benchrest-level accuracy groups at 100 yards.

Shooting a series of groups based on several brands, bullet types and weights, the overall performance of the rifle was, as previously indicated, within limits we would associate with a single MOA grouping rifle. However, the M&P 10 definitely had its preferred go-to loads. Shooting Hornady 178-grain Match ammunition the rifle shot single-hole two shots out of three-round 100-yard groups. The last shot was a stringer that measured a total group size of .475 inch. I can't say that shooting those groups was easy, but with more luck than skill based on that heavy trigger, I did manage to get it done.

Shooting some remanufactured 150-grain SP loads produced about a rough minute-of-deer accuracy. The Hornady 168-grain A-Max stood tall, as had been the case in Utah, and like the company's Match 178's, tended to drill single-hole two-shot impact points quite often. Again, as set up, this is the go-to round for the rifle based on both accuracy and its applied sight system. Future aftermarket applications will include a Timney fully adjustable target trigger of a single-stage type.

Predator hunting is a popular field application for the M&P 10, as shown with this coyote.

M&P 10 / MULTI-USE HIGH-POWER RIFLE

SPECIFICATIONS

CALIBER:	.308 Win./7.62x51 NATO
ACTION:	Gas-operated semiautomatic
CAPACITY:	five or 20-round magazine
BARREL LENGTH:	18 inches
BARREL TWIST:	1-in-10-inch 5R rifling
TRIGGER PULL WEIGHT:	6.15 pounds
GRIP:	Synthetic
STOCK:	Six-position CAR
OVERALL LENGTH:	40.9 inches
WEIGHT:	7.71 pounds
BARREL MATERIAL:	4140 Steel
UPPER/LOWER MATERIAL:	7075 T6 Aluminum
FINISH:	Matte Black
MAGAZINE RELEASE, BOLT CATCH:	Ambidextrous
SAFETY:	Reversible ambidextrous
MSRP:	$1,619

Tom Hanson with a nice 5x5-plus mule deer taken in the river hills of South Dakota. From steel long-range targets to game at responsible ranges – this rifle works.

Based on the fact that the rifle's weight was elevated a bit, all of its field applications were directed to still-hunting tactics. A better alternative would be to locate a good position for deer or varmints and stay still for long periods of time. During five weeks of general field use the M&P 10 never displayed any element of failure. The double set of controls was often a real nice feature to have, especially when the rifle was over a set of sticks, then set in place for a shot that demanded as little shooter movement as possible, such as with coyotes. With the addition of the suppressor the rifle became muzzle heavy, but this was an aid when

A variety of ammunition was tested during the rifle's review period. Here is a small sample that went downrange.

settling in for long-range shots. Just like at the NRA Utah shoot, I applied the rifle to some medium-range 200- through 600-yard steel back home in South Dakota with very positive results – as would be expected. The following is a complete overview of the rifle accuracy performance with a variety of ammunition based on benchrest shooting for groups.

With all of the current LAR receiver ARs that are built of quality materials, shoot well and cost upward of $2,000 to $4,000, the Smith & Wesson M&P 10 is a solid buy with a current MSRP of $1,619. At this price you can afford to tack on a workable scope for long-range shooting, change out the front or rear furniture, or tack on any number of other LAR/AR options. Remove the add-on elements and stay with an ACOG sight, standard factory stock and five-round magazine and you have a perfect walking/long-range varmint and deer rifle. Upgrade the sights and some special extras and the rifle turns into a tack-driving, long-range gunning system. Flexibility and performance are the key to this rifle's success.

RUGER'S .45/
.45 Redhawk

A Double Duty Redhawk that handles both the .45 ACP and .45 Colt

BY Dick Williams

GARRETT CARTRIDGES OF TEXAS
45 LFR +P HAMMERHEADS
365-gr SuperHardCast Hammerhead
UNSAFE/DO NOT FIRE IN ANY REVOLVER CHAMBERED IN .410/45COLT
1250-fps 7.5" 1.735 O.A.L.
ONLY RECOMMENDED FOR: RUGER LARGE FRAME REVOLVERS CHAMBERED FOR 45 COLT

TEST FIRE

450 SMC
255gr SWC Hardcast
1030fps / 5.0" 1911
601 ft/lbs ENERGY

The new Redhawk .45/.45 sets two new standards for double-action revolvers; it's the first gun to chamber both .45 ACP and .45 Colt in the same cylinder, and it will handle the most powerful loads in both calibers. And all of this in an easily carried 4-inch barrel handgun.

Like many of today's shooters, I spent part of my youth reading gun magazines. As I read more and acquired some knowledge of handgun history, the year 1873 struck me as the most interesting time of the 19th century. Admittedly, movies and TV Westerns fueled my enthusiasm (if not my education), but I absorbed two undeniable facts. First, in 1873 Colt introduced the most beautiful revolver of all time, and second, the gun was chambered in the most effective fight-stopping caliber of all time, the .45. What made my facts undeniable was the U.S. Army's selection of both the gun and cartridge as the new standard issue sidearm. Commercial sales soared as the civilian population wanted to have both the gun and the caliber. Those settling the western frontier were especially fond of the .45 for its decisive fight-stopping abilities.

However, sometime during the next 20 years, the real soldiers must have been replaced by political appointees and accountants because the .45 cartridge was replaced by a smaller caliber, the .38 Long Colt. This foolishness lasted until a fight broke out in the Philippines and Americans suffered numerous casualties inflicted by men who had been shot multiple times, but remained unimpressed. Both gun and cartridge were re-issued. Since serious handgun ammo development efforts and terminal ballistic research studies were still in the future, the heavy, large-diameter lead bullet remained supreme in personal conflict resolution.

By 1911, military organizations around the world were acknowledging the enhanced efficiencies of smokeless powder and the advantages of semiauto pistols. The U.S. Army officially adopted John Browning's more compact 1911 pistol chambering the rimless .45 ACP round, a shorter case than the old Colt cartridge but still firing a .45-caliber bullet. When World War I erupted and America finally decided to participate, there weren't enough 1911s on hand for all of our troops, so our major handgun manufacturers started producing .45 ACP versions of their large-frame revolvers. The .45 ACP ammo had to be contained in half moon clips that would allow proper ejection of fired rounds and a quick reload of fresh ammo. Once again, it came as no surprise to anyone that at war's end Americans wanted the weapons their doughboys had used in the quest to preserve freedom. Popularity of the large revolvers was further boosted when the government sold many of the Army issue revolvers as surplus material.

There was one problem with the .45 ACP revolvers. Inserting loaded ammo into and removing empty ACP cases from the half moon clips was not an easy task, with the clips frequently getting bent and becoming unusable.

This was particularly a problem for civilians who did not have Army financed convoys providing resupply of preloaded clips. So in the early 1920s, ammo manufacturers developed and produced the Auto Rim cartridge, which is basically a .45 ACP case with a rim thickness equal to the combined thickness of the ACP rim and the half moon clip. The old revolvers could not distinguish between three loose AR rounds and three ACP rounds in a half moon clip. The new .45-caliber round worked perfectly in the surplus Colt and S&W revolvers and basically matched the performance level of the original ACP load. In addition, one fired AR round could be replaced by a fresh single AR round rather than having to replace three ACP rounds at a time. Perhaps this was the official birth of the "tactical reload." Three decades later, S&W's introduction of the stronger Models 1950 and 1955 allowed the use of more powerful Auto Rim loads,

although case capacity was still limited by the short (less than .9 inch long) case.

As it sometimes does, time plodded (rather than flew) forward for six decades to 2015 when Ruger made some modifications to its incredibly robust Redhawk revolver. This fully magnum-compliant stainless steel workhorse is capable of handling both .45 ACP ammo (in Ruger's full moon clips), plus some exotic magnum performance .45 Colt rounds featuring bullets weighing up to 400 grains.

Given the amount of metal used to build the Redhawk, there was never a question about whether the gun could handle serious magnum performance. Now, firing conventional ACP ammunition in the big sixshooter felt more like firing a smaller magnum. With its heavy, 4.2-inch long barrel, large machined frame and 1.78-inch diameter six-shot cylinder, the Redhawk is an impressive stainless steel revolver. A crane lock in front of the cylinder provides additional lock-up strength to the big double action, yet the small, rounded grip frame and nicely fitted grip panels allow one to carry the Redhawk comfortably, and with easy access under an outer jacket or vest. The adjustable rear sight and dovetail-mounted front sight with red insert are quite functional

for both precise long-range shooting and fast acquisition for close encounters of the dangerous kind, including any threats occurring in low-light conditions. You can fire the revolver either single or double action, your choice, as required by circumstances.

As you would expect, the Redhawk's cylinder, which was designed to handle .44 Magnum and heavy .45 Colt loads, is much longer than those on the older, dual-caliber revolvers that fired both .45 ACP and Auto Rim rounds. Also, the extractor face has been modified and is thinner than those on the regular Ruger Redhawks. The new Redhawk will handle both ACPs in Ruger's new full moon clips and individual rounds, but the cylinder will not close on the thicker rims of AR ammo. Due to the slightly different shape of the Redhawk's extractor face, neither can you use the existing full moon clips that were originally designed for the older S&W revolvers years ago. Bear in mind the Auto Rim round was designed to fit in existing revolvers chambered for the equally short ACP round, whereas the Redhawk revolver was designed for .44 Magnums and Colt rounds and had to be modified to accept the short, rimless ACP ammo. The end result is a pretty good trade; you can shoot

With accessories like Elzetta's powerful handheld flashlight and a durable Ruger knife from CRKT, a Redhawk loaded with .45 ACP rounds provides all the right tools for urban social calls. A box of heavyweight Garret loads rounds out your ensemble so that you're properly dressed for all occasions.

Like the .45 ACP cases, the rims of the .45 Colt rounds protrude slightly from the cylinder.

Ruger Redhawk .45 ACP/.45 Colt Velocities

Garrett Cartridges of TX		
.45 Colt	265 grains	Hard Cast: AV = 947 fps
.45 Colt	365 grains	Hard Cast: AV = 1056 fps
.45 Colt	405 grains	Hard Cast: AV = 1,146 fps
.45 Colt	Buffalo Bore 255 grains	Keith Cast: AV = 965 fps
.45 Colt	DoubleTap 255 grains	Cast: AV = 776 fps
.45 Colt	Winchester 250-grain lead	Cowboy: AV = 633 fps
.45 Colt with 6 grains of TiteGroup	255-grain lead	SWC: AV = 764 fps
.45 ACP	230 grains	Ball: AV = 684 fps

The extractor on the new Redhawk has been relieved enough that the special Ruger moon clips slide into the cylinder – but the .45 ACP cases protrude slightly.

one of the world's most popular defense rounds in either gun, but with the Redhawk you have a power option well beyond anything that can be managed in the shorter cylinder revolvers.

Rifling twist rate in the new Redhawk is 1-in-16, which is much faster than the 1-in-24 rate in the Super Redhawk and Super Blackhawk Bisley. This permits the use and stabilization of heavier weight bullets like 400-grain slugs that can be driven at velocities generating power levels comparable to those delivered by the original '70 Trapdoor Springfield.

Since Garrett Cartridges of Texas now offers three different loads of Colt ammunition and is known for heavy, hard-cast, deep-penetrating bullets, I decided to take one of their loads pig hunting. Unfortunately as I've aged, I'm not the stud I used to be, and my tolerance for recoil has dramatically diminished. Using the Redhawk as delivered with the small, concealable wood grips, I couldn't handle the recoil generated by the heavier bullets, so I settled on the 265-grain load for my pig hunt. In fact, most of my big-bore shooting and hunting is now done with slightly heavy-for-caliber hardcast bullets with a muzzle velocity of somewhere around 1,000 fps. With bigger, softer grips

An older model Redhawk (top) chambered in .45 Colt served as the inspiration for Garrett's heavy bullet loads. They work equally well in the newer, dual-purpose Redhawk (bottom).

on the Redhawk, I might be able to manage Garrett's 365- and 400-grain Colt loads, but keep in mind the new Ruger is a dual-purpose revolver, and the smaller grip frame makes it easier to manage and conceal in a defensive situation where ACP ammo will most likely be used. Velocities of the Garrett ammunition and some other heavy Colt loads are shown in the table at left.

The heavyweight Garrett loads (365- and 405-grain bullets) fill the space in the Redhawk's long cylinder and make you appreciate the revolver's mass when you pull the trigger. These loads are designed for large, dangerous game animals or any situation where deep penetration is required.

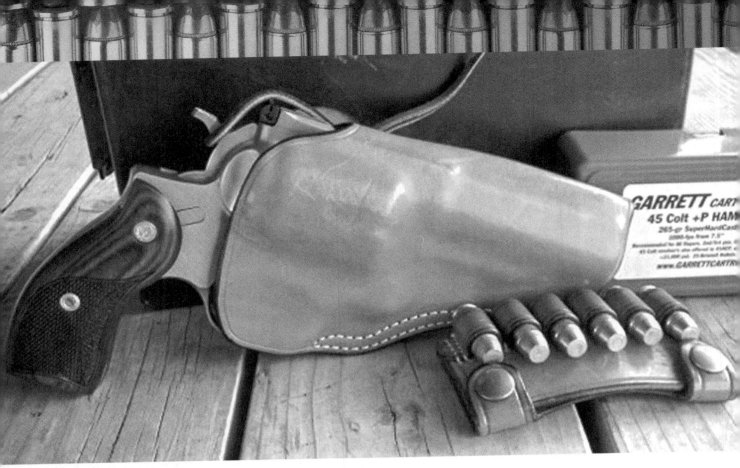

The author doesn't think of the Redhawk as a concealed carry handgun, but with a proper holster and spare cartridge carrier from Rafter-L Combat Leather, there's no need to advertise the gun's presence unless you want to. A loose shirt or lightweight jacket easily keeps the entire rig hidden.

A general-purpose round adequate for almost every occasion is Garrett's 265-grain hardcast bullet. There's little it won't penetrate, but recoil is considerably reduced, something you might appreciate with the revolver's small grip.

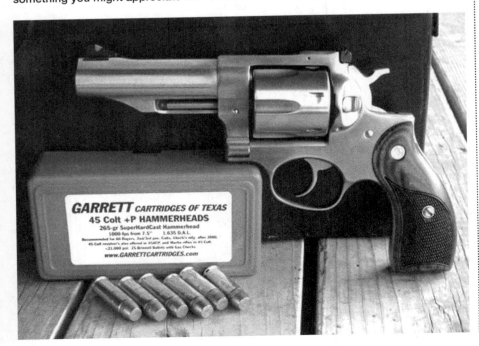

On a visit to the Chain Ranch in Oklahoma I did get an opportunity at a nasty looking boar just before sunset. I was set up in one of the Chain's blinds in late afternoon with one of Garrett's 265-grain hardcast loads. The 250-pound old boar came sniffing his way slowly through the heavy brush with just a few minutes of light remaining in the day. He had some pretty good gristle plate "armor" running from the front shoulders back to his flanks, and had added another protective layer of caked mud to much of his body. His mistake was pausing in a small opening in the midst of the thick cover briefly offering a clear broadside shot. At 35 yards, the 265-grain hardcast Garrett bullet penetrated both shoulders and exited the far side leaving an impressive hole clear through the chest area. He didn't go far before dropping.

If for any reason you don't want or need the extra-heavy Colt bullets, there are plenty of excellent cast bullet loads (in both ACP and AR) suitable for pig hunting. Check the ammo listings from Double Tap, Buffalo Bore and CorBon to see what's being offered for the smaller, defensive caliber in your new Ruger Redhawk .45 ACP/.45 Colt or older S&W .45 ACP/.45 AR. The old ACP-size round may still have a few surprises for you.

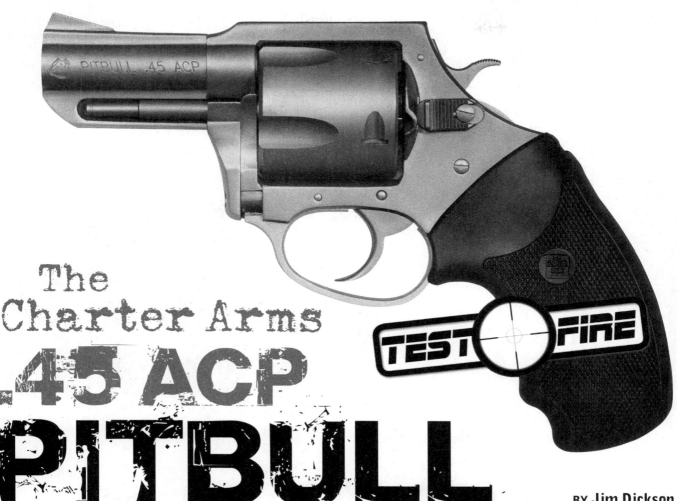

The Charter Arms .45 ACP PITBULL

BY **Jim Dickson**

The long-awaited Charter Arms .45 ACP version of their popular Bulldog series is finally here. Dubbed the Pitbull, it is a pocket revolver that can also do double-duty as a regular service revolver.

When I first picked up the Pitbull at David's Gunroom in Norcross, Ga. I was immediately impressed with it's steadiness in the hand and the exquisite trigger pull in both double action and single action. The molded rubber grips locked into the hand and the full shroud around the ejector rod added sufficient weight to the 2½-inch barrel to provide steadiness. Here was a gun meant to be shot – and shot accurately. Balance and pointing were all that you could desire, and the sights were rugged and well pronounced. The hammer spur was in perfect relationship to the grips for easy cocking for single-action fire, and the gun had little tendency

to want to move in fast double-action fire. The stainless steel pistol is glass beaded to a nice Confederate Gray color that won't catch light like a polished stainless finish will.

A lot of people these days are buying .45 Colt revolvers with long cylinders that can take a .410 shotgun shell. That's fine if you want to shoot snakes, but if you are looking for something to stop man or beast you had better load up with .45s. The FMJ .45 ACP has never been found lacking in stopping power, and has the penetration you need to get through cover in a gunfight or reach the vitals of a big bear or wild hog. You won't catch me shooting a grizzly with a .410 buckshot load, but when Betty and I had Alaskan trappers licenses years ago we found that M1911A1 .45 automatics loaded with G.I. ball ammo would kill anything in the Alaskan interior quickly, and there were no shots outside of close pistol range in that thick bush country.

The Pitbull is one of the smallest bear stoppers you can carry and it is more than adequate providing you stick to FMJ ammo so you have the penetration you need. If you don't want .410 birdshot shells for snakes you have an awful long, heavy cylinder on those .45/.410 revolvers, making the gun heavier and hard to conceal for nothing in return. I would rather have that extra length applied to the barrel's length.

The heart of the .45 ACP Pitbull are the extractors that snap into the groove of the rimless case the same way the extractors do on a double rifle made for a rimless case. This enables you to use the rimless .45 ACP without resorting to half moon or full moon clips. These clips have never been made for a five-shot revolver like this one anyway. You will encounter a slight resistance when loading the cylinder as you push the cartridges past the extractor, but unloading is like any other revolver.

With an overall length of 7.3 inches and a height of 5.2 inches the Pitbull is a true pocket pistol, easily riding in an inside-the-pants or an inside-the-waistband holster. It will even ride in the pocket of a T-shirt, though its 22-ounce weight makes it push the pocket out too much. Charter Arms also sells a fine molded pancake holster for it made by the famed holster maker DeSantis. It is very concealable and enables the Pitbull to fill the role of a service revolver as well as a pocket pistol. Like all tightly molded holsters it is highly resistant to having someone else snatch it from your holster, as it only wants to come out one way – and not at an angle. This holster's gun-retention feature is highly prized by some law enforcement officers. For those who want to be able to draw the gun out at any angle, El Paso Saddlery makes a pancake holster, called the Double Duty, that is not so tightly molded, enabling the gun to be easily

DeSantis makes a fine pancake holster for the Pitbull. It is molded to fit the gun and is highly resistant to allowing someone else to snatch the gun from the holster.

The Pitbull's extractors snap into the groove of the rimless .45 ACP case, negating the use of half moon or full moon clips. Charter Arms has patented the extractor system.

INSTINCT SHOOTING

To hit accurately with fast double-action fire you need to master instinct shooting. You must learn to fix your eyes on the target, ignoring the gun and it's sights as you point the gun at the target. Do not look at the gun or think about what you are doing. Just look, point and pull the trigger. To learn to hit this way, lay a row of matchsticks or spent .22 cases out as far away as you can easily see them. Strict form is important while learning, but not necessary after you have mastered the art. Begin by assuming the classic duelist's stance with your body sideways to the target. This also presents the smallest possible target for return fire. Extend the arm fully with wrist and elbow straight. Lay your chin against your shoulder and look at the target intently – ignoring the gun that you have fully extended and pointing at what you are looking at. Fire at each matchstick or .22 shell in turn. If you miss one keep going or you will just miss again in the same spot. You will soon get the hang of it.

drawn under all conditions. That's important for men like me who tend to drag the gun out of the holster.

The Pitbull is everything you want a pocket revolver to be, and best of all it is in a true manstopper caliber. Now, here is a handgun powerful enough to do the job in such a small, light package that no one has any excuse to leave it behind. With a manufacturers suggested retail price of only $489 – most everyone could afford it. When violence threatens, this is the cheapest life insurance you can buy.

It is very important that you carry a gun that you can hit with. Too many guns are chosen just because they are light and easy to carry. Most everyone buying a modern version of the old Remington double derringer accepts that it is only a belly gun for point blank range, but the modern crop of ultralight, polymer-frame, double-action-only, small-caliber automatics are a lot harder to hit with than even the old fashioned double derringer. They task an expert at any range beyond point blank and are impossible for the average shooter to hit with at any distance. Having an accurate, easy-to-shoot weapon can save your life. Remember that if an assailant is close he can be on you in the blink of an eye. Having a gun that you can't hit with while your enemy is still out of reach puts you in a very dangerous position. This is a gun you can hit with and it has five shots, only one of which is required per attacker. This is critical in a gunfight because if you have to put two shots or more in each attacker and you have multiple attackers, one will either shoot you or reach you before you can get to him. That's just one more way a small caliber can get you killed. One hit in the vitals with a .45 ACP FMJ and the job is done. You can move on to the next one without waiting to observe the effect of your slug. This is how you stay alive in a gunfight against multiple opponents.

The .45 ACP Pitbull was extensively test fired with the following ammo:

- 100 rounds of Black Hills 230-grain FMJ

The author fired almost 1,500 rounds through the Pitbull from a wide variety of ammunition manufacturers.

- 100 rounds of Black Hills 230-grain JHP
- 20 rounds CorBon 160-grain DPX @ 1,095 fps
- 40 rounds of Barnes 185-grain TAC-XPD +P
- 200 rounds of Federal Premium 230-grain FMJ
- 100 rounds of Federal Premium 185-grain SWC
- 80 rounds Hornady 185-grain FTX Critical Defense
- 80 rounds Hornady 185-grain XTP
- 170 rounds of Winchester Train & Defend 230-grain JHP
- 100 rounds of Aguila 230-grain FMJ
- 500 rounds of Armscor 230-grain FMJ

That's a total of 1,490 rounds fired through the little gun. Like all light-weight, powerful pistols the 22-ounce Pitbull has a sharp recoil, but not enough to prevent accurate and fast double-action fire. The best groups at 25 yards were 2 inches, with some groups going 3 to 4 inches in rapid double-action fire as fatigue set in. If the sharp recoil bothers you try a trick I learned years ago when dealing with heavy kicking pistols. Put

on a deerskin driving glove. End of problem. Just try it, never mind the theory, and you will see it works.

For a house pistol the Pitbull is hard to beat. It is light enough for any family member to easily use. Revolvers are often chosen for this role because there is nothing more required in an emergency than to point and pull the trigger. Police preferred the revolver as long as "bring 'em back alive" was the order of the day, since the long double-action trigger pull was less likely to go off accidentally when holding a gun on a suspect than a light single-action trigger pull on an automatic. This safety feature can be more or less important depending on which member of the family has to grab the pistol in an emergency.

As a carry pistol its light weight may help ensure that you always have it on you. I know a man who left his gun at home because he was only going to the convenience store around the corner. A robber was just coming out as he arrived and the robber shot him. He survived but hasn't left his pistol at home since. That's a tough way to learn.

Anyone looking for a powerful, compact, easy to carry and easy to hit with double-action revolver will be well served by the Pitbull. If you need more than its five shots it's time for something with a 20- or 30-shot magazine, not a handgun.

Many manufacturers do not supply suggested retail prices. Others did not get their pricing to us before press time. All pricing can vary dependent on the exact brand and style of ammo selected and/or the retail outlet from which you make your purchase. Pricing has been rounded to the nearest dollar and represents our best estimate of average pricing. An * after the cartridge means these loads are available with Nosler Partition or Swift A-Frame bullets. Listed pricing may or may not reflect this bullet type. ** = these are packed 50 to box, all others are 20 to box. Wea. Mag.= Weatherby Magnum. Spfd. = Springfield. A-Sq. = A-Square. N.E.=Nitro Express.

Cartridge	Bullet Wgt. Grs.	VELOCITY (fps)					ENERGY (ft. lbs.)					TRAJ. (in.)				Est. Price/box
		Muzzle	100 yds.	200 yds.	300 yds.	400 yds.	Muzzle	100 yds.	200 yds.	300 yds.	400 yds.	100 yds.	200 yds.	300 yds.	400 yds.	
17, 22																
17 Hornet	15.5	3860	2924	2159	1531	1108	513	294	160	81	42	1.4	0.0	-9.1	-33.7	NA
17 Hornet	20	3650	3078	2574	2122	1721	592	421	294	200	131	1.10	0.0	-6.4	-20.6	NA
17 Remington Fireball	20	4000	3380	2840	2360	1930	710	507	358	247	165	1.6	1.5	-2.8	-13.5	NA
17 Remington Fireball	25	3850	3280	2780	2330	1925	823	597	429	301	206	0.9	0.0	-5.4	NA	NA
17 Remington	20	4200	3544	2978	2477	2029	783	558	394	272	183	0	-1.3	-6.6	-17.6	NA
17 Remington	25	4040	3284	2644	2086	1606	906	599	388	242	143	+2.0	+1.7	-4.0	-17.0	$17
4.6x30 H&K	30	2025	1662	1358	1135	1002	273	184	122	85	66	0	-12.7	-44.5	—	NA
4.6x30 H&K	40	1900	1569	1297	1104	988	320	218	149	108	86	0	-14.3	-39.3	—	NA
204 Ruger (Hor)	24	4400	3667	3046	2504	2023	1032	717	494	334	218	0.6	0	-4.3	-14.3	NA
204 Ruger (Fed)	32 Green	4030	3320	2710	2170	1710	1155	780	520	335	205	0.9	0.0	-5.7	-19.1	NA
204 Ruger	32	4125	3559	3061	2616	2212	1209	900	666	486	348	0	-1.3	-6.3	—	NA
204 Ruger	32	4225	3632	3114	2652	2234	1268	937	689	500	355	.6	0.0	-4.2	-13.4	NA
204 Ruger	40	3900	3451	3046	2677	2336	1351	1058	824	636	485	.7	0.0	-4.5	-13.9	NA
204 Ruger	45	3625	3188	2792	2428	2093	1313	1015	778	589	438	1.0	0.0	-5.5	-16.9	NA
5.45x39mm	60	2810	2495	2201	1927	1677	1052	829	645	445	374	1.0	0.0	-9.2	-27.7	NA
221 Fireball	40	3100	2510	1991	1547	1209	853	559	352	212	129	0	-4.1	-17.3	-45.1	NA
221 Fireball	50	2800	2137	1580	1180	988	870	507	277	155	109	+0.0	-7.0	-28.0	0.0	$14
22 Hornet (Fed)	30 Green	3150	2150	1390	990	830	660	310	130	65	45	0.0	-6.6	-32.7	NA	NA
22 Hornet	34	3050	2132	1415	1017	852	700	343	151	78	55	+0.0	-6.6	-15.5	-29.9	NA
22 Hornet	35	3100	2278	1601	1135	929	747	403	199	100	67	+2.75	0.0	-16.9	-60.4	NA
22 Hornet	40	2800	2397	2029	1698	1413	696	510	366	256	177	0	-4.6	-17.8	-43.1	NA
22 Hornet	45	2690	2042	1502	1128	948	723	417	225	127	90	+0.0	-7.7	-31.0	0.0	$27**
218 Bee	46	2760	2102	1550	1155	961	788	451	245	136	94	+0.0	-7.2	-29.0	0.0	$46**
222 Rem.	35	3760	3125	2574	2085	1656	1099	759	515	338	213	1.0	0.0	-6.3	-20.8	NA
222 Rem.	50	3345	2930	2553	2205	1886	1242	953	723	540	395	1.3	0	-6.7	-20.6	NA
222 Remington	40	3600	3117	2673	2269	1911	1151	863	634	457	324	+1.07	0.0	-6.13	-18.9	NA
222 Remington	50	3140	2602	2123	1700	1350	1094	752	500	321	202	+2.0	-0.4	-11.0	-33.0	$11
222 Remington	55	3020	2562	2147	1773	1451	1114	801	563	384	257	+2.0	-0.4	-11.0	-33.0	$12
222 Rem. Mag.	40	3600	3140	2726	2347	2000	1150	876	660	489	355	1.0	0	-5.7	-17.8	NA
222 Rem. Mag.	50	3340	2917	2533	2179	1855	1238	945	712	527	382	1.3	0	-6.8	-20.9	NA
222 Rem. Mag.	55	3240	2748	2305	1906	1556	1282	922	649	444	296	+2.0	-0.2	-9.0	-27.0	$14
22 PPC	52	3400	2930	2510	2130	NA	1335	990	730	525	NA	+2.0	1.4	-5.0	0.0	NA
223 Rem.	35	3750	3206	2725	2291	1899	1092	799	577	408	280	1.0	0	-5.7	-18.1	NA
223 Rem.	35	4000	3353	2796	2302	1861	1243	874	607	412	269	0.8	0	-5.3	-17.3	NA
223 Rem.	64	2750	2368	2018	1701	1427	1074	796	578	411	289	2.4	0	-11	-34.1	NA
223 Rem.	75	2790	2562	2345	2139	1943	1296	1093	916	762	629	1.5	0	-8.2	-24.1	NA
223 Remington	40	3650	3010	2450	1950	1530	1185	805	535	340	265	+2.0	+1.0	-6.0	-22.0	$14
223 Remington	40	3800	3305	2845	2424	2044	1282	970	719	522	371	0.84	0.0	-5.34	-16.6	NA
223 Remington (Rem)	45 Green	3550	2911	2355	1865	1451	1259	847	554	347	210	2.5	2.3	-4.3	-21.1	NA
223 Remington	50	3300	2874	2484	2130	1809	1209	917	685	504	363	1.37	0.0	-7.05	-21.8	NA
223 Remington	52/53	3330	2882	2477	2106	1770	1305	978	722	522	369	+2.0	+0.6	-6.5	-21.5	$14
223 Remington (Win)	55 Green	3240	2747	2304	1905	1554	1282	921	648	443	295	1.9	0.0	-8.5	-26.7	NA
223 Remington	55	3240	2748	2305	1906	1556	1282	922	649	444	296	+2.0	-0.2	-9.0	-27.0	$12
223 Remington	60	3100	2712	2355	2026	1726	1280	979	739	547	397	+2.0	+0.2	-8.0	-24.7	$16
223 Remington	62	3000	2700	2410	2150	1900	1240	1000	800	635	495	1.60	0.0	-7.7	-22.8	NA
223 Remington	64	3020	2621	2256	1920	1619	1296	977	723	524	373	+2.0	-0.2	-9.3	-23.0	$14
223 Remington	69	3000	2720	2460	2210	1980	1380	1135	925	750	600	+2.0	+0.8	-5.8	-17.5	$15
223 Remington	75	2790	2554	2330	2119	1926	1296	1086	904	747	617	2.37	0.0	-8.75	-25.1	NA
223 Rem. Super Match	75	2930	2694	2470	2257	2055	1429	1209	1016	848	703	1.20	0.0	-6.9	-20.7	NA
223 Remington	77	2750	2584	2354	2169	1992	1293	1110	948	804	679	1.93	0.0	-8.2	-23.8	NA
223 WSSM	55	3850	3438	3064	2721	2402	1810	1444	1147	904	704	0.7	0.0	-4.4	-13.6	NA
223 WSSM	64	3600	3144	2732	2356	2011	1841	1404	1061	789	574	1.0	0.0	-5.7	-17.7	NA
5.56 NATO	55	3130	2740	2382	2051	1750	1196	917	693	514	372	1.1	0	-7.3	-23.0	NA
5.56 NATO	75	2910	2676	2543	2242	2041	1410	1192	1002	837	693	1.2	0	-7.0	-21.0	NA
224 Wea. Mag.	55	3650	3192	2780	2403	2057	1627	1244	943	705	516	+2.0	+1.2	-4.0	-17.0	$32
225 Winchester	55	3570	3066	2616	2208	1838	1556	1148	836	595	412	+2.0	+1.0	-5.0	-20.0	$19

Cartridge	Bullet Wgt. Grs.	VELOCITY (fps)					ENERGY (ft. lbs.)					TRAJ. (in.)				Est. Price/box
		Muzzle	100 yds.	200 yds.	300 yds.	400 yds.	Muzzle	100 yds.	200 yds.	300 yds.	400 yds.	100 yds.	200 yds.	300 yds.	400 yds.	
22-250 Rem.	35	4450	3736	3128	2598	2125	1539	1085	761	524	351	6.5	0	-4.1	-13.4	NA
22-250 Rem.	40	4000	3320	2720	2200	1740	1420	980	660	430	265	+2.0	+1.8	-3.0	-16.0	$14
22-250 Rem.	40	4150	3553	3033	2570	2151	1530	1121	817	587	411	0.6	0	-4.4	-14.2	NA
22-250 Rem.	45 Green	4000	3293	2690	2159	1696	1598	1084	723	466	287	1.7	1.7	-3.2	-15.7	NA
22-250 Rem.	50	3725	3264	2641	2455	2103	1540	1183	896	669	491	0.89	0.0	-5.23	-16.3	NA
22-250 Rem.	52/55	3680	3137	2656	2222	1832	1654	1201	861	603	410	+2.0	+1.3	-4.0	-17.0	$13
22-250 Rem.	60	3600	3195	2826	2485	2169	1727	1360	1064	823	627	+2.0	+2.0	-2.4	-12.3	$19
22-250 Rem.	64	3425	2988	2591	2228	1897	1667	1269	954	705	511	1.2	0	-6.4	-20.0	NA
220 Swift	40	4200	3678	3190	2739	2329	1566	1201	904	666	482	+0.51	0.0	-4.0	-12.9	NA
220 Swift	50	3780	3158	2617	2135	1710	1586	1107	760	506	325	+2.0	+1.4	-4.4	-17.9	$20
220 Swift	50	3850	3396	2970	2576	2215	1645	1280	979	736	545	0.74	0.0	-4.84	-15.1	NA
220 Swift	50	3900	3420	2990	2599	2240	1688	1298	992	750	557	0.7	0	-4.7	-14.5	NA
220 Swift	55	3800	3370	2990	2630	2310	1765	1390	1090	850	650	0.8	0.0	-4.7	-14.4	NA
220 Swift	55	3650	3194	2772	2384	2035	1627	1246	939	694	506	+2.0	+2.0	-2.6	-13.4	$19
220 Swift	60	3600	3199	2824	2475	2156	1727	1364	1063	816	619	+2.0	+1.6	-4.1	-13.1	$19
22 Savage H.P.	70	2868	2510	2179	1874	1600	1279	980	738	546	398	0	-4.1	-15.6	-37.1	NA
22 Savage H.P.	71	2790	2340	1930	1570	1280	1225	860	585	390	190	+2.0	-1.0	-10.4	-35.7	NA
6mm (24)																
6mm BR Rem.	100	2550	2310	2083	1870	1671	1444	1185	963	776	620	+2.5	-0.6	-11.8	0.0	$22
6mm Norma BR	107	2822	2667	2517	2372	2229	1893	1690	1506	1337	1181	+1.73	0.0	-7.24	-20.6	NA
6mm PPC	70	3140	2750	2400	2070	NA	1535	1175	895	665	NA	+2.0	+1.4	-5.0	0.0	NA
243 Winchester	55	4025	3597	3209	2853	2525	1978	1579	1257	994	779	+0.6	0.0	-4.0	-12.2	NA
243 Win.	58	3925	3465	3052	2676	2330	1984	1546	1200	922	699	0.7	0	-4.4	-13.8	NA
243 Winchester	60	3600	3110	2660	2260	1890	1725	1285	945	680	475	+2.0	+1.8	-3.3	-15.5	$17
243 Win.	70	3400	3020	2672	2350	2050	1797	1418	1110	858	653	0	-2.5	-9.7	—	NA
243 Winchester	70	3400	3040	2700	2390	2100	1795	1435	1135	890	685	1.1	0.0	-5.9	-18.0	NA
243 Winchester	75/80	3350	2955	2593	2259	1951	1993	1551	1194	906	676	+2.0	+0.9	-5.0	-19.0	$16
243 Win.	80	3425	3081	2763	2468	2190	2984	1686	1357	1082	852	1.1	0	-5.7	-17.1	NA
243 Win.	87	2800	2574	2359	2155	1961	1514	1280	1075	897	743	1.9	0	-8.1	-23.8	NA
243 Win.	95	3185	2908	2649	2404	2172	2140	1784	1480	1219	995	1.3	0	-6.3	-18.6	NA
243 W. Superformance	80	3425	3080	2760	2463	2184	2083	1684	1353	1077	847	1.1	0.0	-5.7	-17.1	NA
243 Winchester	85	3320	3070	2830	2600	2380	2080	1770	1510	1280	1070	+2.0	+1.2	-4.0	-14.0	$18
243 Winchester	90	3120	2871	2635	2411	2199	1946	1647	1388	1162	966	1.4	0.0	-6.4	-18.8	NA
243 Winchester*	100	2960	2697	2449	2215	1993	1945	1615	1332	1089	882	+2.5	+1.2	-6.0	-20.0	$16
243 Winchester	105	2920	2689	2470	2261	2062	1988	1686	1422	1192	992	+2.5	+1.6	-5.0	-18.4	$21
243 Light Mag.	100	3100	2839	2592	2358	2138	2133	1790	1491	1235	1014	+1.5	0.0	-6.8	-19.8	NA
243 WSSM	55	4060	3628	3237	2880	2550	2013	1607	1280	1013	794	0.6	0.0	-3.9	-12.0	NA
243 WSSM	95	3250	3000	2763	2538	2325	2258	1898	1610	1359	1140	1.2	0.0	-5.7	-16.9	NA
243 WSSM	100	3110	2838	2583	2341	2112	2147	1789	1481	1217	991	1.4	0.0	-6.6	-19.7	NA
6mm Remington	80	3470	3064	2694	2352	2036	2139	1667	1289	982	736	+2.0	+1.1	-5.0	-17.0	$16
6mm R. Superformance	95	3235	2955	2692	2443	3309	2207	1841	1528	1259	1028	1.2	0.0	-6.1	-18.0	NA
6mm Remington	100	3100	2829	2573	2332	2104	2133	1777	1470	1207	983	+2.5	+1.6	-5.0	-17.0	$16
6mm Remington	105	3060	2822	2596	2381	2177	2105	1788	1512	1270	1059	+2.5	+1.1	-3.3	-15.0	$21
240 Wea. Mag.	87	3500	3202	2924	2663	2416	2366	1980	1651	1370	1127	+2.0	+2.0	-2.0	-12.0	$32
240 Wea. Mag.	100	3150	2894	2653	2425	2207	2202	1860	1563	1395	1082	1.3	0	-6.3	-18.5	NA
240 Wea. Mag.	100	3395	3106	2835	2581	2339	2559	2142	1785	1478	1215	+2.5	+2.8	-2.0	-11.0	$43
25-20 Win.	86	1460	1194	1030	931	858	407	272	203	165	141	0.0	-23.5	0.0	0.0	$32**
25-45 Sharps	87	3000	2677	2385	2112	1859	1739	1384	1099	862	668	1.1	0	-7.4	-22.6	$25
25-35 Win.	117	2230	1866	1545	1282	1097	1292	904	620	427	313	+2.5	-4.2	-26.0	0.0	$24
250 Savage	100	2820	2504	2210	1936	1684	1765	1392	1084	832	630	+2.5	+0.4	-9.0	-28.0	$17
257 Roberts	100	2980	2661	2363	2085	1827	1972	1572	1240	965	741	+2.5	-0.8	-5.2	-21.6	$20
257 Roberts	122	2600	2331	2078	1842	1625	1831	1472	1169	919	715	+2.5	0.0	-10.6	-31.4	$21
257 Roberts+P	100	3000	2758	2529	2312	2105	1998	1689	1421	1187	984	1.5	0	-7.0	-20.5	NA
257 Roberts+P	117	2780	2411	2071	1761	1488	2009	1511	1115	806	576	+2.5	-0.2	-10.2	-32.6	$18
257 Roberts+P	120	2780	2560	2360	2160	1970	2060	1750	1480	1240	1030	+2.5	+1.2	-6.4	-23.6	$22
257 R. Superformance	117	2946	2705	2478	2265	2057	2253	1901	1595	1329	1099	1.1	0.0	-5.7	-17.1	NA
25-06 Rem.	87	3440	2995	2591	2222	1884	2286	1733	1297	954	686	+2.0	+1.1	-2.5	-14.4	$17
25-06 Rem.	90	3350	3001	2679	2378	2098	2243	1790	1434	1130	879	1.2	0	-6.0	-18.3	NA
25-06 Rem.	90	3440	3043	2680	2344	2034	2364	1850	1435	1098	827	+2.0	+1.8	-3.3	-15.6	$17
25-06 Rem.	100	3230	2893	2580	2287	2014	2316	1858	1478	1161	901	+2.0	+0.8	-5.7	-18.9	$17
25-06 Rem.	117	2990	2770	2570	2370	2190	2320	2000	1715	1465	1246	+2.5	+1.0	-7.9	-26.6	$19
25-06 Rem.*	120	2990	2730	2484	2252	2032	2382	1985	1644	1351	1100	+2.5	+1.2	-5.3	-19.6	$17

Cartridge	Bullet Wgt. Grs.	VELOCITY (fps)					ENERGY (ft. lbs.)					TRAJ. (in.)				Est. Price/box
		Muzzle	100 yds.	200 yds.	300 yds.	400 yds.	Muzzle	100 yds.	200 yds.	300 yds.	400 yds.	100 yds.	200 yds.	300 yds.	400 yds.	
25-06 Rem.	122	2930	2706	2492	2289	2095	2325	1983	1683	1419	1189	+2.5	+1.8	-4.5	-17.5	$23
25-06 R. Superformance	117	3110	2861	2626	2403	2191	2512	2127	1792	1500	1246	1.4	0.0	-6.4	-18.9	NA
25 WSSM	85	3470	3156	2863	2589	2331	2273	1880	1548	1266	1026	1.0	0.0	-5.2	-15.7	NA
25 WSSM	115	3060	2844	2639	2442	2254	2392	2066	1778	1523	1398	1.4	0.0	-6.4	-18.6	NA
25 WSSM	120	2990	2717	2459	2216	1987	2383	1967	1612	1309	1053	1.6	0.0	-7.4	-21.8	NA
257 Wea. Mag.	87	3825	3456	3118	2805	2513	2826	2308	1870	1520	1220	+2.0	+2.7	-0.3	-7.6	$32
257 Wea. Mag.	90	3550	3184	2848	2537	2246	2518	2026	1621	1286	1008	1.0	0	-5.3	-16.0	NA
257 Wea. Mag.	100	3555	3237	2941	2665	2404	2806	2326	1920	1576	1283	+2.5	+3.2	0.0	-8.0	$32
257 Wea. Mag.	110	3330	3069	2823	2591	2370	2708	2300	1947	1639	1372	1.1	0	-5.5	-16.1	NA
257 Scramjet	100	3745	3450	3173	2912	2666	3114	2643	2235	1883	1578	+2.1	+2.77	0.0	-6.93	NA
6.5																
6.5 Grendel	123	2590	2420	2256	2099	1948	1832	1599	1390	1203	1037	1.8	0	-8.6	-25.1	NA
6.5x47 Lapua	123	2887	NA	2554	NA	2244	2285	NA	1788	NA	1380	NA	4.53	0.0	-10.7	NA
6.5x50mm Jap.	139	2360	2160	1970	1790	1620	1720	1440	1195	985	810	+2.5	-1.0	-13.5	0.0	NA
6.5x50mm Jap.	156	2070	1830	1610	1430	1260	1475	1155	900	695	550	+2.5	-4.0	-23.8	0.0	NA
6.5x52mm Car.	139	2580	2360	2160	1970	1790	2045	1725	1440	1195	985	+2.5	0.0	-9.9	-29.0	NA
6.5x52mm Car.	156	2430	2170	1930	1700	1500	2045	1630	1285	1005	780	+2.5	-1.0	-13.9	0.0	NA
6.5x52mm Carcano	160	2250	1963	1700	1467	1271	1798	1369	1027	764	574	+3.8	0.0	-15.9	-48.1	NA
6.5x55mm Swe.	93	2625	2350	2090	1850	1630	1425	1140	905	705	550	2.4	0.0	-10.3	-31.1	NA
6.5x55mm Swe.	123	2750	2570	2400	2240	2080	2065	1810	1580	1370	1185	1.9	0.0	-7.9	-22.9	NA
6.5x55mm Swe.*	139/140	2850	2640	2440	2250	2070	2525	2170	1855	1575	1330	+2.5	+1.6	-5.4	-18.9	$18
6.5x55mm Swe.	140	2550	NA	NA	NA	NA	2020	NA	NA	NA	NA	0.0	0.0	0.0	0.0	$18
6.5x55mm Swe.	140	2735	2563	2397	2237	2084	2325	2041	1786	1556	1350	1.9	0	-8.0	-22.9	NA
6.5x55mm Swe.	156	2650	2370	2110	1870	1650	2425	1950	1550	1215	945	+2.5	0.0	-10.3	-30.6	NA
260 Rem.	100	3200	2917	2652	2402	2165	2273	1889	1561	1281	1041	1.3	0	-6.3	-18.6	NA
260 Rem.	130	2800	2613	2433	2261	2096	2262	1970	1709	1476	1268	1.8	0	-7.7	-22.2	NA
260 Remington	125	2875	2669	2473	2285	2105	2294	1977	1697	1449	1230	1.71	0.0	-7.4	-21.4	NA
260 Remington	140	2750	2544	2347	2158	1979	2351	2011	1712	1448	1217	+2.2	0.0	-8.6	-24.6	NA
6.5 Creedmoor	120	3020	2815	2619	2430	2251	2430	2111	1827	1574	1350	1.4	0.0	-6.5	-18.9	NA
6.5 Creedmoor	120	3050	2850	2659	2476	2300	2479	2164	1884	1634	1310	1.4	0	-6.3	-18.3	NA
6.5 Creedmoor	140	2550	2380	2217	2060	1910	2021	1761	1527	1319	1134	2.3	0	-9.4	-27.0	NA
6.5 Creedmoor	140	2710	2557	2410	2267	2129	2283	2033	1805	1598	1410	1.9	0	-7.9	-22.6	NA
6.5 Creedmoor	140	2820	2654	2494	2339	2190	2472	2179	1915	1679	1467	1.7	0.0	-7.2	-20.6	NA
6.5 C. Superformance	129	2950	2756	2570	2392	2221	2492	2175	1892	1639	1417	1.5	0.0	-6.8	-19.7	NA
6.5x52R	117	2208	1856	1544	1287	1104	1267	895	620	431	317	0	-8.7	-32.2	—	NA
6.5x57	131	2543	2295	2060	1841	1638	1882	1532	1235	986	780	0	-5.1	-18.5	-42.1	NA
6.5-284 Norma	142	3025	2890	2758	2631	2507	2886	2634	2400	2183	1982	1.13	0.0	-5.7	-16.4	NA
6.5-284 Norma	156	2790	2531	2287	2056	-	2697	2220	1812	1465	-	1.9	0	-8.6	-	NA
6.71 (264) Phantom	120	3150	2929	2718	2517	2325	2645	2286	1969	1698	1440	+1.3	0.0	-6.0	-17.5	NA
6.5 Rem. Mag.	120	3210	2905	2621	2353	2102	2745	2248	1830	1475	1177	+2.5	+1.7	-4.1	-16.3	Disc.
264 Win. Mag.	100	3400	3104	2828	2568	2322	2566	2139	1775	1464	1197	1.1	0	-5.4	-16.1	NA
264 Win. Mag.	125	3200	2978	2767	2566	2373	2841	2461	2125	1827	1563	1.2	0	-5.8	-16.8	NA
264 Win. Mag.	130	3100	2900	2709	2526	2350	2773	2427	2118	1841	1594	1.3	0	-6.1	-17.6	NA
264 Win. Mag.	140	3030	2782	2548	2326	2114	2854	2406	2018	1682	1389	+2.5	+1.4	-5.1	-18.0	$24
6.5 Nosler	129	3400	3213	3035	2863	2698	3310	2957	2638	2348	2085	0.9	0	-4.7	-13.6	NA
6.5 Nosler	140	3300	3118	2943	2775	2613	3119	2784	2481	2205	1955	1.0	0	-5.0	-14.6	NA
6.71 (264) Blackbird	140	3480	3261	3053	2855	2665	3766	3307	2899	2534	2208	+2.4	+3.1	0.0	-7.4	NA
6.5-300 Weatherby Magnum	127	3531	3309	3099	2898	2706	-	3088	2707	2368	2065	0	-1.68	-6.98	-16.43	NA
6.5-300 Weatherby Magnum	130	3476	3267	3084	2901	2726	-	3097	2746	2430	2145	0	-1.74	-7.14	-16.68	NA
6.5-300 Weatherby Magnum	140	3395	3122	2866	2624	2394	-	3030	2552	2139	1781	0	-2.04	-8.24	-19.36	NA
6.8 REM SPC	90	2840	2444	2083	1756	1469	1611	1194	867	616	431	2.2	0	-3.9	-32.0	NA
6.8 REM SPC	110	2570	2338	2118	1910	1716	1613	1335	1095	891	719	2.4	0.0	-6.3	-20.8	NA
6.8 REM SPC	120	2460	2250	2051	1863	1687	1612	1349	1121	925	758	2.3	0	-10.5	-31.1	NA
6.8mm Rem.	115	2775	2472	2190	1926	1683	1966	1561	1224	947	723	+2.1	0.0	-3.7	-9.4	NA
27																
270 Win. (Rem.)	115	2710	2482	2265	2059	NA	1875	1485	1161	896	NA	0.0	4.8	-17.3	0.0	NA
270 Win.	120	2675	2288	1935	1619	1351	1907	1395	998	699	486	2.6	0	-12.0	-37.4	NA
270 Win.	140	2940	2747	2563	2386	2216	2687	2346	2042	1770	1526	1.8	0	-6.8	-19.8	NA
270 Win. Supreme	130	3150	2881	2628	2388	2161	2865	2396	1993	1646	1348	1.3	0.0	-6.4	-18.9	NA
270 Win. Supreme	150	2930	2693	2468	2254	2051	2860	2416	2030	1693	1402	1.7	0.0	-7.4	-21.6	NA
270 W. Superformance	130	3200	2984	2788	2582	2393	2955	2570	2228	1924	1653	1.2	0.0	-5.7	-16.7	NA
270 Winchester	100	3430	3021	2649	2305	1988	2612	2027	1557	1179	877	+2.0	+1.0	-4.9	-17.5	$17

Cartridge	Bullet Wgt. Grs.	VELOCITY (fps)					ENERGY (ft. lbs.)					TRAJ. (in.)				Est. Price/box
		Muzzle	100 yds.	200 yds.	300 yds.	400 yds.	Muzzle	100 yds.	200 yds.	300 yds.	400 yds.	100 yds.	200 yds.	300 yds.	400 yds.	
270 Winchester	130	3060	2776	2510	2259	2022	2702	2225	1818	1472	1180	+2.5	+1.4	-5.3	-18.2	$17
270 Winchester	135	3000	2780	2570	2369	2178	2697	2315	1979	1682	1421	+2.5	+1.4	-6.0	-17.6	$23
270 Winchester*	140	2940	2700	2480	2260	2060	2685	2270	1905	1590	1315	+2.5	+1.8	-4.6	-17.9	$20
270 Winchester*	150	2850	2585	2336	2100	1879	2705	2226	1817	1468	1175	+2.5	+1.2	-6.5	-22.0	$17
270 WSM	130	3275	3041	2820	2609	2408	3096	2669	2295	1564	1673	1.1	0.0	-5.5	-16.1	NA
270 WSM	140	3125	2865	2619	2386	2165	3035	2559	2132	1769	1457	1.4	0.0	-6.5	-19.0	NA
270 WSM	150	3000	2795	2599	2412	2232	2997	2601	2250	1937	1659	1.5	0	-6.6	-19.2	NA
270 WSM	150	3120	2923	2734	2554	2380	3242	2845	2490	2172	1886	1.3	0.0	-5.9	-17.2	NA
270 Wea. Mag.	100	3760	3380	3033	2712	2412	3139	2537	2042	1633	1292	+2.0	+2.4	-1.2	-10.1	$32
270 Wea. Mag.	130	3375	3119	2878	2649	2432	3287	2808	2390	2026	1707	+2.5	-2.9	-0.9	-9.9	$32
270 Wea. Mag.	130	3450	3194	2958	2732	2517	3435	2949	2525	2143	1828	1.0	0	-4.9	-14.5	NA
270 Wea. Mag.*	150	3245	3036	2837	2647	2465	3507	3070	2681	2334	2023	+2.5	+2.6	-1.8	-11.4	$47
7mm																
7mm BR	140	2216	2012	1821	1643	1481	1525	1259	1031	839	681	+2.0	-3.7	-20.0	0.0	$23
7mm Mauser*	139/140	2660	2435	2221	2018	1827	2199	1843	1533	1266	1037	+2.5	0.0	-9.6	-27.7	$17
7mm Mauser	139	2740	2556	2379	2209	2046	2317	2016	1747	1506	1292	1.9	0	-8.1	-23.3	NA
7mm Mauser	154	2690	2490	2300	2120	1940	2475	2120	1810	1530	1285	+2.5	+0.8	-7.5	-23.5	$17
7mm Mauser	175	2440	2137	1857	1603	1382	2313	1774	1340	998	742	+2.5	-1.7	-16.1	0.0	$17
7x30 Waters	120	2700	2300	1930	1600	1330	1940	1405	990	685	470	+2.5	-0.2	-12.3	0.0	$18
7mm-08 Rem.	120	2675	2435	2207	1992	1790	1907	1579	1298	1057	854	2.2	0	-9.4	-27.5	NA
7mm-08 Rem.	120	3000	2725	2467	2223	1992	2398	1979	1621	1316	1058	+2.0	0.0	-7.6	-22.3	$18
7mm-08 Rem.	139	2840	2608	2387	2177	1978	2489	2098	1758	1463	1207	1.8	0	-7.9	-23.2	NA
7mm-08 Rem.*	140	2860	2625	2402	2189	1988	2542	2142	1793	1490	1228	+2.5	+0.8	-6.9	-21.9	$18
7mm-08 Rem.	154	2715	2510	2315	2128	1950	2520	2155	1832	1548	1300	+2.5	+1.0	-7.0	-22.7	$23
7-08 R. Superformance	139	2950	2857	2571	2393	2222	2686	2345	2040	1768	1524	1.5	0.0	-6.8	-19.7	NA
7x64mm	173	2526	2260	2010	1777	1565	2452	1962	1552	1214	941	0	-5.3	-19.3	-44.4	NA
7x64mm Bren.	140	2950	2710	2483	2266	2061	2705	2283	1910	1597	1320	1.5	0.0	-2.9	-7.3	$24.50
7x64mm Bren.	154	2820	2610	2420	2230	2050	2720	2335	1995	1695	1430	+2.5	+1.4	-5.7	-19.9	NA
7x64mm Bren.*	160	2850	2669	2495	2327	2166	2885	2530	2211	1924	1667	+2.5	+1.6	-4.8	-17.8	$24
7x64mm Bren.	175	2650	2445	2248	2061	1883	2728	2322	1964	1650	1378	2.2	0	-9.1	-26.4	$24.50
7x65mmR	173	2608	2337	2082	1844	1626	2613	2098	1666	1307	1015	0	-4.9	-17.9	-41.9	NA
275 Rigby	139	2680	2456	2242	2040	1848	2217	1861	1552	1284	1054	2.2	0	-9.1	-26.5	NA
284 Winchester	150	2860	2595	2344	2108	1886	2724	2243	1830	1480	1185	+2.5	+0.8	-7.3	-23.2	$24
280 R. Superformance	139	3090	2890	2699	2516	2341	2946	2578	2249	1954	1691	1.3	0.0	-6.1	-17.7	NA
280 Rem.	139	3090	2891	2700	2518	2343	2947	2579	2250	1957	1694	1.3	0	-6.1	-17.7	NA
280 Remington	140	3000	2758	2528	2309	2102	2797	2363	1986	1657	1373	+2.5	+1.4	-5.2	-18.3	$17
280 Remington*	150	2890	2624	2373	2135	1912	2781	2293	1875	1518	1217	+2.5	+0.8	-7.1	-22.6	$17
280 Remington	160	2840	2637	2442	2556	2078	2866	2471	2120	1809	1535	+2.5	+0.8	-6.7	-21.0	$20
280 Remington	165	2820	2510	2220	1950	1701	2913	2308	1805	1393	1060	+2.5	+0.4	-8.8	-26.5	$17
280 Ack. Imp.	140	3150	2946	2752	2566	2387	3084	2698	2354	2047	1772	1.3	0	-5.8	-17.0	NA
280 Ack. Imp.	150	2900	2712	2533	2360	2194	2800	2450	2136	1855	1603	1.6	0	-7.0	-20.3	NA
280 Ack. Imp.	160	2950	2751	2561	2379	2205	3091	2686	2331	2011	1727	1.5	0	-6.9	-19.9	NA
7x61mm S&H Sup.	154	3060	2720	2400	2100	1820	3200	2520	1965	1505	1135	+2.5	+1.8	-5.0	-19.8	NA
7mm Dakota	160	3200	3001	2811	2630	2455	3637	3200	2808	2456	2140	+2.1	+1.9	-2.8	-12.5	NA
7mm Rem. Mag.	139	3190	2986	2791	2605	2427	3141	2752	2405	2095	1817	1.2	0	-5.7	-16.5	NA
7mm Rem. Mag. (Rem.)	140	2710	2482	2265	2059	NA	2283	1915	1595	1318	NA	0.0	-4.5	-1.57	0.0	NA
7mm Rem. Mag.*	139/140	3150	2930	2710	2510	2320	3085	2660	2290	1960	1670	+2.5	+2.4	-2.4	-12.7	$21
7mm Rem. Mag.	150/154	3110	2830	2568	2320	2085	3221	2667	2196	1792	1448	+2.5	+1.6	-4.6	-16.5	$21
7mm Rem. Mag.*	160/162	2950	2730	2520	2320	2120	3090	2650	2250	1910	1600	+2.5	+1.8	-4.4	-17.8	$34
7mm Rem. Mag.	165	2900	2699	2507	2324	2147	3081	2669	2303	1978	1689	+2.5	+1.2	-5.9	-19.0	$28
7mm Rem Mag.	175	2860	2645	2440	2244	2057	3178	2718	2313	1956	1644	+2.5	+1.0	-6.5	-20.7	$21
7 R.M. Superformance	139	3240	3033	2836	2648	2467	3239	2839	2482	2163	1877	1.1	0.0	-5.5	-15.9	NA
7 R.M. Superformance	154	3100	2914	2736	2565	2401	3286	2904	2560	2250	1970	1.3	0.0	-5.9	-17.2	NA
7mm Rem. SA ULTRA MAG	140	3175	2934	2707	2490	2283	3033	2676	2277	1927	1620	1.3	0.0	-6	-17.7	NA
7mm Rem. SA ULTRA MAG	150	3110	2828	2563	2313	2077	3221	2663	2188	1782	1437	2.5	2.1	-3.6	-15.8	NA
7mm Rem. SA ULTRA MAG	160	2850	2676	2508	2347	2192	2885	2543	2235	1957	1706	1.7	0	-7.2	-20.7	NA
7mm Rem. SA ULTRA MAG	160	2960	2762	2572	2390	2215	3112	2709	2350	2029	1743	2.6	2.2	-3.6	-15.4	NA
7mm Rem. WSM	140	3225	3008	2801	2603	2414	3233	2812	2438	2106	1812	1.2	0.0	-5.6	-16.4	NA
7mm Rem. WSM	160	2990	2744	2512	2081	1883	3176	2675	2241	1864	1538	1.6	0.0	-7.1	-20.8	NA
7mm Wea. Mag.	139	3300	3091	2891	2701	2519	3361	2948	2580	2252	1958	1.1	0	-5.2	-15.2	NA
7mm Wea. Mag.	140	3225	2970	2729	2501	2283	3233	2741	2315	1943	1621	+2.5	+2.0	-3.2	-14.0	$35
7mm Wea. Mag.	140	3340	3127	2925	2732	2546	3467	3040	2659	2320	2016	0	-2.1	-8.2	-19	NA

Cartridge	Bullet Wgt. Grs.	VELOCITY (fps)					ENERGY (ft. lbs.)					TRAJ. (in.)				Est. Price/box
		Muzzle	100 yds.	200 yds.	300 yds.	400 yds.	Muzzle	100 yds.	200 yds.	300 yds.	400 yds.	100 yds.	200 yds.	300 yds.	400 yds.	
7mm Wea. Mag.	150	3175	2957	2751	2553	2364	3357	2913	2520	2171	1861	0	-2.5	-9.6	-22	NA
7mm Wea. Mag.	154	3260	3023	2799	2586	2382	3539	3044	2609	2227	1890	+2.5	+2.8	-1.5	-10.8	$32
7mm Wea. Mag.*	160	3200	3004	2816	2637	2464	3637	3205	2817	2469	2156	+2.5	+2.7	-1.5	-10.6	$47
7mm Wea. Mag.	165	2950	2747	2553	2367	2189	3188	2765	2388	2053	1756	+2.5	+1.8	-4.2	-16.4	$43
7mm Wea. Mag.	175	2910	2693	2486	2288	2098	3293	2818	2401	2033	1711	+2.5	+1.2	-5.9	-19.4	$35
7.21(.284) Tomahawk	140	3300	3118	2943	2774	2612	3386	3022	2693	2393	2122	2.3	3.2	0.0	-7.7	NA
7mm STW	140	3300	3086	2889	2697	2513	3384	2966	2594	2261	1963	0	-2.1	-8.5	-19.6	NA
7mm STW	140	3325	3064	2818	2585	2364	3436	2918	2468	2077	1737	+2.3	+1.8	-3.0	-13.1	NA
7mm STW	150	3175	2957	2751	2553	2364	3357	2913	2520	2171	1861	0	-2.5	-9.6	-22	NA
7mm STW	175	2900	2760	2625	2493	2366	3267	2960	2677	2416	2175	0	-3.1	-11.2	-24.9	NA
7mm STW Supreme	160	3150	2894	2652	2422	2204	3526	2976	2499	2085	1727	1.3	0.0	-6.3	-18.5	NA
7mm Rem. Ultra Mag.	140	3425	3184	2956	2740	2534	3646	3151	2715	2333	1995	1.7	1.6	-2.6	-11.4	NA
7mm Rem. Ultra Mag.	160	3225	3035	2854	2680	2512	3694	3273	2894	2551	2242	0	-2.3	-8.8	-20.2	NA
7mm Rem. Ultra Mag.	174	3040	2896	2756	2621	2490	3590	3258	2952	2669	2409	0	-2.6	-9.9	-22.2	NA
7mm Firehawk	140	3625	3373	3135	2909	2695	4084	3536	3054	2631	2258	+2.2	+2.9	0.0	-7.03	NA
7.21 (.284) Firebird	140	3750	3522	3306	3101	2905	4372	3857	3399	2990	2625	1.6	2.4	0.0	-6.0	NA
.28 Nosler	160	3300	3114	2930	2753	2583	3883	3444	3049	2693	2371	1.1	0	-5.1	-14.9	$78
30																
300 ACC Blackout	110	2150	1886	1646	1432	1254	1128	869	661	501	384	0	-8.3	-29.6	-67.8	NA
300 AAC Blackout	125	2250	2031	1826	1636	1464	1404	1145	926	743	595	0	-7	-24.4	-54.8	NA
300 AAC Blackout	220	1000	968	-	-	-	488	457	-	-	-	0	-	-	-	-
30 Carbine	110	1990	1567	1236	1035	923	977	600	373	262	208	0.0	-13.5	0.0	0.0	$28**
30 Carbine	110	2000	1601	1279	1067	—	977	626	399	278	—	0	-12.9	-47.2	—	NA
300 Whisper	110	2375	2094	1834	1597	NA	1378	1071	822	623	NA	3.2	0.0	-13.6	NA	NA
300 Whisper	208	1020	988	959	NA	NA	480	451	422	NA	NA	0.0	-34.10	NA	NA	NA
303 Savage	190	1890	1612	1327	1183	1055	1507	1096	794	591	469	+2.5	-7.6	0.0	0.0	$24
30 Remington	170	2120	1822	1555	1328	1153	1696	1253	913	666	502	+2.5	-4.7	-26.3	0.0	$20
7.62x39mm Rus.	123	2360	2049	1764	1511	1296	1521	1147	850	623	459	3.4	0	-14.7	-44.7	NA
7.62x39mm Rus.	123/125	2300	2030	1780	1550	1350	1445	1125	860	655	500	+2.5	-2.0	-17.5	0.0	$13
30-30 Win.	55	3400	2693	2085	1570	1187	1412	886	521	301	172	+2.0	0.0	-10.2	-35.0	$18
30-30 Win.	125	2570	2090	1660	1320	1080	1830	1210	770	480	320	-2.0	-2.6	-19.9	0.0	$13
30-30 Win.	140	2500	2198	1918	1662	—	1943	1501	1143	858	—	2.9	0	-12.4	—	NA
30-30 Win.	150	2390	2040	1723	1447	1225	1902	1386	989	697	499	0.0	-7.5	-27.0	-63.0	NA
30-30 Win. Supreme	150	2480	2095	1747	1446	1209	2049	1462	1017	697	487	0.0	-6.5	-24.5	0.0	NA
30-30 Win.	160	2300	1997	1719	1473	1268	1879	1416	1050	771	571	+2.5	-2.9	-20.2	0.0	$18
30-30 Win. Lever Evolution	160	2400	2150	1916	1699	NA	2046	1643	1304	1025	NA	3.0	0.2	-12.1	NA	NA
30-30 PMC Cowboy	170	1300	1198	1121	—	—	638	474	—	—	—	0.0	-27.0	0.0	0.0	NA
30-30 Win.*	170	2200	1895	1619	1381	1191	1827	1355	989	720	535	+2.5	-5.8	-23.6	0.0	$13
300 Savage	150	2630	2354	2094	1853	1631	2303	1845	1462	1143	886	+2.5	-0.4	-10.1	-30.7	$17
300 Savage	150	2740	2499	2272	2056	1852	2500	2081	1718	1407	1143	2.1	0	-8.8	-25.8	NA
300 Savage	180	2350	2137	1935	1754	1570	2207	1825	1496	1217	985	+2.5	-1.6	-15.2	0.0	$17
30-40 Krag	180	2430	2213	2007	1813	1632	2360	1957	1610	1314	1064	+2.5	-1.4	-13.8	0.0	$18
7.65x53mm Arg.	180	2590	2390	2200	2010	1830	2685	2280	1925	1615	1345	+2.5	0.0	-27.6	0.0	NA
7.5x53mm Argentine	150	2785	2519	2269	2032	1814	2583	2113	1714	1376	1096	+2.0	0.0	-8.8	-25.5	NA
308 Marlin Express	140	2800	2532	2279	2040	1818	2437	1992	1614	1294	1207	2.0	0	-8.7	-25.8	NA
308 Marlin Express	160	2660	2430	2226	2026	1836	2513	2111	1761	1457	1197	3.0	1.7	-6.7	-23.5	NA
307 Winchester	150	2760	2321	1924	1575	1289	2530	1795	1233	826	554	+2.5	-1.5	-13.6	0.0	Disc.
7.5x55 Swiss	180	2650	2450	2250	2060	1880	2805	2390	2020	1700	1415	+2.5	+0.6	-8.1	-24.9	NA
7.5x55mm Swiss	165	2720	2515	2319	2132	1954	2710	2317	1970	1665	1398	+2.0	0.0	-8.5	-24.6	NA
30 Remington AR	123/125	2800	2465	2154	1867	1606	2176	1686	1288	967	716	2.1	0.0	-9.7	-29.4	NA
308 Winchester	55	3770	3215	2726	2286	1888	1735	1262	907	638	435	-2.0	+1.4	-3.8	-15.8	$22
308 Win.	110	3165	2830	2520	2230	1960	2447	1956	1551	1215	938	1.4	0	-6.9	-20.9	NA
308 Win. PDX1	120	2850	2497	2171	NA	NA	2164	1662	1256	NA	NA	0.0	-2.8	NA	NA	NA
308 Winchester	150	2820	2533	2263	2009	1774	2648	2137	1705	1344	1048	+2.5	+0.4	-8.5	-26.1	$17
308 W. Superformance	150	3000	2772	2555	2348	1962	2997	2558	2173	1836	1540	1.5	0.0	-6.9	-20.0	NA
308 Win.	155	2775	2553	2342	2141	1950	2650	2243	1887	1577	1308	1.9	0	-8.3	-24.2	NA
308 Win.	155	2850	2640	2438	2247	2064	2795	2398	2047	1737	1466	1.8	0	-7.5	-22.1	NA
308 Winchester	165	2700	2440	2194	1963	1748	2670	2180	1763	1411	1199	+2.5	0.0	-9.7	-28.5	$20
308 Winchester	168	2680	2493	2314	2143	1979	2678	2318	1998	1713	1460	+2.5	0.0	-8.9	-25.3	$18
308 Win. Super Match	168	2870	2647	2462	2284	2114	3008	2613	2261	1946	1667	1.7	0.0	-7.5	-21.6	NA
308 Win. (Fed.)	170	2000	1740	1510	NA	NA	1510	1145	860	NA	NA	0.0	0.0	0.0	0.0	NA
308 Winchester	178	2620	2415	2220	2034	1857	2713	2306	1948	1635	1363	+2.5	0.0	-9.6	-27.6	$23

Cartridge	Bullet Wgt. Grs.	VELOCITY (fps)					ENERGY (ft. lbs.)					TRAJ. (in.)				Est. Price/box
		Muzzle	100 yds.	200 yds.	300 yds.	400 yds.	Muzzle	100 yds.	200 yds.	300 yds.	400 yds.	100 yds.	200 yds.	300 yds.	400 yds.	
308 Win. Super Match	178	2780	2609	2444	2285	2132	3054	2690	2361	2064	1797	1.8	0.0	-7.6	-21.9	NA
308 Winchester*	180	2620	2393	2178	1974	1782	2743	2288	1896	1557	1269	+2.5	-0.2	-10.2	-28.5	$17
30-06 Spfd.	55	4080	3485	2965	2502	2083	2033	1483	1074	764	530	+2.0	+1.9	-2.1	-11.7	$22
30-06 Spfd. (Rem.)	125	2660	2335	2034	1757	NA	1964	1513	1148	856	NA	0.0	-5.2	-18.9	0.0	NA
30-06 Spfd.	125	2700	2412	2143	1891	1660	2023	1615	1274	993	765	2.3	0	-9.9	-29.5	NA
30-06 Spfd.	125	3140	2780	2447	2138	1853	2736	2145	1662	1279	953	+2.0	+1.0	-6.2	-21.0	$17
30-06 Spfd.	150	2910	2617	2342	2083	1853	2820	2281	1827	1445	1135	+2.5	+0.8	-7.2	-23.4	$17
30-06 Superformance	150	3080	2848	2617	2417	2216	3159	2700	2298	1945	1636	1.4	0.0	-6.4	-18.9	NA
30-06 Spfd.	152	2910	2654	2413	2184	1968	2858	2378	1965	1610	1307	+2.5	+1.0	-6.6	-21.3	$23
30-06 Spfd.*	165	2800	2534	2283	2047	1825	2872	2352	1909	1534	1220	+2.5	+0.4	-8.4	-25.5	$17
30-06 Spfd.	168	2710	2522	2346	2169	2003	2739	2372	2045	1754	1497	+2.5	+0.4	-8.0	-23.5	$18
30-06 M1 Garand	168	2710	2523	2343	2171	2006	2739	2374	2048	1758	1501	2.3	0	-8.6	-24.6	NA
30-06 Spfd. (Fed.)	170	2000	1740	1510	NA	NA	1510	1145	860	NA	NA	0.0	0.0	0.0	0.0	NA
30-06 Spfd.	178	2720	2511	2311	2121	1939	2924	2491	2111	1777	1486	+2.5	+0.4	-8.2	-24.6	$23
30-06 Spfd.*	180	2700	2469	2250	2042	1846	2913	2436	2023	1666	1362	-2.5	0.0	-9.3	-27.0	$17
30-06 Superformance	180	2820	2630	2447	2272	2104	3178	2764	2393	2063	1769	1.8	0.0	-7.6	-21.9	NA
30-06 Spfd.	220	2410	2130	1870	1632	1422	2837	2216	1708	1301	988	+2.5	-1.7	-18.0	0.0	$17
30-06 High Energy	180	2880	2690	2500	2320	2150	3315	2880	2495	2150	1845	+1.7	0.0	-7.2	-21.0	NA
30 T/C	150	2920	2696	2483	2280	2087	2849	2421	2054	1732	1450	1.7	0	-7.3	-21.3	NA
30 T/C Superformance	150	3000	2772	2555	2348	2151	2997	2558	2173	1836	1540	1.5	0.0	-6.9	-20.0	NA
30 T/C Superformance	165	2850	2644	2447	2258	2078	2975	2560	2193	1868	1582	1.7	0.0	-7.6	-22.0	NA
300 Rem SA Ultra Mag	150	3200	2901	2622	2359	2112	3410	2803	2290	1854	1485	1.3	0.0	-6.4	-19.1	NA
300 Rem SA Ultra Mag	165	3075	2792	2527	2276	2040	3464	2856	2339	1898	1525	1.5	0.0	-7	-20.7	NA
300 Rem SA Ultra Mag	180	2960	2761	2571	2389	2214	3501	3047	2642	2280	1959	2.6	2.2	-3.6	-15.4	NA
300 Rem. SA Ultra Mag	200	2800	2644	2494	2348	2208	3841	3104	2761	2449	2164	0	-3.5	-12.5	-27.9	NA
7.82 (308) Patriot	150	3250	2999	2762	2537	2323	3519	2997	2542	2145	1798	+1.2	0.0	-5.8	-16.9	NA
300 RCM	150	3265	3023	2794	2577	2369	3550	3043	2600	2211	1870	1.2	0	-5.6	-16.5	NA
300 RCM Superformance	150	3310	3065	2833	2613	2404	3648	3128	2673	2274	1924	1.1	0.0	-5.4	-16.0	NA
300 RCM Superformance	165	3185	2964	2753	2552	2360	3716	3217	2776	2386	2040	1.2	0.0	-5.8	-17.0	NA
300 RCM Superformance	180	3040	2840	2649	2466	2290	3693	3223	2804	2430	2096	1.4	0.0	-6.4	-18.5	NA
300 WSM	150	3300	3061	2834	2619	2414	3628	3121	2676	2285	1941	1.1	0.0	-5.4	-15.9	NA
300 WSM	180	2970	2741	2524	2317	2120	3526	3005	2547	2147	1797	1.6	0.0	-7.0	-20.5	NA
300 WSM	180	3010	2923	2734	2554	2380	3242	2845	2490	2172	1886	1.3	0	-5.9	-17.2	NA
300 WSM	190	2875	2729	2588	2451	2319	3486	3142	2826	2535	2269	0	3.2	-11.5	-25.7	NA
308 Norma Mag.	180	2975	2787	2608	2435	2269	3536	3105	2718	2371	2058	0	-3	-11.1	-25.0	NA
308 Norma Mag.	180	3020	2820	2630	2440	2270	3645	3175	2755	2385	2050	+2.5	+2.0	-3.5	-14.8	NA
300 Dakota	200	3000	2824	2656	2493	2336	3996	3542	3131	2760	2423	+2.2	+1.5	-4.0	-15.2	NA
300 H&H Mag.	180	2870	2678	2494	2318	2148	3292	2866	2486	2147	1844	1.7	0	-7.3	-21.6	NA
300 H&H Magnum*	180	2880	2640	2412	2196	1990	3315	2785	2325	1927	1583	+2.5	+0.8	-6.8	-21.7	$24
300 H&H Mag.	200	2750	2596	2447	2303	2164	3357	2992	2659	2355	2079	1.8	0	-7.6	-21.8	NA
300 H&H Magnum	220	2550	2267	2002	1757	NA	3167	2510	1958	1508	NA	-2.5	-0.4	-12.0	0.0	NA
300 Win. Mag.	150	3290	2951	2636	2342	2068	3605	2900	2314	1827	1424	+2.5	+1.9	-3.8	-15.8	$22
300 WM Superformance	150	3400	3150	2914	2690	2477	3850	3304	2817	2409	2043	1.0	0.0	-5.1	-15.0	NA
300 Win. Mag.	165	3100	2877	2665	2462	2269	3522	3033	2603	2221	1897	+2.5	+2.4	-3.0	-16.9	$24
300 Win. Mag.	178	2900	2760	2568	2375	2191	3509	3030	2606	2230	1897	+2.5	+1.4	-5.0	-17.6	$29
300 Win. Mag.	178	2960	2770	2588	2413	2245	3463	3032	2647	2301	1992	1.5	0	-6.7	-19.4	NA
300 WM Super Match	178	2960	2770	2587	2412	2243	3462	3031	2645	2298	1988	1.5	0.0	-6.7	-19.4	NA
300 Win. Mag.*	180	2960	2745	2540	2344	2157	3501	3011	2578	2196	1859	+2.5	+1.2	-5.5	-18.5	$22
300 WM Superformance	180	3130	2927	2732	2546	2366	3917	3424	2983	2589	2238	1.3	0.0	-5.9	-17.3	NA
300 Win. Mag.	190	2885	1691	2506	2327	2156	3511	3055	2648	2285	1961	+2.5	+1.2	-5.7	-19.0	$26
300 Win. Mag.	195	2930	2760	2596	2438	2286	3717	3297	2918	2574	2262	1.5	0	-6.7	-19.4	NA
300 Win. Mag.*	200	2825	2595	2376	2167	1970	3545	2991	2508	2086	1742	-2.5	+1.6	-4.7	-17.2	$36
300 Win. Mag.	220	2680	2448	2228	2020	1823	3508	2927	2424	1993	1623	+2.5	0.0	-9.5	-27.5	$23
30 Nosler	180	3200	3004	2815	2635	2462	4092	3606	3168	2774	2422	0	-2.4	-9.1	-20.9	NA
30 Nosler	210	3000	2868	2741	2617	2497	4196	3836	3502	3193	2906	0	-2.7	-10.1	-22.5	NA
300 Rem. Ultra Mag.	150	3450	3208	2980	2762	2556	3964	3427	2956	2541	2175	1.7	1.5	-2.6	-11.2	NA
300 Rem. Ultra Mag.	150	2910	2686	2473	2279	2077	2820	2403	2037	1716	1436	1.7	0.0	-7.4	-21.5	NA
300 Rem. Ultra Mag.	165	3350	3099	2862	2938	2424	4110	3518	3001	2549	2152	1.1	0	-5.3	-15.6	NA
300 Rem. Ultra Mag.	180	3250	3037	2834	2640	2454	4221	3686	3201	2786	2407	2.4	0.0	-3.0	-12.7	NA
300 Rem. Ultra Mag.	180	2960	2774	2505	2294	2093	3501	2971	2508	2103	1751	2.7	2.2	-3.8	-16.4	NA
300 Rem. Ultra Mag.	200	3032	2791	2562	2345	2138	4083	3459	2916	2442	2030	1.5	0.0	-6.8	-19.9	NA
300 Rem. Ultra Mag.	210	2920	2790	2665	2543	2424	3975	3631	3311	3015	2740	1.5	0	-6.4	-18.1	NA

Cartridge	Bullet Wgt. Grs.	VELOCITY (fps)					ENERGY (ft. lbs.)					TRAJ. (in.)				Est. Price/box
		Muzzle	100 yds.	200 yds.	300 yds.	400 yds.	Muzzle	100 yds.	200 yds.	300 yds.	400 yds.	100 yds.	200 yds.	300 yds.	400 yds.	
300 Wea. Mag.	100	3900	3441	3038	2652	2305	3714	2891	2239	1717	1297	+2.0	+2.6	-0.6	-8.7	$32
300 Wea. Mag.	150	3375	3126	2892	2670	2459	3794	3255	2786	2374	2013	1.0	0	-5.2	-15.3	NA
300 Wea. Mag.	150	3600	3307	3033	2776	2533	4316	3642	3064	2566	2137	+2.5	+3.2	0.0	-8.1	$32
300 Wea. Mag.	165	3140	2921	2713	2515	2325	3612	3126	2697	2317	1980	1.3	0	-6.0	-17.5	NA
300 Wea. Mag.	165	3450	3210	3000	2792	2593	4360	3796	3297	2855	2464	+2.5	+3.2	0.0	-7.8	NA
300 Wea. Mag.	178	3120	2902	2695	2497	2308	3847	3329	2870	2464	2104	+2.5	-1.7	-3.6	-14.7	$43
300 Wea. Mag.	180	3330	3110	2910	2710	2520	4430	3875	3375	2935	2540	+1.0	0.0	-5.2	-15.1	NA
300 Wea. Mag.	190	3030	2830	2638	2455	2279	3873	3378	2936	2542	2190	+2.5	+1.6	-4.3	-16.0	$38
300 Wea. Mag.	220	2850	2541	2283	1964	1736	3967	3155	2480	1922	1471	+2.5	+0.4	-8.5	-26.4	$35
300 Pegasus	180	3500	3319	3145	2978	2817	4896	4401	3953	3544	3172	+2.28	+2.89	0.0	-6.79	NA
31																
32-20 Win.	100	1210	1021	913	834	769	325	231	185	154	131	0.0	-32.3	0.0	0.0	$23**
303 British	150	2685	2441	2211	1993	1789	2401	1985	1628	1323	1066	2.2	0	-9.3	-27.4	NA
303 British	180	2460	2124	1817	1542	1311	2418	1803	1319	950	687	+2.5	-1.8	-16.8	0.0	$18
303 Light Mag.	150	2830	2570	2325	2094	1884	2667	2199	1800	1461	1185	+2.0	0.0	-8.4	-24.6	NA
7.62x54mm Rus.	146	2950	2730	2520	2320	NA	2820	2415	2055	1740	NA	+2.5	+2.0	-4.4	-17.7	NA
7.62x54mm Rus.	174	2800	2607	2422	2245	2075	3029	2626	2267	1947	1664	1.8	0	-7.8	-22.4	NA
7.62x54mm Rus.	180	2580	2370	2180	2000	1820	2650	2250	1900	1590	1100	+2.5	0.0	-9.8	-28.5	NA
7.7x58mm Jap.	150	2640	2399	2170	1954	1752	2321	1916	1568	1271	1022	+2.3	0.0	-9.7	-28.5	NA
7.7x58mm Jap.	180	2500	2300	2100	1920	1750	2490	2105	1770	1475	1225	+2.5	0.0	-10.4	-30.2	NA
8mm																
8x56 R	205	2400	2188	1987	1797	1621	2621	2178	1796	1470	1196	+2.9	0.0	-11.7	-34.3	NA
8x57mm JS Mau.	165	2850	2520	2210	1930	1670	2965	2330	1795	1360	1015	+2.5	+1.0	-7.7	0.0	NA
32 Win. Special	165	2410	2145	1897	1669	NA	2128	1685	1318	1020	NA	2.0	0.0	-13.0	-19.9	NA
32 Win. Special	170	2250	1921	1626	1372	1175	1911	1393	998	710	521	+2.5	-3.5	-22.9	0.0	$14
8mm Mauser	170	2360	1969	1622	1333	1123	2102	1464	993	671	476	+2.5	-3.1	-22.2	0.0	$18
8mm Mauser	196	2500	2338	2182	2032	1888	2720	2379	2072	1797	1552	2.4	0	-9.8	-27.9	NA
325 WSM	180	3060	2841	2632	2432	2242	3743	3226	2769	2365	2009	+1.4	0.0	-6.4	-18.7	NA
325 WSM	200	2950	2753	2565	2384	2210	3866	3367	2922	2524	2170	+1.5	0.0	-6.8	-19.8	NA
325 WSM	220	2840	2605	2382	2169	1968	3941	3316	2772	2300	1893	+1.8	0.0	-8.0	-23.3	NA
8mm Rem. Mag.	185	3080	2761	2464	2186	1927	3896	3131	2494	1963	1525	+2.5	+1.4	-5.5	-19.7	$30
8mm Rem. Mag.	220	2830	2581	2346	2123	1913	3912	3254	2688	2201	1787	+2.5	+0.6	-7.6	-23.5	Disc.
33																
338 Federal	180	2830	2590	2350	2130	1930	3200	2670	2215	1820	1480	1.8	0.0	-8.2	-23.9	NA
338 Marlin Express	200	2565	2365	2174	1992	1820	2922	2484	2099	1762	1471	3.0	1.2	-7.9	-25.9	NA
338 Federal	185	2750	2550	2350	2160	1980	3105	2660	2265	1920	1615	1.9	0.0	-8.3	-24.1	NA
338 Federal	210	2630	2410	2200	2010	1820	3225	2710	2265	1880	1545	2.3	0.0	-9.4	-27.3	NA
338 Federal MSR	185	2680	2459	2230	2020	1820	2950	2460	2035	1670	1360	2.2	0.0	-9.2	-26.8	NA
338-06	200	2750	2553	2364	2184	2011	3358	2894	2482	2118	1796	+1.9	0.0	-8.22	-23.6	NA
330 Dakota	250	2900	2719	2545	2378	2217	4668	4103	3595	3138	2727	+2.3	+1.3	-5.0	-17.5	NA
338 Lapua	250	2900	2685	2481	2285	2098	4668	4002	2416	2899	2444	1.7	0	-7.3	-21.3	NA
338 Lapua	250	2963	2795	2640	2493	NA	4842	4341	3881	3458	NA	+1.9	0.0	-7.9	0.0	NA
338 Lapua	285	2745	2616	2491	2369	2251	4768	4331	3926	3552	3206	1.8	0.0	-7.4	-21	NA
338 Lapua	300	2660	2544	2432	2322	-	4715	4313	3940	3592	-	1.9	0	-7.8	-	NA
338 RCM Superformance	185	2980	2755	2542	2338	2143	3647	3118	2653	2242	1887	1.5	0.0	-6.9	-20.3	NA
338 RCM Superformance	200	2950	2744	2547	2358	2177	3846	3342	2879	2468	2104	1.6	0.0	-6.9	-20.1	NA
338 RCM Superformance	225	2750	2575	2407	2245	2089	3778	3313	2894	2518	2180	1.9	0.0	-7.9	-22.7	NA
338 WM Superformance	185	3080	2850	2632	2424	2226	3896	3337	2845	2413	2034	1.4	0.0	-6.4	-18.8	NA
338 Win. Mag.	200	3030	2820	2620	2429	2246	4077	3532	3049	2621	2240	1.4	0	-6.5	-18.9	NA
338 Win. Mag.*	210	2830	2590	2370	2150	1940	3735	3130	2610	2155	1760	+2.5	+1.4	-6.0	-20.9	$33
338 Win. Mag.*	225	2785	2517	2266	2029	1808	3871	3165	2565	2057	1633	+2.5	+0.4	-8.5	-25.9	$27
338 WM Superformance	225	2840	2758	2582	2414	2252	4318	3798	3331	2911	2533	1.5	0.0	-6.8	-19.5	NA
338 Win. Mag.	230	2780	2573	2375	2186	2005	3948	3382	2881	2441	2054	+2.5	+1.2	-6.3	-21.0	$40
338 Win. Mag.*	250	2660	2456	2261	2075	1898	3927	3348	2837	2389	1999	+2.5	+0.2	-9.0	-26.2	$27
338 Ultra Mag.	250	2860	2645	2440	2244	2057	4540	3882	3303	2794	2347	1.7	0.0	-7.6	-22.1	NA
338 Lapua Match	250	2900	2760	2625	2494	2366	4668	4229	3825	3452	3108	1.5	0.0	-6.6	-18.8	NA
338 Lapua Match	285	2745	2623	2504	2388	2275	4768	4352	3966	3608	3275	1.8	0.0	-7.3	-20.8	NA
8.59(.338) Galaxy	200	3100	2899	2707	2524	2347	4269	3734	3256	2829	2446	3	3.8	0.0	-9.3	NA
340 Wea. Mag.*	210	3250	2991	2746	2515	2295	4924	4170	3516	2948	2455	+2.5	+1.9	-1.8	-11.8	$56
340 Wea. Mag.*	250	3000	2806	2621	2443	2272	4995	4371	3812	3311	2864	+2.5	+2.0	-3.5	-14.8	$56
338 A-Square	250	3120	2799	2500	2220	1958	5403	4348	3469	2736	2128	+2.5	+2.7	-1.5	-10.5	NA
338-378 Wea. Mag.	225	3180	2974	2778	2591	2410	5052	4420	3856	3353	2902	3.1	3.8	0.0	-8.9	NA

Cartridge	Bullet Wgt. Grs.	VELOCITY (fps)					ENERGY (ft. lbs.)					TRAJ. (in.)				Est. Price/box
		Muzzle	100 yds.	200 yds.	300 yds.	400 yds.	Muzzle	100 yds.	200 yds.	300 yds.	400 yds.	100 yds.	200 yds.	300 yds.	400 yds.	
338 Titan	225	3230	3010	2800	2600	2409	5211	4524	3916	3377	2898	+3.07	+3.8	0.0	-8.95	NA
338 Excalibur	200	3600	3361	3134	2920	2715	5755	5015	4363	3785	3274	+2.23	+2.87	0.0	-6.99	NA
338 Excalibur	250	3250	2922	2618	2333	2066	5863	4740	3804	3021	2370	+1.3	0.0	-6.35	-19.2	NA
34, 35																
348 Winchester	200	2520	2215	1931	1672	1443	2820	2178	1656	1241	925	+2.5	-1.4	-14.7	0.0	$42
357 Magnum	158	1830	1427	1138	980	883	1175	715	454	337	274	0.0	-16.2	-33.1	0.0	$25**
35 Remington	150	2300	1874	1506	1218	1039	1762	1169	755	494	359	+2.5	-4.1	-26.3	0.0	$16
35 Remington	200	2080	1698	1376	1140	1001	1921	1280	841	577	445	+2.5	-6.3	-17.1	-33.6	$16
35 Remington	200	2225	1963	1722	1505	—	2198	1711	1317	1006	—	3.8	0	-15.6	—	NA
35 Rem. Lever Evolution	200	2225	1963	1721	1503	NA	2198	1711	1315	1003	NA	3.0	-1.3	-17.5	NA	NA
356 Winchester	200	2460	2114	1797	1517	1284	2688	1985	1434	1022	732	+2.5	-1.8	-15.1	0.0	$31
356 Winchester	250	2160	1911	1682	1476	1299	2591	2028	1571	1210	937	+2.5	-3.7	-22.2	0.0	$31
358 Winchester	200	2475	2180	1906	1655	1434	2720	2110	1612	1217	913	2.9	0	-12.6	-37.9	NA
358 Winchester	200	2490	2171	1876	1619	1379	2753	2093	1563	1151	844	+2.5	-1.6	-15.6	0.0	$31
358 STA	275	2850	2562	2292	2039	NA	4958	4009	3208	2539	NA	+1.9	0.0	-8.6	0.0	$33
350 Rem. Mag.	200	2710	2410	2130	1870	1631	3261	2579	2014	1553	1181	+2.5	-0.2	-10.0	-30.1	$33
35 Whelen	200	2675	2378	2100	1842	1606	3177	2510	1958	1506	1145	+2.5	-0.2	-10.3	-31.1	$20
35 Whelen	200	2910	2585	2283	2001	1742	3760	2968	2314	1778	1347	1.9	0	-8.6	-25.9	NA
35 Whelen	225	2500	2300	2110	1930	1770	3120	2650	2235	1870	1560	+2.6	0.0	-10.2	-29.9	NA
35 Whelen	250	2400	2197	2005	1823	1652	3197	2680	2230	1844	1515	+2.5	-1.2	-13.7	0.0	$20
358 Norma Mag.	250	2800	2510	2230	1970	1730	4350	3480	2750	2145	1655	+2.5	+1.0	-7.6	-25.2	NA
358 STA	275	2850	2562	229*2	2039	1764	4959	4009	3208	2539	1899	+1.9	0.0	-8.58	-26.1	NA
9.3mm																
9.3x57mm Mau.	286	2070	1810	1590	1390	1110	2710	2090	1600	1220	955	+2.5	-2.6	-22.5	0.0	NA
370 Sako Mag.	286	3550	2370	2200	2040	2880	4130	3570	3075	2630	2240	2.4	0.0	-9.5	-27.2	NA
9.3x62mm	232	2625	2302	2002	1728	-	2551	2731	2066	1539	-	2.6	0	-11.3	—	NA
9.3x62mm	250	2550	2376	2208	2048	—	3609	3133	2707	2328	—	0	-5.4	-17.9	—	NA
9.3x62mm	286	2360	2155	1961	1778	1608	3537	2949	2442	2008	1642	0	-6.0	-21.1	-47.2	NA
9.3x62mm	286	2400	2163	1941	1733	—	3657	2972	2392	1908	—	0	-6.7	-22.6	—	NA
9.3x64mm	286	2700	2505	2318	2139	1968	4629	3984	3411	2906	2460	+2.5	+2.7	-4.5	-19.2	NA
9.3x72mmR	193	1952	1610	1326	1120	996	1633	1112	754	538	425	0	-12.1	-44.1	—	NA
9.3x74mmR	250	2550	2376	2208	2048	—	3609	3133	2707	2328	—	0	-5.4	-17.9	—	NA
9.3x74Rmm	286	2360	2136	1924	1727	1545	3536	2896	2351	1893	1516	0.0	-6.1	-21.7	-49.0	NA
375																
375 Winchester	200	2200	1841	1526	1268	1089	2150	1506	1034	714	527	+2.5	-4.0	-26.2	0.0	$27
375 Winchester	250	1900	1647	1424	1239	1103	2005	1506	1126	852	676	+2.5	-6.9	-33.3	0.0	$27
376 Steyr	225	2600	2331	2078	1842	1625	3377	2714	2157	1694	1319	2.5	0.0	-10.6	-31.4	NA
376 Steyr	270	2600	2372	2156	1951	1759	4052	3373	2787	2283	1855	2.3	0.0	-9.9	-28.9	NA
375 Dakota	300	2600	2316	2051	1804	1579	4502	3573	2800	2167	1661	+2.4	0.0	-11.0	-32.7	NA
375 N.E. 2-1/2"	270	2000	1740	1507	1310	NA	2398	1815	1362	1026	NA	+2.5	-6.0	-30.0	0.0	NA
375 Flanged	300	2450	2150	1886	1640	NA	3998	3102	2369	1790	NA	+2.5	-2.4	-17.0	0.0	NA
375 Ruger	250	2890	2675	2471	2275	2088	4636	3973	3388	2873	2421	1.7	0	-7.4	-21.5	NA
375 Ruger	260	2900	2703	2514	2333	—	4854	4217	3649	3143	—	0	-4.0	-13.4	—	NA
375 Ruger	270	2840	2600	2372	2156	1951	4835	4052	3373	2786	2283	1.8	0.0	-8.0	-23.6	NA
375 Ruger	300	2660	2344	2050	1780	1536	4713	3660	2800	2110	1572	2.4	0.0	-10.8	-32.6	NA
375 Flanged NE	300	2400	2103	1829	NA	NA	3838	2947	2228	NA	NA	0	-6.4	-	-	NA
375 H&H Magnum	250	2890	2675	2471	2275	2088	4636	3973	3388	2873	2421	1.7	0	-7.4	-21.5	NA
375 H&H Magnum	250	2670	2450	2240	2040	1850	3955	3335	2790	2315	1905	+2.5	-0.4	-10.2	-28.4	NA
375 H&H Magnum	270	2690	2420	2166	1928	1707	4337	3510	2812	2228	1747	+2.5	0.0	-10.0	-29.4	$28
375 H&H Mag.	270	2800	2562	2337	2123	1921	4700	3936	3275	2703	2213	1.9	0	-8.3	-24.3	NA
375 H&H Magnum*	300	2530	2245	1979	1733	1512	4263	3357	2608	2001	1523	+2.5	-1.0	-10.5	-33.6	$28
375 H&H Mag.	300	2660	2345	2052	1782	1539	4713	3662	2804	2114	1577	2.4	0	-10.8	-32.6	NA
375 H&H Hvy. Mag.	270	2870	2628	2399	2182	1976	4937	4141	3451	2150	1845	+1.7	0.0	-7.2	-21.0	NA
375 H&H Hvy. Mag.	300	2705	2386	2090	1816	1568	4873	3793	2908	2195	1637	+2.3	0.0	-10.4	-31.4	NA
375 H&H Mag.	350	2300	2052	1821	-	-	4112	3273	2578	-	-	0	-6.7	-	-	NA
375 Rem. Ultra Mag.	270	2900	2558	2241	1947	1678	5041	3922	3010	2272	1689	1.9	2.7	-8.9	-27.0	NA
375 Rem. Ultra Mag.	260	2950	2750	2560	2377	—	5023	4367	3783	3262	—	0	-3.8	-12.9	—	NA
375 Rem. Ultra Mag.	300	2760	2505	2263	2035	1822	5073	4178	3412	2759	2210	2.0	0.0	-8.8	-26.1	NA
375 Wea. Mag.	260	3000	2798	2606	2421	—	5195	4520	3920	3384	—	0	-3.6	-12.4	—	NA
375 Wea. Mag.	300	2700	2420	2157	1911	1685	4856	3901	3100	2432	1891	+2.5	-.04	-10.7	0.0	NA
378 Wea. Mag.	260	3100	2894	2697	2509	—	5547	4834	4199	3633	—	0	-4.2	-14.6	—	NA
378 Wea. Mag.	270	3180	2976	2781	2594	2415	6062	5308	4635	4034	3495	+2.5	+2.6	-1.8	-11.3	$71

Cartridge	Bullet Wgt. Grs.	VELOCITY (fps)					ENERGY (ft. lbs.)					TRAJ. (in.)				Est. Price/box
		Muzzle	100 yds.	200 yds.	300 yds.	400 yds.	Muzzle	100 yds.	200 yds.	300 yds.	400 yds.	100 yds.	200 yds.	300 yds.	400 yds.	
378 Wea. Mag.	300	2929	2576	2252	1952	1680	5698	4419	3379	2538	1881	+2.5	+1.2	-7.0	-24.5	$77
375 A-Square	300	2920	2626	2351	2093	1850	5679	4594	3681	2917	2281	+2.5	+1.4	-6.0	-21.0	NA
38-40 Win.	180	1160	999	901	827	764	538	399	324	273	233	0.0	-33.9	0.0	0.0	$42**
40, 41																
400 A-Square DPM	400	2400	2146	1909	1689	NA	5116	2092	3236	2533	NA	2.98	0.0	-10.0	NA	NA
400 A-Square DPM	170	2980	2463	2001	1598	NA	3352	2289	1512	964	NA	2.16	0.0	-11.1	NA	NA
408 CheyTac	419	2850	2752	2657	2562	2470	7551	7048	6565	6108	5675	-1.02	0.0	1.9	4.2	NA
405 Win.	300	2200	1851	1545	1296		3224	2282	1589	1119		4.6	0.0	-19.5	0.0	NA
450/400-3"	400	2050	1815	1595	1402	NA	3732	2924	2259	1746	NA	0.0	NA	-33.4	NA	NA
416 Ruger	400	2400	2151	1917	1700	NA	5116	4109	3264	2568	NA	0.0	-6.0	-21.6	0.0	NA
416 Dakota	400	2450	2294	2143	1998	1859	5330	4671	4077	3544	3068	+2.5	-0.2	-10.5	-29.4	NA
416 Taylor	400	2350	2117	1896	1693	NA	4905	3980	3194	2547	NA	+2.5	-1.2	15.0	0.0	NA
416 Hoffman	400	2380	2145	1923	1718	1529	5031	4087	3285	2620	2077	+2.5	-1.0	-14.1	0.0	NA
416 Rigby	350	2600	2449	2303	2162	2026	5253	4661	4122	3632	3189	+2.5	-1.8	-10.2	-26.0	NA
416 Rigby	400	2370	2210	2050	1900	NA	4990	4315	3720	3185	NA	+2.5	-0.7	-12.1	0.0	NA
416 Rigby	400	2400	2115	1851	1611	—	5115	3973	3043	2305	—	0	-6.5	-21.8	—	NA
416 Rigby	400	2415	2156	1915	1691	—	5180	4130	3256	2540	—	0	-6.0	-21.6	—	NA
416 Rigby	410	2370	2110	1870	1640	NA	5115	4050	3165	2455	NA	+2.5	-2.4	-17.3	0.0	$110
416 Rem. Mag.*	350	2520	2270	2034	1814	1611	4935	4004	3216	2557	2017	+2.5	-0.8	-12.6	-35.0	$82
416 Rem. Mag.	400	2400	2142	1901	1679	—	5116	4076	3211	2504	—	3.1	0	-12.7	—	NA
416 Rem. Mag.	450	2150	1925	1716	-	-	4620	3702	2942	-	-	0	-7.8	-	-	NA
416 Wea. Mag.*	400	2700	2397	2115	1852	1613	6474	5104	3971	3047	2310	+2.5	0.0	-10.1	-30.4	$96
10.57 (416) Meteor	400	2730	2532	2342	2161	1987	6621	5695	4874	4147	3508	+1.9	0.0	-8.3	-24.0	NA
500/416 N.E.	400	2300	2092	1895	1712	—	4697	3887	3191	2602	—	0	-7.2	-24.0	—	NA
500/416 N.E.	410	2325	2062	1817	-	-	4620	3735	2996	NA	NA	0	-6.7	-	-	NA
404 Jeffrey	400	2150	1924	1716	1525	NA	4105	3289	2614	2064	NA	+2.5	-4.0	-22.1	0.0	NA
404 Jeffrey	400	2300	2053	1823	1611	—	4698	3743	2950	2306	—	0	-6.8	-24.1	—	NA
404 Jeffery	400	2350	2020	1720	1458	—	4904	3625	2629	1887	—	0	-6.5	-21.8	—	NA
404 Jeffery	450	2150	1946	1755	-	-	4620	3784	3078	-	-	0	-7.6	-	-	NA
425, 44																
425 Express	400	2400	2160	1934	1725	NA	5115	4145	3322	2641	NA	+2.5	-1.0	-14.0	0.0	NA
44-40 Win.	200	1190	1006	900	822	756	629	449	360	300	254	0.0	-33.3	0.0	0.0	$36**
44 Rem. Mag.	210	1920	1477	1155	982	880	1719	1017	622	450	361	0.0	-17.6	0.0	0.0	$14
44 Rem. Mag.	240	1760	1380	1114	970	878	1650	1015	661	501	411	0.0	-17.6	0.0	0.0	$13
444 Marlin	240	2350	1815	1377	1087	941	2942	1753	1001	630	472	+2.5	-15.1	-31.0	0.0	$22
444 Marlin	265	2120	1733	1405	1160	1012	2644	1768	1162	791	603	+2.5	-6.0	-32.2	0.0	Disc.
444 Mar. Lever Evolution	265	2325	1971	1652	1380	NA	3180	2285	1606	1120	NA	3.0	-1.4	-18.6	NA	NA
444 Mar. Superformance	265	2400	1976	1603	1298	NA	3389	2298	1512	991	NA	4.1	0.0	-17.8	NA	NA
45																
45-70 Govt.	250	2025	1616	1285	1068	—	2276	1449	917	634	—	6.1	0	-27.2	—	NA
45-70 Govt.	300	1810	1497	1244	1073	969	2182	1492	1031	767	625	0.0	-14.8	0.0	0.0	$21
45-70 Govt. Supreme	300	1880	1558	1292	1103	988	2355	1616	1112	811	651	0.0	-12.9	-46.0	-105.0	NA
45-70 Govt.	325	2000	1685	1413	1197	—	2886	2049	1441	1035	—	5.5	0	-23.0	—	NA
45-70 Lever Evolution	325	2050	1729	1450	1225	NA	3032	2158	1516	1083	NA	3.0	-4.1	-27.8	NA	NA
45-70 Govt. CorBon	350	1800	1526	1296			2519	1810	1307			0.0	-14.6	0.0	0.0	NA
45-70 Govt.	405	1330	1168	1055	977	918	1590	1227	1001	858	758	0.0	-24.6	0.0	0.0	$21
45-70 Govt. PMC Cowboy	405	1550	1193	—	—	—	1639	1280	—	—	—	0.0	-23.9	0.0	0.0	NA
45-70 Govt. Garrett	415	1850	—	—	—	—	3150	—	—	—	—	3.0	-7.0	0.0	0.0	NA
45-70 Govt. Garrett	530	1550	1343	1178	1062	982	2828	2123	1633	1327	1135	0.0	-17.8	0.0	0.0	NA
450 Bushmaster	250	2200	1831	1508	1480	1073	2686	1860	1262	864	639	0.0	-9.0	-33.5	0.0	NA
450 Marlin	325	2225	1887	1587	1332	—	3572	2570	1816	1280	—	4.2	0	-18.1	—	NA
450 Marlin	350	2100	1774	1488	1254	1089	3427	2446	1720	1222	922	0.0	-9.7	-35.2	0.0	NA
450 Mar. Lever Evolution	325	2225	1887	1585	1331	NA	3572	2569	1813	1278	NA	3.0	-2.2	-21.3	NA	NA
457 Wild West Magnum	350	2150	1718	1348	NA	NA	3645	2293	1413	NA	NA	0.0	-10.5	NA	NA	NA
450/500 N.E.	400	2050	1820	1609	1420	—	3732	2940	2298	1791	—	0	-9.7	-32.8	—	NA
450 N.E. 3-1/4"	465	2190	1970	1765	1577	NA	4952	4009	3216	2567	NA	+2.5	-3.0	-20.0	0.0	NA
450 N.E.	480	2150	1881	1635	1418	—	4927	3769	2850	2144	—	0	-8.4	-29.8	—	NA
450 N.E. 3-1/4"	500	2150	1920	1708	1514	NA	5132	4093	3238	2544	NA	+2.5	-4.0	-22.9	0.0	NA
450 No. 2	465	2190	1970	1765	1577	NA	4952	4009	3216	2567	NA	+2.5	-3.0	-20.0	0.0	NA
450 No. 2	500	2150	1920	1708	1514	NA	5132	4093	3238	2544	NA	+2.5	-4.0	-22.9	0.0	NA
450 Ackley Mag.	465	2400	2169	1950	1747	NA	5947	4857	3927	3150	NA	+2.5	-1.0	-13.7	0.0	NA
450 Ackley Mag.	500	2320	2081	1855	1649	NA	5975	4085	3820	3018	NA	+2.5	-1.2	-15.0	0.0	NA

Cartridge	Bullet Wgt. Grs.	VELOCITY (fps)					ENERGY (ft. lbs.)					TRAJ. (in.)				Est. Price/box
		Muzzle	100 yds.	200 yds.	300 yds.	400 yds.	Muzzle	100 yds.	200 yds.	300 yds.	400 yds.	100 yds.	200 yds.	300 yds.	400 yds.	
450 Rigby	500	2350	2139	1939	1752	—	6130	5079	4176	3408	—	0	-6.8	-22.9	—	NA
450 Rigby	550	2100	1887	1690	–	–	5387	4311	3425	–	–	0	-8.3	–	–	NA
458 Win. Magnum	400	2380	2170	1960	1770	NA	5030	4165	3415	2785	NA	+2.5	-0.4	-13.4	0.0	$73
458 Win. Magnum	465	2220	1999	1791	1601	NA	5088	4127	3312	2646	NA	+2.5	-2.0	-17.7	0.0	NA
458 Win. Magnum	500	2040	1823	1623	1442	1237	4620	3689	2924	2308	1839	+2.5	-3.5	-22.0	0.0	$61
458 Win. Mag.	500	2140	1880	1643	1432	—	5084	3294	2996	2276	—	0	-8.4	-29.8	—	NA
458 Win. Magnum	510	2040	1770	1527	1319	1157	4712	3547	2640	1970	1516	+2.5	-4.1	-25.0	0.0	$41
458 Lott	465	2380	2150	1932	1730	NA	5848	4773	3855	3091	NA	+2.5	-1.0	-14.0	0.0	NA
458 Lott	500	2300	2029	1778	1551	—	5873	4569	3509	2671	—	0	-7.0	-25.1	—	NA
458 Lott	500	2300	2062	1838	1633	NA	5873	4719	3748	2960	NA	+2.5	-1.6	-16.4	0.0	NA
460 Short A-Sq.	500	2420	2175	1943	1729	NA	6501	5250	4193	3319	NA	+2.5	-0.8	-12.8	0.0	NA
460 Wea. Mag.	500	2700	2404	2128	1869	1635	8092	6416	5026	3878	2969	+2.5	+0.6	-8.9	-28.0	$72
475																
500/465 N.E.	480	2150	1917	1703	1507	NA	4926	3917	3089	2419	NA	+2.5	-4.0	-22.2	0.0	NA
470 Rigby	500	2150	1940	1740	1560	NA	5130	4170	3360	2695	NA	+2.5	-2.8	-19.4	0.0	NA
470 Nitro Ex.	480	2190	1954	1735	1536	NA	5111	4070	3210	2515	NA	+2.5	-3.5	-20.8	0.0	NA
470 N.E.	500	2150	1885	1643	1429	—	5132	3945	2998	2267	—	0	-8.9	-30.8	—	NA
470 Nitro Ex.	500	2150	1890	1650	1440	1270	5130	3965	3040	2310	1790	+2.5	-4.3	-24.0	0.0	$177
475 No. 2	500	2200	1955	1728	1522	NA	5375	4243	3316	2573	NA	+2.5	-3.2	-20.9	0.0	NA
50, 58																
50 Alaskan	450	2000	1729	1492	NA	NA	3997	2987	2224	NA	NA	0.0	-11.25	NA	NA	NA
500 Jeffery	570	2300	1979	1688	1434	—	6694	4958	3608	2604	—	0	-8.2	-28.6	—	NA
505 Gibbs	525	2300	2063	1840	1637	NA	6166	4922	3948	3122	NA	+2.5	-3.0	-18.0	0.0	NA
505 Gibbs	570	2100	1893	1701	-	-	5583	4538	3664	-	-	0	-8.1	-	-	NA
505 Gibbs	600	2100	1899	1711	-	-	5877	4805	3904	-	-	0	-8.1	-	-	NA
500 N.E.	570	2150	1889	1651	1439	—	5850	4518	3450	2621	—	0	-8.9	-30.6	—	NA
500 N.E.-3"	570	2150	1928	1722	1533	NA	5850	4703	3752	2975	NA	+2.5	-3.7	-22.0	0.0	NA
500 N.E.-3"	600	2150	1927	1721	1531	NA	6158	4947	3944	3124	NA	+2.5	-4.0	-22.0	0.0	NA
495 A-Square	570	2350	2117	1896	1693	NA	5850	4703	3752	2975	NA	+2.5	-1.0	-14.5	0.0	NA
495 A-Square	600	2280	2050	1833	1635	NA	6925	5598	4478	3562	NA	+2.5	-2.0	-17.0	0.0	NA
500 A-Square	600	2380	2144	1922	1766	NA	7546	6126	4920	3922	NA	+2.5	-3.0	-17.0	0.0	NA
500 A-Square	707	2250	2040	1841	1567	NA	7947	6530	5318	4311	NA	+2.5	-2.0	-17.0	0.0	NA
500 BMG PMC	660	3080	2854	2639	2444	2248	13688		500 yd. zero			+3.1	+3.9	+4.7	+2.8	NA
577 Nitro Ex.	750	2050	1793	1562	1360	NA	6990	5356	4065	3079	NA	+2.5	-5.0	-26.0	0.0	NA
577 Tyrannosaur	750	2400	2141	1898	1675	NA	9591	7633	5996	4671	NA	+3.0	0.0	-12.9	0.0	NA
600, 700																
600 N.E.	900	1950	1680	1452	NA	NA	7596	5634	4212	NA	NA	+5.6	0.0	0.0	0.0	NA
700 N.E.	1200	1900	1676	1472	NA	NA	9618	7480	5774	NA	NA	+5.7	0.0	0.0	0.0	NA
50 BMG																
50 BMG	624	2952	2820	2691	2566	2444	12077	11028	10036	9125	8281	0	-2.9	-10.6	-23.5	NA
50 BMG Match	750	2820	2728	2637	2549	2462	13241	12388	11580	10815	10090	1.5	0.0	-6.5	-18.3	NA

Notes: Blanks are available in 32 S&W, 38 S&W and 38 Special. "V" after barrel length indicates test barrel was vented to produce ballistics similar to a revolver with a normal barrel-to-cylinder gap. Ammo prices are per 50 rounds except when marked with an ** which signifies a 20 round box; *** signifies a 25-round box. Not all loads are available from all ammo manufacturers. Listed loads are those made by Remington, Winchester, Federal, and others. DISC. is a discontinued load. Prices are rounded to the nearest whole dollar and will vary with brand and retail outlet.

Cartridge	Bullet Wgt. Grs.	VELOCITY (fps)			ENERGY (ft. lbs.)			Mid-Range Traj. (in.)		Bbl. Lgth. (in).	Est. Price/ box
		Muzzle	50 yds.	100 yds.	Muzzle	50 yds.	100 yds.	50 yds.	100 yds.		
22, 25											
221 Rem. Fireball	50	2650	2380	2130	780	630	505	0.2	0.8	10.5"	$15
25 Automatic	35	900	813	742	63	51	43	NA	NA	2"	$18
25 Automatic	45	815	730	655	65	55	40	1.8	7.7	2"	$21
25 Automatic	50	760	705	660	65	55	50	2.0	8.7	2"	$17
30											
7.5mm Swiss	107	1010	NA	NA	240	NA	NA	NA	NA	NA	NEW
7.62x25 Tokarev	85	1647	1458	1295	512	401	317	0	-3.2	4.75	
7.62mmTokarev	87	1390	NA	NA	365	NA	NA	0.6	NA	4.5"	NA
7.62 Nagant	97	790	NA	NA	134	NA	NA	NA	NA	NA	NEW
7.63 Mauser	88	1440	NA	NA	405	NA	NA	NA	NA	NA	NEW
30 Luger	93	1220	1110	1040	305	255	225	0.9	3.5	4.5"	$34
30 Carbine	110	1790	1600	1430	785	625	500	0.4	1.7	10"	$28
30-357 AeT	123	1992	NA	NA	1084	NA	NA	NA	NA	10"	NA
32											
32 NAA	80	1000	933	880	178	155	137	NA	NA	4"	NA
32 S&W	88	680	645	610	90	80	75	2.5	10.5	3"	$17
32 S&W Long	98	705	670	635	115	100	90	2.3	10.5	4"	$17
32 Short Colt	80	745	665	590	100	80	60	2.2	9.9	4"	$19
32 H&R	80	1150	1039	963	235	192	165	NA	NA	4"	NA
32 H&R Magnum	85	1100	1020	930	230	195	165	1.0	4.3	4.5"	$21
32 H&R Magnum	95	1030	940	900	225	190	170	1.1	4.7	4.5"	$19
327 Federal Magnum	85	1400	1220	1090	370	280	225	NA	NA	4-V	NA
327 Federal Magnum	100	1500	1320	1180	500	390	310	-0.2	-4.50	4-V	NA
32 Automatic	60	970	895	835	125	105	95	1.3	5.4	4"	$22
32 Automatic	60	1000	917	849	133	112	96			4"	NA
32 Automatic	65	950	890	830	130	115	100	1.3	5.6	NA	NA
32 Automatic	71	905	855	810	130	115	95	1.4	5.8	4"	$19
8mm Lebel Pistol	111	850	NA	NA	180	NA	NA	NA	NA	NA	NEW
8mm Steyr	112	1080	NA	NA	290	NA	NA	NA	NA	NA	NEW
8mm Gasser	126	850	NA	NA	200	NA	NA	NA	NA	NA	NEW
9mm, 38											
380 Automatic	56	1315	–	–	215	–	–	–	–	–	NA
380 Automatic	60	1130	960	NA	170	120	NA	1.0	NA	NA	NA
380 Automatic	75	950	NA	NA	183	NA	NA	NA	NA	3"	$33
380 Automatic	85/88	990	920	870	190	165	145	1.2	5.1	4"	$20
380 Automatic	90	1000	890	800	200	160	130	1.2	5.5	3.75"	$10
380 Automatic	95/100	955	865	785	190	160	130	1.4	5.9	4"	$20
38 Super Auto +P	115	1300	1145	1040	430	335	275	0.7	3.3	5"	$26
38 Super Auto +P	125/130	1215	1100	1015	425	350	300	0.8	3.6	5"	$26
38 Super Auto +P	147	1100	1050	1000	395	355	325	0.9	4.0	5"	NA
38 Super Auto +P	115	1130	1016	938	326	264	225	1	-9.5	-	NA
9x18mm Makarov	95	1000	930	874	211	182	161	NA	NA	4"	NEW
9x18mm Ultra	100	1050	NA	NA	240	NA	NA	NA	NA	NA	NEW
9x21	124	1150	1050	980	365	305	265	NA	NA	4"	NA
9x21 IMI	123	1220	1095	1010	409	330	281	-3.15	–	5.0	NA
9x23mm Largo	124	1190	1055	966	390	306	257	0.7	3.7	4"	NA
9x23mm Win.	125	1450	1249	1103	583	433	338	0.6	2.8	NA	NA
9mm Steyr	115	1180	NA	NA	350	NA	NA	NA	NA	NA	NEW
9mm Luger	80	1445	–	–	–	385	–	–	–	–	NA
9mm Luger	88	1500	1190	1010	440	275	200	0.6	3.1	4"	$24
9mm Luger	90	1360	1112	978	370	247	191	NA	NA	4"	$26
9mm Luger	92	1325	1117	991	359	255	201	-3.2	–	4.0	NA
9mm Luger	95	1300	1140	1010	350	275	215	0.8	3.4	4"	NA
9mm Luger	100	1180	1080	NA	305	255	NA	0.9	NA	4"	NA
9mm Luger Guard Dog	105	1230	1070	970	355	265	220	NA	NA	4"	NA

Cartridge	Bullet Wgt. Grs.	VELOCITY (fps)			ENERGY (ft. lbs.)			Mid-Range Traj. (in.)		Bbl. Lgth. (in.)	Est. Price/ box
		Muzzle	50 yds.	100 yds.	Muzzle	50 yds.	100 yds.	50 yds.	100 yds.		
9mm Luger	115	1155	1045	970	340	280	240	0.9	3.9	4"	$21
9mm Luger	123/125	1110	1030	970	340	290	260	1.0	4.0	4"	$23
9mm Luger	124	1150	1040	965	364	298	256	-4.5	—	4.0	NA
9mm Luger	135	1010	960	918	306	276	253	—	—	4.0	NA
9mm Luger	140	935	890	850	270	245	225	1.3	5.5	4"	$23
9mm Luger	147	990	940	900	320	290	265	1.1	4.9	4"	$26
9mm Luger +P	90	1475	NA	NA	437	NA	NA	NA	NA	NA	NA
9mm Luger +P	115	1250	1113	1019	399	316	265	0.8	3.5	4"	$27
9mm Federal	115	1280	1130	1040	420	330	280	0.7	3.3	4"V	$24
9mm Luger Vector	115	1155	1047	971	341	280	241	NA	NA	4"	NA
9mm Luger +P	124	1180	1089	1021	384	327	287	0.8	3.8	4"	NA
38											
38 S&W	146	685	650	620	150	135	125	2.4	10.0	4"	$19
38 S&W Short	145	720	689	660	167	153	140	-8.5	—	5.0	NA
38 Short Colt	125	730	685	645	150	130	115	2.2	9.4	6"	$19
39 Special	100	950	900	NA	200	180	NA	1.3	NA	4"V	NA
38 Special	110	945	895	850	220	195	175	1.3	5.4	4"V	$23
38 Special	110	945	895	850	220	195	175	1.3	5.4	4"V	$23
38 Special	130	775	745	710	175	160	120	1.9	7.9	4"V	$22
38 Special Cowboy	140	800	767	735	199	183	168			7.5" V	NA
38 (Multi-Ball)	140	830	730	505	215	130	80	2.0	10.6	4"V	$10**
38 Special	148	710	635	565	165	130	105	2.4	10.6	4"V	$17
38 Special	158	755	725	690	200	185	170	2.0	8.3	4"V	$18
38 Special +P	95	1175	1045	960	290	230	195	0.9	3.9	4"V	$23
38 Special +P	110	995	925	870	240	210	185	1.2	5.1	4"V	$23
38 Special +P	125	975	929	885	264	238	218	1	5.2	4"	NA
38 Special +P	125	945	900	860	250	225	205	1.3	5.4	4"V	#23
38 Special +P	129	945	910	870	255	235	215	1.3	5.3	4"V	$11
38 Special +P	130	925	887	852	247	227	210	1.3	5.50	4"V	NA
38 Special +P	147/150	884	NA	NA	264	NA	NA	NA	NA	4"V	$27
38 Special +P	158	890	855	825	280	255	240	1.4	6.0	4"V	$20
357											
357 SIG	115	1520	NA	NA	593	NA	NA	NA	NA	NA	NA
357 SIG	124	1450	NA	NA	578	NA	NA	NA	NA	NA	NA
357 SIG	125	1350	1190	1080	510	395	325	0.7	3.1	4"	NA
357 SIG	135	1225	1112	1031	450	371	319	—	—	4.0	NA
357 SIG	147	1225	1132	1060	490	418	367	—	—	4.0	NA
357 SIG	150	1130	1030	970	420	355	310	0.9	4.0	NA	NA
356 TSW	115	1520	NA	NA	593	NA	NA	NA	NA	NA	NA
356 TSW	124	1450	NA	NA	578	NA	NA	NA	NA	NA	NA
356 TSW	135	1280	1120	1010	490	375	310	0.8	3.5	NA	NA
356 TSW	147	1220	1120	1040	485	410	355	0.8	3.5	5"	NA
357 Mag., Super Clean	105	1650									NA
357 Magnum	110	1295	1095	975	410	290	230	0.8	3.5	4"V	$25
357 (Med.Vel.)	125	1220	1075	985	415	315	270	0.8	3.7	4"V	$25
357 Magnum	125	1450	1240	1090	585	425	330	0.6	2.8	4"V	$25
357 Magnum	125	1500	1312	1163	624	478	376	—	—	8.0	NA
357 (Multi-Ball)	140	1155	830	665	420	215	135	1.2	6.4	4"V	$11**
357 Magnum	140	1360	1195	1075	575	445	360	0.7	3.0	4"V	$25
357 Magnum FlexTip	140	1440	1274	1143	644	504	406	NA	NA	NA	NA
357 Magnum	145	1290	1155	1060	535	430	360	0.8	3.5	4"V	$26
357 Magnum	150/158	1235	1105	1015	535	430	360	0.8	3.5	4"V	$25
357 Mag. Cowboy	158	800	761	725	225	203	185				NA
357 Magnum	165	1290	1189	1108	610	518	450	0.7	3.1	8-3/8"	NA
357 Magnum	180	1145	1055	985	525	445	390	0.9	3.9	4"V	$25
357 Magnum	180	1180	1088	1020	557	473	416	0.8	3.6	8"V	NA
357 Mag. CorBon F.A.	180	1650	1512	1386	1088	913	767	1.66	0.0		NA
357 Mag. CorBon	200	1200	1123	1061	640	560	500	3.19	0.0		NA
357 Rem. Maximum	158	1825	1590	1380	1170	885	670	0.4	1.7	10.5"	$14**
40, 10mm											
40 S&W	107	1320	-	-	414	-	-	-	-	-	NA

Cartridge	Bullet Wgt. Grs.	VELOCITY (fps)			ENERGY (ft. lbs.)			Mid-Range Traj. (in.)		Bbl. Lgth. (in).	Est. Price/ box
		Muzzle	50 yds.	100 yds.	Muzzle	50 yds.	100 yds.	50 yds.	100 yds.		
40 S&W	120	1150	–	–	352	–	–	–	—	–	$38
40 S&W	125	1265	1102	998	444	337	276	-3.0	–	4.0	NA
40 S&W	135	1140	1070	NA	390	345	NA	0.9	NA	4"	NA
40 S&W Guard Dog	135	1200	1040	940	430	325	265	NA	NA	4"	NA
40 S&W	155	1140	1026	958	447	362	309	0.9	4.1	4"	$14***
40 S&W	165	1150	NA	NA	485	NA	NA	NA	NA	4"	$18***
40 S&W	175	1010	948	899	396	350	314	–	–	4.0	NA
40 S&W	180	985	936	893	388	350	319	1.4	5.0	4"	$14***
40 S&W	180	1000	943	896	400	355	321	4.52	–	4.0	NA
40 S&W	180	1015	960	914	412	368	334	1.3	4.5	4"	NA
400 Cor-Bon	135	1450	NA	NA	630	NA	NA	NA	NA	5"	NA
10mm Automatic	155	1125	1046	986	436	377	335	0.9	3.9	5"	$26
10mm Automatic	155	1265	1118	1018	551	430	357	–	–	5.0	NA
10mm Automatic	170	1340	1165	1145	680	510	415	0.7	3.2	5"	$31
10mm Automatic	175	1290	1140	1035	650	505	420	0.7	3.3	5.5"	$11**
10mm Auto. (FBI)	180	950	905	865	361	327	299	1.5	5.4	4"	$16**
10mm Automatic	180	1030	970	920	425	375	340	1.1	4.7	5"	$16**
10mm Auto H.V.	180	1240	1124	1037	618	504	430	0.8	3.4	5"	$27
10mm Automatic	200	1160	1070	1010	495	510	430	0.9	3.8	5"	$14**
10.4mm Italian	177	950	NA	NA	360	NA	NA	NA	NA	NA	NEW
41 Action Exp.	180	1000	947	903	400	359	326	0.5	4.2	5"	$13**
41 Rem. Magnum	170	1420	1165	1015	760	515	390	0.7	3.2	4"V	$33
41 Rem. Magnum	175	1250	1120	1030	605	490	410	0.8	3.4	4"V	$14**
41 (Med. Vel.)	210	965	900	840	435	375	330	1.3	5.4	4"V	$30
41 Rem. Magnum	210	1300	1160	1060	790	630	535	0.7	3.2	4"V	$33
41 Rem. Magnum	240	1250	1151	1075	833	706	616	0.8	3.3	6.5V	NA
44											
44 S&W Russian	247	780	NA	NA	335	NA	NA	NA	NA	NA	NA
44 Special	210	900	861	825	360	329	302	5.57	–	6.0	NA
44 Special FTX	165	900	848	802	297	263	235	NA	NA	2.5"	NA
44 S&W Special	180	980	NA	NA	383	NA	NA	NA	NA	6.5"	NA
44 S&W Special	180	1000	935	882	400	350	311	NA	NA	7.5"V	NA
44 S&W Special	200	875	825	780	340	302	270	1.2	6.0	6"	$13**
44 S&W Special	200	1035	940	865	475	390	335	1.1	4.9	6.5"	$13**
44 S&W Special	240/246	755	725	695	310	285	265	2.0	8.3	6.5"	$26
44-40 Win.	200	722	698	676	232	217	203	-3.4	-23.7	4.0	NA
44-40 Win.	205	725	689	655	239	216	195	–	–	7.5	NA
44-40 Win.	210	725	698	672	245	227	210	-11.6	–	5.5	NA
44-40 Win.	225	725	697	670	263	243	225	-3.4	-23.8	4.0	NA
44-40 Win. Cowboy	225	750	723	695	281	261	242				NA
44 Rem. Magnum	180	1610	1365	1175	1035	745	550	0.5	2.3	4"V	$18**
44 Rem. Magnum	200	1296	1193	1110	747	632	548	-.5	-6.2	6.0	NA
44 Rem. Magnum	200	1400	1192	1053	870	630	492	0.6	NA	6.5"	$20
44 Rem. Magnum	200	1500	1332	1194	999	788	633	–	–	7.5	NA
44 Rem. Magnum	210	1495	1310	1165	1040	805	635	0.6	2.5	6.5"	$18**
44 Rem. Mag. FlexTip	225	1410	1240	1111	993	768	617	NA	NA	NA	NA
44 (Med. Vel.)	240	1000	945	900	535	475	435	1.1	4.8	6.5"	$17
44 R.M. (Jacketed)	240	1180	1080	1010	740	625	545	0.9	3.7	4"V	$18**
44 R.M. (Lead)	240	1350	1185	1070	970	750	610	0.7	3.1	4"V	$29
44 Rem. Magnum	250	1180	1100	1040	775	670	600	0.8	3.6	6.5"V	$21
44 Rem. Magnum	250	1250	1148	1070	867	732	635	0.8	3.3	6.5"V	NA
44 Rem. Magnum	275	1235	1142	1070	931	797	699	0.8	3.3	6.5"	NA
44 Rem. Magnum	300	1150	1083	1030	881	781	706	–	–	7.5	NA
44 Rem. Magnum	300	1200	1100	1026	959	806	702	NA	NA	7.5"	$17
44 Rem. Magnum	330	1385	1297	1220	1406	1234	1090	1.83	0.00	NA	NA
44 Webley	262	850	–	–	–	–	–	–	–	–	NA
440 CorBon	260	1700	1544	1403	1669	1377	1136	1.58	NA	10"	NA
45, 50											
450 Short Colt/450 Revolver	226	830	NA	NA	350	NA	NA	NA	NA	NA	NEW
45 S&W Schofield	180	730	NA	NA	213	NA	NA	NA	NA	NA	NA
45 S&W Schofield	230	730	NA	NA	272	NA	NA	NA	NA	NA	NA

Cartridge	Bullet Wgt. Grs.	VELOCITY (fps)			ENERGY (ft. lbs.)			Mid-Range Traj. (in.)		Bbl. Lgth. (in).	Est. Price/ box
		Muzzle	50 yds.	100 yds.	Muzzle	50 yds.	100 yds.	50 yds.	100 yds.		
45 G.A.P.	165	1007	936	879	372	321	283	-1.4	-11.8	5.0	NA
45 G.A.P.	185	1090	970	890	490	385	320	1.0	4.7	5"	NA
45 G.A.P.	230	880	842	NA	396	363	NA	NA	NA	NA	NA
45 Automatic	118	1307	–	–	448	–	–	–	–	–	NA
45 Automatic	150	1050	NA	NA	403	NA	NA	NA	NA	NA	$40
45 Automatic	165	1030	930	NA	385	315	NA	1.2	NA	5"	NA
45 Automatic Guard Dog	165	1140	1030	950	475	390	335	NA	NA	5"	NA
45 Automatic	185	1000	940	890	410	360	325	1.1	4.9	5"	$28
45 Auto. (Match)	185	770	705	650	245	204	175	2.0	8.7	5"	$28
45 Auto. (Match)	200	940	890	840	392	352	312	2.0	8.6	5"	$20
45 Automatic	200	975	917	860	421	372	328	1.4	5.0	5"	$18
45 Automatic	230	830	800	675	355	325	300	1.6	6.8	5"	$27
45 Automatic	230	880	846	816	396	366	340	1.5	6.1	5"	NA
45 Automatic +P	165	1250	NA	NA	573	NA	NA	NA	NA	NA	NA
45 Automatic +P	185	1140	1040	970	535	445	385	0.9	4.0	5"	$31
45 Automatic +P	200	1055	982	925	494	428	380	NA	NA	5"	NA
45 Super	185	1300	1190	1108	694	582	504	NA	NA	5"	NA
45 Win. Magnum	230	1400	1230	1105	1000	775	635	0.6	2.8	5"	$14**
45 Win. Magnum	260	1250	1137	1053	902	746	640	0.8	3.3	5"	$16**
45 Win. Mag. CorBon	320	1150	1080	1025	940	830	747	3.47			NA
455 Webley MKII	262	850	NA	NA	420	NA	NA	NA	NA	NA	NA
45 Colt FTX	185	920	870	826	348	311	280	NA	NA	3"V	NA
45 Colt	200	1000	938	889	444	391	351	1.3	4.8	5.5"	$21
45 Colt	225	960	890	830	460	395	345	1.3	5.5	5.5"	$22
45 Colt + P CorBon	265	1350	1225	1126	1073	884	746	2.65	0.0		NA
45 Colt + P CorBon	300	1300	1197	1114	1126	956	827	2.78	0.0		NA
45 Colt	250/255	860	820	780	410	375	340	1.6	6.6	5.5"	$27
454 Casull	250	1300	1151	1047	938	735	608	0.7	3.2	7.5"V	NA
454 Casull	260	1800	1577	1381	1871	1436	1101	0.4	1.8	7.5"V	NA
454 Casull	300	1625	1451	1308	1759	1413	1141	0.5	2.0	7.5"V	NA
454 Casull CorBon	360	1500	1387	1286	1800	1640	1323	2.01	0.0		NA
460 S&W	200	2300	2042	1801	2350	1851	1441	0	-1.60	NA	NA
460 S&W	260	2000	1788	1592	2309	1845	1464	NA	NA	7.5"V	NA
460 S&W	250	1450	1267	1127	1167	891	705	NA	NA	8.375-V	NA
460 S&W	250	1900	1640	1412	2004	1494	1106	0	-2.75	NA	NA
460 S&W	300	1750	1510	1300	2040	1510	1125	NA	NA	8.4-V	NA
460 S&W	395	1550	1389	1249	2108	1691	1369	0	-4.00	NA	NA
475 Linebaugh	400	1350	1217	1119	1618	1315	1112	NA	NA	NA	NA
480 Ruger	325	1350	1191	1076	1315	1023	835	2.6	0.0	7.5"	NA
50 Action Exp.	300	1475	1251	1092	1449	1043	795	-	-	6"	NA
50 Action Exp.	325	1400	1209	1075	1414	1055	835	0.2	2.3	6"	$24**
500 S&W	275	1665	1392	1183	1693	1184	854	1.5	NA	8.375	NA
500 S&W	300	1950	1653	1396	2533	1819	1298	—	—	8.5	NA
500 S&W	325	1800	1560	1350	2340	1755	1315	NA	NA	8.4-V	NA
500 S&W	350	1400	1231	1106	1523	1178	951	NA	NA	10"	NA
500 S&W	400	1675	1472	1299	2493	1926	1499	1.3	NA	8.375	NA
500 S&W	440	1625	1367	1169	2581	1825	1337	1.6	NA	8.375	NA
500 S&W	500	1300	1178	1085	1876	1541	1308	—	—	8.5	NA
500 S&W	500	1425	1281	1164	2254	1823	1505	NA	NA	10"	NA

Note: The actual ballistics obtained with your firearm can vary considerably from the advertised ballistics.
Also, ballistics can vary from lot to lot with the same brand and type load.

Cartridge	Bullet Wt. Grs.	Velocity (fps) 22-1/2" Bbl.		Energy (ft. lbs.) 22-1/2" Bbl.		Mid-Range Traj. (in.)	Muzzle Velocity
		Muzzle	100 yds.	Muzzle	100 yds.	100 yds.	6" Bbl.
17 Aguila	20	1850	1267	NA	NA	NA	NA
17 Hornady Mach 2	15.5	2050	1450	149	75	NA	NA
17 Hornady Mach 2	17	2100	1530	166	88	0.7	NA
17 HMR Lead Free	15.5	2550	1901	NA	NA	.90	NA
17 HMR TNT Green	16	2500	1642	222	96	NA	NA
17 HMR	17	2550	1902	245	136	NA	NA
17 HMR	20	2375	1776	250	140	NA	NA
17 Win. Super Mag.	20 Tipped	3000	2504	400	278	0.0	NA
17 Win. Super Mag.	20 JHP	3000	2309	400	237	0.0	NA
17 Win. Super Mag.	25 Tipped	2600	2230	375	276	0.0	NA
5mm Rem. Rimfire Mag.	30	2300	1669	352	188	NA	24
22 Short Blank	—	—	—	—	—	—	—
22 Short CB	29	727	610	33	24	NA	706
22 Short Target	29	830	695	44	31	6.8	786
22 Short HP	27	1164	920	81	50	4.3	1077
22 Colibri	20	375	183	6	1	NA	NA
22 Super Colibri	20	500	441	11	9	NA	NA
22 Long CB	29	727	610	33	24	NA	706
22 Long HV	29	1180	946	90	57	4.1	1031
22 LR Pistol Match	40	1070	890	100	70	4.6	940
22 LR Shrt. Range Green	21	1650	912	127	NA	NA	NA
CCI Quiet 22 LR	40	710	640	45	36	NA	NA
22 LR Sub Sonic HP	38	1050	901	93	69	4.7	NA
22 LR Segmented HP	40	1050	897	98	72	NA	NA
22 LR Standard Velocity	40	1070	890	100	70	4.6	940
22 LR AutoMatch	40	1200	990	130	85	NA	NA
22 LR HV	40	1255	1016	140	92	3.6	1060
22 LR Silhoutte	42	1220	1003	139	94	3.6	1025
22 SSS	60	950	802	120	86	NA	NA
22 LR HV HP	40	1280	1001	146	89	3.5	1085
22 Velocitor GDHP	40	1435	–	–	–	NA	NA
22LR CCI Copper	21	1850	–	–	–	–	–
22 LR Segmented HP	37	1435	1080	169	96	2.9	NA
22 LR Hyper HP	32/33/34	1500	1075	165	85	2.8	NA
22 LR Expediter	32	1640	NA	191	NA	NA	NA
22 LR Stinger HP	32	1640	1132	191	91	2.6	1395
22 LR Lead Free	30	1650	NA	181	NA	NA	NA
22 LR Hyper Vel	30	1750	1191	204	93	NA	NA
22 LR Shot #12	31	950	NA	NA	NA	NA	NA
22 WRF LFN	45	1300	1015	169	103	3	NA
22 Win. Mag. Lead Free	28	2200	NA	301	NA	NA	NA
22 Win. Mag.	30	2200	1373	322	127	1.4	1610
22 Win. Mag. V-Max BT	33	2000	1495	293	164	0.60	NA
22 Win. Mag. JHP	34	2120	1435	338	155	1.4	NA
22 Win. Mag. JHP	40	1910	1326	324	156	1.7	1480
22 Win. Mag. FMJ	40	1910	1326	324	156	1.7	1480
22 Win. Mag. Dyna Point	45	1550	1147	240	131	2.60	NA
22 Win. Mag. JHP	50	1650	1280	300	180	1.3	NA
22 Win. Mag. Shot #11	52	1000	–	NA	–	—	NA

NOTES: * = 10 rounds per box. ** = 5 rounds per box. Pricing variations and number of rounds per box can occur with type and brand of ammunition. Listed pricing is the average nominal cost for load style and box quantity shown. Not every brand is available in all shot size variations. Some manufacturers do not provide suggested list prices. All prices rounded to nearest whole dollar. The price you pay will vary dependent upon outlet of purchase. # = new load spec this year; "C" indicates a change in data.

10 Gauge 3-1/2" Magnum

Dram Equiv.	Shot Ozs.	Load Style	Shot Sizes	Brands	Avg. Price/box	Velocity (fps)
Max	2-3/8	magnum blend	5, 6, 7	Hevi-shot	NA	1200
4-1/2	2-1/4	premium	BB, 2, 4, 5, 6	Win., Fed., Rem.	$33	1205
Max	2	premium	4, 5, 6	Fed., Win.	NA	1300
4-1/4	2	high velocity	BB, 2, 4	Rem.	$22	1210
Max	18 pellets	premium	00 buck	Fed., Win.	$7**	1100
Max	1-7/8	Bismuth	BB, 2, 4	Bis.	NA	1225
Max	1-3/4	high density	BB, 2	Rem.	NA	1300
4-1/4	1-3/4	steel	TT, T, BBB, BB, 1, 2, 3	Win., Rem.	$27	1260
Mag	1-5/8	steel	T, BBB, BB, 2	Win.	$27	1285
Max	1-5/8	Bismuth	BB, 2, 4	Bismuth	NA	1375
Max	1-1/2	hypersonic	BBB, BB, 2	Rem.	NA	1700
Max	1-1/2	heavy metal	BB, 2, 3, 4	Hevi-Shot	NA	1500
Max	1-1/2	steel	T, BBB, BB, 1, 2, 3	Fed.	NA	1450
Max	1-3/8	steel	T, BBB, BB, 1, 2, 3	Fed., Rem.	NA	1500
Max	1-3/8	steel	T, BBB, BB, 2	Fed., Win.	NA	1450
Max	1-3/4	slug, rifled	slug	Fed.	NA	1280
Max	24 pellets	Buckshot	1 Buck	Fed.	NA	1100
Max	54 pellets	Super-X	4 Buck	Win.	NA	1150

12 Gauge 3-1/2" Magnum

Dram Equiv.	Shot Ozs.	Load Style	Shot Sizes	Brands	Avg. Price/box	Velocity (fps)
Max	2-1/4	premium	4, 5, 6	Fed., Rem., Win.	$13*	1150
Max	2	Lead	4, 5, 6	Fed.	NA	1300
Max	2	Multi combo	5, 6, 7	Fed.	NA	1250
Max	2	Copper plated turkey	4, 5	Rem.	NA	1300
Max	2	Coated lead	4, 5, 6	Win.	NA	1200
Max	18 pellets	premium	00 buck	Fed., Win., Rem.	$7**	1100
Max	1-7/8	Wingmaster HD	4, 6	Rem.	NA	1225
Max	1-7/8	heavyweight	5, 6	Fed.	NA	1300
Max	1-3/4	high density	BB, 2, 4, 6	Rem.		1300
Max	1-7/8	Bismuth	BB, 2, 4	Bis.	NA	1225
Max	1-5/8	blind side	Hex, 1, 3	Win.	NA	1400
Max	1-5/8	Hevi-shot	T	Hevi-shot	NA	1350
Max	1-5/8	Wingmaster HD	T	Rem.	NA	1350
Max	1-5/8	high density	BB, 2	Fed.	NA	1450
Max	1-5/8	Blind side	Hex, BB, 2	Win.	NA	1400
Max	1-3/8	Heavyweight	2, 4, 6	Fed.	NA	1450
Max	1-3/8	steel	T, BBB, BB, 2, 4	Fed., Win., Rem.	NA	1450
Max	1-1/2	FS steel	BBB, BB, 2	Fed.	NA	1500
Max	1-1/2	Supreme H-V	BBB, BB, 2, 3	Win.	NA	1475

12 Gauge 3-1/2" Magnum (cont.)

Dram Equiv.	Shot Ozs.	Load Style	Shot Sizes	Brands	Avg. Price/box	Velocity (fps)
Max	1-3/8	H-speed steel	BB, 2	Rem.	NA	1550
Max	1-1/4	Steel	BB, 2	Win.	NA	1625
Max	24 pellets	Premium	1 Buck	Fed.	NA	1100
Max	54 pellets	Super-X	4 Buck	Win.	NA	1050

12 Gauge 3" Magnum

Dram Equiv.	Shot Ozs.	Load Style	Shot Sizes	Brands	Avg. Price/box	Velocity (fps)
4	2	premium	BB, 2, 4, 5, 6	Win., Fed., Rem.	$9*	1175
4	1-7/8	premium	BB, 2, 4, 6	Win., Fed., Rem.	$19	1210
4	1-7/8	duplex	4x6	Rem.	$9*	1210
Max	1-3/4	turkey	4, 5, 6	Fed., Fio., Win., Rem.	NA	1300
Max	1-3/4	Coated lead	4, 5, 6	Win.	NA	1200
Max	1-3/4	Multi combo	5, 6, 7	Fed.	NA	1250
Max	1-3/4	high density	BB, 2, 4	Rem.	NA	1450
Max	1-5/8	high density	BB, 2	Fed.	NA	1450
Max	1-5/8	Wingmaster HD	4, 6	Rem.	NA	1227
Max	1-5/8	high velocity	4, 5, 6	Fed.	NA	1350
4	1-5/8	premium	2, 4, 5, 6	Win., Fed., Rem.	$18	1290
Max	1-1/2	Wingmaster HD	T	Rem.	NA	1300
Max	1-1/2	Hevi-shot	T	Hevi-shot	NA	1300
Max	1-1/2	high density	BB, 2, 4	Rem.	NA	1300
Max	1-1/2	Coated lead	BB	Win.	NA	1300
Max	1-1/2	slug	slug	Bren.	NA	1604
Max	1-5/8	Bismuth	3, 4, 5, 6	Rio	NA	1350
4	24 pellets	buffered	1 buck	Win., Fed., Rem.	$5**	1040
4	15 pellets	buffered	00 buck	Win., Fed., Rem.	$6**	1210
4	10 pellets	buffered	000 buck	Win., Fed., Rem.	$6**	1225
4	41 pellets	buffered	4 buck	Win., Fed., Rem.	$6**	1210
Max	1-3/8	heavyweight	5, 6	Fed.	NA	1300
Max	1-3/8	high density	B, 2, 4, 6	Rem. Win.	NA	1450
Max	1-3/8	slug	slug	Bren.	NA	1476
Max	1-3/8	blind side	Hex, 1, 3, 5	Win.	NA	1400
Max	1-1/4	slug, rifled	slug	Fed.	NA	1600
Max	1-3/16	saboted slug	copper slug	Rem.	NA	1500
Max	7/8	slug, rifled	slug	Rem.	NA	1875
Max	1-1/8	low recoil	BB	Fed.	NA	850
Max	1-1/8	steel	BB, 2, 3, 4	Fed., Win., Rem.	NA	1550
Max	1-1/16	high density	2, 4	Win.	NA	1400
Max	1	steel	4, 6	Fed.	NA	1330

Dram Equiv.	Shot Ozs.	Load Style	Shot Sizes	Brands	Avg. Price/box	Velocity (fps)
12 Gauge 3" Magnum *(cont.)*						
Max	1-3/8	buckhammer	slug	Rem.	NA	1500
Max	1	TruBall slug	slug	Fed.	NA	1700
Max	1	slug, rifled	slug, magnum	Win., Rem.	$5**	1760
Max	1	saboted slug	slug	Rem., Win., Fed.	$10**	1550
Max	385 grs.	partition gold	slug	Win.	NA	2000
Max	1-1/8	Rackmaster	slug	Win.	NA	1700
Max	300 grs.	XP3	slug	Win.	NA	2100
3-5/8	1-3/8	steel	BBB, BB, 1, 2, 3, 4	Win., Fed., Rem.	$19	1275
Max	1-1/8	snow goose FS	BB, 2, 3, 4	Fed.	NA	1635
Max	1-1/8	steel	BB, 2, 4	Rem.	NA	1500
Max	1-1/8	steel	T, BBB, BB, 2, 4, 5, 6	Fed., Win.	NA	1450
Max	1-1/8	steel	BB, 2	Fed.	NA	1400
Max	1-1/8	FS lead	3, 4	Fed.	NA	1600
Max	1-3/8	Blind side	Hex, BB, 2	Win.	NA	1400
4	1-1/4	steel	T, BBB, BB, 1, 2, 3, 4, 6	Win., Fed., Rem.	$18	1400
Max	1-1/4	FS steel	BBB, BB, 2	Fed.	NA	1450
12 Gauge 2-3/4"						
Max	1-5/8	magnum	4, 5, 6	Win., Fed.	$8*	1250
Max	1-3/8	lead	4, 5, 6	Fiocchi	NA	1485
Max	1-3/8	turkey	4, 5, 6	Fio.	NA	1250
Max	1-3/8	steel	4, 5, 6	Fed.	NA	1400
Max	1-3/8	Bismuth	BB, 2, 4, 5, 6	Bis.	NA	1300
3-3/4	1-1/2	magnum	BB, 2, 4, 5, 6	Win., Fed., Rem.	$16	1260
Max	1-1/4	blind side	Hex, 2, 5	Win.	NA	1400
Max	1-1/4	Supreme H-V	4, 5, 6, 7-1/2	Win. Rem.	NA	1400
3-3/4	1-1/4	high velocity	BB, 2, 4, 5, 6, 7-1/2, 8, 9	Win., Fed., Rem., Fio.	$13	1330
Max	1-1/4	high density	B, 2, 4	Win.	NA	1450
Max	1-1/4	high density	4, 6	Rem.	NA	1325
3-1/4	1-1/4	standard velocity	6, 7-1/2, 8, 9	Win., Fed., Rem., Fio.	$11	1220
Max	1-1/4	Bismuth	3, 4, 5, 6	Rio	NA	1350
Max	1-1/8	Hevi-shot	5	Hevi-shot	NA	1350
3-1/4	1-1/8	standard velocity	4, 6, 7-1/2, 8, 9	Win., Fed., Rem., Fio.	$9	1255
Max	1-1/8	steel	2, 4	Rem.	NA	1390
Max	1	steel	BB, 2	Fed.	NA	1450
3-1/4	1	standard velocity	6, 7-1/2, 8	Rem., Fed., Fio., Win.	$6	1290
3-1/4	1-1/4	target	7-1/2, 8, 9	Win., Fed., Rem.	$10	1220

Dram Equiv.	Shot Ozs.	Load Style	Shot Sizes	Brands	Avg. Price/box	Velocity (fps)
12 Gauge 2-3/4" *(cont.)*						
3	1-1/8	spreader	7-1/2, 8, 8-1/2, 9	Fio.	NA	1200
3	1-1/8	target	7-1/2, 8, 9, 7-1/2x8	Win., Fed., Rem., Fio.	$7	1200
2-3/4	1-1/8	target	7-1/2, 8, 8-1/2, 9, 7-1/2x8	Win., Fed., Rem., Fio.	$7	1145
2-3/4	1-1/8	low recoil	7-1/2, 8	Rem.	NA	1145
2-1/2	26 grams	low recoil	8	Win.	NA	980
2-1/4	1-1/8	target	7-1/2, 8, 8-1/2, 9	Rem., Fed.	$7	1080
Max	1	spreader	7-1/2, 8, 8-1/2, 9	Fio.	NA	1300
3-1/4	28 grams (1 oz)	target	7-1/2, 8, 9	Win., Fed., Rem., Fio.	$8	1290
3	1	target	7-1/2, 8, 8-1/2, 9	Win., Fio.	NA	1235
2-3/4	1	target	7-1/2, 8, 8-1/2, 9	Fed., Rem., Fio.	NA	1180
3-1/4	24 grams	target	7-1/2, 8, 9	Fed., Win., Fio.	NA	1325
3	7/8	light	8	Fio.	NA	1200
3-3/4	8 pellets	buffered	000 buck	Win., Fed., Rem.	$4**	1325
4	12 pellets	premium	00 buck	Win., Fed., Rem.	$5**	1290
3-3/4	9 pellets	buffered	00 buck	Win., Fed., Rem., Fio.	$19	1325
3-3/4	12 pellets	buffered	0 buck	Win., Fed., Rem.	$4**	1275
4	20 pellets	buffered	1 buck	Win., Fed., Rem.	$4**	1075
3-3/4	16 pellets	buffered	1 buck	Win., Fed., Rem.	$4**	1250
4	34 pellets	premium	4 buck	Fed., Rem.	$5**	1250
3-3/4	27 pellets	buffered	4 buck	Win., Fed., Rem., Fio.	$4**	1325
		PDX1	1 oz. slug, 3-00 buck	Win.	NA	1150
Max	1 oz	segmenting, slug	slug	Win.	NA	1600
Max	1	saboted slug	slug	Win., Fed., Rem.	$10**	1450
Max	1-1/4	slug, rifled	slug	Fed.	NA	1520
Max	1-1/4	slug	slug	Lightfield		1440
Max	1-1/4	saboted slug	attached sabot	Rem.	NA	1550
Max	1	slug, rifled	slug, magnum	Rem., Fio.	$5**	1680
Max	1	slug, rifled	slug	Win., Fed., Rem.	$4**	1610
Max	1	sabot slug	slug	Sauvestre		1640
Max	7/8	slug, rifled	slug	Rem.	NA	1800
Max	400	plat. tip	sabot slug	Win.	NA	1700
Max	385 grains	Partition Gold Slug	slug	Win.	NA	1900
Max	385 grains	Core-Lokt bonded	sabot slug	Rem.	NA	1900

Dram Equiv.	Shot Ozs.	Load Style	Shot Sizes	Brands	Avg. Price/box	Velocity (fps)

12 Gauge 2-3/4" *(cont.)*

Dram Equiv.	Shot Ozs.	Load Style	Shot Sizes	Brands	Avg. Price/box	Velocity (fps)
Max	325 grains	Barnes Sabot	slug	Fed.	NA	1900
Max	300 grains	SST Slug	sabot slug	Hornady	NA	2050
Max	3/4	Tracer	#8 + tracer	Fio.	NA	1150
Max	130 grains	Less Lethal	.73 rubber slug	Lightfield	NA	600
Max	3/4	non-toxic	zinc slug	Win.	NA	NA
3	1-1/8	steel target	6-1/2, 7	Rem.	NA	1200
2-3/4	1-1/8	steel target	7	Rem.	NA	1145
3	1#	steel	7	Win.	$11	1235
3-1/2	1-1/4	steel	T, BBB, BB, 1, 2, 3, 4, 5, 6	Win., Fed., Rem.	$18	1275
3-3/4	1-1/8	steel	BB, 1, 2, 3, 4, 5, 6	Win., Fed., Rem., Fio.	$16	1365
3-3/4	1	steel	2, 3, 4, 5, 6, 7	Win., Fed., Rem., Fio.	$13	1390
Max	7/8	steel	7	Fio.	NA	1440

16 Gauge 2-3/4"

Dram Equiv.	Shot Ozs.	Load Style	Shot Sizes	Brands	Avg. Price/box	Velocity (fps)
3-1/4	1-1/4	magnum	2, 4, 6	Fed., Rem.	$16	1260
3-1/4	1-1/8	high velocity	4, 6, 7-1/2	Win., Fed., Rem., Fio.	$12	1295
2-3/4	1-1/8	standard velocity	6, 7-1/2, 8	Fed., Rem., Fio.	$9	1185
2-1/2	1	dove	6, 7-1/2, 8, 9	Fio., Win.	NA	1165
2-3/4	1		6, 7-1/2, 8	Fio.	NA	1200
Max	1	Bismuth	4, 6	Rio	NA	1200
Max	15/16	steel	2, 4	Fed., Rem.	NA	1300
Max	7/8	steel	2, 4	Win.	$16	1300
3	12 pellets	buffered	1 buck	Win., Fed., Rem.	$4**	1225
Max	4/5	slug, rifled	slug	Win., Fed., Rem.	$4**	1570
Max	.92	sabot slug	slug	Sauvestre	NA	1560

20 Gauge 3" Magnum

Dram Equiv.	Shot Ozs.	Load Style	Shot Sizes	Brands	Avg. Price/box	Velocity (fps)
3	1-1/4	premium	2, 4, 5, 6, 7-1/2	Win., Fed., Rem.	$15	1185
Max	1-1/4	Wingmaster HD	4, 6	Rem.	NA	1185
3	1-1/4	Multi shot	5, 6, 7 combo	Fed.	NA	1100
3	1-1/4	turkey	4, 6	Fio.	NA	1200
Max	1-1/4	Hevi-shot	2, 4, 6	Hevi-shot	NA	1250

20 Gauge 3" Magnum *(cont.)*

Dram Equiv.	Shot Ozs.	Load Style	Shot Sizes	Brands	Avg. Price/box	Velocity (fps)
Max	1-1/8	high density	4, 6	Rem.	NA	1300
Max	18 pellets	buck shot	2 buck	Fed.	NA	1200
Max	24 pellets	buffered	3 buck	Win.	$5**	1150
2-3/4	20 pellets	buck	3 buck	Rem.	$4**	1200
Max	1	hypersonic	2, 3, 4	Rem.	NA	Rem.
3-1/4	1	steel	1, 2, 3, 4, 5, 6	Win., Fed., Rem.	$15	1330
Max	1	blind side	Hex, 2, 5	Win.	NA	1300
Max	7/8	steel	2, 4	Win.	NA	1300
Max	7/8	FS lead	3, 4	Fed.	NA	1500
Max	1-1/16	high density	2, 4	Win.	NA	1400
Max	1-1/16	Bismuth	2, 4, 5, 6	Bismuth	NA	1250
Mag	5/8	saboted slug	275 gr.	Fed.	NA	1900
Max	3/4	TruBall slug	slug	Fed.	NA	1700

20 Gauge 2-3/4"

Dram Equiv.	Shot Ozs.	Load Style	Shot Sizes	Brands	Avg. Price/box	Velocity (fps)
2-3/4	1-1/8	magnum	4, 6, 7-1/2	Win., Fed., Rem.	$14	1175
2-3/4	1	high velocity	4, 5, 6, 7-1/2, 8, 9	Win., Fed., Rem., Fio.	$12	1220
Max	1	Bismuth	4, 6	Bis.	NA	1200
Max	1	Hevi-shot	5	Hevi-shot	NA	1250
Max	1	Supreme H-V	4, 6, 7-1/2	Win. Rem.	NA	1300
Max	1	FS lead	4, 5, 6	Fed.	NA	1350
Max	7/8	Steel	2, 3, 4	Fio.	NA	1500
2-1/2	1	standard velocity	6, 7-1/2, 8	Win., Rem., Fed., Fio.	$6	1165
2-1/2	7/8	clays	8	Rem.	NA	1200
2-1/2	7/8	promotional	6, 7-1/2, 8	Win., Rem., Fio.	$6	1210
2-1/2	1	target	8, 9	Win., Rem.	$8	1165
Max	7/8	clays	7-1/2, 8	Win.	NA	1275
2-1/2	7/8	target	8, 9	Win., Fed., Rem.	$8	1200
Max	3/4	steel	2, 4	Rem.	NA	1425
2-1/2	7/8	steel - target	7	Rem.	NA	1200
1-1/2	7/8	low recoil	8	Win.	NA	980
Max	1	buckhammer	slug	Rem.	NA	1500
Max	5/8	Saboted Slug	Copper Slug	Rem.	NA	1500

20 Gauge 2-3/4" (cont.)

Dram Equiv.	Shot Ozs.	Load Style	Shot Sizes	Brands	Avg. Price/box	Velocity (fps)
Max	20 pellets	buffered	3 buck	Win., Fed.	$4	1200
Max	5/8	slug, saboted	slug	Win.,	$9**	1400
2-3/4	5/8	slug, rifled	slug	Rem.	$4**	1580
Max	3/4	saboted slug	copper slug	Fed., Rem.	NA	1450
Max	3/4	slug, rifled	slug	Win., Fed., Rem., Fio.	$4**	1570
Max	.9	sabot slug	slug	Sauvestre		1480
Max	260 grains	Partition Gold Slug	slug	Win.	NA	1900
Max	260 grains	Core-Lokt Ultra	slug	Rem.	NA	1900
Max	260 grains	saboted slug	platinum tip	Win.	NA	1700
Max	3/4	steel	2, 3, 4, 6	Win., Fed., Rem.	$14	1425
Max	250 grains	SST slug	slug	Hornady	NA	1800
Max	1/2	rifled, slug	slug	Rem.	NA	1800
Max	67 grains	Less lethal	2/.60 rubber balls	Lightfield	NA	900

28 Gauge 3"

Dram Equiv.	Shot Ozs.	Load Style	Shot Sizes	Brands	Avg. Price/box	Velocity (fps)
Max	7/8	tundra tungsten	4, 5, 6	Fiocchi	NA	TBD

28 Gauge 2-3/4"

Dram Equiv.	Shot Ozs.	Load Style	Shot Sizes	Brands	Avg. Price/box	Velocity (fps)
2	1	high velocity	6, 7-1/2, 8	Win.	$12	1125
2-1/4	3/4	high velocity	6, 7-1/2, 8, 9	Win., Fed., Rem., Fio.	$11	1295
2	3/4	target	8, 9	Win., Fed., Rem.	$9	1200
Max	3/4	sporting clays	7-1/2, 8-1/2	Win.	NA	1300
Max	3/4	Bismuth	5, 7	Rio	NA	1250
Max	5/8	steel	6, 7	NA	NA	1300
Max	5/8	slug		Bren.	NA	1450

410 Bore 3"

Dram Equiv.	Shot Ozs.	Load Style	Shot Sizes	Brands	Avg. Price/box	Velocity (fps)
Max	11/16	high velocity	4, 5, 6, 7-1/2, 8, 9	Win., Fed., Rem., Fio.	$10	1135
Max	9/16	Bismuth	5, 7	Rio	NA	1175
Max	3/8	steel	6	NA	NA	1400
		judge	5 pellets 000 Buck	Fed.	NA	960
		judge	9 pellets #4 Buck	Fed.	NA	1100
Max	Mixed	Per. Defense	3DD/12BB	Win.	NA	750

410 Bore 2-1/2"

Dram Equiv.	Shot Ozs.	Load Style	Shot Sizes	Brands	Avg. Price/box	Velocity (fps)
Max	1/2	high velocity	4, 6, 7-1/2	Win., Fed., Rem.	$9	1245
Max	1/5	slug, rifled	slug	Win., Fed., Rem.	$4**	1815
1-1/2	1/2	target	8, 8-1/2, 9	Win., Fed., Rem., Fio.	$8	1200
Max	1/2	sporting clays	7-1/2, 8, 8-1/2	Win.	NA	1300
Max		Buckshot	5-000 Buck	Win.	NA	1135
		judge	12-bb's, 3 disks	Win.	NA	TBD
Max	Mixed	Per. Defense	4DD/16BB	Win.	NA	750
Max	42 grains	Less lethal	4/.41 rubber balls	Lightfield	NA	1150

ACCU-TEK AT-380 II ACP
Caliber: 380 ACP, 6-shot magazine. **Barrel:** 2.8" **Weight:** 23.5 oz.
Length: 6.125" overall. **Grips:** Textured black composition. **Sights:**
Blade front, rear adjustable for windage. **Features:** Made from 17-4
stainless steel, has an exposed hammer, manual firing-pin safety
block and trigger disconnect. Magazine release located on the
bottom of the grip. American made, lifetime warranty. Comes with
two 6-round stainless steel magazines and a California-approved
cable lock. Introduced 2006. Made in U.S.A. by Excel Industries.
Price: Satin stainless **$289.00**

ACCU-TEK HC-380
Simlar to AT-380 II except has a 13-round magazine.
Price: **$330.00**

ACCU-TEK LT-380
Simlar to AT-380 II except has a lightweight aluminum frame.
Weight: 15 ounces.
Price: **$324.00**

AMERICAN CLASSIC 1911-A1
Caliber: .45 ACP. 7+1 magazine capacity. **Barrel:** 5" **Grips:**
Checkered walnut. **Sights:** Fixed. **Finish:** Blue or hard chromed.
A .22 LR version is also available. Other variations include Trophy
model with adjustable sights, two-tone finish.
Price: .... **$579.00 to $811.00**

AMERICAN CLASSIC COMMANDER
Caliber: .45 ACP. Same features as 1911-A1 model except is
Commander size with 4.25" barrel.
Price: **$616.00**

AMERICAN TACTICAL IMPORTS MILITARY 1911
Caliber: .45 ACP. 7+1 magazine capacity. **Barrel:** 5" **Grips:** Textured
mahogany. **Sights:** Fixed military style. **Finish:** Blue. Also offered in
Commander and Officer's sizes and Enhanced model with additional
features.
Price: .... **$500.00 to $585.00**

AMERICAN TACTICAL IMPORTS GSG 1911
Caliber: .22 LR. 10+1 magazine capacity. **Weight:** 34 oz. Other
features and dimensions similar to centerfire 1911.
Price: **$299.95**

ARMALITE AR-24
Caliber: 9mm Para., 10- or 15-shot magazine. **Barrel:** 4.671"
6-groove, right-hand cut rifling. **Weight:** 34.9 oz. **Length:** 8.27"
overall. **Grips:** Black polymer. **Sights:** Dovetail front, fixed rear,
3-dot luminous design. **Features:** Machined slide,
frame and barrel. Serrations on forestrap and backstrap, external
thumb safety and internal firing pin box, half cock. Two 15-round
magazines, pistol case, pistol lock, manual and cleaning brushes.
Manganese phosphate finish. Compact comes with two 13-round
magazines, 3.89 barrel, weighs 33.4 oz. Made in U.S.A. by
ArmaLite.
Price: AR-24 Full Size **$550.00**
Price: AR-24K Compact **$550.00**

Prices given are believed to be accurate at time of publication however, many factors affect retail pricing so exact prices are not possible.

71ST EDITION, 2017 ✦ **369**

AUTO-ORDNANCE 1911A1

Caliber: 45 ACP, 7-shot magazine. **Barrel:** 5" **Weight:** 39 oz. **Length:** 8.5" overall. **Grips:** Brown checkered plastic with medallion. **Sights:** Blade front, rear drift-adjustable for windage. **Features:** Same specs as 1911A1 military guns-parts interchangeable. Frame and slide blued; each radius has non-glare finish. Introduced 2002. Made in U.S.A. by Kahr Arms.
Price: 1911PKZSE Parkerized, plastic grips **$688.00**
Price: 1911PKZSEW Parkerized, wood grips **$705.00**

BAER H.C. 40

Caliber: 40 S&W, 18-shot magazine. **Barrel:** 5" **Weight:** 37 oz. **Length:** 8.5" overall. **Grips:** Wood. **Sights:** Low-mount adjustable rear sight with hidden rear leaf, dovetail front sight. **Features:** Double-stack Caspian frame, beavertail grip safety, ambidextrous thumb safety, 40 S&W match barrel with supported chamber, match stainless steel barrel bushing, lowered and flared ejection port, extended ejector, match trigger fitted, integral mag well, bead blast blue finish on lower, polished sides on slide. Introduced 2008. Made in U.S.A. by Les Baer Custom, Inc.
Price: **$2,960.00**

BAER 1911 BOSS .45

Caliber: .45 ACP, 8+1 capacity. **Barrel:** 5" **Weight:** 37 oz. **Length:** 8.5" overall. **Grips:** Premium Checkered Cocobolo Grips. **Sights:** Low-Mount LBC Adj Sight, Red Fiber Optic Front. **Features:** Speed Trgr, Beveled Mag Well, Rounded for Tactical. Rear cocking serrations on the slide, Baer fiber optic front sight (red), flat mainspring housing, checkered at 20 lpi, extended combat safety, Special tactical package, chromed complete lower, blued slide, (2) 8-round premium magazines.
Price: **$2,560.00**

BAER 1911 CUSTOM CARRY

Caliber: .45 ACP, 7- or 10-shot magazine. **Barrel:** 5" **Weight:** 37 oz. **Length:** 8.5" overall. **Grips:** Checkered walnut. **Sights:** Baer improved ramp-style dovetailed front, Novak low-mount rear. **Features:** Baer forged NM frame, slide and barrel with stainless bushing. Baer speed trigger with 4-lb. pull. Partial listing shown. Made in U.S.A. by Les Baer Custom, Inc.
Price: Custom Carry 5, blued **$2,190.00**
Price: Custom Carry 5, stainless **$2,290.00**
Price: Custom Carry 4 Commanche length, blued **$2,190.00**

Price: Custom Carry 4 Commanche length, .38 Super **$2,550.00**

BAER 1911 ULTIMATE RECON

Caliber: .45 ACP, 7- or 10-shot magazine. **Barrel:** 5" **Weight:** 37 oz. **Length:** 8.5" overall. **Grips:** Checkered cocobolo. **Sights:** Baer improved ramp-style dovetailed front, Novak low-mount rear. **Features:** NM Caspian frame, slide and barrel with stainless bushing. Baer speed trigger with 4-lb. pull. Includes integral Picatinny rail and Sure-Fire X-200 light. Made in U.S.A. by Les Baer Custom, Inc. Introduced 2006.
Price: Bead blast blued **$2,650.00**
Price: Bead blast chrome **$2,910.00**

BAER 1911 PREMIER II

Caliber: .38 Super, 400 Cor-Bon, .45 ACP, 7- or 10-shot magazine. **Barrel:** 5" **Weight:** 37 oz. **Length:** 8.5" overall. **Grips:** Checkered rosewood, double diamond pattern. **Sights:** Baer dovetailed front, low-mount Bo-Mar rear with hidden leaf. **Features:** Baer NM forged steel frame and barrel with stainless bushing, deluxe Commander hammer and sear, beavertail grip safety with pad, extended ambidextrous safety; flat mainspring housing; 30 lpi checkered front strap. Made in U.S.A. by Les Baer Custom, Inc.
Price: 5" .45 ACP **$2,180.00**
Price: 5" 400 Cor-Bon **$2,380.00**
Price: 5" .38 Super **$2,620.00**
Price: 6" .45 ACP, 400 Cor-Bon, .38 Super, from **$2,390.00**
Price: Super-Tac, .45 ACP, 400 Cor-Bon, .38 Super, from **$2,650.00**

BAER 1911 S.R.P.

Caliber: .45 ACP. **Barrel:** 5" **Weight:** 37 oz. **Length:** 8.5" overall. **Grips:** Checkered walnut. **Sights:** Trijicon night sights. **Features:** Similar to the F.B.I. contract gun except uses Baer forged steel frame. Has Baer match barrel with supported chamber, complete tactical action. Has Baer Ultra Coat finish. Introduced 1996. Made in U.S.A. by Les Baer Custom, Inc.
Price: Government or Commanche length **$2,840.00**

BAER 1911 STINGER

Caliber: .45 ACP or .38 Super, 7-round magazine. **Barrel:** 5" **Weight:** 34 oz. **Length:** 8.5" overall. **Grips:** Checkered cocobolo. **Sights:** Baer dovetailed front, low-mount Bo-Mar rear with hidden leaf. **Features:** Baer NM frame. Baer Commanche slide, Officer's style grip frame, beveled mag well. Made in U.S.A. by Les Baer Custom, Inc.
Price: .45 ACP ....**$2,240.00 to $2,310.00**
Price: .38 Super **$2,840.00**

BAER 1911 PROWLER III

Caliber: .45 ACP, 8-round magazine. **Barrel:** 5" **Weight:** 34 oz. **Length:** 8.5" overall. **Grips:** Checkered cocobolo. **Sights:** Baer dovetailed front, low-mount Bo-Mar rear with hidden leaf. **Features:** Similar to Premier II with tapered cone stub weight, rounded corners. Made in U.S.A. by Les Baer Custom, Inc.
Price: Blued **$2,910.00**

BAER HEMI 572

Caliber: .45 ACP. Based on Les Baer's 1911 Premier I pistol and inspired by Chrysler 1970 Hemi Cuda muscle car. **Features:** Double serrated slide, Baer fiber optic front sight with green insert, VZ black recon grips with hexhead screws, hard chrome finish on all major components, Dupont S coating on barrel, trigger, hammer, ambi

Prices given are believed to be accurate at time of publication however, many factors affect retail pricing so exact prices are not possible.

safety and other controls.

Price: $2,690.00

BAER ULTIMATE MASTER COMBAT

Caliber: .45 ACP or .38 Super. A full house competition 1911 offered in 8 variations including 5 or 6-inch barrel, PPC Distinguished or Open class, Bullseye Wadcutter class and others. Features include double serrated slide, fitted slide to frame, checkered front strap and trigger guard, serrated rear of slide, extended ejector, tuned extractor, premium checkered grips, blued finish and two 8-round magazines.

Price: Compensated .45................................$3,240.00
Price: Compensated. 38 Super........................$3,390.00

BERETTA M92/96 A1 SERIES

Caliber: 9mm, 15-round magazine; .40 S&W, 12 rounds (M96 A1). **Barrel:** 4.9 inches. **Weight:** 33-34 oz. **Length:** 8.5 inches. **Sights:** Fiber optic front, adjustable rear. **Features:** Same as other models in 92/96 family except for addition of accessory rail.

Price: $775.00

BERETTA MODEL 92FS

Caliber: 9mm Para., 10-shot magazine. **Barrel:** 4.9", 4.25" (Compact). **Weight:** 34 oz. **Length:** 8.5" overall. **Grips:** Checkered black plastic. **Sights:** Blade front, rear adjustable for windage. Tritium night sights available. **Features:** Double action. Extractor acts as chamber loaded indicator, squared trigger guard, grooved front and backstraps, inertia firing pin. Matte or blued finish. Introduced 1977. Made in U.S.A.

Price: $699.00
Price: Inox $850.00

BERETTA M9 .22 LR

Caliber: .22 LR. 10 or 15-shot magazine. Black Brunitron finish, interchangeable grip panels. Similar to centerfire 92/M9 with same operating controls, lighter weight (26 oz.).

Price: $430.00

BERETTA MODEL 21 BOBCAT

Caliber: .22 LR or .25 ACP. Both double action. **Barrel:** 2.4" **Weight:** 11.5 oz.; 11.8 oz. **Length:** 4.9" overall. **Grips:** Plastic. **Features:** Available in matte black or stainless. Introduced in 1985.

Price: Black matte $410.00
Price: Stainless $450.00

BERETTA MODEL 3032 TOMCAT

Caliber: .32 ACP, 7-shot magazine. **Barrel:** 2.45" **Weight:** 14.5 oz. **Length:** 5" overall. **Grips:** Checkered black plastic. **Sights:** Blade front, drift-adjustable rear. **Features:** Double action with exposed hammer; tip-up barrel for direct loading/unloading; thumb safety; Inox stainless or matte blue finish. Made in U.S.A. Introduced 1996.

Price: Matte $390.00
Price: Inox $485.00

BERETTA MODEL U22 NEOS

Caliber: .22 LR, 10-shot magazine. **Barrel:** 4.5" and 6" **Weight:** 32 oz.; 36 oz. **Length:** 8.8"/ 10.3" **Sights:** Target. **Features:** Integral rail for standard scope mounts, light, perfectly weighted, 100 percent American made by Beretta.

Price: Blue $325.00
Price: Inox $350.00

BERETTA MODEL PX4 STORM

Caliber: 9mm Para., 40 S&W. **Capacity:** 17 (9mm Para.); 14 (40 S&W). **Barrel:** 4" **Weight:** 27.5 oz. **Grips:** Black checkered w/3 interchangeable backstraps. **Sights:** 3-dot system coated in Superluminova; removable front and rear sights. **Features:** DA/SA, manual safety/hammer decocking lever (ambi) and automatic firing pin block safety. Picatinny rail. Comes with two magazines (17/10 in 9mm Para. and 14/10 in 40 S&W). Removable hammer unit. American made by Beretta. Introduced 2005.

Price: 9mm or .40 ....$575.00
Price: .45 ACP $650.00
Price: .45 ACP SD (Special Duty) $1,150.00

BERETTA MODEL PX4 STORM SUB-COMPACT

Caliber: 9mm, 40 S&W. **Capacity:** 13 (9mm); 10 (40 S&W). **Barrel:** 3" **Weight:** 26.1 oz. **Length:** 6.2" overall. **Grips:** NA. **Sights:** NA. **Features:** Ambidextrous manual safety lever, interchangeable

Prices given are believed to be accurate at time of publication however, many factors affect retail pricing so exact prices are not possible.

71ST EDITION, 2017 ✦ **371**

backstraps included, lock breech and tilt barrel system, stainless steel barrel, Picatinny rail.

Price: $600.00

BERETTA MODEL M9

Caliber: 9mm Para. **Capacity:** 15. **Barrel:** 4.9" **Weight:** 32.2-35.3 oz. **Grips:** Plastic. **Sights:** Dot and post, low profile, windage adjustable rear. **Features:** DA/SA, forged aluminum alloy frame, delayed locking-bolt system, manual safety doubles as decocking lever, combat-style trigger guard, loaded chamber indicator. Comes with two magazines (15/10). American made by Beretta. Introduced 2005.

Price: $675.00

BERETTA MODEL M9A1

Caliber: 9mm Para. **Capacity:** 15. **Barrel:** 4.9" **Weight:** 32.2-35.3 oz. **Grips:** Plastic. **Sights:** Dot and post, low profile, windage adjustable rear. **Features:** Same as M9, but also includes integral Mil-Std-1913 Picatinny rail, has checkered frontstrap and backstrap. Comes with two magazines (15/10). American made by Beretta. Introduced 2005.

Price: $775.00

BERETTA NANO

Caliber: 9mm Para. Six-shot magazine. **Barrel:** 3.07". **Weight:** 17.7 oz. **Length:** 5.7" overall. **Grips:** Polymer. Sights: 3-dot low profile. **Features:** Double-action only, striker fired. Replaceable grip frames.

Price: $475.00

BERETTA PICO

Caliber: .380 ACP, 6 rounds. **Barrel:** 2.7" **Weight:** 11.5 oz. **Length:** 5.1" overall. **Grips:** Integral with polymer frame. Interchangeable backstrap. **Sights:** White outline rear. **Features:** Adjustable, quick-change. Striker-fired, double-action only operation. Ambidextrous magazine release and slide release. Ships with two magazines, one flush, one with grip extension. Made in the USA.

Price: $399.00

BERSA THUNDER 45 ULTRA COMPACT

Caliber: .45 ACP. **Barrel:** 3.6" **Weight:** 27 oz. **Length:** 6.7" overall. **Grips:** Anatomically designed polymer. **Sights:** White outline rear. **Features:** Double action; firing pin safeties, integral locking system. Available in matte, satin nickel, gold, or duo-tone. Introduced 2003. Imported from Argentina by Eagle Imports, Inc.

Price: Thunder 45, matte blue $500.00
Price: Thunder 45, duo-tone $550.00

BERSA THUNDER 380 SERIES

Caliber: .380 ACP, 7 rounds. **Barrel:** 3.5" **Weight:** 23 oz. **Length:** 6.6" overall. **Features:** Otherwise similar to Thunder 45 Ultra Compact. 380 DLX has 9-round capacity. 380 Concealed Carry has 8-round capacity. Imported from Argentina by Eagle Imports, Inc.

Price: Thunder Matte $335.00

Price: Thunder Satin Nickel $355.00
Price: Thunder Duo-Tone $355.00
Price: Thunder Duo-Tone with Crimson Trace Laser Grips $555.00

BERSA THUNDER 9 ULTRA COMPACT/40 SERIES
Caliber: 9mm Para., 40 S&W. **Barrel:** 3.5" **Weight:** 24.5 oz. **Length:** 6.6" overall. **Features:** Otherwise similar to Thunder 45 Ultra Compact. 9mm Para. High Capacity model has 17-round capacity. 40 High Capacity model has 13-round capacity. Imported from Argentina by Eagle Imports, Inc.
Price: $500.00

BERSA THUNDER 22
Caliber: .22 LR, 10-round magazine. **Weight:** 19 oz. **Features:** Similar to Thunder .380 Series except for caliber. Alloy frame and slide. Finish: Matte black, satin nickel or duo-tone.
Price: $320.00

BROWNING 1911-22 COMPACT
Caliber: .22 L.R., 10-round magazine. **Barrel:** 3.625" **Weight:** 15 oz. **Length:** 6.5" overall. **Grips:** Brown composite. **Sights:** Fixed. **Features:** Slide is machined aluminum with alloy frame and matte blue finish. Blowback action and single action trigger with manual thumb and grip safetys. Works, feels and functions just like a full size 1911. It is simply scaled down and chambered in the best of all practice rounds: .22 LR for focus on the fundamentals.
Price: $600.00

BROWNING 1911-22 A1
Caliber: .22 L.R., 10-round magazine. **Barrel:** 4.25" **Weight:** 16 oz. **Length:** 7.0625" overall. **Grips:** Brown composite. **Sights:** Fixed. **Features:** Slide is machined aluminum with alloy frame and matte blue finish. Blowback action and single action trigger with manual thumb and grip safetys. Works, feels and functions just like a full size 1911. It is simply scaled down and chambered in the best of all practice rounds: .22 LR for focus on the fundamentals.
Price: $600.00

BROWNING 1911-22 BLACK LABEL
Caliber: .22 L.R.,10-round magazine. **Barrel:** 4.25" or 3.625" (Compact model). **Weight:** 14 oz. overall. **Features:** Other features are similar to standard 1911-22 except for this model's composite/polymer frame, extended grip safety, stipled black laminated grip, skeleton trigger and hammer. Available with accessory rail (shown). Suppressor Ready model has threaded muzzle protector, 4 7/8-inch barrel.
Price: $640.00
Price: With Rail $670.00
Price: Suppressor Ready model $740.00

BROWNING 1911-22 POLYMER DESERT TAN
Caliber: .22 L.R.,10-round magazine. **Barrel:** 4.25" or 3.625" **Weight:** 13-14 oz. overall. **Features:** Other features are similar to standard 1911-22 except for this model's composite/polymer frame. Also available with pink composite grips.
Price: $580.00

BROWNING 1911-380
Caliber: ..380 ACP. 8-round magazine. **Barrel:** 4.25" **Weight:** 18 oz.

Prices given are believed to be accurate at time of publication however, many factors affect retail pricing so exact prices are not possible.

71ST EDITION, 2017 ◈ **373**

Features: Aluminum slide, polymer frame. Features are virtually identical to those on the 1911-22.
Price: $670.00

BROWNING HI-POWER

Caliber: 9mm, 13-round magazine. **Barrel:** 4.625 inches. **Weight:** 32 oz. **Length:** 7.75 inches. **Grips:** Checkered walnut (standard model), textured and grooved polymer (Mark III). **Sights:** Fixed low-profile 3-dot (Mark III), fixed or adjustable low profile (standard model).
Features: Single-action operation with ambidextrous thumb safety, forged steel frame and slide. Made in Belgium.
Price: Mark III...$1,070.00
Price: Fixed Sights...$1,080.00

Price: Standard, Adjustable sights $1,160.00

BROWNING BUCK MARK CAMPER UFX

Caliber: .22 LR with 10-shot magazine. **Barrel:** 5.5" tapered bull. **Weight:** 34 oz. **Length:** 9.5" overall. **Grips:** Overmolded Ultragrip Ambidextrous. **Sights:** Pro-Target adjustable rear, ramp front. **Features:** Matte blue receiver, matte blue or stainless barrel.
Price: Camper UFX.. $390.00
Price: Camper UFX stainless $430.00

BROWNING BUCK MARK HUNTER

Caliber: .22 LR with 10-shot magazine. **Barrel:** 7.25" heavy tapered

---

bull. **Weight:** 38 oz. **Length:** 11.3" overall. **Grips:** Cocobolo target. **Sights:** Pro-Target adjustable rear, Tru-Glo/Marble's fiber-optic front. Integral scope base on top rail. Scope in photo is not included. **Features:** Matte blue.
Price: $500.00

BROWNING BUCK PRACTICAL URX

Caliber: .22 LR with 10-shot magazine. **Barrel:** 5.5" tapered bull. **Weight:** 34 oz. **Length:** 9.5" overall. **Grips:** Ultragrip RX Ambidextrous. **Sights:** Pro-Target adjustable rear, Tru-Glo/Marble's fiber-optic front. **Features:** Matte gray receiver, matte blue barrel.
Price: $440.00

BROWNING BUCK MARK PLUS UDX

Caliber: .22 LR with 10-shot magazine. **Barrel:** 5.5" slab sided. **Weight:** 34 oz. **Length:** 9.5" overall. **Grips:** Walnut Ultragrip DX Ambidextrous or rosewood. **Sights:** Pro-Target adjustable rear, Tru-Glo/Marble's fiber-optic front. **Features:** Matte blue or stainless.
Price: $540.00
Price: Stainless $580.00

BUSHMASTER XM-15 PATROLMAN'S AR PISTOL

Caliber: 5.56/223, 30-round. **Barrel:** 7" or 10.5" stainless steel with A2-type flash hider, knurled free-float handguard. **Weight:** 5.2 to 5.7 lbs. (4.9 to 5.5 lbs., Enhanced model). **Length:** 23" to 26.5" **Grips:** A2 pistol grip with standard triggerguard. **Features:** AR-style semi-auto pistol. Enhanced model has Barnes Precision free-float lightweight quad rail, Magpul MOE pistol grip and triggerguard.
Price: $973.00
Price: Enhanced...$1,229.00

CHIAPPA 1911-22
A faithful replica of the famous John Browning 1911A1 pistol. **Caliber:** .22 LR. **Barrel:** 5". **Weight:** 33.5 oz. **Length:** 8.5". **Grips:** Two-piece wood. **Sights:** Fixed. **Features:** Fixed barrel design, 10-shot magazine. Available in black, OD green or tan finish. Target and Tactical models have adjustable sights.
Price: From .... $269.00 to $408.00

CHIAPPA M9-22 STANDARD
Caliber: .22 LR. **Barrel:** 5" **Weight:** 2.3 lbs. **Length:** 8.5" **Grips:** Black molded plastic or walnut. **Sights:** Fixed front sight and windage adjustable rear sight. **Features:** The M9-9mm has been a U.S. standard-issue service pistol since 1990. Chiappa's M9-22 is a replica of this pistol in 22 LR. The M9-22 has the same weight and feel as its 9mm counterpart but has an affordable 10 shot magazine for the 22 long rifle cartridge which makes it a true rimfire reproduction. Comes standard with steel trigger, hammer assembly and a 1/2-28 threaded barrel.
Price: $339.00

CHIAPPA M9-22 TACTICAL
Caliber: .22 LR. **Barrel:** 5" **Weight:** 2.3 lbs. **Length:** 8.5" **Grips:** Black molded plastic. **Sights:** Fixed front sight and Novak style rear sites. **Features:** The M9-22 Tactical model has Novak style rear sites and comes with a fake suppressor (this ups the "cool factor" on the range and extends the barrel to make it even more accurate). It also has a 1/2 x 28 thread adaptor which can be used by those with a legal suppressor.
Price: $419.00

CHRISTENSEN ARMS 1911 SERIES
Caliber: .45 ACP, .40 S&W, 9mm. **Barrel:** 3.7", 4.3", 5.5" **Features:** All models are built on a titanium frame with hand-fitted slide, match-

grade barrel, tritium night sights, G10 Operator grip panels.
Price: .... $2,599.00 to $3,799.00

CITADEL M-1911
Caliber: .45 ACP, .38 Super, 9mm, .22 LR. **Capacity:** 7 (.45), 8 (9mm, .38), or 10 rounds (.22). **Barrel:** 5 or 3.5 inches (.45 & 9mm only). **Weight:** 2.3 lbs. **Length:** 8.5" **Grips:** Checkered wood or Hogue wrap-around polymer. **Sights:** Low-profile combat fixed rear, blade front. **Finish:** Matte black, brushed or polished nickel. **Features:** Extended grip safety, ambidextrous safety and slide release. Built by Armscor (Rock Island Armory) in the Philippines and imported by Legacy Sports.
Price: Matte black..$592.00
Price: Matte black, Hogue grips $630.00
Price: Brushed nickel..$681.00
Price: Polished nickel..$700.00
Price: Matte black, .22 LR $310.00
Price: Matte black, .22 LR, Hogue grips, fiber-optic sights......$592.00

CIMARRON MODEL 1911
Caliber: .45 ACP **Barrel:** 5 inches. **Weight:** 37.5 oz. **Length:** 8.5" overall. **Grips:** Checkered walnut. **Features:** A faithful reproduction of the original pattern of the Model 1911 with Parkerized finish and lanyard ring. Polished or nickel finish available.
Price: $541.00

COBRA ENTERPRISES FS32, FS380
Caliber: .32 ACP, .380 ACP, 7-shot magazine. **Barrel:** 3.5" **Weight:** 2.1 lbs. **Length:** 6-3/8" overall. **Grips:** Black composition. **Sights:** Fixed. **Features:** Choice of bright chrome, satin nickel or black finish. Introduced 2002. Made in U.S.A. by Cobra Enterprises of Utah, Inc.
Price: .... $138.00 to $250.00

COBRA ENTERPRISES PATRIOT SERIES
Caliber: .380, 9mm or .45 ACP; 6, 7, or 10-shot magazine. **Barrel:** 3.3" **Weight:** 20 oz. **Length:** 6" overall. **Grips:** Black polymer. **Sights:** Rear adjustable. **Features:** Stainless steel or black melonite slide with load indicator; Semi-auto locked breech, DAO. Made in U.S.A. by Cobra Enterprises of Utah, Inc.
Price: .... $349.00 to $395.00

COBRA ENTERPRISES CA32, CA380
Caliber: .32 ACP, .380 ACP. **Barrel:** 2.8" **Weight:** 17 oz. **Length:** 5.4" **Grips:** Black molded synthetic. **Sights:** Fixed. **Features:** Choice of black, satin nickel, or chrome finish. Made in U.S.A. by Cobra Enterprises of Utah, Inc.
Price: $157.00

COBRA DENALI
Caliber: .380 ACP, 5 rounds. **Barrel:** 2.8" **Weight:** 22 oz. **Length:** 5.4" **Grips:** Black molded synthetic integral with frame. **Sights:** Fixed. **Features:** Made in U.S.A. by Cobra Enterprises of Utah, Inc.
Price: $179.00

COLT MODEL 1991 MODEL O
Caliber: .45 ACP, 7-shot magazine. **Barrel:** 5" **Weight:** 38 oz. **Length:** 8.5" overall. **Grips:** Checkered black composition. **Sights:** Ramped blade front, fixed square notch rear, high profile. **Features:** Matte finish. Continuation of serial number range used on original G.I. 1911A1 guns. Comes with one magazine and molded carrying case. Introduced 1991.
Price: Blue $799.00
Price: Stainless $879.00

COLT XSE SERIES MODEL O
Caliber: .45 ACP, 8-shot magazine. **Barrel:** 5" **Grips:** Checkered, double diamond rosewood. **Sights:** Drift-adjustable 3-dot combat. **Features:** Brushed stainless finish; adjustable, two-cut aluminum trigger; extended ambidextrous thumb safety; upswept beavertail with palm swell; elongated slot hammer. Introduced 1999. From Colt's Mfg. Co., Inc.
Price: XSE Government **$1,104.00**

COLT XSE LIGHTWEIGHT COMMANDER
Caliber: .45 ACP, 8-shot. **Barrel:** 4.25" **Weight:** 26 oz. **Length:** 7.75" overall. **Grips:** Double diamond checkered rosewood. **Sights:** Fixed, glare-proofed blade front, square notch rear; 3-dot system. **Features:** Brushed stainless slide, nickeled aluminum frame; McCormick elongated slot enhanced hammer, McCormick two-cut adjustable aluminum hammer. Made in U.S.A. by Colt's Mfg. Co., Inc.
Price: **$1,104.00**

COLT DEFENDER
Caliber: .45 ACP (7-round magazine), 9mm (8-round). **Barrel:** 3" **Weight:** 22-1/2 oz. **Length:** 6.75 overall. **Grips:** Pebble-finish rubber wraparound with finger grooves. **Sights:** White dot front, snag-free Colt competition rear. **Features:** Stainless finish; aluminum frame; combat-style hammer; Hi Ride grip safety, extended manual safety, disconnect safety. Introduced 1998. Made in U.S.A. by Colt's Mfg. Co., Inc.
Price: 07000D, stainless **$899.00**

COLT SERIES 70
Caliber: .45 ACP. **Barrel:** 5" **Weight:** 37.5 oz. **Length:** 8.5" **Grips:** Rosewood with double diamond checkering pattern. **Sights:** Fixed. **Features:** Custom replica of the Original Series 70 pistol with a Series 70 firing system, original rollmarks. Introduced 2002. Made in U.S.A. by Colt's Mfg. Co., Inc.
Price: Blued **$899.00**
Price: Stainless **$979.00**

COLT 38 SUPER
Caliber: .38 Super. **Barrel:** 5" **Weight:** 36.5 oz. **Length:** 8.5" **Grips:** Checkered rubber (stainless and blue models); wood with double diamond checkering pattern (bright stainless model). **Sights:** 3-dot. **Features:** Beveled magazine well, standard thumb safety and service-style grip safety. Introduced 2003. Made in U.S.A. by Colt's Mfg. Co., Inc.
Price: Blued **$849.00**
Price: Stainless **$929.00**

COLT MUSTANG POCKETLITE
Caliber: .380 ACP. Six-shot magazine. **Barrel:** 2.75". **Weight:** 12.5 oz. **Length:** 5.5". **Grips:** Black composite. **Finish:** Brushed stainless. **Features:** Thumb safety, firing-pin safety block. Introduced 2012.
Price: **$599.00**

COLT MUSTANG LITE
Caliber: .380 ACP. Similar to Mustang Pocketlite except has black tactical polymer frame.
Price: **$499.00**

COLT MUSTANG XSP
Caliber: .380 ACP. **Features:** Similar to Mustang Pocketlite except has polymer frame, black diamond or bright stainless slide, squared triggerguard, accessory rail, electroless nickel finished controls.
Price: Bright Stainless..**$528.00**
Price: Black Diamond-Like Carbon finish..............................**$672.00**

COLT RAIL GUN
Caliber: .45 ACP (8+1). **Barrel:** NA. **Weight:** NA. **Length:** 8.5" **Grips:** Rosewood double diamond. **Sights:** White dot front and Novak rear. **Features:** 1911-style semi-auto. Stainless steel frame and slide, front and rear slide serrations, skeletonized trigger, integral; accessory rail, Smith & Alexander upswept beavertail grip palm swell safety, tactical thumb safety, National Match barrel.
Price: ....**$1,199.00 to $1,699.00**

COLT SPECIAL COMBAT GOVERNMENT CARRY MODEL
Caliber: .45 ACP (8+1), .38 Super (9+1). **Barrel:** 5" **Weight:** NA. **Length:** 8.5". **Grips:** Black/silver synthetic. **Sights:** Novak front and rear night. **Features:** 1911-style semi-auto. Skeletonized three-hole trigger, slotted hammer, Smith & Alexander upswept beavertail grip palm swell safety and extended magazine well, Wilson tactical ambidextrous safety. Available in blued, hard chrome, or blue/satin nickel finish, depending on chambering. Marine Pistol has Desert

Tan Cerakoted stainless steel finish, lanyard loop.
Price: $2,095.00

COLT GOVERNMENT MODEL 1911A1 .22
Caliber: .22 LR. 12-round magazine. **Barrel:** 5" **Weight:** 36 oz. **Features:** Made in Germany by Walther under exclusive arrangement with Colt Manufacturing Company. Blowback operation. All other features identical to original including manual and grip safeties, drift-adjustable sights.
Price: $399.00

COLT COMPETITION PISTOL
Caliber: .45 ACP or 9mm Para. Full-size Government Model with 5-inch National Match barrel, dual spring recoil operating system, adjustable rear and fiber optic front sights, custom G10 Colt logo grips.
Price: $899.00

CZ 75 B
Caliber: 9mm Para., .40 S&W, 10-shot magazine. **Barrel:** 4.7" **Weight:** 34.3 oz. **Length:** 8.1" overall. **Grips:** High impact checkered plastic. **Sights:** Square post front, rear adjustable for windage; 3-dot system. **Features:** Single action/double action design; firing pin block safety; choice of black polymer, matte or high-polish blue finishes. All-steel frame. B-SA is a single action with a drop-free magazine. Imported from the Czech Republic by CZ-USA.
Price: 75 B $625.00
Price: 75 B, stainless $783.00
Price: 75 B-SA $661.00

CZ 75 BD DECOCKER
Similar to the CZ 75B except has a decocking lever in place of the safety lever. All other specifications are the same. Introduced 1999. Imported from the Czech Republic by CZ-USA.
Price: 9mm Para., black polymer $612.00

CZ 75 B COMPACT
Similar to the CZ 75 B except has 14-shot magazine in 9mm Para., 3.9 barrel and weighs 32 oz. Has removable front sight; non-glare ribbed slide top. Trigger guard is squared and serrated; combat hammer. Introduced 1993. Imported from the Czech Republic by CZ-USA.
Price: 9mm Para., black polymer $631.00
Price: 9mm Para., dual tone or satin nickel $651.00
Price: 9mm Para. D PCR Compact, alloy frame $651.00

CZ P-07 DUTY
Caliber: .40 S&W, 9mm Luger (16+1). **Barrel:** 3.8" **Weight:** 27.2 oz. **Length:** 7.3" overall. **Grips:** Polymer black polycoat. **Sights:** Blade front, fixed groove rear. **Features:** The ergonomics and accuracy of the CZ 75 with a totally new trigger system. The new Omega trigger system simplifies the CZ 75 trigger system, uses fewer parts and improves the trigger pull. In addition, it allows users to choose between using the handgun with a decocking lever (installed) or a manual safety (included) by a simple parts change. The polymer frame design of the Duty and a new sleek slide profile (fully machined from bar stock) reduce weight, making the P-07 Duty a great choice for concealed carry.
Price: $524.00

CZ P-09 DUTY
High-capacity version of P-07. **Caliber:** 9mm, .40 S&W. **Magazine capacity:** 19 rounds (9mm), 15 (.40). **Features:** Accessory rail, interchangeable grip backstraps, ambidextrous decocker can be converted to manual safety.
Price: $544.00

CZ 75 TACTICAL SPORT
Similar to the CZ 75 B except the CZ 75 TS is a competition ready pistol designed for IPSC standard division (USPSA limited division). Fixed target sights, tuned single-action operation, lightweight polymer match trigger with adjustments for take-up and overtravel, competition hammer, extended magazine catch, ambidextrous manual safety, checkered walnut grips, polymer magazine well, two tone finish. Introduced 2005. Imported from the Czech Republic by CZ-USA.

Price: 9mm Para., 20-shot mag. $1,310.00
Price: .40 S&W, 16-shot mag. $1,310.00

CZ 75 SP-01

Similar to NATO-approved CZ 75 Compact P-01 model. Features an integral 1913 accessory rail on the dust cover, rubber grip panels, black polycoat finish, extended beavertail, new grip geometry with checkering on front and back straps, and double or single action operation. Introduced 2005. The Shadow variant designed as an IPSC "production" division competition firearm. Includes competition hammer, competition rear sight and fiber-optic front sight, modified slide release, lighter recoil and main spring for use with "minor power factor" competition ammunition. Includes polycoat finish and slim walnut grips. Finished by CZ Custom Shop. Imported from the Czech Republic by CZ-USA.
Price: SP-01 Standard.. $680.00
Price: SP-01 **Shadow Target II**.. $1,638.00

CZ 85 B/85 COMBAT

Same gun as the CZ 75 except has ambidextrous slide release and safety levers; non-glare, ribbed slide top; squared, serrated trigger guard; trigger stop to prevent overtravel. Introduced 1986. The CZ 85 Combat features a fully adjustable rear sight, extended magazine release, ambidextrous slide stop and safety catch, drop free magazine and overtravel adjustment. Imported from the Czech Republic by CZ-USA.
Price: 9mm Para., black polymer $628.00
Price: Combat, black polymer $664.00

CZ 97 B

Caliber: .45 ACP, 10-shot magazine. **Barrel:** 4.85" **Weight:** 40 oz. **Length:** 8.34" overall. **Grips:** Checkered walnut. **Sights:** Fixed.

Features: Single action/double action; full-length slide rails; screw-in barrel bushing; linkless barrel; all-steel construction; chamber loaded indicator; dual transfer bars. Introduced 1999. Imported from the Czech Republic by CZ-USA.
Price: Black polymer $707.00
Price: Glossy blue $727.00

CZ 97 BD DECOCKER

Similar to the CZ 97 B except has a decocking lever in place of the safety lever. Tritium night sights. Rubber grips. All other specifications are the same. Introduced 1999. Imported from the Czech Republic by CZ-USA.
Price: 9mm Para., black polymer $816.00

CZ 2075 RAMI/RAMI P

Caliber: 9mm Para., .40 S&W. **Barrel:** 3". **Weight:** 25 oz. **Length:** 6.5" overall. **Grips:** Rubber. **Sights:** Blade front with dot, white outline rear drift adjustable for windage. **Features:** Single-action/double-action; alloy or polymer frame, steel slide; has laser sight mount. Imported from the Czech Republic by CZ-USA.
Price: 9mm Para., alloy frame, 10 and 14-shot magazines $671.00
Price: 40 S&W, alloy frame, 8-shot magazine $671.00
Price: RAMI P, polymer frame, 9mm Para., 40 S&W $612.00

CZ P-01

Caliber: 9mm Para., 14-shot magazine. **Barrel:** 3.85". **Weight:** 27 oz. **Length:** 7.2" overall. **Grips:** Checkered rubber. **Sights:** Blade front with dot, white outline rear drift adjustable for windage. **Features:** Based on the CZ 75, except with forged aircraft-grade aluminum alloy frame. Hammer forged barrel, decocker, firing-pin block, M3 rail, dual slide serrations, squared triggerguard, re-contoured trigger, lanyard loop on butt. Serrated front and back strap. Introduced 2006. Imported from the Czech Republic by CZ-USA.
Price: CZ P-01 .... $627.00

CZ 1911A1

Caliber: .45 ACP. 7+1 capacity. **Barrel:** 5 inches. **Grips:** Checkered walnut. **Sights:** High profile fixed. **Features:** Made in the USA, this model pays homage to the classic 1911 A1. Other features and dimensions identical to the original Colt Government Model.
Price: $849.00

CZ SCORPION EVO

Caliber: : 9mm Para. 20-round magazine. Semi-automatic version

of CZ Scorpion Evo submachine gun. **Features:** Ambidextrous controls, adjustable sights, accessory rails.
Price: $849.00

DAN WESSON DW RZ-10
Caliber: 10mm, 9-shot. **Barrel:** 5". **Grips:** Diamond checkered cocobolo. **Sights:** Bo-Mar style adjustable target sight. **Weight:** 38.3 oz. **Length:** 8.8" overall. **Features:** Stainless-steel frame and serrated slide. Series 70-style 1911, stainless-steel frame, forged stainless-steel slide. Commander-style match hammer. Reintroduced 2005. Made in U.S.A. by Dan Wesson Firearms, distributed by CZ-USA.
Price: 10mm, 8+1 ....$1,480.00

DAN WESSON DW RZ-45 HERITAGE
Similar to the RZ-10 Auto except in .45 ACP with 7-shot magazine. Weighs 36 oz., length is 8.8" overall.
Price: 10mm, 8+1 ....$1,298.00

DAN WESSON VALOR 1911
Caliber: .45 ACP, 8-shot. **Barrel:** 5". **Grips:** Slim Line G10. **Sights:** Heinie ledge straight eight adjustable night sights. **Weight:** 2.4 lbs. **Length:** 8.8" overall. **Features:** The defensive style Valor, is a base stainless 1911 with our matte black "Duty" finish. This finish is a ceramic base coating that has set the standard for all coating tests. Other features include forged stainless frame and match barrel with 25 LPI checkering and undercut triggerguard, adjustable defensive night sites, and Slim line VZ grips. Silverback model has polished stainless slide and matte black frame Made in U.S.A. by Dan Wesson Firearms, distributed by CZ-USA.
Price: $2,012.00
Price: Silverback..$2,012.00

DAN WESSON SPECIALIST
Caliber: .45 ACP, 8-shot magazine. **Barrel:** 5". **Grips:** G10 VZ Operator II. **Sights:** Single amber tritium dot rear, green lamp with white target ring front sight. **Features:** Integral Picatinny rail, 25 lpi front strap checkering, undercut triggerguard, ambidextrous thumb safety, extended mag release and detachable two-piece mag well.
Price: $1,701.00

DAN WESSON V-BOB
Caliber: .45 ACP 8-shot magazine. **Barrel:** 4.25". **Weight:** 34 oz. **Length:** 8". **Grips:** Slim Line G10. **Sights:** Heinie Ledge Straight-Eight Night Sights. **Features:** Black matte or stainless finish. Bobtail forged grip frame with 25 lpi checkering front and rear.
Price: $2,077.00

DAN WESSON VALKYRIE
Caliber: .45 ACP. **Barrel:** 4.25". **Length:** 7.75". **Grips:** Slim Line G10. **Sights:** Tritium Night Sights. **Features:** Similar to V-Bob except has Commander-size slide on Officer-size frame.
Price: $2,012.00

DAN WESSON POINTMAN
Caliber: .9mm, .38 Super, .45 ACP. 8 or 9-shot magazine. **Barrel:** 5". **Length:** 8.5". **Grips:** Double-diamond cocobolo. **Sights:** Adjustable rear and fiber optic front. **Features:** Undercut trigger guard, checkered front strap, serrated rib on top of slide.
Price: .45, .38 Super $1,597.00
Price: 9mm...$1,558.00

DESERT EAGLE 1911 G
Caliber: .45 ACP 8-shot magazine. **Barrel:** 5" or 4.33" (DE1911C Commander size), or 3.0" (DE1911U Undercover). **Grips:** Double diamond checkered wood. **Features:** Extended beavertail grip safety, checkered flat mainspring housing, skeletonized hammer and trigger, extended mag release and thumb safety, stainless full-length guide road, enlarged ejection port, beveled mag well and high profile sights. Comes with two 8-round magazines.

Prices given are believed to be accurate at time of publication however, many factors affect retail pricing so exact prices are not possible.

71ST EDITION, 2017 ✛ **379**

Price: $904.00
Price: Undercover $1,019.00

DESERT EAGLE MARK XIX
Caliber: .357 Mag., 9-shot; .44 Mag., 8-shot; .50 AE, 7-shot. **Barrel:** 6", 10", interchangeable. **Weight:** .357 Mag.-62 oz.; .44 Mag.-69 oz.; .50 AE-72 oz. **Length:** 10.25" overall (6" bbl.). **Grips:** Polymer; rubber available. **Sights:** Blade on ramp front, combat-style rear. Adjustable available. **Features:** Interchangeable barrels; rotating three-lug bolt; ambidextrous safety; adjustable trigger. Military epoxy finish. Satin, bright nickel, chrome, brushed, matte or black-oxide finishes available. 10 barrel extra. Imported from Israel by Magnum Research, Inc.
Price: Black-6, 6" barrel..$1,742.00
Price: Black-10, 10" barrel $1,793.00

BABY DESERT EAGLE III
Caliber: 9mm Para., .40 S&W, .45 ACP; 10-, 12- or 15-round magazines. **Barrel:** 3.85" or 4.43". **Weight:** 28 to 37.9 oz. **Length:** 7.25 to 8.25 overall. **Grips:** Ergonomic polymer. **Sights:** White 3-dot system. **Features:** Choice of steel or polymer frame with integral rail; slide-mounted decocking safety. Upgraded design of Baby Eagle II series.
Price: ....$646.00 to $691.00

DESERT EAGLE L5
Caliber: .357 Magnum, 9+1-shot capacity. **Barrel:** 5". **Weight:** 50 oz. **Length:** 9.7". Features: Steel barrel, frame and slide with full Weaver-style accessory rail and integral muzzlebrake. Gas-operated rotating bolt, single-action trigger, fixed sights.
Price: From $1,790.00

DESERT EAGLE MR9, MR40
Caliber: 9mm Para., (15-round magazine) or .40 S&W (11 rounds). **Barrel:** 4.5". **Weight:** 25 oz. **Length:** 7.6" overall. **Sights:** Three-dot rear sight adjustable for windage, interchangeable front sight blades of different heights. **Features:** Polymer frame, locked breech, striker-fired design with decocker/safety button on top of slide, three replaceable grip palm swells, Picatinny rail. Made in Germany by Walther and imported by Magnum Research. Introduced in 2014.
Price: $559.00

DIAMONDBACK DB380
Caliber: .380, 6+1-shot capacity. **Barrel:** 2.8". **Weight:** 8.8 oz. **Features:** A "ZERO-Energy" striker firing system with a mechanical firing pin block, steel magazine catch, windage-adjustable sights.
Price: $328.00

DIAMONDBACK DB9
Caliber: 9mm, 6+1-shot capacity. **Barrel:** 3". **Weight:** 11 oz. **Length:** 5.60". **Features:** Other features similar to DB380 model.
Price: $359.00

DIAMONDBACK DB FS NINE
Caliber: 9mm, 15+1-shot capacity. **Barrel:** 4.75". **Weight:** 21.5 oz. **Length:** 7.8". Double-action, striker-fired model with polymer frame and stainless steel slide. **Features:** Flared magwell, extended magazine base pad, ergonomically contoured grip, fixed 3-dot sights, front and rear slide serrations, integral MIL-STD 1913 Picatinny rail.
Price: $483.00

DOUBLESTAR 1911
Caliber: .45 ACP, 8-shot magazine. **Barrel:** 5". **Weight:** 40 oz. **Grips:**

Cocobolo wood. **Sights:** Novak LoMount 2 white-dot rear, Novak white-dot front. **Features:** Single-action, M1911-style with forged frame and slide of 4140 steel, stainless steel barrel machined from bar stock by Storm Lake, funneled mag well, accessory rail, black Nitride or nickel plated finish.
Price: Black..$2,000.00
Price: Nickel plated...$2,150.00

EAA WITNESS FULL SIZE
Caliber: 9mm Para., .38 Super, 18-shot magazine; .40 S&W, 10mm, 15-shot magazine; .45 ACP, 10-shot magazine. **Barrel:** 4.5". **Weight:** 35.33 oz. **Length:** 8.1" overall. **Grips:** Checkered rubber. **Sights:** Undercut blade front, open rear adjustable for windage. **Features:** Double-action/single-action trigger system; round triggerguard; frame-mounted safety. Available with steel or polymer frame. Also available with interchangeable .45 ACP and .22 LR slides. Steel frame introduced 1991. Polymer frame introduced 2005. Imported from Italy by European American Armory.
Price: Steel frame $607.00
Price: Polymer frame $571.00
Price: 45/22 .22 LR, full-size steel frame, blued $752.00

EAA WITNESS COMPACT
Caliber: 9mm Para., 14-shot magazine; .40 S&W, 10mm, 12-shot magazine; .45 ACP, 8-shot magazine. **Barrel:** 3.6" **Weight:** 30 oz. **Length:** 7.3" overall. **Features:** Available with steel or polymer frame (shown). All polymer frame Witness pistols are capable of being converted to other calibers. Otherwise similar to Full Size Witness. Imported from Italy by European American Armory.
Price: Polymer frame $571.00
Price: Steel frame $607.00

EAA WITNESS-P CARRY
Caliber: 9mm, 17-shot magazine; 10mm, 15-shot magazine; .45 ACP, 10-shot magazine. **Barrel:** 3.6". **Weight:** 27 oz. **Length:** 7.5" overall. **Features:** Otherwise similar to Full Size Witness. Polymer frame introduced 2005. Imported from Italy by European American Armory.
Price: $691.00

EAA WITNESS PAVONA COMPACT POLYMER
Caliber: .380 ACP (13-round magazine), 9mm (13) or .40 S&W (9). **Barrel:** 3.6". **Weight:** 30 oz. **Length:** 7" overall. **Features:** Designed primarily for women with fine-tuned recoil and hammer springs for easier operation, a polymer frame with integral checkering, contoured lines and in black, charcoal, blue, purple, or magenta with silver or gold sparkle.
Price: .... $476.00 to $528.00

EAA WITNESS ELITE 1911
Caliber: .45 ACP (8-round magazine). **Barrel:** 5". **Weight:** 32 oz. **Length:** 8.58" overall. **Features:** Full-size 1911-style pistol with either steel or polymer frame.
Price: $580.00

ED BROWN CLASSIC CUSTOM
Caliber: .45 ACP, 7 shot. **Barrel:** 5". **Weight:** 40 oz. **Grips:** Cocobolo wood. **Sights:** Bo-Mar adjustable rear, dovetail front. **Features:** Single-action, M1911 style, custom made to order, stainless frame and slide available. Special mirror-finished slide.
Price: $3,695.00

ED BROWN KOBRA AND KOBRA CARRY
Caliber: .45 ACP, 7-shot magazine. **Barrel:** 5" (Kobra); 4.25" (Kobra Carry). **Weight:** 39 oz. (Kobra); 34 oz. (Kobra Carry). **Grips:** Hogue exotic wood. **Sights:** Ramp, front; fixed Novak low-mount night sights, rear. **Features:** Has snakeskin pattern serrations on forestrap and mainspring housing, dehorned edges, beavertail grip safety.
Price: Kobra K-SS $2,695.00
Price: Kobra Carry $2,945.00

Prices given are believed to be accurate at time of publication however, many factors affect retail pricing so exact prices are not possible.

71ST EDITION, 2017 ✦ **381**

ED BROWN KOBRA CARRY LIGHTWEIGHT

Caliber: .45 ACP, 7-shot magazine. **Barrel:** 4.25" (Commander model slide). **Weight:** 27 oz. **Grips:** Hogue exotic wood. **Sights:** 10-8 Performance U-notch plain black rear sight with .156 notch, for fast aquisition of close targets. Fixed dovetail front night sight with high visibility white outlines. **Features:** Aluminum frame and Bobtail™ housing. Matte finished Gen III coated slide for low glare, with snakeskin on rear of slide only. Snakeskin pattern serrations on forestrap and mainspring housing, dehorned edges, beavertail grip safety. "LW" insignia on slide, which stands for "Lightweight".
Price: Kobra Carry Lightweight $3,320.00

ED BROWN EXECUTIVE

Similar to other Ed Brown products, but with 25-lpi checkered frame and mainspring housing.
Price: .... $2,895.00 - $3,145.00

ED BROWN SPECIAL FORCES

Similar to other Ed Brown products, but with ChainLink treatment on forestrap and mainspring housing. Entire gun coated with Gen III finish. "Square cut" serrations on rear of slide only. Dehorned. Introduced 2006.
Price: From $2,695.00

ED BROWN SPECIAL FORCES CARRY

Similar to the Special Forces basic models. Features a 4.25" Commander model slide, single stack commander Bobtail frame. Weighs approx. 35 oz. Fixed dovetail 3-dot night sights with high visibility white outlines.
Price: From $2,945.00

EXCEL ARMS MP-22

Caliber: .22 WMR, 9-shot magazine. **Barrel:** 8.5" bull barrel. **Weight:** 54 oz. **Length:** 12.875" overall. **Grips:** Textured black composition. **Sights:** Fully adjustable target sights. **Features:** Made from 17-4 stainless steel, comes with aluminum rib, integral Weaver base, internal hammer, firing-pin block. American made, lifetime warranty. Comes with two9-round stainless steel magazines and a California-approved cable lock. .22 WMR Introduced 2006. Made in U.S.A. by Excel Arms.
Price: $477.00

EXCEL ARMS MP-5.7

Caliber: 5.7x28mm, 9-shot magazine. Blow-back action. Other features similar to MP-22. Red-dot optic sights, scope and rings are optional.
Price: $615.00
Price: With optic sights..$685.00
Price: With scope and rings...$711.00

FMK 9C1 G2

Caliber: 9mm. Magazine capacity 10+1 or 14+1. Available in either single action or double-action only. **Barrel:** 4". **Overall length:** 6.85". **Weight:** 23.45 oz. **Finish:** Black, Dark Earth or pink. **Sights:** Interchangeable Glock compatible. **Features:** Polymer frame, high-carbon steel slide, stainless steel barrel. Very low bore axis and shock absorbing backstrap are said to result in low felt recoil. DAO model has Fast Action Trigger (FAT) with shorter pull and reset. Made in the U.S.A.
Price: $409.95

FN FNS SERIES

Caliber: 9mm, 17-shot magazine, .40 S&W (14-shot magazine). **Barrel:** 4" or 3.6" (Compact). **Weight:** 25 oz. (9mm), 27.5 oz. (.40). **Length:** 7.25". **Grips:** Integral polymer with two interchangeable backstrap inserts. **Features:** Striker-fired, double action with manual safety, accessory rail, ambidextrous controls, 3-dot Night Sights.
Price: $599.00

FN FNX SERIES

Caliber: 9mm, 17-shot magazine, .40 S&W (14-shot), .45 ACP (10 or 14-shot). **Barrel:** 4" (9mm and .40), 4.5" .45. **Weight:** 22 to 32 oz (.45). **Length:** 7.4, 7.9" (.45). **Features:** Double-action/single-action operation with decocking/manual safety lever. Has external extractor with loaded-chamber indicator, front and rear cocking serrations, fixed 3-dot combat sights.
Price: $699.00

FN FNX .45 TACTICAL

Similar to standard FNX .45 except with 5.3" barrel with threaded muzzle, polished chamber and feed ramp, enhanced high-profile night sights, slide cut and threaded for red-dot sight (not included), MIL-STD 1913 accessory rail, ring-style hammer.
Price: $1,400.00

FN FIVE-SEVEN

Caliber: 5.7x28mm, 10- or 20-round magazine capacity. **Barrel:** 4.8". **Weight:** 23 oz. **Length:** 8.2" **Features:** Adjustable three-dot system. Single-action polymer frame model chambered for low-recoil 5.7x28mm cartridge.
Price: $1,349.00

GLOCK 17/17C

Caliber: 9mm Para., 17/19/33-shot magazines. **Barrel:** 4.49". **Weight:**
22.04 oz. (without magazine). **Length:** 7.32" overall. **Grips:** Black polymer. **Sights:** Dot on front blade, white outline rear adjustable for windage. **Features:** Polymer frame, steel slide; double-action trigger with "Safe Action" system; mechanical firing pin safety, drop safety; simple takedown without tools; locked breech, recoil operated action. ILS designation refers to Internal Locking System. Adopted by Austrian armed forces 1983. NATO approved 1984. Model 17L has 6-inch barrel, ported or non ported, slotted and relieved slide, checkered grip with finger grooves, no accessory rail. Imported from Austria by Glock, Inc. USA.
Price: From $599.00
Price: 17L..$750.00
Price: 17 Gen 4..$649.00

GLOCK GEN4 SERIES

In 2010 a new series of Generation Four pistols was introduced with several improved features. These included a multiple backstrap system offering three different size options, short, medium or large frame; reversible and enlarged magazine release; dual recoil springs; and RTF (Rough Textured Finish) surface. Some recent models are only available in Gen 4 configuration.

GLOCK 19/19C

Caliber: 9mm Para., 15/17/19/33-shot magazines. **Barrel:** 4.02". **Weight:** 20.99 oz. (without magazine). **Length:** 6.85" overall. Compact version of Glock 17. Imported from Austria by Glock, Inc.
Price: $599.00
Price: 19 Gen 4 ....$649.00

GLOCK 20/20C 10MM

Caliber: 10mm, 15-shot magazines. **Barrel:** 4.6". **Weight:** 27.68 oz. (without magazine). **Length:** 7.59" overall. **Features:** Otherwise similar to Model 17. Imported from Austria by Glock, Inc. Introduced 1990.
Price: From $637.00
Price: 20 Gen 4..$687.00

GLOCK MODEL 20 SF SHORT FRAME

Caliber: 10mm. **Barrel:** 4.61" with hexagonal rifling. **Weight:** 27.51 oz. **Length:** 8.07" overall. **Sights:** Fixed. **Features:** Otherwise similar to Model 20 but with short-frame design, extended sight radius.
Price: $637.00

GLOCK 21/21C

Caliber: .45 ACP, 13-shot magazines. **Barrel:** 4.6". **Weight:** 26.28 oz. (without magazine). **Length:** 7.59" overall. **Features:** Otherwise similar to Model 17. Imported from Austria by Glock, Inc. Introduced 1991. SF version has tactical rail, smaller diameter grip, 10-round magazine capacity. Introduced 2007.
Price: From $637.00
Price: 21 Gen 4..$687.00

GLOCK 22/22C

Caliber: .40 S&W, 15/17-shot magazines. **Barrel:** 4.49". **Weight:** 22.92 oz. (without magazine). **Length:** 7.32" overall. **Features:** Otherwise similar to Model 17, including pricing. Imported from Austria by Glock, Inc. Introduced 1990.
Price: From $599.00
Price: 22C $649.00
Price: 22 Gen 4......................................$649.00

Prices given are believed to be accurate at time of publication however, many factors affect retail pricing so exact prices are not possible.

71ST EDITION, 2017 ✦ **383**

GLOCK 23/23C
Caliber: .40 S&W, 13/15/17-shot magazines. **Barrel:** 4.02". **Weight:** 21.16 oz. (without magazine). **Length:** 6.85" overall. **Features:** Otherwise similar to Model 22, including pricing. Compact version of Glock 22. Imported from Austria by Glock, Inc. Introduced 1990.
Price: $599.00
Price: 23C Compensated $621.00
Price: 23 Gen 4..$649.00

GLOCK 24/24C
Caliber: .40 S&W, 10/15/17 or 22-shot magazine. Similar to Model 22 except with 6.02-inch barrel, ported or non-ported, trigger pull recalibrated to 4.5 lbs.
Price: From...$750.00

GLOCK 26
Caliber: 9mm Para. 10/12/15/17/19/33-shot magazines. **Barrel:** 3.46". **Weight:** 19.75 oz. **Length:** 6.29" overall. Subcompact version of Glock 17. Imported from Austria by Glock, Inc.
Price: $599.00
Price: 26 Gen 4..$649.00

GLOCK 27
Caliber: .40 S&W, 9/11/13/15/17-shot magazines. **Barrel:** 3.46". **Weight:** 19.75 oz. (without magazine). **Length:** 6.29 overall. **Features:** Otherwise similar to Model 22, including pricing. Subcompact version of Glock 22. Imported from Austria by Glock, Inc. Introduced 1996.
Price: From...$599.00
Price: 27 Gen 4..$649.00

GLOCK 29 GEN 4
Caliber: 10mm, 10/15-shot magazines. **Barrel:** 3.78". **Weight:** 24.69 oz. (without magazine). **Length:** 6.77" overall. **Features:** Otherwise similar to Model 20, including pricing. Subcompact version of Glock 20. Imported from Austria by Glock, Inc. Introduced 1997.
Price: Fixed sight $637.00

GLOCK MODEL 29 SF SHORT FRAME
Caliber: 10mm. **Barrel:** 3.78" with hexagonal rifling. **Weight:** 24.52 oz. **Length:** 6.97" overall. **Sights:** Fixed. **Features:** Otherwise similar to Model 29 but with short-frame design, extended sight radius.
Price: $637.00

GLOCK 30
Caliber: .45 ACP, 9/10/13-shot magazines. **Barrel:** 3.78". **Weight:** 23.99 oz. (without magazine). **Length:** 6.77" overall. **Features:** Otherwise similar to Model 21, including pricing. Subcompact version of Glock 21. Imported from Austria by Glock, Inc. Introduced

1997. SF version has tactical rail, octagonal rifled barrel with a 1:15.75 rate of twist, smaller diameter grip, 10-round magazine capacity. Introduced 2008.
Price: $637.00
Price: 30 SF (short frame) $637.00

GLOCK 30S
Variation of Glock 30 with a Model 36 slide on a Model 30SF frame (short frame). **Caliber:** .45 ACP, 10-round magazine. **Barrel:** 3.78 inches. **Weight:** 20 oz. **Length:** 7 inches.
Price: $637.00

GLOCK 31/31C
Caliber: .357 Auto, 15/17-shot magazines. **Barrel:** 4.49". **Weight:** 23.28 oz. (without magazine). **Length:** 7.32" overall. **Features:** Otherwise similar to Model 17. Imported from Austria by Glock, Inc.
Price: From $599.00
Price: 31 Gen 4..$649.00

GLOCK 32/32C
Caliber: .357 Auto, 13/15/17-shot magazines. **Barrel:** 4.02". **Weight:** 21.52 oz. (without magazine). **Length:** 6.85" overall. **Features:** Otherwise similar to Model 31. Compact. Imported from Austria by Glock, Inc.
Price: $599.00
Price: 32 Gen 4..$649.00

GLOCK 33
Caliber: .357 Auto, 9/11/13/15/17-shot magazines. **Barrel:** 3.46". **Weight:** 19.75 oz. (without magazine). **Length:** 6.29" overall. **Features:** Otherwise similar to Model 31. Subcompact. Imported from Austria by Glock, Inc.
Price: From $599.00
Price: 33 Gen 4..$614.00

GLOCK 34
Caliber: 9mm Para. 17/19/33-shot magazines. **Barrel:** 5.32". **Weight:** 22.9 oz. **Length:** 8.15" overall. **Features:** Competition version of Glock 17 with extended barrel, slide, and sight radius dimensions. Available with MOS (Modular Optic System).
Price: From $679.00
Price: MOS $840.00
Price: 34 Gen 4..$729.00

GLOCK 35
Caliber: .40 S&W, 15/17-shot magazines. **Barrel:** 5.32. **Weight:** 24.52 oz. (without magazine). **Length:** 8.15 overall. **Sights:** Adjustable. **Features:** Otherwise similar to Model 22. Competition version of Glock 22 with extended barrel, slide, and sight radius dimensions. Available with MOS (Modular Optic System). Introduced 1996.
Price: From...$679.00
Price: MOS $840.00
Price: 35 Gen 4..$729.00

GLOCK 36
Caliber: .45 ACP, 6-shot magazines. **Barrel:** 3.78. **Weight:** 20.11 oz. (without magazine). **Length:** 6.77 overall. **Sights:** Fixed. **Features:** Single-stack magazine, slimmer grip than Glock 21/30. Subcompact. Imported from Austria by Glock, Inc. Introduced 1997.
Price: $637.00

GLOCK 37
Caliber: .45 GAP, 10-shot magazines. **Barrel:** 4.49. **Weight:** 25.95 oz. (without magazine). **Length:** 7.32 overall. **Features:** Otherwise similar

to Model 17. Imported from Austria by Glock, Inc. Introduced 2005.

Price: $614.00

Price: 37 Gen 4..$664.00

GLOCK 38

Caliber: .45 GAP, 8/10-shot magazines. **Barrel:** 4.02. **Weight:** 24.16 oz. (without magazine). **Length:** 6.85 overall. **Features:** Otherwise similar to Model 37. Compact. Imported from Austria by Glock, Inc.

Price: $614.00

GLOCK 39

Caliber: .45 GAP, 6/8/10-shot magazines. **Barrel:** 3.46. **Weight:** 19.33 oz. (without magazine). **Length:** 6.3 overall. **Features:** Otherwise similar to Model 37. Subcompact. Imported from Austria by Glock, Inc.

Price: $614.00

GLOCK 40 GEN 4

Caliber: 10mm. Similar features as Model 41 except for 6.01" barrel. Includes MOS optics.

Price: $840.00

GLOCK 41 GEN 4

Caliber: .45 ACP, 13-round magazine capacity. **Barrel:** 5.31". **Weight:** 27 oz. **Length:** 8.9" overall. **Features:** This is a long-slide .45 ACP Gen4 model introduced in 2014. Operating features are the same as other Glock models. Available with MOS (Modular Optic System).

Price: $749.00

Price: MOS $840.00

GLOCK 42

Caliber: .380 ACP, 6-round magazine capacity. **Barrel:** 3.25" **Weight:** 13.8 oz. **Length:** 5.9" overall. **Features:** This single-stack, slimline sub-compact is the smallest pistol Glock has ever made. This is also the first Glock pistol made in the USA.

Price: $499.00

GLOCK 43

Caliber: 9mm. 6+1 capacity. **Barrel:** 3.39" **Weight:** 17.95 oz. **Length:** 6.26". **Height:** 4.25". **Width:** 1.02". **Features:** Newest member of Glock's Slimline series with single-stack magazine.

Price: $599.00

GRAND POWER P-1 MK7

Caliber: 9mm. 15+1 magazine. Compact DA/SA pistol featuring a 3.7-inch barrel, frame-mounted safety, steel slide and frame, polymer grips and weight of 26 ounces. Offered in several variations and sizes. Made in Slovakia and imported by Eagle Imports.

Price: $449.99

GUNCRAFTER INDUSTRIES NO. 1

Caliber: .45 ACP or .50 GI. **Features:** 1911-style series of pistols best known for the proprietary .50 GI chambering. Offered in several common 1911 variations. No. 1 has 5-inch heavy match-grade barrel, 7-round magazine, Parkerized or hard chrome finish, checkered grips and front strap, Heinie slant tritium sights, 7-round magazine. Other models include Commander style, Officer's Model, Long Slide w/6-inch barrel and several 9mm versions.

Price: ....$2,695.00 to $4,125.00

HECKLER & KOCH USP

Caliber: 9mm Para., 15-shot magazine; .40 S&W, 13-shot magazine; 45 ACP, 12-shot magazine. **Barrel:** 4.25-4.41. **Weight:** 1.65 lbs. **Length:** 7.64-7.87 overall. **Grips:** Non-slip stippled black polymer. **Sights:** Blade front, rear adjustable for windage. **Features:** New HK design with polymer frame, modified Browning action with recoil reduction system, single control lever. Special "hostile environment" finish on all metal parts. Available in SA/DA, DAO, left- and right-hand versions. Introduced 1993. 45 ACP Introduced 1995. Imported from Germany by Heckler & Koch, Inc.
Price: USP .45 ....$1,033.00
Price: USP .40 and USP 9mm $952.00

HECKLER & KOCH USP COMPACT

Caliber: 9mm Para., 13-shot magazine; .40 S&W and .357 SIG, 12-shot magazine; .45 ACP, 8-shot magazine. Similar to the USP except the 9mm Para., 357 SIG, and 40 S&W have 3.58 barrels, measure 6.81 overall, and weigh 1.47 lbs. (9mm Para.). Introduced 1996. 45 ACP measures 7.09 overall. Introduced 1998. Imported from Germany by Heckler & Koch, Inc.
Price: USP Compact .45 ....$1,040.00
Price: USP Compact 9mm
Para., .40 S&W $992.00

HECKLER & KOCH USP45 TACTICAL

Caliber: .40 S&W, 13-shot magazine; .45 ACP, 12-shot magazine. **Barrel:** 4.90-5.09. **Weight:** 1.9 lbs. **Length:** 8.64 overall. **Grips:** Non-slip stippled polymer. **Sights:** Blade front, fully adjustable target rear. **Features:** Has extended threaded barrel with rubber O-ring; adjustable trigger; extended magazine floorplate; adjustable trigger stop; polymer frame. Introduced 1998. Imported from Germany by Heckler & Koch, Inc.
Price: USP Tactical .45 ....$1,352.00
Price: USP Tactical .40 ....$1,333.00

HECKLER & KOCH USP COMPACT TACTICAL

Caliber: .45 ACP, 8-shot magazine. Similar to the USP Tactical except measures 7.72 overall, weighs 1.72 lbs. Introduced 2006. Imported from Germany by Heckler & Koch, Inc.
Price: USP Compact Tactical $1,352.00

HECKLER & KOCH HK45

Caliber: .45 ACP, 10-shot magazine. **Barrel:** 4.53". **Weight:** 1.73 lbs. **Length:** 7.52" overall. **Grips:** Ergonomic with adjustable grip panels. **Sights:** Low profile, drift adjustable. **Features:** Polygonal rifling, ambidextrous controls, operates on improved Browning linkless recoil system. Available in Tactical and Compact variations.
Price: USP Tactical .45 .... **$1,193.00 to $1,392.00**

HECKLER & KOCH MARK 23 SPECIAL OPERATIONS

Caliber: .45 ACP, 12-shot magazine. **Barrel:** 5.87. **Weight:** 2.42 lbs. **Length:** 9.65 overall. **Grips:** Integral with frame; black polymer. **Sights:** Blade front, rear drift adjustable for windage; 3-dot. **Features:** Civilian version of the SOCOM pistol. Polymer frame; double action; exposed hammer; short recoil, modified Browning action. Introduced 1996. Imported from Germany by Heckler & Koch, Inc.
Price: $2,299.00

HECKLER & KOCH P30 AND P30L

Caliber: 9mm and .40 S&W with 13 or 15-shot magazines. **Barrel:** 3.86" or 4.45" (P30L). **Weight:** 26 to 27.5 oz. **Length:** 6.95, 7.56" overall. **Grips:** Interchangeable panels. **Sights:** Open rectangular notch rear sight with contrast points (no radioactive). **Features:** Ergonomic features include a special grip frame with interchangeable backstraps inserts and lateral plates, allowing the pistol to be individually adapted to any user. Browning type action with modified short recoil operation. Ambidextrous controls include dual slide releases, magazine

Prices given are believed to be accurate at time of publication however, many factors affect retail pricing so exact prices are not possible.

release levers, and a serrated decocking button located on the rear of the frame (for applicable variants). A Picatinny rail molded into the front of the frame. The extractor serves as a loaded-chamber indicator.

Price: P30 .... **$1,099.00**
Price: P30L Variant 2 Law Enforcement Modification
      (LEM) enhanced DAO **$1,149.00**
Price: P30L Variant 3 Double Action/Single Action
      (DA/SA) with Decocker **$1,108.00**

HECKLER & KOCH P2000
Caliber: 9mm Para., 13-shot magazine; .40 S&W, 12-shot magazine. **Barrel:** 3.62. **Weight:** 1.5 lbs. **Length:** 7 overall. **Grips:** Interchangeable panels. **Sights:** Fixed Patridge style, drift adjustable for windage, standard 3-dot. **Features:** Incorporates features of HK USP Compact pistol, including Law Enforcement Modification (LEM) trigger, double-action hammer system, ambidextrous magazine release, dual slide-release levers, accessory mounting rails, recurved, hook trigger guard, fiber-reinforced polymer frame, modular grip with exchangeable back straps, nitro-carburized finish, lock-out safety device. Introduced 2003. Imported from Germany by Heckler & Koch, Inc.
Price: **$799.00**

HECKLER & KOCH P2000 SK
Caliber: 9mm Para., 10-shot magazine; .40 S&W and .357 SIG, 9-shot magazine. **Barrel:** 3.27. **Weight:** 1.3 lbs. **Length:** 6.42 overall. **Sights:** Fixed Patridge style, drift adjustable. **Features:** Standard accessory rails, ambidextrous slide release, polymer frame, polygonal bore profile. Smaller version of P2000. Introduced 2005. Imported from Germany by Heckler & Koch, Inc.
Price: **$799.00**

HECKLER & KOCH VP9/VP 40
Caliber: 9mm Para., 10 or 15-shot magazine. .40 S&W (10 or 13). **Barrel:** 4.09". **Weight:** 25.6 oz. **Length:** 7.34 overall. **Sights:** Fixed 3-dot, drift adjustable. **Features:** Striker-fired system with HK enhanced light pull trigger. Ergonomic grip design with interchangeable backstraps and side panels.
Price: **$719.00**

HI-POINT FIREARMS MODEL 9MM COMPACT
Caliber: 9mm Para., 8-shot magazine. **Barrel:** 3.5. **Weight:** 25 oz.

Length: 6.75 overall. **Grips:** Textured plastic. **Sights:** Combat-style adjustable 3-dot system; low profile. **Features:** Single-action design; frame-mounted magazine release; polymer frame. Scratch-resistant matte finish. Introduced 1993. Comps are similar except they have a 4 barrel with muzzle brake/compensator. Compensator is slotted for laser or flashlight mounting. Introduced 1998. Made in U.S.A. by MKS Supply, Inc.
Price: C-9 9mm **$189.00**

HI-POINT FIREARMS MODEL 380 POLYMER
Similar to the 9mm Compact model except chambered for .380 ACP, 8-shot magazine, adjustable 3-dot sights. Weighs 25 oz. Polymer frame. Action locks open after last shot. Includes 10-shot and 8-shot magazine; trigger lock.
Price: CF-380 .... **$151.00**

HI-POINT FIREARMS 40 AND 45 SW/POLY
Caliber: .40 S&W, 8-shot magazine; .45 ACP (9-shot). **Barrel:** 4.5. **Weight:** 32 oz. **Length:** 7.72 overall. **Sights:** Adjustable 3-dot. **Features:** Polymer frames, last round lock-open, grip mounted magazine release, magazine disconnect safety, integrated accessory rail, trigger lock. Introduced 2002. Made in U.S.A. by MKS Supply, Inc.
Price: **$199.00**

HIGH STANDARD VICTOR .22
Caliber: .22 Long Rifle (10 rounds) or .22 Short (5 rounds). **Barrel:** 4.5"-5.5". **Weight:** 45 oz.-46 oz. **Length:** 8.5"-9.5" overall. **Grips:** Freestyle wood. **Sights:** Frame mounted, adjustable. **Features:** Semi-auto with drilled and tapped barrel, tu-tone or blued finish.
Price: **$965.00**

HIGH STANDARD 10X CUSTOM .22
Similar to the Victor model but with precision fitting, black wood grips, 5.5 barrel only. High Standard Universal Mount, 10-shot magazine, barrel drilled and tapped, certificate of authenticity. Overall length is 9.5". Weighs 44 oz. to 46 oz. From High Standard Custom Shop.
Price: **$1,375.00**

HIGH STANDARD SUPERMATIC TROPHY .22
Caliber: .22 Long Rifle (10 rounds) or .22 Short (5 rounds/Citation version), not interchangable. **Barrel:** 5.5", 7.25". **Weight:** 44 oz., 46 oz. **Length:** 9.5", 11.25" overall. **Grips:** Wood. **Sights:** Adjustable. **Features:** Semi-auto with drilled and tapped barrel, tu-tone or blued finish with gold accents.
Price: 5.5 .... **$965.00**

HIGH STANDARD OLYMPIC MILITARY .22
Similar to the Supermatic Trophy model but in .22 Short only with 5.5" bull barrel, five-round magazine, aluminum alloy frame, adjustable sights. Overall length is 9.5", weighs 42 oz.
Price: **$1,050.00**

HIGH STANDARD SUPERMATIC CITATION SERIES .22
Similar to the Supermatic Trophy model but with heavier trigger pull, 10" barrel, and nickel accents. 22 Short conversion unit available. Overall length 14.5", weighs 52 oz.
Price: **$975.00**

Prices given are believed to be accurate at time of publication however, many factors affect retail pricing so exact prices are not possible.

71ST EDITION, 2017 ✣ **387**

HIGH STANDARD SUPERMATIC TOURNAMENT .22

Caliber: .22 LR. **Barrel:** 5.5" bull barrel. **Weight:** 44 oz. **Length:** 9.5"
overall. **Features:** Limited edition; similar to High Standard Victor
model but with rear sight mounted directly to slide.
Price: **$1,025.00**

HIGH STANDARD SPORT KING .22

Caliber: .22 LR. **Barrel:** 4.5" or 6.75" tapered barrel. **Weight:** 40 oz.
to 42 oz. **Length:** 8.5" to 10.75". **Features:** Sport version of High
Standard Supermatic. Two-tone finish, fixed sights.
Price: **$835.00**

HI-STANDARD SPACE GUN

Semiauto pistol chambered in .22 LR. Recreation of famed competition
"Space Gun" from 1960s. Features include 6.75- 8- or 10-inch barrel;
10-round magazine; adjustable sights; barrel weight; adjustable
muzzle brake; blue-black finish with gold highlights.
Price: **$1,350.00**

ITHACA 1911

Caliber: .45 ACP, 7-round capacity. **Barrel:** 5". **Weight:** 41 oz.
Length: 8.75" **Sights:** Fixed combat or fully adjustable target.
Grips: Checkered cocobolo with Ithaca logo. **Features:** Classic
1911A1-style pistol with enhanced features including match-grade
barrel, lowered and flared ejection port, skeletonized hammer and
trigger, full-length two-piece guide rod, hand-fitted barrel bushing,
extended beavertail grip safety, checkered front strap. Made 100
percent in the U.S.A.
Price: **$1,799.00**
Price: Adjustable sights, ambidextrous safety **$1,949.00**

IVER JOHNSON EAGLE

Series of 1911-style pistols made in typical variations including full-
size (Eagle), Commander (Hawk), Officer's (Thrasher) sizes in .45
ACP and 9mm. Many finishes available including Cerakote, polished
stainless, pink and several "snakeskin" variations.
Price: .... **$608.00 to $959.00**

KAHR CM SERIES

Caliber: 9mm (6+1), .40 S&W (6+1). .45 ACP (5+1). CM45 Model is
shown. **Barrel:** 3", 3.25"(45). **Weight:** 15.9 to 17.3 oz. **Length:** 5.42
overall. **Grips:** Textured polymer with integral steel rails molded into
frame. **Sights:** CM9093 - Pinned in polymer sight; PM9093 - Drift
adjustable, white bar-dot combat. **Features:** A conventional rifled
barrel instead of the match grade polygonal barrel on Kahr's PM series;
the CM slide stop lever is MIM (metal-injection-molded) instead of
machined; the CM series slide has fewer machining operations and
uses simple engraved markings instead of roll marking and finally the
CM series are shipped with one magazine instead of two magazines.
The slide is machined from solid 416 stainless slide with a matte finish,
each gun is shipped with one 6-round stainless steel magazine with a
flush baseplate. Magazines are USA made, plasma welded, tumbled to
remove burrs and feature Wolff Gunsprings. The magazine catch in the
polymer frame is all metal and will not wear out on the stainless steel
magazine after extended use.
Price: **$460.00**

KAHR CT40/CT45 SERIES

Caliber: .40 S&W (6+1) .45 ACP (7+1). **Barrel:** 4 inches. **Weight:** 23.7 oz. **Length:** 5.42 overall. **Grips:** Textured polymer with integral steel rails molded into frame. **Sights:** Drift adjustable, white bar-dot combat. **Features:** A conventional rifled barrel instead of the match grade polygonal barrel on Kahr's PM series; the CM slide stop lever is MIM (metal-injection-molded) instead of machined; the CM series slide has fewer machining operations and uses simple engraved markings instead of roll marking and finally the CM series are shipped with one magazine instead of two magazines. The slide is machined from solid 416 stainless slide with a matte finish, each gun is shipped with one 6-round stainless steel magazine with a flush baseplate. Magazines are USA made, plasma welded, tumbled to remove burrs and feature Wolff Gunsprings. The magazine catch in the polymer frame is all metal and will not wear out on the stainless steel magazine after extended use
Price: $460.00

KAHR K SERIES

Caliber: K9: 9mm Para., 7-shot; K40: .40 S&W, 6-shot magazine. **Barrel:** 3.5. **Weight:** 25 oz. **Length:** 6 overall. **Grips:** Wraparound textured soft polymer. **Sights:** Blade front, rear drift adjustable for windage; bar-dot combat style. **Features:** Trigger-cocking double-action mechanism with passive firing pin block. Made of 4140 ordnance steel with matte black finish. Contact maker for complete price list. Introduced 1994. Made in U.S.A. by Kahr Arms.
Price: K9093C K9, matte stainless steel $855.00
Price: K9093NC K9, matte stainless steel w/tritium
night sights $985.00
Price: K9094C K9 matte blackened stainless steel $891.00
Price: K9098 K9 Elite 2003, stainless steel $932.00
Price: K4043 K40, matte stainless steel $855.00
Price: K4043N K40, matte stainless steel w/tritium
night sights $985.00
Price: K4044 K40, matte blackened stainless steel $891.00
Price: K4048 K40 Elite 2003, stainless steel $932.00

KAHR MK SERIES MICRO

Similar to the K9/K40 except is 5.35 overall, 4 high, with a 3.08 barrel. Weighs 23.1 oz. Has snag-free bar-dot sights, polished feed ramp, dual recoil spring system, DA-only trigger. Comes with 5-round flush baseplate and 6-shot grip extension magazine. Intro-

duced 1998. Made in U.S.A. by Kahr Arms.
Price: M9093 MK9, matte stainless steel $855.00
Price: M9093N MK9, matte stainless steel, tritium
night sights $958.00
Price: M9098 MK9 Elite 2003, stainless steel $932.00
Price: M4043 MK40, matte stainless steel $855.00
Price: M4043N MK40, matte stainless steel, tritium
night sights $958.00
Price: M4048 MK40 Elite 2003, stainless steel $932.00

KAHR P SERIES

Caliber: 380 ACP, 9x19, 40 S&W, 45 ACP. Similar to K9/K40 steel frame pistol except has polymer frame, matte stainless steel slide. Barrel length 3.5"; overall length 5.8"; weighs 17 oz. Includes two 7-shot magazines, hard polymer case, trigger lock. Introduced 2000. Made in U.S.A. by Kahr Arms.
Price: KP9093 9mm Para. $739.00
Price: KP4043 .40 S&W $739.00
Price: KP4543 .45 ACP..$805.00
Price: KP3833 .380 ACP (2008)...$649.00

KAHR KP GEN 2 PREMIUM SERIES

Caliber: KP9 9mm (7 shot magazine), KP45 .45 ACP (6 shots). **Barrel:** 3.5". **Features:** Black polymer frame, matte stainless slide, Tru-Glo Tritium fiber optic sights, short trigger, accessory rail.
Price: $976.00

KAHR TP GEN 2 PREMIUM SERIES

Caliber: TP9 9mm (8-shot magazine), TP45 .45 ACP (7 or 8 shots). **Barrel:** 4, 5, or 6". Four-inch barrel model has features similar to KP GEN 2. Five-inch has front and rear slide serrations, white 3-dot sights, mount for reflex sights. Six-inch model has same features plus comes with Leupold Delta Point Reflex sight.
Price: $976.00
Price: 5-inch bbl...$1,015.00
Price: 6-inch bbl...$1,566.00

KAHR PM SERIES

Caliber: 9x19, .40 S&W, .45 ACP. Similar to P-Series pistols except has smaller polymer frame (Polymer Micro). Barrel length 3.08"; overall length 5.35"; weighs 17 oz. Includes two 7-shot magazines, hard polymer case, trigger lock. Introduced 2000. Made in U.S.A. by Kahr Arms.
Price: PM9093 PM9 ....$810.00
Price: PM4043 PM40 ....$810.00
Price: PM4543 PM45...$880.00

KAHR T SERIES

Caliber: T9: 9mm Para., 8-shot magazine; T40: .40 S&W, 7-shot

magazine. **Barrel:** 4". **Weight:** 28.1-29.1 oz. **Length:** 6.5" overall. **Grips:** Checkered Hogue Pau Ferro wood grips. **Sights:** Rear: Novak low profile 2-dot tritium night sight, front tritium night sight. **Features:** Similar to other Kahr makes, but with longer slide and barrel upper, longer butt. Trigger cocking DAO; lock breech; "Browning-type" recoil lug; passive striker block; no magazine disconnect. Comes with two magazines. Introduced 2004. Made in U.S.A. by Kahr Arms.
Price: KT9093 T9 matte stainless steel **$857.00**
Price: KT9093-NOVAK T9, "Tactical 9," Novak night sight **$980.00**
Price: KT4043 40 S&W **$857.00**

KAHR CW SERIES
Caliber: 9mm Para., 7-shot magazine; .40 S&W and .45 ACP, 6-shot magazine. **Barrel:** 3.5-3.64". **Weight:** 17.7-18.7 oz. **Length:** 5.9-6.36" overall. **Grips:** Textured polymer. Similar to P-Series, but CW Series have conventional rifling, metal-injection-molded slide stop lever, no front dovetail cut, one magazine. CW40 introduced 2006. Made in U.S.A. by Kahr Arms.
Price: CW9093 CW9 ....**$449.00**
Price: CW4043 CW40 ....**$449.00**
Price: CW4543 CW45 ....**$449.00**

KAHR P380
Very small double action only semiauto pistol chambered in .380 ACP. Features include 2.5-inch Lothar Walther barrel; black polymer frame with stainless steel slide; drift adjustable white bar/dot combat/ sights; optional tritium sights; two 6+1 magazines. Overall length 4.9 inches, weight 10 oz. without magazine.
Price: Standard sights **$667.00**
Price: Night sights **$792.00**

KAHR CW380
Caliber: .380 ACP, six-round magazine. **Barrel:** 2.58 inches. **Weight:** 11.5 oz. **Length:** 4.96 inches. **Grips:** Textured integral polymer. **Sights:** Fixed white-bar combat style. **Features:** Double-action only. Black or purple polymer frame, stainless slide.
Price: **$419.00**

KEL-TEC P-11
Caliber: 9mm Para., 10-shot magazine. **Barrel:** 3.1. **Weight:** 14 oz. **Length:** 5.6 overall. **Grips:** Checkered black polymer. **Sights:** Blade front, rear adjustable for windage. **Features:** Ordnance steel slide, aluminum frame. Double-action-only trigger mechanism. Introduced 1995. Made in U.S.A. by Kel-Tec CNC Industries, Inc.
Price: From **$340.00**

KEL-TEC PF-9
Caliber: 9mm Para.; 7 rounds. **Weight:** 12.7 oz. **Sights:** Rear sight adjustable for windage and elevation. **Barrel Length:** 3.1. **Length:** 5.85. **Features:** Barrel, locking system, slide stop, assembly pin, front sight, recoil springs and guide rod adapted from P-11. Trigger system with integral hammer block and the extraction system adapted from P-3AT. MIL-STD-1913 Picatinny rail. Made in U.S.A. by Kel-Tec CNC Industries, Inc.
Price: From **$340.00**

KEL-TEC P-32
Caliber: .32 ACP, 7-shot magazine. **Barrel:** 2.68. **Weight:** 6.6 oz. **Length:** 5.07 overall. **Grips:** Checkered composite. **Sights:** Fixed. **Features:** Double-action-only mechanism with 6-lb. pull; internal slide stop. Textured composite grip/frame.
Price: From **$326.00**

KEL-TEC P-3AT
Caliber: .380 ACP; 7-rounds. **Weight:** 7.2 oz. **Length:** 5.2. **Features:** Lightest .380 ACP made; aluminum frame, steel barrel.
Price: From **$331.00**

KEL-TEC PLR-16
Caliber: 5.56mm NATO; 10-round magazine. **Weight:** 51 oz. **Sights:** Rear sight adjustable for windage, front sight is M-16 blade. **Barrel:** 9.2. **Length:** 18.5. **Features:** Muzzle is threaded 1/2-28 to accept standard attachments such as a muzzle brake. Except for the

barrel, bolt, sights, and mechanism, the PLR-16 pistol is made of high-impact glass fiber reinforced polymer. Gas-operated semi-auto. Conventional gas-piston operation with M-16 breech locking system. MIL-STD-1913 Picatinny rail. Made in U.S.A. by Kel-Tec CNC Industries, Inc.
Price: Blued **$682.00**

KEL-TEC PLR-22
Semi-auto pistol chambered in .22 LR; based on centerfire PLR-16 by same maker. Blowback action, 26-round magazine. Open sights and picatinny rail for mounting accessories; threaded muzzle. Overall length is 18.5", weighs 40 oz.
Price: **$400.00**

KEL-TEC PMR-30
Caliber: .22 Magnum (.22WMR) 30-rounds. **Barrel:** 4.3. **Weight:** 13.6 oz. **Length:** 7.9 overall. **Grips:** Glass reinforced Nylon (Zytel). **Sights:** Dovetailed aluminum with front & rear fiber optics. **Features:** Operates on a unique hybrid blowback/locked-breech system. It uses a double stack magazine of a new design that holds 30 rounds and fits completely in the grip of the pistol. Dual opposing extractors for reliability, heel magazine release to aid in magazine retention, Picatinny accessory rail under the barrel, Urethane recoil buffer, captive coaxial recoil springs. The barrel is fluted for light weight and effective heat dissipation. PMR30 disassembles for cleaning by removal of a single pin.
Price: **$455.00**

KIMBER MICRO CDP
Caliber: .380 ACP, 6-shot magazine. **Barrel:** 2.75". **Weight:** 17 oz. **Grips:** Double diamond rosewood. Mini 1911-style single action with no grip safety.
Price: **$951.00**

KIMBER MICRO CARRY
Caliber: .380 ACP, 6-round magazine. **Barrel:** 2.75 inches. **Weight:** 13.4 oz. **Length:** 5.6 inches **Grips:** Black synthetic, double diamond.

Sights: Fixed low profile. **Finish:** Blue or stainless. **Features:** Aluminum frame, steel slide, carry-melt treatment, full-length guide rod.
Price: **$651.00**

KIMBER MICRO RAPTOR
Caliber: .380 ACP, 6-round magazine. **Sights:** Tritium night sights. **Finish:** Stainless. **Features:** Variation of Micro Carry with Raptor style scalloped "feathered" slide serrations and grip panels.
Price: **$960.00**

KIMBER AEGIS II
Caliber: 9mm (9-shot magazine, 8-shot (Ultra model). **Barrel:** 3", 4" or 5". **Weight:** 25 to 38 oz. **Grips:** Scale-textured zebra wood. **Sights:** Tactical wedge 3-dot green night sights. **Features:** Made in the Kimber Custom Shop. Two-tone satin silver/matte black finish. Service Melt treatment that rounds and blends edges. Available in three frame sizes: Custom (shown), Pro and Ultra.
Price: **$1,331.00**

KIMBER COVERT II
Caliber: .45 ACP (7-shot magazine). **Barrel:** 3", 4" or 5". **Weight:** 25 to 31 oz. **Grips:** Crimson Trace laser with camo finish. **Sights:** Tactical wedge 3-dot night sights. **Features:** Made in the Kimber Custom Shop. Desert tan frame and matte black slide finishes. Available in three frame sizes: Custom, Pro (shown) and Ultra.
Price: **$1,657.00**

KIMBER CUSTOM II
Caliber: .45 ACP. **Barrel:** 5". **Weight:** 38 oz. **Length:** 8.7" overall. **Grips:** Checkered black rubber, walnut, rosewood. **Sights:** Dovetailed front and rear, Kimber low profile adj. or fixed sights. **Features:** Slide, frame and barrel machined from steel or stainless steel. Match grade barrel, chamber and trigger group. Extended

Prices given are believed to be accurate at time of publication however, many factors affect retail pricing so exact prices are not possible.

71ST EDITION, 2017 ✦ **391**

thumb safety, beveled magazine well, beveled front and rear slide serrations, high ride beavertail grip safety, checkered flat mainspring housing, kidney cut under triggerguard, high cut grip, match grade stainless steel barrel bushing, polished breech face, Commander-style hammer, lowered and flared ejection port, Wolff springs, bead blasted black oxide or matte stainless finish. Introduced in 1996. Custom TLE II (Tactical Law Enforcement) has tritium night sights, threaded barrel. Made in U.S.A. by Kimber Mfg., Inc.

Price: Custom II $871.00
Price: Custom TLE II...$905.00

KIMBER CUSTOM TLE II

Caliber: .45 ACP or 10mm. TLE (Tactical Law Enforcement) version of Custom II model plus night sights, front strap checkering, threaded barrel, Picatinny rail.

Price: .45 ACP $1,250.00
Price: 10mm $1,324.00

KIMBER STAINLESS II

Same features as Custom II except has stainless steel frame.

Price: Stainless II .45 ACP $998.00
Price: Stainless II 9mm Para. $1,016.00
Price: Stainless II .45 ACP w/night sights............................$1,141.00
Price: Stainless II Target .45 ACP (stainless, adj. sight) $1,108.00

KIMBER PRO CARRY II

Similar to Custom II, has aluminum frame, 4 bull barrel fitted directly to the slide without bushing. Introduced 1998. Made in U.S.A. by Kimber Mfg., Inc.

Price: Pro Carry II, .45 ACP $919.00
Price: Pro Carry II, 9mm $969.00
Price: Pro Carry II
w/night sights $1,039.00

KIMBER SAPPHIRE PRO II

Similar to Pro Carry II, chambered in 9mm with 9-shot magazine, 4-inch match-grade barrel. Striking two-tone appearance with satin silver aluminum frame and high polish bright blue slide. Grips are blue/black G-10 with grooved texture. Fixed Tacical Edge night sights. From the Kimber Custom Shop.

Price: $1,652.00

KIMBER RAPTOR II

Caliber: .45 ACP (8-shot magazine, 7-shot (Ultra and Pro models). **Barrel:** 3", 4" or 5". **Weight:** 25 to 31 oz. **Grips:** Thin milled rosewood. **Sights:** Tactical wedge 3-dot night sights. **Features:** Made in the Kimber Custom Shop. Matte black or satin silver finish. Available in three frame sizes: Custom (shown), Pro and Ultra.

Price: .... $1,434.00 to $1,568.00

KIMBER SOLO CARRY

Caliber: 9mm, 6-shot magazine. **Barrel:** 2.7. **Weight:** 17 oz. **Length:** 5.5 overall. **Grips:** Black synthetic, Checkered/smooth. **Sights:** Fixed low-profile dovetail-mounted 3-dot system. **Features:** Single action striker-fired trigger that sets a new standard for small pistols. A premium finish that is self-lubricating and resistant to salt and moisture. Ergonomics that ensure comfortable shooting. Ambidextrous thumb safety, slide release lever and magazine release button are pure 1911 – positive, intuitive and fast. The thumb safety provides additional security not found on most small pistols. Available with Crimson Trace Laser grips. Also available in stainless.

Price: $815.00

KIMBER COMPACT STAINLESS II

Similar to Pro Carry II except has stainless steel frame, 4-inch bbl., grip is .400 shorter than standard, no front serrations. Weighs 34 oz. 45 ACP only. Introduced in 1998. Made in U.S.A. by Kimber Mfg., Inc.

Price: $1,052.00

Prices given are believed to be accurate at time of publication however, many factors affect retail pricing so exact prices are not possible.

KIMBER ULTRA CARRY II

Lightweight aluminum frame, 3 match grade bull barrel fitted to slide without bushing. Grips .4 shorter. Low effort recoil spring. Weighs 25 oz. Introduced in 1999. Made in U.S.A. by Kimber Mfg., Inc.

Price: Stainless Ultra Carry II .45 ACP **$919.00**
Price: Stainless Ultra Carry II 9mm Para. **$1,016.00**
Price: Stainless Ultra Carry II .45 ACP
with night sights **$1,039.00**

KIMBER GOLD MATCH II

Similar to Custom II models. Includes stainless steel barrel with match grade chamber and barrel bushing, ambidextrous thumb safety, adjustable sight, premium aluminum trigger, hand-checkered double diamond rosewood grips. Barrel hand-fitted for target accuracy. Made in U.S.A. by Kimber Mfg., Inc.

Price: Gold Match II **$1,393.00**
Price: Gold Match Stainless II .45 ACP **$1,574.00**
Price: Gold Match Stainless II
9mm Para. (2008) **$1,653.00**

KIMBER CDP II SERIES

Similar to Custom II, but designed for concealed carry. Aluminum frame. Standard features include stainless steel slide, fixed Meprolight tritium 3-dot (green) dovetail-mounted night sights, match grade barrel and chamber, 30 LPI front strap checkering, two-tone finish, ambidextrous thumb safety, hand-checkered double diamond rosewood grips. Introduced in 2000. Made in U.S.A. by Kimber Mfg., Inc.

Price: Ultra CDP II 9mm Para. (2008) **$1,359.00**

Price: Ultra CDP II .45 ACP **$1,318.00**
Price: Compact CDP II .45 ACP **$1,318.00**
Price: Pro CDP II .45 ACP **$1,318.00**
Price: Custom CDP II
(5" barrel, full length grip) **$1,318.00**

KIMBER ECLIPSE II SERIES

Caliber: .45 ACP, 10mm (Target II only). Similar to Custom II and other stainless Kimber pistols. Stainless slide and frame, black oxide, two-tone finish. Gray/black laminated grips. 30 lpi front strap checkering. All models have night sights; Target versions have Meprolight adjustable Bar/Dot version. Made in U.S.A. by Kimber Mfg., Inc.

Price: Eclipse Ultra II (3" barrel, short grip) **$1,350.00**
Price: Eclipse Pro II (4" barrel, full-length grip) **$1,350.00**
Price: Eclipse Custom II 10mm **$1,350.00**
Price: Eclipse Target II (5" barrel, full-length grip,
adjustable sight) **$1,393.00**

KIMBER TACTICAL ENTRY II

Caliber: 45 ACP, 7-round magazine. **Barrel:** 5". **Weight:** 40 oz. **Length:** 8.7" overall. **Features:** 1911-style semiauto with checkered frontstrap, extended magazine well, night sights, heavy steel frame, tactical rail.

Price: **$1,490.00**

KIMBER TACTICAL CUSTOM HD II

Caliber: .45 ACP, 7-round magazine. **Barrel:** 5" match-grade. **Weight:** 39 oz. **Length:** 8.7" overall. **Features:** 1911-style semiauto with night sights, heavy steel frame.

Price: **$1,387.00**

KIMBER SUPER CARRY PRO

1911-syle semiauto pistol chambered in .45 ACP. Features include 8-round magazine; ambidextrous thumb safety; carry melt profiling; full length guide rod; aluminum frame with stainless slide; satin silver finish; super carry serrations; 4-inch barrel; micarta laminated grips; tritium night sights.

Price: **$1,596.00**

KIMBER SUPER CARRY HD SERIES

Designated as HD (Heavy Duty), each is chambered in .45 ACP and features a stainless steel slide and frame, premium KimPro II™ finish and night sights with cocking shoulder for one-hand operation. Like the original Super Carry pistols, HD models have directional serrations on slide, front strap and mainspring housing for unequaled control under recoil. A round heel frame and Carry Melt treatment make them comfortable to carry and easy to conceal.

Prices given are believed to be accurate at time of publication however, many factors affect retail pricing so exact prices are not possible.

71ST EDITION, 2017 ⊕ **393**

KIMBER SUPER CARRY ULTRA HD™
Caliber: .45 ACP, 7-shot magazine. **Barrel:** 3. **Weight:** 32 oz. **Length:** 6.8 overall. **Grips:** G-10, Checkered with border. **Sights:** Night sights with cocking shoulder radius (inches): 4.8. **Features:** Rugged stainless steel slide and frame with KimPro II finish. Aluminum match grade trigger with a factory setting of approximately 4-5 pounds.
Price: $1,699.00

KIMBER SUPER CARRY PRO HD™
Caliber: .45 ACP, 8-shot magazine. **Barrel:** 4. **Weight:** 35 oz. **Length:** 7.7 overall. **Grips:** G-10, Checkered with border. **Sights:** Night sights with cocking shoulder radius (inches): 5.7. **Features:** Rugged stainless steel slide and frame with KimPro II finish. Aluminum match grade trigger with a factory setting of approximately 4-5 pounds.
Price: $1,699.00

KIMBER SUPER CARRY CUSTOM HD™
Caliber: .45 ACP, 8-shot magazine. **Barrel:** 5. **Weight:** 38 oz. **Length:** 8.7 overall. **Grips:** G-10, Checkered with border. **Sights:** Night sights with cocking shoulder radius (inches): 4.8. **Features:** Rugged stainless steel slide and frame with KimPro

II finish. Aluminum match grade trigger with a factory setting of approximately 4-5 pounds.
Price: $1,625.00

KIMBER ULTRA CDP II
Compact 1911-syle pistol chambered in .45 ACP or 9mm. Features include 7-round magazine (9 in 9mm); ambidextrous thumb safety; carry melt profiling; full length guide rod; aluminum frame with stainless slide; satin silver finish; checkered frontstrap; 3-inch barrel; rosewood double diamond Crimson Trace lasergrips grips; tritium 3-dot night sights.
Price: $1,603.00

KIMBER STAINLESS ULTRA TLE II
1911-syle semiauto pistol chambered in .45 ACP. Features include 7-round magazine; full-length guide rod; aluminum frame with stainless slide; satin silver finish; checkered frontstrap; 3-inch barrel; tactical gray double diamond grips; tritium 3-dot night sights.
Price: $1,136.00

KIMBER ROYAL II
Caliber: .45 ACP, 7-shot magazine. **Barrel:** 5". **Weight:** 38 oz.

Prices given are believed to be accurate at time of publication however, many factors affect retail pricing so exact prices are not possible

Length: 8.7" overall. **Grips:** Solid bone-smooth. **Sights:** Fixed low profile. **Features:** A classic full-size pistol wearing a charcoal blue finish complimented with solid bone grip panels. Front and rear serrations. Aluminum match-grade trigger with a factory setting of approximately 4-5 pounds.
Price: $2,020.00

Novak LoMount sights available. **Finish:** Cerakote Graphite Black or Patriot Brown. **Features:** Hammer-forged heat-treated steel slide, hammer-forged aluminum frame. Double-action PLUS action.
Price: $695.00
Price: Novak sights... $749.00

KIMBER MASTER CARRY PRO
Caliber: .45 ACP, 8-round magazine. **Barrel:** 4 inches. **Weight:** 28 oz. **Length:** 7.7 inches **Grips:** Crimson Trace Laser. **Sights:** Fixed low profile. **Features:** Matte black KimPro slide, aluminum round heel frame, full-length guide rod.
Price: $1,568.00

KIMBER WARRIOR SOC
Caliber: .45 ACP, 7-round magazine. **Barrel:** 5 inches threaded for suppression. **Sights:** Fixed Tactical Wedge tritium. **Finish:** Dark Green frame, Flat Dark Earth slide. **Features:** Full-size 1911 based on special series of pistols made for USMC. Service melt, ambidextrous safety.
Price: $1.738.00

LIONHEART LH9 MKII
Caliber: 9mm, 15-round magazine. LH9C Compact, 10 rounds. **Barrel:** 4.1 inches. **Weight:** 26.5 oz. **Length:** 7.5 inches **Grips:** One piece black polymer with textured design. **Sights:** Fixed low profile.

NIGHTHAWK CUSTOM T4
Manufacturer of a wide range of 1911-style pistols in Government Model (full-size), Commander and Officer's frame sizes. **Caliber:** .45 ACP, 7 or 8-round magazine; 9mm, 9 or 10 rounds; 10mm, 9 or 10 rounds. **Barrel:** 3.8, 4.25 or 5 inches. **Weight:** 28 to 41 ounces, depending on model. Shown is T4 model, introduced in 2013 and available only in 9mm.
Price: From .... $2,995.00 to $3,995.00

NIGHTHAWK CUSTOM GRP
Caliber: 9mm, 10mm, .45 ACP. 8-shot magazine. Global Response Pistol (GRP). **Features:** Black, Sniper Gray, green, Coyote Tan or Titanium Blue finish. Match-grade barrel and trigger, choice of Heinie or Novak adjustable night sights.
Price: $2,995.00

NIGHTHAWK CUSTOM SHADOW HAWK
Caliber: 9mm only. 5 or 4.25-inch barrel. **Features:** Stainless steel frame with black Nitride finish, flat-faced trigger, high beavertail grip safety, checkered front strap, Heinie Straight Eight front and rear titanium night sights.
Price: $3,795.00

NIGHTHAWK CUSTOM WAR HAWK
Caliber: .45 ACP. 5 or 4.25-inch barrel. **Features:** One-piece mainspring housing and magwell, Everlast Recoil System, Hyena Brown G10 grips.
Price: $3,895.00

NIGHTHAWK CUSTOM BOB MARVEL 1911
Caliber: 9mm or .45 ACP. 4.25-inch bull barrel, Everlast Recoil System, adjustable sights, match trigger, black Melonite finish.
Price: .45 ACP $3,995.00
Price: 9mm.. $4,195.00

NIGHTHAWK CUSTOM DOMINATOR
Caliber: .45 ACP. 8-shot magazine. **Features:** Stainless frame, black Perma Kote slide, cocobolo double-diamond grips,, front and rear slide serrations, adjustable sights.
Price: $3,450.00

NIGHTHAWK CUSTOM SILENT HAWK
Caliber: .45 ACP. 8-shot magazine. **Features:** 4.25-inch barrel, Commander recon frame, G10 black and gray grips. Designed to match Silencerco silencer, not included with pistol.
Price: $4,295.00

NIGHTHAWK CUSTOM HEINIE LONG SLIDE
Caliber: 10mm or .45 ACP. Long slide 6-inch barrel. **Features:** Cocobolo wood grips, black Perma Kote finish, adjustable or fixed sights, front strap checkering.
Price: $3,795.00

Prices given are believed to be accurate at time of publication however, many factors affect retail pricing so exact prices are not possible.

71ST EDITION, 2017 ◆ **395**

NORTH AMERICAN ARMS GUARDIAN DAO

Caliber: .25 NAA, .32 ACP, .380 ACP, .32 NAA, 6-shot magazine. **Barrel:** 2.49. **Weight:** 20.8 oz. **Length:** 4.75 overall. **Grips:** Black polymer. **Sights:** Low profile fixed. **Features:** Double-action only mechanism. All stainless steel construction. Introduced 1998. Made in U.S.A. by North American Arms. The .25 NAA is based on a bottle-necked .32 ACP case, and the .32 NAA is on a bottle-necked .380 ACP case.
Price: .25 NAA, 32 ACP **$409.00**
Price: .32 NAA, .380 ACP **$486.00**

OLYMPIC ARMS OA-93 AR

Caliber: 5.56 NATO. **Barrel:** 6.5" button-rifled stainless steel. **Weight:** 4.46 lbs. **Length:** 17" overall. **Sights:** None. **Features:** Olympic Arms integrated recoil system on the upper receiver eliminates the buttstock, flat top upper, free floating tubular match handguard, threaded muzzle with flash suppressor. Made in U.S.A. by Olympic Arms, Inc.
Price: **$1,202.00**

OLYMPIC ARMS K23P AR

Caliber: 5.56 NATO. **Barrel:** 6.5" button-rifled chrome-moly steel. **Length:** 22.25" overall. **Weight:** 5.12 lbs. **Sights:** Adjustable A2 rear, elevation adjustable front post. **Features:** A2 upper with rear sight, free floating tubular match handguard, threaded muzzle with flash suppressor, receiver extension tube with foam cover, no bayonet lug. Made in U.S.A. by Olympic Arms, Inc. Introduced 2007.
Price: **$973.70**

OLYMPIC ARMS K23P-A3-TC AR

Caliber: 5.56 NATO. **Barrel:** 6.5" button-rifled chrome-moly steel. **Length:** 22.25" overall. **Weight:** 5.12 lbs. **Sights:** Adjustable A2 rear, elevation adjustable front post. **Features:** Flat-top upper with detachable carry handle, free floating FIRSH rail handguard, threaded muzzle with flash suppressor, receiver extension tube with

foam cover, no bayonet lug. Made in U.S.A. by Olympic Arms, Inc. Introduced 2007.
Price: **$1,118.20**

OLYMPIC ARMS WHITNEY WOLVERINE

Caliber: .22 LR, 10-shot magazine. **Barrel:** 4.625" stainless steel. **Weight:** 19.2 oz. **Length:** 9" overall. **Grips:** Black checkered with fire/safe markings. **Sights:** Ramped blade front, dovetail rear. **Features:** Polymer frame with natural ergonomics and ventilated rib. Barrel with 6-groove 1x16 twist rate. All metal magazine shell. Made in U.S.A. by Olympic Arms.
Price: **$291.00**

PHOENIX ARMS HP22, HP25

Caliber: .22 LR, 10-shot (HP22), .25 ACP, 10-shot (HP25). **Barrel:** 3". **Weight:** 20 oz. **Length:** 5.5" overall. **Grips:** Checkered composition. **Sights:** Blade front, adjustable rear. **Features:** Single action, exposed hammer; manual hold-open; button magazine release. Available in satin nickel, matte blue finish. Introduced 1993. Made in U.S.A. by Phoenix Arms.
Price: With gun lock **$150.00**
Price: HP Range kit with 5" bbl., locking case and accessories (1 Mag) **$194.00**
Price: HP Deluxe Range kit with 3" and 5" bbls., 2 mags, case **$232.00**

REMINGTON R1

Caliber: .45 (7-shot magazine). **Barrel:** 5". **Weight:** 38.5 oz. **Grips:**

Double diamond walnut. **Sights:** Fixed, dovetail front and rear, 3-dot. **Features:** Flared and lowered ejection port. Comes with two magazines.
Price: **$744.00**
Price: (stainless) **$837.00**

REMINGTON R1 ENHANCED

Same features as standard R1 except 8-shot magazine, stainless satin black oxide finish, wood laminate grips and adjustable rear sight. Other features include forward slide serrations, fiber optic front sight. Available with threaded barrel.
Price: **$903.00**
Price: Stainless **$990.00**
Price: Threaded barrel **$959.00**

REMINGTON R1 CARRY

Caliber: .45 ACP. **Barrel:** 5 or 4.25 inches (Carry Commander). **Weight:** 35 to 39 oz. **Grips:** Cocobolo. **Sights:** Novak-type drift-adjustable rear, tritium-dot front sight. **Features:** Skeletonized trigger. Comes with one 8-round and one 7-round magazine.
Price: **$1,067.00**

REMINGTON RM380

Caliber: .380 ACP, 6-shot magazine + 1. **Barrel:** 2.9". **Length:** 5.27". **Height:** 3.86". **Weight:** 12.2 oz. **Sights:** Fixed and contoured. **Grips:** Glass-filled nylon with replaceable panels. **Features:** Double-action-only operation, all-metal construction with aluminum frame, stainless steel barrel, light dual recoil spring system, extended beavertail. Introduced in 2015.
Price: **$436.00**

REPUBLIC FORGE 1911

Caliber: .45 ACP, 9mm, .38 Super, .40 S&W, 10mm. A manufacturer of custom 1911-style pistols offered in a variety of configurations, finishes and frame sizes, including single and double-stack models with many options. Made in Texas.
Price: From **$2,795.00**

ROBERTS DEFENSE 1911 SERIES

Caliber: : .45 ACP (8+1 rounds). **Barrel:** 5, 4.25 or 3.5 inches. **Weight:** 26 to 38 oz. **Sights:** Novak-type drift-adjustable rear, tritium-dot or fiber optic front sight. **Features:** Skeletonized trigger. Offered in three model variants with many custom features and options. Made in Wisconsin by Roberts Defense.
Price: Recon **$1,499.00**
Price: Super Grade **$1,549.00**
Price: Operator **$1,649.00**

ROCK ISLAND ARMORY 1911A1-45 FSP

1911-style semiauto pistol chambered in .45 ACP (8 rounds), 9mm Parabellum, .38 Super (9 rounds). Features include hard rubber grips, 5-inch barrel, blue, Duracoat or two-tone finish, drift adjustable sights. Nickel finish or night sights available.
Price: From **$470.00**

ROCK ISLAND ARMORY 1911A1-FS MATCH

1911 Match-style pistol chambered in .45 ACP. Features fiber optic front and adjustable rear sights, skeletonized trigger and hammer, extended beavertail, double diamond checkered walnut grips, 5 or 6-inch barrel.
Price: **$877.00**

ROCK ISLAND ARMORY 1911A1-.22 TCM

Caliber: .22 TCM, 17-round magazine. **Barrel:** 5 inches. **Weight:** 36 oz. **Length:** 8.5 inches. **Grips:** Polymer. **Sights:** Adjustable rear. **Features:** Chambered for high velocity .22 TCM rimfire cartridge. Comes with interchangeable 9mm barrel.
Price: **$820.00**

ROCK ISLAND ARMORY PRO MATCH ULTRA "BIG ROCK"

Caliber: 10mm, 8 or 16-round magazine. **Barrel:** 6 inches. **Weight:** 40 oz. **Length:** 8.5 inches. **Grips:** VZ G10. **Sights:** Fiber optic front, adjustable rear. **Features:** Two magazines, upper and lower accessory rails, extended beavertail safety.
Price: **$1,187.00**
Price: High capacity model **$1,340.00**

ROCK ISLAND ARMORY MAP & MAPP

Caliber: 9mm, 16-round magazine. **Barrel:** 3.5 (MAPP) or 4 inches (MAP). Browning short recoil action style pistols with: integrated front sight; snag-free rear sight; single & double-action trigger; standard or ambidextrous rear safety; polymer frame with accessory rail.
Price: **$500.00**

ROCK ISLAND ARMORY XT22

Caliber: .22 LR, or .22 Magnum. 10 or 15-round magazine. **Barrel:** 5 **Weight:** 38 oz. The XT-22 is the only .22 1911 with a forged 4140 steel slide and a one piece 4140 chrome moly barrel. Available as a .22/.45 ACP combo.
Price: **$600.00**
Price: .22 LR/.45 combo **$900.00**

ROCK ISLAND ARMORY BABY ROCK 380

Caliber: .380 ACP, 7-round magazine. Blowback operation. An 85 percent-size version of 1911-A1 design with features identical to full-size model.
Price: **$460.00**

Prices given are believed to be accurate at time of publication however, many factors affect retail pricing so exact prices are not possible.

71ST EDITION, 2017 ✦ **397**

ROCK RIVER ARMS LAR-15/LAR-9

Caliber: .223/5.56mm NATO or 9mm Para. **Barrel:** 7", 10.5". Wilson chrome moly, 1:9 twist, A2 flash hider, 1/2-28 thread. **Weight:** 5.1 lbs. (7" barrel), 5.5 lbs. (10.5" barrel). **Length:** 23" overall. **Stock:** Hogue rubber grip. **Sights:** A2 front. **Features:** Forged A2 or A4 upper, single stage trigger, aluminum free-float tube, one magazine. Similar 9mm Para. LAR-9 also available. From Rock River Arms, Inc.

Price: LAR-15 7" A2 AR2115 ....$955.00
Price: LAR-15 10.5" A4 AR2120 ....$945.00
Price: LAR-9 7" A2 9mm2115 ....$1,125.00

ROCK RIVER ARMS 1911 POLY

Caliber: .45 ACP, 7-round magazine. Full-size 1911-style model with polymer frame and steel slide. **Barrel:** 5". **Weight:** 33 oz. **Sights:** Fixed.

Price: $925.00

RUGER AMERICAN PISTOL

Caliber: 9mm, .45 ACP. **Magazine capacity:** 10 or 17 (9), 10 (.45). **Barrel:** 4.2" (9), 4.5" (.45). **Length:** 7.5 or 8". **Weight:** 30 to 31.5 oz. **Sights:** Novak LoMount Carry 3-Dot. **Finish:** Stainless steel slide with black Nitride finish. **Grip:** One-piece ergonomic wrap-around module with adjustable palm swell and trigger reach. **Features:** Short take-up trigger with positive re-set, ambidextrous mag release and slide stop, integrated trigger safety, automatic sear block system, easy takedown. Introduced in 2016.

Price: $579.00

RUGER SR9 /SR40

Caliber: 9mm Para. (17 round magazine), .40 S&W (15). **Barrel:** 4.14". **Weight:** 26.25, 26.5 oz. **Grips:** Glass-filled nylon in two color options—black or OD Green, w/flat or arched reversible backstrap. **Sights:** Adjustable 3-dot, built-in Picatinny-style rail. **Features:** Semi-auto in six configurations, striker-fired, through-hardened stainless steel slide, brushed or blackened stainless slide with black grip frame or blackened stainless slide with OD Green grip frame, ambidextrous manual 1911-style safety, ambi. mag release, mag disconnect, loaded chamber indicator, Ruger camblock design to absorb recoil, comes with two magazines. 10-shot mags available. Introduced 2008. Made in U.S.A. by Sturm, Ruger & Co.

Price: SR9 (17-Round), SR9-10 (SS) $569.00

RUGER SR9C /SR40C COMPACT

Caliber: 9mm or .40 S&W. **Barrel:** 3.4 " (SR9C), 3.5" (SR40C). **Features:** Features include 1911-style ambidextrous manual safety; internal trigger bar interlock and striker blocker; trigger safety; magazine disconnector; loaded chamber indicator; two magazines, one 10-round and the other 17-round; 3.5-inch barrel; 3-dot sights; accessory rail; brushed stainless or blackened allow finish. Weight 23.40 oz.

Price: $569.00

RUGER 9E

Caliber: 9mm. A value-priced variation of the SR9 with black oxide finish, drift-adjustable sights. Other features similar to SR9.

Price: $459.00

RUGER SR45

Caliber: .45 ACP, 10-round magazine. **Barrel:** 4.5 inches. **Weight:** 30 oz. **Length:** 8 inches. **Grips:** Glass-filled nylon with reversible flat/arched backstrap. **Sights:** Adjustable 3-dot. **Features:** Same features as SR9.

Price: $569.00

RUGER LC9

Caliber: 9mm luger, 7+1 capacity. **Barrel:** 3.12 **Weight:** 17.10 oz. **Grips:** Glass-filled nylon. **Sights:** Adjustable 3-dot. **Features:**

Prices given are believed to be accurate at time of publication however, many factors affect retail pricing so exact pricing are not possible.

Double-action-only, hammer-fired, locked-breech pistol with a smooth trigger pull. Control and confident handling of the Ruger LC9 are accomplished through reduced recoil and aggressive frame checkering for a positive grip in all conditions. The Ruger LC9 features smooth "melted" edges for ease of holstering, carrying and drawing. Made in U.S.A. by Sturm, Ruger & Co.
Price: $479.00

RUGER LC9S
Caliber: 9mm luger, 7+1 capacity. **Barrel:** 3.12 **Grips:** Glass-filled nylon. **Sights:** Adjustable 3-dot. **Features:** Identical to the LC9 but with a striker-fired design.
Price: $479.00

RUGER LC380
Caliber: .380 ACP. Other specifications and features identical to LC9.
Price: $479.00

Price: LaserMax laser grips $529.00
Price: Crimson Trace Laserguard $629.00

RUGER LCP
Caliber: .380 (6-shot magazine). **Barrel:** 2.75". **Weight:** 9.4 oz.
Length: 5.16". **Grips:** Glass-filled nylon. **Sights:** Fixed, drift adjustable or integral Crimson Trace Laserguard.
Price: Blued $259.00
Price: Stainless steel slide $289.00
Price: Crimson Trace Laserguard $429.00
Price: Custom w/drift adjustable rear sight $269.00

RUGER CHARGER
Caliber: .22 LR, 10-shot BX-15 magazine. Based on famous 10/22 rifle design with pistol grip stock and fore-end, scope rail, bipod. Brown laminate (standard model) or Green Mountain laminate stock (takedown model). Reintroduced with improvements and enhancements in 2015.
Price: Standard $409.00
Price: Takedown $509.00

RUGER MARK III SERIES
Caliber: .22 LR, 10-shot magazine. **Barrel:** 4.5, 4.75, 5.5, 6, or 6-7/8". **Weight:** 33 oz. (4.75" bbl.). **Length:** 9" (4.75" bbl.). **Grips:** Checkered composition grip panels. **Sights:** Fixed, fiber-optic front, fixed rear. **Features:** Updated design of original Standard Auto and Mark II series. Hunter models have lighter barrels. Target models have cocobolo grips; bull, target, competition, and hunter barrels; and adjustable sights. Introduced 2005. Modern successor of the first Ruger pistol of 1949.
Price: Standard $429.00
Price: Target (blue) $499.00
Price: Target (stainless) $629.00
Price: Hunter $729.00
Price: Competition $729.00

RUGER 22/45 MARK III PISTOL
Similar to other .22 Mark III autos except has Zytel grip frame that matches angle and magazine latch of Model 1911 .45 ACP pistol.

Prices given are believed to be accurate at time of publication however, many factors affect retail pricing so exact prices are not possible.

71ST EDITION, 2017 ✦ **399**

Available in 4.0, 4.4, 4.5, 5.5 inch bull barrels. Comes with extra magazine, plastic case, lock. Molder polymer or replaceable laminate grips. **Weight:** 31 to 33 oz. **Sights:** Adjustable.
Price: 4.5" bull threaded barrel w/rails or adj. sights $499.00
Price: Lite w/rail and adj. sights $549.00

RUGER SR22
Caliber: .22 LR (10-shot magazine). **Barrel:** 3.5". **Weight:** 17.5 oz. **Length:** 6.4". **Sights:** Adjustable 3-dot. **Features:** Ambidextrous manual safety/decocking lever and mag release. Comes with two interchangeable rubberized grips and two magazines. Black or silveranodize finish. Available with threaded barrel.
Price: Black $439.00
Price: Silver $459.00
Price: Threaded barrel $479.00

RUGER SR1911
Caliber: .45 (8-shot magazine). **Barrel:** 5". **Weight:** 39 oz. **Length:** 8.6". **Grips:** Slim checkered hardwood. **Sights:** Novak LoMount Carry rear, standard front. **Features:** Based on Series 70 design. Flared and lowed ejection port. Extended mag release, thumb safety and slide-stop lever, oversized grip safety, checkered backstrap on the flat mainspring housing. Comes with one 7-shot and one 8-shot magazine.
Price: $939.00

RUGER SR1911 CMD
Commander-size version of SR1911. **Caliber:** .45 ACP. **Barrel:** 4.25 inches. **Weight:** 29.3 (aluminum), 36.4 oz. (stainless). Other specifications and features are identical to SR1911.
Price: Low glare stainless $939.00
Price: Anodized aluminum two tone $979.00

SCCY CPX
Caliber: 9mm, 10-round magazine. **Barrel:** 3.1". **Weight:** 15 oz. **Length:** 5.7" overall. **Grips:** Integral with polymer frame. **Sights:**

3-dot system, rear adjustable for windage. **Features:** Zytel polymer frame, steel slide, aluminum alloy receiver machined from bar stock. Double-action only with consistent 9-pound trigger pull. Concealed hammer. Available with (CPX-1) or without (CPX-2) manual thumb safety. Introduced 2014. Made in U.S.A. by SCCY Industries.
Price: Black carbon $334.00
Price: Stainless/blue two-tone................................. $339.00

SEECAMP LWS 32/380 STAINLESS DA
Caliber: .32 ACP, .380 ACP Win. Silvertip, 6-shot magazine. **Barrel:** 2", integral with frame. **Weight:** 10.5 oz. **Length:** 4-1/8" overall. **Grips:** Glass-filled nylon. **Sights:** Smooth, no-snag, contoured slide and barrel top. **Features:** Aircraft quality 17-4 PH stainless steel. Inertia-operated firing pin. Hammer fired double-action-only. Hammer automatically follows slide down to safety rest position after each shot, no manual safety needed. Magazine safety disconnector. Polished stainless. Introduced 1985. From L.W. Seecamp.
Price: .32 .... $446.25
Price: .380... $795.00

SIG SAUER 1911
Caliber: .45 ACP, .40 S&W. 8-10 shot magazine. **Barrel:** 5". **Weight:** 40.3 oz. **Length:** 8.65" overall. **Grips:** Checkered wood grips. **Sights:** Novak night sights. Blade front, drift adjustable rear for windage. **Features:** Single-action 1911. Hand-fitted dehorned stainless-steel frame and slide; match-grade barrel, hammer/sear set and trigger; 25-lpi front strap checkering, 20-lpi mainspring housing checkering. Beavertail grip safety with speed bump, extended thumb safety, firing pin safety and hammer intercept notch. Introduced 2005. XO series has contrast sights, Ergo Grip XT textured polymer grips. Target line features adjustable target night sights, match barrel, custom wood grips, non-railed frame in stainless or Nitron finishes. TTT series is two-tone 1911 with Nitron slide and black controls on stainless frame. Includes burled maple grips, adjustable combat night sights. STX line available from Sig Sauer Custom Shop; two-tone 1911, non-railed, Nitron slide, stainless frame, burled maple grips. Polished cocking serrations, flat-top slide, magwell. Carry line has Novak night sights, lanyard attachment point, gray diamondwood or

rosewood grips, 8+1 capacity. Compact series has 6+1 capacity, 7.7 OAL, 4.25" barrel, slim-profile wood grips, weighs 30.3 oz. RCS line (Compact SAS) is Customs Shop version with anti-snag dehorning. Stainless or Nitron finish, Novak night sights, slim-profile gray diamondwood or rosewood grips. 6+1 capacity. 1911 C3 (2008) is a 6+1 compact .45 ACP, rosewood custom wood grips, two-tone and Nitron finishes. Weighs about 30 ounces unloaded, lightweight alloy frame. Length is 7.7. Now offered in more than 30 different models with numerous options for frame size, grips, finishes, sight arrangements and other features. From SIG SAUER, Inc.

Price: Nitron $1,174.00
Price: Tacops $1,174.00
Price: XO Black $1,010.00
Price: STX $1,174.00
Price: Nightmare $1,195.00
Price: CarryNightmare $1,195.00
Price: Compact C3 .... $1,010.00
Price: Max $1,663.00
Price: Spartan $1,304.00
Price: Super Target $1,609.00
Price: Traditional Stainless Match Elite........................ $1,141.00
Price: Traditional Engraved Texas.............................. $1,522.00

SIG SAUER P210
Caliber: 9mm, 8-shot magazine. **Barrel:** 4.7". **Weight:** 37.4 oz. **Length:** 8.5" overall. **Grips:** Custom wood. **Sights:** Post and notch and adjustable target sights. **Features:** The carbon steel slide, machined from solid billet steel, now features a durable Nitron® coating, and the improved beavertail adorns the Nitron coated, heavy-style, carbon steel frame. The P210 Legend also offers an improved manual safety, internal drop safety, side magazine release, and custom wood grips.
Price: P210-9-LEGEND $2,428.00
Price: P210-9-LEGEND-TGT
w/adjustable target sights $2,642.00

SIG SAUER P220
Caliber: .45 ACP, (7- or 8-shot magazine). **Barrel:** 4.4". **Weight:** 27.8 oz. **Length:** 7.8" overall. **Grips:** Checkered black plastic. **Sights:**

Blade front, drift adjustable rear for windage. Optional Siglite night sights. **Features:** Double action. Stainless-steel slide, Nitron finish, alloy frame, M1913 Picatinny rail; safety system of decocking lever, automatic firing pin safety block, safety intercept notch, and trigger bar disconnector. Squared combat-type trigger guard. Slide stays open after last shot. Introduced 1976. P220 SAS Anti-Snag has dehorned stainless steel slide, front Siglite Night Sight, rounded trigger guard, dust cover, Custom Shop wood grips. Equinox line is Custom Shop product with Nitron stainless-steel slide with a black hard-anodized alloy frame, brush-polished flats and nickel accents. Truglo tritium fiber-optic front sight, rear Siglite night sight, gray laminated wood grips with checkering and stippling. From SIG SAUER, Inc.

Price: $1,087.00
Price: $1,087.00
Price: P220 Elite 10mm $1,422.00
Price: P220 Elite Stainless $1,359.00
Price: P220 Super Match...................................... $1,467.00
Price: P220 Combat Threaded Barrel....................... $1,282.00

SIG SAUER P220 CARRY
Caliber: .45 ACP, 8-shot magazine. **Barrel:** 3.9". **Weight:** NA. **Length:** 7.1" overall. **Grips:** Checkered black plastic. **Sights:** Blade front, drift adjustable rear for windage. Optional Siglite night sights. **Features:** Similar to full-size P220, except is "Commander" size. Single stack, DA/SA operation, Nitron finish, Picatinny rail, and either post and dot contrast or 3-dot Siglite night sights. Introduced 2005. Many variations availble. From SIG SAUER, Inc.
Price: P220 Carry, from $1,087.00
Price: P220 Carry Elite Stainless $1,356.00

SIG SAUER P225 A-1
Caliber: 9mm. 8-shot magazine. **Barrel:** 3.6 or 5". **Weight:** 30.5 oz. Shorter and slim-profile version of P226 with enhanced short reset trigger, single-stack magazine.
Price: $1,122.00
Price: Night sights.. $1,236.00

Prices given are believed to be accurate at time of publication however, many factors affect retail pricing so exact prices are not possible.

71ST EDITION, 2017 ✦ **401**

SIG SAUER P227

Same general specifications and features as P226 except chambered for .45 ACP and has double-stack magazine. **Magazine Capacity:** 10 rounds.

Price: .... **$1,087.00 to $1,350.00**

SIG SAUER P229 DA

Similar to the P220 except chambered for 9mm Para. (10- or 15-round magazines), .40 S&W, (10- or 12-round magazines). Has 3.86" barrel, 7.1" overall length and 3.35" height. Weight is 32.4 oz. Introduced 1991. Snap-on modular grips. Frame made in Germany, stainless steel slide assembly made in U.S.; pistol assembled in U.S. Many variations available. Legion series has improved short reset trigger, contoured and shortened beavertail, relieved trigger guard, higher grip, other improvements. From SIG SAUER, Inc.

Price: P229, from **$1,085.00**
Price: P229 Stainless Elite **$1,396.00**
Price: P229 Scorpion Elite **$1,312.00**
Price: P229 Legion **$1,359.00**

SIG SAUER SP2022

Caliber: 9mm Para., .357 SIG, .40 S&W, 10-, 12-, or 15-shot magazines. **Barrel:** 3.9". **Weight:** 30.2 oz. **Length:** 7.4" overall. **Grips:** Composite and rubberized one-piece. **Sights:** Blade front, rear adjustable for windage. Optional Siglite night sights. **Features:** Polymer frame, stainless steel slide; integral frame accessory rail; replaceable steel frame rails; left- or right-handed magazine release, two interchangeable grips. From SIG SAUER, Inc.

Price: **$642.00**

SIG SAUER P238

Caliber: .380 ACP, 6-7-shot magazine. **Barrel:** 2.7". **Weight:** 15.4 oz. **Length:** 5.5" overall. **Grips:** Hogue® G-10 and Rosewood grips. **Sights:** Contrast / SIGLITE night sights. **Features:** All metal beavertail-style frame.

Price: **$723.00**
Price: Gambler w/rosewood grip **$752.00**
Price: Extreme w/X-Grip extended magazine **$752.00**
Price: Equinox.. **$752.00**

SIG SAUER P226

Similar to the P220 pistol except has 4.4 barrel, measures 7.7 overall, weighs 34 oz. Chambered in 9mm, .357 SIG, or .40 S&W. X-Five series has factory tuned single-action trigger, 5 slide and barrel, ergonomic wood grips with beavertail, ambidextrous thumb safety and stainless slide and frame with magwell, low-profile adjustable target sights, front cocking serrations and a 25-meter factory test target. Many variations available. Snap-on modular grips. Legion series has improved short reset trigger, contoured and shortened beavertail, relieved trigger guard, higher grip, other improvements. From SIG SAUER, Inc.

Price: From **$1,108.00**
Price: Elite from **$1,243.00**
Price: Combat.. **$1,289.00**
Price: Tactical Operations (TACOPS) **$1,329.00**
Price: Engraved **$1,631.00**
Price: Legion... **$1,428.00**

Prices given are believed to be accurate at time of publication however, many factors affect retail pricing so exact pricing is not possible.

SIG SAUER P290 RS

Caliber: 9mm, or .380 ACP. 6/8-shot magazine. **Barrel:** 2.9".
Weight: 20.5 oz. **Length:** 5.5" overall. **Grips:** Polymer. **Sights:**
Contrast / SIGLITE night sights. **Features:** Unlike many small
pistols, the P290 features drift adjustable sights in the standard
SIG SAUER dovetails. This gives shooters the option of either
standard contrast sights or SIGLITE® night sights. The slide is
machined from a solid billet of stainless steel and is available in a
natural stainless or a durable Nitron® coating. A reversible magazine
catch is left-hand adjustable. Interchangeable grip panels allow for
personalization as well as a custom fit. In addition to the standard
polymer inserts, optional panels will be available in aluminum, G10
and wood.

Price: Model 290 RS $570.00
Price: Model 290 RS Enhanced...............................$613.00
Price: Model 290 RS Two-Tone with laser sight $685.00
Price: Model 290 RS Rainbow or Pink with
laser sights...$613.00

SIG SAUER P239

Caliber: 9mm Para., 8-shot, .357 SIG, .40 S&W, 7-shot magazine.
Barrel: 3.6". **Weight:** 25.2 oz. **Length:** 6.6" overall. **Grips:**
Checkered black composite. **Sights:** Blade front, rear adjustable for
windage. Optional Siglite night sights. **Features:** SA/DA or DAO;
blackened stainless steel slide, aluminum alloy frame. Compact
model designed for concealed carry or backup. Introduced 1996.
Made in U.S.A. by SIG SAUER, Inc.

Price: $993.00
Price: Night sights..$1,108.00

SIG SAUER 250 SERIES

Caliber: 9mm Para. (16-round magazine), 357 SIG, .40 S&W and .45
ACP. **Barrel:** 4.7, 3.9, 3.6. **Weight:** : 24.9 to 29.4 oz. **Length:** 7.2"
overall. **Grips:** Interchangeable polymer. **Sights:** Siglite night sights.
Features: Modular polymer frame design allows for immediate
change in caliber. Available in full, compact and subcompact sizes.
Six different grip combinations for each size. Introduced 2008. A
compact version is available in .22 LR. From SIG Sauer, Inc.

Price: P250 ....$480.00
Price: P250 .22 LR $434.00

SIG SAUER P320

Caliber: 9mm, .357 SIG, .40 S&W, .45 ACP. Magazine capacity 15
or 16 rounds (9mm), 13 or 14 rounds (.357 or .40). **Barrel:** 3.9
(Carry model) or 4.7" (Full size). **Weight:** 26 to 30 oz. **Length:** 7.2
or 8.0 inches overall. **Grips:** Interchangeable black composite.
Sights: Blade front, rear adjustable for windage. Optional Siglite
night sights. **Features:** Striker-fired double-action only, Nitron
finish slide, black polymer frame. Frame size and calibers are
interchangeable. Introduced 2014. Made in U.S.A. by SIG
SAUER, Inc.

Price: Full size $713.00
Price: Carry (shown) $713.00

SIG SAUER P556 SWAT

Caliber: 5.56 NATO. Pistol version of P556 rifle. **Barrel:** 10 inches.
Capacity: 10 rounds. **Weight:** 7.2 lbs. **Length:** 27.25 inches.
Price: From $1,794.00

SIG SAUER MPX

Caliber: 9mm, .357 SIG, .40 S&W. **Capacity:** 10, 20 or 30 rounds.
Barrel: 8 inches. Semi-auto AR-style gun with closed, fully locked
short-stroke pushrod gas sytem. **Weight:** 5 lbs.
Price: $1,500.00

SIG SAUER P938

Caliber: 9mm (6-shot magazine), .22 LR (10). **Barrel:** 3.0". **Weight:** 16
oz. **Length:** 5.9". **Grips:** Rosewood, Blackwood, Hogue Extreme,
Hogue Diamondwood. **Sights:** Siglite night sights or Siglite rear with
Tru-Glo front. **Features:** Slightly larger version of P238.
Price: .... $809.00 to $823.00
Price: .22 LR $656.00

Prices given are believed to be accurate at time of publication however, many factors affect retail pricing so exact prices are not possible.

71ST EDITION, 2017 ✦ **403**

SMITH & WESSON M&P SERIES

Caliber: .22 LR, 9mm, .357 Sig, .40 S&W. **Magazine capacity, full-size models:** 12 rounds (.22), 17 rounds (9mm), 15 rounds (.40). **Compact models:** 12 (9mm), 10 (.40). **Barrel:** 4.25, 3.5 inches. **Weight:** 24, 22 oz. **Length:** 7.6, 6.7 inches. **Grips:** Polymer with three interchangeable palmswell grip sizes. **Sights:** 3 white-dot system with low-profile rear. **Features:** Zytel polymer frame with stainless steel slide, barrel and structural components. VTAC (Viking Tactics) model has Flat Dark Earth finish, VTAC Warrior sights. Compact models available with Crimson Trace Lasergrips. Numerous options for finishes, sights, operating controls.

Price: $569.00
Price: (VTAC) $799.00
Price: (Crimson Trace) ....$699.00 to $829.00

Price: M&P 22.............................$389.00 to $419.00

SMITH & WESSON M&P PRO SERIES C.O.R.E.

Caliber: 9mm, .40 S&W. **Magazine capacity:** 17 rounds (9mm), 15 rounds (.40). **Barrel:** 4.25" (M&P9, M&P40), or 5" (M&P9L, M&P40L.) **Features:** Based on the Pro series line of competition-ready firearms, the C.O.R.E. models (Competition Optics Ready Equipment) feature a slide engineered to accept six popular competition optics (Trijicon RMR, Leupold Delta Point, Jpoint, Doctor, C-More STS, Insight MRDS). Sight not included. Other features identical to standard M&P9 and M&P40 models.

Price: $769.00

SMITH & WESSON M&P 45

M&P model offered in three frame sizes and chambered in .45 ACP. **Magazine capacity:** 8 or 10 rounds. **Barrel length:** 4 or 4.5 inches. **Weight:** 26, 28 or 30 oz. Available with or without thumb safety. **Finish:** Black or Dark Earth Brown.

Price: ....$599.00 to $619.00
Price: Threaded barrel kit............................$719.00

SMITH & WESSON M&P 9/40 SHIELD

Ultra-compact, single-stack variation of M&P series. **Caliber:** 9mm, .40 S&W. Comes with one 7 and one 8-round magazine (9mm), one 6-round and one 7-round magazine (.40). **Barrel:** 3.1 inches. **Length:** 6.l inches. **Weight:** 19 oz. **Sights:** 3-white-dot system with low-profile rear. Available with or without thumb safety.

Price: $449.00

SMITH & WESSON MODEL SD9 VE/SD40 VE

Caliber: .40 S&W and 9mm, 10+1, 14+1 and 16+1 round capacities. **Barrel:** 4 inches. **Weight:** 39 oz. **Length:** 8.7". **Grips:** Wood or rubber. **Sights:** Front: Tritium Night Sight, Rear: Steel Fixed 2-Dot. **Features:** SDT™ - Self Defense Trigger for optimal, consistent pull first round to Last, standard picatinny-style rail, slim ergonomic textured grip, textured finger locator and aggressive front and back strap texturing with front and rear slide serrations.

Price: From $389.00

SMITH & WESSON MODEL SW1911

Caliber: .45 ACP, 9mm. **Magazine capacity:** 8 rounds (.45), 7 rounds (sub compact .45), 10 rounds (9mm). **Barrel:** 3, 4.25, 5 inches. **Weight:** 26.5 to 41.7 oz. **Length:** 6.9 to 8.7 inches. **Grips:** Wood, wood laminate or synthetic. Crimson Trace Lasergrips available. **Sights:** Low profile white dot, tritium night sights or adjustable. **Finish:** Black matte, stainless or two-tone. **Features:** Offered in three different frame sizes. Skeletonized trigger. Accessory rail on some models. Compact models have round butt frame. Pro Series have 30 lpi checkered front strap, oversized external extractor, extended mag well, full-length guide rod, ambidextrous safety.

Price: Standard model E Series, from $979.00
Price: Compact SC series $1,449.00
Price: Crimson Trace grips $1,149.00
Price: Pro Series ....$1,459.00 to $1,609.00

SMITH & WESSON BODYGUARD® 380

Caliber: .380 Auto, 6+1 round capacity. **Barrel:** 2.75". **Weight:** 11.85 oz. **Length:** 5.25". **Grips:** Polymer. **Sights:** Integrated laser plus drift-adjustable front and rear. **Features:** The frame of the Bodyguard is made of reinforced polymer, as is the magazine base plate and follower, magazine catch, and the trigger. The slide, sights, and guide rod are made of stainless steel, with the slide and sights having a Melonite hard coating.
Price: $449.00

SPHINX SDP

Caliber: 9mm (15-shot magazine). **Barrel:** 3.7". **Weight:** 27.5 oz. **Length:** 7.4". **Sights:** Defiance Day & Night Green fiber/tritium front, tritium 2-dot red rear. **Features:** Double/single action with ambidextrous decocker, integrated slide position safety, aluminum MIL-STD 1913 Picatinny rail, Blued alloy/steel or stainless. Aluminum and polymer frame, machined steel slide. Offered in several variations. Made in Switzerland and imported by Kriss USA.
Price: From $949.00

SPRINGFIELD ARMORY EMP ENHANCED MICRO

Caliber: 9mm Para., 40 S&W; 9-round magazine. **Barrel:** 3-inch stainless steel match grade, fully supported ramp, bull. **Weight:** 26 oz. **Length:** 6.5" overall. **Grips:** Thinline cocobolo hardwood.

Sights: Fixed low profile combat rear, dovetail front, 3-dot tritium. **Features:** Two 9-round stainless steel magazines with slam pads, long aluminum match-grade trigger adjusted to 5 to 6 lbs., forged aluminum alloy frame, black hardcoat anodized; dual spring full-length guide rod, forged satin-finish stainless steel slide. Introduced 2007.
Price: $1,320.00
Price: Champion $1,179.00

SPRINGFIELD ARMORY XD SERIES

Caliber: 9mm Para., .40 S&W, .45 ACP. **Barrel:** 3, 4, 5 inches. **Weight:** 20.5-31 oz. **Length:** 6.26-8 overall. **Grips:** Textured polymer. **Sights:** Varies by model; Fixed sights are dovetail front and rear steel 3-dot units. **Features:** Three sizes in X-Treme Duty (XD) line: Sub-Compact (3" barrel), Service (4" barrel), Tactical (5" barrel). Three ported models available. Ergonomic polymer frame, hammer-forged barrel, no-tool disassembly, ambidextrous magazine release, visual/tactile loaded chamber indicator, visual/tactile striker status indicator, grip safety, XD gear system included. Introduced 2004. XD 45 introduced 2006. Compact line introduced 2007. Compact is shipped with one extended magazine (13) and one compact magazine (10). XD Mod.2 Sub-Compact has newly contoured slide and redesigned serrations, stippled grip panels, fiber-optic front sight. From Springfield Armory.

Prices given are believed to be accurate at time of publication however, many factors affect retail pricing so exact prices are not possible.

71ST EDITION, 2017 ⊕ **405**

Price: Sub-Compact OD Green 9mm Para./40 S&W,
fixed sights **$508.00**
Price: Compact .45 ACP, 4 barrel, Bi-Tone finish (2008) **$607.00**
Price: Service Black 9mm Para./40 S&W, fixed sights **$541.00**
Price: Service Black .45 ACP, external thumb safety
(2008)... **$638.00**
Price: V-10 Ported Black 9mm Para./40 S&W **$608.00**
Price: XD Mod.2.. **$565.00**

SPRINGFIELD ARMORY XDM SERIES
Calibers: 9mm, .40 S&W, .45 ACP. **Barrel:** 3.8 or 4.5". **Sights:**
Fiber optic front with interchangeable red and green filaments,
adjustable target rear. **Grips:** Integral polymer with three optional
backstrap designs. **Features:** Variation of XD design with improved
ergonomics, deeper and longer slide serrations, slightly modified
grip contours and texturing. Black polymer frame, forged steel slide.
Black and two-tone finish options.
Price: .... **$697.00 to $732.00**

SPRINGFIELD ARMORY XD-S
Caliber: 9mm, .45 ACP. Same features as XDM except has single-
stack magazine for thinner profile. **Capacity:** 7 rounds (9mm), 5
rounds (.45). An extra extended-length magazine is included (10
rounds, 9mm; 7 rounds, .45). **Barrel:** 3.3 inches. **Weight:** 21.5 oz.
Features: Black or two-tone finish.
Price: (two-tone) .... **$599.00 to $669.00**

SPRINGFIELD ARMORY MIL-SPEC 1911A1
Caliber: .45 ACP, 7-shot magazine. **Barrel:** 5". **Weight:** 35.6- 39 oz.
Length: 8.5-8.625" overall. **Finish:** Stainless steel. **Features:** Similar
to Government Model military .45.
Price: Mil-Spec Parkerized, 7+1, 35.6 oz. **$785.00**
Price: Mil-Spec Stainless Steel, 7+1, 36 oz. **$889.00**

SPRINGFIELD ARMORY TACTICAL RESPONSE
Similar to 1911A1 except .45 ACP only, checkered front strap and
main-spring housing, Novak Night Sight combat rear sight and
matching dove-tailed front sight, tuned, polished extractor, oversize
barrel link; lightweight speed trigger and combat action job, match
barrel and bushing, extended ambidextrous thumb safety and fitted
beavertail grip safety. Checkered cocobolo wood grips, comes with
two Wilson 7-shot magazines. Frame is engraved "Tactical" both
sides of frame with "TRP." Introduced 1998. TRP-Pro Model meets
FBI specifications for SWAT Hostage Rescue Team.
Price: **$1,646.00**
Price: Operator with adjustable Trijicon night sights **$1,730.00**

Prices given are believed to be accurate at time of publication however, many factors affect retail pricing so exact prices are not possible.

SPRINGFIELD ARMORY RANGE OFFICER

Caliber: 9mm or .45 ACP. **Barrel:** 5" stainless match grade. Compact model has 4" barrel. **Sights:** Adjustable target rear, post front. **Grips:** Double diamond checkered walnut. **Weight:** 40 oz. 28 oz. (compact). Operator model has fiber optic sights.

Price: $936.00
Price: Compact $899.00
Price: Stainless finish...$1,045.00
Price: Operator $1,029.00

SPRINGFIELD ARMORY CHAMPION OPERATOR LIGHTWEIGHT

Caliber: .45 ACP. **Barrel:** 4" stainless match grade bull barrel. **Sights:** 3-dot Tritum combat profile. **Grips:** Double diamond checkered cocobolo with Cross Cannon logo. **Features:** Alloy frame with integral rail, extended ambi thumb safety and trigger, lightweight Delta hammer.

Price: $1,050.00

STEYR M-A1 SERIES

Caliber: 9mm (15 or 17-round capacity) or .40 S&W (10-12). **Barrel:** 3.5" (MA-1), 4.5" (L-A1), 3" (C-A1). **Weight:** 27 oz. **Sights:** Fixed with white outline triangle. **Grips:** Black synthetic. Ergonomic low-profile for reduced muzzle lift. DAO striker-fired operation.

Price: M-A1 ....$560.00
Price: C-A1 compact model $560.00
Price: L-A1 full-size model...................................$560.00

STOEGER COMPACT COUGAR

Caliber: 9mm, 13+1 round capacity. **Barrel:** 3.6". **Weight:** 32 oz.

Length: 7". **Grips:** Wood or rubber. **Sights:** Quick read 3-dot. **Features:** Double/single action with a matte black finish. The ambidextrous safety and decocking lever is easily accessible to the thumb of a right-handed or left-handed shooter.

Price: $469.00

STI DUTY ONE

This company manufactures a wide selection of 1911-style semiauto pistols chambered in .45 ACP, 9mm, .357 SIG, 10mm and .38 Super. Barrel lengths are offered from 3.0 to 6.0 inches. Listed here are several of the company's more than 20 current models. Numerous finish, grip and sight options are available. Duty One series features include government size frame with integral tactical rail and 30 lpi checkered front strap; milled tactical rail on the dust cover of the frame; ambidextrous thumb safeties; high rise beavertail grip safety; lowered and flared ejection port; fixed rear sight; front and rear cocking serrations; 5-inch fully supported STI International ramped bull barrel.

Price: $1,384.00

STI EAGLE

1911-style semiauto pistol chambered in .45 ACP, .38 Super, .357 SIG, 9mm, .40 S&W. Features include modular steel frame with polymer grip; high capacity double-stack magazines; scalloped slide with front and rear cocking serrations; dovetail front sight and STI adjustable rear sight; stainless steel STI hi-ride grip safety and stainless steel STI ambi-thumb safety; 5- or 6-inch STI stainless steel fully supported, ramped bull barrel or the traditional bushing barrel; blued or stainless finish.

Price: $2,123.00

Prices given are believed to be accurate at time of publication however, many factors affect retail pricing so exact prices are not possible.

71ST EDITION, 2017 ⬦ **407**

STI TOTAL ECLIPSE

Compact 1911-style semiauto pistol chambered in 9x19, .40 S&W, and .45 ACP. Features include 3-inch slide with rear cocking serrations, oversized ejection port; 2-dot tritium night sights recessed into the slide; high-capacity polymer grip; single-sided blued thumb safety; bobbed, high-rise, blued, knuckle relief beavertail grip safety; 3-inch barrel.
Price: $1,870.00

STI ESCORT

Similar to STI Eclipse but with aluminum alloy frame and chambered in .45 ACP only.
Price: $1,233.00

TAURUS CURVE

Caliber: .380 ACP. 6+1 capacity. Unique curved design to fit contours of the body for comfortable concealed carry with no

visible "printing" of the firearm. **Barrel:** 2.5 inches. **Weight:** 10.2 oz. **Length:** 5.2 inches. Double-action only. Light and laser are integral with frame.
Price: $392.00

TAURUS MODEL 1911

Caliber: .45 ACP, 8+1 capacity, 9mm, 9+1 capacity. **Barrel:** 5". **Weight:** 33 oz. **Length:** 8.5". **Grips:** Checkered black. **Sights:** Heinie straight 8. **Features:** SA. Blue, stainless steel, duotone blue, and blue/gray finish. Standard/picatinny rail, standard frame, alloy frame, and alloy/picatinny rail. Introduced in 2007. Imported from Brazil by Taurus International.
Price: 1911B, Blue $719.00
Price: 1911B, Walnut grips $866.00
Price: 1911SS, Stainless Steel $907.00
Price: 1911SS-1, Stainless Steel w/rail $945.00
Price: 1911 DT, Duotone Blue $887.00

TAURUS MODEL PT-22/PT-25

Caliber: .22 LR, 8-shot (PT-22); .25 ACP, 9-shot (PT-25). **Barrel:** 2.75". **Weight:** 12.3 oz. **Length:** 5.25" overall. **Grips:** Smooth rosewood or mother-of-pearl. **Sights:** Fixed. **Features:** Double action. Tip-up barrel for loading, cleaning. Blue, nickel, duo-tone or blue with gold accents. Introduced 1992. Made in U.S.A. by Taurus International.
Price: PT-22B or PT-25B, checkered
wood grips $282.00

TAURUS PT2011 DT

Caliber: 9mm, .40 S&W. **Magazine capacity:** 9mm (13 rounds), .40 S&W (11 rounds). **Barrel:** 3.2 inches. **Weight:** 24 oz. Features: Single/double-action with trigger safety.
Price: $589.00
Price: (stainless) $605.00

TAURUS MODEL 22PLY SMALL POLYMER FRAME

Similar to Taurus Models PT-22 and PT-25 but with lightweight polymer frame. Features include .22 LR (9+1) or .25 ACP (8+1)

chambering. 2.33" tip-up barrel, matte black finish, extended magazine with finger lip, manual safety. Overall length is 4.8". Weighs 10.8 oz.
Price: **$276.00**

TAURUS 24/7 G2 SERIES
Double/single action semiauto pistol chambered in 9mm Parabellum (15+1), .40 S&W (13+1), and .45 ACP (10+1). Features include blued or stainless finish; "Strike Two" capability; new trigger safety; low-profile adjustable rear sights for windage and elevation; ambidextrous magazine release; 4.2-inch barrel; Picatinny rail; polymer frame; polymer grip with metallic inserts and three interchangeable backstraps. Also offered in compact model with shorter grip frame and 3.5-inch barrel.
Price: .... **$523.00 to $543.00**

TAURUS MODEL 92
Caliber: 9mm Para., 10- or 17-shot mags. **Barrel:** 5". **Weight:** 34 oz. **Length:** 8.5" overall. **Grips:** Checkered rubber, rosewood, mother-of-pearl. **Sights:** Fixed notch rear. 3-dot sight system. Also offered with micrometer-click adjustable night sights. **Features:** Double action, ambidextrous 3-way hammer drop safety, allows cocked & locked carry. Blue, stainless steel, blue with gold highlights, stainless steel with gold highlights, forged aluminum frame, integral key-lock. .22 LR conversion kit available. Imported from Brazil by Taurus International.
Price: 92B **$638.00**
Price: 92SS **$653.00**

TAURUS MODEL 111 G2
Caliber: 9mm Para., 10- or 12-shot mags. **Barrel:** 3.25. **Weight:** 18.7 oz. **Length:** 6-1/8 overall. **Grips:** Checkered polymer. **Sights:** 3-dot fixed; night sights available. Low profile, 3-dot combat. **Features:** Double action only, polymer frame, matte stainless or blue steel slide, manual safety, integral key-lock. Deluxe models with wood grip inserts.
Price: Blued **$436.00**
Price: Stainless **$450.00**

TAURUS SLIM 700 SERIES
Compact double/single action semiauto pistol chambered in 9mm Parabellum (7+1), .40 S&W (6+1), and .380 ACP (7+1). Features include polymer frame; blue or stainless slide; single action/double action trigger pull; low-profile fixed sights. Weight 19 oz., length 6.24 inches, width less than an inch.
Price: **$404.00**
Price: Stainless **$504.00**

TAURUS MODEL 709 G2 SLIM
Caliber: 9mm., 7+1-shot magazine. **Barrel:** 3". **Weight:** 19 oz. **Length:** 6" overall. **Grips:** Black. **Sights:** Low profile. **Features:** Single-action only operation.
Price: Matte black **$404.00**
Price: Stainless **$504.00**

TAURUS SLIM 740
Caliber: .40 cal., 6+1-shot magazine. **Barrel:** 3.2". **Weight:** 19 oz. **Length:** 6.24" overall. **Grips:** Polymer Grips. **Features:** Double action with stainless steel finish.
Price: **$504.00**

THOMPSON CUSTOM 1911A1
Caliber: .45 ACP, 7-shot magazine. **Barrel:** 4.3". **Weight:** 34 oz. **Length:** 8" overall. **Grips:** Checkered laminate grips with a Thompson bullet logo inlay. **Sights:** Front and rear sights are black with serrations and are dovetailed into the slide. **Features:** Machined from 420 stainless steel, matte finish. Thompson bullet logo on slide. Flared ejection port, angled front and rear serrations on slide, 20-lpi checkered mainspring housing and frontstrap. Adjustable trigger, combat hammer, stainless steel full-length recoil guide rod, extended beavertail grip safety; extended magazine release; checkered slide-stop lever. Made in U.S.A. by Kahr Arms.
Price: 1911TC **$866.00**

THOMPSON TA5 1927A-1 LIGHTWEIGHT DELUXE
Caliber: .45 ACP, 50-round drum magazine. **Barrel:** 10.5", 1:16 right-

hand twist. **Weight:** 94.5 oz. **Length:** 23.3" overall. **Grips:** Walnut, horizontal foregrip. **Sights:** Blade front, open rear adjustable. **Features:** Based on Thompson machine gun design. Introduced 2008. Made in U.S.A. by Kahr Arms.
Price: TA5 (2008)...$1,323.00

TRISTAR 100 /120 SERIES
Caliber: 9mm, .40 S&W (C-100 only). **Magazine capacity:** 15 (9mm), 11 (.40). **Barrel:** 3.7 to 4.7 inches. **Weight:** 26 to 30 oz. **Grips:** Checkered polymer. **Sights:** Fixed. **Finish:** Blue or chrome. **Features:** Alloy or steel frame. Single/double action. A series of pistols based on the CZ-75 design. Imported from Turkey.
Price: $459.00

TURNBULL MODEL 1911
Caliber: .45 ACP. An accurate reproduction of 1918-era Model 1911 pistol. **Features:** Forged slide with appropriate shape and style. Later style sight with semi-circle notch. Early style safety lock with knurled undercut thumb piece. Short, wide checkered spur hammer. Hand checkered double-diamond American Black Walnut grips. Hand polished with period correct Carbonia charcoal bluing. Custom made to order with many options. Made in the USA by Doug Turnbull Manufacturing Co.
Price: $2,250.00

WALTHER P99 AS
Caliber: 9mm, .40 S&W. Offered in two frame sizes, standard and compact. **Magazine capacity:** 15 or 10 rounds (9mm), 10 or 8 rounds (.40). **Barrel:** 3.5 or 4 inches. **Weight:** 21 to 26 oz.

Length: 6.6 to 7.1 inches. **Grips:** Polymer with interchangeable backstrap inserts. **Sights:** Adjustable rear, blade front with three interchangeable inserts of different heights. **Features:** Double action with trigger safety, decocker, internal striker safety, loaded chamber indicator. Made in Germany.
Price: $629.00

WALTHER PK380
Caliber: .380 ACP (8-shot magazine). **Barrel:** 3.66". **Weight:** 19.4 oz. **Length:** 6.5". **Sights:** Three-dot system, drift adjustable rear. **Features:** Double action with external hammer, ambidextrous mag release and manual safety. Picatinny rail. Black frame with black or nickel slide.
Price: $399.00
Price: Nickel slide $449.00

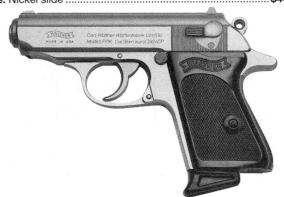

WALTHER PPK
Caliber: .380 ACP. **Capacity:** 6+1. **Barrel:** 3.3 inches **Weight:** 22 oz. **Length:** 6.1 inches **Grips:** Checkered plastic. **Sights:** Fixed. **Features:** Available in blue or stainless finish. Made in the U.S.A.
Price: $699.00

WALTHER PPK/S
Caliber: .22 LR or .380 ACP. **Capacity:** 10+1 (.22), 7+1 (.380). Made in Germany. **Features:** identical to PPK except for grip length and magazine capacity.
Price: (.380)..$699.00
Price: (.22 blue)..$400.00
Price: (.22 stainless)...$430.00

WALTHER PPQ M2
Caliber: 9mm, (15 round magazine), .40 S&W (11). .45 ACP, 22 LR (PPQ M2 .22). 12-shot magazine. **Barrel:** 4 or 5". **Weight:** 24 oz. **Length:** 7.1, 8.1". **Sights:** Drift adjustable. **Features:** Quick Defense trigger, firing pin block, ambidextrous slide lock and mag release, Picatinny rail. Comes with two extra magazines, two interchangeable frame backstraps and hard case. Navy SD model has threaded 4.6" barrel. M2 .22 has aluminum slide, blowback operation, weighs 19 ounces.
Price: 9mm, .40 .... $649.00 to $749.00
Price: M2 .22...$429.00
rice: .45 .... $699.00 to $799.00

WALTHER CCP

Caliber: 9mm, 8-shot magazine. **Barrel:** 3.5 inches. **Weight:** 22 oz. **Length:** 6.4 inches. **Features:** Thumb operated safety, reversible mag release, loaded chamber indicator. Delayed blowback gas-operated action provides less recoil and muzzle jump, and easier slide operation. Available in all black or black/stainless two-tone finish.
Price: From .... **$469.00 to $499.00**

WALTHER PPS

Caliber: 9mm Para., 40 S&W. 6-, 7-, 8-shot magazines for 9mm Para.; 5-, 6-, 7-shot magazines for 40 S&W. **Barrel:** 3.2". **Weight:** 19.4 oz. **Length:** 6.3" overall. **Stocks:** Stippled black polymer. **Sights:** Picatinny-style accessory rail, 3-dot low-profile contoured sight. **Features:** PPS–"Polizeipistole Schmal," or Police Pistol Slim. Measures 1.04 inches wide. Ships with 6- and 7-round magazines. Striker-fired action, flat slide stop lever, alternate backstrap sizes. QuickSafe feature decocks striker assembly when backstrap is removed. Loaded chamber indicator. Introduced 2008.
Price: **$629.00**

WALTHER PPX

Caliber: 9mm, .40 S&W. **Capacity:** 16 rounds (9mm), 14 rounds (.40). **Barrel:** 4 inches. **Weight:** 27.2 oz. **Length:** 7.3 inches. **Grips:**

Textured polymer integral with frame. **Sights:** Fixed. **Finish:** Black or black/stainless two-tone. Threaded barrel is optional. Made in Ulm, Germany.
Price: **$449.00**
Price: (threaded barrel) **$499.00**

WALTHER P22

Caliber: .22 LR. **Barrel:** 3.4, 5". **Weight:** 19.6 oz. (3.4), 20.3 oz. (5). **Length:** 6.26, 7.83". **Sights:** Interchangeable white dot, front, 2-dot adjustable, rear. **Features:** A rimfire version of the Walther P99 pistol, available in nickel slide with black frame, or Desert Camo or Digital Pink Camo frame with black slide.
Price: From **$379.00**
Price: Nickel slide/black frame, or black slide/camo frame **$449.00**

WILSON COMBAT ELITE SERIES

Caliber: 9mm Para., .38 Super, .40 S&W; .45 ACP. **Barrel:** Compensated 4.1" hand-fit, heavy flanged cone match grade. **Weight:** 36.2 oz. **Length:** 7.7" overall. **Grips:** Cocobolo. **Sights:** Combat Tactical yellow rear tritium inserts, brighter green tritium front insert. **Features:** High-cut front strap, 30-lpi checkering on front strap and flat mainspring housing, High-Ride Beavertail grip safety. Dehorned, ambidextrous thumb safety, extended ejector, skeletonized ultralight hammer, ultralight trigger, Armor-Tuff finish on frame and slide. Introduced 1997. Made in U.S.A. by Wilson Combat. This manufacturer offers more than 100 different 1911 models ranging in price from about $2,800 to $5,000. XTAC and Classic 6-inch models shown. Prices show a small sampling of available models.
Price: Classic from..**$3,300.00**
Price: CQB from..**$2,865.00**
Price: Hackathorn Special **$3,750.00**
Price: Tactical Carry...**$3,750.00**
Price: Tactical Supergrade..**$5,045.00**
Price: Bill Wilson Carry Pistol **$3,205.00**
Price: Ms. Sentinel...**$3,875.00**
Price: Hunter 10mm, .460 Rowland.....................................**$4,100.00**
Price: Beretta Brigadier Series from **$1,095.00**

Prices given are believed to be accurate at time of publication however, many factors affect retail pricing so exact prices are not possible.

71ST EDITION, 2017 ✦ **411**

BAER 1911 ULTIMATE MASTER COMBAT

Caliber: .38 Super, 400 Cor-Bon, .45 ACP (others available), 10-shot magazine. **Barrel:** 5, 6"; Baer NM. **Weight:** 37 oz. **Length:** 8.5" overall. **Grips:** Checkered cocobolo. **Sights:** Baer dovetail front, low-mount Bo-Mar rear with hidden leaf. **Features:** Full-house competition gun. Baer forged NM blued steel frame and double serrated slide; Baer triple port, tapered cone compensator; fitted slide to frame; lowered, flared ejection port; Baer reverse recoil plug; full-length guide rod; recoil buff; beveled magazine well; Baer Commander hammer, sear; Baer extended ambidextrous safety, extended ejector, checkered slide stop, beavertail grip safety with pad, extended magazine release button; Baer speed trigger. Made in U.S.A. by Les Baer Custom, Inc.
Price: .45 ACP Compensated $2,880.00
Price: .38 Super Compensated $3,140.00

BAER 1911 NATIONAL MATCH HARDBALL

Caliber: .45 ACP, 7-shot magazine. **Barrel:** 5". **Weight:** 37 oz. **Length:** 8.5" overall. **Grips:** Checkered walnut. **Sights:** Baer dovetail front with under-cut post, low-mount Bo-Mar rear with hidden leaf. **Features:** Baer NM forged steel frame, double serrated slide and barrel with stainless bushing; slide fitted to frame; Baer match trigger with 4-lb. pull; polished feed ramp, throated barrel; checkered front strap, arched mainspring housing; Baer beveled magazine well; lowered, flared ejection port; tuned extractor; Baer extended ejector, checkered slide stop; recoil buff. Made in U.S.A. by Les Baer Custom, Inc.
Price: $1,960.00

BAER 1911 PPC OPEN CLASS

Designed for NRA Police Pistol Combat matches. **Caliber:** .45 ACP, 9mm. **Barrel:** 6 inches, fitted to frame. **Sights:** Adjustable PPC rear, dovetail front. **Grips:** Checkered cocobola. **Features:** Lowered and flared ejection port, extended ejector, polished feed ramp, throated barrel, front strap checkered at 30 lpi, flat serrated mainspring housing, Commander hammer, front and rear slide serrations. 9mm has supported chamber.
Price: $2,350.00

BAER 1911 BULLSEYE WADCUTTER

Similar to National Match Hardball except designed for wadcutter loads only. Polished feed ramp and barrel throat; Bo-Mar rib on slide; full length recoil rod; Baer speed trigger with 3-1/2-lb. pull; Baer deluxe hammer and sear; Baer beavertail grip safety with pad; flat mainspring housing checkered 20 lpi. Blue finish; checkered walnut grips. Made in U.S.A. by Les Baer Custom, Inc.
Price: From $2,140.00

COLT GOLD CUP SERIES

Caliber: .45 ACP, 8-shot + 1 magazine. **Barrel:** 5-inch National Match. **Weight:** 37 oz. **Length:** 8.5. **Grips:** Checkered wraparound rubber composite with silver-plated medallions or checkered walnut grips with gold medallions. **Sights:** Target post dovetail front, Bomar fully adjustable rear. **Features:** Adjustable aluminum wide target trigger, beavertail grip safety, full length recoil spring and target recoil spring, available in blued finish or stainless steel.
Price: (blued) $1,217.00
Price: (stainless) $1,250.00

COLT COMPETITION PISTOL

Caliber: .45 ACP or 9mm. 8 or 9-shot magazine. **Barrel:** 5" National Match. **Weight:** 39 oz. **Length:** 8.5". **Grips:** Custom Blue Colt G10. **Sights:** Novak adjustable rear, fiber optic front. A competition-ready pistol out of the box at a moderate price. Blue or satin nickel finish. Series 80 firing system. Introduced 2016.
Price: $899.00

COMPETITOR SINGLE-SHOT

Caliber: .22 LR through .50 Action Express, including belted magnums. **Barrel:** 14" standard; 10.5" silhouette; 16" optional. **Weight:** About 59 oz. (14 bbl.). **Length:** 15.12" overall. **Grips:** Ambidextrous; synthetic (standard) or laminated or natural wood. **Sights:** Ramp front, adjustable rear. **Features:** Rotary cannon-type action cocks on opening; cammed ejector; interchangeable barrels, ejectors. Adjustable single stage trigger, sliding thumb safety and trigger safety. Matte blue finish. Introduced 1988. From Competitor Corp., Inc.
Price: 14, standard calibers, synthetic grip $660.00

Prices given are believed to be accurate at time of publication however, many factors affect retail pricing so exact prices are not possible.

CZ 75 TS CZECHMATE

Caliber: 9mm Luger, 20-shot magazine. **Barrel:** 130mm. **Weight:** 1360 g **Length:** 266 mm overall. **Features:** The handgun is custom-built, therefore the quality of workmanship is fully comparable with race pistols built directly to IPSC shooters wishes. Individual parts and components are excellently match fitted, broke-in and tested. Every handgun is outfitted with a four-port compensator, nut for shooting without a compensator, the slide stop with an extended finger piece, the slide stop without a finger piece, ergonomic grip panels from aluminium with a new type pitting and side mounting provision with the C-More red dot sight. For the shooting without a red dot sight there is included a standard target rear sight of Tactical Sports type, package contains also the front sight.
Price: $3,317.00

CZ 75 TACTICAL SPORTS

Caliber: 9mm Luger and .40 S&W, 17-20-shot magazine capacity. **Barrel:** 114mm. **Weight:** 1270 g **Length:** 225 mm overall. **Features:** semi-automatic handgun with a locked breech. This pistol model is designed for competition shooting in accordance with world IPSC (International Practical Shooting Confederation) rules and regulations. The pistol allow rapid and accurate shooting within a very short time frame. The CZ 75 TS pistol model design stems from the standard CZ 75 model. However, this model feature number of special modifications, which are usually required for competitive handguns: - single-action trigger mechanism (SA) - match trigger made of plastic featuring option for trigger travel adjustments before discharge (using upper screw), and for overtravel (using bottom screw). The adjusting screws are set by the manufacturer - sporting hammer specially adapted for a reduced trigger pull weight - an extended magazine catch - grip panels made of walnut wood - guiding funnel made of plastic for quick inserting of the magazine into pistol's frame. Glossy blue slide, silver polycoat frame. Packaging includes 3 pcs of magazines.
Price: $1,310.00

CZ 85 COMBAT

Caliber: 9mm Luger, 16-shot magazine. **Barrel:** 114mm. **Weight:** 1000 g **Length:** 206 mm overall. **Features:** The CZ 85 Combat modification was created as an extension to the CZ 85 model in its standard configuration with some additional special elements. The rear sight is adjustable for elevation and windage, and the trigger for overtravel regulation. An extended magazine catch, elimination of the magazine brake and ambidextrous controlling elements directly predispose this model for sport shooting

competitions. Characteristic features of all versions A universal handgun for both left-handers and right-handers,. The selective SA/DA firing mechanism, a large capacity double-column magazine, a comfortable grip and balance in either hand lead to good results at instinctive shooting (without aiming). Low trigger pull weight and high accuracy of fire. A long service life and outstanding reliability - even when using various types of cartridges. The slide stays open after the last cartridge has been fired, suitable for combat shooting. The sights are fitted with a three-dot illuminating system for better aiming in poor visibility conditions. The combat version features an adjustable rear sight by means of micrometer screws.

Price: $664.00

DAN WESSON CHAOS

Caliber: 9mm Luger, 21-shot magazine capacity. **Barrel:** 5". **Weight:** 3.20 lbs. **Length:** 8.75" overall. **Features:** A double-stack 9mm designed for three-gun competition.
Price: $3,829.00

DAN WESSON HAVOC

Caliber: 9mm Luger & .38 Super, 21-shot magazine capacity. **Barrel:** 4.25". **Weight:** 2.20 lbs. **Length:** 8" overall. **Features:** The HAVOC is based on an "All Steel" Hi-capacity version of the 1911 frame. It comes ready to dominate Open IPSC/USPSA division. The C-more mounting system offers the lowest possible mounting configuration possible, enabling extremely fast target acquisition. The barrel and compensator arrangement pairs the highest level of accuracy with the most effective compensator available.
Price: $4,299.00

Prices given are believed to be accurate at time of publication however, many factors affect retail pricing so exact prices are not possible.

71ST EDITION, 2017 ✛ **413**

DAN WESSON MAYHEM

Caliber: .40 S&W, 18-shot magazine capacity. **Barrel:** 6". **Weight:** 2.42 lbs. **Length:** 8.75" overall. **Features:** The MAYHEM is based on an "All Steel" Hi-capacity version of the 1911 frame. It comes ready to dominate Limited IPSC/USPSA division or fulfill the needs of anyone looking for a superbly accurate target grade 1911. Taking weight away from where you don't want it and adding it to where you do want it was the first priority in designing this handgun. The 6" bull barrel and the tactical rail add to the static weight "good weight". We wanted a 6" long slide for the added sight radius and the enhanced pointability, but that would add to the "bad weight" so the 6" slide has been lightened to equal the weight of a 5". The result is a 6" long slide that balances and feels like a 5" but shoots like a 6". The combination of the all steel frame with industry leading parts delivers the most well balanced, softest shooting 6" limited gun on the market.
Price: $3,899.00

DAN WESSON TITAN

Caliber: 10mm, 21-shot magazine capacity. **Barrel:** 4.25". **Weight:** 1.62 lbs. **Length:** 8" overall. **Features:** The TITAN is based on an "All Steel" Hi-capacity version of the 1911 frame. Turning the most well known defensive pistol "1911" into a true combat handgun was no easy task. The rugged HD night sights are moved forward and recessed deep in the slide yielding target accuracy and extreme durability. The Snake Scale serrations' aggressive 25 lpi checkering, and the custom competition G-10 grips ensure controllability even in the harshest of conditions. The combination of the all steel frame, bull barrel, and tactical rail enhance the balance and durability of the most formidable target grade Combat handgun on the market.
Price: $3,829.00

EAA WITNESS ELITE GOLD TEAM

Caliber: 9mm Para., 9x21, .38 Super, .40 S&W, .45 ACP. **Barrel:** 5.1". **Weight:** 44 oz. **Length:** 10.5" overall. **Grips:** Checkered walnut, competition-style. **Sights:** Square post front, fully adjustable rear. **Features:** Triple-chamber cone compensator; competition SA trigger; extended safety and magazine release; competition hammer; beveled magazine well; beavertail grip. Hand-fitted major components. Hard chrome finish. Match-grade barrel. From E.A.A. Custom Shop. Introduced 1992. Limited designed for IPSC Limited Class competition. Features include full-length dust-cover frame, funneled magazine well, interchangeable front sights. Stock (2005) designed for IPSC Production Class competition. Match introduced 2006. Made in Italy, imported by European American Armory.
Price: Gold Team $2,336.00
Price: Pro Limited, 4.75" barrel $1,216.00
Price: Stock, 4.5" barrel, hard-chrome finish $1,102.00
Price: Match, 4.75" barrel, two-tone finish $778.00
Price: Limited Custom Xtreme $1,961.00
Price: Witness Match Xtreme $1,879.00
Price: Witness Stock III Xtreme $1,404.00

FREEDOM ARMS MODEL 83 .22 FIELD GRADE SILHOUETTE CLASS

Caliber: .22 LR, 5-shot cylinder. **Barrel:** 10". **Weight:** 63 oz. **Length:** 15.5" overall. **Grips:** Black micarta. **Sights:** Removable Patridge front blade; Iron Sight Gun Works silhouette rear, click adjustable for windage and elevation (optional adj. front sight and hood). **Features:** Stainless steel, matte finish, manual sliding-bar safety system; dual firing pins, lightened hammer for fast lock time, pre-set trigger stop. Introduced 1991. Made in U.S.A. by Freedom Arms.
Price: Silhouette Class $2,603.00

FREEDOM ARMS MODEL 83 CENTERFIRE SILHOUETTE MODELS

Caliber: 357 Mag., .41 Mag., .44 Mag.; 5-shot cylinder. **Barrel:** 10", 9" (.357 Mag. only). **Weight:** 63 oz. (41 Mag.). **Length:** 15.5", 14.5" (.357 only). **Grips:** Pachmayr Presentation. **Sights:** Iron Sight Gun Works silhouette rear sight, replaceable adjustable front sight blade with hood. **Features:** Stainless steel, matte finish, manual sliding-bar safety system. Made in U.S.A. by Freedom Arms.
Price: Silhouette Models, from $2,318.00

HIGH STANDARD SUPERMATIC TROPHY TARGET

Caliber: .22 LR, 9-shot mag. **Barrel:** 5.5" bull or 7.25" fluted. **Weight:** 44-46 oz. **Length:** 9.5-11.25" overall. **Stock:** Checkered hardwood with thumbrest. **Sights:** Undercut ramp front, frame-mounted micro-click rear adjustable for windage and elevation; drilled and tapped for scope mounting. **Features:** Gold-plated trigger, slide lock, safety-lever and magazine release; stippled front grip and backstrap; adjustable trigger and sear. Barrel weights optional. From

High Standard Manufacturing Co., Inc.
Price: 5.5" barrel $1,070.00
Price: 7.25" barrel $1,205.00

HIGH STANDARD VICTOR TARGET
Caliber: .22 LR, 10-shot magazine. **Barrel:** 4.5" or 5.5" polished blue; push-button takedown. **Weight:** 46 oz. **Length:** 9.5" overall. **Stock:** Checkered walnut with thumbrest. **Sights:** Undercut ramp front, micro-click rear adjustable for windage and elevation. Also available with scope mount, rings, no sights. **Features:** Stainless steel frame. Full-length vent rib. Gold-plated trigger, slide lock, safety-lever and magazine release; stippled front grip and backstrap; polished blue slide; adjustable trigger and sear. Comes with barrel weight. From High Standard Manufacturing Co., Inc.
Price: 4.5" or 5.5" barrel, vented sight rib,
scope base $1,050.00

KIMBER SUPER MATCH II
Caliber: .45 ACP, 8-shot magazine. **Barrel:** 5". **Weight:** 38 oz. **Length:** 8.7" overall. **Grips:** Rosewood double diamond. **Sights:** Blade front, Kimber fully adjustable rear. **Features:** Guaranteed to shoot 1" groups at 25 yards. Stainless steel frame, black KimPro slide; two-piece magazine well; premium aluminum match-grade trigger; 30 lpi front strap checkering; stainless match-grade barrel; ambidextrous safety; special Custom Shop markings. Introduced 1999. Made in U.S.A. by Kimber Mfg., Inc.
Price: $2,313.00

KIMBER RIMFIRE TARGET
Caliber: .22 LR, 10-shot magazine. **Barrel:** 5". **Weight:** 23 oz. **Length:** 8.7" overall. **Grips:** Rosewood, Kimber logo, double diamond checkering, or black synthetic double diamond. **Sights:** Blade front, Kimber fully adjustable rear. **Features:** Bumped

beavertail grip safety, extended thumb safety, extended magazine release button. Serrated flat top slide with flutes, machined aluminum slide and frame, matte black or satin silver finishes, 30 lines-per-inch checkering on frontstrap and under trigger guard; aluminum trigger, test target, accuracy guarantee. No slide lock-open after firing the last round in the magazine. Introduced 1999. Made in U.S.A. by Kimber Mfg., Inc.
Price: $871.00

RUGER MARK III TARGET
Caliber: .22 LR, 10-shot magazine. **Barrel:** 5.5" to 6-7/8". **Weight:** 41 to 45 oz. **Length:** 9.75" to 11-1/8" overall. **Grips:** Checkered cocobolo/laminate. **Sights:** .125 blade front, micro-click rear, adjustable for windage and elevation, loaded chamber indicator; integral lock, magazine disconnect. Plastic case with lock included.
Price: (bull barrel, blued) $499.00
Price: (bull barrel, stainless) $629.00
Price: (stainless slabside barrel) $659.00
Price: Target Govt. Competition $729.00

SMITH & WESSON MODEL 41 TARGET
Caliber: .22 LR, 10-shot clip. **Barrel:** 5.5", 7". **Weight:** 41 oz. (5.5" barrel). **Length:** 10.5" overall (5.5" barrel). **Grips:** Checkered walnut with modified thumbrest, usable with either hand. **Sights:** 1/8" Patridge on ramp base; micro-click rear adjustable for windage and elevation. **Features:** 3/8" wide, grooved trigger; adjustable trigger stop drilled and tapped.
Price: .... $1,369.00 to $1,619.00

STI APEIRO
1911-style semiauto pistol chambered in 9x19, .40 S&W, and .45 ACP. Features include Schuemann "Island" barrel; patented modular steel frame with polymer grip; high capacity double-stack magazine; stainless steel ambidextrous thumb safeties and knuckle relief high-rise beavertail grip safety; unique sabertooth rear cocking serrations; 5-inch fully ramped, fully supported "island" bull barrel, with the sight milled in to allow faster recovery to point of aim; custom engraving on the polished sides of the (blued) stainless steel slide; stainless steel magwell; STI adjustable rear sight and Dawson fiber optic front sight; blued frame.
Price: $2,699.00

STI EAGLE 5.0, 6.0
Caliber: 9mm Para., 9x21, .38 & .40 Super, .40 S&W, 10mm, .45 ACP, 10-shot magazine. **Barrel:** 5", 6" bull. **Weight:** 34.5 oz. **Length:** 8.62" overall. **Grips:** Checkered polymer. **Sights:** STI front, Novak or Heinie rear. **Features:** Standard frames plus 7 others; adjustable match trigger; skeletonized hammer; extended grip safety with locator pad. Introduced 1994. Made in U.S.A. by STI International.
Price: (5.0 Eagle) $2,099.00

Prices given are believed to be accurate at time of publication however, many factors affect retail pricing so exact prices are not possible.

71ST EDITION, 2017 ✛ **415**

HANDGUNS Competition

STI EXECUTIVE
Caliber: .40 S&W. **Barrel:** 5" bull. **Weight:** 39 oz. **Length:** 8-5/8".
Grips: Gray polymer. **Sights:** Dawson fiber optic, front; STI
adjustable rear. **Features:** Stainless mag. well, front and rear
serrations on slide. Made in U.S.A. by STI.
Price: $2,599.00

STI STEELMASTER
Caliber: 9mm minor, comes with one 126mm magazine. **Barrel:**
4.15". **Weight:** 38.9 oz. **Length:** 9.5" overall. **Features:** Based
on the renowned STI race pistol design, the SteelMaster is a
shorter and lighter pistol that allows for faster target acquisition
with reduced muzzle flip and dip. Designed to shoot factory 9mm
(minor) ammo, this gun delivers all the advantages of a full size
race pistol in a smaller, lighter, faster reacting, and less violent
package. The Steelmaster is built on the patented modular steel
frame with polymer grip. It has a 4.15" classic slide which has
been flat topped. Slide lightening cuts on the front and rear further

reduce weight while "Sabertooth" serrations further enhance
the aesthtics of this superior pistol. It also uses the innovative
Trubor compensated barrel which has been designed to eliminate
misalignment of the barrel and compensator bore or movement of
the compensator on the barrel. The shorter Trubor barrel system
in the SteelMaster gives an even greater reduction in muzzle flip,
and the shorter slide decreases overall slide cycle time allowing
the shooter to achieve faster follow up shots. The SteelMaster is
mounted with a C-More, 6-minute, red-dot scope with blast shield
and thumb rest. Additional enhancements include aluminum
magwell, stainless steel ambidextrous safeties, stainless steel high
rise grip safety, STI's "Spur" hammer, STI's RecoilMaster guide rod
system, and checkered front strap and mainspring housing.
Price: $2,799.00

STI TROJAN
Caliber: 9mm Para., .38 Super, .40 S&W, .45 ACP. **Barrel:** 5", 6".
Weight: 36 oz. **Length:** 8.5". **Grips:** Rosewood. **Sights:** STI front with
STI adjustable rear. **Features:** Stippled front strap, flat top slide, one-
piece steel guide rod.
Price: (Trojan 5) $1,299.00
Price: (Trojan 6, not available in .38 Super) $1,555.00

STI TRUBOR
Caliber: 9mm 'Major', 9x23, .38 Super - USPSA, IPSC. **Barrel:** 5"
with integrated compensator. **Weight:** 41.3 oz. (including scope
and mount) **Length:** 10.5" overall. **Features:** Built on the patented
modular steel frame with polymer grip, the STI Trubor utilizes the
Trubor compensated barrel which is machined from ONE PIECE of
416, Rifle Grade, Stainless Steel. The Trubor is designed to eliminate
misalignment of the barrel and compensator bore or movement
of the compensator along the barrel threads, giving the shooter a
more consistent performance and reduced muzzle flip. True to 1911
tradition, the Trubor has a classic scalloped slide with front and
rear cocking serrations on a forged steel slide (blued) with polished
sides, aluminum magwell, stainless steel ambidextrous safeties,
stainless steel high rise grip safety, full length guide rod, checkered
front strap, and checkered mainspring housing. With mountedC-
More Railway sight included with the pistol.
Price: $2,999.00

CHARTER ARMS BULLDOG

Caliber: .44 Special. **Barrel:** 2.5". **Weight:** 21 oz. **Sights:** Blade front, notch rear. **Features:** 5-round cylinder, soft-rubber pancake-style grips, shrouded ejector rod, wide trigger and hammer spur. American made by Charter Arms.
Price: Blued $409.00
Price: Stainless $422.00
Price: Target Bulldog, 4 barrel, 23 oz. $479.00

CHARTER ARMS POLICE BULLDOG

Caliber: .38 Special, 6-shot cylinder. **Barrel:** 4.2" **Weight:** 26 oz. **Sights:** Blade front, notch rear. Large frame version of Bulldog design.
Price: Blued $408.00

CHARTER ARMS CHIC LADY & CHIC LADY DAO

Caliber: .38 special - 5-round cylinder. **Barrel:** 2". **Weight:** 12 oz. **Grip:** Combat. **Sights:** Fixed. **Features:** 2-tone pink or lavender & stainless with aluminum frame. American made by Charter Arms.
Price: Chic Lady $473.00
Price: Chic Lady DAO $483.00

CHARTER UNDERCOVER LITE

Caliber: .38 special +P - 5-round cylinder. **Barrel:** 2". **Weight:** 12 oz. **Grip:** Full. **Sights:** Fixed. **Features:** 2-tone pink & stainless with aluminum frame. Constructed of tough aircraft-grade aluminum and steel, the Undercover Lite offers rugged reliability and comfort. This ultra-lightweight 5-shot .38 Special features a 2" barrel, fixed sights and traditional spurred hammer. American made by Charter Arms.
Price: $397.00

CHARTER ARMS CRIMSON UNDERCOVER

Caliber: .38 special +P - 5-round cylinder. **Barrel:** 2". **Weight:** 16 oz.

Grip: Crimson Trace™. **Sights:** Fixed. **Features:** Stainless finish & frame. American made by Charter Arms.
Price: $577.00

CHARTER ARMS OFF DUTY

Caliber: .38 Spec. **Barrel:** 2". **Weight:** 12.5 oz. **Sights:** Blade front, notch rear. **Features:** 5-round cylinder, aluminum casting, DAO with concealed hammer. Also available with semi-concealed hammer. American made by Charter Arms.
Price: Aluminum $404.00
Price: Crimson Trace Laser grip $657.00

CHARTER ARMS MAG PUG

Caliber: .357 Mag. **Barrel:** 2.2" **Weight:** 23 oz. **Sights:** Blade front, notch rear. **Features:** Five-round cylinder. American made by Charter Arms.
Price: Blued or stainless $400.00
Price: 4.4" full-lug barrel $470.00
Price: Crimson Trace Laser Grip.............................$609.00

CHARTER ARMS PIT BULL

Caliber: 9mm, 40 S&W, .45 ACP. 5-round cylinder. **Barrel:** 2.2". **Weight:** 20-22 oz. **Sights:** Fixed rear, ramp front. **Grips:** Rubber. **Features:** Matte stainless steel frame or Nitride frame. Moon clips not required for 9mm, .45 ACP.
Price: 9mm..$502.00
Price: .40 S&W...$489.00
Price: .45 ACP $489.00

CHARTER ARMS SOUTHPAW

Caliber: .38 Special +P. **Barrel:** 2". **Weight:** 12 oz. **Grips:** Rubber Pachmayr-style. **Sights:** NA. **Features:** Snubnose, five-round cylinder, matte black aluminum alloy frame with stainless steel cylinder. Cylinder latch and crane assembly are on right side of frame for convenience to left-hand shooters.
Price: $419.00

CHARTER ARMS PATHFINDER

Caliber: .22 LR or .22 Mag. - 6-round cylinder. **Barrel:** 2", 4". **Weight:** 20 oz. (12 oz. Lite model). **Grip:** Full. **Sights:** Fixed or adjustable (Target). **Features:** Stainless finish & frame.
Price .22 LR $365.00

Price .22 Mag...**$367.00**
Price: Lite **$379.00**
Price: Target **$409.00**

CHARTER ARMS UNDERCOVER
Caliber: .38 Spec. +P. **Barrel:** 2". **Weight:** 12 oz. **Sights:** Blade front, notch rear. **Features:** 6-round cylinder. American made by Charter Arms.
Price: Blued **$346.00**

CHARTER ARMS UNDERCOVER SOUTHPAW
Caliber: .38 Spec. +P. **Barrel:** 2". **Weight:** 12 oz. **Sights:** NA. **Features:** Cylinder release is on the right side and the cylinder opens to the right side. Exposed hammer for both single and double-action firing. 5-round cylinder. American made by Charter Arms.
Price: **$419.00**

CHIAPPA RHINO
Caliber: .357 Magnum, 9mm, .40 S&W. **Features:** 2-, 4-, 5- or 6-inch barrel; fixed or adjustable sights; visible hammer or hammerless design. **Weight:** 24 to 33 oz. Walnut or synthetic grips with black frame; hexagonal-shaped cylinder. Unique design fires from bottom chamber of cylinder.
Price: From **$1,139.00**

COBRA SHADOW
Caliber: .38 Spec. +P. **Capacity:** 5 rounds. **Barrel:** 1-7/8". **Weight:** 15 oz. Aluminum frame with stainless steel barrel and cylinder. **Length:** 6 3/8". **Grips:** Rosewood, black rubber or Crimson Trace Laser. **Features:** Black anodized, titanium anodized, or custom colors including gold, red, pink and blue.
Price: **$369.00**
Price: Rosewood grips **$434.00**
Price: Crimson Trace Laser grips...................**$625.00**

COMANCHE II-A
Caliber: .38 Special, 6 shot. **Barrel:** 3 or 4". **Weight:** 33, 35 oz. **Length:** 8, 8.5" overall. **Grips:** Rubber. **Sights:** Fixed. **Features:**

Blued finish, alloy frame. Distributed by SGS Importers.
Price: **$236.95**

DAN WESSON 715
Caliber: .357 Magnum, 6-shot cylinder. **Barrel:** Six-inch heavy barrel with full lug. **Weight:** 38 oz. **Length:** 8, 8.5" overall. **Grips:** Hogue rubber with finger grooves. **Sights:** Adjustable rear, interchangeable front blade. **Features:** Stainless steel. Interchangeable barrel assembly. Reintroduced in 2014.
Price: **$1,168.00**

EAA WINDICATOR
Caliber: .38 Spec., 6-shot; .357 Mag., 6-shot. **Barrel:** 2", 4". **Weight:** 30 oz. (4"). **Length:** 8.5" overall (4" bbl.). **Grips:** Rubber with finger grooves. **Sights:** Blade front, fixed rear. **Features:** Swing-out cylinder; hammer block safety; blue or nickel finish. Introduced 1991. Imported from Germany by European American Armory.
Price: .38 Spec. 2" barrel, alloy frame **$325.00**
Price: .38 Spec. 4" barrel, alloy frame **$342.00**
Price: .357 Mag. 2" barrel, steel frame **$343.00**
Price: .357 Mag. 4" barrel, steel frame **$360.00**
Price: .357 Mag. 2" barrel, steel frame, nickel finish **$405.00**
Price: .357 Mag. 4" barrel, steel frame, nickel finish **$422.00**

KIMBER K6S
Caliber: .357 Magnum. 6-round cylinder. **Barrel:** 2-inch full lug. **Grips:** Gray rubber. **Finish:** Satin stainless. Kimber's first revolver, claimed to be world's lightest production 6-shot .357 Magnum. Double-action-only design with non-stacking match-grade trigger.
Price: $899.00

KORTH USA
Caliber: .22 LR, .22 WMR, .32 S&W Long, .38 Spec., .357 Mag., 9mm Para. **Barrel:** 3", 4", 5.25", 6". **Weight:** 36-52 oz. Grips, Combat, Sport: Walnut, Palisander, Amboinia, Ivory. Grips, Target: German Walnut, matte with oil finish, adjustable ergonomic competition style. **Sights:** Adjustable Patridge (Sport) or Baughman (Combat), interchangeable and adjustable rear w/Patridge front (Target) in blue and matte. **Features:** DA/SA, 3 models, over 50 configurations, externally adjustable trigger stop and weight, interchangeable cylinder, removable wide-milled trigger shoe on Target model. Deluxe models are highly engraved editions. Available finishes include high polish blue finish, plasma coated in high polish or matted silver, gold, blue, or charcoal. Many deluxe options available. 6-shot. From Korth USA.
Price: From $8,000.00
Price: Deluxe Editions, from $12,000.00

ROSSI R461/R462
Caliber: .357 Mag. **Barrel:** 2". **Weight:** 26-35 oz. **Grips:** Rubber. **Sights:** Fixed. **Features:** DA/SA, +P rated frame, blue carbon or high polish stainless steel, patented Taurus Security System, 6-shot.
Price: Blue carbon finish...$391.00
Price: Stainless finish..$455.00

Brazil by Amadeo Rossi. Imported by BrazTech/Taurus.
Price: Model R971 (blued finish, 4" bbl.) $455.00
Price: Model R972 (stainless steel finish, 6" bbl.) $511.00

ROSSI MODEL 351/851
Similar to Model R971/R972, chambered for .38 Spec. +P. Blued finish, 4-inch barrel. Introduced 2001. Made in Brazil by Amadeo Rossi. From BrazTech/Taurus.
Price: $389.00

ROSSI MODEL R971/R972
Caliber: 357 Mag. +P, 6-shot. **Barrel:** 4", 6". **Weight:** 32 oz. **Length:** 8.5 or 10.5" overall. **Grips:** Rubber. **Sights:** Blade front, adjustable rear. **Features:** Single/double action. Patented key-lock Taurus Security System; forged steel frame. Introduced 2001. Made in

RUGER GP-100
Caliber: .357 Mag., 6-shot cylinder. , .22 LR, 10-shot. **Barrel:** 3" full shroud, 4" full shroud, 6" full shroud. **Weight:** 36 to 45 oz. **Sights:** Fixed; adjustable on 4" and 6" full shroud barrels. **Grips:** Ruger Santoprene Cushioned Grip with Goncalo Alves inserts. **Features:**

Prices given are believed to be accurate at time of publication however, many factors affect retail pricing so exact prices are not possible.

71ST EDITION, 2017 ◆ **419**

HANDGUNS Double-Action Revolvers

Uses action, frame features of both the Security-Six and Redhawk revolvers. Full length, short ejector shroud. Satin blue and stainless steel.

Price: Blued **$769.00**
Price: Satin stainless **$799.00**
Price: .22 LR **$829.00**

ounce, small frame revolver with a smooth, easy-to-control trigger and highly manageable recoil. Packed with the latest technological advances and features required by today's most demanding shooters.

Price: .22 LR, .22 WMR, .38 Spl., iron sights **$579.00**
Price: 9mm, .357, iron sights **$669.00**

RUGER GP-100 MATCH CHAMPION
Caliber: .357 Mag., 6-shot cylinder. **Barrel:** 4.2" half shroud, slab sided. **Weight:** 38 oz. **Sights:** Fixed rear, fiber optic front. **Grips:** Hogue Stippled Hardwood. **Features:** Satin stainless steel finish.
Price: Blued **$969.00**

RUGER LCRX
.38 Special+P, Barrel: 1 7/8 or 3 inches. Features similar to LCR except this model has visible hammer, adjustable rear sight. Three-inch barrel model has longer grip.
Price: **$579.00**

RUGER LCR
Caliber: .22 LR (8-shot cylinder), .22 WMR, .38 Special and .357 Mag., 5-shot cylinder. **Barrel:** 1-7/8". **Weight:** 13.5 oz. –17.10 oz. **Length:** 6-1/2" overall. **Grips:** Hogue® Tamer™ or Crimson Trace® Lasergrips®. **Sights:** Pinned ramp front, U-notch integral rear. **Features:** The Ruger Lightweight Compact Revolver (LCR), a 13.5

Prices given are believed to be accurate at time of publication however, many factors affect retail pricing so exact prices are not possible

RUGER SP-101

Caliber: .22 LR (6 shot); .327 Federal Mag. (6-shot), .38 Spl, .357 Mag. (5-shot). **Barrel:** 2.25, 3-1/16, 4.2 inches (.327 Mag.). **Weight:** 25-30 oz. **Sights:** Adjustable or fixed, rear; fiber-optic or black ramp front. **Grips:** Ruger Cushioned Grip with inserts. **Features:** Compact, small frame, double-action revolver. Full-length ejector shroud. Stainless steel only.
Price: Fixed sights $719.00
Price: Adjustable rear, fiber optic front sights $769.00

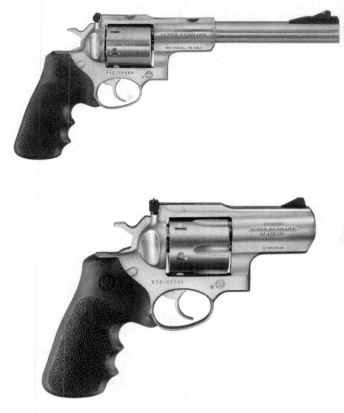

RUGER SUPER REDHAWK

Caliber: .44 Rem. Mag., .454 Casull, .480 Ruger, 5 or 6-shot. **Barrel:** 2.5" (Alaskan), 5.5" 7.5" or 9.5". **Weight:** 44 to 58 oz. **Length:** 13" overall (7.5" barrel). **Grips:** Hogue Tamer Monogrip. **Features:** Similar to standard Redhawk except has heavy extended frame with Ruger Integral Scope Mounting System on wide topstrap. Wide hammer spur lowered for better scope clearance. Incorporates mechanical design features and improvements of GP-100. Ramp front sight base has Redhawk-style Interchangeable Insert sight blades, adjustable rear sight. Alaskan model has 2.5-inch barrel. Satin stainless steel and low-glare stainless finishes. Introduced 1987.
Price: .44 Magnum $1,159.00
Price: .454 Casull, .480 Ruger $1,199.00

RUGER REDHAWK

Caliber: .44 Rem. Mag., .45 Colt and .45 ACP/.45 Colt combo. 6-shot cylinder. **Barrel:** 2.75, 4.2, 5.5, 7.5 inches. (.45 Colt in 4.2" only.) **Weight:** 54 oz. (7.5 bbl.). **Length:** 13 overall (7.5 barrel). **Grips:** Square butt cushioned grip panels. TALO Distributor exclusive 2.75" barrel stainless model has round butt, wood grips. **Sights:** Interchangeable Patridge-type front, rear adjustable for windage and elevation. **Features:** Stainless steel, brushed satin finish, blued ordnance steel. 9.5 sight radius. Introduced 1979.
Price: $1,079.00
Price: Hunter Model 7.5" bbl. $1,159.00
Price: TALO 2.75" model $1,069.00

SMITH & WESSON GOVERNOR™

Caliber: .410 Shotshell (2 1/2"), .45 ACP, .45 Colt; 6 rounds. **Barrel:** 2.75". **Length:** 7.5", (2.5" barrel). **Grip:** Synthetic. **Sights:** Front: Dovetailed tritium night sight or black ramp, rear: fixed. **Grips:** Synthetic. **Finish:** Matte Black or matte silver (Silver Edition). **Weight:** 29.6 oz. **Features:** Capable of chambering a mixture of .45 Colt, .45 ACP and .410 gauge 2½-inch shotshells, the Governor is suited for both close and distant encounters, allowing users to customize the load to their preference. Scandium Alloy frame, stainless steel cylinder. Packaged with two full-moon clips and three 2-shot clips.

Price: **$869.00**
Price: w/Crimson Trace® Laser Grip **$1,179.00**

SMITH & WESSON J-FRAME

The smallest S&W wheelguns come in a variety of chamberings, barrel lengths, and materials, as noted in the individual model listings.

SMITH & WESSON 60LS/642LS LADYSMITH

Caliber: .38 Spec. +P, .357 Mag., 5-shot. **Barrel:** 1-7/8" (642LS); 2-1/8" (60LS); **Weight:** 14.5 oz. (642LS); 21.5 oz. (60LS); **Length:** 6.6" overall (60LS). **Grips:** Wood. **Sights:** Black blade, serrated ramp front, fixed notch rear. 642 CT has Crimson Trace Laser Grips. **Features:** 60LS model has a Chiefs Special-style frame. 642LS has Centennial-style frame, frosted matte finish, smooth combat wood grips. Introduced 1996. Comes in a fitted carry/storage case. Introduced 1989. Made in U.S.A. by Smith & Wesson.

Price: (642LS) **$499.00**
Price: (60LS) **$759.00**
Price: (642 CT) **$699.00**

SMITH & WESSON MODEL 63

Caliber: .22 LR, 8-shot. **Barrel:** 3". **Weight:** 26 oz. **Length:** 7.25" overall. **Grips:** Black synthetic. **Sights:** Hi-Viz fiber optic front sight, adjustable black blade rear sight. **Features:** Stainless steel construction throughout. Made in U.S.A. by Smith & Wesson.

Price: **$769.00**

SMITH & WESSON MODELS 637 CT/638 CT/642 CT

Similar to Models 637, 638 and 642 but with Crimson Trace Laser Grips.

Price: **$699.00**

SMITH & WESSON MODEL 317 AIRLITE

Caliber: .22 LR, 8-shot. **Barrel:** 1-7/8". **Weight:** 10.5 oz. **Length:** 6.25" overall (1-7/8" barrel). **Grips:** Rubber. **Sights:** Serrated ramp front, fixed notch rear. **Features:** Aluminum alloy, carbon and stainless steels, Chiefs Special-style frame with exposed hammer. Smooth combat trigger. Clear Cote finish. Model 317 Kit Gun has adjustable rear sight, fiber optic front. Introduced 1997.

Price: Model 317, 1-7/8 barrel.................................**$759.00**

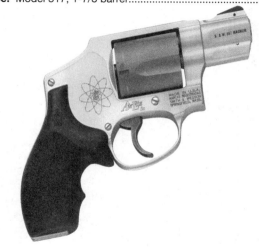

SMITH & WESSON MODEL 442/637/638/642 AIRWEIGHT

Caliber: .38 Spec. +P, 5-shot. **Barrel:** 1-7/8", 2-1/2". **Weight:** 15 oz. **Length:** 6-3/8" overall. **Grips:** Soft rubber. **Sights:** Fixed, serrated ramp front, square notch rear. **Features:** A family of J-frame .38 Special revolvers with aluminum-alloy frames. Model 637; Chiefs Special-style frame with exposed hammer. Introduced 1996. Models 442, 642; Centennial-style frame, enclosed hammer. Model 638, Bodyguard style, shrouded hammer. Comes in a fitted carry/storage case. Introduced 1989. Made in U.S.A. by Smith & Wesson.

Price: From **$469.00**
Price: Laser Max Frame Mounted Red Laser sight **$539.00**

Prices given are believed to be accurate at time of publication however, many factors affect retail pricing so exact prices are not possible.

HANDGUNS Double-Action Revolvers

SMITH & WESSON MODEL 340/340PD AIRLITE SC CENTENNIAL
Caliber: .357 Mag., 38 Spec. +P, 5-shot. **Barrel:** 1-7/8". **Weight:** 12 oz. **Length:** 6-3/8" overall (1-7/8" barrel). **Grips:** Rounded butt rubber. **Sights:** Black blade front, rear notch **Features:** Centennial-style frame, enclosed hammer. Internal lock. Matte silver finish. Scandium alloy frame, titanium cylinder, stainless steel barrel liner. Made in U.S.A. by Smith & Wesson.
Price: Model 340 ....$1,019.00

SMITH & WESSON MODEL 351PD
Caliber: .22 Mag., 7-shot. **Barrel:** 1-7/8". **Weight:** 10.6 oz. **Length:** 6.25" overall (1-7/8" barrel). **Sights:** HiViz front sight, rear notch. **Grips:** Wood. **Features:** Seven-shot, aluminum-alloy frame. Chiefs Special-style frame with exposed hammer. Nonreflective matte-black finish. Internal lock. Made in U.S.A. by Smith & Wesson.
Price: $759.00

SMITH & WESSON MODEL 360/360PD AIRLITE CHIEF'S SPECIAL
Caliber: .357 Mag., .38 Spec. +P, 5-shot. **Barrel:** 1-7/8". **Weight:** 12 oz. **Length:** 6-3/8" overall (1-7/8" barrel). **Grips:** Rounded butt rubber. **Sights:** Black blade front, fixed rear notch. **Features:** Chief's Special-style frame with exposed hammer. Internal lock. Scandium alloy frame, titanium cylinder, stainless steel barrel. Made in U.S.A. by Smith & Wesson.
Price: 360PD $988.00

SMITH & WESSON BODYGUARD® 38
Caliber: .38 S&W Special +P; 5 rounds. **Barrel:** 1.9". **Weight:** 14.3 oz. **Length:** 6.6". **Grip:** Synthetic. **Sights:** Front: Black ramp, Rear: fixed, integral with backstrap. **Plus:** Integrated laser sight. **Finish:** Matte Black. **Features:** The first personal protection series that comes with an integrated laser sight.
Price: $539.00

SMITH & WESSON MODEL 640 CENTENNIAL DA ONLY
Caliber: .357 Mag., .38 Spec. +P, 5-shot. **Barrel:** 2-1/8". **Weight:** 23 oz. **Length:** 6.75" overall. **Grips:** Uncle Mike's Boot grip. **Sights:** Tritium Night Sights. **Features:** Stainless steel. Fully concealed hammer, snag-proof smooth edges. Internal lock.
Price: $839.00

SMITH & WESSON MODEL 649 BODYGUARD
Caliber: .357 Mag., .38 Spec. +P, 5-shot. **Barrel:** 2-1/8". **Weight:** 23 oz. **Length:** 6-5/8" overall. **Grips:** Uncle Mike's Combat. **Sights:** Black pinned ramp front, fixed notch rear. **Features:** Stainless steel construction, satin finish. Internal lock. Bodyguard style, shrouded hammer. Made in U.S.A. by Smith & Wesson.
Price: $729.00

SMITH & WESSON K-FRAME/L-FRAME
The K-frame series are mid-size revolvers and the L-frames are slightly larger.

SMITH & WESSON MODEL 10 CLASSIC
Caliber: .38 Special, 6-round cylinder. Features include a bright blue steel frame and cylinder, checkered wood grips, 4-inch barrel, and fixed sights. The oldest model in the Smith & Wesson line, its basic design goes back to the original Military & Police Model of 1905.
Price: $739.00

SMITH & WESSON MODEL 17 MASTERPIECE CLASSIC
Caliber: .22 LR. **Capacity:** 6 rounds. **Barrel:** 6 inches. **Weight:** 40 oz. **Grips:** Checkered wood. **Sights:** Pinned Patridge front, Micro Adjustable rear. Updated variation of K-22 Masterpiece of the 1930s.
Price: $989.00

Prices given are believed to be accurate at time of publication however, many factors affect retail pricing so exact prices are not possible.

71ST EDITION, 2017   423

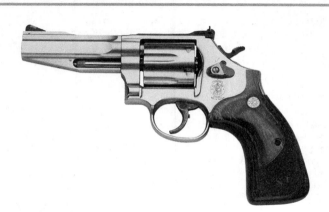

SMITH & WESSON MODEL 48 CLASSIC

Same specifications as Model 17 excet chambered in .22 Magnum (.22 WMR) and is available with a 4 or 6-inch barrel.
Price: .... $949.00 to $989.00

SMITH & WESSON MODEL 64/67

Caliber: .38 Spec. +P, 6-shot. **Barrel:** 3". **Weight:** 33 oz. **Length:** 8-7/8" overall. **Grips:** Soft rubber. **Sights:** Fixed, 1/8 serrated ramp front, square notch rear. Model 67 issimilar to Model 64 except for adjustable sights. **Features:** Satin finished stainless steel, square butt.
Price: From .... $689.00 to $749.00

SMITH & WESSON MODEL 66

Caliber: .357 Magnum. **Capacity:** 6 rounds. **Barrel:** 4.25". **Weight:** 36.6 oz. **Grips:** Synthetic. **Sights:** White outline adjustable rear, red ramp front. **Features:** Return in 2014 of the famous K-frame "Combat Magnum" with stainless finish.
Price: $849.00

SMITH & WESSON MODEL 686/686 PLUS

Caliber: .357 Mag/.38 Special. **Capacity:** 6 (686) or 7 rounds (Plus). **Barrel:** 6 (686), 3 or 6" (686 Plus), 4" (SSR). **Weight:** 35 oz. (3" barrel). **Grips:** Rubber. **Sights:** White outline adjustable rear, red ramp front. **Features:** Satin stainless frame and cylinder. Stock Service Revolver (SSR) has tapered underlug, interchangeable front sight, high-hold ergonomic wood grips, chamfered charge holes, custom barrel w/ recessed crown, bossed mainspring.
Price: 686 .... $829.00
Price: Plus $849.00
Price: SSR $999.00

SMITH & WESSON MODEL 986 PRO

Single/double-action L-frame revolver chambered in 9mm. Features similar to 686 PLUS Pro Series including 7-round cylinder, 5-inch tapered underlug barrel, satin stainless finish, synthetic grips, adjustable rear and Patridge blade front sight.
Price: $1,149.00

SMITH & WESSON MODEL 69

Caliber: ..44 Magnum. **Capacity:** 5 rounds. **Barrel:** 4.25". **Weight:** 37 oz. **Grips:** Checkered wood. **Sights:** White outline adjustable rear, red ramp front. **Features:** L-frame with stainless finish, 5-shot cylinder, introduced in 2014.
Price: $989.00

SMITH & WESSON MODEL 617

Caliber: .22 LR, 10-shot cylinder **Barrel:** 6". **Weight:** 44 oz. **Length:** 11-1/8". **Grips:** Soft rubber. **Sights:** Patridge front, adjustable rear. Drilled and tapped for scope mount. **Features:** Stainless steel with satin finish. Introduced 1990.
Price: From $829.00

SMITH & WESSON M&P R8

Caliber: .357 Mag., 8-round cylinder. **Barrel:** 5", half lug with accessory rail. **Weight:** 36.3 oz. **Length:** 10.5" **Grips:** Black synthetic. **Sights:** Adjustable v-notch rear, interchangeable front. **Features:** Scandium alloy frame, stainless steel cylinder.
Price: $1,329.00

Prices given are believed to be accurate at time of publication however, many factors affect retail pricing so exact prices are not possible.

SMITH & WESSON N-FRAME

These large-frame models introduced the .357, .41 and .44 Magnums to the world.

SMITH & WESSON MODEL 25 CLASSIC

Caliber: .45 Colt. **Capacity:** Six rounds. **Barrel:** 6.5 inches. **Weight:** 45 oz. **Grips:** Checkered wood. **Sights:** Pinned Patridge front, Micro Adjustable rear.
Price: $1,019.00

SMITH & WESSON MODEL 27 CLASSIC

Caliber: .357 Magnum. **Capacity:** Six rounds. **Barrel:** 4 or 6.5 inches. **Weight:** 41.2 oz. **Grips:** Checkered wood. **Sights:** Pinned Patridge front, Micro Adjustable rear. Updated variation of the first magnum revolver, the .357 Magnum of 1935.
Price: (4") $1,019.00
Price: (6.5") $1,059.00

SMITH & WESSON MODEL 29 CLASSIC

Caliber: .44 Mag, 6-round. **Barrel:** 4 or 6.5". **Weight:** 48.5 oz. **Length:** 12". **Grips:** Altamont service walnut. **Sights:** Adjustable white-outline rear, red ramp front. **Features:** Carbon steel frame, polished-blued or nickel finish. Has integral key lock safety feature to prevent accidental discharges. Original Model 29 made famous by "Dirty Harry" character created in 1971 by Clint Eastwood.
Price: .... $999.00 to $1,169.00

SMITH & WESSON MODEL 57 CLASSIC

Caliber: .41 Magnum. Six rounds. **Barrel:** 6 inches. **Weight:** 48 oz. **Grips:** Checkered wood. **Sights:** Pinned red ramp, Micro Adjustable rear.
Price: $1,009.00

SMITH & WESSON MODEL 329PD ALASKA BACKPACKER

Caliber: .44 Mag., 6-round. **Barrel:** 2.5". **Weight:** 26 oz. **Length:** 9.5". **Grips:** Synthetic. **Sights:** Adj. rear, HiViz orange-dot front. **Features:** Scandium alloy frame, blue/black finish, stainless steel cylinder.
Price: From $1,159.00

SMITH & WESSON MODEL 625/625JM

Caliber: .45 ACP, 6-shot. **Barrel:** 4", 5". **Weight:** 43 oz. (4" barrel). **Length:** 9-3/8" overall (4" barrel). **Grips:** Soft rubber; wood optional. **Sights:** Patridge front on ramp, S&W micrometer click rear adjustable for windage and elevation. **Features:** Stainless steel construction with .400 semi-target hammer, .312 smooth combat trigger; full lug barrel. Glass beaded finish. Introduced 1989. Jerry Miculek Professional (JM) Series has .265-wide grooved trigger, special wooden Miculek Grip, five full moon clips, gold bead Patridge front sight on interchangeable front sight base, bead blast finish. Unique serial number run. Mountain Gun has 4" tapered barrel, drilled and tapped, Hogue Rubber Monogrip, pinned black ramp front sight, micrometer click-adjustable rear sight, satin stainless frame and barrel, weighs 39.5 oz.
Price: 625 or 625JM $1,074.00

SMITH & WESSON MODEL 629

Caliber: .44 Magnum, .44 S&W Special, 6-shot. **Barrel:** 4", 5", 6.5". **Weight:** 41.5 oz. (4" bbl.). **Length:** 9-5/8" overall (4" bbl.). **Grips:** Soft rubber; wood optional. **Sights:** 1/8 red ramp front, white outline rear, internal lock, adjustable for windage and elevation. Classic similar to standard Model 629, except Classic has full-lug 5" barrel, chamfered front of cylinder, interchangeable red ramp front sight with adjustable white outline rear, Hogue grips with S&W monogram, drilled and tapped for scope mounting. Factory accurizing and endurance packages. Introduced 1990. Classic Power Port has Patridge front sight and adjustable rear sight. Model 629CT has 5" barrel, Crimson Trace Hoghunter Lasergrips, 10.5 OAL, 45.5 oz. weight. Introduced 2006.
Price: From $949.00

SMITH & WESSON MODEL 329 XL HUNTER

Similar to Model 386 XL Hunter but built on large N-frame and chambered in .44 Magnum. Other features include 6-round cylinder and 6.5"-barrel.
Price: $1,138.00

SMITH & WESSON X-FRAME

These extra-large X-frame S&W revolvers push the limits of bigbore handgunning.

SMITH & WESSON MODEL 500

Caliber: 500 S&W Mag., 5 rounds. **Barrel:** 4", 6-1/2", 8-3/8". **Weight:** 72.5 oz. **Length:** 15" (8-3/8" barrel). **Grips:** Hogue Sorbothane Rubber. **Sights:** Interchangeable blade, front, adjustable rear. **Features:** Recoil compensator, ball detent cylinder latch, internal lock. 6.5"-barrel model has orange-ramp dovetail

Millett front sight, adjustable black rear sight, Hogue Dual Density Monogrip, .312 chrome trigger with over-travel stop, chrome tear-drop hammer, glassbead finish. 10.5"-barrel model has red ramp front sight, adjustable rear sight, .312 chrome trigger with overtravel stop, chrome tear drop hammer with pinned sear, hunting sling. Compensated Hunter has .400 orange ramp dovetail front sight, adjustable black blade rear sight, Hogue Dual Density Monogrip, glassbead finish w/black clear coat. Made in U.S.A. by Smith & Wesson.
Price: From **$1,299.00**

SMITH & WESSON MODEL 460V

Caliber: 460 S&W Mag., 5-shot. Also chambers .454 Casull, .45 Colt. **Barrel:** 7-1/2", 8-3/8" gain-twist rifling. **Weight:** 62.5 oz. **Length:** 11.25". **Grips:** Rubber. **Sights:** Adj. rear, red ramp front. **Features:** Satin stainless steel frame and cylinder, interchangeable compensator. 460XVR (X-treme Velocity Revolver) has black blade front sight with interchangeable green Hi-Viz tubes, adjustable rear sight. 7.5"-barrel version has Lothar-Walther barrel, 360-degree recoil compensator, tuned Performance Center action, pinned sear, integral Weaver base, non-glare surfaces, scope mount accessory kit for mounting full-size scopes, flashed-chromed hammer and trigger, Performance Center gun rug and shoulder sling. Interchangeable Hi-Viz green dot front sight, adjustable black rear sight, Hogue Dual Density Monogrip, matte-black frame and shroud finish with glass-bead cylinder finish, 72 oz. Compensated Hunter has tear drop chrome hammer, .312 chrome trigger, Hogue Dual Density Monogrip, satin/matte stainless finish, HiViz interchangeable front sight, adjustable black rear sight. XVR introduced 2006.
Price: 460V **$1,369.00**
Price: 460XVR, from **$1,369.00**

SUPER SIX CLASSIC BISON BULL

Caliber: .45-70 Government, 6-shot. **Barrel:** 10" octagonal with 1:14 twist. **Weight:** 6 lbs. **Length:** 17.5"overall. **Grips:** NA. **Sights:** Ramp front sight with dovetailed blade, click-adjustable rear. **Features:** Manganese bronze frame. Integral scope mount, manual crossbolt safety.
Price: **$1,500.00**

TAURUS MODEL 17 TRACKER

Caliber: .17 HMR, 7-shot. **Barrel:** 6.5". **Weight:** 45.8 oz. **Grips:** Rubber. **Sights:** Adjustable. **Features:** Double action, matte stainless, integral key-lock.
Price: From **$539.00**

TAURUS MODEL 992 TRACKER

Caliber: .22 LR with interchangeable .22 WMR cylinder. 9-shot capacity. **Barrel:** 4 or 6.5 inches with ventilated rib, adjustable rear sight, blue or stainless finish.
Price: Blue **$591.00**
Price: Stainless **$627.00**

TAURUS MODEL 44SS

Caliber: .44 Mag., 5-shot. **Barrel:** 4" ported. **Weight:** 34 oz. **Grips:** Rubber. **Sights:** Adjustable. **Features:** Double-action. Integral key-lock. Introduced 1994. Finish: Matte stainless. Imported from Brazil by Taurus International Manufacturing, Inc.
Price: From **$648.00**

TAURUS MODEL 65

Caliber: .357 Mag., 6-shot. **Barrel:** 4" full underlug. **Weight:** 38 oz. **Length:** 10.5" overall. **Grips:** Soft rubber. **Sights:** Fixed. **Features:** Double action, integral key-lock. Matte blue or stainless. Imported by Taurus International.
Price: Blue **$488.00**
Price: Stainless **$536.00**

TAURUS MODEL 66

Similar to Model 65, 4" or 6" barrel, 7-shot cylinder, adjustable rear sight. Integral key-lock action. Imported by Taurus International.
Price: Blue **$543.00**
Price: Stainless **$591.00**

TAURUS MODEL 82 HEAVY BARREL

Caliber: .38 Spec., 6-shot. **Barrel:** 4", heavy. **Weight:** 36.5 oz. **Length:** 9-1/4" overall. **Grips:** Soft black rubber. **Sights:** Serrated ramp front, square notch rear. **Features:** Double action, solid rib, integral key-lock. Imported by Taurus International.
Price: From **$473.00**

TAURUS MODEL 85

Caliber: .38 Spec., 5-shot. **Barrel:** 2". **Weight:** 17-24.5 oz., titanium 13.5-15.4 oz. **Grips:** Rubber, rosewood or mother-of-pearl. **Sights:** Ramp front, square notch rear. **Features:** Blue, matte stainless, blue with gold accents, stainless with gold accents; rated for +P ammo. Integral keylock. Some models have titantium frame. Introduced 1980. Imported by Taurus International.
Price: From **$403.00**

TAURUS 380 MINI

Caliber: .380 ACP (5-shot cylinder w/moon clip). **Barrel:** 1.75". **Weight:** 15.5 oz. **Length:** 5.95". **Grips:** Rubber. **Sights:** Adjustable rear, fixed front. **Features:** Double-action-only. Available in blued or stainless finish. Five Star (moon) clips included.

Price: Blued **$443.00**
Price: Stainless **$447.00**

TAURUS MODEL 45-410 JUDGE
Caliber: 2-1/2"-.410/.45 LC, 3"-.410/.45 LC. **Barrel:** 3", 6.5" (blued finish). **Weight:** 35.2 oz., 22.4 oz. **Length:** 7.5". **Grips:** Ribber rubber. **Sights:** Fiber Optic. **Features:** DA/SA. Matte Stainless and Ultra-Lite Stainless finish. Introduced in 2007. Imported from Brazil by Taurus International.
Price: From **$653.00**

TAURUS JUDGE PUBLIC DEFENDER POLYMER
Single/double action revolver chambered in .45 Colt/.410 (2-1/2"). Features include 5-round cylinder; polymer frame; Rubber rubber-feel grips; fiber-optic front sight; adjustable rear sight; blued or stainless cylinder; shrouded hammer with cocking spur; blued finish; 2.5-inch barrel. Weight 27 oz.
Price: .... **$515.00 to $653.00**

TAURUS RAGING JUDGE MAGNUM
Single/double-action revolver chambered for .454 Casull, .45 Colt, 2.5-inch and 3-inch .410. Features include 3- or 6-inch barrel; fixed sights with fiber-optic front; blued or stainless steel finish; vent rib for scope

mounting (6-inch only); cushioned Raging Bull grips.
Price: **$1,038.00**

TAURUS MODEL 627 TRACKER
Caliber: .357 Mag., 7-shot. **Barrel:** 4 or 6.5". **Weight:** 28.8, 41 oz. **Grips:** Rubber. **Sights:** Fixed front, adjustable rear. **Features:** Double-action. Stainless steel, Shadow Gray or Total Titanium; vent rib (steel models only); integral key-lock action. Imported by Taurus International.
Price: From **$670.00**

TAURUS MODEL 444 ULTRA-LIGHT
Caliber: .44 Mag, 5-shot. **Barrel:** 2.5 or 4". **Weight:** 28.3 oz. **Grips:** Cushioned inset rubber. **Sights:** Fixed red-fiber optic front, adjustable rear. **Features:** UltraLite titanium blue finish, titanium/alloy frame built on Raging Bull design. Smooth trigger shoe, 1.760 wide, 6.280 tall. Barrel rate of twist 1:16, 6 grooves. Introduced 2005. Imported by Taurus International.
Price: **$792.00**

TAURUS MODEL 444/454 RAGING BULL SERIES
Caliber: .44 Mag., .454 Casull. **Barrel:** 2.25, 5, 6.5, 8-3/8". **Weight:** 53-63 oz. **Length:** 12" overall (6.5" barrel). **Grips:** Soft black rubber. **Sights:** Patridge front, adjustable rear. **Features:** Double-action, ventilated rib, integral key-lock. Most models have ported barrels. Introduced 1997. Imported by Taurus International.
Price: 444 .... **$753.00**
Price: 454 .... **$1,055.00**

Prices given are believed to be accurate at time of publication however, many factors affect retail pricing so exact prices are not possible.

71ST EDITION, 2017 ✦ **427**

TAURUS MODEL 605 PLY

Caliber: .357 Mag., 5-shot. **Barrel:** 2". **Weight:** 20 oz. **Grips:** Rubber. **Sights:** Fixed. **Features:** Polymer frame steel cylinder. Blued or stainless. Introduced 1995. Imported by Taurus International.
Price: Blue $460.00
Price: Stainless $507.00

TAURUS MODEL 608

Caliber: .357 Mag., 38 Spec., 8-shot. **Barrel:** 4, 6.5, 8-3/8". **Weight:** 44-57 oz. **Length:** 9-3/8" overall. **Grips:** Soft black rubber. **Sights:** Adjustable. **Features:** Double-action, integral key-lock action. Available in blue or stainless. Introduced 1995. Imported by Taurus International.
Price: From $608.00

TAURUS MODEL 617

Caliber: .357 Mag., 7-shot. **Barrel:** 2". **Weight:** 28.3 oz. **Length:** 6.75" overall. **Grips:** Soft black rubber. **Sights:** Fixed. **Finish:** Stainless steel. **Features:** Double-action, polished or matte stainless steel, integral key-lock. Available with porting, concealed hammer. Introduced 1998. Imported by Taurus International.
Price: $560.00

TAURUS MODEL 650 CIA

Caliber: .357 Mag., or .38 Special +P only. 5-shot. **Barrel:** 2". **Weight:** 24.5 oz. **Grips:** Rubber. **Sights:** Ramp front, square notch rear. **Features:** Double-action only, blue finish, integral key-lock, internal hammer. Introduced 2001. From Taurus International.
Price: : From $513.00

TAURUS MODEL 941

Caliber: .22 WMR, 8-shot. **Barrel:** 2", 4", 5". **Weight:** 27.5 oz. (4" barrel). **Grips:** Soft black rubber. **Sights:** Serrated ramp front, rear adjustable. **Features:** Double-action, integral key-lock. Blued or stainless finish. Introduced 1992. Imported by Taurus International.
Price: From $465.00

TAURUS MODEL 970 TRACKER

Caliber: .22 LR, 7-shot. **Barrel:** 6". **Weight:** 53.6 oz. **Grips:** Rubber. **Sights:** Adjustable. **Features:** Double barrel, heavy barrel with ventilated rib; matte stainless finish, integral key-lock. Introduced 2001. From Taurus International.
Price: $472.00

TAURUS MODEL 905

Caliber: 9mm, 5-shot. **Barrel:** 2". Small-frame revolver with rubber boot grips, fixed sights, choice of exposed or concealed hammer Blue or stainless finish.
Price: Blue $481.00
Price: Stainless $528.00

CIMARRON 1872 OPEN TOP

Caliber: .38, .44 Special, .44 Colt, .44 Russian, .45 LC, .45 S&W Schofield. **Barrel:** 5.5" and 7.5". **Grips:** Walnut. **Sights:** Blade front, fixed rear. **Features:** Replica of first cartridge-firing revolver. Blue finish; Navy-style brass or steel Army-style frame. Introduced 2001 by Cimarron F.A. Co.

Price: Navy model...$508.00
Price: Army $550.00

CIMARRON 1875 OUTLAW

Caliber: .357, .38 Special, .44 W.C.F., .45 Colt, .45 ACP. **Barrel:** 5-1/2" and 7-1/2". **Weight:** 2.5-2.6 lbs. **Grip:** 1-piece walnut. **Features:** Standard blue finish with color case hardened frame. Replica of 1875 Remington model. Available with dual .45 Colt/.45 ACP cylinder.

Price: $578.00
Price: Dual Cyl. $686.00

CIMARRON MODEL 1890

Caliber: .357, .38 special, .44 W.C.F., .45 Colt, .45 ACP. **Barrel:** 5-1/2". **Weight:** 2.4-2.5 lbs. **Grip:** 1-piece walnut. **Features:** Standard blue finish with standard blue frame. Replica of 1890 Remington model. Available with dual .45 Colt/.45 ACP cylinder.

Price: $606.00
Price: Dual Cyl. $702.00

CIMARRON BISLEY MODEL SINGLE-ACTION

Caliber: .357 Mag., .44 WCF, .44 Spl., .45. Similar to Colt Bisley, special grip frame and triggerguard, knurled wide-spur hammer, curved trigger. Introduced 1999. Imported by Cimarron F.A. Co.

Price: From $615.00

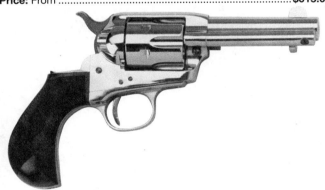

CIMARRON LIGHTNING SA

Caliber: .22 LR, .32-20/32 H&R dual cyl. combo, .38 Special, .41 Colt. **Barrel:** 3.5", 4.75", 5.5". **Grips:** Smooth or checkered walnut. **Sights:** Blade front. **Features:** Replica of the Colt 1877 Lightning DA. Similar to Cimarron Thunderer, except smaller grip frame to fit smaller hands. Standard blue, charcoal blue or nickel finish with forged, old model, or color case-hardened frame. Dual cylinder model available with .32-30/.32 H&R chambering. Introduced 2001. From Cimarron F.A. Co.

Price: From .... $503.00 to $565.00
Price: .32-20/.32 H&R dual cylinder $649.00

CIMARRON MAN WITH NO NAME

Caliber: .45 LC. **Barrel:** 4-3/4" and 5-1/2". **Weight:** 2.66-2.76 lbs.
Grip: 1-piece walnut with silver rattle snake inlay in both sides.

Features: Standard blue finish with case hardened pre-war frame. An accurate copy of the gun used by our nameless hero in the classic Western movies "Fist Full Of Dollars" & "For A Few Dollars More".
Price: Conversion Model $818.00
Price: SAA Model...$774.00

CIMARRON MODEL P SAA

Caliber: .32 WCF, .38 WCF, .357 Mag., .44 WCF, .44 Spec., .45 Colt, and .45 ACP. **Barrel:** 4.75, 5.5, 7.5". **Weight:** 39 oz. **Length:** 10" overall (4.75" barrel). **Grips:** Walnut. **Sights:** Blade front. **Features:** Old model black-powder frame with Bullseye ejector, or New Model frame. Imported by Cimarron F.A. Co.

Price: From $550.00

CIMARRON MODEL "P" JR.

Caliber: .32-20, .32 H&R. **Barrel:** 3.5, 4.75, 5.5". **Grips:** Checkered walnut. **Sights:** Blade front. **Features:** Styled after 1873 Colt Peacemaker, except 20 percent smaller. Blue finish with color case-hardened frame; Cowboy action. Introduced 2001. From Cimarron F.A. Co.

Price: $550.00

CIMARRON ROOSTER SHOOTER

Caliber: .357, .45 Colt and .44 W.C.F. **Barrel:** 4-3/4". **Weight:** 2.5 lbs. **Grip:** 1-piece orange finger grooved. **Features:** A replica of John Wayne's Colt Single Action Army model used in many of his great Westerns including his Oscar winning performance in "True Grit", where he brings the colorful character Rooster Cogburn to life.

Price: $909.00

CIMARRON THUNDERER

Caliber: .357 Mag., .44 WCF, .45 Colt, 6-shot. Combo comes with leather shoulder holster, ivory handled dagger. Gun and knife have matching serial numbers. Made by Uberti.
Price: .... $723.00 to $948.00
Price: Combo...$1,754,00

CIMARRON THUNDERSTORM

Caliber: .45 Colt. **Barrel:** 3.5 or 4.75 inches. **Grips:** Model P or Thunderer, checkered wood. **Finish:** Blue or stainless. Action job including U.S. made competition springs. Designed for Cowboy Action Shooting. Available with Short Stroke action.
Price: Blue $753.00

Prices given are believed to be accurate at time of publication however, many factors affect retail pricing so exact pricing are not possible.

71ST EDITION, 2017 ✛ **429**

Price: Stainless $948.00
Price: Short Stroke Action $779.00

CIMARRON FRONTIER
Caliber: .357 Mag., .44 WCF, .45 Colt. **Barrel:** 3.5, 4.75, 5.5 or 7.5 inches. Basic SAA design. Choice of Old Model or Pre-War frame. Blue or stainless finish. Available with Short Stroke action.
Price: Blue $530.00
Price: Stainless $723.00
Price: Short Stroke Action $598.00

CIMARRON U.S.V. ARTILLERY MODEL SINGLE-ACTION
Caliber: .45 Colt. **Barrel:** 5.5". **Weight:** 39 oz. **Length:** 11.5" overall. **Grips:** Walnut. **Sights:** Fixed. **Features:** U.S. markings and cartouche, case-hardened frame and hammer. Imported by Cimarron F.A. Co.
Price: Blue finish $594.00
Price: Original finish $701.00

COLT NEW FRONTIER
Caliber: .44 Special and .45 Colt. **Barrel:** 4-3/4", 5-1/2",and 7-1/2". **Grip:** Walnut. **Features:** The legend of Colt continues in the New Frontier®, Single Action Army. From 1890 to 1898, Colt manufactured a variation of the venerable Single Action Army with a uniquely different profile. The "Flattop Target Model" was fitted with an adjustable leaf rear sight and blade front sights. Colt has taken this concept several steps further to bring shooters a reintroduction of a Colt classic. The New Frontier has that sleek flattop design with an adjustable rear sight for windage and elevation and a target ready ramp style front sight. The guns are meticulously finished in Colt Royal Blue on both the barrel and cylinder, with a case-colored frame.
Price: $1,599.00

COLT SINGLE-ACTION ARMY
Caliber: .357 Mag., .45 Colt, 6-shot. **Barrel:** 4.75", 5.5", 7.5". **Weight:** 40 oz. (4.75" barrel). **Length:** 10.25" overall (4.75" barrel).

Grips: Black Eagle composite. **Sights:** Blade front, notch rear. **Features:** Available in full nickel finish with nickel grip medallions, or Royal Blue with color case-hardened frame. Reintroduced 1992.
Price: Blue $1,499.00
Price: Stainless $1,699.00

EAA BOUNTY HUNTER SA
Caliber: .22 LR/.22 WMR, .357 Mag., .44 Mag., .45 Colt, 6-shot. 10-shot cylinder available for .22LR/.22WMR. **Barrel:** 4.5", 7.5". **Weight:** 2.5 lbs. **Length:** 11" overall (4-5/8" barrel). **Grips:** Smooth walnut. **Sights:** Blade front, grooved topstrap rear. **Features:** Transfer bar safety; 3-position hammer; hammer-forged barrel. Introduced 1992. Imported by European American Armory
Price: Centerfire, blue or case-hardened $478.00
Price: Centerfire, nickel $515.00
Price: .22 LR/.22 WMR, blue $343.00
Price: .22LR/.22WMR, nickel $380.00
Price: .22 LR/.22WMR, 10-round cylinder $465.00

EMF 1875 OUTLAW
Caliber: .357 Mag., .44-40, .45 Colt. **Barrel:** 7.5", 9.5". **Weight:** 46 oz. **Length:** 13.5" overall. **Grips:** Smooth walnut. **Sights:** Blade front, fixed groove rear. **Features:** Authentic copy of 1875 Remington with firing pin in hammer; color case-hardened frame, blue cylinder, barrel, steel backstrap and triggerguard. Also available in nickel, factory engraved. Imported by E.M.F. Co.
Price: All calibers $520.00
Price: Laser Engraved $800.00

EMF 1873 GREAT WESTERN II
Caliber: .357, .45 Colt, .44/40. **Barrel:** 3.5, 4.75, 5.5, 7.5". **Weight:** 36 oz. **Length:** 11" (5.5" barrel). **Grips:** Walnut. **Sights:** Blade front, notch rear. **Features:** Authentic reproduction of the original 2nd Generation Colt single-action revolver. Standard and bone case hardening. Coil hammer spring. Hammer-forged barrel.
Price: 1873 Californian .... $545.00 to $560.00

Prices given are believed to be accurate at time of publication however, many factors affect retail pricing so exact prices are not possible.

HANDGUNS Single-Action Revolvers

Price: 1873 Custom series, bone or nickel, ivory-like grips ... **$689.90**
Price: 1873 Stainless steel, ivory-like grips **$589.90**
Price: 1873 Paladin **$560.00**
Price: Deluxe Californian with checkered walnut grips **$660.00**
Price: Buntline with stag grips **$810.00**

EMF 1873 DAKOTA II
Caliber: .357, 45 Colt. **Barrel:** 4¾ inches. **Grips:** Walnut. **Finish:** black.
Price: **$400.00**

FREEDOM ARMS MODEL 97 PREMIER GRADE
Caliber: .17 HMR, .22 LR, .32 H&R, .327 Federal, .357 Mag., 6-shot; .41 Mag., .44 Special, .45 Colt, 5-shot. **Barrel:** 4.25", 5.5", 7.5", 10" (.17 HMR, .22 LR, .32 H&R). **Weight:** 40 oz. (5.5" .357 Mag.). **Length:** 10.75" (5.5" bbl.). **Grips:** Impregnated hardwood; Micarta optional. **Sights:** Adjustable rear, replaceable blade front. Fixed rear notch and front blade. **Features:** Stainless steel construction, brushed finish, automatic transfer bar safety system. Introduced in 1997. Lifetime warranty. Made in U.S.A. by Freedom Arms.
Price: From **$2,055.00**

FREEDOM ARMS MODEL 83 PREMIER GRADE
Caliber: .357 Mag., 41 Mag., .44 Mag., .454 Casull, .475 Linebaugh, .500 Wyo. Exp., 5-shot. **Barrel:** 4.75", 6", 7.5", 9" (.357 Mag. only), 10" (except .357 Mag. and 500 Wyo. Exp.) **Weight:** 53 oz. (7.5" bbl. in .454 Casull). **Length:** 13" (7.5" bbl.). **Grips:** Impregnated hardwood. **Sights:** Adjustable rear with replaceable front sight. Fixed rear notch and front blade. **Features:** Stainless steel construction with brushed finish; manual sliding safety bar. Micarta grips optional. 500 Wyo. Exp. Introduced 2006. Lifetime warranty. Made in U.S.A. by Freedom Arms, Inc.
Price: From **$2,583.00**

HERITAGE ROUGH RIDER
Caliber: .17 HMR, .22 LR, 22 LR/22 WMR combo,.32 H&R, .357 Mag, .45 Colt, 6-shot. **Barrel:** 2.75, 3.5, 4.75, 5.5, 6.5, 7.5, 9. **Weight:** 31 to 38 oz. **Grips:** Exotic cocobolo laminated wood or mother-of-pearl; bird's-head models offered. **Sights:** Blade front, fixed rear. Adjustable sight on 4, 6 and 9 models. **Features:** Hammer block safety. Transfer bar with Big Bores. High polish blue, black satin, silver satin, case-hardened and stainless finish. Introduced 1993. Made in U.S.A. by Heritage Mfg., Inc.
Price: Rimfire calibers, from... **$301.00**
Price: Centerfire calibers, from **$467.00**

FREEDOM ARMS MODEL 83 FIELD GRADE
Caliber: .22 LR, .357 Mag., 41 Mag., .44 Mag., .454 Casull, .475 Linebaugh, .500 Wyo. Exp., 5-shot. **Barrel:** 4.75", 6", 7.5", 9" (.357 Mag. only), 10" (except .357 Mag. and .500 Wyo. Exp.) **Weight:** 56 oz. (7.5" bbl. in .454 Casull). **Length:** 13.1" (7.5" bbl.). **Grips:** Pachmayr standard, impregnated hardwood or Micarta optional. **Sights:** Adjustable rear with replaceable front sight. Model 83 frame. All stainless steel. Introduced 1988. Made in U.S.A. by Freedom Arms Inc.
Price: From **$2,199.00**

MAGNUM RESEARCH BFR SINGLE ACTION
Caliber: .44 Magnum, .444 Marlin, .45/70, .45 Colt/.410, .450 Marlin, .454 Casull, .460 S&W Magnum, .480 Ruger/.475 Linebaugh, .500 S&W, .30/30 Winchester. **Barrel:** 6.5", 7.5" and 10". **Weight:** 3.6 lbs. - 5.3 lbs. **Grips:** Black rubber. **Sights:** Rear sights are the same configuration as the Ruger revolvers. Many aftermarket rear sights will fit the BFR. Front sights are machined by Magnum in four heights and anodized flat black. The four heights accommodate all shooting styles, barrel lengths and calibers. All sights are interchangeable with each BFR's. **Features:** Crafted in the U.S.A., the BFR single action 5-shot stainless steel

Prices given are believed to be accurate at time of publication however, many factors affect retail pricing so exact prices are not possible.

71ST EDITION, 2017 ◆ **431**

revolver frames are CNC machined inside and out from a "pre-heat treated" investment casting. This is done to prevent warping and dimensional changes or shifting that occurs during the heat treat process. Magnum Research designed the frame with large calibers and large recoil in mind, built to close tolerances to handle the pressure of true big-bore calibers. The BFR is equipped with a transfer bar safety feature that allows the gun to be carried safely with all five chambers loaded.
Price: **$1,184.00**

NORTH AMERICAN ARMS MINI
Caliber: .22 Short, 22 LR, 22 WMR, 5-shot. **Barrel:** 1-1/8", 1-5/8". **Weight:** 4 to 6.6 oz. **Length:** 3-5/8" to 6-1/8" overall. **Grips:** Laminated wood. **Sights:** Blade front, notch fixed rear. **Features:** All stainless steel construction. Polished satin and matte finish. Engraved models available. From North American Arms.
Price: .22 Short, .22 LR **$209.00**
Price: .22 WMR **$219.00**

NORTH AMERICAN ARMS MINI-MASTER
Caliber: .22 LR, .22 WMR, 5-shot cylinder. **Barrel:** 4" **Weight:** 10.7 oz. **Length:** 7.75" overall. **Grips:** Checkered hard black rubber. **Sights:** Blade front, white outline rear adjustable for elevation, or fixed. **Features:** Heavy vented barrel; full-size grips. Non-fluted cylinder. Introduced 1989.
Price: ....**$284.00 to $349.00**

NORTH AMERICAN ARMS BLACK WIDOW
Similar to Mini-Master, 2" heavy vent barrel. Built on .22 WMR frame. Non-fluted cylinder, black rubber grips. Available with Millett Low Profile fixed sights or Millett sight adjustable for elevation only. Overall length 5-7/8", weighs 8.8 oz. From North American Arms.
Price: Adjustable sight, .22 LR or .22 WMR **$309.00**
Price: Fixed sight, .22 LR or .22 WMR **$274.00**

NORTH AMERICAN ARMS "THE EARL" SINGLE-ACTION
Caliber: .22 Magnum with .22 LR accessory cylinder, 5-shot cylinder.

Barrel: 4" octagonal. **Weight:** 6.8 oz. **Length:** 7-3/4" overall. **Grips:** Wood. **Sights:** Barleycorn front and fixed notch rear. **Features:** Single-action mini-revolver patterned after 1858-style Remington percussion revolver. Includes a spur trigger and a faux loading lever that serves as cylinder pin release.
Price: ....**$289.00, $324.00** (convertible)

RUGER NEW MODEL SINGLE-SIX SERIES
Caliber: .22 LR, .17 HMR. **Capacity:** Six rounds. Convertible and Hunter models come with extra cylinder for .22 WMR. **Barrel:** 4.62, 5.5, 6.5 or 9.5 inches. **Weight:** 35 to 42 ounces. **Finish:** Blue or stainless. **Grips:** Black checkered hard rubber, black laminate or hardwood (stainless model only). Single-Six .17 Model available only with 6.5-inch barrel, blue finish, rubber grips. Hunter Model available only with 7.5-inch barrel, black laminate grips and stainless finish.
Price: (blue)...**$629.00**
Price: (stainless)..**$699.00**
Price: (Hunter) **$879.00**

RUGER SINGLE-TEN AND RUGER SINGLE-NINE SERIES
Caliber: .22 LR, .22 WMR. **Capacity:** 10 (.22 LR Single-Ten), 9 (.22 Mag Single-Nine). **Barrel:** 5.5 inches (Single-Ten), 6.5 inches (Single-Nine). **Weight:** 38 to 39 ounces. **Grips:** Hardwood Gunfighter. **Sights:** Williams Adjustable Fiber Optic.
Price: **$699.00**

RUGER NEW MODEL BLACKHAWK/ BLACKHAWK CONVERTIBLE
Caliber: .30 Carbine, .357 Mag./.38 Spec., .41 Mag., .44 Special, .45 Colt, 6-shot. **Barrel:** 4-5/8", 5.5", 6.5", 7.5" (.30 carbine and .45 Colt). **Weight:** 36 to 45 oz. **Lengths:** 10-3/8" to 13.5" **Grips:** Rosewood or black checkered. **Sights:** 1/8 ramp front, micro-click rear adjustable for windage and elevation. **Features:** Rosewood grips, Ruger transfer bar safety system, independent firing pin, hardened chrome-moly steel frame, music wire springs through-out. Case and lock included. Convertibles come with extra cylinder.
Price: (blue)..**$669.00**
Price: (Convertible, .357/9mm)..**$699.00**
Price: (Convertible, .45 Colt/.45 ACP) **$699.00**
Price: (stainless, .357 only) **$799.00**

RUGER BISLEY SINGLE-ACTION
Similar to standard Blackhawk, hammer is lower with smoothly

Prices given are believed to be accurate at time of publication however, many factors affect retail pricing so exact prices are not possible.

curved, deeply checkered wide spur. The trigger is strongly curved with wide smooth surface. Longer grip frame. Adjustable rear sight, ramp-style front. Unfluted cylinder and roll engraving, adjustable sights. Chambered for .44 Mag. and .45 Colt; 7.5" barrel; overall length 13.5"; weighs 48-51 oz. Plastic lockable case. Orig. fluted cylinder introduced 1985; discontinued 1991. Unfluted cylinder introduced 1986.

Price: RB-44W (.44 Mag.), RB45W (.45 Colt) **$825.00**

RUGER NEW MODEL SUPER BLACKHAWK

Caliber: .44 Mag., 6-shot. Also fires 44 Spec. **Barrel:** 4-5/8", 5.5", 7.5", 10.5" bull. **Weight:** 45-55 oz. **Length:** 10.5" to 16.5" overall. **Grips:** Rosewood. **Sights:** 1/8 ramp front, micro-click rear adjustable for windage and elevation. **Features:** Ruger transfer bar safety system, fluted or unfluted cylinder, steel grip and cylinder frame, round or square back trigger guard, wide serrated trigger, wide spur hammer. With case and lock.

Price: **$829.00**

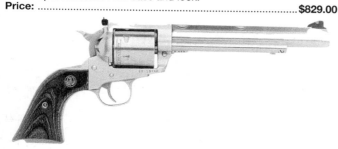

RUGER NEW MODEL SUPER BLACKHAWK HUNTER

Caliber: .44 Mag., 6-shot. **Barrel:** 7.5", full-length solid rib, unfluted cylinder. **Weight:** 52 oz. **Length:** 13-5/8" **Grips:** Black laminated wood. **Sights:** Adjustable rear, replaceable front blade. **Features:** Reintroduced Ultimate SA revolver. Includes instruction manual, high-impact case, set 1 medium scope rings, gun lock, ejector rod as standard. Bisley-style frame available.

Price: (Hunter, Bisley Hunter) **$959.00**

RUGER NEW VAQUERO SINGLE-ACTION

Caliber: .357 Mag., .45 Colt, 6-shot. **Barrel:** 4-5/8", 5.5", 7.5". **Weight:** 39-45 oz. **Length:** 10.5" overall (4-5/8" barrel). **Grips:** Rubber with Ruger medallion. **Sights:** Fixed blade front, fixed notch rear. **Features:** Transfer bar safety system and loading gate interlock. Blued model color case-hardened finish on frame, rest polished and blued. Engraved model available. Gloss stainless. Introduced 2005.

Price: **$829.00**

RUGER NEW MODEL BISLEY VAQUERO

Similar to New Vaquero but with Bisley-style hammer and grip frame. Chambered in .357 and .45 Colt. Features include a 5.5" barrel, simulated ivory grips, fixed sights, six-shot cylinder. Overall length is 11.12", weighs 45 oz.

Price: **$899.00**

RUGER NEW BEARCAT SINGLE-ACTION

Caliber: .22 LR, 6-shot. **Barrel:** 4" **Weight:** 24 oz. **Length:** 9" overall. **Grips:** Smooth rosewood with Ruger medallion. **Sights:** Blade front, fixed notch rear. Distributor special edition available with adjustable sights. **Features:** Reintroduction of the Ruger Bearcat with slightly lengthened frame, Ruger transfer bar safety system. Available in blue only. Rosewood grips. Introduced 1996 (blued), 2003 (stainless). With case and lock.

Price: SBC-4, blued **$639.00**
Price: KSBC-4, satin stainless **$689.00**

UBERTI 1851-1860 CONVERSION

Caliber: .38 Spec., .45 Colt, 6-shot engraved cylinder. **Barrel:** 4.75, 5.5, 7.5, 8" **Weight:** 2.6 lbs. (5.5" bbl.). **Length:** 13" overall (5.5" bbl.). **Grips:** Walnut. **Features:** Brass backstrap, triggerguard; color case-hardened frame, blued barrel, cylinder. Introduced 2007. Imported from Italy by Stoeger Industries.

Price: 1851 Navy **$569.00**
Price: 1860 Army **$589.00**

UBERTI 1871-1872 OPEN TOP

Caliber: .38 Spec., .45 Colt, 6-shot engraved cylinder. **Barrel:** 4.75, 5.5, 7.5". **Weight:** 2.6 lbs. (5.5" bbl.). **Length:** 13" overall (5.5" bbl.). **Grips:** Walnut. **Features:** Blued backstrap, triggerguard; color case-

Prices given are believed to be accurate at time of publication however, many factors affect retail pricing so exact prices are not possible.

71ST EDITION, 2017 ⊕ **433**

hardened frame, blued barrel, cylinder. Introduced 2007. Imported from Italy by Stoeger Industries.
Price: .... **$539.00 to $569.00**

UBERTI 1873 CATTLEMAN SINGLE-ACTION
Caliber: .45 Colt; 6-shot fluted cylinder. **Barrel:** 4.75, 5.5, 7.5". **Weight:** 2.3 lbs. (5.5" bbl.). **Length:** 11" overall (5.5" bbl.). **Grips:** Styles: Frisco (pearl styled); Desperado (buffalo horn styled); Chisholm (checkered walnut); Gunfighter (black checkered); Cody (ivory styled), one-piece walnut. **Sights:** Blade front, groove rear. **Features:** Steel or brass backstrap, triggerguard; color case-hardened frame, blued barrel, cylinder. NM designates New Model plunger style frame; OM designates Old Model screw cylinder pin retainer. Imported from Italy by Stoeger Industries.
Price: 1873 Cattleman Frisco $809.00
Price: 1873 Cattleman Desperado (2006) $819.00
Price: 1873 Cattleman Chisholm (2006) $549.00
Price: 1873 Cattleman NM, blued 4.75" barrel $619.00
Price: 1873 Cattleman NM, Nickel finish, 7.5" barrel ...$819.00
Price: 1873 Cattleman Cody...................................$819.00

UBERTI 1873 CATTLEMAN BIRD'S HEAD SINGLE ACTION
Caliber: .357 Mag., .45 Colt; 6-shot fluted cylinder. **Barrel:** 3.5, 4, 4.75, 5.5". **Weight:** 2.3 lbs. (5.5" bbl.). **Length:** 10.9" overall (5.5" bbl.). **Grips:** One-piece walnut. **Sights:** Blade front, groove rear. **Features:** Steel or brass backstrap, triggerguard; color case-hardened frame, blued barrel, cylinder. Imported from Italy by Stoeger Industries.
Price: $569.00

UBERTI CATTLEMAN .22
Caliber: .22 LR. **Capacity:** 6 or 12 rounds. **Barrel:** 5.5 inches **Grips:** One-piece walnut. **Sights:** Fixed. **Features:** Blued and case hardened finish, steel or brass backstrap/triggerguard.
Price: (brass backstrap, triggerguard) $509.00
Price: (steel backstrap, triggerguard).......................$529.00
Price: (12-shot model, steel backstrap, triggerguard) ..$559.00

UBERTI 1873 BISLEY SINGLE-ACTION
Caliber: .357 Mag., .45 Colt (Bisley); .22 LR and .38 Spec. (Stallion), both with 6-shot fluted cylinder. **Barrel:** 4.75, 5.5, 7.5". **Weight:** 2 to 2.5 lbs. **Length:** 12.7" overall (7.5" barrel). **Grips:** Two-piece walnut. **Sights:** Blade front, notch rear. **Features:** Replica of Colt's Bisley Model. Polished blue finish, color case-hardened frame. Introduced 1997. Imported by Stoeger Industries.
Price: 1873 Bisley, 7.5" barrel $599.00

UBERTI 1873 BUNTLINE AND REVOLVER CARBINE SINGLE-ACTION
Caliber: .357 Mag., .44-40, .45 Colt; 6-shot fluted cylinder **Barrel:** 18" **Length:** 22.9 to 34" **Grips:** Walnut pistol grip or rifle stock. **Sights:** Fixed or adjustable. **Features:** Imported from Italy by Stoeger Industries.
Price: 1873 Revolver Carbine, 18" barrel, 34" OAL $729.00
Price: 1873 Catttleman Buntline Target, 18" barrel, 22.9" OAL $639.00

UBERTI OUTLAW, FRONTIER, AND POLICE
Caliber: .45 Colt, 6-shot fluted cylinder. **Barrel:** 5.5", 7.5". **Weight:** 2.5 to 2.8 lbs. **Length:** 10.8" to 13.6" overall. **Grips:** Two-piece smooth walnut. **Sights:** Blade front, notch rear. **Features:** Cartridge version of 1858 Remington percussion revolver. Nickel and blued finishes. Imported by Stoeger Industries.
Price: 1875 Outlaw, nickel finish $629.00
Price: 1875 Frontier, blued finish $539.00
Price: 1890 Police, blued finish $549.00

UBERTI 1870 SCHOFIELD-STYLE TOP BREAK
Caliber: .38, .44 Russian, .44-40, .45 Colt, 6-shot cylinder. **Barrel:** 3.5, 5, 7". **Weight:** 2.4 lbs. (5" barrel) **Length:** 10.8" overall (5" barrel). **Grips:** Two-piece smooth walnut or pearl. **Sights:** Blade front, notch rear. **Features:** Replica of Smith & Wesson Model 3 Schofield. Single-action, top break with automatic ejection. Polished blue finish (first model). Introduced 1994. Imported by Stoeger Industries.
Price: No. 3-2nd Model, nickel finish $1,509.00

Prices given are believed to be accurate at time of publication however, many factors affect retail pricing so exact prices are not possible.

AMERICAN DERRINGER MODEL 1
Caliber: All popular handgun calibers plus .45 Colt/.410 Shotshell. **Capacity:** Two rounds, (.45-70 model is single shot). **Barrel:** 3 inches. **Overall length:** 4.82 inches. **Weight:** 15 oz. **Features:** Manually operated hammer-block safety automatically disengages when hammer is cocked.
Price: .... $635.00 to $735.00
Price: Texas Commemorative $835.00

AMERICAN DERRINGER MODEL 8
Caliber: .45 Colt/.410 shotshell. **Capacity:** Two rounds. **Barrel:** 8 inches. **Weight:** 24 oz.
Price: $915.00
Price: High polish finish $1,070.00

AMERICAN DERRINGER DA38
Caliber: .38 Special, .357 Magnum, 9mm Luger. **Barrel:** 3.3 inches. **Weight:** 14.5 oz. **Features:** Double-action operation with hammer-block thumb safety. Barrel, receiver and all internal parts are made from stainless steel.
Price: .... $690.00 to $740.00

BOND ARMS TEXAS DEFENDER DERRINGER
Caliber: Available in more than 10 calibers, from .22 LR to .45 LC/.410 shotshells. **Barrel:** 3". **Weight:** 20 oz. **Length:** 5". **Grips:** Rosewood. **Sights:** Blade front, fixed rear. **Features:** Interchangeable barrels, stainless steel firing pins, cross-bolt safety, automatic extractor for rimmed calibers. Stainless steel construction, brushed finish. Right or left hand.
Price: $493.00
Price: Interchangeable barrels, .22 LR thru .45 LC, 3" $139.00
Price: Interchangeable barrels, .45 LC, 3.5" .... $159.00 to $189.00

BOND ARMS RANGER II
Caliber: .45 LC/.410 shotshells or .357/.38 Spl. **Barrel:** 4.25" **Weight:** 23.5 oz. **Length:** 6.25" **Features:** This model has a triggerguard. Intr. 2011. From Bond Arms.
Price: $673.00

BOND ARMS CENTURY 2000 DEFENDER
Caliber: .45 LC/.410 shotshells. or .357/.38 Spl. **Barrel:** 3.5" **Weight:**

21 oz. **Length:** 5.5". **Features:** Similar to Defender series.
Price: $517.00

BOND ARMS COWBOY DEFENDER
Caliber: From .22 LR to .45 LC/.410 shotshells. **Barrel:** 3". **Weight:** 19 oz. **Length:** 5.5". **Features:** Similar to Defender series. No trigger guard.
Price: $493.00

BOND ARMS SNAKE SLAYER
Caliber: .45 LC/.410 shotshell (2.5" or 3"). **Barrel:** 3.5". **Weight:** 21 oz. **Length:** 5.5". **Grips:** Extended rosewood. **Sights:** Blade front, fixed rear. **Features:** Single-action; interchangeable barrels; stainless steel firing pin. Introduced 2005.
Price: $568.00

BOND ARMS SNAKE SLAYER IV
Caliber: .45 LC/.410 shotshell (2.5" or 3"). **Barrel:** 4.25". **Weight:** 22 oz. **Length:** 6.25". **Grips:** Extended rosewood. **Sights:** Blade front, fixed rear. **Features:** Single-action; interchangeable barrels; stainless steel firing pin. Introduced 2006.
Price: $613.00

COBRA BIG-BORE DERRINGERS
Caliber: .22 WMR, .32 H&R Mag., .38 Spec., 9mm Para., .380 ACP. **Barrel:** 2.75". **Weight:** 14 oz. **Length:** 4.65" overall. **Grips:** Textured black or white synthetic or laminated rosewood. **Sights:** Blade front, fixed notch rear. **Features:** Alloy frame, steel-lined barrels, steel breech block. Plunger-type safety with integral hammer block. Black, chrome or satin finish. Introduced 2002. Made in U.S.A. by Cobra Enterprises of Utah, Inc.
Price: $187.00

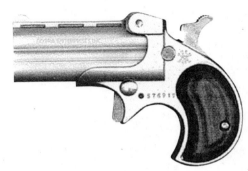

COBRA STANDARD SERIES DERRINGERS
Caliber: .22 LR, .22 WMR, .25 ACP, .32 ACP. **Barrel:** 2.4". **Weight:** 9.5 oz. **Length:** 4" overall. **Grips:** Laminated wood or pearl. **Sights:** Blade front, fixed notch rear. **Features:** Choice of black powder coat, satin nickel or chrome finish. Introduced 2002. Made in U.S.A. by Cobra Enterprises of Utah, Inc.
Price: $169.00

COBRA LONG-BORE DERRINGERS
Caliber: .22 WMR, .38 Spec., 9mm Para. **Barrel:** 3.5". **Weight:** 16 oz. **Length:** 5.4" overall. **Grips:** Black or white synthetic or rosewood. **Sights:** Fixed. **Features:** Chrome, satin nickel, or black Teflon finish.

Prices given are believed to be accurate at time of publication however, many factors affect retail pricing so exact prices are not possible.

71ST EDITION, 2017 ⊕ **435**

Introduced 2002. Made in U.S.A. by Cobra Enterprises of Utah, Inc.

Price: **$187.00**

COBRA TITAN
.45 LC/.410 DERRINGER
Caliber: .45 LC, .410 or 9mm, 2-round capacity. **Barrel:** 3-1/2". **Weight:** 16.4 oz. **Grip:** Rosewood. **Features:** Standard finshes include: satin stainless, black stainless, and brushed stainless. Made in U.S.A. by Cobra Enterprises of Utah, Inc.

Price: **$399.00**

COMANCHE SUPER SINGLE-SHOT
Caliber: .45 LC/.410 **Barrel:** 10". **Sights:** Adjustable. **Features:** Blue finish, not available for sale in CA, MA. Distributed by SGS Importers International, Inc.

Price: **$225.00**

DOUBLETAP DERRINGER
Caliber: .45 Colt or 9mm **Barrel:** 3". **Weight:** 12 ozs. **Length:** 5.5"

Sights: Adjustable. **Features:** Over/under, two-barrel design. Rounds are fired individually with two separate trigger pulls. Tip-up design, aluminum or titanium frame.

Price: Aluminum **$499.00**
Price: Titanium **$799.00**

HEIZER PS1 POCKET SHOTGUN
Caliber: .45 Colt or .410 shotshell. Single-shot. **Barrel:** Tip-up, 3.25 inches. **Weight:** 22 oz. **Length:** 5.6 inches. **Width:** .742 inches **Height:** 3.81 inches. **Features:** Available in several finishes. Standard model is matte stainless or black. Also offered in Hedy Jane series for the women in pink or in two-tone combinations of stainless and pink, blue, green, purple. Made in the U.S.A. by Heizer Industries.

Price: **$499.00**

HEIZER POCKET AR
Caliber: : .223 Rem./5.56 NATO. Similar to PS1 Pocket Shotgun but chambered for .223/5.56 rifle cartridge. Single shot. **Length:** 6-3/8 inches. **Weight:** 23 oz.

Price: **$499.00**

HENRY MARE'S LEG
Caliber: : .22 LR, .22 WMR, .357 Mag., .44 Mag., .45 Colt. **Capacity:** 10 rounds (.22 LR), 8 rounds (.22 WMR), 5 rounds (others). **Barrel:** 12.9 inches. **Length:** 25 inches. **Weight:** 4.5 lbs (rimfire) to 5.8 lbs. (centerfire calibers). Lever-action operation based on Henry rifle series and patterned after gun made famous in Steve McQueen '50s TV show, "Wanted: Dead or Alive." Made in the U.S.A. .
Price: .22 LR **$440.00**
Price: .22 WMR **$450.00**
Price: Centerfire calibers **$975.00**

HANDGUNS Miscellaneous

MAXIMUM SINGLE-SHOT

Caliber: .22 LR, .22 Hornet, .22 BR, .22 PPC, 223 Rem., 22-250, 6mm BR, 6mm PPC, 243, 250 Savage, 6.5mm-35M, 270 MAX, 270 Win., 7mm TCU, 7mm BR, 7mm-35, 7mm INT-R, 7mm-08, 7mm Rocket, 7mm Super-Mag., 30 Herrett, 30 Carbine, 30-30, 308 Win., 30x39, 32-20, 350 Rem. Mag., .357 Mag., .357 Maximum, 358 Win., 375 H&H, .44 Mag., .454 Casull. **Barrel:** 8.75", 10.5", 14". **Weight:** 61 oz. (10.5" bbl.); 78 oz. (14" bbl.). **Length:** 15", 18.5" overall (with 10.5" and 14" bbl., respectively). **Grips:** Smooth walnut stocks and fore-end. Also available with 17-finger-groove grip. **Sights:** Ramp front, fully adjustable open rear. **Features:** Falling block action; drilled and tapped for M.O.A. scope mounts; integral grip frame/receiver; adjustable trigger; Douglas barrel (interchangeable). Introduced 1983. Made in U.S.A. by M.O.A. Corp.
Price: $1,062.00

ROSSI MATCHED PAIR , "DUAL THREAT PERFORMER"

Caliber: .22LR, .44 Mag., .223, .243. .410, 20 gauge, single shot. Interchangeable rifle and shotgun barrels in various combinations. **Sights:** Fiber optic front sights, adjustable rear. **Features:** Two-in-one pistol system with sinle-shot simplicity. Removable choke and cushioned grip with a Taurus Security System.
Price: .22/.410 from $245.00
Price: .44 Mag/20 ga. from $352.00

ROSSI RANCH HAND

Caliber: .38/.357, .45 Colt or .44 magnum, 6-shot. **Weight:** 4 lbs. **Length:** 24" overall. **Stock:** Brazilian hardwood. **Sights:** Adjustable buckhorn. **Features:** Matte blue or case hardened finish with oversized lever loop to accomodate gloved hands. Equipped with classic buckhorn sights for fast target aquisition and a Taurus Security Sytem.
Price: .... $597.00 to $661.00

THOMPSON/CENTER ENCORE

Calibers: .17 HMR, .22 LR, .204 Ruger, .223, .22-250, .243, .270., 7mm-08, .308, .20-06, .44 Mag., .45 Colt/.410, .45-70 Govt., .460 S&W, .500 S&W. Single shot, break-open design. **Barrel:** 15 inches, 12 inches (.44 Mag., .45 Colt). **Weight:** 4.25 to 4.5 lbs. **Grip:** Walnut on blued models, rubber on stainless. Matching fore-end. **Sights:** Adjustable rear, ramp front. **Features:** Interchangeable barrels, adjustable trigger. Pro Hunter has "Swing Hammer" to allow reaching the hammer when the gun is scoped. Other Pro Hunter features include fluted barrel.
Price: From $779.00

THOMPSON/CENTER G2 CONTENDER

A second generation Contender pistol maintaining the same barrel interchangeability with older Contender barrels and their corresponding forends (except Herrett fore-end). The G2 frame will not accept old-style grips due to the change in grip angle. Incorporates an automatic hammer block safety with built-in interlock. Features include trigger adjustable for overtravel, adjustable rear sight; ramp front sight blade, blued steel finish.
Price: From $729.00

Prices given are believed to be accurate at time of publication however, many factors affect retail pricing so exact prices are not possible.

71ST EDITION, 2017 ✦ 437

ALEXANDER ARMS AR SERIES

Caliber: .17 HMR, 5.56 NATO, 6.5 Grendel, .300 AAC, .338 Lapua Mag., .50 Beowulf. This manufacturer produces a wide range of AR-15 type rifles and carbines. **Barrel:** 16, 18, 20 or 24 inches. Models are available for consumer, law enforcement and military markets. Depending on the specific model, features include forged flattop receiver with Picatinny rail, button-rifled stainless steel barrels, composite free-floating handguard, A2 flash hider, M4 collapsible stock, gas piston operating system.
Price: .17 HMR **$1,210.00**
Price: 5.56 NATO **$1,349.00**
Price: 6.5 Grendel .... **$1,540.00 to $1,750.00**
Price: .300 AAC **$1,349.00**
Price: .50 Beowulf.......................... **$1,375.00 to $1,750.00**

ALEXANDER ARMS ULFBERHT

Caliber: .338 Lapua Mag. Custom-designed adjustable gas-piston operating system. **Barrel:** 27.5-inch chrome moly with three-prong flash hider. **Stock:** Magpul PRS. **Length:** 41.25 inches (folded), 50 inches (extended stock). **Weight:** 19.8 lbs.
Price: Ulfberht .338 Lapua Mag.............................**$6,850.00**

ARMALITE M15A4 CARBINE

Caliber: .223 Rem., 30-round magazine. **Barrel:** 16" heavy chrome lined; 1:7" twist, flash suppressor. **Weight:** 6.8 lbs. **Length:** 36" overall. **Stock:** Green or black composition. **Sights:** Standard A2. **Features:** Forged flattop receiver with Picatinny rail, 8-inch handguard, anodize aluminum supper/lower receiver, flip-up sights.
Price: **$1,073.00**

ARMALITE AR-10A4 SPECIAL PURPOSE

Caliber: .243, .308 Win., 10- and 20-round magazine. **Barrel:** 20" chrome-lined, 1:11.25" twist. **Weight:** 9.6 lbs. **Length:** 41" overall. **Stock:** Green or black composition. **Sights:** Detachable handle, front sight, or scope mount available; comes with international style flattop receiver with Picatinny rail. **Features:** Forged upper receiver with case deflector. Receivers are hard-coat anodized. Introduced 1995. Made in U.S.A. by ArmaLite, Inc.
Price: **$1,571.00**

ARMALITE AR-10A2

Utilizing the same 20" double-lapped, heavy barrel as the ArmaLite AR10A4 Special Purpose Rifle. Offered in .308 Win. only. Made in U.S.A. by ArmaLite, Inc.
Price: AR-10A2 rifle or carbine **$1,561.00**

ARMALITE AR-10 SUPER SASS

Caliber: 7.62 NATO/.308 Win. **Barrel:** 20-inch ceramic coated stainless steel threaded with flash suppressor. **Weight:** 9.4 to 11.8 lbs. **Features:** Upper receiver has Picatinny rail, forward assist, adjustable sniper stock, Super Sass quad rail, floating handguard. Many optional accessories and variants.
Price: From **$3,100.00**

ARSENAL, INC. SLR-107F

Caliber: 7.62x39mm. **Barrel:** 16.25". **Weight:** 7.3 lbs. **Stock:** Left-side folding polymer stock. **Sights:** Adjustable rear. **Features:** Stamped receiver, 24mm flash hider, bayonet lug, accessory lug, stainless steel heat shield, two-stage trigger. Introduced 2008. Made in U.S.A. by Arsenal, Inc.
Price: SLR-107FR, includes scope rail **$1,099.00**

ARSENAL, INC. SLR-107CR

Caliber: 7.62x39mm. **Barrel:** 16.25". **Weight:** 6.9 lbs. **Stock:** Left-side folding polymer stock. **Sights:** Adjustable rear. **Features:** Stamped receiver, front sight block/gas block combination, 500-meter rear sight, cleaning rod, stainless steel heat shield, scope rail, and removable muzzle attachment. Introduced 2007. Made in U.S.A. by Arsenal, Inc.
Price: SLR-107CR **$1,119.00**

ARSENAL, INC. SLR-106CR

Caliber: 5.56 NATO. **Barrel:** 16.25", Steyr chrome-lined barrel, 1:7 twist rate. **Weight:** 6.9 lbs. **Stock:** Black polymer folding stock with cutout for scope rail. Stainless-steel heatshield handguard. **Sights:** 500-meter rear sight and rear sight block calibrated for 5.56 NATO. Warsaw Pact scope rail. **Features:** Uses Arsenal, Bulgaria, Mil-Spec receiver, two-stage trigger, hammer and disconnector. Polymer magazines in 5- and 10-round capacity in black and green, with Arsenal logo. Others are 30-round black waffles, 20- and 30-round versions in clear/smoke waffle, featuring the "10" in a double-circle logo of Arsenal, Bulgaria. Ships with 5-round magazine, sling, cleaning kit in a tube, 16" cleaning rod, oil bottle. Introduced 2007. Made in U.S.A. by Arsenal, Inc.
Price: SLR-106CR **$1,200.00**

AUTO-ORDNANCE 1927A-1 THOMPSON

Caliber: .45 ACP. **Barrel:** 16.5". **Weight:** 13 lbs. **Length:** About 41" overall (Deluxe). **Stock:** Walnut stock and vertical fore-end. **Sights:** Blade front, open rear adjustable for windage. **Features:** Recreation of Thompson Model 1927. Semiauto only. Deluxe model has finned barrel, adjustable rear sight and compensator; Standard model has plain barrel and military sight. Available with 100-round drum or 30-round stick magazine. From Auto-Ordnance Corp
Price: Deluxe w/stick magazine............................**$1,461.00**
Price: Deluxe w/drum magazine............................**$2,061.00**
Price: Lightweight model w/stick mag.................**$1,325.00**

AUTO-ORDNANCE THOMPSON M1/M1-C

Similar to the 1927 A-1 except is in the M-1 configuration with side cocking knob, horizontal fore-end, smooth unfinned barrel, sling swivels on butt and fore-end. Matte-black finish. Introduced 1985.
Price: M1 semiauto carbine.................................**$1,375.00**
Price: M1-C lightweight semiauto **$1,241.00**

AUTO-ORDNANCE 1927 A-1 COMMANDO

Similar to the 1927 A-1 except has Parkerized finish, black-finish wood butt, pistol grip, horizontal fore-end. Comes with black nylon sling. Introduced 1998. Made in U.S.A. by Auto-Ordnance Corp.
Price: T1-C...**$1,393.00**

AUTO ORDNANCE M1 CARBINE

Caliber: .30 Carbine (15-shot magazine). **Barrel:** 18". **Weight:** 5.4 to 5.8 lbs. **Length:** 36.5". **Stock:** Wood or polymer. **Sights:** Blade front, flip-style rear. A faithful recreation of the military carbine.
Price: **$846.00**

BARRETT MODEL 82A-1 SEMI-AUTOMATIC

Caliber: .416 Barret, 50 BMG, 10-shot detachable box magazine. **Barrel:** 29". **Weight:** 28.5 lbs. **Length:** 57" overall. **Stock:** Composition with energy-absorbing recoil pad. **Sights:** Scope optional. **Features:** Semiautomatic, recoil operated with recoiling barrel. Three-lug locking bolt; muzzle brake. Adjustable bipod. Introduced 1985. Made in U.S.A. by Barrett Firearms.
Price: From **$9,119.00**

BARRETT M107A1

Caliber: 50 BMG. 10-round detachable magazine. **Barrel:** 20 or 29 inches. **Sights:** 27-inch optics rail with flip-up iron sights. **Weight:** 30.9 lbs. **Finish:** Flat Dark Earth. Features: Four-port cylindrical muzzle brake. Quick-detachable Barrett QDL Suppressor. Adjustable bipod and monopod.
Price: **$12,281.00**

BARRETT MODEL REC7 GEN II

Caliber: 5.56 (.223), 6.8 Rem. SPC. 30-round magazine. **Barrel:** 16 inches. **Sights:** ARMS rear, folding front. Weight: 28.7 lbs. **Features:** AR-style configuration with standard 17-4 stainless piston system, two-position forward venting gas plug, chrome-lined gas block, A2 flash hider, 6-postion MOE stock.
Price: **$2,759.00**

BENELLI R1

Caliber: .30-06 (4+1), .300 Win Mag (3+1), .338 Win Mag (3+1). **Weight:** 7.1 lbs. **Length:** 43.75" to 45.75". **Stock:** Select satin walnut or synthetic. **Sights:** None. **Features:** Auto-regulating gas-operated system, three-lug rotary bolt, interchangeable barrels, optional recoil pads. Introduced 2003. Imported from Italy by Benelli USA.
Price: **$1,019.00**

BENELLI MR1

Gas-operated semiauto rifle chambered in 5.56 NATO. Features include 16-inch, 1:9 twist, hard chrome-lined barrel, synthetic stock with pistol grip, rotating bolt, military-style aperture sights with picatinny rail. Comes equipped with 5-round detachable magazine but accepts M16 magazines.
Price: **$1,339.00**

BROWNING BAR SAFARI AND SAFARI W/BOSS SEMI-AUTO

Caliber: Safari: .25-06 Rem., .270 Win., 7mm Rem. Mag., .30-06 Spfl., .308 Win., .300 Win. Mag., .338 Win. Mag. Safari w/BOSS: .270 Win., 7mm Rem. Mag., .30-06 Spfl., .300 Win. Mag., .338 Win. Mag. **Barrel:** 22-24" round tapered. **Weight:** 7.4-8.2 lbs. **Length:** 43-45" overall. **Stock:** French walnut pistol grip stock and fore-end, hand checkered. **Sights:** No sights. **Features:** Has new bolt release lever; removable trigger assembly with larger triggerguard; redesigned gas and buffer systems. Detachable 4-round box magazine. Scroll-engraved receiver is tapped for scope mounting. BOSS barrel vibration modulator and muzzle brake system available. Mark II Safari introduced 1993. Made in Belgium.
Price: BAR MK II Safari, from **$1,230.00**
Price: BAR Safari w/BOSS, from **$1,400.00**

BROWNING BAR SHORTTRAC/LONGTRAC

Caliber: (ShortTrac models) .270 WSM, 7mm WSM, .300 WSM, .243 Win., .308 Win., .325 WSM; (LongTrac models) .270 Win., .30-06 Spfl., 7mm Rem. Mag., .300 Win. Mag. **Barrel:** 23". **Weight:** 6 lbs. 10 oz. to 7 lbs. 4 oz. **Length:** 41.5" to 44". **Stock:** Satin-finish walnut, pistol-grip, fluted fore-end. **Sights:** Adj. rear, bead front standard, no sights on BOSS models (optional). **Features:** Designed to handle new WSM chamberings. Gas-operated, blued finish, rotary bolt design (LongTrac models).
Price: BAR ShortTrac, .243 Win., .308 Win. from **$1,230.00**
Price: BAR ShortTrac Left-Hand, intr. 2007, from **$1,270.00**
Price: BAR ShortTrac Mossy Oak New Break-up
.... **$1,260.00 to $1,360.00**
Price: BAR LongTrac Left Hand, .270 Win., .30-06 Spfl.,
from **$1,270.00**
Price: BAR LongTrac, from **$1,200.00**
Price: BAR LongTrac Mossy Oak Break Up, from **$1,360.00**

BROWNING BAR STALKER

Caliber: .243 Win., 7mm-08, .308 Win., .270 Win., .30-06 Spfl., .270 WSM, 7mm WSM, .300 WSM, .300 Win. Mag., .338 Win. Mag. **Barrel:** 20-24". **Weight:** 7.1-7.75 LBS. **Length:** 41-45" overall. **Stock:** Black composite stock and forearm. **Sights:** Hooded front and adjustable rear. **Features:** Gas-operated action with seven-lug rotary bolt; dual action bars; 2-, 3- or 4-shot magazine (depending on cartridge). Introduced 2001. Imported by Browning.
Price: BAR ShortTrac or LongTrac Stalker, from.................... **$1,350.00**
Price: BAR Lightweight Stalker, from.................................... **$1,260.00**

BUSHMASTER 308 HUNTER

Caliber: .308 Win / 7.62 NATO., 5-round magazine. **Barrel:** 20". **Weight:** 8-1/2 lbs. **Length:** 38-1/4" overall. **Stock:** Standard A2 stock with Hogue® rubberized pistol grip. **Sights:** Two ¾" mini-risers for optics mounting. **Features:** Bushmaster .308 Rifles

Prices given are believed to be accurate at time of publication however, many factors affect retail pricing so exact prices are not possible.

71ST EDITION, 2017 ✛ **439**

were developed for the Hunter who intends to immediately add optics (scope, red dot or holographic sight) to the rifle. The premium 20" heavy fluted profile barrel is chrome lined in both bore and chamber to provide Bushmaster accuracy, durability and maintenance ease.
Price: .308 Hunter. **$1,685.00**

BUSHMASTER ACR
Caliber: 5.56mm, 6.5mm, 6.8mm., 30-round polymer magazine. **Barrel:** All three calibers are availaible with 10-1/2", 14-1/2", 16-1/2" and 18" barrels. **Weight:** 14-1/2" bbl. 7 lbs.. **Length:** 14-1/5" bbl. with stock folded: 25-3/4", with stock deployed (mid) 32-5/8", 10.5" bbl. with stock folded: 21-5/16", with stock deployed (mid): 27-7/8", with stock deployed and extended: 31-3/4". Folding Stock Length of Pull - 3". **Stock:** Fixed high-impact composite A-frame stock with rubber buttpad and sling mounts. **Features:** Cold hammer-forged barrels with melonite coating for extreme long life. A2 birdcage-type hider to control muzzle flash and adjustable, two-position, gas piston-driven system for firing suppressed or unsuppressed, supported by hardened internal bearing rails. The Adaptive Combat Rifle (ACR) features a tool-less, quick-change barrel system available in 10.5", 14.5" and 16.5" and in multiple calibers. Multi-caliber bolt carrier assembly quickly and easily changes from .223/5.56mm NATO to 6.8mm Rem SPC (spec II chamber). Free-floating MIL-STD 1913 monolithic top rail for optic mounting. Fully ambidextrous controls including magazine release, bolt catch and release, fire selector and nonreciprocating charging handle. High-impact composite handguard with heat shield – accepts rail inserts. High-impact composite lower receiver with textured magazine well and modular grip storage. Fire Control – Semi and Full Auto two-stage standard AR capable of accepting drop-in upgrade. Magazine – Optimized for MagPul PMAG Accepts standard NATO/M-16 magazines.
Price: Basic Folder Configuration...**$2,149.00**
Price: ACR Enhanced **$2,249.00**

BUSHMASTER HEAVY-BARRELED CARBINE
Caliber: 5.56/.223. **Barrel:** 16". **Weight:** 6.93 lbs. to 7.28 lbs. **Length:** 32.5" overall. **Features:** AR-style carbine with chrome-lined heavy profile vanadium steel barrel, fixed or removable carry handle, six-position telestock.
Price: **$895.00**
Price: A3 with removable handle **$1,420.00**

BUSHMASTER MODULAR CARBINE
Caliber: 5.56/.223, 30-shot mag. **Barrel:** 16". **Weight:** 7.3 lbs. **Length:** 36.25" overall. **Features:** AR-style carbine with chrome-lined chrome-moly vanadium steel barrel, skeleton stock or six-position telestock, clamp-on front sight and detachable flip-up dual aperature rear.
Price: **$1,745.00**

BUSHMASTER 450 RIFLE AND CARBINE
Caliber: .450 Bushmaster. **Barrel:** 20" (rifle), 16" (carbine), five-round mag. **Weight:** 8.3 lbs. (rifle), 8.1 lbs. (carbine). **Length:** 39.5" overall (rifle), 35.25" overall (carbine). **Features:** AR-style with chrome-lined chrome-moly barrel, synthetic stock, Izzy muzzlebrake.
Price: Carbine **$1,285.00**
Price: Rifle **$1,300.00**

BUSHMASTER TARGET
Caliber: 5.56/.223, 30-shot mag. **Barrel:** 20 or 24-inch heavy or standard. **Weight:** 8.43 lbs. to 9.29 lbs. **Length:** 39.5" or 43.5" overall. **Features:** Semiauto AR-style with chrome-lined or stainless steel 1:9" twist barrel, fixed or removable carry handle, manganese phosphate finish.
Price: .... **$969.00 to $1,000.00**

BUSHMASTER M4A3 TYPE CARBINE
Caliber: 5.56/.223, 30-shot mag. **Barrel:** 16". **Weight:** 6.22 to 6.7 lbs. **Length:** 31 to 32.5 inches overall. **Features:** AR-style carbine with

chrome-moly vanadium steel barrel, Izzy-type flash hider, six-position telestock, various sight options, standard or multi-rail handguard, fixed or removable carry handle.
Price: **$1,100.00**

BUSHMASTER QUICK RESPONSE CARBINE
Caliber: 5.56/223, 10-shot mag. **Barrel:** 16" chromemoly superlight contour with Melonite finish. **Features:** Mini red dot detachable sight, 6-position collapsible stock, A2 type flash hider. Introduced in 2016.
Price: **$769.00**

CENTURY INTERNATIONAL AES-10 HI-CAP
Caliber: 7.62x39mm. 30-shot magazine. **Barrel:** 23.2". **Weight:** NA. **Length:** 41.5" overall. **Stock:** Wood grip, fore-end. **Sights:** Fixed notch rear, windage-adjustable post front. **Features:** RPK-style, accepts standard double-stack AK-type mags. Side-mounted scope mount, integral carry handle, bipod. Imported by Century Arms Int'l.
Price: AES-10, from **$450.00**

CENTURY INTERNATIONAL GP WASR-10 HI-CAP
Caliber: 7.62x39mm. 30-shot magazine. **Barrel:** 16.25", 1:10 right-hand twist. **Weight:** 7.2 lbs. **Length:** 34.25" overall. **Stock:** Wood laminate or composite, grip, forend. **Sights:** Fixed notch rear, windage-adjustable post front. **Features:** Two 30-rd. detachable box magazines, cleaning kit, bayonet. Version of AKM rifle; U.S.-parts added for BATFE compliance. Threaded muzzle, folding stock, bayonet lug, compensator, Dragunov stock available. Made in Romania by Cugir Arsenal. Imported by Century Arms Int'l.
Price: GP WASR-10, from..**$450.00**

CENTURY INTERNATIONAL M70AB2 SPORTER
Caliber: 7.62x39mm. 30-shot magazine. **Barrel:** 16.25". **Weight:** 7.5 lbs. **Length:** 34.25" overall. **Stocks:** Metal grip, wood fore-end. **Sights:** Fixed notch rear, windage-adjustable post front. **Features:** Two 30-rd. double-stack magazine, cleaning kit, compensator, bayonet lug and bayonet. Paratrooper-style Kalashnikov with under-folding stock. Imported by Century Arms Int'l.
Price: M70AB2, from **$480.00**

COLT LE6920
Caliber: 5.56 NATO. **Barrel:** 16.1-inch chrome lined. **Sights:** Adjustable. Based on military M4. Features include Magpul MOE handguard, carbine stock, pistol grip, vertical grip. Direct gas/locking bolt operating system.
Price: From **$1,049.00**

COLT LE6940
Caliber: 5.56 NATO. Similar to LE1920 with Magpul MBUS backup sight, folding front, four accessory rails. One-piece monolithic upper receiver has continuous Mil Spec rail from rear of upper to the front sight. Direct gas (LE6940) or articulating link piston (LE6940P) system.
Price: LE6940 ....**$1,399.00**

COLT EXPANSE M4
Caliber: 5.56 NATO, capacity 30 rounds. **Barrel:** 16.1 inches. **Sights:** Adjustable front post. Comes optic ready. **Weight:** 6.4 lbs. Flattop Picatinny rail. **Stock:** Adjustable M4 with A2 style grip. Economy

priced AR. Introduced in 2016.

Price: $699.00

COLT MARC 901 MONOLITHIC
Caliber: .308. **Capacity:** 20 rounds. **Barrel:** 16.1 or 18" heavy fully floated with bayonet lug, flash hider. **Stock:** Adjustable VLTOR. **Sights:** Mil Spec Flip Up. **Weight:** 9.4 pounds. **Features:** One-piece flattop upper receiver with Picatinny rail, ambidextrous controls, matte black finish. Carbine model has muzzlebrake, retractable B% Bravo stock, full length Picatinny rail. Tubular handguard with 3 rails.

Price: $1,999.00
Price: Carbine $1,399.00

DANIEL DEFENSE AR SERIES
Caliber: 5.56 NATO/.223. 20-round Magpul PMAG magazine. **Barrel:** 16 or 18 inches. Flash suppressor. **Weight:** 7.4 lbs. **Length:** 34.75" to 37.85" overall. **Stock:** Glass-filled polymer with Soft Touch overmolding. Pistol grip. **Sights:** None. **Features:** Lower receiver is Mil Spec with enhanced and flared magazine well, QD swivel attachment point. Upper receiver has M4 feed ramps. Lower and upper CNC machined of 7075-T6 aluminum, hard coat anodized. Shown is MK12, one of many AR variants offered by Daniel Defense. Made in the U.S.A.

Price: From $1,599.00
Price: DD5VI 7.62/.308 ....$2,899.00

DPMS VARMINT SERIES
Caliber: .204 Ruger, .223. **Barrel:** 16", 20" or 24" bull or fluted profile. **Weight:** 7.75 to 11.75 lbs. **Length:** 34.5" to 42.25" overall. **Stock:** Black Zytel composite. **Sights:** None. **Features:** Flattop receiver with Picatinny top rail; hardcoat anodized receiver; aluminum free-float tube handguard; many options. From DPMS Panther Arms.

Price: .... $939.00 to $1,229.00

DPMS PRAIRIE PANTHER
Semiauto AR-style rifle chambered in 5.56 NATO or 6.8 SPC. Features include 20-inch 416 stainless fluted heavy 1:8" barrel; phosphated steel bolt; free-floated carbon fiber handguard; flattop upper with Picatinny rail; aluminum lower; two 30-round magazines; skeletonized Zytel stock; Choice of matte black or one of several camo finishes.

Price: .... $1,269.00 to $1,289.00

DPMS REPR
Semiauto AR-style rifle chambered in .308 Win./7.62 NATO. Features include 18-inch 416 stainless steel 1:10" twist barrel; phosphated steel bolt; 4-rail free-floated handguard; no sights; aluminum lower; bipoad; two 19-round magazines; Coyote Brown camo finish overall. Scope not included.

Price: $2,549.00

DPMS MK12
Caliber: .308 Win./7.62 NATO. **Barrel:** 18 inches. **Weight:** 8.5 lbs. **Sights:** Midwest Industry flip-up. **Features:** 4-rail free floating handguard, flash hider, extruded 7029 T6 A3 Flattop receiver.

Price: $1,759.00

DPMS 3G2
Caliber: .223/5.56. **Barrel:** 16 inches. **Weight:** 7.1 lbs. **Stock:** Magpul STR with Hogue rubber pistol grip. **Sights:** Magpul Gen 2 BUS. **Features:** Miculek Compensator, two-stage fire control. M111 Modular handguard allows placement of sights on top rail or 45-degree angle.

Price: $1,239.00

DPMS LITE HUNTER
Caliber: .243, .260 Rem., .308, .338 Federal. **Barrel:** 20 inches, stainless. **Weight:** 8 pounds. **Stock:** Standard A2. **Features:** Two-stage match trigger. Hogue pistol grip. Optics ready top rail.

Price: $1,499.00

DPMS .300 AAC BLACKOUT
Caliber: .300 AAC Blackout. **Barrel:** 16-inch heavy 4150 chrome-lined. **Weight:** 7 pounds. **Stock:** Adjustable 6-position.

Price: $1,199.00

DPMS ORACLE
Caliber: .223/5.56 or .308/7.62. **Barrel:** 16 inches. **Weight:** 6.2 (.223), 8.3 (308). Standard AR-15 fire control with A3 flattop receiver. **Finish:** Matte black or A-TACS camo.

Price: .223...$739, $849 (A-TACS)
Price: .308................................... $1,099, $1,189 (A-TACS)

Prices given are believed to be accurate at time of publication however, many factors affect retail pricing so exact prices are not possible.

71ST EDITION, 2017 ✦ **441**

DPMS GII SERIES

Caliber: .308 Win./7.62 NATO. **Barrel:** 16, 18 inches. **Weight:** From 7.25 lbs., promoted as the lightest .308 AR available. Features include new extractor and ejector systems, and improved steel feed ramp. New bolt geometry provides better lock-up and strength. Offered in several configurations.

Price: AP4 (shown)	**$1,499.00**
Price: Recon	**$1,759.00**
Price: SASS	**$2,379.00**
Price: Hunter	**$1,699.00**
Price: Bull	**$1,759.00**
Price: MOE	**$1,599.00**

DSA SA58 CONGO, PARA CONGO

Caliber: .308 Win. **Barrel:** 18" w/short Belgian short flash hider. **Weight:** 8.6 lbs. (Congo); 9.85 lbs. (Para Congo). **Length:** 39.75" **Stock:** Synthetic w/military grade furniture (Congo); Synthetic with nonfolding steel para stock (Para Congo). **Sights:** Elevation adjustable protected post front sight, windage adjustable rear peep (Congo); Belgian type Para Flip Rear (Para Congo). **Features:** FAL-style rifle with fully adjustable gas system, high-grade steel upper receiver with carry handle. Made in U.S.A. by DSA, Inc.

Price: Congo	**$1,975.00**
Price: Para Congo	**$2,200.00**

DSA SA58 STANDARD

Caliber: .308 Win. **Barrel:** 21" bipod cut w/threaded flash hider. **Weight:** 8.75 lbs. **Length:** 43" **Stock:** Synthetic, X-Series or optional folding para stock. **Sights:** Elevation-adjustable post front, windage-adjustable rear peep. **Features:** Fully adjustable short gas system, high-grade steel or 416 stainless upper receiver. Made in U.S.A. by DSA, Inc.

Price: From **$1,700.00**

DSA SA58 CARBINE

Caliber: .308 Win. **Barrel:** 16.25" bipod cut w/threaded flash hider. **Features:** Carbine variation of FAL-style rifle. Other features identical to SA58 Standard model. Made in U.S.A. by DSA, Inc.

Price: **$1,700.00**

DSA SA58 TACTICAL CARBINE

Caliber: .308 Win. **Barrel:** 16.25" fluted with A2 flash hider. **Weight:** 8.25 lbs. **Length:** 36.5". **Stock:** Synthetic, X-Series or optional folding para stock. **Sights:** Elevation-adjustable post front, windage-adjustable match rear peep. **Features:** Shortened fully adjustable short gas system, high grade steel or 416 stainless upper receiver. Made in U.S.A. by DSA, Inc.

Price: **$1,975.00**

DSA SA58 MEDIUM CONTOUR

Caliber: .308 Win. **Barrel:** 21" w/threaded flash hider. **Weight:** 9.75 lbs. **Length:** 43". **Stock:** Synthetic military grade. **Sights:** Elevation-adjustable post front, windage-adjustable match rear peep. **Features:** Gas-operated semiauto with fully adjustable gas system, high grade steel receiver. Made in U.S.A. by DSA, Inc.

Price: **$1,700.00**

DSA ZM4 AR SERIES

Caliber: .223/5.56 NATO. Standard Flattop rifle features include 20-inch, chrome moly heavy barrel with A2 flash hider. **Weight:** 9 pounds. **Features:** Mil-Spec forged lower receiver, forged flattop or A2 upper. Fixed A2 stock. Carbine variations are also available with 16-inch barrels and many options.

Price: Standard Flat-Top	**$788.00**
Price: .300 Blackout	**$853.00**
Price: Enhanced Carbine	**$929.00**
Price: Flat-Top with rail	**$1,050.00**

EXCEL ARMS ACCELERATOR

Caliber: .17 HMR, .22 WMR, 5.7x28mm, 9-shot magazine. **Barrel:** 18" fluted stainless steel bull barrel. **Weight:** 8 lbs. **Length:** 32.5" overall. **Grips:** Textured black polymer. **Sights:** Fully adjustable target sights. **Features:** Made from 17-4 stainless steel, aluminum shroud w/ Weaver rail, manual safety, firing-pin block, last-round bolt-hold-open feature. Four packages with various equipment available. American made, lifetime warranty. Comes with one 9-round stainless steel magazine and a California-approved cable lock. Introduced 2006. Made in U.S.A. by Excel Arms.

Price: MR-17 .17 HMR	**$672.00**
Price: MR-22 .22 WMR	**$538.00**

EXCEL ARMS X-SERIES

Caliber: .22 LR, 5.7x28mm (10 or 25-round); .30 Carbine (10 or 20-round magazine). 9mm (10 or 17 rounds). **Barrel:** 18". **Weight:** 6.25 lbs. **Length:** 34 to 38". **Features:** Available with or without adjustable iron sights. Blow-back action (5.57x28) or delayed blow-back (.30 Carbine).

Price: .22 LR	**$504.00**
Price: 5.7x28 or 9mm	**$795.00 to $916.00**

FNH FNAR COMPETITION

Caliber: .308 Win., 10-shot magazine. **Barrel:** 20" fluted. **Weight:** 8.9 lbs. **Length:** 41.25" overall. **Sights:** None furnished. Optical rail atop

receiver, three accessory rails on fore-end. **Stock:** Adjustable for comb height, length of pull, cast-on and cast-off. Blue/gray laminate. Based on BAR design.

Price: $1,767.00

FNH SCAR 16S
Caliber: 5.56mm/.223. **Capacity:** 10 or 30 rounds. **Barrel:** 16.25". **Weight:** 7.25 lbs. **Length:** 27.5 to 37.5 " (extended stock). **Stock:** Telescoping, side-folding polymer. Adjustable cheekpiece, A2 style pistol grip. **Sights:** Adjustable folding front and rear. **Features:** Hard anodized aluminum receiver with four accessory rails. Ambidextrous safety and mag release. Charging handle can be mounted on right or left side. Semiauto version of newest service rifle of U.S. Special Forces.

Price: $2,995.00

FNH SCAR 17S
Caliber: 7.62x51mm/.308. **Capacity:** 10 or 30 rounds. **Barrel:** 16.25". **Weight:** 8 lbs. **Length:** 28.5 to 38.5 " (extended stock). **Features:** Other features the same as SCAR 16S.

Price: $3,349.00

FRANKLIN ARMORY 3 GR-L
Caliber: 5.56mm/.223. **Capacity:** 10 or 30 rounds. **Barrel:** 18" fluted with threaded muzzle crown. **Weight:** 7.25 lbs. **Stock:** Magpul PRS. Adjustable comb and length of pull. **Features:** Hard anodized Desert Smoke upper receiver with full length Picatinny rail. One of many AR type rifles and carbines offered by this manufacturer. Made in the U.S.A.

Price: $2,310.00

HECKLER & KOCH MODEL MR556A1
Caliber: .223 Remington/5.56 NATO, 10+1 capacity. **Barrel:** 16.5". **Weight:** 8.9 lbs. **Length:** 33.9"-37.68". **Stock:** Black Synthetic Adjustable. **Features:** Uses the gas piston system found on the HK 416 and G26, which does not introduce propellant gases and carbon fouling into the rifle's interior.

Price: $3,295.00

HECKLER & KOCH MODEL MR762A1
Caliber: Similar to Model MR556A1 except chambered for 7.62x51mm/.308 Win. cartridge. **Weight:** 10 lbs. w/empty magazine. **Length:** 36 to 39.5". Variety of optional sights are available. Stock has five adjustable positions.

Price: $3,995.00

HIGH STANDARD HSA-15
Caliber: .223 Remington/5.56 NATO or 6x45mm. A2 style with 16 or 20" barrel, 30 capacity magazine, fixed or collapsible stock, adjustable sights. Made by High Standard Manufacturing Co.

Price: $965.00

HI-POINT 9MM CARBINE
Caliber: 9mm Para. .40 S&W, (10-shot magazine); .45 ACP (9-shot). **Barrel:** 16.5" (17.5" for .40 S&W and .45). **Weight:** 4.5 lbs. **Length:** 31.5" overall. **Stock:** Black polymer, camouflage. **Sights:** Protected post front, aperture rear. Integral scope mount. **Features:** Grip-mounted magazine release. Black or chrome finish. Sling swivels. Available with laser or red-dot sights, RGB 4X scope, forward grip. Introduced 1996. Made in U.S.A. by MKS Supply, Inc.

Price: 9mm (995TS) from $286.00
Price: .40 S&W (4095TS) from $315.00
Price: .45 ACP (4595TS) from $319.00

INLAND M1 1945 CARBINE
Caliber: .30 Carbine. **Capacity:** 15 rounds. **Barrel:** 18". **Weight:** 5 lbs. 3 oz. A faithful reproduction of the last model that Inland manufactured in 1945, featuring a type 3 bayonet lug/barrel band, adjustable rear sight, push button safety, and walnut stock. Scout Model has 16.5" barrel, flash hider, synthetic stock with accessory rail. Made in the USA.

Price: $1,079.00
Price: Scout Model $1,199.00

JP ENTERPRISES LRP-07
Caliber: .308 Win., .260 Rem., 6.5 Creedmoor, .338 Federal. **Barrel:** 16 to 22 inches, polished stainless with compensator. **Buttstock:** A2, ACE ARFX, Tactical Tactical Intent Carbine, Magpul MOE. **Grip:** Hogue Pistol Grip. **Features:** Machined upper and lower receivers with left-side charging system. MKIII Hand Guard. Adjustable gas system.

Price: From $3,299.00

JP ENTERPRISES JP-15
Caliber: .223, .204 Ruger, 6.5 Grendel, .300 Blackout, .22 LR. **Barrel:** 18 or 24-inches. **Buttstock:** Synthetic modified thumbhole or laminate thumb-hole. **Grip:** Hogue Pistol grip. Basic AR-type general-purpose rifle with numerous options.

Price: From $1,999.00

KALASHNIKOV USA
Caliber: 7.62x39mm. 30-round magazine. AK-47 series made in the USA in several variants and styles. **Barrel:** 16.25". **Weight:** 7.52 lbs.
Price: US132S Synthetic stock...$799.00
Price: US132W Wood carbine $836.00

KEL-TEC RFB
Caliber: 7.62 NATO/.308. 20-round FAL-type magazine. **Barrel:** 18" with threaded muzzle, A2-style flash hider. **Weight:** 8 lbs.

Features: A bullpup short-stroke gas piston operated carbine with ambidextrous controls, reversible operating handle, Mil-Spec Picatinny rail.
Price: $1,927.00

KEL-TEC SU-16 SERIES
Caliber: 5.56 NATO/.223. 10-round magazine capacity. **Barrel:** 16 or 18.5". **Weight:** 4.5 to 5 lbs. **Features:** Offering in several rifle and carbine variations.
Price: From $682.00

LARUE TACTICAL OBR
Caliber: 5.56 NATO/.223, 7.62 NATO/.308 Win. **Barrel:** 16.1, 18 or 20 inches. **Weight:** 7.5 to 9.25 lbs. **Features:** Manufacturer of several models of AR-style rifles and carbines. Optimized Battle Rifle (OBR) series is made in both NATO calibers. Many AR-type options available. Made in the U.S.A.
Price: OBR 5.56 ....$2,245.00
Price: OBR 7.62 ....$3,370.00

LEWIS MACHINE & TOOL (LMT)
Caliber: 5.56 NATO/.223, 7.62 NATO/.308 Win. **Barrel:** 16.1, 18 or 20 inches. **Weight:** 7.5 to 9.25 lbs. **Features:** Manufacturer of a wide range of AR-style carbines with many options. SOPMOD stock, gas piston operating system, monolithic rail platform, tactical sights. Made in the U.S.A. by Lewis Machine & Tool.
Price: Standard 16 ....$1,594.00
Price: Comp 16, flattop receiver $1,685.00
Price: CQB Series from $2,100.00
Price: Sharpshooter Weapons System $5,198.00

LES BAER CUSTOM ULTIMATE AR 223
Caliber: .223. **Barrel:** 18", 20", 22", 24". **Weight:** 7.75 to 9.75 lb. **Length:** NA. **Stock:** Black synthetic. **Sights:** None furnished; Picatinny-style flattop rail for scope mounting. **Features:** Forged receiver; Ultra single-stage trigger (Jewell two-stage trigger optional); titanium firing pin; Versa-Pod bipod; chromed National Match carrier; stainless steel, hand-lapped and cryo-treated barrel; guaranteed to shoot 1/2 or 3/4 MOA, depending on model. Made in U.S.A. by Les Baer Custom Inc.
Price: Super Varmint Model .... **$2,640.00 to $2870.00**
Price: Super Match Model .... **$2,740.00 to $2960.00**
Price: M4 Flattop model $2,590.00
Price: Police Special 16" (2008) $1,790.00
Price: IPSC Action Model $2,890.00
Price: LBC-AR (.264 LBC-AR) $2,640.00

LES BAER UTIMATE MATCH/SNIPER
Caliber: .308 Win. **Barrel:** 18 or 20 in. Magpul stock, Enforcer

muzzlebrake.
Price: $3,940.00

LR 300S
Caliber: 5.56 NATO, 30-shot magazine. **Barrel:** 16.5"; 1:9" twist. **Weight:** 7.4-7.8 lbs. **Length:** NA. **Stock:** Folding. **Sights:** YHM flip front and rear. **Features:** Flattop receive, full length top picatinny rail. Phantom flash hider, multi sling mount points, field strips with no tools. Made in U.S.A. from Z-M Weapons.
Price: AXL, AXLT $2,139.00
Price: NXL $2,208.00

LWRC INTERNATIONAL M6 SERIES
Caliber: 5.56 NATO or 6.8 SPC, 30-shot magazine. REPR (Rapid Engagement Precision Rifle) chambered in 7.62 NATO/.308 Win. **Barrel:** 16.1 inches (16, 18, 20 inches, REPR). This company makes a complete line of AR-15 type rifles operated by a short-stroke, gas piston system. A wide variety of stock, sight and finishes are available. Colors include black, Flat Dark Earth, Olive Drab Green, Patriot Brown.
Price: M6A2 (shown) $2,217.00
Price: M6-SPR (Special Purpose Rifle) $2,479.00
Price: REPR (7.62 NATO) $3,600.00

MERKEL MODEL SR1 SEMI-AUTOMATIC
Caliber: .223, .308 Win., .30-06, .300 Win Mag., 7x64, 8x57IS, 9.3x62.
Features: Streamlined profile, checkered walnut stock and fore-end, 19.7" (308) or 20.8" (300 SM) barrel, two- or five-shot detachable box magazine. Adjustable front and rear iron sights with Weaver-style optics rail included. Imported from Germany by Merkel USA.
Price: $1,995.00

OLYMPIC ARMS K9, K10, K40, K45 PISTOL-CALIBER AR15 CARBINES
Caliber: 9mm Para., 10mm, .40 S&W, .45 ACP; 32/10-shot modified magazines. **Barrel:** 16" button rifled stainless steel, 1x16" twist rate. **Weight:** 6.73 lbs. **Length:** 31.625" overall. **Stock:** A2 grip, M4 6-point collapsible stock. **Features:** A2 upper with adjustable rear sight, elevation adjustable front post, bayonet lug, sling swivel, threaded muzzle, flash suppressor, carbine length handguards. Made in U.S.A. by Olympic Arms, Inc.
Price: K9GL, 9mm Para., Glock lower $1,157.00
Price: K10, 10mm, modified 10-round Uzi magazine............$1,006.20
Price: K40, .40 S&W, modified 10-round Uzi magazine $1,006.20
Price: K45, .45 ACP, modified 10-round Uzi magazine $1,006.20

OLYMPIC ARMS K3B SERIES AR15 CARBINES
Caliber: 5.56 NATO, 30-shot magazines. **Barrel:** 16" button rifled chrome-moly steel, 1x9" twist rate. **Weight:** 5-7 lbs. **Length:** 31.75" overall. **Stock:** A2 grip, M4 6-point collapsible buttstock. **Features:** A2 upper with adjustable rear sight, elevation adjustable front post, bayonet lug, sling swivel, threaded muzzle, flash suppressor, carbine-length handguards. Made in U.S.A. by Olympic Arms, Inc.
Price: K3B base model, A2 upper $815.00
Price: K3B-M4 M4 contoured barrel & handguards ...$1,103.70
Price: K3B-M4-A3-TC A3 upper, M4 barrel, FIRSH rail handguard $1,246.70
Price: K3B-CAR 11.5" barrel with 5.5" permanent flash

suppressor..$1,033.50
Price: K3B-FAR 16" featherweight contoured barrel............$1,071.20

OLYMPIC ARMS PLINKER PLUS AR15 MODELS
Caliber: 5.56 NATO, 30-shot magazine. **Barrel:** 16" or 20" button-rifled chrome-moly steel, 1x9" twist. **Weight:** 7.5-8.5 lbs. **Length:** 35.5"-39.5" overall. **Stock:** A2 grip, A2 buttstock with trapdoor. **Sights:** A1 windage rear, elevation-adjustable front post. **Features:** A1 upper, fiberlite handguards, bayonet lug, threaded muzzle and flash suppressor. Made in U.S.A. by Olympic Arms, Inc.
Price: Plinker Plus.....................................$727.00
Price: Plinker Plus 20..............................$908.00

OLYMPIC ARMS GAMESTALKER
Sporting AR-style rifle chambered in 5.56 NATO, 6.8 SPC, .243 WSSM, .25 WSSM, .300 WSSM or 7.62x39. Features include forged aluminum upper and lower; flat top receiver with Picatinny rail; gas block front sight; 22-inch stainless steel fluted barrel; free-floating slotted tube handguard; camo finish overall; ACE FX skeleton stock.
Price: $1,364.00

OLYMPIC ARMS ULTIMATE MAGNUM AR
Sporting AR-style rifle chambered in .22-250, .223 WSSM, .243 WSSM, .25 WSSM and .300 WSSM. **Weight:** 9.4 lbs. Features include forged aluminum upper and lower; flat top gas block receiver with Picatinny rail; 24-inch heavy match-grade bull barrel; free-floating slotted-tube handguard; camo finish overall.
Price: $1,359.00

REMINGTON MODEL R-15 VTR PREDATOR
Caliber: .223, five-shot magazine. **Barrel:** 22" **Weight:** 7.75 lbs. **Length:** 36.25" **Stock:** Synthetic with full camo coverage. **Features:** AR-style with optics rail, aluminum alloy upper and lower.
Price: $1,199.00

REMINGTON MODEL R-25 G-II
Caliber: .243, 7mm-08, .308 Win., four-shot magazine. **Barrel:** 20" chrome-moly. **Weight:** 7.75 lbs. **Length:** 38.25" overall. **Features:** AR-style semiauto with single-stage trigger, aluminum alloy upper and lower, Mossy Oak Treestand camo finish overall.
Price: $1,697.00

REMINGTON MODEL 750 WOODSMASTER
Caliber: .243 Win., .270 Win., .308 Win., .30-06 Spfl., .35 Whelen. 4-shot magazine. **Barrel:** 22" round tapered, 18.5" (carbine version). **Weight:** 7.2 to 7.5 lbs. **Length:** 42.6" overall. **Stock:** Restyled American walnut fore-end and stock with machine-cut

checkering. Satin finish. **Sights:** Gold bead front sight on ramp; step rear sight with windage adjustable. **Features:** Gas-operated action, SuperCell recoil pad. Positive cross-bolt safety. Receiver tapped for scope mount. Introduced 2006. The latest variation of the classic semiauto Remington 740 of 1955. Made in U.S.A. by Remington Arms Co.
Price: 750 Woodsmaster $1,024.00
Price: 750 Woodsmaster Carbine (18.5" bbl.) $902.00

ROCK RIVER ARMS LAR SERIES
Caliber: .223/5.56, .308/7.62, 6.8 SPC, .458 SOCOM, 9mm and .40 S&W. These AR-15 type rifles and carbines are available with a very wide range of options. Virtually any AR configuration is offered including tactical, hunting and competition models. Some models are available in left-hand versions.
Price: .... $1,035.00 to $1,845.00

RUGER AR-556
Caliber: 5.56 NATO. Basic AR M4-style Modern Sporting Rifle with direct impingement operation, forged aluminum upper and lower receivers, and cold hammer-forged chrome-moly steel barrel with M4 feed ramp cuts. Other features include Ruger Rapid Deploy folding rear sight, milled F-height gas block with post front sight, telescoping 6-postion stock and one 30-round Magpul magazine. Introduced in 2015.
Price: $799.00

RUGER SR-556
AR-style semiauto rifle chambered in 5.56 NATO or 7.62 NATO/.308. (SR-762 model). Feature include two-stage piston; quad rail handguard; Troy Industries sights; black synthetic fixed or telescoping buttstock; 16.12-inch 1:9" twist steel barrel with birdcage; 10- or 30-round detachable box magazine; black matte finish overall.
Price: $2,049.00
Price: Takedown model $2,199.00
Price: SR-762 ....$2,349.00

Prices given are believed to be accurate at time of publication however, many factors affect retail pricing so exact prices are not possible.

71ST EDITION, 2017   **445**

RUGER MINI-14

Caliber: .223 Rem., 5-shot or 20-shot detachable box magazine. Tactical Rifle is also available in .300 AAC Blackout. **Barrel:** 18.5". Rifling twist 1:9". **Weight:** 6.75 to 7 lbs. **Length:** 37.25" overall. **Stock:** American hardwood, steel reinforced, or synthetic. **Sights:** Protected blade front, fully adjustable Ghost Ring rear. **Features:** Fixed piston gas-operated, positive primary extraction. New buffer system, redesigned ejector system. Ruger S100RM scope rings included on Ranch Rifle. Heavier barrels added in 2008, 20-round magazine added in 2009.

Price: Mini-14/5, Ranch Rifle, blued, wood stock **$999.00**
Price: K-Mini-14/5, Ranch Rifle, stainless, scope rings **$1,069.00**
Price: Mini-14 Target Rifle: laminated thumbhole stock, heavy crowned 22" stainless steel barrel, other refinements **$1,259.00**
Price: Mini-14 ATI Stock: Tactical version of Mini-14 but with six-position collapsible stock or folding stock, grooved pistol grip. Multiple Picatinny optics/accessory rails **$1,089.00**
Price: Mini-14 Tactical Rifle: Similar to Mini-14 but with 16.12" barrel with flash hider, black synthetic stock, adjustable sights **$1,019.00**

RUGER MINI THIRTY

Similar to the Mini-14 rifle except modified to chamber the 7.62x39 Russian service round. **Weight:** 6.75 lbs. Has 6-groove barrel with 1:10" twist, Ruger Integral Scope Mount bases and protected blade front, fully adjustable Ghost Ring rear. Detachable 5-shot staggered box magazine. 20-round magazines available. Stainless or matte black alloy w/synthetic stock. Introduced 1987.

Price: Matte black finish **$1,069.00**
Price: Stainless **$1,089.00**
Price: Stainless w/20-round mag **$1,139.00**

SIG-SAUER MCX

AR-style rifle chambered in 5.56 NATO, 7.62x39mm or .300 Blackout. Modular system allows switching between calibers with conversion kit. Features include a 16" barrel, aluminum KeyMod handguards, amdi controls and charging handle, choice of side-folding or telescoping stock, auto-regulating gas system to all transition between subsonic and supersonic loads.

Price: **$1,866.00**
Price: With conversion kit **$2,138.00**

SIG-SAUER SIG516 GAS PISTON

AR-style rifle chambered in 5.56 NATO. Features include 14.5-, 16-, 18- or 20-inch chrome-lined barrel; free-floating, aluminum quad rail fore-end with four M1913 Picatinny rails; threaded muzzle with a standard (0.5x28TPI) pattern; aluminum upper and lower receiver is machined; black anodized finish; 30-round magazine; flattop upper; various configurations available.

Price: **$1,794.00**

SIG SAUER M400 VARMINTER/PREDATOR SERIES

Caliber: .223/5.56 NATO. AR Flattop design. **Barrel:** 18" (Predator) with Hogue free-floated fore-end. **Features:** Two-stage Geissele match trigger, Hogue grip, ambidextrous controls, Magpul MOE stock.

Price: Predator... **$1,446.00**

SIG-SAUER SIG716 TACTICAL PATROL

AR-10 type rifle chambered in 7.62 NATO/.308 Winchester. Features include gas-piston operation with 3-round-position (4-position optional) gas valve; 16-, 18- or 20-inch chrome-lined barrel with threaded muzzle and nitride finish; free-floating aluminum quad rail fore-end with four M1913 Picatinny rails; telescoping buttstock; lower receiver is machined from a 7075-T6 Aircraft grade aluminum forging; upper receiver, machined from 7075-T6 aircraft grade aluminum with integral M1913 Picatinny rail. DMR has free-floating barrel, two-stage match-grade trigger, short-stroke push rod operating system.

Price: **$2,283.00**
Price: Designated Marksman (DMR).................................... **$2,963.00**

SMITH & WESSON M&P15

Caliber: 5.56mm NATO/.223, 30-shot steel magazine. **Barrel:** 16", 1:9" twist. **Weight:** 6.74 lbs., w/o magazine. **Length:** 32-35" overall. **Stock:** Black synthetic. **Sights:** Adjustable post front sight, adjustable dual aperture rear sight. **Features:** 6-position telescopic stock, thermo-set M4 handguard. 14.75" sight radius. 7-lbs. (approx.) trigger pull. 7075 T6 aluminum upper, 4140 steel barrel. Chromed barrel bore, gas key, bolt carrier. Hard-coat black-anodized receiver and barrel finish. OR (Optics Ready) model has no sights. TS model has Magpul stock and folding sights. Made in U.S.A. by Smith & Wesson.

Price: Sport Model.. **$739.00**
Price: OR Model **$1,069.00**
Price: TS model **$1,569.00**

SMITH & WESSON M&P15-300

Caliber: .300 Whisper/.300 AAC Blackout. Other specifications the same of 5.56 models.

Price: **$1,119.00**

SMITH & WESSON MODEL M&P15 VTAC

Caliber: .223 Remington/5.56 NATO, 30-round magazine. **Barrel:** 16". **Weight:** 6.5 lbs. **Length:** 35" extended, 32" collapsed, overall. **Features:** Six-position CAR stock. Surefire flash-hider and G2 light with VTAC light mount; VTAC/JP handguard; JP single-stage match trigger and speed hammer; three adjustable picatinny rails; VTAC padded two-point adjustable sling.

Price: **$1,949.00**

SMITH & WESSON M&P15PC CAMO

Caliber: 223 Rem/5.56 NATO, A2 configuration, 10-round mag. **Barrel:** 20" stainless with 1:8" twist. **Weight:** 8.2 lbs. **Length:** 38.5" overall. **Features:** AR-style, no sights but integral front and rear optics rails. Two-stage trigger, aluminum lower. Finished in Realtree Advantage Max-1 camo.

Price: **$1,589.00**

SMITH & WESSON M&P10

Caliber: .308 Win. **Capacity:** 10 rounds. **Barrel:** 18 inches. **Weight:** 7.7 pounds. **Features:** 6-position CAR stock, black hard anodized finish. Camo finish hunting model available w/5-round magazine.

Price: **$1,619.00**
Price: (Camo) **$1,729.00**

SPRINGFIELD ARMORY M1A
Caliber: 7.62mm NATO (.308), 5- or 10-shot box magazine. **Barrel:** 25-1/16" with flash suppressor, 22" without suppressor. **Weight:** 9.75 lbs. **Length:** 44.25" overall. **Stock:** American walnut with walnut-colored heat-resistant fiberglass handguard. Matching walnut handguard available. Also available with fiberglass stock. **Sights:** Military, square blade front, full click-adjustable aperture rear. **Features:** Commercial equivalent of the U.S. M-14 service rifle with no provision for automatic firing. From Springfield Armory
Price: SOCOM 16 .... $1,965.00
Price: Scout Squad, from $1,830.00
Price: Standard M1A, from $1,669.00
Price: Loaded Standard, from $1,828.00
Price: National Match, from $2,359.00
Price: Super Match (heavy premium barrel) about $2,956.00
Price: Tactical, from .... $3,619.00 to $4,046.00

STAG ARMS AR-STYLE SERIES
Caliber: 5.56 NATO/.223, 6.8 SPC, 9mm Parabellum. Ten, 20 or 30-shot magazine capacity. This manufacturer offers more than 25 AR-style rifles or carbines with many optional features including barrel length and configurations, stocks, sights, rail systems and both direct impingement and gas piston operating systems. Left-hand models are available on some products. Listed is a sampling of Stag Arms models.
Price: Model 1 .... $949.00
Price: Model 2T Carbine (Tactical) $1,130.00
Price: Model 3 Carbine (shown) $895.00
Price: Model 3G Rifle $1,459.00
Price: Model 5 Carbine (6.8) $1,045.00
Price: Stag 7 Hunter (6.8) $1,055.00
Price: Model 9 (9mm) $990.00

STONER SR-15 MOD2
Caliber: .223. **Barrel:** 18". **Weight:** 7.6 lbs. **Length:** 38" overall. **Stock:** Mag-Pul MOE. **Sights:** Post front, fully adjustable rear (300-meter sight). **Features:** URX-4 upper receiver; two-stage trigger, 30-round magazine. Black finish. Made in U.S.A. by Knight's Mfg.
Price: $2,400.00

STONER SR-25 ACC
Caliber: 7.62 NATO, 10-or 20-shot steel magazine. **Barrel:** 16" with flash hider. **Weight:** 8.5 lbs. **Features:** Shortened, non-slip handguard; drop-in two-stage match trigger, removable carrying handle, ambidextrous controls, matte black finish. Made in U.S.A. by Knight's Mfg. Co.
Price: $5,300.00

STONER SR-30
Caliber: .300 Blackout. **Barrel:** 16" **Weight:** 7.75 lbs. **Features:** QDC flash suppressor, micro front and rear iron sights, ambidextrous controls, fully adjustable stock.
Price: $2,500.00

WILSON COMBAT TACTICAL
Caliber: 5.56mm NATO, accepts all M-16/AR-15 Style Magazines, includes one 20-round magazine. **Barrel:** 16.25", 1:9" twist, match-grade fluted. **Weight:** 6.9 lbs. **Length:** 36.25" overall. **Stock:** Fixed or collapsible. **Features:** Free-float ventilated aluminum quad-rail handguard, Mil-Spec parkerized barrel and steel components, anodized receiver, precision CNC-machined upper and lower receivers, 7075 T6 aluminum forgings, Single stage JP Trigger/Hammer Group, Wilson Combat Tactical Muzzle Brake, nylon tactical rifle case. M-4T version has flat-top receiver for mounting optics, OD green furniture, 16.25" match-grade M-4 style barrel. SS-15 Super Sniper Tactical Rifle has 1-in-8 twist, heavy 20" match-grade fluted stainless steel barrel. Made in U.S.A by Wilson Combat.
Price: .... $2,225.00 to $2,450.00

BIG HORN ARMORY MODEL 89 RIFLE AND CARBINE

Lever action rifle or carbine chambered for .500 S&W Magnum. Features include 22-or 18-inch barrel; walnut or maple stocks with pistol grip; aperture rear and blade front sights; recoil pad; sling swivels; enlarged lever loop; magazine capacity 5 (rifle) or 7 (carbine) rounds.

Price: **$2,424.00**

BIG HORN ARMORY MODEL 90 SERIES

Calibers: .460 S&W, .454 Casull. Features similar to Model 89. Several wood and finish upgrades available.
Price: Rifle .460 w/22" bbl. from.............................**$3,024.00**
Price: Carbine .460 w/18" bbl. From **$2,849.00**
Price: 90A rifle, .454, 22" bbl. From.................................**$2,949.00**
Price: 90A carbine, .454, 18" bbl. From................................**$2,774.00**

BROWNING BLR

Action: Lever action with rotating bolt head, multiple-lug breech bolt with recessed bolt face, side ejection. Rack-and-pinion lever. Flush-mounted detachable magazines, with 4+1 capacity for magnum cartridges, 5+1 for standard rounds. **Barrel:** Button-rifled chrome-moly steel with crowned muzzle. **Stock:** Buttstocks and forends are American walnut with grip and forend checkering. Recoil pad installed. **Trigger:** Wide-groove design, trigger travels with lever. Half-cock hammer safety; fold-down hammer. **Sights:** Gold bead on ramp front; low-profile square-notch adjustable rear. **Features:** Blued barrel and receiver, high-gloss wood finish. Receivers are drilled and tapped for scope mounts, swivel studs included. Action lock provided. Introduced 1996. Imported from Japan by Browning.

BROWNING BLR LIGHTWEIGHT W/PISTOL GRIP, SHORT AND LONG ACTION; LIGHTWEIGHT '81, SHORT AND LONG ACTION

Calibers: Short Action, 20" Barrel: .22-250 Rem., .243 Win., 7mm-08 Rem., .308 Win., .358, .450 Marlin. Calibers: Short Action, 22" Barrel: .270 WSM, 7mm WSM, .300 WSM, .325 WSM. Calibers: Long Action 22" Barrel: .270 Win., .30-06. Calibers: Long Action 24" Barrel: 7mm Rem. Mag., .300 Win. Mag. **Weight:** 6.5-7.75 lbs. **Length:** 40-45" overall. **Stock:** New checkered pistol grip and Schnabel forearm. Lightweight '81 differs from Pistol Grip models with a Western-style straight grip stock and banded forearm. Lightweight w/Pistol Grip Short Action and Long Action introduced 2005. Model '81 Lightning Long Action introduced 1996.
Price: Lightweight w/Pistol Grip Short Action, from..............**$1,020.00**
Price: Lightweight w/Pistol Grip Long Action **$1,100.00**
Price: Lightweight '81 Short Action **$960.00**
Price: Lightweight '81 Long Action **$1,040.00**
Price: Lightweight '81 Takedown Short Action, from **$1,040.00**
Price: Lightweight '81 Takedown Long Action, from **$1,120.00**
Price: Lightweight stainless .... **$1,100.00 to $1,180.00**
Price: Stainless Takedown .... **$1,230.00 to $1,300.00**
Price: Gold Medallion w/nickel finish,
  engraving .... **$1,470.00 to $1,550.00**

CHIAPPA MODEL 1892 RIFLE

Caliber: .38 Spec./.357 Mag., .38-40, .44-40, .44 Mag., .45 Colt. **Barrel:** 16" (Trapper), 20" round and 24" octagonal (Takedown). **Weight:** 7.7 lbs. **Stock:** Walnut. **Sights:** Blade front, buckhorn. Trapper model has interchangeable front sight blades. **Features:** Finishes are blue/case colored. Magazine capacity is 12 rounds with 24" bbl.; 10 rounds with 20" barrel; 9 rounds in 16" barrel. Mare's Leg models have 4-shot magazine, 9 or 12-inch barrel.
Price: **$1,053.00**
Price: Takedown **$1,299.00**
Price: Trapper **$1,169.00**
Price: Mare's Leg, from..**$1,349.00**

CIMARRON 1860 HENRY CIVIL WAR MODEL

Caliber: .44 WCF, .45 LC; 12-shot magazine. **Barrel:** 24" (rifle). **Weight:** 9.5 lbs. **Length:** 43" overall (rifle). **Stock:** European walnut. **Sights:** Bead front, open adjustable rear. **Features:** Brass receiver

and buttplate. Uses original Henry loading system. Copy of the original rifle. Charcoal blue finish optional. Introduced 1991. Imported by Cimarron F.A. Co.
Price: From **$1,579.78**

CIMARRON 1866 WINCHESTER REPLICAS

Caliber: .38 Spec., .357, .45 LC, .32 WCF, .38 WCF, .44 WCF. **Barrel:** 24" (rifle), 20" (short rifle), 19" (carbine), 16" (trapper). **Weight:** 9 lbs. **Length:** 43" overall (rifle). **Stock:** European walnut. **Sights:** Bead front, open adjustable rear. **Features:** Solid brass receiver, buttplate, fore-end cap. Octagonal barrel. Copy of the original Winchester '66 rifle. Introduced 1991. Imported by Cimarron F.A. Co.
Price: 1866 Sporting Rifle, 24" barrel, from **$1,226.00**
Price: 1866 Short Rifle, 20" barrel, from **$1,226.00**
Price: 1866 Carbine, 19" barrel, from **$1,364.00**
Price: 1866 Trapper, 16" barrel, from **$1,203.00**

CIMARRON 1873 SHORT

Caliber: .357 Mag., .38 Spec., .32 WCF, .38 WCF, .44 Spec., .44 WCF, .45 Colt. **Barrel:** 20" tapered octagon. **Weight:** 7.5 lbs. **Length:** 39" overall. **Stock:** Walnut. **Sights:** Bead front, adjustable semi-buckhorn rear. **Features:** Has half "button" magazine. Original-type markings, including caliber, on barrel and elevator and "Kings" patent. Trapper Carbine (.357 Mag., .44 WCF, .45 Colt). From Cimarron F.A. Co.
Price: **$1,272.00**
Price: Trapper Carbine 16" bbl. **$1,242.00**

CIMARRON 1873 DELUXE SPORTING

Similar to the 1873 Short Rifle except has 24" barrel with half-magazine.
Price: **$1,378.00**

CIMARRON 1873 LONG RANGE

Caliber: .44 WCF, .45 Colt. **Barrel:** 30", octagonal. **Weight:** 8.5 lbs. **Length:** 48" overall. **Stock:** Walnut. **Sights:** Blade front, semi-buckhorn ramp rear. Tang sight optional. **Features:** Color case-hardened frame; choice of modern blue-black or charcoal blue for other parts. Barrel marked "Kings Improvement." From Cimarron F.A. Co.
Price: **$1,325.10**

EMF 1866 YELLOWBOY LEVER ACTIONS

Caliber: .38 Spec., .44-40, .45 LC. **Barrel:** 19" (carbine), 24" (rifle). **Weight:** 9 lbs. **Length:** 43" overall (rifle). **Stock:** European walnut. **Sights:** Bead front, open adjustable rear. **Features:** Solid brass frame, blued barrel, lever, hammer, buttplate. Imported from Italy by EMF.
Price: Rifle...**$1,175.00**

EMF MODEL 1873 LEVER-ACTION

Caliber: .32/20, .357 Mag., .38/40, .44-40, .45 Colt. **Barrel:** 18", 20", 24", 30". **Weight:** 8 lbs. **Length:** 43.25" overall. **Stock:** European walnut. **Sights:** Bead front, rear adjustable for windage and elevation. **Features:** Color case-hardened frame (blue on carbine). Imported by EMF.
Price: **$1,250.00**

HENRY ORIGINAL RIFLE

Caliber: .44-40 (13-round magazine). **Barrel:** 24". **Weight:** 9 lbs. **Stock:** Straight-grip fancy American walnut with hardened brass buttplate. **Sights:** Folding ladder rear with blade front. **Finish:** Hardened brass receiver with blued steel barrel. **Features:** Virtually identical to the original 1860 version except for the caliber. Each serial number has prefix "BTH" in honor of Benjamin Tyler Henry, the inventor of the lever-action repeating rifle that went on to become the most legendary firearm in American history. Introduced in 2014 by Henry Repeating Arms. Made in the U.S.A.

Price: $2,300.00

HENRY .45-70
Caliber: .45-70 (4-shot magazine). **Barrel:** 18.5". **Weight:** 7 lbs. **Stock:** Pistol grip walnut. **Sights:** XS Ghost Rings with blade front.

Price: $850.00

HENRY BIG BOY LEVER-ACTION CARBINE
Caliber: .44 Magnum, standard model; .357 Magnum, .45 Colt, Deluxe II only. 10-shot tubular magazine. **Barrel:** 20" octagonal, 1:38" right-hand twist. **Weight:** 8.68 lbs. **Length:** 38.5" overall. **Stock:** Straight-grip American walnut, brass buttplate. **Sights:** Marbles full adjustable semi-buckhorn rear, brass bead front. **Features:** Brasslite receiver not tapped for scope mount. Made in U.S.A. by Henry Repeating Arms.

Price: .44 Magnum, walnut, blued barrel...............................$899.95
Price: Deluxe II .45 Colt, .357 Mag., engraved receiver $1,995.95

HENRY .30/30 LEVER-ACTION CARBINE
Same as the Big Boy except has straight grip American walnut, .30-30 only, 6-shot. Receivers are drilled and tapped for scope mount. Made in U.S.A. by Henry Repeating Arms.

Price: H009 Blued receiver, round barrel...............................$850.00
Price: H009B Brass receiver, octagonal barrel.......................$949.95

HENRY LONG RANGER
Caliber: .223 Rem., .243 Win., 308 Win. **Magazine capacity:** 5 (.223), 4 (.243, .308). **Barrel:** 20". **Stock:** Straight grip, checkered walnut with buttpad, oil finish, swivel studs. **Features:** Geared action, side ejection, chromed steel bolt with 6 lugs, flush fit detachable magazine.

Price: $1,014.95

MARLIN MODEL 336C LEVER-ACTION CARBINE
Caliber: .30-30 or .35 Rem., 6-shot tubular magazine. **Barrel:** 20" Micro-Groove. **Weight:** 7 lbs. **Length:** 38.5" overall. **Stock:** Checkered American black walnut, capped pistol grip. Mar-Shield finish; rubber buttpad; swivel studs. **Sights:** Ramp front with Wide-Scan hood, semi-buckhorn folding rear adjustable for windage and elevation. **Features:** Hammer-block safety. Receiver tapped for scope mount, offset hammer spur; top of receiver sandblasted to prevent glare. Includes safety lock. The latest variation of Marlin's classic lever gun that originated in 1937.

Price: $635.00

MARLIN MODEL 336SS LEVER-ACTION CARBINE
Same as the 336C except receiver, barrel and other major parts are machined from stainless steel. .30-30 only, 6-shot; receiver tapped for scope. Includes safety lock.

Price: $779.00

MARLIN MODEL 336W LEVER-ACTION
Similar to the Model 336C except has walnut-finished, cut-checkered Maine birch stock; blued steel barrel band has integral sling swivel; no front sight hood; comes with padded nylon sling; hard rubber butplate. Introduced 1998. Includes safety lock. Made in U.S.A. by Marlin.

Price: $548.00

MARLIN 336BL
Lever action rifle chambered for .30-30. Features include 6-shot full length tubular magazine; 18-inch blued barrel with Micro-Groove rifling (12 grooves); big-loop finger lever; side ejection; blued steel receiver; hammer block safety; brown laminated hardwood pistol-grip stock with fluted comb; cut checkering; deluxe recoil pad; blued swivel studs.

Price: $667.00

MARLIN MODEL XLR LEVER-ACTION RIFLES
Similar to Model 336C except has an 24" stainless barrel with Ballard-type cut rifling, stainless steel receiver and other parts, laminated hardwood stock with pistol grip, nickel-plated swivel studs. Chambered for .30-30 Win. with Hornady spire-pointed Flex-Tip cartridges. Includes safety lock. Introduced 2006.

Price: Model 336XLR $969.00

MARLIN MODEL 1894
Caliber: .44 Spec./.44 Mag., 10-shot tubular magazine. **Barrel:** 20" Ballard-type rifling. **Weight:** 6 lbs. **Length:** 37.5" overall. **Stock:** Checkered American black walnut, straight grip and forend. Mar-Shield finish. Rubber rifle buttpad; swivel studs. **Sights:** Wide-Scan hooded ramp front, semibuckhorn folding rear adjustable for windage and elevation. **Features:** Hammer-block safety. Receiver tapped for scope mount, offset hammer spur; solid top receiver sand blasted to prevent glare. Includes safety lock.

Price: $789.00

MARLIN MODEL 1894C CARBINE
Similar to the standard Model 1894 except chambered for .38 Spec./.357 Mag. with full-length 9-shot magazine, 18.5" barrel, hammer-block safety, hooded front sight. Introduced 1983. Includes safety lock.

Price: $730.00

MARLIN MODEL 1894 COWBOY
Caliber: .357 Mag., .44 Mag., .45 Colt, 10-shot magazine. **Barrel:** 20" tapered octagon, deep cut rifling. **Weight:** 7.5 lbs. **Length:** 41.5" overall. **Stock:** Straight grip American black walnut, hard rubber buttplate, Mar-Shield finish. **Sights:** Marble carbine front, adjustable Marble semibuckhorn rear. **Features:** Squared finger lever; straight grip stock; blued steel fore-end tip. Designed for Cowboy Shooting events. Introduced 1996. Includes safety lock. Made in U.S.A. by Marlin.

Price: $1,040.00

MARLIN 1894 DELUXE
Lever action rifle chambered in .44 Magnum/.44 Special. Features include 10-shot tubular magazine; squared finger lever; side ejection; richly polished deep blued metal surfaces; solid top receiver; hammer block safety; #1 grade fancy American black walnut straight-grip stock and forend; cut checkering; rubber rifle buttpad; Mar-Shield finish; blued steel fore-end cap: swivel studs; deep-cut Ballard-type rifling (6 grooves).

Price: $950.00

MARLIN MODEL 1895 LEVER-ACTION
Caliber: .45-70 Govt., 4-shot tubular magazine. **Barrel:** 22", round. **Weight:** 7.5 lbs. **Length:** 40.5" overall. **Stock:** Checkered American black walnut, full pistol grip. Mar-Shield finish; rubber buttpad; quick detachable swivel studs. **Sights:** Bead front with Wide-Scan hood, semibuckhorn folding rear adjustable for windage and elevation. **Features:** Hammer-block safety. Solid receiver tapped for scope mounts or receiver sights; offset hammer spur. Includes safety lock.

Price: $745.00

MARLIN MODEL 1895G GUIDE GUN LEVER-ACTION
Similar to Model 1895 with deep-cut Ballard-type rifling; straight-grip walnut stock. Overall length is 37", weighs 7 lbs. Introduced 1998.

Prices given are believed to be accurate at time of publication however, many factors affect retail pricing so exact prices are not possible.

71ST EDITION, 2017 ◆ **449**

Includes safety lock. Made in U.S.A. by Marlin.
Price: $750.00

MARLIN MODEL 1895GS GUIDE GUN
Similar to Model 1895G except receiver, barrel and most metal parts are machined from stainless steel. Chambered for .45-70 Govt., 4-shot, 18.5" barrel. Overall length is 37", weighs 7 lbs. Introduced 2001. Includes safety lock. Made in U.S.A. by Marlin.
Price: $896.00

MARLIN MODEL 1895 SBLR
Similar to Model 1895GS Guide Gun but with stainless steel barrel (18.5"), receiver, large loop lever and magazine tube. Black/gray laminated buttstock and forend, XS ghost ring rear sight, hooded ramp front sight, receiver/barrel-mounted top rail for mounting accessory optics. Chambered in .45-70 Government. Overall length is 42.5", weighs 7.5 lbs.
Price: $1,232.00

MARLIN MODEL 1895 COWBOY LEVER-ACTION
Similar to Model 1895 except has 26" tapered octagon barrel with Ballard-type rifling, Marble carbine front sight and Marble adjustable semi-buckhorn rear sight. Receiver tapped for scope or receiver sight. Overall length is 44.5", weighs about 8 lbs. Introduced 2001. Includes safety lock. Made in U.S.A. by Marlin.
Price: $899.00

MARLIN 1895GBL
Lever action rifle chambered in .45-70 Government. Features include 6-shot, full-length tubular magazine; 18-1/2-inch barrel with deep-cut Ballard-type rifling (6 grooves); big-loop finger lever; side ejection; solid-top receiver; deeply blued metal surfaces; hammer block safety; pistol-grip two-tone brown laminate stock with cut checkering; ventilated recoil pad; Mar-Shield finish, swivel studs.

Price: $786.00

MOSSBERG 464 LEVER ACTION
Caliber: .30-30 Win., 6-shot tubular magazine. **Barrel:** 20" round. **Weight:** 6.7 lbs. **Length:** 38.5" overall. **Stock:** Hardwood with straight or pistol grip, quick detachable swivel studs. **Sights:** Folding rear sight, adjustable for windage and elevation. **Features:** Blued receiver and barrel, receiver drilled and tapped, two-position top-tang safety. Available with straight grip or semi-pistol grip. Introduced 2008. From O.F. Mossberg & Sons, Inc.
Price: $572.00
Price: SPX Model w/tactical stock and features $540.00

NAVY ARMS 1873 RIFLE
Caliber: .357 Mag., .45 Colt, 12-shot magazine. **Barrel:** 20", 24.25", full octagonal. **Stock:** Deluxe checkered American walnut. **Sights:** Gold bead front, semi-buckhorn rear. **Features:** Turnbull color case-hardened frame, rest blued. Full-octagon barrel. Available exclusively from Navy Arms.
Price: $2,500.00

NAVY ARMS 1892 SHORT RIFLE
Caliber: .45 Colt, .44 Magnum. 10-shot magazine. **Barrel:** 20" full octagon. **Stock:** Checkered Grade 1 American walnut. **Sights:** Marble's Semi-Buckhorn rear and gold bead front. **Finish:** Color case hardened.
Price: $2,500.00

NAVY ARMS LIGHTNING RIFLE
Caliber: .45 Colt, .357 Magnum. Replica of the Colt Lightning slide-action rifle of the late 19th and early 20th centuries. **Barrel:** Octagon

20 or 24". **Stock:** Checkered Grade 1 American walnut. **Finish:** Color case hardened.
Price: $2,500.00

REMINGTON MODEL 7600 PUMP ACTION
Caliber: .243 Win., .270 Win., .30-06 Spfl., .308. **Barrel:** 22" round tapered. **Weight:** 7.5 lbs. **Length:** 42.6" overall. **Stock:** Cut-checkered walnut pistol grip and fore-end, Monte Carlo with full cheekpiece. Satin or high-gloss finish. Also, black synthetic. **Sights:** Gold bead front sight on matted ramp, open step adjustable sporting rear. **Features:** Redesigned and improved version of the Model 760. Detachable 4-shot magazine. Crossbolt safety. Receiver tapped for scope mount. Introduced 1981.
Price:7600 Wood $918.00
Price:7600 Synthetic..$771.00

ROSSI R92 LEVER-ACTION CARBINE
Caliber: .38 Special/.357 Mag., .44 Mag., .44-40 Win., .45 Colt, .454 Casull. **Barrel:** 16" or 20" with round barrel, 20" or 24" with octagon barrel. **Weight:** 4.8 lbs. to 7 lbs. **Length:** 34 to 41.5 inches. **Features:** Blued or stainless finish. Various options available in selected chamberings (large lever loop, fiber-optic sights, cheekpiece, etc.).
Price: Blued $624.00
Price: Stainless $650.00
Price: .454 Casull $754.00

ROSSI RIO GRANDE
Caliber: .30-30 or .45-70 or .410 shotshell. **Barrel:** 20". **Weight:** 7 lbs. **Sights:** Adjustable rear, post front. **Stock:** Hardwood or camo.
Price: $643.00

UBERTI 1873 SPORTING RIFLE
Caliber: .357 Mag., .44-40, .45 Colt. **Barrel:** 16.1" round, 19" round or 20", 24.25" octagonal. **Weight:** Up to 8.2 lbs. **Length:** Up to 43.3" overall. **Stock:** Walnut, straight grip and pistol grip. **Sights:** Blade front adjustable for windage, open rear adjustable for elevation. **Features:** Color case-hardened frame, blued barrel, hammer, lever, buttplate, brass elevator. Imported by Stoeger Industries.
Price: Carbine 19" bbl. $1,219.00
Price: Trapper 16.1" bbl. $1,259.00
Price: Carbine 18" half oct. bbl. $1,309.00
Price: Short Rifle 20" bbl. $1,259.00
Price: Sporting Rifle, 24.25" bbl. $1,259.00
Price: Special Sporting Rifle, A-grade walnut $1,399.00

UBERTI 1866 YELLOWBOY CARBINE, SHORT, RIFLE
Caliber: .38 Spec., .44-40, .45 Colt. **Barrel:** 24.25", octagonal. **Weight:** 8.2 lbs. **Length:** 43.25" overall. **Stock:** Walnut. **Sights:** Blade front adjustable for windage, rear adjustable for elevation. **Features:**

Prices given are believed to be accurate at time of publication however, many factors affect retail pricing so exact prices are not possible

CENTERFIRE RIFLES Lever & Slide

Frame, buttplate, fore-end cap of polished brass, balance charcoal blued. Imported by Stoeger Industries.
Price: 1866 Yellowboy Carbine, 19" round barrel.................**$1,119.00**
Price: 1866 Yellowboy Short Rifle, 20" octagonal barrel **$1,169.00**
Price: 1866 Yellowboy Rifle, 24.25" octagonal barrel **$1,169.00**

UBERTI 1860 HENRY
Caliber: .44-40, .45 Colt. **Barrel:** 24.25", half-octagon. **Weight:** 9.2 lbs. **Length:** 43.75" overall. **Stock:** American walnut. **Sights:** Blade front, rear adjustable for elevation. Imported by Stoeger Industries.
Price: 1860 Henry Trapper, 18.5" barrel, brass frame............**$1,429.00**
Price: 1860 Henry Rifle Iron Frame, 24.25" barrel **$1,459.00**

UBERTI LIGHTNING
Caliber: .357 Mag., .45 Colt, 10+1. Slide action operation. **Barrel:** 20" to 24.25". **Stock:** Satin-finished walnut. **Finish:** Case-hardened. Introduced 2006. Imported by Stoeger Industries.
Price: **$1,259.00**

WINCHESTER MODEL 94 SHORT RIFLE
Caliber: .30-30, .38-55. **Barrel:** 20". **Weight:** 6.75 lbs. **Sights:** Semi-buckhorn rear, gold bead front. **Stock:** Walnut with straight grip. Fore-end has black grip cap. Also available in Trail's End takedown design in .450 Marlin or .30-30.
Price: **$1,230.00**
Price: (Takedown)...**$1,460.00**

WINCHESTER MODEL 94 CARBINE
Same general specifications as M94 Short Rifle except for curved buttplate and fore-end barrelband.
Price: **$1,200.00**

WINCHESTER MODEL 94 SPORTER
Caliber: .30-30, .38-55. **Barrel:** 24". **Weight:** 7.5 lbs. **Features:** Same features of Model 94 Short Rifle except for crescent butt and steel buttplate, 24" half-round, half-octagon barrel, checkered stock.
Price: **$1,400.00**

WINCHESTER 1873 SHORT RIFLE
Caliber: .357 Magnum, .44-40, .45 Colt. Tubular magazine holds 10 rounds (.44-40, .45 Colt), 11 rounds (.38 Special). **Barrel:**

20 inches. **Weight:** 7.25 lbs. **Sights:** Marble semi-buckhorn rear, gold bead front. Tang is drilled and tapped for optional peep sight. **Stock:** Satin finished, straight-grip walnut with steel crescent buttplate and steel fore-end cap. Tang safety. A modern version of the "Gun That Won the West."
Price: **$1,300.00**

WINCHESTER MODEL 1886 SHORT RIFLE
Caliber: .45-70 or .49-90. **Barrel:** 24". **Weight:** 8.4 lbs. **Sights:** Adjustable buckhorn rear, blade front. **Stock:** Grade 1 walnut with crescent butt.
Price **$1,340.00**

WINCHESTER MODEL 1892 CARBINE
Caliber: .357 Mag., .44 Mag., .44-40, .45 Colt. **Barrel:** 20 inches. **Weight:** 6 lbs. **Stock:** Satin finished walnut with straight grip, steel fore-end strap. **Sights:** Marble semi-buckhorn rear, gold bead front. Other features include saddle ring and tang safety. Available with large loop lever.
Price: Large loop lever......................................**$1,260.00**
Price: 1892 Short Rifle.......................................**$1,070.00**

ARMALITE AR-30A1

Caliber: .300 Win. Mag., .338 Lapua. Bolt-action with five-round capacity. **Barrel:** 24 inches (.300 Win.), 26 inches (.338 Lapua), competition grade. **Weight:** 12.8 lbs. **Length:** 46 inches. **Stock:** Standard fixed. **Sights:** None. Accessory top rail included. **Features:** Muzzlebrake, ambidextrous magazine release, large ejection port makes single loading easy, V-block patented bedding system, bolt-mounted safety locks firing pin. Target versions have adjustable stock.
Price: .... $3,264.00 to $3,599.00

ARMALITE AR-50A1

Caliber: .50 BMG, .416 Barrett. Bolt-action single-shot. **Barrel:** 30 inches with muzzlebrake. National Match model (shown) has 33-inch fluted barrel. **Weight:** 34.1 lbs. **Stock:** Three-section. Extruded fore-end, machined vertical grip, forged and machined buttstock that is vertically adjustable. National Match model (.50 BMG only) has V-block patented bedding system, Armalite Skid System to ensure straight-back recoil.
Price: $3,359.00
Price: National Match $4,230.00

BARRETT MODEL 95

Caliber: 50 BMG, 5-shot magazine. **Barrel:** 29". **Weight:** 23.5 lbs. **Length:** 45" overall. **Stock:** Energy-absorbing recoil pad. **Sights:** Scope optional. **Features:** Bolt-action, bullpup design. Disassembles without tools; extendable bipod legs; match-grade barrel; muzzlebrake. Introduced 1995. Made in U.S.A. by Barrett Firearms Mfg., Inc.
Price: From $6,500.00

BARRETT MODEL 98B

Caliber: .338 Lapua Magnum (10-shot magazine). **Barrel:** 26" fluted or 20". **Weight:** 13.5 lbs. **Length:** 49.8". Comes with two magazines, bipod, monopod, side accessory rail, hard case. Fieldcraft model chambered in .260 Rem., 6.5 Creedmoor, 7mm Rem., .308Win., .300 Win Mag. Tactical Model in .308, .300 Win Mag., .338 Lapua.
Price: From $4,850.00
Price: Fieldcraft Model from $4,113.00
Price: Tactical Model from $4,419.00

BARRETT MODEL 99 SINGLE SHOT

Caliber: .50 BMG, .416 Barrett. **Barrel:** 33". **Weight:** 25 lbs. **Length:** 50.4" overall. **Stock:** Anodized aluminum with energy-absorbing recoil pad. **Sights:** None furnished; integral M1913 scope rail. **Features:** Bolt action; detachable bipod; match-grade barrel with high-efficiency muzzlebrake. Introduced 1999. Made in U.S.A. by Barrett Firearms.
Price: From .... $3,999.00 to $4,199.00

BARRETT MRAD

Caliber: .260 Rem., 6.5 Creedmoor, .308 Win., .300 Win. Mag., .338 Lapua Magnum. **Magazine capacity:** 10 rounds. **Barrel:** 20, 24 or 26 inches, fluted or heavy. **Features:** User interchangeable barrel system, folding stock, adjustable cheekpiece, 5-position length of pull adjustment button, match-grade trigger, 22-inch optics rail.
Price: .... $5,850.00 to $6,000.00

BERGARA B-14 SERIES

Caliber: 6.5 Creedmoor, .270 Win., 7mm Rem. Mag., .308 Win., .30-06, .300 Win. Mag. **Barrel:** 22 or 24". **Weight:** 7 lbs. **Features:** Synthetic with Soft touch finish, recoil pad, swivel studs, adjustable trigger, choice of detachable mag or hinged floorplate. Made in Spain.
Price: $825.00
Price: Walnut stock... $945.00
Price: Premier series from.. $2,190.00

BERGARA BCR SERIES

Caliber: Most popular calibers from .222 Rem. to .300 Win. Mag **Barrel:** 18, 22, 24 or 26". Various options available.
Price: BCR22 Mountain Hunter from.................................... $2,950.00
Price: BCR23 Sport Hunter from $3,150.00
Price: BCR24 Varmint Hunter from...................................... $3,150.00
Price: BCR25 Long Range Hunter from $3,500.00
Price: BCR27 Competition from $4,100.00

BLASER R93 PROFESSIONAL

Caliber: .22-250 Rem., .243 Win., 6.5x55, .270 Win., 7x57, 7mm-08 Rem., .308 Win., .30-06 Spfl., .257 Wby. Mag., 7mm Rem. Mag., .300 Win. Mag., .300 Wby. Mag., .338 Win. Mag., .375H&H, 416 Rem. Mag. **Barrel:** 22" (standard calibers), 26" (magnum). **Weight:** 7 lbs. **Length:** 40" overall (22" barrel). **Stock:** Two-piece European walnut. **Sights:** None furnished; drilled and tapped for scope mounting. **Features:** Straight pull-back bolt action with thumb-activated safety slide/cocking mechanism; interchangeable barrels and bolt heads. LRS (Long Range Sporter) is competition model with many competition features including fluted barrel, adjustable trigger and stock. Imported from Germany by Blaser USA.
Price: From $3,288.00
Price: LRS from... $4,405.00

BROWNING AB3 COMPOSITE STALKER
Caliber: .270, 7mm Rem. Mag., .30-06, .300 Win. Mag. or .308 Win. **Barrel:** 22 inches, 26 for magnums. **Weight:** 6.8 lbs. **Stock:** Matte black synthetic. **Sights:** None. Picatinny rail scope mount included. **Features:** Based on A-Bolt action. General specifications are the same as A-Bolt Medallion.
Price: **$600.00**

BROWNING A-BOLT MEDALLION
Calibers: 7mm Rem. Mag., .300 Win. Mag. **Barrel:** 26" **Weight:** 7.1 lbs. **Length:** 46.75" overall. **Stock:** Select walnut with rosewood grip cap and fore-end cap. Checkered grip and fore-end. Gloss finish. **Features:** High polish blue metal finish. Sixty-degree bolt lift, top tang safety.
Price: **$700.00**
Price: Left-hand model with synthetic stock **$800.00**

BROWNING X-BOLT HOG STALKER
Caliber: .223 or .308 Win. **Barrel:** 20 inches, medium heavy, threaded for suppressor. **Weight:** 6.8 to 7 pounds. **Stock:** Composite black or Realtree Max-1 camo. **Sights:** None. Picatinny rail scope mount included.
Price: **$1,200.00**

BROWNING X-BOLT HUNTER
Calibers: .223, .22-250, .243 Win., .25-06 Rem., .270 Win., .270 WSM, .280 Rem., 7mm Rem. Mag., 7mm WSM, 7mm-08 Rem., .308 Win., .30-06 Spfl., .300 Win. Mag., .300 WSM, .325 WSM, .338 Win. Mag., .375 H&H Mag. **Barrels:** 22", 23", 24", 26", varies by model. Matte blued or stainless free-floated barrel, recessed muzzle crown. **Weight:** 6.3-7 lbs. **Stock:** Hunter and Medallion models have black walnut stocks; Composite Stalker and Stainless Stalker models have composite stocks. Inflex Technology recoil pad. **Sights:** None, drilled and tapped receiver, X-Lock scope mounts. **Features:** Adjustable three-lever Feather Trigger system, polished hard-chromed steel components, factory pre-set at 3.5 lbs., alloy trigger housing. Bolt unlock button, detachable rotary magazine, 60-degree bolt lift, three locking lugs, top-tang safety, sling swivel studs. Introduced 2008.
Price: Standard calibers **$900.00**
Price: Magnum calibers **$950.00**

BROWNING X-BOLT MICRO MIDAS
Caliber: .243 Win., 7mm-08 Rem., .308 Win., .22-250 Rem. .270 WSM, .300 WSM. **Barrel:** 20" **Weight:** 6 lbs.1 oz. **Length:** 37-5/8" to 38-1/8" overall. **Stock:** Satin finish checkered walnut stock. **Sights:** Hooded front and adjustable rear. **Features:** Steel receiver with low-luster blued finish. Glass bedded, drilled and tapped for scope mounts. Barrel is free-floating and hand chambered with target crown. Bolt-action with adjustable Feather Trigger™ and detachable rotary magazine. Compact 12-1/2" length of pull for smaller shooters, designed to fit smaller-framed shooters like youth and women. This model has all the same features as the full-size model with sling

swivel studs installed and Inflex Technology recoil pad. (Scope and mounts not included).
Price: **$860.00**

BROWNING X-BOLT VARMINT STALKER
Similar to Browning X-Bolt Stalker but with medium-heavy free-floated barrel, target crown, composite stock. Chamberings available: .204 Ruger, .223, .22-250, .243 Winchester and .308 Winchester only
Price: **$1,170.00**

BROWNING X-BOLT MEDALLION
Calibers: Most popular calibers from .223 Rem. to .375 H&H. **Barrel:** 22, 24 or 26" free-floated. **Features:** Engraved receiver with polished blue finish, gloss finished and checkered walnut stock with rosewood grip and fore-end caps, detachable rotary magazine. Medallion Maple model has AAA-grade maple stock.
Price: **$1,040.00**
Price: Medallion Maple **$1,070.00**

BROWNING X-BOLT ECLIPSE HUNTER
Calibers: Most popular calibers from .243 Win. to .300 WSM. Same general features of X-Bolt series except for its laminated thumbhole stock.
Price: **$1,020.00**
Price: Varmint and Target models **$1,070.00**

BROWNING X-BOLT HELL'S CANYON
Calibers: .243 Win., 26 Nosler, 6.5 Creedmoor, .270 Win., .270 WSM, 7mm-08 Rem., 7mm Rem. Mag., .308 Win., .30-06, .300 Win. Mag., .300 WSM. **Barrel:** 22 to 26 inches, fluted and free-floating with muzzlebrake the thread protector. **Stock:** A-TACS AU Camo composite with checkered grip panels. **Features:** Detachable rotary magazine, adjustable trigger, Cerakote Burnt Bronze finish on receiver and barrel.
Price: .... **$1,200.00 to $1,270.00**

BROWNING X-BOLT WHITE GOLD
Calibers: Eighteen popular calibers from .223 Rem. to .338 Win. Mag. Same general features of X-Bolt series plus polished stainless steel barrel, receiver, bolt and trigger. Gloss-finished finely checkered walnut Monte Carlo-style stock with rosewood grip and fore-end caps.
Price: **$1,420.00**

BUSHMASTER BA50 BOLT-ACTION
Caliber: .50 Browning BMG. **Barrel:** 30" (rifle), 22" (carbine), 10-round mag. **Weight:** 30 lbs. (rifle), 27 lbs. (carbine). **Length:** 58" overall (rifle), 50" overall (carbine). **Features:** Free-floated Lothar Walther

Prices given are believed to be accurate at time of publication however, many factors affect retail pricing so exact prices are not possible.

71ST EDITION, 2017 ✦ 453

barrel with muzzlebrake, Magpul PRS adjustable stock.
Price: **$5,657.00**

CHEYTAC M-200
Caliber: 408 CheyTac, 7-round magazine. **Barrel:** 30". **Length:** 55", stock extended. **Weight:** 27 lbs. (steel barrel); 24 lbs. (carbon-fiber barrel). **Stock:** Retractable. **Sights:** None, scope rail provided. **Features:** CNC-machined receiver, attachable Picatinny rail M-1913, detachable barrel, integral bipod, 3.5-lb. trigger pull, muzzlebrake. Made in U.S. by CheyTac, LLC.
Price: **$13,795.00**

CMMG MK SERIES
Caliber: 5.56 NATO, .308 Win., 7.62x39, .300 BLK. This company manufactures a wide range of AR and AK style rifles and carbines. Many AR/AK options offered. Listed are several variations of CMMG's many models. Made in the USA.
Price: MK4 LEM .223 ....**$995.00**
Price: MK3 .308 ....**$1,595.00**
Price: MK47 AKS8 7.62x39 (shown).....................................**$1,650.00**
Price: MK4 RCE .300 BLK **$1,500.00**

COOPER FIREARMS OF MONTANA
This company manufacturers bolt-action rifles in a variety of styles and in almost any factory or wildcat caliber. Features of the major model sub-category/styles are listed below. Several other styles and options are available.
Classic: Available in all models. AA Claro walnut stock with 4-panel hand checkering, hand-rubbed oil-finished wood, Pachmayr pad, steel grip cap and standard sling swivel studs. Barrel is chrome-moly premium match grade Wilson Arms. All metal work has matte finish.
Custom Classic: Available in all models. AAA Claro walnut stock with shadow-line beaded cheek-piece, African ebony tip, Western fleur wrap-around hand checkering, hand-rubbed oil-finished wood, Pachmayr pad, steel grip cap and standard sling swivel studs. Barrel is chrome-moly premium match grade Wilson Arms. All metal work has high gloss finish.
Western Classic: Available in all models. AAA+ Claro walnut stock. Selected metal work is highlighted with case coloring. Other features same as Custom Classic.
Mannlicher: Available in all models. Same features as Western Classic with full-length stock having multi-point wrap-around hand checkering.
Varminter: Available in Models 21, 22, 38, 52, 54 and 57-M. Same features as Classic except heavy barrel and stock with wide fore-end, hand-checkered grip.

COOPER MODEL 21
Caliber: Virtually any factory or wildcat chambering in the .223 Rem. family is available including: .17 Rem., .19-223, Tactical 20, .204 Ruger, .222 Rem., .222 Rem. Mag., .223 Rem, .223 Rem A.I., 6x45, 6x47. Single shot. **Barrel:** 22" or 24" in Classic configurations, 24"-26" in Varminter configurations. **Weight:** 6.5-8.0 lbs., depending on type. **Stock:** AA-AAA select claro walnut, 20 lpi checkering. **Sights:** None furnished. **Features:** Three front locking-lug, bolt-action, single-shot.

Action: 7.75" long, Sako extractor. Button ejector. Fully adjustable single-stage trigger. Options include wood upgrades, case-color metalwork, barrel fluting, custom LOP, and many others.
Price: Classic **$2,225.00**
Price: Custom Classic. **$2,595.00**
Price: Western Classic..**$3,455.00**
Price: Varminter **$2,295.00**
Price: Mannlicher...**$4,395.00**

COOPER MODEL 22
Caliber: Virtually any factory or wildcat chambering in the mid-size cartridge length including: .22-250 Rem., .22-250 Rem. AI, .25-06 Rem., .25-06 Rem. AI, .243 Win., .243 Win. AI, .220 Swift, .250/3000 AI, .257 Roberts, .257 Roberts AI, 7mm-08 Rem., 6mm Rem., .260 Rem., 6x284, 6.5x284, .22 BR, 6mm BR, .308 Win. Single shot. **Barrel:** 24" or 26" stainless match in Classic configurations. 24" or 26" in Varminter configurations. **Weight:** 7.5 to 8.0 lbs. depending on type. **Stock:** AA-AAA select claro walnut, 20 lpi checkering. **Sights:** None furnished. **Features:** Three front locking-lug bolt-action single shot. Action: 8.25" long, Sako-style extractor. Button ejector. Fully adjustable single-stage trigger. Options include wood upgrades, case-color metalwork, barrel fluting, custom LOP, and many others.
Price: Classic **$2,225.00**
Price: Custom Classic. **$2,595.00**
Price: Western Classic...**$3,455.00**
Price: Varminter **$2,225.00**
Price: Mannlicher...**$4,495.00**

COOPER MODEL 38
Caliber: .22 Hornet family of cartridges including the.17 Squirrel, 17 He Bee, 17 Ackley Hornet, 17 Mach IV, 19 Calhoon, 20 VarTarg, 221 Fireball, .22 Hornet, .22 K-Hornet, .22 Squirrel, 218 Bee, 218 Mashburn Bee. Single shot. **Barrel:** 22" or 24" in Classic configurations, 24" or 26" in Varminter configurations. **Weight:** 6.5-8.0 lbs. depending on type. **Stock:** AA-AAA select claro walnut, 20 lpi checkering. **Sights:** None furnished. **Features:** Three front locking-lug bolt-action single shot. Action: 7" long, Sako-style extractor. Button ejector. Fully adjustable single-stage trigger. Options include wood upgrades, case-color metalwork, barrel fluting, custom LOP, and many others.
Price: Classic..**$2,195.00**
Price: Custom Classic. **$2,595.00**
Price: Western Classic...**$3,455.00**
Price: Varminter **$2,225.00**
Price: Mannlicher...**$4,395.00**

COOPER MODEL 52
Caliber: .30-06, .270 Win., .280 Rem, .25-06, .284 Win.,.257 Weatherby Mag., .264 Win. Mag., .270 Weatherby Mag., 7mm Remington Mag., 7mm Weatherby Mag., 7mm Shooting Times Westerner, .300 Holland & Holland, .300 Winchester Mag., .300 Weatherby Mag., .308 Norma Mag., 8mm Rem. Mag., .338 Win. Mag., .340 Weatherby V. Three-shot magazine. **Barrel:** 22" or 24" in Classic configurations, 24" or 26" in Varminter configurations. **Weight:** 7.75 - 8 lbs. depending on type. **Stock:** AA-AAA select claro walnut, 20 lpi checkering. **Sights:** None furnished. **Features:** Three front locking-lug bolt-action single shot. Action: 7" long, Sako style extractor. Button ejector. Fully adjustable single-stage trigger. Options include wood upgrades, case-color metalwork, barrel fluting, custom LOP, and many others.
Price: Classic. **$2,275.00**
Price: Custom Classic. **$3,195.00**
Price: Western Classic..**$3,895.00**
Price: Jackson Game...**$2,355.00**
Price: Jackson Hunter **$2,225.00**
Price: Excalibur. **$2,275.00**
Price: Mannlicher...**$4,995.00**

COOPER MODEL 54
Caliber: .22-250, .243 Win., .250 Savage, .260 Rem., 7mm-08, .308 Win. and similar length cartridges. Features are similar to those of the Model 52.
Price: Classic. **$2,275.00**
Price: Custom Classic. **$3,195.00**
Price: Western Classic..**$3,895.00**
Price: Jackson Game...**$2,355.00**
Price: Jackson Hunter **$2,225.00**
Price: Excalibur. **$2,275.00**

Price: Mannlicher $4,995.00

COOPER MODEL 57-M

Caliber: .17 HMR, .22 LR, .22 WMR. Capacity 3 or 4 rounds. Cooper Firearms series of rimfire rifles, available in most of the company's popular styles.

Price: Classic $2,245.00
Price: Custom Classic $2,595.00
Price: Western Classic $3,445.00
Price: Schnabel $2,395.00
Price: Jackson Squirrel $2,355.00
Price: Jackson Hunter $2,195.00
Price: Mannlicher $4,395.00

COOPER MODEL 58 DANGEROUS GAME

Caliber: .404 Jeffery, .416 Rigby, .458 Lott, .505 Gibbs. Built for the world's most dangerous game. Controlled round feed, Timney trigger, AA or AAA Claro checkered walnut stock, rollover cheek piece, ebony fore-end tip, color case hardened finish and other high-grade features available on various models.

Price: Classic $3,095.00
Price: Custom Classic $4,255.00
Price: Western Classic $4,595.00
Price: Jackson Game $3,195.00
Price: Mannlicher $5,695.00

CZ 527 LUX BOLT-ACTION

Caliber: .17 Hornet, .204 Ruger, .22 Hornet, .222 Rem., .223 Rem., detachable 5-shot magazine. **Barrel:** 23.5"; standard or heavy barrel. **Weight:** 6 lbs., 1 oz. **Length:** 42.5" overall. **Stock:** European walnut with Monte Carlo. **Sights:** Hooded front, open adjustable rear. **Features:** Improved mini-Mauser action with non-rotating claw extractor; single set trigger; grooved receiver. Imported from the Czech Republic by CZ-USA.

Price: Brown laminate stock $733.00
Price: Model FS, full-length stock, cheekpiece $827.00

CZ 527 AMERICAN BOLT-ACTION

Similar to the CZ 527 Lux except has classic-style stock with 18 lpi checkering; free-floating barrel; recessed target crown on barrel. No sights furnished. Introduced 1999. Imported from the Czech Republic by CZUSA.

Price: From $733.00

CZ 550 FS MANNLICHER

Caliber: .22-250 Rem., .243 Win., 6.5x55, 7x57, 7x64, .308 Win., 9.3x62, .270 Win., 30-06. **Barrel:** Free-floating barrel; recessed target crown. **Weight:** 7.48 lbs. **Length:** 44.68" overall. **Stock:** American classic style stock with 18 lpi checkering or FS (Mannlicher). **Sights:** No sights furnished. **Features:** Improved Mauser-style action with claw extractor, fixed ejector, square bridge dovetailed receiver; single set trigger. Introduced 1999. Imported from the Czech Republic by CZ-USA.

Price: FS (full stock) $894.00
Price: American, from $827.00

CZ 550 SAFARI MAGNUM/AMERICAN SAFARI MAGNUM

Similar to CZ 550 American Classic. Chambered for .375H&H Mag., .416 Rigby, .458 Win. Mag., .458 Lott. Overall length is 46.5"; barrel length 25"; weighs 9.4 lbs., 9.9 lbs (American). Hooded front sight, express rear with one standing, two folding leaves. Imported from the Czech Republic by CZ-USA.

Price: Safari Magnum $1,215.00

Price: American Safari Field .... $1,215.00 to $1,348.00
Price: American Kevlar $1,714.00

CZ 550 VARMINT

Similar to CZ 550 American Classic. Chambered for .308 Win. and .22-250. Kevlar, laminated stocks. Overall length is 46.7"; barrel length 25.6"; weighs 9.1 lbs. Imported from the Czech Republic by CZ-USA.

Price: $865.00
Price: Kevlar $1,037.00
Price: Laminated $966.00

CZ 550 MAGNUM H.E.T.

Similar to CZ 550 American Classic. Chambered for .338 Lapua, .300 Win. Mag., .300 RUM. Overall length is 52"; barrel length 28"; weighs 14 lbs. Adjustable sights, satin blued barrel. Imported from the Czech Republic by CZ-USA.

Price: $3,929.00

CZ 550 ULTIMATE HUNTING

Similar to CZ 550 American Classic. Chambered for .300 Win Mag. Overall length is 44.7"; barrel length 23.6"; weighs 7.7 lbs. Kevlar stock. Nightforce 5.5-20x50mm scope included. Imported from the Czech Republic by CZ-USA.

Price: $4,242.00

CZ 557

Caliber: .243 Win., 6.5x55, .270 Win., .308 Win., .30-06. **Capacity:** 5+1. **Barrel:** 20.5". **Stock:** Satin finished walnut or Manners carbon fiber with textured grip and fore-end. **Sights:** None on Sporter model; Carbine has fixed rear and fiber optic front. Forged steel receiver has integral scope mounts. Magazine has hinged floorplate. Trigger is adjustable. Push-feed action features short extractor and plunger style ejector.

Price: Carbine, walnut stock (shown) $812.00
Price: Sporter, walnut stock $792.00

DAKOTA 76 TRAVELER TAKEDOWN

Caliber: .257 Roberts, .25-06 Rem., 7x57, .270 Win., .280 Rem., .30-06 Spfl., .338-06, .35 Whelen (standard length); 7mm Rem. Mag., .300 Win. Mag., .338 Win. Mag., .416 Taylor, .458 Win. Mag. (short magnums); 7mm, .300, .330, .375 Dakota Magnums. **Barrel:** 23". **Weight:** 7.5 lbs. **Length:** 43.5" overall. **Stock:** Medium fancy-grade walnut in classic style. Checkered grip and fore-end; solid buttpad. **Sights:** None furnished; drilled and tapped for scope mounts. **Features:** Threadless disassembly. Uses modified Model 76 design with many features of the Model 70 Winchester. Left-hand model also available. Introduced 1989. African chambered for .338 Lapua Mag., .404 Jeffery, .416 Rigby, .416 Dakota, .450 Dakota, 4-round magazine, select wood, two stock cross-bolts. 24" barrel, weighs 9-10 lbs. Ramp front sight, standing leaf rear. Introduced 1989. Made in U.S.A. by Dakota Arms, Inc.

Price: Traveler $7,240.00
Price: Safari Traveler $9,330.00
Price: African Traveler $10,540.00

DAKOTA 76 CLASSIC

Caliber: .257 Roberts, .270 Win., .280 Rem., .30-06 Spfl., 7mm Rem. Mag., .338 Win. Mag., .300 Win. Mag., .375H&H, .458 Win. Mag.

Prices given are believed to be accurate at time of publication however, many factors affect retail pricing so exact prices are not possible.

71ST EDITION, 2017 ✛ 455

Barrel: 23". Weight: 7.5 lbs. Length: 43.5" overall. Stock: Medium fancy grade walnut in classic style. Checkered pistol grip and fore-end; solid buttpad. Sights: None furnished; drilled and tapped for scope mounts. Features: Has many features of the original Winchester Model 70. One-piece rail triggerguard assembly; steel gripcap. Model 70-style trigger. Many options available. Left-hand rifle available at same price. Introduced 1988. From Dakota Arms, Inc.

Price: From $6,030.00
Price: Professional Hunter $7,995.00
Price: Safari Grade $8,010.00

DAKOTA MODEL 97

Caliber: .22-250 to .330. Barrel: 22" to 24". Weight: 6.1 to 6.5 lbs. Length: 43" overall. Stock: Fiberglass. Sights: Optional. Features: Matte blue finish, black stock. Right-hand action only. Introduced 1998. Made in U.S.A. by Dakota Arms, Inc.

Price: From $3,720.00
Price: All Weather (stainless)..................................$4,050.00
Price: Outfitter Takedown $5,150.00
Price: Varminter $4,820.00

HOWA M-1500 RANCHLAND COMPACT

Caliber: .223 Rem., .22-250 Rem., .243 Win., .308 Win. and 7mm-08. Barrel: 20" #1 contour, blued finish. Weight: 7 lbs. Stock: Hogue Overmolded in black, OD green, Coyote Sand colors. 13.87" LOP. Sights: None furnished; drilled and tapped for scope mounting. Features: Three-position safety, hinged floorplate, adjustable trigger, forged one-piece bolt, M-16 style extractor, forged flat-bottom receiver. Also available with Nikko-Stirling Nighteater 3-9x42 riflescope. Introduced in 2008. Imported from Japan by Legacy Sports International.

Price: Rifle Only, (2008)..$762.00
Price: Rifle with 3-9x42 Nighteater scope (2008) $872.00

HOWA/AXIOM M-1500 VARMINTER

Caliber: .204, .223 Rem., .22-250 Rem., .243 Win., 6.5x55 (2008), .25-06 Rem. (2008), .270 Win., .308 Win., .30-06 Spfl., 7mm Rem., .300 Win. Mag., .338 Win. Mag., .375 Ruger standard barrel; .204, .223 Rem., .243 Win. and .308 Win. heavy barrel. Barrel: Howa barreled action, 22" contour standard barrel, 20" #6 contour heavy barrel, and 24" #6 contour heavy barrel. Weight: 8.6-10 lbs. Stock: Knoxx Industries Axiom V/S synthetic, black or camo. Adjustable length of pull from 11.5" to 15.5". Sights: None furnished; drilled and tapped for scope mounting. Features: Three-position safety, adjustable trigger, hinged floorplate, forged receiver with large recoil lug, forged one-piece bolt with dual locking lugs. Introduced in 2007. Standard-barrel scope packages come with 3-10x42 Nikko-Stirling Nighteater scope, rings, bases (2008). Heavy barrels come with 4-16x44 Nikko-Stirling scope. Imported from Japan by Legacy Sports International.

Price: From $915.00
Price: Varminter Package, camo stock w/scope from...........$1,065.00

HOWA/HOGUE KRYPTEK RIFLE

Caliber: Most popular calibers from .204 Ruger to .375 Ruger. Barrel: 20, 22 or 24", blue or stainless. Hogue overmolded stock in Kryptek Camo. Features include three-position safety, two-stage match trigger, one piece bolt with two locking lugs.

Price: $672.00
Price: Magnum calibers $700.00
Price: Stainless from...$736.00

HOWA ALPINE MOUNTAIN RIFLE

Caliber: .243 Win., 6.5 Creedmoor, 7mm-08, .308 Win. Barrel: 20". Weight: 5.7 lbs. Stock: OD Green synthetic. Features: Two-stage HACT trigger, Cerakote finish on barrel and action, Pachmyr Decelerator pad.

Price: Stainless from...$1,188.00

H-S PRECISION PRO-SERIES 2000

Caliber: Offered in about 30 different chamberings including virtually all popular calibers. Made in hunting, tactical and competition styles with many options. Barrel: 20", 22", 24" or 26", depending on model and caliber. Hunting models include the Pro-Hunter Rifle (PHR) designed for magnum calibers with built-in recoil reducer and heavier barrel; Pro-Hunter Lightweight (PHL) with slim, fluted barrel; Pro-Hunter Sporter (SPR) and Pro-Hunter Varmint (VAR). Takedown,

Competition and Tactical variations are available. Stock: H-S Precision synthetic stock in many styles and colors with full-length bedding block chassis system. Made in U.S.A.

Price: PHR $3,695.00
Price: PHL $3,795.00
Price: SPR $3,395.00
Price: SPL Sporter $3,495.00
Price: VAR $3,495.00
Price: PTD Hunter Takedown.......................................$3,495.00
Price: STR Short Tactical $3,795.00
Price: HTR Heavy Tactical $3,795.00
Price: Competition $3,795.00

KENNY JARRETT RIFLES

Caliber: Custom built in virtually any chambering including .223 Rem., .243 Improved, .243 Catbird, 7mm-08 Improved, .280 Remington, .280 Ackley Improved, 7mm Rem. Mag., .284 Jarrett, .30-06 Springfield, .300 Win. Mag., .300 Jarrett, .323 Jarrett, .338 Jarrett, .375 H&H, .416 Rem., .450 Rigby, other modern cartridges. Numerous options regarding barrel type and weight, stock styles and material. Features: Tri-Lock receiver. Talley rings and bases. Accuracy guarantees and custom loaded ammunition. Newest series is the Shikar featuring 28-year aged American Black walnut hand-checkered stock with Jarrett-designed stabilizing aluminum chassis. Accuracy guaranteed to be ½ MOA with standard calibers, 7/10 MOA with magnums.

Price: Shikar Series...$10,320.00
Price: Signature Series $8,320.00
Price: Long Ranger Series $8,320.00
Price: Ridge Walker Series $8,320.00
Price: Wind Walker $8,320.00
Price: Original Beanfield (customer's receiver) $6,050.00
Price: Professional Hunter $11,070.00
Price: SA/Custom $7,000.00

KIMBER MODEL 8400

Caliber: .25-06 Rem., .270 Win., 7mm, .30-06 Spfl., .300 Win. Mag., .338 Win. Mag., or .325 WSM, 4 shot. Barrel: 24". Weight: 6 lbs., 3 oz. to 6 lbs., 10 oz. Length: 43.25". Stock: Claro walnut or Kevlar-reinforced fiberglass. Sights: None; drilled and tapped for bases. Features: Mauser claw extractor, two-position wing safety, action bedded on aluminum pillars and fiberglass, free-floated barrel, match-grade adjustable trigger set at 4 lbs., matte or polished blue or matte stainless finish. Introduced 2003. Sonora model (2008) has brown laminated stock, hand-rubbed oil finish, chambered in .25-06 Rem., .30-06 Spfl., and .300 Win. Mag. Weighs 8.5 lbs., measures 44.50" overall length. Front swivel stud only for bipod. Stainless steel bull barrel, 24" satin stainless steel finish. Made in U.S.A. by Kimber Mfg. Inc.

Price: Classic $1,223.00
Price: Classic Select Grade, French walnut stock (2008)......$1,427.00
Price: SuperAmerica, AAA walnut stock............................$2,240.00
Price: Patrol Tactical $2,447.00
Price: Montana $1,427.00

KIMBER MODEL 8400 ADVANCED TACTICAL II

Caliber: 6.5 Creedmoor, .308 Win., .300 Win Mag. Five-round detachable box. Barrel: 22", 27", threaded and fitted with SureFire muzzlebrake/suppressor adaptor. Stock: Manners MCS-TS4 Folding. Weight: 10.6 to 11.3 lbs.
Price: $4,351.00

KIMBER MODEL 8400 CAPRIVI

Similar to 8400 bolt rifle, but chambered for .375 H&H, .416 Remington and .458 Lott, 4-shot magazine. Stock is Claro walnut or Kevlar-reinforced fiberglass. Features twin steel crossbolts in stock, AA French walnut, pancake cheekpiece, 24 lines-per-inch wrap-around checkering, ebony forend tip, hand-rubbed oil finish, barrel-mounted sling swivel stud, 3-leaf express sights, Howell-type rear sling swivel stud and a Pachmayr Decelerator recoil pad in traditional orange color. Introduced 2008. Made in U.S.A. by Kimber Mfg. Inc.

Price: From $3,263.00
Price: Special Edition from $5,031.00

KIMBER MODEL 8400 TALKEETNA

Similar to 8400 bolt rifle, but chambered for .375 H&H, 4-shot magazine. Weighs 8 lbs., overall length is 44.5". Stock is synthetic. Features free-floating match-grade barrel with tapered match-grade chamber and target crown, three-position wing safety acts directly on the cocking piece for greatest security, and Pachmayr Decelerator. Made in U.S.A. by Kimber Mfg. Inc

Price: $2,175.00

KIMBER MODEL 84M

Caliber: .22-250 Rem., .204 Ruger, .223 Rem., .243 Win., .257 Robts., .260 Rem., 7mm-08 Rem., .308 Win., 5-shot. **Barrel:** 22", 24", 26". **Weight:** 5 lbs., 10 oz. to 10 lbs. **Length:** 41" to 45". **Stock:** Claro walnut, checkered with steel gripcap; synthetic or gray laminate. **Sights:** None; drilled and tapped for bases. **Features:** Mauser claw extractor, three-position wing safety, action bedded on aluminum pillars, free-floated barrel, match-grade trigger set at 4 lbs., matte blue finish. Includes cable lock. Introduced 2001. Montana (2008) has synthetic stock, Pachmayr Decelerator recoil pad, stainless steel 22" sporter barrel. Adirondak has Kevlar white/black Optifade Forest camo stock, 18" barrel with threaded muzzle, weighs less than 5 lbs. Made in U.S.A. by Kimber Mfg. Inc.

Price: Classic $1,223.00
Price: Varmint $1,291.00
Price: Montana $1,427.00
Price: Adirondak $1,768.00

KIMBER MODEL 84M HUNTER

Caliber: .243 Win., .257 Robts., 6.5 Creedmoor, 7mm-08, .308 Win. Magazine capacity 3 + 1, removable box type. **Barrel:** 22 inches. **Weight:** 6.5 lbs. **Stock:** FDE Polymer with recoil pad, pillar bedding. **Finish:** Stainless. Other features include Mauser-type claw extractor, M70-type 3-position safety, adjustable trigger.
Price: $885.00

KIMBER MODEL 84L CLASSIC

Bolt-action rifle chambered in .270 Win. and .30-06. Features include 24-inch sightless matte blue sporter barrel; hand-rubbed A-grade walnut stock with 20 lpi panel checkering; pillar and glass bedding; Mauser claw extractor; 3-position M70-style safety; 5-round magazine; adjustable trigger.
Price: $1,427.00

MERKEL RX HELIX

Caliber: .223 Rem., .243 Rem., 6.5x55, 7mm-08, .308 Win., .270 Win., .30-06, 9.3x62, 7mm Rem. Mag., .300 Win. Mag., .270 WSM, .300 WSM, .338 Win. Mag. **Features:** Straight-pull bolt action. Synthetic stock on Explorer model. Walnut stock available in several grades. Factory engraved models available. Takedown system allows switching calibers in minutes.
Price: Explorer, synthetic stock, from $3,295.00
Price: Walnut stock, from $3,795.00

MOSSBERG MVP SERIES

Caliber: .223/5.56 NATO. 10-round capacity. Uses AR-style magazines. **Barrel:** 16.25 inches medium bull, 20-inch fluted sporter. **Weight:** 6.5 to 7 lbs. **Stock:** Classic black textured polymer. **Sights:** Adjustable folding rear, adjustable blade front. **Features:** Available

with factory mounted 3-9x32mm scope, (4-16x50mm on Varmint model). FLEX model has 20-inch fluted sporter barrel, FLEX AR-style 6-position adjustable stock. Varmint model has laminated stock, 24-inch barrel. Thunder Ranch model has 18-inch bull barrel, OD Green synthetic stock.

Price: Patrol model $709.00
Price: Patrol model w/scope......................... $863.00
Price: FLEX model $966.00
Price: FLEX MODEL w/scope........................ $1,142.00
Price: Thunder Ranch model $748.00
Price: Predator model................................. $709.00
Price: Predator model w/scope..................... $758.00
Price: Varmint Model.................................. $732.00
Price: Varmint Model w/scope...................... $912.00

MOSSBERG PATRIOT

Caliber: .22-250, .243 Win., .25-06, .270 Win., 7mm-08, .7mm Rem., .308 Win., .30-06, .300 Win. Mag., .38 Win. Mag., .375 Ruger. **Capacity:** 4 or 5 rounds. Detachable box magazine. **Barrel:** 22" sporter or fluted. **Stock:** Walnut, laminate, camo or synthetic black. **Weight:** 7.5 - 8 lbs. **Finish:** Matte blue. **Sights:** Adjustable or none. Some models available with 3-9x40mm scope. Other features include patented Lightning Bolt Action Trigger adjustable from 2 to 7 pounds, spiral-fluted bolt. Not all variants available in all calibers. Introduced in 2015.
Price: Walnut stock.................................... $438.00
Price: Walnut with premium Vortex Crossfire scope $649.00
Price: Synthetic stock................................. $386.00
Price: Synthetic stock with standard scope $426.00
Price: Laminate stock w/iron sights................ $584.00
Price: Deer THUG w/Mossy Oak Infinity Camo stock $500.00

MOSSBERG PATRIOT NIGHT TRAIN

Caliber: .308 Win. or .300 Win. Mag. Tactical model with Silencerco Saker Muzzlebrake, 6-24x50mm scope with tactical turrets, green synthetic stock with Neoprene comb-raising kit. **Weight:** 9 lbs.
Price: Night Train with 6-24x50mm $811.00

NESIKA SPORTER RIFLE

Caliber: .260 Rem., 6.5x284, 7mm-08, .280 Rem., 7mm Rem. Mag., 308 Win., .30-06, .300 Win. Mag. **Barrel:** 24 or 26" Douglas air-gauged stainless. **Stock:** Composite with aluminum bedding block. **Sights:** None, Leupold QRW bases. **Weight:** 8 lbs. **Features:** Timney trigger set at 3 pounds, receiver made from 15-5 stainless steel, one-piece bolt from 4340 CM steel. Guaranteed accuracy at 100 yards.
Price: $3,499.00
Price: Long Range w/heavy bbl., varmint stock $3,999.00
Price: Tactical w/28î bbl., muzzle brake, adj. stock............. $4,499.00

NEW ULTRA LIGHT ARMS

Caliber: Custom made in virtually every current chambering. **Barrel:**

Prices given are believed to be accurate at time of publication however, many factors affect retail pricing so exact prices are not possible.

71ST EDITION, 2017 ✦ **457**

Douglas, length to order. **Weight:** 4.75 to 7.5 lbs. **Length:** Varies. **Stock:** Kevlar graphite composite, variety of finishes. **Sights:** None furnished; drilled and tapped for scope mounts. **Features:** Timney trigger, hand-lapped action, button-rifled barrel, hand-bedded action, recoil pad, sling-swivel studs, optional Jewell trigger. Made in U.S.A. by New Ultra Light Arms.

Price: Model 20 Ultimate Mountain Rifle $3,240.00
Price: Model 20 Ultimate Varmint Rifle $3,500.00
Price: Model 24 Ultimate Plains Rifle $3,325.00
Price: Model 28 Ultimate Alaskan Rifle $3,475.00
Price: Model 40 Ultimate African Rifle $3,475.00
Price: Model 20 Rimfire Rifle $1,600.00

NOSLER MODEL 48 SERIES
Caliber: Offered in most popular calibers including .280 Ackley Improved and 6.5-284 wildcats. **Barrel:** 24". **Weight:** 7.25 to 8 lbs. **Stock:** Walnut or composite. Custom Model is made to order with several optional features.

Price: Patriot $1,795.00
Price: Heritage $1,895.00
Price: Custom Model from $3,795.00

REMINGTON MODEL 700 CDL CLASSIC DELUXE
Caliber: .243 Win., .25-06 Rem., .270 Win., 7mm-08 Rem., .280 Remington, 7mm Rem. Mag., 7mm Rem. Ultra Mag., .30-06 Spfl., .300 Win. Mag. **Barrel:** 24" or 26" round tapered. **Weight:** 7.4 to 7.6 lbs. **Length:** 43.6" to 46.5" overall. **Stock:** Straight-comb American walnut stock, satin finish, checkering, right-handed cheekpiece, black fore-end tip and grip cap, sling swivel studs. **Sights:** None. **Features:** Satin blued finish, jeweled bolt body, drilled and tapped for scope mounts. Hinged-floorplate magazine capacity: 4, standard calibers; 3, magnum calibers. SuperCell recoil pad, cylindrical receiver, integral extractor. Introduced 2004. CDL SF (stainless fluted) chambered for .260 Rem., .257 Wby. Mag., .270 Win., .270 WSM, 7mm-08 Rem., 7mm Rem. Mag., .30-06 Spfl., .300 WSM. Left-hand versions introduced 2008 in six calibers. Made in U.S. by Remington Arms Co., Inc.

Price: Standard Calibers from .... $1,029.00 to $1,089.00
Price: CDL SF from $1,180.00

REMINGTON MODEL 700 BDL
Caliber: .243 Win., .270 Win., 7mm Rem. Mag., .30-06 Spfl., .300 Rem Ultra Mag. **Barrel:** 22, 24, 26" round tapered. **Weight:** 7.25-7.4 lbs. **Length:** 41.6-46.5" overall. **Stock:** Walnut. Gloss-finish pistol grip stock with skip-line checkering, black forend tip and gripcap with white line spacers. **Sights:** Gold bead ramp front; hooded ramp, removable step-adjustable rear with windage screw. **Features:** Side safety, receiver tapped for scope mounts, matte receiver top, quick detachable swivels. 200th Year Anniversary edition is limited to 2,016 rifles with C grade walnut stock, special engraving and medallion. Introduced in 2016.

Price: Standard Calibers $994.00
Price: Magnum Calibers $1,020.00
Price: 50th Anniversary Edition, 7mm Rem. Mag. $1,399.00
Price: 200th Year Anniversary Limited Edition $2,399.00

REMINGTON MODEL 700 SPS
Caliber: : .22-250 Rem., 6.8 Rem SPC, .223 Rem., .243 Win., .270 Win., .270 WSM, 7mm-08 Rem., 7mm Rem. Mag., 7mm Rem. Ultra Mag., .30-06 Spfl., .308 Win., .300 WSM, .300 Win. Mag., .300 Rem. Ultra Mag. **Barrel:** 20", 24" or 26" carbon steel. **Weight:** 7 to 7.6 lbs. **Length:** 39.6" to 46.5" overall. **Stock:** Black synthetic, sling swivel studs, SuperCell recoil pad. Woodtech model has walnut decorated synthetic stock with overmolded grip patterns. Camo stock available. **Sights:** None. Introduced 2005. SPS Stainless replaces Model 700 BDL Stainless Synthetic. **Barrel:**

Bead-blasted 416 stainless steel. **Features:** Plated internal fire control component. SPS DM features detachable box magazine. SPS Varmint includes X-Mark Pro trigger, 26" heavy contour barrel, vented beavertail fore-end, dual front sling swivel studs. Made in U.S. by Remington Arms Co., Inc.

Price: From .... $724.00 to $838.00

REMINGTON 700 SPS TACTICAL
Caliber: :.223 .300 AAC Blackout and .308 Win. **Features:** Features include 20-inch heavy-contour tactical-style barrel; dual-point pillar bedding; black synthetic stock with Hogue overmoldings; semi-beavertail fore-end; X-Mark Pro adjustable trigger system; satin black oxide metal finish; hinged floorplate magazine; SuperCell recoil pad.

Price: From .... $788.00 to $842.00

REMINGTON 700 VTR A-TACS CAMO
Caliber: :.223 and .308 Win. **Features:** Features include ATACS camo finish overall; triangular contour 22-inch barrel has an integral muzzlebrake; black overmold grips; 1:9" twist (.223 caliber), or 1:12" (.308) twist.

Price: $930.00

REMINGTON MODEL 700 VLS
Caliber: .204 Ruger, .223 Rem., .22-250 Rem., .243 Win., .308 Win. **Barrel:** 26" heavy contour barrel (0.820" muzzle O.D.), concave target-style barrel crown. **Weight:** 9.4 lbs. **Length:** 45.75" overall. **Stock:** Brown laminated stock, satin finish, with beavertail fore-end, gripcap, rubber buttpad. **Sights:** None. **Features:** Introduced 1995. Made in U.S. by Remington Arms Co., Inc.

Price: $1,056.00

REMINGTON MODEL 700 SENDERO SF II
Caliber: 7mm Rem. Mag., .300 Win. Mag., .300 Rem. Ultra Mag. **Barrel:** Satin stainless 26" heavy contour fluted. **Weight:** 8.5 lbs. **Length:** 45.75" overall. **Stock:** Black composite reinforced with aramid fibers, beavertail fore-end, palm swell. **Sights:** None. **Features:** Aluminum bedding block, drilled and tapped for scope mounts, hinged floorplate magazines. Introduced 1996. Made in U.S. by Remington Arms Co., Inc.

Price: $1,465.00

REMINGTON MODEL 700 TARGET TACTICAL
Caliber: .308 Win. **Barrel:** 26" triangular counterbored, 1:11-1/2" rifling. **Weight:** 11.75 lbs. **Length:** 45-3/4" overall. **Features:** Textured green Bell & Carlson varmint/tactical stock with adjustable comb and length of pull, adjustable trigger, satin black oxide finish on exposed metal surfaces, hinged floorplate, SuperCell recoil pad, matte blue on exposed metal surfaces.

Price: $2,138.00

REMINGTON MODEL 700 VTR SERIES
Caliber: .204 Ruger, .22-250, .223 Rem., .243 Win., .308 Win. **Barrel:** 22" triangular counterbored with integrated muzzlebrake. **Weight:** 7.5 lbs. **Length:** 41-5/8" overall. **Features:** Olive drab overmolded or Digital Tiger TSP Desert Camo stock with vented semi-beavertail fore-end, tactical-style dual swivel mounts for bipod, matte blue on exposed metal surfaces.

Price: From .... $825.00 to $980.00

Prices given are believed to be accurate at time of publication however, many factors affect retail pricing so exact prices are not possible.

CENTERFIRE RIFLES Bolt-Action

REMINGTON MODEL 700 VARMINT SF
Caliber: .22-250, .223, .220 Swift, .308 Win. **Barrel:** 26" stainless steel fluted. **Weight:** 8.5 lbs. **Length:** 45.75 inches. **Features:** Synthetic stock with ventilated forend, stainless steel/triggerguard/floorplate, dual tactical swivels for bipod attachment.
Price: **$991.00**

REMINGTON MODEL 700 MOUNTAIN SS
Calibers: .25-06, .270 Win., .280 Rem., 7mm-08, .308 Win., .30-06. **Barrel:** 22". **Length:** 40.6". **Weight:** 6.5 lbs. Satin stainless finish, Bell & Carlson Aramid Fiber stock.
Price: **$1,135.00**

REMINGTON MODEL 700 XCR TACTICAL
Caliber: .308 Win., .300 Win. Mag., 338 Lapua Mag. Detachable box magazine. **Barrel:** 26-inch varmint contour, fluted and free floating. Tactical, long-range precision rifle with Bell & Carlson Tactical stock in OD Green, full-length aluminum bedding, adjustable X-Mark Pro trigger. Muzzlebrake on .338 Lapua model.
Price: **$1,525.00**

REMINGTON MODEL 783
Calibers: .223 Rem., .22-250, .243 Win., .270 Win., 7mm Rem. Mag., .308 Win., .30-06 Sprg., .300 Win. Mag. **Barrel:** 22 inches. **Stock:** Synthetic. **Weight:** 7 to 7.25 lbs. **Finish:** Matte black. **Features:** Adjustable trigger with two-position trigger-block safety, magnum contour button-rifle barrel, cylindrical receiver with minimum-size ejection port, pillar-bedded stock, detachable box magazine, 90-degree bolt throw.
Price: **$399.00**
Price: Compact with 18¼" or 20" bbl.................... **$399.00**
Price: Mossy Oak Breakup Camo stock.................... **$451.00**

REMINGTON MODEL SEVEN CDL
Calibers: .243, .260 Rem., 7mm-08, .308 Win. **Barrel:** 20". **Weight:** 6.5 lbs. **Length:** 39.25". **Stock:** Walnut with black fore-end tip, satin finish. Predator model in .223, .22-250 and .243 has Mossy Oak Brush camo stock, 22" barrel.
Price: CDL **$1,039.00**
Price: Predator **$895.00**
Price: Synthetic stock **$731.00**

REMINGTON 40-XB TACTICAL
Caliber: .308 Winchester. **Features:** Features include stainless steel bolt with Teflon coating; hinged floorplate; adjustable trigger; 27-1/4-inch tri-fluted 1:14" twist barrel; H-S precision pro series tactical stock, black color with dark green spiderweb; two front swivel studs; one rear swivel stud; vertical pistol grip. From the Remington Custom Shop.
Price: **$2,995.00**

REMINGTON 40-XB RANGEMASTER
Caliber: Almost any caliber from .22 BR Rem. to .300 Rem. Ultra Mag. Single-shot or repeater. **Features:** Features include stainless steel bolt with Teflon coating; hinged floorplate; adjustable trigger; 27-1/4-inch tri-fluted 1:14" twist barrel; walnut stock. From the Remington Custom Shop.
Price: **$2,595.00**

REMINGTON 40-XS TACTICAL SERIES
Caliber: .338 Lapua Magnum. **Features:** Features include 416 stainless steel Model 40-X 24-inch 1:12" twist barreled action;

black polymer coating; McMillan A3 series stock with adjustable length of pull and adjustable comb; adjustable trigger and Sunny Hill heavy-duty, all-steel triggerguard; Tactical Weapons System has Harris bi-pod with quick adjust swivel lock, Leupold Mark IV 3.5-10x40mm long range M1 scope with Mil Dot reticle, Badger Ordnance all-steel Picatinny scope rail and rings, military hard case, Turner AWS tactical sling. From the Remington Custom Shop.
Price: .308 Win.. **$4,400.00**
Price: .338 Lapua.. **$4,950.00**
Price: Tactical Weapons System from **$7,731.00**

ROCK ISLAND ARMORY TCM
Caliber: .22 TCM. 5-round capacity magazine, interchangeable with .22 TCM 17-round pistol magazine. **Barrel:** 22.75 inches. **Weight:** 6 pounds. Chambered for .22 TCM cartridge introduced in 2013. Manufactured in the Philippines and imported by Armscor Precision International.
Price: **$450.00**

RUGER PRECISION RIFLE
Calibers: .243 Win., 6.5 Creedmoor, .308 Win. Magazine capacity 10 rounds. **Barrel:** Medium contour, 20" (.308), 24" (6.5), 26" (.243). **Stock:** Folding with adjustable length of pull and comb height. Soft rubber buttplate, sling attachment points, Picatinny bottom rail. **Weight:** 9.7 to 11 lbs. **Features:** Three lug one-piece CNC-machined bolt with oversized handle, dual cocking cams; multi magazine interface works with Magpul, DPMS, SR-25, M110, AICS and some M14 magazines; CNC-machined 4140 chrome-moly steel upper; Ruger Marksman adjustable trigger with wrench stored in bolt shroud; comes with two 10-round Magpul magazines. Introduced in 2016.
Price: **$1,399.00**

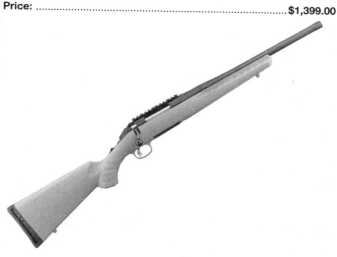

Prices given are believed to be accurate at time of publication however, many factors affect retail pricing so exact prices are not possible.

71ST EDITION, 2017 ✦ **459**

CENTERFIRE RIFLES Bolt-Action

RUGER AMERICAN RIFLE

Caliber: .22-250, .243, 7mm-08, .308, .270 Win., .30-06 (4-shot rotary magazine). **Barrel:** 22" or 18" (Compact). **Length:** 42.5". **Weight:** 6.25 lbs. **Stock:** Black composite. **Finish:** Matte black or matte stainless (All Weather model). **Features:** Tang safety, hammer-forged free-floating barrel. Available with factory mounted Redfield Revolution 4x scope. Ranch model has Flat Dark Earth composite stock, Predator has Moss Green composite stock, both chambered in several additional calibers to standard model.

Price: Standard or compact...$489.00
Price: All-weather model, standard or compact.....................$629.00
Price: With scope...$639.00
Price: Ranch or Predator model $529.00

RUGER GUNSITE SCOUT RIFLE

Caliber: .308 Win., 10-shot magazine capacity. **Barrel:** 16.5". **Weight:** 7 lbs. **Length:** 38-39.5". **Stock:** Black laminate. **Sights:** Front post sight and rear adjustable. **Features:** Gunsite Scout Rifle is a credible rendition of Col. Jeff Cooper's "fighting carbine" Scout Rifle. The Ruger Gunsite Scout Rifle is a platform in the Ruger M77 family. While the Scout Rifle has M77 features such as controlled round feed and integral scope mounts (scope rings included), the 10-round detachable box magazine is the first clue this isn't your grandfather's Ruger rifle. The Ruger Gunsite Scout Rifle has a 16.5 medium contour, cold hammer-forged, alloy steel barrel with a Mini-14 protected nonglare post front sight and receiver mounted, adjustable ghost ring rear sight for out-of-the-box usability. A forward mounted Picatinny rail offers options in mounting an assortment of optics – including Scout Scopes available from Burris and Leupold, for "both eyes open" sighting and super-fast target acquisition.

Price: $1,075.00
Price: (stainless)..$1,139.00

RUGER ROTARY MAGAZINE RIFLE

Caliber: .17 Hornet, .22 Hornet, .357 Magnum, . 44 Magnum (capacity 4 to 6 rounds). **Barrel:** 18.5" (.357 and .44 Mag.), 20 or 24" (.17 Hornet and .22 Hornet). **Weight:** 5.5 to 7.5 lbs. **Stock:** American walnut, black synthetic, Next G1 Vista Camo or Green Mountain laminate.

Price: 77/17, Green Mtn. Laminate stock $969.00
Price: 77/22, Green Mtn. Laminate stock $969.00
Price: 77/22, walnut stock $939.00
Price: 77/357, 77/44, black synthetic stock $999.00
Price: 77/44, Next G1 Vista Camo $1,060.00

RUGER GUIDE GUN

Calibers: .30-06, .300 Ruger Compact Mag., .300 Win. Mag., .338 RCM, .338 Win. Mag., .375 Ruger. **Capacity:** 3 or 4 rounds. **Barrel:** 20 inches with barrelband sling swivel and removable muzzlebrake. **Weight:** 8 to 8.12 pounds. **Stock:** Green Mountain Laminate. **Finish:** Hawkeye matte stainless. **Sights:** Adjustable rear, bead front. Introduced 2013.

Price: $1,269.00

RUGER HAWKEYE

Caliber: .204 Ruger, .223 Rem., .22-250 Rem., .243 Win., .25-06 Rem., .270 Win., .280 Rem., 6.5 Creedmoor, 7mm/08, 7mm Rem. Mag., .308 Win., .30-06 Spfl., .300 Win. Mag., .338 Win. Mag., .375 Ruger, .416 Ruger. 4-shot magazine, except 3-shot magazine for magnums; 5-shot magazine for .204 Ruger and .223 Rem. **Barrel:** 22", 24". **Weight:** 6.75 to 8.25 lbs. **Length:** 42-44.4" overall. **Stock:** American walnut, laminate or synthetic. Magnum Hunter has Green Hogue stock. **Sights:** None furnished. Receiver has Ruger integral scope mount base, Ruger 1" rings. **Features:** Includes Ruger LC6 trigger, new red rubber recoil pad, Mauser-type controlled feeding, claw extractor, 3-position safety, hammer-forged steel barrels, Ruger scope rings. Walnut stocks have wrap-around cut checkering on the forearm, and more rounded contours on stock and top of pistol grips. Matte stainless all-weather version features synthetic stock. Hawkeye African chambered in .375 Ruger and has 23" blued barrel, checkered walnut stock, windage-adjustable shallow "V" notch rear sight, white bead front sight. Introduced 2007.

Price: Standard, right- and left-hand.......................................$939.00
Price: All-Weather $939.00
Price: Compact $939.00
Price: Laminate Compact $999.00
Price: Compact Magnum $969.00
Price: Magnum Hunter $1,139.00
Price: VT Varmint Target $1,139.00
Price: Predator $1,139.00
Price: African with muzzlebrake...$1,279.00

SAKO TRG-22 TACTICAL RIFLE

Caliber: .308 Winchester (TRG-22). **Features:** Features include target grade Cr-Mo or stainless barrels with muzzlebrake; three locking lugs; 60° bolt throw; adjustable two-stage target trigger; adjustable or folding synthetic stock; receiver-mounted integral 17mm axial optics rails with recoil stop-slots; tactical scope mount for modern three-turret tactical scopes (30 and 34 mm tube diameter); optional bipod.

Price: TRG-22 ....$3,495.00
Price: TRG-42 ....$4,550.00

SAKO MODEL 85

Caliber: .22-250 Rem., .243 Win., .25-06 Rem., .260, 6.5x55mm, .270 Win., .270 WSM, 7mm-08 Rem., 7x64, .308 Win., .30-06; 7mm WSM, .300 WSM, .338 Federal, 8x57IS, 9.3x62. **Barrel:** 22.4", 22.9", 24.4".

Weight: 7.75 lbs. Length: NA. Stock: Polymer, laminated or high-grade walnut, straight comb, shadow-line cheekpiece. Sights: None furnished. Features: Controlled-round feeding, adjustable trigger, matte stainless or nonreflective satin blue. Offered in a wide range of variations and models. Introduced 2006. Imported from Finland by Beretta USA.

Price: Grey Wolf $1,725.00
Price: Black Bear $1,850.00
Price: Kodiak $1,950.00
Price: Varmint Laminated $2,025.00
Price: Classic...$2,275.00
Price: Bavarian ....$2,200.00 - $2,300.00
Price: Bavarian carbine, Full-length stock $2,400.00
Price: Brown Bear $2,175.00

SAKO 85 FINNLIGHT
Similar to Model 85 but chambered in .243 Win., .25-06, .260 Rem., .270 Win., .270 WSM, .300 WSM, .30-06, .300 WM, .308 Win., 6.5x55mm, 7mm Rem Mag., 7mm-08. Weighs 6 lbs., 3 oz. to 6 lbs. 13 oz. Stainless steel barrel and receiver, black synthetic stock
Price: $1,800.00

SAVAGE AXIS SERIES
Caliber: .243 WIN., 7mm-08 REM., .308 WIN., .25-06 REM., .270 WIN, .30-06 SPFLD., .223 REM., .22-250 REM. Barrel: 22". Weight: 6.5 lbs. Length: 43.875". Stock: Black synthetic or camo, including pink/black Muddy Girl. Sights: Drilled and tapped for scope mounts. Several models come with factory mounted Weaver Kaspa 3-9x40 scope. Features: Available with black matte or stainless finish
Price: From ....$363.00 to $525.00

SAVAGE MODEL 25
Caliber: .17 Hornet, .22 Hornet, .222 Rem., .204 Ruger, .223 Rem., 4-shot magazine. Barrel: 24", medium-contour fluted barrel with recessed target crown, free-floating sleeved barrel, dual pillar bedding. Weight: 8.25 lbs. Length: 43.75" overall. Stock: Brown laminate with beavertail-style fore-end. Sights: Weaver-style bases installed. Features: Diameter-specific action built around the .223 Rem. bolthead dimension. Three locking lugs, 60-degree bolt lift, AccuTrigger adjustable from 2.5 to 3.25 lbs. Model 25 Classic Sporter has satin lacquer American walnut with contrasting fore-end tip, wraparound checkering, 22" blued barrel. Weight: 7.15 lbs. Length: 41.75". Introduced 2008. Made in U.S.A. by Savage Arms, Inc.
Price: From ....$620.00 to $824.00

SAVAGE CLASSIC SERIES MODEL 14/114
Caliber: .243 Win., 7mm-08 Rem., .308 Win., .270 Win., 7mm Rem. Mag., .30-06 Spfl., .300 Win. Mag., 3- or 4-shot magazine. Barrel: 22" or 24". Weight: 7 to 7.5 lbs. Length: 41.75" to 43.75" overall (Model 14 short action); 43.25" to 45.25" overall (Model 114 long action). Stock: Satin lacquer American walnut with ebony fore-end, wraparound checkering, Monte Carlo Comb and cheekpiece. Sights: None furnished. Receiver drilled and tapped for scope mounting. Features: AccuTrigger, matte blued barrel and action, hinged floorplate.
Price: $922.00

SAVAGE MODEL 12 VARMINT/TARGET SERIES
Caliber: .204 Ruger, .223 Rem., .22-250 Rem.; 4-shot magazine. Barrel: 26" stainless barreled action, heavy fluted, free-floating

and button-rifled barrel. Weight: 10 lbs. Length: 46.25" overall. Stock: Dual pillar bedded, low profile, black synthetic or laminated stock with extra-wide beavertail fore-end. Sights: None furnished; drilled and tapped for scope mounting. Features: Recessed target-style muzzle. AccuTrigger, oversized bolt handle, detachable box magazine, swivel studs. Model 112BVSS has heavy target-style prone laminated stock with high comb, Wundhammer palm swell, internal box magazine. Model 12VLP DBM has black synthetic stock, detachable magazine, and additional chamberings in .243, .308 Win., .300 Win. Mag. Model 12FV has blued receiver. Model 12BTCSS has brown laminate vented thumbhole stock. Made in U.S.A. by Savage Arms, Inc.

Price: 12 FV $732.00
Price: 12 FCV $904.00
Price: 12 BVSS $1,146.00
Price: 12 Varminter Low Profile (VLP) $1,181.00
Price: 12 Long Range Precision $1,288.00
Price: 12 BTCSS Thumbhole stock $1,293.00
Price: 12 Long Range Precision Varminter $1,554.00
Price: 12 F Class $1,648.00
Price: 12 Palma...$2,147.00

SAVAGE MODEL 16/116 WEATHER WARRIORS
Caliber: .204 Ruger, .223 Rem., .22-250 Rem., .243 Win., 6.5 Creedmoor, 6.5-284 Norma, 7mm-08 Rem., .308 Win., .270 WSM, 7mm WSM, .300 WSM (short action Model 16), 2- or 4-shot magazine; .270 Win., 7mm Rem. Mag., .30-06 Spfl., .300 Win. Mag., .338 Win. Mag. (long action Model 114), 3- or 4-shot magazine. Barrel: 22", 24"; stainless steel with matte finish, free-floated barrel. Weight: 6.5 to 6.75 lbs. Length: 41.75" to 43.75" overall (Model 16); 42.5" to 44.5" overall (Model 116). Stock: Graphite/fiberglass filled composite. Sights: None furnished; drilled and tapped for scope mounting. Features: Quick-detachable swivel studs; laser-etched bolt. Left-hand models available. Model 116FSS introduced 1991; 116FSAK introduced 1994. Made in U.S.A. by Savage Arms, Inc.
Price: From ....$885.00 to $966.00

SAVAGE MODEL 11/111 HUNTER SERIES
Caliber: .223 Rem., .22-250 Rem., .243 Win., 6.5 Creedmoor, .260 Rem., 6.5x284 Norma, .338 Lapua, 7mm-08 Rem., .308 Win., 2- or 4-shot magazine; .25-06 Rem., .270 Win., 7mm Rem. Mag., .30-06 Spfl., .300 Win. Mag., (long action Model 111), 3- or 4-shot magazine. Barrel: 20", 22" or 24"; blued free-floated barrel. Weight: 6.5 to 6.75 lbs. Length: 41.75" to 43.75" overall (Model 11); 42.5" to 44.5" overall (Model 111). Stock: Graphite/fiberglass filled composite or hardwood. Sights: Ramp front, open fully adjustable rear; drilled and tapped for scope mounting. Features: Three-position top tang safety, double front locking lugs. Introduced 1994. Made in U.S.A. by Savage Arms, Inc.
Price: From ....$595.00 to $1,171.00

SAVAGE MODEL 10 BAS LAW ENFORCEMENT
Caliber: .308 Win., (10 BAS), .300 Win., .338 Lapua (110 BA). Barrel: 24" or 26" fluted heavy with muzzlebrake Weight: 13.4 to 15.6 lbs. Length: 45". Features: Bolt-action repeater based on Model 10 action but with M4-style collapsible buttstock, pistol grip with palm swell, all-

Prices given are believed to be accurate at time of publication however, many factors affect retail pricing so exact prices are not possible.

71ST EDITION, 2017 ✦ **461**

aluminum Accustock, Picatinny rail for mounting optics.
Price: 10 BAS... **$2,446.00**
Price: 110 BA... **$2,638.00**

SAVAGE MODEL 10FP/110FP LAW ENFORCEMENT SERIES
Caliber: .223 Rem., .308 Win. (Model 10), 4-shot magazine; .25-06 Rem., .300 Win. Mag., (Model 110), 3- or 4-shot magazine. **Barrel:** 24"; matte blued free-floated heavy barrel and action. **Weight:** 6.5 to 6.75 lbs. **Length:** : 41.75" to 43.75" overall (Model 10); 42.5" to 44.5" overall (Model 110). **Stock:** Black graphite/fiberglass composition, pillar-bedded, positive checkering. **Sights:** None furnished. Receiver drilled and tapped for scope mounting. **Features:** Black matte finish on all metal parts. Double swivel studs on the forend for sling and/or bipod mount. Right- or left-hand. Model 110FP introduced 1990. Model 10FP introduced 1998. Model 10FCP HS has HS Precision black synthetic tactical stock with molded alloy bedding system, Leupold 3.5-10x40mm black matte scope with Mil Dot reticle, Farrell Picatinny Rail Base, flip-open lens covers, 1.25" sling with QD swivels, Harris bipod, Storm heavy-duty case. Made in U.S.A. by Savage Arms, Inc.
Price: Model 10FCP McMillan, McMillan fiberglass tactical
  stock...**$1,591.00**
Price: Model 10FCP-HS HS Precision, HS Precision tactical
  stock...**$1,315.00**
Price: Model 10FCP **$925.00**
Price: Model 10FLCP, left-hand model, standard stock
  or Accu-Stock **$975.00**
Price: Model 10FCP SR.. **$785.00**
Price: Model 10 Precision Carbine **$952.00**

SAVAGE MODEL 10 PREDATOR SERIES
Caliber: .204 Ruger. .223, .22-250, .243, .260 Rem., 6.5 Creedmoor, 6.5x284 Norma. **Barrel:** 22", medium-contour. **Weight:** 7.25 lbs. **Length:** 43" overall. **Stock:** Synthetic with rounded fore-end and oversized bolt handle. **Features:** Entirely covered in either Mossy Oak Brush or Realtree Hardwoods Snow pattern camo. Also features AccuTrigger, AccuStock, detachable box magazine.
Price: **$999.00**

SAVAGE MODEL 12 PRECISION TARGET SERIES
BENCHREST
Caliber: .308 Win., 6.5x284 Norma, 6mm Norma BR. **Barrel:** 29" ultra-heavy. **Weight:** 12.75 lbs. **Length:** 50" overall. **Stock:** Gray laminate. **Features:** New Left-Load, Right-Eject target action, Target AccuTrigger adjustable from approx 6 oz. to 2.5 lbs, oversized bolt handle, stainless extra-heavy free-floating and button-rifled barrel.
Price: **$1,629.00**

SAVAGE MODEL 12 PRECISION TARGET PALMA
Similar to Model 12 Benchrest but in .308 Win. only, 30" barrel, multi-adjustable stock, weighs 13.3 lbs.
Price: **$2,147.00**

SAVAGE MODEL 12 F CLASS TARGET RIFLE
Similar to Model 12 Benchrest but chambered in 6 Norma BR, 30" barrel, weighs 13.3 lbs.
Price: **$1,648.00**

SAVAGE MODEL 12 F/TR TARGET RIFLE
Similar to Model 12 Benchrest but in .308 Win. only, 30" barrel, weighs 12.65 lbs.
Price: **$1,538.00**

STEYR MANNLICHER CLASSIC
Caliber: .222 Rem., .223 Rem., .243 Win., .25-06 Rem., .308 Win., 6.5x55, .270 Win., .270 WSM, 7x64 Brenneke, 7mm-08 Rem., .30-06 Spfl., 8x57IS, 9.3x62, 7mm Rem. Mag., .300 WSM, .300 Win. Mag., .330 Wby. Mag.; 4-shot magazine. **Barrel:** 23.6" standard; 26" magnum; 20" full stock standard calibers. **Weight:** 7 lbs. **Length:** 40.1" overall. **Stock:** Hand-checkered fancy European oiled walnut with standard fore-end. **Sights:** Ramp front adjustable for elevation, V-notch rear adjustable for windage. **Finish:** Deep blue with case colors. **Features:** Single adjustable trigger; 3-position roller safety with "safe-bolt" setting; drilled and tapped for Steyr factory scope mounts. Introduced 1997. Imported from Austria by Steyr Arms, Inc.
Price: Half stock **$2,495.00**
Price: Full stock **$2,695.00**

STEYR PRO HUNTER
Similar to the Classic Rifle except has ABS synthetic stock with adjustable butt spacers, straight comb without cheekpiece, palm swell, Pachmayr 1" swivels. Special 10-round magazine conversion kit available. Introduced 1997. Imported from Austria by Steyr Arms, Inc.
Price: From .... **$1,150.00 to $1,377.00**

STEYR SCOUT
Caliber: .308 Win., 5-shot magazine. **Barrel:** 19", fluted. **Weight:** NA. **Length:** NA. **Stock:** Gray Zytel. **Sights:** Pop-up front & rear, Leupold M8 2.5x28 IER scope on Picatinny optic rail with Steyr mounts. **Features:** luggage case, scout sling, two stock spacers, two magazines. Introduced 1998. Imported from Austria by Steyr Arms, Inc.
Price: From **$2,199.00**

STEYR SSG08
Caliber: 7.62x51mmNATO (.308Win) or 7.62x63B (.300 Win Mag)., 10-shot magazine capacity. **Barrel:** 508mm or 600mm. **Weight:** 5.5 kg - 5.7 kg. **Length:** 1090mm - 1182mm. **Stock:** Dural aluminium foldingstock black with .280 mm long UIT-rail and various Picatinny rails. **Sights:** Front post sight and rear adjustable. **Features:** The STEYR SSG 08 features high-grade alumnium folding stock, adjustable cheekpiece and buttplate with height marking, and an ergonomical exchangeable pistol grip. The STEYR SSG 08 also features a Versa-Pod, a muzzlebrake, a Picatinny rail, a UIT rail on stock and various Picatinny rails on fore-end, and a 10-round HC-magazine. SBSrotary

Prices given are believed to be accurate at time of publication however, many factors affect retail pricing so exact prices are not possible

bolt action with four frontal locking lugs, arranged in pairs. Cold-hammer-forged barrels are available in standard or compact lengths.
Price: **$5,899.00**

STEYR SSG 69 PII
Caliber: .22-250 Rem., .243 Win., .308 Win., detachable 5-shot rotary magazine. **Barrel:** 26". **Weight:** 8.5 lbs. **Length:** 44.5" overall. **Stock:** Black ABS Cycolac with spacers for length of pull adjustment. **Sights:** Hooded ramp front adjustable for elevation, V-notch rear adjustable for windage. **Features:** Sliding safety; NATO rail for bipod; 1" swivels; Parkerized finish; single or double-set triggers. Imported from Austria by Steyr Arms, Inc.
Price: **$1,889.00**

THOMPSON/CENTER DIMENSION
Caliber: .204 Ruger, .223 Rem., .22-250 Rem., .243 Win., .270 Win., 7mm Rem. Mag., .308 Win., .30-06 Springfield, .300 Win. Mag., 3-round magazine. **Barrel:** 22 or 24". **Weight:** NA. **Length:** NA. **Stock:** Textured grip composite with adjustment spacers. **Features:** Calibers are interchangeable between certain series or "families" – .204/.223; .22-250/.243/7mm-08/.308; .270/.30-06; 7mm Rem. Mag./.300 Win. Mag. Introduced in 2012.
Price: **$689.00**

THOMPSON/CENTER VENTURE
Caliber: .270 Win., 7mm Rem. Mag., .30-06 Springfield, .300 Win. Mag. Standard length action with 3-round magazine. **Barrel:** 24", 20" (Compact). **Weight:** 7.5 lbs. **Stock:** Composite. **Sights:** None, Weaver-style base. **Features:** Nitride fat bolt design, externally adjustable trigger, two-position safety, textured grip. Introduced 2009.
Price: **$537.00**

THOMPSON/CENTER VENTURE MEDIUM ACTION
Bolt action rifle chambered in .204, .22-250, .223, .243, 7mm-08, .308 and 30TC. Features include a 24-inch crowned medium weight barrel, classic styled composite stock with inlaid traction grip panels, adjustable 3.5 to 5-pound trigger along with a drilled and tapped receiver (bases included). 3+1 detachable nylon box magazine. **Weight:** 7 lbs. **Length:** 43.5 inches.
Price: **$537.00**

THOMPSON/CENTER VENTURE PREDATOR PDX
Bolt action rifle chambered in .204, .22-250, .223, .243, .308. Similar to Venture Medium action but with heavy, deep-fluted 22-inch barrel and Max-1 camo finish overall. **Weight:** 8 lbs. **Length:** 41.5 inches.
Price: From **$638.00**

TIKKA T3 HUNTER
Caliber: .243 Win., .270 Win., 7mm Rem. Mag., .308 Win., .30-06 Spfl., .300 Win. Mag. **Stock:** Walnut. **Sights:** None furnished. **Barrel:** 22-7/16", 24-3/8". **Features:** Detachable magazine, aluminum scope

rings. Left-hand model available. Introduced 2005. Imported from Finland by Beretta USA.
Price: **$825.00**

TIKKA T3 STAINLESS SYNTHETIC
Similar to the T3 Hunter except stainless steel, synthetic stock. Available in .243 Win., .25-06, .270 Win., .308 Win., .30-06 Spfl., .270 WSM, .300 WSM, 7mm Rem. Mag., .300 Win. Mag., .338 Win. Mag. Introduced 2005.
Price: **$740.00**

TIKKA T3 LITE
Similar to the T3 Hunter, available in .204 Ruger, .222 Rem., .223 Rem., .22-250 Rem., .243 Win., .25-06 Rem., .260 Rem., 6.5x66, 7mm-08, 7x64, 7mm. Rem. Mag., 8x57IS, .270 Win., .270 WSM, .308 Win., .30-06 Sprg., .300 Win. Mag., .300 WSM, .338 Federal, .338 Win. Mag., 9.3x62. Synthetic stock. Barrel lengths vary from 22-7/16" to 24-3/8". Made in Finland by Sako. Imported by Beretta USA.
Price: **$675.00**
Price: Left-hand **$875.00**

ULTRA LIGHT ARMS
Caliber: Custom made in virtually every current chambering. **Barrel:** Douglas, length to order. **Weight:** 4.75 to 7.5 lbs. **Length:** Varies. **Stock:** Kevlar graphite composite, variety of finishes. **Sights:** None furnished; drilled and tapped for scope mounts. **Features:** Timney trigger, hand-lapped action, button-rifled barrel, hand-bedded action, recoil pad, sling-swivel studs, optional Jewell trigger. Made in U.S.A. by New Ultra Light Arms.
Price: Model 20 (short action) **$3,500.00**
Price: Model 24 (long action) **$3,600.00**
Price: Model 28 (magnum action) **$3,900.00**
Price: Model 32 (long action magnum action) **$3,900.00**
Price: Model 40 (.416 Rigby) **$3,900.00**

WEATHERBY MARK V
Caliber: Deluxe version comes in all Weatherby calibers plus .243 Win., .270 Win., 7mm-08 Rem., .30-06 Spfl., .308 Win. **Barrel:** 24", 26", 28". **Weight:** 6.75 to 10 lbs. **Length:** 44" to 48.75" overall. **Stock:** Walnut, Monte Carlo with cheekpiece; high luster finish; checkered pistol grip and fore-end; recoil pad. **Sights:** None furnished. **Features:** 4 models with Mark V action and wood stocks; other common elements include cocking indicator; adjustable trigger; hinged floorplate, thumb safety; quick detachable sling swivels. Lazermark same as Mark V Deluxe except stock has extensive oak leaf pattern laser carving on pistol grip and fore-end; chambered in Wby. Magnums—.257, .270 Win., 7mm., .300, .340, with 26" barrel. Introduced 1981. Sporter is same as the Mark V Deluxe without the embellishments. Metal has low-luster blue, stock is Claro walnut with matte finish, Monte Carlo comb, recoil pad. Chambered for these Wby. Mags: .257, .270 Win., 7mm, .300, .340. Other chamberings: 7mm Rem. Mag., .300 Win. Introduced 1993. Six Mark V models come with synthetic stocks. Ultra Lightweight rifles weigh 5.75 to 6.75 lbs.; 24", 26" fluted stainless barrels with recessed target crown; Bell & Carlson stock with CNC-machined aluminum bedding plate and tan "spider web" finish, skeletonized handle and sleeve. Available in .243 Win., .25-06 Rem., .270 Win., 7mm-08 Rem., 7mm Rem. Mag., .280 Rem, .308 Win., .30-06 Spfl., .300 Win. Mag. Wby. Mag chamberings: .240, .257, .270 Win., 7mm, .300. Introduced 1998. Accumark uses Mark V action with heavy-contour 26" and 28" stainless barrels with black oxidized flutes, muzzle diameter of .705". No sights, drilled and tapped for scope mounting. Stock is composite with matte gel-coat finish, full-length aluminum bedding Hasblock. Weighs 8.5 lbs. Chambered for these Wby. Mags: .240, .257, .270, 7mm, .300, .340, .338-378, .30-378. Other chamberings: .22-250, .243 Win., .25-06 Rem., .270 Win., .308 Win., 7mm Rem. Mag., .300 Win. Mag. Introduced 1996. Made in U.S.A. From Weatherby.
Price: Mark V Deluxe **$2,600.00**
Price: Mark V Lazermark **$2,800.00**

Prices given are believed to be accurate at time of publication however, many factors affect retail pricing so exact prices are not possible.

71ST EDITION, 2017 ✦ **463**

Price: Mark V Sporter $1,800.00
Price: Mark V Ultra Lightweight............................$2,300.00
Price: Mark V Accumark .... **$2,300.00 to $2,700.00**

WEATHERBY VANGUARD II SERIES

Caliber: .240, .257, and .300 Wby Mag. **Barrel:** 24" barreled action, matte black. **Weight:** 7.5 to 8.75 lbs. **Length:** 44" to 46-3/4" overall. **Stock:** Raised comb, Monte Carlo, injection-molded composite stock. **Sights:** None furnished. **Features:** One-piece forged, fluted bolt body with three gas ports, forged and machined receiver, adjustable trigger, factory accuracy guarantee. Vanguard Stainless has 410-Series stainless steel barrel and action, bead blasted matte metal finish. Vanguard Deluxe has raised comb, semi-fancy-grade Monte Carlo walnut stock with maplewood spacers, rosewood fore-end and grip cap, polished action with high-gloss-blued metalwork. Vanguard Synthetic Package includes Vanguard Synthetic rifle with Bushnell Banner 3-9x40mm scope mounted and boresighted, Leupold Rifleman rings and bases, Uncle Mikes nylon sling, and Plano PRO-MAX injection-molded case. Sporter has Monte Carlo walnut stock with satin urethane finish, fineline diamond point checkering, contrasting rosewood fore-end tip, matte-blued metalwork. Sporter SS metalwork is 410 Series bead-blasted stainless steel. Vanguard Youth/Compact has 20" No. 1 contour barrel, short action, scaled-down nonreflective matte black hardwood stock with 12.5" length of pull, and full-size, injection-molded composite stock. Chambered for .223 Rem., .22-250 Rem., .243 Win., 7mm-08 Rem., .308 Win. Weighs 6.75 lbs.; OAL 38.9". Sub-MOA Matte and Sub-MOA Stainless models have pillar-bedded Fiberguard composite stock (Aramid, graphite unidirectional fibers and fiberglass) with 24" barreled action; matte black metalwork, Pachmayr Decelerator recoil pad. Sub-MOA Stainless metalwork is 410 Series bead-blasted stainless steel. Sub-MOA Varmint guaranteed to shoot 3-shot group of .99" or less when used with specified Weatherby factory or premium (non-Weatherby calibers) ammunition. Hand-laminated, tan Monte Carlo composite stock with black spiderwebbing; CNC-machined aluminum bedding block, 22" No. 3 contour barrel, recessed target crown. Varmint Special has tan injection-molded Monte Carlo composite stock, pebble grain finish, black spiderwebbing. 22" No. 3 contour barrel (.740" muzzle dia.), bead blasted matte black finish, recessed target crown. Back Country has two-stage trigger, pillar-bedded Bell & Carlson stock, 24-in. fluted barrel, three-position safety. WBY-X Series comes with choice of several contemporary camo finishes (Bonz, Black Reaper, Kryptek, Hog Reaper, Whitetail Bonz, Blaze, GH2 "Girls Hunt Too") and is primarily targeted to younger shooters. Made in U.S.A. From Weatherby.
Price: Vanguard Synthetic $649.00
Price: Vanguard Synthetic DBM .... $749.00 to $899.00
Price: Vanguard Stainless $799.00
Price: Vanguard Deluxe, 7mm Rem. Mag., .300 Win. Mag. ..$1,149.00
Price: Vanguard Synthetic Package, .25-06 Rem......................$999.00
Price: Vanguard Sporter $849.00
Price: Vanguard Youth/Compact $599.00
Price: Vanguard S2 Back Country $1,399.00
Price: Vanguard WBY-X Series $749.00
Price: Vanguard Black Reaper $749.00
Price: Vanguard RC (Range Certified)....................$1,199.00
Price: Vanguard Varmint Special $849.00
Price: Camilla (designed for women shooters).......................$849.00
Price: Lazerguard (Laser carved AA-grade walnut stock) $1,199.00
Price: H-Bar (tactical series) from.................... **$1,149.00 to $1,449.00**

WINCHESTER MODEL 70

Caliber: Varies by model. Available in virtually all popular calibers. **Barrel:** Blued, or free-floating, fluted stainless hammer-forged barrel, 22", 24", 26". Recessed target crown. **Weight:** 6.75 to 7.25 lbs. **Length:** 41" to 45.75 " overall. **Stock:** Walnut (three models) or Bell and Carlson composite; textured charcoal-grey matte finish, Pachmayr Decelerator recoil pad. Super Grade offered with maple stock. **Sights:** None. **Features:** Claw extractor, three-position safety, M.O.A. three-lever trigger system, factory-set at 3.75 lbs. Super Grade features fancy grade walnut stock, contrasting black fore-end tip and pistol grip cap, and sculpted shadowline cheekpiece. Featherweight Deluxe has angled-comb walnut stock,

Schnabel fore-end, satin finish, cut checkering. Extreme Weather SS has composite stock, drop @ comb, 0.5"; drop @ heel, 0.5". Made in U.S.A. From Winchester Repeating Arms.
Price: Extreme Weather SS...................................$1,270.00
Price: Super Grade $1,360.00
Price: Super Grade Maple stock .... **$1,600.00 to $1,640.00**

WINCHESTER MODEL 70 COYOTE LIGHT

Caliber: .22-250, .243 Winchester, .308 Winchester, .270 WSM, .300 WSM and .325 WSM, five-shot magazine (3-shot in .270 WSM, .300 WSM and .325 WSM). **Barrel:** 22" fluted stainless barrel (24" in .270 WSM, .300 WSM and .325 WSM). **Weight:** 7.5 lbs. **Length:** NA. **Features:** Composite Bell and Carlson stock, Pachmayr Decelerator pad. Controlled round feeding. No sights but drilled and tapped for mounts.
Price: .... **$1,200.00 to $1,240.00**

WINCHESTER MODEL 70 FEATHERWEIGHT

Caliber: .22-250, .243, 7mm-08, .308, .270 WSM, 7mm WSM, .300 WSM, .325 WSM, .25-06, .270, .30-06, 7mm Rem. Mag., .300 Win. Mag., .338 Win. Mag. Capacity 5 rounds (short action) or 3 rounds (long action). **Barrel:** 22" blued barrel (24" in magnum chamberings). **Weight:** 6-1/2 to 7-1/4 lbs. **Length:** NA. **Features:** Satin-finished checkered Grade I walnut stock, controlled round feeding. Pachmayr Decelerator pad. No sights but drilled and tapped for scope mounts.
Price: .... **$940.00 to $980.00**

WINCHESTER MODEL 70 SPORTER

Caliber: .270 WSM, 7mm WSM, .300 WSM, .325 WSM, .25-06, .270, .30-06, 7mm Rem. Mag., .300 Win. Mag., .338 Win. Mag. Capacity 5 rounds (short action) or 3 rounds (long action). **Barrel:** 22", 24" or 26" blued. **Weight:** 6-1/2 to 7-1/4 lbs. **Length:** NA. **Features:** Satin-finished checkered Grade I walnut stock with sculpted cheekpiece, controlled round feeding. Pachmayr Decelerator pad. No sights but drilled and tapped for scope mounts.
Price: .... **$940.00 to $980.00**

WINCHESTER MODEL 70 ULTIMATE SHADOW

Caliber: .243, .308, .270 WSM, 7mm WSM, .300 WSM, .325 WSM, .270, .30-06, 7mm Rem. Mag., .300 Win. Mag. Capacity 5 rounds (short action) or 3 rounds (long action). **Barrel:** 22" matte stainless (24" or 26" in magnum chamberings). **Weight:** 6-1/2 to 7-1/4 lbs. **Length:** NA. **Features:** Synthetic stock with WinSorb recoil pad, controlled round feeding. Pachmayr Decelerator pad. No sights but drilled and tapped for scope mounts.
Price: .... **$760.00 to $1,040.00**

WINCHESTER MODEL 70 ALASKAN

Caliber: .30-06, .300 Win. Mag., .338 Win. Mag., .375 H&H Magnum. **Barrel:** 25 inches. **Weight:** 8.8 pounds. **Sights:** Folding adjustable rear, hooded brass bead front. **Stock:** Satin finished Monte Carlo with cut checkering. **Features:** Integral recoil lug, Pachmayr Decelerator recoil pad.
Price: $1,270.00

WINCHESTER MODEL 70 SAFARI EXPRESS

Caliber: .375 H&H Magnum, .416 Remington, .458 Winchester. **Barrel:** 24 inches. **Weight:** 9 pounds. **Sights:** Fully adjustable rear, hooded brass bead front. **Stock:** Satin finished Monte Carlo with cut checkering, deluxe cheekpiece. **Features:** Forged steel receiver with double integral recoil lugs bedded front and rear, dual steel crossbolts, Pachmayr Decelerator recoil pad.
Price: $1,420.00

WINCHESTER XPR

Caliber: .270 Win., .30-06, .300 Win. Mag., .338 Win. Mag. Detachable box magazine holds 3 to 5 rounds. **Barrel:** 24 or 26". **Stock:** Black polymer with Inflex Technology recoil pad. **Weight:** Approx. 7 lbs. **Finish:** Matte blue. **Features:** Bolt unlock button, nickel coated Teflon bolt.
Price: $549.99
Price: Mossy Oak Break-Up Country camo stock...................$600.00
Price: With Vortex II 3-9x40 scope $710.00

Prices given are believed to be accurate at time of publication however, many factors affect retail pricing so exact prices are not possible.

ARMALITE AR-50

Caliber: .50 BMG **Barrel:** 31". **Weight:** 33.2 lbs. **Length:** 59.5" **Stock:** Synthetic. **Sights:** None furnished. **Features:** A single-shot bolt-action rifle designed for long-range shooting. Available in left-hand model. Made in U.S.A. by Armalite.
Price: $3,359.00

BALLARD 1875 1 1/2 HUNTER

Caliber: Various calibers. **Barrel:** 26-30". **Weight:** NA **Length:** NA. **Stock:** Hand-selected classic American walnut. **Sights:** Blade front, Rocky Mountain rear. **Features:** Color case-hardened receiver, breechblock and lever. Many options available. Made in U.S.A. by Ballard Rifle & Cartridge Co.
Price: $3,250.00

BALLARD 1875 #3 GALLERY SINGLE SHOT

Caliber: Various calibers. **Barrel:** 24-28" octagonal with tulip. **Weight:** NA. **Length:** NA. **Stock:** Hand-selected classic American walnut. **Sights:** Blade front, Rocky Mountain rear. **Features:** Color case-hardened receiver, breechblock and lever. Many options available. Made in U.S.A. by Ballard Rifle & Cartridge Co.
Price: $3,300.00

BALLARD 1875 #4 PERFECTION

Caliber: Various calibers. **Barrel:** 30" or 32" octagon, standard or heavyweight. **Weight:** 10.5 lbs. (standard) or 11.75 lbs. (heavyweight bbl.) **Length:** NA. **Stock:** Smooth walnut. **Sights:** Blade front, Rocky Mountain rear. **Features:** Rifle or shotgun-style buttstock, straight grip action, single or double-set trigger, "S" or right lever, hand polished and lapped Badger barrel. Made in U.S.A. by Ballard Rifle & Cartridge Co.
Price: $3,950.00

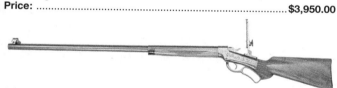

BALLARD 1875 #7 LONG RANGE

Caliber: .32-40, .38-55, .40-65, .40-70 SS, .45-70 Govt., .45-90, .45-110. **Barrel:** 32", 34" half-octagon. **Weight:** 11.75 lbs. **Length:** NA. **Stock:** Walnut; checkered pistol grip shotgun butt, ebony fore-end cap. **Sights:** Globe front. **Features:** Designed for shooting up to 1,000 yards. Standard or heavy barrel; single or double-set trigger; hard rubber or steel buttplate. Introduced 1999. Made in U.S.A. by Ballard Rifle & Cartridge Co.
Price: From $3,600.00

BALLARD 1875 #8 UNION HILL

Caliber: Various calibers. **Barrel:** 30" half-octagon. **Weight:** About 10.5 lbs. **Length:** NA. **Stock:** Walnut; pistol grip butt with cheekpiece. **Sights:** Globe front. **Features:** Designed for 200-yard offhand shooting. Standard or heavy barrel; double-set triggers; full loop lever; hook Schuetzen buttplate. Introduced 1999. Made in U.S.A. by Ballard Rifle & Cartridge Co.
Price: From $4,175.00

BALLARD MODEL 1885 LOW WALL SINGLE SHOT RIFLE

Caliber: Various calibers. **Barrel:** 24-28". **Weight:** NA. **Length:** NA. **Stock:** Hand-selected classic American walnut. **Sights:** Blade front, sporting rear. **Features:** Color case-hardened receiver, breechblock and lever. Many options available. Made in U.S.A. by Ballard Rifle & Cartridge Co.
Price: $3,300.00

BALLARD MODEL 1885 HIGH WALL STANDARD SPORTING SINGLE SHOT

Caliber: Various calibers. **Barrel:** Lengths to 34". **Weight:** NA. **Length:** NA. **Stock:** Straight-grain American walnut. **Sights:** Buckhorn or flattop rear, blade front. **Features:** Faithful copy of original Model 1885 High Wall; parts interchange with original rifles; variety of options available. Introduced 2000. Made in U.S.A. by Ballard Rifle & Cartridge Co.
Price: $3,300.00

BALLARD MODEL 1885 HIGH WALL SPECIAL SPORTING SINGLE SHOT

Caliber: Various calibers. **Barrel:** 28-30" octagonal. **Weight:** NA. **Length:** NA. **Stock:** Hand-selected classic American walnut. **Sights:** Blade front, sporting rear. **Features:** Color case-hardened receiver, breechblock and lever. Many options available. Made in U.S.A. by Ballard Rifle & Cartridge Co.
Price: $3,600.00

BROWN MODEL 97D SINGLE SHOT

Caliber: Available in most factory and wildcat calibers from .17 Ackley Hornet to .375 Winchester. **Barrel:** Up to 26", air gauged match grade. **Weight:** About 5 lbs., 11 oz. **Stock:** Sporter style with pistol grip, cheekpiece and Schnabel fore-end. **Sights:** None furnished; drilled and tapped for scope mounting. **Features:** Falling-block action gives rigid barrel-receiver matting; polished blue/black finish. Hand-fitted action. Standard and custom made-to-order rifles with many options. Made in U.S.A. by E. Arthur Brown Co., Inc.
Price: Standard model $1,695.00

C. SHARPS ARMS MODEL 1875 TARGET & SPORTING RIFLE

Caliber: .38-55, .40-65, .40-70 Straight or Bottlenecks, .45-70, .45-90. **Barrel:** 30" heavy tapered round. **Weight:** 11 lbs. **Length:** NA. **Stock:** American walnut. **Sights:** Globe with post front sight. **Features:** Long Range Vernier tang sight with windage adjustments. Pistol grip stock with cheek rest; checkered steel buttplate. Introduced 1991. From C. Sharps Arms Co.
Price: Without sights...$1,425.00
Price: With blade front & Buckhorn rear barrel sights $1,525.00
Price: With standard Tang & Globe w/post & ball front sights $1,725.00
Price: With deluxe vernier Tang & Globe w/spirit level & aperture sights $1,825.00
Price: With single set trigger, add $125.00

C. SHARPS ARMS 1875 CLASSIC SHARPS

Similar to New Model 1875 Sporting Rifle except 26", 28" or 30" full octagon barrel, crescent buttplate with toe plate, Hartford-style fore-end with cast German silver nose cap. Blade front sight, Rocky Mountain buckhorn rear. Weighs 10 lbs. Introduced 1987. From C. Sharps Arms Co.
Price: $1,775.00

C. SHARPS ARMS 1874 BRIDGEPORT SPORTING

Caliber: .38-55 to .50-3.25. **Barrel:** 26", 28", 30" tapered octagon. **Weight:** 10.5 lbs. **Length:** 47". **Stock:** American black walnut; shotgun butt with checkered steel buttplate; straight grip, heavy fore-end with Schnabel tip. **Sights:** Blade front, buckhorn rear. Drilled and tapped for tang sight. **Features:** Double-set triggers. Made in U.S.A. by C. Sharps Arms.

CENTERFIRE RIFLES Single Shot

Price: $1,995.00

C. SHARPS ARMS NEW MODEL 1885 HIGHWALL
Caliber: .22 LR, .22 Hornet, .219 Zipper, .25-35 WCF, .32-40 WCF, .38-55 WCF, .40-65, .30-40 Krag, .40-50 ST or BN, .40-70 ST or BN, .40-90 ST or BN, .45-70 Govt. 2-1/10" ST, .45-90 2-4/10" ST, .45-100 2-6/10" ST, .45-110 2-7/8" ST, .45-120 3-1/4" ST. **Barrel:** 26", 28", 30", tapered full octagon. **Weight:** About 9 lbs., 4 oz. **Length:** 47" overall. **Stock:** Oil-finished American walnut; Schnabel-style forend. **Sights:** Blade front, buckhorn rear. Drilled and tapped for optional tang sight. **Features:** Single trigger; octagonal receiver top; checkered steel buttplate; color case-hardened receiver and buttplate, blued barrel. Many options available. Made in U.S.A. by C. Sharps Arms Co.
Price: From $1,975.00

C. SHARPS ARMS 1885 HIGHWALL SCHUETZEN RIFLE
Caliber: .30-30, .32-40, .38-55, .40-50. **Barrel:** 24, 26, 28 or 30". Full tapered octagon. **Stock:** Straight grain American walnut with oil finish, pistol grip, cheek rest. **Sights:** Globe front with aperture set, long range fully adjustable tang sight with Hadley eye cup. **Finish:** Color case hardened receiver group, buttplate and bottom tang, matte blue barrel. Single set trigger.
Price: From $2,875.00

CIMARRON BILLY DIXON 1874 SHARPS SPORTING
Caliber: .45-70, .45-90, .50-70. **Barrel:** 32" tapered octagonal. **Weight:** NA. **Length:** NA. **Stock:** European walnut. **Sights:** Blade front, Creedmoor rear. **Features:** Color case-hardened frame, blued barrel. Hand-checkered grip and fore-end; hand-rubbed oil finish. Made by Pedersoli. Imported by Cimarron F.A. Co.
Price: From $2,141.70

CIMARRON MODEL 1885 HIGH WALL
Caliber: .38-55, .40-65, .45-70 Govt., .45-90, .45-120, .30-40 Krag, .348 Winchester, .405 Winchester. **Barrel:** 30" octagonal. **Weight:** NA. **Length:** NA. **Stock:** European walnut. **Sights:** Bead front, semi-buckhorn rear. **Features:** Replica of the Winchester 1885 High Wall rifle. Color case-hardened receiver and lever, blued barrel. Curved buttplate. Optional double-set triggers. Introduced 1999. Imported by Cimarron F.A. Co.
Price: From $1,065.00
Price: With pistol grip, adj. sights, from $1,277.00

CIMARRON MODEL 1885 LOW WALL
Caliber: .22 Hornet, .32-20, .38-40, .44-40, .45 Colt. **Barrel:** 30" octagonal. **Weight:** NA. **Length:** NA. **Stock:** European walnut. **Sights:** Bead front, semi-buckhorn rear. **Features:** Replica of the Winchester 1885 Low Wall rifle. Color case-hardened receiver, blued barrel. Curved buttplate. Optional double-set triggers. Introduced 1999. Imported by Cimarron F.A. Co.
Price: From $1,023.00

CIMARRON ADOBE WALLS ROLLING BLOCK
Caliber: .45-70 Govt. **Barrel:** 30" octagonal. **Weight:** 10-1/3 lbs. **Length:** NA. **Stock:** Hand-checkered European walnut. **Sights:** Bead front, semi-buckhorn rear. **Features:** Color case-hardened receiver, blued barrel. Curved buttplate. Double-set triggers. Made by Pedersoli. Imported by Cimarron F.A. Co.
Price: From $1,805.00

DAKOTA ARMS MODEL 10
Caliber: Most rimmed and rimless commercial calibers. **Barrel:** 23". **Weight:** 6 lbs. **Length:** 39.5" overall. **Stock:** Medium fancy grade walnut in classic style. Standard or full-length Mannlicher-style.

Checkered grip and fore-end. **Sights:** None furnished. Drilled and tapped for scope mounting. **Features:** Falling block action with underlever. Top tang safety. Removable trigger plate for conversion to single set trigger. Introduced 1990. Made in U.S.A. by Dakota Arms.
Price: From $5,260.00
Price: Deluxe from $6,690.00

DAKOTA ARMS SHARPS
Calibers: Virtually any caliber from .17 Ackley Hornet to .30-40 Krag. Features include a 26" octagon barrel, XX-grade walnut stock with straight grip and tang sight. Many options and upgrades are available.
Price: From $4,490.00

EMF PREMIER 1874 SHARPS
Caliber: .45-70, .45-110, .45-120. **Barrel:** 32", 34". **Weight:** 11-13 lbs. **Length:** 49", 51" overall. **Stock:** Pistol grip, European walnut. **Sights:** Blade front, adjustable rear. **Features:** Superb quality reproductions of the 1874 Sharps Sporting Rifles; case-hardened locks; double-set triggers; blue barrels. Imported from Pedersoli by EMF.
Price: Business Rifle $1,499.90
Price: Down Under Sporting Rifle, Patchbox, heavy barrel ..$2,249.90
Price: Silhouette, pistol-grip $1,799.90
Price: Super Deluxe Hand Engraved $3,500.00

EMF ROLLING BLOCK SPORTING TARGET
Caliber: .45/70. **Barrel:** 30" octagonal. **Weight:** 9 lbs. **Finish:** Polished blue with case hardened frame. Accurate reproduction of Remington Rolling Block rifle. Imported from Pedersoli by EMF.
Price: $1,350.00

EMF ROLLING BLOCK SUPER MATCH
Caliber: .45/70. **Barrel:** 34" round. **Weight:** 12 lbs. **Sights:** Adjustable Creedmoor rear, adjustable front with interchangeable inserts. **Stock:** Checkered walnut. **Finish:** Polished blue with case hardened frame. Imported from Pedersoli by EMF.
Price: $1,635.00

EMF SPRINGFIELD TRAPDOOR RIFLE/CARBINE
Caliber: .45/70. **Barrel:** Round 22" (Carbine) or 26" (Officer's Model). **Weight:** 7 or 8 lbs. **Features:** Officer's Model has Creedmoor adjustable sight, checkered walnut stock, steel fore-end cap. Carbine has saddle ring, oil-finished walnut stock. Both models have single set trigger, case hardened frame, blued barrel. Imported from Pedersoli by EMF.
Price: Carbine $1,540.00
Price: Officer's $1,890.00

H&R BUFFALO CLASSIC
Caliber: .45 Colt or .45-70 Govt. **Barrel:** 32" heavy. **Weight:** 8 lbs. **Length:** 46" overall. **Stock:** Cut-checkered American black walnut. **Sights:** Williams receiver sight; Lyman target front sight with 8 aperture inserts. **Features:** Color case-hardened Handi-Rifle action with exposed hammer; color case-hardened crescent buttplate; 19th century checkering pattern. Introduced 1995. Made in U.S.A. by H&R 1871, Inc.
Price: Buffalo Classic Rifle.....................................$479.00

H&R HANDI-RIFLE
Caliber: .204 Ruger, .22 Hornet, .223 Rem., .243 Win., .30-30, .270 Win., .280 Rem., 7mm-08 Rem., .308 Win., 7.62x39 Russian,

.30-06 Spfl., .357 Mag., .35 Whelen, .44 Mag., .45-70 Govt., .500 S&W. **Barrel:** From 20" to 26", blued or stainless. **Weight:** 5.5 to 7 lbs. **Stock:** Walnut-finished hardwood or synthetic. **Sights:** Vary by model, but most have ramp front, folding rear, or are drilled and tapped for scope mount. **Features:** Break-open action with side-lever release. Swivel studs on all models. Blue finish. Introduced 1989. From H&R 1871, Inc.

Price: $314.00
Price: Synthetic stock $323.00

H&R SURVIVOR
Caliber: 223 Rem., .308 Win. **Barrel:** 20" to 22" bull contour. **Weight:** 6 lbs. **Length:** 34.5" to 36" overall. **Stock:** Black polymer, thumbhole design. **Sights:** None furnished; scope mount provided. **Features:** Receiver drilled and tapped for scope mounting. Stock and fore-end have storage compartments for ammo, etc.; comes with integral swivels and black nylon sling. Introduced 1996. Made in U.S.A. by H&R 1871, Inc.
Price: Blue or nickel finish $327.00

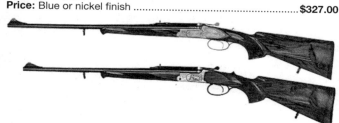

KRIEGHOFF HUBERTUS SINGLE-SHOT
Caliber: .222, .22-250, .243 Win., .270 Win., .308 Win., .30-06 Spfl., 5.6x50R Mag., 5.6x52R, 6x62R Freres, 6.5x57R, 6.5x65R, 7x57R, 7x65R, 8x57JRS, 8x75RS, 9.3x74R, 7mm Rem. Mag., .300 Win. Mag. **Barrel:** 23.5". Shorter lengths available. **Weight:** 6.5 lbs. **Length:** 40.5" **Stock:** High-grade walnut. **Sights:** Blade front, open rear. **Features:** Break-open loading with manual cocking lever on top tang; takedown; extractor; Schnabel forearm; many options. Imported from Germany by Krieghoff International Inc.
Price: Hubertus single shot, from $7,295.00
Price: Hubertus, magnum calibers $8,295.00

MERKEL K1 MODEL LIGHTWEIGHT STALKING
Caliber: .243 Win., .270 Win., 7x57R, .308 Win., .30-06 Spfl., 7mm Rem. Mag., .300 Win. Mag., 9.3x74R. **Barrel:** 23.6". **Weight:** 5.6 lbs. unscoped. **Stock:** Satin-finished walnut, fluted and checkered; sling-swivel studs. **Sights:** None (scope base furnished). **Features:** Franz Jager single-shot break-open action, cocking/uncocking slide-type safety, matte silver receiver, selectable trigger pull weights, integrated, quick detach 1" or 30mm optic mounts (optic not included). Extra barrels are an option. Imported from Germany by Merkel USA.
Price: Jagd Stalking Rifle $3,795.00
Price: Jagd Stutzen Carbine $4,195.00
Price: Extra barrels $1,195.00

MILLER ARMS
Calibers: Virtually any caliber from .17 Ackley Hornet to .416

Remington. Falling block design with 24" premium match-grade barrel, express sights, XXX-grade walnut stock and fore-end with 24 lpi checkering. Made in several styles including Classic, Target and Varmint. Many options and upgrades are available. From Dakota Arms.
Price: From $5,590.00

ROSSI SINGLE-SHOT SERIES
Caliber: .223 Rem., .243 Win., .44 Magnum. **Barrel:** 22". **Weight:** 6.25 lbs. **Stocks:** Black Synthetic Synthetic with recoil pad and removable cheek piece. **Sights:** Adjustable rear, fiber optic front, scope rail. Some models have scope rail only. **Features:** Single-shot break open, positive ejection, internal transfer bar mechanism, manual external safety, trigger block system, Taurus Security System, Matte blue finish.
Price: $307.00

ROSSI MATCHED PAIRS
Gauge/Caliber: .410-bore or 20-gauge shotgun barrel with interchangeable rifle barrel in either .223 Rem., .243 Win. or .44 Mag. caliber. **Barrel:** 23" shotgun, 28" rifle. **Weight:** 5-6.3 lbs. **Stock:** Black synthetic. **Sights:** Bead front on shotgun barrel, fully adjustable front and rear on rifle barrel, top rail mounted for scope, fully adjustable fiber optic sights. **Features:** Single-shot break open, internal transfer bar mechanism, manual external safety, blue finish, trigger block system, Taurus Security System. Rimfire models are also available.
Price: $352.00

RUGER NO. 1-A LIGHT SPORTER
Caliber: 7mm-08 Rem. **Barrel:** 22". **Weight:** 7.25 lbs. **Length:** 38.5". **Stock:** Checkered American walnut with Alexander Henry style fore-end. **Sights:** Adjustable rear, bead front. **Features:** Under-lever falling-block design with automatic ejector, top tang safety. Ruger currently chambers each No. 1 variation only in one caliber, which will change every year.
Price: $1,449.00

RUGER NO. 1-V VARMINTER
Caliber: .223 Rem. **Barrel:** 26" heavy barrel. **Weight:** 8.5 lbs. **Length:** 38.5". **Stock:** Checkered American walnut with semi-beaver-tail fore-end. **Sights:** None. Barrel ribbed for target scope block, with 1" Ruger scope rings. **Features:** Under-lever falling-block design with automatic ejector, top tang safety. Ruger currently chambers each No. 1 variation only in one caliber, which will change every year.
Price: $1,449.00

Prices given are believed to be accurate at time of publication however, many factors affect retail pricing so exact prices are not possible.

71ST EDITION, 2017 ◆ **467**

CENTERFIRE RIFLES Single Shot

RUGER NO. 1 RSI INTERNATIONAL
Caliber: 6.5x55mm. **Barrel:** 20 inches. **Weight:** 7 lbs. **Length:** 38.5". **Stock:** Checkered American walnut with full-length International-style fore-end with loop sling swivel. **Sights:** Adjustable folding leaf rear sight on quarter-rib, ramp front with gold bead. **Features:** Under-lever falling-block design with automatic ejector, top tang safety. Ruger currently chambers each No. 1 variation only in one caliber, which will change every year.
Price: $1,449.00

RUGER NO. 1-H TROPICAL RIFLE
Caliber: .375 H&H Magnum. **Barrel:** 24" heavy contour. **Weight:** 9.25 lbs. **Length:** 38.5". **Stock:** Checkered American walnut with Alexander Henry-style fore-end. **Sights:** Adjustable folding leaf rear sight on quarter-rib, ramp front with dovetail gold bead. **Features:** Under-lever falling-block design with automatic ejector, top tang safety. Ruger currently chambers each No. 1 variation only in one caliber, which will change every year.
Price: $1,449.00

RUGER NO. 1-S MEDIUM SPORTER
Caliber: .30-06. **Barrel:** 20" **Weight:** 7.25 lbs. **Length:** 38.5". **Stock:** Checkered American walnut with Alexander Henry-style fore-end. **Sights:** Adjustable folding leaf rear sight on quarter-rib, ramp front sight base and dovetail-type gold bead front sight. **Features:** Under-lever falling-block design with automatic ejector, top tang safety. Ruger currently chambers each No. 1 variation only in one caliber, which will change every year.
Price: $1,449.00

NO. 1-B STANDARD
Caliber: .257 Weatherby. **Barrel:** 28". **Stock:** Checkered American walnut with Alexander Henry-style fore-end, **Sights:** None. **Barrel:** Ribbed for target scope block, with 1" Ruger scope rings. **Weight:** 8.5 lbs. Under-lever falling-block design with automatic ejector, top tang safety. Ruger currently chambers each No. 1 variation only in one caliber, which will change every year.
Price: $1,449.00

SHILOH CO. SHARPS 1874 LONG RANGE EXPRESS
Caliber: .38-55, .40-50 BN, .40-70 BN, .40-90 BN, .40-70 ST, .40-90 ST, .45-70 Govt. ST, .45-90 ST, .45-110 ST, .50-70 ST, .50-90 ST. **Barrel:** 34" tapered octagon. **Weight:** 10.5 lbs. **Length:** 51" overall. **Stock:** Oil-finished walnut (upgrades available) with pistol grip, shotgun-style butt, traditional cheek rest, Schnabel forend. **Sights:** Customer's choice. **Features:** Re-creation of the Model 1874 Sharps rifle. Double-set triggers. Made in U.S.A. by Shiloh Rifle Mfg. Co.
Price: $2,018.00
Price: Sporter Rifle No. 1 (similar to above except with 30" barrel, blade front, buckhorn rear sight) $2,018.00
Price: Sporter Rifle No. 3 (similar to No. 1 except straight-grip stock, standard wood) $1,910.00

SHILOH CO. SHARPS 1874 QUIGLEY
Caliber: .45-70 Govt., .45-110. **Barrel:** 34" heavy octagon. **Stock:** Military-style with patch box, standard-grade American walnut. **Sights:** Semi-buckhorn, interchangeable front and midrange vernier tang sight with windage. **Features:** Gold inlay initials, pewter tip, Hartford collar, case color or antique finish. Double-set triggers.
Price: $3,464.00

SHILOH CO. SHARPS 1874 SADDLE
Caliber: .38-55, .40-50 BN, .40-65 Win., .40-70 BN, .40-70 ST, .40-90 BN, .40-90 ST, .44-77 BN, .44-90 BN, .45-70 Govt. ST, .45-90 ST, .45-100 ST, .45-110 ST, .45-120 ST, .50-70 ST, .50-90 ST. **Barrel:** 26" full or half octagon. **Stock:** Semi-fancy American walnut. Shotgun style with cheek rest. **Sights:** Buckhorn and blade. **Features:** Double-set trigger, numerous custom features can be added.
Price: $1,964.00

SHILOH CO. SHARPS 1874 MONTANA ROUGHRIDER
Caliber: .38-55, .40-50 BN, .40-65 Win., .40-70 BN, .40-70 ST, .40-90 BN, .40-90 ST, .44-77 BN, .44-90 BN, .45-70 Govt. ST, .45-90 ST, .45-100 ST, .45-110 ST, .45-120 ST, .50-70 ST, .50-90 ST. **Barrel:** 30" full or half octagon. **Stock:** American walnut in shotgun or military style. **Sights:** Buckhorn and blade. **Features:** Double-set triggers, numerous custom features can be added.
Price: $2,018.00

SHILOH CO. SHARPS CREEDMOOR TARGET
Caliber: .38-55, .40-50 BN, .40-65 Win., .40-70 BN, .40-70 ST, .40-90 BN, .40-90 ST, .44-77 BN, .44-90 BN, .45-70 Govt. ST, .45-90 ST, .45-100 ST, .45-110 ST, .45-120 ST, .50-70 ST, .50-90 ST. **Barrel:** 32" half round-half octagon. **Stock:** Extra fancy American walnut. Shotgun style with pistol grip. **Sights:** Customer's choice. **Features:** Single trigger, AA finish on stock, polished barrel and screws, pewter tip.
Price: $2,966.00

THOMPSON/CENTER ENCORE PROHUNTER PREDATOR RIFLE
Caliber: .204 Ruger, .223 Remington, .22-250 and .308 Winchester. **Barrel:** 28-inch deep-fluted interchangeable. **Length:** 42.5 inches. **Weight:** 7 3/4 lbs. **Stock:** Composite buttstock and fore-end with non-slip inserts in cheekpiece, pistol grip and fore-end. Realtree Advantage Max-1 camo finish overall. Scope is not included.
Price: $882.00

THOMPSON/CENTER ENCORE PRO HUNTER KATAHDIN CARBINE
Caliber: .45-70 Govt., .460 S&W Mag., .500 S&W Mag. **Barrel:** 28-inch deep-fluted interchangeable. **Length:** 34.5 inches. **Weight:** 7 lbs. **Stock:** Flex-Tech with Simms recoil pad. Grooved and textured grip

surfaces. **Sights:** Adjustable rear peep, fiber optic front.
Price: $852.00

Price: Long Range Sharps................................ $2,579.00
Price: Buffalo Hunter Sharps $2,469.00
Price: Sharps Cavalry Carbine......................... $1,809.00
Price: Sharps Extra Deluxe.............................. $4,999.00
Price: Sharps Hunter $1,639.00

THOMPSON/CENTER G2 CONTENDER
Caliber: .204 Ruger, .223 Rem., 6.8 Rem. 7-30 Waters, .30-30 Win. **Barrel:** 23-inch interchangeable with blued finish. **Length:** 36.75 inches. **Stock:** Walnut. **Sights:** None. **Weight:** 5.5 pounds. Reintroduced in 2015. Interchangeable barrels available in several centerfire and rimfire calibers.
Price: $729.00

UBERTI 1885 HIGH-WALL SINGLE-SHOT
Caliber: .45-70 Govt., .45-90, .45-120. **Barrel:** 28" to 32". **Weight:** 9.3 to 9.9 lbs. **Length:** 44.5" to 47" overall. **Stock:** Walnut stock and fore-end. **Sights:** Blade front, fully adjustable open rear. **Features:** Based on Winchester High-Wall design by John Browning. Color case-hardened frame and lever, blued barrel and buttplate. Imported by Stoeger Industries.
Price: From .... $1,009.00 to $1,279.00

UBERTI 1874 SHARPS SPORTING
Caliber: .45-70 Govt. **Barrel:** 30", 32", 34" octagonal. **Weight:** 10.57 lbs. with 32" barrel. **Length:** 48.9" with 32" barrel. **Stock:** Walnut. **Sights:** Dovetail front, Vernier tang rear. **Features:** Cut checkering, case-colored finish on frame, buttplate, and lever. Imported by Stoeger Industries.
Price: Standard Sharps..................................... $1,809.00
Price: Special Sharps $2,019.00
Price: Deluxe Sharps $3,129.00
Price: Down Under Sharps $2,579.00

UBERTI SPRINGFIELD TRAPDOOR RIFLE/CARBINE
Caliber: .45-70 Govt., single shot **Barrel:** 22 or 32.5 inches. **Features:** Blue steel receiver and barrel, case-hardened breechblock and buttplate. **Sights:** Creedmoor style.
Price: Springfield Trapdoor Carbine, 22" barrel $1,669.00
Price: Springfield Trapdoor Army, 32.5" barrel $1,949.00

Prices given are believed to be accurate at time of publication however, many factors affect retail pricing so exact prices are not possible.

71ST EDITION, 2017 ⊕ **469**

BAIKAL MP94 COMBO GUN

Caliber/Gauge: Over/under style with 12-gauge shotgun barrel over either a .223 or .308 rifle barrel. **Barrels:** 19.7". **Stock:** Checkered walnut. **Sights:** Adjustable rear, ramp front with bead. Picatinny or 11mm scope rail. **Features:** Four choke tubes for shotgun barrel. Double triggers. Made in Russia by Baikal and imported by U.S. Sporting Goods Inc.
Price: **$592.00**

BAIKAL MP221 DOUBLE RIFLE

Caliber: .30-06 or .45-70 side-by-side double rifle. **Barrels:** 23.5". **Stock:** Checkered walnut. **Sights:** Adjustable rear, ramp front with bead. Picatinny or 11mm scope rail. **Features:** Double triggers, extractors, adjustable barrel regulation. Made in Russia by Baikal and imported by U.S. Sporting Goods Inc.
Price: **$1,155.00**

BERETTA S686/S689 O/U RIFLE SERIES

Calibers: .30-06, 9.3x74R. **Barrels:** 23 inches. O/U boxlock action. Single or double triggers. EELL Grade has better wood, moderate engraving.
Price: ....**$4,200.00 to $9,000.00**
Price: EELL Diamond Sable grade, from **$12,750.00**

BRNO MODEL 802 COMBO GUN

Caliber/Gauge: .243 Win./12 ga. Over/under. **Barrels:** 23.6". **Weight:** 7.6 lbs. **Length:** 41". **Stock:** European walnut. **Features:** Double trigger, shotgun barrel is improved-modified chokes. Imported by CZ USA.
Price: **$2,181.00**

FAUSTI CLASS EXPRESS

Caliber: .30-06, .30R Blaser, 8x57 JRS, 9.3x74R, .444 Marlin, .45-70 Govt. Over/under. **Barrels:** 24". **Weight:** 7.5 lbs. **Length:** 41". **Stock:** Oil-finished Grade A walnut. Pistol grip, Bavarian or Classic. **Sights:** Folding leaf rear, fiber optic front adjustable for elevation. **Features:** Inertia single or double trigger, automatic ejectors. Made in Italy and imported by Fausti USA.
Price: **$4,990.00**
Price: SL Express w/hand engraving, AA wood **$7,600.00**

HOENIG ROTARY ROUND ACTION DOUBLE

Caliber: Most popular calibers. Over/under design. **Barrel:** 22" to 26". **Stock:** English Walnut; to customer specs. **Sights:** Swivel hood front with button release (extra bead stored in trap door gripcap), express-style rear on quarter-rib adjustable for windage and elevation; scope mount. **Features:** Round action opens by rotating barrels, pulling forward. Inertia extractor system, rotary safety blocks strikers. Single lever quick-detachable-e scope mount. Simple takedown without removing fore-end. Introduced 1997. Custom rifle made in U.S.A. by George Hoenig.
Price: From **$22,500.00**

HOENIG ROTARY ROUND ACTION COMBINATION

Caliber: Most popular calibers and shotgun gauges. Over/under design with rifle barrel atop shotgun barrel. **Barrel:** 26". **Weight:** 7 lbs. **Stock:** English Walnut to customer specs. **Sights:** Front ramp with button release blades. Foldable aperture tang sight windage and elevation adjustable. Quarter-rib with scope mount. **Features:** Round action opens by rotating barrels, pulling forward. Inertia extractor; rotary safety blocks strikers. Simple takedown without removing forend. Custom rifle made in U.S.A. by George Hoenig.
Price: **$27,500.00**

HOENIG VIERLING FOUR-BARREL COMBINATION

Caliber/gauge: Two 20-gauge shotgun barrels with one rifle barrel chambered for .22 Long Rifle and another for .223 Remington. Custom rifle made in U.S.A. by George Hoenig.
Price: **$50,000.00**

KRIEGHOFF CLASSIC DOUBLE

Caliber: 7x57R, 7x65R, .308 Win., .30-06 Spfl., 8x57 JRS, 8x75RS, 9.3x74R, 375NE, 500/416NE, 470NE, 500NE. **Barrel:** 23.5". **Weight:** 7.3 to 11 lbs. **Stock:** High grade European walnut. Standard model has conventional rounded cheekpiece, Bavaria model has Bavarian-style cheekpiece. **Sights:** Bead front with removable, adjustable wedge (.375 H&H and below), standing leaf rear on quarter-rib. **Features:** Boxlock action; double triggers; short opening angle for fast loading; quiet extractors; sliding, self-adjusting wedge for secure bolting; Purdey-style barrel extension; horizontal firing pin placement. Many options available. Introduced 1997. Imported from Germany by Krieghoff International.
Price: **$10,995.00**
Price: Engraved sideplates, add **$4,000.00**
Price: Extra set of rifle barrels, add **$6,300.00**
Price: Extra set of 20-ga., 28" shotgun barrels, add **$4,400.00**

KRIEGHOFF CLASSIC BIG FIVE DOUBLE RIFLE

Similar to the standard Classic except available in .375 H&H, .375 Flanged Mag. N.E., .416 Rigby, .458 Win., 500/416 NE, 470 NE, 500 NE. Has hinged front trigger, nonremovable muzzle wedge, Universal Trigger System, Combi Cocking Device, steel triggerguard, specially weighted stock bolt for weight and balance. Many options available. Introduced 1997. Imported from Germany by Krieghoff International.
Price: **$13,995.00**
Price: Engraved sideplates, add **$4,000.00**
Price: Extra set of 20-ga. shotgun barrels, add **$5,000.00**
Price: Extra set of rifle barrels, add **$6,300.00**

LEBEAU-COURALLY EXPRESS SXS

Caliber: 7x65R, 8x57JRS, 9.3x74R, .375 H&H, .470 N.E. **Barrel:** 24" to 26". **Weight:** 7.75 to 10.5 lbs. **Stock:** Fancy French walnut with cheekpiece. **Sights:** Bead on ramp front, standing left express rear on quarter-rib. **Features:** Holland & Holland-type sidelock with automatic ejectors; double triggers. Built to order only. Imported from Belgium by Wm. Larkin Moore and Griffin & Howe.
Price: **$45,000.00**

MERKEL DRILLINGS

Caliber/Gauge: : 12, 20, 3" chambers, 16, 2-3/4" chambers; .22 Hornet, 5.6x50R Mag., 5.6x52R, .222 Rem., .243 Win., 6.5x55, 6.5x57R, 7x57R, 7x65R, .308 Win., .30-06 Spfl., 8x57JRS, 9.3x74R, .375 H&H. **Barrel:** 25.6". **Weight:** 7.9 to 8.4 lbs. depending upon caliber. **Stock:** Oil-finished walnut with pistol grip; cheekpiece on 12-, 16-gauge. **Sights:** Blade front, fixed rear. **Features:** Double barrel locking lug with Greener crossbolt; scroll-engraved, case-hardened receiver; automatic trigger safety; Blitz action; double triggers. Imported from Germany by Merkel USA.
Price: Model 96K (manually cocked rifle system), from.........**$8,495.00**
Price: Model 96K engraved (hunting series on receiver) **$9,795.00**

MERKEL BOXLOCK DOUBLE

Caliber: 5.6x52R, .243 Winchester, 6.5x55, 6.5x57R, 7x57R, 7x65R, .308 Win., .30-06 Springfield, 8x57 IRS, 9.3x74R. **Barrel:** 23.6". **Weight:** 7.7 oz. **Length:** NA. **Stock:** Walnut, oil finished, pistol grip. **Sights:** Fixed 100 meter. **Features:** Anson & Deeley boxlock action with cocking indicators, double triggers, engraved color case-hardened receiver. Introduced 1995. Imported from Germany by Merkel USA.

Price: Model 140-2, from...**$11,995.00**
Price: Model 141 Small Frame SXS Rifle; built on smaller frame, chambered for 7mm Mauser, .30-06, or 9.3x74R **$8,195.00**
Price: Model 141 Engraved; fine hand-engraved hunting scenes on silvered receiver **$9,495.00**

RIZZINI EXPRESS 90L
Caliber: .308 Win., .30-06 Spfl., 7x65R, 9.3x74R, 8x57 JRS, .444 Marlin. **Barrel:** 24". **Weight:** 7.5 lbs. **Length:** 40" overall. **Stock:** Select European walnut with satin oil finish; English-style

cheekpiece. **Sights:** Ramp front, quarter-rib with express sight.
Features: Over/under with color case-hardened boxlock action; automatic ejectors; single selective trigger; polished blue barrels. Extra 20-gauge shotgun barrels available. Imported from Italy by Fierce Products.
Price: With case...**$4,500.00**

SAVAGE MODEL 42
Caliber/Gauge: Break-open over/under design with .22 LR or .22 WMR barrel over a .410 shotgun barrel. Under-lever operation.
Barrel: 20 inches. **Stock:** Synthetic black matte. **Weight:** 6.1 lbs.
Sights: Adjustable rear, bead front. Updated variation of classic Stevens design from the 1940s.
Price: **$485.00**

ANSCHUTZ RX22

Caliber: .22 LR. AR-style semiautomatic rifle with blowback operation. **Barrel:** 16.5". **Features:** Available in several styles and colors including black, Desert Tan. Fixed or folding stock, adjustable trigger, military-type folding iron sights. Made in Germany and imported by Steyr Arms Inc.

Price: **$895.00**

AMERICAN TACTICAL IMPORTS GSG-522

Semiauto tactical rifle chambered in .22 LR. Features include 16.25-inch barrel; black finish overall; polymer fore-end and buttstock; backup iron sights; receiver-mounted Picatinny rail; 10-round magazine. Several other rifle and carbine versions available.

Price: **$451.00**

BROWNING BUCK MARK SEMI-AUTO

Caliber: .22 LR, 10+1. **Action:** A rifle version of the Buck Mark Pistol; straight blowback action; machined aluminum receiver with integral rail scope mount; manual thumb safety. **Barrel:** Recessed crowns. **Stock:** Stock and forearm with full pistol grip. **Features:** Action lock provided. Introduced 2001. Four model name variations for 2006, as noted below. **Sights:** FLD Target, FLD Carbon, and Target models have integrated scope rails. Sporter has Truglo/Marble fiber-optic sights. Imported from Japan by Browning.

Price: FLD Target, 5.5 lbs., bull barrel, laminated stock **$720.00**
Price: Target, 5.4 lbs., blued bull barrel, wood stock **$700.00**
Price: Sporter, 4.4 lbs., blued sporter barrel w/sights **$700.00**

BROWNING SA-22 SEMI-AUTO 22

Caliber: .22 LR. Tubular magazine in buttstock hold 11 rounds. **Barrel:** 19.375". **Weight:** 5 lbs. 3 oz. **Length:** 37" overall. **Stock:** Checkered select walnut with pistol grip and semi-beavertail fore-end. **Sights:** Gold bead front, folding leaf rear. **Features:** Engraved receiver with polished blue finish; crossbolt safety; easy takedown for carrying or storage. The Grade VI is available with either grayed or blued receiver with extensive engraving with gold-plated animals: right side pictures a fox and squirrel in a woodland scene; left side shows a beagle chasing a rabbit. On top is a portrait of the beagle. Stock and fore-end are of high-grade walnut with a double-bordered cut checkering design. . Introduced 1956. Made in Belgium until 1974. Currently made in Japan by Miroku.

Price: Grade I, scroll-engraved blued receiver **$700.00**
Price: Grade VI BL, gold-plated engraved blued receiver **$1,580.00**

COLT TACTICAL RIMFIRE M4 OPS CARBINE

Blowback semiauto rife chambered in .22 LR, styled to resemble Colt M16. Features include 16.2-inch barrel; front sight adjustable for elevation; adjustable rear sight; alloy lower; adjustable telestock; flattop receiver with removable carry handle; 10- or 30-round detachable magazine. Made in Germany by Walther, under license from Colt, and imported by Umarex.

Price: **$599.00**

COLT TACTICAL RIMFIRE M4 CARBINE

Blowback semiauto rifle chambered in .22 LR, styled to resemble

Colt M4. Features include 16.2-inch barrel; front sight adjustable for elevation; adjustable rear sight; alloy lower; adjustable telestock; flattop receiver with optics rail; 10- or 30-round detachable magazine. M4 Ops model has four-position collapsible stock, muzzle brake, inline design. Made in Germany by Walther under license from Colt, and imported by Umarex.

Price: **$569.00**

CITADEL M-1 CARBINE

Caliber: .22LR., 10-round magazines. **Barrel:** 18". **Weight:** 4.8 lbs. **Length:** 35". **Stock:** Wood or synthetic in black or several camo patterns. **Features:** Built to the exacting specifications of the G.I. model used by U.S. infantrymen in both WWII theaters of battle and in Korea. Used by officers as well as tankers, drivers, artillery crews, mortar crews, and other personnel. Weight, barrel length and OAL are the same as the "United States Carbine, Caliber .30, M1," its official military designation. Made in Italy by Chiappa. Imported by Legacy Sports.

Price: Synthetic stock, black. **$316.00**
Price: Synthetic stock, camo................................... **$368.00**
Price: Wood stock. **$400.00**

CZ MODEL 512

Caliber: .22 LR/.22 WMR, 5-round magazines. **Barrel:** 20.5". **Weight:** 5.9 lbs. **Length:** 39.3". **Stock:** Beech. **Sights:** Adjustable. **Features:** The modular design is easily maintained, requiring only a coin as a tool for field stripping. The action of the 512 is composed of an aluminum alloy upper receiver that secures the barrel and bolt assembly and a fiberglass reinforced polymer lower half that houses the trigger mechanism and detachable magazine. The 512 shares the same magazines and scope rings with the CZ 455 bolt-action rifle.

Price: .22 LR **$480.00**
Price: .22 WMR.. **$510.00**

H&K 416-22

Blowback semiauto rife chambered in .22 LR, styled to resemble H&K 416. Features include metal upper and lower receivers; rail interface system; retractable stock; pistol grip with storage compartment; on-rail sights; rear sight adjustable for wind and elevation; 16.1-inch barrel; 10- or 20-round magazine. Also available in pistol version with 9-inch barrel. Made in Germany by Walther under license from Heckler & Koch and imported by Umarex.

Price: **$599.00**

H&K MP5 A5

Blowback semiauto rifle chambered in .22 LR, styled to resemble H&K MP5. Features include metal receiver; compensator; bolt catch; NAVY pistol grip; on-rail sights; rear sight adjustable for wind and elevation; 16.1-inch barrel; 10- or 25-round magazine. Also available in pistol version with 9-inch barrel. Also available with SD-type fore-end. Made in Germany by Walther under license from Heckler & Koch. Imported by Umarex.

Price: **$499.00**
Price: MP5 SD **$599.00**

HENRY U.S. SURVIVAL AR-7 22

Caliber: .22 LR, 8-shot magazine. **Barrel:** 16" steel lined. **Weight:** 2.25 lbs. **Stock:** ABS plastic. **Sights:** Blade front on ramp, aperture rear. **Features:** Takedown design stores barrel and action in hollow stock. Light enough to float on water. Dark gray or camo finish. Comes with

two magazines. Introduced 1998. From Henry Repeating Arms Co.
Price: H002B Black finish **$290.00**
Price: H002C Camo finish **$350.00**

KEL-TEC SU-22CA
Caliber: .22 LR. 26-round magazine. **Barrel:** 16.1". **Weight:** 4 lbs.
Length: 34" **Features:** Blowback action, crossbolt safety, adjustable
front and rear sights with integral picatinny rail. Threaded muzzle,
26-round magazine.
Price: **$547.00**

MAGNUM RESEARCH MLR22 SERIES
Caliber: .22 WMR or .22 LR, 10-shot magazine. **Barrel:** 17" graphite.
Weight: 4.45 lbs. **Length:** 35.5" overall. **Stock:** Hogue OverMolded
synthetic or Laminated Thumbhole (Barracuda model). **Sights:**
Integral scope base. **Features:** French grey anodizing, match bolt,
target trigger. .22 LR rifles use factory Ruger 10/22 magazines. 4-5
lbs. average trigger pull. Barracuda model has Laminated Thumbhole
stock, 19" barrel. Introduced: 2007. From Magnum Research, Inc.
Price: .22 LR Hogue OverMolded stock **$669.00**
Price: .22 LR Barracuda w/Thumbhole stock........................**$819.00**
Price: .22 WMR Hogue OverMolded stock **$791.00**
Price: .22 WMR Barracuda w/Thumbhole stock **$935.00**

MARLIN MODEL 60
Caliber: .22 LR, 14-shot tubular magazine. **Barrel:** 19" round tapered.
Weight: About 5.5 lbs. **Length:** 37.5" overall. **Stock:** Press-checkered,
laminated Maine birch with Monte Carlo, full pistol grip; black synthetic
or Realtree Camo. **Sights:** Ramp front, open adjustable rear. Matted
receiver is grooved for scope mount. **Features:** Last-shot bolt hold-
open. Available with factory mounted 4x scope.
Price: Laminate...**$199.00**
Price: Model 60C camo **$232.00**
Price: Synthetic **$191.00**

MARLIN MODEL 60SS SELF-LOADING RIFLE
Same as the Model 60 except breech bolt, barrel and outer magazine
tube are made of stainless steel; most other parts are either nickel-
plated or coated to match the stainless finish. Monte Carlo stock is of
black/gray Maine birch laminate, and has nickel-plated swivel studs,
rubber buttpad. Introduced 1993.
Price: **$300.00**

MARLIN 70PSS PAPOOSE STAINLESS
Caliber: .22 LR, 7-shot magazine. **Barrel:** 16.25" stainless steel,
Micro-Groove rifling. **Weight:** 3.25 lbs. **Length:** 35.25" overall.
Stock: Black fiberglass-filled synthetic with abbreviated forend,
nickel-plated swivel studs, molded-in checkering. **Sights:** Ramp
front with orange post, cut-away Wide Scan hood; adjustable open
rear. Receiver grooved for scope mounting. **Features:** Takedown
barrel; crossbolt safety; manual bolt hold-open; last shot bolt hold-
open; comes with padded carrying case. Introduced 1986. Made in
U.S.A. by Marlin.
Price: **$345.00**

MARLIN MODEL 795
Caliber: .22. **Barrel:** 18" with 16-groove Micro-Groove rifling. **Sights:**
Ramp front sight, adjustable rear. Receiver grooved for scope mount.
Stock: Black synthetic, hardwood, synthetic thumbhole, solid pink,
pink camo, or Mossy Oak New Break-up camo finish. **Features:**
10-round magazine, last shot hold-open feature. Introduced 1997. SS
is similar to Model 795 except stainless steel barrel. Most other parts
nickel-plated. Adjustable folding semi-buckhorn rear sights, ramp front
high-visibility post and removable cutaway wide scan hood. Made in
U.S.A. by Marlin Firearms Co.

Price:
Price: Stainless **$183.00**
Price: Stainless **$262.00**

MOSSBERG BLAZE SERIES
Caliber: .22 LR. **Magazine capacity:** 10 or 25 rounds. **Barrel:** 16½".
Sights: Adjustable. **Weight:** 3½ to 4¾ lbs. A series of lightweight
polymer rifles with several finish options and styles. Green Dot
Combo model has Dead Ringer greet dot sight. Blaze 47 has
AK-profile with adjustable fiber optic rear and raised front sight,
ambidextrous safety, and a choice of wood or synthetic stock.
Price: **$196.00**
Price: Muddy Girl camo **$262.00**
Price: Wildfire camo **$262.00**
Price: Kryptek Highlander camo **$283.00**
Price: Blaze 47 synthetic stock..**$346.00**
Price: Blaze 47 wood stock **$397.00**

MOSSBERG MODEL 702 PLINKSTER
Caliber: .22 LR, 10-round detachable magazine. **Barrel:** 18" free-
floating. **Weight:** 4.1 to 4.6 lbs. **Sights:** Adjustable rifle. Receiver
grooved for scope mount. **Stock:** Wood or black synthetic.
Features: Ergonomically placed magazine release and safety
buttons, crossbolt safety, free gun lock. Made in U.S.A. by O.F.
Mossberg & Sons, Inc.
Price: From **$190.00**

MOSSBERG MODEL 715T SERIES
Caliber: .22 LR with 10 or 25-round magazine. AR-style offered
in several models. **Barrel:** 16.25 or 18 inches with A2-style
muzzlebrake. **Weight:** 5.5 lbs. **Features:** Flattop or A2 style carry
handle.
Price: Black finish **$375.00**
Price: Muddy Girl camo **$430.00**

REMINGTON MODEL 552 BDL DELUXE SPEEDMASTER
Caliber: : .22 Short (20 rounds), Long (17) or LR (15) tubular magazine.
Barrel: 21" round tapered. **Weight:** 5.75 lbs. **Length:** 40" overall.
Stock: Walnut. Checkered grip and fore-end. **Sights:** Adjustable rear,
ramp front. **Features:** Positive crossbolt safety in triggerguard, receiver
grooved for tip-off mount. Operates with .22 Short, Long or Long Rifle
cartridges. Classic design introduced in 1957.
Price: **$707.00**

REMINGTON 597
Caliber: .22 LR, 10-shot clip; or .22 WMR, 8-shot clip. **Barrel:** 20".
Weight: 5.5 lbs. **Length:** 40" overall. **Stock:** Black synthetic or
camo coverage in several patterns. TVP has laminated, contoured
thumbhole stock. **Sights:** Big game. **Features:** Matte black metal
finish or stainless, nickel-plated bolt. Receiver is grooved and drilled
and tapped for scope mounts. Introduced 1997. Made in U.S.A. by
Remington.
Price: Standard model, synthetic stock **$213.00**
Price: Synthetic w/Scope **$257.00**
Price: Camo from **$306.00**

RUGER 10/22 AUTOLOADING CARBINE
Caliber: .22 LR, 10-shot rotary magazine. **Barrel:** 18.5" round tapered

Prices given are believed to be accurate at time of publication however, many factors affect retail pricing so exact prices are not possible.

71ST EDITION, 2017 ◈ **473**

(16.12", compact model). **Weight:** 5 lbs. (4.5, compact). **Length:** 37.25", 34" (compact) overall. **Stock:** American hardwood with pistol grip and barrelband, or synthetic. **Sights:** Brass bead front, folding leaf rear adjustable for elevation. **Features:** Available with satin black or stainless finish on receiver and barrel. Detachable rotary magazine fits flush into stock, crossbolt safety, receiver tapped and grooved for scope blocks or tip-off mount. Scope base adaptor furnished with each rifle. Made in U.S.A. by Sturm, Ruger & Co.

Price: Wood stock $309.00
Price: Synthetic stock $309.00
Price: Stainless, synthetic stock $339.00
Price: Compact model, fiber-optic front sight $359.00

RUGER 10/22 TAKEDOWN RIFLE

Caliber: .22 LR, 10-shot rotary magazine. **Barrel:** 18.5" stainless, or 16.6" satin black threaded with suppressor. Easy takedown feature enables quick separation of the barrel from the action by way of a recessed locking lever, for ease of transportation and storage. **Stock:** Black synthetic. **Sights:** Adjustable rear, gold bead front. **Weight:** 4.66 pounds. Comes with backpack carrying bag.

Price: Stainless $439.00
Price: Satin black w/flash suppressor $459.00
Price: Threaded barrel $629.00
Price: With Silent-SR suppressor $1,078.00

RUGER 10/22 SPORTER

Same specificaions as 10/22 Carbine except has American walnut stock with hand-checkered pistol grip and fore-end, straight buttplate, sling swivels, 18.9" barrel, and no barrelband.

Price: $419.00

RUGER 10/22-T TARGET RIFLE

Similar to the 10/22 except has 20" heavy, hammer-forged barrel with tight chamber dimensions, improved trigger pull. **Weight:** 7.5 lbs. **Stock:** Black or brown laminated hardwood, dimensioned for optical sights. No iron sights supplied. Introduced 1996.

Price: From $550.00
Price: Stainless from.................................. $589.00

RUGER SR-22 RIFLE

AR-style semiauto rifle chambered in .22 LR, based on 10/22 action. Features include all-aluminum chassis replicating the AR-platform dimensions between the sighting plane, buttstock height and grip;

Picatinny rail optic mount includes a six-position, telescoping M4-style buttstock (on a Mil-Spec diameter tube); Hogue Monogrip pistol grip; buttstocks and grips interchangeable with any AR-style compatible option; round, mid-length handguard mounted on a standard-thread AR-style barrel nut; precision-rifled, cold hammer forged 16-1/8-inch alloy steel barrel capped with an SR-556/Mini-14 flash suppressor.

Price: $709.00

SAVAGE A17 SERIES

Caliber: .17 HMR. 10-shot rotary magazine. **Barrel:** 22". **Weight:** 5.4 to 5.6 lbs. **Features:** Delayed blowback action, Savage AccuTrigger, synthetic or laminated stock. Target model has heavy barrel, sporter or thumbhole stock. Also available in .22 WMR (A22 Model.) Introduced in 2016.

Price: Standard model $473.00
Price: Sporter (Gray laminate stock)..................... $574.00
Price: Target Sporter $571.00
Price: Target Thumbhole $631.00
Price: A22 .22 WMR.............................. $465.00

SAVAGE MODEL 64G

Caliber: .22 LR, 10-shot magazine. **Barrel:** 20", 21". **Weight:** 5.5 lbs. **Length:** 40", 41". **Stock:** Walnut-finished hardwood with Monte Carlo-type comb, checkered grip and fore-end. **Sights:** Bead front, open adjustable rear. Receiver grooved for scope mounting. **Features:** Thumb-operated rotating safety. Blue finish. 64 SS has stainless finish. Side ejection, bolt hold-open device. Introduced 1990. Made in Canada, from Savage Arms.

Price: 64 G...................................... $221.00
Price: 64 F....................................... $175.00
Price: 64 FSS.................................... $264.00
Price: 64 TR-SR................................. $360.00

SMITH & WESSON M&P15-22 SERIES

Caliber: .22 LR. 10 or 25-round magazine. **Barrel:** 15.5", 16" or 16.5". **Stock:** 6-position telescoping or fixed. **Features:** A rimfire verson of AR-derived M&P tactical autoloader. Operates with blowback action. Quad-mount picatinny rails, plain barrel or compensator, alloy upper and lower, matte black metal finish. Kryptek Highander or Muddy Girl camo finishes available.

Price: Standard $449.00
Price: Kryptek Highlander or Muddy Girl camo...................... $499.00
Price: MOE Model with Magpul sights, stock and grip $609.00
Price: Performance Center upgrades, threaded barrel............. $789.00

BROWNING BL-22

Action: Short-throw lever action, side ejection. Rack-and-pinion lever. Tubular magazines, with 15+1 capacity for .22 LR. **Barrel:** Recessed muzzle. **Stock:** Walnut, two-piece straight-grip Western style. **Trigger:** Half-cock hammer safety; fold-down hammer. **Sights:** Bead post front, folding-leaf rear. Steel receiver grooved for scope mount. **Weight:** 5-5.4 lbs. **Length:** 36.75-40.75" overall. **Features:** Action lock provided. Introduced 1996. FLD Grade II Octagon has octagonal 24" barrel, silver nitride receiver with scroll engraving, gold-colored trigger. FLD Grade I has satin-nickel receiver, blued trigger, no stock checkering. FLD Grade II has satin-nickel receivers with scroll engraving; gold-colored trigger, cut checkering. Both introduced 2005. Grade I has blued receiver and trigger, no stock checkering. Grade II has gold-colored trigger, cut checkering, blued receiver with scroll engraving. Imported from Japan by Browning.

Price: BL-22 Grade I/II, from.................................. $620.00 to $700.00
Price: BL-22 FLD Grade I/II, from .... $660.00 to $750.00
Price: BL-22 FLD, Grade II Octagon $980.00

HENRY LEVER-ACTION RIFLES

Caliber: .22 Long Rifle (15 shot), .22 Magnum (11 shots), .17 HMR (11 shots). **Barrel:** 18.25" round. **Weight:** 5.5 to 5.75 lbs. **Length:** 34" overall (.22 LR). **Stock:** Walnut. **Sights:** Hooded blade front, open adjustable rear. **Features:** Polished blue finish; full-length tubular magazine; side ejection; receiver grooved for scope mounting. Introduced 1997. Made in U.S.A. by Henry Repeating Arms Co.

Price: H001 Carbine .22 LR.. $360.00
Price: H001L Carbine .22 LR, Large Loop Lever..................... $375.00
Price: H001Y Youth model (33" overall, 11-round .22 LR) $360.00
Price: H001M .22 Magnum, 19.25" octagonal barrel, deluxe
    walnut stock $500.00
Price: H001V .17 HMR, 20" octagonal barrel, Williams Fire
    Sights.. $500.00

HENRY LEVER-ACTION OCTAGON FRONTIER MODEL

Same as Lever rifles except chambered in .17 HMR, .22 Short/Long/LR, .22 Magnum. **Barrel:** 20" octagonal. **Sights:** Marble's full adjustable semi-buckhorn rear, brass bead front. **Weight:** 6.25 lbs. Made in U.S.A. by Henry Repeating Arms Co.

Price: H001T Lever Octagon $450.00
Price: H001TM Lever Octagon .22 Magnum $550.00

HENRY GOLDEN BOY SERIES

Caliber: .17 HMR, .22 LR (16-shot), .22 Magnum. **Barrel:** 20" octagonal. **Weight:** 6.25 lbs. **Length:** 38" overall. **Stock:** American walnut. **Sights:** Blade front, open rear. **Features:** Brasslite receiver, brass buttplate, blued barrel and lever. Introduced 1998. Made in U.S.A. from Henry Repeating Arms Co.

Price: H004 .22 LR.. $550.00
Price: H004M .22 Magnum $595.00
Price: H004V .17 HMR $615.00
Price: H004DD .22 LR Deluxe, engraved receiver................ $1,585.00

HENRY SILVER BOY

Caliber: 17 HMR, .22 S/L/LR, .22 WMR. Tubular magazine capacity: 12 rounds (.17 HMR and .22 WMR), 16 rounds (.22 LR), 21 rounds (.22 Short). **Barrel:** 20 inches. **Stock:** American walnut with curved

buttplate. **Finish:** Nickel receiver, barrel band and buttplate. **Sights:** Adjustable buckhorn rear, bead front. Silver Eagle model has engraved scroll pattern from early original Henry rifle. Offered in same calibers as Silver Boy. Made in U.S.A. from Henry Repeating Arms Company.

Price: .22 S/L/LR $600.00
Price: .22 WMR.. $650.00
Price: .17 HMR $675.00
Price: Silver Eagle................................ $850.00 to $900.00

HENRY PUMP ACTION

Caliber: .22 LR, 15-shot. **Barrel:** 18.25". **Weight:** 5.5 lbs. **Length:** NA. **Stock:** American walnut. **Sights:** Bead on ramp front, open adjustable rear. **Features:** Polished blue finish; receiver grooved for scope mount; grooved slide handle; two barrelbands. Introduced 1998. Made in U.S.A. from Henry Repeating Arms Co.

Price: H003T .22 LR.. $550.00
Price: H003TM .22 Magnum................................... $595.00

MARLIN MODEL GOLDEN 39A

Caliber: .22, S (26), L (21), LR (19), tubular magazine. **Barrel:** 24" Micro-Groove. **Weight:** 6.5 lbs. **Length:** 40" overall. **Stock:** Checkered American black walnut; Mar-Shield finish. Swivel studs; rubber buttpad. **Sights:** Bead ramp front with detachable Wide-Scan hood, folding rear semi-buckhorn adjustable for windage and elevation. **Features:** Hammer block safety; rebounding hammer. Takedown action, receiver tapped for scope mount (supplied), offset hammer spur, gold-colored steel trigger. The 39 series certainly deserve the term "classic" since it has been in continuous production longer than any other rifle in America, since 1922.

Price: $709.00

MOSSBERG MODEL 464 RIMFIRE

Caliber: .22 LR. **Barrel:** 20" round blued. **Weight:** 5.6 lbs. **Length:** 35-3/4" overall. **Features:** Adjustable sights, straight grip stock, 14-shot tubular magazine, plain hardwood straight stock and fore-end.

Price: $485.00
Price: SPX $513.00

REMINGTON 572 BDL DELUXE FIELDMASTER PUMP

Caliber: .22 S (20), L (17) or LR (15), tubular magazine. **Barrel:** 21" round tapered. **Weight:** 5.5 lbs. **Length:** 40" overall. **Stock:** Walnut with checkered pistol grip and slide handle. **Sights:** Big game. **Features:** Crossbolt safety; removing inner magazine tube converts rifle to single shot; receiver grooved for tip-off scope mount. Another classic rimfire, this model was been in production since 1955.

Price: $723.00

Prices given are believed to be accurate at time of publication however, many factors affect retail pricing so exact pricing is not possible.

71ST EDITION, 2017 ✦ **475**

ANSCHUTZ MODEL 64 MP
Caliber: .22 LR. Magazine capacity: 5 rounds. **Barrel:** 25.6 inch heavy match. **Weight:** About 9 pounds. **Stock:** Multipurpose hardwood with beavertail fore-end. **Sights:** None. Drilled and tapped for scope or receiver sights. **Features:** Model 64S BR (benchrest) has 20" heavy barrel, adjustable two-stage match-grade trigger, flat beavertail stock, weighs 9.5 pounds. Imported from Germany by Steyr Arms
Price: $1,399.00
Price: Model 64 S BR $1,539.00

ANSCHUTZ 1416D/1516D CLASSIC
Caliber: .22 LR (1416D888), .22 WMR (1516D), 5-shot clip. **Barrel:** 22.5". **Weight:** 6 lbs. **Length:** 41" overall. **Stock:** European hardwood with walnut finish; classic style with straight comb, checkered pistol grip and fore-end. **Sights:** Hooded ramp front, folding leaf rear. **Features:** Uses Match 64 action. Adjustable single-stage trigger. Receiver grooved for scope mounting. Imported from Germany by Steyr Arms.
Price: 1416D KL, .22 LR $1,099.00
Price: 1416D KL Classic left-hand $1,199.00
Price: 1516D KL, .22 WMR $1,169.00
Price: 1416D, thumbhole stock $1,599.00

ANSCHUTZ 1710D CUSTOM
Caliber:.22 LR, 5-shot clip. **Barrel:** : 23.75 or 24.25" heavy contour. **Weight:** 6.5 to 7-3/8 lbs. **Length:** 42.5" overall. **Stock:** Select European walnut. **Sights:** Hooded ramp front, folding leaf rear; drilled and tapped for scope mounting. **Features:** Match 54 action with adjustable single-stage trigger; roll-over Monte Carlo cheekpiece, slim fore-end with Schnabel tip, Wundhammer palm swell on pistol grip, rosewood gripcap with white diamond insert; skip-line checkering on grip and fore-end. Introduced 1988. Imported from Germany by Steyr Arms.
Price: From $2,195.00
Price: Meistergrade w/high grade walnut stock $2,595.00

BROWNING T-BOLT RIMFIRE
Caliber: .22 LR, .17 HMR, .22 WMR, 10-round rotary box Double Helix magazine. **Barrel:** 22", free-floating, semi-match chamber, target muzzle crown. **Weight:** 4.8 lbs. **Length:** 40.1" overall. **Stock:** Walnut, maple or composite. **Sights:** None. **Features:** Straight-pull bolt-action, three-lever trigger adjustable for pull weight, dual action screws, sling swivel studs. Crossbolt lockup, enlarged bolt handle, one-piece dual extractor with integral spring and red cocking indicator band, gold-tone trigger. Top-tang, thumb-operated two-position safety, drilled and tapped for scope mounts. Varmint model has raised Monte Carlo comb, heavy barrel, wide forearm. Introduced 2006. Imported from Japan by Browning. Left-hand models added in 2009.
Price: .22 LR, from................................ $750.00 to $780.00
Price: Composite Target .... $780.00 to $800.00
Price: .17 HMR/.22 WMR, from .... $790.00 to $830.00

COOPER MODEL 57-M REPEATER
Caliber: .22 LR, .22 WMR, .17 HMR, .17 Mach 2. **Barrel:** 22" or 24".

Weight: 6.5-7.5 lbs. **Stock:** Claro walnut, 22 lpi hand checkering. **Sights:** None furnished. **Features:** Three rear locking lug, repeating bolt-action with 5-shot magazine for .22 LR; 4-shot magazine for .22 WMR and 17 HMR. Fully adjustable trigger. Left-hand models add $150 to base rifle price. 1/4"-group rimfire accuracy guarantee at 50 yards; 0.5"-group centerfire accuracy guarantee at 100 yards. Options include wood upgrades, case-color metalwork, barrel fluting, custom LOP, and many others.

Price: Classic $2,295.00
Price: Custom Classic $2,695.00
Price: Western Classic $3,455.00
Price: Schnabel $2,455.00
Price: Jackson Squirrel $2,395.00
Price: Jackson Hunter $2,255.00
Price: Mannlicher...$4,395.00

CZ 452 AMERICAN
Similar to the CZ 452 M 2E Lux except has classic-style stock of Circassian walnut; 22.5" free-floating barrel with recessed target crown; receiver dovetail for scope mounting. No open sights furnished. Introduced 1999. Imported from the Czech Republic by CZ-USA.
Price: .22 LR, .22 WMR $463.00
Price: Scout/Youth model w/16" barrel $312.00

CZ 455 AMERICAN
Caliber: .17 HMR, .22 LR, .22 WMR (5-round magazine). **Barrel:** 20.5". **Weight:** 6.1 lbs. **Length:** 38.2". **Stock:** Walnut. **Sights:** None. Intergral 11mm dovetail scope base. **Features:** Adjustable trigger. Six versions available including blue laminate with thumbhole stock, Varmint model with .866" heavy barrel, full-length Mannlicher walnut stock, and others. American Combo Package includes interchangeable barrel to switch calibers.
Price: from .... $421.00 to $565.00

DAVEY CRICKETT SINGLE SHOT
Caliber: .22 LR, 122 WMR, single-shot. **Barrel:** 16-1/8". **Weight:** About 2.5 lbs. **Length:** 30" overall. **Stock:** American walnut. **Sights:** Post on ramp front, peep rear adjustable for windage and elevation. **Features:** Drilled and tapped for scope mounting using special Chipmunk base ($13.95). Engraved model also available. Made in U.S.A. Introduced 1982. Formerly Chipmunk model. From Keystone Sporting Arms.
Price: From $171.00

HENRY MINI BOLT YOUTH RIFLE
Caliber: .22 LR, single-shot youth gun. **Barrel:** 16" stainless, 8-groove rifling. **Weight:** 3.25 lbs. **Length:** 30", LOP 11.5". **Stock:** Synthetic, pistol grip, wraparound checkering and beavertail forearm. Available in black finish or bright colors. **Sights:** William Fire sights. **Features:** One-piece bolt configuration manually operated safety.
Price: $275.00

MARLIN MODEL XT-17 SERIES
Caliber: .17 HRM. **Magazine capacity:** 4 and 7-shot, two magazines included. **Barrel:** 22 inches. **Weight:** 6 pounds. **Stock:** Black synthetic with palm swell, stippled grip areas, or walnut-finished hardwood with Monte Carlo comb. Laminated stock available. **Sights:** Adjustable rear, ramp front. Drilled and tapped for scope mounts. **Features:** Adjustable trigger. Blue or stainless finish.
Price: .... $269.00 to $429.00

Prices given are believed to be accurate at time of publication however, many factors affect retail pricing so exact prices are not possible.

MARLIN MODEL XT-22 SERIES

Caliber: .22 Short, Long, Long Rifle. Available with 7-shot detachable box magazine or tubular magazine (17 to 22 rounds). **Barrel:** 22 inches. Varmint model has heavy barrel. **Weight:** 6 lbs. **Stock:** Black synthetic, walnut-finished hardwood, walnut or camo. Tubular model available with two-tone brown laminated stock. **Finish:** Blue or stainless. **Sights:** Adjustable rear, ramp front. Some models have folding rear sight with a hooded or high visibility orange front sight. **Features:** Pro-Fire Adjustable Trigger, Micro-Groove rifling, thumb safety with red cocking indicator. The XT-22M series is chambered for .22 WMR. Made in U.S.A. by Marlin Firearms Co.
Price: From .... **$221.00 to $340.00**
Price: XT-22M .... **$240.00 to $270.00**

MEACHAM LOW-WALL

Caliber: Any rimfire cartridge. **Barrel:** 26-34". **Weight:** 7-15 lbs. **Sights:** none. Tang drilled for Win. base, 3/8" dovetail slot front. **Stock:** Fancy eastern walnut with cheekpiece; ebony insert in forearm tip. **Features:** Exact copy of 1885 Winchester. With most Winchester factory options available including double-set triggers. Introduced 1994. Made in U.S.A. by Meacham T&H Inc.
Price: From **$4,999.00**

MOSSBERG MODEL 817

Caliber: .17 HMR, 5-round magazine. **Barrel:** 21"; free-floating bull barrel, recessed muzzle crown. **Weight:** 4.9 lbs. (black synthetic), 5.2 lbs. (wood). **Stock:** Black synthetic or wood; length of pull, 14.25". **Sights:** Factory-installed Weaver-style scope bases. **Features:** Blued or brushed chrome metal finishes, crossbolt safety, gun lock. Introduced 2008. Made in U.S.A. by O.F. Mossberg & Sons, Inc.
Price: .... **$212.00 to $253.00**

MOSSBERG MODEL 801/802

Caliber: .22 LR, 10-round detachable magazine. **Barrel:** 18" free-floating. Varmint model has 21" heavy barrel. **Weight:** 4.1 to 4.6 lbs. **Sights:** Adjustable rifle. Receiver grooved for scope mount. **Stock:** Black synthetic. **Features:** Ergonomically placed magazine release and safety buttons, crossbolt safety, free gun lock. 801 Half Pint has 12.25" length of pull, 16" barrel, and weighs 4 lbs. Hardwood stock; removable magazine plug.
Price: Plinkster....................................... **$223.00**
Price: Half Pint....................................... **$223.00**
Price: Varmint....................................... **$223.00**

NEW ULTRA LIGHT ARMS 20RF

Caliber: .22 LR, single-shot or repeater. **Barrel:** Douglas, length to order. **Weight:** 5.25 lbs. **Length:** Varies. **Stock:** Kevlar/graphite composite, variety of finishes. **Sights:** None furnished; drilled and tapped for scope mount. **Features:** Timney trigger, hand-lapped action, button-rifled barrel, hand-bedded action, recoil pad, sling-swivel studs, optional Jewell trigger. Made in U.S.A. by New Ultra Light Arms.
Price: 20 RF single shot....................................... **$1,800.00**
Price: 20 RF repeater **$1,850.00**

ROSSI MATCHED PAIR SINGLE-SHOT/SHOTGUN

Caliber: .17 HMR rifle with interchangeable 12 or 20-gauge shotgun barrel. **Barrel:** 23" (rifle), 28" (shotgun). **Weight:** 5.25 to 6.25 lbs. **Stock:** Hardwood (brown or black finish). **Sights:** Fully adjustable front and rear. **Features:** Break-open breech, transfer-bar manual safety. Youth Model has .17 HMR or .22 LR rifle barrel with interchangeable .410 shotgun. Introduced 2001. Imported by BrazTech International.
Price: From **$298.00**
Price: Youth model from **$245.00**

RUGER 77/22 RIMFIRE

Caliber: .22 LR, 10-shot magazine; .22 WMR, 9-shot magazine. **Barrel:** 20" or 24" (stainless model only). **Weight:** 6.0 to 6.5 lbs. (20" bbl.); 7.5 lbs. (24" bbl.). **Length:** 39.25" overall (20" bbl.). **Stock:** Checkered American walnut or synthetic, stainless sling swivels. **Sights:** Plain barrel with integral scope mounting system complete with 1-inch Ruger rings. **Features:** Mauser-type action uses Ruger's famous rotary magazine. Three-position safety, simplified bolt stop, patented bolt-locking system. Uses the dual-screw barrel attachment system of the 10/22 rifle.
Price: Blue finish w/walnut or synthetic stock **$979.00**
Price: Stainless steel w/walnut stock **$1,069.00**

RUGER 77/17 RIMFIRE

Caliber: .17 HMR, 9-shot rotary magazine. **Barrel:** 22" to 24". **Weight:** 6.5-7.5 lbs. **Length:** 41.25-43.25" overall. **Stock:** Checkered American walnut, laminated hardwood; stainless sling swivels. **Sights:** None. Integral scope mounting system with 1-inch Ruger rings. **Features:** Mauser-type action uses Ruger's rotary magazine. Three-position safety, simplified bolt stop, patented bolt-locking system. Uses the dual-screw barrel attachment system of the 10/22 rifle. Introduced 2002.
Price: Blue finish w/walnut stock.. **$979.00**
Price: Stainless steel w/laminate stock **$1,069.00**

SAKO FINNFIRE II

Caliber: .22 LR or .17 HMR, 6-shot detachable magazine. **Barrel:** 22". **Weight:** 6.3 lbs. **Stock:** Checkered American walnut, oil-finished with cheekpiece, rubber buttpad, sling swivels. **Sights:** Adjustable or fixed rear, bead front. Made in Finland and imported by Beretta USA.
Price: **$1,100.00**

SAVAGE MARK II BOLT-ACTION

Caliber: .22 LR, .17 HMR, 10-shot magazine. **Barrel:** 20.5". **Weight:** 5.5 lbs. **Length:** 39.5" overall. **Stock:** Walnut-finished hardwood with Monte Carlo-type comb, checkered grip and fore-end. Camo or OD Green stock available. **Sights:** Bead front, open adjustable rear. Receiver grooved for scope mounting. **Features:** Thumb-operated rotating safety. Blue finish. Introduced 1990. Made in Canada, from Savage Arms, Inc.
Price: .... **$228.00 to $280.00**
Price: Varmint w/heavy barrel....................................... **$242.00**
Price: Camo stock....................................... **$280.00**
Price: OD Green stock....................................... **$291.00**

SAVAGE MARK II-FSS STAINLESS RIFLE

Similar to the Mark II except has stainless steel barreled action and black synthetic stock with positive checkering, swivel studs, and 20.75" free-floating and button-rifled barrel with detachable magazine. Weighs 5.5 lbs. Introduced 1997. Imported from Canada by Savage Arms, Inc.
Price: **$336.00**

SAVAGE MODEL 93G MAGNUM BOLT-ACTION

Caliber: .22 WMR, 5-shot magazine. **Barrel:** 20.75". **Weight:** 5.75 lbs. **Length:** 39.5" overall. **Stock:** Walnut-finished hardwood with Monte Carlo-type comb, checkered grip and fore-end. **Sights:** Bead front, adjustable open rear. Receiver grooved for scope mount. **Features:** Thumb-operated rotary safety. Blue finish. Introduced 1994. Made in Canada, from Savage Arms.
Price: Model 93G....................................... **$285.00**
Price: Model 93F (as above with black graphite/fiberglass stock) **$364.00**
Price: Model 93 BSEV, thumbhole stock **$646.00**

Prices given are believed to be accurate at time of publication however, many factors affect retail pricing so exact prices are not possible.

71ST EDITION, 2017 ✦ **477**

SAVAGE MODEL 93FSS MAGNUM RIFLE

Similar to Model 93G except stainless steel barreled action and black synthetic stock with positive checkering. Weighs 5.5 lbs. Introduced 1997. Imported from Canada by Savage Arms, Inc.

Price: $353.00

SAVAGE MODEL 93FVSS MAGNUM

Similar to Model 93FSS Magnum except 21" heavy barrel with recessed target-style crown, satin-finished stainless barreled action, black graphite/fiberglass stock. Drilled and tapped for scope mounting; comes with Weaver-style bases. Introduced 1998. Imported from Canada by Savage Arms, Inc.

Price: $364.00

SAVAGE B-MAG

Caliber: .17 Winchester Super Magnum. Rotary magazine holds 8 rounds. **Stock:** Synthetic. **Weight:** 4.5 pounds. Chambered for new Winchester .17 Super Magnum rimfire cartridge that propels a 20-grain bullet at approximately 3,000 fps. **Features:** Adjustable AccuTrigger, rear locking lugs, new and different bolt-action rimfire design that cocks on close of bolt. New in 2013.

Price: $402.00

Price: Stainless steel receiver and barrel................................$433.00

SAVAGE BRJ SERIES

Similar to Mark II, Model 93 and Model 93R17 rifles but features spiral fluting pattern on a heavy barrel, blued finish and Royal Jacaranda wood laminate stock.

Price: Mark II BRJ, .22 LR $519.00

Price: Model 93 BRJ, .22 Mag...$527.00

Price: Model 93 R17 BRJ, .17 HMR $527.00

SAVAGE TACTICAL RIMFIRE SERIES

Similar to Savage Model BRJ series semiauto rifles but with matte finish and a tactical-style wood stock.

Price: Mark II TR, .22 LR $533.00

Price: Mark II TRR, .22 LR, three-way accessory rail $627.00

Price: Model 93R17 TR, .17 HMR $541.00

Price: Model 93R17 TRR, .17 HMR, three-way accessory rail $635.00

ANSCHUTZ 1903 MATCH

Caliber: .22 LR, single-shot. **Barrel:** 21.25". **Weight:** 8 lbs. **Length:** 43.75" overall. **Stock:** Walnut-finished hardwood with adjustable cheekpiece; stippled grip and fore-end. **Sights:** None furnished. **Features:** Uses Anschutz Match 64 action. A medium weight rifle for intermediate and advanced Junior Match competition. Available from Champion's Choice.
Price: Right-hand...$1,195.00

ANSCHUTZ 64-MP R SILHOUETTE

Caliber: .22 LR, 5-shot magazine. **Barrel:** 21.5", medium heavy; 7/8" diameter. **Weight:** 8 lbs. **Length:** 39.5" overall. **Stock:** Walnut-finished hardwood, silhouette-type. **Sights:** None furnished. **Features:** Uses Match 64 action. Designed for metallic silhouette competition. Stock has stippled checkering, contoured thumb groove with Wundhammer swell. Two-stage #5098 trigger. Slide safety locks sear and bolt. Introduced 1980. Available from Champion's Choice.
Price: 64-MP R $1,100.00
Price: 64-S BR Benchrest......................................$1,327.00

ANSCHUTZ 2007 MATCH RIFLE

Uses same action as the Model 2013, but has a lighter barrel. European walnut stock in right-hand, true left-hand or extra-short models. Sights optional. Available with 19.6" barrel with extension tube, or 26", both in stainless or blue. Introduced 1998. Available from Champion's Choice.
Price: Right-hand, blue, no sights $2,595.00

ANSCHUTZ 1827BT FORTNER BIATHLON

Caliber: .22 LR, 5-shot magazine. **Barrel:** 21.7". **Weight:** 8.8 lbs. with sights. **Length:** 40.9" overall. **Stock:** European walnut with cheekpiece, stippled pistol grip and fore-end. **Sights:** Optional globe front specially designed for Biathlon shooting, micrometer rear with hinged snow cap. **Features:** Uses Super Match 54 action and nine-way adjustable trigger; adjustable wooden buttplate, biathlon butthook, adjustable hand-stop rail. Uses Anschutz/Fortner system straight-pull bolt action, blued or stainless steel barrel. Introduced 1982. Available from Champion's Choice.
Price: From about $3,195.00

ANSCHUTZ SUPER MATCH SPECIAL MODEL 2013

Caliber: .22 LR, single-shot. **Barrel:** 25.9". **Weight:** 13 lbs. **Length:** 41.7" to 42.9". **Stock:** Adjustable aluminum. **Sights:** None furnished. **Features:** 2313 aluminum-silver/blue stock, 500mm barrel, fast lock time, adjustable cheekpiece, heavy action and muzzle tube, w/ handstop and standing riser block. Introduced in 1997. Available from Champion's Choice.
Price: From about $3,995.00

ANSCHUTZ 1912 SPORT

Caliber: .22 LR. **Barrel:** 26" match. **Weight:** 11.4 lbs. **Length:** 41.7" overall. **Stock:** Non-stained thumbhole stock adjustable in length with adjustable buttplate and cheekpiece adjustment. Flat fore-end raiser block 4856 adjustable in height. Hook buttplate. **Sights:** None furnished. **Features:** "Free rifle" for women. Smallbore model 1907 with 1912 stock: Match 54 action. Delivered with: Hand stop 6226, fore-end raiser block 4856, screwdriver, instruction leaflet with test target. Available from Champion's Choice.
Price: $2,795.00

ANSCHUTZ 1913 SUPER MATCH RIFLE

Same as the Model 1911 except European walnut International-type stock with adjustable cheekpiece, or color laminate, both available with straight or lowered fore-end, adjustable aluminum hook buttplate, adjustable hand stop, weighs 13 lbs., 46" overall. Stainless or blue barrel. Available from Champion's Choice.
Price: Right-hand, blue, no sights, walnut stock..................$3,290.00

ANSCHUTZ 1907 STANDARD MATCH RIFLE

Same action as Model 1913 but with 7/8" diameter 26" barrel (stainless or blue). Length is 44.5" overall, weighs 10.5 lbs. Choice of stock configurations. Vented fore-end. Designed for prone and position shooting ISU requirements; suitable for NRA matches. Also available with walnut flat-forend stock for benchrest shooting. Available from Champion's Choice.
Price: Right-hand, blue, no sights $2,185.00

ARMALITE AR-10(T)

Caliber: .308 Win., 10-shot magazine. **Barrel:** 24" target-weight Rock 5R custom. **Weight:** 10.4 lbs. **Length:** 43.5" overall. **Stock:** Green or black composition; N.M. fiberglass handguard tube. **Sights:** Detachable handle, front sight, or scope mount available. Comes with international-style flattop receiver with Picatinny rail. **Features:** National Match two-stage trigger. Forged upper receiver. Receivers hard-coat anodized. Introduced 1995. Made in U.S.A. by ArmaLite, Inc.
Price: Black $1,912.00
Price: AR-10, .338 Federal $1,992.00

ARMALITE AR-10 NATIONAL MATCH

Caliber: .308/7.62 NATO. **Barrel:** 20", triple-lapped Match barrel, 1:10" twist rifling. **Weight:** 11.5 lbs. **Length:** 41". **Features:** Stainless steel flash suppressor, two-stage National Match trigger. Forged flattop receiver with Picatinny rail and forward assist.
Price: $2,365.00

ARMALITE M14A4(T)

Caliber: .223 Rem., 10-round magazine. **Barrel:** 24" heavy stainless; 1:8" twist. **Weight:** 9.2 lbs. **Length:** 42-3/8" overall. **Stock:** Green or black butt, N.M. fiberglass handguard tube. **Sights:** One-piece international-style flattop receiver with Weaver-type rail, including case deflector. **Features:** Detachable carry handle, front sight and scope mount (30mm or 1") available. Upper and lower receivers have push-type pivot pin, hard coat anodized. Made in U.S.A. by ArmaLite, Inc.
Price: From .... **$1,318.00 to $1,449..00**

ARMALITE M15 A4 CARBINE 6.8 & 7.62X39

Caliber: 6.8 Rem., 7.62x39. **Barrel:** 16" chrome-lined with flash suppressor. **Weight:** 7 lbs. **Length:** 26.6". **Features:** Front and rear picatinny rails for mounting optics, two-stage tactical trigger, anodized aluminum/phosphate finish.
Price: $1,107.00

BLASER R93 LONG RANGE SPORTER 2

Caliber: .308 Win., 10-shot detachable box magazine. **Barrel:** 24". **Weight:** 10.4 lbs. **Length:** 44" overall. **Stock:** Aluminum with synthetic lining. **Sights:** None furnished; accepts detachable scope mount. **Features:** Straight-pull bolt action with adjustable trigger; fully adjustable stock; quick takedown; corrosion resistant finish. Introduced 1998. Imported from Germany by Blaser USA.
Price: $4,400.00

BUSHMASTER A2/A3 TARGET

Caliber: 5.56mm, .223 Rem., 30-round magazine. **Barrel:** 20", 24". **Weight:** 8.43 lbs. (A2); 8.78 lbs. (A3). **Length:** 39.5" overall (20" barrel). **Stock:** Black composition; A2 type. **Sights:** Adjustable post front, adjustable aperture rear. **Features:** Patterned after Colt M-16A2. Chrome-lined barrel with manganese phosphate exterior. Available in stainless barrel. Made in U.S.A. by Bushmaster Firearms Co.
Price: A2 ....$969.00
Price: A3 with carrying handle $999.00

OLYMPIC ARMS UM ULTRAMATCH AR15

Caliber: .223 Rem. minimum SAAMI spec, 30-shot magazine. **Barrel:**

20" or 24" bull broach-cut Ultramatch stainless steel 1x10" twist rate. **Weight:** 8-10 lbs. **Length:** 38.25" overall. **Stock:** A2 grip, A2 buttstock with trapdoor. **Sights:** None, flattop upper and gas block with rails. **Features:** Flattop upper, free-floating tubular match handguard, Picatinny gas block, crowned muzzle and factory trigger job. Premium model adds pneumatic recoil buffer, Harris S-series bipod, hand selected premium receivers and William Set Trigger. Made in U.S.A. by Olympic Arms, Inc

Price: UM-1, 20" Ultramatch **$1,332.50**
Price: UM-1P **$1,623.70**

OLYMPIC ARMS ML-2 MULTIMATCH AR15 CARBINES

Caliber: .223 Rem. minimum SAAMI spec, 30-shot magazine. **Barrel:** 16" broach-cut Ultramatch stainless steel 1x10" twist rate. **Weight:** 7-8 lbs. **Length:** 34-36" overall. **Stock:** A2 grip and varying buttstock. **Sights:** None. **Features:** The ML-2 includes bull diameter barrel, flattop upper, free-floating tubular match handguard, Picatinny gas block, crowned muzzle and A2 buttstock with trapdoor. Made in U.S.A. by Olympic Arms, Inc.

Price: ML-2 .... **$1,253.20**

OLYMPIC ARMS K8 TARGETMATCH AR15

Caliber: 5.56 NATO, .223 WSSM, .243 WSSM, .25 WSSM, 30/7-shot magazine. **Barrel:** 20", 24" bull button-rifled stainless/chrome-moly steel 1x9"/1x10" twist rate. **Weight:** 8-10 lbs. **Length:** 38"-42" overall. **Stock:** A2 grip, A2 buttstock with trapdoor. **Sights:** None. **Features:** Barrel has satin bead-blast finish; flattop upper, free-floating tubular match handguard, Picatinny gas block, crowned muzzle and "Targetmatch" pantograph on lower receiver. K8-MAG model uses Winchester Super Short Magnum cartridges. Includes 24" bull chrome-moly barrel, flattop upper, free-floating tubular match handguard, Picatinny gas block, crowned muzzle and 7-shot magazine. Made in U.S.A. by Olympic Arms, Inc.

Price: K8 .... **$908.70**
Price: K8-MAG **$1,363.70**

REMINGTON 40-XB RANGEMASTER TARGET

Caliber: 15 calibers from .22 BR Remington to .300 Win. Mag. **Barrel:** 27.25". **Weight:** 11.25 lbs. **Length:** 47" overall. **Stock:** American walnut, laminated thumbhole or Kevlar with high comb and beavertail fore-end stop. Rubber nonslip buttplate. **Sights:** None. Scope blocks installed. **Features:** Adjustable trigger. Stainless barrel and action. Receiver drilled and tapped for sights. Model 40-XB Tactical (2008) chambered in .308 Win., comes with guarantee of 0.75-inch maximum 5-shot groups at 100 yards. **Weight:** 10.25 lbs. Includes Teflon-coated stainless button-rifled barrel, 1:14" twist, 27.25-inch long, three longitudinal flutes. Bolt-action repeater, adjustable 40-X trigger and precision machined aluminum bedding block. Stock is H-S Precision Pro Series synthetic tactical stock, black with green web finish, vertical pistol grip. From Remington Custom Shop.

Price: 40-XB KS, aramid fiber stock, single shot **$2,863.00**
Price: 40-XB KS, aramid fiber stock, repeater **$3,014.00**
Price: 40-XB Tactical .308 Win. **$2,992.00**

REMINGTON 40-XBBR KS

Caliber: Five calibers from .22 BR to .308 Win. **Barrel:** 20" (light varmint class), 24" (heavy varmint class). **Weight:** 7.25 lbs. (light varmint class); 12 lbs. (heavy varmint class). **Length:** 38" (20" bbl.), 42" (24"bbl.). **Stock:** Aramid fiber. **Sights:** None. Supplied with scope blocks. **Features:** Unblued benchrest with stainless steel barrel, trigger adjustable from 1-1/2 lbs. to 3.5 lbs. Special

2-oz. trigger extra cost. Scope and mounts extra. From Remington Custom Shop.

Price: Single shot **$3,950.00**

REMINGTON 40-XC KS TARGET

Caliber: 7.62 NATO, 5-shot. **Barrel:** 24", stainless steel. **Weight:** 11 lbs. without sights. **Length:** 43.5" overall. **Stock:** Aramid fiber. **Sights:** None furnished. **Features:** Designed to meet the needs of competitive shooters. Stainless steel barrel and action. From Remington Custom Shop.

Price: **$3,067.00**

REMINGTON 40-XR CUSTOM SPORTER

Caliber: .22 LR, .22 WM. **Barrel:** 24" stainless steel, no sights. **Weight:** 9.75 lbs. **Length:** 40". **Features:** Model XR-40 Target rifle action. Many options available in stock, decoration or finish.

Price: Single shot **$4,500.00**

SAKO TRG-22 BOLT-ACTION

Caliber: .308 Win., 10-shot magazine, .338 Lapua, 5-shot magazine. **Barrel:** 26". **Weight:** 10.25 lbs. **Length:** 45.25" overall. **Stock:** Reinforced polyurethane with fully adjustable cheekpiece and buttplate. **Sights:** None furnished. Optional quick-detachable, one-piece scope mount base, 1" or 30mm rings. **Features:** Resistance-free bolt, free-floating heavy stainless barrel, 60-degree bolt lift. Two-stage trigger is adjustable for length, pull, horizontal or vertical pitch. TRG-42 has similar features but has long action and is chambered for .338 Lapua. Imported from Finland by Beretta USA.

Price: TRG-22 .... **$3,495.00**
Price: TRG-22 with folding stock **$6,075.00**
Price: TRG-42 .... **$4,445.00**
Price: TRG-42 with folding stock **$7,095.00**

SPRINGFIELD ARMORY M1A SUPER MATCH

Caliber: .308 Win. **Barrel:** 22", heavy Douglas Premium. **Weight:** About 11 lbs. **Length:** 44.31" overall. **Stock:** Heavy walnut competition stock with longer pistol grip, contoured area behind the rear sight, thicker butt and fore-end, glass bedded. **Sights:** National Match front and rear. **Features:** Has figure-eight-style operating rod guide. Introduced 1987. From Springfield Armory.

Price: About **$2,956.00**

SPRINGFIELD ARMORY M1A/M-21 TACTICAL MODEL

Similar to M1A Super Match except special sniper stock with adjustable cheekpiece and rubber recoil pad. Weighs 11.6 lbs. From Springfield Armory.

Price: **$3,619.00**

STI SPORTING COMPETITION

AR-style semiauto rifle chambered in 5.56 NATO. Features include 16-inch 410 stainless 1:8" twist barrel; mid-length gas system; Nordic Tactical Compensator and JP Trigger group; custom STI Valkyrie handguard and gas block; flattop design with picatinny rail; anodized finish with black Teflon coating. Also available in Tactical configuration.

Price: **$1,455.00**

TIME PRECISION .22 RF BENCH REST

Caliber: .22 LR, single-shot. **Barrel:** Shilen match-grade stainless. **Weight:** 10 lbs. with scope. **Length:** NA. **Stock:** Fiberglass. Pillar bedded. **Sights:** None furnished. **Features:** Shilen match trigger removable trigger bracket, full-length steel sleeve, aluminum receiver. Introduced 2008. Made in U.S.A. by Time Precision.

Price: **$2,833.00**

BENELLI ETHOS
Gauge: 12, 20, 28. 3" chamber. Magazine capacity 4+1. **Barrel:** 28" (Full, Mod., Imp. Cyl., Imp. Mod., Cylinder choke tubes). **Weight:** 6.5 lbs. (12 ga.), 5.3 to 5.7 (20 & 28 ga.). **Length:** 49.5" overall (28" barrel). **Stock:** Select AA European walnut with satin finish. **Sights:** Red bar fiber optic front, with three interchangeable inserts, metal middle bead. **Features:** Utilizes Benelli's Intertia Driven system. Recoil is reduced by Progressive Comfort recoil reduction system within the buttstock. Twelve and 20-gauge models cycle all 3-inch loads from light 7/8 oz. up to 3-inch magnums. Also available with nickel-plated engraved receiver. Imported from Italy by Benelli USA, Corp.

Price: $1,999.00
Price: Engraved nickel-plated (shown) $2,199.00
Price: 20 or 28 ga. (engraved, nickel plated only) $2,199.00

BENELLI LEGACY
Gauge: 12, 20, 28. 3" chamber (12, 20), 2 ¾" (28). **Barrel:** 24", 26", 28" (Full, Mod., Imp. Cyl., Imp. Mod., cylinder choke tubes). Mid-bead sight. **Weight:** 5.8 to 7.4 lbs. Length: 49-5/8" overall (28" barrel). **Stock:** Select AA European walnut with satin finish. **Features:** Uses the rotating bolt inertia recoil operating system with a two-piece steel/aluminum etched receiver (bright on lower, blue upper). Drop adjustment kit allows the stock to be custom fitted without modifying the stock. Introduced 1998. Ultralight model has gloss-blued finish receiver. Weight is 6.0 lbs., 24" barrel, 45.5" overall length. WeatherCoat walnut stock. Introduced 2006. Imported from Italy by Benelli USA, Corp.

Price: Legacy (12 and 20 gauge) $1,799.00
Price: Legacy (28 gauge) $2,039.00

BENELLI LEGACY SPORT
Gas-operated semiauto shotgun chambered for 12, 20 (2-3/4- and 3-inch) gauge. Features include Inertia Driven system; sculptured nickel finished lower receiver with classic game scene etchings; highly polished blued upper receiver; AA-Grade walnut stock; (A-grade on Sport II); gel recoil pad; ported 24- or 26-inch barrel, Crio chokes. Weight 6.3 (20 ga.) to 7.4 to 7.5 lbs.

Price: $2,439.00
Price: Legacy Sport II $1,899.00

BENELLI ULTRA LIGHT
Gauge: 12, 20, 28. 3" chamber (12, 20), 2 ¾" (28). **Barrel:** 24", 26". Mid-bead sight. **Weight:** 5.2 to 6 lbs. **Features:** Similar to Legacy line. Drop adjustment kit allows the stock to be custom fitted without modifying the stock. WeatherCoat walnut stock. Lightened receiver, shortened magazine tube, carbon-fiber rib and grip cap. Introduced 2008. Imported from Italy by Benelli USA, Corp.

Price: 12 and 20 gauge..$1,699.00
Price: 28 gauge..$1,799.00

BENELLI M2 FIELD
Gauge: 20 ga., 12 ga., 3" chamber. **Barrel:** 21", 24", 26", 28". **Weight:** 5.4 to 7.2 lbs. **Length:** 42.5 to 49.5" overall. **Stock:** Synthetic, Advantage Max-4 HD, Advantage Timber HD, APG HD. **Sights:** Red bar. **Features:** Uses the Inertia Driven bolt mechanism. Vent rib. Comes

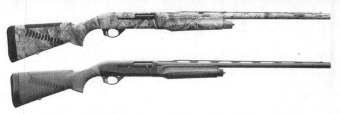

with set of five choke tubes. Imported from Italy by Benelli USA.
Price: Synthetic stock 12 ga. $1,499.00
Price: Camo stock 12 ga. $1,549.00
Price: Synthetic stock 20 ga. $1,499.00
Price: Camo stock 20 ga. $1,599.00
Price: Rifled slug ....$1,469.00 to $1,589.00
Price: Left-hand 12 ga. $1409.00
Price: Left-hand model 20 ga. $1519.00

BENELLI MONTEFELTRO
Gauge: 12 and 20 ga. Full, Imp. Mod, Mod., Imp. Cyl., Cyl. choke tubes. **Barrel:** 24", 26", 28". **Weight:** 5.3 to 7.1 lbs. **Stock:** Checkered walnut with satin finish. Length: 43.6 to 49.5" overall. **Features:** Uses the Inertia Driven rotating bolt system with a simple inertia recoil design. Finish is blue. Introduced 1987.
Price: Standard Model $1,139.00
Price: Left Hand Model $1,229.00
Price: Silver $1,779.00

BENELLI SUPER BLACK EAGLE II
Gauge: 12, 3 ½-inch chamber. **Barrel:** 24", 26", 28" (Cyl. Imp. Cyl., Mod., Imp. Mod., Full choke tubes). **Weight:** 7.1 to 7.3 lbs. Length: 45.6 to 49.6" overall. **Stock:** European walnut with satin finish, polymer, or camo. Adjustable for drop. **Sights:** Red bar front. **Features:** Uses Benelli inertia recoil bolt system. Vent rib. Advantage Max-4 HD, Advantage Timber HD camo patterns. Features ComforTech stock. Introduced 1991. Left-hand models available. Imported from Italy by Benelli USA.
Price: Satin walnut $1,569.00
Price: Camo stock ....$1,680.00 to $1,899.00
Price: Black Comfortech synthetic stock $1,799.00
Price: Left hand, camo stock $1,999.00
Price: Left hand, Comfortech synthetic $1,899.00
Price: Turkey edition w/pistol grip stock.....................$1,999.00

BENELLI SUPER BLACK EAGLE II WATERFOWL EDITION
Gauge: 12, (3+1 capacity), chambered for 2 ¾", 3" and 3 ¼" ammunition. **Barrel:** 28". **Weight:** 7.3 lbs. **Length:** 49.6". **Features:** Lengthened and polished forcing cone, Rob Roberts Custom choke tubes, Realtree Max-4 camo finish, Hi Viz front sight, metal middle bead. From the Benelli Performance Shop.
Price: $2,669.00

BENELLI CORDOBA
Gauge: 20; 12; 3" chamber. **Barrel:** 28" and 30", ported, 10mm sporting rib. **Weight:** 7.2 to 7.3 lbs. **Length:** 49.6 to 51.6". **Features:** Designed

for high-volume sporting clays and Argentina dove shooting. Inertia-driven action, Extended Sport CrioChokes, 4+1 capacity. Ported. Imported from Italy by Benelli USA.
Price: Field Models .... **$2,069.00 to $2,099.00**
Price: Performance Shop Model .... **$2,719.00 to $2,829.00**

BENELLI SUPERSPORT & SPORT II
Gauge: 20; 12; 3" chamber. **Barrel:** 28" and 30", ported, 10mm sporting rib. **Weight:** 7.2 to 7.3 lbs. **Length:** 49.6 to 51.6". **Stock:** Carbon fiber, ComforTech (Supersport) or walnut (Sport II). **Sights:** Red bar front, metal midbead. Sport II is similar to the Legacy model except has nonengraved dual tone blue/silver receiver, ported wide-rib barrel, adjustable buttstock, and functions with all loads. Walnut stock with satin finish. Introduced 1997. **Features:** Designed for high-volume sporting clays. Inertia-driven action, Extended CrioChokes, 4+1 capacity. Ported. Imported from Italy by Benelli USA.
Price: Supersport $2,199.00
Price: Sport II **$1,899.00**

BENELLI VINCI
Gauge: 12, 3-inch chamber. Gas-operated action. Features include modular disassembly; interchangeable choke tubes; 24- to 28-inch ribbed barrel; black, MAX-4HD or APG HD finish; synthetic contoured stocks; optional Steady-Grip model. Weight is 6.7 to 6.9 lbs. Tactical model available with 18.5-" barrel, Picatinny rail, pistol grip, ghost ring sight.
Price: .... **$1,449.00 to $2,199.00**

BENELLI SUPER VINCI
Gauge: 12 - 2-3/4", 3" and 3-1/2" chamber. **Barrel:** 26" and 28" barrels. **Weight:** 6.9-7 lbs. **Length:** 48.5"-50.5". **Stock:** Black synthetic, Realtree Max4 and Realtree APG. **Features:** 3+1 capacity, Crio Chokes: C,IC,M,IM,F. Length of Pull: 14-3/8". Drop at Heel: 2". Drop at Comb: 1-3/8". Type of **Sights:** Red bar front sight and metal bead mid-sight. Minimum recommended load: 3-dram, 1-1/8 oz. loads (12-ga.). Receiver drilled and tapped for scope mounting. Imported from Italy by Benelli USA., Corp.
Price: Black Synthetic Comfortech **$1,799.00**
Price: Camo **$1,899.00**

BERETTA A300 OUTLANDER
Gauge: 12, 3-inch chamber. **Capacity:** 3+1. Operates with 2 ¾" shells. **Barrel:** 28 inches with Mobilechoke system. **Stock:** Synthetic, camo or wood. **Weight:** 7.1 pounds. Based on A400 design but at a lower price.
Price: .... **$775.00 to $850.00**

BERETTA A400 XPLOR UNICO
Self-regulation gas-operated shotgun chambered to shoot all 12-ga. loads from 2-3/4 to 3.5 inches. Features include optional Kick-Off hydraulic damper; 26- or 28-inch "Steelium" barrel with interchangeable choke tubes; anodized aluminum receiver; sculpted, checkered walnut buttstock and fore-end.
Price: **$1,755.00**
Price: With Kick-Off recoil reduction system **$1,855.00**

BERETTA A400 XCEL SPORTING
Gauge: 12-gas operated, 3" chamber. **Barrel:** 28, 30 or 32". **Weight:** 7.5 lbs. **Stock:** Walnut and polymer. **Features:** In addition to A400 specifications and features, the Sporting model has aqua blue receiver. Optional Gun Pod electronic system gives digital read-out of air temperature, ammunition pressure, number of rounds fired.
Price: **$1,745.00**
Price: With Gun Pod **$1,895.00**
Price: With Kick-Off system.. **$1,845.00**

BERETTA A400 ACTION
Gauge: 12, 20 (3") or 28 (2 ¾" chamber). **Barrel:** 28, 30 barrel. **Weight:** 5.3 (28 ga.) to 6.7 lbs. **Stock:** Walnut and polymer combination. **Features:** Gas-operating Blink operating system can reportedly fire 4 rounds in less than one second. Kick-Off hydraulic recoil reduction system reduces felt recoil up to 70 percent.
Price: **$1,550.00**
Price: With Kick-Off system...................................**$1,655.00**

BROWNING A5
Gauge: 12, 3- or 3.5-inch chamber, 16 2¾" chamber (Sweet Sixteen). **Barrel:** 26, 28 or 30". **Weight:** 6.6 to 7 lbs. **Length:** 47.25 to 51.5". **Stock:** Gloss finish walnut with 22 lpi checkering, black synthetic or camo. Adjustable for cast and drop. **Features:** Operates on Kinematic short-recoil system, totally different than the classic Auto-5 long-recoil action manufactured from 1903-1999. Lengthened forcing cone, three choke tubes (IC, M, F), flat ventilated rib, brass bead front sight, ivory middle bead. Available in Mossy Oak Duck Blind or Break-up Infinity camo. Ultimate Model has satin finished aluminum alloy receiver with light engraving of pheasants on left side, mallards on the right. Glossy blue finish, Grade III oil-finished walnut stock,
Price: A5 Hunter **$1,630.00**
Price: A5 Hunter 3.5" **$1,700.00**
Price: A5 Stalker (synthetic) **$1,500.00**
Price: A5 Stalker 3.5" **$1,580.00**
Price: A5 Ultimate **$1,990.00**
Price: A5 Sweet Sixteen **$1,700.00**

BROWNING MAXUS HUNTER
Gauge: 12 ga., 3" & 3-1/2" chamber. **Barrel:** 26", 28" & 30" flat ventilated rib with fixed cylinder choke; stainless Steel; Matte finish. **Weight:** 7 lbs. 2 ozs. **Length:** 40.75". **Stock:** Gloss finish walnut stock with close radius pistol grip, sharp 22 lines-per-inch checkering, speed Lock Forearm, shim adjustable for length of pull, cast and drop. **Features:** Vector Prolengthened forcing cone, three Invector-Pluschoke tubes, Inflex Technology recoil pad, ivory front bead sight, One 1/4" stock spacer. Strong, lightweight aluminum alloy receiver with durable satin nickel finish & laser engraving (pheasant on the right, mallard on the left). All Purpose Hunter has Mossy Oak Break-Up Country Camo, Duratouch coated composite stock.
Price: 3" chamber..**$1,550.00**
Price: 3-1/2" chamber **$1,700.00**
Price: All Purpose Hunter **$1,740.00**

BROWNING MAXUS SPORTING
Gauge: 12 ga., 3" chamber. **Barrel:** 28" & 30" flat ventilated rib. **Weight:** 7 lbs. 2 ozs. **Length:** 49.25"-51.25". **Stock:** Gloss finish high grade walnut stock with close radius pistol grip , Speed Lock forearm, shim adjustable for length of pull, cast and drop. **Features:** This new model is sure to catch the eye, with its laser engraving of game birds transforming into clay birdson the lightweight alloy receiver. Quail are on the right side, and a mallard duck on the left. The Power Drive Gas System reduces recoil and cycles a wide array of loads. It's available in a 28" or 30" barrel length. The high grade walnut stock and forearm are generously checkered, finished with a deep, high gloss. The stock is adjustable and one 1/4" stock spacer is included. For picking up either clay or live birds quickly, the HiViz Tri-Comp fiber-optic front sight with mid-bead ivory sight does a great job, gathering light on the most overcast days. Vector Prolengthened forcing cone, five Invector-

Prices given are believed to be accurate at time of publication however, many factors affect retail pricing so exact prices are not possible.

Pluschoke tubes, Inflex Technology recoil pad ,HiViz Tri-Comp fiber-optic front sight, ivory mid-bead sight, one ¼" stock spacer.

Price: **$1,760.00**
Price: Golden Clays **$2,070.00**

BROWNING MAXUS SPORTING CARBON FIBER

Gauge: 12 ga., 3" chamber. **Barrel:** 28" & 30" flat ventilated rib. **Weight:** 6 lbs. 15 ozs. - 7 lbs. **Length:** 49.25"-51.25". **Stock:** Composite stock with close radius pistol grip, Speed Lock forearm, textured gripping surfaces, shim adjustable for length of pull, cast and drop, carbon fiber finish, Dura-Touch Armor Coating. **Features:** Strong, lightweight aluminum alloy, carbon fiber finish on top and bottom The stock is finished with Dura-Touch Armor Coating for a secure, non-slip grip when the gun is wet. It has the Browning exclusive Magazine Cut-Off, a patented Turn-Key Magazine Plug and Speed Load Plus. It will be an impossible task to locate an autoloading shotgun for the field with such shooter-friendly features as the Browning Maxus, especially with this deeply finished look of carbon fiber and the Dura-Touch Armor Coating feel. Vector Prolengthened forcing cone, five Invector-Pluschoke tubes, Inflex Technology recoil pad, HiViz Tri-Comp fiber-optic front sight, ivory mid-bead sight, one 1/4" stock spacer.

Price: **$1,550.00**

BROWNING MAXUS RIFLED DEER STALKER

Gauge: 12 ga., 3" chamber. **Barrel:** 22" thick-walled, fully rifled for slug ammunition only. **Weight:** 7 lbs. 3 ozs. **Length:** 43.25". **Stock:** Composite stock with close radius pistol grip, Speed Lock forearm, textured gripping surfaces, shim adjustable for length of pull, cast and drop, matte black finish Dura-Touch Armor Coating. **Features:** Stock is adjustable for length of pull, cast and drop. Cantilever scope mount, one 1/4" stock spacer. Available with Mossy Oak Break-up Country camo full coverage.

Price: **$1,520.00**
Price: Mossy Oak Break-Up Country camo **$1,640.00**

BROWNING GOLD LIGHT 10 GAUGE

Gauge: 10, 3-1/2". **Capacity:** 4 rounds. **Barrel:** 24 (NWTF), 26 or 28 inches. **Stock:** Composite with Dura-Cote Armor coating. Mossy Oak camo (Break-Up Country or Shadow Grass Blades). **Weight:** Approx. 9.5 pounds. Gas operated action, aluminum receiver, three standard Invector choke tubes. Receiver is drilled and tapped for scope mount. National Wild Turkey Foundation model has Hi-Viz 4-in-1 fiber optic sight, NWTF logo on buttstock.

Price: Mossy Oak Camo finishes **$1,740.00**
Price: NWTF Model **$1,870.00**

BROWNING SILVER

Gauge: 12, 3" or 3-1/2" chamber; 20, 3" chamber. **Barrel:** 12 ga.-26", 28", 30", Invector Plus choke tubes. **Weight:** 7 lbs., 9 oz. (12 ga.), 6 lbs., 7 oz. (20 ga.). **Stock:** Satin finish walnut. **Features:** Active Valve

gas system, semi-humpback receiver. Invector Plus choke system, three choke tubes. Imported by Browning.

Price: Silver Hunter, 12 ga., 3.5" chamber **$1,360.00**
Price: Silver Hunter, 20 ga., 3" chamber, intr. 2008 .... **$1,200.00**
Price: Silver Sporting, 12 ga., 2-3/4" chamber,
intr. 2009 .... **$1,320.00**
Price: Silver Sporting Micro, 12 ga., 2-3/4" chamber,
intr. 2008 .... **$1,320.00**
Price: Silver Rifled Deer, Mossy Oak New Break-Up,
12 ga., 3" chamber, intr. 2008 .... **$1,460.00**
Price: Silver Rifled Deer Stalker, 12 ga., 3" chamber,
intr. 2008 .... **$1,310.00**

CHARLES DALY MODEL 600

Gauge: 12 or 20 (3" chamber) or 28 (2 3/4") with magazine capacity of 5+1. **Barrel:** 26 or 28" (20 and 28 ga.), 26, 28 or 30 inches (12 ga.). Three choke tubes provided (Rem-Choke pattern). **Stock:** Synthetic, wood or camo. Comes in several variants including Field, Sporting Clays, Tactical and Trap. Left-hand models available. Uses gas-assisted recoil operation. Imported from Turkey.

Price: Field .... **$523.00 to $633.00**
Price: Superior w/walnut stock (shown) **$597.00**
Price: Sporting **$739.00**
Price: Tactical **$685.00**
Price: Trap **$769.00**

CHARLES DALY MODEL 635 MASTER MAG

Gauge: 12, 3.5-inch chamber. **Barrel:** 24, 26 or 28 inches. Ported. **Stock:** Synthetic with full camo coverage. Other features similar to Model 600 series.

Price: From **$595.00**

CZ MODEL 712/720

Gauge: 12, 20 (4+1 capacity). **Barrel:** 26". **Weight:** 6.3 lbs. **Stock:** Turkish walnut with 14.5" length of pull. **Features:** Chrome-lined barrel with 3-inch chamber, ventilated rib, five choke tubes. Matte black finish.

Price: 712 12 ga. .... **$499.00 to $699.00**
Price: 720 20 ga. .... **$516.00 to $599.00**

ESCORT WATERFOWL EXTREME SEMIAUTO

Gauge: 12 or 20 ga., 2-3/4" through 3-1/2" chamber, multi 5+1 capacity. **Barrel:** 28". **Weight:** 7.4 lbs. **Length:** 48". **Stock:** Composite stock with close radius pistol grip; Speed Lock forearm; textured gripping surfaces; shim adjustable for length of pull and cast and drop; Realtree Max4 or AP camo finish; Dura-Touch Armor Coating. **Sights:** HiVis MagniSightfiber optic, magnetic sight to enhance sight acquisition in low light conditions. **Features:** The addition of non-slip grip pads on the fore-end and pistol grip provide a superior hold in all weather conditions. Smart-Valve gas pistons regulate gas blowback to cycle every round – from 2.75 inch range loads through 3.5 inch heavy magnums. Escorts also have Fast-loading systems that allow one-handed round changes without changing aiming position. Left-hand models available at no increase in price.

Price: Black/Synthetic **$551.00**
Price: Realtree Camo **$736.00**
Price: 3.5" Black/Synthetic **$649.00**
Price: 3.5" Realtree Camo **$815.00**

ESCORT SEMI-AUTO

Gauge: 12, 20; 3" or 3.5" chambers. **Barrel:** 22" (Youth), 26" and 28". **Weight:** 6.7-7.8 lbs. **Stock:** Polymer in black, Shadow Grass or Obsession camo finish, Turkish walnut, select walnut. **Sights:** Optional HiViz Spark front. **Features:** Black-chrome or dipped-camo metal parts, top of receiver dovetailed for sight mounts, gold plated trigger, trigger guard safety, magazine cut-off. Three choke tubes (IC, M, F) except the Waterfowl/Turkey Combo, which adds a .665 turkey choke to the standard three. Waterfowl/Turkey combo is two-barrel

SHOTGUNS Autoloaders

set, 24"/26" and 26"/28". Several models have Trio recoil pad. Models are: AS, AS Select, AS Youth, AS Youth Select, PS, PS Spark and Waterfowl/Turkey. Introduced 2002. Camo introduced 2003. Youth, Slug and Obsession camo introduced 2005. Imported from Turkey by Legacy Sports International.
Price: .... **$425.00 to $589.00**

FABARM XLR5 VELOCITY AR
Gauge: 12. **Barrel:** 30 or 32". **Weight:** 8.25 lbs. Gas-operated model designed for competition shooting. Features include a unique adjustable rib that allows a more upright shooting position. There is also an adjustable trigger shoe, magazine cap adjustable weight system. Five interchangeable choke tubes. Imported from Italy by Fabarm USA.
Price: From .... **$2,755.00 to $3,300.00**
Price: FR Sporting .... **$1,990.00 to $2,165.00**
Price: LR (Long Rib) .... **$2,260.00 to $2,800.00**

FRANCHI AFFINITY
Gauge: 12, 20. Three-inch chamber also handles 2 ¾ inch shells. **Barrel:** 26, 28 inches or 30 inches (12 ga.), 26 inches (20 ga.). 30-inch barrel available only on 12-gauge Sporting model. **Weight:** 5.6 to 6.8 pounds. **Stock:** Black synthetic or Realtree Camo. Left-hand versions available.
Price: Synthetic **$849.00**
Price: Synthetic left-hand action **$899.00**
Price: Camo **$949.00**
Price: Sporting **$1,149.00**

FRANCHI INTENSITY
Gauge: 12, 3.5" chamber. **Barrel:** 26", 28", 30" (IC, Mod., Full choke tubes). **Weight:** 6.8 lbs. **Stock:** Black synthetic or camo.
Price: Synthetic **$1,099.00**
Price: Camo **$1,199.00**

FRANCHI FENICE
Gauge: 20 or 28. **Barrel:** 26", 28". **Weight:** 5.5 to 5.7. lbs. **Stock:** Oil finished, checkered AA walnut. **Features:** Light scroll engraving on silver finish receiver. Limited availability.
Price: Camo **$1,399.00**

FRANCHI 48AL FIELD AND DELUXE
Gauge: 20 or 28, 2-3/4" chamber. **Barrel:** 24", 26", 28" (Full, Cyl., Mod., choke tubes). **Weight:** 5.4 to 5.7 lbs. **Length:** 42.25" to 48". **Stock:** Walnut with checkered grip and fore-end. **Features:** Long recoil-operated action. Chrome-lined bore; cross-bolt safety. Imported from Italy by Benelli USA.
Price: Al Field 20 ga. **$999.00**
Price: Al Field 28 ga. **$1,049.00**
Price: Al Field Deluxe 20 ga. **$1,199.00**
Price: Al Field Deluxe 28 ga. **$1,349.00**

MOSSBERG 930
Gauge: 12, 3" chamber, 4-shot magazine. **Barrel:** 24", 26", 28", over-bored to 10-gauge bore dimensions; factory ported, Accu-Choke tubes. **Weight:** 7.5 lbs. **Length:** 44.5" overall (28" barrel). **Stock:**

Walnut or synthetic. Adjustable stock drop and cast spacer system. **Sights:** Turkey Taker fiber-optic, adjustable windage and elevation. Front bead fiber-optic front on waterfowl models. **Features:** Self-regulating gas system, dual gas-vent system and piston, EZ-Empty magazine button, cocking indicator. Interchangeable Accu-Choke tube set (IC, Mod, Full) for waterfowl and field models. XX-Full turkey Accu-Choke tube included with turkey models. Ambidextrous thumb-operated safety, Uni-line stock and receiver. Receiver drilled and tapped for scope base attachment, free gun lock. Introduced 2008. From O.F. Mossberg & Sons, Inc.
Price: Turkey, from **$782.00**
Price: Waterfowl, from **$782.00**
Price: Combo, from **$744.00**
Price: Field, from **$685.00**
Price: Slugster, from **$645.00**
Price: Turkey Pistolgrip; Mossy Oak Infinity camo ... **$896.00**
Price: Tactical; 18.5" tactical barrel, black synthetic stock and matte black finish **$739.00**
Price: SPX; no muzzlebrake, M16-style front sight, ghost ring rear sight, full pistol grip stock, eight-round extended magazine **$1,012.00**
Price: Home Security/Field Combo; 18.5" Cylinder bore barrel and 28" ported Field barrel; black synthetic stock and matte black finish **$735.00**
Price: Duck Commander Series **$928.00**
Price: High Performance (13-round magazine) **$974.00**

MOSSBERG MODEL 935 MAGNUM
Gauge: 12; 3" and 3.5» chamber, interchangeable. **Barrel:** 22", 24», 26», 28». **Weight:** 7.25 to 7.75 lbs. **Length:** 45" to 49" overall. **Stock:** Synthetic. **Features:** Gas-operated semiauto models in blued or camo finish. Fiber optics sights, drilled and tapped receiver, interchangeable Accu-Mag choke tubes.
Price: 935 Magnum Turkey: Realtree Hardwoods, Mossy Oak New Break-up or Mossy Oak Obsession camo overall, 24" barrel **$866.00**
Price: 935 Magnum Turkey Pistol grip; full pistol grip stock **$1,000.00**
Price: 935 Magnum Grand Slam: 22" barrel **$900.00**
Price: 935 Magnum Flyway: 28" barrel and Advantage Max-4 camo overall **$924.00**
Price: 935 Magnum Waterfowl: 26"or 28" barrel **$725.00**
Price: 935 Magnum Turkey/Deer Combo: interchangeable 24" Turkey barrel, Mossy Oak New Break-up camo overall **$974.00**
Price: 935 Magnum Waterfowl/Turkey Combo: 24" Turkey and 28" Waterfowl barrels, Mossy Oak New Break-up finish overall **$974.00**

MOSSBERG SA-20
Gauge: 20. 20" (Tactical), 26" or 28". **Weight:** 5.5 to 6 lbs. **Stock:** Black synthetic. Gas operated action, matte blue finish. Tactical model has ghost-ring sight, accessory rail.

Price: From .... **$580.00 to $633.00**

REMINGTON MODEL 11-87 SPORTSMAN
Gauge: 12, 20, 3" chamber. **Barrel:** 26", 28", RemChoke tubes. Standard contour, vent rib. **Weight:** About 7.75 to 8.25 lbs. **Length:** 46" to 48" overall. **Stock:** Black synthetic or Mossy Oak Break Up Mossy Oak Duck Blind, and Realtree Hardwoods HD and AP Green HD camo finishes. **Sights:** Single bead front. **Features:** Matte-black metal finish, magazine cap swivel studs. Sportsman Deer gun has 21-inch fully rifled barrel, cantilever scope mount.
Price: .... **$734.00 to $1,010.00**

REMINGTON MODEL 1100 CLASSIC
Gauge: 12, 20 or 28. Part of the Remington American Classics

Collection honoring Remington's most enduring firearms. **Barrel:** 28" (12 ga.), 26" (20), 25" (28). Features include American walnut B-grade stock with classic white line spacer and grip caps, ventilated recoil pad the white line spacer and white diamond grip cap. Machine-cut engraved receiver has tasteful scroll pattern with gold inlayed retriever and "American Classic" label.

Price: $1,686.00

REMINGTON MODEL 1100 200TH YEAR ANNIVERSARY

Gauge: 12. **Barrel:** 28". Features include C-grade American walnut stock with fleur-de-lis checkering. Receiver has classic engraving pattern, gold inlay. Limited edition of 2,016 guns to honor the Remington company's 200th anniversary — the oldest firearms manufacturer in the USA.

Price: $1,999.00

REMINGTON MODEL 1100 COMPETITION MODELS

Gauge: .410 bore, 28, 20, 12. **Barrel:** 26", 27", 28", 30" light target contoured vent rib barrel with twin bead target sights. **Stock:** Semi-fancy American walnut stock and fore-end, cut checkering, high gloss finish. **Features:** Classic Trap has 30-inch barrel and weighs approximately 8.25 pounds. Sporting Series is available in all four gauges with 28-inch barrel in 12 and 20 gauge, 27 inch in 28 and .410. **Weight:** 6.25 to 8 pounds. Competion Synthetic model has synthetic stock with adjustable comb, case and length. Five Briley Target choke tubes. High-gloss blued barrel, Nickel-Teflon finish on receiver and internal parts. **Weight:** 8.1 pounds.

Price: Classic Trap $1,334.00
Price: Sporting Series, from $1,252.00
Price: Competition Synthetic: $1,305.00

REMINGTON VERSA MAX SERIES

Gauge: 12 ga., 2 3/4", 3", 3 1/2" chamber. **Barrel:** 26" and 28" flat ventilated rib. **Weight:** 7.5 lbs.-7.7 lbs. **Length:** 40.25". **Stock:** Synthetic. **Features:** Reliably cycles 12-gauge rounds from 2 3/4" to 3 1/2" magnum. Versaport gas system regulates cycling pressure based on shell length. Reduces recoil to that of a 20-gauge. Self-cleaning - Continuously cycled thousands of rounds in torture test. Synthetic stock and fore-end with grey overmolded grips. Drilled and tapped receiver. Enlarged trigger guard opening and larger safety for easier use with gloves. TriNyte Barrel and Nickel Teflon plated internal components offer extreme corrosion resistance. Includes 5 Flush Mount Pro Bore Chokes (Full, Mod, Imp Mod Light Mod, IC)

Price: Sportsman, from $1,066.00
Price: Synthetic, from $1,427.00
Price: Tactical, from $1,456.00
Price: Waterfowl, from $1,765.00
Price: Camo, from $1,664.00

REMINGTON MODEL V3

Gauge: 12, 3-inch chamber. Magazine capacity 3+1. **Barrel:** 26 or 28 inches. The newest addition to the Remington shotgun family operates on an improved VersaPort gas system, claimed to offer the least recoil of any 12-gauge autoloader. Operating system is located in front of the receiver instead of the fore-end, resulting in better weight distribution than other autoloaders, and improved handling qualities. **Stock:** Walnut, black synthetic, or camo. Designed to function with any 2¾ or 3-inch ammo. Made in the U.S.A. by Remington.

Price: Synthetic black..$895.00
Price: Walnut or camo $995.00

SKB MODEL IS300

Gauge: 12, 2-3/4 and 3-inch loads. Magazine capacity: 4+1. Inertia-driven operating system. **Barrel:** 26, 28 or 30 inches with 3 choke tubes IC, M, F. **Stock:** Black synthetic, oil-finished walnut or camo. **Weight:** 6.7 to 7.3 pounds. **Features:** Target models have adjustable stock dimensions including cast and drop. Made in Turkey and imported by GU, Inc.

Price: Synthetic $625.00
Price: Walnut or Camo Field $715.00
Price: Walnut Target..$870.00
Price: RS300 Target with adjustable stock $1,000.00

STEVENS S1200

Gauge: 12, 3-inch chamber. Five-round capacity. **Barrel:** 26" with ventilated rib, 5 choke tubes. **Weight:** 6.8 lbs. **Stock:** Black synthetic or walnut. **Features:** Inertia operating system, bottom loading. Introduced in 2016.

Price: Synthetic stock..$571.00
Price: Walnut $685.00

STOEGER MODEL 3000

Gauge: 12, 2-3/4 and 3-inch loads. Minimum recommended load 3-dram, 1-1/8 ounces. **Magazine capacity:** 4+1. Inertia-driven operating system. **Barrel:** 26 or 28 inches with 3 choke tubes IC, M, XF. **Weight:** 7.4 to 7.5 pounds. **Finish:** Black synthetic or camo (Realtree APG or Max-4). M3K model is designed for three-gun competition and has synthetic stock, 24-inch barrel, modified loading port.

Price: Synthetic $599.00
Price: Walnut or Camo $649.00
Price: M3K $699.00
Price: 3000R rifled slug model................................$649.00

STOEGER MODEL 3020

Gauge: 20, 2¾ or 3-inch loads. This model has the same general specifications as the Model 3000 except for its chambering and weight of 5.5 to 5.8 pounds.

Price: Synthetic...$599.00
Price: Camo $649.00

STOEGER MODEL 3500

Gauge: 12. 2 3/4, 3 and 3 1/2-inch loads. Minimum recommended load 3-dram, 1-1/8 ounces. **Barrel:** 24, 26 or 28 inches. Other features similar to Model 3000. Choke tubes for IC, M, XF. **Weight:** 7.4 to 7.5 pounds. **Finish:** Black synthetic or camo (Realtree APG or Max-4).

Price: Synthetic $679.00
Price: Camo $799.00

TRISTAR VIPER G2

Gauge: 12, 20; shoots 2-3/4" or 3" interchangeably. **Barrel:** 26", 28" barrels (carbon fiber only offered in 12-ga. 28" and 20-ga. 26"). **Stock:** Wood, black synthetic, Mossy Oak Duck Blind camouflage, faux carbon fiber finish (2008) with the new Comfort Touch technology. **Features:** Magazine cut-off, vent rib with matted sight plane, brass front bead (camo models have fiber-optic front sight), five round magazine-shot plug included, and 3 Beretta-style choke tubes (IC, M, F). Viper synthetic, Viper camo have swivel studs. Five-year warranty. Viper Youth models have shortened length of pull and 24" barrel. Imported by Tristar Sporting Arms Ltd.

Price: From $519.00
Price: Camo models from...$609.00
Price: Silver model................................... $639.00 to $689.00

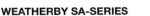

WEATHERBY SA-SERIES

Gauge: 12 ga. & 20 ga., 3" chamber. **Barrel:** 26" and 28" flat ventilated rib. **Weight:** 6.5 lbs. **Stock:** Wood and synthetic. **Features:** The SA-08 is a reliable workhorse that lets you move from early season dove loads to late fall's heaviest waterfowl loads

Prices given are believed to be accurate at time of publication however, many factors affect retail pricing so exact prices are not possible.

71ST EDITION, 2017 ⊕ **485**

in no time. Available with wood and synthetic stock options in 12 and 20 gauge models, including a scaled-down youth model to fit 28 ga. Comes with 3 application-specific choke tubes (SK/IC/M). Made in Turkey.

Price: SA-08 Upland **$799.00**
Price: SA-08 Synthetic **$649.00**
Price: SA-08 Waterfowler 3.0 ....**$799.00**
Price: SA-08 Synthetic Youth **$649.00**
Price: SA-08 Deluxe..**$849.00**
Price: Element Deluxe w/inertia operated action, AA walnut **$1,099.00**

WEATHERBY SA-459

Gauge: 12 or 20, 3-inch chamber. Five or 8-shot capacity. **Barrel:** 18 ½ (Tactical) or 21 ¼ inches (Turkey). Tactical model has Pica tinny rail, pistol grip synthetic stock, ghost ring rear and M16 type front sight. Turkey model has fiber optic front sight, RealtreeXtra Green camo finish full coverage.

Price: Tactical model...**$699.00**
Price: Turkey model **$799.00**

WINCHESTER SUPER X3

Gauge: 12, 3" and 3.5" chambers. **Barrel:** 26", 28", .742" back-bored; Invector Plus choke tubes. **Weight:** 7 to 7.25 lbs. **Stock:** Composite, 14.25"x1.75"x2". Mossy Oak New Break-Up camo with Dura-Touch Armor Coating. Pachmayr Decelerator buttpad with hard heel insert, customizable length of pull. **Features:** Alloy magazine tube, gunmetal grey Perma-Cote UT finish, self-adjusting Active Valve gas action, lightweight recoil spring system. Electroless nickel-plated bolt, three choke tubes, two length-of-pull stock spacers, drop and cast adjustment spacers, sling swivel studs. Introduced 2006. Made in Belgium, assembled in Portugal by U.S. Repeating Arms Co.

Price: Field **$1,070.00**
Price: Black Shadow ....**$1,000.00 to $1,070.00 (3.5")**
Price: Universal Hunter ....**$1,160.00 to $1,230.00 (3.5")**
Price: Waterfowl Hunter **$1,200.00**
Price: Sporting, Adj. comb **$1,700.00**
Price: Cantilever Buck **$1,150.00**
Price: Coyote, pistol grip composite stock **$1,200.00**
Price: Long Beard, pistol grip camo stock **$1,270.00**

BENELLI SUPERNOVA

Gauge: 12; 3.5" chamber. **Barrel:** 24", 26", 28". Length: 45.5-49.5". **Stock:** Synthetic; Max-4 , Timber, APG HD (2007). **Sights:** Red bar front, metal midbead. **Features:** 2-3/4", 3" chamber (3-1/2" 12 ga. only). Montefeltro rotating bolt design with dual action bars, magazine cut-off, synthetic trigger assembly, adjustable combs, shim kit, choice of buttstocks. 4-shot magazine. Introduced 2006. Imported from Italy by Benelli USA.
Price: $549.00
Price: Camo stock $669.00
Price: Rifle slug model .... **$829.00 to $929.00**

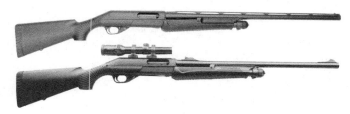

BENELLI NOVA

Gauge: 12, 20. **Barrel:** 24", 26", 28". **Stock:** Black synthetic, Max-4, Timber and APG HD. **Sights:** Red bar. **Features:** 2-3/ 4", 3" chamber (3-1/2" 12 ga. only). Montefeltro rotating bolt design with dual action bars, magazine cut-off, synthetic trigger assembly, 4-shot magazine. Introduced 1999. Field & Slug Combo has 24" barrel and rifled bore; open rifle sights; synthetic stock; weighs 8.1 lbs. Imported from Italy by Benelli USA.
Price: Max-5 camo stock......................................$559.00
Price: H20 model, black synthetic, matte nickel finish............$669.00
Price: Tactical, 18.5" barrel, Ghost Ring sight $459.00
Price: Black synthetic youth stock, 20 ga. $469.00

BROWNING BPS

Gauge: 10, 12, 3-1/2" chamber; 12, 16, or 20, 3" chamber (2-3/4" in target guns), 28, 2-3/4" chamber, 5-shot magazine, .410, 3" chamber. **Barrel:** 10 ga.-24" Buck Special, 28", 30", 32" Invector; 12, 20 ga.-22", 24", 26", 28", 30", 32" (Imp. Cyl., Mod. or Full), .410-26" barrel. (Imp. Cyl., Mod. and Full choke tubes.) Also available with Invector choke tubes, 12 or 20 ga.; Upland Special has 22" barrel with Invector tubes. BPS 3" and 3-1/2" have back-bored barrel. **Weight:** 7 lbs., 8 oz. (28" barrel). Length: 48.75" overall (28" barrel). **Stock:** 14.25"x1.5"x2.5". Select walnut, semi-beavertail fore-end, full pistol grip stock. **Features:** All 12 gauge 3" guns except Buck Special and game guns have back-bored barrels with Invector Plus choke tubes. Bottom feeding and ejection, receiver top safety, high post vent rib. Double action bars eliminate binding. Vent rib barrels only. All 12 and 20 gauge guns with 3" chamber available with fully engraved receiver flats at no extra cost. Each gauge has its own unique game scene. Introduced 1977. Stalker is same gun as the standard BPS except all exposed metal parts have a matte blued finish and the stock has a black finish with a black recoil pad. Available in 10 ga. (3-1/2") and 12 ga. with 3" or 3-1/2" chamber, 22", 28", 30" barrel with Invector choke system. Introduced 1987. Rifled Deer Hunter is similar to the standard BPS except has newly designed receiver/magazine tube/barrel mounting system to eliminate play, heavy 20.5" barrel with rifle-type sights with adjustable rear, solid receiver scope mount, "rifle" stock dimensions for scope or open sights, sling swivel studs. Gloss or matte finished wood with checkering, polished blue metal. Medallion model has additional engraving on receiver, polished blue finish,

AA/AAA grade walnut stock with checkering. All Purpose model has Realtree AP camo on stock and fore-end, HiVis fiber optic sights. Introduced 2013. Imported from Japan by Browning.
Price: Field, Stalker models $700.00
Price: Camo coverage $820.00
Price: Deer Hunter $830.00
Price: Deer Hunter Camo..$870.00
Price: Magnum Hunter (3.5") .... **$800.00 to $1,030.00**
Price: Medallion $830.00
Price: Trap $840.00

BROWNING BPS 10 GAUGE SERIES

Similar to the standard BPS except completely covered with Mossy Oak Shadow Grass camouflage. Available with 26" and 28" barrel. Introduced 1999. Imported by Browning
Price: Mossy Oak camo..$950.00
Price: Synthetic stock, Stalker...$800.00

BROWNING BPS NWTF TURKEY SERIES

Similar to the standard BPS except has full coverage Mossy Oak Break-Up Infinity camo finish on synthetic stock, fore-end and exposed metal parts. Offered in 12 gauge, 3" or 3-1/2" chamber, or 10 gauge; 24" bbl. has extra-full choke tube and HiViz fiber-optic sights. Introduced 2001. From Browning.
Price: 12 ga., 3" $950.00
Price: 3.5" $1,030.00

BROWNING BPS MICRO MIDAS

Gauge: 12, 20, 28 ga. or .410 bore, 24 or 26". Three Invector choke tubes for 12 and 20 gauge, standard tubes for 28 and .410. **Stock:** Walnut with pistol grip and recoil pad. Satin finished and scaled down to fit smaller statured shooters. Length of pull is 13.25". Two spacers included for stock length adjustments. **Weight:** 7 to 7.8 lbs.
Price: .... **$700.00 to $740.00**

BROWING BPS HIGH CAPACITY

Gauge: .410 bore. 3" chamber. 5-round magazine. **Barrel:** 20" fixed Cylinder choke; stainless Steel; Matte finish. **Weight:** 6 lbs. Length: 40.75". **Stock:** Black composite on All Weather with matte finish. **Features:** Forged and machined steel; satin nickel finish. Bottom ejection; dual steel action bars; top tang safety. HiViz Tactical fiber-optic front sight; stainless internal mechanism; swivel studs installed.
Price: Synthetic...$800.00

CHARLES DALY 300 SERIES

Gauge: 12, 20 or 28 gauge. Chambered for 3" and 2¾" shells (12 and 20), 2¾" (28 ga.). Model 335 Master Mag is chambered for 12-ga. 3½-inch shells. **Barrel:** 24, 26, 28 and 30 inches, depending upon specific model. Ventilated rib. Three choke tubes (REM-Choke pattern) are provided. **Stock:** Synthetic, walnut or camo. **Weight:** 7 to 8 lbs. Left-hand models available. Imported from Turkey.
Price: Field .... $365.00 to $495.00
Price: Tactical.. $423.00 to $503.00
Price: Turkey $553.00

CZ 612

Gauge: 12. Chambered for all shells up to 3 ½ inches. **Capacity:** 5+1, magazine plug included with Wildfowl Magnum. **Barrel length:** 18.5 inches (Home Defense), 20 (HC-P), 26 inches (Wildfowl Mag). **Weight:** 6 to 6.8 pounds. **Stock:** Polymer. **Finish:** Matte black or full camo (Wildfowl Mag.) HC-P model has pistol grip stock, fiber optic front sight and ghost-ring rear. Home Defense Combo comes with extra 26-inch barrel.
Price: Wildfowl Magnum $428.00
Price: Home Defense .... $304.00 to $409.00

ESCORT PUMP SERIES

Gauge: 12, 20; 3" chamber. **Barrel:** 18" (AimGuard, Home Defense and MarineGuard), 22" (Youth Pump), 26", and 28" lengths. **Weight:** 6.7-7.0 lbs. **Stock:** Polymer in black, Shadow Grass camo or Obsession camo finish. Two adjusting spacers included. Youth model

Prices given are believed to be accurate at time of publication however, many factors affect retail pricing so exact prices are not possible.

71ST EDITION, 2017 ⊕ 487

SHOTGUNS Pumps

has Trio recoil pad. **Sights:** Bead or Spark front sights, depending on model. AimGuard and MarineGuard models have blade front sights. **Features:** Black-chrome or dipped camo metal parts, top of receiver dovetailed for sight mounts, gold plated trigger, trigger guard safety, magazine cut-off. Three choke tubes (IC, M, F) except AimGuard/ MarineGuard which are cylinder bore. Models include: FH, FH Youth, AimGuard and Marine Guard. Introduced in 2003. Imported from Turkey by Legacy Sports International.

Price: $379.00
Price: Youth model..$393.00
Price: Model 87 w/wood stock.................................$350.00

HARRINGTON & RICHARDSON (H&R) PARDNER PUMP
Gauge: 12, 20.3-inch chamber. **Barrel:** 21 to 28 inches. **Weight:** 6.5 to 7.5 lbs. **Stock:** Synthetic or hardwood. Ventilated recoil pad and grooved fore-end. **Features:** Steel receiver, double action bars, cross-bolt safety, easy takedown, ventilated rib, screw-in choke tubes.
Price: From ....$231.00 to $259.00

IAC MODEL 97T TRENCH GUN
Gauge: 12, 2 ¾" chamber. Replica of Winchester Model 1897 Trench Gun. **Barrel:** 20" with cylinder choke. **Stock:** Hand rubbed American walnut. **Features:** Metal hand guard, bayonet lug. Imported from China by Interstate Arms Corp.
Price: $465.00

IAC HAWK SERIES
Gauge: 12, 2 ¾" chamber. This series of tactical/home defense shotguns is based on the Remington 870 design. **Barrel:** 18 ½ inches with cylinder choke. **Stock:** Sythetic. **Features:** 981 model has top Picatinny rail and bead front sight. 982 has adjustable ghost ring sight with post front. 982T has same sights as 982 plus a pistol grip stock. Imported from China by Interstate Arms Corporation.
Price: 981..$275.00
Price: 982..$285.00
Price: 982T..$300.00

ITHACA MODEL 37 FEATHERWEIGHT
Gauge: 12, 20, 16, 28 (4+1 capacity). **Barrel:** 26, 28 or 30" with 3" chambers (12 and 20 ga.), plain or ventiltated rib. **Weight:** 6.1 to 7.6 lbs. **Stock:** Fancy grade black walnut with Pachmayr Decelerator recoil pad. Checkered fore-end made of matching walnut. **Features:** Receiver machined from a single block of steel or aluminum. Barrel is steel shot compatible. Three Briley choke tubes provided. Available in several variations including turkey, home defense, tactical and high-grade.
Price: 12, 16 or 20 ga. from $895.00
Price: 28 ga. from $1,149.00
Price: Turkey Slayer w/synthetic stock from................$925.00
Price: Trap Series 12 ga..$999.00
Price: Waterfowl...$885.00
Price: Home Defense 18 or 20" bbl $784.00

ITHACA DEERSLAYER III SLUG
Gauge: 12, 20; 3" chamber. **Barrel:** 26" fully rifled, heavy fluted with 1:28 twist for 12 ga.; 1:24 for 20 ga. **Weight:** 8.14 lbs. to 9.5 lbs.

with scope mounted. Length: 45.625" overall. **Stock:** Fancy black walnut stock and fore-end. **Sights:** NA. **Features:** Updated, slug-only version of the classic Model 37. Bottom ejection, blued barrel and receiver.
Price: $1,350.00

MAVERICK ARMS MODEL 88
Gauge: 12, 20. 3" chamber. **Barrel:** 26" or 28", Accu-Mag choke tubes for steel or lead shot. **Weight:** 7.25 lbs. **Stock:** Black synthetic with recoil pad. **Features:** Crossbolt safety, aluminum alloy receiver. Economy model of Mossberg Model 500 series. Available in several variations including Youth, Slug and Special Purpose (home defense) models.
Price: $298.00

MOSSBERG MODEL 835 ULTI-MAG
Gauge: 12, 3-1/2" chamber. **Barrel:** Ported 24" rifled bore, 24", 28", Accu-Mag choke tubes for steel or lead shot. Combo models come with interchangeable second barrel. **Weight:** 7.75 lbs. **Length:** 48.5" overall. **Stock:** 14"x1.5"x2.5". Dual Comb. Cut-checkered hardwood or camo synthetic; both have recoil pad. **Sights:** White bead front, brass mid-bead; fiber-optic rear. Turkey Thug has red dot sight. **Features:** Shoots 2-3/4", 3" or 3-1/2" shells. Back-bored and ported barrel to reduce recoil, improve patterns. Ambidextrous thumb safety, twin extractors, dual slide bars. Mossberg Cablelock included. Introduced 1988.
Price: Turkey ....$601.00 to $617.00
Price: Turkey Thug $708.00
Price: Waterfowl ....$503.00 to $585.00
Price: Slugster $638.00
Price: Turkey/Deer combo $641.00
Price: Turkey/Waterfowl combo....................................$641.00

MOSSBERG MODEL 500 SPORTING SERIES
Gauge: 12, 20, .410, 3" chamber. **Barrel:** 18.5" to 28" with fixed or Accu-Choke, plain or vent rib. Combo models come with interchangeable second barrel. **Weight:** 6-1/4 lbs. (.410), 7-1/4 lbs. (12). **Length:** 48" overall (28" barrel). **Stock:** 14"x1.5"x2.5". Walnut-stained hardwood, black synthetic, Mossy Oak Advantage camouflage. Cut-checkered grip and fore-end. **Sights:** White bead front, brass mid-bead; fiber-optic. **Features:** Ambidextrous thumb safety, twin extractors, disconnecting safety, dual action bars. Quiet Carry fore-end. Many barrels are ported. FLEX series has many modular options and accessories including barrels and stocks. From Mossberg. Left-hand versions (L-series) available in most models.
Price: Turkey, from $466.00
Price: Waterfowl, from $537.00
Price: Combo, from $593.00
Price: FLEX Hunting..$702.00
Price: FLEX All Purpose...$561.00
Price: Field, from $406.00
Price: Slugster, from $447.00
Price: FLEX Deer/Security combo $763.00

MOSSBERG MODEL 500 SUPER BANTAM PUMP
Same as the Model 500 Sporting Pump except 12 or 20 gauge, 22" vent rib Accu-Choke barrel with choke tube set; has 1" shorter stock, reduced length from pistol grip to trigger, reduced fore-end reach. Introduced 1992.
Price: $414.00
Price: Combo with extra slug barrel, camo finish....................$534.00

MOSSBERG 510 MINI BANTAM
Gauge: 20 & .410 ga., 3" chamber. **Barrel:** 18 1/2 " vent-rib. **Weight:** 5 lbs. Length: 34 3/4". **Stock:** Synthetic with optional Mossy Oak Break-Up Infinity, Muddy Girl pink/black camo. **Features:** Available in either 20 gauge or .410 bore, the Mini features an 18 1/2 " vent-rib barrel with dual-bead sights. Parents don't have to worry about their young shooter growing out of this gun too quick, the adjustable classic stock can be adjusted from 10 1/2" to 11 1/2" length of pull so the Mini can grow with your youngster. This adjustability also helps provide a proper fit for young shooters and allowing for a more safe and enjoyable shooting experience.
Price: From $466.00

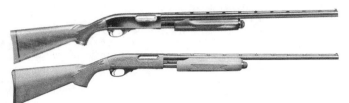

REMINGTON MODEL 870 WINGMASTER
Gauge: 12, 20, 28 ga., .410 bore. **Barrel:** 25", 26", 28", 30" (RemChokes). **Weight:** 7-1/4 lbs. Length: 46", 48". **Stock:** Walnut, hardwood. **Sights:** Single bead (Twin bead Wingmaster). **Features:** Light contour barrel. Double action bars, cross-bolt safety, blue finish. LW is 28 gauge and .410-bore only, 25" vent rib barrel with RemChoke tubes, high-gloss wood finish. Gold-plated trigger, American B Grade walnut stock and fore-end, high-gloss finish, fleur-de-lis checkering. A classic American shotgun first introduced in 1950.
Price: .... $830.00 to $929.00

REMINGTON MODEL 870 AMERICAN CLASSIC
Gauge: 12, 20 or 28 gauge. **Barrel:** 25" (28 ga.), 26" (20 ga.), 28" (12 ga.) with ventilated rib and Rem Choke system. **Weight:** 6 to 7 lbs. Commemorating one of the most popular firearms in history, this model features a B-grade American walnut stock, a high polish blue finish, and machine-cut engraved receiver with gold filled banner reading "American Classic." Other features in keeping with those that were popular in the 1950s include ventilated recoil pad with white line spacer and a diamond grip cap.
Price: $1,249.00

REMINGTON MODEL 870 200TH ANNIVERSARY LIMITED EDITION
Gauge: 12. **Barrel:** 26 inches with ventilated rib and Rem Choke system. C-grade American walnut stock with fleur-de-lis checkering, medallion in grip cap. Receiver features engraving and gold inlay. Limited to 2,016 guns to commemorate the 200th anniversary of America's oldest firearms manufacturing company.
Price: $1,499.00

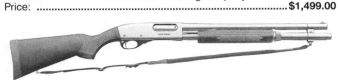

REMINGTON MODEL 870 MARINE MAGNUM
Similar to 870 Wingmaster except all metal plated with electroless nickel, black synthetic stock and fore-end. Has 18" plain barrel (cyl.), bead front sight, 7-shot magazine. Introduced 1992. XCS version with TriNyte corrosion control introduced 2007.
Price: $841.00

REMINGTON MODEL 870 CLASSIC TRAP
Similar to Model 870 Wingmaster except has 30" vent rib, light contour barrel, singles, mid- and long-handicap choke tubes, semi-fancy American walnut stock, high-polish blued receiver with engraving. Chamber 2.75". From Remington Arms Co.
Price: $1,098.00

REMINGTON MODEL 870 EXPRESS
Similar to Model 870 Wingmaster except laminate, synthetic black, or camo stock with solid, black recoil pad and pressed checkering on grip and fore-end. Outside metal surfaces have black oxide finish. Comes with 26" or 28" vent rib barrel with mod. RemChoke tube. ShurShot Turkey (2008) has ShurShot synthetic pistol-grip thumbhole design, extended fore-end, Mossy Oak Obsession camouflage, matte black metal finish, 21" vent rib barrel, twin beads, Turkey Extra Full Rem Choke tube. Receiver drilled and tapped for mounting optics. ShurShot FR CL (Fully Rifled Cantilever, 2008) includes compact 23" fully-rifled barrel with integrated cantilever scope mount.
Price: .... $417.00 to $629.00

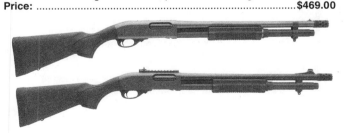

REMINGTON MODEL 870 EXPRESS SUPER MAGNUM
Similar to Model 870 Express except 28" vent rib barrel with 3-1/2" chamber, vented recoil pad. Introduced 1998. Model 870 Express Super Magnum Waterfowl (2008) is fully camouflaged with Mossy Oak Duck Blind pattern, 28-inch vent rib Rem Choke barrel, "Over Decoys" Choke tube (.007") fiber-optic HiViz single bead front sight; front and rear sling swivel studs, padded black sling.
Price: $469.00

REMINGTON MODEL 870 EXPRESS TACTICAL
Similar to Model 870 but in 12 gauge only (2-2/4" and 3" interchangeably) with 18.5" barrel, Tactical RemChoke extended/ported choke tube, black synthetic buttstock and fore-end, extended magazine tube, gray powdercoat finish overall. 38.5" overall length, weighs 7.5 lbs.
Price: $601.00
Price: Model 870 TAC Desert Recon; desert camo stock and sand-toned metal surfaces $692.00

Prices given are believed to be accurate at time of publication however, many factors affect retail pricing so exact prices are not possible.

SHOTGUNS Pumps

Price: Tactical Magpul **$898.00**

REMINGTON MODEL 870 SPS SHURSHOT SYNTHETIC SUPER SLUG
Gauge: 12; 2-3/4" and 3" chamber, interchangeable. **Barrel:** 25.5" extra-heavy, fully rifled pinned to receiver. **Weight:** 7-7/8 lbs. Length: 47" overall. **Features:** Pump-action model based on 870 platform. SuperCell recoil pad. Drilled and tapped for scope mounts with Weaver rail included. Matte black metal surfaces, ShurShot pistol grip buttstock with Mossy Oak Treestand camo.
Price: **$829.00**
Price: 870 SPS ShurShot Synthetic Turkey; adjustable
sights and APG HD camo buttstock and fore-end **$681.00**

REMINGTON 870 EXPRESS SYNTHETIC SUPER MAG TURKEY-WATERFOWL CAMO
Pump action shotgun chambered in 12-ga., 2-3/4 to 3-1/2 inch. Features include full Mossy Oak Bottomland camo coverage; 26-inch barrel with HiViz fiber-optics sights; Wingmaster HD Waterfowl and Turkey Extra Full RemChokes; SuperCell recoil pad; drilled and tapped receiver.
Price: **$629.00**

REMINGTON 870 EXPRESS SYNTHETIC TURKEY CAMO
Pump action shotgun chambered for 2-3/4 and 3-inch 12-ga. Features include 21-inch vent rib bead-sighted barrel; standard Express finish on barrel and receiver; Turkey Extra Full RemChoke; synthetic stock with integrated sling swivel attachment.
Price: **$492.00**

REMINGTON 870 SUPER MAG TURKEY-PREDATOR CAMO WITH SCOPE
Pump action shotgun chambered in 12-ga., 2-3/4 to 3-1/2 inch. Features include 20-inch barrel; TruGlo red/green selectable illuminated sight mounted on pre-installed Weaver-style rail; black padded sling; Wingmaster HDTurkey/Predator RemChoke; full Mossy Oak Obsession camo coverage; ShurShot pistol grip stock with black overmolded grip panels; TruGlo 30mm Red/Green Dot Scope pre-mounted.
Price: **$710.00**

REMINGTON MODEL 887 NITRO MAG
Gauge: 12; 3.5", 3", and 2-3/4" chambers. **Barrel:** 28". **Features:** Pump-action model based on the Model 870. Interchangeable shells, black matte ArmoLokt rustproof coating throughout. SuperCell recoil pad. Solid rib and Hi-Viz front sight with interchangeable light tubes. Black synthetic stock with contoured grip panels.
Price: **$445.00**
Price: Model 887 Nitro Mag Waterfowl, camo **$594.00**

REMINGTON 887 NITRO MAG CAMO COMBO
Pump action shotgun chambered in 12-ga., 2-3/4 to 3-1/2 inch. Features include 22-inch turkey barrel with HiViz fiber-optic rifle sights and 28-inch waterfowl with a HiViz sight; extended Waterfowl and Super Full Turkey RemChokes are included; SuperCell recoil pad; synthetic stock and fore-end with specially contoured grip panels; full camo coverage.
Price: **$728.00**

STEVENS MODEL 350/320
Gauge: 12, 3-inch chamber, 5+1 capacity. **Barrel:** 18.25" with interchangeable choke tubes. Features include all-steel barrel and receiver; bottom-load and ejection design; black synthetic stock.
Price: Security Model **$276.00**
Price: Field Model 320 with 28-inch barrel **$251.00**
Price: Combo Model with Field and Security barrels **$307.00**

STOEGER P-350
Gauge: 12. Designed to fire any 12-gauge ammunition. **Capacity:** 4+1. **Barrel:** 18.5, 20, 24, 26 or 28 inches, with ventilated rib. **Weight:** 6.6 to 7 pounds. **Stock:** Black synthetic, or Realtree APG or Max-4 camo in standard stock configuration. Also available with vertical pistol-style handgrip.
Price: .... **$349.00 to $479.00**

WEATHERBY PA-08 SERIES
Gauge: 12 ga. chamber. **Barrel:** 26" and 28" flat ventilated rib. **Weight:** 6.5 lbs. -7 lbs. **Stock:** Walnut. **Features:** The PA-08 # Walnut stock with gloss finish, all metalwork is gloss black for a distinctive look, vented top rib dissipates heat and aids in target acquisition. Comes with 3 application-specific choke tubes (IC/M/F). Upland/Slug Gun combo includes 24" rifled barrel. Made in Turkey.
Price: PA-08 Upland **$449.00**
Price: PA-08 Upland/Slug combo.............................**$649.00**
Price: PA-08 Turkey **$429.00**
Price: PA-08 Synthetic...**$399.00**
Price: PA-08 Synthetic Waterfowler.......................**$399.00**
Price: PA-08 Synthetic Turkey **$399.00**

WEATHERBY PA-459 TURKEY
Gauge: 12, 3-inch chamber. **Barrel:** 21.25 inches. **Stock:** Synthetic with

Mothwing Spring Mimicry camo, rubber texturized grip areas. Vertical pistol grip. **Sights:** Ghost ring rear, fiber optic front. Picatinny rail. Features: Mothwing Spring Mimicry camo. TR Model has 18½" barrel, ported with removeable cylinder-choke tube.
Price: **$549.00**
Price: PA-459 TR Tactical rifle **$599.00**

WINCHESTER SUPER X (SXP)
Gauge: 12, 3" or 3.5" chambers; 20 gauge, 3". **Barrel:** 18"; 26" and 28" barrels are .742" back-bored, chrome plated; Invector Plus choke tubes. **Weight:** 6 .5 to 7 lbs. **Stock:** Walnut or composite.

Features: Rotary bolt, four lugs, dual steel action bars. Walnut Field has gloss-finished walnut stock and forearm, cut checkering. Black Shadow Field has composite stock and forearm, non-glare matte finish barrel and receiver. SXP Defender has composite stock and forearm, chromed plated, 18" cylinder choked barrel, non-glare metal surfaces, five-shot magazine, grooved forearm. Some models offered in left-hand versions. Reintroduced 2009. Made in U.S.A. from Winchester Repeating Arms Co.
Price: Black Shadow Field, 3" **$380.00**
Price: Black Shadow Field, 3.5" **$430.00**
Price: SXP Defender.............................**$350.00 to $400.00**
Price: Waterfowl Hunter 3" **$460.00**
Price: Waterfowl Hunter 3.5" **$500.00**
Price: Turkey Hunter 3.5" **$520.00**
Price: Black Shadow Deer **$520.00**
Price: Trap...**$480.00**
Price: Field, walnut stock.......................**$400.00 to $430.00**

Prices given are believed to be accurate at time of publication however, many factors affect retail pricing so exact prices are not possible.

71ST EDITION, 2017 ⊕ **491**

BENELLI 828U
Gauge: 12. 3-inch chambers **Barrels:** 26 or 28 inches. **Weight:** 6.5 to 7 lbs. **Stock:** AA-grade satin walnut, fully adjustable for both drop and cast. New patented locking system allows use of aluminum frame. Features include carbon fiber rib, fiber optic sight, removable trigger group, and Benelli's Progressive Comfort recoil reduction system.
Price: Matte black...$2,499.00
Price: Nickel..$2,999.00

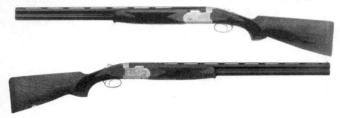

BERETTA 686/687 SILVER PIGEON SERIES
Gauge: 12, 20, 28, 3" chambers (2-3/4" 28 ga.). .410 bore, 3" chamber. **Barrel:** 26", 28". **Weight:** 6.8 lbs. **Stock:** Checkered walnut. **Features:** Interchangeable barrels (20 and 28 ga.), single selective gold-plated trigger, boxlock action, auto safety, Schnabel fore-end.
Price: 686 Silver Pigeon Grade I..$2,350.00
Price: 686 Silver Pigeon Grade I, Sporting............................$2,400.00
Price: 687 Silver Pigeon Grade III.......................................$3,430.00
Price: 687 Silver Pigeon Grade V...$4,075.00

BERETTA MODEL 687 EELL
Gauge: 12, 20, 28, 410. Premium grade model with decorative sideplates featuring lavish hand-chased engraving with a classic game scene enhanced by detailed leaves and flowers that also cover the triggerguard, trigger plate and fore-end lever. Stock has high-grade, specially selected European walnut with fine-line checkering, Offered in three actions size with scaled-down 28 gauge and .410 receivers. Combo models are available with extra barrel sets in 20/28 or 28/.410.
Price: $7,995.00
Price: Combo model..$9,695.00

BERETTA MODEL 690
Gauge: 12. 3-inch chambers. **Barrels:** 26, 28 or 30 inches with OptimaChoke HP system. Similar features of the 686/687 series with minor improvements. Stock has higher grade oil-finished walnut. Re-designed barrel/fore-end attachment reduces weight.
Price: $3,475.00

BERETTA MODEL 692 SPORTING
Gauge: 12, 3-inch chamber. **Barrels:** 30 inches with long forcing cones of approximately 14 inches. Receiver is ½-inch wider than 682 model for improved handling. **Stock:** Hand rubbed oil finished select walnut with Schnabel fore-end. Features include selective single adjustable trigger, manual safety, tapered 8mm to 10mm rib.
Price: $4,800.00
Price: Skeet $5,275.00

BERETTA DT11
Gauge: 12. 3-inch chambers. Competition model offered in Sporting, Skeet and Trap models. **Barrels:** 30, 32, 34 inches. Top rib has hollowed bridges. **Stock:** Hand-checkered buttstock and fore-end. Hand-rubbed oil, Tru-Oil or wax finish. Adjustable comb on

skeet and trap models. Newly designed receiver, top lever, safety/selector button. ACS (All Competition Shotgun) has adjustable rib, OptimaChoke HP system.
Price: From $8,999
Price: ACS $9,750.00

BLASER F3 SUPERSPORT
Gauge: 12 ga., 3" chamber. **Barrel:** 32". **Weight:** 9 lbs. **Stock:** Adjustable semi-custom, Turkish walnut wood grade: 4. **Features:** The latest addition to the F3 family is the F3 SuperSport. The perfect blend of overall weight, balance and weight distribution make the F3 SuperSport the ideal competitor. Briley Spectrum-5 chokes, free floating barrels, adjustable barrel hanger system on o/u, chrome plated barrels full length, revolutionary ejector ball system, barrels finished in a powder coated nitride, selectable competition trigger.
Price: SuperSport from...$9,076.00
Price: Competition Sporting $7,951.00
Price: Superskeet American Super Trap.............................$9,076.00

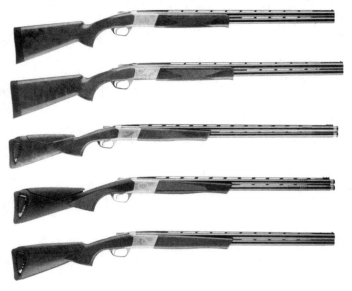

BROWNING CYNERGY
Gauge: .410, 12, 20, 28. **Barrel:** 26", 28", 30", 32". **Stock:** Walnut or composite. **Sights:** White bead front most models; HiViz Pro-Comp sight on some models; mid bead. **Features:** Mono-Lock hinge, recoil-reducing interchangeable Inflex recoil pad, silver nitride receiver; striker-based trigger, ported barrel option. Browning repositioned the Cynergy series with lower prices in 2015. Imported from Japan by Browning.
Price: Field Grade Model, 12 ga. $1,870.00
Price: Field, small gauges...$1,940.00
Price: Feather model, from $2,140.00
Price: Sporting, from..$2,400.00
Price: Sporting w/adjustable comb $2,670.00
Price: Camo, Mossy Oak Shadow Grass or Realtree Max 5.$2,000.00

BROWNING CITORI SERIES
Gauge: 12, 20, 28 and .410. **Barrel:** 26", 28" in 28 and .410. Offered with Invector choke tubes. All 12 and 20 gauge models have back-bored barrels and Invector Plus choke system. **Weight:** 6 lbs., 8 oz. (26" .410) to 7 lbs., 13 oz. (30" 12 ga.). **Length:** 43" overall (26" bbl.). **Stock:** Dense walnut, hand checkered, full pistol grip, beavertail fore-end. Field-type recoil pad on 12 ga. field guns and trap and skeet models. **Sights:** Medium raised beads, German nickel silver. **Features:** Barrel selector integral with safety, automatic ejectors, three-piece takedown. Imported from Japan by Browning.
Price: Lightning, from $1,990.00
Price: White Lightning, from $2,070.00

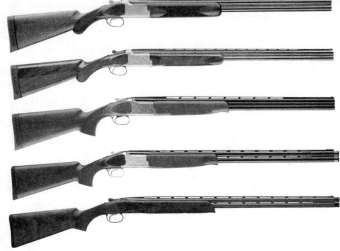

Price: Superlight Feather $2,390.00
Price: Lightning Feather, combo 20 and 28 ga. $3,580.00
Price: Crossover Target $2,000.00
Price: Micro Midas Satin Hunter w/13" stock.......................$1,650.00

BROWNING 725 CITORI

Gauge: 12, 20, 28 or .410 bore. **Barrel:** 26, 28, 30". **Weight:** 5.7 to 7.6 lbs. **Length:** 43.75 to 50". **Stock:** Gloss oil finish grade II/III walnut. Features include a new receiver that is significantly lower in profile than other 12-gauge Citori models. Other features include a mechanical trigger, Vector Pro lengthened forcing cones, three Invector-DS choke tubes, silver nitride finish with high relief engraving.

Price: 725 Field (12 or 20)......................................$2,470.00
Price: 725 Field (28 or .410)..................................$2,540.00
Price: 725 Feather (12 or 20) $2,550.00
Price: 725 Sporting, from $3,070.00
Price: 725 Sporting w/adjustable comb $3,530.00
Price: 725 Skeet, from $3,140.00
Price: 725 Trap, from $3,340.00

BROWNING CITORI XT TRAP

Gauge: 12. **Barrels:** 30" or 32", Invector-Plus choke tubes, adjustable comb and buttplate. **Features:** Engraved silver nitride receiver with gold highlights, vented side barrel rib. Introduced 1999. Imported by Browning.

Price: XT Trap $2,650.00
Price: XT Trap w/adjustable comb........................$3,000.00

CAESAR GUERINI

Gauge: 12, 20, 28 gauge, also 20/28 gauge combo. Some models are available in .410 bore. **Barrels:** All standard lengths from 26 to 32 inches. **Weight:** 5.5 to 8.8 lbs. **Stock:** High grade walnut with hand-rubbed oil finish. **Features:** A wide range of over/under models designed for the field, sporting clays, skeet and trap shooting. The models listed below are representative of some of the different models and variants. Many optional features are offered including high grade wood and engraving, and extra sets of barrels. Made it Italy and imported by Caesar Guerini USA.

Price: Ellipse $4,450.00
Price: Ellipse Curve...................................$6,900.00
Price: Ellipse EVO Sporting $6,800.00
Price: Magnus...$4,600.00

Price: Maxum...$6,295.00
Price: Forum $10,500.00
Price: Woodlander...$3,450.00
Price: Invictus Sporting...$6,850.00

CONNECTICUT SHOTGUN A10 AMERICAN

Gauge: 12, 20, 28, 2 ¾" chambers, .410, 3-inches. Sidelock design. **Barrels:** 26, 28, 30 or 32" with choice of fixed or interchangeable chokes. **Weight:** 6.3 lbs. **Stock:** Hand rubbed oil finished, hand checkered at 24 lines per inch. Black, English or Turkish walnut offered in numerous grades. Pistol or Price of Wales grip, short or long tang. **Features:** Low profile, shallow frame full sidelock. Single-selective trigger, automatic ejectors. Engraved models available. Made in the U.S.A. by Connecticut Shotgun Mfg. Co.

Price: 12 gauge from $7,995.00
Price: Smaller gauges from $9,045.00

CONNECTICUT SHOTGUN MODEL 21 O/U

Gauge: 20, 3" chambers. **Barrels:** 26" to 32" chrome-lined, back-bored with extended forcing cones. **Weight:** 6.3 lbs. **Stock:** A Fancy (2X) American walnut, standard point checkering, choice of straight or pistol grip. Higher grade walnut is optional. **Features:** The over/under version of Conn. Shotgun's replica of the Winchester Model 21 side-by-side, built using the same machining, tooling, techniques and finishes. Low profile shallow frame with blued receiver. Pigeon and Grand American grades are available. Made in the U.S.A. by Connecticut Shotgun Mfg. Co.

Price: From $3,995.00

CZ SPORTER

Gauge: 12, 3" chambers. **Barrel:** 30", 32" chrome-lined, back-bored with extended forcing cones. **Weight:** 8.5 lbs. **Length:** NA. **Stock:** Neutral cast stock with an adjustable comb, trap style fore-end, pistol grip and ambidextrous palm swells. No. 3 grade Circassian walnut. At lowest position, drop at comb: 1-5/8"; drop at heel: 2-3/8"; length of pull: 14-1⁄2". **Features:** Designed for Sporting Clays and FITASC competition. Hand engraving, satin black-finished receiver. Tapered adjustable rib with center bead and a red fiber-optic front bead, 10 choke tubes with wrench, single selective trigger, automatic ejectors, thin rubber pad with slick plastic top. Introduced 2008. Made in the Czech Repubic and imported by CZ-USA.

Price: G2 grade...$2,497.00
Price: Standard grade.....................................$1,899.00

CZ MALLARD

Gauge: 12, 20, 28, .410, 3" chambers. **Barrel:** 26". **Weight:** 7.7 lbs. **Length:** NA. **Stock:** Round-knob pistol grip, Schnabel fore-end, Turkish walnut. **Features:** Double triggers and extractors, coin finished receiver, multi chokes. From CZ-USA.

Price: $583.00

CZ REDHEAD PREMIER

Gauge: 12, 20, .410 (3" chambers), 28 (2 3/4"). **Barrel:** 28". **Weight:** 7.4 lbs. **Length:** NA. **Stock:** Round-knob pistol grip, Schnabel fore-end, Turkish walnut. **Features:** Single selective triggers and extractors (12 & 20 ga.), screw-in chokes (12, 20, 28 ga.) choked IC and Mod (.410), coin finished receiver, multi chokes. From CZ-USA.

Price: Deluxe $953.00
Price: Mini (28, .410) $960.00
Price: Target $1,389.00

CZ SUPER SCROLL COMBO

Gauge: 20 and 28 combo. **Barrels:** 30 inches for both gauges with five choke tubes for each set. **Stock:** Grave V Turkish walnut with Schnabel fore-end, rounded grip. **Weight:** 6.7 pounds. **Features:** Ornate hand-engraved scrollwork on receiver, faux sideplates, triggerguard and mono-block. Comes in a custom-fitted aluminum case.

Price: $3,899.00

CZ UPLAND STERLING
Gauge: 12, 3-inch chambers. **Barrels:** 28 inches with ventilated rib, fiber optic sight, five choke tubes. **Stock:** Turkish walnut with stippled gripping surfaces. **Weight:** 7.5 pounds. Lady Sterling has smaller stock dimensions.
Price: $999.00
Price: Lady Sterling.. $1,281.00

CZ WINGSHOOTER ELITE
Gauge: 12, 20 ga., 2-3/4" chamber. **Barrel:** 28" flat ventilated rib. **Weight:** 6.3 lbs. **Length:** 45.5". **Stock:** Turkish walnut. **Features:** This colorful Over and Under shotgun has the same old world craftsmanship as all of our shotguns but with a new stylish look. This elegant hand engraved work of art is available in four gauges and its eye-catching engraving will stand alone in the field or range. 12 and 20 gauge models have auto ejectors, while the 28 gauge and .410 have extractors only. Heavily engraved scroll work with special side plate design, mechanical selective triggers, box Lock frame design, 18 LPI checkering, coil spring operated hammers, chrome lined, 5 interchangeable choke tubes and special engraved skeleton butt plate.
Price: 12 or 20 ga. $1,059.00

ESCORT OVER/UNDER
Gauge: 12, 3" chamber. **Barrel:** 28". **Weight:** 7.4 lbs. **Stock:** Walnut or select walnut with Trio recoil pad; synthetic stock with adjustable comb. Three adjustment spacers. **Sights:** Bronze front bead. **Features:** Blued barrels, blued or nickel receiver. Trio recoil pad. Five interchangeable chokes (SK, IC, M, IM, F); extractors or ejectors (new, 2008), barrel selector. Hard case available. Introduced 2007. Imported from Turkey by Legacy Sports International.
Price: From $641.00

FAUSTI CLASS ROUND BODY
Gauge: 16, 20, 28. **Barrels:** 28 or 30". **Weight:** 5.8 to 6.3 lbs. **Length:** 45.5 to 47.5". **Stock:** Turkish walnut Prince of Wales style with oil finish. Features include automatic ejectors, single selective trigger, laser-engraved receiver.
Price: From $5,399.00

FAUSTI CALEDON
Gauge: 12, 16, 20, 28 and .410 bore. **Barrels:** 26, 28 or 30". **Weight:** 5.8 to 7.3 lbs. **Stock:** Turkish walnut with oil finish, round pistol grip. **Features:** Automatic ejectors, single selective trigger, laser-engraved receiver. Coin finish receiver with gold inlays.
Price: 12 or 20 ga. $1,999.00
Price: 16, 28, .410 ....$2,569.00

FN SC-1
Gauge: 12. 2-3/4" chamber. **Barrels:** 28 or 30 inches, ported with ventilated rib, Invector-Plus extended choke tubes. **Stock:** Laminated black or blue with adjustable comb and length-of-pull. **Weight:** 8 pounds.
Price: $2,449.00

FRANCHI INSTINCT SERIES
Gauge: 12, 20 with 3" chambers. Barrels: 26 or 28". **Weight:** 5.3 to 6.4 lbs. **Length:** 42.5 to 44.5". **Stock:** AA-grade satin walnut (LS), A-grade (L) with rounded pistol grip and recoil pad. Single trigger, automatic ejectors, tang safety, choke tubes. L model has steel receiver, SL has aluminum alloy receiver. Sporting model has higher grade wood, extended choke tubes.

Price: L..$1,349.00
Price: SL $1,699.00
Price: Sporting $1,899.00

KOLAR SPORTING CLAYS
Gauge: 12, 2-3/4" chambers. **Barrel:** 30", 32", 34"; extended choke tubes. **Stock:** 14-5/8"x2.5"x1-7/8"x1-3/8". French walnut. Four stock versions available. **Features:** Single selective trigger, detachable, adjustable for length; overbored barrels with long forcing cones; flat tramline rib; matte blue finish. Made in U.S. by Kolar.
Price: Standard $11,995.00
Price: Prestige.. $14,190.00
Price: Elite Gold $16,590.00
Price: Legend $17,090.00
Price: Select $22,590.00
Price: Custom .... **Price on request**

KOLAR AAA COMPETITION TRAP
Gauge: 12. Similar to the Sporting Clays gun except has 32" O/U /34" Unsingle or 30" O/U /34" Unsingle barrels as an over/under, unsingle, or combination set. Stock dimensions are 14.5"x2.5"x1.5"; American or French walnut; step parallel rib standard. Contact maker for full listings. Made in U.S.A. by Kolar.
Price: Single bbl. from $8,495.00
Price: O/U from $11,695.00

KOLAR AAA COMPETITION SKEET
Similar to the Sporting Clays gun except has 28" or 30" barrels with Kolarite AAA sub gauge tubes; stock of American or French walnut with matte finish; flat tramline rib; under barrel adjustable for point of impact. Many options available. Contact maker for complete listing. Made in U.S.A. by Kolar.
Price: Max Lite, from..$13,995.00

KRIEGHOFF K-80 SPORTING CLAYS
Gauge: 12. **Barrel:** 28", 30", 32", 34" with choke tubes. **Weight:** About 8 lbs. **Stock:** #3 Sporting stock designed for gun-down shooting. **Features:** Standard receiver with satin nickel finish and classic scroll engraving. Selective mechanical trigger adjustable for position. Choice of tapered flat or 8mm parallel flat barrel rib. Free-floating barrels. Aluminum case. Imported from Germany by Krieghoff International, Inc.
Price: Standard grade with five choke tubes, from $11,395.00

KRIEGHOFF K-80 SKEET
Gauge: 12, 2-3/4" chambers. **Barrel:** 28", 30", 32", (skeet & skeet), optional choke tubes). **Weight:** About 7.75 lbs. **Stock:** American skeet or straight skeet stocks, with palm-swell grips. Walnut. **Features:** Satin gray receiver finish. Selective mechanical trigger adjustable for position. Choice of ventilated 8mm parallel flat rib or ventilated 8-12mm tapered flat rib. Introduced 1980. Imported from Germany by Krieghoff International, Inc.
Price: Standard, skeet chokes.................................$10,595.00
Price: Skeet Special (28", 30", 32" tapered flat rib,
    skeet & skeet choke tubes) $9,100.00

KRIEGHOFF K-80 TRAP
Gauge: 12, 2-3/4" chambers. **Barrel:** 30", 32" (Imp. Mod. & Full or choke tubes). **Weight:** About 8.5 lbs. **Stock:** Four stock dimensions or adjustable stock available; all have palm-swell grips. Checkered European walnut. **Features:** Satin nickel receiver. Selective mechanical trigger, adjustable for position. Ventilated step rib. Introduced 1980. Imported from Germany by Krieghoff International, Inc.
Price: K-80 O/U (30", 32", Imp. Mod. & Full), from................$8,850.00
Price: K-80 Unsingle (32", 34", Full), standard, from..........$10,080.00
Price: K-80 Combo (two-barrel set), standard, from $13,275.00

KRIEGHOFF K-20
Similar to the K-80 except built on a 20-gauge frame. Designed for skeet, sporting clays and field use. Offered in 20, 28 and .410; 28", 30" and 32" barrels. Imported from Germany by Krieghoff International Inc.
Price: K-20, 20 gauge, from..$11,395.00
Price: K-20, 28 gauge, from..$12,395.00
Price: K-20, .410, from...$12,395.00

LEBEAU-COURALLY BOSS-VEREES
Gauge: 12, 20, 2-3/4" chambers. **Barrel:** 25" to 32". **Weight:** To customer specifications. **Stock:** Exhibition-quality French walnut. **Features:** Boss-type sidelock with automatic ejectors; single or double triggers; chopper lump barrels. A custom gun built to customer specifications. Imported from Belgium by Wm. Larkin Moore.
Price: From $96,000.00

MERKEL MODEL 2001EL O/U
Gauge: 12, 20, 3" chambers, 28, 2-3/4" chambers. **Barrel:** 12-28"; 20, 28 ga.-26.75". **Weight:** About 7 lbs. (12 ga.). **Stock:** Oil-finished walnut; English or pistol grip. **Features:** Self-cocking Blitz boxlock action with cocking indicators; Kersten double cross-bolt lock; silver-grayed receiver with engraved hunting scenes; coil spring ejectors; single selective or double triggers. Imported from Germany by Merkel USA.
Price: $9,995.00
Price: Model 2001EL Sporter; full pistol grip stock $9,995.00

MERKEL MODEL 2000CL
Similar to Model 2001EL except scroll-engraved case-hardened receiver; 12, 20, 28 gauge. Imported from Germany by Merkel USA.
Price: $8,495.00
Price: Model 2016 CL; 16 gauge $8,495.00

MOSSBERG SILVER RESERVE II
Gauge: 12, 3-inch chambers. **Barrels:** 28 inches with ventilated rib, choke tubes. **Stock:** Select black walnut with satin finish. **Sights:** Metal bead. Available with extractors or automatic ejectors. Also offered in Sport model with ported barrels with wide rib, fiber optic front and middle bead sights. Super Sport has extra wide high rib, optional adjustable comb.
Price: Field $773.00
Price: Sport $950.00
Price: Sport w/ejectors $1,070.00
Price: Super Sport w/ejectors..$1,163.00
Price: Super Sport w/ejectors, adj. comb $1,273.00

PERAZZI MX8/MX8 TRAP/SKEET
Gauge: 12, 20 2 ¾" chambers. **Barrel:** Trap: 29.5" (Imp. Mod. & Extra Full), 31.5" (Full & Extra Full). Choke tubes optional. Skeet: 27-5/8" (skeet & skeet). **Weight:** About 8.5 lbs. (trap); 7 lbs., 15 oz. (skeet). **Stock:** Interchangeable and custom made to customer specs. **Features:** Has detachable and interchangeable trigger group with flat V springs. Flat 7/16" vent rib. Many options available. Imported from Italy by Perazzi U.S.A., Inc.
Price: Trap from $9,861.00
Price: Skeet from $9,861.00

PERAZZI MX8
Gauge: 12, 20 2 ¾" chambers. **Barrel:** 28-3/8" (Imp. Mod. & Extra Full), 29.5" (choke tubes). **Weight:** 7 lbs., 12 oz. **Stock:** Special specifications. **Features:** Has single selective trigger; flat 7/16" x 5/16" vent rib. Many options available. Imported from Italy by Perazzi U.S.A., Inc.
Price: Standard, from $9,861.00
Price: Sporting, from $9,861.00

Price: SC3 Grade (variety of engraving patterns) from $21,000.00
Price: SCO Grade (more intricate engraving/inlays) from ...$36,000.00

PERAZZI MX12 HUNTING
Gauge: 12, 2-3/4" chambers. **Barrel:** 26.75", 27.5", 28-3/8", 29.5" (Mod. & Full); choke tubes available in 27-5/8", 29.5" only (MX12C). **Weight:** 7 lbs., 4 oz. **Stock:** To customer specs; interchangeable. **Features:** Single selective trigger; coil springs used in action; Schnabel fore-end tip. Imported from Italy by Perazzi U.S.A., Inc.
Price: From $11,698.00
Price: MX12C (with choke tubes) from $12,316.00

PERAZZI MX20 HUNTING
Similar to the MX12 except 20 ga. frame size. Non-removable trigger group. Available in 20, 28, .410 with 2-3/4" or 3" chambers. 26" standard, and choked Mod. & Full. Weight is 6 lbs., 6 oz. Imported from Italy by Perazzi U.S.A., Inc.
Price: From $11,900.00
Price: MX20C (with choke tubes) from $13,700.00

PERAZZI MX10
Gauge: 12, 2-3/4" chambers. **Barrel:** 29.5", 31.5" (fixed chokes). **Weight:** NA. **Stock:** Walnut; cheekpiece adjustable for elevation and cast. **Features:** Adjustable rib; vent side rib. Externally selective trigger. Available in single barrel, combo, over/under trap, skeet, pigeon and sporting models. Introduced 1993. Imported from Italy by Perazzi U.S.A., Inc.
Price: From $11,900.00

PERAZZI MX2000S
Gauge: 12, 20. **Barrels:** 29.5, 30.75, 31.5 inches with fixed I/M and Full chokes, or interchangeable. Competition model with features similar to MX8.
Price: $12,500.00

PERAZZI MX15 UNSINGLE TRAP
Gauge: 12. **Barrel:** 34 inches with fixed Full choke. **Features:** Bottom single barrel with 6-notch adjustable rib, adjustable stock, drop-out trigger. , or interchangeable. Competition model with features similar to MX8.
Price: $9,175.00

PIOTTI BOSS
Gauge: 12, 20. **Barrel:** 26" to 32", chokes as specified. **Weight:** 6.5 to 8 lbs. **Stock:** Dimensions to customer specs. Best quality figured walnut. **Features:** Essentially a custom-made gun with many options. Introduced 1993. Imported from Italy by Wm. Larkin Moore.
Price: From $69,500.00

RIZZINI OMNIUM
Gauge: 12, 20. **Barrels:** 26.5, 28 or 30 inches with choke tubes, ventilated rib. **Stock:** Walnut with pistol grip, Schnabel fore-end. **Features:** Entry level Rizzini over/under boxlock with blue or coin finish, scroll engraving, automatic ejectors and single-selective trigger. Made in Italy by Battista Rizzini and distributed by Rizzini USA.
Price: From $2,632.00

RIZZINI S790 EMEL
Gauge: 20, 28, .410. **Barrel:** 26", 27.5" (Imp. Cyl. & Imp. Mod.). **Weight:** About 6 lbs. **Stock:** 14"x1.5"x2-1/8". Extra fancy select walnut. **Features:** Boxlock action with profuse engraving; automatic ejectors; single selective trigger; silvered receiver. Comes with Nizzoli leather case. Introduced 1996. Made in Italy by Battista Rizzini and distributed by Wm. Larkin Moore & Co.
Price: From $14,600.00

RIZZINI S792 EMEL
Similar to S790 EMEL except dummy sideplates with extensive engraving coverage. Nizzoli leather case. Introduced 1996. Made in Italy by Battista Rizzini and distributed by Wm. Larkin Moore & Co.
Price: From $15,500.00

RIZZINI UPLAND EL
Gauge: 12, 16, 20, 28, .410. **Barrel:** 26", 27.5", Mod. & Full, Imp. Cyl. & Imp. Mod. choke tubes. **Weight:** About 6.6 lbs. **Stock:** 14.5"x1-1/2"x2.25". **Features:** Boxlock action; single selective trigger; ejectors;

profuse engraving on silvered receiver. Comes with fitted case. Introduced 1996. Made in Italy by Battista Rizzini and distributed by Wm. Larkin Moore & Co.
Price: From $6,595.00

RIZZINI ARTEMIS
Gauge: 12, 16, 20, 28, .410. Same as Upland EL model except dummy sideplates with extensive game scene engraving. Fancy European walnut stock. Fitted case. Introduced 1996. Imported from Italy by Fierce Products and by Wm. Larkin Moore & Co.
Price: From $4,250.00
Price: Artemis Light $4,395.00

RIZZINI S782 EMEL
Gauge: 12, 2-3/4" chambers. **Barrel:** 26", 27.5" (Imp. Cyl. & Imp. Mod.). **Weight:** About 6.75 lbs. **Stock:** 14.5"x1.5"x2.25". Extra fancy select walnut. **Features:** Boxlock action with dummy sideplates, extensive engraving with gold inlaid game birds, silvered receiver, automatic ejectors, single selective trigger. Nizzoli leather case. Introduced 1996. Made in Italy by Battista Rizzini and distributed by Wm. Larkin Moore & Co.
Price: From $18,800.00

SKB 590 FIELD
Gauge: 12, 20 with 3" chambers. **Barrel:** 26", 28", 30". Three SKB Competition choke tubes (IC, M, F). Lengthened forcing cones. **Stock:** Oil finished walnut with Pachmayr recoil pad. **Weight:** 7.1 to 7.9 lbs. **Sights:** NA. **Features:** Boxlock action, bright blue finish with laser engraved receiver. Automatic ejectors, single trigger with selector switch incorporated in thumb-operated tang safety. Youth Model has 13" length of pull. Imported from Turkey by GU, Inc.
Price: $1,300.00

SKB 90TSS
Gauge: 12, 20 with 2 ¾-inch chambers. **Barrel:** 28, 30, 32 inches. Three SKB Competition choke tubes (SK, IC, M for Skeet and Sporting Models; IM, M, F for Trap). Lengthened forcing cones. **Stock:** Oil finished walnut with Pachmayr recoil pad. **Weight:** 7.1 to 7.9 lbs. **Sights:** Ventilated rib with target sights. **Features:** Boxlock action, bright blue finish with laser engraved receiver. Automatic ejectors, single trigger with selector switch incorporated in thumb-operated tang safety. Sporting and Trap models have adjustable comb and buttpad system. Imported from Turkey by GU, Inc.
Price: Skeet $1,470.00
Price: Sporting Clays, Trap..$1,720.00

STEVENS MODEL 555
Gauge: 12, 20, 28, .410; 2-3/4" and 3" chambers. **Barrel:** 26", 28". **Weight:** 5.5 to 6 lbs. **Features:** Five screw-in choke tubes with 12, 20, and 28 gauge; .410 has fixed M/IC chokes. Turkish walnut stock and Schnabel fore-end. Single selective mechanical trigger with extractors.
Price: $694.00

STOEGER CONDOR
Gauge: 12, 20, 2-3/4" 3" chambers; 16, .410. **Barrel:** 22", 24", 26", 28", 30". **Weight:** 5.5 to 7.8 lbs. **Sights:** Brass bead. **Features:** IC, M, or F screw-in choke tubes with each gun. Oil finished hardwood with pistol grip and fore-end. Auto safety, single trigger, automatic extractors.
Price: From ....$449.00 to $669.00
Price: Combo with 12 and 20 ga. barrel sets $899.00
Price: Competition...$669.00

TRISTAR HUNTER EX
Gauge: 12, 20, 28, .410. **Barrel:** 26", 28". **Weight:** 5.7 lbs. (.410); 6.0 lbs. (20, 28), 7.2-7.4 lbs. (12). Chrome-lined steel mono-block barrel, five Beretta-style choke tubes (SK, IC, M, IM, F). Length: NA. **Stock:** Walnut, cut checkering. 14.25"x1.5"x2-3/8". **Sights:** Brass front sight. **Features:** All have extractors, engraved receiver, sealed actions, self-adjusting locking bolts, single selective trigger, ventilated rib. 28 ga. and .410 built on true frames. Five-year warranty. Imported from Italy by Tristar Sporting Arms Ltd.
Price: From $630.00

TRISTAR SETTER
Gauge: 12, 20 with 3-inch chambers. **Barrels:** 28" (12 ga.), 26" (20 ga.) with ventilated rib, three Beretta-style choke tubes. **Weight:** 6.3 to 7.2 pounds. **Stock:** High gloss wood. Single selective trigger, extractors.
Price: $559.00

WEBLEY & SCOTT O/U SERIES
Gauge: 12, 20, 28, .410. **Barrels:** 26, 28, 30", five interchangeable choke tubes. **Weight:** 5.5 to 7.5 lbs. **Stock:** Checkered Turkish walnut with recoil pad. **Features:** Automatic ejectors, single selective trigger, ventilated rib, tang selector/safety. 2000 Premium Model has higher-grade select walnut stock, color case hardening. 3000 Sidelock Model is a high-grade gun with 7-pin sidelocks, oil-finished premium-grade walnut stock with checkered butt, jeweled monobloc walls, and comes with high quality, fleeced line lockable case. Made in Turkey and imported by Centurion International.
Price: 900 Sporting..$1,250.00
Price: 2000 Premium $2,500.00
Price: 3000 Sidelock..$6,000.00

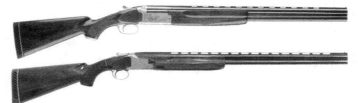

WINCHESTER MODEL 101
Gauge: 12, 2-3/4", 3" chambers. **Barrel:** 28", 30", 32", ported, Invector Plus choke system. **Weight:** 7 lbs. 6 oz. to 7 lbs. 12. oz. **Stock:** Checkered high-gloss grade II/III walnut stock, Pachmayr Decelerator sporting pad. **Features:** Chrome-plated chambers; back-bored barrels; tang barrel selector/safety; Signature extended choke tubes. Model 101 Field comes with solid brass bead front sight, three tubes, engraved receiver. Model 101 Sporting has adjustable trigger, 10mm runway rib, white mid-bead, Tru-Glo front sight, 30" and 32" barrels. Camo version of Model 101 Field comes with full-coverage Mossy Oak Duck Blind pattern. Model 101 Pigeon Grade Trap has 10mm steel runway rib, mid-bead sight, interchangeable fiber-optic front sight, porting and vented side ribs, adjustable trigger shoe, fixed raised comb or adjustable comb, Grade III/IV walnut, 30" or 32" barrels, molded ABS hard case. Reintroduced 2008. Made in Belgium by FN. Winchester 150th Anniversary Commemorative model has grade IV/V stock, deep relief scrolling on a silver nitride finish receiver.
Price: Field $1,900.00
Price: Sporting..$2,300.00
Price: Pigeon Grade Trap..$2,520.00
Price: Pigeon Grade Trap w/adj. comb...................................$2,680.00
Price: 150th Anniversary Commemorative $3,070.00

Prices given are believed to be accurate at time of publication however, many factors affect retail pricing so exact prices are not possible.

ARRIETA SIDELOCK DOUBLE
Gauge: 12, 16, 20, 28, .410. **Barrel:** Length and chokes to customer specs. **Weight:** To customer specs. **Stock:** To customer specs. Straight English with checkered butt (standard), or pistol grip. Select European walnut with oil finish. **Features:** Essentially custom gun with myriad options. H&H pattern hand-detachable sidelocks, selective automatic ejectors, double triggers (hinged front) standard. Some have self-opening action. Finish and engraving to customer specs. Imported from Spain by Quality Arms, Wm. Larking Moore and others.
Price: Model 557...$6,970.00
Price: Model 570...$7,350.00
Price: Model 578...$8,200.00
Price: Model 600 Imperial.............................$12,125.00
Price: Model 801...$19,850.00
Price: Model 802...$19,850.00
Price: Model 803...$15,000.00
Price: Model 931...$36,000.00

AYA MODEL 4/53
Gauge: 12, 16, 20, 28, 410. **Barrel:** 26", 27", 28", 30". **Weight:** To customer specifications. **Length:** To customer specifications. **Features:** Hammerless boxlock action; double triggers; light scroll engraving; automatic safety; straight grip oil finished walnut stock; checkered butt. Made in Spain. Imported by New England Custom Gun Service.
Price: $3,895.00
Price: No. 2 ....$5,895.00
Price: No. 2 Rounded Action $6,299.00

AYA MODEL ADARRA
Gauge: 12, 16, 20, 28, 410. **Barrel:** 26", 28". **Weight:** Approx. 6.7 lbs. **Features:** Hammerless boxlock action; double triggers; light scroll engraving; automatic safety; straight grip oil finished walnut stock; checkered butt. Made in Spain. Imported by New England Custom Gun Service.
Price: $4,800.00

BERETTA 486 PARALELLO
Gauge: 12 or 20, 3" chamber, or 28 with 2¾" chamber. **Barrel:** 26", 28", 30". **Weight:** 7.1 lbs. **Stock:** English-style straight grip, splinter fore-end. Select European walnut, checkered, oil finish. **Features:** Round action, Optima-Choke Tubes. Automatic ejection or mechanical extraction. Firing-pin block safety, manual or automatic, open top-lever safety. Imported from Italy by Beretta U.S.A.
Price: From $5,350.00

CIMARRON 1878 COACH GUN
Gauge: 12. 3-inch chambers. **Barrels:** 20 or 26 inches. **Weight:** 8 to 9 pounds. **Stock:** Hardwood. External hammers, double triggers. **Finish:** Blue, Cimarron "USA", Cimarron "Original."
Price: Blue .... $575.00 (20") to $594.00 (26")
Price: Original .... $675.00 to $694.00
Price: USA .... $832.00 to $851.00

CIMARRON 1881 HAMMERLESS
Gauge: 12. 3-inch chambers. **Barrels:** 20, 22, 26, 28 or 30 inches. **Stock:** Standard or Deluxe wood with rounded pistol grip. Single trigger, extractors, bead front sight.
Price: Deluxe............................ $722.00 to $761.00

CONNECTICUT SHOTGUN MANUFACTURING CO. RBL
Gauge: 12, 16, 20. **Barrel:** 26", 28", 30", 32". **Weight:** NA. **Length:** NA. **Stock:** NA. **Features:** Round-action SxS shotguns made in the USA. Scaled frames, five TruLock choke tubes. Deluxe fancy grade walnut

buttstock and fore-end. Quick Change recoil pad in two lengths. Various dimensions and options available depending on gauge.
Price: 12 gauge $3,795.00
Price: 16 gauge $3,795.00
Price: 20 gauge Special Custom Model $7,995.00

CONNECTICUT SHOTGUN MANUFACTURING CO. MODEL 21
Gauge: 12, 16, 20, 28, .410. A faithful re-creation of the famous Winchester Model 21. Many options and upgrades are available. Each frame is machined from specially produced proof steel. The 28 and .410 guns are available on the standard frame or on a newly engineered small frame. These are custom guns and are made to order to the buyer's individual specifications, wood, stock dimensions, barrel lengths, chokes, finishes and engraving.
Price: 12, 16 or 20 gauge from $15,000.00
Price: 28 or .410 from $18,000.00

CZ BOBWHITE, SHARP-TAIL
Gauge: 12, 20, 28, .410. (5 screw-in chokes in 12 and 20 ga. and fixed chokes in IC and Mod in .410). **Barrel:** 26 or 28". **Weight:** 6.5 lbs. **Stock:** Turkish walnut with straight English-style grip and double triggers (Bobwhite) or conventional American pistol grip with a single trigger (Ringneck). Both are hand checkered 20 lpi. **Features:** Both color case-hardened shotguns are hand engraved.
Price: Bobwhite $789.00
Price: Bobwhite 28 or .410 ....$974.00
Price: Sharp-Tail $1,022.00
Price: Sharp-Tail Target.............................$1,298.00

CZ HAMMER COACH
Gauge: 12, 3" chambers. **Barrel:** 20". **Weight:** 6.7 lbs. **Features:** Following in the tradition of the guns used by the stagecoach guards of the 1880's, this cowboy gun features double triggers, 19th century color case-hardening and fully functional external hammers.
Price: $922.00
Price: Classic model w/30" bbls............................$963.00

EMF MODEL 1878 WYATT EARP
Gauge: 12. **Barrel:** 20". **Weight:** 8 lbs. **Length:** 37" overall. **Stock:** Smooth walnut with steel butt place. **Sights:** Large brass bead. **Features:** Colt-style exposed hammers rebounding type; blued receiver and barrels; cylinder bore. Based on design of Colt Model 1878 shotgun. Made in Italy by Pedersoli.
Price: $1,590.00

FAUSTI DEA SERIES
Gauge: 12, 16, 20, 28, .410. **Barrel:** 26, 28, or 30 inches. **Weight:** 6 to 6.8 lbs. **Stock:** AAA walnut, oil finished. Straight grip, checkered butt, classic fore-end. **Features:** Automatic ejectors, single non-selective trigger. Duetto model is in 28 gauge with extra set of .410 barrels. Made in Italy and imported by Fausti, USA.
Price: 12 or 20 ....$3,518.00
Price: 16, 28, .410............................$4,190.00
Price: Duetto...$5,790.00

FOX, A.H.
Gauge: 16, 20, 28, .410. **Barrel:** Length and chokes to customer specifications. Rust-blued Chromox or Krupp steel. **Weight:** 5-1/2 to 6.75 lbs. **Stock:** Dimensions to customer specifications. Hand-checkered Turkish Circassian walnut with hand-rubbed oil finish. Straight, semi or full pistol grip; splinter, Schnabel or beavertail fore-end; traditional pad, hard rubber buttplate or skeleton butt. **Features:** Boxlock action with automatic ejectors;

Prices given are believed to be accurate at time of publication however, many factors affect retail pricing so exact prices are not possible.

71ST EDITION, 2017 ✦ **497**

double or Fox single selective trigger. Scalloped, rebated and color case-hardened receiver; hand finished and handengraved. Grades differ in engraving, inlays, grade of wood, amount of hand finishing. Introduced 1993. Made in U.S. by Connecticut Shotgun Mfg.

Price: CE Grade $19,500.00
Price: XE Grade $22,000.00
Price: DE Grade $25,000.00
Price: FE Grade $30,000.00
Price: 28/.410 CE Grade...$21,500.00
Price: 28/.410 XE Grade...$24,000.00
Price: 28/.410 DE Grade...$27,000.00
Price: 28/.410 FE Grade...$32,000.00

GARBI MODEL 101
Gauge: 12, 16, 20, 28. **Barrel:** 26", 28", choked to customer specs. **Weight:** 5-1/2 to 7.5 lbs. **Stock:** 14.5"x2.25"x1.5". Select European walnut. Straight grip, checkered butt, classic fore-end. **Features:** Sidelock action, automatic ejectors, double triggers standard. Color case-hardened action, coin finish optional. Single trigger; beavertail fore-end, etc. optional. Hand engraved with scroll engraving. Imported from Spain by Wm. Larkin Moore.
Price: From $15,950.00

GARBI MODEL 103A, 103B
Similar to the Garbi Model 101 except has Purdey-type fine scroll and rosette engraving. Model 103B has nickel-chrome steel barrels, H&H-type easy opening mechanism; other mechanical details remain the same. Imported from Spain by Wm. Larkin Moore.
Price: Model 103A. From...$21,000.00
Price: Model 103B. From...$28,000.00

GARBI MODEL 200
Similar to the Garbi Model 101 except has heavy-duty locks, magnum proofed. Very fine Continental-style floral and scroll engraving, well figured walnut stock. Other mechanical features remain the same. Imported from Spain by Wm. Larkin Moore.
Price: $24,000.00

MERKEL MODEL 47E, 147E
Gauge: 12, 3" chambers, 16, 2.75" chambers, 20, 3" chambers. **Barrel:** 12, 16 ga.-28"; 20 ga.-26.75" (Imp. Cyl. & Mod., Mod. & Full). **Weight:** About 6.75 lbs. (12 ga.). **Stock:** Oil-finished walnut; straight English or pistol grip. **Features:** Anson & Deeley-type boxlock action with single selective or double triggers, automatic safety, cocking indicators. Color case-hardened receiver with standard arabesque engraving. Imported from Germany by Merkel USA.
Price: Model 47E (H&H ejectors) $4,595.00
Price: Model 147E (as above with ejectors)..........................$7,695.00

MERKEL MODEL 47EL, 147EL
Similar to Model 47E except H&H style sidelock action with cocking indicators, ejectors. Silver-grayed receiver and sideplates have arabesque engraving, engraved border and screws (Model 47E), or fine hunting scene engraving (Model 147E). Limited edition. Imported from Germany by Merkel USA.
Price: Model 47EL $8,995.00
Price: Model 147EL $8,795.00

MERKEL MODEL 280EL, 360EL
Similar to Model 47E except smaller frame. Greener cross bolt with double under-barrel locking lugs, fine engraved hunting scenes on silver-grayed receiver, luxury-grade wood, Anson and Deeley boxlock action. H&H ejectors, single-selective or double triggers. Introduced 2000. Imported from Germany by Merkel USA.
Price: Model 280EL (28 gauge, 28" barrel, Imp. Cyl. and Mod. chokes)..$8,695.00
Price: Model 360EL (.410, 28" barrel, Mod. and Full chokes)...$7,695.00
Price: Model 280EL Combo $12,995.00

MERKEL MODEL 280SL AND 360SL
Similar to Model 280EL and 360EL except has sidelock action, double triggers, English-style arabesque engraving. Introduced 2000. Imported from Germany by Merkel USA.
Price: Model 280SL (28 gauge, 28" barrel, Imp. Cyl. and Mod. chokes)...$12,995.00
Price: Model 360SL (.410, 28" barrel, Mod. and Full chokes)...$12,995.00

MERKEL MODEL 1620
Gauge: 16. **Features:** Greener crossbolt with double under-barrel locking lugs, scroll-engraved case-hardened receiver, Anson and Deeley boxlock action, Holland & Holland ejectors, English-style stock, single selective or double triggers, or pistol grip stock with single selective trgger. Imported from Germany by Merkel USA.
Price: $4,995.00
Price: Model 1620E; silvered, engraved receiver $5,995.00
Price: Model 1620 Combo; 16- and 20-gauge two-barrel set $8,695.00
Price: Model 1620EL; upgraded wood $8,695.00
Price: Model 1620EL Combo; 16- and 20-gauge two-barrel set $12,195.00

MERKEL MODEL 40E
Gauge: 12, 20. **Barrels:** 28" (12), 26 ¾" (20). **Weight:** 6.2 lbs. **Features:** Anson & Deeley locks, Greener-style crossbolt, automatic ejectors, choice of double or single trigger, blue finish, checkered walnut stock with cheekpiece.
Price: $4,795.00

MOSSBERG SILVER RESERVE II SXS
Gauge: 12, 20, 28. **Barrels:** 26 or 28 inches with front bead sight, five choke tubes. **Stock:** Select black walnut. **Weight:** 6.5 to 7.5 pounds. Side-by-side companion to over/under model with same Silver Reserve name. Blue barrels, silver receiver with scroll engraving. Single non-selective trigger with standard extractors.
Price: $1,067.00

PIOTTI KING NO. 1
Gauge: 12, 16, 20, 28, .410. **Barrel:** 25" to 30" (12 ga.), 25" to 28" (16, 20, 28, .410). To customer specs. Chokes as specified. **Weight:** 6.5 lbs. to 8 lbs. (12 ga. to customer specs.). **Stock:** Dimensions to customer specs. Finely figured walnut; straight grip with checkered butt with classic splinter fore-end and hand-rubbed oil finish standard. Pistol grip, beavertail fore-end. **Features:** Holland & Holland pattern sidelock action, automatic ejectors. Double trigger; non-selective single trigger optional. Coin finish standard; color case-hardened optional. Top rib; level, file-cut; concave, ventilated optional. Very fine, full coverage scroll engraving with small floral bouquets. Imported from Italy by Wm. Larkin Moore.
Price: From $37,900.00

PIOTTI LUNIK SIDE-BY-SIDE SHOTGUN
Similar to the Piotti King No. 1 in overall quality. Has Renaissance-style large scroll engraving in relief. Best quality Holland & Holland-pattern sidelock ejector double with chopper lump (demi-bloc) barrels. Other mechanical specifications remain the same. Imported from Italy by Wm. Larkin Moore.
Price: From $40,825.00

PIOTTI PIUMA
Gauge: 12, 16, 20, 28, .410. **Barrel:** 25" to 30" (12 ga.), 25" to 28" (16, 20, 28, .410). **Weight:** 5-1/2 to 6-1/4 lbs. (20 ga.). **Stock:** Dimensions to customer specs. Straight grip stock with walnut checkered butt, classic splinter fore-end, hand-rubbed oil finish are standard; pistol grip, beavertail fore-end, satin luster finish optional. **Features:** Anson & Deeley boxlock ejector double with chopper lump barrels. Level, file-cut rib, light scroll and rosette engraving, scalloped frame. Double triggers; single non-selective optional. Coin finish standard, color case-hardened optional. Imported from Italy by Wm. Larkin Moore.
Price: From $19,800.00

Prices given are believed to be accurate at time of publication however, many factors affect retail pricing so exact prices are not possible.

SHOTGUNS Side-by-Side

SKB 200 SERIES
Gauge: 12, 20, .410, 3" chambers; 28, 2¾-inches. **Barrel:** 26", 28". Five choke tubes provided (F, IM, M, IC, SK). **Stock:** Hand checkered and oil finished Turkish walnut. Price of Wales grip and beavertail fore-end. **Weight:** 6 to 7 lbs. **Sights:** Brass bead. **Features:** Boxlock with platform lump barrel design. Polished bright blue finish with charcoal color case hardening on receiver. Manual safety, automatic ejectors, single selective trigger. 200 HR target model has high ventilated rib, full pistol grip. 250 model has decorative color case hardened sideplates. Imported from Turkey by GU, Inc.

Price: 12, 20 ga...$2,100.00
Price: 28, .410..$2,250.00
Price: 200 HR 12, 20 ga.............................$2,500.00
Price: 200 HR 28, .410..............................$2,625.00
Price: 250 12, 20 ga.................................$2,600.00
Price: 250 28, .410...................................$2,725.00

SKB 7000SL SIDELOCK
Gauge: 12, 20. **Barrel:** 28", 30". Five choke tubes provided (F, IM, M, IC, SK). **Stock:** Premium Turkish walnut with hand-rubbed oil finish, fine-line hand checkering, Price of Wales grip and beavertail fore-end. **Weight:** 6 to 7 lbs. **Sights:** Brass bead. **Features:** Sidelock design with Holland & Holland style seven-pin removable locks with safety sears. Bison Bone Charcoal case hardening, hand engraved sculpted sidelock receiver. Manual safety, automatic ejectors, single selective trigger. Available by special order only. Imported from Turkey by GU, Inc.

Price: From $6,700.00

STOEGER UPLANDER
Gauge: 12, 20, .410, 3" chambers; 28, 2-3/4 chambers. **Barrel:** 22", 24", 26", 28". **Weight:** 6.5 to 7.3 lbs. **Sights:** Brass bead. **Features:** Double trigger, IC & M choke tubes included with gun. Other choke tubes available. Tang auto safety, extractors, black plastic buttplate.

Imported by Benelli USA.
Price: Standard..$499.00
Price: Supreme (single trigger, AA-grade wood) $539.00
Price: Longfowler (12 ga., 30" bbl.) $499.00
Price: Home Defense (20 or 12 ga., 20" bbl., tactical sights) ..$499.00
Price: Double Defense (20 ga.) fiber optic sight, accessory rail.$499.00

STOEGER COACH GUN
Gauge: 12, 20, 2-3/4", 3" chambers. **Barrel:** 20". **Weight:** 6.5 lbs. **Stock:** Brown hardwood, classic beavertail fore-end. **Sights:** Brass bead. **Features:** Double or single trigger, IC & M choke tubes included, others available. Tang auto safety, extractors, black plastic buttplate. Imported by Benelli USA.

Price: .... $449.00 to $499.00

WEBLEY & SCOTT SXS SERIES
Gauge: 12, 20. **Barrels:** 28 inches, five interchangeable choke tubes. **Weight:** 6.5 to 7.5 lbs. **Stock:** Oil finished, hand-checkered Turkish walnut with recoil pad, splinter fore-end. **Features:** Automatic ejectors, single selective trigger, ventilated rib, tang selector/safety, charcoal case hardened receiver, English scroll engraving. 3000 Model is a high-grade gun with hand-rubbed oil-finished premium-grade walnut stock with checkered butt, jeweled monobloc walls, higher grade English scroll engraving, and comes with high quality, fleeced line lockable case. Made in Turkey and imported by Centurion International.

Price: Model 2000...$2,500.00
Price: Model 3000...$6,000.00

BERETTA DT10 TRIDENT TRAP TOP SINGLE
Gauge: 12, 3" chamber. **Barrel:** 34"; five Optima Choke tubes (Full, Full, Imp. Modified, Mod. and Imp. Cyl.). **Weight:** 8.8 lbs. **Stock:** High-grade walnut; adjustable. **Features:** Detachable, adjustable trigger group; Optima Bore for improved shot pattern and reduced recoil; slim Optima Choke tubes; raised and thickened receiver for long life. Introduced 2000. Imported from Italy by Beretta USA.
Price: $8,650.00

BROWNING BT-99 TRAP
Gauge: 12. **Barrel:** 30", 32", 34". **Stock:** Walnut; standard or adjustable. **Weight:** 7 lbs. 11 oz. to 9 lbs. **Features:** Back-bored single barrel; interchangeable chokes; beavertail forearm; extractor only; high rib.
Price: BT-99 w/conventional comb, 32" or 34" barrels $1,430.00
Price: BT-99 w/adjustable comb, 32" or 34" barrels $1,680.00
Price: BT-99 Golden Clays w/adjustable comb, 32" or 34" barrels $4,340.00
Price: BT-99 Grade III .... $2,540.00 to $2,840.00

BROWNING A-BOLT SHOTGUN HUNTER
Gauge: 12 ga. 3" chamber. **Barrel:** 22". **Weight:** 7 lbs. 2 ozs. **Length:** 43.75". **Stock:** Satin finish walnut stock and forearm – checkered. **Features:** Drilled and tapped for scope mounts, 60° bolt action lift, detachable two-round magazine, and top-tang safety. Sling swivel studs installed, recoil pad, TRUGLO/Marble's fiber-optic front sight with rear sight adjustable for windage and elevation.
Price: $1,280.00

BROWNING A-BOLT SHOTGUN, MOSSY OAK BREAK-UP INFINITY
Gauge: 12 ga. 3" chamber. **Barrel:** 22". **Weight:** 7 lbs. 2 ozs. **Length:** 43.75". **Stock:** Composite stock and forearm, textured gripping surfaces, Mossy Oak Break-Up Infinitycamo finish • Dura-Touch Armor Coating. **Features:** Drilled and tapped for scope mounts, 60° bolt action lift, detachable two-round magazine, and top-tang safety. Sling swivel studs installed, rrecoil pad, TRUGLO/Marble's fiber-optic front sight with rear sight adjustable for windage and elevation.
Price: From $1,300.00

BROWNING A-BOLT SHOTGUN STALKER
Gauge: 12 ga. 3" chamber. **Barrel:** 22". **Weight:** 7 lbs. **Length:** 43.75". **Stock:** Composite stock and forearm, textured gripping surfaces, Dura-Touch Armor Coating. **Features:** Drilled and tapped for scope mounts, 60° bolt action lift, detachable two-round magazine, and top-tang safety. Sling swivel studs installed, rrecoil pad, TRUGLO/Marble's fiber-optic front sight with rear sight adjustable for windage and elevation.
Price: From $1,150.00

HARRINGTON & RICHARDSON ULTRA SLUG HUNTER/TAMER
Gauge: 12, 20 ga., 3" chamber, .410. **Barrel:** 20" to 24" rifled. **Weight:** 6 to 9 lbs. **Length:** 34.5" to 40". **Stock:** Hardwood, laminate, or polymer with full pistol grip; semi-beavertail fore-end. **Sights:** Gold bead front. **Features:** Break-open action with side-lever release,

automatic ejector. Introduced 1994. From H&R 1871, LLC.
Price: Ultra Slug Hunter, blued, hardwood $291.00
Price: Ultra Slug Hunter Youth, blued, hardwood, 13-1/8" LOP..$291.00
Price: Ultra Slug Hunter Deluxe, blued, laminated $291.00
Price: Tamer .410 bore, stainless barrel, black polymer stock..$193.00

HARRINGTON & RICHARDSON ULTRA LITE SLUG HUNTER
Gauge: 12, 20 ga., 3" chamber. **Barrel:** 24" rifled. **Weight:** 5.25 lbs. **Length:** 40". **Stock:** Hardwood with walnut finish, full pistol grip, recoil pad, sling swivel studs. **Sights:** None; base included. **Features:** Youth Model, available in 20 ga. has 20" rifled barrel. Deluxe Model has checkered laminated stock and fore-end. From H&R 1871, LLC.
Price: $194.00

HARRINGTON & RICHARDSON ULTRA SLUG HUNTER THUMBHOLE STOCK
Similar to the Ultra Lite Slug Hunter but with laminated thumbhole stock and weighs 8.5 lbs.
Price: $401.00

HARRINGTON & RICHARDSON PARDNER AND TRACKER II
Gauge: 10, 12, 16, 20, 28, .410, up to 3.5" chamber for 10 and 12 ga. 16, 28, 2-3/4" chamber. **Barrel:** 24" to 30". **Weight:** Varies from 5 to 9.5 lbs. **Length:** Varies from 36" to 48". **Stock:** Walnut-finished hardwood with full pistol grip, synthetic, or camo finish. **Sights:** Bead front on most. **Features:** Transfer bar ignition; break-open action with side-lever release.
Price: Pardner, all gauges, hardwood stock, 26" to 32" blued barrel, Mod. or Full choke....................................$206.00
Price: Turkey model, 10/12 ga., camo finish or black....................................$277.00 to $322.00
Price: Youth Turkey, 20 ga., camo finish or black....................$192.00
Price: Waterfowl, 10 ga., camo finish or hardwood.................$227.00
Price: Tracker II slug gun, 12/20 ga., hardwood......................$291.00

KRIEGHOFF K-80 SINGLE BARREL TRAP GUN
Gauge: 12, 2-3/4" chamber. **Barrel:** 32" or 34" Unsingle. Fixed Full or choke tubes. **Weight:** About 8-3/4 lbs. **Stock:** Four stock dimensions or adjustable stock available. All hand-checkered European walnut. **Features:** Satin nickel finish. Selective mechanical trigger adjustable for finger position. Tapered step vent rib. Adjustable point of impact.
Price: Standard grade Full Unsingle, from...........................$10,595.00

KRIEGHOFF KX-6 TRAP GUN
Gauge: 12, 2-3/4" chamber. **Barrel:** 32", 34"; choke tubes. **Weight:** About 8.5 lbs. **Stock:** Factory adjustable stock. European walnut. **Features:** Ventilated tapered step rib. Adjustable position trigger, optional release trigger. Fully adjustable rib. Satin gray electroless nickel receiver. Fitted aluminum case. Imported from Germany by

Krieghoff International, Inc.
Price: $5,495.00

LJUTIC MONO GUN SINGLE BARREL

Gauge: 12 only. **Barrel:** 34", choked to customer specs; hollow-milled rib, 35.5" sight plane. **Weight:** Approx. 9 lbs. **Stock:** To customer specs. Oil finish, hand checkered. **Features:** Custom gun. Pull or release trigger; removable trigger guard contains trigger and hammer mechanism; Ljutic pushbutton opener on front of trigger guard. From Ljutic Industries.
Price: Std., med. or Olympic rib, custom bbls.,
  fixed choke. $7,495.00
Price: Stainless steel mono gun $8,495.00

LJUTIC LTX PRO 3 DELUXE MONO GUN

Deluxe, lightweight version of the Mono gun with high quality wood, upgrade checkering, special rib height, screw-in chokes, ported and cased.
Price: $8,995.00
Price: Stainless steel model................................... $9,995.00

ROSSI CIRCUIT JUDGE

Revolving shotgun chambered in .410 (2-1/2- or 3-inch/.45 Colt. Based on Taurus Judge handgun. Features include 18.5-inch barrel; fiber optic front sight; 5-round cylinder; hardwood Monte Carlo stock.
Price: $669.00

ROSSI SINGLE-SHOT

Gauge: 12, 20, .410. **Barrel:** 22" (Youth), 28". **Weight:** 3.75-5.25 lbs. Stocks: Wood. **Sights:** Bead front sight, fully adjustable fiber optic sight on Slug and Turkey. **Features:** Single-shot break open, 8

models available, positive ejection, internal transfer bar mechanism, trigger block system, Taurus Security System, blued finish, Rifle Slug has ported barrel.
Price: From $171.00

SKB CENTURY III TRAP

Single-shot, break-open 12 gauge with 2 ¾" chamber, SKB Competition Choke Tube System with three choke tubes. **Barrel:** 30 or 32 inches with lengthened forcing cone. **Stock:** Oil finished Grade II Turkish walnut, right or left-hand cast, Pachmayr SXT recoil pad. Adjustable comb and buttplate system is available. Imported from Turkey by GU, Inc.
Price: $1,150.00
Price: Adjustable comb $1,300.00
Price: Adjustable comb and buttstock $1,430.00

TAR-HUNT RSG-12 PROFESSIONAL RIFLED SLUG GUN

Gauge: 12, 2-3/4" or 3" chamber, 1-shot magazine. **Barrel:** 23", fully rifled with muzzle brake. **Weight:** 7.75 lbs. **Length:** 41.5" overall. **Stock:** Matte black McMillan fiberglass with Pachmayr Decelerator pad. **Sights:** None furnished; comes with Leupold windage or Weaver bases. **Features:** Uses rifle-style action with two locking lugs; two-position safety; Shaw barrel; single-stage, trigger; muzzle brake. Many options available. All models have area-controlled feed action. Introduced 1991. Made in U.S. by Tar-Hunt Custom Rifles, Inc.
Price: 12 ga. Professional model $2,895.00
Price: Left-hand model $3,000.00

TAR-HUNT RSG-16 ELITE

Similar to RSG-12 Professional except 16 gauge; right- or left-hand versions.
Price: $2,895.00

TAR-HUNT RSG-20 MOUNTAINEER SLUG GUN

Similar to the RSG-12 Professional except chambered for 20 gauge (2-3/4" and 3" shells); 23" Shaw rifled barrel, with muzzle brake; two-lug bolt; one-shot blind magazine; matte black finish; McMillan fiberglass stock with Pachmayr Decelerator pad; receiver drilled and tapped for Rem. 700 bases. Right- or left-hand versions. Weighs 6.5 lbs. Introduced 1997. Made in U.S.A. by Tar-Hunt Custom Rifles, Inc.
Price: $2,895.00

BENELLI M3 CONVERTIBLE
Gauge: 12, 2-3/4", 3" chambers, 5-shot magazine. **Barrel:** 19.75" (Cyl.). **Weight:** 7 lbs., 4oz. **Length:** 41" overall. **Stock:** High-impact polymer with sling loop in side of butt; rubberized pistol grip on stock. **Sights:** Open rifle, fully adjustable. Ghost ring and rifle type. **Features:** Combination pump/auto action. Alloy receiver with inertia recoil rotating locking lug bolt; matte finish; automatic shell release lever. Introduced 1989. Imported by Benelli USA. Price with pistol grip, open rifle sights.
Price: With ghost ring sights, pistol grip stock **$1,589.00**

BENELLI M2 TACTICAL
Gauge: 12, 2-3/4", 3" chambers, 5-shot magazine. **Barrel:** 18.5" IC, M, F choke tubes. **Weight:** 6.7 lbs. **Length:** 39.75" overall. **Stock:** Black polymer. **Sights:** Rifle type ghost ring system, tritium night sights optional. **Features:** Semiauto intertia recoil action. Cross-bolt safety; bolt release button; matte-finish metal. Introduced 1993. Imported from Italy by Benelli USA.
Price: from .... **$1,239.00 to $1,359.00**

BENELLI M4 TACTICAL
Gauge: 12, 3" chamber. **Barrel:** 18.5". **Weight:** 7.8 lbs. **Length:** 40" overall. **Stock:** Synthetic. **Sights:** Ghost Ring rear, fixed blade front. **Features:** Auto-regulating gas-operated (ARGO) action, choke tube, Picatinny rail, standard and collapsible stocks available, optional LE tactical gun case. Introduced 2006. Imported from Italy by Benelli USA.
Price: From **$1,899.00**

KEL-TEC KSG BULL-PUP TWIN-TUBE
Gauge: 12. **Capacity:** 13+1. **Barrel:** 18.5". **Overall Length:** 26.1". **Weight:** 8.5 lbs. (loaded). Pump action shotgun with two magazine tubes. The shotgun bears a resemblance to the South African designed Neostead pump-action gun. The operator is able to move a switch located near the top of the grip to select the right or left tube, or move the switch to the center to eject a shell without chambering another round. Optional accessories include a factory installed Picatinny rail with flip-up sights and a pistol grip.
Price: **$990.00**

MOSSBERG MODEL 500 SPECIAL PURPOSE
Gauge: 12, 20, .410, 3" chamber. **Barrel:** 18.5", 20" (Cyl.). **Weight:** 7 lbs. **Stock:** Walnut-finished hardwood or black synthetic. **Sights:** Metal bead front. **Features:** Available in 6- or 8-shot models. Top-mounted safety, double action slide bars, swivel studs, rubber recoil pad. Blue, Parkerized, Marinecote finishes. Mossberg Cablelock included. The HS410 Home Security model chambered for .410 with 3" chamber; has pistol grip fore-end, thick recoil pad, muzzle brake and has special spreader choke on the 18.5" barrel. Overall length is 37.5", weight is 6.25 lbs. Blue finish; synthetic field stock. Mossberg Cablelock and video included. Mariner model has Marinecote metal

finish to resist rust and corrosion. Synthetic field stock; pistol grip kit included. 500 Tactical 6-shot has black synthetic tactical stock. Introduced 1990.
Price: 500 Mariner **$616.00**
Price: HS410 Home Security **$502.00**
Price: FLEX Tactical ....**$583.00 to $630.00**
Price: 500 Chainsaw pistol grip only; removable top handle ...**$525.00**
Price: JIC **$484.00**
Price: Thunder Ranch **$498.00**

MOSSBERG MODEL 590 SPECIAL PURPOSE
Gauge: 12, 20, .410 3" chamber, 9 shot magazine. **Barrel:** 20" (Cyl.). **Weight:** 7.25 lbs. **Stock:** Synthetic field or Speedfeed. **Sights:** Metal bead front or Ghost Ring. **Features:** Top-mounted safety, double slide action bars. Comes with heat shield, bayonet lug, swivel studs, rubber recoil pad. Blue, Parkerized or Marinecote finish. Mossberg Cablelock included. From Mossberg.
Price: From **$542.00**
Price: Flex Tactical..**$652.00**
Price: Tactical Tri-Rail Adjustable **$853.00**
Price: Mariner **$734.00**

MOSSBERG 930 SPECIAL PURPOSE SERIES
Gauge: 12 ga., 3" chamber. **Barrel:** 28" flat ventilated rib. **Weight:** 7.3 lbs. **Length:** 49". **Stock:** Composite stock with close radius pistol grip; Speed Lock forearm; textured gripping surfaces; shim adjustable for length of pull, cast and drop; Mossy Oak Bottomland camo finish; Dura-Touch Armor Coating. **Features:** 930 Special Purpose shotguns feature a self-regulating gas system that vents excess gas to aid in recoil reduction and eliminate stress on critical components. All 930 autoloaders chamber both 2 3/4 inch and 3-inch 12-gauge shotshells with ease—from target loads, to non-toxic magnum loads, to the latest sabot slug ammo. Magazine capacity is 7+1 on models with extended magazine tube, 4+1 on models without. To complete the package, each Mossberg 930 includes a set of specially designed spacers for quick adjustment of the horizontal and vertical angle of the stock, bringing a custom-feel fit to every shooter. All 930 Special Purpose models feature a drilled and tapped receiver, factory-ready for Picatinny rail, scope base or optics installation. 930 SPX models conveniently come with a factory-mounted Picatinny rail and LPA/M16-Style Ghost Ring combination sight right out of the box. Other sighting options include a basic front bead, or white-dot front sights. Mossberg 930 Special Purpose shotguns are available in a variety of configurations; 5-shot tactical barrel, 5-shot with muzzle brake, 8-shot pistol-grip, and even a 5-shot security / field combo.
Price: Tactical 5-Shot..**$714.00**
Price: Home Security **$662.00**
Price: Standard Stock **$787.00**
Price: Pistol Grip 8-shot **$883.00**
Price: 5-shot Combo w/extra 18.5" barrel...................**$679.00**

REMINGTON MODEL 870 PUMP AND MODEL 1100 AUTOLOADER TACTICAL SHOTGUNS
Gauge: 870: 12, 2-3/4 or 3" chamber; 1100: 2-3/4". **Barrel:** 18", 20", 22" (Cyl or IC). **Weight:** 7.5-7.75 lbs. **Length:** 38.5-42.5" overall. **Stock:** Black synthetic, synthetic Speedfeed IV full pistol-grip stock, or Knoxx

SHOTGUNS Military & Police

Industries SpecOps stock w/recoil-absorbing spring-loaded cam and adjustable length of pull (12" to 16", 870 only). **Sights:** Front post w/ dot only on 870; rib and front dot on 1100. **Features:** R3 recoil pads, LimbSaver technology to reduce felt recoil, 2-, 3- or 4-shot extensions based on barrel length; matte-olive-drab barrels and receivers. Model 1100 Tactical is available with Speedfeed IV pistol grip stock or standard black synthetic stock and fore-end. Speedfeed IV model has an 18" barrel with two-shot extension. Standard synthetic-stocked version is equipped with 22" barrel and four-shot extension. Introduced 2006. From Remington Arms Co.

Price: 870 Express Tactical Knoxx 20 ga. $555.00
Price: 870 Express Magpul...$898.00
Price: 870 Special Purpose Marine (nickel) $841.00
Price: 1100 TAC-4 ....$1,015.00

REMINGTON 870 EXPRESS TACTICAL A-TACS CAMO
Pump action shotgun chambered for 2-3/4- and 3-inch 12-ga. Features include full A-TACS digitized camo; 18-1/2-inch barrel; extended ported Tactical RemChoke; SpeedFeed IV pistol-grip stock with SuperCell recoil pad; fully adjustable XS Ghost Ring Sight rail with removable white bead front sight; 7-round capacity with factory-installed 2-shot extension; drilled and tapped receiver; sling swivel stud.
Price: $720.00

REMINGTON 887 NITRO MAG TACTICAL
Pump action shotgun chambered in 12-ga., 2-3/4 to 3-1/2 inch. Features include 18-1/2-inch barrel with ported, extended tactical RemChoke; 2-shot magazine extension; barrel clamp with integral Picatinny rails; ArmorLokt coating; synthetic stock and fore-end with specially contour grip panels.
Price: $534.00

TACTICAL RESPONSE STANDARD MODEL
Gauge: 12, 3" chamber, 7-shot magazine. **Barrel:** 18" (Cyl.). **Weight:** 9 lbs. **Length:** 38" overall. **Stock:** Fiberglass-filled polypropolene with non-snag recoil absorbing butt pad. Nylon tactical fore-end houses flashlight. **Sights:** Trak-Lock ghost ring sight system. Front sight has Tritium insert. **Features:** Highly modified Remington 870P with Parkerized finish. Comes with nylon three-way adjustable sling, high visibility non-binding follower, high performance magazine spring, Jumbo Head safety, and Side Saddle extended 6-shot shell carrier on left side of receiver. Introduced 1991. From Scattergun Technologies, Inc.
Price: Standard model, from.................................$1,540.00
Price: Border Patrol model, from $1,135.00
Price: Professional Model 13" bbl. (Law enf., military only)...$1,550.00

TRISTAR COBRA
Gauge: 12, 3". **Barrel:** 28". **Weight:** 6.7 lbs. Three Beretta-style choke tubes (IC, M, F). **Length:** NA. **Stock:** Matte black synthetic stock and forearm. **Sights:** Vent rib with matted sight plane. **Features:** Five-year warranty. Cobra Tactical Pump Shotgun magazine holds 7, return spring in forearm, 20" barrel, Cylinder choke. Introduced 2008. Imported by Tristar Sporting Arms Ltd.
Price: Tactical.. $319.00 to $429.00

TRISTAR TEC12 AUTO/PUMP
Gauge: 12. 3-inch chamber. 20-inch ported barrel with fixed cylinder choke. Capable of operating in pump-action or semi-auto model with the turn of a dial. **Stock:** Pistol-grip synthetic with matte black finish. **Weight:** 7.4 lbs. **Sights:** Ghost-ring rear, raised bridge fiber-optic front. Picatinny rail.
Price: $689

WINCHESTER SXP EXTREME DEFENDER
Gauge: 12. 3-inch chamber. Pump action. **Barrel:** 18-inches with chrome-plated chamber and bore, "door breaching" ported choke tube. **Stock:** Adjustable military-style buttstock with vertical pistol grip. **Sights:** Ghost-ring rear integrated with Picatinny rail. Matte black finish.
Price: $560.00
Price: Marine Model with hard chrome metal finish $620.00

Prices given are believed to be accurate at time of publication however, many factors affect retail pricing so exact prices are not possible.

71ST EDITION, 2017 — **503**

CARLETON UNDERHAMMER MATCH PERCUSSION PISTOL

Caliber: .36. **Barrel:** 9.5 in., browned octagonal, rifled. **Weight:** 2.25 lbs. **Length:** 16.75 in. overall. **Stocks:** Walnut grip. **Sights:** Blade front, open rear, adjustable for elevation. **Features:** Percussion, under-hammer ignition, adjustable trigger, no half cock. No ramrod. Made by Pedersoli. Imported by Dixie Gun Works.
Price: Dixie, FH0332 .... **$915.00**

CVA OPTIMA PISTOL

Caliber: .50. **Barrel:** 14 in., 1:28-in. twist, Cerakote finish. **Weight:** 3.7 lbs. **Length:** 19 in. **Stocks:** Black synthetic, Realtree Xtra Green. **Ramrod:** Aluminum. **Sights:** Scope base mounted. **Features:** Break-open action, all stainless construction, quick-removal breech plug for 209 primer. From CVA.
Price: PP222SM Stainless/Realtree Xtra, rail mount **$318.00**
Price: PP221SM Stainless/black, rail mount **$378.00**

FRENCH AN IX, AN XIII AND GENDARMERIE NAPOLEONIC PISTOLS

Caliber: .69. **Barrel:** 8.25 in. **Weight:** 3 lbs. **Length:** 14 in. overall. **Stocks:** Walnut. **Sights:** None. **Features:** Flintlock, case-hardened lock, brass furniture, buttcap, lock marked "Imperiale de S. Etienne." Steel ramrod. Other Napoleonic pistols include half-stocked "AN XIII" and Gendarmerie with 5.25-inch barrel. Made by Pedersoli. Imported by Dixie Gun Works.
Price: Dixie Gun Works FH0890 .... **$740.00**
Price: Dixie Gun Works AN XIII FHO895................................ **$710.00**
Price: Dixie Gun Works Gendarmerie FHO954........................ **$665.00**

HARPER'S FERRY 1805 PISTOL

Caliber: .58. **Barrel:** 10 in. **Weight:** 2.5 lbs. **Length:** 16 in. overall. **Stocks:** Walnut. **Sights:** Fixed. **Features:** Flintlock. Case-hardened lock, brass-mounted German silver-colored barrel. Wooden ramrod. Replica of the first U.S. government made flintlock pistol. Made by Pedersoli. Imported by Dixie Gun Works.
Price: Dixie Gun Works RH0225 .... **$565.00**
Price: Dixie Gun Works Kit RH0411.. **$433.00**

HOWDAH HUNTER PISTOLS

Caliber: .50, 20 gauge, .58 **Barrels:** 11.25 in., blued, rifled in .50 and .58 calibers **Weight:** 4.25 to 5 lbs. **Length:** 17.25 in. **Stocks:** American walnut with checkered grip. **Sights:** Brass bead front sight. **Features:** Blued barrels, swamped barrel rib, engraved, color case-hardened locks and hammers, captive steel ramrod. Available with detachable shoulder stock, case, holster and mold. Made by Pedersoli. Imported by Dixie Gun Works, and individual models by Cabela's, Taylor's and others.
Price: Dixie, 50X50, PH0572 .... **$850.00**

Price: Dixie, 58XD58, PH09024 .... **$875.00**
Price: Dixie, 20X20 gauge, PH0581 .... **$815.00**
Price: Dixie, 50X20 gauge, PH0581 .... **$850.00**
Price: Dixie, 50X50, Kit, PK0952 .... **$640.00**
Price: Dixie, 50X20, Kit, PK1410.. **$675.00**
Price: Dixie, 20X20, Kit, PK0954.. **$640.00**

KENTUCKY PISTOL

Caliber: .45, .50, .54 **Barrel:** 10.25 in. **Weight:** 2.5 lbs. **Length:** 15.4 in. overall. **Stocks:** Walnut with smooth rounded birds-head grip. **Sights:** Fixed. **Features:** Available in flint or percussion ignition in various calibers. Case-hardened lock, blued barrel, drift-adjustable rear sights, blade front. Wooden ramrod. Kit guns of all models available from Dixie Gun Works. Made by Pedersoli. Imported by Dixie Gun Works, EMF and others.
Price: .45 Percussion, Dixie, PH0440 .... **$350.00**
Price: .45 Flint, Dixie, PH0430 .... **$375.00**
Price: .45 Flint, Dixie, Kit FH0320 .... **$299.00**
Price: .50 Flint, Dixie, PH0935 .... **$435.00**
Price: .50 Percussion, Dixie, PH0930 .... **$395.00**
Price: .54 Flint, Dixie, PH0080 .... **$440.00**
Price: .54 Percussion, Dixie,PH0330 .... **$395.00**
Price: .54 Percussion, Dixie, Kit PK0436 .... **$283.00**
Price: .45 Flint, Navy Moll, brass buttcap,
Dixie, PK0436 .... **$610.00**
Price: .45 Percussion, Navy Moll, brass buttcap,
Dixie, PK0903 ....**$565.00**

LE PAGE PERCUSSION DUELING PISTOL

Caliber: .44 (Pedersoli), .45 (Armi, Chiappa). **Barrel:** 10.25 in. browned octagon, rifled. **Weight:** 2.5 lbs. **Length:** 16.6 in. overall. **Stocks:** Walnut, rounded checkered butt (Pedersoli), fluted butt (Armi). **Sights:** Blade front, open-style rear. **Features:** Single set trigger (Pedersoli), double set (Armi) trigger. Browned barrel (Dixie International). Bright barrel, silver-plated brass furniture (Armi). External ramrod. Made by Pedersoli, Armi, Chiappa. Imported by Dixie Gun Works.
Price: Dixie, Pedersoli, PH0431 ....**$925.00**
Price: Dixie, International, Pedersoli, PH0231 ....**$1,250.00**
Price: Dixie, Armi, PH0310 .... **$627.00**

LYMAN PLAINS PISTOL

Caliber: .50 or .54. **Barrel:** 8 in.; 1:30-in. twist, both calibers. **Weight:** 50 oz. **Length:** 15 in. overall. **Stocks:** Walnut. **Sights:** Blade front, square-notch rear adjustable for windage. **Features:** Polished brass triggerguard and ramrod tip, color case-hardened coil spring lock, spring-loaded trigger, stainless steel nipple, blackened iron furniture. Hooked patent breech, detachable belt hook. Introduced 1981. From Lyman Products.
Price: 6010608 .50-cal.. **$419.95**
Price: 6010609 .54-cal..**$419.95**
Price: 6010610 .50-cal Kit **$349.95**
Price: 6010611 .54-cal. Kit... **.$349.95**

Prices given are believed to be accurate at time of publication however, many factors affect retail pricing so exact prices are not possible.

MAMELOUK
Caliber: .54. **Barrel:** 7-5/8 in., bright. **Weight:** 1.61 lbs. **Length:** 13 in. overall. **Stocks:** Walnut, with brass end cap and medallion. **Sights:** Blade front. **Features:** Flint, lanyard ring, wooden ramrod. Made by Davide Pedersoli. Available on order from IFG (Italian Firearms Group)
Price: $445.00

MORTIMER TARGET PISTOL
Caliber: .44. **Barrel:** 10 in., bright octagonal on Standard, browned on Deluxe, rifled. **Weight:** 2.25 lbs. **Length:** 16 in. overall. Stocks: Walnut, checkered saw-handle grip on Deluxe. **Sights:** Blade front, open-style rear. **Features:** Percussion or flint, single set trigger, sliding hammer safety, engraved lock on Deluxe. Wooden ramrod. Made by Pedersoli. Imported by Dixie Gun Works
Price: Dixie, Flint, FH0316 ....**$1,175.00**
Price: Dixie, Percussion, PH0231 ....**$1,095.00**
Price: Dixie, Deluxe, FH0950 ....**$2,200.00**

PEDERSOLI MANG TARGET PISTOL
Caliber: .38. **Barrel:** 10.5 in., octagonal; 1:15-in. twist. **Weight:** 2.5 lbs. **Length:** 17.25 in. overall. Stocks: Walnut with fluted grip. **Sights:** Blade front, open rear adjustable for windage. **Features:** Browned barrel, polished breech plug, remainder color case-hardened. Made by Pedersoli. Imported by Dixie Gun Works.
Price: PH0503.. **$1,750.00**

PHILADELPHIA DERRINGER
Caliber: .45, browned, rifled. **Weight:** .5 lbs. **Length:** 6.215 in. Grips: European walnut checkered. **Sights:** V-notch rear, blade front. **Features:** Back-hammer percussion lock with engraving, single trigger. From Pedersoli. Sold by Dixie Gun Works.
Price: Dixie, PH0913 .... **$550.00**
Price: Dixie, Kit PK0863 .... **$385.00**

QUEEN ANNE FLINTLOCK PISTOL

Caliber: .50. **Barrel:** 7.5 in., smoothbore. Stocks: Walnut. **Sights:** None. **Features:** Flintlock, German silver-colored steel barrel, fluted brass triggerguard, brass mask on butt. Lockplate left in the white. No ramrod. Introduced 1983. Made by Pedersoli. Imported by Dixie Gun Works.
Price: Dixie, RH0211.. **$495.00**
Price: Dixie, Kit, FH0421 .... **$470.00**

REMINGTON RIDER DERRINGER
Caliber: 4.3 mm (BB lead balls only). **Barrel:** 2.1 in., blued, rifled. **Weight:** .25 lbs. **Length:** 4.75 in. Grips: All-steel construction. **Sights:** V-notch rear, bead front. **Features:** Fires percussion cap only – no powder. Available as case-hardened frame or polished white. From Pedersoli. Sold by Dixie Gun Works.
Price: Dixie, Casehardened PH0923 . ... **$210.00**

SCREW BARREL PISTOL
Caliber: .44. **Barrel:** 2.35 in., blued, rifled. **Weight:** .5 lbs. **Length:** 6.5 in. Grips: European walnut. **Sights:** None. **Features:** Percussion,

boxlock with center hammer, barrel unscrews for loading from rear, folding trigger, external hammer, combination barrel and nipple wrench furnished. From Pedersoli. Sold by Dixie Gun Works.
Price: Dixie, PH0530 .... **$210.00**
Price: Dixie, PH0545 .... **$165.00**

TRADITIONS CROCKETT PISTOL
Caliber: .32. **Barrel:** 10 in., 1:48 in. twist. **Weight:** 2.75 lbs. **Length:** 15 in. **Stocks:** Hardwood full stock. **Sights:** Notched rear brass blade front. **Features:** Polished brass triggerguard and ramrod tip, blued leaf spring lock, spring-loaded trigger, No. 11 percussion nipple, no ramrod. From Traditions.
Price: P1060 Finished **$249.00**

TRADITIONS KENTUCKY PISTOL
Caliber: .50. **Barrel:** 10 in., 1:20 in. twist. **Weight:** 2.75 lbs. **Length:** 15 in. Stocks: Hardwood full stock. **Sights:** Brass blade front, square notch rear adjustable for windage. **Features:** Polished brass finger spur-style triggerguard, stock cap and ramrod tip, color case-hardened leaf spring lock, spring-loaded trigger, No. 11 percussion nipple, brass furniture. From Traditions, and as kit from Bass Pro and others.
Price: P1060 Finished.. **$244.00**
Price: KPC50602 Kit **$209.00**

TRADITIONS PIRATE PISTOL
Caliber: .50. **Barrel:** 10 in., round armory-bright steel, 1:20 in. twist. **Weight:** 2.75 lbs. **Length:** 15 in. Stocks: Hardwood rounded bag-style grip with skull-crushing brass grip cap, fullstock. **Sights:** Square-notched rear adjustable for windage, brass blade front. **Features:** Flint, armory-bright polished lock, single trigger, polished brass triggerguard, stock cap and ramrod tip, color case-hardened leaf spring lock, spring-loaded trigger. From Traditions, and as kit from Bass Pro and others.
Price: P1430 Finished, flint **$404.00**
Price: KPC 5400 Kit, flint **$330.00**

TRADITIONS TRAPPER PISTOL
Caliber: .50. **Barrel:** 9.75 in., octagonal, blued, hooked patent breech, 1:20 in. twist. **Weight:** 2.75 lbs. **Length:** 15.5 in. Stocks: Hardwood, modified saw-handle style grip, halfstock. **Sights:** Brass blade front, rear sight adjustable for windage and elevation. **Features:** Percussion or flint, double set triggers, polished brass triggerguard, stock cap and ramrod tip, color case-hardened leaf spring lock, spring-loaded trigger, No. 11 percussion nipple, brass furniture. From Traditions and as a kit from Bass Pro and others.
Price: P1100 Finished, percussion **$329.00**
Price: P1090 Finished, flint **$355.00**
Price: KPC51002 Kit, percussion **$299.00**
Price: KPC50902 Kit, flint **$359.00**

TRADITIONS VEST POCKET DERRINGER
Caliber: .31. **Barrel:** 2.35 in., round brass, smoothbore. **Weight:** .75 lbs. **Length:** 4.75 in. Grips: Simulated ivory. **Sights:** Front bead. **Features:** Replica of riverboat gambler's derringer. No. 11 percussion cap nipple, brass frame and barrel, spur trigger, external hammer. From Traditions.
Price: P1381, Brass **$189.00**
Price: Dixie, White, PH0920 .... **$210.00**

TRADITIONS VORTEK PISTOL
Caliber: .50. **Barrel:** 13 in., 1:28 in. twist, Cerakote finish. **Weight:** 3.25 lbs. **Length:** 18 in. Stocks: Hardwood, black synthetic, Reaper Buck camo. Ramrod: Solid aluminum. **Sights:** LPA steel, 1-4X24mm scope. **Features:** Vortek break-open action with removable trigger group, quick-removal breech plug for 209 primer, over-molded stocks. From Traditions.
Price: P1-151178 Scope, select hardwood, Cerakote......... ..**$469.00**
Price: P1-151178 No sights, select hardwood, Cerakote.......**$383.00**
Price: P1-151170 Scope, Black synthetic, Cerakote **$479.00**
Price: P1-151170 No sights, Black synthetic, Cerakote.........**$324.00**

Prices given are believed to be accurate at time of publication however, many factors affect retail pricing so exact prices are not possible.

71ST EDITION, 2017 ◆ **505**

COLT ARMY 1860 PERCUSSION REVOLVER

Caliber: .44. **Barrel:** 8 in. **Weight:** 2.75 lbs. **Length:** 13.25 in. overall. Grips: One-piece walnut. **Sights:** Brass blade front, hammer notch rear. **Features:** Steel or case-hardened frame, brass triggerguard, case-hardened creeping loading lever. Many models and finishes are available for this pistol. Made by Pietta and Uberti. Imported by Cabela's, Cimarron, Dixie Gun Works, EMF, Taylor's, Uberti U.S.A. and others.
Price: Dixie, standard model with brass triggerguard RH0705 **$260.00**
Price: Dixie, standard model kit RK0965 .... **$234.00**
Price: Dixie, half-fluted cylinder cut for shoulder stock RH0125........... **$295.00**
Price: Dixie, 5.5 in. Sheriff's model RH0975 .... **$325.00**

COLT ARMY 1862 POLICE SNUBNOSE (THUNDERER) PERCUSSION REVOLVER

Caliber: .44, six-shot. **Barrel:** 3 in. **Weight:** 1.5 lbs. **Length:** 9.2 in. overall. Grips: Varnished birds-head walnut. **Sights:** Brass pin front, hammer notch rear. **Features:** Steel or case-hardened frame, steel triggerguard, no loading. Ramrod: Brass loading rod. Made by Uberti. Imported by EMF, Taylor's, Uberti U.S.A.
Price: Pietta CPPSNB44MYLC.. **$398.00**

COLT BABY DRAGOON 1848, 1849 POCKET, WELLS FARGO PERCUSSION REVOLVER

Caliber: .31. **Barrel:** 3 in., 4 in., 5 in., 6 in.; seven-groove; RH twist. **Weight:** About 21 oz. Grips: Varnished walnut. **Sights:** Brass pin front, hammer notch rear. **Features:** No loading lever on Baby Dragoon or Wells Fargo models. Unfluted cylinder with stagecoach holdup scene, cupped cylinder pin, no grease grooves, one safety pin on cylinder and slot in hammer face, straight (flat) mainspring. Made by Uberti. Imported by Cimarron, Dixie Gun Works, EMF, Uberti U.S.A. and others.
Price: from .... **$310.00 to $346.00**

COLT 1847 WALKER PERCUSSION REVOLVER

Caliber: .44 **Barrel:** 9 in. **Weight:** 4.5 lbs. **Length:** 15.7 in. overall. Grips: One-piece hardwood. **Sights:** Brass blade front, hammer notch rear. **Features:** Copy of Sam Colt's first U.S. contract revolver. Engraved cylinder, case-hardened hammer and loading lever. Blued finish. Made by Uberti, imported by Cabela's, Cimarron, Dixie Gun Works, EMF, Taylor's, Uberti U.S.A. and others.
Price: Dixie, standard model, blued steel RH0450.................. **$399.00**
Price: Dixie, standard model, blued steel kit RH0450 .... **$299.00**

COLT 1848 DRAGOON PERCUSSION REVOLVERS

Caliber: .44 **Barrel:** 7.5 in. **Weight:** 4.1 lbs. Grips: One-piece walnut. **Sights:** Brass blade front, hammer notch rear. **Features:** Copy of Eli Whitney's design for Colt using Walker parts and improved loading lever latch. Blued barrel, backstrap and triggerguard. Made in Italy by Uberti. Imported by Dixie Gun Works, Taylor's, Uberti U.S.A. and others.
Price: 1848 Dragoon, 1st-3rd models, ... **$385.00**
Price: 1848 Dragoon, 3rd. model, cut for stock RH0234 .... **$410.00**

COLT TEXAS PATTERSON PERCUSSION REVOLVER

Caliber: .36 **Barrel:** 9 in. tapered octagon. **Weight:** 2.75 lbs. **Length:** 13.75 in. **Grips:** One-piece walnut. **Sights:** Brass pin front, hammer notch rear. **Features:** Folding trigger, blued steel furniture, frame and barrel; engraved scene on cylinder. Ramrod: Loading tool provided. Made by Pietta. Imported by Dixie Gun Works.
Price: Dixie RH0600.. **$595.00**

COLT NAVY MODEL 1851 PERCUSSION REVOLVER

Caliber: .36, .44, 6-shot. **Barrel:** 7.5 in. **Weight:** 44 oz. **Length:** 13 in. overall. Grips: Walnut. **Sights:** Post front, hammer notch rear. **Features:** Many authentic and non-authentic variations are offered that include, brass backstrap and triggerguard, steel or brass frame options, some have 1st Model square-back triggerguard, engraved cylinder with navy battle scene; case-hardened hammer, loading lever. Cartridge conversion pistols and cylinders are also available from Cimarron and Taylor's. Made by Uberti and Pietta. Imported by Cabela's, Cimarron, EMF, Dixie Gun Works, Taylor's, Traditions (.44 only), Uberti U.S.A. and others.
Price: Brass frame (Dixie Gun Works RH0100)........................**$290.00**
Price: Steel frame (Dixie Gun Works RH844)..........................**$275.00**
Price: Confederate Navy (Cabela's) **$179.99**
Price: Cartridge conversion cylinders .38 Spl. and .45 LC .... **$240-$300.00**

COLT SHERIFF MODEL 1851 PERCUSSION REVOLVER

Caliber: .44, 6-shot. **Barrel:** 5.5 in. **Weight:** 40 oz. **Length:** 10.5 in. overall. Grips: Walnut. **Sights:** Fixed. **Features:** Steel frame, brass backstrap and triggerguard; engraved navy scene; case-hardened frame, hammer, loading lever. Made by Uberti. Imported by EMF.
Price: PF51CH44512 Steel frame **$235.00**
Price: PF51BR44512 Brassframe.....................................**$200.00**

COLT NAVY 1861 PERCUSSION REVOLVER

Caliber: .36 **Barrel:** 8 in. **Weight:** 2.75 lbs. **Length:** 13.25 in. overall. Grips: One-piece walnut. **Sights:** Brass blade front, hammer notch rear. **Features:** Steel or case-hardened frame, brass triggerguard, case-hardened creeping loading lever. Many models and finishes are available for this pistol. Made by Pietta and Uberti. Imported by Cabela's, Cimarron, Dixie Gun Works, EMF, Taylor's, Uberti U.S.A. and others.
Price: Dixie, standard model with brass triggerguard RH0841 **$295.00**

Price: Dixie, Sheriff's 5.5 in. barrel RK0975 .... **$325.00**

COLT POCKET POLICE 1862 PERCUSSION REVOLVER

Caliber: .36, 5-shot. **Barrel:** 4.5 in., 5.5 in., 6.5 in., 7.5 in. **Weight:** 26 oz. **Length:** 12 in. overall (6.5 in. bbl.). Stocks: Walnut. **Sights:** Fixed. **Features:** Round tapered barrel; half-fluted and rebated cylinder; case-hardened frame, loading lever and hammer; silver or brass triggerguard and backstrap. Made by Uberti. Imported by Cimarron, Dixie Gun Works, Taylor's, Uberti U.S.A. and others.
Price: Dixie Gun Works RH0422 .... **$340.00**

Prices given are believed to be accurate at time of publication however, many factors affect retail pricing so exact prices are not possible.

BLACKPOWDER REVOLVERS

NAVY YANK PEPPERBOX
Caliber: .36, six-shot. **Cylinder-Barrel:** 3.1 in. **Weight:** 2.2 lbs. **Length:** 7 in. overall. **Grips:** European walnut. **Sights:** Hammer notch rear. **Features:** Case-hardened frame, brass triggerguard, no loading lever or ramrod. Made by Pietta. Imported by Dixie, Taylor's.
Price: Pietta YAN36PP **$225.00**

DRAGOON PISTOL U.S. MODEL OF 1858 WITH DETACHABLE SHOULDER STOCK
Caliber: .58. **Barrel:** 12 in. **Weight:** 3.75 lbs., with shoulder stock 5.5 lbs. **Length:** 18.25 in. overall pistol. **Stocks:** Walnut pistol and shoulder stock. **Sights:** Flip-up blued steel rear, blade steel front. **Features:** Percussion, musket-cap nipple, case-hardened lock, brass furniture. Captive steel ramrod. Shoulder stock included. Made by Palmetto. Imported by Dixie Gun Works.
Price: Dixie Gun Works, with shoulder stock PH1000............... **$600.00**

DANCE AND BROTHERS PERCUSSION REVOLVER
Caliber: .44 **Barrel:** 7.4 in., round. **Weight:** 2.5 lbs. **Length:** 13 in. overall. **Grip:** Two-piece walnut. **Sights:** Fixed. **Features:** Reproduction of the C.S.A. revolver. Brass frame and triggerguard. Made by Pietta. From Dixie Gun Works, Cabela's and others.
Price: Dixie Gun Works RH0120 .... **$343.00**

DIXIE REMINGTON ARMY SHOOTERS REVOLVER
Caliber: .44 **Barrel:** 8 in., tapered octagon progressive twist. **Weight:** 2.75 lbs. **Length:** 13-3/4 in. overall. **Grips:** One-piece hardwood. **Sights:** V-notch on top strap, blued steel blade front. **Features:** Silver plated brass triggerguard, blued steel backstrap and frame, case-hardened hammer, trigger and loading lever. Navy size shoulder stock requires minor fitting. A higher grade gun for international match shooting. Won gold medals in 1987 and 1989. Made by Pietta. From Dixie Gun Works.
Price: RH0135 .... **$950.00**

DIXIE TEXAS OR BUFFALO PERCUSSION REVOLVER
Caliber: .44 **Barrel:** 12 in., octagon. **Weight:** 46 oz. **Length:** 18 in. overall. **Grips:** One-piece hardwood. **Sights:** Rear adjustable. **Features:** Highly polished Remington-style brass frame, backstrap and triggerguard; blued barrel and cylinder; case-hardened hammer, trigger and loading lever. Made by Pietta. From Dixie Gun Works, EMF.
Price: SS1039 .... **$275.00**

DIXIE WYATT EARP PERCUSSION REVOLVER
Caliber: .44 **Barrel:** 12 in., octagon. **Weight:** 46 oz. **Length:** 18 in. overall. **Grips:** One-piece hardwood. **Sights:** Fixed. **Features:** Highly polished brass frame, backstrap and triggerguard; blued barrel and cylinder; case-hardened hammer, trigger and loading lever. Navy size shoulder stock requires minor fitting. Made by Pietta. From Dixie Gun Works, EMF.
Price: RH0130 .... **$225.00**

GRISWOLD AND GUNNISON PERCUSSION REVOLVER
Caliber: .36 **Barrel:** 7.5 in., round. **Weight:** 2.5 lbs. **Length:** 13.25 in. **Grip:** One-piece walnut. **Sights:** Fixed. **Features:** Reproduction of the C.S.A. revolver. Brass frame and triggerguard. Made by Pietta. From Cabela's and others.
Price: Cabelas JC-21-7650 .... **$209.99**

LEACH AND RIGDON PERCUSSION REVOLVER
Caliber: .36. **Barrel:** 7.5 in., octagon to round. **Weight:** 2.75 lbs. **Length:** 13 in. **Grip:** One-piece walnut. **Sights:** Hammer notch and pin front. **Features:** Steel frame. Reproduction of the C.S.A. revolver. Brass backstrap and triggerguard. Made by Uberti. From Dixie Gun Works and others.
Price: Dixie Gun Works RH0611 .... **$340.00**

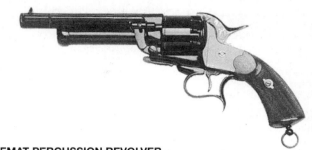

LEMAT PERCUSSION REVOLVER
Caliber: .44/20 ga. **Barrel:** 6.75 in. (revolver); 4-7/8 in. (single shot). **Weight:** 3 lbs., 7 oz. **Length:** 14 in. overall. **Grips:** Hand-checkered walnut. **Sights:** Post front, hammer notch rear. **Features:** Exact reproduction with all-steel construction; 44-cal. 9-shot cylinder, 20-gauge single barrel; color case-hardened hammer with selector; spur triggerguard; ring at butt; lever-type barrel release. Made by Pietta. From Dixie Gun Works.
Price: LeMat Navy with knurled pin barrel release **$1,095.00**
Price: LeMat Calvary with trigger spur and lanyard ring **$995.00**
Price: LeMat Army with cross pin barrel selector **$995.00**

NEW MODEL 1858 REMINGTON ARMY PERCUSSION REVOLVER
Caliber: .36 or .44, 6-shot. **Barrel:** Standard 8 in., and 5.5 to 12 in. **Weight:** Standard 2 lbs. **Length:** Standard 13.5 in. **Grips:** Walnut, two-piece. **Sights:** Standard blade front, groove-in-frame rear; adjustable on some models. **Features:** Many variations of this gun are available. Also available as the Army Model Belt Revolver in .36 cal., a shortened and lightened version of the .44 model. Target Model (Uberti U.S.A.) has fully adjustable target rear sight, target front, .36 or .44. Imported by Cabela's, Cimarron F.A. Co., EMF, Taylor's, Traditions (.44 only), Uberti U.S.A. and others.
Price: Steel frame, Dixie RH0424 .... **$285.00**
Price: Steel frame kit, Dixie, oversized grips
    and frame RV0440 .... **$245.00**
Price: Stainless steel Model 1858, Cabela's, Traditions **$389.99**
Price: Target Model, adj. rear sight (Cabela's, Traditions) **$479.99**
Price: Sheriff's Model, .44, steel frame (Cabela's, Traditions) . **$229.99**
Price: Brass frame Cabela's, Traditions, ... **$219.99**
Price: Buffalo model, brass frame, .44-cal. (Cabela's) **$249.99**
Price: Buffalo model, blued steel, .44-cal., 12-in barrel limited
    numbers, (Old South Firearms FR185822).... .... **$365.00**
Price: Traditions Redi-Pak, steel frame, accessories **$336.00**
Price: 1858 Target Carbine 18-in. barrel Dixie PR0338 .... **$525.00**

NEW MODEL REMINGTON POCKET PERCUSSION REVOLVER
Caliber: .31, 5-shot. **Barrel:** 3.5 in. **Weight:** 1 lb. **Length:** 7.6 in. **Grips:** Walnut, two-piece. **Sights:** Pin front, groove-in-frame rear. **Features:** Spur trigger; iron, brass or nickel-plated frame. Made by Pietta. Imported by Dixie Gun Works, EMF, Taylor's and others.
Price: Brass frame, Dixie PH0407 .... **$245.00**
Price: Steel frame, Dixie PH0370 .... **$275.00**
Price: Nickel-plated, Dixie PH0409 .... **$285.00**

Prices given are believed to be accurate at time of publication however, many factors affect retail pricing so exact prices are not possible.

71ST EDITION, 2017 ✛ **507**

NORTH AMERICAN COMPANION PERCUSSION REVOLVER
Caliber: .22 **Barrel:** 1-1/8 in. **Weight:** 5.1 oz. **Length:** 4 in. overall. **Grips:** Laminated wood. **Sights:** Blade front, notch rear. **Features:** All stainless steel construction. Uses No. 11 percussion caps. Comes with bullets, powder measure, bullet seater, leather clip holster, gun rag. Long Rifle frame. Introduced 1996. Made in U.S. by North American Arms.
Price: NAA-22LR-CB Long Rifle frame..................................... $251.00

NORTH AMERICAN EARL PERCUSSION REVOLVER
Caliber: .22 **Barrel:** 4 in. **Weight:** 9.4 oz. **Length:** 7.75 in. **Sights:** Post front, notch rear. **Features:** All stainless steel construction. No. 11 percussion caps. Nonfunctional loading lever. Comes with bullets, powder measure, bullet seater, leather clip holster, gun rag. Introduced 1996. Magnum frame. Introduced 2012. Made in U.S. by North American Arms.
Price: NAA-1860-4-CB Magnum frame.................................. $322.00

NORTH AMERICAN SUPER COMPANION PERCUSSION REVOLVER
Caliber: .22 **Barrel:** 1-5/8 in. **Weight:** 7.2 oz. **Length:** 5-1/8 in. **Grips:** Laminated wood. **Sights:** Blade font, notched rear. **Features:** All stainless steel construction. No. 11 percussion caps. Comes with bullets, powder measure, bullet seater, leather clip holster, gun rag. Introduced 1996. Larger "Magnum" frame. Made in U.S. by North American Arms.
Price: NAA-Mag-CB Magnum frame $261.00

ROGERS & SPENCER PERCUSSION REVOLVER
Caliber: .44 **Barrel:** 7.5 in. **Weight:** 47 oz. **Length:** 13.75 in. overall. **Stocks:** Walnut. **Sights:** Cone front, integral groove-in-frame for rear. **Features:** Accurate reproduction of a Civil War design. Solid frame, extra-large nipple cut-out on rear of cylinder; loading lever and cylinder easily removed for cleaning. From Dixie Gun Works and others.
Price: $500.00

SPILLER & BURR PERCUSSION REVOLVER
Caliber: .36 **Barrel:** 7 in., octagon. **Weight:** 2.5 lbs. **Length:** 12.5 in. overall. **Grip:** Two-piece walnut. **Sights:** Fixed. **Features:** Reproduction of the C.S.A. revolver. Brass frame and triggerguard. Also available as a kit. Made by Pietta. From Dixie Gun Works, Traditions and others.
Price: Dixie RH0120.. $250.00
Price: Dixie kit RH0300... $225.00

STARR DOUBLE-ACTION 1858 ARMY REVOLVER
Caliber: .44 **Barrel:** 6 in. tapered round. **Weight:** 3 lbs. **Length:** 11.75 in. Stocks: Walnut one-piece. **Sights:** Hammer notch rear, dovetailed front. **Features:** Double-action mechanism, round tapered barrel, all blued frame and barrel. Made by Pietta. Imported by Dixie Gun Works and others.
Price: Dixie RH460... $565.00

STARR SINGLE-ACTION ARMY REVOLVER
Caliber: .44 **Barrel:** 8 in. tapered round. **Weight:** 3 lbs. **Length:** 13.5 in. Stocks: Walnut one-piece. **Sights:** Hammer notch rear, dovetailed front. **Features:** Single-action mechanism, round tapered barrel, all blued frame and barrel. Made by Pietta. Imported by Cabela's, Dixie Gun Works and others.
Price: Dixie RH460...$550.00

Prices given are believed to be accurate at time of publication however, many factors affect retail pricing so exact prices are not possible.

BROWN BESS MUSKET, SECOND MODEL
Caliber: .75. **Barrel:** 42 in., round, smoothbore. **Weight:** 9 lbs. **Length:** 57.75 in. **Stock:** European walnut, fullstock. **Sights:** Steel stud on front serves as bayonet lug. **Features:** Flintlock using one-inch flint with optional brass flash guard (SCO203), steel parts all polished armory bright, brass furniture. Lock marked Grice, 1762 with crown and GR. Made by Pedersoli. Imported by Cabela's, Dixie Gun Works, others.
Price: Dixie Complete gun FR0810.................................... $1,099.00
Price: Dixie Kit Gun FR0825 .... $1,050.00
Price: Cabela's Complete gun $1,200.00
Price: Dixie Trade Gun, 30.5-in. barrel, browned FR0665 .... $1,495.00
Price: Dixie Trade Gun Kit FR0600 .... $950.00
Price: Dixie Trade Musket , 30.5-in. barrel,
browned FR0665 .... $1,495.00
Price: Dixie Trade Musket Kit FR3370 .... $695.00

CABELA'S BLUE RIDGE RIFLE
Caliber: .32, .36, .45, .50, .54. **Barrel:** 39 in., octagon. **Weight:** 7.75 lbs. **Length:** 55 in. overall. **Stock:** American black walnut. **Sights:** Blade front, rear drift adjustable for windage. **Features:** Color case-hardened lockplate and cock/hammer, brass triggerguard and buttplate; double set, double-phased triggers. From Cabela's.
Price: Percussion.. $649.99
Price: Flintlock $699.99

CABELA'S KODIAK EXPRESS DOUBLE RIFLE
Caliber: .50, .54, .58, .72. **Barrel:** 1:48 in. twist. **Weight:** 9.3 lbs. **Length:** 45.25 in. overall. **Stock:** European walnut, oil finish. **Sights:** Fully adjustable double folding-leaf rear, ramp front. **Features:** Percussion. Barrels regulated to point of aim at 75 yards; polished and engraved lock, top tang and triggerguard. From Cabela's.
Price: .54-cal... $1,299.99

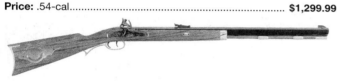

CABELA'S TRADITIONAL HAWKEN
Caliber: .50, 54. **Barrel:** 29 in. **Weight:** 9 lbs. **Stock:** Walnut. **Sights:** Blade front, open adjustable rear. **Features:** Flintlock or percussion. Adjustable double-set triggers. Polished brass furniture, color case-hardened lock. Imported by Cabela's.
Price: Percussion, right hand or left hand $499.99
Price: Flintlock, right hand $649.99

CVA OPTIMA V2 STAINLESS BREAK-ACTION RIFLE
Caliber: .50. **Barrel:** 28 in. fluted. **Weight:** 8.8 lbs. **Stock:** Ambidextrous solid composite in standard or thumbhole. **Sights:** Adj. fiber-optic. **Features:** Break-action, quick release breech plug, aluminum loading rod, cocking spur, lifetime warranty. Also available with exposed ignition as a Northwest Model.
Price: PR2029NM (.50-cal., Nitride stainless/Realtree Xtra,
thumbhole, scope mount) $448.00
Price: PR2023N (.50-cal., Nitride stainless/Realtree Xtra, fib. opt.
sight) $416.00
Price: PR2023NM (.50-cal., Nitride stainless/Realtree Xtra,
thumbhole, scope mount) $426.00
Price: PR2028SM (.50-cal, stainless/ Realtree Xtra,
scope mount) $400.00
Price: PR2022SM (.50-cal, stainless/Realtree Xtra,
fib. opt. sight) $378.00
Price: PR2022S (.50-cal, stainless/Realtree Xtra,
scope mount) $368.00
Price: PR2020SM (.50-cal, stainless/black, scope mount) $328.00
Price: PR2020S (.50-cal, stainless/black, fib. opt. sight)....... $318.00

CVA WOLF 209 MAGNUM BREAK-ACTION RIFLE
Caliber: .50 **Barrel:** 24 in. **Weight:** 6.23 lbs. **Stock:** Ambidextrous composite. **Sights:** Dead-On Scope Mounts or Fiber Optic. **Features:** Break-Action, quick detachable breech plug for 209 primer, aluminum loading road, cocking spur, lifetime warranty. Also available with exposed ignition as a Northwest model.
Price: PR2112SM (.50-cal, stainless/Realtree
Hardwoods HD, scope mount) $309.00
Price: PR2112S (50-cal, stainless/Realtree
Hardwoods HD, fib. opt. sight) $301.00
Price: PR2110SM (.50-cal, stainless/black, scope mount)...... $261.00
Price: PR2110S
(.50-cal, stainless/black, fib. opt. sight) $253.00
Price: PR2110M
(.50-cal, blued/black, scope mount) $224.00
Price: PR2110
(.50-cal, blued/black, fig. opt. sight)............................ $224.00

CVA APEX
Caliber: .45, .50. **Barrel:** 27 in., 1:28 in. twist. **Weight:** 8 lbs. **Length:** 42 in. **Stock:** Synthetic. **Features:** Ambidextrous with rubber grip panels in black or Realtree APG camo, crush-zone recoil pad, reversible hammer spur, quake claw sling, lifetime warranty.
Price: CR4013s (.45-cal., stainless/Realtree APG) $738.00
Price: CR4012S (.50-cal., stainless/Realtree APG)............. .. $695.00
Price: CR4011S (.45-cal., stainless/black)........................ ..$615.00
Price: CR4010S (.50-cal., stainless/black)........................ $615.00

CVA ACCURA V2 LR
Caliber: .50 **Barrel:** 27 or 30-in. **Weight:** 7.3 lbs. **Length:** 42 or 45-in. **Stock:** Synthetic. **Features:** Ambidextrous stock, quick release breech plug, crush-zone recoil pad, reversible hammer spur quake claw sling, lifetime warranty. Also available with exposed ignition as a Northwest model.
Price: PR3124NM (.50-cal, Nitride stainless/Realtree
Max-1 thumbhole, scope mount) $624.00
Price: PR3122SNM (.50-cal., stainless/Realtree
APG thumbhole) $608.00
Price: PR3116SM (.50-cal., stainless/Realtree HD
thumbhole, scope mount) $560.00
Price: PR3125N (.50-cal., Nitride, stainless/Realtree
HD, fib. opt. sight).. $574.00
Price: PR3125NM (.50-cal., Nitride,stainless/black/RFealtree
HD, scope mount) $584.00
Price: PR3112SM
(.50-cal., stainless/Realtree APG, scope mount)........... $536.00
Price: PR3112S
(.50-cal., stainless/Realtree APG. fib. opt. sights) $526.00
Price: PR3110S (.50-cal, stainless/black, fib. opt. sights)........ $464.00

CVA ACCURA MOUNTAIN RIFLE
Caliber: .50. **Barrel:** 25-in. **Weight:** 6.35 lbs. **Length:** 40-in. **Stock:** Synthetic. **Features:** Ambidextrous stock, quick release breech plug, crush-zone recoil pad, reversible hammer spur quake claw sling, lifetime warranty
Price: PR3121SNM (.50-cal, Nitride stainless/Realtree
Max-1,scope mount) $584.00
Price: PR3120SM (.50-cal, stainless/black) $472.00

DIXIE 1803 HARPERS FERRY FLINTLOCK RIFLE
Caliber: .54. **Barrel:** 35.5 in., smoothbore. **Weight:** 9.5 lbs. **Length:** 29.5 in. overall. **Stock:** Halfstock, walnut w/oil finish. **Sights:** Blade front, notched rear. **Features:** Color case-hardened lock, browned barrel, with barrel key. Made by Euro Arms. Imported by Dixie Gun Works.
Price: FR0171 .... $1,050.00

DIXIE 1816 FLINTLOCK MUSKET
Caliber: .69. **Barrel:** 42 in., smoothbore. **Weight:** 9.75 lbs. **Length:** 56-7/8 in. overall. **Stock:** Walnut w/oil finish. **Sights:** Blade front. **Features:** All metal finished in "National Armory Bright," three

Prices given are believed to be accurate at time of publication however, many factors affect retail pricing so exact pricing is not possible.

71ST EDITION, 2017 ✛ **509**

BLACKPOWDER MUSKETS & RIFLES

barrelbands w/springs, steel ramrod w/button-shaped head. Made by Pedersoli. Imported by Dixie Gun Works.
Price: PR3180, Percussion conversion.....................................$875.00

DIXIE DELUXE CUB RIFLE
Caliber: .32, .36, .45. **Barrel:** 28 in. octagonal. **Weight:** 6.5 lbs. **Length:** 44 in. overall. **Stock:** Walnut. **Sights:** Fixed. **Features:** Each gun available in either flint or percussion ignition. Short rifle for small game and beginning shooters. Brass patchbox and furniture. Kit guns available in .32 or .36 calibers in percussion ($690) or flint ($710). From Dixie Gun Works.
Price: Deluxe Cub (.32-cal. flint) PR3130 ....$890.00
Price: Deluxe Cub (.36-cal. flint) FR3135..............................$890.00
Price: Deluxe Cub kit (.32-cal. percussion) PK3360...............$690.00
Price: Deluxe Cub kit (.36-cal. percussion) PK3365...............$690.00
Price: Deluxe Cub (.45-cal. percussion) PR0768.....................$850.00
Price: Deluxe Cub (.32-cal. percussion) PR3140.....................$850.00
Price: Deluxe Cub (.36-cal. percussion) PR3145.....................$850.00

DIXIE EARLY AMERICAN JAEGER RIFLE
Caliber: .54. **Barrel:** 27.5 in. octagon, 1:24 in. twist. **Weight:** 8.25 lbs. **Length:** 43.5 in. overall. **Stock:** American walnut; sliding wooden patchbox on butt. **Sights:** Notch rear, blade front. **Features:** Flintlock or percussion. Conversion kits available, and recommended converting percussion guns to flintlocks using kit LO1102 at $209.00. Browned steel furniture. Made by Pedersoli. Imported by Dixie Gun Works.
Price: Percussion, PR0835 .... $1,295.00
Price: Flint, PR0835 .... $1,375.00
Price: Percussion, kit gun, PK0146 .... $1,075.00
Price: Flint, kit gun, PKO143.. $1,075.00

DIXIE HAWKEN RIFLE
Caliber: .50 and .54. **Barrel:** 29.5 in. octagonal, 1:48 in. twist. **Weight:** 9 or 8.5 lbs. **Length:** 45.5 in. overall. **Stock:** European walnut, halfstock. **Sights:** Rear click adjustable for windage and elevation, blade front. **Features:** Percussion and flintlock, brass patchbox, double-set triggers, one barrel key. Flint gun available for left-handed shooters. Both flint and percussion guns available as kit guns. Made by Pedersoli. Imported by Dixie Gun Works.
Price: Percussion, .50 PR0502 ....$495.00
Price: Percussion, .54 PR0507 ....$495.00
Price: Flint, .50 FR1332 ....$515.00
Price: Flint, .50 left hand, FR1336.....................................$515.00
Price: Flint, .50 left hand, kit, FR1345..............................$450.00

DIXIE JAPANESE TANEGASHIMA MATCHLOCK
Caliber: .50. **Barrel:** 53 in. **Weight:** 8.75 lbs. **Length:** 53 in. overall. **Stock:** Japanese cherry with drilled hole on bottom for wooden ramrod. **Sights:** Post front, block rear. **Features:** A replica of the snapping matchlock guns used in Japan from the 17th to 19th centuries. Brass lock with ball trigger, and brass lockplate and hammer. Pan has pivoting cover. Browned barrel. Case-hardened lock. Made by Miroku. Imported by Dixie Gun Works.
Price: Dixie MM0005 ....$1,100.00

DIXIE J.P. MURRAY ARTILLERY CARBINE
Caliber: .58. **Barrel:** 23.5 in. **Weight:** 8 lbs. **Length:** 39.5 in. **Stock:** European walnut. **Sights:** Blade front, fixed notch rear. **Features:** Percussion musket-cap ignition. Reproduction of the original Confederate carbine. Lock marked "J.P. Murray, Columbus, Georgia." Blued barrel. Made Euro Arms. Imported by Dixie Gun Works and others.
Price: Dixie, PRO173 ....$1,100.00

DIXIE PEDERSOLI 1857 MAUSER RIFLE
Caliber: .54. **Barrel:** 39.75 in. **Weight:** 9.5 lbs. **Length:** 52 in. overall. **Stock:** European walnut. **Sights:** Blade front, rear steel adjustable for windage and elevation. **Features:** Percussion musket-cap ignition. Color case-hardened lockplate marked "Konigi.Wurt Fabrik." Armory bright steel barrel. Made by Pedersoli. Imported by Dixie Gun Works.
Price: Dixie PR1330..$1,650.00

DIXIE PENNSYLVANIA RIFLE
Caliber: .45 and .50. **Barrel:** 41.5 in. octagonal, .45/1:48, .50/1:56 in. twist. **Weight:** 8.5, 8.75 lbs. **Length:** 56 in. overall. **Stock:** European walnut, full-length stock. **Sights:** Notch rear, blade front. **Features:** Flintlock or percussion, brass patchbox, double-set triggers. Also available as kit guns for both calibers and ignition systems. Made by Pedersoli. Imported by Dixie Gun Works.
Price: Percussion, .45, PF1070................................$775.00
Price: Flint, .45, PF1060 ....$925.00
Price: Percussion, .50, PR3205................................$825.00
Price: Flint, .45, PR3200 ....$975.00

DIXIE POTSDAM 1809 PRUSSIAN MUSKET
Caliber: .75 **Barrel:** 41.2 in. round, smoothbore. **Weight:** 9 lbs. **Length:** 56 in. **Stock:** European walnut, fullstock. **Sights:** Brass lung on upper barrelband. **Features:** Flintlock using one-inch flint. Steel parts all polished armory bright, brass furniture. Lock marked "Potsdam over G.S." Made by Pedersoli. Imported by Dixie Gun Works.
Price: Dixie FR3175 ....$1,495.00

DIXIE SHARPS NEW MODEL 1859 MILITARY RIFLE AND CARBINE
Caliber: .54. **Barrel:** 30 in., 6-groove, 1:48 in. twist. **Weight:** 9 lbs. **Length:** 45.5 in. overall. **Stock:** Oiled walnut. **Sights:** Blade front, ladder-style rear. **Features:** Blued barrel, color case-hardened barrelbands, receiver, hammer, nose cap, lever, patchbox cover and buttplate. Introduced 1995. Rifle made by Armi Sport (Chiappa) and carbine by Pedersoli. Rifle imported from Italy by Dixie Gun Works and carbine by Dixie and Cabela's.
Price: Rifle PR0107 (Chiappa)...$1,150.00
Price: Rifle PR0862 (Pedersoli) $1,400.00
Price: Carbine (22-in. barrel, 39-1/4 in. long, 8 lbs.) PR0982 $1,400.00

DIXIE SMITH CARBINE
Caliber: .50. **Barrel:** 21.5 in., 3-groove, 1:66 in. twist. **Weight:** 7.75 lbs. **Length:** 39 in. **Stock:** Oiled walnut. **Sights:** Blade front, ladder-style rear. **Features:** Hinged breech that drops barrel to allow loading of pre-loaded brass or plastic cartridges fired by a musket cap. Blued barrel, color case-hardened receiver and hammer. Cavalry Carbine has saddle bar and ring, Artillery Carbine has sling swivel on buttstock and barrelband. Rifle made by Pietta. Imported from Italy by Dixie Gun Works.
Price: Dixie Cavalry Carbine PR0220 .... $995.00

DIXIE TRYON RIFLE
Caliber: .50. **Barrel:** 32 in. octagonal, 1:48 in. twist. **Weight:** 9.5 lbs. **Length:** 49 in. overall. **Stock:** European walnut, halfstock. **Sights:** Elevation-adjustable rear with stair-step notches, blade front. **Features:** Percussion, brass patchbox, double-set triggers, two barrel keys. Made by Pedersoli. Imported by Dixie Gun Works.
Price: Percussion, PR0860 ....$1,075.00
Price: Percussion, kit, PR0255 ....$890.00

DIXIE ZOUAVE RIFLE
Caliber: .58. **Barrel:** 33 in. **Weight:** 9.5 lbs. **Length:** 49 in. **Stock:** European walnut. **Sights:** Blade front, three-leaf military rear. **Features:** Percussion musket-cap ignition. Case-hardened lock and blued barrel. One-piece solid barrel and bolster. Made in Italy by Armi Sport. Imported by Dixie Gun Works, others.
Price: PF0340 ....$975.00

ENFIELD MUSKETOON P1861
Caliber: .58. **Barrel:** 33 in. **Weight:** 9 lbs. **Length:** 35 in. overall. **Stock:** European walnut. **Sights:** Blade front, flip-up rear with elevator marked to 700 yards. **Features:** Reproduction of the original cavalry version of the Enfield rifle. Percussion musket-cap ignition. Blued barrel with steel barrelbands, brass furniture. Case-hardened lock. Euro Arms version marked London Armory with crown. Pedersoli

BLACKPOWDER MUSKETS & RIFLES

version has Birmingham stamp on stock and Enfield and Crown on lockplate. Made by Euro Arms, Pedersoli. Imported by Cabela's, Dixie Gun Works and others.
Price: Dixie Euro Arms PR0343 ....**$1,050.00**

ENFIELD THREE-BAND P1853 RIFLE
Caliber: .58. **Barrel:** 39 in. **Weight:** 10.25 lbs. **Length:** 52 in. overall. **Stock:** European walnut. **Sights:** Blade front, flip-up rear with elevator marked to 800 yards. **Features:** Reproduction of the original three-band rifle. Percussion musket-cap ignition. Blued barrel with steel barrelbands, brass furniture. Case-hardened lock. Lockplate marked "London Armory Co. and Crown." Made by Euro Arms, Armi Sport (Chiappa), Pedersoli. Imported by Cabela's, Dixie Gun Works and others.
Price: Cabela's, Pedersoli **$949.99**
Price: Dixie Armi Sport/Chiappa PR1130 ....**$825.00**
Price: Dixie Euro Arms PR0340 ....**$800.00**

ENFIELD TWO-BAND P1858 RIFLE
Caliber: .58. **Barrel:** 24 in. **Weight:** 7.75 lbs. **Length:** 43.25 in. overall. **Stock:** European walnut. **Sights:** Blade front, flip-up rear with elevator marked to 1,000 yards. **Features:** Reproduction of the original two-band rifle. Percussion musket-cap ignition. Blued barrel with steel barrelbands, brass furniture. Case-hardened lock. Lockplate marked "1858 Enfield and Crown." Made by Euro Arms, Pedersoli, Chiappa. Imported by Cabela's, Dixie Gun Works and others.
Price: Cabela's, Pedersoli **$930.00**
Price: Dixie Euro Arms PR1135 ....**$895.00**
Price: Dixie Chiappa 150th Aniv. Mod. PR0106 ....**$750.00**

KNIGHT BIGHORN
Caliber: .50. **Barrel:** 26 in., 1:28 in. twist. **Weight:** 7 lbs. 3 oz. **Length:** 44.5 in. overall. **Stock:** G2 straight or thumbhole, Carbon Knight straight or thumbhole or black composite thumbhole with recoil pad, sling swivel studs. **Ramrod:** Carbon core with solid brass extendable jag. **Sights:** Fully adjustable metallic fiber optic. **Features:** Uses four different ignition systems (included): #11 nipple, musket nipple, bare 208 shotgun primer and 209 Extreme shotgun primer system (Extreme weatherproof full plastic jacket system); vented breech plug, striker fired with one-piece removable hammer assembly. With recommended loads, guaranteed to have 4-inch, three-shot groups at 200 yards. Also available as Western gun with exposed ignition. Made in U.S. by Knight Rifles.
Price: Standard stock **$454.99**
Price: With maximum available options, scope.....................**$1,074.99**

KNIGHT DISC EXTREME
Caliber: .50, .52. **Barrel:** 26 in., fluted stainless, 1:28 in. twist. **Weight:** 7 lbs. 14 oz. to 8 lbs. **Length:** 45 in. overall. **Stock:** Carbon Knight straight or thumbhole with blued or SS; G2 thumbhole; left-handed Nutmeg thumbhole. **Ramrod:** Solid brass extendable jag. **Sights:** Fully adjustable metallic fiber optics. **Features:** Bolt-action rifle, full plastic jacket ignition system, #11 nipple, musket nipple, bare 208 shotgun primer. With recommended loads, guaranteed to have 4-inch, three-shot groups at 200 yards. Also available as Western gun with exposed ignition. Made in U.S. by Knight Rifles.
Price: Standard **$392.99**
Price: With maximum available options, scope.................**$1,184.99**

KNIGHT HPX
Caliber: .50, .45-70 Govt. or .444 Marlin. **Barrel:** 26 in. as muzzleloader, 24 in. as centerfire. **Length:** 43.5 in./muzzleloader, 39.5 in./centerfire. Ignition: Full Plastic Jacket or bare 209 primer. **Stock:** Shadow gray laminated wood, G2 Camo or composite straight. **Weight:** 8 lbs./muzzleloader, 7.8 lbs./cartridge. **Features:** Break-open rifle with stainless steel action, quick-release trigger assembly, vented breech plug and stainless steel Dyna-coated barrel. **Ramrod:** Carbon core with solid brass extendable jag. **Sights:** Williams fiber-optic sights. **Finish:** Stainless steel. With recommended loads, guaranteed to have 4-inch, three-shot groups at 200 yards. Made in U.S. by Knight Rifles.
Price: : To be Introduced 2015-16, about................**$900.00**

KNIGHT LITTLEHORN
Caliber: .50. **Barrel:** 22 in., 1:28 in. twist. **Weight:** 6.7 lbs. **Length:** 39 in. overall. **Stock:** 12.5-in. length of pull, G2 straight or pink Realtree AP HD. **Ramrod:** Carbon core with solid brass extendable jag. **Sights:** Fully adjustable Williams fiber optic. **Features:** Uses four different ignition systems (included): Full Plastic Jacket, #11 nipple, musket

nipple or bare 209 shotgun primer; vented breech plug, striker-fired with one-piece removable hammer assembly. **Finish:** Stainless steel. With recommended loads, guaranteed to have 4-inch, three-shot groups at 200 yards. Also available as Western gun with exposed ignition. Made in U.S. by Knight Rifles.
Price: Standard **$489.99**
Price: With maximum available options, scope.................**$1,059.99**

KNIGHT MOUNTAINEER FOREST GREEN
Caliber: .45, .50, .52. **Barrel:** 27 in. fluted stainless steel, free floated. **Weight:** 8 lbs. (thumbhole stock), 8.3 lbs. (straight stock). **Length:** 45.5 inches. **Sights:** Fully adjustable metallic fiber optic. **Features:** Bolt-action rifle, adjustable match-grade trigger, aluminum ramrod with carbon core, solid brass extendable jag, vented breech plug. Ignition: Full plastic jacket, #11 nipple, musket nipple, bare 208 shotgun primer. With recommended loads, guaranteed to have 4-inch, three-shot groups at 200 yards. Also available as Western gun with exposed ignition. Made in U.S. by Knight Rifles.
Price: Standard **$730.99**
Price: Maximum available options, scope.....................**$1,408.99**

KNIGHT ULTRA-LITE
Caliber: .50. **Barrel:** 24 in. Ignition: 209 Primer with Full Plastic Jacket, musket cap or #11 nipple, bare 208 shotgun primer; vented breech plug. **Stock:** Black, tan or olive green Kevlar spider web. **Weight:** 6 lbs. **Features:** Bolt-action rifle. **Ramrod:** Carbon core with solid brass extendable jag. **Sights:** With or without Williams fiber-optic sights, drilled and tapped for scope mounts. **Finish:** Stainless steel. With recommended loads, guaranteed to have 4-inch, three-shot groups at 200 yards. Also available as Western version with exposed ignition. Made in U.S. by Knight Rifles.
Price: Standard **$886.99**
Price: Maximum available options, scope.....................**$1,456.99**

KNIGHT VISION
Caliber: .50. **Barrel:** 24 in. **Length:** 44 in. Ignition: Full Plastic Jacket. **Stock:** Black composite. **Weight:** 7.9 lbs. **Features:** Break-open rifle with carbon-steel barrel and all new machined steel action. With recommended loads, guaranteed to have 4-inch, three-shot groups at 200 yards. **Ramrod:** Carbon core with solid brass extendable jag. **Sights:** Weaver sight bases attached and Williams fiber-optic sights provided. **Finish:** Blued steel. Made in U.S. by Knight Rifles.
Price: **$504.99**
Price: Maximum available options scope.....................**$1,131.99**

KNIGHT WOLVERINE
Caliber: .50. **Barrel:** 22 in. stainless steel, 1:28 in. twist. **Weight:** 6.9 lbs. **Length:** 40.5 overall. **Stock:** Realtree Hardwoods straight, CarbonKnight straight. **Ramrod:** Carbon core with solid brass extendable jag. **Sights:** Fully adjustable Williams fiber optic. **Features:** Ignition systems (included): #11 nipple, musket nipple, bare 208 shotgun primer; vented breech plug, striker fired with one-piece removable hammer assembly. **Finish:** Stainless steel. With recommended loads, guaranteed to have 4-inch, three-shot groups at 200 yards. Also available as Western gun with exposed ignition. Made in U.S. by Knight Rifles.
Price: **$499.99**
Price: Thumbhole stock **$479.99**

Prices given are believed to be accurate at time of publication however, many factors affect retail pricing so exact prices are not possible.

71ST EDITION, 2017 ⬦ **511**

LYMAN DEERSTALKER RIFLE
Caliber: .50, .54. **Barrel:** 24 in., octagonal, 1:48 in. rifling. **Weight:** 10.4 lbs. **Stock:** Walnut with black rubber buttpad. **Sights:** Lyman #37MA beaded front, fully adjustable fold-down Lyman #16A rear. **Features:** Percussion and flintlock ignition. Stock has less drop for quick sighting. All metal parts are blackened, with color case-hardened lock, single trigger. Comes with sling and swivels. Available in flint or percussion. Introduced 1990. From Lyman.
Price: 6033140 .50-cal. percussion $565.00
Price: 6033141 .54-cal. percussion $565.00
Price: 6033185 .50-cal. percussion stainless $669.95
Price: 6033146 .50-cal. flintlock blue $614.95
Price: 6033147 .54-cal. flintlock blue..................................$614.95
Price: 6033148 .50-cal. flintlock left hand...........................$654.95

LYMAN GREAT PLAINS RIFLE
Caliber: .50, .54. **Barrel:** 32 in., 1:60in. twist. **Weight:** 11.6 lbs. **Stock:** Walnut. **Sights:** Steel blade front, buckhorn rear adjustable for windage and elevation, and fixed notch primitive sight included. **Features:** Percussion or flint ignition. Blued steel furniture. Stainless steel nipple. Coil spring lock, Hawken-style triggerguard and double-set triggers. Round thimbles recessed and sweated into rib. Steel wedge plates and toe plate. Introduced 1979. From Lyman.
Price: 6031102/3 .50-cal./.54-cal percussion...........................$769.95
Price: 6031105/6 .50-ca./.54-cal flintlock.............................$829.95
Price: 6031125/6 .50-ca./.54-cal left-hand percussion $809.95
Price: 6031137 .50-cal. left-hand flintlock $670.00
Price: 6031111/2 .50/.54-cal. percussion kit...........................$625.00
Price: 6031114/5 .50/.54-cal. flintlock kit.............................$675.00

LYMAN GREAT PLAINS HUNTER MODEL
Similar to Great Plains model except 1:32 in. twist, shallow-groove barrel and comes drilled and tapped for Lyman 57GPR peep sight.
Price: 6031120/1 .50-cal./.54-cal percussion...........................$769.95
Price: 6031148/9 .50-cal./.54-cal flintlock $824.95
Price: 6031142 .50-cal left-hand percussion...........................$769.95

LYMAN MUSTANG BREAKAWAY 209
Caliber: .50. **Barrel:** 26 in., 1:28 twist. **Ignition:** 209 primer. **Weight:** 7 lbs. **Stock:** Ultra Grade wood finish, checkered, rubber recoil pad. **Ramrod:** Solid aluminum. **Sights:** Fiber-optic front and rear. **Features:** Hammerless break-open action for 209 shotshell primer and up to 150-grain charges. Imported by Lyman.
Price: 6032113...$579.95

LYMAN TRADE RIFLE
Caliber: .50, .54. **Barrel:** 28 in. octagon, 1:48 in. twist. **Weight:** 10.8 lbs. **Length:** 45 in. overall. **Stock:** European walnut. **Sights:** Blade front, open rear adjustable for windage, or optional fixed sights. **Features:** Fast-twist rifling for conical bullets. Polished brass furniture with blue steel parts, stainless steel nipple. Hook breech, single trigger, coil spring percussion lock. Steel barrel rib and ramrod ferrules. Introduced 1980. From Lyman.
Price: 6032125/6 .50-cal./.54-cal. percussion...........................$565.00
Price: 6032129/30 .50-cal/.54-cal. flintlock $619.00

NAVY ARMS PARKER-HALE VOLUNTEER RIFLE
Caliber: .451. **Barrel:** 32 in., round interior bore 1:20 in. twist. **Weight:** 9.5 lbs. **Length:** 49 in. **Stock:** Oiled Grade 1 American walnut. **Sights:** Blade front, ladder-style rear. **Features:** Checkered stock wrist and fore end. . Blued barrel, steel ramrod, bone charcoal case-hardened receiver and hammer. Designed for .451 conical bullet. Compare to hexagonal-bored Whitworth Rifle below. Hand fitted and finished.
Price: $1,499.95

NAVY ARMS PARKER-HALE WHITWORTH RIFLE
Caliber: .451. **Barrel:** 36 in., hexagonal interior bore 1:20 in. twist. **Weight:** 9.6 lbs. **Length:** 52.5 in. **Stock:** Oiled Grade 1 American walnut. **Sights:** Blade front, ladder-style rear. **Features:** Checkered stock wrist and fore end. . Blued barrel, steel ramrod, bone charcoal case-hardened receiver and hammer. Designed for .451 conical hexagonal bullet. Compare to round-bored Volunteer Rifle above. Hand fitted to original specifications using original Enfield arsenal gauges.
Price: $1,499.95

NAVY ARMS SMITH CARBINE
Caliber: .50. **Barrel:** 21.5 in., 3-groove, 1:66 in. twist. **Weight:** 7.75 lbs. **Length:** 39 in. **Stock:** Oiled Grade 1 American walnut. **Sights:** Blade front, ladder-style rear. **Features:** Hinged breech that drops barrel to allow loading of pre-loaded brass or plastic cartridges fired by a musket cap. Blued U.S.-made barrel, bone charcoal case-hardened receiver and hammer. Cavalry Carbine has saddle bar and ring, Artillery Carbine has sling swivel on buttstock and barrel band. Hand fitted and finished.
Price: Cavalry Carbine $1,499.95
Price: Artillery Model..$1,499.95

PEDERSOLI 1776 CHARLEVILLE MUSKET
Caliber: .69. **Barrel:** 44.75 in. round, smoothbore. **Weight:** 10.5 lbs. **Length:** 60 in. **Stock:** European walnut, fullstock. **Sights:** Steel stud on upper barrelband. **Features:** Flintlock using one-inch flint. Steel parts all polished armory bright, brass furniture. Lock marked Charleville. Made by Pedersoli. Imported by Cabela's, Dixie Gun Works, others.
Price: Dixie Complete gun FR1045................................$1,425.00
Price: Dixie Kit Gun FK3440 ....$1,140.00
Price: Dixie French Model 1777 Complete gun FR0930 ......$1,450.00
Price: Dixie French Currige An IX Charleville FR0157 ....$1,450.00

PEDERSOLI 1795 SPRINGFIELD MUSKET
Caliber: .69. **Barrel:** 44.75 in., round, smoothbore. **Weight:** 10.5 lbs. **Length:** 57.25 in. **Stock:** European walnut, fullstock. **Sights:** Brass stud on upper barrelband. **Features:** Flintlock using one-inch flint. Steel parts all polished armory bright, brass furniture. Lock marked US Springfield. Made by Pedersoli. Imported by Cabela's, Dixie Gun Works, others.
Price: Dixie Complete gun FR3210..................................$1,495.00

PEDERSOLI 1841 MISSISSIPPI RIFLE
Caliber: .58. **Barrel:** 33 inches. **Weight:** 9.5 lbs. **Length:** 48.75 in. overall. **Stock:** European walnut. **Sights:** Blade front, notched rear. **Features:** Percussion musket-cap ignition. Reproduction of the original one-band rifle with large brass patchbox. Color case-hardened lockplate with browned barrel. Made by Pedersoli. Imported by Cabela's.
Price: Cabela's...$850.00

PEDERSOLI 1861 SPRINGFIELD RIFLE
Caliber: .58. **Barrel:** 40 inches. **Weight:** 10 lbs. **Length:** 55.5 in. overall. **Stock:** European walnut. **Sights:** Blade front, three-leaf military rear. **Features:** Reproduction of the original three-band rifle. Percussion musket-cap ignition. Lockplate marked 1861 with eagle and U.S. Springfield. Armory bright steel. Made by Armi Sport/Chiappa, Pedersoli. Imported by Cabela's, Dixie Gun Works, others.
Price: Cabela's, Pedersoli...$1,149.99
Price: Dixie Armi Sport/Chiappa PR3180 ....$875.00

PEDERSOLI BRISTLEN MORGES AND WAADTLANDER TARGET RIFLES
Caliber: .44, .45. **Barrel:** 29.5 in. tapered octagonal, hooked breech. **Weight:** 15.5 lbs. **Length:** 48.5 in. overall. **Stock:** European walnut, halfstock with hooked buttplate and detachable palm rest. **Sights:** Creedmoor rear on Morges, Swiss Diopter on Waadtlander, hooded front sight notch. **Features:** Percussion back-action lock, double set, double-phase triggers, one barrel key, muzzle protector. Specialized bullet molds for each gun. Made by Pedersoli. Imported by Dixie Gun Works.
Price: Percussion, .44 Bristlen Morges PR0165 ....$2,995.00
Price: Percussion, .45 Waadtlander PR0183 ....$2,995.00

PEDERSOLI COOK & BROTHER CONFEDERATE CARBINE / ARTILLERY/RIFLE
Caliber: .58 **Barrel:** 24/33/39 inches. **Weight:** 7.5/8.4/8.6 lbs. **Length:**

40.5/48/54.5 in. **Stock:** Select oil-finished walnut. **Features:** Percussion musket-cap ignition. Color case-hardened lock, browned barrel. Buttplate, triggerguard, barrelbands, sling swivels and nose cap of polished brass. Lock marked with stars and bars flag on tail and Athens, Georgia. Made by Pedersoli. Imported by Dixie Gun Works, others.
Price: Dixie Carbine PR0830 ....**$1,100.00**
Price: Artillery/Rifle PR3165..................................... **$925.00**
Price: Dixie Artillery Carbine PR0223 .... **$925.00**

PEDERSOLI COUNTRY HUNTER
Caliber: .50. **Barrel:** 26 in. octagonal. **Weight:** 6 lbs. **Length:** 41.75 in. overall. **Stock:** European walnut, halfstock. **Sights:** Rear notch, blade front. **Features:** Percussion, one barrel key. Made by Pedersoli. Imported by Dixie Gun Works.
Price: Percussion, .50 PR3155 .... **$625.00**

PEDERSOLI KENTUCKY RIFLE
Caliber: .32, .45 and .50. **Barrel:** 35.5 in. octagonal. **Weight:** 7.5 (.50 cal.) to 7.75 lbs. (.32 cal.) **Length:** 51 in. overall. **Stock:** European walnut, full-length stock. **Sights:** Notch rear, blade front. **Features:** Flintlock or percussion, brass patchbox, double-set triggers. Also available as kit guns for all calibers and ignition systems. Made by Pedersoli. Imported by Dixie Gun Works.
Price: Percussion, .32, PR3115 .... **$625.00**
Price: Flint, .32, FR3100 .... **$595.00**
Price: Percussion, .45, FR3120 .... **$625.00**
Price: Flint, .45, FR3105 .... **$595.00**
Price: Percussion, .50, FR3125 .... **$625.00**
Price: Flint, .50, FR3110 .... **$650.00**

PEDERSOLI KODIAK DOUBLE RIFLES AND COMBINATION GUN
Caliber: .50, .54 and .58 **Barrel:** 28.5 in.; 1:24/1:24/1:48 in. twist. **Weight:** 11.25/10.75/10 lbs. **Stock:** Straight grip European walnut. **Sights:** Two adjustable rear, steel ramp with brass bead front. **Features:** Percussion ignition, double triggers, sling swivels. A .72-caliber express rifle and a .50-caliber/12-gauge shotgun combination gun are also available. Blued steel furniture. Stainless steel nipple. Made by Pedersoli. Imported by Dixie Gun Works and some models by Cabela's and others.
Price: Rifle 50X50 PR0970 ....**$1,495.00**
Price: Rifle 54X54 PR0975 ....**$1,495.00**
Price: Rifle 58X58 PR0980 ....**$1,495.00**
Price: Combo 50X12 gauge PR0990 ....**$1,150.00**
Price: Express Rifle .72 caliber PR0916 ....**$1,525.00**

PEDERSOLI MORTIMER RIFLE & SHOTGUN
Caliber: .54, 12 gauge. **Barrel:** 36 in., 1:66 in. twist, and cylinder bore. **Weight:** 10 lbs. rifle, 9 lbs. shotgun. **Length:** 52.25 in. **Stock:** Halfstock walnut. **Sights:** Blued steel rear with flip-up leaf, blade front. **Features:** Percussion and flint ignition. Blued steel furniture. Single trigger. Lock with hammer safety and "waterproof pan" marked Mortimer. A percussion .45-caliber target version of this gun is available with a peep sight on the wrist, and a percussion shotgun version is also offered. Made by Pedersoli. Imported by Dixie.
Price: Flint Rifle, FR0151 ....**$1,525.00**
Price: Flint Shotgun FS0155.................................**$1,495.00**
Price: Percussion Shotgun PS3160.........................**$995.00**

PEDERSOLI ROCKY MOUNTAIN & MISSOURI RIVER HAWKEN RIFLES
Caliber: .54 (Rocky Mountain), .45 and .50 in Missouri River. **Barrel:** 34.75 in. octagonal with hooked breech; Rocky Mountain 1:65 in. twist; Missouri River 1:47 twist in .45 cal., and 1:24 twist in .50 cal. **Weight:** 10 lbs. **Length:** 52 in. overall. **Stock:** Maple or walnut, halfstock. **Sights:** Rear buckhorn with push elevator, silver blade front. **Features:** Percussion, brass furniture, double triggers, two barrel keys. Made by Pedersoli. Imported by Dixie Gun Works, others.
Price: Rocky Mountain, Maple PR3430 ....**$1,125.00**
Price: Rocky Mountain, Walnut PR3435................. **$975.00**
Price: Missouri River, .50 Walnut PR3415 .... **$925.00**
Price: Missouri River, .50 Maple PR3410 ....**$1,050.00**
Price: Missouri River, .45 Walnut PR3405 .... **$995.00**
Price: Missouri River, .45 Maple PR3080 ....**$1,050.00**

PEDERSOLI ZOUAVE RIFLE
Caliber: .58 percussion. **Barrel:** 33 inches. **Weight:** 9.5 lbs. **Length:**

49 inches. **Stock:** European walnut. **Sights:** Blade front, three-leaf military rear. **Features:** Percussion musket-cap ignition. One-piece solid barrel and bolster. Brass-plated patchbox. Made in Italy by Pedersoli. Imported by Cabela's, others.
Price: **$975.00**

RICHMOND 1861 RIFLE
Caliber: .58. **Barrel:** 40 inches. **Weight:** 9.5 lbs. **Length:** 55.5 in. overall. **Stock:** European walnut. **Sights:** Blade front, three-leaf military rear. **Features:** Reproduction of the original three-band rifle. Percussion musket-cap ignition. Lock marked C. S. Richmond, Virginia. Armory bright. Made by Pedersoli, Euro Arms. Imported by Cabela's, Dixie Gun Works and others.
Price: Cabela's **$950.00**
Price: From Dixie Gun Works, Made by Euro Arms
PR0846 ....**$1,150.00**

REMINGTON MODEL 700 ULTIMATE MUZZLELOADER
Caliber: .50 percussion. **Barrel:** 26 in., 1:26-in twist, satin stainless steel, fluted. **Length:** 47 in. **Stock:** Bell & Carlson black synthetic or laminated wood. **Sights:** None on synthetic stocked model, Williams peep and blade front on laminated-wood model. **Ramrod:** Stainless steel. **Weight:** 8.5 lbs. **Features:** Remington single shot Model 700 bolt action, Reprimable cartridge-case ignition using Remington Magnum Large Rifle Primer., sling studs.
Price: 86960 .50-cal. synthetic black, no sights **$999.00**
Price: 86950 . 50-caliber laminated wood,
Willliams peep sights **$949.00**

THOMPSON/CENTER ENCORE PRO HUNTER FX
Caliber: .50 as muzzleloading barrel. **Barrel:** 26 in., Weather Shield with relieved muzzle on muzzleloader; interchangeable with 14 centerfire calibers. **Weight:** 7 lbs. **Length:** 40.5 in. overall. **Stock:** Interchangeable American walnut butt and forend, black composite, FlexTech recoil-reducing camo stock as thumbhole or straight, rubber over-molded stock and fore-end. **Ramrod:** Solid aluminum. **Sights:** TruGlo fiber optic front and rear. **Features:** Blue or stainless steel. Uses the frame of the Encore centerfire pistol; break-open design using triggerguard spur; stainless steel universal breech plug; uses #209 shotshell primers. Made in U.S. by Thompson/Center Arms.
Price: .50-cal Stainless/Black FlexTech Stock Model 5800 .... **$649.00**
Price: .50-cal Stainless/Engraved frame FlexTech
RT-AP camo **$709.00**

THOMPSON/CENTER IMPACT MUZZLELOADING RIFLE
Caliber: .50-caliber. **Barrel:** 26 in., 1:28 twist, Weather Shield finish. **Weight:** 6.5 lbs. **Length:** 41.5 in. **Stock:** Straight Realtree Hardwoods HD or black composite. **Features:** Sliding-hood, break-open action, #209 primer ignition, removable breech plug, synthetic stock adjustable from 12.5 to 13.5 in., adjustable fiber-optic sights, aluminum ramrod, camo, QLA relieved muzzle system.
Price: .50-cal Stainless/Realtree Hardwoods,
Weather Shield **$324.00**
Price: .50-cal Blued/Black/scope, case...........................**$263.99**

THOMPSON/CENTER TRIUMPH MUZZLELOADER
Caliber: .50. **Barrel:** 28 in. Weather Shield coated. **Weight:** 6.5 lbs. **Stock:** FlexTech recoil-reducing. Black composite or Realtree AP HD

Prices given are believed to be accurate at time of publication however, many factors affect retail pricing so exact prices are not possible.

71ST EDITION, 2017 ✛ **513**

camo straight, rubber over-molded stock and fore-end. **Sights:** Fiber optic. **Ramrod:** Solid aluminum. **Features:** Break-open action. Quick Detachable Speed Breech XT plug, #209 shotshell primer ignition, easy loading QLA relieved muzzle, Cabela's, Bass Pro. Made in U.S. by Thompson/Center Arms.

Price:.50 cal. Blued/Black composite................................**$456.00**
Price: .50 cal. Weather Shield/Black composite..................**$517.00**
Price: .50 cal. Weather Shield/AP Camo stock....................**$578.00**

THOMPSON/CENTER TRIUMPH BONE COLLECTOR

Similar to the Triumph but with added FlexTech technology and Energy Burners to a shorter stock. Also added is Thompson/Center's premium fluted barrel with Weather Shield and their patented Power Rod.

Price: .50-cal Synthetic Realtree AP, fiber optics.….............. **$720.00**
Price: .50-cal Synthetic/Weather Shield Black.....................**$638.00**
Price: .50 cal. Weather Shield/AP Camo..........................**$679.00**
Price: .50 cal. Silver Weather Shield/AP Camo....................**$689.00**

THOMPSON/CENTER STRIKE

Caliber: .50. **Barrel:** 24 or 20 in. nitride finished, tapered barrel. **Weight:** 6.75 or 6.25 lbs. **Length:** 44 in. or 40 in. **Stock:** Walnut, black synthetic, G2-Vista Camo. **Finish:** Armornite nitride. **Features:** Break-open action, sliding hammerless cocking mechanism, optional pellet or loose powder primer holders, easy removable breech plugs retained by external collar, aluminum frame with steel mono-block to retain barrel, recoil pad. **Sights:** Williams fiber-optic sights furnished, drilled and tapped for scope. Made in the U.S. Introduced by Thompson/Center in 2015.

Price: .50 cal. 24-in. barrel, black synthetic stock **$499.00**
Price: .50 cal. 24-in. barrel, walnut stock **$599.00**
Price: .50 cal. 24-in. barrel, G2 camo stock **$549.00**

TRADITIONS BUCKSTALKER

Caliber: .50. **Barrel:** 24 in., Cerakote finished, Accelerator Breech Plug. **Weight:** 6 lbs. **Length:** 40 in. **Stock:** Synthetic, G2 Vista camo or black. **Sights:** Fiber-optic rear. **Features:** Break-open action, matte-finished action and barrel. **Ramrod:** Solid aluminum.

Price: R72003540 .50-cal. Synthetic stock /blued...............**$215.00**
Price: R72103540 .50-cal. Synthetic stock/Cerakote **$245.00**
Price: R72103547 .50-cal. Synthetic stock/G2-Vista **$289.00**
Price: R5-72003540 .50-cal. Synthetic stock/blued, scope....**$279.00**
Price: R5-72103547 .50-cal. Synthetic stock/Cerakote,
    scope. **$355.00**
Price: RY7223540 .50-cal. 13-in. pull, synthetic stock/
    blued..**$215.00**

TRADITIONS CROCKETT RIFLE

Caliber: .32. **Barrel:** 32 in., 1:48 in. twist. **Weight:** 6.75 lbs. **Length:** 49 in. overall. **Stock:** Beech, inletted toe plate. **Sights:** Blade front, fixed rear. **Features:** Set triggers, hardwood halfstock, brass furniture, color case-hardened lock. Percussion. From Traditions.

Price: R26128101 .32-cal. Percussion, finished **$494.00**
Price: RK52628100 .32-cal. Kit, percussion, hardwood,
    Armory bright, unfinished brass **$438.00**

TRADITIONS DEERHUNTER RIFLE SERIES

Caliber: .50. **Barrel:** 24 in., Cerakote finish, octagonal, 15/16 in. flats, 1:48 in. twist. **Weight:** 6 lbs. **Length:** 40 in. overall. **Stock:** Stained hardwood or All-Weather composite with rubber buttpad, sling swivels. **Ramrod:** Synthetic polymer. **Sights:** Fiber Optic blade front, adjustable rear fiber optics, offset hammer spur. **Features:** Flint or percussion with color case-hardened lock. Hooked breech, oversized triggerguard, blackened furniture, PVC ramrod. Drilled and tapped for scope mounting. Imported by Traditions, Inc.

Price: R36128101 .50-cal. Percussion hardwood, fib.opt **$304.00**
Price: R3590801 .50-cal. Flintlock, hardwood/blued, fib.opt. .**$365.00**
Price: R3690801 .50-cal. Flintlock, hardwood/blued,
    fiber optic L.H.…..**$389.00**
Price: R36108101 .50-cal. Percussion, hardwood/blued
    fiber optic …...**$295.00**
Price: R3500850 .50-cal. Flintlock, synthetic Cerakote
    fiber optic …...**$299.00**

Price: R3670856 .50-cal. Flintlock, synthetic Realtree,
    fiber optic……...**$374.00**
Price: R35108150 .50-cal. Percussion, blued, synthetic black
    fiber optic...**$249.00**

TRADITIONS EVOLUTION BOLT-ACTION BLACKPOWDER RIFLE

Caliber: .50 percussion. **Barrel:** 26 in., 1:28 in. twist, Cerakote finished barrel and action. **Length:** 39 in. **Sights:** Steel Williams fiber-optic sights. **Weight:** 7 to 7.25 lbs. **Length:** 45 in. overall. **Features:** Bolt action, cocking indicator, thumb safety, shipped with adaptors for No. 11 caps, musket caps and 209 shotgun primer ignition, sling swivels. Ramrod: Aluminum, sling studs. Available with exposed ignition as a Northwest Gun.

Price: R67113350 .50-cal. synthetic black, Cerakote **$304.00**
Price: R67113353 .50-cal. synthetic Realtree AP camo...... ...**$355.00**

TRADITIONS HAWKEN WOODSMAN RIFLE

Caliber: .50. **Barrel:** 28 in., blued, 15/16 in. flats. **Weight:** 7 lbs., 11 oz. **Length:** 44.5 in. overall. **Stock:** Walnut stained hardwood. **Sights:** Beaded blade front, hunting-style open rear adjustable for windage and elevation. **Features:** Brass patchbox and furniture. Double-set triggers. Flint or percussion. From Traditions.

Price: R2390801 .50-cal. Flintlock............................... **$519.00**
Price: R24008 .50-cal. Percussion **$479.00**
Price: KRC5208 .50-cal. Kit, percussion, hardwood/
    Armory bright, unfinished brass **$374.00**
Price: R3300801 ,50-cal. Percussion, .50 cal.,
    hardwood/blued **$324.00**
Price: R3200850 .50-cal. Flintlock,synthetic/blued,
    fib.opt…… **$329.00**
Price: RKC53008 .50-cal. Percussion Kit,
    hardwood, Armory bright, unfinished brass **$299.00**

TRADITIONS KENTUCKY RIFLE

Caliber: .50. **Barrel:** 33.5 in., 7/8 in. flats, 1:66 in. twist. **Weight:** 7 lbs. **Length:** 49 in. overall. **Stock:** Beech, inletted toe plate. **Sights:** Blade front, fixed rear. **Features:** Full-length, two-piece stock; brass furniture; color case-hardened lock. Flint or percussion. From Traditions, Bass Pro and others.

Price: R2010 .50-cal. Flintlock,1:66 twist **$489.00**
Price: R2020 .50-cal. Percussion, 1:66 twist...................... **$429.00**
Price: KRC52206 .50-cal. Kit, percussion, hardwood/Armory bright,
    unfinished brass **$355.00**

TRADITIONS PA PELLET FLINTLOCK

Caliber: .50. **Barrel:** 26 in., blued, 1:48 in. twist., Cerakote. **Weight:** 7 lbs. **Length:** 45 in. **Stock:** Hardwood, synthetic and synthetic break-up, sling swivels. **Sights:** Fiber optic. **Features:** New flintlock action, removable breech plug, available as left-hand model with hardwood stock.

Price: R3800501 .50-cal. Hardwood, blued, fib.opt **$459.00**
Price: R3890501 .50-cal. Hardwood, left-hand, blued **$459.00**
Price: R3800550 .50-cal. Synthetic/blued, fib. opt................ **$399.00**
Price: R3810556 .50-cal. Synthetic/Cerakote, fib. opt........... **$465.00**
Price: R3840556 .50-cal. Synthetic/Realtree Xtra.,
    fib.opt **$489.00**

TRADITIONS PENNSYLVANIA RIFLE

Caliber: .50. **Barrel:** 40.25 in., 7/8 in. flats, 1:66 in. twist, octagon.

Weight: 9 lbs. **Length:** 57.5 in. overall. **Stock:** Walnut. **Sights:** Blade front, adjustable rear. **Features:** Single-piece walnut stock, brass patchbox and ornamentation. Double-set triggers. Flint or percussion. From Traditions.
Price: R2090 .50-cal. Flintlock, 1:66 twist **$799.00**
Price: R2100 .50-cal. Percussion, 1:66 twist **$754.00**

TRADITIONS PURSUIT ULTRALIGHT MUZZLELOADER

Caliber: .50. **Barrel:** 26 in., chromoly tapered, fluted barrel with premium Cerakote finish, Accelerator Breech Plug. **Weight:** 5.5 lbs. **Length:** 42 in. **Stock:** Rubber over-molded Soft Touch camouflage, straight and thumbhole stock options. **Sights:** 3-9x40 scope with medium rings and bases, mounted and bore sighted by a factory trained technician. **Features:** Break-open action, Williams fiber-optic sights.
Price: R741140 .50-cal. Synthetic/Cerakote fib.opt..... .... **$309.00**
Price: R7411415 .50-cal. Synthetic/Cerakote/
   Mossy Oak Infinity, fib. opt...... .... **$385.00**
Price: R741140NS .50-cal. synthetic/black Steel,
   no sights **$309.00**
Price: R7411415NS .50-cal. Synthetic/Cerakote,
   no sights **$370.00**
Price: R741140 .50-cal.Synthetic/Cerakote,
   3x9 scope **$404.00**
Price: R741148NS .50-cal. Synthetic/Cerakote,
   Buck Camo, 3x9 scope... .... **$439.00**
Price: R74446NS .50-cal. Synthetic/Realtree Xtra
   stock and barrel, 3x9 range-finding scope **$515.00**

TRADITIONS TENNESSEE RIFLE

Caliber: .50. **Barrel:** 24 in., octagon, 15/16 in. flats, 1:66 in. twist. **Weight:** 6 lbs. **Length:** 40.5 in. overall. **Stock:** Stained beech. **Sights:** Blade front, fixed rear. **Features:** One-piece stock has brass furniture, cheekpiece, double-set trigger, V-type mainspring. Flint or percussion. From Traditions.
Price: R2310 .50-cal. Flintlock/hardwood stock **$539.00**
Price: R2320 .50-cal. Percussion/hardwood stock **$479.00**

TRADITIONS TRACKER 209 IN-LINE RIFLE

Caliber: .50. **Barrel:** 24 in., blued or Cerakote, 1:28 in. twist. **Weight:** 6 lbs., 4 oz. **Length:** 43 in. **Stock:** Black synthetic. **Ramrod:** Synthetic, high-impact polymer. **Sights:** Lite Optic blade front, adjustable rear. **Features:** Striker-fired action, thumb safety, adjustable trigger, rubber buttpad, sling swivel studs. Takes 150 grains of Pyrodex pellets, one-piece musket cap and 209 ignition systems. Drilled and tapped for scope. Legal for use in Northwest. From Traditions.
Price: R44003470 .50-cal. Synthetic/blued **$184.00**

TRADITIONS VORTEK STRIKERFIRE

Caliber: .50. **Barrel:** 28 in., chromoly, tapered, fluted barrel. **Weight:** 6.25 lbs. **Length:** 44 in. **Stock:** Over-molded soft-touch straight stock, removable buttplate for in-stock storage. Finish: Premium Cerakote and Realtree Xtra. **Features:** Break-open action, sliding hammerless cocking mechanism, drop-out trigger assembly, speed load system, accelerator breech plug, recoil pad. **Sights:** Optional 3-9x40 muzzleloader scope.

Price: R561140NS .50-cal. Synthetic/black Hogue Over-mold,
   Cerakote barrel **$493.00**
Price: R561146NS .50-cal. Synthetic/Realtree Xtra camo, Cerakote
   barrel **$569.00**
Price: R29564446 .50-cal. Synthetic Realtree Xtra camo stock and
   barrel, 3X9 scope.. **$649.00**

TRADITIONS VORTEK STRIKERFIRE LDR

Caliber: .50 **Barrel:** 30 in., chromoly, tapered, fluted barrel. **Weight:** 6.8 lbs. **Length:** 46 in. **Stock:** Over-molded soft-touch straight stock, removable buttplate for in-stock storage. **Finish:** Premium Cerakote and Realtree Xtra. **Features:** Break-open action, sliding hammerless cocking mechanism, drop-out trigger assembly, speed load system, accelerator breech plug, recoil pad. **Sights:** Optional 3-9x40 muzzleloader scope.
Price: R491120NS .50-cal, Synthetic/black Hogue Over-mold,
   Cerakote barrel, no sights............................... **$459.00**
Price: R491128NS .50-cal Synthetic/Realtree Xtra camo,
   Cerakote barrel **$530.00**
Price: R29-594446 .50-cak, Synthetic Realtree Xtra camo on stock
   and barrel, 3X9 scope Cerakote barrel......................... **$629.00**

TRADITIONS VORTEK STRIKERFIRE LDR NORTHWEST MODEL

Caliber: .50. **Barrel:** 28 or 30 in. chromoly tapered, fluted barrel. **Weight:** 6.25 or 6.8 lbs. **Length:** 46 or 48 in. **Stock:** Synthetic black, over-molded soft-touch straight stock, removable buttplate for in-stock storage. **Finish:** Premium Cerakote. **Features:** Break-open action, sliding hammerless cocking mechanism, drop-out trigger assembly, speed load system, accelerator breech plug, recoil pad. **Sights:** Williams fiber-optic sights.
Price: R401120WM .50-cal. Northwest,
   synthetic/black, LDR Model, 30-in. Cerakote barrel **$489.00**
Price: R461123WM .50-cal. Northwest, synthetic/Realtree Xtra
   Camo, soft touch Hogue overmold,
   28-in. Cerakote barrel **$625.00**
Price: 481123WM .50-cal. Thumbhole stock, Hogue overmold,
   Realtree AP camo.. .**$525.00**

TRADITIONS VORTEK ULTRALIGHT

Caliber: .50. **Barrel:** 28 in., chromoly, tapered, fluted barrel. **Weight:** 6.25 lbs. **Length:** 44 in. **Stock:** Over-molded soft-touch straight stock. **Finish:** Premium Cerakote, Realtree AP, Reaper Buck. **Features:** Break-open action, hammer cocking mechanism, drop-out trigger assembly, speed load system, accelerator breech plug, recoil pad. **Sights:** Optional 3-9x40 muzzleloader scope.
Price: R461120 .50-cal. Synthetic/black Hogue Over-mold,
   Cerakote barrel, fib. opt…................................... **$449.00**
Price: R461123 .50-cal Synthetic/Realtree AP camo
   Hogue, Cerakote barrel, fib. opt…. **$515.00**
Price: R461128 .50-cal Synthetic/Reaper Buck camo,
   Cerakote barrel, fib. opt…,.................................. **$515.00**
Price: R461140NS .50-cal. Synthetic/Reaper Buck camo,
   Hogue
   Over-mold, no sights **$515.00**
Price: R481128NS .50-cal. Synthetic/Realtree AP
   camo Hogue, Cerakote barrel, no sights........................**$519.00**
Price: R461120 NS .50-cal. Synthetic/Reaper
   Buck camo, Cerakote barrel, no sights **$519.00**
Price: R20-464423NS .50-cal. Synthetic/Realtree AP
   camo stock and barrel, 2x9 rangefinder scope.............**$599.00**
Price: R26-464428 NS .50.cal. Synthetic/Reaper Buck
   camo stock and barrel, 2x9 rangefinder scope.............**$599.00**
Price: R461146WA .50-cal. Synthetic/Realtree AP, Hogue,
   Cerakote barrel, fib. opt.................................**$529.00**
Price: R481146WA .50-cal. Synthetic Thumbhole/Realtree
   Xtra camo, Cerakote barrel, fib. opt. **$529.00**
Price: R491140WA (LDR) , Synthetic/Black, Hogue,
   30-in. barrel, Cerakote barrel, fib. opt **$499.00**

TRADITIONS VORTEK ULTRALIGHT NORTHWEST MAGNUM
Caliber: .50. **Barrel:** 28 or 30 in. chromoly tapered, fluted barrel. **Weight:** 6.25 or 6.8 lbs. **Length:** 44 or 46 in. **Stock:** Over-molded, soft-touch, straight or thumbhole stock. **Finish:** Premium Cerakote and Realtree AP. **Features:** Break-open action, hammer cocking mechanism, musket-cap ignition, drop-out trigger assembly, speed load system, accelerator breech plug, recoil pad. **Sights:** Williams fiber-optic sights.
Price: R461140WA .50-cal. Synthetic/black Hogue
Over-mold, Cerakote barrel, fib. opt. $469.00
Price: R461146WA .50-cal. Synthetic/Realtree AP, Hogue,
Cerakote barrel, fib. opt..$529.00
Price: R481146WA .50-cal. Synthetic Thumbhole/Realtree
Xtra camo, Cerakote barrel, fib. opt. $529.00
Price: R491140WA (LDR) , Synthetic/Black, Hogue,
30-in. barrel, Cerakote barrel, fib. opt $499.00

WOODMAN ARMS PATRIOT
Caliber: .45, .50. **Barrel:** 24 in., nitride coated 416 stainless, 1:24 twist in .45, 1:28 twist in .50. **Weight:** 5.75 lbs. **Length:** 43-in,. **Stocks:** Laminated, walnut or hydrographic dipped. Synthetic black, over-molded soft-touch straight stock. **Finish:** Nitride black and black anodized. **Features:** Break-open action, hammerless cocking mechanism, match-grade patented trigger assembly, speed load system, recoil pad. **Sights:** Picatinny rail with built-in rear and 1-inch or 30 mm scope mounts, red fiber-optic front bead.
Price: Patriot .45 or .50-cal...$899.00

BAKER CAVALRY SHOTGUN

Gauge: 20. **Barrels:** 11.25 inches. **Weight:** 5.75 pounds. **Length:** 27.5 in. overall. **Stock:** American walnut. **Sights:** Bead front. **Features:** Reproduction of shotguns carried by Confederate cavalry. Single non-selective trigger, back-action locks. No. 11 percussion musket-cap ignition. Blued barrel with steel furniture. Case-hardened lock. Pedersoli also makes a 12-gauge coach-length version of this back-action-lock shotgun with 20-inch barrels, and a full-length version in 10, 12 and 20 gauge. Made by Pedersoli. Imported by Cabela's and others.
Price: Cabela's, Pedersoli..$899.99

CABELA'S HOWDAH HUNTER 20-GAUGE PISTOL

Gauge: 20. **Barrels:** Cylinder bored, 11.25 in. **Weight:** 4.5 lbs. **Length:** 17.25 in. **Stock:** American walnut with checkered grip. **Sights:** Brass bead front sight. **Features:** Blued barrels, swamped barrel rib, engraved, color case-hardened locks and hammers, captive steel ramrod. Available with detachable shoulder stock, case, holster and mold. Made by Pedersoli. Imported by Cabela's, Dixie Gun Works, Taylor's and others.
Price: Cabela's 20-gauge $749.99
Price: Cabela's 20-gauge presentation box
    and accessories..$1,199.99

KNIGHT TK-2000 TURKEY SHOTGUN

Gauge: 12. **Ignition:** #209 primer with Full Plastic Jacket, musket cap or No. 11. Striker-fired with one-piece removable hammer assembly. **Barrel:** 26 inches. **Choke:** Extra-full and improved cylinder available. **Stock:** Realtree Xtra Green straight or thumbhole. **Weight:** 7.7 pounds. **Sights:** Williams fully adjustable rear, fiber-optic front. **Features:** Striker-fired action, receiver is drilled and tapped for scope, adjustable trigger, removable breech plug, double-safety system. Made in U.S. by Knight Rifles.
Price: Standard......................................$523.99 to $733.99
Price: Thumbhole stock................................$504.99 to $714.99

PEDERSOLI KODIAK MK III RIFLE-SHOTGUN COMBINATION GUN

Gauge: .50 caliber/12 gauge. **Barrels:** 28.5 in. **Weight:** 10.75 lbs. **Stock:** Straight grip, European walnut. **Sights:** Two adjustable rear, steel ramp with brass bead. **Features:** Percussion ignition, double triggers, sling swivels, 12-gauge cylinder bored barrel. Blued steel furniture. Stainless steel nipple. Made by Pedersoli. Imported by Dixie Gun Works, and some models by Cabela's and others.
Price: Combo 50X12 gauge PR0990 ....$1,150.00
Price: Combo .58X12 gauge PR0995 ....$1,150.00

PEDERSOLI MAGNUM PERCUSSION SHOTGUN & COACH GUN

Gauge: 10, 12, 20 **Barrel:** Chrome-lined blued barrels, 25.5 in. Imp. cyl. and Mod. **Weight:** 7.25, 7, 6.75 lbs. **Length:** 45 in. overall. **Stock:** Hand-checkered walnut, 14-in. pull. **Features:** Double triggers, light hand engraving, case-hardened locks, sling swivels. Made by Pedersoli. From Dixie Gun Works, others.
Price: 10-ga. PS1030 .... $995.00
Price: 10-ga. kit PS1040 .... $895.00
Price: 12-ga. PS0930.. $1,125.00
Price: 12-ga. Kit PS0940 .... $875.00
Price: 12-ga. Coach gun, 25.5-in. barrels, CylXCyl.
    PS0914... $1,050.00
Price: 20-ga. PS0334.. $1,000.00

PEDERSOLI MORTIMER SHOTGUN

Gauge: 12. **Barrel:** 36 in., 1:66 in., cylinder bore. **Weight:** 9 pounds. **Length:** 52.25 in. **Stock:** Halfstock walnut. **Sights:** Bead front. **Features:** Percussion and flint ignition. Blued steel furniture. Single trigger. Lock with hammer safety and "waterproof pan" on flintlock gun. Lock marked Mortimer. Rifle versions of this gun are also available. Made by Pedersoli. Imported by Dixie.
Price: Flint Shotgun FS0155....................................$1,495.00
Price: Percussion Shotgun PS3160..$995.00

PEDERSOLI OLD ENGLISH SHOTGUN

Gauge: 12 **Barrels:** Browned, 28.5 in. Cyl. and Mod. **Weight:** 7.5 lbs. **Length:** 45 in. overall. **Stock:** Hand-checkered American maple, cap box, 14-in. pull. **Features:** Double triggers, light hand engraving on lock, cap box and tang, swivel studs for sling attachment. Made by Pedersoli. From Dixie Gun Works, others.
Price: PR4090 .... $1,750.00

AIR ARMS ALFA PROJ COMP PCP PISTOL
Caliber: .177 Pellets. **Barrel:** Rifled. **Weight:** 1.94 lbs. **Length:** 15.5 inches. **Power:** Pre-charged pneumatic. **Sights:** Front post, fully adjustable rear blade. **Features:** 10 Meter competition class pistol, highly adjustable trigger, **Velocity:** 500 fps.
Price: **$850.00**

AIRFORCE TALON P

AIRFORCE TALON P
Caliber: .25. **Barrel:** Rifled 12.0 inches. **Weight:** 3.5 lbs. **Length:** 23.25". **Sights:** None, grooved for scope. **Features:** Quick-detachable air tank with adjustable power. Match grade Lothar Walther, massive power output in a highly compact size **Velocity:** 900 fps.
Price: **$479.95**

ASG CZ P-09 PELLET GUN
Caliber: .177 pellets and steel BBs. **Barrel:** Rifled and threaded for barrel extension. **Power:** CO2. **Weight:** 1.6 lbs. **Length:** 8.2 inches. **Sights:** Fixed. **Features:** Polymer frame, blowback **Velocity:** 412 fps.
Price: **$104.95**

ASG CZ SP-01 NON-BLOWBACK AIR PISTOL
Caliber: .177 steel BBs. **Barrel:** Smoothbore threaded for barrel extension. **Power:** CO2. **Weight:** 1.3 1lbs. **Length:** 8.27 inches. **Sights:** Fiber optics front and rear. **Features:** Replica based on the CZ- 75 series pistols. **Velocity:** 380 fps.
Price: **$59.95**

ASG CZ 75 BLOWBACK AIR PISTOL
Caliber: .177 BBs. **Barrel:** Smoothbore. **Weight:** 2.09 lbs. **Length:** 8.72 inches. **Power:** CO2. **Sights:** Fixed. **Features:** Full metal construction, blowback. **Velocity:** 312 fps.
Price: **$159.95**

ASG CZ 75 P-07 DUTY
BLOWBACK AIR PISTOL

ASG CZ 75 P-07 DUTY BLOWBACK AIR PISTOL
Caliber: .177 steel BBs. **Barrel:** Smoothbore threaded for barrel extension. **Weight:** 1.81 lbs. **Length:** 7.32 inches. **Power:** CO2. **Sights:** Fixed. **Features:** Full metal construction, weaver rail, blowback. **Velocity:** 320 fps.
Price: **$99.95**

ASG CZ 75 P-07 DUTY NON-BLOWBACK AIR PISTOL
Caliber: .177 Steel BBs. **Barrel:** Smoothbore, threaded for barrel extension. **Weight:** 1.8 lbs. **Length:** 7.5 inches. **Power:** CO2. **Sights:** Fixed. **Features:** Realistic look and feel **Velocity:** 377 fps.
Price: **$79.95**

ASG CZ 75 P-07 DUTY DUAL TONE AIR PISTOL
Caliber: .177 Steel BBs. **Barrel:** Smoothbore, threaded for barrel extension. **Weight:** 1.81 lbs. **Length:** 7.32 inches. **Power:** CO2 **Sights:** Fixed. **Features:** Metal slide, front rail. **Velocity:** 320.
Price: **$119.95**

ASG CZ 75D COMPACT AIR PISTOL
Caliber: .177 Steel BBs. **Barrel:** Smoothbore. **Weight:** 1.46 lbs. **Length:** 7.28 inches. **Power:** CO2. **Sights:** Adjustable rear sight and blade front sight. **Features: Compact** design. **Velocity:** 380 fps.
Price: **$90.00**

ASG DAN WESSON 715 6" PELLET REVOLVER AIR PISTOL
Caliber: .177 Pellets. **Barrel:** Rifled. **Weight:** 2.3 lbs. **Length:** 11.73 inches. **Power:** CO2. **Sights:** Blade front and adjustable rear sight. **Features:** Rifled barrel and comes with a magazine capacity of 6 rounds and includes a speed loader. **Velocity:** 430 fps.
Price: **$179.95**

ASG BERSA BP9CC

ASG BERSA BP9CC DUAL TONE BLOWBACK AIR PISTOL
Caliber: .177 Steel BBs. **Barrel:** Smoothbore **Weight:** 1.35 lbs. **Length:** 6.61 inches. **Power:** CO2. **Sights:** Fixed 3-dot system. **Features:** Blowback, metal slide, weaver accessory rail. **Velocity:** 350 fps.
Price: **$119.95**

ASG STI INTERNATIONAL DUTY ONE BLOWBACK AIR PISTOL
Caliber: .177 Steel BBs. **Barrel:** Smoothbore **Weight:** 1.82 lbs. **Length:** 8.66 inches. **Power:** CO2. **Sights:** Fixed. **Features:** Blowback, accessory rail, and metal slide. **Velocity:** 383 fps.
Price: **$120.00**

        Prices given are believed to be accurate at time of publication however, many factors affect retail pricing so exact prices are not possible.

AIRGUNS—Handguns

ASG STEYR MANNLICHER M9-A1 AIR PISTOL
Caliber: .177 Steel BBs. **Barrel:** Smoothbore **Weight:** 1.17 lbs. **Length:** 7.36 inches. **Power:** CO2. **Sights:** Fixed. **Features:** Non-Blowback design, accessory rail, extremely high shot count per CO2. **Velocity:** 449 fps.
Price: $44.95

BEEMAN P17 MAGNUM AIR PISTOL
Caliber: .177 Pellets. **Barrel:** Rifled. **Weight:** 1.7 lbs. **Length:** 9.6 inches. **Power:** Single stroke pneumatic. **Sights:** Front and rear fiber-optic sights, rear sight fully adjustable. **Features:** Exceptional trigger, Grooved for scope mounting with dry-fire feature for practice. **Velocity:** 410 fps.
Price: $44.99

BEEMAN P1 MAGNUM AIR PISTOL
Caliber: .177, .20, .22. Pellets. **Barrel:** Rifled. **Weight:** 2.5 lbs. **Length:** 11 inches. **Power:** Single stroke, spring-piston. **Grips:** Checkered walnut. **Sights:** Blade front, square notch rear with click micrometer adjustments for windage and elevation. Grooved for scope mounting. **Features:** Dual power for .177 and 20 cal.; Compatible with all Colt 45 auto grips. Dry-firing feature for practice. **Velocity:** varies by caliber and power setting
Price: .... $529.95 to $564.95

BEEMAN P3 PNEUMATIC AIR PISTOL
Caliber: .177. Pellets. **Barrel:** Rifled **Weight:** 1.7 lbs. **Length:** 9.6 inches. **Power:** Single-stroke pneumatic. **Sights:** Front and rear fiber-optic sights, rear sight fully adjustable. **Features:** Groved for scope mounting, exceptional trigger, automatic safety. **Velocity:** 410 fps.
Price: $290.00

BEEMAN P11 AIR PISTOL
Caliber: .177 & .22. **Barrel:** Rifled. **Weight:** 2.6 lbs. **Length:** 10.75 inches. **Power:** Single-stroke pneumatic with high & low settings. **Sights:** front ramp sight, fully adjustable rear sight. **Features:** 2-stage adjustable trigger and automatic safety. **Velocity:** Up to 600 fps in .177 caliber and Up to 460 fps in .22 caliber.
Price: .... $614.95 to $634.95

BEEMAN HW70A AIR PISTOL
Caliber: .177. Pellets **Barrel:** Rifled. **Weight:** 2.4 lbs. **Length:** 12.8 inches. **Power:** Single stroke, spring-piston. **Sights:** Hooded post front, square notch rear adjustable for windage and elevation. **Features:** Adjustable trigger, 31-lb. cocking effort, automatic barrel safety. **Velocity:** 440 fps.
Price: $334.95

BENJAMIN MARAUDER PCP PISTOL
Caliber: .22 **Barrel:** Rifled. **Weight:** 2.7 lbs. **Length:** Pistol length 18 inches / Carbine length 29.75 inches. **Power:** Pre-charged pneumatic **Sights:** none - grooved for optics. **Features:** Multi-shot (8-round rotary magazine) bolt action, shrouded steel barrel, two-stage adjustable trigger, includes both pistol grips and a carbine stock and is built in America. **Velocity:** 700 fps.
Price: $500.00

BENJAMIN MARAUDER WOODS WALKER PCP PISTOL
Caliber: .22 **Barrel:** Rifled. **Weight:** 2.7 lbs. **Length:** Pistol length 18 inches / Carbine length 29.75 inches. **Power:** Pre-charged pneumatic **Sights:** Includes CenterPoint Multi-TAC Quick Aim Sight. **Features:** Multi-shot (8-round rotary magazine) bolt action, shrouded steel barrel, two-stage adjustable trigger, includes both pistol grips and a carbine stock and is built in America. **Velocity:** 700 fps.
Price: $550.00

BENJAMIN TRAIL NP BREAK BARREL PISTOL
Caliber: .177 Pellets **Barrel:** Rifled. **Weight:** 3.43 lbs. **Length:** 16 inches. **Power:** Single cock, nitro piston. **Sights:** Fiber-optic front, fully adjustable rear. **Features:** Grooved for scope, **Velocity:** To 625 fps
Price: $90.00

BERETTA MODEL 84FS AIR PISTOL
Caliber: .177 Steel BBs. **Barrel:** Smoothbore **Weight:** 1.4 lbs. **Length:** 7 inches. **Power:** CO2. **Sights:** Fixed. **Features:** Highly realistic replica action pistol, blowback operation, full metal construction. **Velocity:** To 360 fps.
Price: $119.95

BERETTA MODEL 84FS

BERETTA MODEL PX4 AIR PISTOL
Caliber: .177 Pellet / .177 Steel BBs. **Barrel:** Rifled **Weight:** 1.6 lbs. **Length:** 7.6 inches. **Power:** CO2. **Sights:** Blade front sight and fixed rear sight. **Features:** Semi-automatic, 16-shot capacity with maximum of 40-shots per fill, dual ammo capable. **Velocity:** To 380 fps.
Price: $119.99

BERETTA ELITE II CO2 PISTOL
Caliber: .177 Steel BBs. **Barrel:** Smoothbore **Weight:** 1.5 lbs. **Length:** 8.5 inches. **Power:** CO2. **Sights:** Blade front sight and fixed rear sight. **Features:** Semi-automatic, 19-shot capacity. **Velocity:** Up to 410 fps.
Price: $49.99

BERETTA 90TWO CO2 BB PISTOL & LASER
Caliber: .177 Steel BBs. **Barrel:** Smoothbore **Weight:** 1.99 lbs. **Length:** 8.5 inches. **Power:** CO2. **Sights:** Blade front sight and fixed rear sight. **Features:** Includes rail mounted tactical laser, semi-automatic, 21-shot capacity. **Velocity:** To 375 fps.
Price: $69.90

BERETTA MODEL 92A1 CO2 BB PISTOL
Caliber: .177 Steel BBs. **Barrel:** Smoothbore **Weight:** 2.4 lbs. **Length:** 8.5 inches. **Power:** CO2. **Sights:** Fixed. **Features:** Highly realistic replica action pistol, 18 shot semi-automatic, full metal construction, selectable fire semi-automatic & full-automatic. **Velocity:** To 330 fps.
Price: $149.99

BROWNING 800 EXPRESS AIR PISTOL
Caliber: .177 Pellets. **Barrel:** Rifled. **Weight:** 3.9 lbs. **Length:** 18 inches. **Power:** Single cock, spring-piston. **Sights:** Fiber optic front sight and adjustable fiber optic rear sight. **Features:** Automatic safety, 11mm dovetail rail scope mounting possible. **Velocity:** 700 fps.
Price: $168.00

BROWNING BUCK MARK URX

BROWNING BUCK MARK URX AIR PISTOL
Caliber: .177 Pellet **Barrel:** Rifled **Weight:** 1.5 lbs. **Length:** 12.0 inches. **Power:** Single cock, spring-piston. **Sights:** Front ramp sight, fully adjustable rear notch sight. **Features:** Weaver rail for scope mounting, light cocking force. **Velocity:** 360 fps.
Price: $50.00

COLT PYTHON CO2 PISTOL
Caliber: .177 Steel BBs. **Barrel:** Smoothbore **Weight:** 2.6 lbs. **Length:** 11.25 inches. **Power:** CO2. **Sights:** Fixed. **Features:** High quality **replica,** swing-out cylinder, removable casings and functioning

Prices given are believed to be accurate at time of publication however, many factors affect retail pricing so exact prices are not possible.

71ST EDITION, 2017 ⊕ **519**

COLT PYTHON

COLT DEFENDER

ejector, multiple finishes other options, **Velocity:** To 400 fps.
Price: **$149.99**

COLT DEFENDER BB AIR PISTOL
Caliber: .177 Steel BBs. **Barrel:** Smoothbore **Weight:** 1.6-lbs. **Length:** 6.75 inches. **Power:** CO2. **Sights:** Fixed with blade ramp front sight. **Features:** Semi-automatic, 16-shot capacity, all metal construction, realistic weight and feel. **Velocity:** 410 fps.
Price: **$75.00**

COLT 1911 SPECIAL COMBAT CLASSIC BB AIR PISTOL
Caliber: .177 Steel BBs. **Barrel:** Smoothbore. **Weight:** 2.05 lbs. **Length:** 8.58 inches. **Power:** CO2. **Sights:** Blade front sight and adjustable rear sight. **Features:** Semi-automatic, 20-shot capacity, realistic action, weight and feel. **Velocity:** 400 fps.
Price: **$120.00**

COLT 1911 A1 CO2 PELLET PISTOL
Caliber: .177 Pellets. **Barrel:** Rifled **Weight:** 2.4 lbs. **Length:** 9.0 inches. **Power:** CO2. **Sights:** Blade ramp front sight and adjustable rear sight. **Features:** Semi-automatic, 8-shot capacity, all metal construction, realistic weight and feel. **Velocity:** 425 fps.
Price: **$259.99**

COLT COMMANDER CO2 PISTOL
Caliber: .177 Steel BBs. **Barrel:** Smoothbore. **Weight:** 2.1 lbs. **Length:** 8.5 inches. **Power:** CO2. **Sights:** Blade front sight and fixed rear sight. **Features:** Semi-automatic, 18-shot capacity, highly realistic replica pistol. **Velocity:** 325 fps.
Price: **$119.99**

COLT SINGLE ACTION ARMY CO2 REVOLVER
Caliber: .177 Steel BBs. **Barrel:** Smoothbore. **Weight:** 2.1 lbs. **Length:** 11 inches. **Power:** CO2. **Sights:** Blade front sight and fixed rear sight. **Features:** Full metal revolver with manual safety, realistic loading, 6 individual shells, highly accurate, full metal replica pistol, multiple finishes, grips and custom engraved, special editions available. **Velocity:** 410 fps.
Price: . . . . **$149.99 to $449.99**

COLT SINGLE ACTION ARMY CO2 PELLET REVOLVER
Caliber: .177 Pellets. **Barrel:** Rifled. **Weight:** 2.1 lbs. **Length:** 11 inches. **Power:** CO2. **Sights:** Blade front sight and fixed rear sight. **Features:** Full metal revolver with manual safety, realistic loading, 6 individual shells, highly accurate, full metal replica pistol, multiple finishes and grips available. **Velocity:** 380 fps.
Price: **$179.99**

CROSMAN 2240
Caliber: .22. **Barrel:** Rifled. **Weight:** 1.8 lbs. **Length:** 11.13 inches. **Power:** CO2. **Sights:** Blade front, rear adjustable. **Features:** Single

shot bolt action, ambidextrous grip, all metal construction. **Velocity:** 460 fps.
Price: **$79.95**

CROSMAN 2300S CO2 TARGET PISTOL
Caliber: .177 Pellets **Barrel:** Rifled. **Weight:** 2.66 lbs. **Length:** 16 inches. **Power:** CO2. **Sights:** Front fixed sight and Williams notched rear sight. **Features:** Meets IHMSA rules for Production Class Silhouette Competitions. Lothar Walter match grade barrel, adjustable trigger, adjustable hammer, stainless steel bolt, 60 shots per CO2 cartridge. **Velocity:** 520 fps.
Price: **$299.99**

CROSMAN 2300T CO2 TARGET PISTOL
Caliber: .177 Pellets. **Barrel:** Rifled. **Weight:** 2.66 lbs. **Length:** 13.25 inches. **Power:** CO2. **Sights:** Single-shot, bolt action, front fixed sight and LPA rear sight. **Features:** Adjustable trigger, designed for shooting clubs and organizations that teach pistol shooting and capable of firing 40 shots per CO2 cartridge. **Velocity:** 420 fps.
Price: **$190.00**

CROSMAN SR .357 REVOLVER
Caliber: .177 Steel BBs. **Barrel:** Smoothbore. **Weight:** 2 lbs. **Length:** 11.38 inches. **Power:** CO2. **Sights:** Blade front, rear adjustable. **Features:** Semi-auto (10-shot pellet / 6 shot BBs) with revolver styling and finger-molded grip design. Multiple finishes available. **Velocity:** 450 fps.
Price: . . . . **$129.95 to 149.95**

CROSMAN C11
Caliber: .177 Steel BBs. **Barrel:** Smoothbore **Weight:** 1.4 lbs. **Length:** 7.0 inches. **Power:** CO2. **Sights:** Fixed. **Features:** Compact semi-automatic BB pistol, front accessory rail. **Velocity:** 480 fps
Price: **$49.99**

CROSMAN C41 CO2 PISTOL
Caliber: .177 Steel BBs. **Barrel:** Smoothbore **Weight:** 2 lbs. **Length:** 6.75 inches. **Power:** CO2. **Sights:** Fixed. **Features:** Compact, realistic weight and feel. **Velocity:** To 495 fps.
Price: **$90.00**

CROSMAN 1377C / P1377
Caliber: .177 Pellets. **Barrel:** Rifled **Weight:** 2 lbs. **Length:** 13.63 inches. **Power:** Multi-pump pneumatic. **Sights:** Front fixed sight and adjustable rear sight. **Features:** Single shot, bolt action. **Velocity:** 600 fps.
Price: **$76.95**

CROSMAN 1322
Caliber: .22. **Barrel:** Rifled **Weight:** 2 lbs. **Length:** 13.63 inches. **Power:** Multi-pump pneumatic. **Sights:** Front fixed sight and adjustable rear sight. **Features:** Single shot, bolt action. **Velocity:** To 460 fps.
Price: **$76.95**

DAISY MODEL 717

DAISY AVANTI 717 TRIUMPH MATCH AIR PISTOL
Caliber: .177 Pellets. **Barrel:** Rifled. **Weight:** 2.25 lbs. **Length:** 13.5 inches. **Power:** Single-stroke pneumatic. **Sights:** Blade and ramp front, open rear with windage and elevation adjustments. **Features:** Single pump pneumatic pistol. **Velocity:** 360 fps.
Price: **$203.99**

DAISY AVANTI MODEL 747 TRIUMPH AIR PISTOL
Caliber: .177 Pellets. **Barrel:** Rifled. **Weight:** 2.35 lbs. **Length:** 13.5 inches. **Power:** Single-stroke pneumatic. **Sights:** Blade and ramp front, open rear with windage and elevation adjustments. **Features:**

Single pump pneumatic pistol. Lothar Walther rifled high-grade steel barrel; crowned 12 lands and grooves, right-hand twist. Precision bore sized for match pellets. **Velocity:** 360 fps.
Price: **$264.99**

DAISY POWERLINE 340 AIR PISTOL
Caliber: .177 Steel BBs. **Barrel:** Smoothbore, **Weight:** 1.0 lbs. **Length:** 8.5 inches. **Power:** Single cock, spring-piston. **Sights:** Fixed. **Features:** Spring-air action, 200-shot BB reservoir with a 13-shot Speed-load Clip located in the grip. **Velocity:** 230 fps.
Price: **$23.99**

DAISY POWERLINE 415 AIR PISTOL
Caliber: .177 Steel BBs. **Barrel:** Smoothbore, **Weight:** 1.0 lbs. **Length:** 8.6 inches. **Power:** CO2. **Sights:** Fiber optic front, fixed open rear. **Features:** Semi-automatic 21 shot BB pistol. **Velocity:** 500 fps.
Price: **$35.99**

DAISY POWERLINE 5170

DAISY POWERLINE 5170 AIRSTRIKE
Caliber: .177 Steel BBs. **Barrel:** Smoothbore. **Weight:** 1.0 lbs. **Length:** 9.5 Inches. **Power:** CO2. **Sights:** Blade and ramp front, open rear. **Features:** Semi-automatic, 21 shot capacity, upper and lower rails for mounting sights and other accessories. **Velocity:** 520 fps.
Price: **$59.99**

DAISY POWERLINE 5501 CO2 BLOWBACK PISTOL
Caliber: .177 Steel BBs. **Barrel:** Smoothbore. **Weight:** 1.0 lbs. **Length:** 6.8 Inches. **Power:** CO2. **Sights:** Blade and ramp front, open rear. **Features:** CO2 semi-automatic blow-back action **Velocity:** 430 fps.
Price: **$59.99**

EAA/BAIKAL IZH-46M MATCH TARGET AIR PISTOL
Caliber: .177 Pellets. **Barrel:** Rifled **Weight:** 2.86 lbs. **Length:** 16.53 inches. **Power:** Underlever single-stroke pneumatic. **Sights:** Micrometer fully adjustable rear, blade front. **Features:** Hammer-forged match barrel, adjustable wooden target grips, match grade adjustable trigger. **Velocity:** 500 fps.
Price: **$745.00**

EAA/BAIKAL IZH-53M AIR PISTOL
Caliber: .177 Pellets. **Barrel:** Rifled **Weight:** 2.67 lbs. **Length:** 16.02 inches. **Power:** Single cock, spring-pistol **Sights:** Fully adjustable rear, blade front. **Features:** 2 stage trigger. **Velocity:** 360 fps.
Price: **$95.00**

EVANIX HUNTING MASTER AR6 AIR PISTOL
Caliber: .22. **Barrel:** Rifled. **Weight:** 3.05 lbs. **Length:** 17.3 overall. **Power:** Pre-charged Pneumatic. **Sights:** Adjustable rear, blade front. **Features:** Checkered Hardwood grips, 6 shot repeater with rotary magazine, single or double action, receiver grooved for scope **Velocity:** .22 cal with 3,000 psi charge: 922 fps to 685 fps (10-shot range starting with shot #1 to shot #10 using 11.9-grian RWS Hobby pellets) and 423 fps to 701 fps (10-shot range starting with shot #1 to shot #10 using 28-grain Eun Jin pellets).
Price: **$659.99**

FWB P11 PICCOLO AIR PISTOL
Caliber: .177 Pellets. **Barrel:** Rifled. **Weight:** 1.52 lbs. **Length:** 12.4 inches. **Power:** Pre-charged pneumatic. **Sights:** Front post, fully adjustable rear blade, **Features:** 10 Meter competition class pistol, meets ISSF requirements, highly adjustable match trigger, **Velocity:** 492 fps.
Price: **$1,600.00**

GAMO COMPACT 10M TARGET AIR PISTOL
Caliber: .177 Pellets. **Barrel:** Rifled **Weight:** 1.95 lbs. **Length:** 12.6

inches. **Power:** Single-stroke pneumatic. **Sights:** Micrometer fully adjustable rear, blade front. **Features:** Adjustable wooden target grips, match grade trigger. **Velocity:** 400 fps.
Price: **$300.00**

GAMO MP-9 CO2 PISTOL
Caliber: .177 Steel BBs, .177 Pellets. **Barrel:** Rifled. **Weight:** 3.0 lbs. **Length:** 21.0 inches. **Power:** CO2. **Sights:** Fixed. **Features:** Blow-back semiautomatic replica of the B&T MP-9 9mm submachine gun. Shoots both pellets or BBs using the same magazine, Weaver-style tactical rails, ambidextrous compact design, foldable stock, 16-shot double magazine and manual safety. **Velocity:** 450 fps.
Price: **$159.95**

GAMO P-900 IGT AIR PISTOL
Caliber: .177 Pellets. **Barrel:** Rifled. **Weight:** 1.3 lbs. **Length:** 12.6 inches. **Power:** Single cock, gas-pistol. **Sights:** Fiber optic front and fully adjustable fiber optic rear sight. **Features:** Break-barrel single-shot, ergonomic design, rubberized grip. **Velocity:** 508 fps.
Price: **$79.95**

GAMO PT-25 BLOWBACK CO2 PISTOL
Caliber: .177 Pellets. **Barrel:** Rifled. **Weight:** 1.55 lbs. **Length:** 7.75 inches. **Power:** CO2. **Sights:** Fixed. **Features:** Semiautomatic, 16-shot capacity, realistic blowback action. **Velocity:** 450 fps.
Price: **$109.95**

GAMO PT-25 BLOWBACK TACTICAL CO2 PISTOL
Caliber: .177 Pellets. **Barrel:** Rifled. **Weight:** 2.8 lbs. **Length:** 14.75 inches. **Power:** CO2. **Sights:** Fixed / Red dot optical sight included. **Features:** Quad accessory rail system, light and red dot scope bundled, semiautomatic, 16-shot capacity, realistic blowback action **Velocity:** 560 fps.
Price: **$189.95**

GAMO PT-85 BLOWBACK CO2 PISTOL
Caliber: .177 Pellets. **Barrel:** Rifled. **Weight:** 1.50 lbs. **Length:** 7.8 inches. **Power:** CO2. **Sights:** Fixed. **Features:** Semiautomatic, 16-shot capacity, realistic blowback action **Velocity:** 450 fps.
Price: **$119.95**

GAMO PT-85 BLOWBACK TACTICAL CO2 PISTOL
Caliber: .177 Pellets. **Barrel:** Rifled. **Weight:** 3.3 lbs. **Length:** 14.93 inches. **Power:** CO2. **Sights:** Fixed / Red dot optical sight included **Features:** Semiautomatic design, compensator, rifled steel barrel, manual safety, 16-shot double magazine, quad rail, laser and light included. **Velocity:** 560 fps.
Price: . . . . **$ 269.95**

HATSAN USA MOD 25 SUPERCHARGER VORTEX PISTOL

HATSAN USA MOD 25 SUPERCHARGER VORTEX PISTOL
Caliber: .177 Pellets. **Barrel:** Rifled. **Weight:** 3.3 lbs. **Length:** 14.93 inches. **Power:** Single cock, air-piston **Sights:** Fiber optic front and fully adjustable fiber optic rear sight **Features:** Molded right handed grips, left handed grips available, fully adjustable "Quattro," integrated anti-recoil system. **Velocity:** 700 fps with lead pellets.
Price: **$189.99**

HATSAN USA AT P1 QUIET ENERGY PCP PISTOL

Prices given are believed to be accurate at time of publication however, many factors affect retail pricing so exact prices are not possible.

71ST EDITION, 2017 ✦ **521**

HATSAN USA AT P1 QUIET ENERGY PCP PISTOL
Caliber: .177, .22, .25. **Barrel:** Rifled. **Weight:** 4.7 lbs. **Length:** 23.2 inches. **Power:** Pre-charged pneumatic. **Sights:** N/A - grooved for scope mounting. **Features:** Multi-shot magazine feed, integrated suppressor, muzzle energy suitable for pest control and small game hunting. **Velocity:** .177, 870 fps / .22, 780 fps / .25, 710 fps.
Price: From $479.99

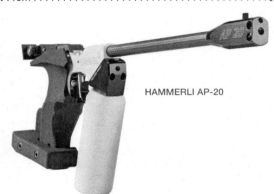

HAMMERLI AP-20

HAMMERLI AP-20 AIR PISTOL
Caliber: .177 Pellets. **Barrel:** Rifled. **Weight:** 1.2 lbs. **Length:** 16.34 inches. **Power:** Pre-charged pneumatic **Sights:** Fully adjustable micrometer. **Features:** 2-stage adjustable trigger factory set to 500 grams pull weight, single shot, bolt action, up to 120 shots per fill. **Velocity:** 492 fps.
Price: $999.99

MAGNUM RESEARCH DESERT EAGLE
Caliber: .177 Pellets. **Barrel:** Rifled. **Weight:** 2.5 lbs. **Length:** 10.8 inches. **Power:** CO2. **Sights:** Fixed front, fully adjustable rear. **Features:** 8-shot rotary clip. Double or single action, realistic size, blowback action. **Velocity:** 425 fps.
Price: $229.99

MAGNUM BABY DESERT EAGLE
Caliber: .177 Steel BBs. **Barrel:** Smoothbore. **Weight:** 1.0 lbs. **Length:** 8.3 inches. **Power:** CO2. **Sights:** Fixed. **Features:** Extremely realistic replica pistol, top and bottom weaver/picatinny rails. **Velocity:** 420 fps.
Price: $59.99

MARKSMAN 1010 CLASSIC AIR PISTOL
Caliber: .177 Steel BBs, .177 Darts. **Barrel:** Smoothbore. **Weight:** 1.5 lbs. **Length:** 8.5 inches. **Power:** Single cock, spring-piston. **Sights:** Fixed front, adjustable rear. **Features:** 18-shot BB reservoir. **Velocity:** 200 fps.
Price: $29.75

MORINI MOR-162EL MATCH AIR PISTOL
Caliber: .177 Pellets. **Barrel:** Rifled. **Weight:** 2.5 lbs. **Length:** 16.14 inches. **Power:** Pre-charged pneumatic **Sights:** Front post, rear adjustable for windage. **Features:** Adjustable electronic trigger, single-shot bolt action, extreme match grade accuracy, over 200 regulated shots per 200 bar fill. **Velocity:** 500 fps.
Price: $2,200.00

REMINGTON 1911 RAC
CO2 BB PISTOL

REMINGTON 1911 RAC CO2 BB PISTOL
Caliber: .177 Steel BBs. **Barrel:** Smoothbore. **Weight:** 2.0 lbs. **Length:** 8.0 inches. **Power:** CO2. **Sights:** Fixed. **Features:** All metal, blowback, extremely realistic replica pistol, bottom weaver/picatinny accessory rail. **Velocity:** 320 fps.
Price: $119.99

SMITH & WESSON 586 & 686
Caliber: .177 Pellets. **Barrel:** Rifled. **Weight:** Model 586 4" 2.50 lbs. / Model 586 & 686 6" 2.8 lbs. **Length:** Model 586 9.5 inches / Model 686 11.5 inches. **Power:** CO2. **Sights:** Fixed front, adjustable rear **Features:** Extremely accurate, full metal, replica revolvers.
Price: 586 4" barrel. Velocity - 400 fps $300.00
Price: 586 6" barrel. Velocity - 425 fps $295.95
Price: 685 6" barrel. Velocity - 425 fps $329.95

SMITH & WESSON M&P CO2 PISTOL
Caliber: .177 Steel BBs. **Barrel:** Smoothbore. **Weight:** 1.5 lbs. **Length:** 7.5 inches. **Power:** CO2. **Sights:** Blade front and ramp rear fiber optic. **Features:** Integrated accessory rail, drop-free 19-shot BB magazine, double-action only, synthetic frame available in dark earth brown or black color. **Velocity:** 480 fps.
Price: (black) $50.00
Price: (dark earth brown) $45.99

SMITH & WESSON M&P 40
CO2 BB PISTOL

SMITH & WESSON M&P 40 CO2 BB PISTOL
Caliber: .177 Steel BBs. **Barrel:** Smoothbore. **Weight:** 1.61 lbs. **Length:** 7.75 inches. **Power:** CO2. **Sights:** Fixed. **Features:** All metal replica action pistol, blowback, 15-shot semiautomatic. **Velocity:** 300 fps.
Price: $119.99

SMITH & WESSON M&P 45 CO2 BB PISTOL
Caliber: .177 Steel BBs, .177 Pellets. **Barrel:** Rifled. **Weight:** 1.35 lbs. **Length:** 8.1 inches. **Power:** CO2. **Sights:** Fixed front sight, fully adjustable rear sight. **Features:** Double and single action, 8-shot semiautomatic. **Velocity:** 370 fps.
Price: $80.00

SMITH & WESSON 327 TRR8 CO2 BB PISTOL
Caliber: .177 Steel BBs. **Barrel:** Smoothbore **Weight:** 2.0 lbs. **Length:** 12 inches. **Power:** CO2. **Sights:** Fiber optic front sight, fully adjustable fiber optic rear sight. **Features:** High quality replica, top mounted weaver scope rail, weaver accessory rail under the barrel, swing-out cylinder, removable casings and functioning ejector. **Velocity:** 400 fps.
Price: $120.00

SMITH & WESSON DOMINANT TRAIT (TRR8) CO2 BB PISTOL
Caliber: .177 Steel BBs. **Barrel:** Smoothbore **Weight:** 2.0 lbs. **Length:** 12 inches. **Power:** CO2. **Sights:** Fiber-optic front sight, fully adjustable fiber optic rear sight. **Features:** High-quality replica, top mounted weaver scope rail, weaver accessory rail under the barrel, swing-out cylinder, removable casings and functioning ejector, Includes speedloader, 6 shells, 12 Walther 12-gram CO2 cartridges & 1500 Walther steel BBs. **Velocity:** 400 fps.
Price: $170.00

Prices given are believed to be accurate at time of publication however, many factors affect retail pricing so exact prices are not possible.

WALTHER CP88 4-INCH BARREL

Caliber: .177 Pellet. **Barrel:** Rifled. **Weight:** 2.3 lbs. **Length:** 7 inches. **Power:** CO2. **Sights:** Blade ramp front sight and adjustable rear sight. **Features:** Manual safety, semi-auto repeater, single or double action, available in multiple finishes and grip materials. **Velocity:** 400 fps.
Price: . . . . **$229.99 to $300.00**

WALTHER CP88 6-INCH BARREL

Caliber: .177 Pellet. **Barrel:** Rifled. **Weight:** 2.5 lbs. **Length:** 9 inches. **Power:** CO2. **Sights:** Blade ramp front sight and adjustable rear sight. **Features:** Manual safety, semiauto repeater, single or double action, available in multiple finishes and grip materials. **Velocity:** 450 fps.
Price: . . . . **$229.99 to $329.99**

WALTHER CP99 CO2 PELLET PISTOL

Caliber: .177 Pellet. **Barrel:** Rifled **Weight:** 1.6 lbs. **Length:** 7.1 inches. **Power:** CO2. **Sights:** Fixed front and fully adjustable rear sight. **Features:** Extremely realistic replica pistol, single and double action, 8-shot rotary magazine. **Velocity:** 360 fps.
Price: **$200.00**

WALTHER CP99 COMPACT

WALTHER CP99 COMPACT

Caliber: .177 Steel BBs. **Barrel:** Smoothbore **Weight:** 1.7 lbs. **Length:** 6.6 inches. **Power:** CO2. **Sights:** Fixed front and rear. **Features:** Extremely realistic replica pistol, semi-automatic 18-shot capacity, available in various configurations including a nickel slide. **Velocity:** 345 fps.
Price: . . . . **$105.99 to $100.00**

WALTHER PPQ

WALTHER PPQ

Caliber: .177 Steel BBs, .177 Pellets. **Barrel:** Rifled **Weight:** 1.37 lbs. **Length:** 7.0 inches. **Power:** CO2. **Sights:** Fixed front and fully adjustable rear sight. **Features:** Extremely realistic replica pistol, semiautomatic 8-shot rotary magazine. **Velocity:** 360 fps.
Price: **$70.00**

WALTHER NIGHTHAWK

Caliber: .177 Pellet. **Barrel:** Rifled. **Weight:** 1.47 lbs. **Length:** 7.0 inches. **Power:** CO2. **Sights:** Blade ramp front sight and adjustable rear sight. **Features:** Quad accessory rail, red-dot optic, tactical light. **Velocity:** 400 fps.
Price: **$250.00**

WALTHER P38 PISTOL

Caliber: .177 Steel BBs. **Barrel:** Smoothbore. **Weight:** 1.9 lbs. **Length:** 8.5 inches. **Power:** CO2. **Sights:** Fixed. **Features:** Authentic replica action pistol, blowback action, semiautomatic 20-shot magazine. **Velocity:** 400 fps.
Price: **$120.00**

WALTHER PPS

WALTHER PPS PISTOL

Caliber: .177 Steel BBs. **Barrel:** Smoothbore. **Weight:** 1.2 lbs. **Length:** 6.38 inches. **Power:** CO2. **Sights:** Fixed. **Features:** Authentic replica action pistol, blowback action, semiautomatic 18-shot capacity. **Velocity:** 350 fps.
Price: **$89.99**

WINCHESTER MODEL 11

WINCHESTER MODEL 11

Caliber: .177 Steel BBs. **Barrel:** Smoothbore. **Weight:** 1.9 lbs. **Length:** 8.5 inches. **Power:** CO2. **Sights:** Fixed. **Features:** All metal replica action pistol, blowback action, 4-lb. 2-stage trigger, semiautomatic 15-shot capacity. **Velocity:** 410 fps.
Price: **$110.00**

AIR ARMS TX200 MKIII
Caliber: .177, .22 **Barrel:** Rifled, Lothar Walter match-grade barrel, 13.19 inches. **Weight:** 9.3 lbs. **Length:** 41.34 inches. **Power:** Single cock, spring-piston **Stock:** Various; right and left handed versions, multiple wood options. **Sights:** 11mm dovetail. **Features:** Fixed barrel, heirloom quality craftsmanship, holds the record for the most winning spring powered airgun in international field target competitions. **Velocity:** .177, 930 fps / .22, 755 fps.
Price: **$749.99**

AIR ARMS PRO SPORT
Caliber: .177, .22 **Barrel:** Rifled, Lothar Walter match-grade barrel, 9.5 inches. **Weight:** 9.03 lbs. **Length:** 40.5 inches. **Power:** Single cock, spring-piston **Stock:** Various; right and left handed versions, multiple wood options. **Sights:** 11mm dovetail. **Features:** Fixed barrel, Heirloom quality craftsmanship, unique inset cocking arm. **Velocity:** .177, 950 fps / .22, 750 fps.
Price: **$929.99**

AIR ARMS S510 XTRA FAC
Caliber: .177, .22, .25 **Barrel:** Rifled, Lothar Walter match-grade barrel, 19.45 inches. **Weight:** 7.65 lbs. **Length:** 43.75 inches. **Power:** Pre-charged pneumatic **Stock:** Right handed, multiple wood options. **Sights:** 11mm dovetail. **Features:** Side lever action, 10-shot magazine, shrouded barrel, variable power, Heirloom quality craftsmanship **Velocity:** .177, 1050 fps / .22, 920 fps / .25, 780 fps.
Price: **$1450.99**

AIR ARMS S510 ULTIMATE SPORTER
Caliber: .177, .22, .25 **Barrel:** Rifled, Lothar Walter match-grade barrel, 19.5 inches. **Weight:** 8.6 lbs. **Length:** 44.25 inches. **Power:** Pre-charged pneumatic **Stock:** Fully adjustable, ambidextrous laminate stock. **Sights:** 11mm dovetail. **Features:** Side lever action, 10-shot magazine, integrated suppressor, variable power, Heirloom quality craftsmanship. **Velocity:** .177, 1050 fps / .22, 920 fps / .25, 780 fps.
Price: **$1900.00**

AIR ARMS S200 FT
Caliber: .177 Pellets, **Barrel:** Rifled, match-grade barrel, 19.09 inches. **Weight:** 8.17 lbs. **Length:** 35.7 inches. **Power:** Pre-charged pneumatic **Stock:** Ambidextrous hardwood stock. **Sights:** 11mm dovetail. **Features:** Single-shot, designed for international field target competition. **Velocity:** 800 fps.
Price: **$850.00**

AIRFORCE CONDOR

AIRFORCE CONDOR RIFLE
Caliber: .177, .20, .22, .25. **Barrel:** Rifled, Lothar Walther match barrel, 24 inches. **Weight:** 6.1 lbs. **Length:** 38.75 inches. **Power:** Pre-charged pneumatic. **Stock:** Synthetic pistol grip, tank acts as butt stock. **Sights:** Grooved for scope mounting. **Features:** Single shot, adjustable power, automatic safety, large 490cc tank volume, extended scope rail allows easy mounting of the largest air-gun scopes, optional CO2 power system available, manufactured in the U.S.A. by AirForce Airguns. **Velocity:** .177, 1450 fps / .20, 1150 fps / .22, 1250 fps / .25, 1100 fps.
Price: **$744.95**

AIRFORCE CONDOR SS AIR RIFLE
Caliber: .177, .20, .22, .25. **Barrel:** Rifled, Lothar Walther match barrel, 18 inches. **Weight:** 6.1 lbs. **Length:** 38.13 inches. **Power:** Pre-charged pneumatic. **Stock:** Synthetic pistol grip, tank acts as butt stock. **Sights:** Grooved for scope mounting. **Features:** Fully shrouded barrel with integrated suppressor, single shot, adjustable power, automatic safety, large 490cc tank volume, extended scope rail allows easy mounting of the largest air-gun scopes, multiple color options available, optional CO2 power system available, manufactured in the U.S.A. by AirForce Airguns. **Velocity:** .177, 1300 fps / .20, 1000 / fps / .22, 1100 fps / .25, 950 fps.
Price: **$774.95**

AIRFORCE ESCAPE AIR RIFLE
Caliber: .22, .25. **Barrel:** Rifled, Lothar Walther match barrel, 24 inches. **Weight:** 5.3 lbs. **Length:** 39.13 inches. **Power:** Pre-charged pneumatic. **Stock:** Synthetic pistol grip, tank acts as butt stock. **Sights:** Grooved for scope mounting. **Features:** Single shot, adjustable power, automatic safety, extended scope rail allows easy mounting of the largest air-gun scopes, manufactured in the U.S.A. by AirForce Airguns. **Velocity:** .22, 1300 fps / .25, 1145 fps.
Price: **$684.95**

AIRFORCE ESCAPE SS AIR RIFLE
Caliber: .22, .25. **Barrel:** Rifled, Lothar Walther match barrel, 12 inches. **Weight:** 4.3 lbs. **Length:** 32.25 inches. **Power:** Pre-charged pneumatic. **Stock:** Synthetic pistol grip, tank acts as butt stock. **Sights:** Grooved for scope mounting. **Features:** Fully shrouded barrel with integrated suppressor, single shot, adjustable power, automatic safety, extended scope rail allows easy mounting of the largest air-gun scopes, manufactured in the U.S.A. by AirForce Airguns. **Velocity:** .22, 1054 fps / .25, 900 fps.
Price: **$694.95**

AIRFORCE ESCAPE UL AIR RIFLE
Caliber: .22, .25. **Barrel:** Rifled, Lothar Walther match barrel, 18 inches. **Weight:** 4.25 lbs. **Length:** 33.0 inches. **Power:** Pre-charged pneumatic. **Stock:** Synthetic pistol grip, tank acts as butt stock. **Sights:** Grooved for scope mounting. **Features:** Single-shot, adjustable power, automatic safety, extended scope rail allows easy mounting of the largest air-gun scopes, manufactured in the U.S.A. by AirForce Airguns. **Velocity:** .22, 1200 fps / .25, 1041 fps.
Price: **$642.95**

AIRFORCE TALON AIR RIFLE
Caliber: .177, .22, .25. **Barrel:** Rifled, Lothar Walther match barrel, 18 inches. **Weight:** 5.5 lbs. **Length:** 32.6 inches. **Power:** Pre-charged pneumatic, **Stock:** Synthetic pistol grip, tank acts as butt stock. **Sights:** Grooved for scope mounting. **Features:** Single shot, adjustable power, automatic safety, large 490cc tank volume, extended scope rail allows easy mounting of the largest air-gun scopes, optional CO2 power system available, manufactured in the U.S.A. by AirForce Airguns. **Velocity:** .177, 1100 fps / fps / .22, 950 fps / .25, 850 fps.
Price: **$609.95**

AIRFORCE TALON SS AIR RIFLE
Caliber: .177, .20, .22, .25. **Barrel:** Rifled, Lothar Walther match barrel, 12 inches. **Weight:** 5.25 lbs. **Length:** 32.75 inches. **Power:** Pre-charged pneumatic. **Stock:** Synthetic pistol grip, tank acts as butt stock. **Sights:** Grooved for scope mounting. **Features:** Fully shrouded barrel with integrated suppressor, single shot, adjustable power, automatic safety, large 490cc tank volume, extended scope rail allows easy mounting of the largest air-gun scopes, multiple color options available, optional CO2 power system available, manufactured in the U.S.A. by AirForce Airguns. **Velocity:** .177, 1000 fps / .20, 800 fps / .22, 800 fps / .25, 665 fps.
Price: **$774.95**

BAIKAL IZH-61 MULTI-SHOT AIR RIFLE
Caliber: .177 **Barrel:** Rifled, 18.5 inches. **Weight:** 4.3 lbs. **Length:** 33 inches. **Power:** Single cock, spring-piston **Stock:** Adjustable, ambidextrous pistol grip synthetic. **Sights:** Globe front sight, fully adjustable rear sight **Features:** Automatic pellet advance system, very accurate and easy to shoot. **Velocity:** .177, 490 fps.
Price: **$165.96**

BEEMAN HW100 S FSB PRECHARGE PNEUMATIC AIR RIFLE
Caliber: .177, .20 **Barrel:** Rifled 23.63 inches. **Weight:** 8.6 lbs. **Length:** 42.13 inches. **Power:** Pre-charged pneumatic. **Stock:** Right handed hardwood stock. **Sights:** Grooved for scope mounting. **Features:** Multi-shot side lever, 14 round magazine, shrouded barrel. **Velocity:** .177, 1135 fps / .20, 865 fps.
Price: **$1,769.95**

BEEMAN HW100 T FSB PRECHARGE PNEUMATIC AIR RIFLE
Caliber: .177, **Barrel:** Rifled 23.63 inches. **Weight:** 8.6 lbs. **Length:** 42.13 inches. **Power:** Pre-charged pneumatic. **Stock:** Ambidextrous thumbhole hardwood stock. **Sights:** Grooved for scope mounting. **Features:** Multi-shot side lever, 14-round magazine, shrouded barrel.

AIRGUNS—Long Guns

Velocity: .177, 1135 fps.
Price: $1,729.95

BEEMAN RS-2 DUAL CALIBER GAS RAM AIR RIFLE COMBO
Caliber: .177, .22. Barrel: Rifled Weight: 6.9 lbs. Length: 45.5 inches. Power: Break-barrel, gas-piston. Stock: Ambidextrous hardwood stock. Sights: Fiber optic front and rear, includes 4x32 scope and rings. Features: Single-shot, easily exchangeable .177 and .22 cal barrels, two stage trigger. Velocity: .177, 1000 fps / .22, 830 fps.
Price: $179.99

BEEMAN QUIET TEK DUAL CALIBER GAS RAM AIR RIFLE COMBO
Caliber: .177, .22. Barrel: Rifled Weight: 6.7 lbs. Length: 47 inches. Power: Break-barrel, spring-piston. Stock: Ambidextrous synthetic stock. Sights: none, grooved for scope mounting, includes 4x32 scope and rings. Features: Integrated suppressor, single shot, easily exchangeable .177- and .22-cal. barrels, two-stage trigger. Velocity: .177, 1000 fps / .22, 830 fps.
Price: $179.99

BEEMAN MACH 12.5 AIR RIFLE
Caliber: .177, .22. Barrel: Rifled Weight: 10 lbs. Length: 49 inches. Power: Break-barrel, spring-piston. Stock: Ambidextrous hardwood stock. Sights: none, grooved for scope mounting, includes 3-9x40AO scope and rings. Features: Single shot, adjustable two stage trigger. Velocity: .177, 1250 fps / .22, 1000 fps.
Price: $269.99

BEEMAN R1 SUPERMAGNUM AIR RIFLE
Caliber: .177, .20, .22. Barrel: Rifled 19.75 inches. Weight: 8.8 lbs. Length: 45.5 inches. Power: Break-barrel, spring-piston. Stock: Walnut-stained beech, cut-checkered pistol grip, Monte Carlo comb and rubber buttpad. Sights: None, grooved for scope. Features: German quality, limited lifetime warranty, highly adjustable match grade trigger. The .22-caliber rifle is available in both right and left hand versions. Extremely accurate. Velocity: .177, 1100 fps / fps / .20, 950 fps / .22, 850 fps.
Price: . . . . $749.95 to $849.95

BEEMAN R7 AIR RIFLE
Caliber: .177, .20 Barrel: Rifled 13.5 inches. Weight: 6.1 lbs. Length: 37 inches. Power: Break-barrel, spring-piston. Stock: Ambidextrous walnut-stained beech, cut-checkered pistol grip, Monte Carlo comb and rubber buttpad. Sights: None, grooved for scope. Features: German quality, limited lifetime warranty, highly adjustable match grade trigger, very easy to cock and shoot, extremely accurate. Velocity: .177, 700 fps / .20, 620 fps.
Price: . . . . $419.95 to $449.95

BEEMAN R9 AIR RIFLE
Caliber: . 177, .20, .22. Barrel: Rifled 16.33 inches. Weight: 7.3 lbs. Length: 43 inches. Power: Break-barrel, spring-piston. Stock: Ambidextrous walnut-stained beech, cut-checkered pistol grip, Monte Carlo comb and rubber buttpad. Sights: None, grooved for scope. Features: German quality, limited lifetime warranty, highly adjustable match-grade trigger, extremely accurate. Velocity: .177, 935 fps / .20, 800 fps / .22, 740 fps.
Price: . . . . $549.95 to $579.95

BEEMAN RAM COMBO AIR RIFLE
Caliber: .177, .22. Barrel: Rifled 20 inches. Weight: 7.9 lbs. Length: 46.5 inches. Power: Break-barrel, spring-piston. Stock: Ambidextrous hardwood stock. Sights: none, grooved for scope mounting, includes 3-9x32 scope and rings. Features: Muzzlebrake for extra cocking leverage, single-shot, adjustable two-stage trigger. Velocity: .177, 1000 fps / .22, 850 fps.
Price: $220.00

BEEMAN R11 MKII AIR RIFLE
Caliber: .177 Pellets Barrel: Rifled 16.25 inches. Weight: 8.6 lbs. Length: 43.5 inches. Power: Break-barrel, spring-piston. Stock: Adjustable ambidextrous hardwood stock. Sights: None, grooved

BEEMAN R11 MKII

for scope. Features: German quality, limited lifetime warranty, highly adjustable match-grade trigger, this rifle is optimized for competitive field target. Velocity: 925 fps.
Price: $799.95

BEEMAN WOLVERINE CARBINE COMBO AIR RIFLE
Caliber: .177 Pellets Barrel: Rifled Weight: 8.5 lbs. Length: 45.5 inches. Power: Break-barrel, spring-piston. Stock: Ambidextrous synthetic stock. Sights: Fiber-optic front sight, fully adjustable fiber-optic rear sight, grooved for scope, includes 4x32 scope and mounts. Features: Single-shot, two-stage trigger. Velocity: 1000 fps.
Price: $129.99

BEEMAN GUARDIAN COMBO AIR RIFLE
Caliber: .177 Pellets Barrel: Rifled Weight: 5.85 lbs. Length: 37 inches. Power: Break-barrel, spring-piston. Stock: Monte Carlo style synthetic stock. Sights: None, grooved for scope, includes mounted 4x20 scope and mounts. Features: Lightweight youth airgun. Velocity: 550 fps.
Price: $59.99

BEEMAN SPORTSMAN RANGER COMBO AIR RIFLE
Caliber: .177 Pellets Barrel: Rifled Weight: 4.15 lbs. Length: 40 inches. Power: Break-barrel, spring-piston. Stock: Lightweight skeleton, synthetic stock. Sights: None, grooved for scope, includes 4x20 scope and mounts. Features: Lightweight youth airgun. Velocity: 480 fps.
Price: $79.99

BEEMAN SILVER KODIAK X2 COMBO AIR RIFLE
Caliber: .177, .22. Barrel: Rifled Weight: 8.75 lbs. Length: 47.75 inches. Power: Break-barrel, spring-piston. Stock: Ambidextrous synthetic stock. Sights: None includes 4x32 scope and rings. Features: Satin finish nickel plated receiver and barrels, single-shot, easily exchangeable .177 and .22 cal barrels, two-stage trigger. Velocity: .177, 1000 fps / .22, 830 fps.
Price: $169.99

BEEMAN HW97K AIR RIFLE
Caliber: .177, .20, .22. Barrel: Rifled 11.81 inches. Weight: 9.2 lbs. Length: 40.25 inches. Power: Under-lever, spring-piston. Stock: Ambidextrous beech stock with checkering on the forearm and grip. Sights: None, grooved for scope. Features: German quality, limited lifetime warranty, highly adjustable match-grade trigger. Extremely accurate fixed barrel design. Velocity: .177, 930 fps / .20, 820 fps / .22, 750 fps.
Price: . . . . $679.95 to $749.95

BEEMAN HW97K THUMBHOLE STOCK AIR RIFLE
Caliber: .177, .20, .22. Barrel: Rifled 11.81 inches. Weight: 9.37 lbs. Length: 40.35 inches. Power: Under-lever, spring-piston. Stock: Ambidextrous thumbhole beech stock with checkering on the fore-end and grip. Sights: None, grooved for scope. Features: German quality, limited lifetime warranty, highly adjustable match-grade trigger. Extremely accurate fixed barrel design. Velocity: .177, 930 fps / .20, 820 fps / .22, 750 fps.
Price: $890.00

BEEMAN HW97K BLUE AIR RIFLE
Caliber: .177, .20, .22. Barrel: Rifled 11.81 inches. Weight: 9.2 lbs. Length: 40.25 inches. Power: Under-lever, spring-piston. Stock: Right handed blue laminate stock with checkering on the fore-end and grip. Sights: None, grooved for scope. Features: German quality, limited lifetime warranty, highly adjustable match-grade trigger. Extremely accurate fixed barrel design. Velocity: .177, 930 fps / .20, 820 fps / .22, 750 fps.
Price: . . . . $839.95 to $869.95

BEEMAN RX-2 AIR RIFLE
Caliber: .177, .20, .22., .25 Barrel: Rifled 19.63 inches. Weight: 9.8 lbs. Length: 45.7 inches. Power: Break-barrel, gas-piston. Stock: Ambidextrous laminated stock. Sights: None, grooved for scope mounting. Features: German quality, limited lifetime warranty, highly adjustable match-grade trigger. Extremely accurate. Velocity: .177, 1000 fps / .22, 850 fps. / .25, 725 fps.
Price: . . . . $949.95 to $999.95

BENJAMIN ARMADA, BASE, TACTICAL, & MAGPUL EDITION AIR RIFLE
Caliber: .177, .22, .25 Barrel: Rifled, 20 inches. Weight: 7.3 lbs. (10.3

Prices given are believed to be accurate at time of publication however, many factors affect retail pricing so exact prices are not possible.

71ST EDITION, 2017 525

BENJAMIN ARMADA, BASE, TACTICAL, & MAGPUL EDITION AIR RIFLE

pounds with scope and bipod) **Length:** 42.8 inches. **Power:** Pre-charged pneumatic **Stock:** Adjustable mil-spec AR15 style buttstock, all metal M-LOK compatible handguard with 15 inches of picatinny rail space. **Sights:** None, weaver/picatinny rail for scope mounting. **Features:** Core features include: fully shrouded barrel with integrated suppressor, depinger device, bolt action, multi shot, choked barrel for maximum accuracy. Variations: Base configuration includes the rifle only. Tactical version includes a bipod and CenterPoint 4-16x56 side focus scope with 4" sunshade. Magpul edition (available in .22 caliber only) includes a Magpul MOE grip and 6-posistion butstock, standard bipod and 4-16x56 side focus scope with 4" sunshade, **Velocity:** .177, 1100 fps / .22, 1000 fps / .25, 900 fps.
Price: . . . . $750.00 to $1,200.00

BENJAMIN BULLDOG .357 BULLPUP

BENJAMIN BULLDOG .357 BULLPUP
Caliber: .357 **Barrel:** Rifled 28 inches. **Weight:** 7.7 lbs. **Length:** 36 inches. **Power:** Pre-charged pneumatic. **Stock:** Synthetic bullpup stock with pistol grip. **Sights:** Full top picatinny rail. **Features:** Innovative bullpup design, massive power output of up to 180 foot-pounds, 5-shot magazine, shrouded barrel for noise reduction, large cylinder delivers up to 10 usable shots, available in multiple bundled configurations and stock finishes. **Velocity:** Up to 900 fps based on the weight of the projectile.
Price: . . . . $1,199.99 to $1,549.99

BENJAMIN EVA SHOCKEY STEEL EAGLE (NP2) BREAK BARREL AIR RIFLE
Caliber: .177. **Barrel:** Rifled. **Weight:** 8 lbs. **Length:** 45.8 inches. **Power:** Break-barrel, 2nd generation gas-piston. **Stock:** Ambidextrous synthetic stock **Sights:** None, weaver/picatinny rail for scope mounting, includes Crosman CenterPoint 4x32 scope and mounts. **Features:** Very quiet due to the shrouded barrel with integrated suppressor, extremely easy cocking, single-shot, advanced adjustable two-stage trigger, innovative sling mounts for optional Benjamin break-barrel rifle sling. **Velocity:** 1400 fps.
Price: $249.99

BENJAMIN JIM SHOCKEY STEEL EAGLE (NP2) BREAK BARREL AIR RIFLE
Caliber: .22. **Barrel:** Rifled. **Weight:** 8 lbs. **Length:** 45.8 inches. **Power:** Break-barrel, 2nd generation gas-piston. **Stock:** Ambidextrous synthetic stock **Sights:** None, weaver/picatinny rail for scope mounting, includes Crosman CenterPoint 3-9x32 scope and mounts. **Features:** Very quiet due to the shrouded barrel with integrated suppressor, extremely easy cocking, single shot, advanced adjustable two stage trigger, innovative sling mounts for optional

BENJAMIN JIM SHOCKEY STEEL EAGLE (NP2) BREAK BARREL AIR RIFLE

Benjamin break-barrel rifle sling. **Velocity:** 1100 fps.
Price: $279.99

BENJAMIN MARAUDER PCP AIR RIFLE
Caliber: .177, .22, .25 **Barrel:** Rifled 20 inches. **Weight:** Synthetic 7.3 lbs. / Hardwood 8.2 lbs. **Length:** 42.8 inches. **Power:** Pre-charged pneumatic. **Stock:** Ambidextrous stock available in hardwood or synthetic, adjustable cheek riser. **Sights:** None, grooved for scope mounting. **Features:** Multi-shot bolt action, 10-shot in .177 and .22, 8-shot in .25, user adjustable performance settings for power and shot count. **Velocity:** .177, 1100 fps / .22, 1000 fps. / .25, 900 fps.
Price: . . . . $499.99 to $529.99

BENJAMIN TITAN GP BREAK BARREL AIR RIFLE
Caliber: .177, .22. **Barrel:** Rifled 15 inches. **Weight:** 6.75 lbs. **Length:** 43.5 inches. **Power:** Break-barrel, gas-piston. **Stock:** Ambidextrous thumbhole wood stock with dual raised cheekpieces. **Sights:** none, grooved for scope mounting, includes 4x32 scope and rings. **Features:** Muzzlebrake for extra cocking leverage, single-shot, adjustable two-stage trigger. **Velocity:** .177, 1200 fps / .22, 950 fps.
Price: $199.99

BENJAMIN TITAN XS BREAK BARREL AIR RIFLE
Caliber: .177 **Barrel:** Rifled. **Weight:** 8.3 lbs. **Length:** 44.5 inches. **Power:** Break-barrel, gas-piston. **Stock:** Ambidextrous thumbhole synthetic with dual raised cheekpieces. **Sights:** None, grooved for scope mounting, includes 3-9x32 scope and rings. **Features:** Muzzlebrake for extra cocking leverage, single-shot, adjustable two-stage trigger, innovative sling mounts for optional Benjamin break-barrel rifle sling. **Velocity:** .177, 1200 fps
Price: $199.99

BENJAMIN TRAIL NITRO PISTON 2 (NP2) BREAK BARREL AIR RIFLE
Caliber: .177, .22. **Barrel:** Rifled 15.75 inches. **Weight:** 8.3 lbs. **Length:** 46.25 inches. **Power:** Break-barrel, 2nd generation gas-piston. **Stock:** Ambidextrous thumbhole stock available in wood and synthetic options as well as multiple finishes and patterns. **Sights:** None, picatinny rail for scope mounting, multiple Crosman CenterPoint scope options available as factory bundles. **Features:** Very quiet due to the shrouded barrel with integrated suppressor, extremely easy cocking, single-shot, advanced adjustable two-stage trigger, innovative sling mounts for optional Benjamin break-barrel rifle sling. **Velocity:** .177, 1400 fps / .22, 1100 fps.
Price: . . . . $299.95 to $349.95

BENJAMIN VARMINT POWER PACK BREAK BARREL
Caliber: .22. **Barrel:** Rifled. **Weight:** 7.38 lbs. **Length:** 44.5 inches. **Power:** Break-barrel, gas-piston. **Stock:** Ambidextrous synthetic stock. **Sights:** none, weaver rail for scope mounting, includes a Crosman CenterPoint 4x32 scope with laser and light attachments complete with intermittent pressure switches. **Features:** Shrouded barrel, easy cocking, single-shot, adjustable two-stage trigger. **Velocity:** 950 fps.
Price: $249.95

BERETTA CX4 STORM

BERETTA CX4 STORM
Caliber: .177 Pellets. **Barrel:** Rifled 17.5 inches. **Weight:** 5.25 lbs. **Length:** 30.75 inches. **Power:** CO_2. **Stock:** Synthetic

thumbole. **Sights:** Adjustable front and rear. **Features:** Multi-shot semiautomatic with 30-round belt-fed magazine, highly realistic replica, utilizes large 88/90 gram disposable CO2 canisters for high shot count and uninterrupted shooting sessions. Available bundled with a Walther red-dot optics. **Velocity:** 600 fps.
Price: . . . . **$375.95 to $400.00**

BROWNING LEVERAGE AIR RIFLE
Caliber: .177, .22 **Barrel:** Rifled 18.9 inches. **Weight:** 8.6 lbs. **Length:** 44.8 inches. **Power:** Under-lever cock, spring-piston **Stock:** Hardwood right handed with raised cheekpiece. **Sights:** Front fiber-optic sight and fully adjustable rear fiber-optic sight, weaver/picatinny rail for scope mounting, includes 3-9x40 scope. **Features:** Fixed barrel accuracy, easy cocking, two-stage trigger. **Velocity:** .177, 1000 fps / .22, 800 fps.
Price: **$230.00**

BSA SUPERSPORT SE AIR RIFLE
Caliber: .177, .22. **Barrel:** Rifled 18.5 inches. **Weight:** 6.6 lbs. **Length:** 42 inches. **Power:** Break-barrel, spring-piston. **Stock:** Right-handed beech stock with raised cheekpiece. **Sights:** Front fiber-optic sight and fully adjustable rear fiber-optic sight, grooved for scope mounting. **Features:** European quality, adjustable two-stage trigger, single-shot, manufactured to stringent quality control and testing. **Velocity:** .177, 1000 fps / .22, 730 fps.
Price: **$295.95**

BSA METEOR EVO AIR RIFLE
Caliber: .177, .22. **Barrel:** Rifled 17.5 inches. **Weight:** 6.1 lbs. **Length:** 43.5 inches. **Power:** Break-barrel, spring-piston. **Stock:** Ambidextrous beech stock. **Sights:** Front fiber optic sight and fully adjustable rear fiber optic sight, grooved for scope mounting. **Features:** European quality, fitted with BSA-Made cold hammer forged barrel known for precision and accuracy, adjustable two-stage trigger, single-shot, manufactured to stringent quality control and testing. **Velocity:** .177, 950 fps / .22, 722 fps.
Price: **$295.95**

BSA R-10 MK2 PCP AIR RIFLE

BSA R-10 MK2 PCP AIR RIFLE
Caliber: .177, .22. **Barrel:** Rifled, BSA-made cold hammer forged precision barrel, 18 inches. **Weight:** 7.3 lbs. **Length:** 43 inches. **Power:** Pre-charged pneumatic. **Stock:** Right-hand, walnut stock or right-hand soft-touch coated beech. **Sights:** None, grooved for scope mounting. **Features:** Multi-shot bolt action, 10-shot magazine, fully regulated valve for maximum accuracy and shot consistency, free-floating, shrouded barrel. **Velocity:** .177, 1000 fps / .22, 900 fps.
Price: **$1,299.99**

BSA BUCCANEER SE AIR RIFLE
Caliber: .177, .22. **Barrel:** Rifled, BSA-made cold hammer forged precision barrel, 24 inches. **Weight:** 7.7 lbs. **Length:** 42.5 inches. **Power:** Pre-charged pneumatic. **Stock:** Ambidextrous beech stock or hardwood stock wrapped in innovative black soft-touch. **Sights:** None, grooved for scope mounting. **Features:** Multi-shot bolt action, 10-shot magazine, enhanced valve system for maximum shot count and consistency, integrated suppressor, adjustable two-stage trigger. **Velocity:** .177, 1000 fps / .22, 800 fps.
Price: **$649.99**

BSA GOLD STAR SE HUNTER FIELD TARGET PCP AIR RIFLE
Caliber: .177 **Barrel:** Rifled, BSA-made enhanced cold hammer forged precision barrel, 15.2 inches. **Weight:** 7 lbs. **Length:** 35.8 inches. **Power:** Pre-charged pneumatic. **Stock:** Highly adjustable gray laminate field target competition stock. **Sights:** None, grooved for scope mounting. **Features:** Multi-shot bolt action, 10-shot magazine, fully regulated valve for maximum accuracy and shot consistency, 70

consistent shots per charge, free-floating barrel with ½ UNF threaded muzzle, includes adjustable air stripper, adjustable match-grade trigger. **Velocity:** 800 fps.
Price: **$1,949.95**

BSA SCORPION 1200 SE AIR RIFLE

BSA SCORPION 1200 SE AIR RIFLE
Caliber: .177, .22. **Barrel:** Rifled, BSA-made cold hammer forged precision barrel, 24 inches. **Weight:** 8.75 lbs. **Length:** 44.5 inches. **Power:** Pre-charged pneumatic **Stock:** Ambidextrous synthetic stock. **Sights:** None, grooved for scope mounting. **Features:** Multi-shot bolt action, 10-shot magazine, high-capacity cylinder and enhanced valve capable of up to 80 shots per fill in .177 and 45 shots per fill in .22, free-floating shrouded barrel, adjustable two-stage trigger. **Velocity:** .177, 1200 fps / .22, 1000 fps.
Price: **$979.95**

BSA SCORPION SE AIR RIFLE
Caliber: .25 **Barrel:** Rifled, BSA-made cold hammer forged precision barrel, 18.5 inches. **Weight:** 7.7 lbs. **Length:** 36.5 inches. **Power:** Pre-charged pneumatic **Stock:** Ambidextrous Monte Carlo synthetic and beech stock options. **Sights:** None, grooved for scope mounting. **Features:** Multi-shot bolt action, 8-shot magazine, enhanced valve for high shot count in such a small platform, free-floating barrel with ½ UNF threads, included threaded muzzlebrake, adjustable two-stage trigger. **Velocity:** 700 fps.
Price: **$949.99**

CROSMAN CHALLENGER PCP COMPETITION

CROSMAN CHALLENGER PCP COMPETITION AIR RIFLE
Caliber: .177 **Barrel:** Match-grade Lothar Walther rifled barrel. **Weight:** 7.3 lbs. **Length:** 41.75 inches. **Power:** Pre-charged pneumatic / CO2 **Stock:** Highly adjustable synthetic competition stock. **Sights:** Globe front sight and Precision Diopter rear sight. **Features:** Innovative dual fuel design alows this rifle to run on HPA or CO2, single-shot, adjustable match-grade trigger, approved by the Civilian Marksmanship Program (CMP) for 3-position air rifle Sporter Class

competition. **Velocity:** 530 fps.
Price: $649.99

CROSMAN GENESIS NP AIR RIFLE
Caliber: .177, .22. **Barrel:** Rifled. **Weight:** 7.44 lbs. **Length:** 44.5 inches. **Power:** Break-barrel, gas-piston. **Stock:** Ambidextrous wood stock with dual raised cheekpieces and checkered grip and forearm. **Sights:** None, weaver/picatinny rail for scope mounting, includes 4x32 scope and rings. **Features:** Shrouded barrel with integrated suppressor, extremely easy cocking, single-shot, adjustable two-stage trigger, innovative sling mounts for optional Benjamin break-barrel rifle sling. **Velocity:** .177, 1200 fps / .22, 950 fps.
Price: $220.00

CROSMAN M4-177

CROSMAN M4-177 (VARIOUS STYLES AND KITS AVAILABLE)
Caliber: .177 Steel BBs, .177 pellet. **Barrel:** Rifled 17.25 inches. **Weight:** 3.75 lbs. **Length:** 41.75 inches. **Power:** Multi-pump pneumatic. **Stock:** M4 style adjustable plastic stock. **Sights:** Weaver/picatinny rail for scope mounting and flip-up sights. Bundled packages include various included sighting options. **Features:** Single-shot bolt action, lightweight and very accurate, multiple colors available. "Ready to go" kits available complete with ammo, safety glasses, targets and extra 5-shot pellet magazines. **Velocity:** 660 fps.
Price: . . . . $99.99 to $149.99

CROSMAN MODEL 760 PUMPMASTER AIR RIFLE
Caliber: .177 Steel BBs, .177 pellet. **Barrel:** Rifled 16.75 inches. **Weight:** 2.75 lbs. **Length:** 33.5 inches. **Power:** Multi-pump pneumatic. **Stock:** Ambidextrous plastic stock. **Sights:** Blade and ramp, rear sight adjustable for elevation, grooved for scope mounting. **Features:** Single-shot pellet, BB repeater, bolt action, lightweight, accurate and easy to shoot. Multiple colors available and configurations avalable. "Ready to go" kits available complete with ammo, safety glasses, targets and extra 5-shot pellet magazines. **Velocity:** 620 fps.
Price: . . . . $50.00 to $60.00

CROSMAN MODEL 1077 REPEATAIR RIFLE
Caliber: .177 pellet. **Barrel:** Rifled 20.38 inches. **Weight:** 3.75 lbs. **Length:** 36.88 inches. **Power:** SO2. **Stock:** Ambidextrous plastic stock. **Sights:** Blade and ramp, rear sight adjustable for windage and elevation, grooved for scope mounting. **Features:** Multi-shot, semi-automatic, 12-shot magazine, lightweight, fun and easy to shoot. "Ready to go" kits available complete with ammo, CO2, targets, target trap, etc. **Velocity:** 625 fps.
Price: . . . . $94.95 to $120.00

CROSMAN MODEL 2100 CLASSIC AIR RIFLE
Caliber: .177 Steel BBs, .177 pellet. **Barrel:** Rifled 20.84 inches. **Weight:** 4.81 lbs. **Length:** 39.75 inches. **Power:** Multi-pump pneumatic. **Stock:** Ambidextrous plastic stock with simulated wood grain. **Sights:** Blade and ramp, rear sight adjustable for windage and elevation, grooved for scope mounting. **Features:** Adult-size inexpensive airgun, single-shot, bolt action, lightweight, accurate and easy to shoot. **Velocity:** 755 fps.
Price: $69.99

CROSMAN MODEL NITRO VENOM

CROSMAN NITRO VENOM AIR RIFLE
Caliber: .177, .22. **Barrel:** Rifled 18.63 inches. **Weight:** 7.4 lbs. **Length:** 44.25 inches. **Power:** Break-barrel, gas-piston. **Stock:** Ambidextrous wood stock with dual raised cheekpieces and checkered grip and

forearm. **Sights:** None, weaver/picatinny rail for scope mounting, includes 3-9x32 scope and rings. **Features:** Muzzle break action for extra cocking leverage, single-shot, adjustable two-stage trigger. **Velocity:** .177, 1200 fps / .22, 950 fps.
Price: $220.00

CROSMAN MODEL NITRO VENOM DUSK

CROSMAN NITRO VENOM DUSK AIR RIFLE
Caliber: .177, .22. **Barrel:** Rifled 18.63 inches. **Weight:** 7.4 lbs. **Length:** 44.25 inches. **Power:** Break-barrel, gas-piston. **Stock:** Ambidextrous synthetic stock with dual raised cheekpieces and grooved grip and forearm. **Sights:** None, weaver/picatinny rail for scope mounting, includes 3-9x32 scope and rings. **Features:** Muzzle break for extra cocking leverage, single-shot, adjustable two-stage trigger. **Velocity:** .177, 1200 fps / .22, 950 fps.
Price: $220.00

CROSMAN MTR77 NP TACTICAL BREAK BARREL AIR RIFLE
Caliber: .177 Pellets **Barrel:** Rifled 15 inches. **Weight:** 7 lbs. **Length:** 40 inches. **Power:** Break-barrel, gas-piston. **Stock:** Ambidextrous AR15 styled stock. **Sights:** none, weaver/picatinny rail for flip up sights and scope mounting, includes 4x32 scope and rings. **Features:** Aggressive and realistic AR15 styling. Sling mounts, single-shot, adjustable two-stage trigger. **Velocity:** 1200 fps.
Price: $199.99

CROSMAN TR77 NPS BREAK BARREL AIR RIFLE
Caliber: .177 Pellets. **Barrel:** Rifled 12 inches. **Weight:** 5.8 lbs. **Length:** 40 inches. **Power:** Break-barrel, gas-piston. **Stock:** Ambidextrous synthetic skeleton stock. **Sights:** None, grooved for scope mounting, includes 4x32 scope and rings. **Features:** Aggressive styling, single-shot, adjustable two-stage trigger. **Velocity:** 1200 fps.
Price: $179.00

DAISY 1938 RED RYDER

DAISY 1938 RED RYDER AIR RIFLE
Caliber: .177 Steel BBs. **Barrel:** Smoothbore 10.85 inches. **Weight:** 2.2 lbs. **Length:** 35.4 inches. **Power:** Single-cock, lever action, spring-piston. **Stock:** Solid wood stock and fore-end. **Sights:** Blade front sight, adjustable rear sight. **Features:** 650 BB reservoir, single-stage trigger, designed for all day fun and backyard pliking, exceptional first airgun for young shooters. **Velocity:** 350 fps.
Price: $56.99

DAISY AVANTI MODEL 887 GOLD MEDALIST
Caliber: .177 Pellets. **Barrel:** Rifled, match-grade Lothar Walther barrel, 20.88 inches. **Weight:** 6.9 lbs. **Length:** 38.5 inches. **Power:** CO2. **Stock:** Ambidextrous laminated wood stock. **Sights:** Globe front sight and Precision Diopter rear sight. **Features:** Precision bored and crowned barrel for match accuracy, bulk fill CO2 is capable of up to 300 shots, additional inserts available for front sight, ideal entry level rifle for all 10-meter shooting disciplines. **Velocity:** 500 fps.
Price: $563.99

DAISY AVANTI MODEL 888 MEDALIST
Caliber: .177 Pellets. **Barrel:** Rifled, match-grade Lothar Walther barrel, 20.88 inches. **Weight:** 6.9 lbs. **Length:** 38.5 inches. **Power:** CO2. **Stock:** Ambidextrous laminated colorful wood stock. **Sights:** Globe front sight and micrometer adjustable rear peep sight. **Features:** Precision bored and crowned barrel for match accuracy, bulk fill CO2 is capable of up to 300 shots, additional inserts available for front sight, ideal entry level rifle for all 10-meter shooting disciplines. **Velocity:** 560 fps.
Price: $563.99

DAISY MODEL 105 BUCK AIR RIFLE
Caliber: .177 Steel BBs. **Barrel:** Smoothbore 7.97 inches. **Weight:** 1.6

lbs. **Length:** 29.84 inches. **Power:** Single-cock, lever action, spring-piston. **Stock:** Solid wood buttstock. **Sights:** Fixed front and rear sights. **Features:** 400 BB reservoir, single-stage trigger, designed for all day fun and backyard pliking. **Velocity:** 275 fps.
Price: **$35.99**

DAISY MODEL 753 ELITE

DAISY MODEL 753
Caliber: .177 Pellets. **Barrel:** Rifled, Lothar Walther, 20.88 inches. **Weight:** 6.4 lbs. **Length:** 39.75 inches. **Power:** Single-stroke pneumatic. **Stock:** Ambidextrous wood stock **Sights:** Globe front sight and Precision Diopter rear sight. **Features:** Full-size wood stock, additional inserts available for front sight, fully self contained power system, excellent "first" rifle for all 10-meter shooting disciplines. **Velocity:** 510 fps.
Price: **$479.99**

DAISY MODEL 4841 GRIZZLY AIR RIFLE
Caliber: .177 Steel BBs, .177 pellet. **Barrel:** Smoothbore 19.07 inches. **Weight:** 2.25 lbs. **Length:** 36.8 inches. **Power:** Single-stroke pneumatic. **Stock:** Ambidextrous plastic stock, Mossy Oak Break-Up pattern. **Sights:** Blade and ramp, rear sight adjustable for elevation, grooved for scope mounting, includes 4x15 scope and mounts. **Features:** Single-shot, lightweight, easy to shoot. **Velocity:** 350 fps.
Price: **$59.99**

DAISY MODEL 853
Caliber: .177 Pellets. **Barrel:** Rifled, Lothar Walther barrel, 20.88 inches. **Weight:** 5.5 lbs. **Length:** 38.5 inches. **Power:** Single-stroke pneumatic. **Stock:** Ambidextrous wood stock. **Sights:** Globe front sight and micrometer adjustable rear sight. **Features:** Full-size wood stock with spacers to adjust length of pull, additional inserts available for front sight, fully self-contained power system, classic NRA Junior Competition Rifle. **Velocity:** 510 fps.
Price: **$419.99**

DAISY MODEL 10 CARBINE AIR RIFLE
Caliber: .177, Steel BBs. **Barrel:** Smoothbore. **Weight:** 1.6 lbs. **Length:** 29.84 inches. **Power:** Single-cock, lever action, spring-piston. **Stock:** Solid wood stock and forearm. **Sights:** Fixed front and rear sights. **Features:** 400 BB reservoir, single-stage trigger, designed for all day fun and backyard pliking, lightweight youth airgun. **Velocity:** 350 fps.
Price: **$41.99**

DAISY 1938 PINK CARBINE AIR RIFLE
Caliber: .177, Steel BBs. **Barrel:** Smoothbore 10.85 inches. **Weight:** 2.2 lbs. **Length:** 35.4 inches. **Power:** Single-cock, lever action, spring-piston. **Stock:** Solid wood stock and forearm painted pink. **Sights:** Blade front sight, adjustable rear sight. **Features:** 650 BB reservoir, single-stage trigger, designed for all day fun and backyard pliking, great option for young ladies just starting out. **Velocity:** 350 fps.
Price: **$47.99**

DAISY POWERLINE MODEL 35 AIR RIFLE
Caliber: .177 Steel BBs, .177 pellet. **Barrel:** Smoothbore. **Weight:** 2.25 lbs. **Length:** 34.5 inches. **Power:** Multi-pump pneumatic. **Stock:** Ambidextrous plastic stock, available in black and pink camo. **Sights:** Blade and ramp, rear sight adjustable for elevation, grooved for scope mounting. **Features:** Single-shot pellet, BB rep, lightweight, accurate and easy to shoot. **Velocity:** 625 fps.
Price: . . . . $41.99 to $69.95

DAISY POWERLINE® 880
AIR RIFLE

DAISY POWERLINE® 880 AIR RIFLE
Caliber: .177 Steel BBs, .177 pellet. **Barrel:** Rifled 21 inches. **Weight:** 3.1 lbs. **Length:** 37.65 inches. **Power:** Multi-pump pneumatic. **Stock:** Ambidextrous brown wood grain plastic stock and black wood grain plastic stock options. **Sights:** Blade and ramp, rear sight adjustable for elevation, grooved for scope mounting. **Features:** Full-size young adult airgun, single-shot pellet, BB repeater, bolt action, lightweight, accurate and easy to shoot. "Ready to go" kit available complete with ammo, safety glasses, 4x15 scope and mounts. **Velocity:** 750 fps.
Price: . . . . $55.99 to $71.99

DAISY POWERLINE® 901 AIR RIFLE
Caliber: .177 Steel BBs, .177 pellet. **Barrel:** Rifled 20.8 inches. **Weight:** 3.2 lbs. **Length:** 37.75 inches. **Power:** Multi-pump pneumatic **Stock:** Ambidextrous black wood grain plastic stock. **Sights:** Front fiber-optic sight, rear blade sight adjustable for elevation, grooved for scope mounting. **Features:** Full-size adult airgun, single-shot pellet, BB repeater, bolt action, lightweight, accurate and easy to shoot. "Ready to go" kit available complete with ammo, safety glasses, shatterblast targets, 4x15 scope and mounts. **Velocity:** 750 fps.
Price: . . . . $71.99 to $95.99

DIANA MODEL 34 AIR RIFLE
Caliber: .177, .22. **Barrel:** Rifled 19.0 inches. **Weight:** 7.5 lbs. **Length:** 45 inches. **Power:** Break-barrel, spring-piston. **Stock:** Ambidextrous beech stock. **Sights:** Front fiber-optic sight and fully adjustable rear fiber-optic sight, grooved for scope mounting. **Features:** European quality, exceptional two-stage adjustable match trigger, single-shot, German manufactured to stringent quality control and testing, limited lifetime warranty. Various bundled configurations available. **Velocity:** .177, 1000 fps / .22, 800 fps.
Price: **$322.00**

DIANA MODEL 340
AIR RIFLE

DIANA MODEL 340 AIR RIFLE
Caliber: .177, .22. **Barrel:** Rifled 19.5 inches. **Weight:** 8.6 lbs. **Length:** 46 inches. **Power:** Break-barrel, German gas-piston. **Stock:** Ambidextrous beech stock. **Sights:** Front fiber-optic sight and fully adjustable rear fiber-optic sight, grooved for scope mounting. **Features:** European quality, exceptional two-stage adjustable match trigger, single-shot, German manufactured to stringent quality control and testing, limited lifetime warranty. The new N-TEC gas-piston power plant boasts smoother cocking and shooting, making the N-TEC line of Diana guns the most refined Diana airguns to date. Various bundled configurations available. **Velocity:** .177, 1000 fps / .22, 800 fps.
Price: **$500.00**

DIANA MODEL 350 MAGNUM AIR RIFLE
Caliber: .177, .22. **Barrel:** Rifled 19.25 inches. **Weight:** 8.2 lbs. **Length:** 48 inches. **Power:** Break-barrel, spring-piston. **Stock:** Right handed beech stock with grip and forearm checkering. **Sights:** Post and globe front sight and fully adjustable rear sight, grooved for scope mounting. **Features:** European quality, exceptional two-stage adjustable match trigger, single-shot, German manufactured to stringent quality control and testing, limited lifetime warranty. Various bundled configurations available. **Velocity:** .177, 1100 fps / .22, 900 fps.
Price: **$490.00**

DIANA MODEL 48 AIR RIFLE

DIANA MODEL 48 AIR RIFLE
Caliber: .177, .22. **Barrel:** Rifled 17 inches. **Weight:** 8.5 lbs. **Length:** 42.13 inches. **Power:** Single-cock, side-lever, spring-piston. **Stock:** Ambidextrous beech thumbhole stock. **Sights:** Blade front sight, fully adjustable rear sight, grooved for scope mounting. **Features:** European quality, exceptional two-stage match trigger, single-shot,

Prices given are believed to be accurate at time of publication however, many factors affect retail pricing so exact prices are not possible.

71ST EDITION, 2017 ✛ **529**

German manufactured to stringent quality control and testing, limited lifetime warranty. **Velocity:** .177, 1100 fps / .22, 900 fps.
Price: **$322.00**

DIANA MODEL 430 AIR RIFLE
Caliber: .177, .22. **Barrel:** Rifled 15.4 inches. **Weight:** 7.9 lbs. **Length:** 41 inches. **Power:** Under-lever, spring-piston. **Stock:** Right-handed beech stock with grip and forearm checkering. **Sights:** Blade front sight and fully adjustable rear sight, grooved for scope mounting. **Features:** European quality, exceptional two-stage adjustable match trigger, single-shot, German manufactured to stringent quality control and testing **Velocity:** .177, 870 fps / .22, 670 fps.
Price: **$650.00**

DIANA MODEL 460 MAGNUM AIR RIFLE
Caliber: .177, .22. **Barrel:** Rifled 19.25 inches. **Weight:** 8.2 lbs. **Length:** 48 inches. **Power:** Under-lever, spring-piston. **Stock:** Right-hand hardwood stock with grip and fore-end checkering. **Sights:** Post front sight and fully adjustable rear sight, grooved for scope mounting. **Features:** European quality, exceptional two-stage adjustable match trigger, single-shot, German manufactured to stringent quality control and testing, limited lifetime warranty. Various bundled configurations available. **Velocity:** .177, 1200 fps / .22, 1000 fps.
Price: **$600.00**

DIANA MODEL 470 TARGET HUNTER AIR RIFLE
Caliber: .177, .22 **Barrel:** 18" **Weight:** 9.4 lbs. **Length:** 45 inches overall. **Power:** Break-barrel, single-shot. **Stock:** Ambidextrous thumbhole hardwood, adjustable buttplate for elevation. **Features:** Upgraded two-stage adjustable trigger assembly with all-metal parts, rifled barrel. 1,150 fps in .177 and 930 fps in .22.
Price: **$725.50**

DIANA MODEL 56TH TARGET HUNTER AIR RIFLE
Caliber: .177, .22. **Barrel:** Rifled 17.3 inches. **Weight:** 11.1 lbs. **Length:** 44 inches. **Power:** Single-cock, side-lever, spring-piston. **Stock:** Ambidextrous beech thumbhole stock. **Sights:** None, grooved for scope mounting. **Features:** European quality, exceptional two-stage match trigger, single-shot, German manufactured to stringent quality control and testing. **Velocity:** .177, 1100 fps / .22, 900 fps.
Price: **$969.99**

DIANA MODEL P1000 PCP AIR RIFLE
Caliber: .177 Pellets. **Barrel:** Rifled 17.5 inches. **Weight:** 7.9 lbs. **Length:** 38 inches. **Power:** Pre-charged pneumatic. **Stock:** Right-hand hardwood stock. **Sights:** None, grooved for scope mounting. **Features:** Multi-shot side lever, 14-round magazine, 300 Bar max. fill yields up to 70 powerful shots. **Velocity:** 1150 fps.
Price: **$1,499.95**

DIANA MODEL P1000TH PCP AIR RIFLE
Caliber: .177 Pellets. **Barrel:** Rifled 17.7 inches. **Weight:** 8.2 lbs. **Length:** 38 inches. **Power:** Pre-charged pneumatic. **Stock:** Right-hand hardwood thumbhole stock. **Sights:** None, grooved for scope mounting. **Features:** Multi-shot side lever, 14-round magazine, 300 Bar max. fill yields up to 70 powerful shots. **Velocity:** 1150 fps.
Price: **$1,595.95**

EVANIX TACTIAL SNIPER AIR RIFLE

EVANIX TACTIAL SNIPER AIR RIFLE
Caliber: .22, .25, .30, .357, .45, .50. **Barrel:** Rifled 18.5 inches. **Weight:** 8.4 lbs. **Length:** 46 inches. **Power:** Pre-charged pneumatic. **Stock:** Adjustable skeleton tactical aluminum stock with lower accessory rail and foregrip. **Sights:** None, weaver/picatinny optics rail compatible for scope mounting. **Features:** Available in 6 calibers,

multi-shot side-lever action, 11-shot .22 magazine, 10-shot .25 magazine, 8-shot .30 magazine, 7-shot .357/9mm magazine, 6-shot .45 magazine, 6-shot .50 magazine. Amazing styling and function make the Evanix Tactical sniper a one-of-a-kind airgun. **Velocity:** .22, 1200 fps / .25, 910 fps, .30, 910 fps, .357/9mm, 800 fps / .45, 720 fps / .50, 720 fps.
Price: . . . . **$1,200.00 to $1,799.99**

EVANIX MAX-ML BULLPUP AIR RIFLE
Caliber: .22, .25, .30, .357, .45, .50. **Barrel:** Rifled 19.5 inches. **Weight:** 8.16 lbs. **Length:** 29.3 inches. **Power:** Pre-charged pneumatic. **Stock:** Bullpup synthetic with aluminum foregrip. **Sights:** None, weaver/picatinny optics rail compatible for scope mounting. **Features:** Available in 6 calibers, multi-shot side-lever action, 11-shot .22 magazine, 10-shot .25 magazine, 8-shot .30 magazine, 7-shot .357/9mm magazine, 6-shot .45 magazine, 6-shot .50 magazine. Evanix pioneered the high-powered, big-bore bullpup airgun. Shrouded barrel helps reduce shot noise, extremely accurate, compact, and easy to shoot with consistent accuracy. **Velocity:** .22, 1050 fps / .25, 910 fps / .30, 910 fps / .357/9mm, 730 fps / .45, 805 fps / .50, 690 fps.
Price: . . . . **$1,299.00 to $1,599.99**

GAMO ACCU PREMIUM COMBO
Caliber: .177, .22. **Barrel:** Rifled 17.8 inches. **Weight:** 6.6 lbs. **Length:** 45.6 inches. **Power:** Under-lever, spring-piston. **Stock:** Ambidextrous lightweight composite with dual raised cheekpieces. **Sights:** Front globe fiber-optic sight, fully adjustable rear fiber-optic sight, grooved for scope mounting, includes 3-9x40AO scope and mounts. **Features:** Enhanced fixed barrel accuracy, lightweight, single-shot, adjustable two-stage trigger. **Velocity:** .177, 1200 fps / .22, 900 fps.
Price: **$229.99**

GAMO BIG CAT 1250
Caliber: .177, .22. **Barrel:** Rifled 18 inches. **Weight:** 6.1 lbs. **Length:** 43.3 inches. **Power:** Break-barrel, spring-piston. **Stock:** Ambidextrous lightweight composite. **Sights:** None, grooved for scope mounting, includes 4x32 or 3-9x40 scope and mounts based on bundle. **Features:** Very lightweight, single-shot, easy cocking, adjustable two-stage trigger, all-weather fluted barrel. **Velocity:** .177, 1250 fps / .22, 950 fps.
Price: **$179.95**

GAMO BIG CAT .25 CALIBER
Caliber: .25. **Barrel:** Rifled 18 inches. **Weight:** 6.1 lbs. **Length:** 43.3 inches. **Power:** Break-barrel, spring-piston. **Stock:** Ambidextrous lightweight composite. **Sights:** Front globe fiber-optic sight, fully adjustable rear fiber-optic sight, grooved for scope mounting, includes 4x32 scope and mounts. **Features:** Very lightweight, single-shot, easy cocking, adjustable two-stage trigger, all-weather stock. **Velocity:** 800 fps.
Price: **$249.99**

GAMO BIG CAT 1400 AIR RIFLE
Caliber: .177 Pellets. **Barrel:** Rifled 18 inches. **Weight:** 6.61 lbs. **Length:** 44.7 inches. **Power:** Break-barrel, spring-piston. **Stock:** Ambidextrous lightweight composite. **Sights:** None, grooved for scope mounting, includes recoil reducing rail, 4x32 scope and mounts. **Features:** Very lightweight, single-shot, easy cocking, adjustable two-stage trigger, all-weather fluted barrel. **Velocity:** 1400 fps.
Price: **$239.99**

GAMO CFR AIR RIFLE COMBO
Caliber: .177 Pellets. **Barrel:** Rifled 20 inches. **Weight:** 8 lbs. **Length:** 46.85 inches. **Power:** Under-lever, spring-piston. **Stock:** Ambidextrous lightweight composite with adjustable cheekpiece. **Sights:** Front globe fiber-optic sight, fully adjustable rear fiber-optic sight, grooved for scope mounting, includes 3-9x40 scope and mounts. **Features:** Enhanced fixed barrel accuracy, integrated Gamo "Whisper" noise dampening system lightweight, single-shot, easy cocking, adjustable two-stage trigger. **Velocity:** 1100 fps.
Price: **$349.95**

GAMO HORNET AIR RIFLE
Caliber: .177 Pellets. **Barrel:** Rifled 18 inches. **Weight:** 6.1 lbs. **Length:** 43.3 inches. **Power:** Break-barrel, spring-piston. **Stock:** Ambidextrous lightweight composite. **Sights:** None, grooved for

Prices given are believed to be accurate at time of publication however, many factors affect retail pricing so exact prices are not possible.

scope mounting, includes 4x32 scope and mounts. **Features:** Very lightweight, single-shot, easy cocking, adjustable two-stage trigger, all-weather fluted barrel. **Velocity:** 1200 fps.
Price: **$179.95**

GAMO BONE COLLECTOR BULL WHISPER IGT AIR RIFLE
Caliber: .177, .22. **Barrel:** Rifled 19.13 inches. **Weight:** 5.95 lbs. **Length:** 43.75 inches. **Power:** Break-barrel, gas-piston. **Stock:** Ambidextrous lightweight composite with rubberized inserts for grip. **Sights:** None, grooved for scope mounting, includes recoil-reducing rail, 4x32 scope and mounts. **Features:** Very lightweight, single-shot, easy cocking, adjustable two-stage trigger, all-weather bull barrel with integrated suppressor technology. **Velocity:** .177, 1300 fps / .22, 975 fps.
Price: **$289.95**

GAMO BONE COLLECTOR IGT AIR RIFLE
Caliber: .177 pellets. **Barrel:** Rifled 18 inches. **Weight:** 6.1 lbs. **Length:** 43.3 inches. **Power:** Break-barrel, gas-piston. **Stock:** Ambidextrous lightweight composite with rubberized inserts for grip. **Sights:** None, grooved for scope mounting, includes recoil-reducing rail, 4x32 scope and mounts. **Features:** Very lightweight, single-shot, easy cocking, adjustable two-stage trigger, all-weather fluted barrel. **Velocity:** 1300 fps.
Price: **$289.95**

GAMO BUCKMASTER SQUIRREL TERMINATOR AIR RIFLE
Caliber: .177 Pellets. **Barrel:** Rifled 18 inches. **Weight:** 6.61 lbs. **Length:** 45 inches. **Power:** Break-barrel, spring-piston. **Stock:** Ambidextrous lightweight composite. **Sights:** None, grooved for scope mounting, includes 4x32 scope and mounts. **Features:** Very lightweight, single-shot, easy cocking, adjustable two-stage trigger, innovative turbo stabilizing system helps manage recoil, all-weather fluted barrel. **Velocity:** 1275 fps.
Price: **$239.99**

GAMO CAMO ROCKET IGT AIR RIFLE
Caliber: .177 pellets. **Barrel:** Rifled 18 inches. **Weight:** 6.6 lbs. **Length:** 43 inches. **Power:** Break-barrel, gas-piston. **Stock:** Ambidextrous lightweight composite camo stock. **Sights:** None, grooved for scope mounting, includes 4x32 scope and mounts. **Features:** Very lightweight, single-shot, easy cocking, adjustable two-stage trigger, all-weather fluted barrel. **Velocity:** 1300 fps.
Price: **$249.95**

GAMO HUNTER BIG CAT
Caliber: .177 pellets. **Barrel:** Rifled 18 inches. **Weight:** 6.1 lbs. **Length:** 43.3 inches. **Power:** Break-barrel, spring-piston. **Stock:** Ambidextrous wood stock with grip and fore-end checkering. **Sights:** Globe fiber-optic front sight and fully adjustable fiber-optic rear sight, grooved for scope mounting. **Features:** High-quality traditional European hardwood and steel design, single-shot, easy cocking, adjustable two-stage trigger. **Velocity:** 1250 fps.
Price: **$199.99**

GAMO HUNTER EXTREME SE (SPECIAL EDITION) AIR RIFLE
Caliber: .177, .22, .25. **Barrel:** Rifled 18 inches. **Weight:** 9 lbs. **Length:** 45.8 inches. **Power:** Break-barrel, spring-piston. **Stock:** Ambidextrous wood stock with grip and fore-end checkering. **Sights:** None, grooved for scope mounting, includes 3-9x50 illuminated dot reticle scope with heavy duty mount. **Features:** High-quality traditional European hardwood and steel design, single-shot, bull barrel with metal jacket, adjustable two-stage trigger. **Velocity:** .177, 1650 fps / .22, 1300 fps / .25, 730 fps.
Price: . . . . **$529.95 to $550.00**

GAMO SHAWN MICHAELS SHOWSTOPPER AIR RIFLE
Caliber: .177 pellets. **Barrel:** Rifled 18 inches. **Weight:** 6.1 lbs. **Length:** 43.8 inches. **Power:** Break-barrel, spring-piston. **Stock:** Ambidextrous lightweight composite stock with dual raised cheekpieces. **Sights:** None, grooved for scope mounting, includes recoil-reducing rail, 4x32 scope and mounts. **Features:** Very lightweight, single-shot, easy cocking, adjustable two-stage trigger, all-weather fluted barrel. **Velocity:** 1400 fps.
Price: **$259.95**

GAMO SILENT STALKER WHISPER IGT AIR RIFLE
Caliber: .177, .22. **Barrel:** Rifled 18 inches. **Weight:** 7.15 lbs. **Length:** 43 inches. **Power:** Break-barrel, gas-piston. **Stock:** Ambidextrous

GAMO SILENT STALKER
WHISPER IGT AIR RIFLE

lightweight composite skeleton stock. **Sights:** Globe fiber-optic front sight and fully adjustable fiber-optic rear sight, grooved for scope mounting, includes recoil reducing rail, 3-9x40 scope and heavy duty mount. **Features:** Integrated Gamo "Whisper" noise dampening system, lightweight, single-shot, easy cocking, adjustable two-stage trigger, all-weather fluted barrel. **Velocity:** .177, 1300 fps / .22, 975 fps.
Price: **$329.95**

GAMO VARMINT HUNTER HP AIR RIFLE
Caliber: .177 Pellets. **Barrel:** Rifled 18 inches. **Weight:** 6.61 lbs. **Length:** 43.78 inches. **Power:** Break-barrel, spring-piston. **Stock:** Ambidextrous lightweight composite with dual raised cheekpieces. **Sights:** None, grooved for scope mounting, includes recoil-reducing rail, 4x32 scope and mounts, laser and light with intermittent pressure switches included. **Features:** Lightweight, single-shot, easy cocking, adjustable two-stage trigger, all-weather fluted barrel. **Velocity:** 1400 fps.
Price: **$309.95**

GAMO VARMINT STALKER AIR RIFLE
Caliber: .177 pellets. **Barrel:** Rifled 18 inches. **Weight:** 7.15 lbs. **Length:** 43 inches. **Power:** Break-barrel, spring-piston. **Stock:** Ambidextrous lightweight composite stock with dual raised cheekpieces. **Sights:** None, grooved for scope mounting, includes 4x32 scope and mounts. **Features:** Very lightweight, single-shot, easy cocking, adjustable two-stage trigger, all-weather fluted bull barrel. **Velocity:** 1250 fps.
Price: **$250.00**

GAMO WHISPER FUSION IGT AIR RIFLE
Caliber: .177, .22. **Barrel:** Rifled 18 inches. **Weight:** 8 lbs. **Length:** 43 inches. **Power:** Break-barrel, gas-piston. **Stock:** Ambidextrous lightweight composite stock with adjustable cheekpiece. **Sights:** Globe fiber-optic front sight and fully adjustable fiber-optic rear sight, grooved for scope mounting, includes recoil reducing rail, 3-9x40 scope and heavy duty mount. **Features:** Integrated Gamo "Whisper" noise dampening system and bull barrel noise suppression system for maximum stealth, lightweight, single-shot, easy cocking, adjustable two-stage trigger. **Velocity:** .177, 1300 fps / .22, 975 fps.
Price: **$329.95**

GAMO WHISPER FUSION PRO AIR RIFLE
Caliber: .22. **Barrel:** Rifled 18 inches. **Weight:** 8 lbs. **Length:** 46.5 inches. **Power:** Break-barrel, spring-piston. **Stock:** Ambidextrous lightweight composite stock with dual raise cheekpieces. **Sights:** Globe fiber-optic front sight and fully adjustable fiber-optic rear sight, grooved for scope mounting, includes recoil reducing rail, 3-9x40AO scope and mounts. **Features:** Integrated Gamo "Whisper" noise dampening system and bull barrel noise suppression system for maximum stealth, lightweight, single-shot, easy cocking, adjustable two-stage trigger. **Velocity:** 1000 fps.
Price: **$349.95**

GAMO WHISPER

GAMO WHISPER G2 AIR RIFLE
Caliber: .177, .22. **Barrel:** Rifled 18 inches. **Weight:** 8 lbs. **Length:** 43 inches. **Power:** Break-barrel, spring-piston. **Stock:** Ambidextrous lightweight composite stock with adjustable cheekpiece. **Sights:** Globe fiber-optic front sight and fully adjustable fiber-optic rear sight, grooved for scope mounting, includes 4x32 scope and mounts. **Features:** Integrated Gamo "Whisper" noise dampening system, very lightweight, single-shot, easy cocking, adjustable two-stage trigger, all-weather fluted barrel. **Velocity:** .177, 1275 fps / .22, 975 fps.
Price: **$279.95**

Prices given are believed to be accurate at time of publication however, many factors affect retail pricing so exact prices are not possible.

71ST EDITION, 2017 ✦ **531**

AIRGUNS—Long Guns

GAMO WHISPER SILENT CAT AIR RIFLE
Caliber: .177 pellets. **Barrel:** Rifled 18 inches. **Weight:** 5.28 lbs. **Length:** 46 inches. **Power:** Break-barrel, spring-piston. **Stock:** Ambidextrous lightweight composite skeleton stock. **Sights:** Globe fiber-optic front sight and fully adjustable fiber-optic rear sight, grooved for scope mounting, includes 4x32 scope and mounts. **Features:** Integrated Gamo "Whisper" noise dampening system, very lightweight, single-shot, easy cocking, adjustable two-stage trigger, all-weather fluted barrel. **Velocity:** 1200 fps.
Price: **$259.95**

HAMMERLI 850 AIR MAGNUM
Caliber: .177, .22. **Barrel:** Rifled 23.62 inches. **Weight:** 5.65 lbs. **Length:** 41 inches. **Power:** CO2. **Stock:** Ambidextrous lightweight composite stock with dual raised cheekpieces. **Sights:** Globe fiber-optic front sight and fully adjustable fiber-optic rear sight, grooved for scope mounting. **Features:** Multi-shot bolt action, 8-shot rotary magazine, utilizes 88 gram disposable CO_2 canisters delivering up to 200 shots per cartridge. Extremely accurate, very easy to shoot. German manufacturing. **Velocity:** .177, 760 fps / .22, 655 fps.
Price: **$329.99**

HATSAN USA STRIKER & EDGE CLASS AIRGUNS

HATSAN USA STRIKER & EDGE CLASS AIRGUNS
Caliber: .177, .22, .25. **Barrel:** Rifled 17.7 inches. **Weight:** 6.4 to 6.6 lbs. **Length:** 43 inches. **Power:** Break-barrel, spring-piston and gas-spring variations. **Stock:** Multiple synthetic and synthetic skeleton stock options. Available in different colors such as black, muddy girl camo, moon camo, etc. **Sights:** Fiber-optic front sight and fully adjustable fiber-optic rear sight, grooved for scope mounting, includes 3-9x32 scope and mounts. **Features:** European manufacturing with German Steel, single-shot, adjustable two-stage trigger, performance tested at the factory with lead pellets for accurate velocity specifications. **Velocity:** .177, 1000 fps / .22, 800 fps / .25, 650 fps.
Price: . . . . **$150.00 to $180.00**

HATSAN USA MOD 87 QE VORTEX AIRGUN

HATSAN USA MOD 87 QE VORTEX AIRGUN
Caliber: .177, .22, .25. **Barrel:** Rifled 10.6 inches. **Weight:** 7.4 lbs. **Length:** 44.5 inches. **Power:** Break-barrel, gas-spring. **Stock:** Synthetic all-weather stock with adjustable cheekpiece. **Sights:** Fiber-optic front sight and fully adjustable fiber-optic rear sight, grooved for scope mounting, includes 3-9x32 scope and mounts. **Features:** "Quiet Energy" barrel shroud with integrated suppressor, European manufacturing with German Steel, single-shot, fully adjustable two-stage "Quattro" trigger, performance tested at the factory with lead pellets for accurate velocity specifications. **Velocity:** .177, 1000 fps / .22, 800 fps / .25, 650 fps.
Price: **$219.99**

HATSAN USA MOD 95 QE VORTEX AIRGUN

HATSAN USA MOD 95 QE VORTEX AIRGUN
Caliber: .177, .22, .25. **Barrel:** Rifled 10.6 inches. **Weight:** 7.6 lbs. **Length:** 44.5 inches. **Power:** Break-barrel, gas-spring. **Stock:** Turkish walnut stock with grip and fore-end checkering. **Sights:** Fiber-optic front sight and fully adjustable fiber-optic rear sight, grooved for scope mounting, includes 3-9x32 scope and mounts. **Features:** "Quiet Energy" barrel shroud with integrated suppressor, European manufacturing with German Steel, single-shot, fully adjustable two-

stage "Quattro" trigger, performance tested at the factory with lead pellets for accurate velocity specifications. **Velocity:** .177, 1000 fps / .22, 800 fps / .25, 650 fps.
Price: **$229.99**

HATSAN USA MOD 125 SNIPER VORTEX AIRGUN

HATSAN USA MOD 125 SNIPER VORTEX AIRGUN
Caliber: .177, .22, .25. **Barrel:** Rifled 19.6 inches. **Weight:** 9 lbs. **Length:** 48.8 inches. **Power:** Break-barrel, gas-spring. **Stock:** Synthetic all-weather stock with adjustable cheekpiece, available in black or camo options. **Sights:** Fiber-optic front sight and fully adjustable fiber-optic rear sight, grooved for scope mounting, includes 3-9x32 scope and mounts. **Features:** Integrated suppressor, European manufacturing with German Steel, single-shot, fully adjustable two-stage "Quattro" trigger, performance tested at the factory with lead pellets for accurate velocity specifications. **Velocity:** .177, 1250 fps / .22, 1000 fps / .25, 750 fps.
Price: . . . . **$319.99 to $359.99**

HATSAN USA MOD 135 QE VORTEX AIRGUN

HATSAN USA MOD 135 QE VORTEX AIRGUN
Caliber: .177, .22, .25., .30 **Barrel:** Rifled 10.6 inches. **Weight:** 9.9 lbs. **Length:** 48.8 inches. **Power:** Break-barrel, gas-spring. **Stock:** Turkish walnut stock with grip and fore-end checkering, adjustable buttplate and cheekpiece. **Sights:** Fiber-optic front sight and fully adjustable fiber-optic rear sight, innovative dual rail 11mm dovetail and Weaver compatible for scope mounting. **Features:** The most powerful break barrel in the world. Worlds first "big-bore" break-barrel airgun, "Quiet Energy" barrel shroud with integrated suppressor, European manufacturing with German Steel, single-shot, fully adjustable two-stage "Quattro" trigger, performance tested at the factory with lead pellets for accurate velocity specifications. **Velocity:** .177, 1250 fps / .22, 1000 fps / .25, 750 fps. / .30, 550 fps.
Price: . . . . **$299.95 to $329.99**

HATSAN USA MOD "TORPEDO" 150 SNIPER VORTEX AIRGUN
Caliber: .177, .22, .25. **Barrel:** Rifled 13 inches. **Weight:** 9.4 lbs. **Length:** 48.4 inches. **Power:** Under-lever, gas-spring. **Stock:** Synthetic all-weather stock with adjustable cheekpiece. **Sights:** Fiber-optic front sight and fully adjustable fiber-optic rear sight, innovative dual rail 11mm dovetail and Weaver compatible for scope mounting. **Features:** Integrated suppressor, enhanced fixed barrel accuracy, European manufacturing with German steel, single-shot, fully adjustable two-stage "Quattro" trigger, performance tested at the factory with lead pellets for accurate velocity specifications. **Velocity:** .177, 1250 fps / .22, 1000 fps / .25, 750 fps.
Price: **$359.99**

HATSAN USA AT44 QE PCP AIRGUN

HATSAN USA AT44 QE PCP AIRGUN
Caliber: .177, .22, .25. **Barrel:** Rifled 19.5 inches. **Weight:** 8 lbs. **Length:** 45.4 inches. **Power:** Pre-charged pneumatic. **Stock:** Various configurations, synthetic all-weather stock with front accessory rail and sling mounts. Turkish hardwood with sling mounts, full tactical stock with soft rubber grip inserts, adjustable buttstock and cheek riser. **Sights:** None, innovative dual rail 11mm dovetail and Weaver compatible for scope mounting. **Features:** Multi-shot

side-lever action, 10-shot .177 and .22 magazines / 9-shot .25 magazine, "Quiet Energy" barrel shroud with integrated suppressor, European manufacturing with German steel, removable air cylinder, fully adjustable two-stage "Quattro" trigger, performance tested at the factory with lead pellets for accurate velocity specifications. **Velocity:** .177, 1070 fps / .22, 970 fps / .25, 870 fps.
Price: **$599.99**

HATSAN USA CARNIVORE BIG BORE

HATSAN USA CARNIVORE BIG BORE AIR RIFLE
Caliber: ..30, .35. **Barrel:** Rifled 23 inches. **Weight:** 9.3 lbs. **Length:** 48.9 inches. **Power:** Pre-charged pneumatic. **Stock:** Synthetic all-weather stock with sling mounts, front accessory rail, adjustable cheekpiece and buttpad. **Sights:** None, innovative dual rail 11mm dovetail and Weaver compatible for scope mounting. **Features:** Multi-shot bolt action, 6-shot .35 magazine / 7-shot .30 magazine, "Quiet Energy" barrel shroud with integrated suppressor, European manufacturing with German steel, removable air cylinder, fully adjustable two-stage "Quattro" trigger, performance tested at the factory with lead pellets for accurate velocity specifications. **Velocity:** .30, 860 fps / .35, 730 fps.
Price: **$800.00**

HATSAN USA GALATIAN QE SERIES
Caliber: .177, .22, .25. **Barrel:** Rifled 17.7 inches. **Weight:** 8.6 lbs. **Length:** 43.3 inches. **Power:** Pre-charged pneumatic. **Stock:** Synthetic all-weather stock with extra mag storage, sling mounts, tri-rail front accessory rails, adjustable cheek riser and buttstock. **Sights:** None, innovative dual rail 11mm dovetail and Weaver compatible for scope mounting. **Features:** Multi-shot side-lever action, 17-shot .177 magazine, 14-shot .22 magazine, 13-shot .25 magazine, "Quiet Energy" barrel shroud with integrated suppressor, European manufacturing with German steel, removable air cylinder, fully adjustable two-stage "Quattro" trigger, performance tested at the factory with lead pellets for accurate velocity specifications. **Velocity:** .177, 1130 fps / .22, 1050 fps / .25, 950 fps.
Price: **$999.99**

HATSAN USA GLADIUS BULLPUP QE SERIES (LONG VERSION)
Caliber: .177, .22, .25. **Barrel:** Rifled 23 inches. **Weight:** 10.6 lbs. **Length:** 38 inches. **Power:** Pre-charged pneumatic. **Stock:** Synthetic bullpup all-weather stock with extra mag storage, sling mounts, tri-rail front accessory rails, adjustable cheek riser and buttstock. **Sights:** None, innovative dual rail 11mm dovetail and Weaver compatible for scope mounting. **Features:** 6-way indexing power selector makes selecting the right energy for the job as easy as turning a knob to the right number, multi-shot side-lever action, 10-shot .177 and .22 magazines / 9-shot .25 magazine, "Quiet Energy" barrel shroud with integrated suppressor, European manufacturing with German steel, large removable air cylinder delivers industry leading shot counts, fully adjustable two-stage "Quattro" trigger, performance tested at the factory with lead pellets for accurate velocity specifications. **Velocity:** .177, 1170 fps / .22, 1070 fps / .25, 970 fps.
Price: **$999.99**

HATSAN USA HURCULES QE SERIES
Caliber: .177, .22, .25, .30, .35, .45 **Barrel:** Rifled 23 inches. **Weight:** 13 lbs. **Length:** 48.4 inches. **Power:** Pre-charged pneumatic. **Stock:** Fully adjustable synthetic all-weather stock, with sling mounts. **Sights:** None, innovative dual rail 11mm dovetail and Weaver compatible for scope mounting. **Features:** Available in 6 calibers, 1000cc of air on board provides industry leading shot count and energy on target. Multi-shot side-lever action, 17-shot .177 magazine, 14-shot .22 magazine, 13-shot .25 magazine, 10-shot .30 magazine, 9-shot .35 magazine, 7-shot .45 magazine, "Quiet Energy" barrel shroud with integrated suppressor, European manufacturing with German steel, fully adjustable two-stage "Quattro" trigger, performance tested at the factory with lead pellets for accurate velocity specifications. **Velocity:** .177, 1300 fps / .22, 1230 fps / .25, 1200 fps / .30, 990 fps / .35, 890 fps / .45, TBA fps.
Price: . . . . **TBA 4th quarter 2016**

MARKSMAN 2040 AIR RIFLE
Caliber: .177 Steel BBs, **Barrel:** Smoothbore 10.5 inches. **Weight:** 4 lbs. **Length:** 33.5 inches. **Power:** Single-cock, spring-piston **Stock:** Ambidextrous plastic stock. **Sights:** Blade and ramp, adjustable rear sight adjustable for elevation, grooved for scope mounting, includes 4x20 scope and mounts. **Features:** BB repeater, lightweight, easy to shoot. **Velocity:** 300 fps.
Price: **$59.50**

REMINGTON EXPRESS

REMINGTON EXPRESS AIR RIFLE W/ SCOPE COMBOS
Caliber: .177, .22. **Barrel:** Rifled, 19 inches. **Weight:** 8 lbs. **Length:** 45 inches. **Power:** Break-barrel, spring-piston **Stock:** Available in ambidextrous wood with grip and fore-end checkering and textured synthetic options. **Sights:** Fiber-optic front sight and fully adjustable fiber-optic rear sight, grooved for scope mounting, includes 4x32 scope and mounts. **Features:** Single-shot, two-stage trigger. **Velocity:** .177, 1150 fps / .22, 800 fps.
Price: **$179.95**

REMINGTON EXPRESS XP AIR RIFLE W/ SCOPE COMBOS
Caliber: .177 Pellets **Barrel:** Rifled. **Weight:** 8.8 lbs. **Length:** 47.5 inches. **Power:** Break-barrel, spring-piston **Stock:** Available in ambidextrous wood with grip and fore-end checkering and textured synthetic options. **Sights:** None, grooved for scope mounting, includes 3-9x32 scope and mounts. **Features:** Single-shot, integrated suppressor, two-stage trigger. **Velocity:** 1150 fps.
Price: **$199.95**

RUGER AIR MAGNUM COMBO

RUGER AIR MAGNUM COMBO AIR RIFLE
Caliber: .177, .22. **Barrel:** Rifled 19.5 inches. **Weight:** 9.5 lbs. **Length:** 48.5 inches. **Power:** Break-barrel, spring-piston. **Stock:** Ambidextrous Monte Carlo synthetic stock with textured grip and fore-end. **Sights:** Fiber-optic front sight and fully adjustable fiber-optic rear sight, Weaver scope rail, includes 4x32 scope and mounts. **Features:** Single-shot, two-stage trigger. **Velocity:** .177, 1400 fps / .22, 1200 fps.
Price: **$220.00**

RUGER BLACKHAWK COMBO AIR RIFLE
Caliber: .177 Pellets. **Barrel:** Rifled 18.7 inches. **Weight:** 6.95 lbs. **Length:** 44.8 inches. **Power:** Break-barrel, spring-piston. **Stock:** Ambidextrous synthetic stock with checkering on the grip and fore-end. **Sights:** Fiber-optic front sight and fully adjustable fiber-optic rear sight, grooved for scope mounting, includes 4x32 scope and mounts. **Features:** Single-shot, two-stage trigger. **Velocity:** 1000 fps.
Price: **$130.00**

RUGER EXPLORER AIR RIFLE
Caliber: .177 Pellets. **Barrel:** Rifled 15 inches. **Weight:** 4.55 lbs. **Length:** 37.13 inches. **Power:** Break-barrel, spring-piston **Stock:** Ambidextrous synthetic skeleton stock. **Sights:** Fiber-optic front sight and fully adjustable fiber-optic rear sight, grooved for scope mounting.

Prices given are believed to be accurate at time of publication however, many factors affect retail pricing so exact prices are not possible.

71ST EDITION, 2017 ⊕ **533**

Features: Designed as an entry level youth break-barrel rifle, easy to shoot and accurate, single-shot, two-stage trigger. **Velocity:** 1000 fps.
Price: $79.99

RUGER TARGIS HUNTER AIR RIFLE COMBO
Caliber: .22. **Barrel:** Rifled 18.7 inches. **Weight:** 9.85 lbs. **Length:** 44.85 inches. **Power:** Break-barrel, spring-piston. **Stock:** Ambidextrous synthetic stock with texture grip and fore-end, includes rifle sling. **Sights:** Fiber-optic front sight and fully adjustable fiber-optic rear sight, picatinny optics rail, includes 3-9x40AO scope and mounts. **Features:** Integrated "SilencAIR" suppressor, single-shot, two-stage trigger. **Velocity:** 1000 fps.
Price: $210.00

RUGER YUKON GAS-PISTON COMBO AIR RIFLE
Caliber: .177, .22. **Barrel:** Rifled 18.7 inches. **Weight:** 9 lbs. **Length:** 44.8 inches. **Power:** Break-barrel, gas-piston **Stock:** Ambidextrous Monte Carlo wood stock with dual raised cheekpieces. **Sights:** Fiber-optic front sight and fully adjustable fiber-optic rear sight, Weaver/picatinny scope rail, includes 4x32 scope and mounts. **Features:** Integrated "SilencAIR" suppressor, single-shot, two-stage trigger. **Velocity:** .177, 1250 fps / .22, 1050 fps.
Price: $220.00

RUGER TARGIS AIR RIFLE
Caliber: .177. **Barrel:** Rifled 18.7" inches **Weight:** 9.85 lbs. **Length:** 44.85 inches. **Power:** Break-barrel, spring-piston, single-shot. **Stock:** Black colored synthetic with ventilated comb. **Sights:** Fiber-optic front sight and adjustable rear sight with Weaver/Picatinny rail system. **Features:** Two-stage trigger with 3.3-lb. trigger pull weight and rubber buttplate. **Velocity:** 1,200 fps with alloy pellets and 1,000 fps with lead pellets.
Price: $176.00

STOEGER A30 AIR RIFLE
Caliber: .177, .22. **Barrel:** Rifled 16.5 inches. **Weight:** 8.2 lbs. **Length:** 42.5 inches. **Power:** Break-barrel, gas-piston **Stock:** Ambidextrous synthetic stock with textured grip and fore-end. **Sights:** None, picatinny optics rail, includes 4x32 scope and mounts. **Features:** Single-shot, two-stage trigger. **Velocity:** .177, 1200 fps / .22, 1000 fps.
Price: $220.00

STOEGER X50

STOEGER X50 AIR RIFLE
Caliber: .177, .22. **Barrel:** Rifled 19.7 inches. **Weight:** 8.3 lbs. **Length:** 50 inches. **Power:** Break-barrel, spring-piston. **Stock:** Ambidextrous Monte Carlo synthetic stock. **Sights:** Fiber-optic front sight and fully adjustable fiber-optic rear sight, grooved for scope mounting, includes 3-9x40AO scope and heavy duty mount. **Features:** Single-shot, two-stage trigger. **Velocity:** .177, 1500 fps / .22, 1200 fps.
Price: $350.00

STOEGER X20S SUPPRESSOR AIR RIFLE
Caliber: .177, .22. **Barrel:** Rifled 16.3 inches. **Weight:** 7 lbs. **Length:** 43 inches. **Power:** Break-barrel, spring-piston. **Stock:** Ambidextrous Monte Carlo synthetic stock. **Sights:** None, grooved for scope mounting, includes compact 4x32 scope and mounts. **Features:** Industry leading dual-stage noise reduction technology makes the X20s perhaps the quietest spring-powered magnum airgun on the market. Single-shot, two-stage trigger. **Velocity:** .177, 1200 fps / .22, 1000 fps.
Price: $300.00

STOEGER X20 WOOD AIR RIFLE
Caliber: .177, .22. **Barrel:** Rifled 16.5 inches. **Weight:** 7 lbs. **Length:** 43 inches. **Power:** Break-barrel, spring-piston. **Stock:** Ambidextrous Monte Carlo wood stock with dual raised cheekpieces. **Sights:** Fiber-optic front sight and fully adjustable fiber-optic rear sight, grooved for scope mounting, includes 3-9x40AO scope and heavy duty mount. **Features:** Single-shot, two-stage trigger. **Velocity:** .177, 1200 fps / .22, 1000 fps.
Price: $200.00

STOEGER ATAC GAS RAM AIR RIFLE
Caliber: .177, .22. **Barrel:** Rifled 13 inches. **Weight:** 9 lbs. **Length:** 43 inches. **Power:** Break-barrel, gas-piston **Stock:** Advanced tactical ambidextrous synthetic stock with side accessory rails. **Sights:** None, picatinny optics rail, includes 4-16x40AO scope and mounts. **Features:** Industry leading dual-stage noise reduction technology, optional bipod accessory, optional picatinny sling mount adaptor, single-shot, two-stage trigger. **Velocity:** .177, 1200 fps / .22, 1000 fps.
Price: $295.95

STOEGER X3-TAC AIR RIFLE
Caliber: .177. **Barrel:** Rifled 14.5 inches. **Weight:** 5.6 lbs. **Length:** 36.25 inches. **Power:** Break-barrel, spring-piston. **Stock:** Ambidextrous synthetic skeleton stock. **Sights:** Fiber-optic front sight and fully adjustable fiber-optic rear sight, grooved for scope mounting. **Features:** Easy cocking, designed for younger shooters, single-shot. **Velocity:** 550 fps.
Price: $119.99

TECH FORCE M8 AIR RIFLE & COMBO PACKAGE
Caliber: .177. **Barrel:** Rifled 9 inches. **Weight:** 6.5 lbs. **Length:** 40 inches. **Power:** Break-barrel, spring-piston. **Stock:** Ambidextrous wood stock. **Sights:** None, grooved for scope mounting, includes 4x32AO scope and mounts. **Features:** Easy cocking, designed for younger shooters, single-shot, unique dual-blade trigger. **Velocity:** 800 fps.
Price: $195.95

TECH FORCE M12 AIR RIFLE & COMBO PACKAGES
Caliber: .177, .22. **Barrel:** Rifled 15.7 inches. **Weight:** 8.6 lbs. **Length:** 43.1 inches. **Power:** Break-barrel, spring-piston. **Stock:** Ambidextrous wood stock. **Sights:** None, grooved for scope mounting, various scope and mounting options available as bundles. **Features:** Single-shot. **Velocity:** .177, 1000 fps / .22, 800 fps.
Price: . . . . $249.99 to $299.99

WALTHER LGV
COMPETITION ULTRA

WALTHER LGV ULTRA
Caliber: .177, .22. **Barrel:** Rifled 16.5 inches. **Weight:** 7 lbs. **Length:** 43 inches. **Power:** Single-cock, spring-piston. **Stock:** Ambidextrous synthetic stock. **Sights:** Fiber-optic front sight and fully adjustable fiber-optic rear sight, grooved for scope mounting. **Features:** German engineered and manufactured, highly advanced anti-recoil and vibration technology, easy cocking and shooting, locking barrel joint, ½ UNF threaded muzzle, weighted muzzlebrake, single-shot, adjustable two-stage trigger, limited lifetime warranty. **Velocity:** .177, 1000 fps / .22, 700 fps.
Price: $649.95

WALTHER LGU AIR RIFLE
Caliber: .177, .22. **Barrel:** Rifled 11.81 inches. **Weight:** 9.5 lbs. **Length:** 41.89 inches. **Power:** Single-cock, spring-piston. **Stock:** Ambidextrous beech stock with dual raised cheekpieces. **Sights:** None, grooved for scope mounting. **Features:** German engineered and manufactured, highly advanced anti-recoil and vibration technology, enhanced fixed barrel accuracy, easy cocking and shooting, weighted muzzlebrake, single-shot, adjustable two-stage trigger, limited lifetime warranty. **Velocity:** .177, 1000 fps / .22, 700 fps.
Price: $650.00

WALTHER LG400 UNIVERSAL AIR RIFLE
Caliber: .177. **Barrel:** Advanced match-grade rifled barrel 16.53 inches. **Weight:** 8.6 lbs. **Length:** 43.7 inches. **Power:** Pre-charged pneumatic. **Stock:** Ambidextrous competition, highly adjustable wood stock. **Sights:** Olympic-grade, match Diopter/Micrometer adjustable sights. **Features:** True professional class 10-meter target rifle, meets ISSF requirements. **Velocity:** 577 fps.
Price: $2,500.00

WALTHER LEVER ACTION
Caliber: .177. **Barrel:** Rifled 18.9 inches. **Weight:** 6.2 lbs. **Length:** 39.2 inches. **Power:** CO_2 **Stock:** Ambidextrous wood stock. **Sights:** Blade front sight, adjustable rear sight. **Features:** Lever-action repeater,

WALTHER LEVER ACTION

8-shot rotary magazine, great wild west replica airgun. **Velocity:** 600 fps.
Price: $500.00

WALTHER 1250 DOMINATOR AIR RIFLE
Caliber: .177, .22. **Barrel:** Rifled 23.62 inches. **Weight:** 8 lbs. **Length:** 40.94 inches. **Power:** Pre-charged pneumatic. **Stock:** Ambidextrous synthetic stock with dual raised cheekpieces. **Sights:** None, grooved for scope mounting, includes 8-32x56 side focus mil-dot scope and mounts. **Features:** German engineered and manufactured, bolt-action repeater, 8-shot rotary magazine, adjustable two-stage trigger. Ships with hard case, bipod and muzzlebrake. **Velocity:** .177, 1200 fps / .22, 1000 fps.
Price: $650.00

WALTHER LG300-XT JUNIOR AIR RIFLE
Caliber: .177. **Barrel:** Advanced match-grade rifled barrel, 16.54 inches. **Weight:** 7.72 lbs. **Length:** 39.76 inches. **Power:** Pre-charged pneumatic. **Stock:** Ambidextrous highly adjustable competition laminate wood stock. **Sights:** Olympic-grade, match Diopter/Micrometer adjustable sights. **Features:** 10-meter competition target rifle, meets ISSF requirements, removable air cylinder delivers up to 400 shots per fill. **Velocity:** 570 fps.
Price: $1,725.95

WALTHER TERRUS
Caliber: .177, .22. **Barrel:** Rifled 17.75 inches. **Weight:** 7.52 lbs. **Length:** 44.25 inches. **Power:** Single-cock, spring-piston. **Stock:** Ambidextrous beech and synthetic stock options available. **Sights:** Front fiber-optic sight and fully adjustable rear fiber-optic sight, grooved for scope mounting. **Features:** German engineered and manufactured, very easy cocking and shooting, ½ UNF threaded muzzle, single-shot, two-stage target trigger, limited lifetime warranty. **Velocity:** .177, 1050 fps / .22, 800 fps.
Price: $650.00

WINCHESTER AIR RIFLE MODEL 77XS
Caliber: .177 Steel BBs, .177 Pellet. **Barrel:** Rifled 20.8 inches. **Weight:** 3.1 lbs. **Length:** 37.6 inches. **Power:** Multi-pump pneumatic. **Stock:** Ambidextrous synthetic thumbhole stock. **Sights:** Blade front sight, adjustable rear sight, grooved for scope mounting, includes 4x32 scope and mounts. **Features:** Single-shot pellet, 50-round BB repeater, bolt action, lightweight, accurate and easy to shoot. **Velocity:** 800 fps.
Price: $95.45

WINCHESTER AIR RIFLE MODEL 500S
Caliber: .177. **Barrel:** Rifled. **Weight:** 6 lbs. **Length:** 39.38 inches. **Power:** Break-barrel, spring-piston. **Stock:** Ambidextrous synthetic stock with textured grip and fore-end. **Sights:** Fiber-optic front sight and fully adjustable fiber-optic rear sight, grooved for scope mounting. **Features:** Easy cocking, designed for younger shooters, single-shot. **Velocity:** 490 fps.
Price: $119.99

WINCHESTER AIR RIFLE MODEL 1100SS AND 1100WS
Caliber: .177. **Barrel:** Rifled. **Weight:** 9.1 lbs. **Length:** 46.25 inches. **Power:** Break-barrel, spring-piston. **Stock:** Ambidextrous synthetic stock and wood stock options, textured grip and fore-end on both stock types. **Sights:** Fixed front sight and fully adjustable rear sight, grooved for scope mounting, includes 4x32 scope and mounts. **Features:** Single-shot, aggressive pricing. **Velocity:** 1100 fps.
Price: $143.99

WINCHESTER AIR RIFLE MODEL 1250 CS
Caliber: .177. **Barrel:** Rifled. **Weight:** 8.7 lbs. **Length:** 46.5 inches. **Power:** Break-barrel, spring-piston. **Stock:** Ambidextrous synthetic thumbhole camo pattern stock. **Sights:** Fixed fiber-optic front sight and fully adjustable fiber-optic rear sight, grooved for scope mounting, includes 3-9x32 scope and mounts. **Features:** Integrated suppressor, single-shot, includes web sling, integrated bipod. **Velocity:** 1400 fps.
Price: $215.99

WINCHESTER MODEL 1400 CS

WINCHESTER MODEL 1400 CS AIR RIFLE
Caliber: .177. **Barrel:** Rifled. **Weight:** 9 lbs. **Length:** 51.2 inches. **Power:** Break-barrel, spring-piston. **Stock:** Ambidextrous synthetic thumbhole Mossy Oak camo pattern stock. **Sights:** None, grooved for scope mounting, includes 3-9x32 scope and mounts. **Features:** Single-shot, includes web sling, integrated bipod. **Velocity:** 1100 fps.
Price: $239.99

WINCHESTER AIR RIFLE .22 CAL. MODEL 1052
Caliber: .22. **Barrel:** Rifled. **Weight:** 8.2 lbs. **Length:** 46.25 inches. **Power:** Break-barrel, spring-piston. **Stock:** Ambidextrous synthetic thumbhole stock. **Sights:** None, grooved for scope mounting, includes 3-9x32 scope and mounts. **Features:** Single-shot, includes web sling, all-weather fluted barrel jacket. **Velocity:** 1000 fps.
Price: $219.99

WINCHESTER MODEL MP4

WINCHESTER MODEL MP4 CO2 RIFLE
Caliber: .177 Steel BBs, .177 Pellet. **Barrel:** Rifled. **Weight:** 4.4 lbs. **Length:** 38.5 inches. **Power:** CO2. **Stock:** Ambidextrous AR15-style synthetic stock with adjustable buttstock, quad rail fore-end. **Sights:** Flip-up adjustable sights, Weaver/picatinny optics rail. **Features:** Semiautomatic, 16-shot magazine, utilizes dual 12-gram CO2 cartridges for high shot count and better consistency, can shoot BBs and pellets. **Velocity:** 1000 fps.
Price: $203.99

THE 2017 GUN DIGEST
web directory

      This is the 18th year of our web directory and, as usual, there are changes, additions and a few deletions.

The directory is offered to our readers as a guide to the major companies in the firearms industry, and also as convenient jumping-off point. After all, half the fun is just exploring what's out there. Considering that most of the web pages have hot links to other firearms-related web pages, the Internet trail just goes on and on once you've taken the initial step to go online.

If the website you are looking for is not listed here, just try using the full name of the company or product between www. and .com. Probably 95 percent of current websites are based on this simple, self-explanatory format.

Another option is to go directly to the popular search engines, such as www.google.com., www.yahoo.com or www.bing.com, and enter the name of the company or product for which you are searching. This is also an invaluable method for finding new companies or those that have changed their web addresses.

Finally, make it a point to access YouTube, www.YouTube.com, for short videos on the subjects you are pursuing. Firearms enthusiasts and companies have posted literally thousands of firearms-related videos—some good, some bad—but always interesting. Many of the how-to gunsmithing videos, in particular, are excellent. Just be very specific when you type in the subject to be searched.

—The Editors

AMMUNITION AND COMPONENTS

2 Monkey Trading **www.2monkey.com**

2nd Amendment Ammunition **www.secondammo.com**

Accurate Reloading Powders **www.accuratepowder.com**

Advanced Tactical **www.advancedtactical.com**

Aguila Ammunition **www.aguilaammo.com**

Alexander Arms **www.alexanderarms.com**

Allegiance Ammunition **www.allegianceammunition.com**

Alliant Powder **www.alliantpowder.com**

American Derringer Co. **www.amderringer.com**

American Eagle **www.federalpremium.com**

American Pioneer Powder **www.americanpioneerpowder.com**

American Specialty Ammunition
www.americanspecialityammo.com

Ammo Depot **www.ammodepot.com**

Ammo Importers **www.ammoimporters.com**

Ammo-Up **www.ammoupusa.com**

Applied Ballistics Munitions **www.buyabmammo.com**

Arizona Ammunition, Inc. **www.arizonaammunition.net**

Armscor **www.us.armscor.com**

ASYM Precision Ammunition **www.asymammo.com**

Atesci **www.atesci.com**

Australian Munitions **www.australian-munitions.com**

B&T (USA) **www.bt-ag.ch**

Ballistic Products Inc. **www.ballisticproducts.com**

Barnes Bullets **www.barnesbullets.com**

Baschieri & Pellagri **www.baschieri-pellagri.com**

Berger Bullets, Ltd. **www.bergerbullets.com**

Berry's Mfg., Inc. **www.berrysmfg.com**

Big Bore Express **www.powerbeltbullets.com**

Black Hills Ammunition, Inc. **www.black-hills.com**

BlackHorn209 **www.blackhorn209.com**

Brenneke of America Ltd. **www.brennekeusa.com**

Browning **www.browning.com**

Buffalo Arms **www.buffaloarms.com**

Buffalo Bore Ammunition **www.buffalobore.com**

Calhoon, James, Bullets **www.jamescalhoon.com**

Cartuchos Saga **www.saga.es**

Cast Performance Bullet **www.grizzlycartridge.com**

CCI **www.cci-ammunition.com**

Centurion Ordnance **www.centurionammo.com**

Century International Arms **www.centuryarms.com**

Cheaper Than Dirt **www.cheaperthandirt.com**

Cheddite France **www.cheddite.com**

Claybuster Wads **www.claybusterwads.com**

Combined Tactical Systems **www.combinedsystems.com**

Cor-Bon/Glaser **www.corbon.com**

Cutting Edge Bullets **www.cuttingedgebullets.com**
DDupleks, Ltd. **www.ddupleks.com**
Defense Technology Corp. **www.defense-technology.com**
Denver Bullets **www.denverbullets.com**
Desperado Cowboy Bullets **www.cowboybullets.com**
Dillon Precision **www.dillonprecision.com**
Double Tap Ammunition **www.doubletapammo.net**
Down Range Mfg. **www.downrangemfg.com**
Dynamic Research Technologies **www.drtammo.com**
Dynamit Nobel RWS Inc. **www.dnrws.com**
EcoSlug **www.eco-slug.com**
Eley Ammunition **www.eley.co.uk**
Environ-Metal **www.hevishot.com**
Estate Cartridge **www.estatecartridge.com**
Federal Cartridge Co. **www.federalpremium.com**
Fiocchi of America **www.fiocchiusa.com**
Fowler Bullets **www.benchrest.com/fowler**
Gamebore Cartridge **www.gamebore.com**
GaugeMate **www.gaugemate.com**
Glaser Safety Slug, Inc. **www.corbon.com**
GOEX Inc. **www.goexpowder.com**
Graf & Sons **www.grafs.com**
Grizzly Cartridge Co. **www.grizzlycartridge.com**
Haendler & Natermann **www.hn-sport.de**
Hawk Bullets **www.hawkbullets.com**
Herter's Ammuniition **www.cabelas.com**
Hevi.Shot **www.hevishot.com**
High Precision Down Range **www.hprammo.com**
Hodgdon Powder **www.hodgdon.com**
Hornady **www.hornady.com**
HSM Ammunition **www.thehuntingshack.com**
Huntington Reloading Products **www.huntingtons.com**
IMR Smokeless Powders **www.imrpowder.com**
International Cartridge Corp **www.iccammo.com**
James Calhoon **www.jamescalhoon.com**
Kent Cartridge America **www.kentgamebore.com**
Knight Bullets **www.benchrest.com/knight/**
Lapua **www.lapua.com**
Lawrence Brand Shot **www.lawrencebrandshot.com**
Leadheads Bullets **www.proshootpro.com**
Lehigh Defense **www.lehighdefense.com**
Lightfield Ammunition Corp **www.litfld.com**
Lomont Precision Bullets **www.klomont.com/kent**
Lyman **www.lymanproducts.com**
Magnum Muzzleloading Products **www.mmpsabots.com**
Magnus Bullets **www.magnusbullets.com**
Magtech **www.magtechammunition.com**
Meister Bullets **www.meisterbullets.com**
Midway USA **www.midwayusa.com**
Mitchell's Mausers **www.mauser.net**
National Bullet Co. **www.nationalbullet.com**

Navy Arms **www.navyarms.com**
Nobel Sport **www.nobelsportammo.com**
Norma **www.norma.cc**
North Fork Technologies **www.northforkbullets.com**
Nosler Bullets, Inc. **www.nosler.com**
Pattern Control **www.patterncontrol.com**
PCP Ammunition **www.pcpammo.com**
Piney Mountain Ammunition
   www.pineymountainammunitionco.com
PMC **www.pmcammo.com**
PolyCase Ammunition **www.polycaseammo.com**
Polywad **www.polywad.com**
PowerBelt Bullets **www.powerbeltbullets.com**
PPU Ammunition **www.prvipartizan.com**
PR Bullets **www.prbullet.com**
Precision Reloading **www.precisionreloading.com**
Pro Load Ammunition **www.proload.com**
Prvi Partizan Ammunition **www.prvipartizan.com**
Rainier Ballistics **www.rainierballistics.com**
Ram Shot Powder **www.ramshot.com**
Rare Ammunition **www.rareammo.com**
Reloading Specialties Inc. **www.reloadingspecialtiesinc.com**
Remington **www.remington.com**
Rio Ammunition **www.rioammo.com**
Rocky Mountain Cartridge **www.rockymountaincartride.com**
RUAG Ammotec **www.ruag.com/ammotec**
RWS **www.ruag-usa.com**
Sauvestre Ammunition **www.centuryarms.com**
SBR Ammunition **www.sbrammunition.com**
Schuetzen Powder **www.schuetzenpowder.com**
Sellier & Bellot **www.sellier-bellot.cz**
Shilen **www.shilen.com**
Sierra **www.sierrabullets.com**
SIG Sauer **www.sigammo.com**
Silver State Armory **www.ssarmory.com**
Simunition **www.simunition.com**
SinterFire, Inc. **www.sinterfire.com**
Spectra Shot **www.spectrashot.com**
Speer Ammunition **www.speer-ammo.com**
Speer Bullets **www.speer-bullets.com**
Sporting Supplies Int'l Inc. **www.wolfammo.com**
Starline **www.starlinebrass.com**
Stealth Gunpowder **www.stealthgunpowder.com**
Swift Bullets Co. **www.swiftbullets.com**
Tannerite **www.tannerite.com**
Tascosa Cartridge Co. **www.tascosacartridge.com**
Ted Nugent Ammunition **www.americantactical.us**
Ten-X Ammunition **www.tenxammo.com**
Top Brass **www.topbrass-inc.com**
TulAmmo **www.tulammousa.com**
Velocity Tactics **www.velocitytactics.com**

Vihtavuori **www.vihtavuori.com**
Weatherby **www.weatherby.com**
Western Powders Inc. **www.westernpowders.com**
Widener's Reloading & Shooters Supply **www.wideners.com**
Winchester Ammunition **www.winchester.com**
Windjammer Tournament Wads **www.windjammer-wads.com**
Wolf Ammunition **www.wolfammo.com**
Woodleigh Bullets **www.woodleighbullets.com.au**
Xtreme Bullets **www.xtremebullets.com**
Zanders Sporting Goods **www.gzanders.com**

CASES, SAFES, GUN LOCKS AND CABINETS

Ace Case Co. **www.acecase.com**
AG English Sales Co. **www.agenglish.com**
Dee Zee **www.deezee.com**
American Security Products **www.amsecusa.com**
Americase **www.americase.com**
Assault Systems **www.elitesurvival.com**
Avery Outdoors, Inc. **www.averyoutdoors.com**
Bore-Stores **www.borestores.com**
Boyt Harness Co. **www.boytharness.com**

Gardall Safes **www.gardall.com**
Campbell Industrial Supply **www.gun-racks.com**
Cannon Safe Co. **www.cannonsafe.com**
Fort Knox Safes **www.ftknox.com**
Franzen Security Products **www.securecase.com**
Goldenrod Dehumidifiers **www.goldenroddehumidifiers.com**
Gunlocker Phoenix USA Inc. **www.gunlocker.com**
Gun Storage Solutions **www.storemoreguns.com**
GunVault **www.gunvault.com**
Hakuba USA Inc. **www.hakubausa.com**
Heritage Safe Co. **www.heritagesafe.com**
Hide-A-Gun **www.hide-a-gun.com**
Homak Safes **www.homak.com**
Hunter Company **www.huntercompany.com**
Liberty Safe & Security **www.libertysafe.com**
Morton Enterprises **www.uniquecases.com**
New Innovative Products **www.starlightcases.com**
Phoenix USA Inc. **www.gunlocker.com**
Plano Molding Co. **www.planomolding.com**
Plasticase, Inc. **www.nanuk.com**
Rhino Safe **www.rhinosafe.com**
Rotary Gun Racks **www.gun-racks.com**
Sack-Ups **www.sackups.com**

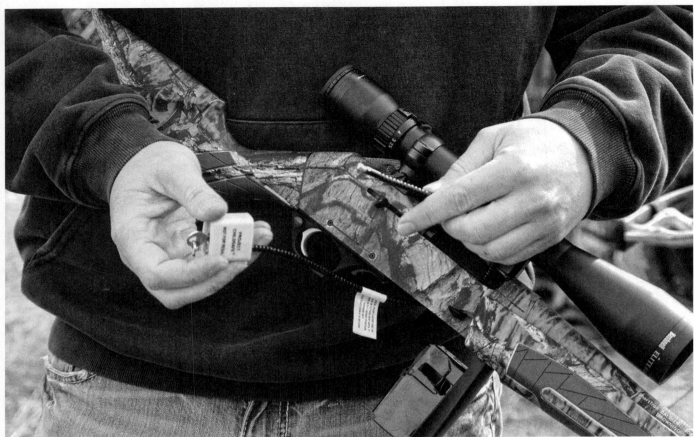

Safe Tech, Inc. **www.safrgun.com**

Secure Firearm Products **www.securefirearmproducts.com**

Securecase **www.securecase.com**

Shot Lock Corp. **www.shotlock.com**

SKB Cases **www.skbcases.com**

Smart Lock Technology Inc. **www.smartlock.com**

Snap Safe **www.snapsafe.com**

Sportsmans Steel Safe Co. **www.sportsmansteelsafes.com**

Starlight Cases **www.starlightcases.com**

Strong Case **www.strongcasebytnb.com**

Technoframes **www.technoframes.com**

Titan Gun Safes **www.titangunsafes.com**

Tracker Safe **www.trackersafe.com**

T.Z. Case Int'l **www.tzcase.com**

U.S. Explosive Storage **www.usexplosivestorage.com**

Versatile Rack Co. **www.versatilegunrack.com**

V-Line Industries **www.vlineind.com**

Winchester Safes **www.winchestersafes.com**

Ziegel Engineering **www.ziegeleng.com**

CHOKE DEVICES, RECOIL REDUCERS, SUPPRESSORS AND ACCURACY DEVICES

ACT Tactical **www.blackwidowshooters.com**

Advanced Armament Corp. **www.advanced-armament.com**

100 Straight Products **www.100straight.com**

Briley Mfg. **www.briley.com**

Carlson's **www.choketube.com**

Colonial Arms **www.colonialarms.com**

Comp-N-Choke **www.comp-n-choke.com**

Elite Iron **www.eliteiron.net**, Gemtech **www.gem-tech.com**

Great Lakes Tactical **www.gltactical.com**

KDF, Inc. **www.kdfguns.com**

Kick's Industries **www.kicks-ind.com**

LimbSaver **www.limbsaver.com**

Mag-Na-Port Int'l Inc. **www.magnaport.com**

Metro Gun **www.metrogun.com**

Patternmaster Chokes **www.patternmaster.com**

Poly-Choke **www.poly-choke.com**

SilencerCo **www.silencerco.com**

Sims Vibration Laboratory **www.limbsaver.com**

SRT Arms **www.srtarms.com**

SureFire **www.surefire.com**

Teague Precision Chokes **www.teaguechokes.com**

Truglo **www.truglo.com**

Trulock Tool **www.trulockchokes.com**

Vais Arms, Inc. **www.muzzlebrakes.com**

CHRONOGRAPHS AND BALLISTIC SOFTWARE

Barnes Ballistic Program **www.barnesbullets.com**
Ballisticard Systems **www.ballisticards.com**
Competition Electronics **www.competitionelectronics.com**
Competitive Edge Dynamics **www.cedhk.com**
Hodgdon Shotshell Program **www.hodgdon.com**
Lee Shooter Program **www.leeprecision.com**
NECO **www.neconos.com**
Oehler Research Inc. **www.oehler-research.com**
PACT **www.pact.com**
ProChrony **www.competitionelectronics.com**
Quickload **www.neconos.com**
RCBS Load **www.rcbs.com**
Shooting Chrony Inc **www.shootingchrony.com**
Sierra Infinity Ballistics Program **www.sierrabullets.com**
Winchester Ballistics Calculator **www.winchester.com**

CLEANING PRODUCTS

Accupro **www.accupro.com**
Ballistol USA **www.ballistol.com**
Birchwood Casey **www.birchwoodcasey.com**
Bore Tech **www.boretech.com**
Break-Free, Inc. **www.break-free.com**
Bruno Shooters Supply **www.brunoshooters.com**
Butch's Bore Shine **www.butchsboreshine.com**
C.J. Weapons Accessories **www.cjweapons.com**
Clenzoil **www.clenzoil.com**
Corrosion Technologies **www.corrosionx.com**
Dewey Mfg. **www.deweyrods.com**
DuraCoat **www.lauerweaponry.com**
Emby Enterprises **www.alltemptacticallube.com**
Extreme Gun Care **www.extremeguncare.com**
G96 **www.g96.com**
Gun Butter **www.gunbutter.com**
Gun Cleaners **www.guncleaners.com**
Gunslick Gun Care **www.gunslick.com**
Gunzilla **www.topduckproducts.com**
Hoppes **www.hoppes.com**
Hydrosorbent Products **www.dehumidify.com**
Inhibitor VCI Products **www.theinhibitor.com**
Jag Brush **www.jagbrush.com**
KG Industries **www.kgcoatings.com**
L&R Ultrasonics **www.ultrasonics.com**
Lyman **www.lymanproducts.com**
Mil-Comm Products **www.mil-comm.com**
Montana X-Treme **www.montanaxtreme.com**
MPT Industries **www.mptindustries.com**
Mpro7 Gun Care **www.mp7.com**

Old West Snake Oil **www.oldwestsnakeoil.com**
Otis Technology, Inc. **www.otisgun.com**
Outers **www.outers-guncare.com**
Prolix Lubricant **www.prolixlubricant.com**
ProShot Products **www.proshotproducts.com**
ProTec Lubricants **www.proteclubricants.com**
Rigel Products **www.rigelproducts.com**
Sagebrush Products **www.sagebrushproducts.com**
Sentry Solutions Ltd. **www.sentrysolutions.com**
Shooters Choice Gun Care **www.shooters-choice.com**
Slip 2000 **www.slip2000.com**
Southern Bloomer Mfg. **www.southernbloomer.com**
Stony Point Products **www.unclemikes.com**
www.topduckproducts.com
Triangle Patch **www.trianglepatch.com**
Wipe-Out **www.sharpshootr.com**
World's Fastest Gun Bore Cleaner **www.michaels-oregon.com**

FIREARM AUCTION SITES

Alderfer Austion **www.alderferauction.com**
Amoskeag Auction Co. **www.amoskeagauction.com**
Antique Guns **www.antiqueguns.com**
Auction Arms **www.auctionarms.com**
Batterman's Auctions **www.battermans.com**
Bonhams & Butterfields **www.bonhams.com/usarms**
Cowan's **www.cowans.com**
Fontaine's Auction Gallery **www.fontainesauction.net**
Guns America **www.gunsamerica.com**
Gun Broker **www.gunbroker.com**
Guns International **www.gunsinternational.com**
Heritage Auction Galleries **www.ha.com**
James D. Julia, Inc. **www.jamesdjulia.com**
Lock, Stock & Barrel Investments **www.lsbauctions.com**
Morphy Auctions **www.morphyauctions.com**
Poulin Auction Co. **www.poulinantiques.com**
Rock Island Auction Co. **www.rockislandauction.com**
Wallis & Wallis **www.wallisandwallis.org**

FIREARM MANUFACTURERS AND IMPORTERS

Accu-Tek **www.accu-tekfirearms.com**
Accuracy Int'l North America **www.accuracyinternational.com**
Adcor Defense **www.adcorindustries.com**
AIM **www.aimsurplus.com**
AirForce Airguns **www.airforceairguns.com**
Air Gun Inc. **www.airrifle-china.com**
Air Ordnance/Tippmann Armory **www.tippmannarmory.com**
Airguns of Arizona **www.airgunsofarizona.com**
Alexander Arms **www.alexanderarms.com**

America Remembers **www.americaremembers.com**
American Classic **www.americanclassic1911.com**
American Derringer Corp. **www.amderringer.com**
American Spirit Arms **www.americanspirtarms.com**
American Tactical Imports **www.americantactical.us**
American Classic **www.eagleimportsinc.com**
American Western Arms **www.awaguns.com**
Angstadt Arms **www.angstadtarms.com**
Anschutz **www.anschutz-sporters.com**
AR-7 Industries **www.ar-7.com**
Ares Defense Systems **www.aresdefense.com**
Armalite **www.armalite.com**
Armi Sport **www.armisport.com**
Armscor Precision Internationl **www.armscor.com**
Armscorp USA Inc. **www.armscorpusa.com**
Arrieta **www.arrietashotguns.com**
Arsenal Inc. **www.arsenalinc.com**
Atlanta Cutlery Corp. **www.atlantacutlery.com**
ATA Arms **www.ataarms.com**
Auto-Ordnance Corp. **www.tommygun.com**
Aya **www.aya-fineguns.com**
B&T (USA) **www.bt-ag.ch**
Ballard Rifles **www.ballardrifles.com**
Barrett Firearms Mfg. **www.barrettrifles.com**
Bat Machine Co. **www.batmachine.com**
Battle Arms Development **www.battlearmsdevelopment.com**
Beeman Precision Airguns **www.beeman.com**
Benelli USA Corp. **www.benelliusa.com**
Benjamin Sheridan **www.crosman.com**
Beretta U.S.A. Corp. **www.berettausa.com**
Bergara Rifles **www.bergararifles.com**
Bernardelli **www.bernardelli.com**
Bersa **www.bersa.com**
Big Horn Armory **www.bighornarmory.com**
Blaser Jagdwaffen Gmbh **www.blaser.de**
Bleiker **www.bleiker.ch**
Bond Arms **www.bondarms.com**
Borden Rifles, Inc. **www.bordenrifles.com**
Boss & Co. **www.bossguns.co.uk**
Bowen Classic Arms **www.bowenclassicarms.com**
Breda **www.bredafucili.com**
Briley Mfg. **www.briley.com**
BRNO Arms **www.cz-usa.com**
Brown, E. Arthur **www.eabco.com**
Brown, Ed Products **www.edbrown.com**
Brown, McKay **www.mckaybrown.com**
Browning **www.browning.com**
BRP Corp. **www.brpguns.com**
BUL Ltd. **www.bultransmark.com**
Bushmaster Firearms **www.bushmaster.com**
BWE Firearms **www.bwefirearms.com**

Cabot Guns **www.cabotguns.com**
Caesar Guerini USA **www.gueriniusa.com**
Caracal **www.caracal-usa.com**
Carolina Arms Group **www.carolinaarmsgroup.com**
Caspian Arms, Ltd. **www.caspianarmsltd.com**
CDNN Sports **www.cdnnsports.com**
Century Arms **www.centuryarms.com**
Champlin Firearms **www.champlinarms.com**
Charter Arms **www.charterfirearms.com**
CheyTac USA **www.cheytac.com**
Chiappa Firearms **www.chiappafirearms.com**
Christensen Arms **www.christensenarms.com**
Cimarron Firearms Co. **www.cimarron-firearms.com**
CK Arms/Freedom Gunworks **www.ckarms.com**
Clark Custom Guns **www.clarkcustomguns.com**
Cobalt Kinetics **www.cobaltarms.com**
Cobra Enterprises **www.cobrapistols.net**
Cogswell & Harrison **www.cogswellandharrison.com**
Collector's Armory, Ltd. **www.collectorsarmory.com**
Colt's Mfg Co. **www.colt.com**
Comanche **www.eagleimportsinc.com**
Competitor Pistols **www.competitor-pistol.com**
Connecticut Shotgun Mfg. Co. **www.connecticutshotgun.com**
Connecticut Valley Arms **www.cva.com**
Coonan, Inc. **www.coonaninc.com**
Cooper Firearms **www.cooperfirearms.com**
Core Rifle Systems **www.core15.com**
Corner Shot **www.cornershot.com**
CPA Rifles **www.singleshotrifles.com**
Crickett Rifles **www.crickett.com**
Crosman **www.crosman.com**
CVA **www.cva.com**
Cylinder & Slide Shop **www.cylinder-slide.com**
Czechp Int'l **www.czechpoint-usa.com**
CZ USA **www.cz-usa.com**
Daisy Mfg Co. **www.daisy.com**
Dakota Arms Inc. **www.dakotaarms.com**
Desert Eagle **www.magnumresearch.com**
Detonics USA **www.detonicsdefense.com**
Devil Dog Arms **www.devildogarms.com**
Diamondback **www.diamondbackfirearms.com**
Diana **www.diana-airguns.de**
Dixie Gun Works **www.dixiegunworks.com**
Double D Armory **www.ddarmory.com**
DoubleStar **www.star15.com**
DPMS, Inc. **www.dpmsinc.com**
DSA Inc. **www.dsarms.com**
Dumoulin **www.dumoulin-herstal.com**
EAA Corp. **www.eaacorp.com**
Eagle Imports, Inc. **www.eagleimportsinc.com**
Ed Brown Products **www.edbrown.com**

EDM Arms **www.edmarms.com**
EMF Co. **www.emf-company.com**
E.R. Shaw **www.ershawbarrels.com**
European American Armory Corp. **www.eaacorp.com**
Evans, William **www.williamevans.com**
Excel Arms **www.excelarms.com**
Fabarm **www.fabarm.com**
Fausti USA **www.faustiusa.com**
Flodman Guns **www.flodman.com**
FMK **www.fmkfirearms.com**
FN Herstal **www.fnherstal.com**
FN America **www.fnamerica.com**
FNH USA **www.fnhusa.com**
Franchi **www.franchiusa.com**
Franklin Armory **www.franklinarmory.com**
Freedom Arms **www.freedomarms.com**
Freedom Group, Inc. **www.freedom-group.com**
Galazan **www.connecticutshotgun.com**
Gambo Renato **www.renatogamba.it**
Gamo **www.gamo.com**
Gary Reeder Custom Guns **www.reedercustomguns.com**
German Sport Guns **www.german-sport-guns.com**
Gibbs Rifle Company **www.gibbsrifle.com**

Glock **www.glock.com**
Griffin & Howe **www.griffinhowe.com**
Gunbroker.com **www.gunbroker.com**
Guncrafter Industries **www.guncrafterindustries.com**
Gun Room Co. **www.onlylongrange.com**
Hammerli **www.carl-walther.com**
Hatsan Arms Co. **www.hatsan.com.tr**
Heckler and Koch **www.hk-usa.com**
Heizer Defense **www.heizerdefense.com**
Henry Repeating Arms Co. **www.henryrepeating.com**
Heritage Mfg. **www.heritagemfg.com**
High Standard Mfg. **www.highstandard.com**
Hi-Point Firearms **www.hi-pointfirearms.com**
Holland & Holland **www.hollandandholland.com**
Honor Defense **www.honordefense.com**
H&R 1871 Firearms **www.hr1871.com**
H-S Precision **www.hsprecision.com**
Hunters Lodge Corp. **www.hunterslodge.com**
Inland Arms **www.inland-mfg.com**
International Military Antiques, Inc. **www.ima-usa.com**
Inter Ordnance **www.interordnance.com**
ISSC, LLC **www.issc-austria.com**
Ithaca Gun Co. **www.ithacagun.com**

Iver Johnson Arms **www.iverjohnsonarms.com**
Izhevsky Mekhanichesky Zavod **www.baikalinc.ru**
James River Armory **www.jamesriverarmory.com**
Jarrett Rifles, Inc. **www.jarrettrifles.com**
Jesse James Firearms **www.jjfu.com**
J&G Sales, Ltd. **www.jgsales.com**
Johannsen Express Rifle **www.johannsen-jagd.de**
JP Enterprises, Inc. **www.jprifles.com**
Kahr Arms/Auto-Ordnance **www.kahr.com**
Kalashnikov USA www.kalashnikov-usa.com
KDF, Inc. **www.kdfguns.com**
KE Arms **www.kearms.com**
Keystone Sporting Arms **www.keystonesportingarmsllc.com**
Kifaru **www.kifaru.net**
Kimber **www.kimberamerica.com**
Kingston Armory **www.kingstonarmory.com**
Knight's Armament Co. **www.knightarmco.com**
Knight Rifles **www.knightrifles.com**
Kolar **www.kolararms.com**
Korth **www.korthwaffen.de**
Krebs Custom Guns **www.krebscustom.com**
Kriss **www.kriss-usa.com**
Krieghoff Int'l **www.krieghoff.com**
KY Imports, Inc. **www.kyimports.com**
K-VAR **www.k-var.com**
Larue **www.laruetactical.com**
Lazzeroni Arms Co. **www.lazzeroni.com**
Legacy Sports International **www.legacysports.com**
Legendary Arms Works **www.legendaryarmsworks.com**
Les Baer Custom, Inc. **www.lesbaer.com**
Lewis Machine & Tool Co. **www.lewismachine.net**
Linebaugh Custom Sixguns **www.customsixguns.com**
Lionheart **www.lionheartindustries.com**
Ljutic **www.ljuticgun.com**
Llama **www.eagleimportsinc.com**
LMT Defense **www.lmtdefense.com**
LRB Arms **www.lrbarms.com**
Lyman **www.lymanproducts.com**
LWRC Int'l **www.lwrci.com**
MAC **www.eagleimportsinc.com**
Magnum Research **www.magnumresearch.com**
Majestic Arms **www.majesticarms.com**
Marksman Products **www.marksman.com**
Marlin **www.marlinfirearms.com**
MasterPiece Arms **www.masterpiecearms.com**
Mauser **www.mauser.com**
McMillan Firearms **www.mcmillanfirearms.com**
Meacham Rifles **www.meachamrifles.com**
Milkor USA **www.milkorusainc.com**
Miltech **www.miltecharms.com**
MOA Maximum **www.moaguns.com**

MOA Precision **www.moaprecision.com**
Modern Weapon Systems **www.modernweaponsystems**
Montana Rifle Co. **www.montanarifleco.com**
Mossberg **www.mossberg.com**
Navy Arms **www.navyarms.com**
New England Arms Corp. **www.newenglandarms.com**
New England Custom Gun **www.newenglandcustomgun.com**
New Ultra Light Arms **www.newultralight.com**
Nighthawk Custom **www.nighthawkcustom.com**
North American Arms **www.northamericanarms.com**
Nosler **www.nosler.com**
Nowlin Mfg. Inc. **www.nowlinguns.com**
O.F. Mossberg & Sons **www.mossberg.com**
Ohio Ordnance Works **www.ohioordnanceworks.com**
Olympic Arms **www.olyarms.com**
Osprey Defense **www.gaspiston.com**
Panther Arms **www.dpmsinc.com**
Pedersoli Davide & Co. **www.davide-pedersoli.com**
Perazzi **www.perazzi.com**
Pietta **www.pietta.it**
Piotti **www.piotti.com/en**
Pistol Dynamics **www.pistoldynamics.com**
PKP Knife-Pistol **www.sanjuanenterprise.com**
Power Custom **www.powercustom.com**
Precision Small Arm Inc. **www.precisionsmallarms.com**
Primary Weapons Systems **www.primaryweapons.com**
Proof Research **www.proofresearch.com**
PTR 91,Inc. **www.ptr91.com**
Purdey & Sons **www.purdey.com**
Pyramyd Air **www.pyramydair.com**
Remington **www.remington.com**
Republic Forge **www.republicforge.com**
Rigby **www.johnrigbyandco.com**
Riverman Gun Works **www.rivermangunworks.com**
Rizzini USA **www.rizziniusa.com**
RM Equipment, Inc. **www.40mm.com**
Robar Companies, Inc. **www.robarguns.com**
Roberts Defense **www.robertsdefense.com**
Robinson Armament Co. **www.robarm.com**
Rock Island Armory **www.armscor.com**
Rock River Arms, Inc. **www.rockriverarms.com**
Rossi Arms **www.rossiusa.com**
RUAG Ammotec **www.ruag.com**
Ruger **www.ruger.com**
Safety Harbor Firearms **www.safetyharborfirearms.com**
Sarco **www.sarcoinc.com**
Sarsilmaz Silah San **www.sarsilmaz.com**
Sauer & Sohn **www.sauer.de**
Savage Arms Inc. **www.savagearms.com**
Scattergun Technologies Inc. **www.wilsoncombat.com**
SCCY Firearms **www.sccy.com**

Schmeisser Gmbh **www.schmeisser-germany.de**
SD Tactical Arms **www.sdtacticalarms.com**
Searcy Enterprises **www.searcyent.com**
Seecamp **www.seecamp.com**
Shaw **www.ershawbarrels.com**
Shilen Rifles **www.shilen.com**
Shiloh Rifle Mfg. **www.shilohrifle.com**
Sig Sauer, Inc. **www.sigsauer.com**
Simpson Ltd. **www.simpsonltd.com**
SKB Shotguns **www.skbshotguns.com**
Smith & Wesson **www.smith-wesson.com**
Sphinx System **www.sphinxarms.com**
Springfield Armory **www.springfield-armory.com**
SPS **www.eagleimportsinc.com**
SSK Industries **www.sskindustries.com**
Stag Arms **www.stagarms.com**
Stevens **www.savagearms.com**
Steyr Arms, Inc. **www.steyrarms.com**
STI International **www.stiguns.com**
Stoeger Industries **www.stoegerindustries.com**
Strayer-Voigt Inc. **www.sviguns.com**
Sturm, Ruger & Company **www.ruger.com**
Surgeon Rifles **www.surgeonrifles.com**
Tactical Solutions **www.tacticalsol.com**
Tar-Hunt Slug Guns, Inc. **www.tarhunt.com**
Taser Int'l **www.taser.com**
Taurus **www.taurususa.com**
Taylor's & Co., Inc. **www.taylorsfirearms.com**
Tempco Mfg. Co. **www.tempcomfg.com**
Tennessee Guns **www.tennesseeguns.com**
TG Int'l **www.tnguns.com**
Thompson/Center Arms **www.tcarms.com**
Tikka **www.tikka.fi**
Time Precision **www.benchrest.com/timeprecision**
TNW, Inc. **www.tnwfirearms.com**
Traditions **www.traditionsfirearms.com**
Tristar Sporting Arms **www.tristarsportingarms.com**
Turnbull Mfg. Co. **www.turnbullmfg.com**
Uberti **www.ubertireplicas.com**
Ultra Light Arms **www.newultralight.com**
Umarex **www.umarex.com**
U.S. Armament Corp. **www.usarmamentcorp.com**
Uselton Arms, Inc. **www.useltonarmsinc.com**
Valkyrie Arms **www.valkyriearms.com**
Vektor Arms **www.vektorarms.com**
Verney-Carron **www.verney-carron.com**
Volquartsen Custom Ltd. **www.volquartsen.com**
Warrior **www.warrior.co**
Walther USA **www.waltherarms.com**
Weatherby **www.weatherby.com**
Webley and Scott Ltd. **www.webley.co.uk**

Westley Richards **www.westleyrichards.com**
Wild West Guns **www.wildwestguns.com**
William Larkin Moore & Co. **www.williamlarkinmoore.com**
Wilson Combat **www.wilsoncombat.com**
Winchester Rifles and Shotguns **www.winchesterguns.com**

GUN PARTS, BARRELS, AFTERMARKET ACCESSORIES

300 Below **www.300below.com**
Accuracy International of North America
　　www.accuracyinternational.us
Accuracy Speaks, Inc. **www.accuracyspeaks.com**
Accuracy Systems **www.accuracysystemsinc.com**
Accurate Airguns **www.accurateairguns.com**
Advantage Arms **www.advantagearms.com**
AG Composites **www.agcomposites.com**
Aim Surplus **www.aimsurplus.com**
AK-USA **www.ak-103.com**
American Spirit Arms Corp. **www.americanspiritarms.com**
Amhurst-Depot **www.amherst-depot.com**
Apex Gun Parts **www.apexgunparts.com**
Armaspec **www.armaspec.com**
Armatac Industries **www.armatac.com**
Arthur Brown Co. **www.eabco.com**
Asia Sourcing Corp. **www.asiasourcing.com**
Barnes Precision Machine **www.barnesprecision.com**
Bar-Sto Precision Machine **www.barsto.com**
Bellm TC's **www.bellmtcs.com**
Belt Mountain Enterprises **www.beltmountain.com**
Bergara Barrels **www.bergarabarrels.com**
Beyer Barrels **www.beyerbarrels.com**
Bighorn Arms **www.bighornarms.com**
Bill Wiseman & Co. **www.wisemanballistics.com**
Bluegrass Gun Works **www.rocksolidind.com**
Bravo Company USA **www.bravocompanyusa.com**
Briley **www.briley.com**
Brownells **www.brownells.com**
B-Square **www.b-square.com**
Buffer Technologies **www.buffertech.com**
Bullberry Barrel Works **www.bullberry.com**
Bulldog Barrels **www.bulldogbarrels.com**
Bullet Central **www.bulletcentral.com**
Bushmaster Firearms/Quality Parts **www.bushmaster.com**
Butler Creek Corp **www.butlercreek.com**
Cape Outfitters Inc. **www.capeoutfitters.com**
Cavalry Arms **www.cavalryarms.com**
Caspian Arms Ltd. **www.caspianarms.com**
CDNN Sports **www.cdnnsports.com**
Cheaper Than Dirt **www.cheaperthandirt.com**
Chesnut Ridge **www.chestnutridge.com/**

Choate Machine & Tool Co. **www.riflestock.com**
Christie's Products **www.1022cental.com**
CJ Weapons Accessories **www.cjweapons.com**
Colonial Arms **www.colonialarms.com**
Comp-N-Choke **www.comp-n-choke.com**
Custom Gun Rails **www.customgunrails.com**
Cylinder & Slide Shop **www.cylinder-slide.com**
Dave Manson Precision Reamers **www.mansonreamers.com**
DC Machine **www.dcmachine.net**
Digi-Twist **www.fmtcorp.com**
Dixie Gun Works **www.dixiegun.com**
DPMS **www.dpmsinc.com**
D.S. Arms **www.dsarms.com**
E. Arthur Brown Co. **www.eabco.com**
Ed Brown Products **www.edbrown.com**
EFK Marketing/Fire Dragon Pistol Accessories
   www.efkfiredragon.com
E.R. Shaw **www.ershawbarrels.com**
FJ Fedderson Rifle Barrels **www.gunbarrels.net**
FTF Industries **www.ftfindustries.com**
Fulton Armory **www.fulton-armory.com**
Galazan **www.connecticutshotgun.com**
Gemtech **www.gem-tech.com**

Gentry, David **www.gentrycustom.com**
GG&G **www.gggaz.com**
Great Lakes Tactical **www.gltactical.com**
Green Mountain Rifle Barrels **www.gmriflebarrel.com**
Gun Parts Corp. **www.e-gunpartscorp.com**
Guntec USA **www.guntecusa.com**
Harris Engineering **www.harrisbipods.com**
Hart Rifle Barrels **www.hartbarrels.com**
Hastings Barrels **www.hastingsbarrels.com**
Heinie Specialty Products **www.heinie.com**
High Performance Firearms/Hiperfire **www.hiperfire.com**
HKS Products **www.hksspeedloaders.com**
Holland Shooters Supply **www.hollandguns.com**
H-S Precision **www.hsprecision.com**
100 Straight Products **www.100straight.com**
I.M.A. **www.ima-usa.com**
Jarvis, Inc. **www.jarvis-custom.com**
J&T Distributing **www.jtdistributing.com**
JP Enterprises **www.jprifles.com**
Keng's Firearms Specialities **www.versapod.com**
KG Industries **www.kgcoatings.com**
Kick Eez **www.kickeezproducts.com**
Kidd Triggers **www.coolguyguns.com**

Knoxx Industries **www.impactguns.com**
Krieger Barrels **www.kriegerbarrels.com**
K-VAR Corp. **www.k-var.com**
LaRue Tactical **www.laruetactical.com**
Legend Armory **www.legend-armory.com**
Les Baer Custom, Inc. **www.lesbaer.com**
Lilja Barrels **www.riflebarrels.com**
Lone Wolf Dist. **www.lonewolfdist.com**
Lothar Walther Precision Tools Inc. **www.lothar-walther.de**
M&A Parts, Inc. **www.mapartsinc.com**
Magna-Matic Defense **www.magna-matic-defense.com**
Magpul Industries Corp. **www.magpul.com**
Majestic Arms **www.majesticarms.com**
MEC-GAR USA **www.mec-gar.com**
Mech Tech Systems **www.mechtechsys.com**
Mesa Tactical **www.mesatactical.com**
Midway USA **www.midwayusa.com**
Model 1 Sales **www.model1sales.com**
New England Custom Gun Service
    www.newenglandcustomgun.com
NIC Industries **www.nicindustries.com**
North Mfg. Co. **www.rifle-barrels.com**
Numrich Gun Parts Corp. **www.e-gunparts.com**
Osprey Defense LLC **www.gaspiston.com**
Pachmayr **www.pachmayr.com**
Pac-Nor Barrels **www.pac-nor.com**
Power Custom, Inc. **www.powercustom.com**
Precision Reflex **www.pri-mounts.com**
Promag Industries **www.promagindustries.com**
RCI-XRAIL **www.xrailbyrci.com**
Red Star Arms **www.redstararms.com**
River Bank Armory **www.riverbankarmory.com**
Riverman Gun Works **www.rivermangunworks.com**
Rock Creek Barrels **www.rockcreekbarrels.com**
Royal Arms Int'l **www.royalarms.com**
R.W. Hart **www.rwhart.com**
Sage Control Ordnance **www.sageinternationalltd.com**
Sarco Inc. **www.sarcoinc.com**
Scattergun Technologies Inc. **www.wilsoncombat.com**
Schuemann Barrels **www.schuemann.com**
Score High Gunsmithing **www.scorehi.com**
Shaw Barrels **www.ershawbarrels.com**
Shilen **www.shilen.com**
SilencerCo **www.silencerco.com**
Sims Vibration Laboratory **www.limbsaver.com**
Slide Fire **www.slidefire.com**
Smith & Alexander Inc. **www.smithandalexander.com**
Springfield Sporters, Inc. **www.ssporters.com**
STI Int'l **www.stiguns.com**
S&S Firearms **www.ssfirearms.com**
SSK Industries **www.sskindustries.com**

Sun Devil Mfg. **www.sundevilmfg.com**
Sunny Hill Enterprises **www.sunny-hill.com**
Tac Star **www.lymanproducts.com**
Tactical Innovations **www.tacticalinc.com**
Tactical Solutions **www.tacticalsol.com**
Tactilite **www.tactilite.com**
Tapco **www.tapco.com**
Triple K Manufacturing Co. Inc. **www.triplek.com**
Ultimak **www.ultimak.com**
Verney-Carron SA **www.verney-carron.com**
Vintage Ordnance **www.vintageordnance.com**
Vltor Weapon Systems **www.vltor.com**
Volquartsen Custom Ltd. **www.volquartsen.com**
W.C. Wolff Co. **www.gunsprings.com**
Weigand Combat Handguns **www.jackweigand.com**
Western Gun Parts **www.westerngunparts.com**
Wilson Arms **www.wilsonarms.com**
Wilson Combat **www.wilsoncombat.com**

GUNSMITHING SUPPLIES AND INSTRUCTION

4-D Products **www.4-dproducts.com**
American Gunsmithing Institute
    www.americangunsmith.com
Baron Technology **www.baronengraving.com**
Battenfeld Technologies **www.battenfeldtechnologies.com**
Bellm TC's **www.bellmtcs.com**
Blue Ridge Machinery & Tools
    www.blueridgemachinery.com
Brownells, Inc. **www.brownells.com**
B-Square Co. **www.b-square.com**
Cerakote Firearm Coatings **www.ncindustries.com**
Clymer Mfg. Co. **www.clymertool.com**
Dem-Bart **www.dembartco.com**
Doug Turnbull Restoration **www.turnbullrestoration.com**
Du-Lite Corp. **www.dulite.com**
DuraCoat Firearm Finishes **www.lauerweaponry.com**
Dvorak Instruments **www.dvorakinstruments.com**
Gradiant Lens Corp. **www.gradientlens.com**
Grizzly Industrial **www.grizzly.com**
Gunline Tools **www.gunline.com**
Harbor Freight **www.harborfreight.com**
JGS Precision Tool Mfg. LLC **www.jgstools.com**
Mag-Na-Port International **www.magnaport.com**
Manson Precision Reamers **www.mansonreamers.com**
Midway USA **www.midwayusa.com**
Murray State College **www.mscok.edu**
New England Custom Gun Service
    www.newenglandcustomgun.com
Olympus America Inc. **www.olympus.com**

Pacific Tool & Gauge **www.pacifictoolandgauge.com**
Penn Foster Career School **www.pennfoster.edu**
Pennsylvania Gunsmith School **www.pagunsmith.edu**
Piedmont Community College **www.piedmontcc.edu**
Precision Metalsmiths, Inc.
   www.precisionmetalsmiths.com
Sonoran Desert Institute **www.sdi.edu**
Trinidad State Junior College **www.trinidadstate.edu**

HANDGUN GRIPS

Ajax Custom Grips, Inc. **www.ajaxgrips.com**
Altamont Co. **www.altamontco.com**
Aluma Grips **www.alumagrips.com**
Barami Corp. **www.hipgrip.com**
Crimson Trace Corp. **www.crimsontrace.com**
Decal Grip **www.decalgrip.com**
Eagle Grips **www.eaglegrips.com**
Falcon Industries **www.ergogrips.net**
Handgun Grips **www.handgungrips.com**
Herrett's Stocks **www.herrettstocks.com**
Hogue Grips **www.hogueinc.com**
Kirk Ratajesak **www.kgratajesak.com**
N.C. Ordnance **www.gungrip.com**
Nill-Grips USA **www.nill-grips.com**
Pachmayr **www.pachmayr.com**
Pearce Grips **www.pearcegrip.com**
Rio Grande Custom Grips **www.riograndecustomgrips.com**
Talon Grips **www.talongrips.com**
Uncle Mike's **www.unclemikes.com**

HOLSTERS AND LEATHER PRODUCTS

Active Pro Gear **www.activeprogear.com**
Akah **www.akah.de**
Aker Leather Products **www.akerleather.com**
Alessi Distributor R&F Inc. **www.alessigunholsters.com**
Armor Holdings **www.holsters.com**
Bagmaster **www.bagmaster.com**
Bianchi International **www.safariland.com/our-brands/bianchi**
Black Dog Machine **www.blackdogmachinellc.net**
Blackhawk Outdoors **www.blackhawk.com**
Blackhills Leather **www.blackhillsleather.com**
Boyt Harness Co. **www.boytharness.com**
Brigade Gun Leather **www.brigadegunleather.com**
Center of Mass **www.comholsters.com**
Clipdraw **www.clipdraw.com**
Comp-Tac Victory Gear **www.comp-tac.com**
Concealed Carrie **www.concealedcarrie.com**
Concealment Shop Inc. **www.theconcealmentshop.com**
Coronado Leather Co. **www.coronadoleather.com**

Creedmoor Sports, Inc. **www.creedmoorsports.com**
Cross Breed Holsters **www.crossbreedholsters.com**
Deep Conceal **www.deepconceal.com**
Defense Security Products **www.thunderwear.com**
DeSantis Holster **www.desantisholster.com**
Dillon Precision **www.dillonprecision.com**
Don Hume Leathergoods, Inc. **www.donhume.com**
Duty Smith **www.dutysmith.com**
Elite Survival **www.elitesurvival.com**
El Paso Saddlery **www.epsaddlery.com**
Fobus USA **www.fobusholster.com**
Frontier Gun Leather **www.frontiergunleather.com**
Galco **www.usgalco.com**
Gilmore's Sports Concepts **www.gilmoresports.com**
Gould & Goodrich **www.gouldusa.com**
Hide-A-Gun **www.hide-a-gun.com**
High Noon Holsters **www.highnoonholsters.com**
Holsters.com **www.holsters.com**
Houston Gun Holsters **www.houstongunholsters.com**
Hunter Co. **www.huntercompany.com**
JBP/Master's Holsters **www.jbpholsters.com**
KJ Leather **www.kbarjleather.com**
KNJ **www.knjmfg.com**
Kramer Leather **www.kramerleather.com**
K-Rounds Holsters **www.krounds.com**
Mernickle Holsters **www.mernickleholsters.com**
Michaels of Oregon Co. **www.michaels-oregon.com**
Milt Sparks Leather **www.miltsparks.com**
Mitch Rosen Extraordinary Gunleather **www.mitchrosen.com**
N82 Tactical **www.n82tactical.com**
Pacific Canvas & Leather Co. **paccanadleather@directway.com**
Pager Pal **www.pagerpal.com**
Phalanx Corp. **www.smartholster.com**
Purdy Gear **www.purdygear.com**
PWL **www.pwlusa.com**
Safariland Ltd. Inc. **www.safariland.com**
Shooting Systems Group Inc. **www.shootingsystems.com**
Sneaky Pete Holsters **www.sneakypete.com**
Skyline Tool Works **www.clipdraw.com**
Stellar Rigs **www.stellarrigs.com**
Strong Holster Co. **www.badgecase.com**
Tex Shoemaker & Sons **www.texshoemaker.com**
The Outdoor Connection **www.outdoorconnection.com**
Tuff Products **www.tuffproducts.com**
Triple K Manufacturing Co. **www.triplek.com**
Wilson Combat **www.wilsoncombat.com**
Wright Leatherworks **www.wrightleatherworks.com**

MISCELLANEOUS SHOOTING PRODUCTS

ADCO Sales **www.adcosales.com**

Aero Peltor **www.aearo.com**

American Body Armor **www.americanbodyarmor.com**

Ammo-Up **www.ammoupusa.com**

Battenfeld Technologies **www.battenfeldtechnologies.com**

Beartooth **www.beartoothproducts.com**

Burnham Brothers **www.burnhambrothers.com**

Collectors Armory **www.collectorsarmory.com**

Dead Ringer Hunting **www.deadringerhunting.com**

Deben Group Industries Inc. **www.deben.com**

E.A.R., Inc. **www.earinc.com**

ESP **www.espamerica.com**

Gunstands **www.gunstands.com**

Howard Leight Hearing Protectors **www.howardleight.com**

Hunters Specialities **www.hunterspec.com**

Johnny Stewart Wildlife Calls **www.hunterspec.com**

Joseph Chiarello Gun Insurance **www.guninsurance.com**

Mec-Gar USA **www.mec-gar.com**

Merit Corporation **www.meritcorporation.com**

Michaels of Oregon Co. **www.michaels-oregon.com**

Midway USA **www.midwayusa.com**

MT2, LLC **www.mt2.com**

MTM Case-Gard **www.mtmcase-gard.com**

Natchez Shooters Supplies **www.natchezss.com**

Oakley, Inc. **www.usstandardissue.com**

Plano Molding **www.planomolding.com**

Practical Air Rifle Training Systems **www.smallarms.com**

Pro-Ears **www.pro-ears.com**

Quantico Tactical **www.quanticotactical.com**

Second Chance Body Armor Inc. **www.secondchance.com**

SilencerCo **www.silencerco.com**

Smart Lock Technologies **www.smartlock.com**

SportEAR **www.sportear.com**

Surefire **www.surefire.com**

Taser Int'l **www.taser.com**

Walker's Game Ear Inc. **www.walkersgameear.com**

MUZZLELOADING FIREARMS AND PRODUCTS

American Pioneer Powder **www.americanpioneerpowder.com**

Armi Sport **www.armisport.com**

Barnes Bullets **www.barnesbullets.com**

Black Powder Products **www.bpiguns.com**
Buckeye Barrels **www.buckeyebarrels.com**
Cabin Creek Muzzleloading **www.cabincreek.net**
CVA **www.cva.com**
Caywood Gunmakers **www.caywoodguns.com**
Davide Perdsoli & Co. **www.davide-pedersoli.com**
Dixie Gun Works, Inc. **www.dixiegun.com**
Goex Black Powder **www.goexpowder.com**
Green Mountain Rifle Barrel Co. **www.gmriflebarrel.com**
Gunstocks Plus **www.gunstocksplus.com**
Gun Works **www.thegunworks.com**
Honorable Company of Horners **www.hornguild.org**
Hornady **www.hornady.com**
Jedediah Starr Trading Co. **www.jedediah-starr.com**
Jim Chambers Flintlocks **www.flintlocks.com**
Knight Rifles **www.knightrifles.com**
Knob Mountain **www.knobmountainmuzzleloading.com**
The Leatherman **www.blackpowderbags.com**
Log Cabin Shop **www.logcabinshop.com**
L&R Lock Co. **www.lr-rpl.com**
Lyman **www.lymanproducts.com**
MSM, Inc. **www.msmfg.com**
Muzzleload Magnum Products **www.mmpsabots.com**
Navy Arms **www.navyarms.com**
Northwest Trade Guns **www.northstarwest.com**

Nosler, Inc. **www.nosler.com**
Palmetto Arms **www.palmetto.it**
Pecatonica River **www.longrifles-pr.com**
Pietta **www.pietta.it**
Powerbelt Bullets **www.powerbeltbullets.com**
Precision Rifle Dead Center Bullets **www.prbullet.com**
R.E. Davis Co. **www.redaviscompany.com**
Rightnour Mfg. Co. Inc. **www.rmcsports.com**
Savage Arms, Inc. **www.savagearms.com**
Schuetzen Powder **www.schuetzenpowder.com**
TDC **www.tdcmfg.com**
Tennessee Valley Muzzleloading
    www.tennesseevalleymuzzleloading.com
Thompson Center Arms **www.tcarms.com**
Tiger Hunt Stocks **www.gunstockwood.com**
Track of the Wolf **www.trackofthewolf.com**
Traditions Performance Muzzleloading **www.traditionsfirearms. com**
Turnbull Restoration & Mfg. **www.turnbullmfg.com**
Vernon C. Davis & Co. **www.stonewallcreekoutfitters.com**

PUBLICATIONS, VIDEOS AND CD'S

Arms and Military Press **www.skennerton.com**
A&J Arms Booksellers **www.ajarmsbooksellers.com**
American Cop **www.americancopmagazine.com**

PHOTO COURTESY OF THE NATIONAL SHOOTING SPORTS FOUNDATION

American Gunsmithing Institute **www.americangunsmith.com**
American Handgunner **www.americanhandgunner.com**
American Hunter **www.nrapublications.org**
American Pioneer Video **www.americanpioneervideo.com**
American Rifleman **www.nrapublications.org**
Backwoodsman **www.backwoodsmanmag.com**
Blue Book Publications **www.bluebookinc.com**
Combat Handguns **www.combathandguns.com**
Concealed Carry **www.uscca.us**
Cornell Publications **www.cornellpubs.com**
Deer & Deer Hunting **www.deeranddeerhunting.com**
Field & Stream **www.fieldandstream.com**
Firearms News **www.firearmsnews.com**
FMG Publications **www.fmgpubs.com**
Fouling Shot **www.castbulletassoc.org**
Fur-Fish-Game **www.furfishgame.com**
George Shumway Publisher **www.shumwaypublisher.com**
Grays Sporting Journal **www.grayssportingjournal.com**
Gun Digest, The Magazine **www.gundigest.com**
Gun Digest Books **www.gundigeststore.com**
Gun Dog **www.gundogmag.com**
Gun Mag **www.thegunmag.com**
Gun Tests **www.gun-tests.com**
Gun Video **www.gunvideo.com**
Gun World **www.gunworld.com**
Guns & Ammo **www.gunsandammo.com**
GUNS Magazine **www.gunsmagazine.com**
Guns of the Old West **www.gunsoftheoldwest.com**
Handloader **www.riflemagazine.com**
Handguns **www.handguns.com**
Hendon Publishing Co. **www.hendonpub.com**
Heritage Gun Books **www.gunbooks.com**
Krause Publications **www.krause.com**
Law and Order **www.hendonpub.com**
Man at Arms **www.manatarmsbooks.com**
Muzzle Blasts **www.nmlra.org**
Muzzleloader **www.muzzleloadermag.com**
North American Whitetail **www.northamericanwhitetail.com**
On-Target Productions **www.ontargetdvds.com**
Outdoor Channel **www.outdoorchannel.com**
Outdoor Life **www.outdoorlife.com**
Paladin Press **www.paladin-press.com**
Petersen's Hunting **www.petersenshunting.com**
Police and Security News **www.policeandsecuritynews.com**
Police Magazine **www.policemag.com**
Primitive Arts Video **www.primitiveartsvideo.com**
Pursuit Channel **www.pursuitchannel.com**
Recoil Gun Magazine **www.recoilweb.com**
Rifle Magazine **www.riflemagazine.com**
Rifle Shooter Magazine **www.rifleshootermag.com**
Safari Press Inc. **www.safaripress.com**

Shoot! Magazine **www.shootmagazine.com**
Shooting Illustrated **www.nrapublications.org**
Shooting Industry **www.shootingindustry.com**
Shooting Times Magazine **www.shootingtimes.com**
Shooting Sports Retailer **www.shootingsportsretailer.com**
Shooting Sports USA **www.nrapublications.org**
Shop Deer Hunting **www.shopdeerhunting.com**
Shotgun Report **www.shotgunreport.com**
Shotgun Sports Magazine **www.shotgunsportsmagazine.com**
Single Shot Exchange **www.singleshotexchange.com**
Single Shot Rifle Journal **www.assra.com**
Skyhorse Publishing **www.skyhorsepublishing.com**
Small Arms Review **www.smallarmsreview.com**
Sporting Classics **www.sportingclassics.com**
Sporting Clays **www.sportingclays.net**
Sports Afield **www.sportsafield.com**
Sportsman Channel **www.thesportsmanchannel.com**
Sportsmen on Film **www.sportsmenonfilm.com**
Standard Catalog of Firearms **www.gundigeststore.com**
Successful Hunter **www.riflemagazine.com**
SWAT Magazine **www.swatmag.com**
Trapper & Predator Caller **www.trapperpredatorcaller.com**
Turkey & Turkey Hunting **www.turkeyandturkeyhunting.com**
Varmint Hunter **www.varminthunter.com**
VSP Publications **www.gunbooks.com**
Wildfowl **www.wildfowlmag.com**

RELOADING TOOLS

21st Century Shooting **www.21stcenturyshooting.com**
Ballisti-Cast Mfg. **www.ballisti-cast.com**
Battenfeld Technologies **www.battenfeldtechnologies.com**
Black Hills Shooters Supply **www.bhshooters.com**
Bruno Shooters Supply **www.brunoshooters.com**
Buffalo Arms **www.buffaloarms.com**
CabineTree **www.castingstuff.com**
Camdex, Inc. **www.camdexloader.com**
CH/4D Custom Die **www.ch4d.com**
Corbin Mfg & Supply Co. **www.corbins.com**
Dillon Precision **www.dillonprecision.com**
Forster Precision Products **www.forsterproducts.com**
Gracey Trimmer **www.matchprep.com**
Harrell's Precision **www.harrellsprec.com**
Hornady **www.hornady.com**
Hunter's Supply, Inc. **wwwhunters-supply.com**
Huntington Reloading Products **www.huntingtons.com**
J & J Products Co. **www.jandjproducts.com**
Lead Bullet Technology **www.lbtmoulds.com**
Lee Precision, Inc. **www.leeprecision.com**
L.E. Wilson **www.lewilson.com**
Little Crow Gun Works **www.littlecrowgunworks.com**

Littleton Shotmaker **www.littletonshotmaker.com**
Load Data **www.loaddata.com**
Lyman **www.lymanproducts.com**
Mayville Engineering Co. (MEC) **www.mecreloaders.com**
Midway USA **www.midwayusa.com**
Montana Bullet Works **www.montanabulletworks.com**
NECO **www.neconos.com**
NEI **www.neihandtools.com**
Neil Jones Custom Products **www.neiljones.com**
New Lachaussee SA **www.lachaussee.com**
Ponsness/Warren **www.reloaders.com**
Precision Reloading **www.precisionreloading.com**
Quinetics Corp. **www.quineticscorp.com**
RCBS **www.rcbs.com**
Redding Reloading Equipment **www.redding-reloading.com**
Russ Haydon's Shooting Supplies **www.shooters-supply.com**
Sinclair Int'l Inc. **www.sinclairintl.com**
Stealth Gunpowder **www.stealthgunpowder.com**

Stoney Point Products Inc. **www.stoneypoint.com**
Vickerman Seating Die **www.castingstuff.com**

RESTS— BENCH, PORTABLE, ATTACHABLE

Accu-Shot **www.accu-shot.com**
Battenfeld Technologies **www.battenfeldtechnologies.com**
Bench Master **www.bench-master.com**
B-Square **www.b-square.com**
Center Mass, Inc. **www.centermassinc.com**
Desert Mountain Mfg. **www.benchmasterusa.com**
DOA Tactical **www.doatactical.com**
Harris Engineering Inc. **www.harrisbipods**
KFS Industries **www.versapod.com**
Kramer Designs **www.snipepod.com**
Level-Lok **www.levellok.com**
Midway **www.midwayusa.com**

PHOTO COURTESY OF THE NATIONAL SHOOTING SPORTS FOUNDATION

Rotary Gun Racks **www.gun-racks.com**
R.W. Hart **www.rwhart.com**
Sinclair Intl, Inc. **www.sinclairintl.com**
Shooting Bench USA **www.shootingbenchusa.com**
Stoney Point Products **www.stoneypoint.com**
Target Shooting **www.targetshooting.com**

SCOPES, SIGHTS, MOUNTS AND ACCESSORIES

Accumount **www.accumounts.com**
Accusight **www.accusight.com**
Advantage Tactical Sight **www.advantagetactical.com**
Aimpoint **www.aimpoint.com**
Aim Shot, Inc. **www.aimshot.com**
Aimtech Mount Systems **www.aimtech-mounts.com**
Alpen Outdoor Corp. **www.alpenoutdoor.com**
American Technologies Network, Corp. **www.atncorp.com**
AmeriGlo, LLC **www.ameriglo.net**
ArmaLaser **www.armalaser.com**
Amerigun USA **www.amerigunusa.com**
Armament Technology, Inc. **www.armament.com**
ARMS **www.armsmounts.com**
ATN **www.atncorp.com**
Badger Ordnance **www.badgerordnance.com**
Barrett **www.barrettrifles.com**
Beamshot-Quarton **www.beamshot.com**
BKL Technologies, Inc. **www.bkltech.com**
BSA Optics **www.bsaoptics.com**
B-Square **www.b-square.com**
Burris **www.burrisoptics.com**
Bushnell Performance Optics **www.bushnell.com**
Carl Zeiss Optical Inc. **www.zeiss.com**
CenterPoint Precision Optics **www.centerpointoptics.com**
Centurion Arms **www.centurionarms.com**
C-More Systems **www.cmore.com**
Conetrol Scope Mounts **www.conetrol.com**
Crimson Trace Corp. **www.crimsontrace.com**
D&L Sports **www.disports.com**
DuraSight Scope Mounting Systems **www.durasight.com**
EasyHit, Inc. **www.easyhit.com**
EAW **www.eaw.de**
Elcan Optical Technologies **www.elcan. com**
Electro-Optics Technologies **www.eotech.com**
EoTech **www.eotech-inc.com**
Eurooptik Ltd. **www.eurooptik.com**
Field Sport Inc. **www.fieldsportinc.com**
GG&G **www.gggaz.com**
Gilmore Sports **www.gilmoresports.com**
Gradient Lens Corp. **www.gradientlens.com**
Guangzhou Bosma Corp. **www.bosmaoptics.com**

Hahn Precision **www.hahn-precision.com**
Hi-Lux Optics **www.hi-luxoptics.com**
HIVIZ **www.hivizsights.com**
Horus Vision **www.horusvision.com**
Huskemaw Optics **www.huskemawoptics.com**
Insight **www.insighttechnology.com**
Ironsighter Co. **www.ironsighter.com**
KenSight **www.kensight.com**
Knight's Armament **www.knightarmco.com**
LaRue Tactical **www.laruetactical.com**
Lasergrips **www.crimsontrace.com**
LaserLyte **www.laserlytesights.com**
LaserMax Inc. **www.lasermax.com**
Laser Products **www.surefire.com**
Leapers, Inc. **www.leapers.com**
Leatherwood **www.hi-luxoptics.com**
Leica Camera Inc. **www.leica-camera.com**
Leupold **www.leupold.com**
Lewis Machine & Tool **www.lewismachine.net**
LightForce/NightForce USA **www.nightforceoptics.com**
LUCID LLC **www.mylucidgear.com**
Lyman **www.lymanproducts.com**
Lynx **www.b-square.com**
Matech **www.matech.net**
Marble's Gunsights **www.marblearms.com**
Meopta **www.meopta.com**
Meprolight **www.meprolight.com**
Mini-Scout-Mount **www.amegaranges.com**
Minox USA **www.minox.com**
Montana Vintage Arms **www.montanavintagearms.com**
Mounting Solutions Plus **www.mountsplus.com**
NAIT **www.nait.com**
Newcon International Ltd. **www.newcon-optik.com**
Night Force Optics **www.nightforceoptics.com**
Night Optics USA, Inc. **www.nightoptics.com**
Night Owl Optics **www.nightowloptics.com**
Nikon Inc. **www.nikonhunting.com**
Nitehog **www.nitehog.com**
North American Integrated Technologies **www.nait.com**
Novak Sights **www.novaksights.com**
O.K. Weber, Inc. **www.okweber.com**
Optolyth-Optic **www.optolyth.de**
Precision Reflex **www.pri-mounts.com**
Pride Fowler, Inc. **www.rapidreticle.com**
Redfield **www.redfield.com**
Schmidt & Bender **www.schmidtundbender.de**
Scopecoat **www.scopecoat.com**
Scopelevel **www.scopelevel.com**
SIG Sauer **www.sigsauer.com**
Sightmark **www.sightmark.com**
Simmons **www.simmonsoptics.com**

S&K **www.scopemounts.com**
Springfield Armory **www.springfield-armory.com**
Sun Optics USA **www.sunopticsusa.com**
Sure-Fire **www.surefire.com**
SWATSCOPE **www.swatscope.com**
Talley Mfg. Co. **www.talleyrings.com**
Steve Earle Scope Blocks **www.steveearleproducts.com**
Tasco **www.tasco.com**
Tech Sights **www.tech-sights.com**
Trijicon Inc. **www.trijicon.com**
Trinity Force **www.trinityforce.com**
Troy Industries **www.troyind.com**
Truglo Inc. **www.truglo.com**
Ultimak **www.ultimak.com**
UltraDot **www.ultradotusa.com**
U.S. Night Vision **www.usnightvision.com**
U.S. Optics Technologies Inc. **www.usoptics.com**
Valdada-IOR Optics **www.valdada.com**
Viridian Green Laser Sights **www.viridiangreenlaser.com**
Vortex Optics **www.vortexoptics.com**
Warne **www.warnescopemounts.com**
Weaver Scopes **www.weaveroptics.com**
Wilcox Industries Corp **www.wilcoxind.com**
Williams Gun Sight Co. **www.williamsgunsight.com**
Wilson Combat **www.wilsoncombat.com**

XS Sight Systems **www.xssights.com**
Zeiss **www.zeiss.com**

SHOOTING ORGANIZATIONS, SCHOOLS AND MUSEUMS

Amateur Trapshooting Assoc. **www.shootata.com**
American Custom Gunmakers Guild **www.acgg.org**
American Gunsmithing Institute **www.americangunsmith.com**
American Pistolsmiths Guild **www.americanpistol.com**
American Single Shot Rifle Assoc. **www.assra.com**
American Snipers **www.americansnipers.org**
Assoc. of Firearm & Tool Mark Examiners **www.afte.org**
Autry National Center of the American West **www.theautry.org**
BATFE **www.atf.gov**
Boone and Crockett Club **www.boone-crockett.org**
Browning Collectors Association **www.browningcollectors.com**
Buffalo Bill Center of the West **www.centerofthewest.org**
Buckmasters, Ltd. **www.buckmasters.com**
Cast Bullet Assoc. **www.castbulletassoc.org**
Citizens Committee for the Right to Keep & Bear Arms
    www. ccrkba.org
Civilian Marksmanship Program **www.odcmp.com**
Colorado School of Trades **www.schooloftrades.edu**
Contemporary Longrifle Assoc. **www.longrifle.com**

Colt Collectors Assoc. **www.coltcollectors.com**
Cylinder & Slide Pistolsmithing Schools **www.cylinder-slide. com**
Ducks Unlimited **www.ducks.org**
4-H Shooting Sports Program **www.4-hshootingsports.org**
Fifty Caliber Institute **www.fiftycaliberinstitute.org**
Fifty Caliber Shooters Assoc. **www.fcsa.org**
Firearms Coalition **www.nealknox.com**
Front Sight Firearms Training Institute **www.frontsight.com**
Garand Collectors Assoc. **www.thegca.org**
German Gun Collectors Assoc. **www.germanguns.com**
Gibbs Military Collectors Club **www.gibbsrifle.com**
Gun Clubs **www.associatedgunclubs.org**
Gun Owners Action League **www.goal.org**
Gun Owners of America **www.gunowners.org**
Gun Trade Asssoc. Ltd. **www.gtaltd.co.uk**
Gunsite Training Center, Inc. **www.gunsite.com**
Hunting and Shooting Sports Heritage Fund **www.hsshf.org**
I.C.E. Training **www.icetraining.us**
International Ammunition Assoc. **www.cartridgecollectors.org**
IWA **www.iwa.info**
International Defensive Pistol Assoc. **www.idpa.com**
International Handgun Metallic Silhouette Assoc. **www.ihmsa.org**
International Hunter Education Assoc. **www.ihea.com**
Int'l Law Enforcement Educators and Trainers Assoc.
   www. ileeta.com
International Single Shot Assoc. **www.issa-schuetzen.org**
Ithaca Owners **www.ithacaowners.com**
Jews for the Preservation of Firearms Ownership **www.jpfo.org**
L.C. Smith Collectors Assoc. **www.lcsmith.org**
Lefever Arms Collectors Assoc. **www.lefevercollectors.com**
Mannlicher Collectors Assoc. **www.mannlicher.org**
Marlin Firearms Collectors Assoc. **www.marlin-collectors.com**
Mule Deer Foundation **www.muledeer.org**
Muzzle Loaders Assoc. of Great Britain **www.mlagb.com**
National 4-H Shooting Sports **www.4-hshootingsports.org**
National Association of Sporting Goods Wholesalers
   www.nasgw.org
National Benchrest Shooters Assoc. **www.nbrsa.com**
National Defense Industrial Assoc. **www.ndia.org**
National Cowboy & Western Heritage Museum
   www.nationalcowboymuseum.org
National Firearms Museum **www.nramuseum.org**
National Mossberg Collectors Assoc.
   www.mossbergcollectors.org
National Muzzle Loading Rifle Assoc. **www.nmlra.org**
National Rifle Association **www.nra.org**
National Rifle Association ILA **www.nraila.org**
National Shooting Sports Foundation **www.nssf.org**
National Tactical Officers Assoc. **www.ntoa.org**
National Wild Turkey Federation **www.nwtf.com**
NICS/FBI **www.fbi.gov**
North American Hunting Club **www.huntingclub.com**

Order of Edwardian Gunners (Vintagers) **www.vintagers.org**
Outdoor Industry Foundation
   www.outdoorindustryfoundation.org
Parker Gun Collectors Assoc. **www.parkerguns.org**
Pennsylvania Gunsmith School **www.pagunsmith.com**
Pheasants Forever **www.pheasantsforever.org**
Piedmont Community College **www.piedmontcc.edu**
Quail & Upland Wildlife Federation **www.quwf.net**
Quail Forever **www.quailforever.org**
Remington Society of America **www.remingtonsociety.com**
Right To Keep and Bear Arms **www.rkba.org**
Rocky Mountain Elk Foundation **www.rmef.org**
Ruffed Grouse Society **www.ruffedgrousesociety.org**
Ruger Collectors Assoc. **www.rugercollectorsassociation.com**
Ruger Owners & Collectors Society **www.rugersociety.com**
SAAMI **www.saami.org**
Safari Club International **www.scifirstforhunters.org**
Sako Collectors Club **www.sakocollectors.com**
Scholastic Clay Target Program
   www.sssfonline.org/scholasti-clay-target-program
Scholastic Shooting Sports Foundation **www.sssfonline.org**
Second Amendment Foundation **www.saf.org**
Shooting for Women Alliance
   www.shootingforwomenalliance. com
Sig Sauer Academy **www.sigsauer.com**
Single Action Shooting Society **www.sassnet.com**
Smith & Wesson Collectors Assoc. **www.theswca.org**
L.C. Smith Collectors Assoc. **www.lcsmith.org**
Steel Challenge Pistol Tournament **www.steelchallenge.com**
Students for Second Amendment **www.sf2a.org**
Sturgis Economic Development Corp.
   www.sturgisdevelopment.com
Suarez Training **www.warriortalk.com**
Tactical Defense Institute **www.tdiohio.com**
Tactical Life **www.tactical-life.com**
Thompson/Center Assoc.
   www.thompsoncenterassociation.org
Thunder Ranch **www.thunderranchinc.com**
Trapshooters Homepage **www.trapshooters.com**
Trinidad State Junior College **www.trinidadstate.edu**
United Sportsmen's Youth Foundation **www.usyf.com**
Universal Shooting Academy
   www.universalshootingacademy.com
U.S. Concealed Carry Association **www.uscca.us**
U.S. Fish and Wildlife Service **www.fws.gov**
U.S. Practical Shooting Assoc. **www.uspsa.org**
U.S. Sportsmen's Alliance **www.ussportsmen.org**
USA Shooting **www.usashooting.com**
Weatherby Collectors Assoc. **www.weatherbycollectors.com**
Wild Sheep Foundation **www.wildsheepfoundation.org**
Winchester Arms Collectors Assoc.
   www.winchestercollector.com

STOCKS, GRIPS, FOREARMS

10/22 Fun Gun **www.1022fungun.com**
Advanced Technology **www.atigunstocks.com**
AG Composites **www.agcomposites.com**
Battenfeld Technologies **www.battenfeldtechnologies.com**
Bell & Carlson, Inc. **www.bellandcarlson.com**
Butler Creek Corp **www.butlercreek.com**
Cadex **www.vikingtactics.com**
Calico Hardwoods, Inc. **www.calicohardwoods.com**
Choate Machine **www.riflestock.com**
Command Arms **www.commandarms.com**
C-More Systems **www.cmore.com**
D&L Sports **www.dlsports.com**
Duo Stock **www.duostock.com**
E. Arthur Brown Co. **www.eabco.com**
Fajen **www.battenfeldtechnologies.com**
Great American Gunstocks **www.gunstocks.com**
Grip Pod **www.grippod.com**

Gun Stock Blanks **www.gunstockblanks.com**
Herrett's Stocks **www.herrettstocks.com**
High Tech Specialties **www.hightech-specialties.com**
Hogue Grips **www.getgrip.com**
Knight's Mfg. Co. **wwwknightarmco.com**
Knoxx Industries **www.blackhawk.com**
KZ Tactical **www.kleyzion.com**
LaRue Tactical **www.laruetactical.com**
Lewis Machine & Tool **www.lewismachine.net**
Lone Wolf **www.lonewolfriflestocks.com**
Magpul **www.magpul.com**
Manners Composite Stocks **www.mannersstocks.com**
McMillan Fiberglass Stocks **www.mcmfamily.com**
MPI Stocks **www.mpistocks.com**
Phoenix Technology/Kicklite **www.kicklitestocks.com**
Precision Gun Works **www.precisiongunstocks.com**
Ram-Line **www.outers-guncare.com**
Richards Microfit Stocks **www.rifle-stocks.com**
Rimrock Rifle Stock **www.bordenrifles.com**

Royal Arms Gunstocks **www.royalarmsgunstocks.com**
Speedfeed **www.safariland.com**
TacStar/Pachmayr **www.tacstar.com**
Tango Down **www.tangodown.com**
TAPCO **www.tapco.com**
Slide Fire **www.slidefire.com**
Stocky's **www.newriflestocks.com**
Surefire **www.surefire.com**
Tiger-Hunt Curly Maple Gunstocks **www.gunstockwood.com**
UTG Pro **www.leapers.com**
Wenig Custom Gunstocks Inc. **www.wenig.com**
Wilcox Industries **www.wilcoxind.com**
Yankee Hill **www.yhm.net**

TARGETS AND RANGE EQUIPMENT

Action Target Co. **www.actiontarget.com**
Advanced Training Systems **www.atsusa.biz**
Alco Target **www.alcotarget.com**
Arntzen Targets **www.arntzentargets.com**
Birchwood Casey **www.birchwoodcasey.com**
Caswell Meggitt Defense Systems **www.mds-caswell.com**
Champion Traps & Targets **www.championtarget.com**
Custom Metal Products **www.custommetalprod.com**
Laser Shot **www.lasershot.com**
MGM Targets **www.mgmtargets.com**
MTM Products **www.mtmcase-gard.com**
National Muzzleloading Rifle Assoc. **www.nmlra.org**
National Target Co. **www.nationaltarget.com**
Newbold Target Systems **www.newboldtargets.com**
Paragon Tactical **www.paragontactical.com**
PJL Targets **www.pjltargets.com**
Rolling Steel Targets **www.rollingsteeltargets.com**
Savage Range Systems **www.savagerangesystems.com**
ShatterBlast Targets **www.daisy.com**
Super Trap Bullet Containment Systems **www.supertrap.com**
Thompson Target Technology **www.thompsontarget.com**
Unique Tek **www.uniquetek.com**
Visible Impact Targets **www.crosman.com**
White Flyer **www.whiteflyer.com**

TRAP AND SKEET SHOOTING EQUIPMENT AND ACCESSORIES

Atlas Trap Co **www.atlastraps.com**
Auto-Sporter Industries **www.auto-sporter.com**
Do-All Traps, Inc. **www.doalloutdoors.com**
Gamaliel Shooting Supply **www.gamaliel.com**
Howell Shooting Supplies **www.howellshootingsupplies.com**
Promatic, Inc. **www.promatic.biz**
White Flyer **www.whiteflyer.com**

TRIGGERS

American Trigger Corp. **www.americantrigger.com**
Brownells **www.brownells.com**
Huber Concepts **www.huberconcepts.com**
Jard, Inc. **www.jardinc.com**
Kidd Triggers **www.coolguyguns.com**
Shilen **www.shilen.com**
Spec-Tech Industries, Inc. **www.spec-tech-industries.com**
Timney Triggers **www.timneytriggers.com**
Williams Trigger Specialties **www.williamstriggers.com**

MAJOR SHOOTING WEBSITES AND LINKS

24 Hour Campfire **www.24hourcampfire.com**
Accurate Shooter **www.6mmbr.com**
Alphabetic Index of Links **www.gunsgunsguns.com**
Ammo Guide **www.ammoguide.com**
Auction Arms **www.auctionarms.com**
Benchrest Central **www.benchrest.com**
Big Game Hunt **www.biggamehunt.net**
Bullseye Pistol **www.bullseyepistol.com**
Firearms History **www.researchpress.co.uk**
Glock Talk **www.glocktalk.com**
Gun Broker Auctions **www.gunbroker.com**
Gun Blast **www.gunblast.com**
Gun Boards **www.gunboards.com**
Gun Digest **www. gundigest.com**
Guns & Ammo Forum **www.gunsandammo.com**
GunsAmerica **www.gunsamerica.com**
Gun Shop Finder **www.gunshopfinder.com**
Guns and Hunting **www.gunsandhunting.com**
Hunt and Shoot (NSSF) **www.huntandshoot.org**
Keep and Bear Arms **www.keepandbeararms.com**
Leverguns **www.leverguns.com**
Load Swap **www.loadswap.com**
Long Range Hunting **www.longrangehunting.com**
Real Guns **www.realguns.com**
Ruger Forum **www.rugerforum.com**
Savage Shooters **www.savageshooters.com**
Shooters Forum **www.shootersforum.com**
Shotgun Sports Resource Guide **www.shotgunsports.com**
Shotgun World **www.shotgunworld.com**
Sniper's Hide **www.snipershide.com**
Sportsman's Web **www.sportsmansweb.com**
Tactical-Life **www.tactical-life.com**
The Gun Room **www.doublegun.com**
Wing Shooting USA **www.wingshootingusa.org**

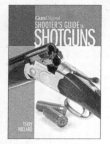

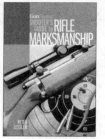

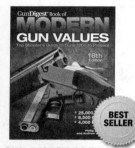

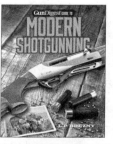

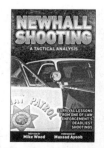

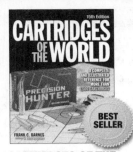
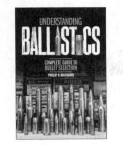

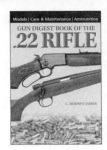

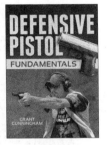

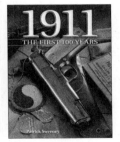
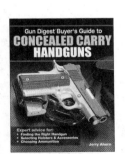
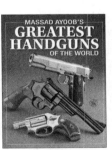
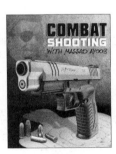

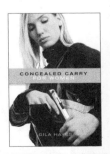

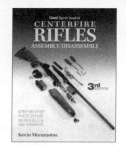

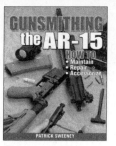

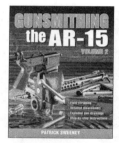
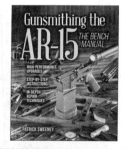

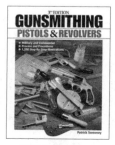
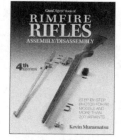

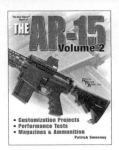
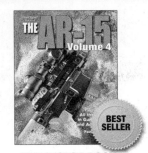
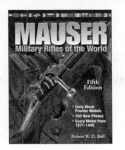
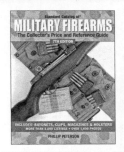
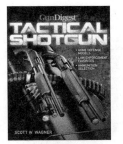
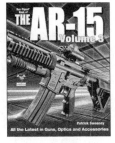
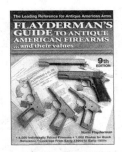

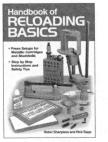

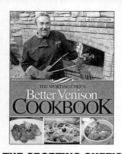

**THE SPORTING CHEF'S
BETTER VENISON
COOKBOOK**
U1948 • $24.99

COOKING GAME
U2929 • $9.99

BIG BUCK SECRETS
T4648 • $24.99

**WE KILL IT
WE GRILL IT**
V6707 • $9.99

**301
VENISON RECIPES**
VR01 • $10.95

**ADVENTURE
BOWHUNTER**
V9708 • $34.99

**WHITE-TAILED DEER
MANAGEMENT AND
HABITAT IMPROVEMENTS**
S3321 • $34.99

**DEER & DEER
HUNTING'S GUIDE
TO BETTER
BOW HUNTING**
V6706 • $9.99

**STRATEGIES FOR
WHITETAILS**
WTLDD • $24.99

**TOM DOKKEN'S
ADVANCED RETRIEVER
TRAINING**
U1863 • $22.99

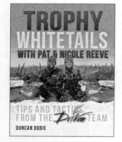

**TROPHY WHITETAILS WITH
PAT AND NICOLE REEVE**
U3680 • $31.99

**LEGENDARY
WHITETAILS**
W7618 • $29.99

GUT IT. CUT IT. COOK IT.
Z5014 • $24.99

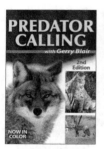

**PREDATOR CALLING
WITH GERRY BLAIR**
Z0740 • $19.99

THE RUT HUNTERS
U7573 • $31.99

GAME COOKERY
U7125 • $24.99

**THE MOUNTAIN MAN
COOKBOOK**
U9370 • $12.99

**TOM DOKKEN'S
RETRIEVER TRAINING**
Z3235 • $19.99

**TROPHY BUCKS
IN ANY WEATHER**
Z1781 • $21.99

To order, go to www.GunDigestStore.com.

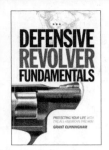

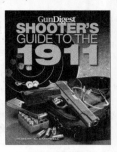

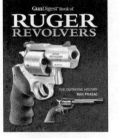
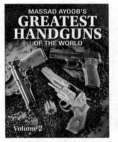
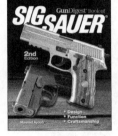

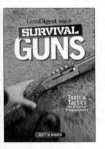

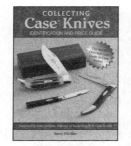

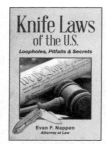

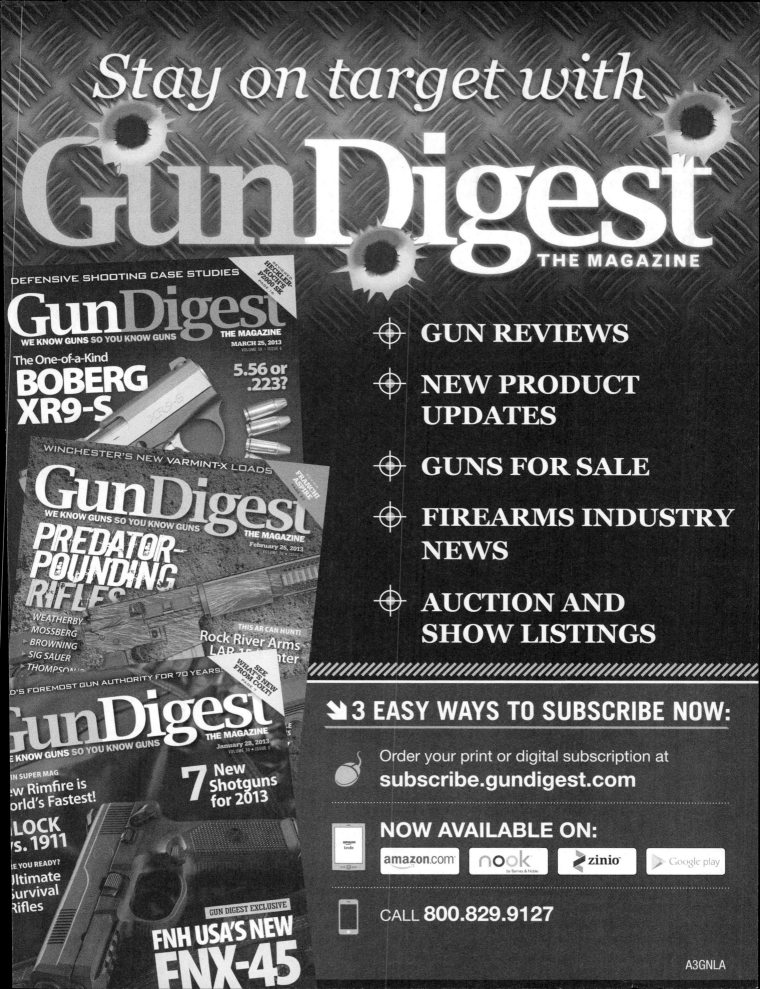